THE
MAFIA
ENCYCLOPEDIA

Third Edition

Carl Sifakis

Checkmark Books®

An imprint of Facts On File, Inc.

For Dieter Kohlenberger

A special acknowledgment to Ingrid Hagard,
who is equally adept at researching Jane Austen and the Mob

The Mafia Encyclopedia, Third Edition

Copyright © 2005, 1999, 1987 by Carl Sifakis

Checkmark Books
An imprint of Facts On File, Inc.
132 West 31st Street
New York NY 10001

ISBN 0-8160-5695-1

Text design by Erika K. Arroyo
Cover design by Cathy Rincon

Printed in the United States of America

Contents

Preface to the Third Edition*

It was the big con in the world of organized crime. Perhaps *con* is the wrong word. *Delusion* might be more accurate. A delusion of course is a con that fools just about everybody, often its perpetrators as well. And that was very true about the so-called decline and fall of the American Mafia. In the final years of the 20th century many a family boss, underboss, and consigliere were imprisoned by law enforcement campaigns, and as successors took over, they too were neutralized. From the law enforcement viewpoint it was glorious doings. U.S. Attorney for the Southern District of New York Rudolph Giuliani was widely quoted for predicting that the Mafia crime families were on the way out and that the Gambino crime family would soon be reduced to a mere street gang, its major unlawful activities eliminated. Other prosecutors and leading investigators predicted the same dire fate for other crime families in New York and elsewhere around the country. By sheer numbers the claims had considerable logic. Only a few cynics saw the triumphal bowing out of these successful law enforcers as a ploy like the one that had been suggested in Vietnam where it was said that the United States should declare it had won the war and was pulling out.

Of course, these law enforcement leaders were not acting cynically but truly believed organized crime could be eliminated by lopping off the leadership. Long sentences were handed down to the top mafiosi, who became doomed to spend the rest of their years behind bars, sometimes being denied contact with their outside cohorts. The idea was that eventually the mobs would simply wither away. Overlooked in this so-called strategy was that a boss is just a boss, an underboss is just an underboss, a consigliere just a consigliere. Mob guys can be described many ways. Many are illiterate, downright stupid, have no sense of conscience, or are murderous, but above all they are ambitious. It does not matter how many of them fall to the wayside under attack from the law or from other mobsters. The supply for bosses down to capos is without end, and the race to the top is clearly Darwinian. The real power of the mobs are the wise guys and soldiers, even those who do not qualify as superbrains. They are shooters, the final arbiter in the Mafia, and they understand their own power. They know how to resurrect powers that are lost. They can do whatever the job demands. They have the Mafia "gift" for exercising the process of corruption and influencing and convincing people with promises that may never be delivered or by lecturing a victim while holding him feet-first out a high window.

Still it cannot be denied that the 1990s, give or take a few years in special situations, marked the low point of organized crime since the 1920s. Those observers who insisted the Mafia was not dead were in a distinct minority. The author of the second edition of the *Mafia Encyclopedia*, which appeared in 1999, was asked by an interviewer, "Aren't you beating a dead horse?"—a circumspect way of saying the author was trying to milk a few bucks out of a criminal enterprise whose time has passed? Certainly that evaluation of the Mafia was held by the general public, but some investigators were not buying into the dead or dying Mafia. One of the most perceptive law enforcers in the Federal Bureau of Investigation (FBI) and for a time the head of the New York office, Lewis J. Schiliro, declared, "The families are in transition, trying to figure out how to redirect their criminal activities in a

---

*The introduction to the second edition of *The Mafia Encyclopedia* is reprinted below for its historical overview of the development of the American Mafia. This preface picks up the story from about 1999 to capture the new history of the new American Mafia.

new environment." (Have they succeeded? In recent years a low estimate of $200 million was given for a few Gambino wise guys, who insinuated fake charges on the telephone bills of unsuspecting consumers. The racket is called "cramming." And when that basic fraud is noted by the law, the boys, as they put it, "sophisticate" the money-producing scheme up a notch and keep on operating.)

Finally by the first few years of the new century, more observers have come to the conclusion that "the Mafia ain't dead" and in fact is not even close to expiration. As proof there are all the new rackets the mobs have come up with, and there is the troubling matter of the numbers. Law enforcement agents can pronounce the death of the families but shortly thereafter may also have to announce the arrests of 45 Gambinos here and some 35 Genoveses or Luccheses there. In 2003 the *New York Times* concluded, some might say belatedly, that "Reports of its death have been greatly exaggerated. For more than two decades, law enforcement officials have declared that the latest round of mob indictments would put the nail in the coffin of the Mafia." The *Times* now conceded the mob is not ready for burial. The *Times* also had to note the death of a different canard, concluding, "As other bands of ethnic criminals come and go, the old Mafia persists." Despite all the recent colorful accounts and dire predictions about the "new Mafias," the truth is that no other ethnic group or collection of criminals has been able to replace the traditional mobs.

Then there is the expert opinion of a longtime Mafia fighter, Robert J. Castelli, formerly of the New York state police and now in the halls of academia: "As much as we'd like to think we've broken the back of organized crime, we have only stubbed its toe." The reality of the situation is that two decades after the major war against the Mafia was undertaken, it is now clear that the Mafia business model (which one prosecutor described as turning fear into money) is tenaciously resilient. The mob quickly reassembles its techniques of imposing a "tax" of sorts across its domain, with a firm grip on legitimate businesses ranging from small coin laundries to unions and companies in construction and the waterfront.

Mark E. Feldman, the chief of organized crime prosecution for the U.S. attorney's office in Brooklyn, recognized that the command structure of the mob allows leadership succession because what is always paramount is the machinery for illegal profit and the durability of the operations. "Above all things," Feldman noted, "it is a money-making enterprise." More than anyone else, the motto of the mobsters is "show us the money."

Sent reeling by legal prosecution, the mobs managed to survive because the promise of huge financial rewards could not be extinguished. In exchange for that the average wise guy tolerates repression from within the organization. Wise guys are filled with fear of their superiors. By around 2000 the mobs had more or less righted themselves. Part of this success was due to the new leaders, who developed a bunker mentality. Their answer to all problems was twofold: inspire fear and kill. In that sense they were prepared to exceed the internal bloodletting of the mob's early days. Back then Carlo Gambino, the most celebrated godfather of his era, wiped out all opposition within what was then the Anastasia crime family by killing some 20 rebels against his potential rule on the same day and burying their bodies so well that they were never found. From the Mafia view of morality this was the norm, and the new leaders of the new century have seen the merits of the way. The new leaders were ready to follow the Gambino way, but when it came to eliminating challengers they also had help from law enforcement. Many wise guys who feared they would be eliminated surrendered to the government either for refuge in prison or safety within the witness protection program. But there was no mistake—the new leaders believed in killing not only their enemies within but those without as well, sometimes even if they offered no real threat.

Remarkably, the wise guys are rallying to the new leaders and accepting their firm edicts. The new bosses are more brutal than those who ran the mobs a decade or two ago. Why do the wise guys follow? They seek resiliency in their organizations, and if that means more brutality toward some of their own, they accept the situation. Law enforcement has made much of the way officials can strip wise guys away from the families by making them willing turncoats in exchange for leniency. The situation is hardly new for the mobs. Informers have always been a problem, often a most pressing one. One would think that recent, relatively large-scale defections would have a chilling effect on mob membership, but the fact is that it has not. In 1999 the imprisoned John Gotti complained to his visitors that he couldn't recognize many new members of the Gambino crime family.

When a slew of codefendants showed up in indictments along with John Gotti Jr., the elder Gotti was bewildered. "I can't even identify two people. I don't even know Sigmund the Sea Monster, Tony the One-Handed Leprechaun, Philly Jump Over the Fence Moon. Where did these people come from? I'm not away 100 years! I'm only away seven years! Where did these creatures emerge from?"

At a time when the press and authorities regarded the Gambinos as being on their last legs, the fact was that new recruits were a dime a dozen. In other words, it was obvious that these new recruits were attracted by the lure of big money rewards and were not about to be distracted by worrying that they would be caught. It is part of the mindset of most wise guy wanna-bes that they believe they can survive the pitfalls of crime family membership and be more competent than others. And should things go wrong? Well then they could turn to witness protection, but for the present they accept the brutality of the new bosses as a necessity and a prescription for success. In the 1990s as these new bosses came to the fore, some leaders proved too brutal. The prime example was Gas Pipe Casso and Vic Amuso, who were in effect the cobosses of the decimated Lucchese crime family. They purged the ranks relentlessly to a point where no one in the crime family felt safe. In an obvious case of overkill, Gas Pipe showed some of his adherents a list of 49 men he and Amuso intended to eliminate, including about 25 respected charter members of the crime family. When asked why they had to go, Casso swelled to his full intellectual prowess and said they were all "creeps." Even more frightening to some of his supporters was Casso's plan to carry out a most bizarre plot when he was free of government watchdogs. He would, he said, invite all the creeps to a party and kill them. There was clear dissent in the ranks, but it was all about money and the lack of new revenues. Casso and Amuso brought no new loot to the mob, instead merely squeezing the various capos and soldiers to bring more tribute to the top. In due course Amuso and Casso went on the lam to avoid arrest, yet Amuso was caught while walking on a street, clearly an indication that some members of the mob may have tipped off the law. In short order authorities also nabbed Casso and the weird reign of terror was over.

Other bosses have shown a bit more circumspection, even while instilling their men with paralyzing terror. When Joel Cacace achieved status as acting boss of the Colombo family he was very properly feared, within the acceptable limits of mob etiquette. He allegedly had two hitmen take out a victim and when they killed the wrong party, he ordered two other hit men to take out the bungling pair. Then, said the authorities, he played it extra safe by having the second set of hit men put to sleep as well. In an apparent affair of the heart, Cacace then married the widow of one of the first two hit men. After they separated, the lady married an ex-policeman who ended up later being murdered, perhaps sort of a morality tale of Mafia romance. All that may have fed considerable gossip in the family, but it merely ascribed more awe for Cacace. He was to most of the boys a peerless leader by new Mafia standards.

The new Mafia is not exactly the version portrayed on television in *The Sopranos*. The wise guys generally have a warm spot for *The Sopranos* but they are prone to point out weaknesses in the show. As one said, "There's not enough fear in the ranks. They ain't afraid of none of their own people. But in real life, there are some guys in charge that you had to be afraid of. [Philadelphia boss] Nicky Scarfo, he'd turn on you in a minute." Clearly, the Soprano family could not survive in the new meaner Mafia.

It takes a discerning discipline to accept the principle of the very tough boss. Wise guys do accept the exercise of fear and force. They employ such tactics themselves and can accept them employed against them. That in part is the internal mystique of the mob. It touches almost everyone, especially the public. Many tourists go to Las Vegas and Atlantic City still expecting to encounter mobsters. It may not be a completely vain hope, despite the new cleaned-up facilities offered by the gambling establishments. Into recent times William F. Roemer Jr., a leading expert on organized crime, especially in Vegas, held that while most casinos were now free of Mafia taint, there were a couple still suspect. Other observers have noted that while the casinos seem to be clean, almost none of the casino operators will even talk about the mob activities, past or possibly present. Still the mob in Vegas now may be little more than mystique.

The public's appetite for that mystique is insatiable. A fatal shooting in December 2003 of one alleged mob guy by another at Rao's, an East Harlem restaurant hot spot and in the past an upscale mob hangout, sparked headlines that the Mafia was back.

Actually the motive was that one mobster had shown "disrespect" for the other at the bar. It has been more than a few years since mobsters per se could not get into Rao's dining room where by contrast such celebrities as film director Martin Scorsese, who today is said to bring fellow film people for a treat there, could. There can be a year's wait for a reservation. But the mob guys frequent the bar, and in this instance the survivor insisted he had shot his victim, a higher-ranking figure in another family, for badmouthing the female singer and then showing him disrespect after telling the victim to be quiet. There was a comic element too, as the shooter said he had not carried a gun in years but had packed one that night because the government had raised the terrorist alert level to orange the previous day. The shooter confessed willingly but was really appealing to the mob to spare him for violating the rules against killing or even striking another wise guy. The resolution in this case, which could have taken months, might have indicated how firmly the mobs are back in control of their members, and whether they can even consider easing up on violators. The matter was settled with a guilty plea and a 15-year sentence. Again the mystique is the thing.

The mobs' growing returning power is fundamentally based on leaders who provide them with chances of making money. Thus, within the Lucchese family, leaders who can reestablish their basic revenues in construction and other rackets and save them from the continuous madness of the Casso-Amuso era are embraced. Members of the Bonanno crime family can accept the tough rule of Joe Massino under which a capo who criticized a capo appointed by Massino ended up with six bullets in him. According to turncoats, Massino said this was as good as criticizing him and thus he deserved to die. Yet the Bonannos boosted their boss, who raised the family to new heights of power and deserved even having the organization named after him, although there was common agreement that the families would retain the names that existed in the early 1960s.

The bosses understand the mystique their followers attribute to them. That is nothing new. The last fabled leader of the Luccheses, Tony Ducks Carollo, thrived on the mystique. In a reality switch on *The Godfather,* a couple from Carollo's old neighborhood came to him for Mafia justice, explaining a Lucchese hood had raped their son. Tony Ducks replied, "You will have justice." The offending hood was snatched and subjected to horrendous tortures for several hours and dismantled piece by piece until he was dead. Tony Ducks then summoned the couple and announced that justice had been done, describing the Mafia's traditional use of a broomstick in meting out the proper punishment. Whereupon the couple dropped to their knees and kissed Carollo's hand.

Aside from the money and powers of the ordinary crime leader, the mystique of playing god is equally potent. All mafiosi up and down the crime chain look to gather that intoxicating power for themselves. They will use it on their enemies, their victims, their competitors, and those who rise to the top savor the hypnotic sensation. Only the stupid few think the feeling will last forever. In recent years most bosses are likely to last six or seven years. For all his notoriety John Gotti lasted only seven years on top. But the thirst for money and the lure of power is overwhelming as they circle the flame. It explains why the Mafia keeps coming back, advertised or unadvertised.

There is an additional fillip on how leaders in the resurrected Mafia win power. They have to become hands-on killers, something the soldiers not only respect but praise. Even a turncoat who would later testify against Massino described with considerable awe the murder of three crime family rivals. Massino had four shooters with him, and they fled when the shooting stopped. Still standing there alone with blood all about was Massino. He was cool as could be and when a cleanup crew arrived to sanitize the place, they informed Massino it couldn't be done. Massino considered the situation only briefly and then decided to burn down the place. It wasn't long after this that the Bonannos started calling their outfit the Massino family, which the other families hated, but they were not about to challenge one who was perceived to be a rising stone killer.

In short, Massino's outfit remained the model of the successful Mafia mob. The other families continued to wallow in the chaos of prosecutions. Oddly, as some families crashed in modest or massive declines in the 1990s, it grew more difficult for prosecutors and serious researchers to develop accurate measures of the Mafia's remaining muscle. While there was a parade of turncoats, a strong cultural code remained in effect influencing people to tell investigators nothing. This code even applied to a wise guy's family relationships, ages, and so on. "Mafia juniors" were schooled to lie about their age when pinched. Thus a 15- or 16-year-old would tearfully claim to be 12 or 13 in hope of drawing a lighter charge or even getting booted out of the station house. A half century later the same offenders would muddy their age the other way, again looking for lighter treatment and in some cases being able to draw retirement pensions while doing time.

Deaths have also become harder to track as many aged mobsters simply slip through the cracks or are buried under obscure family surnames unknown to authorities. Such was the case of the notorious Johnny Dio who went to prison in 1973 and later died in a Pennsylvania hospital, where authorities had moved him. Dio's death drew no media attention for a time,

even though a paid death notice appeared in a New York paper. It was as if the name Dioguardi had meant nothing to younger newspaper hands.

There is no complete record kept of the demise of wise guys, and families feel no obligation to inform the public. Even the government's records are incomplete as Freedom of Information requests are often denied on the basis that the facts cannot be released until the request is accompanied by proof that the person is dead. Some researchers see this as a ploy by the government as a way to update its files with the public's work. As a result some researchers then accept the statements of dubious Internet sources whose attitude has been described as: "You want a date, we'll give you a date." In short, a Mafia researcher's lot is not a happy one.

Introduction

Had this book appeared a few years earlier, the introduction would have focused on the question of whether or not there really was a "Mafia." In previous decades there had been a multi-pronged drive to deny the existence not only of the Mafia, but also, in some cases, of organized crime. Italian-American groups denied the existence of the Mafia. J. Edgar Hoover and many other law officials did the same, and so did a number of scholars. Naturally, the mafiosi agreed with them. But by late 1986 such arguments had all but ceased. Lawyers for leading mafiosi, brought to trial for being bosses of organized crime, went before juries and conceded that the Mafia did exist and that their clients might even have been members of it.

Ethnic Italian Americans and others have since changed their position. Rather than deny the existence of the Mafia, they argue instead that organized crime is bigger than the Mafia and that by focusing on the Mafia alone, the government and writers on the subject perpetuate anti-Italian sentiment. Certainly bigotry has in the past been a motive in the exposure of the Mafia. There can be little doubt that many politicians since the days of the unsavory New Orleans mayor Joseph A. Shakespeare in the 1890s have used fear of the Mafia and the Camorra in an attempt to undermine the growing economic and political power of Italian Americans.

If this is so, why then a book called *The Mafia Encyclopedia?* Is the glib rationale by Joe Valachi (perhaps spoon-fed to him by his prompters)—"I'm not writing about Italians. I'm writing about mob guys."—really a sufficient response? Of course not. The Mafia has been an integral part of organized crime since the latter's inception in the 1920s. Well then, why not *The Organized Crime Encyclopedia?* Not a "sexy" enough title? That would be a valid observation except for the inescapable truth, contrary to the long-held views of the few sociologist-scholars who have ventured into studying the field, that the Mafia is not withering away in the face of something called "ethnic succession in organized crime." Within syndicated crime, *the ethnic balance has actually shifted more than ever to the Mafia.*

Most crime, save for white-collar crime, springs from ethnic situations, determined almost completely by which ethnics occupy the ghetto, itself generally subdivided into smaller ethnic areas. There is an ethnic succession in the ghetto—and an ethnic succession in crime. And for this reason any study of crime of necessity becomes an ethnic study. Thus the great criminals of 19th-century America were the Irish. Until the 1880s or 1890s almost all the great criminal street gangs were Irish. And the WASP fear of being a crime victim—being mugged, perhaps having one's eyes gouged out, or murdered—was a reflection of the "Irish menace."

In time, as the Irish vacated the worst ghettos, their experience in crime was to be repeated by ethnic newcomers, the Jews and Italians, who, over a period of decades savaged most of the remaining organized Irish gangs and gained dominance. Then, street-crime activities by Jews and Italians dropped when they too vacated many of their ghettos as they gained affluence. Taking their place in the ghettos were the blacks and the Hispanics, and inexorably crime statistics took on a new ethnic flavor, determined by the new have-nots of society.

All such crime, however, has little to do with *organized crime.* That too had an origin in a sort of ethnicity, but it was an aberration of history and place. Why is the United States the *only* industrialized country in the world with a pervasive organized crime problem? It was the confluence of three important forces that allowed organized crime to develop and to achieve its power. In fact, before 1920, organized crime, in its truest sense, did not exist in this country; we had huge, organized gangs of criminals, but crime itself was not organized. It did not embrace the vast interplay of a network of gangs with certain territorial rights but an obligation to handle matters within their territory for other gangs—up to and including murders. Such rules, discussed in detail in the "Mafia" entry, were not restricted, in the new picture, to the Italian criminal gangs. For example, the Jewish Purple Mob in Detroit handled assignments in its area for the Capone Mob, and if it needed certain chores taken care of in Cleveland it could rely on the Jewish mobsters under Moe Dalitz or his Mafia allies in the Mayfield Road Mob.

After 1920, in a stunning development, the ethnic criminals of the day—the Italians and Jews (as it happens, the successors to the Irish in the criminal breeding grounds of the ghettos)—were catapulted to new heights of power, accumulating such great wealth that they were no longer the lackeys of the political bosses and their police puppets but rather the new masters. Indeed, Prohibition created something very new in history—the millionaire criminal, the beneficiary of bootlegging.

By the early 1930s a purge within organized crime had eliminated the less foresighted among the vastly enriched criminal leaders. The two most important criminals of the day—Lucky Luciano, Sicilian-born, and Meyer Lansky, a Polish-born Jew, but both Americans to the core—successfully unified the great criminal gangs into a vast national crime syndicate. It was they who set up a board of directors of organized crime, who apportioned territories and rights and duties among the gangs, and who even set up an enforcement arm that was to become known as Murder, Incorporated.

Still, the end of Prohibition could have spelled the end to organized crime in America but for the Depression and the law (or frequent lack in enforcement thereof). The syndicate had become so rich it could suffer through some lean Depression years as it moved into other rackets. But, perhaps more important, the economic climate itself helped the organization achieve stability. With Repeal the Italians and Jews should have reverted to their prior condition as ethnics about to step out from the ghettos, but the Great Depression froze these groups in place. Only

those talented in the entertainment and sports worlds, and a few through better education, could avoid the realities of a battered economic system. Most youths were trapped in the ghettos and for them the only avenue of escape was crime. Thus organized crime had a steady supply of new recruits from its own ethnic ranks. This allowed organized crime to further sophisticate its own appreciation and understanding of crime.

The wisecracking, loud-dressing, obscene and violent criminals of the 1920s did not disappear but more and more became the followers of more intelligent criminal leaders. Meyer Lansky saw the potentials in new rackets; Luciano had a superb ability to activate such plans. And Frank Costello, Longy Zwillman and others knew how to corrupt a political system to achieve substantial non-interference by the law.

Ironically, some elements of the law itself cooperated, remarkably, without prompting and without bribery. The national syndicate came into being because it had no problem corrupting the criminal justice system on a local or often a statewide basis. And as its tentacles lengthened nationally, it felt little resistance from the federal government. The Federal Bureau of Narcotics had only its one sphere of interest. What was required was the energetic employment of the Federal Bureau of Investigation to battle organized crime, especially in the infancy of the national crime syndicate. However, under the iron-fisted rule of J. Edgar Hoover, the FBI was nowhere to be found, and it would remain in the main outside the fray for some three and a half decades—an astonishing period of malfeasance (or nonfeasance) in leadership with tragic consequences (see J. Edgar Hoover entry).

Thus Prohibition, the Depression and the invisible Mr. Hoover were all midwives in the birth and nurturing of organized crime in America.

Aiding this growth was a lack of scholarly study and hence understanding of organized crime and particularly of the Mafia's role within the syndicate. Yet scholars had good reason to be faint-hearted since their knowledge of organized crime was culled heavily, as one researcher put it, from "unsubstantiated accounts of informers or the ideological preoccupations of law enforcement agencies." Predictably, journalistic accounts often extended into the sensational, with false "facts" introduced for want of fresh angles. Sociologists John F. Galliher and James

A. Cain noted (*American Sociologist,* May 1974): "There are two troublesome aspects to this reliance on such sources, one empirical, the other political. In arriving at conclusions and statements of fact, the journalist or political investigator is not bound by the canons of scientific investigation as is the social scientist." Still other researchers were frightened off by the realization that their findings might smack of reactionary ethnic bias. Thus most scholars gravitated to a line that one hard-bitten journalist refers to disdainfully as the "there-ain't-no-Mafia school of thought no matter how many corpses litter the streets."

Proponents of the theory that the Mafia is but legend or myth had their heyday in the early 1970s. Some used what can only be described as empirical trivia to "prove" that not only was there no American Mafia but also that there never was one in Sicily. It would take another volume to refute all their claims and sort out all their terms, but history has in its own way resolved the problem. It is now impossible—with the wealth of eavesdropping evidence—to deny the existence of an American Mafia and a national commission. The war declared on the Italian Mafia by Pope John Paul II and the onset of trials for hundreds of mafiosi in Italy in 1986 similarly eliminate the basic argument about the existence of the Honored Society in that country, reducing the claims of critics to a matter of semantics.

In many respects, however, the proof is still sketchy. Written records, especially the self-serving memoirs and reminiscences of criminals, must be scrutinized carefully. Errors and deliberate misrepresentations in such reminiscences are to be suspected. Thus the serious student of crime must constantly search for correlating documentation when drawing from such sources—not always an easy task from material proclaimed to be "exclusive revelations." Not surprisingly, also, there is a certain contentiousness among the authors of rival books and in their critical evaluations of each other's works. The problems in documentation and the confusions of fact are apparent in numerous examples.

Indeed, such confusion surrounds probably the most controversial, yet among the most important, crime books published in recent years—*The Last Testament of Lucky Luciano,* written in 1974 by Martin A. Gosch and Richard Hammer, formerly a reporter for the *New York Times.* On December 17, 1974, Nicholas Gage, in a front-page article in the *Times,* questioned the authenticity of the book by citing errors of fact. This creates a serious problem for a crime historian. Is the Luciano testament to be thrown out wholesale or are Gage's and others' criticisms merely limited to specific details, misrepresentations or even lapses of memory by an aging and ill Luciano, or poor research by one or both of the authors? (The claim by many writers of true crime that their subjects had camera-like memories and were never caught in a lie need hardly be accepted at face value. Errors in crime biographies as well as those in books written by law-enforcement officials are probably greater than in any other field.)

Penthouse magazine, which excerpted the Luciano book before publication, made a serious misrepresentation, acknowledged in part by the book's publisher, Little, Brown, that the book was based on tapes made by Luciano. Author Hammer (by the time the book appeared Gosch had died) never claimed there were tapes of Luciano talking but rather that Gosch had taped his notes which Hammer found impossible to read. Hammer was quoted by the *Times* as saying, "Luciano would have had to be out of his mind to sit with a tape recorder. What guy in his position would . . ."

As a counterpoint, Gage wrote: "According to Peter Maas, Frank Costello, Luciano's successor as the top Mafia boss, agreed to such an arrangement shortly before he died in 1973. Mr. Maas, author of 'The Valachi Papers' said Mr. Costello agreed to recount his life on tape and sign verifying documents for a prospective memoir Mr. Maas would write.

"Mr. Costello's death cut short the collaboration and Mr. Maas said he abandoned the project."

In any evaluation of Gage's methodology, it must be noted that if there had been any Luciano tapes, the mob boss would have, as the book indicated, admitted complicity in a number of murders—for which there was no statute of limitations. There is nothing contributed on the record by Gage or Maas that puts the Costello tapes on the same qualitative level.

The question remains: Does the Luciano testament, backed up by basically similar reminiscences by such important Jewish syndicate criminals as Lansky and Doc Stacher, as Hammer put it, "hang" together, even though parts of it were angry, scurrilous, defamatory and self-serving on Luciano's part? The answer comes only after a meticulous search through the crime literature.

A major contradiction between the Luciano testament and *The Valachi Papers* involves the murder of Peter "The Clutching Hand" Morello. While obviously the facts as to "whodunit" are of significance, such contradictions also offer an opportunity for evaluations of sources.

Valachi credits a picturesque gunman he called "Buster from Chicago" as having killed Morello, the top adviser to Joe the Boss Masseria. He knew because Buster told him. (Buster was, according to Valachi, a quaint character who lugged his armaments about in a violin case.) Luciano by contrast says the murder was carried out on his orders by Albert Anastasia and Frank Scalise.

Valachi offered a vivid scene of Buster shooting Morello once, only to have his victim jump up and dance about trying to avoid being hit again. Buster took this as a sporting challenge and backed off, trying to wing Morello as though he was an amusement-park shooting gallery target before he finally polished him off. Obviously, the Buster-Valachi account is "exclusive" and not subject to confirmation. Yet a diligent researcher might well come across the older tale of the jumping murder victim, one that involved an unsuccessful attempt against Joe the Boss himself and was well documented in news accounts of the time.

It is possible Valachi made up the story, or the ubiquitous Buster appropriated the old Masseria tale and simply pulled the gullible Valachi's leg. But the story must be weighed against Luciano's version. First of all, Joe the Boss, Morello, Luciano, Anastasia and Scalise were allied at the time. According to Luciano, his two assassins had no trouble penetrating the protection around Morello's loan shark headquarters. Buster, according to Valachi, was a hit man for the enemy forces of Salvatore Maranzano, and he offers no explanation of how Buster, a rival gunman, simply was able to walk into enemy territory and do his shooting.

Luciano's memoir raises yet another argument, another stumbling block for serious crime scholars. The "Night of the Sicilian Vespers," taken as a standard article of faith for many popular writers, was, according to *The Valachi Papers,* "an intricate painstakingly executed mass execution. . . . On the day Maranzano died, some forty Cosa Nostra leaders allied with him were slain across the country, practically all of them Italian-born oldtimers eliminated by a younger generation making its bid for power."

Apparently the publicizing of the supposed purge originated with Richard "Dixie" Davis, a corrupt underworld lawyer who worked for Dutch Schultz. In 1939 he related in *Collier's* magazine details of the Maranzano killing. Davis's source turned out to be Abe "Bo" Weinberg, a top Schultz gunner. According to Weinberg, Maranzano's murder triggered a nationwide attack on the "oldtimers." In fact, "at the same hour . . . there was about ninety guineas [Italians] knocked off all over the country. That was the time we Americanized the mobs." Yet, in his memoirs, Luciano wonders why no one ever named any of these victims.

Following publication of the Luciano memoirs, a number of studies were made of the Night of the Sicilian Vespers (or what others called "Purge Day"). In *The Business of Crime* (Oxford University Press, 1976), a work funded by grants from the National Endowment for the Humanities and the Kentucky Research Foundation, Humbert S. Nelli reports on a survey made of newspapers issued during September, October and November 1931 in 12 cities—Boston, Philadelphia, Pittsburgh, Baltimore, New Orleans, Cleveland, Detroit, Chicago, Kansas City, Denver, Los Angeles and San Francisco. Evidence was found of only one killing concurrent with the Maranzano murder that could even be remotely connected to him. Nelli himself concluded this murder, in Denver, was actually tied to the Colorado bootleg wars of the period. (According to Virgil Peterson, the respected longtime former head of the Chicago Crime Commission, his organization's records showed only two gangland-type killings in the Chicago area during the month of September, and they were not of top-flight underworld figures and "obviously were unrelated to it [Maranzano's murder] in any way.")

Other researchers in the late 1970s supported the Luciano thesis, pointing out the logistical problems facing such "an intricate, painstakingly executed mass execution." They estimated each murder would have required at least 10 conspirators: hit men, drivers, backup men, spotters, lookouts and even "shovel men" in case of burials. The idea of 40 or 60 or 90 executions being carried out to precision in such a short time frame is mindboggling, especially when underworld hits frequently take days or weeks to set up.

Clearly, Valachi himself knew nothing about the Night of the Sicilian Vespers, and whatever he may have said merely repeated an old refrain made by

Dixie Davis. This hardly dismisses Valachi's revelations as trivial, but makes them, like Luciano's, candidates for scrutiny. Valachi was a low-echelon street soldier, and as Peterson notes in *The Mob* (Greenhill, 1983), "Obviously, his credentials for providing a blueprint of organized crime and its structure throughout America were not overly impressive." In some cases, Peterson further noted, Valachi's Senate subcommittee testimony "was considerably less than forthright."

When other gangster tales are examined, not all of their claims are credible. The revelations made by informer Vincent Teresa in part contradict information from Valachi. Teresa, who served as an aide to New England boss Raymond Patriarca and his underboss Henry Tameleo, certainly had far more knowledge of organized crime than Joe Valachi. As a government informer Teresa gave testimony that resulted in the convictions of scores of mafiosi, and his books, *My Life in the Mafia* and *Vinnie Teresa's Mafia,* written with Thomas Renner, contain mother lodes of information for the crime historian. Confirmability of other facts presents problems.

A federal jury acquitted mob genius Meyer Lansky despite Teresa's testimony against him. Teresa said in *My Life in the Mafia* and later at the trial that he had twice brought money from London gambling junkets, once over $40,000 and the second time over $50,000, and given it to Lansky in Florida. Unfortunately, it turned out that at the time of Teresa's alleged second visit to Lansky—he described Lansky "fingering through" the money—the gangster was actually up in Boston recovering from an operation, a fact confirmed by Lansky's wife, a surgeon, and hospital and hotel records.

Problems develop when Teresa's considerable contributions about the mob's gambling activities are subjected to searches for confirmation. The view expressed in gambling literature is one of doubt and even derision. Gambling expert John Scarne found that Teresa knew "little or nothing about crooked casinos."

In discussing the mob's deal with Papa Doc Duvalier in Haiti, Teresa declares the dictator's cut was "10 percent of all the money bet—not just the profits, but the money bet—and it was to be delivered to him each night by one of his secret policemen." This author failed to find a single gambling authority who gave any credence to such an arrangement. Experts point out that no major gambling casino game offers an edge of 10 percent, and that paying off bribes at 10 percent of the money bet becomes a mathematical impossibility.

Similarly professionals did not take seriously Teresa's account of some of the fixes he said took place at foreign casinos under mob dominance.

Of one on Antigua Teresa stated: "Everything at the casino was in the bag. Card sharks, dice manipulators, all kinds of crooks worked for [mob boss] Charlie the Blade. They had women dealers handling the Twenty-One card games with marked cards; switchmen who moved mercury-loaded dice in and out of the game to control it."

Gambling expert John Scarne pointed out, "Mercury-load dice . . . don't work . . . and . . . casinos all over the world use .750-inch transparent dice." Mercury loads can only be used, if inefficiently, with opaque dice. No high roller, and certainly not a losing one, would play in a casino using anything but transparent dice, which are infinitely harder to fix.

Confirmation becomes crucial when dealing with possible whitewashes of the protagonist in crime "confessions." If skepticism should characterize the approach to Luciano's memoirs, it is equally important in evaluating the content of *A Man of Honor,* the autobiography of crime family boss Joe Bonanno, a source relied upon by the federal government in the mid-1980s to make its case in the so-called Commission Trial of a number of New York crime-family bosses. The Bonanno book is remarkable in its omissions. There is, for instance, no acknowledgement of Bonanno's longtime underboss, Carmine Galante.

How reliably can a researcher trust Bonanno's descriptions of machinations within the national commission? Factual confirmation of his narrative of the dethroning of Frank Costello and the assassination of Albert Anastasia is not forthcoming. In Bonanno's account he is the self-proclaimed hero, author of what he termed "Pax Bonanno"—which kept underworld peace for more than two years. The Pax began with the attempted assassination of Frank Costello in 1955 at the instigation of Vito Genovese. Enraged by this, Anastasia prepared to have his crime family make war on Genovese. Instead, Bonanno claimed, he himself rushed into the breach, warning Anastasia, "If war breaks out, there'll be no winners. We're all going to lose." Bonanno assures his readers he thus brought about peace and "Albert and Vito kissed each other on the cheek."

In August 1956 Bonanno's son, Salvatore (Bill), married Rosalie Profaci, daughter of New York don Joe Profaci. Mob bosses from all around the country attended, including Genovese and Anastasia. Bonanno said he saw to it that they were seated at opposite sides of the hall. "But at least they came. They were making an effort to be nice." He complimented himself on the Pax Bonanno he had established after the attempt on Costello's life.

Pax Bonanno broke down in October 1957 when Anastasia was murdered. Bonanno at the time had been on what he described as a sentimental trip to Italy, and he adds, "In fact, if I had not gone off to Italy I doubt whether anyone would have felt bold enough to make an attempt on Albert's life."

It was a sad ending for Pax Bonanno. But was there any Pax Bonanno at all?

The facts do not confirm Bonanno's statements. The two-year-old Pax Bonanno hangs on the attempt on Costello's life, which is dated as 1955 in Bonanno's book. Actually, the attempt occurred in May 1957. The Anastasia assassination took place a little over five months later. Thus there could have been no Pax Bonanno, no Bonanno handwringing, at the time of the Bonanno-Profaci wedding in 1956.

In fairness to Bonanno and his collaborator, the 1955 date for the Costello murder try pops up regularly in many accounts. After they were so led astray, it is easy to see how Pax Bonanno could represent a sort of historical revisionism.

If *A Man of Honor*, like *The Last Testament of Lucky Luciano*, suffers from some inaccuracies, it does not render the book valueless to the serious student of crime. It is enlightening to discover how important clairvoyance can be within the Mafia— that is, the ability of certain crime bosses to be far away, often thousands of miles, even continents away, whenever a major mob hit occurs.

Inaccuracies, errors, misstatements and whitewashes are par for the course in works on crime, whether the story is told by a criminal or a lawman. The reality the crime historian faces is rather akin to a situation faced by Canada Bill Jones, the celebrated 19th-century gambler and conman who was himself a sucker at losing his money at faro.

Marooned in a small Louisiana river town before the Civil War, he diligently hunted up a faro game at which he proceeded to lose consistently. His partner

tried to get him to stop. "The game's crooked," he whispered.

"I know it," Canada Bill replied, "but it's the only one in town."

Mafioso confessions are not the only game in town, but buggings and wiretaps are subject to various interpretations, and stool pigeon accounts tend to reflect what the informer feels investigators want to hear.

The crime historian has to deal with uncertain material, recognize biases, and reach certain conclusions based on the relevancies.

Valid analysis of crime facts is seldom possible in quickie interpretations and with only partial knowledge. Information and facts are to be culled from material that "hangs together." In the case of the Luciano book, other sources have since confirmed many of the facts contained therein. Interviews given to three highly respected Israeli journalists by Jewish mobster Doc Stacher and the same writers' biography of Meyer Lansky, who gave them a number of interviews, back up a number of facts in the Luciano book, such as the role of Frank Costello, the mob's chief briber, in seeing to it that Murder, Inc., informer Abe Reles "went out the window."

Fitting together this jigsaw of twists and turns in organized crime and the Mafia makes it possible to understand the deep changes that continue to develop within the syndicate. There has been a marked decrease of Jewish gangsters in the top echelon of the mob—not due to an ethnic purge, but rather to the simple dying off of top Jewish mobsters. In the early 1930s the syndicate may have been more Jewish than Italian; despite individual flare-ups, the combination was highly peaceful, even affectionate.

There is little need to hammer away at what every Mafia entry says about the lack of nepotism on the part of Jewish mobsters. They were empire builders, not dynasty builders. The same in large measure was true about the individual mafioso, as far as nepotism was concerned. But the Mafia's very structure, its organization, automatically engendered a dynasty. Whether we call it the combination, the Mafia or even Cosa Nostra is unimportant. What matters is that by its very nature, with crime families and a system of bosses, underbosses, capos, soldiers and associates, the Mafia became a dynamic organization existing in a sense on its own, independent of its own members—indeed in spite of them.

And as their Jewish compatriots—using the term in a most generic sense—retired or died off, the Mafia was forced to fill the vacuum in order to carry on the more sophisticated aspects of syndicate operations. The mafiosi were ready, having spent several decades learning the ropes. This has led to what may be called Lansky's First Law: Retreat to the background, turn over the high-visibility street activities to others. Let the blacks and Hispanics work the streets, sell the dope, peddle the female flesh. In New York the pimps of Manhattan are virtually all black, but how many blacks *own* the massage parlors? Similarly it is the Mafia that collects "franchise fees" for those ghetto gambling rackets it does not actively run. It is the Mafia that provides the protection for such operations.

Today, "ethnic succession in organized crime" seems the banner of only a small band of confused observers and, of course, the Mafia itself. Mob guys are the first to say they aren't there.

And it does not appear that the Mafia is a dying institution. Many a hoodlum still clamors to become a "made man" or "wise guy." He hangs around the mob, doing their chores and hoping for the big break that will propel him to the top. As former New York chief of detectives Albert Seedman put it, a mob hopeful still labors at "fencing stolen goods for family members with only a small cut for himself, or even dirty work like burying bodies." His goal: being made a hijacker instead of a peddler, a hit man instead of a mere shoveler. And as a reward he might even get a loan-sharking or numbers territory where, as a "made man," he will have no fear of competition.

Not even the worst sort of treachery can sour eager new recruits for Mafia duty. New York hoodlum Tommy DeSimone never gave up hope of making it. He figured he had the credentials, having been involved in major robberies at Kennedy Airport and in handling a number of hits. But he wasn't in; he wasn't a "made man." Then at last he got the good word; he was going to be inducted into the Honored Society.

What he didn't know was that the Gambinos had actually marked him for death, suspecting him of killing one of their members. Tommy DeSimone suspected nothing. He got himself dolled up for the big occasion and got in a car with some of the boys to be driven to the secret rites—in his case, the Mafia-style last rites. Such tales however do not frighten off other Mafia aspirants. As one longtime Mafia-watching cop explained, "Even a simple soldier these days can wind up a millionaire. With those kind of odds, everybody wants in."

Years ago, Meyer Lansky bragged about the syndicate: "We're bigger than U.S. Steel." Apparently little but the players has changed.

In the late 1980s, as well as in almost every previous decade, there were official claims that at last we have organized crime and the Mafia on the run. Yet Thomas Dewey and others in the 1930s claimed they had sounded the death knell of organized crime with massive convictions. Indeed Dewey probably achieved the most impressive record in conviction of top mobsters and their political allies. In the 1940s the smashing of Murder, Incorporated was supposed to at last destroy organized crime. In the 1950s the Kefauver investigation triggered many more convictions and deportations of scores of criminals. In the aftermath of the Apalachin Conference and the revelations of Joe Valachi, it was the same story. The mobs would soon be crippled beyond repair.

In the 1980s there were mass convictions of Mafia bosses. However, there has been no important motion to adjourn by any of the crime families. While officials say that if we maintain "a full court press," the Mafia will be gone within a decade.

Other observers are less sanguine. There is the very real possibility that prosecution of top mafiosi will result in a form of social Darwinism. forcing the mobs to bring newer and better leaders to the fore, those who can develop immunity to detection.

The Mafia in various forms has existed in America for at least a century. When an institution becomes as rich and powerful as the Mafia, it is hard to believe that mere harassment of the leadership will destroy it. In the late 1980s most of the bosses of the New York families were either convicted or facing likely conviction and long prison sentences. A real crisis in the Mafia was building there and around the country. By the 1990s the crisis reached the point where no one wanted to seize the mantle of leadership—at least it was so theorized by prosecutors. The reality was, however, that as the old mob leaders disappeared to assassination or law enforcement crackdowns, replacements were always at the ready. Typical of the crisis was the situation in Chicago where the Outfit was reeling after the wipeout of the top bosses on charges of murder, conspiracy and the looting of Las Vegas casinos.

Forced to do as he had often done before, Tony Accardo emerged from semi-retirement to bring order to the mob. A meeting of the top capos was called for Accardo to anoint a new day-to-day boss. Through inside informers, the FBI learned the details of the meeting. Accardo reminded the capos that since the formation of the Outfit in the 1920s by Johnny Torrio and Al Capone, every boss had either fallen to the gun or ended up in prison. There had been only one exception—Accardo himself. Now he had a man able and willing to take charge. Under the circumstances, Accardo said, "we got to count this guy as one hell of a man. We got to give him every fuckin' thing we got. . . . So I want every one of you to pledge to Joe Ferriola that you will work your ass off for him and that you will keep him as protected as you can."

Ferriola rose and took charge, announcing the only item on his agenda for the meeting—deciding the fate of Tony Spilotro. The mob held Spilotro, their enforcer in Las Vegas, responsible for the collapse of the Outfit's dominant status there. Ferriola announced Spilotro would be hit, the standard punishment for such failure. The new boss had exercised his first godlike moment. It is often said that the only thing that counts in the Mafia is money, but the right to play god and pass death sentences on other men is one of the most tantalizing elements of Mafia power.

Ferriola lasted less than two years, expiring of a heart condition while under the care of the famed Dr. Michael DeBakey. Ferriola may have known of his ill health when he accepted the position of boss. If so, he had little to lose and much to gain. The boss always reaped millions in tribute from his mobsters, but more important Ferriola gained the ultimate perk of being the top man, the right to decide who lived and who died.

The combination of money and power explains why, despite the risk of death or imprisonment, someone is always ready to step into the breach. In reality, the candidates are prepared to kill to make it to the top. The fact is the average Mafia godfather maintains power for six to eight years. Al Capone fell into that category, as did Lucky Luciano, Albert Anastasia, Carmine Galante and John Gotti. Many others had even shorter reigns. Some of the brighter ones lasted much longer, such as the brilliant Carlo Gambino, the tough Tony Accardo and the careful and devious Chin Gigante. When Gigante went to prison, he tapped Quiet Dom Cirillo as his successor. Inside sources remarked that Cirillo became the top guy reluc-

tantly. More likely, he grabbed the power with both hands, or it grew on him in any case.

Of the above only Gambino and Accardo died in bed. The rest went to prison or perished under their opponents' guns. As Accardo put it, the average top guy these days is "lookin' at a few good years and then the rest of his life in prison."

What is the main impetus for the embrace of power by top mobsters or their chief aides? They would all tell you it is just the money and that the killings are "strictly business." The last point is debatable, as monotonously attested to by mobsters' habitual acts of violence meant to demonstrate their own omnipotence over life and death, committed often for the most trivial of reasons. Little Nicky Scarfo, onetime boss of the Philadelphia family, ordered hits willy-nilly to satisfy his blood lust. Often his victims had done little else than to show, in Scarfo's eyes, a secret disrespect to Little Nicky. John Gotti revealed on tape similar reasons for why a certain mobster had to die: "You know why he's dying?" he told an aide. "He's going to die because he refused to come in when I called."

More damning on the Gotti tapes were his statements about what was necessary to get a hit done: "You go to the Boss, and your Boss kills him. He kills 'em. He okays it. Says it's all right, good." Clearly, Gotti relished the power over life and death. Not surprisingly his longtime role model for the operations of a boss was the violent Albert Anastasia, the "Lord High Executioner" of the infamous Murder, Inc., which had been active in the 1930s and 1940s.

The true code of the Mafia states that a boss must be willing to oblige his underlings. When Jackie Cerone informed Accardo that Johnny Whales, a hit man with whom Cerone had done many gang killings in the "old days," had started to wig out, Accardo obligingly asked if he wanted Whales killed. Cerone was too fond of Whales to do that but said he would have nothing more to do with Whales. Accardo let it pass, but it was clear the offer was there if Cerone ever wanted it. He apparently never did, and Whales eventually went off the deep end and disappeared. However, one should not perceive Cerone as a gentle soul. Details of some of his authenticated killings demonstrated a savage blood lust. Pathological violence from which final death is a blessed release often typifies Mafia killings. Enforcer Tony Spilotro enjoyed torturing victims by squeezing their heads in a vise until an eye popped out. When Spilotro himself was summoned to his own execution, his killers batted him unconscious at a prepared grave and then covered him up for the final blackness while he was still alive.

Mob killers surrender themselves to both the need and joy of killing. After completing his first contract Sammy "the Bull" Gravano reflected in *Underboss*: ". . . I felt a surge of power. I realized that I had taken a human life, that I had the power over life and death. I was a predator. I was an animal. I was Cosa Nostra."

The feeling of power is common to the cold-blooded "stone killers" of the Mafia. Roy DeMeo, the stone killer and body dissembler for the Gambinos, murdered at least 37 people and perhaps many times that. He believed a similar philosophy, here repeated almost certainly word for word by one of his apt "disciples": "No one understands what it's like to kill. The power you possess when you kill someone, it's like being God. Do I want this guy to continue living, or should I kill him? No one can understand it unless you do it."

When the boss orders a hit, it reflects the total power of the Mafia, a power to be celebrated for the ease and matter-of-factness with which it can be executed. Carlo Gambino had but to arch an eyebrow and a killing would be done. Sam Giancana, the Chicago boss, had what was called "the look." He could be with several of his men and the potential victim, and say nothing, merely give the look, and his men knew what to do.

Killing is part of what mobsters call "the life." Sonny Black, who plotted and killed his way to the position of acting boss of the Bonanno family, told undercover FBI agent "Donnie Brasco": "Every day is a fucking struggle, because you don't know who's looking to knock you off, especially when you become a captain or boss. Every day somebody's looking to dispose of you and take your position. You always got to be on your toes. Every fucking day is a scam to keep your power and position."

That too is the romance—for want of a better word—of Mafia life.

From the 1980s to the 1990s law enforcement authorities led a string of successful prosecutions. A key figure, New York mayor Rudy Giuliani, predicted that in time the crime families would be reduced to little more than street gangs. Clearly, the prosecutions left many of the crime families in various levels of dis-

array. Certainly that was true of the Gambino family, which after the disastrous Gotti era saw its wise guy membership drop from about 250 or 300 to a mere 150. (On a bottom-line basis, John Gotti may have been the worst Gambino family leader of all.)

It seemed only a matter of time before further degeneration set in. The mainstream press bought wholeheartedly into the theory. Thus it was something of a shock when John Gotti Jr. was arrested in January 1998 along with 39 others in what was alleged to be a massive strike at the Gambino family.

The *New York Times* (January 22, 1998) observed, "Although prosecutors portrayed the indictments as a triumphant blow to organized crime, the allegations also testified to the resiliency of the Mafia, which despite repeated indictments has been able to continue its hold on lucrative ventures and enter into new ones, like telecommunications fraud." Even the triumphant Mary Jo White, the U.S. attorney for Manhattan, noted, "What this case graphically shows is the power, profit and reach of the Gambino crime family in business and industries, both legitimate and illegitimate, throughout the metropolitan New York area."

The families have lost considerable clout and power in the fish and construction industries and to a lesser but growing extent in trash hauling and the garment industry, but the Gambinos and the other families are still around. Officials concede that even as the Mafia loses ground in some areas, it gains ground in others. Certain mainstays, such as loan-sharking, chop-shop rings and gambling, are still there. A new crop of mobsters, however, is focusing on lucrative white-collar crimes, such as stock swindles, the sale of fake prepaid telephone cards, and medical-insurance frauds. Said Lewis D. Schiliro, the head of the FBI's New York office, "The families are in transition, trying to figure out how to redirect their criminal activities in a new environment."

If John Gotti bossed the Gambinos down in power, other families have thrived. Typical was the Bonanno family, which had fallen into disrepute among mafiosi. They were deeply involved in drug trafficking and fought numerous brutal turf wars among themselves for internal rackets and spots in the power structure. Yet under boss Joseph Massino, the Bonannos staged a stunning resurgence with 100 active members and no top leaders in prison or even under indictment. By 1998 they had gained so much

Ia

strength that they were close to rivaling the Gambinos as the second most powerful crime group in the East. Law-enforcement agents shifted major attention to the Bonannos. Clearly the family's growing strength also indicated organized crime's resilience.

Undoubtedly the law will continue to harass the mobs and imprison deserving criminals, and RICO (the 1970 Racketeer Influenced and Corrupt Organizations Acts) will continue to offer the way to big-time sentences. On another level, the effect of confiscation of mob profits may be rather underwhelming. As wise guys themselves note, there are more riches where the previous came from.

It is doubtful that the war on the Mafia can simply be proclaimed won. The profit motive remains, and so do the romantic attractions of "the life." The Mafia's kill-or-be-killed ways continue to draw mobsters. Admittedly, each mobster believes he is Mr. Smart, the guy who will never be tripped up. And the blood lust is a hard temptation to resist.

After Sammy the Bull made his first hit he met with Junior Persico, soon to be anointed the head of the Colombo family. Persico was clearly impressed by how Gravano had handled the job. Later an intermediary informed Gravano that Persico thought he had done a fine piece of work and that "Junior loves you. He's real proud of you." One can only imagine Sammy's exhilaration. Certainly Persico was satisfied by the blood lust involved.

Some mafiosi are prepared to abide by the code of the life even unto death. After "Donnie Brasco" was revealed as an overwhelmingly effective undercover agent and Sonny Black was exposed as one of his chief victims, it was obvious to all that Sonny would have to die. He had introduced Brasco to such top bosses as Santo Trafficante in Tampa and Frank Balistrieri in Milwaukee. He had betrayed the mob, even if unwittingly. There was no way out for Black other than flipping and joining the witness protection program after aiding in the prosecution of other top mafiosi. Black refused to do this. When summoned, he went to a mob meeting, hardly ignorant about his ultimate fate. He was of course executed. But that again was "the life," the only life Sonny Black knew or understood.

The same can be said of John Gotti, doing life in 23-hours-a-day solitary lockup in one of the government's toughest prisons. He tries to direct the Gambinos' affairs, with uncertain results. He remains doomed to his cell, doing, as age permits, his 1,000 push-ups a day. That now is his life, one that he can only escape by flipping, which hardly any observer thinks will happen. Gotti remains defiant, his motto still "Cosa Nostra forever." He is consumed by his chosen Cosa Nostra life. If Gotti ever thought he had godlike powers, he faces the fact, whether he grasps the idea or not, that the life controls him. He is a prisoner not only of the federal government, but of "the life."

John Gotti's personal fate is of minor moment (although it reportedly cost $75 million to convict him). The important question remains whether or not the life will continue to be the driving force of crime in America. So far the mobs remain and the players abound. The lure of huge profits and the exercise of unlimited power may be incentives unrivaled by any other motivations or fears.

A

ACCARDO, Anthony Joseph (1906–1992): Chicago mob leader

Although known to Chicago crime intimates as Tony, to lesser lieutenants as "Mr. Accardo," to syndicate supporters as having "more brains before breakfast than Al Capone had all day," Anthony Joseph Accardo slugged his way to syndicate power as "Joe Batters."

That Accardo rose to such heights is rather amazing considering his comparatively humble mob beginning. A young tough, Accardo served as an enforcer for Capone and established an early notoriety for his proficient use of the baseball bat. But, brainy and adroit, he knew how to balance brute force and velvet glove, a talent not overlooked by Capone.

When Big Al went to jail for a brief time in 1929, he named a triumvirate to rule in his place: Jake Guzik in charge of administration, Frank Nitti in operations, and Accardo as head of enforcement. Under Accardo were such brutal worthies as Machine Gun Jack McGurn, Tough Tony Capezio, Sam "Golf Bag" Hunt, Screwy John Moore, Red Forsyth and Jimmy Belcastro, the King of the Bombers. Accardo's stature grew when Capone was put away for good. In 1943, when Nitti committed suicide rather than go to prison, Accardo became the acknowledged head of the mob.

Over the years, Accardo shared power with his good friend Paul Ricca, one of the few underworld

Tony Accardo, nicknamed Joe Batters for his proficient use of a baseball bat in the service of Al Capone, became the most enduring boss of the Chicago outfit.

relationships that never resulted in any doublecrosses. Accardo was a firm believer in power sharing at the top, but strict obedience in the lower ranks.

Accardo and Ricca, a brilliant leader until his last senile years, extended Chicago's influence far beyond the Windy City, something Capone showed no inclination to do. It was Accardo as much as any one man who proclaimed Chicago's influence as far west and south of the city as California, Arizona, Colorado, Texas and Nevada, among other sunny sites. And the Eastern mobs made no protest, asking only that they also be granted rights in Nevada and California. In exchange Chicago got juicy rewards in Florida, Cuba and the Bahamas.

Some writers have tended to downplay Chicago's importance, noting that it frequently does not have membership on the national commission that supposedly runs organized crime. What they fail to understand is that there are *two* national crime syndicates in the United States—Chicago and the rest. This influence was the achievement of Accardo and Ricca and has been extended by their successors, Sam Giancana and, especially, Joey Aiuppa.

Never one to concern himself too much with day-to-day matters, Accardo gladly brought a Ricca favorite, Sam Giancana, into a leadership role in the 1940s. Whenever he wished, Accardo stepped back in to take control. Eventually, Giancana became too hot and Accardo and Ricca had to return to active leadership in the mid-1960s. With Ricca's death in 1972, Accardo brought in an old gunman buddy, Joe Aiuppa, boss of the Cicero rackets, to run things, thus allowing Accardo a life of leisure in his 22-room mansion with its indoor pool, two bowling alleys, pipe organ and gold-plated bathroom fixtures (described as being worth a half a million dollars).

It would be wrong, however, to believe that his aloof ministering meant Accardo ever lost any of his hardness. Never forgetting his enforcer past, Accardo presided over the Chicago Outfit's relentless reign of brutality.

The fate of one William "Action" Jackson, a collector for the mob who forgot who he was collecting for, bore the Accardo trademark. Found stripped naked and hanging by his chained feet from a meat hook in a Cicero basement, he had been beaten on the lower body and genitals with Accardo's trusty old weapon, a baseball bat, then carved up with a razor, his eyes burned out with a blowtorch. Following those tortures he was further dissected; he died, the coroner reported, not of his wounds but of shock. Pictures of the body were distributed later in

mob circles as an admonishment against theft within the organization.

When Sam Giancana was assassinated in 1975, it was obvious that the move could only have been made with Accardo's approval, if it were a mob operation. A number of gangsters earnestly informed the press that Accardo was not behind the murder, that the Giancana killing was "a CIA operation all the way" to prevent him from revealing details of the agency's use of the underworld in a bizarre and childish Castro assassination plot.

Accardo, who looked upon the death sentence as a solution to pesky problems, was nonetheless known for his fairness, a characteristic that won him considerable affection from gangsters. Once, Jackie the Lackey Cerone complained to him that an old hit man buddy of his, Johnny Whales, had gone soft in the head and that the "Dagos" in the mob would knock him off. Cerone said he tried to reassure Whales that he had nothing to fear from Italians, that the mob had a great many "Jews and Pollacks also. I told him this but he was still afraid." Accardo, a firm believer in the old Capone tenet of multi-ethnic membership, was sympathetic and asked Cerone if he wanted Whales killed. Cerone said he liked Whales too much for that but assured Accardo he would have no more to do with Whales in the future. Accardo was said to have magnanimously accepted this view.

Noted as an excellent pool player, Accardo was once victimized in a $1,000 game by a pool hustler who had wedged up the table and then adjusted his technique accordingly to win the match. When the trick was spotted, Accardo accorded all the blame to himself. "Let the bum go," he ordered. "He cheated me fair and square."

By the late 1970s, Accardo had returned to a multi-millionaire semi-retirement in which Joey Aiuppa was said to be joining in with Cerone to take over active leadership. However, there was no doubt that if the circumstances warranted, old Joe Batters would come back.

And he did return when the Outfit's Las Vegas empire fell apart and the top leadership went to prison. Accardo proceeded to juggle the remaining leaders' roles and gave mobsters new assignments as he saw fit, with never a word of objection from the admiring ranks. He continued to administer control right up till his death of natural causes in 1992.

He never served a night in jail.

ACE of Diamonds: Mafioso "bad luck" card

Newspaper photos captured the macabre scene of Joe the Boss Masseria slumped over the table, six bullet holes in his body streaming blood onto the white tablecloth—and the ace of diamonds dangling from his right hand. Assassinated in April 1931 in a Coney Island, Brooklyn, restaurant, he had been playing cards with his top aide, Lucky Luciano, who had set him up for death. Luciano excused himself from the table and went to the men's room. In the ensuing moments, four armed gunmen rushed in and shot Masseria to death. Since that time the ace of diamonds has been dubbed the Mafia's hard-luck card.

The legend is strictly manufactured. As newsman Leonard Katz revealed in his book, *Uncle Frank, The Biography of Frank Costello,* "Irving Lieberman, a veteran reporter for the *New York Post,* covered the murder of Joe the Boss and was at the scene. An imaginative reporter from a rival newspaper, he said, decided to make the story even better. He surveyed things and then picked up the ace of diamonds from the floor and stuck it in Joe's hand. He reported the extra-added ingredient to his newspaper."

ADONIS, Joe (1902–1972): Syndicate leader

One of the most powerful members of the national crime syndicate, Joe Adonis had been a longtime associate of such stalwart racket bosses as Lucky Luciano, Frank Costello and Meyer Lansky. He headed up the Broadway Mob, the most powerful Prohibition bootleg gang in Manhattan.

While Adonis always claimed to have been born in the United States, he was, as the law finally determined in deportation hearings, actually born in Montemarano, Italy, on November 22, 1902. He had entered the country illegally and taken the name of Adonis (his real name was Doto) to pay himself proper homage for what he regarded as his handsome looks.

Like many of his youthful associates—Luciano, Vito Genovese and Albert Anastasia—he soared up the criminal ladder of success during the get-rich-quick days of Prohibition. By the late 1920s Adonis had moved the center of his operations to Brooklyn. He became the virtual boss of much of that borough's criminal activities, taking over the Frankie Yale interests after that leading gangster was assassinated in 1928. The key to Adonis's success appears to have been his loyalty and modest ambitions. He was one of the gunners who killed Joe the Boss Masseria, the murder that put Luciano only one killing away from becoming the foremost Italian-American syndicate leader in the nation.

In Brooklyn, Adonis moved on two fronts. He was a trusted member of the board of the syndicate, settling disputes between various criminal factions and issuing murder contracts. While Albert Anastasia, Lord High Executioner of Murder, Inc., carried out tasks assigned by Louis Lepke, Adonis was also Anastasia's superior and kept a tight rein on him. Otherwise the mad-hatter murder boss could well have run amok, ordering too many hits. Abe Reles, the informer in the Murder, Inc., case, told authorities: "Cross Joey Adonis and you cross the national combination."

While Adonis was active in purely criminal matters, he was also becoming a very influential figure in Brooklyn's political life. A restaurant he owned in downtown Brooklyn, Joe's Italian Kitchen, became a

Joe Adonis, a longtime power in organized crime and sidekick of Lucky Luciano and Meyer Lansky, took "voluntary deportation" to Italy in the aftermath of revelations at the Kefauver hearings. He abandoned his real name, Joseph Doto, for the Adonis moniker in honor of his self-proclaimed good looks.

rendezvous point for the most eminent political figures in Brooklyn—as well as members of the underworld. Among those he courted was a county judge, William O'Dwyer, later district attorney and mayor of New York. Adonis was often seen conferring with O'Dwyer and James J. Moran, a venal assistant, later regarded as O'Dwyer's bagman.

When Luciano was sent away in prison, he left Frank Costello in charge of his own crime family and Adonis in nominal charge of the combination's affairs, but he told Adonis, "Cooperate with Meyer." Meyer was Meyer Lansky, who was to become the guiding genius of the syndicate. Adonis understood both his role and Lansky's and proved smart enough to take orders.

After the end of Prohibition, Adonis extended his interests over waterfront rackets both in Brooklyn and New Jersey and became a power in syndicate gambling enterprises as well. Despite the fact he had moved up to multimillionaire class, Adonis also masterminded a string of jewelry thefts. For a man in his position, it was foolhardy and an activity his bigwig associates viewed with considerable amusement. But Adonis was a thief at heart and happiest when handling an old-fashioned heist.

In 1944 Adonis moved the center of his activities to New Jersey and there presided over the affairs of the syndicate in what was to become a famous mob headquarters, Duke's Restaurant in Cliffside Park. The political and police situation in New Jersey had become far more hospitable than in Brooklyn, and Adonis readily switched from Democratic politics to Republican, the dominant power in Jersey.

Despite a long and dishonorable career in crime, Adonis avoided prison until 1951 when, in the aftermath of the Kefauver hearings, so much heat was generated that he was forced to plead guilty to violation of state gambling laws. He was hit with a two-year sentence. In 1956, pressed hard by the federal government and facing perjury charges, Adonis agreed to accept a deportation order once his foreign birth was established. Adonis lived out his days in lavish comfort in exile in Milan. Occasionally he met with Luciano who was in exile in Naples, but relationships between the two men deteriorated badly. Adonis was in far better financial shape than Luciano but pointedly never asked Lucky if there ever was anything he needed. More important, he did not aid Luciano's efforts to prevent Vito Genovese from making a play for preeminence in the Mafia in America.

By the 1960s the two men had more or less fallen out of touch. However, when Luciano died in 1962 Adonis procured permission from Italian authorities to attend a requiem mass for Lucky in Naples. Tears flowed down his cheeks as Adonis presented in final tribute to his old criminal leader: a huge floral wreath with the obligatory mob farewell, "So Long, Pal."

See also BROADWAY MOB; DUKE'S RESTAURANT

AGRON, Evsei (?–1985): Self-proclaimed "godfather" of the Russian Mafia

He was a dreamer, or at least a perverted dreamer. Evsei Agron emerged on the list of suspects as part of what was then an alleged "Russian Mafia" operating in the United States. By the early 1980s Agron was acting big-time in the rackets in the Russian-Jewish section of Brighton Beach in Brooklyn, New York, as well as in other localities around the country with a similar populace. In *Organized Crime in America*, professors Dennis J. Kenney and James O. Finckenauer quote an account by an independent journalist declaring Argon "made his reputation through several years spent in Soviet jails, and claimed to be an experienced killer. . . . [According to one source], Agron was supposedly one of the top people. When he came to this country he must have picked up with some of his old cronies." The independent journalist went on: "Like most real-life mobsters, Agron was a low-life thug. . . . He kept an electric cattle-prod in his car, and specialized in extortion and blackmail. . . . In his prime, he opened up the gasoline racket that would net millions, possibly billions of dollars for the Russians. He made contacts with emigre criminals in Europe."

While many crime experts doubt that the Russian Mafia exists as an organized crime group, there is no doubt that Agron was dreaming big. It was to be an impossible dream. His biggest idea, of course, was the gasoline racket, or more accurately the fuel tax fraud. The lucrative gimmick amounted to an estimated tax loss of more than $1 billion annually, and it cost New Jersey alone about $40 million a year. The plan was simplicity itself. Diesel fuel is taxable as a motor fuel, while home heating oil is not taxed, although it is basically the same product. As a result Agron was selling what was essentially a legal product in an illegal market. Agron had hit on a gold mine, but the dodge invited competition. Pretty soon members of the Gambino crime family were in as partners. The mob had the muscle to control the "no brand" distribution and retail markets. Soon other mafiosi declared in, and Agron had other woes. A group labeled by federal prosecutors as the "Goldberg crime group" under one Boris Goldberg attempted to branch out in a number of illegitimate areas. (The government referred to the outfit as a "crime group," not regarding it as a major organized criminal organization.) In 1991 the government used the RICO statute to name Goldberg as the head of a racketeering enterprise, engaging in drug trafficking, armed robbery, extortion, illegal deals with weapons and attempted murder. There was also a conspiracy charge that the Goldberg group had discussed killing Agron. They tailed him for close to a year, and in January 1984 Agron was shot but did not die. Eight years later Goldberg pleaded guilty to a number of charges including the attempt on Agron's life, but he apparently was not involved in a later hit that sealed Agron's fate. In May 1985 Agron was shot dead by two hit men posing as joggers.

Thus ended Evsei Agron's dream of establishing a grand crime empire. His murder has not been solved. Some believe one of his lieutenants murdered him but others suspect one of any of the five Mafia families looking to eliminate him from any share of the great fraud he had originated.

See also RUSSIAN MAFIA

AIELLO, Joseph (1891–1930): Chicago Mafia leader and Capone foe

Just as Lucky Luciano wiped out the Mustache Pete influences in New York to create a new Mafia along multiethnic syndicate lines, Al Capone did the same in Chicago, wiping out the Aiello family—especially Joe Aiello, often described as the Mafia boss of the city. Aiello was a Castellammarese and sided with Salvatore Maranzano in the great New York Mafia War against the then-dominant forces of Joe the Boss Masseria. Aiello dutifully forwarded the Maranzano forces $5,000 a week for the war chest. According to informer Joe Valachi, this meant Capone was supporting Masseria and what happened to Aiello was determined by the Chicago gang wars.

As Aiello and Capone jockeyed for supremacy Aiello and his brothers, Dominick, Antonio and Andrew, fought hard and allied themselves with other Capone enemies, especially the North Side

Mob, the O'Banions, then under the control of Bugs Moran. Aiello carried the murder campaign against Capone to intriguing heights, once trying to persuade the chef of a favorite Capone restaurant, Diamond Joe Esposito's Bella Napoli Cafe, to put prussic acid in Capone's minestrone soup. Although the fee escalated from $10,000 to $35,000, the chef shrewdly figured that if the fatal recipe did the job, he would not live long enough to enjoy his money. He reported the poison plot to Big Al. The frustrated Aiello promptly spread the word that $50,000 awaited anyone who killed Capone.

These hostile efforts proved annoying to Capone and stoked his own determination that Aiello get his "real good."

One October evening Aiello stepped outside his expensive West Side apartment building, on North Kolmar Avenue, right into the cross fire of a sawed-off shotgun and two Thompson submachine guns. They dug 59 slugs weighing well over a pound out of the ventilated corpse.

See also CAMPAGNA, LOUIS "LITTLE NEW YORK"

AIUPPA, Joseph John (1907–1997): Chicago Outfit leader

Although he never got beyond the third grade in school, Joe Aiuppa had plenty of criminal smarts as well as old-style Capone muscle. These traits propelled him to the top position in the Chicago Outfit, where he bowed to no one except the semi-retired Tony Accardo. Operating out of Cicero, always the Chicago mob's stronghold, he started out as a gunner for the Capones and so was questioned in several murder investigations.

Aiuppa may have used raw power to maintain the mob's rackets in Cicero but, at the same time, he mastered the big fix. He was once thought to be paying $500 a month to have secret copies of intelligence reports, from the Chicago Crime Commission to the sheriff's office, sent to him. And he was once recorded in a conversation with a "wired" police officer as saying he could obtain secret grand jury testimony. The extent of Aiuppa's fixing ability was further highlighted in another taped conversation, when an underworld aide informed the same officer that Aiuppa had learned the lawman had been wired for sound.

Aiuppa bore two nicknames. One was "Ha Ha" because he was a dour-looking, menacing mobster who seldom cracked a smile. The other was

"Mourning Doves" since one of his few convictions was three months in a federal prison for illegally possessing and transporting more than 500 mourning doves from Kansas to Chicago. In the underworld he developed a reputation for hunting rabbits and ducks with a shotgun.

When Sam Giancana was removed from active control of the syndicate in the mid-1960s, leadership reverted to the semi-retired leaders, Paul Ricca and Tony Accardo, who in time brought in Aiuppa to run the mob. After Ricca's death, Aiuppa was in active control, with Accardo as an adviser. Aiuppa joined Accardo in semi-retirement and adopted a similar adviser role with the new active leader in Chicago, Jackie the Lackey Cerone.

If the murder of Sam Giancana was a mob job and not a CIA caper as some in the underworld insist, it is obvious it had to have been okayed by Aiuppa—as was the steady elimination of Giancana supporters both before and after the murder. According to an FBI theory, Aiuppa and Accardo were angered at Giancana's refusal to share the proceeds from gambling ship operations he had set up in Mexico using mob money.

After Giancana's closest mob associate, Johnny Roselli, was murdered in Florida, underworld informer Jimmy "the Weasel" Fratianno had a conversation with Aiuppa. The boss said with exaggerated casualness, "By the way, do you remember that guy, what the fuck's his name, you know, the guy they found in a barrel in Florida?"

Fratianno, who, as Aiuppa knew, had been very close to Roselli, was very casual as well, suspecting that Aiuppa would have him killed on the spot if he said anything favorable about Roselli.

The incident emphasized a point made often in the underworld: If Joey Aiuppa considers you a has-been, you're as good as dead.

It may well be that is what happened to Anthony Spilotro in 1986 after Aiuppa was convicted for conspiring to skim money from Las Vegas casinos. Spilotro, long described as figuring in more than 25 execution-style killings, had been since 1971 the Chicago Outfit's representative in Las Vegas and California; the speculation was that Aiuppa felt Spilotro's carelessness had caused his conviction.

Two bludgeoned bodies were found buried in a cornfield near Enos, Indiana. They were those of 48-year-old Tony Spilotro and his 41-year-old brother Michael. They had been beaten to death with heavy blows to their heads, necks and chests. The burial spot was five miles from a farm owned by Joe Aiuppa.

In 1986 Aiuppa was convicted of, among other charges, the multimillion dollar skimming of Las Vegas casinos. He was sentenced to a long prison term from which he did not emerge alive.

ALDERISIO, Felix "Milwaukee Phil" (1912–1971): Mob "bogeyman"

Debt collector and hit man, Felix "Milwaukee Phil" Alderisio was the genuine bogeyman for the Chicago mob. He controlled the prostitution racket in nearby Milwaukee and figured largely in the gambling, loan-sharking and narcotics rackets there.

As a debt collector, Phil was once sent, in tandem with another Chicago torpedo, to the offices of a Colorado lawyer named Sunshine. Sunshine had allegedly mishandled some investments, causing significant monetary losses for Phil's bosses. "We're here to kill you." Phil announced blithely to the petrified attorney.

Sunshine pleaded with his would-be killers, explaining that he had not cheated his and their clients and that it was an honest loss. Milwaukee Phil was contemptuous of such delaying tactics. He said the only way for the lawyer to avoid death was to hand over the dough instantly or the execution would go forward.

Still the lawyer persisted, and for 90 minutes he brought out ledger after ledger to demonstrate his honesty. Even the likes of Milwaukee Phil could be swayed by argument and logic at times. "It's a little irregular," he said, "but just to show you there's no hard feelings, I'll do it. If he [Phil's mob superior] wants to cancel the hit, it's okay with me. I'll get paid anyway."

Then and there a long-distance call was placed and Phil came up with one less-than-lethal offer: If the lawyer would agree to pay back the principal of $68,000 plus interest at the rate of $2,000 a month, he would be permitted to continue breathing.

It was an offer Sunshine could not refuse—and a happy ending all around. As one mob leader put it gleefully, the deal Milwaukee Phil had arranged meant "we'll be collecting from this sucker for the rest of his life."

As a hit man Milwaukee Phil was suspected by authorities to have carried out contracts on 13 or 14 victims. He also has been credited with designing what some journalists labeled the "hitmobile," a car equipped with all the necessities for the commission of efficient homicide. Among the extras with which Alderisio fitted his vehicle were such devices as switches that would turn off front or rear lights to confuse police tailers. A secret compartment in a backrest not only carried an array of lethal weapons but also contained clamps into anchor down rifles, shotguns or handguns for more steady aiming while the car was moving.

Although Phil was arrested 36 times for burglary, gambling, assault and battery and murder, he avoided any major conviction or sentencing until his last arrest in the 1960s. He was convicted of extortion and died in prison in 1971.

When Milwaukee Phil's body was shipped back to suburban Chicago for burial, top mobster Tony Accardo attended the funeral. Accardo always loved how Milwaukee Phil had handled Sunshine and, going to the funeral—a regular Accardo chore as his longtime buddies died off—he whistled as the hearse went by, "You are my sunshine. . . ."

Both Accardo's bodyguard and the FBI agents who tailed him were appalled at such a display of poor taste, but Accardo had no doubt that Milwaukee Phil would have loved the joke.

ALDERMAN, Israel "Ice Pick Willie" See ICE PICK MURDERS

ALEX, Gus (1916–): Chicago mob leader

The myth of the all-Italian Mafia is soon dispelled when one looks at the Chicago mob founded by Al Capone. Its ability to absorb other ethnics started with Capone, who readily took in and trusted everyone, from WASPs and Jews to Poles, blacks and others. Thus Jake "Greasy Thumb" Guzik, a Jew, could rise to what could only be described as the number two position in the outfit; and each of Capone's successors—Nitti, Ricca, Accardo, Giancana—gave Guzik the widest leeway and trust. The same was true of Gus Alex, Guzik's protégé and role successor with the mob. A Greek, Gussie Alex ran the Loop vice rackets for the family for years and worked the liaison between the mob and various supposedly respectable figures in the business and political world. He also has been identified as the man who

handled the Las Vegas skim for the Chicago family. The Swiss government came to recognize him as the man who salted away Chicago money in that Alpine banking haven.

Alex, an avid skier, made annual trips to Switzerland until the mid-1960s, when the Swiss tabbled him as a courier bearing loads of underworld cash and barred him from their country for 10 years. It was clear that the Swiss were being pressured by the U.S. government. However, Alex had his own political artillery. Coming to his aid were Illinois' then senior senator, Republican Everett M. Dirksen, and the state's then senior congressman, Democrat William L. Dawson.

Both informed the Swiss what a swell guy Gussie really was. Though he had often been arrested, he had never been convicted. (Gussie's record included more than two dozen arrests for bribery, assault, manslaughter and kidnapping. He was identified as a suspect in several murders, two victims contributing deathbed statements; three other individuals, who testified that Alex had threatened them with death, were later killed. Alex also appeared before the McClellan Committee and took the Fifth Amendment 39 times. Dirksen had not been quite as forgiving to "Fifth Amendment communists.")

Despite Alex's reluctance to talk about himself, Dirksen and Dawson clearly agreed he had "a good reputation."

Alex's influence with politicians, public officials, members of the judiciary and labor leaders made him extremely valuable to the Chicago Outfit. In fact, as death, retirement, arrest and flight from jurisdiction played hob with much of the Chicago mob's leadership in the 1970s, there was pressure on Alex to take up the reins. Alex begged off, spending more and more time in Florida and insisting he wanted to retire. Instead, he simply kept performing his high-level role. Had Gussie accepted, it would certainly have been rather disconcerting to those writers and professional informers who insist the Mafia is strictly Italian. Perhaps they would have been forced to observe that, after all, it was the Greeks who first settled in Sicily.

Law enforcement officials had long abandoned any hope of putting Alex away. But they finally convicted him of extortion, thanks to the evidence provided by a longtime Outfit member, Lenny Patrick, who wore a wire in hopes of winning a shorter sentence for himself. In 1994 Alex was sentenced to 15 years and eight months with no chance of parole. At 78, it was unlikely that Alex, till then a true teflon mobster, would survive the jail term, which had a special fillip that he had to pay $1,400 a month for the cost to the taxpayers for his prison cell.

ALIBIS and the Mafia

On the last day of his life, October 4, 1951, Willie Moretti granted Albert Anastasia a special favor: He let Anastasia borrow his chauffeur, Harry Shepherd, to drive him to a hospital in Passaic, New Jersey, where Anastasia was to have his back x-rayed. While Anastasia was at the hospital, Moretti, conveniently minus his driver, was lured into Joe's Elbow Room in Cliffside Park by several of Anastasia's gunners. There Willie Moretti was shot to death.

The police most certainly could not blame Anastasia for the murder; he had an iron-clad alibi. Indeed, Anastasia was the kind of careful executioner who always covered his tracks. As a rule of thumb, some experts determined that when Anastasia was absolutely in the clear personally he was almost positively deeply involved.

Like fedoras and fancy cars, airtight alibis are practically synonymous with the Mafia. Al Capone would almost invariably be in Florida taking the sun whenever a particularly noteworthy hit took place in Chicago. He was there when reporter Jake Lingle was murdered, when Frankie Yale was killed in Brooklyn, and when the St. Valentine's Day Massacre occurred. "I get blamed for everything that goes on here," Capone once moaned, having returned to Chicago to face extensive police grilling.

Sometimes Capone did his killings personally when he felt particularly affronted by his victims-to-be, but he, like most bosses, usually farmed out the chores. The murder of Big Jim Colosimo allowed Capone's mentor, Johnny Torrio, to seize control of the Colosimo organization and start syndicating Chicago crime. Both Torrio and Capone were prime suspects—Capone would probably have enjoyed doing the hit—but each presented unassailable alibis for the time of the murder. Frankie Yale imported by Torrio and Capone from New York, actually made the hit.

Perhaps the champion at alibis among the recent-vintage Mafia dons was Joe Bonanno. He seemed to have developed a sort of clairvoyance that got him out of town whenever big doings were about to occur—such as the erasure of another crime boss, an event that more often than not required an exchange of information between New York crime families.

Bonanno's autobiography, *A Man of Honor*, is replete with examples of being away at the right time. When crime family boss Vince Mangano disappeared permanently, Bonanno could do nothing but read about it in the newspapers "at my winter residence in Tucson, Arizona." It is nigh unto impossible to get much farther away from New York City in the continental United States than Tucson. When Albert Anastasia was murdered in a conspiracy that included Vito Genovese, Carlo Gambino, most likely Meyer Lansky, and certainly with Tommy Lucchese's okay, only Frank Costello—who needed Anastasia as a shield—could have been deemed free of motive. Bonanno? He was on an international jaunt that took him to France, Sicily and far-off India.

But sometimes alibis aren't quite good enough. When Joe Profaci's successor, Joe Magliocco, sought to have a number of crime bosses murdered—the general theory is that it was under Bonanno's influence and orders—Bonanno pointed out he was on the move at the time to avoid legal summonses and subpoenas. The national commission did not buy that line, being all too familiar with Bonanno's "I wasn't around" patter, and moved to strip him of control of his crime family.

Today, some crime experts say, alibis are not considered important by crime big shots. It is generally conceded by the press, public and police that they seldom carry out their own executions. On the rare occasions when they do, usually out of personal pique, care is taken that the victim's corpse is never found, making time and place of the murder obscure and the need for an alibi obsolete.

ALO, Vincent "Jimmy Blue Eyes" (?–2001): Syndicate gangster

Vincent Alo, nicknamed Jimmy Blue Eyes, was a giant among mafiosi, a sort of Paul Bunyan in organized crime. The Mafia is a society of myth builders and above all myth believers. One of the more astonishing myths held among low-level mafiosi (the higher-ups have always known better) is that Alo was the boss over Meyer Lansky, the Jewish criminal mastermind who together with Lucky Luciano set up organized crime in America as we know it today.

Alo was a close, lifelong friend of Lansky's, but his mythical elevation over Lansky is attributable solely to the psyche of the Mafia's lower levels, where it is important to believe that Italians are superior in all matters and always in control. After all, it was the exclusive privilege of Italians to be mafiosi. (These lowly soldiers were convinced accordingly that Lansky could not vote at mob confabs because he was Jewish. In fact Lansky voted from a position of power; his word often carried the force of law. When Luciano in exile in Italy once thought of allowing a motion picture of his life to be made, Mafia couriers brought word to forget the project. Their clincher: "The Little Man [Lansky] says so.")

Some of the most famous informers to come out of the Mafia also perpetrated the Alo myth, thereby confirming that their disclosures were from a low-level view in organized crime. In *My Life in the Mafia* Vinnie Teresa says of Alo: "He's got one job in life. He's the mob's watchdog. He watches Lansky to make sure he doesn't short shrift the crime bosses." Significantly, Teresa has to add: "He protects Lansky from any mob guy who thinks he can shake Lansky down. Anyone in the mob who had any ideas about muscling Lansky would have Jimmy Blue Eyes on his back in a second." In *The Last Mafioso* Jimmy "the Weasel" Fratianno quotes and believes the word from higher-ups that "Meyer makes no move without clearing it with Jimmy Blue Eyes."

The fact is that Alo always functioned as a liaison between Lansky and the various crime families. Everyone knew that because of Lansky's friendship and trust in Alo, he could be relied on and that he always bore the true word and orders of Lansky.

Because of his warm feelings for Alo, Lansky took care of him, allowed him part ownership in various gambling enterprises in Florida and Las Vegas. After all, they had been youthful allies in crime. In 1930 Meyer's wife Anna gave birth to a son who was born a cripple. Anna Lansky suffered a breakdown over this and blamed her husband for calling down the wrath of God on the child to punish him for his wicked way of life.

It was too much for Lansky and he fled New York for a hideout in Boston where he drank himself into oblivion. Only his buddy Jimmy Blue Eyes was with him, consoling him and helping through his week-long crisis. Finally, Lansky came out of it, and he and Alo drove back to the New York gang wars.

Since that time Alo prospered under Lansky or, as an investigation by Robert M. Morgenthau when he was U.S. attorney for the Southern District of New York demonstrated, Lansky closely guarded the interests of Jimmy Blue Eyes. Morgenthau never did nail Lansky but, in 1970, he had the satisfaction of seeing Alo go to prison for obstructing justice. U.S. attorney Gary Naftalis informed the court: "Alo is one of the most significant organized crime figures in the United States. He is closely associated with Meyer Lansky of Miami, who is at the apex of organized crime."

In the final analysis, the true pecking order in the Lansky-Alo alliance can be seen in the ultimate rating system used by the mob—money. When Lansky died in 1983, his personal net worth was placed at between $300 and $400 million. Alo could barely qualify as a mere millionaire.

ALTERIE, Louis "Two Gun" (1892–1935): Gangster

A prelude to establishing a national crime syndicate in America was the purging from the underworld of unorganizable pathological types. Of course, the Mafia still has its pathological members, and such traits are still highly valuable to the masters of organized crime. But the brass could retain only those brutes who took orders and conformed to orderly criminality. If they did not, they were more dangerous than a loose cannon on the battlefield.

The Dion O'Banion Gang, which dominated Chicago's North Side during the early Prohibition years, were considered the zanies of the underworld. (Deanie himself may be described as a charming psychopath, as could many of his followers in the mainly Irish gang.) However, even by standard O'Banion measurements, Louis "Two Gun" Alterie was a "bedbug."

Alterie, born Leland Verain, owned a ranch in Colorado, but came east to join up with O'Banion's booze and gambling operations. Wearing two pistols, one on each hip, he boasted of his perfect marksmanship with either left or right hand, often shooting out the lights in saloons to prove his point. Quite naturally the press dubbed him Two Gun Alterie, which pleased him most of the time. However, at times he carried three pieces and was disappointed that he was not generally rechristened as the more-imposing "Three Gun" Alterie.

Alterie reputedly masterminded the hit on a horse guilty of transgressions against the mob. A leading member of the O'Banion Gang, Nails Morton, had been thrown by a horse in a riding mishap in Lincoln Park and kicked to death. Alterie demanded that vengeance be done and he led the gang to the riding stable. The boys kidnapped the horse, led it to the exact spot of Morton's demise and executed it. Alterie was so worked up by the "murder" of good old Nails that he first punched the hapless horse in the snout before filling it with lead.

When Dion O'Banion was murdered by Capone gunmen in 1924, Two Gun Alterie went on an hysterical tear. In a tearful performance at the funeral, Alterie raged to reporters: "I have no idea who killed Deanie, but I would die smiling if only I had a chance to meet the guys who did, any time, any place they mention and I would get at least two or three of them before they got me. If I knew who killed Deanie, I'd shoot it out with the gang of killers before the sun rose in the morning." Asked where in his opinion the shootout should occur, he said Chicago's busiest intersection, Madison and State Streets, at high noon. Mayor William E. Dever countered, "Are we still abiding by the code of the Dark Ages?"

Hymie Weiss, who took over leadership of the O'Banions, tried to get Alterie to tone down, explaining that his ranting was forcing politicians and police to put pressure on the gang's operations on the North Side. Alterie responded with a knowing wink and managed to shut his mouth for an entire week. Then he turned up, swaggering into a Loop nightclub brandishing his two pistols and announcing to gangster and reporters who frequented the joint: "All 12 bullets in these rods have Capone's initials carved on their noses. And if I don't get him, Bugs, Hymie or Schemer will."

Weiss, trying to put on a peaceful front while planning an attack on Capone, was livid. He told Bugs Moran to "move him." Moran went to the cowboy gangster and growled, "You're getting us in bad. You run off at the mouth too much."

Alterie took Moran's words for precisely what they were, an invitation to get out of town. Alterie went back to Colorado and played no further role in the Chicago gang wars. He thus escaped the virtual extinction of the O'Banion Gang, save for Moran, who in the 1930s was reduced to insignificance.

In 1935 Alterie showed up in Chicago for a visit. Was it possible Alterie still lived by his old words? Almost certainly not. But perhaps out of respect for his old days with O'Banion apparently he was bumped off.

Further reading: *Capone* by John Kobler.

AMATUNA, Samuzzo "Samoots" (1898–1925): Chicago mafioso

Samuzzo "Samoots" Amatuna, a prime example of the old-line mafiosi, failed to embrace the concept of organized crime and the so-called American Mafia. Nevertheless, Samoots—colorful, brutal and cunning—for a time held a power base from which he actually challenged Capone's control of crime in Chicago.

Samoots was a professional fiddler and may well have been the first gangster to conceal a weapon in an instrument case, choosing the technique for his attempted murder of a musicians' union business agent. Also a fop, Samoots was the proud owner of a wardrobe that included 200 monogrammed silk shirts. Once, gun in hand, he chased after a Chinese laundry wagon driver who had returned one of his shirts scorched. Samoots was ready to plug the Asian man but evidently was overwhelmed with an uncharacteristic burst of humanity. He spared the man but shot his delivery horse.

For a time Samoots functioned as the chief bodyguard for the notorious Terrible Gennas, a mafioso family that controlled much of Little Italy's homemade moonshine production. As the Genna brothers were exterminated or scattered one by one, Samoots moved up in power. In 1925 he seized control of the huge Chicago chapters of the Unione Siciliane. The organization had been a lawful fraternal group at the turn of the century, but from then on, it came more and more under the control of Mafia criminals. Chicago boasted the largest number of branches of the Unione, whose 40,000 members represented a potent force as well as an organization ripe for looting through various rackets, such as the manipulation of pension funds. For years the Unione had been dominated by Mike Merlo, who used his influence to keep peace among the various criminal forces, but after his death in 1924 the Unione presidency became a hot seat. Bloody Angelo Genna took over as president, only to be murdered in May 1925.

Capone, himself a non-Sicilian and ineligible for membership, sought to put in his consigliere, Tony Lombardo, as president. He made plans for the next election. Samoots didn't see what elections had to do with the matter. Together with two confederates, Eddie Zion and Abe "Bummy" Goldstein, Samoots marched into the Unione's offices and declared himself elected. Capone raged and got even more furious as Samoots proceeded to gouge his booze and other operations.

Old-fashioned mafiosi, in Capone's view, were greed personified. He realized that old Mafia traditions had to be eradicated, a position that eventually brought him closer to Lucky Luciano in New York.

Meanwhile, happily, Samoots had many other enemies. The O'Banion Irish gang of the North Side, still mighty despite the murder of their leader, did not care for Samoots's moves against them. On November 13, 1925, Samoots, planning to go to the opera with his fiancée, Rose Pecorara, stopped off at a Cicero barbershop for a shave. He was reclining in the chair with a towel over his face when two gunmen, reputedly Jim Doherty and Schemer Drucci of the North Siders, stormed in. One of the gunners opened up with four shots and, incredibly, missed with each of them. The startled Samoots catapulted out of the barber's chair and tried to dance around the shots of the second gunner. The second assassin hit Samoots with each of his four shots, and the hit men walked out, their victim bleeding profusely. Samoots was rushed to a hospital and lived long enough to request that he marry his fiancée from his hospital bed. He expired before the ceremony could get started.

Within a short time Samoots's two aides, Zion and Goldstein, were also murdered, and, having preserved democracy, Capone was able to put across his man Lombardo to take charge of the Unione.

Since Samoots's murder was the second barbershop slaying in a very short time, nervous barbers with a gangster clientele ceased the hot towel treatment and positioned their chair to face the shop entrance. The Chicago custom did not make its way to New York, where a little over three decades later Albert Anastasia fell victim in a barber chair ambush.

AMBERG, Louis "Pretty" (1898–1935): Independent racketeer and killer

When Pretty Amberg, often said to be the worst Jewish criminal ever raised in America, departed this world, it was hard to tell who had done the grisly chore. One theory holds that the Lucky Luciano–Meyer Lansky

combination, realizing there was no way Amberg could fit into a syndicate concept of crime, had him "put to sleep" to allow organized crime to function in some organized fashion.

If the mob didn't kill Amberg it was only because someone else may have beaten them to it. Surely *everybody* hated Pretty—with the possible exception of newspaper columnist and short story writer Damon Runyon. In a number of short stories, a thinly disguised Amberg stuffs victims into laundry bags in an ingeniously trussed-up form that causes them to strangle themselves to death. In reality, Louis Amberg is believed to have murdered at least 100 people; yet, as he deposited corpses all over the streets of Brooklyn, he was never so much as hit with a littering violation.

Amberg came to America from Russia with his mother and father, a fruit peddler, and settled in the Brownsville section of Brooklyn. By the age of 10

"Pretty" Amberg, often described as the worst Jewish criminal ever raised in America, was immortalized by Damon Runyon in his short stories as the racketeer who bought a laundry business because he needed bags to stuff all his corpses in.

little Louis was peddling fruit on his own. He had a unique style of selling, going from door-to-door, kicking until someone opened up. With his hands filled with fruits and vegetables, he'd shove them forward and snarl: "Buy." Somehow, after staring into the wells of madness that were little Louis's eyes, people bought.

By the age of 20 Pretty was the terror of Brownsville, not only because he was mean, but also because he was very ugly. In fact, a representative from Ringling Brothers offered him a job with the circus as the missing link. Remarkably, Louis did not kill the man; instead he bragged about the offer.

Pretty Amberg however had no time for show-biz. There was too much money to be made in loan-sharking. Unlike the banks of Brownsville that hesitated to loan money to new immigrants, Pretty and his brother Joe never turned down an applicant. Of course they did charge interest, a mere 20 percent per week, and as Joe counted out the money, Pretty would snarl at the borrower, "I will kill you if you don't pay us back on time." He wasn't kidding.

The Ambergs were so successful that they expanded their loan-sharking activities to Borough Hall in downtown Brooklyn, but Pretty's malicious heart remained in Brownsville. He was the king of Pitkin Avenue where his idea of fun was to stroll into a cafeteria and spit in people's soup. If a diner raised an objection, Pretty would tilt the whole bowl on his lap. Even Buggsy Goldstein, who would soon become one of the more deadly killers in the fledgling Murder, Inc., silently took Pretty's abuse. Famous Murder, Inc., stool pigeon Abe Reles later told the law, "The word was that Pretty was nutty."

Pretty expanded his control of Brownsville to include bootlegging. The speakeasy that did not take Pretty's booze got bombed. Soon Pretty was awash with money, and he became a well-known gorilla-about-town. Waiters vied to tend him since he never tipped less than $100. (We owe the following special intelligence to Damon Runyon, that the first time New York's playboy mayor, Jimmy Walker, saw Pretty at his favorite watering hole, the Central Park Casino, His Honor vowed to stay off booze.)

Amberg further expanded his criminal activities to include laundry services for Brooklyn businesses. Although his charges were steep, he offered businessmen a deal they couldn't refuse—they used his laundry and they stayed in business.

Some dark-humored journalists insisted Pretty got into the laundry racket just so he would have a supply of laundry bags for all his stiffs. It is a fact that laundry bags stuffed with corpses started littering the streets of Brooklyn about this time. One victim turned out to be an Amberg loan shark client who was in arrears for $80. Pretty was picked up on a murder charge, but he laughed it off, stating, "I tip more than that. Why'd I kill a bum for a lousy 80 bucks?"

Actually that was Pretty Amberg for you. His credo was to knock off customers who were behind in their payments for small total sums. That way their demise would cost him very little on his original investment and at the same time serve as a powerful warning to bigger debtors. The police knew all about this but could prove nothing. Pretty had to be let loose.

Pretty projected his domain from other gangsters in the early 1930s. The Depression had hit criminal operations and most crime leaders were looking for more ways to make a buck. Big-time racketeer Owney Madden once told Pretty that he'd never been in Brownsville in his life and suggested he come out and "let you show me the sights." Ever the diplomat, Pretty, who was carving up a steak at the moment, replied, "Tell you what, Owney, if I ever see you in Brownsville, I'll cut your heart out on the spot."

Next, Legs Diamond made noise about moving into the area. Pretty informed him, "We'll be pals, Jack, but if you ever set foot in Brownsville, I'll kill you and your girlfriend and your missus and your whole damn family."

With the end of Prohibition the financial stresses got worse. Dutch Schultz, by then down to little more than a multimillion dollar numbers racket centered in Harlem, told Amberg, "Pretty, I think I'm going to come in as your partner in Brooklyn."

"Arthur," Pretty said, "why don't you put a gun in your mouth and see how many times you can pull the trigger."

Pithy comments were not enough to put off a tough like Schultz. In 1935 he put a couple of his boys, Benny Holinsky and Frank Dolak, in a new loan office in Borough Hall, just a block away from the Amberg operation. Within 24 hours the two Schultz men were bullet-riddled corpses.

The Schultz-Amberg war broke out in earnest, and the next victim was Joey Amberg, killed in an ambush. Later, in October 1935, both Pretty Amberg and Schultz died. Schultz's execution had been ordered by the Luciano-Lansky crime syndicate. It may well be that the boys also had Amberg put out of the way. However, there is a quainter story told by some observers. According to this version, each man was responsible for having the other knocked off. Amberg supposedly paid some hit men $25,000 down to murder Schultz with another $25,000 payable on completion of the contract.

In the meantime Amberg was murdered, supposedly on Schultz's orders. His body was pulled from a blazing automobile on a Brooklyn street, charred beyond all recognition. There was wire wrapped around his neck, arms and legs and it took several days for an identification to be made. In the meantime some gunmen blasted Dutch Schultz in a Newark chop house. Poor Schultz may have died never knowing Pretty Amberg had gone to his reward.

Actually, it was never determined whether Amberg's death was a Schultz job or a Luciano-Lansky caper. There was even a third theory that Amberg had been murdered by an angry gang of armed robbers with whom he had joined in a major job and then taken most of the loot for himself.

In Brooklyn, most everyone thought it was about time somebody did something about Pretty Amberg.

AMUSO, Vic See CASSO, GAS PIPE, AND AMUSO, VIC

ANASTASIA, Albert (1903–1957): Executioner and crime family boss

Albert Anastasia, chief executioner of Murder, Inc., found his unbridled brutality could land him leadership of one of the most important Mafia families in the country. But, preoccupied with killing, he was not really a competent godfather, a fact decisively indicated by the efficient and prosperous operation of the family under Anastasia's underboss and successor, Carlo Gambino.

One of nine brothers, Italian-born Anastasia jumped ship in the United States sometime between 1917 and 1920. He became active in Brooklyn's dock operations and rose to a position of authority in the longshoreman's union. It was here that Anastasia first demonstrated his penchant for murder at the slightest provocation, killing a fellow longshore-

man in the early 1920s. Nor was his executioner's behavior pattern altered by a consequent 18-month stay in the death house in Sing Sing. He went free when, at a new trial, the four most important witnesses turned up missing, a situation that proved permanent.

Dead witnesses forever littered Anastasia's trail. In the mid-1950s Anastasia was prosecuted for income tax evasion. The first trial ended in a hung jury. A second trial was scheduled for 1955. Charles Ferri, a Fort Lee, New Jersey, plumbing contractor who had collected $8,700 for work he had performed on Anastasia's home, was expected to be a key witness. In April, about a month before the retrial, Ferri and his wife disappeared from their blood-splattered home in a Miami, Florida, suburb. Some time earlier Vincent Macri, an Anastasia associate, had been found shot to death, his body stuffed in the trunk of a car in the Bronx. A few days after that, Vincent's brother Benedicto was declared missing, his body supposedly dumped in the Passaic River. The erasure of the two Ferris and the two Macris was seen as part of a plot to eliminate all possible witnesses against Anastasia. At Anastasia's trial the crime boss suddenly entered a guilty plea and was sentenced to one year in federal prison. It was unlikely the government would have accepted what amounted to a plea bargain had it still had a full arsenal of witnesses against him.

Considering Anastasia's lifelong devotion to homicide as the solution to any problem it was not surprising that he and Louis "Lepke" Buchalter were installed as the operating heads of the national crime syndicate's enforcement arm, Murder, Inc. Some estimates have it that Murder, Inc., may have taken in a decade of operation a toll of between 400 and 500 victims. Unlike Lepke and many other members of Murder, Inc., Anastasia was never prosecuted for any of the crimes. There was a "perfect case" against him, but the main prosecution witness not surprisingly disappeared.

Anastasia was always a devoted follower of others, primarily Lucky Luciano and Frank Costello. His devotion to Luciano knew no bounds. When in 1930 Luciano finalized plans to take over crime in America by destroying the two old-line Mafia factions headed by Joe the Boss Masseria and Salvatore Maranzano, he outlined his plot to Anastasia. He knew the Mad Hatter, as Anastasia had become known, would enthusiastically kill for him. Anastasia responded by

Albert Anastasia, Lord High Executioner of Murder, Inc., was assassinated in a Manhattan barbershop. Crime experts agreed Anastasia would have approved of the efficiency of the operation, matching that of many of his own kills.

seizing Luciano in a bear hug and kissing him on both cheeks. "Charlie," he said, "I been waiting for this day for at least eight years. You're gonna be on top if I have to kill everybody for you. With you there, that's the only way we can have any peace and make the real money." Anastasia was personally part of the four-man death squad that mowed down Masseria in a Coney Island restaurant in 1931.

During World War II Anastasia appears to have been the originator of a plan to free Luciano from prison by winning him a pardon for "helping the war effort." To accomplish the goal, Anastasia set out to create problems on the New York waterfront so the Navy would agree to any kind of deal to stop sabotage. The French luxury liner S.S. *Normandie*, in the process of being converted into a troopship, burned

and capsized in New York harbor. Anastasia was credited with ordering his brother, Tough Tony Anastasio (different spelling of the last name), to carry out the sabotage. Afterward, a deal was made for Luciano to get lighter treatment in prison, and Anastasia was informed to cease waterfront troubles. Lansky years later told his Israeli biographers: "I told him face to face that he mustn't burn any more ships. He was sorry—not sorry he'd had the *Normandie* burned but sorry he couldn't get at the Navy again. Apparently he had learned in the Army to hate the Navy. 'Stuck-up bastards' he called them."

Anastasia's violent ways could be contained as long as Luciano and Costello pulled the strings. In 1951 Costello may well have been the prime mover in Anastasia's rise to boss of the Mangano crime family in which he was technically an underling. Through the years boss Vince Mangano had fumed at Anastasia's closeness to Luciano, Costello, Adonis and others and that they used him without first seeking Mangano's approval. Frequently Mangano and Anastasia almost came to blows over family affairs, and it was considered only a matter of time until one or the other was killed. In 1951 Vince's brother, Phil Mangano, was murdered and Vince himself became another in Anastasia's legion of the permanently missing. Anastasia then claimed control of the family with Costello's active support. At a meeting of all the bosses of New York families, Costello backed up Anastasia's claim that Mangano was planning to kill Anastasia and that Albert had a right to act in self-defense. Faced with a fait accompli the other bosses could do nothing but accept Anastasia's elevation.

It appears Costello had other motivation for wanting Anastasia in control of the crime family. Costello at the time was facing a concentrated challenge from Vito Genovese for control of the Luciano family now that Luciano was in exile. Up until 1951 Costello had depended for muscle on New Jersey crime family boss Willie Moretti, but Moretti was in the process of losing his mind and would soon be a rubout in a "mercy killing" by the mob. That meant Costello needed new muscle and Anastasia, with a family of gunmen behind him, would make a strong foil to Genovese.

Unfortunately, as a crime boss Anastasia turned even more kill-crazy than ever. In 1952 he even ordered the murder of a young Brooklyn salesman named Arnold Schuster after watching Schuster bragging on television about his role as primary witness in bank robber Willie Sutton's arrest. "I can't stand squealers!" Anastasia raged to his men. "Hit that guy!"

In killing Schuster, Anastasia had violated a cardinal crime syndicate rule which ran, as Bugsy Siegel once quaintly put it, "We only kill each other." Outsiders—prosecutors, reporters, the public in general—were not to be killed. Members of the general public could only be hit if the very life of the organization or some of its top leaders were threatened. This certainly was not the case with Arnold Schuster, a man whose killing generated much heat on the mob. Like other members of the syndicate, even Luciano in Italy and Costello were horrified, but they could not disavow Anastasia because they needed

him to counter Genovese's growing ambitions and power. Genovese cunningly used Anastasia's kill-crazy behavior against him, wooing supporters away from Anastasia on that basis. Secretly over a few years time Genovese won the cooperation of Anastasia's underboss, Carlo Gambino. Gambino in turn recruited crime boss Joe Profaci to oppose Anastasia.

Still, Genovese dared not move against Anastasia and his real target, Costello, because of Meyer Lansky, the highest-ranking and the most powerful member of the national syndicate. Normally Lansky would not have supported Genovese under any circumstances, their dislike for each other going back to the 1920s. But in recent years Lansky was riding high as the king of casino gambling in Cuba, cutting in other syndicate bosses for lesser shares. When Anastasia leaned on him for a piece of the action, Lansky refused. So Anastasia started working on plans to bring his own gambling setup into Cuba. That was not something Lansky took lightly. Anyone messing with his gambling empire went. That applied to Lansky's good friend Bugsy Siegel and it certainly applied to Anastasia. Up until then Lansky had preferred to let Anastasia and Genovese bleed each other to death, but now he gave his approval to the former's eradication.

Anastasia's rubout was carried out with an efficiency that the former lord high executioner of Murder, Inc., would have approved. On the morning of October 25, 1957, Anastasia entered the barbershop of the Park Sheraton Hotel in New York for a quick going over. Anastasia's bodyguard parked the car in an underground garage and then most conveniently decided to take a little stroll. Anastasia relaxed in the barber chair, closing his eyes. Suddenly two men, scarves covering their faces, marched in. One told the shop owner, Arthur Grasso, who was standing by the cash register: "Keep your mouth shut if you don't want your head blown off."

The pair moved on Anastasia's chair, shoving the attending barber out of the way. Anastasia still did not open his eyes. Both men shot Anastasia, who after the first volley jumped to his feet. Anastasia lunged at his killers or what he thought were his killers, trying to get them with his bare hands. Actually he attacked their reflection in the mirror. It took several more shots to drop him, but he finally fell to the floor dead.

Like virtually all gang killings, the Anastasia murder remains unsolved. It is known, though, that the contract was given to Joe Profaci who passed it on to the three homicidal Gallo brothers from Brooklyn. Whether they did it themselves or let others handle the actual gunning was never determined.

The double-dealing did not cease with Anastasia's death. Gambino now secretly deserted Genovese and joined with Lansky, Luciano and Costello in a plot that would entrap Genovese in a narcotics conviction and send him away to prison for the rest of his life. In that sense Anastasia was avenged, but it was not with the abrupt finality that the kill-crazy executioner would likely have preferred.

See also *NORMANDIE*, S.S., TENUTO, FREDERICK J.

ANASTASIA Crime Family See GAMBINO CRIME FAMILY

ANASTASIO, Anthony "Tough Tony" (1906–1963): Waterfront racketeer

For about three decades, until his death in 1963, Tough Tony Anastasio ruled the New York waterfront with an iron fist. A vice president of the International Longshoremen's Association and head of Local 1814, he had other, more important, unofficial offices. Although never officially connected to Murder, Inc., and brother Albert, Tony rarely had to say more than "my brother Albert" to make a point. (Albert Anastasia, the notorious lord high executioner of Murder, Inc., was head of one of New York's five Mafia crime families. Tony kept the original spelling of the family name but he was always ready to invoke Anastasia's name to make a point and solidify his position on the docks. It worked like a charm.)

Tony was ever loyal to Albert. He once confronted a reporter for the *New York World-Telegram and Sun* and demanded: "How come you keep writing all those bad things about my brother Albert? He ain't killed nobody in your family . . . yet."

Because dock rivals knew Tough Tony had the full weight of the mob behind him, they never seriously challenged him. As a result, Tony's word was supreme. During World War II, as part of a Mafia plot he orchestrated the sabotage of the French luxury liner S.S. *Normandie*, demonstrating to federal authorities that the docks weren't safe unless the Mafia received concessions. "Concessions" equalled the transfer of Lucky Luciano, then imprisoned in

Dock racketeer "Tough Tony" Anastasio leaves a morgue in tears after identifying the body of his murdered brother, the dreaded Albert Anastasia.

Dannemora, the "Siberia" of New York state's penal system, to a far less restrictive prison. The demand met, Luciano saw to it that no other ships were burned in New York and did other "good works" for the war effort. In 1946, he was pardoned by Governor Thomas E. Dewey. On February 9 Luciano was escorted aboard the *Laura Keene*, docked in Brooklyn's Bush Terminal. A mob of reporters tried to follow but some 50 longshoremen carrying menacing-looking bailing hooks kept them away. Tough Tony saw to it that only top gangland figures were permitted on board to bid Luciano farewell on his deportation to Italy. It was, observers said, Tough Tony's finest hour.

The fact remained that Anastasio only rose as far as his brother's clout permitted. When Albert was murdered in 1957, Tony raced to the barbershop in Manhattan to identify the body. Then, it developed, he rushed to Frank Costello's apartment where a visitor found them embracing each other and sobbing. Costello expressed a fear that he would be the next one marked for death. It went without saying Tough Tony's power would wane. How much did not become known for many years.

Carlo Gambino succeeded as head of the Anastasia crime family and in due course Tough Tony was reduced to figurehead status. The assault on Anastasio's ego was enough to loosen his tongue and he started talking to the Justice Department. Before he could be developed into a full scale informant, he died of natural causes in 1963.

See also LUCIANO, CHARLES "LUCKY"; *NOR-MANDIE, S.S.*

ANGIULO, Gennaro J. (1919–): Boss of Boston Mafia

Gennaro "Jerry" Angiulo, the boss of the Boston Mafia, was reminiscing one day in 1981, in his North End headquarters, about the gang wars of the 1960s. He told how he and his brothers "buried 20 Irishmen to take this town over. We can't begin to dig up half we got rid of," he said, adding, "And I'm not bragging, either."

As is not uncommon on FBI tapes, the conversation was an excellent case of criminal bragging. The Irish War was actually prosecuted by Angiulo's superior, Raymond Patriarca. There were those who never thought of Angiulo as tough enough to fight a Mafia-style war. The Mafia in New England, as distinguished from many crime families elsewhere, pretty much stuck to the requirement that a "made" member had to have committed at least one murder. There were only a few exceptions and Angiulo was one of them. (He bought his way into the organization with a $50,000 payoff to Patriarca.)

Jerry Angiulo's rise to power was not within the Mafia itself, but instead was a result of the Kefauver hearings of 1950–1951. At the time, Joseph Lombardo, then crime boss of Massachusetts, decided, what with the Senate probers planning to come to town, it would be a good idea to shut down Boston gambling. He was most interested in preventing any Kefauver heat from affecting the business of the mob's racing wire. For that reason he wanted the probers to have as few targets as possible and pulled his men in Boston out of the numbers racket. The ploy worked. Lombardo came off unscathed but, deciding the heat would be around for a while, he remained out of numbers.

Then Jerry Angiulo, a lowly runner in mob activities, made his move, asking Lombardo's permission to take over the numbers. Lombardo agreed, provided Angiulo understood he had no organization protection, that he was on his own. Well, perhaps not completely on his own—Lombardo got himself a cut of the numbers action while suffering no exposure himself.

Angiulo operated safely until Lombardo was succeeded by new boss Philip Bruccola. Bruccola took so much heat from investigations that he finally fled to Sicily. Now Angiulo was operating without a patron and soon individual mobsters started pressuring him for payoffs. Unable to fight, Angiulo paid until the demands became too great. Finally, he went to Providence where Raymond Patriarca was emerging as the new boss of all New England. He got Patriarca's protection by paying him $50,000 down and guaranteeing him an even larger annual cut from the Boston numbers racket. Patriarca simply placed some phone calls to mobsters in Boston, announcing that "Jerry's with me now" and for them to lay off.

The mobsters had to obey Patriarca and a new setup came to Boston. Angiulo became not only a "made" mafioso, but also the boss of Boston. And Ilario Zannino, one of the mobsters who had been shaking him down, was designated his number two man.

In time, Angiulo became a multimillionaire and the New England Mafia's money and payoff man. According to informer Vinnie Teresa, Angiulo claimed he could make 300 of Boston's 360-odd detectives follow his directives. It is very possible that Angiulo was exaggerating, a tendency he had, but it is true that, after the 1981 bugging of Angiulo's office, 40 Boston police officers were transferred because many of their names had been mentioned on the tapes.

In 1984 New England boss Patriarca died. His underboss Henry Tameleo was in prison and unlikely ever to be freed. Angiulo, as the number three man in the organization, laid claim to the boss position. He didn't get it.

By that time Angiulo was facing massive federal racketeering prosecutions. If convicted, he could have been sentenced to as much as 170 years. But the threat of imprisonment was not at issue in Angiulo's aborted succession. Many members still smarted over the way he had gotten into the mob. Zannino, his underboss, refused, according to an FBI report, to support him, instead backing Raymond J. Patriarca, the late boss's son, for the leadership. The younger Patriarca, the FBI said, named Zannino his counselor and Angiulo was demoted to the status of a mere soldier. That demotion was not necessarily the worst of Jerry Angiulo's worries. In 1986 Angiulo was convicted on racketeering charges and sentenced to 45 years imprisonment.

ANNENBERG, Moses L. (1878–1942): Gambling information czar

Probably no fortune in America was built on a sturdier foundation of cooperation with organized crime and the Mafia than that of Moses Annenberg. A newspaper circulation man by trade and a gambler to boot, Moe Annenberg rose from poverty in the slums of South Side Chicago to accumulate the largest estimated individual income of any person in the nation—thanks to mob money.

Considered a "circulation genius" by William Randolph Hearst, Moe started out in the circulation department of the *Chicago Tribune*. Later, he was hired away by Hearst's new sheets in town, the *American* and the *Examiner*, serving from 1904 to 1906 as circulation manager. He became a grand operative during the early Chicago newspaper circulation wars, selling newspapers with an army of sluggers, overturning the competition's delivery trucks, burning their papers and roughing up newspaper vendors.

Moe's "genius," in fact, was muscle. His roster of sluggers reads less like a publishing staff than a muster of public enemies. A typical Annenberg employee was Frank McErlane. Former Chicago journalist George Murray later described the Annenberg-McErlane relationship: "McErlane went on to become the most vicious killer of his time. Moe Annenberg went on to become father of the ambassador to the Court of St. James."

Under Hearst, Annenberg was one of the highest-paid circulation men in the nation. Hearst so valued him that he tolerated Moe's myriad private business dealings. More than Hearst himself, Annenberg realized the money to be made in the racing information field, both legally and illegally. In 1922 he bought the *Daily Racing Form* and by 1926 his various private businesses became so big he quit Hearst. In a few years Moe took over the *New York Morning Telegraph*, *Radio Guide*, *Screen Guide* and, most impor-

tant, formed the Nations-Wide News Service in association with the East Coast's gambler, Frank Erickson, a close associate of Lucky Luciano, Meyer Lansky and Frank Costello.

In 1929, Al Capone brought Annenberg into the underworld's famous Atlantic City Conference, the gathering at which the groundwork was laid for the national crime syndicate. Capone and Annenberg ironed out the details of a syndicated racing wire in discussions on the boardwalk.

Nation-Wide brought in a flood of money. The service received its information from telegraph and telephone wires hooked into 29 race tracks and from those tracks into 223 cities in 30 states, where thousands of poolrooms and bookie joints operated in violation of local laws. Annenberg thus became the fifth largest customer of American Telephone and Telegraph, making transmissions only slightly behind RCA and the three press associations of the day. It was with Annenberg's cooperation that Lansky sewed up for himself his pre-eminent gambling position in Miami and Florida's lush East Coast.

In the 1930s Annenberg also took over the century-old *Philadelphia Inquirer* and through it became a power in Republican Party politics—a "respectable" citizen. But Moe was to end up like Al Capone—hauled up for income tax evasion. In 1939, both he and his only son, Walter, were indicted. For the year 1932 the government found Annenberg owed $313,000 and paid only a paltry $308. For 1936 alone Annenberg owed an estimated $1,692,000 and paid $470,000, still not the epitome of civic-mindedness. All told, along with interest and penalties, Moe's unpaid taxes came to $9.5 million.

Annenberg claimed that, because much of his activities came during a period of national Democratic dominance, his legal troubles were politically inspired. More accurate was the evaluation of the *New York Times*, reporting that the money gush became so large "it apparently did not seem worth while to give the government its share."

Walter pleaded not guilty and finally Moe, in what some observers to the conversation regarded as the epitome of paternal devotion, declared: "It's the best gamble. I'll take the rap." Moe was in his 60s and his lawyers advised that a guilty plea by him could well lead to the dropping of charges against his son. The gamble paid off. Moe got a three-year prison term and handed the government $9.5 million in settlement.

Nation-Wide News folded and Moe was succeeded as the country's racing information czar by James M. Ragen, who set up Continental Press Service. Walter Annenberg remained an important publishing king and society figure and under President Richard Nixon went on to become ambassador to England. Moe wasn't around anymore but he would have been proud. "Only in America," he might well have said. And it would have been true. Organized crime and the great fortunes derived from it never flourished as in America.

See also RAGEN, JAMES M.

Further reading: *My Last Million Readers* by Emile Gauvreau

ANSELMI and Scalise: Mafia murder team

The Chicago newspapers referred to Albert Anselmi (squat and bulky) and John Scalise (tall and thin) as "the Mutt and Jeff of Murder." Another writer called them "the Damon and Pythias of Crime." If that appears a rather elegant characterization for two near maniacal killers, it does have a measure of truth to it. It was not until their dying day that either one spoke ill of the other—and that only when he faced certain execution as his partner had already. They grew up together in Sicily, came to America together, became syndicate gangsters together, became the most-feared killers of their day together, betrayed their bosses together, but always to their own selves were true.

Before they departed this world in 1929 they left their mark on the ways of Mafia mayhem. It was they who imported to Chicago the Sicilian custom of rubbing bullets with garlic, based on a theory that if the bullets didn't kill the victim the resultant gangrene would. They also introduced the "handshake hit," whereby the iron-gripped Anselmi would shake hands with an unsuspecting victim, locking the man's gunhand in a death grip, while the taller Scalise would produce a gun and blast him in the head. The pair, together with an imported New York killer, Frankie Yale, "wacked out" the infamous Irish gang boss Dion O'Banion in that fashion.

Both Anselmi and Scalise fled to America in their twenties when murder charges were brought against them in their native Marsala. In the early 1920s they were in Chicago in the employ of the Terrible Gennas, a bloodthirsty Mafia family also from Marsala. The Gennas were at the time the leading producers of illicit liquor in the entire Midwest and as such had a real need for efficient gunmen to guarantee their primacy. Naturally the murder twins fit the Genna specifications just as the Gennas fit the twins' needs. Very earnestly Anselmi and Scalise informed other Sicilian gunners that they had come to the United States in order to accumulate $1 million apiece, which they reckoned would allow them to return to their native land as wealthy men with the means to fix the murder case against them. The Gennas treasured this pair enough to pay them amounts extraordinary for the period. For one murderous caper alone, each was given $10,000 and a $3,000 diamond ring. Scalise promptly sent his ring to his sweetheart in Sicily. Anselmi, less romantic, haggled $4,000 out of a jeweler, at the point of a gun, for the $3,000 ring.

The tales of their killings became the talk of the underworld. When one victim begged mercy with his hands held in prayer, the boys jokingly shot off his hands before shooting him in the head. They gunned down their victims on crowded streets, with absolutely no regard for innocent bystanders.

Anselmi and Scalise finally broke with the Gennas when they were given a contract to hit Al Capone, realizing that even if they succeeded, Capone's followers would sooner or later get them. Instead, they revealed the murder order to Capone and went to work for him—while letting the Gennas think they were still in their employ. That way they were eventually able to set up one Genna brother for assassination and personally dispatch another.

Once the pair became open members of the Capone forces, they were quickly regarded as the gang's most efficient killers, outdoing even Machine Gun McGurn and Golf Bag Hunt. They took part in the most important Chicago murder of the 1920s, that of O'Banion. Later when a peace pact was almost worked out between the Capones and the O'Banions (then under the leadership of Hymie Weiss), the agreement foundered on the Weiss demand that Anselmi and Scalise be turned over to them for execution. Capone who prided himself on loyalty to his men, refused saying, "I wouldn't do that to a yellow dog."

Anselmi and Scalise went about their murdering business. They were arrested many number of times but never convicted; somehow witnesses against them suddenly remembered they did not recognize them. The pair even beat a rap of murdering two police detectives. After three trials, a typical Chicago verdict found that they were just innocent gangsters resisting unwarranted police aggression.

Anselmi and Scalise were finally to die at Al Capone's hands in 1929, shortly after the St. Valentine's Day Massacre, for which they were arrested but did not live long enough to be tried. Capone had learned that Anselmi and Scalise with Joseph "Hop Toad" Giunta, whom he had installed as head of the fraternal Unione Siciliane, were conspiring with another Mafia crime family boss named Joe Aiello to kill him. At first Capone could not believe this of Anselmi and Scalise whom he had refused to sacrifice to Hymie Weiss, but another aide, Frankie Rio, convinced him of the pair's disloyalty with a contrived test. At a dinner Capone and Rio faked an argument and Rio slapped Capone and stormed out. The next day Anselmi and Scalise approached Rio full of sympathy and offered to bring him in on a plan to kill Capone. Rio dickered with the gangsters for three days and then reported back to Capone.

On May 7, 1929, Capone hosted a party to honor Giunta, Anselmi and Scalise. At the height of the banquet, Capone accused them of betraying him and, producing an Indian club, beat Giunta and Scalise with blow after blow until they slumped to the floor, near death. Then Capone turned to the quaking Anselmi, who looked awestruck at his murder partner and for the first time in his life turned on him. "Not me, Al," he begged. "Honest to God. Johnnie. It was his idea. His and Joe's. Believe me, Al, I wouldn't—." Capone cut him off with a barrage of blows. Then Capone was handed a gun and he shot all three, finishing the gory job. Anselmi and Scalise died as they had always worked—together.

ANSLINGER, Harry J. (1892–1975): U.S. narcotics commissioner

One of our most controversial lawmen in this century, Harry J. Anslinger was an implacable foe of the Mafia and consequently a major enemy of the FBI's J. Edgar Hoover, who for more than 30 years maintained the Mafia did not exist. For those same 30 years, Anslinger's men had been gathering names and identities of top gangsters in the United States. Eventually they compiled a list of 800 big names in national and international crime and a black book which was labeled *Mafia*. This can fairly be called the first federal study of the American Mafia and

was done at a time when Hoover's "there-is-no-Mafia" line was generally accepted in law enforcement circles.

The rivalry between Hoover and Anslinger, in his prime a squat, bull-necked, bald, energetic man, was particularly intense. Each considered the other as both incompetent and a threat. But Hoover's disregard of and disrespect for Anslinger was not shared by Hoover's agents. In the early 1950s, Anslinger had provided them with a five-page list, four columns to a page, of the names and cities of over 300 crime family members. There were those who said the specter of organized crime was one that Hoover could not see because it had become visible to Anslinger first.

FBI agents surreptitiously circulated the "List of Mafia Members Obtained From Narcotics Bureau." It had to be done surreptitiously since any agent caught with the list would undoubtedly have been subjected to transfer and, more likely, to dismissal from the service. In his *Inside Hoover's FBI* Special Agent Neal J. Welch describes FBI men "burning' shiny grayish reproductions on primitive office copiers and passing the list secretly from agent to agent like some heretical religious creed—which it was." Welch relates that when he became special agent in charge of the Detroit bureau, he was given a faded old copy of the Narcotics Bureau's list with an astounding notation: "In 1952, the Narcotics Bureau had the answers but no one would listen . . . every LCN [La Cosa Nostra] member we have is on this list, without exception."

Anslinger clearly was a confirmed Mafia fighter long before Hoover finally was forced into the battle, but like Hoover he suffered certain performance defects. His overstated opinion of the dangers of marijuana, for instance, was in the 1960s to raise him to the status of a cult figure in the same way that *Reefer Madness* was and is a cult movie today. Anslinger can also be accused of following the headlines in the administration of his office. In 1942, only after the United States went to war with Japan, Anslinger reported to the secretary of the Treasury that there was ample proof that Japan had violated its international commitments for years by its promotion of the opium trade and had used drugs as an offensive weapon against countries it was trying to conquer. "Wherever the Japanese army goes, the drug traffic follows. In every territory conquered by the Japanese a large part of the people become enslaved with drugs." He noted this had been particularly true in Manchuria and China.

Like the complete bureaucrat, Anslinger followed every twist in American foreign policy and thus in time found the great drug menace was being masterminded by the Red Chinese, who were succeeded, coincidentally during the Korean War, by North Korea.

Anslinger was hewing to the sure road of popularity. With the arrival of the Kennedy administration, he was to embrace Attorney General Robert Kennedy. In his book, *The Protectors,* published shortly after the assassination of John Kennedy, Anslinger could not contain his praise for Bobby Kennedy, even lapsing into overstatement: "He [Bobby Kennedy] traveled over the country, calling special meetings with our agents, exhorting them to nail the big traffickers. He would review every case with them personally. He kept the prosecutors on their toes and promised the utmost effort in court to bring about convictions." Unfortunately Anslinger also proclaimed: "It was, in large measure, due to his forceful encouragement of our men that we knocked off such public enemies as Vito Genovese, the number one gangster in the United States, Big John Ormento, Joe Valachi and Carmine Galante, and numerous others." The sad fact was that all these men, save the last, had been through the entire prosecution process from arrest to conviction to sentencing to incarceration before Robert Kennedy even took office.

Yet whatever his failings in a quest for popularity and headlines, a peril of the profession among lawmen, Harry J. Anslinger still qualified during his lifetime as the nation's number one and, some would say, only Mafia hunter.

ANTINORI, Ignacio (?–1940): Early Florida Mafia boss

One of the more shadowy Mafia figures in U.S. history, Ignacio Antinori was the most powerful early leader in Tampa, Florida, crime family. One of the oldest Mafia groups in the country, the Tampa family, through the years, figured significantly in the narcotics trade and simply ignored requests or directives from other crime families to curtail such activities. And no one ever seriously contemplated going into Tampa to do anything about it.

While Antinori's early history may be cloudy there is no doubt that by the 1920s he was one of the major narcotics bosses in the United States. Antinori, connected through bribery with officials high up in the Cuban government, godfathered a setup in which Tampa became the American end of a drug pipeline extending from Marseilles, France, through Cuba to Florida. Tampa took care of distribution in Florida and sent on supplies to the Midwest, especially to the Kansas City Mafia, where according to the Narcotics Bureau, it passed under the control of such mafiosi as Nicolo Impostato, James De Simone and Joseph De Luca in Kansas City and Thomas Buffa in St. Louis.

It should not be assumed that Antinori's influence within the Tampa organization was unrivaled. Law enforcement knowledge of the affairs of the Tampa family was limited, and by about 1930 Santo Trafficante Sr. may well have taken over as top boss. Certainly, when Antinori was murdered on October 22, 1940, the operations of the Tampa family went on without skipping a beat. Under the senior Trafficante, the family remained a power in narcotics, smuggling of aliens, loan-sharking and Florida Gambling, as well as moving into Cuban gambling.

APACHE Indian job: Mob bombings

The bomb, long an underworld weapon, was used first in this country by Black Handers to terrorize victims. Later, in the labor racketeering field and in political campaigns (organized by the Capones), bombs were used as instruments of persuasion. Bombs also came in handy in convincing some businesses to accept the right beer and booze during Prohibition and others to come through with protection money. But, by the mid-1930s the custom fell into general disuse on a wholesale basis; bombings attracted more attention and public uproar than the politicians and police could ignore.

In the 1970s, firebombing came back into vogue with what the underworld called an Apache Indian job, a bombing so thorough that it is reminiscent of Indian attacks on settlers' cabins—nothing left standing except a chimney and a few smoking timbers.

New York restaurants that failed to pay tribute to the little-known but prosperous parsley racket were threatened with a firebombing. In the 1980s, the Montana State Crime Commission found the parsley racket had moved west under guidance of a New York crime family. Restaurants that failed to buy a large amount of parsley—so much that it would have to be served with every meal and with virtually every mixed drink—were being hit by Apache Indian jobs.

See also PARSLEY RACKET

APALACHIN Conference: Underworld convention

The 1957 Apalachin, New York, Conference of the Mafia was a landmark in the history of crime in America. Ill fated—indeed, something of a comic opera—the conference nonetheless had a profound effect on the FBI's J. Edgar Hoover, who for almost three decades had been denying the existence of both the Mafia and anything called organized crime. (It was a convenient stance for Hoover; after all, he could hardly be expected to combat what did not exist.)

The New York state police raid on the Apalachin meeting created a thunderbolt in FBI headquarters. The late William C. Sullivan, Hoover's former assistant, related in his memoirs, *The Bureau: My Thirty Years in Hoover's FBI:* "Hoover knew he could no longer duck and dodge and weave his way out of a confrontation with the Mafia, and he realized that his policy of non-recognition left him and the FBI open to criticism."

To protect himself, Hoover launched the FBI into a giant game of catch-up, gathering all the information he could about the Mafia and organized crime. Apalachin (and Robert Kennedy's later appointment as attorney general) prompted an agency wiretap and eavesdropping campaign from which, some observers have pointed out, the FBI gained a lot of information, not all of which it understood. FBI surveillance men heard big mafiosi referring to "our thing," and not knowing better, capitalized the words and came up with a "new" criminal organization—La Cosa Nostra. Happily for Hoover this gave him a sort of out. He didn't have to concede the existence of the Mafia and could stick with La Cosa Nostra or the LCN. No matter, it forced Hoover at last into the game, leaving the "there-ain't-no-Mafia" school to a dwindling number of uninformed "experts"—and, of course, to the mafiosi themselves.

But the Apalachin Conference was not intended to incite FBI investigations. By most theories the conference was mainly concerned with Vito Genovese's ascendancy plans in wake of the assassination just 20 days earlier of Albert Anastasia, as well as the earlier attempt on the life of Frank Costello.

The bare-bones history of the conference is easily stated: It never really got off the ground. Some 60 or more underworld leaders were on hand in Joseph Barbara's stone mansion in Apalachin when the sudden appearance of New York State troopers and federal agents disrupted matters. It was something of a modern version of the Keystone Kops in chase of the bad guys, starring immaculately groomed crime bosses, who, in their fifties and older, were hardly fleet of foot but were scurrying about, climbing out windows, bolting through back doors and diving through bushes, burrs and undergrowth while trying to escape. It can only be speculated exactly how many got away, but authorities the next day listed 58 detainees. While most of those arrested were from New York, New Jersey and Pennsylvania, a healthy representation of out-of-towners indicated the national interest of the conference. There were crime leaders from Florida, Texas, California, Illinois and Ohio. The arrest roster bore the names of men whom law enforcement had tried for years to net: Trafficante, Profaci, Genovese, Magliocco, Bonanno, DeSimone, Scalish, Riela, Gambino, Magaddino, Catena, Miranda, Zito, Civello, Ida, Ormento, Coletti, Galante. Of the 58, 50 had arrest records, 35 had convictions and 23 had served prison sentences. Eighteen had been involved in murder investigations, 15 netted for narcotics violations, 30 for gambling and 23 for illegal use of firearms.

The conference might simply have been broken up on account of a state police sergeant who, suspecting that something was up at the Barbara mansion, ordered the raid. However, such an interpretation requires a certain suspension of critical analysis. The fact that Vito Genovese became the emperor caught without his clothes and was destroyed at the meeting suggests a setup. Through hindsight—and the revelations made by such figures as Lucky Luciano and Doc Stacher that the police were tipped off and the meeting sabotaged—it became almost impossible to reject insider foul play.

If Genovese thought he was going to call a meeting of the syndicate—and it wasn't merely a Mafia conference, since among those invited (but not attending) were Meyer Lansky and Doc Stacher—and simply rearrange affairs to suit himself he would be, and was, rudely disillusioned.

Newspaper speculation suggested that the Apalachin meeting was intended as a forum for presenting Genovese with his "boss of bosses" crown. Much was also made of the fact that a total of $300,000 was found on the arrested crime bosses; "envelope money" perhaps to be given to Genovese? More likely the money was a total of typical fat wads carried by dons. And Carlo Gambino did make it known that he brought no money for Genovese. (Gambino had cooperated with Genovese in the Anastasia assassination to get control of the latter's crime family, but had no intention of winding up with Genovese in any sort of superior position.)

If Apalachin had been held, there would have been considerable conflict. It could be avoided if the meeting were boycotted or sabotaged. Unless one embraces the theory that the crime leaders from Chicago, Detroit, New Orleans and San Francisco had escaped during the raid or were still en route, their absence was noteworthy. Luciano, from his exile in Italy, was against the meeting and lobbied with those particular cities where his voice was still powerful. Frank Costello did not show; he had explained that he was under constant surveillance since the attempt on his life. Significantly, no one showed up from New Orleans where Costello had strong authority. As essentially the treasurer for the syndicate, Meyer Lansky was supposed to attend but seemed to develop a throat condition that kept him in the warm Florida climes. Doc Stacher, close to Lansky, also did not appear. There was a clear conspiracy against Genovese by three non-attendees—Luciano, Costello and Lansky. Gambino, who since the murder of Anastasia had been in contact with Luciano and made peace with him, became the "inside man" at the conference.

All these absences undoubtedly were not lost on those who gathered at Apalachin and pointed up the lack of unanimity Genovese faced. Then the raid turned the conference into pure fiasco. Nothing as degrading had ever occurred to the Mafia or the crime syndicate before, and it all came down on Genovese.

There was also a lot of posturing. Chicago boss Sam Giancana, who later informed his associates that he'd just avoided the police net (but actually may well have been tipped off that a raid was coming), was particularly irate. The telephone conversation was recorded between Giancana and Stefano Magaddino, the Buffalo crime family boss:

Magaddino: "It never would've happened in your place."

Giancana: "You're fuckin' right it wouldn't. This is the safest territory in the world for a big meet . . . We got three towns just outside of Chicago with the police chiefs in our pocket. We got this territory locked up tight."

Magaddino's comments were less than gracious considering it was he who had suggested to Genovese that the meeting be staged at Apalachin. The host, Barbara, was a lieutenant in Magaddino's crime family.

Undoubtedly, Genovese realized he had been set up, but there was nothing, immediately, that he could do about it. Nor were foes going to give him any breathing space. Within half a year Genovese and a number of his loyal associates were nailed in a narcotics conspiracy. The principal testimony against Genovese came from a heroin pusher named Nelson Cantellops, who interestingly enough was known in the past to have worked for Lansky and Giancana, two leading Apalachin no-shows. It hardly seemed likely that on his own a two-bit character like Cantellops could be in a position to get incriminating evidence on Genovese. It appeared the government was being used to frame Genovese, but federal officials were positively gleeful about catching the crime boss and didn't wonder too much how it had come about.

Not long before he died, Luciano revealed the secret behind the Cantellops evidence. The pusher had gotten a $100,000 payoff from Luciano, Lansky, Costello and Gambino. As a fillip for his $25,000 Costello had insisted that Vincent "the Chin" Gigante, the triggerman in the Genovese-ordered attempt on Costello's life, also had to be convicted. He was. In interviews still later in Israel, Doc Stacher confirmed the plot and added that Lansky gratefully put Cantellops on a pension of several thousand dollars a month for the rest of his life—which ended in a night club brawl in 1965. "But as far as I know there wasn't anything sinister about his death."

Apalachin started Genovese's rapid decline and the narcotics conviction finished him off. He went to prison in 1959 for 15 years and died there in 1969. He remained powerful enough to have a number of members of his own crime family killed but when he tried to have Luciano and Lansky murdered, nothing much happened. Vito apparently never figured out that he wasn't named boss of bosses at Apalachin.

See also BARBARA, JOSEPH, SR.

ARGOS Lectionary: Capone Gang "Bible"

In 1930 the manager of a Chicago underworld-controlled nightclub offered to sell the University of Chicago what he described as "a Bible with an odd history." When university scholars examined the "Bible" they were ecstatic. It was a ninth- or 10th-century Greek manuscript of parchment leaves with a number of biblical excerpts arranged for church services. Called the Argos Lectionary, it was quickly snapped up by the university and recognized as a stunning historical find.

The nightclub manager thought the item valuable for rather different reasons. It turned out that recruits to the Capone Gang took an oath, with their hand on the "Bible," that they would remain loyal to Scarface Al. In that sense, it did have some historical import in that it showed that the Capone did not practice the mumbo-jumbo blood initiation rites that informer Joe Valachi said were performed in the Costa Nostra.

ARM, on the: Freebies, Mafia style

An enduring myth is that wise guys are notorious big spenders. Actually they are moochers, wanting everything "on the arm"—that is, for free. This is generally the code in mob-owned places, a sort of courtesy from one crime family to another. It is all a matter of esteem among wise guys.

Once undercover cop Donnie Brasco (Joe Pistone) was hitting New York joints with Tough Tony Mirra, who Brasco considered "the nastiest, most intimidating guy I met in the Mafia," and a bunch of wise guys. They occupied half the bar half the night, not paying for a drink and certainly not keeping track of their drinks, which included various offered to assorted wise guys who happened by.

When they finally prepared to depart, Brasco slapped $25 down on the bar, which enraged Mirra. "Take that money off the bar," he snarled. "Nobody pays for nothing when they're with me."

Donnie explained he was just leaving a tip for the bartender, that that was the way he operated. Mirra growled that when he was with him, he operated the way he told him. Brasco picked up the money.

Some topflight establishments become mob joints precisely because they are victimized in this manner by wise guys. In desperation the owner will cut some mob big shot in for some of the action on the assumption that it will cut down the mob depreda-

tions. The mob boss gets his cut of a few grand a week, but the place continues to attract on-the-armers. When it gets too bad, profits suffer, but the mob big shot doesn't care. He wants his cut in full, good times or bad. It's strictly according to mob rules.

ATLANTIC City Conference: Underworld convention prelude to national crime syndicate

It was far more important in criminal history than the notorious Apalachin Conference in 1957. It was more significant than the Havana Convention of 1946. The 1929 Atlantic City Conference represented the first concrete move toward establishment of the national crime syndicate. It started out with screams and curses but ended in the sweetness of reasonable accommodation, unanimously arrived at.

This was demonstrated even by a relatively minute matter in which Al Capone agreed to go from the resort to Philadelphia where he would be arrested on a gun charge and clapped in jail. In the wake of the ruthless St. Valentine's Day Massacre which had outrage the entire nation, something had to be done to soothe the national temperament. It was agreed that Capone clapped in jail, even on a slap-on-the-wrist matter, would be good public relations. Capone saw the light; even the Chicago savage was being tamed by the brains of the underworld.

The Atlantic City confab was hosted by Nucky Johnson, the boss of the city. He was able to guarantee there would be no police interference. However, some of the gangsters were subjected to a grievous affront: Johnson had registered them at the exclusive Break Hotel along the Boardwalk, which was restricted to white Protestants, and he had used proper Anglo-Saxon aliases. Once the management got a look at Capone, Nig Rosen and others, the monikers didn't wash and they were refused admittance. The hotel did not know with whom it was dealing but the gangsters who had to keep their identities secret, had to accept the ignominy of being drummed out of the place. By this time Johnson had joined the group, and Capone screamed at him that he had failed to make the proper arrangements. A loud argument ensued and the gangsters were afraid the pair would come to blows.

Suddenly, Johnson, who was taller and heavier than Capone, shoved him into a limousine and ordered the others to join the caravan. The cars headed for the Ritz and its neighbor, the Ambassador. Still fuming, Capone ripped pictures from the wall of the quiet Ritz lobby and heaved them at Johnson. As Lucky Luciano recalled, "Everybody got over bein' mad and concentrated on keepin' Al quiet. That's the way our convention started."

Amazingly it went on to become a huge success. Deals were struck involving a wide disparity of interests and criminals of varied backgrounds. Among the delegates present were: Greasy Thumb Guzik, in addition to Capone from Chicago: Nig Rosen and Boo-Boo Hoff of Philadelphia; King Solomon of Boston; Abe Bernstein of the Purple Gang from Detroit; Moe Dalitz and Chuck Polizzi of Cleveland; Longy Zwillman of New Jersey; John Lazia (representing Tom Pendergast) of Kansas City; Daniel Walsh of Providence, Rhode Island. New York offered the biggest contingent, including Luciano, Meyer Lansky, Johnny Torrio (with whom Capone had an emotional reunion), Frank Costello, Joe Adonis, Dutch Schultz, Louis Lepke, Vince Mangano, gambler Frank Erickson, Frank Scalise and Albert Anastasia.

Equally important were the two men who weren't there: Joe the Boss Masseria and Salvatore Maranzano, two old-line mafiosi ready to square off in New York in a war to claim the position of boss of bosses. Their obsession with such a claim ran counter to the desires of the Atlantic City conferees who were looking for a confederation of forces that left each supreme in his own area. Above all, the conferees understood the need for working with all ethnics. In fact, almost half of them were Jewish; in terms of the power they represented, they probably composed a more potent force than the Italians.

In reality the conference was the creation of two men of like thoughts—Meyer Lansky and Johnny Torrio—both of whom saw the virtue of establishing a syndicate of cooperation. Plans were laid at the meeting for activities after Prohibition. It was agreed that the gangs would get into the legitimate end of the liquor business by acquiring distilleries, breweries and important franchises. It was agreed there was a big future in gambling and the country was divided into exclusive franchises for both the liquor and gambling campaigns.

Emphasis was laid on the fact that all these activities had to be apportioned peacefully to avoid the sort of gang wars that would inevitably lead to governmental crackdowns. The successful Seven Group that resolved the bootlegging wars was held up as the way of the future.

This, it was agreed, did not mean force would not have to be used to achieve this end. All the conferees understood that the Luciano-Lansky forces would have to employ considerable violence to get rid of the old-line mafiosi. No one at the time articulated the idea but the conference had agreed to kill off the Italian Mafia and replace it with an American Mafia, one that functioned within an all-ethnic combination. Capone certainly understood he had to rid Chicago once and for all of Mafia kingpin Joey Aiello; that task was a accomplished the following year.

Overall, both Torrio and Lansky had hoped the conference would go even further in establishing the crime syndicate, but overall they were satisfied with the results. It had been a conference that started out badly and still managed to end with Capone and Johnson embracing one another.

Never before had so much been accomplished by such a group of important criminals, and it had been done in most unorthodox manner. Many decisions were taken as the leading criminals in America walked barefoot through the water, their pants legs rolled up. In such fashion empires were carved out and decisions made on who would live and who would die.

See also SEVEN GROUP

B

BAGMAN: Payoff man or collector

Although the word *bagman* was first applied in the United States to traveling salesmen who carried their wares in bags, "bagmen" maintained a different livelihood in underworld parlance. Stolen goods were carried off in bags by thieves, who thus became bagmen. Later they sold the loot to fences who also carried the booty around in bags, often to give the appearance of being salesmen. Since fences were always in peril of being caught by police, they carried a supply of money in their bags to pay their way out of trouble. In time, the term *bagman* exclusively connoted an underworld character who carried around money—cash to be used for bribes, or already collected from bribers, or for other illegal enterprises.

The Mafia was always big on using women as bagmen. The most famous of these was Virginia Hill, probably the bedmate of more mafiosi than any other woman in America. During the Kefauver hearings, the senators tried to figure out why she was used so much as a bagman. In executive session, Senator Charles W. Tobey of New Hampshire professed puzzlement why so many men in organized crime were so willing to give her expensive presents and large sums of money.

"Young lady, what makes you the favorite of the underworld?" he asked Hill.

"Senator," a much-sanitized version of her reply went, "I'm the best goddamned lay in the world."

Certainly less outspoken was Ida Devine, the wife of Irving "Nig" Devine, a longtime associate of Meyer Lansky. Dubbed "the Lady in Mink" because she always dressed well, Ida once traveled by plane from Las Vegas to Los Angeles and then by train to Chicago and Hot Springs where she picked up more money before returning to Chicago. She then flew to Miami, her handbag always clutched tightly in her hand. That was hardly surprising since she was carrying $100,000 in cash. At the end of the line she handed over the money to Meyer Lansky.

The top payoff man of the Capone-Chicago syndicate was Greasy Thumb Guzik, so-called because his fingers got greasy from handling so much money. He was the mob's bagman in paying off police and politicians. His duty was to sit nightly at a table at St. Hubert's Old English Grill and Chop House, where district police captains and sergeants could pick up their payoffs. Other visitors to Guzik included bagmen for various Chicago mayors and other high officials. It was entirely fitting that Guzik died at work and with his boots on, at St. Hubert's partaking of a sparse meal of lamb chops and a glass of Mosel. Less philosophical were those who had not made their pick-ups in time.

It was well known that mob payoffs in New York City for years went through Frank Costello, although it seems likely that he seldom handled the money directly. For instance, for many years payoffs to the police department were handled by Joe Cooney, better known as Joe the Coon. Every week he delivered $10,000 in small bills to the commissioner's office, a sum said to have been increased to $20,000 during the regimes of Joseph A. Warren and Grover A. Whalen. Because he was a red-haired, freckle-faced Irishman, Joe the Coon attracted little attention as he walked about with a brown paper bag (stuffed with bills). Still, Lucky Luciano advised Costello to instruct Joe the Coon to change a light-bulb in the building now and then so he blended in even more.

The Kefauver Committee crime hearings in the early 1950s dug up facts on how bagmen operated during the reign of Mayor William O'Dwyer. Frank Bals, always close to O'Dwyer and seventh deputy police commissioner, admitted to the committee—and later retracted—that while he and his 12-man staff were charged with investigating gambling and corruption of the police department, they turned matters completely around. Bals said they were actually bagmen for the police department, collecting payoffs from gamblers and parceling it out at headquarters.

Occasionally, the financial mastermind of the syndicate, Meyer Lansky, personally played bagman when the recipient was very highly placed. He handed over huge sums to Huey Long, the political dictator of Louisiana, and Fulgencio Batista, the dictator of Cuba. In the case of Huey Long, Lansky and his aide, Doc Stacher, arranged to pay the Kingfish three to four million dollars a year, in Switzerland, where the tax men, hot after Long, would never find it.

Stacher explained to him, "You have nothing to worry about. We'll take the money there for you with our special couriers and nobody but you and us will know your number. And only you will be able to draw on the account. Your signature and secret code which you will give the bank—you don't even have to tell us—will be your protection. To put money in, all we need is the number. To draw it out, you need the code that only you will know. You must never write it down. Keep it in your head."

Naturally, Long was deeply impressed and allowed the Lansky-Costello forces to take over gambling activities in his domain. Somehow a bagman loaded with ready cash has a way with people.

BALDWIN Wallace College: "Mafia U."

Within certain law enforcement circles and, most likely, among the ranks of organized crime, small Baldwin Wallace College in Berea, Ohio, is referred to

as "Mafia U." Although the arrangement has never been quite clear, Alfred Bond, the president of the college, was known to have given a commitment to government agents that the school would falsify its records to provide backgrounds for former mafiosi. Neither the U.S. Justice Department nor President Bond ever discussed the number of repentant mafiosi that eventually were added to the alumni lists, but noted television reporter Fred Graham in his book, *The Alias Program*, puts it a shade more kindly than using the Mafia U. sobriquet ". . . it seems possible that this tiny Ohio college could have developed—with Justice Department assistance—one of the largest Italian-American alumni groups in the Midwest."

Eventually, there is little doubt that Mafia snoopers learned to look for a Baldwin Wallace background when tracking possible "new citizens" in the government's witness protection program. It may also be presumed that Mafia U.'s participation in salvaging former mafiosi probably tapered off.

The school's experience in the program may not always have been a happy one. Fabricating a college background is no easy chore; a great many bases at an institution have to be meticulously covered to make the phony background stand up. Justice Department bungling sometimes made the job that much harder.

In one case, a cover history for a prize informer, Gerald Zelmanowitz, assigned him the new name Paul J. Maris. His bogus résumé stated: "9/53–6/55—Baldwin Wallace—Berea, Ohio." However, in answer to inquiries, the registrar's office at one time verified that "Maris" had been awarded a bachelor of science degree in 1957. Yet in other cases the office of admissions reported there was no record of a Paul Maris ever having attended Baldwin Wallace College. Later, President Bond insisted that the Justice Department simply had never included Maris's name as one to be inserted in the records, an oversight that contributed mightily to the many mishaps in the masquerade. Eventually Maris was unmasked as a non-person when his picture failed to turn up in the school yearbook.

All in all it was hardly a stirring example of higher education in action.

BALISTRIERI, Frank P. (1918–1986): Milwaukee Mafia boss

Although feared by his local "button men" (soldiers), Frank Balistrieri never ranked high in nationwide Mafia or crime syndicate councils. This is explained by Milwaukee's proximity to Chicago.

Noted for spreading its Windy City tentacles over much of the country and operating on the proposition that everything west of Chicago belongs to them, the Chicago Outfit's claim is not entirely recognized in Las Vegas, Arizona or California. But other domains, notably Kansas City and Milwaukee, are another matter.

In September 1985 Balistrieri and eight others were tried in federal court on charges of skimming $2 million of the Argent Corporation's gross income from casino operations. Allegedly, the defendants skimmed the money as a tax dodge and then distributed the cash to organized crime interests in Kansas City, Chicago, Milwaukee and Cleveland.

Balistrieri had gotten a share but whether it was a fair share is debatable. Both the late Kansas City don Nick Civella and Balistrieri felt they were entitled to more from the pot in general—and from one another in particular. Finally Civella and Balistrieri requested Chicago crime leaders arbitrate their dispute.

Chicago boss Joey Aiuppa and Jackie the Lackey Cerone, his underboss, served as mediators. Their verdict, a classic, underlined the preeminence of power in the affairs of the "Honored Society." Aiuppa and Cerone decreed that henceforth Chicago itself would take 25 percent of the money skimmed. The case was closed with both Civella and Balistrieri coming out losers.

Perhaps under the circumstances the simplest thing for Balistrieri to do in December 1985 was plead guilty and take a 10-year sentence on the skimming charges.

BANANA War: Fight for dominance in organized crime

From 1964 to about 1969, the last great war in which a leading Mafia crime family sought to take over a king-sized portion of organized crime was fought. If the aggressors had succeeded, they might have altered the underworld nearly as much as Lucky Luciano's purge of the Mustache Petes. This new conflict of the 1960s was triggered by an aging don of towering self-assurance, Joseph C. Bonanno, the head of a relatively small but efficient New York crime family, known by nickname as the "Bananas" family. The war was called the Banana War.

In a sense the war was inevitable. Had Bonanno not struck first, other Mafia leaders would have hit him, having become upset about his "planting flags all over the world." Bonanno had established interests in the West, in Canada and in Italy where, as later related by the Italian Mafia's celebrated informer, Tommaso Buscetta, Bonanno was instrumental in getting Sicilian mafiosi to establish a commission, American style, to deal with disputes among the 30 Italian crime families. If Bonanno had been allowed to develop close contacts in Sicily with this commission, he would have been in a position to tie up the entire drug traffic out of Europe. In a broader sociological sense the Bonanno drive demonstrated that America was being polluted less by Italian criminals than Italy was being corrupted by American criminals.

As Bonanno watched many of the older American dons fade away, he decided it was time to strike out for greater glory and more loot. He developed an attack program for eliminating in one swoop such old-time powers as New York's Carlo Gambino and Tommy Lucchese, Buffalo's Stefano Magaddino and Los Angeles's Frank DeSimone. Bonanno involved in his plot an old ally, Joe Magliocco, who had succeeded another longtime Bonanno friend, the late Joe Profaci, as head of another Brooklyn crime family. Magliocco's loyalty to Bonanno was beyond question and he went along despite misgivings and his own ill health.

The plot began to unravel when Magliocco passed along the hit assignment on Gambino and Lucchese to an ambitious underboss named Joe Colombo, who had been a trusted hit man in the organization for Profaci. Colombo weighed the situation and, not realizing the extent of Bonanno's involvement, decided the Gambino—Lucchese forces looked the stronger. Colombo sold out to them. It did not take Gambino and Lucchese long to determine that Bonanno was behind the plot.

The national commission treaded softly on the matter, realizing that Bonanno could put 100 gunmen on the streets of Brooklyn and Manhattan and produce a bloodbath on a level unwitnessed in this country since the Capone era. Bonanno and Magliocco were summoned to a meeting with the commission, but Bonanno contemptuously refused to attend. Magliocco showed up, confessed and begged for mercy. The syndicate leaders let him live, deciding he lacked the guts to continue the battle and was so ill he'd probably die soon anyway. He was fined $50,000 and stripped of his power, which was given to Colombo. This leniency, not typical for treachery in the Mafia, was aimed at encouraging Bonanno's surrender. Within a matter of months, Magliocco was dead of a heart attack.

Bonanno took off for the safety of his strongholds in the West and in Canada, keeping on the move while avoiding orders from the commission to come in. In October 1964 he returned to Manhattan to appear before a grand jury. On the evening of October 21, he had dinner with his lawyers. Afterward, as he stepped from a car on Park Avenue, he was seized by two gunmen, shoved into another car and taken away. The newspapers assumed Bananas had been executed.

While Bonanno was out of sight, war broke out within the Bonanno organization. The national commission ruled that Bonanno had forfeited his position and installed Gaspar DiGregorio to take charge of the family. This split the family in two with many members backing Bonanno's son, Bill, while still hoping that Joe Bonanno would come back. After considerable shooting. DiGregorio called for a peace meeting with Bill Bonanno. The confab was to be held in a house on Troutman Street in Brooklyn. When Bill arrived, several riflemen and shotgunners opened up on him and his men. The Bananas men returned fire but in the dark, everyone's aim was off. There were no casualties.

Meanwhile Bonanno had been held captive by Buffalo's Magaddino, his older cousin. The rest of the commission apparently did not deal with Bonanno directly but Magaddino conferred regularly with them. It soon became clear to Bonanno that the commission did not want to kill him because that would only lead to further bloodshed. Instead, negotiations were carried on while at the same time Bonanno's foes tried to wipe out Bill Bonanno and his loyalists.

Bonanno offered a deal. He would retire from the rackets, give up control of his crime family and move to Arizona. He wanted his son Bill and his brother-in-law Frank Labruzzo to take charge. The commission would not buy this, realizing they would just be puppets and Bonanno would remain in control. Instead, they said they would name the new family head. Bonanno was in no position to hold out and finally agreed.

Bonanno was released and then surprised the commission by not returning to New York but disappearing again. He was still out of sight when DiGregorio

was named and the Troutman Street ambush was attempted.

In May 1966—19 months after he had been kidnapped—Bonanno reappeared. It soon became obvious to the other Mafia leaders that Bonanno had no intention of sticking to their arrangement. Upset with DiGregorio's failure to prosecute the war successfully, they dumped him and brought in a tougher man, Paul Sciacca. However, Sciacca could not handle a Joe Bonanno–led opposition. Several of his men were badly shot up in gun battles and in the most spectacular incident in the war three Sciacca henchmen were machine-gunned to death in a Queens restaurant. In short order five others on each side died.

Then in 1968 Bonanno, felled by a severe heart attack, flew off to his Tucson, Arizona, home. He sent word now that he was retiring, a statement the commission not surprisingly greeted skeptically. They continued to wage war in Brooklyn and appeared to make some moves against Bonanno and his followers in Arizona. A bomb went off at the Bonanno home, and, in a bizarre development a number of other bombs were exploded at other homes; some or perhaps all of these were planted by a rogue FBI agent.

Finally the conflict petered out and an arrangement was made. The Bonannos kept control of their Western interests but Sciacca (and later Natale Evola) was accepted as the boss of New York. The war was over and with it Bonanno's dreams of vast new powers.

It may be the Banana War made a valuable object lesson for the other Mafia leaders. When Bonanno's long-imprisoned underboss Carmine Galante emerged from prison in the 1970s, took command of the family and started a violent drive to extend his power, he was summarily executed. Galante was accorded no opportunity to come before the board and explain his actions.

BANDIDOS: Outlaw biker gang

The Bandidos is an outlaw biker gang centered in Texas. The group is estimated to be at least 600 strong and generally believed to be involved in carrying out missions for organized crime. The Bandidos is big in the manufacturing and dealing of both methamphetamines and cocaine. As such it is both supplier and client for the mob. It has been said that the Bandidos will deal with not only mafiosi types but even rogue mobsters such as turncoat Sammy "the Bull" Gravano because the gang feels it can deal out whatever punishment is required, no matter who the party is. This may be a bit of bravado as it is also said that the Bandidos is most circumspect in dealing with "big timers." Bandidos members are credited with a full array of criminal activities, including murder for the gang's own account or for organized crime. They are into larceny, arson, armed robbery, dynamite offenses, and weapons dealing. Because of the huge revenues the gang accumulates, the Bandidos looks for "legit outlets," such as massage parlors and escort services.

BANK manipulation by Mafia

The mob's interest in the banking system was undoubtedly triggered by its laundering problems—the need to move safely its huge profits from gambling operations (especially casino skimming) and narcotics and other heavy cash-flow enterprises. With Mafia-financed banks, especially in Florida, this laundering requirement was fulfilled, as was the need for a stolen securities repository against which good-money loans could be written.

As the Mafia became more accustomed to the intricacies of banking, the mobsters began to see the banks as something worth robbing. As Slick Willie Sutton had maintained, they were "where the money is."

Many crime families engage in bank looting on a straight and simple basis. Operating through front men, mafiosi buy up enough shares in a bank to gain effective control and either install their own management or make existing management totally complaint to their wishes. Loans are then made to Mafia applicants and businesses. These loans are never repaid. If the banks have insufficient insurance and supervision, the depositors will take the loss.

Another even more sophisticated manipulation involves keeping the bank healthy and viable and using it to furnish phony statements of worth for mob figures who, in turn, are able to obtain loans from other banks. By scattering the loans to many banks around the country, it can be a long time before the original bank comes under suspicion.

The mob has also found it worthwhile to use a captive bank as an intelligence resource, since a bank can get financial information from other banks regarding any individual or company in the country. Banks share information with each other on a level financial reporting firms are unable to match. With such intelligence the mobster can zero in on logical victims or even check up on individuals ostensibly cooperating with them to make sure they are not enjoying more revenue than the criminals want them to have.

BANKRUPTCY scams

The discovery of the bankruptcy laws must have been to the Mafia what the wheel was to early man. Bankruptcies are used by legitimate businessmen as protection from the collection of debts. Organized crime, having seen how easy it was to pull a bankruptcy scam, moved its operators in. According to one estimate by U.S. Justice Department sources, crime syndicates pull off at least 250 such scams or "bustouts" annually, all netting anywhere from a quarter of a million dollars up to several million.

The bustout is worked either by taking over an established company with a good credit reputation, the preferred method, or by setting up a new firm. To accomplish the latter, the New York crime families use a "front man" who has no criminal record and give him "nut money"—anywhere from $30,000 to $100,000—which is put in a bank to establish credit; the firm orders supplies that are quickly paid for in full. Then, as orders are increased, payments start coming through just a bit slower. It is very difficult for a supplier to turn its back on an account whose orders are increasing. When the orders become king-sized, business greed or hunger on the supplier's part tends to overwhelm its caution.

The mob concentrates on businesses with goods that can be turned over rapidly and thus shipped off to another company, often under control of the mob as well. Liquor supplies frequently go in the front door of a mob restaurant and bar and right out the back door. When the nut money is suddenly pulled out of the bank and the business is shut down, all creditors will find is a bankrupt shell of a company and absolutely no assets.

A mob restaurant-bar in Queens, New York, simply vanished with the placing of a sign in its window, reading: "Closed due to oven fire. Will reopen shortly." Of course, it never reopened and creditors found not a thing on the premises; all liquor, food supplies and furnishings were gone. If there had been an oven fire, it was not evident. The oven had been carted off as well.

Not long ago a conglomerate, stuck with a publishing division some $3 million in debt, was approached by a front man representing New Jersey syndicate operators who offered to take over the publishing company for $10,000 and the assumption of the $3 million debt. The parent firm jumped at the offer. It turned out the $10,000 was paid in the form of two rubber checks, but that very first week the mob got hold of a cash flow of $90,000 and made them good.

Then the publishing firm's creditors were contacted and told the past debts would be paid off over a period of 18 months but that they would have to continue to service the company's printing needs and that current bills would be paid as they came in. The creditors agreed and the operators soon ran up another couple of million in added debts.

The old bills were not paid nor were the newer ones. In the meantime funds continued to be siphoned out of the cash-flow pipeline. Expensive typesetting machines and electronic typewriters were ordered and quickly disappeared. In the end everyone dealing with the firm was stuck, except for the operator of a copy-machine firm who personally appeared to reclaim his machines, wheeling them out of the offices while threatening to run over anyone getting in his way. He had, he told an inquirer, been burned too often by scammers before.

The speed with which the mob can move in such a scam is illustrated by an operation by the Genovese family. They took over a large New York meat wholesaler after getting it in the family's debt and then insisting on putting in their own man as president to watch-dog their money. Over a 10-day period poultry and meat were bought up at high prices and sold off at lower amounts. Then the Genovese man disappeared, leaving the company once more in the hands of the old management—with the advice that it declare immediate bankruptcy. Everyone got stuck except the mob.

BARBARA, Joseph, Sr. (1905–1959): Apalachin Conference host

The fact that the Apalachin Conference of 1957 was broken up by a New York State police raid couldn't help but throw Joseph Barbara Sr. into public attention. The owner of the mansion where the gangsters met, Barbara was dubbed "The Underworld's Host" by journalists. In fact, Barbara's home was the site of many underworld conferences, of national and regional scope. According to Joe Bonanno's memoirs, the Barbara mansion had been the site not only of the underworld's 1956 national convention but also of the election of members to the national commission for the next five years.

Despite the fiasco of 1957, the mob generally held conferences in safe areas, which the Barbara estate had otherwise been. Since Barbara was a regular Mafia host it would have been inconceivable that "protection" had not been taken care of; the underworld slates meetings only at areas deemed police-proof. According to Joe Bonanno, in his autobiography *A Man of Honor* (a work that might be deemed spurious for many of its claims, but credible concerning Apalachin), Barbara's connections with many law enforcement agencies had up until that time assured privacy. But over the year preceding Apalachin, Bonanno said, Barbara had been at odds with some law enforcement people over money matters.

Barbara had come to the United States from Sicily in 1921 when he was 16. He emerged in crime as an enforcer in Buffalo, New York, Mafia circles and was arrested several times in connection with a number of murders in Pennsylvania, then within the influence of the aggressive Buffalo family. One Barbara victim was believed to have been racketeer Sam Wichner, who came to Barbara's home in 1933 apparently to discuss business matters with Barbara, Santo Volpe and Angelo Valente, Wichner's silent partners in bootlegging operations. According to the police, Barbara personally strangled Wichner to death. However, as in all the other murder investigations, nothing that would stand up in court could be produced and Barbara remained free from prosecution. Throughout a criminal career that spanned more than three and a half decades Barbara was only convicted of one crime, the illegal acquisition of 300,000 pounds of sugar in 1946.

After the conviction, Barbara became a beer and soft drink distributor, holding important and exclusive upstate New York franchises, acquired, no doubt, through offers that certain parties could not refuse. After the 1956 national meeting, Barbara suffered a heart attack, and in fact virtually all the mobsters caught at the 1957 Apalachin Conference insisted they had just happened to drop in to pay a visit to a sick friend. It was the merest coincidence, apparently, that all the boys happened to be struck by the same idea at the same time.

While some matters on the agenda for the conference became known, the full story of Apalachin '57 has been shrouded in mystery. Barbara was of little help, insisting he was much too ill to testify. The State Investigation Commission sent its own heart specialist to examine Barbara, and in May 1959 a state supreme court justice ordered him to testify before the commission. Of course, claims of illness by mafiosi always produce two sets of medical men, each with different assessments. In Barbara's case, he proved his doctor correct. A month later he dropped dead of a heart attack.

After the 1957 fiasco, Barbara vacated his Apalachin mansion, now too prominent for a residence. In fact, the 58-acre estate was sold for conversion into a tourist attraction, presumably into some form of Mafia Disneyland. Nothing came of the idea.

See also APALACHIN CONFERENCE

BARNES, Leroy "Nicky" (1933–): Harlem narcotics king

In the words of one New York reporter, Leroy Barnes is "a sort of Muhammed Ali of crime, or even better the black man's Al Capone."

Born to a poor family in Harlem in 1933, Leroy "Nicky" Barnes was for a time the king of Harlem, the first boss of the "Black Mafia," if the term is correctly understood. The *New York Times Magazine* profiled him thusly: "Checking in at Shalimar, the Gold Lounge, or Smalls . . . he will be bowed to, nodded to, but not touched." The juke seemed to always be playing "Baaad, Baaad Leroy Brown," which, according to Barnes's fans, was written specifically for him. "It's like the Godfather movie," said a New York police detective of Barnes wading through mobs of admirers, "being treated like the goddamn Pope."

During his heyday, many writers, the present one included, felt Barnes characterized a shift in organized crime leadership to the newer ghetto minorities. But as it turned out, while Barnes became a multimillionaire and was lionized by fellow blacks as "taking over" the mob, he was really no more effective than other ghetto criminals, ultimately capable of exploit-

Drug kingpin Leroy "Nicky" Barnes cut a romantic figure in Harlem before he was sent to prison for life. Mafiosi with whom he cooperated missed him deeply, having lost the opportunity to insist that the Black Mafia "have taken over and we couldn't run drugs anymore even if we wanted to."

ing only his own kind. Far from taking over from the Mafia, he was used by it, playing the typical role of ghetto criminals, that of visible kingpin of the street rackets—in Barnes's case, the drug racket. He was indeed king of the Harlem narcotics distributors, but little more.

Barnes's success was mainly due to his alliance with Crazy Joey Gallo, a maverick of the Mafia whom he had met in New York's Green Haven Prison. Barnes was serving a narcotics violations sentence, Gallo doing time for extortion. In his past, Gallo handled or knew of the modus operandi in the mob's dealing with Harlem pushers. He showed Barnes how to achieve dominance in the field and so make himself vital to the mob. It was said that when

Gallo was released, the pair agreed to work together. With Gallo's help, Barnes would gain access to large amounts of heroin shipped directly from Italian sources while Barnes, in return, would supply black "troops" to Gallo when he needed them. In time Barnes was the chief distributor of narcotics in black ghetto areas, not only in New York City, but also in upstate New York, New Jersey and Pennsylvania.

Nicky Barnes became more than rich; he became "flamboyantly" rich. He was a walking bank, always with an impressive bankroll on him. During one of his arrests, $130,000 was found in the trunk of his automobile. He had a Mercedes Benz and a Citroen Maserati, and the police themselves admitted they had no idea how many Cadillacs, Lincoln Continentals and Thunderbirds Barnes also owned. Barnes maintained several apartments in Manhattan, plus one in the Riverdale section of the Bronx and at least two in New Jersey.

Although Barnes lived an openly lavish life, he beat the government on its reliable tax evasion gambit—Barnes paid taxes on a quarter of a million dollars in annual "miscellaneous income." The IRS insisted Barnes owed a lot more, but substantiating that was no easy matter. In fact, Barnes seemed more or less immune to prosecution. Although he sported 13 arrests, they all led to only one sentence, a short one, behind bars (where he met Gallo). It was this record that made Barnes a cult figure in Harlem and other black communities. "Sure, that's the reason the kids loved the guy and wanted to be like him," a federal narcotics agent told a newsweekly. "Mr. Untouchable—that's what they called him—was rich, but he was smart, too, and sassy about it. The bastard loved to make us cops look like idiots."

Eventually in 1978 Nicky Barnes fell, thanks to a federal narcotics strike force. He was sentenced to life imprisonment and fined $125,000. Behind bars Barnes found his life less than rewarding. In recent years he has started talking to authorities, handing them his confederates in his drug empire in an effort to win his freedom eventually. What he delivered was about a dozen blacks, men who he said were cheating him of his women and the money he had left behind. But that was all Barnes had to offer. What of his vaunted distribution setup, direct to Sicily, if you will? Barnes could offer nothing because he never had it. Mafiosi control the drug supplies. They delivered to Barnes and then he operated as little more than a high-priced pusher. Barnes

was so insulated from the rest of the operation that he could offer the government little about the flow of narcotics. After Barnes's departure the drug racket continued to flourish in the black ghettos; distributors, small, medium and large, remained a dime a dozen for the Mafia. Eventually Barnes went into the witness protection program for his limited service.

Not that the mob did not miss Leroy. He had been so valuable to them. They could say "the niggers have taken over . . . We couldn't run drugs anymore even if we wanted to." Clearly the best friend the so-called Black Mafia ever had has been and continues to be the Italian-American model.

See also BLACK MAFIA

BARREL murder: Early mafioso execution method

Barrel murder—wherein a corpse was deposited in a barrel and abandoned—came into vogue in this country in the 1870s, especially in New Orleans and New York where the first waves of Italian emigration washed ashore. It was the outbreak of such crimes, in which the victim invariably was an Italian, that first led American authorities to announce the presence of the Mafia in this country.

The barrel was deposited in the ocean if the corpse was not meant to be found or else, rather perversely, shipped off by rail to some distant city—and a non-existent address. In other cases the barrel was simply left in a vacant lot or even on a street corner. This was often done if the purpose of the killing was to carry out a Black Hand murder threat and thus advertise the slaughtering abilities of such extortionists.

The leading exponents of barrel murder were Lupo the Wolf (Ignazio Saietta) and the Morello family, a homicidal pack of cutthroats, brothers, half-brothers and brothers-in-law, from Corleone, Sicily. Together they were believed to have slaughtered and barreled at least 100 victims over three decades.

Eventually the power of the Morellos and of Lupo, who went to prison, was broken and the mobs stopped utilizing the barrel techniques, mainly because it so clearly established the crime as a mob job.

Possibly almost as troubling was the fact that many freelance killers started using the technique in an effort to shift the blame for their acts on the Mafia. Oddly, the technique was revived in 1976 when 71-year-old Johnny Roselli, involved along with Chicago crime boss Sam Giancana in the CIA-underworld plots to assassinate Fidel Castro, was murdered and his body stuffed into a 55-gallon oil drum and dumped into waters off Florida. The drum eventually floated to shore despite the holes punched in its sides and heavy chains weighing it down. Of course, any near-competent hit man should have predicted that gases produced by the body's decomposition would lift the grisly drum to the surface.

Sources in the underworld also pointed out that the barrel technique had long been abandoned, but whoever had disposed of Roselli's body in this fashion either did not know that or perhaps was simply using it as an expedient to label it a mob job. Since the Roselli murder remains unsolved, the possibility cannot be excluded that this method of victim disposal might well have been used to make a mob job look like a CIA job.

BASILE, Tobia (c. 1809–?): Camorra's grand old man

The grand old man of the Camorra, the Neopolitan criminal society, Tobia Basile trained many erstwhile Camorristas who ended up as important members of the American underworld. A seasoned criminal when he first entered prison in Italy in 1860, Basile was to remain behind bars for the next 30 years, there to become Italy's greatest crime teacher, instructing numerous eager inmates in the ways and deeds of the Camorra.

The Italian sociologist G. Alongi, a 19th-century expert on the Camorra, made a detailed study of Basile. He wrote:

His numerous pupils used to go to his lessons regularly to listen to his advice, to learn from him the science of "prudence in crime" for he was a walking encyclopedia on the art of the mala vita. His long stay in the penitentiary, his cold and reflective temperament, his cleverness, and his venerable age made him a much-heeded master. For a few cents he would teach the art of stealing from a puppet entirely covered with numberless tiny bells that would jingle at the slightest touch; he taught the tradition of the Honorable Society and the chief rules to be observed in order to conform to its spirit, the art of dealing a straight or a treacherous blow, the way of slipping along the floor without making any noise, the secrets of the Camorristic jargon, a quantity of methods successful in diverting the attention of the police, the way of behaving in the courts, and the numberless swindles committed

against the emigrant who, coming from the provinces, stops a few days in Naples on his way to America. This extraordinary man was in possession of a complete outfit of false keys, files, and picklocks, and thought the aspirants all that was necessary to know before being initiated into the Honorable Society.

When Basile was released from prison he was a shrunken old man well over 80 and he was, he felt, an old warhorse ready to be set out to graze. He wanted only to contemplate the world, to be consulted from time to time by other Camorristas, but above all to be free of cares. Unfortunately he had a wife who talked endlessly and nagged. It was not right that an honored Camorrista could not enjoy a peaceful retirement. Basile suffered 10 years of torment and then, suddenly, his wife disappeared in May 1900. Newspaper reporters made a big thing of it, wondering if some of Basile's old enemies were exacting vengeance. Not so, Basile insisted. His wife he said had been abducted "for ransom which a poor man like me doesn't have.

Basile grew more senile with the passing years, walking about Naples mumbling of honor and respect and the art of murder. One day Basile was seen packing his belongings onto a cart and then he was gone, never to be seen again.

Then in 1910 the Basile house was torn down by a new owner so that he could build anew. In the Basile bedroom, workers found a shrine of Our Lady of Mount Carmel, whom Camorristas regarded as their special patron. It was removed to reveal a false wall. There behind the wall was the skeleton of Tobia Basile's wife. From the condition of the sealed compartment it was obvious that the woman had been walled up alive and had for many days screamed and tried to claw her way out of her brick and plaster tomb. The position of the bed indicated Basile had lain there with his head no more than two feet from the wall.

It had been the last crime of an honored member of the Camorra asserting his right to the respect of others.

See also CAMORRA

BATISTA, Fulgencio (1901–1973): Cuban dictator and Meyer Lansky partner

When at 2:30 A.M., New Year's Day 1959, Fulgencio Batista, the dictator of Cuba, arrived at Camp Columbia outside Havana with seven carloads of armed guards, it marked the end of the game for him and the American underworld in Cuba. It is not known how many millions of dollars Batista and several of his cronies took with them—after they had already shipped a huge amount of wealth to Swiss banks. Considerably, however, before coming to the airfield, Batista had been on the phone, telling the chosen few that Castro had won, that the rebels would soon take possession of the capital. But Batista's most important call did not go to a fellow Cuban. It went to Polish Jew Maier Suchowljansky—better known as Meyer Lansky—easily at the time the most important gangster in America. And in Cuba, for that matter.

Lansky followed Batista out of the country within a matter of hours, although he did leave representatives at his casino enterprises to see if Castro would be interested in the same financial setup Lansky had provided Batista. Castro's answer was to throw them in jail for a time before kicking them out of the country. Celebrating the demise of the Batista regime, the Cuban populace went on a slot-machine smashing rampage. It might not have been on a par with the storming of the Winter Palace or Versailles, but for Lansky and the American mob the result was devastating.

Lansky had enjoyed a long relationship with Batista, even before he took the Cuban to his hotel room to show him a set of suitcases stuffed with a reported $6 million, just a sort of good-faith demonstration to prove how easily the boys could set up a gambling empire that would make them and Batista rich. Batista knew Lansky was a producer; he had in the past enjoyed the fruits of a rewarding business by supplying Lansky with a steady flow of molasses to keep a mob bootleg operation functioning.

Batista considered Lansky a "genius," a fact he repeatedly demonstrated by laughing off the efforts of other big-time mobsters to muscle in on Lansky. When Santo Trafficante, the Mafia boss of Tampa, Florida, tried to set up his own casinos on the island, Batista waved him off coldly, saying. "You have to get approval from the 'Little Man' [Lansky] before you can get a license on this island."

Magnanimously, Lansky cut Trafficante in for a small piece of the action, more to demonstrate his power with Batista than to placate Trafficante. That hold continued even after Batista fled. Batista kept hoping that Castro would fall so that he and Lansky could return to Cuba. Needless to say, Batista would never do without Lansky who made taking bribes so easy. The Little Man's aide, Doc Stacher, handled the couriers who took all the gambling profits and Batista's cash bribes direct to Switzerland. Stacher exercised the right to make deposits to Batista's account but the Cuban dictator alone had the authority to withdraw funds from the account.

Obviously Batista never wanted for money during the remaining dozen years of his life. And undoubtedly he often considered the truism that if all his supporters had been as remarkably efficient as Lansky, no upstart like Fidel Castro would ever have overthrown him.

See also BAGMAN

BATTAGLIA, Sam "Teets" (1908–1973): Chicago Outfit's narcotics overlord

For many years during the reign of Sam Giancana as boss of the Chicago Outfit, Sam "Teets" Battaglia was regarded as his heir-apparent. Battaglia was also considered Giancana's narcotics overlord, belying the claim by some, including informer Joe Valachi, that Chicago had an edict against dealing in drugs. The fact was that narcotics was so important in mob economics that traffickers had to have approval to operate. Battaglia dispensed or withheld such rights and permission.

Battaglia and Giancana had climbed a long road up from Chicago's notorious juvenile 42 Gang of the late 1920s. Battaglia succeeded because he always exhibited the same vicious outlook as his mentor. In 1924, at age 16, he was arrested for burglary. In all he accumulated more than 25 arrests for burglary, larceny, robbery, assault and attempted murder. He was considered the prime suspect in at least seven homicides.

The simple recitation of Battaglia's criminal record does not capture his essential zaniness. Battaglia—nicknamed "Teets" because of his muscular chest—first came to the public's attention for a bizarre crime in 1930. He was arrested for robbing at gunpoint the wife of the mayor of Chicago, Mrs. William Hale Thompson, of her jewels worth $15,500. Rubbing it in, Teets marched off with the gun and badge of her policeman chauffeur. However, a hitch developed in the police case when a positive identification could not be made and Teets insisted he was watching a movie when the robbery occurred. He also produced a half dozen witnesses who said they were watching him watch the movie.

The robbery took place on November 17 and until the end of the year Teets was a busy criminal, being involved in one fatal killing and one attempted killing. Such remarkable exploits attracted the favorable attention of Capone mobsters and, like Giancana, Teets was on the rise. By 1950s he was involved in, besides narcotics, mob extortion, burglary, fraud and murders. He was also the king of much of the mob's loan shark activities and sat as a "judge" in "debtors court" held in the basement of Casa Madrid. Here Battaglia heard the cases of delinquent juice victims and meted out the appropriate penalties, either severe beatings or death.

Battaglia, a hoodlum with far more brawn than brain, became a major success in organized crime. He was a millionaire several times over and owned a luxurious horse-breeding farm and country estate in Kane County, Illinois. In the mid-1960s when the elders in the Chicago Outfit, Paul Ricca and Tony Accardo, decided that Giancana had to be downgraded in authority because of the intense heat he was taking, Giancana wanted Battaglia named his successor. In that fashion, Giancana knew, he would maintain effective control of the organization. However, Ricca and Accardo decided they favored instead the duo of Cicero boss Joey Aiuppa and Jackie the Lackey Cerone.

The mob infighting on the succession resolved itself in 1967 when Teets was finally ushered off to prison for 15 years on an extortion conviction. He died six years later. It has been suggested by some crime experts that there was no way Sam Giancana could be forcibly removed from the Chicago crime scene until three of his murderous followers had first vanished. The trio were Teets Battaglia, Fifi Buccieri and Mad Sam DeStefano. All three died in 1973, Mad Sam violently. Giancana was murdered in 1975.

See also FORTY-TWO GANG

BATTLE, Jose Miguel, Sr. (?–): Cuban-American godfather

Much is made of the so-called Cuban Mafia as a potent new force on the criminal scene in America. More correctly it should be viewed as an adjunct on franchise operation of organized crime. In the New York–New Jersey area the Cuban-American racketeers operate a $45-million-a-year illegal gambling syndicate that has been dubbed "the Corporation."

According to the President's Commission on Organized Crime, the "godfather" of the Corporation is Jose Miguel Battle Sr., a former Havana anti-vice officer—in the days when Meyer Lansky dominated the vice scene in Cuba—who was recruited by the Central Intelligence Agency to play a major role in the Bay of Pigs invasion. Battle had lived in Union City, New Jersey, and since then has made his home in Miami.

Sworn testimony before the commission indicated that about 2,500 people in New York City worked for the crime group. One informer testified that the Corporation established a foothold in New York through Cuban and other Hispanic-owned groceries and bars. The Corporation's "enforcer" dealt harshly with competitors, assigning men to "kill the people and burn down their stores." He said 10 to 15 other people, not the targets of the hit men, died in such arson incidents.

A profile of the Corporation as sketched by the President's Commission showed it to control legitimate finance and mortgage companies, banks, travel agencies and real estate companies worth "several hundred million dollars." The value of such holdings is that they permit laundering of funds by creating non-existent sales to explain illegitimate income. The Corporation is also big in laundering money through the Puerto Rico lottery, buying up the tickets of big winners for more than real value and then cashing the tickets.

One of the more fanciful tales told by some journalists is that this new activity of the Cuban Mafia is part of the process of replacing and even killing off the traditional mafiosi. The President's Commission demonstrated this was nonsense, pointing out that the Corporation under Battle paid the Mafia a fee to run illegal numbers in its territory of Manhattan, Brooklyn, the Bronx and northern New Jersey. Battle was finally indicted in 2004 for racketeering and other organized crime charges.

Cooperation is the operative word in gambling deals between the Latinos and the mafiosi, as it is in narcotics. Organized crime, unlike big business, is not subject to "takeover bids." Only franchisees need apply.

See also "CUBAN MAFIA"

BAY of Pigs invasion: Mafia's great disappointment

The ill-fated Bay of Pigs invasion on April 17, 1961—an attempt to topple Cuba's Fidel Castro—was a black-letter day not only for U.S. foreign policy and the CIA in particular, but also for the patriotic Mafia. Top mafiosi saw the success of such a campaign as a surefire method for their return to gambling eminence in Havana. After all, neither the U.S. government nor organized crime believed in expropriation of capital and that was what the mob had suffered.

Santo Trafficante Jr.—like his father long kept in check by Meyer Lansky, the top mob power in Havana under Batista—now saw his chance to become the new gambling czar of Cuba. Trafficante was rather fully knowledgeable about the invasion plans, a fact that might have disconcerted U.S. Intelligence but was inevitable since he maintained close liaison with Cuban refugee groups in Florida. (There has always been a sizable group within law enforcement and some organized crime circles that maintains that Trafficante had sold out to Castro, was informing for him and, thus, was playing both ends.)

On the assumption that the Bay of Pigs operation would be successful, Trafficante dispatched an aide to Nassau where the latter waited with a fortune in gold. The Trafficante man was to follow the victorious troops into the Cuban capital and get the roulette wheels and dice tables going immediately. In *Syndicate Abroad*, author Hank Messick cites a secret report of the Bahamas police as identifying the Trafficante operatives as Joe Silesi, better known as Joe Rivers, a veteran of the Havana gambling scene.

For his part, Meyer Lansky was also rooting for the success of the Bay of Pigs, certain that no matter what Trafficante did, he had the connections and knowhow to organize Havana anew.

With the failure of the Bay of Pigs, Lansky moved his action toward Nassau and the Bahamas. Trafficante remained a secondary force, a victim of flawed U.S. government policy.

BENDER, Tony (1899–1962): Genovese lieutenant and murder victim

Who'd have thought that Tony Bender's best man would have him bumped off? But when Bender (real name Anthony Strollo) married Edna Goldenberg, Vito Genovese, as Bender put it, "Stood up for me, and I stood up for him." For the next several decades Bender remained tight with Genovese—until the Mafia boss had him murdered.

Actually it was surprising that Bender lasted as long as he did. Within the councils of the underworld it was no secret that Bender's loyalty was always for sale to the highest bidder. He changed colors and sides like a chameleon. Early in the 1930s he stood with Salvatore Maranzano in the great Mafia War but transferred his allegiance to Lucky Luciano when Luciano looked like a sure winner. Then he allied himself with Genovese, Luciano's right hand man. When Genovese fled to Europe to avoid a murder conviction in the late 1930s, leaving instructions for Bender to "hold things together," Bender just as readily transferred his loyalties to Frank Costello and the murderous Albert Anastasia. On Genovese's return after World War II, Bender decided the future lay with Genovese and followed him like a faithful killer dog for the next decade, among other things running the rackets in Greenwich Village and criminal activities on the New Jersey docks, succeeding the deported Joe Adonis in the latter chore.

During this period Bender probably set up more murder victims than any other mafioso. That was inevitable if you worked for the cunning and ever-plotting Genovese, as he was striving to achieve the position the press labeled "boss of bosses." Friendship meant little to Bender. When he learned in 1959 that Genovese had marked his best friend, Little Augie Pisano, for murder—even Genovese was tenderhearted enough originally to try not to involve Bender—Bender cheerfully volunteered to set up the hit. He broke bread with Little Augie in a Manhattan restaurant while gunmen took up positions in Little Augie's car to shoot him after he left.

Bender played the same role in the 1957 attempted murder of Frank Costello. Bender met Costello at Chandler's restaurant at 5 P.M. and was able to learn the Mafia leader's plans for the rest of the evening.

In 1958 Bender changed camps again, joining the deported Luciano, Meyer Lansky, Carlo Gambino and the same Costello he had earlier tried to set up, in a plot to get rid of Genovese. It involved railroading Genovese into a sucker narcotics deal and then feeding him to federal authorities. Bender's involvement was proposed by Gambino and at first Luciano drew back from the prospect, knowing how twisty Bender was. However Gambino explained to

Tony Bender (foreground, wearing hat and surrounded by newsmen) ran Mafia rackets in Greenwich Village, New York City, and on the New Jersey docks. He was known within the mob as a man whose loyalty could shift to the highest bidder—until Vito Genovese had him "put to sleep."

Luciano that he had had a private talk with Bender who was very much convinced that he, Gambino, was the man of the future, and he swore fealty to him.

The plot worked. In 1959 Genovese was sent to prison for 15 years; he would die behind bars 10 years later. Unfortunately for Bender, Genovese managed his crime family from his prison cell and with machiavellian logic was able to figure out the various twists of the plotting against him. He determined that Bender had to have been a part of the conspiracy, that it was he who advised him to give up, that the most he would get would be a five-year sentence.

On the morning of April 8, 1962, Bender left his home. His wife told him, "You better put on your topcoat. It's chilly."

Bender demurred. "I'm only going out for a few minutes," he said. "Besides, I'm wearing thermal underwear."

Bender strolled down the sidewalk and out of underworld society, never to be seen alive again.

There have been many underworld tales of what happened to him. One was that he became part of the West Side Highway. Another, in Greenwich Village crime circles, was that the Genovese contract on Bender was given to a one-time Jewish boxer-turned loan shark and contract killer. In this version Bender's body was dumped into a cement mixer and is now part of a Manhattan skyscraper. And it was said

that that was the only way an opportunist like Bender could make it to the top.

See also PISANO, LITTLE AUGIE

BERMAN, Otto "Abbadabba" (1880–1935): Policy game fixer

Before Lucky Luciano and Meyer Lansky realized how lucrative it was, Dutch Schultz had in the early 1930s found the way to fix the numbers racket in order to control the winning digits.

Avaricious to the core, Schultz did not like the fact that policy produced a mere 40 percent profit on the money gambled. Every paid-off winner grieved Dutch. If he could only find a way to fix the results, he realized, he could greatly increase profits.

Schultz took over the Harlem rackets, business concerns that took off thanks to a mathematical "magician" named Otto "Abbadabba" Berman. At that time the numbers were determined by the betting statistics at various race tracks. It was impossible for the mob to control the figures at the New York tracks, but when those tracks were closed the numbers were based on the results from tracks that the underworld had successfully infiltrated, such as Chicago's Hawthorne, Cincinnati's Coney Island and New Orleans's Fair Grounds. Berman worked out a system whereby aides could pour money in on some races to manipulate the payoff number. It was believed that

Abbadabba's mathematical wizardry added 10 percent to every million dollars a day the mob took in.

Dutch Schultz, noted as being one of the stingiest crime bosses in New York, paid his top gangster aides—men like Lulu Rosenkrantz and Abe Landau—something like $1,200 a week. By contrast he paid Abbadabba $10,000.

In 1935 a vote by the syndicate's national commission passed the death sentence on Dutch Schultz after he announced plans to bump off Thomas E. Dewey. Then a racket-busting prosecutor, Dewey was closing in on Schultz. The other top mobsters in the syndicate, men like Lucky Luciano, Meyer Lansky, Louis Lepke and Joe Adonis, felt that such a killing would cause a widespread crackdown in which they would all be hurt. So much for criminal statesmanship. It was also a fact that all the mobsters were eager to cut in on Schultz's rackets.

On October 23, 1935, Schultz and two bodyguards, Landau and Rosenkrantz, arrived at the Palace Chop House in Newark, New Jersey. A three-man syndicate hit squad was dispatched to take care of them. Unfortunately, another late arrival joined the Schultz party. It was Abbadabba Berman.

All four were shot to death, Abbadabba included. A final testament to the skills of the magician was contained in the papers the quartet had been going over. They indicated that over a certain period of time the Schultz policy banks had taken in $827,253.43 in bets and paid out only $313,711.99. The difference between that last figure and the approximately $500,000 which should have been paid out to winners was attributed to Abbadabba Berman's skills.

His demise cost the syndicate literally millions of dollars annually. For a time others tried to imitate Berman's technique—as much as could be figured out—but none came within a fraction of his results. Even Vito Genovese, probably the most anti-Semitic crime bigwig in the syndicate, mourned the passing of "the Yid adding machine."

BILOTTI, Thomas (1940–1985): Castellano aide and murder victim

A rule of thumb: The assassination of a top aide of a Mafia boss often presages the boss's murder. The reason: It usually weakens the boss and at the same time eliminates a figure who, if he survives, could rally the crime family to his side.

Thomas Bilotti didn't exactly fit the pattern. Clearly he had moved up to top aide of Paul Castellano, the boss of the Gambino crime family. On the natural death of underboss Aniello Dellacroce (no close ally of Castellano) on December 2, 1985, Bilotti was slated to succeed as No. 2 man in the family—the eventual, logical successor to Castellano.

Under Castellano the Gambino family had been divided into two less than friendly camps. Before his death, Carlo Gambino, who wanted his brother-in-law Castellano to succeed him over the underboss Dellacroce, won his way by giving Dellacroce control of most of the crime family's Manhattan rackets. Dellacroce gained the allegiance of a number of Young Turks, especially John Gotti, said at the time to control the organization's rackets at JFK airport. Gotti, who idolized the murderous Albert Anastasia (a previous boss of the family), was clearly viewed as the ailing Dellacroce's successor and as such the logical heir to the position of underboss. The problem that arose within the Gambino family was that by December 1985 there were two logical heirs to the throne—obviously one too many.

Castellano had cast about among his supporters for someone deemed capable of standing up to the fiery and vicious Gotti. He came up with Bilotti and promoted him to the position of capo—in line with Gotti. What Castellano liked best about Bilotti was his toughness; he was known to smash opponents over the head with a baseball bat as a way of ending disputes. With the 70-year-old Castellano under several indictments and likely facing a long imprisonment, it appeared that Bilotti would jump over Gotti.

But, on December 16, 1985—two weeks to the day after underboss Dellacroce died—Castellano and Bilotti stepped from a limousine on New York's East 46th Street near the Sparks Steak House, where they had reservations to dine with three unknown individuals. The three men who showed up on the sidewalk carried semi-automatic weapons under their trench-coats and put six bullets each in Castellano and his protégé.

For a time authorities believed the motive was to kill Castellano, and Bilotti had to go just because he was there. However, after a period of gleaning information from informers and through electronic eavesdropping, investigators concluded that the Gotti faction had marked Bilotti as a primary target.

Bilotti, it was theorized, was not taken out first, according to custom, since it would alert both

Castellano and the authorities. A protective ring would surround Castellano and make him harder to kill. Castellano and Bilotti had to go together.

In the shifting eddies that mark Mafia power struggles, there are a few who make it to the top and some like Tommy Bilotti who are stopped just short.

See also CASTELLANO, PAUL

BINAGGIO, Charles (1909–1950): Kansas City political-criminal leader

The murder of Charley Binaggio, the political and criminal boss of Kansas City and real successor to Tom Pendergast, was arguably the most important killing in decades. Although the underworld itself might number many other homicides—that of O'Banion, Rothstein, Masseria, Maranzano, Schultz, Reles and Siegel, to name a few—as far more momentous, from the view of law and order, the April 6, 1950, killing of Binaggio and his "enforcer," Charley Gargotta, is paramount. Without those murders it is entirely possible that the famed Kefauver hearings might never have come about.

Even Kansas City, which had seen almost everything during the heyday of the Pendergast Machine, was shocked. Binaggio, at age 41, was found dead, shot four times in the head and stretched out in a swivel chair at his headquarters at the First District Democratic Club. Gargotta, a vicious muscleman and killer, lay on the floor nearby, the same number of bullet wounds in his head. Looking down on the scene were large portraits of President Harry Truman and Governor Forrest Smith, a man for whose recent election Binaggio took much credit.

The method of execution told much about Binaggio, who law enforcement men would speculate was an actual member of the Mafia—and if so, the highest ranked mafioso on any political ladder, a political boss on the brink of national importance.

In death there could be no doubt he had been subjected to Mafia violence. The bullet wounds in the heads of both men were arranged in two straight rows, forming "two deuces." This is called Little Joe in dice parlance, and it has long been the mob's sign for a welsher. When used in a murder it indicates the mob not only did the job but also wanted everyone to know it. Clearly, Binaggio had welshed to the crime syndicate and he was paying for it.

Binaggio was considered a political "comer," steeped in scandal perhaps, but likely to overcome such trivialities through the exercise of raw power. Born in Texas, Binaggio was a drifter with arrests in Denver for vagrancy and carrying a concealed weapon. He landed in Kansas City at 23 and joined the operations of North Side leader Johnny Lazia, probably through the sponsorship of mafioso Jim Balestrere. Lazia delivered the votes of the North Side to Democratic boss Pendergast and was in turn allowed to control all gambling, racing wires, liquor and vice in the area.

Lazia was murdered in 1934 after he got into tax trouble and made signs of informing against the machine in exchange for gentle treatment. This left the way clear for Binaggio's climb up the criminal ladder. By the early 1940s, Binaggio had a lock on the North Side while the Pendergast machine was foundering.

In 1946 President Truman ordered a purge of Congressman Roger C. Slaughter who was consistently voting against the administration. Truman called in Jim Pendergast, the late Tom's nephew successor, and ordered him to get the nomination for Enos Axtell. Slaughter was defeated but the *Kansas City Star* uncovered evidence of wholesale ballot fraud. In the ensuing investigations, a woman election watcher was shot to death on the porch of her home. And just before critical state hearings were scheduled to begin, the safe at City Hall went up in a huge dynamite blast that destroyed the fraudulent ballot evidence.

Binaggio, everyone suspected but could not prove, was the brain behind both the ballot fraud and the City Hall bombing. As a result, only one minor hanger-on, Snags Klein, was punished with a short prison term for the crime.

Now Binaggio was ready to make his move for supremacy against Jim Pendergast. Pendergast was nowhere near as astute as his late uncle and, by 1948, Kansas City, politically and criminally, belonged to Binaggio. However, Binaggio needed a political slush fund to wipe out the Pendergast forces and he appealed to Mafia crime families around the country for financial aid. Many responded, Chicago most generously. More than $200,000 came in from the underworld in exchange for Binaggio's promise that once he got his man in the governorship both Kansas City and St. Louis would become "wide open" for syndicate operations.

Binaggio backed Forrest Smith for the office and Smith won. There was no hard evidence, however, that Binaggio had funneled something like $150,000 into Smith's campaign. But the other crime families had put up the money and expected results. Binaggio failed to deliver. A St. Louis newspaper broke the story about the understanding Binaggio had with the underworld and the St. Louis police commissioner blocked all efforts to open up the city.

Binaggio stalled for time on his deal. It wouldn't wash with the mob. They were troubled with thoughts that Binaggio had merely backed the winner and hadn't put up the money they had advanced him. Like true businessmen the crime families wrote off their investment. They also wrote off Binaggio and Gargotta. Little Joe was the warning to others not to try the same thing.

See also FIVE IRON MEN; LAST CHANCE TAVERN; LITTLE JOE

BIOFF, Willie Morris (1900–1955): Movie extortionist and stool pigeon

In his 55 years Willie Bioff enjoyed many unsavory careers. He was a pimp, a procurer, a strongarm man, a labor racketeer, a stool pigeon, and a friend of leading politicians. But his chief claim to fame was as a Hollywood extortionist, shaking down tough-minded movie moguls, making them quake with fear. It was said that Louis B. Mayer was convinced that Bioff would kill him as readily as he would look at him.

Bioff's life of crime started when he was 10 years old. He lined up some girls and sold their favors atop a pool table to other schoolboys. By the time he was 16, he was a full-scale procurer with a string of hookers working for him in the Levee, Chicago's worst vice area. For a time he worked with Harry Guzik, another notorious procurer, and as such came in contact with The Capone mob. Harry Guzik was the brother of Jake Guzik, Al Capone's closest gang ally, who saw in Bioff greater talents. A man who could whack around prostitutes might well be able to intimidate others. There was plenty of room in the mob's shakedown and union rackets for a man with the brutal talents of beefy Willie Bioff.

Bioff proved he could be a very convincing union slugger and it was decided to put him on more lucrative assignments. Jake Guzik recommended Bioff to Frank Nitti who was running the mob after Capone's imprisonment for income tax violations. Nitti assigned Bioff to provide muscle power for George

Browne whom the mob was promoting from a local union power to presidency of the International Alliance of Theatrical Stage Employees and Motion Picture Operators. The election was in the bag. Chicago was solid for Browne, and in New York Lucky Luciano and Louis Lepke lined up strong support for him as did Al Polizzi in Cleveland.

Bioff became Browne's watchdog. Together the pair at first split 50 percent of all monies they were able to shake out of the movie industry, with the rest going to the Chicago Outfit. Later Browne and Bioff's share was cut to 25 percent, but by then the pie was enormous and they never noticed any loss. Through Bioff and Browne the Chicago mob just about controlled the Hollywood movie industry in the 1930s. In 1936 Bioff informed the head of Loew's, Inc.: "Now your industry is a prosperous industry and I must get two million dollars out of it." They actually did get a million over the next four years.

A later court trial demonstrated Bioff's negotiating ability. He was dealing with Jack Miller, labor representative for an association of Chicago movie exhibitors.

Bioff: "I told Miller the exhibitors . . . would have to have two operators in each booth. Miller said: 'My God! That will close up all my shows.'"

Prosecutor: "And what did you say?"

Bioff: "I said: 'If that will kill grandma—then grandma must die.' Miller said that two men in each booth would cost about $500,000 a year. So I said, well, why don't you make a deal? And we finally agreed on $60,000."

Judge John Bright: "What was this $60,000 paid for?"

Bioff (beaming): "Why, Your Honor, to keep the booth costs down . . . You see, Judge, if they wouldn't pay we'd give them lots of trouble. We'd put them out of business and I mean out."

This trial came about after a right-wing, crusading newspaper columnist, Westbrook Pegler, started digging into Bioff's activities. Pegler discovered Bioff as the "guest of honor" at a lavish Hollywood party and remembered him as a venal little panderer during his own apprentice reporter days in Chicago. When Pegler started attacking Bioff in print, the latter tried to counter by attacking Pegler's anti-union-ism. It didn't wash. Pegler pointed out Bioff had served jail sentences for brutalizing his prostitutes but had in one case not served a six-month sentence, not an unusual situation in a corrupt Chicago law enforcement system. Ultimately, Bioff was forced to do that time, but did it in true crime syndicate style—with a private office in the Chicago House of Correction and a tub of iced beer daily.

Pegler's newspaper assaults finally got Bioff and Browne convicted in 1941 for violation of anti-racketeering laws, and each was sentenced to 10 years. Both men broke under that pressure and agreed to testify against many top leaders of the Chicago Syndicate, among them Frank Nitti, Paul Ricca, Phil D'Andrea, Charlie Gioe, Lou Kaufman and Johnny Roselli.

The defense constantly attacked Bioff's character and his lying testimony before several grand juries. Bioff shook his head when asked to explain himself and said, "I am just a low, uncouth person. I'm a low-type sort of man."

Bioff and Browne's testimony convicted the Chicago crime leaders who went to prison. Nitti was an exception. Fearful of having to do time, the supposed tough successor to Al Capone committed suicide. As the syndicate gangsters entered prison, Bioff and Browne went out. They ran for their lives.

No one ever learned where Browne went. It turned out Bioff had gone to Phoenix, Arizona, after a time, living under the name of William Nelson.

Bioff had tasted power in his Hollywood days, and it was not an appetite he could give up readily. In 1952 Bioff and his wife contributed $5,000 to the senatorial campaign of a department store heir named Barry Goldwater. After the election a warm friendship blossom between the Arizona senator and Bioff-Nelson. In the meantime Bioff also went to work for Gus Greenbaum who was running the Riviera in Las Vegas. It was an unhappy coincidence, since the Riviera was secretly backed by the Chicago Outfit, and the very gangsters that Bioff had sent to prison. It was only a matter of time until the boys in Chicago learned who Willie Nelson was. In October 1955, Goldwater, an accomplished air force pilot, ferried Bioff and his wife to Las Vegas and back to Phoenix in his private plane. On November 4, 1955, Bioff left his house, climbed into his small pickup truck, and waved to his wife who was looking out the kitchen door. When Bioff stepped on the starter, there was a terrific explosion. Pieces of the truck flew in every direction. A little late perhaps, but Chicago had avenged Bioff's betrayal.

A few years later Gus Greenbaum and his wife were murdered in very brutal fashion. Yes, Greenbaum was stealing the mob's casino money, but it was also true that the boys had never really forgiven him for giving the hated Bioff a haven.

See also MOVIE RACKETEERING

BLACK Book: Las Vegas Mafia blacklist

Though heralded as a major weapon against the Mafia, one that would make Las Vegas safe from organized crime, it was largely an exercise in futility.

In 1960 the Nevada Gaming Control Board issued a "Black Book" to all casino licensees. It contained just 11 sheets of letter-sized paper, each sheet bearing a man's photograph and a list of aliases. All with an arrest record, these 11 men were mostly considered to be part of organized crime:

John Louis Battaglia, Los Angeles
Marshal[l] Caifano, Chicago
Carl James Civella, Kansas City
Nichola Civella, Kansas City
Trigger Mike Coppola, Miami
Louis Tom Dragna, Los Angeles
Robert L. "Bobby" Garcia, Southern California
Sam Giancana, Chicago
Motel Grezebrenacy, Kansas City
Murray Llewellyn Humphreys, Chicago
Joe Sica, Los Angeles

The idea was to purge the town of its Mafia and organized crime flavor. The men named were not to be allowed on the premises of the casinos and the casinos were held responsible for keeping them out. An interesting idea, especially since some on the list were probably owners through "front men" of a piece of some of the casinos. The blacklist theoretically would keep casino owners off their own premises.

One of the men, Caifano, also known as Johnny Marshall, challenged the principle of the Black Book in court, claiming among other things that his constitutional rights had been violated, that he had been listed as an "undesirable" without notice or hearing. Caifano, a member of the Chicago Outfit, eventually lost his case, the federal court adding further insult by requiring him to pay court costs. The court held that "the problem of excluding hoodlums from gambling places in the state of Nevada can well be regarded by the state authorities as a matter almost of life or death."

The listing of Chicago mob head Sam Giancana as an undesirable put much pressure on singer Frank Sinatra, who, in the words of the Nevada Gaming Commission, "has for a number of years maintained and continued social association with Sam Giancana well knowing his unsavory and notorious reputation, and has openly stated that he intends to continue such association in defiance. . . ." At first Sinatra made noises that he intended to fight the Black Book but in the end announced he was "withdrawing from the gaming industry in Nevada."

Since then the Black Book has been continued. Its name was changed in 1976 to "The List of Excluded Persons," following a complaint from a black citizen that the original title was a racial slur. However, it has never amounted to much and certainly never made a dent in organized crime's penetration of the casino scene in Nevada. A somewhat harsher judgment is offered by Jerome H. Skolnick, professor of law at the University of California, Berkeley, in *House of Cards,* a study of casino gambling: "It was more a public-relations stunt than a serious control measure. In any event, its existence did nothing to reassure the federal authorities and others that Nevada had succeeded in expelling organized criminal interests from its casinos."

BLACK Hand: Italian extortion racket

What the newspapers called "the Black Hand Society" never really existed in America—or anywhere else. That's cold comfort to the hundreds who number among their victims, forming a bloody trail that makes it easy to understand why there have been and still are today politicians and investigators who speak of the Black Hand as being synonymous with the Mafia or "Cosa Nostra."

The Black Hand racket was extortion, a pay-or-die shakedown of the Italian community in which murders often followed if a victim refused to pay. Victims or their families usually were only maimed since a corpse cannot pay tribute, but if they remained recalcitrant or it was felt that an object-lesson murder or two would shake loose money from other potential victims, death by gun, knife, bomb, rope or poison could well follow. The average victim paid immediately upon receiving a demand for money usually "signed" at the bottom with a hand that had been dipped in black ink (a procedure that was altered as the science of fingerprinting came into vogue). The terror it struck in most targets was simply overwhelming.

In point of fact there was an actual Society of the Black Hand in Europe, but it had nothing to do with either the Mafia or Camorra, the two largest criminal societies in Italy, who practiced extortion rackets there while members immigrated to America. The Society of the Black Hand was of Spanish origin and formed during the Inquisition as a force of good, seeking to prevent the oppression of the day. According to popular theories, the Mafia and Camorra also started out with noble intent and later turned into criminal bodies. The Society of the Black Hand merely withered away. But the name remained, *La Mano Nera,* or Black Hand, and it had an inspiring ring to New York newspapermen who had no intention of losing such a sinister phrase. The Black Hand was simply reborn as an organized force and reporters constantly traced various criminals back to some Black Hand Society.

In actuality the Black Hand was never more than a loosely run extortion racket practiced in the Little Italy sections of many American cities. It was not at all unusual for a businessman in financial trouble to send a Black Hand note to another businessman in hopes of solving his own money woes. When the recipient got such a note threatening him or members of his family, he automatically thought the Black Handers were most likely mafioso or Camorra gangsters. Certainly when the great opera tenor Enrico Caruso got a Black Hand threat with the imprint of a black hand and a dagger, he took the threat seriously and paid the $2,000 demanded. When the extortionists then presented a new demand for $15,000, he realized he had to go to the police or he would be the target of constant demands. The police set a trap and the Black Handers were caught when they tried to retrieve the loot from under the steps of a factory. They turned out to be private businessmen who figured Caruso was a natural for taking. The pair was convicted of extortion and sent to prison, one of the very few successful prosecutions of Black Handers. Thereafter Caruso was considered to be in danger from other Black Handers—a successful prosecution was bad for business—and he was kept under police and private detective protection both in this country and Europe for the rest of his life.

Mafia and Camorra gangsters never struck at Caruso but they did at other uncooperative victims just to demonstrate that it was wise to pay. Often they applied a convincer to a victim by first seizing his child and cutting off a finger. A typical Black Hand case involved a well-to-do Brooklyn butcher named Gaetano Costa who, in 1905, got a Black Hand threat: "You have more money than we have. We know of your wealth and that you are alone in this country. We want $1,000, which you are to put in a loaf of bread and hand to a man who comes in to buy meat and pulls out a red handkerchief." Costa was an exception in his neighborhood; most other businessmen in the area had paid on demand. He ignored the demands. One morning Black Hand killers marched into his shop and shot Costa to death behind his meat counter. No one was ever charged in the case, although it was generally known that the gangsters who did the killing worked for Lupo the Wolf, a Black Hand mafioso headquartered in Italian Harlem.

For many years, Lupo, whose real name was Ignazio Saietta, was the foremost Black Hander in New York City. He remained a notorious "Murder Stable" where more than 60 gangland victims, many recalcitrant Black Hand targets, were buried. Lupo paraded his Black Hand activities openly to the Italian community, thus reinforcing the perception that he was untouchable by the law. It was common for many Italians to cross themselves at the mere mention of his name.

Another Black Hander who considered himself immune from legal interference was Paul Di Cristina. He blithely delivered his Black Hand extortion notes in person to his New Orleans victims. They all paid, trembling in fear. All, that is, save a grocer named Pietro Pepitone. After Di Cristina visited Pepitone he sent his enforcers around later to collect. Pepitone announced he would not pay. For such effrontery Di Cristina sent word he'd come personally to collect his money. When Di Cristina strutted toward the grocer's store, Pepitone wordlessly picked up a shotgun, came out to the sidewalk and blew the Black Hander away.

In 1908 New York police estimated that for every Black Hand extortion they heard about at least 250 went unreported. If that was accurate, Black Hand depredations were truly staggering since there were 424 Black Hand offenses reported that year. Yet as big an industry as Black Handing was in New York,

activities were undoubtedly greater in Chicago where it was estimated that upward of 80 different gangs operated, all unrelated to each other.

By about 1920 the Black Hand operators disappeared. Lupo the Wolf was in prison, albeit for counterfeiting, his second favorite pastime. Many members of the Sam Cardinella Black Hand ring in Chicago went to prison with Sam and his top aides were executed. The Di Giovanni mob in Kansas City suffered a number of convictions as did extortionists in Pittsburgh, Philadelphia and San Francisco. Some credit for the decline in Black Handing is given to federal officials who from 1915 started enforcing the laws prohibiting the use of the U.S. mail to defraud, but this came about only after considerable newspaper pressure. The extortionists shifted to private delivery of their notes.

However, by 1920 the exodus from the profession was enormous. Frankie Yale in Brooklyn, Scarface Di Giovanni in Kansas City, Vincenzo Cosmanno and the Genna brothers in Chicago all quit. They entered the much more profitable booze game, which writer Edward Dean Sullivan described as "No work—slight risk—vast remuneration." By comparison Black Hand setups were penny ante. Only a few unimaginative criminals kept at extortion and they were soon caught by the police, who suddenly got a steady flow of complaints from residents in Little Italies.

Bootlegging had turned the Italian communities into massive moonshine factories, with most families producing liquor for the bootleg gangs to sell. As these cottage industries developed, the Italian immigrants lost their fear of the police and saw they were actually in partnership with them, both being paid off by the bootleg gangs. And when you have a partner, you don't hesitate to ask a favor of him, such as taking care of this Black Hander who is bothering you.

See also CARDINELLA, SALVATORE "SAM"; LUPO THE WOLF; SHOTGUN MAN; WHITE HAND SOCIETY

BLACK Mafia

One of the myths gaining currency about syndicate crime in America is that other ethnic groups will take over the basically Italian-Jewish combination that has ruled the underworld for well over half a century. This overlooks the fact that the development of organized crime (actually "syndicate crime," since any crime involving a gang of two or more members is "organized") was in fact an aberration due to a confluence of socioeconomic forces not like to be repeated.

According to the "take-over" theory and what Ralph Salerno, former head of the organized crime intelligence squad in New York City, called the Black Mafia, the members of syndicated crime have become upwardly mobile and will be replaced by those of lower-class status. It is a theory easily made but difficult to prove.

Crime springs from ghettos and the current occupants of ghettos are increasingly black and Hispanic, thus giving rise to speculation about a Black Mafia and a Cuban, or Latin, Mafia. There is no doubt that, as today's ghetto occupants, these ethnic groups have become the prime criminals—in terms of ordinary crime—that the Jews and Italians were before them and the Irish before that.

However, fundamental differences exist. The 19th-century Irish criminals, the largest such group by far at the time, were "organized" in the sense of having enormous gangs. But these Irish gangs were not syndicated. The Dead Rabbits gang in New York, for instance, did not have any special relationship with the Bloody Tubs in Philadelphia—no special working arrangements dividing up crime territories and activities. They did not sit in council as Angelo Bruno of Philadelphia's 20th-century crime family parleyed with Joe Bonnano of New York or Joe Zerilli of Detroit. The Irish gangs were organized, but there were no special arrangements that a New York gangster had to make with the Bloody Tubs before he killed someone in Philadelphia or Baltimore (to where the Tubs' influence extended).

The Jewish-Italian crime syndicate came about because of very special socioeconomic conditions in the United States. Surely Prohibition and the Great Depression help explain why organized syndicate crime developed in this country, and in a form that is unique throughout the world. Syndicate crime in the United States, in operation, was and is more pervasive than organized criminal activities anywhere in the world, including the Mafia's homeland of Sicily.

Why was this aberration possible only in the United States? Firstly, there was Prohibition, probably the most sweeping social experiment of the 20th century short of social revolution. Without Prohibition the upward mobility of Jewish and Italian gangsters would have proceeded in the normal fashion:

An ethnic group occupies the ghettos, produces crime, matures and moves up the social ladder at least to the extent of turning over the bottom rung to the next ethnic minority. The Irish were succeeded in close proximity by the Jews and the Italians, who became the criminals of their day, as in lesser numbers did the Poles and Russians and others.

By logical progression the Jews and Italians should have moved away from crime. Indeed before the start of World War I, the 1,500-member, Jewish Monk Eastman Gang and the like-numbered Italian Five Points Gang under Paul Kelly (Paolo Vaccarelli) both had splintered. Both groups had been abandoned by the political machines who understood that their use of the gangs was ending under the cutting edge of reform. There simply were no more prospects for such huge organized gangs.

America's entry into the war contributed further to the destruction of the gangs. We should have entered the post-war period with no more than the usual and temporary outbreaks of violence caused by returning soldiers. Instead, within a short time Prohibition lay heavy on the land.

Great new criminal vistas opened. Americans had no intention of being deprived of beer and booze, and the Jewish and Italian gangsters had a great rebirth—even the Irish staged a big comeback. The 1920s, when the Jewish and Italians should have been tapering off on their criminal activities, saw them instead expanding. Money poured in so fast that the criminals no longer needed to curry favor with the politicians. They did, in fact, buy the politicians in a unique reversal of the normal arrangement.

The Italians and Jews combined forces at a new and previously unheard of level of organized crime—after a series of wars eliminated those who resisted syndication. Infusing this new criminal combination was a steady supply of young blood. The Depression of the 1930s froze the ethnic groups in their ghettos. It was perhaps the deepest and most severe economic crisis to afflict the nation, and many youngsters, lacking special talents or abilities, were forced into crime. They were eager to "make it with the mob."

Coupled with these two favorable factors for the new crime syndicate was the lack of police repression. In many cities the syndicate had little trouble buying off the police just as it bought off the politicians. The only hope lay on the federal level and here, incredibly, nothing happened. Through the 1930s and, indeed, for the next two decades the federal government did nothing to curb syndicate crime. The FBI was muzzled by its director, J. Edgar Hoover, who refused even to acknowledge the existence of either the Mafia or organized crime in any way, shape or form.

During the lost years the structure of organized crime solidified to the extent that the demise of any of its players has now become meaningless. The system continues.

Some analysts, failing to appreciate the uniquely favorable climate that gave birth to the American Mafia and the national crime syndicate, have seen the normal criminal development by the now ghettoized blacks and Hispanics as an indication that they will step into power in syndicate crime. But such organized crime is based on a sophistication that does not come to any criminal ethnic group in a single generation. It must be remembered that the Italian mobsters of 1920 were little more than illiterate, hulking, Black Hand–type extortionists whose appreciation of criminal activities was limited to crude shakedowns and murder. It took the schooling of the bootleg years, the forced transition to more advanced crimes after Repeal; gambling, not just to numbers, but legalized casino operations and the sophisticated principles of the skim; the laundering of money, the use of Swiss banks, the infiltration of the banking and business system, the looting of pension funds through well-papered transactions.

Yet the exponents of the Black Mafia in the mid-1970s were talking about a decade that would show huge strides forward for the Black Mafia. It has not happened and if it were to happen—and given the lack of very powerful social and economic events, it cannot—a logical guess would be the rise of a Black Mafia by the 2050s.

The "Bible" of the Black Mafia theory is *Black Mafia, Ethnic Succession in Organized Crime* by Francis A.J. Ianni. While an exceedingly informative and colorful portrayal, the book can't help but go far to demonstrate against the author's very contention. What Ianni calls a Black Mafia, as organized-crime authority Gus Tyler notes, "consists of a pimp with a stable of seven hookers, a dope pusher, a fence who dabbles in loan sharking and gambling, a con man who gets phony insurance policies for gypsy cabs and a numbers racketeer." Tyler grants these activities are organized but "they are not in a class with white

organized crime either qualitatively or quantitatively" and don't conclusively support a theory of "ethnic succession."

It may well be that talk of a Black Mafia or a Cuban Mafia merely makes an excellent cover story for the Mafia and its syndicate mobsters, who in the meantime claim to be "going legit."

Ianni is very impressed with the comments of one Italian crime family leader: ". . . what the Hell, those guys want to make a little, too. We're moving out and they're moving in. I guess it's their turn now." Such a high-flown philosophical attitude is remarkable within an underworld that maimed and murdered in wholesale lots to get where it is. And it may be rather cynical to doubt such sentiments as self-serving. Perhaps the Mafia is going legit. It also may be that we have done Al Capone a grievous injustice. His business card read: "Alphonse Capone, second hand furniture dealer, 2220 South Wabash Avenue."

See also BARNES, LEROY "NICKY"; "CUBAN MAFIA"; FORTY THIEVES; JOHNSON, ELLSWORTH "BUMPY"

BOIARDO, Ruggiero "Richie the Boot" (1891–1984): New Jersey Mafia patriarch

Ruggiero Boiardo may have been the oldest mafioso the law ever tried to bring to trial on organized crime charges. At 89, the state had indicted him in the "Great Mob Trial," an operation instigated by the state of New Jersey to prove the existence of an organized crime network. Richie the Boot Boiardo had been facing a variety of charges—including racketeering, extortion and murder conspiracy—but was released because, it was ruled, his health was too poor for him to stand trial. Richie the Boot told the court he just wanted "St. Peter to bring me to heaven." So the white-haired, hobbled mob boss went back behind the walls of his 30-room estate in Livingston, where he continued for another four years to conduct much of his business from a small vegetable spread that bore the sign: "Godfather's Garden." And authorities kept calling him the patriarch of organized crime in New Jersey.

Born in Italy, Boiardo came to Chicago at the turn of the century when he was nine. In 1910 he was working as a mason in Newark, New Jersey. Bootlegging during Prohibition made Boiardo a big man in Newark, and he established himself as a sort of godfather of the First Ward where he developed a philanthropic side, and entire families came to him in times of need. He satisfied the political elements because people in his area voted the way he thought best.

Police labeled him a gang leader but Boiardo avoided trouble and for a long time was never arrested for anything serious enough to send him to jail. He did have to fight off incursions by other gangsters, however, and to his dying day carried the remains of shotgun pellets that lodged in his chest during a gun battle. By 1930 he had become an associate of Abner "Longy" Zwillman, who was known as "the Al Capone of New Jersey." Through the 1930s and later Boiardo was connected by state and federal investigators with bootlegging, numbers and lottery rackets. His good fortune with the law ended when he did 22 months in jail on a concealed weapons charge.

In theory Boiardo "retired" from all criminal activities in 1941. He moved to a lavish estate in Livingston, the main house constructed of stone imported from Italy. Like the domain of a powerful feudal lord, the estate sported wrought-iron gates, fountains, mosaics, a collection of sculpted busts of the Boiardo family and an impressive statue of Richie the Boot riding a white stallion.

In the 1950s it was clear that Boiardo was still heavily involved in mob gambling and loan-sharking activities; in 1963 informer Joe Valachi named Boiardo as a power in the "Cosa Nostra" or Mafia crime syndicate. Boiardo denied it all, insisting he was just an avid gardener and proud grandfather. However, in the 1980s he escaped prosecution only because of his age. The man who law enforcement officials called the patriarch, one of the most powerful and feared men in the state's underworld, died in November 1984 at the age of 93, still said to be a kingpin in gambling and extortion operations in Essex County.

BOMPENSIERO, Frank "Bomp" (1905–1977): Hit man, San Diego crime boss and FBI informer

In the treacherous world of Mafia hit men, few characters proved shiftier than Frank "Bomp" Bompensiero. Bomp was at the same time a pitiless killer and an FBI informer who betrayed his friends to the FBI and in the end was betrayed by that agency to a certain death at the murderous hands of the mob.

For decades regarded as one of the most efficient hit men in the West Coast mob, Bompensiero was an expert in the so-called Italian rope trick, a surprise garroting that always left the dying victim with a surprised look on his face.

For double-dealing, Bompensiero was without peer. Once the Detroit mob gave him a murder contract involving one of two crime figures who had each approached the leadership with demands that the other be killed. The leadership discussed the matter at a sit-down and decided which man should get it. Bomp was informed and at a party he immediately approached the victim to be, whom he happened to know, and told him, "Look here, you've been having this problem and the old man's given me the contract. I'm going to clip this guy but I'm going to need your help."

Naturally the man was eager to be of aid and was overjoyed when told to help dig a hole for the body in advance. Bomp picked out a lonely spot and they took turns digging. Finally the man asked Bomp if the hole was deep enough. Bomp announced it was perfect and shot his victim in the back of the head.

Bomp was especially close to the late Los Angeles crime boss Jack Dragna and ran a number of rackets with him in San Diego, where he eventually became the chief of the L.A. family's rackets in that city. During the last 10 years of his life, Bomp turned stool pigeon for the FBI after he was charged with conspiracy to defraud. The case was dismissed on the grounds of insufficient evidence after the FBI "turned" Bomp and thereafter Bomp supplied federal officials with a wealth of information about mob activities.

Not that Bomp played straight with the FBI. He continued his own crimes which apparently included the murder of a wealthy San Diego real estate broker, Mrs. Tamara Rand, who had close ties with gangster elements in Las Vegas. Many observers found it inconceivable that the FBI did not learn of Bomp's involvement in the matter. But Bomp had outsmarted himself. He had become a doomed man. Suddenly the L.A. mob put out a contract on him, but Bomp was not an easy man to kill, not a man to be trapped easily. To allay his suspicions the L.A. mob appointed Bomp to the post of consigliere in the hope of catching him off guard. Amazingly, for two years, nothing happened. Even among friends or supposed friends Bomp was on the alert. Nobody could get at him without very obviously being killed in the process.

Finally the FBI had Bomp lead a number of L.A. mobsters into contact with a porno outfit that was really an agency front. When the agency made a number of arrests it had to be apparent to Bomp that he was being tossed to the wolves. Apparently, the FBI concocted the scheme in an effort to draw Jimmy Fratianno into their informer net and, by dooming Bompensiero, they got their way. Now branded by the L.A. family as a stoolie, Bomp still continued to survive—for a time. He stayed close to home, leaving his expensive Pacific Beach apartment only to make his rounds of telephone calls from a phone booth because he was sure his home phone was tapped. Finally, in February 1977, 10 years after Bomp started dealing with the FBI, unknown gunmen caught up with him as he was returning from a phone booth and pumped four bullets into his head with a silencer-equipped automatic pistol.

BONANNO, Joseph (1905–2002): Crime family boss

Although Joseph "Joe Bananas" Bonanno's crime family was, in 1931, the smallest of New York's big five, he still wanted to be the largest power in syndicated crime in America.

Bonanno came to America with his parents from Sicily when he was three years old, but the family returned to their hometown of Castellammare del Golfo. He lived out his teens there, absorbed the Mafia traditions and became an anti-Fascist student radical in Palermo following Mussolini's seizure of power in 1922. Bonanno was forced to flee and reentered America in 1925 after sojourning in Cuba. Although some crime writers say Bonanno went to Chicago and worked under Al Capone, he instead stayed in the Williamsburg section of Brooklyn in a tight-knit area composed mainly of Castellammarese. He made a mark for himself among the mafioso as an enforcer who saw to it that Brooklyn speakeasies bought their whiskey from the proper sources. (In *Honor Thy Father*, a biography of the Bonanno family, Gay Talese writes: "... he did this without resorting to threats and pressure," which would have made Bonanno a most remarkable—and probably a one-of-a-kind—hawker of booze in the era.)

A young man who seized every opportunity he saw, Bonanno grabbed off virgin territories in Brook-

Joe Bonanno, or "Joe Bananas," was a longtime crime family boss, going back to the early 1930s. Revelations he made in his autobiography in the 1980s put him in prison when he refused to say more in court about the Mafia and its ruling commission.

lyn for the Italian lottery. About 1927 Salvatore Maranzano arrived in America and effectively took over the leadership of the Castellammarese mafiosi. He soon launched a war of supremacy with Joe the Boss Masseria. Bonanno proved to be a dedicated and dependable soldier in that struggle which became known as the Castellammarese War.

Eventually, Masseria was murdered and the war ended—although not by the hands of the Maranzano forces. Masseria was killed by combined Italian and Jewish gangsters who had entirely different plans for the underworld. Lucky Luciano, though serving under Masseria, had his own thing going with other mobsters, especially with Jewish gangster Meyer Lansky. Together these two envisioned crime operating in peace and the highest possible profitability by "syndicating" or "organizing" individual crime effort into a national network.

Neither Masseria nor Maranzano, who were closed minded Mustache Petes, wanted to consider working with other gangs, much less with other ethnics. After Maranzano had won the war, he took in Luciano as his number two man, and appointed himself boss of bosses over them all. Neither Luciano nor his followers, including many Young Turks on Maranzano's side whom Luciano secretly courted, cared much for the boss of bosses idea. Luciano vacated the position by having four Lansky gunners assassinate Maranzano less than five months after he'd taken full power.

Luciano kept only the five-family concept and named Bonanno to head up what was originally a large part of Maranzano's Castellammarese crime family. Under Bonanno the crime family's revenues rolled in and he was soon a millionaire. He diversified into a number of businesses and skimmed or covered up the income so adroitly that Internal Revenue could never catch him. Bonanno was into clothing factories and cheese firms and even a funeral parlor. Many police give Bonanno's undertaking activities credit for starting a quaint custom of double-decker coffins, which permitted an extra corpse to be laid under a false bottom to the coffin. It is not known how many missing victims of the Mafia were buried in such communal coffins.

Oddly, although Bonanno was the youngest crime family head in the United States, he was among the most traditional. He took his position as a don—he preferred to call himself the "Father" of his family—most seriously. In his 1983 autobiography, *A Man of Honor*, Bonanno differentiated the attitudes of himself and Luciano, some think amusingly. Luciano, said Bonanno, was so Americanized that he operated on "the most primitive consideration: making money." On the other hand, Bonanno continued, "Men of my Tradition have always considered wealth a by-product of power." Such men of this tradition, Bonanno explained, "were mainly in the people business."

Whatever business Bonanno considered himself in, it became evident over the years that he thought big. To some rival bosses, upset by his moves beyond his traditional territory, he was "planting flags all over the world."

By the 1960s this was very obvious. Bonanno had long since invaded the open Arizona territory and clearly looked to California where the local mafiosi were not considered serious competition. He had had casino investments with Meyer Lansky in pre-Castro Cuba and was working on going it alone in Haiti. He also worked rackets in Canada, which licensed Buffalo's Stefano Magaddino, who considered much of that country his territory.

By the early 1960s Bonanno for the first time faced some internal opposition from his soldiers who complained he was on the road so much checking out these developments elsewhere that he was neglecting family business in New York and that their revenues were suffering. Some New York bosses were also acting tougher with him, especially after Joe Profaci, who had been another longtime crime family boss in Brooklyn, died of cancer in 1962. Profaci had been Bonanno's staunchest ally, but at the same time controlled Bonanno's raging ambitions in the interests of underworld peace.

Without Profaci's restraint, Bonanno decided to make his big move. Profaci had been succeeded as boss by Joe Magliocco who also feared the other New York bosses. Bonanno approached him with a plan to kill off several other bosses, including Carlo Gambino and Tommy Lucchese in New York, Magaddino in Buffalo and Frank DeSimone in Los Angeles. Magliocco agreed to the plot and passed an order to a previously trustworthy hit man, Joe Colombo, to take out the New York chiefs. The plot collapsed when the ambitious Colombo instead revealed it to the intended victims.

Bonanno and Magliocco were ordered to appear before the Mafia commission, of which they themselves were members, to explain their actions. Bonanno refused to appear but Magliocco did and confessed. As punishment—and it was uncommonly light—Magliocco was allowed to retire from his crime family and be replaced as boss by Colombo. The commission had treated him easy because Magliocco was in poor health and likely to die soon (he did within half a year). Also, by showing leniency the commission was hoping to lure Bonanno in.

It didn't work. Bonanno refused to appear. The commission then ordered him stripped of his crime family authority and replaced him with a Bonanno defector, Gaspar DiGregorio. This split the Bonanno family, some members going with the Bonannos, the others with DiGregorio. In October 1964 Joe Bonanno was kidnapped at gunpoint on Park Avenue while in the company of his lawyer. He was to disappear for 19 months during which time war broke out between the DiGregorio forces and Bonanno's son, Bill. Dubbed the Banana War, it produced a goodly number of corpses but no decision.

Meanwhile Bonanno was being held prisoner by Buffalo's Magaddino who was Bonanno's cousin. Magaddino was clearly acting for the commission and tried to get Bonanno to agree to quit the Mafia and go into retirement. While under constant threat of death, Bonanno reasoned that the commission did not feel on safe ground but was worried that really bloody warfare could break out. It also did not wish to establish the precedent of the commission dethroning a boss since members might find themselves in the same position in the future.

Finally, Bonanno offered a compromise. He would retire to Arizona and his son would succeed him. The commission would not buy that one, realizing it would still leave Bonanno in effective control. Stalemated, Bonanno at last agreed to quit and accept the commission's decision on his successor.

Bonanno was released; but forcing an agreement out of Bonanno and making him live up to that agreement were two different things. Bonanno threw himself into the Banana War. The commission had in the meantime replaced the ineffective DiGregorio with a tougher man, Paul Sciacca, but he was no match against the wily elder Bonanno. In the ensuing killings the Bonanno forces inflicted more damage than they received. It is doubtful the commission could ever have won the Banana War, but in 1968 Bonanno suffered a heart attack and was forced into real retirement.

This time an effective compromise was worked out. Bonanno went to Arizona and was allowed to maintain his western interests while giving up the Bonanno holdings in New York. It marked the end of an era. Bonanno was the last of the five original bosses of the 1931 American Mafia still living, but he was now out of action as well. But there were some exceptions. In 1979, when the families decided to rid themselves of the vicious Carmine Galante, a former underboss to Bonanno and at the time the new boss of the family, the Mafia powers thought it wise to get Bonanno's approval. If not, they feared that, agreement or no agreement, Bonanno might launch a comeback in the hopes of promoting one of his sons into the top position in the crime family. Galante was hit, but no Bonanno offspring took over, a situation that undoubtedly left the father frustrated. The truth was there was only one Joe Bananas, and no one could match his cunning.

Bonanno remained in the news. He was prosecuted and convicted on some criminal charges, and in the mid-1980s the federal government sought to make use of his autobiography to prove that there was a Mafia commission and that its present members were part of a criminal conspiracy and thus could be sent to prison. When the aging and ailing Bonanno refused to answer questions to a grand jury about the revelations in his book, he was jailed.

By the time he was approaching 90, Bonanno knew his era had passed. At 94 his son Bill said, "He visits my mother's grave a few times a week, places flowers there, talks to her for a time, and returns to his home, where his keenest interests (aside from talking) are reading old classics—Dante and Homer—and watching vintage black-and-white movies on TV that hearken back to the days of his youth." He died May 11, 2002, at a hospital in Tucson, Arizona, of heart failure at the age of 97.

See also BANANA WAR

BONANNO, Salvatore "Bill" (1932–): Son of Mafia boss

The son of crime boss Joseph Bonanno (Joe Bananas), Bill Bonanno embodies one of the few examples of nepotism in the Mafia—the theme of *The Godfather* notwithstanding. Long dreaming that his son would take over his leadership of the crime family, the elder Bonanno provoked the so-called Banana War, which littered the streets of Brooklyn with corpses. When Bonanno disappeared from the scene for an extended period of time, execution of the conflict was placed in the inexperienced hands of son Bill.

The younger Bonanno was the cooperative subject of a book, *Honor Thy Father* by Gay Talese, which attempts, almost heroically, to counter the general mob belief that Bill was an incompetent. The effort was not wholly convincing to some.

The majority underworld opinion was perhaps best typified by the sentiments revealed in the celebrated "DeCavalcante tapes"—based on an FBI eavesdropping campaign that for almost four years recorded conversations in the offices of New Jersey crime leader Simone Rizzo DeCavalcante (Sam the Plumber). At the height of the troubles between the elder Bonanno and the rest of the members of the commission, the so-called overseers of Mafia affairs, DeCavalcante tried to act as a mediator and met with the younger Bonanno. He was later recorded discussing the meeting with his underboss, Frank Majuri. DeCavalcante said, "His son [Bill] is a bedbug. I'm not afraid of him [Joe Bonanno] so much as I am of his son. . . ."

Despite the elder Bonanno's naming his son consigliere (adviser) of the crime family, young Bill never achieved a position of undisputed leadership. He was convicted on such charges as loan-sharking, perjury, mail fraud and conspiracy but was never accused of having carried out any of these activities with finesse.

See also BANANA WAR; BONANNO, JOSEPH

BONANNO crime family

Although Joe Bonanno has been out of power since the mid-1960s, the family he ran for some three and a half decades is still known by his name, not because of a patrilineal succession, but rather because of inept successors.

Bonanno was put in charge of his Brooklyn family on the assassination of Salvatore Maranzano in 1931. He was at the time only 26 years old, the youngest crime family boss in the country. Traditionally his was one of the smaller of the New York families, but it was for a number of years very tight-knit and extremely profitable under Bonanno. Because of its limited manpower, Bonanno over the years sought consistently to ally himself with another crime boss or two to cement his position. Until they fell out much later, he could rely on support from his cousin Stefano Magaddino, the head of the Buffalo crime family, and in Brooklyn from Joe Profaci, with whom he remained very tight until Profaci's death in 1962. Under Bonanno the major sources of crime revenue derived from numbers, the Italian lottery, bookmaking, loan-sharking and, although he always denied it, narcotics. But when Bonanno underboss Carmine Galante went to prison in the early 1960s, it was for his involvement in drug trafficking, and to this very day the Bonanno family is regarded as one of the major suppliers of drugs to New York City.

By the time of Profaci's death in 1962 Bonanno had become convinced that some of the other family chiefs—especially Carlo Gambino, Tommy Lucchese and even his cousin Magaddino—were plotting his downfall. Feeling isolated, Bonanno developed a counterplot to kill those three and apparently a few other crime leaders around the country. It was viewed as an effort by Bonanno to become a new "Boss of Bosses." Allied with Bonanno was the ailing Joseph Magliocco, the successor to Profaci, and the uncle of Bonanno's eldest son's wife. The plot blew up when Magliocco passed the contract for the hits on Gambino and Lucchese to one of his most proficient hit men, Joe Colombo, who in turn sold out to the other side.

Called before the national commission Magliocco confessed and was allowed to retire from his crime family. (He was in extremely poor health and sure to die shortly.) Bonanno however admitted nothing and refused to appear. Instead, he disappeared and seemed to be concentrating his efforts on expanding the crime family's interests in Arizona, Canada and elsewhere.

Advancing in age himself, Bonanno had already started boosting his son Bill to become the active head of the family, a move that brought stiff resistance within the Bonanno organization, many of whose members felt Bill was incapable of the task. By that time many of the mobsters had become disenchanted with Bonanno's rule in general, feeling his interest in expanding elsewhere was adversely affecting their bread-and-butter—the Brooklyn operations.

Backed by the national commission or, perhaps more accurately, rammed in as family head was Gaspar DiGregorio. The commission ruled that Bonanno by his treachery had lost all rights. As a result a split developed within the family, about half the members going with DiGregorio and the rest with Bill Bonanno. In October 1964 the elder Bonanno was kidnapped at gunpoint in front of a luxury apartment house on Park Avenue. It was unclear whether it was an arranged disappearance by Bonanno, who was due to go before a federal grand jury, or the work of the rival crime families. In any event, Bill Bonanno was on his own. The result was the Banana War, "Banana" being a pet journalistic corruption of the Bonanno name.

In January 1966 the DiGregorio forces lured Bill Bonanno and some of his supporters with the promise of a peace meeting into an ambush and then bungled the attempted assassination. Although well over 100 shots were fired nobody was so much as scratched. Dissatisfied by DiGregorio's inability to handle the war, the commission forced him out in favor of Paul Sciacca, a tougher man and a close friend of Gambino.

In May, however, Joe Bonanno reappeared, refusing to say where he had been the past 19 months. It appeared he had been held by the commission and had only been released on his promise he would leave the crime family permanently and retire to Arizona. Bonanno did no such thing, instead prosecuting the Banana War. The Sciacca forces did not give anywhere near as good as they got, many more falling to Bonanno gunners than the other way around. A heart attack in 1968 finally slowed Bonanno and he shifted back to Arizona while the Banana War petered out. Bonanno held on to his western interests while the Brooklyn holdings shifted to Sciacca, later to Natale Evola and finally to Phil Rastelli.

The national commission's dream, or at least Gambino's dream, of a subservient Bonanno crime family was shattered by the return of Carmine Galante, who quickly took over affairs. If the commission was upset with Bonanno, it was especially unhappy with Galante—all the more so after Gambino died in 1976. Newspaper talk settled on Galante becoming the new boss of bosses, but he was assassinated by the combined agreement not only of all the New York crime families but also of many key dons around the country. It was said that even the hated Bonanno was consulted before Galante was eliminated.

Returning as ruler after Galante was Philip "Rusty" Rastelli. Under him the organization's principal activities were described as home video pornography, pizza parlors (regarded as an excellent business in which to hide illegal aliens), espresso cafés, restaurants and a very large narcotics operation. But Rastelli seemed by the mid-1980s to be in less than total control as one segment of the family pushed it deeper into drug trafficking. With Rastelli facing a long prison term in 1986, he was said by law officials to have placed Joseph Massino in charge of family affairs.

By 1998, under Massino, the Bonanno family was thriving. While the overall strength of the five New York families was said to have been declining, there was no doubt that, much to the chagrin of law enforcement, the Bonannos were clearly gaining strength. The crime family that had been in much disgrace following the Galante period and had even been booted off the National Commission made a remarkable recovery with about 100 active wise guys and was fast approaching the Gambinos under the imprisoned John Gotti as the country's second-most-dangerous Mafia faction.

See also BANANA WAR; MASSINO, JOSEPH C.

BONES, making your: Supposed requirement for being made

There is a popular myth that before someone can become a wise guy, he has to carry out a hit, or professional killing. Actually this is not true. Men get made into the Mafia for other reasons than being a stone killer. (It would be impossible for every made guy to have killed for such exalted status. Since the establishment of the modern American Mafia under Lucky Luciano, there have been, among all the crime families in the country, thousands of made men—far more than the total number of killings attributed to the mob, and there were many stone killers who carried out 10, 20, 30 or more hits by themselves.) A man, for example, can make it as a wise guy because he is a "producer"—that is, one who makes big bucks for the organization through some special expertise. A crime family would not dream of risking a real moneymaker committing murders.

Early in his career Sammy "the Bull" Gravano exhibited no brilliant potential and, so, was required to make his bones to demonstrate his qualifications. To such hoodlums killing is to be regarded as a badge of honor. Sammy shot a man sitting in front of him in a car. Although two companions with him panicked afterward, unable to take the tension, the Bull felt differently. As Gravano relates in *Underboss*, the book on his career: "I felt a surge of power. I realized that I had taken a human life, that I had the power over life and death. I was a predator. I was an animal. I was Cosa Nostra."

Wise guys have an earnest desire to train hit men. "Donnie Brasco"—undercover FBI agent Joe Pistone—related having been asked by Lefty Ruggiero, a top Bonanno hit man, if he'd ever killed anyone, explaining that it would be necessary for him to be made. Brasco lied that he had killed a few guys over arguments. Lefty was not impressed. Those kind of killings, he said, "don't count."

A contract killing, he explained, was much different because you don't have the luxury of genuinely being enraged with the victim. A contract killing was done without feelings, with no concern about the victim one way or the other. A lot of guys, Brasco was informed, think they can handle that but then freeze up. Then Ruggiero made a magnanimous promise to his protégé: "Next time I get a contract, I'll take you with me, show you how to do it."

Ruggiero apparently did a few "pieces of work" after that but had no time to invite Brasco along.

Finally, without any schooling, Brasco was assigned a contract, and the FBI was forced to end his six-year undercover operation, since a federal agent could not be permitted to take part in a homicide.

Donnie did not get to sample the fruits of such murderous endeavors as did Sammy the Bull. After his first successful murder, Gravano went before high-ranking Carmine "Junior" Persico, soon to be made head of the Colombo family. Persico wanted to know how the hit had been carried out. He was very pleased and impressed. Later a Persico underling informed the Bull that it had been "a good piece of work" and that "Junior loves you. He's real proud of you."

Mafia hits are not always as anonymous as popularly believed. In this case the Colombo-controlled area of Brooklyn knew that a crew of the family had handled some work and that Sammy was now the crew's workhorse. It became known that the family intended to have Sammy made when the Mafia books were opened for new members. That entitled him to new respect. Previously the Bull had been just another tough. Going to a club or disco the Bull had always stood in line like anyone else. Now it was different. When bouncers spotted him, he was pulled out of line and ushered inside by the proprietor. Other patrons were bounced from a prized table and Sammy was accommodated with everything on the house.

FBI-er Brasco got no such perks.

BONVENTRE, Cesare (1956–1984): Zip, or young Sicilian mafioso

Of all the Zips, or young Sicilian mafiosi, brought into the United States by the likes of Carlo Gambino and Carmine Galante, no one was more hated or feared than Cesare Bonventre, who killed his way up to underboss of the Zips and their faction within the Colombo family. Many American mobsters viewed the Zips as imported "crazies," who were not to be trusted, Cesare least of all. Nonetheless, the Zips became the key factors in the so-called Pizza Connection, importing millions of dollars of heroin into the country.

The Colombo family boss Galante, recently released from prison, ran the operation. He wanted total control of the heroin trade in America and ultimately meant to take over all five of the New York families. For that he needed the Zips and the unques-

tioning loyalty of the swaggering Cesare Bonventre, at 28 one of the youngest of the weird bunch. Galante felt he could trust the Zips; he was making them rich and powerful. What more could they want?

Trusting no one else in the Mafia, Galante kept only a small group of Zips around him, with Cesare always at his side. He used the Zips for all kinds of murderous work and for handling junk deals. Then in 1979 three masked gunmen shot Galante to death in a Brooklyn restaurant. With him at the time as "bodyguards" were Cesare and his cousin Baldo Amato. Both fled after the shooting. It was clear the assassins had no interest in shooting them.

Inside both mob and law enforcement circles there was little doubt that Bonventre was in on the hit. The other crime families in New York and elsewhere had grown so frightened of Galante that they decided he had to die. They followed an old Mafia custom of involving some of the victim's closest associates in the plot. Cesare Bonventre fit the bill perfectly. He probably didn't even consider it an act of betrayal. He could see how the odds had suddenly swung against his mentor. Farewell, Carmine.

As a reward Cesare became a capo within the Bonanno family, honored if hardly trusted.

Cesare's own downfall was a bare five years off. The Pizza Connection plot, funneling heroin deals through pizza parlors all over Brooklyn and elsewhere, was unraveling. Higher-ups probably blamed Bonventre for at least part of the chaos. And if Cesare had betrayed Galante, might he not also betray them to the authorities?

As arrests were made in the pizza case, Bonventre and Amato disappeared. Amato later turned up alive and was convicted with many others. Cesare Bonventre was not so fortunate. His body was found hacked in two and stuffed into two glue drums in a warehouse in New Jersey. The body had been located through a tip from an unidentified source who knew where the drums were stored pending shipment to the Midwest. It took weeks to identify the corroded and decomposed remains as Cesare. The task was accomplished using dental records and a gaudy gold chain the victim always wore around his neck and bragged was "indestructible."

No arrests ever resulted even though an informant stated that one of the killers was one Cosmo Aiello, who also turned up dead about five weeks after the discovery of Bonventre's body.

Perhaps Bonventre's murder had been ordered by his Zip superior, Sal Catalano, but there were other suspects. Certain forces in Philadelphia hated Cesare for having cheated them with diluted heroin. And there was an endless number of Bonventre's associates who had long chaffed under his rough treatment.

Cesare made a very popular corpse.

See also CATALANO, SALVATORE "SACA"; CATALANO, SALVATORE "TOTO"; ZIPS

BOOK, putting up a: Bringing a Mafia member up on mob charges

Far more threatening to a mafioso than facing legal charges is having a "book" put up against him within his own crime family. This generally involves serious charges, and a guilty verdict allows for no appeal, with death virtually the only possible sentence.

The accused man is summoned to a meeting, often said at first to be planned in a private room at a restaurant or diner. This allays his fears since it is unlikely that he would face any immediate danger there. However, on arriving at the supposed trial scene, he finds no judges present and is then taken by other mafiosi to a new place for the book, usually the basement of a private house. The accused is told the shift was made to avoid any possible law enforcement bugs, but the setting is now far more grim and tension soars.

If the verdict is guilty, the accused is led away never again to be seen alive.

The most common reasons for a book involve a dispute about money or the use of violence, or even the mere threat of violence. Striking a crime family member automatically calls for the death sentence. Usually the best the accused can do is deny the charges and hope it is just one man's word against another's.

One exception was the defiant defense made by Sammy "the Bull" Gravano against charges brought by Louis DiBono. The pair had been running a construction scam gouging the federal government in housing rehabilitation works. The dispute arose when DiBono started stiffing Gravano. The Bull, in his usual violent manner, exploded in a confrontation with DiBono in the latter's Long Island office. The Bull raged, "I guarantee you, if you rob me, you won't enjoy the money. I'll kill."

Against the advice of mob friends, the Bull did not simply deny making threats. Instead he freely admitted doing so and told his judges, headed by family boss Paul Castellano, "This fat scumbag was robbing me. He was robbing the family." He outlined all the ways DiBono was doctoring the financial paperwork. Then he snarled, "Let me kill him. I'll shoot him fucking dead right here and now. He'll never walk away from this table."

Such a performance had never before occurred during the "majesty" of a mob "trial." The Bull wanted to commit murder before all the Gambino family's leaders. Castellano erupted, saying that Gravano was going too far and that maybe he should be executed right on the spot.

It didn't happen. Underboss Neil Dellacroce intervened, pointing out that the Bull could have avoided any serious problem with a simple denial. Certainly this was what the judges had expected. Dellacroce said he believed Gravano and called DiBono "a disgrace to our life."

Castellano opted to calm things. Gravano and DiBono had to end their business relationship. They would shake hands and the matter would be dropped. The Bull promised to do nothing to harm DiBono. When Castellano put the same terms up to DiBono, Sammy did not give him a chance to reply: "Paul, I don't think there's any worry about him hurting me."

The importance of Gravano's effrontery had more lasting repercussions that went beyond its impact on DiBono who was later killed for other infractions. When John Gotti heard of Gravano's defiance, he was already thinking about taking down Castellano, and he decided he wanted Gravano on his side in that war.

BOOTLEGGING

Bootlegging was as essential to organized crime and the Mafia as the chicken is to the egg. And it virtually saved the great criminal gangs that were collapsing in America just prior to and during World War I. Bootlegging became the great source of income that turned around the relationship between criminals and the establishment. Whereas previously criminals were bought and controlled by the politicians, bootlegging made the criminals so rich that they bought the politicians in wholesale lots.

With the end of Prohibition, bootlegging declined but hardly disappeared from the American scene. High liquor taxes saw to that. As a result, bootlegging continued to be a major criminal pastime and the Mafia is deeply involved. Among the crime families in recent years known to have a considerable investment in bootlegging are the Buffalo group; the Erie-Pittston, Pennsylvania, family under Russell Bufalino; and especially the Philadelphia Bruno family. For years, this last group ran in Reading, Pennsylvania, the biggest illegal still since Prohibition and blithely had it tied into the city water supply.

Prohibition had brought to the larger cities powerful bootlegging gangs that fought bloody wars for control of the huge racket. Much of the liquor was smuggled across the border from Mexico or Canada or slipped in by fast boat. Many of the gangs found it necessary to produce their own alcohol to guarantee their supplies; they set up illegal distilleries and breweries—activities that could hardly have been operated without police and political cooperation. In Chicago alone it was estimated that more than 1,000 men died as a result of the bootleg wars. Similar wars produced similar death tolls in such cities as Detroit, New York and Philadelphia. Some of the most brutal battles occurred in Williamson County, Illinois, the site where on November 12, 1926, a farmhouse belonging to a prominent family of bootleggers was bombed from an airplane by another bootlegging group. Although the attack was unsuccessful, it was the first and only time real bombs were dropped from a plane in the United States in an effort to destroy human life and property.

In 1930 a federal grand jury uncovered the largest liquor operation of the era. Thirty-one corporations and 158 individuals were cited in Chicago, New York, Cleveland, Philadelphia, St. Paul, Detroit, St. Louis, Minneapolis, Los Angeles and North Bergen, New Jersey, for having diverted more than 7 million gallons of alcohol in seven years.

Some experts say as much as 20 percent of all alcohol consumed in this country is still illicit moonshine; they base their estimates on the government's open admission that it finds no more than one-third to one-half of all illegal stills (a figure many believe is far too high). The mobs have many ways of bringing their booze to market; they can dispense it through the clubs and bars they own or sell it through the distributorships they control. Control of the waterfront is said to offer the opportunity to substitute their booze for high-priced imports.

See also HAMS; PROHIBITION; RUM ROW

BOSS etiquette: Survival code for wise guys with a new boss

Knowing how to survive when a new family boss takes over has long been a problem for mobsters. Since the late 1990s rapid changes in leadership due to concentrated prosecutions by law enforcement have put more stress than ever on wise guys to give the right answers and exhibit the proper "good works." It is important for crime family members to show the proper deference to the new boss even if they have been bosom buddies and partners in murder in the past. When the new boss appears in his takeover action, nobody puts their feet up on the furniture. Soldiers, even those with 40 years or more in the mob, stand up when the boss makes his entrance. Nobody extends a hand to shake hands. The boss is untouchable. Nobody speaks unless the boss asks them to. The boss may even emphasize his new position by not speaking directly to the common wise guys but passing his comments on through one of his entourage.

Whether the previous boss was murdered or sent away for a prison term, which means he "will never leave the can alive," is of no consequence. It all depends on what the new boss wants. He may decide to eliminate some of the important people in the old regime, or if they are not murdered, they may be reduced in rank or even allowed to remain in place. The surest etiquette for soldiers to survive is to have a track record of bringing in money for the mob and to show they are continuing to do so. Sometimes, to make a point, the new boss may have someone he has doubts about killed on the spot. Other times he may tell the high-risk individual that he is safe and then have him eliminated when the smoke has cleared. In the competition of succession, frequently based on strength rather than popularity or proficiency in running the mob, the new bosses themselves may be eliminated, and a new power struggle ensues. Now wise guys who had demonstrated their loyalty to the departed new boss may find they are under more suspicion than ever. In the Mafia of the new century, the new bosses have felt the need to exhibit more cruelty than their predecessors did. For example, making a comeback is the technique of not simply killing a possible high-risk wise guy but ramming a crowbar up his rectum. This makes very sobering incentive for other wise guys to pledge their loyalty and really mean it.

One of the most successful of the new bosses has been Joe Massino who took over the Bonanno family and ran it with ironclad discipline. In 2003 he was indicted for a number of murders including that of one of his own capos who had complained that a recently promoted capo was a danger because he used cocaine. The merits of the complaint allegedly had little impact on Massino, who according to prosecutors, simply said the complainant "had to go." The reason, said the government, was Massino could abide no "meddling." Massino is supposed to have told an informant, "It served him right for telling me how to run the family." If the allegations are true it is obvious Massino was simply indicating that no questioning of his rule, even indirectly, was allowed.

Easily the biggest purging of crime family ranks in the Mafia's new era was that of Lucchese cobosses Vic Amuso and Gas Pipe Casso who killed a number of potential opponents and apparently had a hit list of 49 others, half of whom were charter members of the Luccheses. Ironically, not all observers of the Mafia find the purges launched by new bosses "unhelpful." The idea that it represented the "survival of the fittest," in a most vile form, is undeniable and will continue unless or until the new Mafia achieves certain durability. It can be added that the average wise guy is not opposed to such purges, one such observer being quoted as saying, "Once we clear up this mess, the sooner we can get back to making money."

BOSS of bosses: Mythical Mafia leader

Capo di tutti capi, boss of all the bosses. The last man to claim the title for himself was Salvatore Maranzano in 1931. He was dead less than five months later. It seems organized crime in America, and the American Mafia, is too diverse, too greedy, too provincial, too ill-organized to follow one man.

That hardly matters to the press, which has, through the years, continued to bestow the boss of bosses crown, sometimes one publication in conflict with another. There was a period in the late 1970s when some insisted the crown belonged to Carmine Galante of the old Bonanno family while others said the mantle should fall to Frank "Funzi" Tieri, the head of the old Luciano-Genovese family.

The first to claim the title of boss of bosses was Joe Masseria, who in the 1920s was the foremost Mafia leader in New York City. Masseria didn't kid around. A pudgy, squat murderous man, he simply started calling himself Joe the Boss—and blasted those who disagreed. That, however, hardly settled that. According to Masseria, all the other gangsters of the era—Luciano, Rothstein, Dwyer, Lansky, Costello, Adonis, Capone, Schultz, Diamond, Genovese, Anastasia, Profaci, Gagliano and a latecomer named Maranzano—had to acknowledge his supremacy. Yet he got a war with some and treachery from within by others, supposedly loyal underlings like Luciano, who actually was busy plotting his downfall.

The great Mafia conflict called the Castellammarese War of 1930–1931 ended in victory for Maranzano following Luciano's assassination of Masseria. Maranzano had plans to be an American boss of bosses and, while it is common for crime scholars to deride the idea of a boss of bosses ruling over the American Mafia from Sicily, it is rather well established that it was attempted. Maranzano was sent to America by the foremost Mafia leader of the Italian island, Don Vito Cascio Ferro, to organize the American underworld so that it would follow the orders of Don Vito. After Maranzano arrived in America, Don Vito was imprisoned by Italian dictator Benito Mussolini and would never see freedom again. This left Maranzano free, he thought, to pick up the boss of bosses mantle himself.

At a celebrated meeting shortly after Joe the Boss's demise, informer Joe Valachi later reported, Maranzano outlined the new organization of the Mafia in New York. There would be five families, under five capos (that grand sentimentalist of the Mafia, Joe Bonanno, called them five Fathers): Luciano, Tom Gagliano, Joe Profaci, Vince Mangano and Maranzano. Maranzano was, in addition, establishing an added post for himself, that of boss of bosses. This produced some gasps from the crowd of gangsters. The man who had led the fight to end boss rule was turning about and making himself the new boss.

Chances are if Maranzano had not been so insistent, Luciano and the others would have let him live somewhat longer. As it was Maranzano was murdered on September 10, 1931. With him died the title of boss of bosses.

The first thing Luciano did on his ascendancy was cancel the position. Luciano knew that Maranzano had aims on the rest of the country and besides having Luciano on his death list, he planned to kill Al Capone, Frank Costello, Joey Adonis, Vito Genovese, Dutch Schultz and Willie Moretti, among others. Luciano knew that the new underworld would not be a strictly Italian setup as Maranzano visualized it, and he most certainly was not about to challenge Capone, although Capone for his part had no nationwide ambitions; he was having trouble enough conquering the Chicago North Side, among other districts, to think any bigger.

Luciano and Meyer Lansky became the most important syndicate criminals of the 1930s. Within the Italian segment of their multiethnic national crime syndicate, important to Luciano as his power base, some of Maranzano's innovations were continued, such as the five-family arrangement in New York, with Joe Bonanno inheriting the essential elements of the Maranzano family.

It could be said quite accurately that Luciano did rule as the de facto boss of bosses in part precisely because he refused the title. When he went to prison on a 30- to 50-year sentence on prostitution charges, Luciano left the affairs of his own family under the control of Frank Costello, with Joe Adonis assigned the nominal custody of syndicate matters—which were more or less under the control of a National Commission of the five family heads and a few other crime bosses from other cities. However, Luciano told Adonis to "listen to Meyer." For all intents and purposes, then, organized crime had a Jewish boss of bosses in Lansky. However, Lansky's influence derived not from any bequeath of power but rather from general recognition of his "smarts."

The constant search for a boss of bosses by the press nevertheless concentrated on Italians and settled for a while on Costello and, later, after his return from Italy, on Genovese. Genovese clearly wanted the title and from 1950 on he started a steady campaign to achieve it, first by convincing everyone that Willie Moretti, a Luciano-Costello loyalist, had to be killed because he was "going off his rocker." In 1957 Genovese tried but failed to have Costello murdered and then succeeded in having Albert Anastasia put down. It fact, some have asserted that the Apalachin Conference of 1957 was called to crown Genovese as the new boss of bosses, but this is untrue or, in any event, never came to pass. A police raid broke up the meeting, and strong evidence later showed the conference was sabotaged by an alliance of Lansky,

Luciano (from exile in Italy) and Frank Costello—all three not present at the meeting—and Carlo Gambino, who succeeded to head of the Anastasia family. According to statements attributed to Luciano, Gambino had gone there in case the meeting somehow proceeded, planning to denounce Genovese's ambitions and to refuse to hand him any envelope of money as a symbol of his authority.

This did not stop the press from calling Genovese the boss of bosses, but if he was, his reign was to prove even less enduring than that of the unfortunate Maranzano. He was arrested and convicted on a narcotics charge—widely believed to have been arranged by the same quartet who stopped Apalachin. With Genovese tucked away, the press turned to Gambino as the new boss of bosses, and there is little doubt he became the most powerful crime leader not only in New York but also across the country. Certainly, his influence extended over some of the other crime families. He dominated the old Profaci family through Joe Colombo and eventually placed his favorite, "Funzi" Tieri, at the head of the Genovese family after Tommy Eboli, who inherited the throne on Genovese's death, was conveniently murdered.

Law enforcement agencies have a keen interest in establishing a boss of bosses, especially if they figure they can bust him, so that they can take credit for dealing organized crime a mighty blow. That was what federal narcotics men claimed when they nailed Genovese; law enforcement officials figured they could do the same to Gambino but he died in 1976.

After some casting about, Carmine Galante, the underboss to Joe Bonanno before doing a long stretch for narcotics smuggling, was next elected to become the boss of bosses. Indeed, the *New York Times*, among others, so dubbed him. Galante was then rearrested for parole violation and the government looked very good again, knocking off yet another boss of bosses.

Next in line for the mythical crown was Tieri, which meant that he too would soon face a serious conviction. He was sentenced to 10 years for violating the Organized Crime Control Act of 1970 but died shortly thereafter in 1981.

After that came Paul Castellano, the head of the Gambino family. The fact that he headed a powerful family may not have been enough to dub him the boss of bosses, especially when one considers that he was taken down so easily by gangster elements within his own family headed by John Gotti. Clearly,

Gotti then became the press's leading candidate for the title boss of bosses. The fact that under Gotti the Gambinos went into deep decline so that the Genovese family once more gained the distinction of becoming more powerful and prosperous was a clear fly in the ointment. Still the press was not ready to name that mob's leader, Chin Gigante, to the grandiose position. When both Gotti and Gigante went to prison, the mythical title remained vacant.

BOSS'S annual income: No limit for the man at the top

It would be hard to estimate accurately the annual income of a Mafia don. In Chicago Tony Accardo's take was known to be enormous, as was that of his associate Sam Giancana. New York's Paul Castellano (and Carlo Gambino before him) and Tough Tony Salerno garnered fortunes, and it was said their annual payola could not be reckoned on just their 10 fingers, each one representing a million—and maybe not even if their 10 toes were counted as well.

Only in the recent case of John Gotti can some ballpark figures be established, thanks to informer Sammy "the Bull" Gravano. Sammy disclosed his own income to show what size slice Gotti took. Rigged construction deals set up by the Bull with the Teamsters and other unions topped $1.2 million a year. The Bull also garnered a number of so-called legit construction contracts, and he and his wife paid $800,000 in taxes. After taxes at least $200,000 went to Gotti. Sammy's operations in nightclubs, discos, and after-hours joints produced another $600,000 a year and again Gotti took his share. The Bull insisted this made him Gotti's biggest producer, which might or might not have been true, as Gotti had numerous sources of money. Tommy Gambino's garment industry operations netted Gotti huge sums. Then there were cuts from hijackings, the carting industry, pier rackets and other rackets. And of course there was also drug money. One mob heroin dealer was good for handing Gotti $100,000 a payment. Officially there was a ban on drug activities, but Gotti took the money and asked no questions.

In *Underboss*, the Bull estimated that Gotti on the very low side was getting $5 million a year—"and probably more like ten or twelve."

It would take time to join the ranks of the wealthiest mob bosses, boasting at least a few hundred million as some dons had done, but Gotti never made it.

He was cut off at the very prime of his money-making years.

BOURG, Frank (1890–1955): "Wrong man" Mafia victim

In April 1955, 64-year-old New Orleans bank teller Frank Bourg suffered a heart attack and was hospitalized. One night as he lay in bed a visitor walked into his room and proceeded to smash his skull with a cleaver. It clearly appeared to be a gang hit although Bourg, evidently an innocent teller for some 30 years, had no record of any sort of criminal involvement.

Later it was concluded that Bourg had been the mistaken victim of a Mafia assassination attempt. It appeared the real target was Sheriff Frank Clancy who had occupied the next hospital room. According to a police report, "from the time Clancy . . . entered the hospital, he . . . had a guard outside of his door but the guard was removed—on the morning of the attack—by somebody representing themselves as the sheriff's wife."

Clancy, an old-style political boss, had been a reluctant witness at the Kefauver Hearings in 1950–1951. He revealed that he had allowed the underworld to place 5,000 slot machines in his parish. In addition, acting New Orleans boss Carlos Marcello opened three gambling casinos on the New Orleans side of the river; it was said that Clancy had a share in the profits. Clancy also maintained the right to hire all personnel below the management level. Clancy's testimony proved embarrassing to Marcello but had little effect on gambling operations.

There was some reason to believe that Clancy was talking to federal agents about Louisiana gambling right up to the time of the Bourg murder. Nothing bad came out of the Bourg murder for the Marcello family. A nurse's aide who had seen the killer and provided police with a detailed description three days later suddenly recalled she had no idea what the man looked like. And as David Leon Chandler noted in *Brothers in Blood*, "As for Sheriff Clancy, he ceased giving information to federal agents."

BRASCO, Donnie (1939–): FBI agent who infiltrated the Mafia

He was the greatest Mafia informer, far more productive than such informers as Sammy "the Bull"

Gravano, Joe Valachi or Abe Reles, the Murder, Inc., canary. He was Donnie Brasco, an informer with a difference. He was an undercover FBI agent who infiltrated the Mafia. His real name was Joe Pistone, and unlike the usual informer, his box score was of record proportions, his exposures sending more than 100 mobsters to prison.

To carry off his dangerous masquerade, Pistone played the Brasco tough-guy role to the hilt. Trusted more and more by key mafiosi, he provided insights into the mob never offered before by others. He took part in potential linkups between crime families in different parts of the country, from the Bonanno crime family in New York to the Trafficante family in Florida and the Balistrieri family in Milwaukee, a group tied closely to the Chicago Outfit.

Brasco worked his way up as an associate of such lower echelon wise guys as Tony Mirra and Lefty Ruggiero. Neither were mental geniuses, but they were vicious and deadly when aroused. In the movie, *Donnie Brasco* (1997), Al Pacino played not the dapper, college-educated Michael Corleone of *The Godfather* (1972) but the ignorant, erratic and frequently homicidal Ruggiero, an average soldier of the mob. Even though Brasco developed a certain affinity for Ruggiero and his superior, Sonny Black, he later explained the difference between *The Godfather* and the real-world Mafia was that the movie gave the hoodlums too much credit. The reality of Mafia life was grubby; petty and venal. Unseen was the infighting, the lying to one another, the scheming against each other to achieve power. Clearly Donnie Brasco found no "Honored Society." As capo Sonny Black, who was finally murdered by his fellow mafiosi, said, "Every day somebody's looking to dispose of you and take your position. You always got to be on your toes. Every fucking day is a scam day to keep your power and position."

Brasco soon learned the Mafia law of the jungle, under which how strong a man is and how much power he can assemble and how mean he can be determines how far he can rise in the mob—right up to the mythical title of "godfather."

For six years starting in 1976 Donnie Brasco worked his way into the higher reaches of the mob. Only when the internal struggles worsened and the FBI feared Brasco would either be found out and killed as a snitch or become a victim of intrafamily warfare did they pull him out. But there was another reason. Brasco, who was up for membership, had been given a contract to murder an enemy of Sonny Black's. The government could not allow this and would not agree with Brasco that he could dodge and weave until the FBI found the murder target and snatched him away.

Once Brasco became Pistone again he spent more than five years in various Mafia trials around the country, aiding in the conviction of wise guys. Some of those imprisoned died in jail, and some have now gotten out, but most remain behind bars.

In retaliation, the mob bosses put out an open-ended contract on Pistone—open to anyone—for $500,000. The bosses generally abide by the rule against killing lawmen, but in Pistone's case they made an exception. Lefty Ruggiero survived because the FBI found him before the mob did and put him in prison for a long term. He was released a few years later suffering from cancer and died in 1989 at the age of 67.

Pistone retired from the FBI in 1997 after 27 years as an agent. For a while he and his family were in the witness protection program, but not in recent years. He does not let his photograph be taken, but he no longer has guards around him. But he remains cautious: "What I do is take proper precautions. What you worry about is some cowboy who recognizes you and wants to make a name for himself."

What Joe Pistone did was make a name for Donnie Brasco, one that scores of mafiosi behind bars still curse.

BRIBERY and the Mafia

In California it is called "juice," in Florida "ice," in New York "grease." It could as well be called a rose or any other name, but what it stands for is bribery. The Mafia bribes in wholesale lots, and it does not stint on the amount.

In *The American Mafia: Genesis of a Legend*, Joseph L. Albini of Wayne State University tells of a former police official who was offered $12,500 cash and $1,000 a week not to interfere with the operation of a single gambling establishment. Some years later he got another offer of $50,000 cash and $5,000 a week to allow two clubs to operate.

Early in his career Lucky Luciano found himself and his partners, Meyer Lansky, Bugsy Siegel and Joe Adonis, with an income one year of $12 million from bootlegging alone. They had a payroll of about 100 men—muscle men, guards, drivers, bookkeepers, messengers, fingermen, etc.—who cost them about $1 million. By contrast their "grease"—protection to police and politicians—totaled about $100,000 a week or about $5 million a year. This left them a profit of $6 million a year. The bribed, one might say, were almost equal partners with the mobsters.

In California, one major gambling racket broken up was the so-called Guarantee Finance Company, which although posing as a loan agency was actually a front for a $6 million bookmaking combine. When Guarantee's books were seized, they disclosed that $108,000 was paid for juice. Since Guarantee was a "50-50 book," meaning that participating bookies had to share equally in expenses, this meant the actual expenditure for police non-interference came to $216,000.

It is true that sometimes only a single cop or official is offered a bribe if he is in a special position to offer the mob a special service, such as obtaining confidential information or even the names of informers. In Cleveland in the late 1970s an FBI file clerk and her husband, an automobile salesman, were sentenced to five years in prison for selling information to the local Mafia crime family. However, far more common is blanket bribery in which all or most cops in a particular precinct are cut in on a piece of the action. It is not a case of a few rotten apples in a good barrel.

For years Gennaro "Jerry" Angiulo, the crime boss of Boston and underboss of the New England family headed by Raymond Patriarca, handled the police fix for the entire group. According to informer Vinnie Teresa, he claimed he could control 300 of Boston's 360-odd detectives. Teresa also stated, "In Providence, Patriarca had half the city on his payroll." From January to May 1981 the FBI maintained a court-approved electronic eavesdropping system at Angiulo's shabby Boston office in the North End. After 850 hours of recorded conversations, 40 Boston police officers were transferred because their names were mentioned on the tapes.

Former FBI agent Neil J. Welch has stated, "Cop cases are never just one cop—it's the captain, the lieutenant, the inspector, the sergeants, the whole pad, as they say in New York."

Special bribery involves special payoffs. If a valued mafioso or syndicate figure is up for possible probation or parole, heavy bribes are offered. In one case a bribe of $100,000 had to be returned by a high-ranking public official because a parole for a major crime figure had to be called off when a newspaper raised too much of a stink.

Bribes are made in an amount commensurate with the value received and there are many low echelon figures who get no more than $25 a month. And bribery costs rise and fall from time to time, depending on how much public tolerance compared to public pressure is exerted in a given area. "Heat" does not cripple organized crime but merely raises the tab.

In Caponeland—Chicago—the tab for many years was quite low because no one seemed capable of stopping corruption. Thus in one of his more loquacious moments, Jake "Greasy Thumb" Guzik—he was so dubbed because his thumb became so greasy from the huge amount of graft money he passed out—could sneer about judges in his domain: "You buy a judge by weight, like iron in a junkyard. A justice of the peace or a magistrate can be had for a five-dollar bill. In municipal court he will cost you ten. In the circuit or superior courts he wants fifteen. The state appellate court or the state supreme court is on a par with the federal courts. By the time a judge reaches such courts he is middle-aged, thick around the middle, fat between the ears. He's heavy. You can't buy a federal judge for less than a twenty-dollar bill."

One must temper Guzik's classic words by allowing for several decades of inflation. And quite possibly he was exaggerating the monies he was able to save for the mob, though the record shows he paid out substantial sums. For years Guzik spent many nights a week seated at the same table at St. Hubert's Old English Grill and Chop House, 316 South Federal Street, in the Loop, there to be visited by district police captains and the sergeants who collected their graft for them, and by the various bagmen for various politicians.

It is perhaps touching that Guzik died of a heart attack at his post at 6:17 P.M., February 21, 1956, while dining at St. Hubert's on a simple meal of broiled lamb chops and a glass of moselle. Equally touching were the comments of Rabbi Noah Ganze at Guzik's orthodox Jewish funeral. The rabbi called the deceased "a fine husband who was good to his children. Jacob Guzik never lost faith in his God. Hundreds benefited by his kindness and generosity. His charities were performed quietly."

A Chicago journalist added the comment: "Some of the police captains and politicians who were among these hundreds who benefited from Jake's generosity looked at the ceiling."

BRIDGE of Sighs: American version

They came from the poverty of Italy to the teeming ghetto of lower New York, in hope of escaping the grimness of life in Italy, a grimness typified for many by the Bridge of Sighs in Venice. The bridge, over which the convicted and condemned were led, directly connected the ducal palace and the state prison.

Many were trapped into a new life of crime, America's standard offer for all "huddled masses" squeezed into crowded criminal breeding areas. Inevitably the exposed bridge at the old Tombs prison in lower New York was dubbed the new Bridge of Sighs. Unfortunately this added to the public conception that most criminals were Italian and led later to further misunderstanding of the organized mobs' multi-ethnicity.

BROADWAY Mob: Prohibition racketeers

There probably was no more important Prohibition gang in New York than the Broadway Mob. Its power and its unique assemblage of criminals helped to forge in the early 1930s the national crime syndicate that remains the basis of organized crime today.

Officially, the Broadway Mob was run by Joe Adonis, but Lucky Luciano and Frank Costello were the brains of the operation. Behind the gang was Broadway millionaire gambler and criminal mastermind, Arnold Rothstein. Rothstein also brought in the Bug and Meyer Mob, run by Meyer Lansky and Bugsy Siegel, to provide protection for the gang's convoys of bootleg liquor. Since Lansky had worked with Luciano previously and each trusted the other, it was easy to see why Adonis and Costello thought it an even better idea to make Lansky and Siegel partners—indeed, it would certainly be cheaper. Lansky and Siegel had to be paid a lot for protection; it was well known they were not above engaging in hijacking if the returns were better.

The new multi-ethnic Broadway Mob soon dominated bootlegging in New York, offering top-quality non-diluted whiskey to all the most renowned speakeasies—the Silver Slipper, Sherman Billingsley's Stork Club, Jack White's, Jack and Charlie's "21" Club and others. Even if all the liquor was not "right off the boat" as claimed but produced in Waxey Gordon's Philadelphia distilleries, it was still far superior to the rotgut offered by most bootlegging gangs. Under Rothstein's tutelage, the Broadway Mob bought interests in a number of leading speakeasies, which in turn, gave the gangsters a vested interest in making sure the liquor they dispensed was top grade. These speakeasy and nightclub investments were the first these mobsters made in Manhattan and, in time, gave them ownership of some prime Manhattan real estate, a situation said to be unchanged today among the New York crime families.

See also ADONIS, JOE; ROTHSTEIN, ARNOLD

BRONFMAN, Samuel (1891–1971): Liquor manufacturer and underworld supplier

No encyclopedic study of the American Mafia would be complete without mention of the likes of Samuel Bronfman and Lewis Rosentiel. Both became in later life important figures in the legalized liquor industry, even philanthropists in the United States. During Prohibition they can be said to have put the dollar sign in organized crime in America.

The Bronfman family, having fled the pogroms of eastern Europe, settled in Canada, where they proceeded to amass a great fortune in the liquor business, the bulk of which came from peddling booze to bootleggers who brought it into the United States. While it may be said that the leader of the family, Sam Bronfman, was doing nothing illegal since the manufacture of whiskey was legal in Canada, he was nevertheless in a dangerous business. His brother-in-law, Paul Matoff, was gunned down in 1922 in Saskatchewan in a battle between two bootlegging gangs.

Most of Bronfman's business was conducted through such crime figures as Arnold Rothstein, Meyer Lansky, Lucky Luciano, the Purple Gang in Detroit and Moe Dalitz in Cleveland. So much booze was run across Lake Erie—primarily to the Dalitz organization—that it was called "the Jewish lake."

If later on Rosentiel and his company, Schenley, were to deny ever having any doings with the underworld, Bronfman was a bit more forthcoming, although he frequently changed the subject when the name of his close friend Meyer Lansky came up.

Bronfman once declared in an interview in *Fortune* magazine: "We loaded a carload of goods, got our cash, and shipped it. We shipped a lot of goods. I never went to the other side of the border to count the empty Seagram's bottles."

The Bronfman Connection entered the United States through a variety of sources, by border-running trucks all the way from New York State to Montana, in ships that docked on both the East and West Coasts, by speedboats darting across the St. Lawrence–Great Lakes waterways.

With the end of Prohibition, a financial dispute broke out between the United States and Canada. The U.S. Treasury Department claimed that Canadian distillers like Bronfman owed $60 million in excise and customs taxes on alcohol shipments. Finally U.S. Treasury Secretary Henry Morgenthau Jr. issued an ultimatum that importation of all Canadian goods would be halted until the bill was paid. Eventually Canada agreed to settle for five cents on the dollar of $3 million. Sam Bronfman sportingly put up half that sum.

Some of the underworld bootlegging kings, like Waxey Gordon, ended up broke after Prohibition. The same could not be said about Sam Bronfman. The American public had drunk his product for 14 years illegally and drank even more when booze became legal again.

See also BOOTLEGGING

BROOKLIER, Dominic (1914–1984): Los Angeles crime boss

Dominic Brooklier was one of a long line of Los Angeles crime bosses who contributed to the demeaning characterization of the crime family as "the Mickey Mouse Mafia." Under Brooklier the L.A. family was big in porno and various forms of extortion, but failed to take over the bookmaking racket in southern California. In a long criminal arrest record dating back to the 1930s, he had been convicted of armed robbery, larceny, interstate transportation of forged documents and racketeering.

Brooklier was originally part of the Mickey Cohen gambling operation in California but defected to the forces of mafioso Jack Dragna and took part in the war against his former mentor. His chief claim to fame as a hit man in that struggle was attempting to shotgun Cohen as he came out of a restaurant. Just as Brooklier, accompanied by another gunman, squeezed the trigger, Cohen noticed a tiny scratch on the fender of his new Cadillac and bent down to inspect it, thereby avoiding a fatal hit.

Over the years Brooklier formed a love-hate relationship with Jimmy "the Weasel" Fratianno. Brooklier was a faithful follower of Los Angeles Nick Licata and when he died in 1974, Brooklier was named to replace him. When he himself was sent to prison for a couple of years, Brooklier named Fratianno as acting boss. Quickly, the ambitious Fratianno appeared to be making a pitch that would allow him to keep control of the family. Brooklier was ailing and the Weasel figured there was an even chance he might not live to complete his prison term.

Brooklier did survive and took over again, edging out the Weasel. He was suspicious of Fratianno on more than one count, not only that he coveted the boss position, but also that he might actually be an informer. Indeed, Fratianno was already giving limited cooperation to the FBI while at the same time trying to carve out a power position for himself in the Mafia. Brooklier eventually put out a contract on Fratianno but was unable to see it through. He had to ask the Chicago crime family for assistance, another sign that he headed an outfit that could not even discipline its own straying members—an open invitation to the greedy Chicago group to move even more heavily into California.

Fratianno avoided assassination by going all the way as an informer and joining the federal witness protection program. The Weasel supplied information on Brooklier's successful order to have another informer eliminated, San Diego mobster Frank "Bomp" Bompensiero, who was shot to death in a telephone booth in February 1977. Brooklier was the man who was at the other end of the line holding Bomp in conversation until the gunners got there. However, Brooklier was acquitted of conspiracy in that murder.

He was convicted along with several others. L.A. crime figures—including Louis Tom Dragna, Jack LoCicero, Mike Rizzitello and Sam Sciortino—on racketeering and conspiracy charges involving extortion of bookmakers and pornography dealers. Brooklier got five years and died of a heart attack at the Federal Metropolitan Correctional Center in Tucson in July 1984.

BROTHERS, Leo Vincent (1899–1951): Alleged murderer of Jake Lingle

Investigations following the murder of *Chicago Tribune* reporter-legman Jake Lingle on June 9, 1930, revealed the cozy relationship the Capone underworld and other gangs had with members of the press. Lingle was no ordinary newsman, but a major criminal go-between for Al Capone (and other Chicago gangs) and Police Commissioner William F. Russell and others in the political structure.

Although he ostensibly earned only $65 a week, an annual income of at least $60,000 was traced to Lingle—that was only what could be definitely established. He had a big chauffeur-driven car, owned a home in the city and a summer home in the country, played the stock market (partly in a $100,000 joint brokerage account with Commissioner Russell), bet heavily at the races (sometimes wagering $1,000 on a single race) and maintained a lavish suite of rooms at one of Chicago's most expensive hotels. Through his police connections Lingle fixed it for gambling joints and speakeasies to operate and was spoken of in knowledgeable underworld circles as the "unofficial chief of police." He himself bragged to friends that he "fixed the price of beer in Chicago."

Lingle was shot by an unknown gunman near a subway entrance to the Washington Park racetrack train. The killer escaped as Lingle crumpled to the ground, dead with a bullet in his head. Lingle's murder shocked the city and the whole country and there were large black headlines, front-page editorials and messages of condolence from newspapers around the country. Rewards totaling more than $55,000 were offered for information that led to the apprehension and conviction of the killer.

Lingle was given a lavish funeral, but shortly thereafter indignation began to give way to suspicion. Why had Lingle been murdered? As details of his high-living were unearthed, suspicion festered. The public learned Lingle was an intimate friend of Capone; he had visited Capone's estate in Florida on a number of occasions and he was the proud owner of a diamond-studded belt buckle given him by the notorious gang lord. Then there were reports of a falling out between Capone and the newsman. Lingle, it developed, was making protection deals with Capone's hated counterparts in the Bugs Moran Gang, and the newsman-fixer was not delivering on deals with Big Al. Capone was heard to state, "Jake is going to get his."

Meanwhile an embarrassed Colonel Robert McCormick and the *Chicago Tribune* waged a running battle with other newspapers concerning the Lingle scandal. McCormick's newspaper ran an exposé series to demonstrate, rather accurately, that a number of newsmen on other papers were "on the take" from the underworld. Still, there was little doubt that the *Tribune* needed an arrest to cool things off. A special investigative committee was formed headed up by Charles F. Rathbun, a *Tribune* lawyer, and Patrick T. Roche, chief investigator for the State's Attorney's office, with the *Tribune* agreeing to cover all expenses beyond what the county could afford. Working with the group was a *Tribune* reporter, John Boettiger, who other newspapers would complain had the job of seeing to it that McCormick and the *Tribune* were cast in the best possible light.

About a half year after the Lingle murder the Rathbun-Roche-Boettiger group was instrumental in capturing and charging one Leo Vincent Brothers, alias Leo Bader, with the crime. Brothers, 31, was from St. Louis, where he was wanted for robbery, arson, bombing and murder. Of 14 witnesses who had seen the murderer leaving the scene, seven identified Brothers while seven did not. The *Tribune* nevertheless congratulated the investigative team and itself. A number of opposition newspapers were not as convinced on the solution and intimated that Brothers was a frame-up victim, either innocent or one who allowed himself to take the fall for money.

There were negotiations between Capone and a representative for the Rathbun-Roche-Boettiger team. Details of a released conversation revealed:

Capone: "Well, I didn't kill Jake Lingle, did I?"
Unidentified representative: "We don't know who killed him."
Capone: "Why didn't you ask me? Maybe I can find out for you."

It is almost certain Capone did know who killed Lingle. In a conversation overheard by Mike Malone, a federal agent who had infiltrated the Capone ranks, Big Al told his top aide, Greasy Thumb Guzik, he did not intend to deliver the real murderer.

Then Brothers was arrested. He was convicted, but the jury found the evidence against him less than overwhelming. He was found guilty on charges that brought him only a 14-year sentence. Brothers was elated. He announced: "I can do that standing on my head."

The trade publication *Editor and Publisher* ran a story, stating:

> The verdict . . . brought a torrent of denunciation upon Chicago courts in newspaper comments from other cities.
>
> The very fact that Brothers received the minimum sentence has given critics a basis for charges which have persisted since the announcement of the arrest. The utter certainty of officials that Brothers was the man who killed Lingle and the fact that not one witness testified he saw Lingle slain, presents at least a groundwork for the ugly rumors that have been circulated.
>
> . . . it is held unreasonable that a jury, finding a man guilty of the cold-blooded murder of Lingle, could impose the minimum sentence on the evidence presented.
>
> It is a question in the mind of the police at large as to the guilt of Brothers.
>
> The Tribune has, from the first, maintained that Brothers is the man. This persistence, in the face of an unwillingness on the part of either the newspaper or officials to strip the case bare, show a motive, reveal gang connections, and thus prove to the world that Brothers had a reason for killing Lingle and did so, has engendered a belief among newspapermen that Brothers is the man who killed Lingle, but it cannot be legitimately proved without entailing a scandal which would prove so devastating as to render the game not worth the candle.
>
> . . . Those dissatisfied with the verdict are of the opinion that from a point of general good, Brothers belongs in jail but they hold that there is still the question left unanswered, "Who killed 'Jake' Lingle, and why?"

Publisher McCormick countered with a fiery protest to the dispatch which had been written by a member of the opposing *Chicago Daily News,* and *Editor and Publisher* issued a retraction and apology. Nevertheless, the view that Brothers was not the key figure in the murder—and that perhaps he demonstrated the ease with which the mob could get stand-ins for their crimes—remained probably the majority view outside the editorial offices of the *Tribune.*

Of course, the newspaper warfare on the Lingle case had to be judged within the confines of unbridled competition, probably unmatched in any other American city. The relationship of many gangsters, both in and out of the Capone organization, with various newspapers was undisputed; the newspapers were involved in a distribution war that decided which papers were sold at what corners and newsstands. The war was waged through the good offices of the baseball bat, brass knuckles, knives and guns.

According to a popular account, Capone came to McCormick's aid by preventing a strike by newspaper deliverers, and McCormick was quoted as telling the gang leader: "You know, you are famous, like Babe Ruth. We can't help printing things about you, but I will see that the *Tribune* gives you a square deal."

McCormick gave a much different version of events. "I arrived late at a publishers' meeting. Capone walked in with some of his hoodlums. I threw him out and after that I traveled around in an armored car with one or two bodyguards. Capone didn't settle anything. And he didn't take over the newspapers as he wanted to do."

Whichever version is closer to the truth, Capone nevertheless had a way of influencing many newspapers. By the sheer virtue of his argument (and the unquestioned criminal ability he had to harass newspapers), he caused Hearst's *Chicago Evening American* to stop printing Capone's nickname of "Scarface" unless it was within a direct quote from someone like a police official.

As for Leo Brothers, he served only eight years of his sentence and was released, refusing to make any comments on the crime or on the sources of the money furnished him for his expensive legal defense. He maintained his silence until his death in 1951.

The Brothers solution has gotten short shrift over the years. In *Barbarians in Our Midst,* the definitive book on Chicago crime, Virgil W. Peterson, longtime head of the Chicago Crime Commission, speculates on various mobsters who might have killed Lingle. Brothers is deemed unworthy of mention. This view, hardly an oversight, apparently led a number of crime writers later to state that the Lingle murder was never officially solved. It was. It was just that hardly anybody paid the solution much mind.

See also LINGLE, ALFRED "JAKE"

BRUNO, Angelo (1910–1980): Philadelphia Mafia boss

Angelo Bruno was called "the Gentle Don." For the two decades that he ruled the Philadelphia crime family, it was one of the most peaceful in the nation.

Sicilian-born Angelo Bruno preached the quiet approach to his men. He ordered very few mob shootings and kept his organization out of the lucrative drug trade, a policy that earned him the approval of his neighbors and at least tacit acceptance by the authorities. Neil Welch, who later became special agent in charge of the FBI's Philadelphia office, said in effect that for years the agency had not pursued Bruno with any great vigor.

Bruno, a truly rare mafioso chieftain, was even capable of turning the other cheek when he was the object of a botched assassination try. He shrugged it off and did not subject the foe to reciprocity but rather merely enforced his retirement from the rackets. Even his own men faced his wrath for their violent ways. When in the mid-1960s family member Little Nicky Scarfo, whom Bruno probably considered a flake, stabbed a longshoreman to death in an argument over a restaurant seat, the godfather banished him to Atlantic City, then a depressed area. (By the mid-1980s it had become a glittering gambling mecca and Little Nicky was cock-of-the-walk.)

The Gentle Don was not around to see Atlantic City develop. On March 21, 1980, Bruno was sitting in his car after dinner when a shotgun blast blew a huge hole behind his right ear, killing him instantly. There was hardly any doubt the motive was Atlantic City. The other eastern families had long recognized Philadelphia's right to Atlantic City, when Philly's main source of revenue there was the numbers business in the ghettos. But the new big money action, they were known to feel, was more than Bruno could handle or, for that matter, deserved. In New York, federal authorities labeled Funzi Tieri, the boss of the Genovese family, as responsible for Bruno's eradication. Both the Genoveses and the Gambinos, then in close alliance under Tierri's leadership, had action in various parts of New Jersey and fully intended to grab the seashore city's gambling action. It may be assumed the Gentle Don objected too gently.

Officially the Bruno murder was unsolved and its consequences were to rip the previously quiet Philly crime family apart with two dozen gang murders in the next few years. Taking over after Bruno was the more violent Phil "Chicken Man" Testa, his underboss. Ten days after the Bruno assassination a local newspaper's resident horoscoper declared: "With Neptune in exact conjunction with his retrograde Jupiter, no matter what's going on, Testa will come out in a better position than he started." Unfortunately, the mafiosi in New York were not big on astrology.

See also TESTA, PHILIP "CHICKEN MAN"

BUCCIERI, Fiore "Fifi" (1904–1973): Chicago syndicate killer

Fiore Buccieri's nickname was Fifi, an unlikely moniker for the lord high executioner of the Chicago syndicate, Albert Anastasia's analog, and boss Sam Giancana's personal hit man. Giancana kept Buccieri very, very busy, not only as a murderer, but also as a bomber, arsonist, terrorist, labor union racketeer and loan shark. Buccieri was also a master of the threat.

Debtors paid up when Buccieri passed the word around to their friends, advising them not to ride in a car with the borrower—because he "is going to get hit." Buccieri sometimes had the "business" cards of his street men placed in employment offices; when a job-hunter was turned down, he was handed the business card of a Buccieri "loan officer." It might not seem too wise to lend money to men out of work, but Buccieri knew no genuinely bad risk—his clients paid up no matter what. If they were made to sweat enough, he explained, the money would come out of their pores. He was right. Men paid, even if they had to steal from their parents, their relatives, their friends, and their bosses. If necessary they would put their wives and daughters out on the street to make money to cover their juice payments.

Buccieri's awesome reputation did not come from threats alone. He was near to being the most monstrous killer in the Chicago Outfit, and that covered a lot of bloodletters. Evidence of his dedication to the art of murder is offered in tapes collected in a wiretapping by federal agents of conversations between Buccieri and a group of his boys. While planning an underworld hit in a rented house in Miami in 1962, Buccieri nostalgically recounted some of his more gruesome kills, especially the 1962 torture-murder of William "Action" Jackson, a 300-pound collector for the mob's loan-sharking operations. Believed guilty of two major offenses—appropriating some of the mob's funds for his personal use and, as Buccieri put it, being a "stoolpigeon for the 'G'"—Jackson was hustled to the "Plant," a mob locale with a large meat hook on the wall. With Buccieri were James "Turk" Torello, Jackie "the Lackey" Cerone, Mad Sam De Stefano and Dave Yaras, credited in recent years as the most prominent Jewish mobster in the Chicago organization. They started off by shooting Jackson "just once in the knee." Then they stripped him naked, bound his hands and feet and proceeded, in Buccieri's words, "to have a little bit of fun." They worked Jackson over with ice picks, baseball bats, and a blow torch. Next Buccieri employed an electric cattle prod. "You should have heard the prick scream," Buccieri recalled. His audience convulsed in laughter as he regaled them with details of what happened next.

A sober moment was then provided by Torello who said, "I still don't understand why he didn't admit he was a pigeon." Buccieri's response was, "I'm only sorry the big slob died so soon." Considering the fact that Jackson's torture on the meat hook lasted two days, Buccieri's regrets were worth another round of laughter. Buccieri had taken photographs of Jackson's mutilated body and passed them around to other mob workers as a reminder of the perils of breaking "Family" trust.

Buccieri had graduated into the Chicago syndicate from the 42 Gang, a notorious Chicago juvenile gang. He was a follower of another 42er, Sam Giancana, who rose to the top post in the outfit. Giancana, who always appreciated first-rate murderers, made Fifi his personal executioner as well as a powerful ally during the power struggle for mob leadership.

If the authorities thought they might get at Giancana through Buccieri, they were always disappointed. Buccieri would never talk. Even the press found Buccieri's stubbornness a source of amusement. Once federal probers tried to elicit intelligence about the mob from Fifi and quizzed him about his brother Frank, also a syndicate stalwart. They even pursued the fact that Fifi's brother had a girlfriend who had done duty as a Playboy bunny. She was a nude centerfold in *Playboy* magazine, and Frank had given her a horse as a present. Fifi's response, still cited with approbation in the underworld, was, "I take the Fifth on the horse and the broad."

Cancer claimed Fifi in 1973, two years before Giancana's assassination. Many claim no mobster would have dared take out Giancana were Fifi still alive. Retribution in the form of a Buccieri-led bloodbath would have been too gruesome, even by Chicago standards.

BUCHALTER, Louis   See Lepke, Louis

BUCKWHEATS: Painful murder methods

Steve Franse died buckwheats. That meant that Vito Genovese ordered that his one-time trusted aide had

to die, but not simply die painlessly. Genovese wanted him to suffer. Mob murders are seldom buckwheats, being instead simple business matters. An exception is made, however, for murders of example, such as in the case of informers, or mobsters who hold out on gang revenues, or, in some cases, loan shark victims whose painful demise could inspire other debtors to pay up promptly.

Franse's sin involved an affair of the heart. Genovese had left America to avoid a murder rap and ordered Franse to watch over some of his funds and his wife. Franse did a good job on the money, but Genovese's wife strayed, and all the worse in a manner involving both sexes. Genovese was outraged. Franse had betrayed him by not stopping it, and for this he died hard.

Joe Valachi told what happened. Two hit men grabbed Franse in a restaurant kitchen. While one got him in an armlock the other started beating him in the mouth and belly. "He gives it to him good. It's what we call 'buckwheats,' meaning spite-work."

After Franse collapsed to the floor, the killers wrapped a chain around his neck; when he started to struggle as the chain was tightened, one of his assailants stomped on his neck to hold him down until the job was finished.

Old Joe Profaci of the Brooklyn crime family was known as a vindictive sort who often had victims die hard. One Profaci gunman was quoted as telling a potential victim: "Sometimes guys really suffer, you know? I once saw a guy get shot right up the ass. Man, did *he* suffer."

When the killers of Murder, Inc., particularly hated a victim they would ice pick him and shoot him several times before burying him in the sand along a beach or a swamp—while he was still breathing.

Undoubtedly the most buckwheats-oriented family in the country was the Chicago Outfit. Once a showgirl named Estelle Carey was suspected of ratting on a gang member. The mob realized that women often knew more than they should about gangsters and that it would be useful to finish Estelle off in a torturous manner that would convince other women that silence meant survival. Most of Chicago's favorite methods were used on her. Her nose was broken, and her face badly bruised. There were knife wounds and throat slashes, and she was badly burned. Among the weapons used were a rolling pin, a flatiron and a blackjack.

Life magazine once recounted the agonizing death of a 300-pound mob loan shark named William Jackson whom the Chicago Outfit suspected of being both a stool pigeon and a knock-down artist. To get him to confess, they took him to a mob meat-rendering place where he was tied up and hung from a meat hook. Bullets were pumped into him and he was worked over with ice picks and baseball bats; an electric cattle prod was used on his rectum. It took two days for Jackson to die. An FBI bug on a mob apartment later caught several of the boys nostalgically discussing Jackson's demise and amid howls of laughter bemoaning the fact that he hadn't survived longer.

A soldier in the Magaddino family in Buffalo, Albert Agueci, once was arrested with his brother in a narcotics case, one which also involved informer Joe Valachi. Agueci got angry when he and his brother got no bail money from the family and let it be known that he was going to "declare" himself unless boss Steve Magaddino came through for him. All he got was silence and finally was released on bail only after his wife sold his house.

Agueci had acted most irresponsibly and compounded his errors by calling on Magaddino and threatening him. He became a buckwheats candidate. An illegal FBI wiretap caught two capos in the family joyfully anticipating taking him to "Mary's farm" and "cutting him up." The FBI concentrated their search for Mary's farm in the Buffalo area but it turned out to be near Rochester, New York. A few weeks later Agueci's body was found in a field. His arms were tied behind his back with wire and he had been strangled with a clothesline. His body was then soaked with gasoline and set ablaze. Identification of the body was made possible because of a single unburned finger. The worst of Agueci's treatment showed up in an autopsy report which found that about 30 pounds of flesh had been stripped from Agueci's body while he was still alive.

Buckwheats is an essential ingredient in organized crime, one in which only the most cunning and/or the most brutal survive. It may be why Mafia gangsters in America triumphed over their Neapolitan Camorra counterparts. As *New York Times* writer Nicholas Gage once noted: ". . . the Camorra punishment for a 'rat' was merely to slit his tongue before killing him, while the Mafia punishment was to cut off his genitals and jam them down his throat before execution." On such nuances are crime empires built.

BUFALINO, Russell A. (1903–1993): Crime family boss

The McClellan Committee dubbed Russ Bufalino, boss of the Pittstown, Pennsylvania, crime family, "one of the most ruthless and powerful leaders of the Mafia in the United States." He might also be described aptly as "shadowy" since, until well into the 1970s, he avoided any major convictions.

A man some have described as having "nervous eyes"—they seem to rotate to opposite corners so that they give others the odd sensation that he is looking around them instead of at them, a condition that can make a threat from him seem matter-of-factly awesome—Bufalino centered his operations through much of Pennsylvania but constantly stretched the boundaries of his power into New Jersey and upstate New York. When the aged Stefano Magaddino, boss of the Buffalo family, died in the mid-1970s, Bufalino made a concerted push in that direction as well.

Strong in labor racketeering and considered a major power behind the scenes in Teamsters Union affairs, Bufalino has been considered by federal authorities as the number one suspect in the disappearance of ex-union head Jimmy Hoffa. The Pittstown family has often been considered active in the peddling of drugs and the fencing of stolen jewelry. Bufalino's arrest record dates back to his mid-20s and includes minor charges such as petty larceny, receiving stolen goods and conspiracy to obstruct justice.

He did not have a serious conviction until 1977 when he got a four-year sentence for extortion after threatening a witness because he owed $25,000 to a diamond fence associated with Bufalino. Unfortunately, the witness was taped at the time and then tucked away in the witness protection program. Bufalino found out where he was hidden and asked hit man Jimmy "the Weasel" Fratianno to arrange to hit him. Fratianno couldn't find him and Bufalino was convicted. An indignant Bufalino told the court: "If you had to deal with an animal like that, Judge, you'd have done the same damn thing."

BUFFALO crime family   See MAGADDINO, STEFANO

BUG and Meyer Mob: Early Lansky-Siegel gang

In the 1970s when Meyer Lansky was in Israel and trying to win permanent residence there, he was questioned about the early Bug and Meyer Mob. He insisted, in an effort to win the sympathy of Israelis, that it was just a little old group of Jewish boys out to protect other Jewish boys from the dirty Irish gangs of the era who were beating up on them. Actually the last thing Bug and Meyer were concerned with was acting as selfless pogrom fighters.

The gang, formed in 1921 by Lansky and Bugsy Siegel, was aptly named the Bug and Meyer Mob. Lansky was the brains and Siegel the star shooter of an expert group of gunmen. They started as a gun-for-hire gang that also supplied mobsters with stolen cars and trucks and expert drivers. Their specialty, however, was as shootists; they performed as hit men on order. Lansky hired out his boys to protect bootleg gangs' convoys and at time helped out in hijacking rival gangs' trucks. It was not always wise to involve Bug and Meyer in hijacking because they might just as readily turn around the grab your own shipments.

The mob's rates came very high under the circumstances, and it was hardly surprising that some bootleggers finally figured out it would be cheaper to bring them into the operation and give them a slice of the take rather than pay them wages.

Lucky Luciano had known both Lansky and Siegel from their teenage years (Siegel at the time the Bug and Meyer mob was formed was a murderously precocious 15-year-old) and was the prime mover in having the Jewish gangster duo join Joe Adonis's Broadway Mob, Manhattan's foremost bootleg outfit. It was Lansky's first regular work with leading Italian mobsters, an arrangement that would continue the whole of his life.

When Lansky and Luciano formed the national crime syndicate in the early 1930s, it was Lansky who pushed hardest for a special outfit to handle "enforcement," that is, murders for the entire syndicate. In that sense the old Bug and Meyer mob served as the model for Murder, Inc., and in fact many of its "graduates" played godfatherly advisers for the Brooklyn extermination troop bossed by Louis Lepke and Albert Anastasia.

See also LANSKY, MEYER; SIEGEL, BENJAMIN "BUGSY"

BULLET eaters: Hard-to-kill victims

"Bullet eaters" are legends of the mob, victims or wise guys who manage to survive being shot several times on one or more occasions. An amazing bullet eater was gangster Legs Diamond who was shot on numerous occasions by underworld gunners and lived. Once he was peppered in the head with shot and took a bullet in the foot but still escaped. Another time his wounds were so bad that doctors predicted his death. They were wrong. Diamond was finally dispatched by killers who found him asleep in bed, and, while one held his head, the other pumped three shots into it. *That* was more than even Legs Diamond could digest.

The most storied bullet eater of all has to have been the now incarcerated Carmine "the Snake" Persico, who during the mob wars for control of the Colombo crime family, won tribute as a man who could catch bullets with his teeth. That was a slight exaggeration. In fact, Snake was ambushed in a car, and bullets rained in on him, through the doors, the frame, the windows, and the motor. One spent bullet lodged in Persico's mouth and teeth. That was good enough for the boys. The Snake could catch bullets with his teeth—real bullet eating!

BURIAL grounds of the Mafia

In August 1985 a tranquil Bensonhurst, Brooklyn, neighborhood, centering around a Mobil station at 86th Street and Bay 7th Street, was shattered by sudden and intensive excavation work. Under the eyes of FBI agents three backhoe units dug a gaping 10-foot-deep hole. At first, journalists got no comment on the reason for the excavation; eventually it came out that the FBI expected to find at least three mob rubout victims buried beneath the gasoline tanks.

One of the owners of the station recalled that the FBI "come up to me a week ago and say, 'We got to dig up your station.' I say, 'Why?' But the FBI says, 'No particular reason.' We take it in stride. They think somebody's going to find some bodies. There's nothing there we know of."

The owners, who had bought the station eight years previously, made an agreement with the FBI that the two massive gas tanks pulled out for the dig would be replaced, the station would be fully restored and compensation would be given for lost business.

An FBI spokesman said it had decided to dig up the station after getting information from two different sources that it was a mob burial ground. The final count: zero bodies. The backhoes started filling up the hole, and the full restoration effort ran to about three weeks.

The hunt for Mafia burial grounds has always tantalized law enforcement officials because it is an established fact that mobsters do seem to form a sentimental attachment to certain spots. The father-and-son Mafia team of Charles and Joe Dippolito, both soldiers in the Los Angeles crime family, planted a great many corpses, each with a sack of lime, in the fertile soil of their vineyard in Cucamonga.

But such capers are very rare and most reports can be attributed to journalistic hype. A recent case in point is the so-called burial ground found in Queens, New York. One body, that of Alphonse Indelicato, was found in a vacant lot in 1981, and the FBI returned in 2004 looking for more bodies and turned up two, Philip and Dominick Trinchera, who like Indelicato were Bonanno capos. Actually all three died at the same time in a battle for control of the crime family. A mob burial ground? Hardly. It was merely a case of victims killed together getting planted together. It was a set of killings that would in time establish Joe Massino as undisputed boss of the family.

One of the sillier aspects of this burial ground tale was that the law expected to find the body of a long-missing neighbor of John Gotti who had killed the mob boss's son in a traffic mishap. The theory was nonsense. The mob doesn't go about putting together unrelated victims so that the law can have a bonus of wholesale solutions.

In one of Al Capone's most celebrated killing sprees, the mob chief personally dispatched three gangsters after a banquet given in their honor. Al had a surprise package opened that contained an Indian club and proceeded to beat their brains out. The matter of disposing of the bodies was left to Capone's favorite enforcer, Machine Gun Jack McGurn. Since Capone wanted the deaths of the trio well advertised, McGurn dumped them where they were sure to be found. Otherwise McGurn had his own private burial ground on some farmland in northern Indiana. Decades later Chicago gangsters still took sightseeing rides through the area to point out to friends and talked openly of planting some additional corpses there; law enforcement agencies have generally assumed they did make use of Machine Gun Jack's private cemetery.

Murder, Inc., had its own graveyard in Lyndhurst, New Jersey, in a chicken yard near the house of a brother-in-law of one of the assassination outfit's top gunners. Stool pigeon Abe Reles revealed the location, and the law, searching for the body of Peter Panto, a young anti-racketeer dockworker, launched a massive steam-shovel hunt. After several weeks of futile probing, a steam shovel hit paydirt. A 600-pound lump of earth, clay, rock and the everpresent quicklime was found. The pile was too fragile to pull apart, but X-rays of the mass revealed an almost complete skeleton of one body and parts of another. The skeleton was believed to be Panto's, but positive identification was not made. In this particular case it did not matter, the death-penalty law in effect at the time in New York provided for execution of kidnappers, unless the victim was returned alive before the start of the abductor's trial. A corpus delicti was not necessary.

Planting bodies in burial grounds was generally done when there was a need to hide the fact that a murder had been committed. In Panto's case it was generally known that his only enemies were waterfront mobsters and simply depositing his corpse in a gutter would put the heat on them. Having Panto "disappear" made the case—to some extent, at least—an enigma.

Burial grounds are still used since they are deemed more permanent than a water grave for unwanted corpses. Such stiffs, no matter how weighted down, have a disturbing habit of floating to the surface. As the mobs became more intimately involved in construction rackets, foundations and cement roadways have become very popular burial sites. There is, to mobsters, something inspiring about planting a victim under a high-rise. "Sort of like a real tombstone," one gangster told police.

BURNING the G: New mob tax dodges

Given the pressure put on the Mafia in recent years, it is hardly surprising that the mob relishes the idea of feeding off tax revenues that should flow to federal or local governments. While the mobs have shown considerable ability to come up with sophisticated swindles, it is probably true that when pulling a "burning the G" scam, the wise guys need all the help in scheming they can get from others. For example, the so-called burn company ripoffs made the Russian Mafia tons of money, at least for a time. Russian mobsters looking for a new racket had found a loophole in the collection of the 7.1¢ federal excise tax on wholesale gasoline. Like many business taxes, this one relied on an "honor system" for the taxes due to be paid by the last wholesaler who sold the gas to retailers. The Russians simply set up a bewildering string of wholesalers, or more accurately a series of paper entries. The last company—the burn company—sold the gasoline, collected the taxes, and then did a vanishing act. Considering the loot when millions of gallons were involved, the burning of Uncle Sam was colossal. To the scheme the American crime families merely added a creative touch of their own: moving in on a moneymaking deal already set up.

The Mafia came onto the racket late, however, and might not have noticed it for a long time had not shooting wars broken out between several groups of Russian mobsters. The wise guys noticed the noise and started worming in on the operations until one group of mobsters approached them with a clear invitation to settle the disputes among the Russians. The first to get involved was the Lucchese family, followed by the Gambinos. Being horribly squeezed at the time by government crackdowns, the two families decided they needed to divide the whole pie among themselves.

The mobs agreed to settle the dispute among the Russians and did it with old-fashioned Mafia flair, inviting two contending groups to a peace meeting and shooting down the criminals on one side. If the victorious side was pleased, it was no surprise to them that the mobs would cut themselves in on the deal, demanding a constantly growing percentage. But that of course was mere Mafia math. Today, it is generally believed, only a few Russians are still active as front men for the Mafia. If there has been, as reported, a decline in total take from the rackets, it is still said to represent a juicy income and more important has led to the mobs' version of "cramming" using various dummy companies, à la the gasoline burners, to bilk $200 million from telephone users for bogus charges. Give the mob a lesson, and the boys learn to apply new wrinkles to new scams.

See also CRAMMING

BUSCETTA, Tommaso (1928–2000): Greatest Mafia turncoat

He was easily the most important turncoat in either the Sicilian or American Mafia. Tommaso Buscetta was the first major Italian mafioso to break the Mafia's vow of silence, becoming an informer in 1984. The American Mafia had long suffered from defectors, but in Sicily turncoats were much harder to flip, largely because the Sicilian Mafia imposed far more frightening vengeance on even suspected defectors. Newcomers were often initiated into the criminal empire at special torture houses where those slated for death would spend the last days or perhaps weeks of their lives in nonstop begging for the relief of death. Seasoned mafiosi took great joy watching many of the new inductees keel over as they watched the tortures.

Buscetta turned informer when he became convinced he faced execution by his Mafia superiors. He had been on the run from the mob until captured in Brazil in 1983. Being sent back to Sicily, he knew, was a death sentence for him, so he talked and talked and talked. It must be said he did not do it out of fear but rather to get his revenge "in advance." He consistently insisted he had no fear of death but was out to kill those who intended to kill him. He carried out his vendetta in wholesale numbers. His testimony in cases both in Italy and the United States convicted mafiosi great and small by the hundreds. Italian leaders tried everything they could to silence the feared informer, and in one case a Sicilian mafioso offered him $5 million not to testify against him. When Buscetta disdained the bribe the crime boss offered $1 million to anyone who could smuggle a gun into the courtroom so that he could personally eliminate his tormentor.

Buscetta provided key testimony in New York in the notorious "pizza connection" heroin smuggling case in the mid-1980s. One journalist described Buscetta as lifting "a trapdoor over an immense and horrible catacomb," revealing more of the workings of both the Sicilian and American contingents of the Mafia. Still Buscetta did not reveal all he knew; he held back on his political connections or knowledge of what has been called the "third, or governmental, level of the Mafia." Buscetta insisted he held back on this because if he revealed all, his stories would be dismissed as the "ravings of a madman." He said if he did so, he would "end up in the loony bin."

If this was a "wart" in Buscetta's behavior, it did not prevent the U.S. government from rewarding this prize turncoat handsomely. He was not only placed in the federal protection program but given U.S. citizenship, remarkable for one with such an unwhole-

Tommaso Buscetta, an alleged Sicilian Mafia leader, is escorted by two uniformed policemen upon his arrival from Brazil to Rome, Italy, on December 3, 1972. Buscetta was deported on orders from the Brazilian president Emilio G. Medici after his arrest by the Brazilian police probing into drug trafficking by the Mafia and the French union core.

some past. In the 1990s Buscetta was sent back to Italy to testify against former premier Giulio Andreotti whom Buscetta linked to the Mafia. However, the Italian courts cleared Andreotti of the charges. Buscetta was returned to the witness protection program in America and remained there until his death in 2000 at the age of 71.

Further reading: *Last Days of the Sicilians: The FBI's War Against the Mafia* by Ralph Blumenthal

BUSINESS penetration by Mafia

For years the claim has been made that the Mafia is going legit. The crime families' take from gambling, narcotics, loan-sharking and labor rackets, to name a few of their major income sectors, has stayed about even in recent years, the argument goes, and so has opened the need for expansion into more honest enterprises. Thus it is known that one crime family owns real estate valued at well over $200 million, while another controls a major hotel chain. New York mafiosi are said to be part owners of several of the city's skyscrapers.

In the 1950s the Kefauver Committee determined that syndicate figures were involved in "approximately 50 areas of business enterprise." Among them, alphabetically, were advertising, appliances, automobile industry, banking, coal,

construction, drug stores and drug companies, electrical equipment, florists, food, garment industry, import-export, insurance, liquor industry, news services, newspapers, oil industry, paper products, radio stations, ranching, real estate, restaurants, scrap, shipping, steel, television, theaters and transportation.

Although the mobsters' moves into such enterprises may seem motivated by a desire to go legit, it is easy, upon closer consideration, to suspect ulterior motives. For example, although they flocked to Las Vegas for legal gambling in the 1940s, they thereafter derived several dishonest dollars for every honest one they extracted from such operations.

And, what was the Gambino family's real interest when they penetrated one of the largest furniture firms in the country? Ettore Zappi, identified by the McClellan subcommittee as a capodecina (captain) of the Gambinos, joined the firm in a minor executive position in New York and later proposed to management that he set up a separate corporation which alone would supply all the company's mattresses. The company brass found the idea attractive, thinking they could dictate price and production standards and yet be free of actually manufacturing the mattresses or paying competitive prices. However, with Zappi's contract came a sole supplier agreement; the furniture company was boxed in since it depended entirely on the new firm for its mattresses. If it couldn't get them, the furniture firm was as good as out of business.

And, in terms of getting the mattresses, they had to be shipped from the mattress maker to the furniture firm's plant. Suddenly an exclusive franchise was awarded to a new trucking firm—more mafiosi going legit—organized by the Gambinos. The trucking firm was in turn tied to a Teamsters local, also by coincidence with close ties to the Gambino family. Going legit or not, the Gambinos came out of the deal with two sweetheart franchises, employment for many family members and a strengthened grip on union affiliations.

An added fillip for the mob's move into legitimate business is that the investment can never go wrong. Should the crime family find itself stuck with a lemon it can turn the company—legit or otherwise—to bankruptcy and still walk away with a solid profit.

See also BANKRUPTCY SCAMS

BUSTER from Chicago (?–1931): Hit man

According to Joseph Valachi, an imported gunman from Chicago may have been the most prolific hit man of the entire underworld. Valachi, remarkably, never even knew his name, insisting the gunner was simply known as "Buster from Chicago."

Brought to New York for the Mafia war of the early 1930s, Buster looked anything but a professional gunman. Valachi described him as a "college boy" in appearance and in the grand Chicago style he carried a tommy gun in a violin case. Valachi was awed at Buster's shooting ability with all types of weapons, from pistols to shotguns and machine guns.

Buster, like Valachi, was at the time allied with Salvatore Maranzano, a brilliant mafioso seeking to wrest control of the New York rackets from Joe the Boss Masseria. Buster was the ace shotgunner in the assassination of two chief Masseria aides, Alfred Mineo and Steve Ferrigno, in the Bronx on November 5, 1930. Hidden in a ground-floor Bronx apartment, Buster cut them down with a 12-gauge shotgun blast into the courtyard. Two other gunmen also fired but Buster took out both victims, killing them instantly. As the assassins scattered, ditching their weapons, Buster ran into a policeman who had been attracted by the gunfire. Excitedly, he told the officer there had been a shooting at the apartment house a block away. As the officer, gun in hand, took off in that direction, Buster ran the other way.

In another killing, Buster quite efficiently took out James Catania, alias Joe Baker, as he and his wife left a building. Buster did not want to kill the woman; he fired only in the split-second he had a clear shot at the husband. He was most proud of the fact that every slug from his gun hit Catania and not his wife.

There is some suspicion that Valachi's version of the exploits of Buster from Chicago was inaccurate or highly colored. For example, Valachi also credits Buster with assassinating Peter "the Clutching Hand" Morello, Masseria's bodyguard and top adviser. Valachi relates that Morello was a tough kill, getting up and dancing about after he was shot once, trying to avoid being hit again. Buster took this as a sporting challenge and backed off; before he finally polished him off, he tried to wing Morello as though he were an amusement-park shooting gallery target.

Almost certainly this is pure nonsense. Valachi either made up facts or more likely was so gullible that he tended to accept as gospel anything related to him. Buster could not have had anything to do with the Morello killing, which was not carried out on Maranzano's orders, but was a crime of treachery from within the Masseria organization, actually done by Albert Anastasia and Frank "Don Cheech" Scalise on orders from Lucky Luciano. It was a necessary prerequisite to Luciano's elimination of Joe the Boss.

Valachi never explained or apparently even wondered how Buster, either a stranger to Morello or a known member of the opposition, could possibly have penetrated Morello's inner sanctum, especially considering Morello (and loan shark Pariano) were counting out $30,000 in racket cash receipts when assassinated. Anastasia and Scalise would have been readily admitted because they were Morello allies.

In any event, Buster lived through the Castellammarese War that put Maranzano on the pinnacle of power, but once Maranzano was eliminated by Luciano, Buster's days were numbered. According to Valachi, Buster wanted to fight Luciano because he believed: "They'll take us anyway, one by one." Before Buster could act, Luciano and Vito Genovese, probably solely as a precaution, gave orders to have Buster taken out. (Being such an expert gunner, he could be recruited by enemies wanting Lucky and Vito killed). In September 1931, Buster was killed in a poolhall on the Lower East Side and his body carted away and discretely disposed of. Buster came to New York a mystery and he went out the same way.

See also VALACHI, JOSEPH M.

C

CACACE, Joel (1941–   ): Fearsome acting boss of Colombo family

With the removal of John Gotti from the Mafia scene, Joel Cacace was among the new breed of mob bosses, one who inspired awesome fear and loathing in both his foes and his own men. Back in the 1980s Cacace was an ambitious mobster who understood that to climb the ranks he had to follow orders to the letter, giving no objections, nothing but strict obedience. The imprisoned boss of the Colombo family, Carmine Persico, passed down word to Cacace that he wanted William Aronwald, a former federal prosecutor, murdered. Persico, according to later charges by prosecutors, wanted Aronwald hit because he had "disrespected" him. At the time of the order, Cacace was not going to point out to Persico that his request was contrary to Mafia rules that no prosecutor was ever to be taken out by the mob, since it would most certainly unleash a reign of terror against the crime family. (Later, William Aronwald would be puzzled by having been singled out for punishment, since he had not personally prosecuted Persico although in his Colombo cases he had handled prosecution against Persico's brother Alphonse, also known as Allie Boy. That case however ended in acquittal.)

Cacace obediently set up the machinery for taking out Aronwald. It was to result in a tangled web of intrigue that probably only wise guys could carry out. Cacace himself traced William Aronwald to a law office in Brooklyn that he shared with his 78-year-old father, George M. Aronwald. Having located the quarry, Cacace turned the contract over to two brothers in the Colombo family, Vincent and Eddie Carini. The Carinis shot Aronwald to death in a laundry near his Brooklyn home. The trouble was they had killed the elder Aronwald rather than their assigned target, William.

Cacace's reaction was predictable fiery white rage. Other crime family bosses also wanted the Carini brothers eliminated. Wise guys who botch up hits know they face retribution. The brothers may not have appreciated their plight or at least the imminence of the punishment. The Carini brothers were hit, according to police, by a second pair of hit men, Carmine Variale and Frank Santora, on orders from Cacace. Then at the funeral of the brothers, investigators said, Cacace pointed out Variale and Santora to two other hit men. These hit men went off in search of a gun, it being considered most improper to attend a sad event armed. The Carini brothers' assassins were shot dead in broad daylight in front of a Brooklyn social club.

Thus, according to the allegations, Cacace had arranged for the killing of the hit men he had hired and then had the second set of hit men hit. If that were all there was to the case, Cacace would have been entitled to a high rank of fear and loathing, even by the new boss standards of dirty dealing, but there were more twists in the web. After the Carini brothers were planted, Cacace married the beautiful

28-year-old widow of Eddie Carini. Sometime later the couple separated and the former widow Carini married a retired police officer named Ralph C. Dois. And later, some might say predictably, of course, Dois ended up murdered. All this could have been mere coincidence based on affairs of the heart; in any event prosecutors have tended not to enter that thicket. The wise guys on the other hand may have seen it as all part of a Cacace mosaic. According to the boys Joel was one cool guy. As one criminal observer said, "With Joel dealing the cards, you never know where the next card is coming from—the top or the bottom or the middle of the deck."

Clearly Cacace was ready to pick up the mantle of the "new wave Don of the 2000s." He was in the eyes of many wise guys a brutal leader who deserved being followed—if a guy can find a way to survive. But in 2003 Cacace was arrested for the usual racketeering charges of extortion, gambling, and murder. The authorities had put together what they felt was a strong case for conviction for the wrong-man murder of George Aronwald. Cacace pleaded guilty to the charges on August 14, 2004. One observer noted that even behind bars, however, "He's the kind of guy the mobsters will still fear and hate and still follow his orders to the letter."

CAIFANO, John Michael "Marshall" (1911–): Chicago Outfit enforcer

A graduate of the juvenile 42 Gang in the 1920s, Marshall Caifano was a playboy enforcer for the Chicago Outfit, serving directly under Sam Giancana and readily available for murder jobs. He was the prime suspect in a number of murders, several on the grisly side, and his arrest record, dating back to 1929, includes 35 collars, with convictions for burglary (reduced to petty larceny), larceny, bank robbery, interstate extortion and interstate fraud. He was also cited for contempt of congress in 1958. He took the Fifth Amendment 73 times before the McClellan Committee.

Caifano shuttled around the country on assignments for Giancana and his successors, Joey Aiuppa and Jackie Cerone. Police investigators connected him with the murder of Estelle Carey, a Chicago cocktail waitress and the beautiful girlfriend of imprisoned Hollywood extortionist Nick Circella. The mob got the notion that Nick might blab to get out of prison early and sent a brutal killer over to visit Estelle. She was tied to a chair, tortured, covered with gasoline and set ablaze. The only witness to the grisly homicide was Estelle's pet poodle cowering in a corner. From the mob's viewpoint the murder had the salutary effect of zipping Nick's lips.

Caifano was also considered a prime suspect in the murder of Richard Cain, a chauffeur, bodyguard and confidante of Giancana until Cain's assassination in December 1973. It remains unclear whether Cain's extermination was ordered by Giancana or by the newer heads of the mob.

A free-spending playboy, Caifano was a regular on the Las Vegas scene, known at times to drop as much as $200,000 at the gaming tables. Whether he ever paid off such debts was a matter between the casinos and Caifano. In his Las Vegas Strip stalking, Caifano was credited with locating Willie Bioff, the old pimp and stool pigeon in the movie shakedown case that sent much of the Chicago leadership to prison. Shortly afterward Bioff got into a small pickup truck and was blown into eternity.

Caifano was one of the first 11 undesirables blacklisted by the Nevada Gaming Control Board from entering any casino in the state. It was like preventing Caifano from visiting his money. He took the matter to court to fight for what he considered his constitutional rights to gamble. He lost.

Still, he left his mark in Las Vegas folklore for his part in the murder and disappearance of a bigtime gambler, Russian Louie Strauss. According to Jimmy "the Weasel" Fratianno, Caifano took part in plotting Russian Louie's demise although, unlike the Weasel, he did not take part in the actual strangling and secret burial. To this day there is a saying in Las Vegas, when you owe someone money, that goes: "I'll pay when Russian Louie hits town."

Caifano did a turn in prison for trying to extort $60,000 from millionaire oilman and gambler Ray Ryan, the owner of a resort in Palm Springs, a gambling casino in Las Vegas and joint owner with actor William Holden in the Mt. Kenya Safari Club in Africa. When Marshall got out he was said to be after Chicago to knock off Ryan in revenge for testifying against him. It was said that Caifano was incensed because Joey Aiuppa sat on the hit for some time. Finally, in October 1977, a bomb in his own car finished off Ryan.

In the 1980s Caifano was doing a 20-year-stretch on a federal racketeering count for the possession and transportation of stolen securities valued at

$4 million. The sentence was extended to 20 years under the Special Offenders Act after the government demonstrated that Caifano was a "special dangerous offender." Taking the witness stand on that point was Caifano's former buddy, Fratianno, who detailed the facts about the Russian Louie killing. Fratianno had special incentive for nailing Caifano. When Los Angeles and Chicago put out a contract on the Weasel's life, Caifano was the fingerman who tried to lure Fratianno to Chicago for a "sit-down," one that he most likely would not have got up from. Instead the Weasel ran to the witness protection program.

See also BLACK BOOK

CALIFORNIA crime family See DRAGNA, JACK

CAMORRA: Neapolitan crime society

Although some claim its origins are Spanish or Arabic, the Camorra (meaning "fight" or "quarrel" in Spanish) first surfaced in Naples and its environs about 1820. Formed in Neapolitan prisons as a protective society for prisoners, the Camorra flourished as convicts were released and settled into Naples and the surrounding countryside. They organized into gangs and preyed on citizens, later offering immunity to those who paid protection money.

The Camorra, even more than the Sicilian Mafia, was very structured, consisting of 12 groups or families, each supervised by a boss. These bosses sometimes met to plan joint policy and strategy, and, like the crime families in the United States, each Camorrista unit enjoyed total supremacy in its own territory.

The families were also divided into subgroups called *paranze*, each supervised by a *caporegime*, or *capo*. The capo was charged with assigning each member to a specific task: robbery, protection, blackmail, kidnapping, loan-sharking, murder for hire or fee collecting at gambling places. The capo also determined the "taxes" to be paid by auctioneers, boatmen and cabdrivers. In effect, the Camorra achieved a sort of second government status.

All revenues were handed over to the boss of the family who then apportioned part for the corruption of the police and courts, another share for pensions of wives of dead or imprisoned members, and the rest as profits, according to the rank of each member.

New recruits to the Camorra came in the form of novices, who were admitted to the Camorra on a sort of probation and, until the 1850s or 1860s, they could not achieve full Camorrist status until they committed a murder on specific order by the society. (There is a belief that this is so in the American Mafia today, but despite the testimony of some informers, this requirement is far more honored in the breach.)

Some authorities have argued that the crime families in America are patterned more after the Camorra form of organization than that of the Sicilian Mafia, but in actuality virtually all secret criminal societies in history have operated in the same general pattern. Joe Valachi testified that when he entered what he called the Cosa Nostra he was told by his boss: "Here are the two most important things you have to remember. Drill them into your head. The first is to betray the secret to Cosa Nostra means death without trial. Second, to violate any member's wife means death without trial." These were, of course, the bylaws of the Camorra too.

Initiation rites of the 19th-century Camorra and the 20th-century Cosa Nostra are similar. Historian C. W. Heckethorn in 1872 described in *Secret Societies of All Ages and Countries* the Camorra initiation:

On the reception of a picciotto [beginning member] into the degree of camorrist, the sectaries assembled around a table on which were placed a dagger, a loaded pistol, a glass of water or wine, and a lancet. The picciotto was introduced, accompanied by a barber who opened one of the candidate's veins. He dipped his hand in the blood and extending it towards the camorristi, he swore for ever to keep the secrets of the society and faithfully to carry out its orders.

In 1964 Joe Valachi, with minor contrast, testified:

I sit down at the table. There is wine. Someone put a gun and knife in front of me. The gun was a .38 and the knife was what we call a dagger. Maranzano [the boss] motions us up and we say some words in Italian. Then Joe Bonanno pricks my finger with a pin and squeezes until the blood comes out. What then happens, Mr. Maranzano says, "This blood means that we are now one Family. You live by the gun and the knife and you die by the gun and the knife."

There is no scientific study available of today's average American mafioso, but in 1890 the Italian sociologist G. Alongi conducted physical examinations and interviews of more than 200 Camorristas. He found,

the majority have naturally great physical strength, though many become syphilitic through habitual intercourse with prostitutes. The courage with which they endure physical pain is so extraordinary as to suggest a profound insensibility; they betray no signs of suffering under the most painful operations, and laugh while they sew up their own wounds. Not a few have epileptic tendencies, which they endeavour for some unknown reason to conceal. Many are, apart from their criminality, strange in character, and have occasional fits of apparent mania, not a few having been actually confined or having relatives who have been confined for insanity.

. . . They are incapable of any work requiring perseverance and are devoted, during the leisure afforded them by the business of the society, to games of all kinds. Their affections are demonstrative but unstable. Religious feeling is general among them, taking the form of a love of ecclesiastical ceremonies and some peculiar superstitions. . . . They have no political feelings, except a detestation of the police, although they are ready in their own interests to serve any political party.

Some historians hold the power of the Camorra was broken, and indeed the death knell of the society sounded in 1911 when 35 Camorra leaders, including Enrico Alfano, the Grand Master, were convicted on murder charges and given long prison terms. Other observers insist the society survived although in a weakened form. Certainly Mussolini in the 1920s vowed to eliminate the Camorra just as he did the Sicilian Mafia. And just as so many mafiosi in that decade fled to the United States, so did Camorristas—too late, unfortunately, to join the once powerful American Camorra.

In its 19th-century heyday the Camorra in America had achieved near parity with the Mafia in New Orleans and certain parity in New York. The Camorra controlled Brooklyn in very large measure through World War I. In New Orleans the Mafia overpowered the Camorra in a bloody war ending after World War I. But, for a time, matters were reversed in New York. Under Don Pelligrino Morano, the Brooklyn Camorra held the upper hand over the Mafia, then largely controlled by Manhattan's Morello family. Greedily, Morano sought to extend Camorra influence into Manhattan and in 1916 in an act of vicious cunning he invited his opposite number, the imposing Nicholas Morello, to

journey to Brooklyn for a peace conference. Morello was a far-sighted criminal with visions of reorganizing the American underworld in a manner that put aside petty Old World prejudices, and although he remained suspicious of Morano, he felt he had no alternative but to go to the meeting.

It was, predictably, a mistake. In broad daylight, Morano had a five-man execution squad dispatch his enemy and his bodyguard as they reached the sidewalk of the cafe where the peace meeting was to be held. Morano dared to commit the murder so openly because he was sure the Camorra could seal the lips of all observers. Such was not the case; a witness talked and the Brooklyn district attorney even got one from the execution squad to talk. This was an amazing breach of omerta, the code of silence; it shook the Italian underworld and Don Morano most particularly. Ultimately, the Mafia proved better able than the Camorra to survive in America. The reason could well be due to the fact, as *New York Times* reporter Nicholas Gage asserts, "that the Camorra punishment for a 'rat' was merely to slit his tongue before killing him, while the Mafia punishment was to cut off his genitals and jam them down his throat before execution."

In any event several Camorrista gunmen went to the electric chair and Don Morano himself got life for conspiracy. After the trial the *Brooklyn Eagle* reported, "Morano was surrounded by a dozen Italians who showered kisses on his face and forehead. On the way to jail other Italians braved the guard and kissed Morano's hands, cheeks and forehead."

But the Camorrista plot, instead of eliminating the Mafia, had managed instead to lose the Camorra's own boss. Although the Camorrista/Mafia war continued for a time to lose many lives, the Neapolitans never recovered from Don Morano's conviction and subsequent absence. By 1920 the surviving Camorristas shifted into various Mafia groups.

See also BASILE, TOBIA; MORELLO, NICHOLAS

CAMPAGNA, Louis "Little New York" (1900–1955): Syndicate enforcer

"Anybody resigns from us resigns feet first." Such was the credo of the Chicago syndicate's Louis Campagna, a gunner who for three decades enforced his "feet first" solution.

It was Al Capone who gave Campagna the nickname of "Little New York" when he imported him in

1927 to help out in the Chicago gang wars. It was slick advertising, informing the underworld that he, Capone, could with little effort bring in all the East Coast firepower he needed to handle things. And Campagna proved to be a most effective enforcer, precisely because he was so zany and unpredictable, ready to do insane stunts. Once, during the Capone gang wars, Campagna led a dozen gunmen to surround a police lockup where a mobster enemy, Joe Aiello, was being held. They clearly intended to lay siege to the building and get Aiello. A score of police detectives foiled the plot by charging out of the building and seizing Campagna and two others before the other startled gunmen realized what was happening and could come to their aid.

Campagna was hardly nonplussed by his arrest. When he was placed in a cell adjacent to his quarry, Aiello, he kept up his threats to him. Overheard by a detective, posing as a prisoner, who understood the Sicilian dialect, Campagna said to Aiello:

"You're dead, dear friend, you're dead. You won't get up to the end of the street still walking."

Trembling, Aiello begged, "Can't we settle this? Give me fourteen days and I'll sell my stores, my house and everything and quit Chicago for good. Can't we settle it? Think of my wife and baby."

Campagna shook off the abject plea. "You dirty rat! You've broke faith with us twice now. You started this. We'll finish it."

The truth of Campagna's words was confirmed on October 28, 1930, when Aiello stepped out of an apartment house on North Kolmar Avenue and was hit by a fusillade of bullets. The coroner extracted 59 slugs from Aiello's body; they were found to weigh well over a pound.

Campagna was known as one of Capone's most devoted gunners. As Big Al's main bodyguard, he slept at night on a cot immediately outside Capone's bedroom door. The only way anyone could have gotten to Capone was over Little New York's dead body.

The roly-poly gangster moved into union rackets and extortion shakedowns against Hollywood movie studios in the 1930s and 1940s—until he was convicted with six others of the Chicago syndicate, in 1943, of conspiring to extort one million dollars from studio executives. Like the others, he went to prison for 10 years. Also like the others, in a scandalous pardon that the Chicago newspapers said

demonstrated the mob's power, the uncouth gangster was freed after doing only three years.

Campagna immediately returned to mob activities and became a devoted associate of Sam Giancana, perhaps the most unstable and murderous of the Chicago mob leaders. The camaraderie was clearly a case of birds of a feather.

In between killings and sundry other misdeeds, Campagna took up the unlikely role of gentleman farmer, owning a picturesque spread of 800 acres in Indiana. He died of a heart attack aboard his pleasure cruiser off Florida at the age of 54.

CAPONE, Alphonse "Scarface Al" (1899–1947): Chicago crime leader

His name—Alphonse Capone—is synonymous worldwide with "Chicago gangster." There were men who did far more than Al Capone to foster organized crime in America, but his remains Public Enemy Number One.

To become that, Capone had to achieve a certain metamorphosis of character and personality. It goes with the territory in bigtime crime. Unless a gangster can make this transition he almost certainly is doomed to fall, more often than not to the underworld itself, since the mob always demands a higher standard of its leaders than it does of itself.

Mug shot of Al Capone, who made his name and the term *Chicago gangster* synonymous worldwide. As the great purveyor of booze during Prohibition, he was cheered at the baseball games while President Herbert Hoover was booed.

By instinct Capone was a heartless, mindless murderer. The gun, young Capone believed, solved all. Yet by the time he was 26 Capone was transformed from a mindless killer into a shrewd criminal executive, bossing an enormous payroll and charged with keeping criminal rewards flowing. At that tender age he had become the most powerful crime boss of the time and he could—and did—boast he "owned" Chicago.

At the zenith of its power the Capone organization numbered upward of 1,000 members, most of them experienced gunmen. Yet this represented only a portion of Capone's strength. "I own the police," Capone announced, and that was gospel. Only a naive observer of the Chicago scene would have concluded that anywhere less than half of the city's police was on the Capone payroll. The payoff proportion for politicians was undoubtedly higher since their value to the mob was greater. Capone had "in his pocket" aldermen, state's attorneys, mayors, legislators, governors and even congressmen.

The Capone organization's domination of Chicago approached the absolute; in such suburban areas as Cicero, Illinois, it was total. When Capone wanted a big vote he got the vote; when he wanted to control the election returns, he unleashed his gangster-animals to intimidate and terrorize voters by the thousand. Politicians Capone put in power were expected to deliver upon demand. Once the mayor of Cicero, in an inexplicable exercise of independence, actually took an action without first clearing it with Scarface. Capone seized His Honor on the steps of City Hall and proceeded to kick and punch him to a pulp. All the while a very embarrassed police officer worked very hard at averting his gaze.

The fourth of nine children of immigrant parents from Naples, Al Capone was born in 1899 in the Williamsburg section of Brooklyn. He attended school through the sixth grade when he proceeded to beat up his teacher, was in turn beaten by the principal and then quit school for good. After that, he learned "street smarts," especially through a tough outfit of teenagers called the James Street Gang. Run by an older criminal, Johnny Torrio, James Street was a youthful subsidiary of the notorious Five Points Gang to which Capone later graduated. Among his closest friends, in school and in the gang, was a kid who was to become a major crime figure,

Lucky Luciano, and the two would remain dear friends the rest of their lives.

In his late teens, Capone was hired by Torrio and his partner, Frankie Yale, as a bouncer in a saloon-brothel they ran in Brooklyn. It was here that Capone picked up his moniker of "Scarface Al," after his left cheek was slashed in an altercation over a girl with a hoodlum named Frank Galluccio. Later Capone would tell acquaintances and reporters that he got the wound serving in the "Lost Battalion" in France in the Great War, but he was never even in the service.

In 1919 Capone was in trouble over a murder or two the law was trying to pin on him. He relocated in Chicago to take on new duties for Torrio, who had been summoned there to help his uncle, Big Jim Colosimo, the city's leading whoremaster, run his empire. By the time Capone arrived Torrio was deeply in dispute with Big Jim. Seeing the huge financial opportunities that came with Prohibition, Torrio wanted Colosimo to shift his organization's main thrust to bootlegging. Big Jim was not interested. He had become rich and fat in the whoring trade and saw no need to expand. He forebade Torrio to get into the new racket. Torrio now realized that Colosimo had to be eradicated so that he could use Big Jim's organization for his criminal plans. Together he and Capone planned Colosimo's murder and sent to New York for the talent to carry out the job. Capone and Torrio meantime would act out airtight alibis.

The Torrio-Capone duo soon was on the move, taking over mobs that bowed to their entreaties or threats and going to war with those that wouldn't cooperate. Their most impressive coup was arranging the killing in 1924 of Dion O'Banion, the head of the largely Irish North Side Gang. Utilizing the murderous abilities of Frankie Yale of Brooklyn, the same man who carried out the Colosimo assassination, O'Banion's death ultimately failed to rout the North Siders who, instead, waged war off and on for several years. Torrio himself was badly shot in an ambush but, after lingering on the edge of death for days, recovered. When he got out of the hospital in February 1925, Torrio told Capone after considerable soul-searching: "Al, it's all yours." Torrio took the $30 million he had squirreled away and retired back to Brooklyn, thereafter to function as a sort of elder statesman and adviser to the leaders of organized crime and the national crime syndicate that would emerge in the 1930s.

In a sense it was dirty trick to play on the 26-year-old Capone who cold turkey found himself in a position calling for a premium on brains rather than on his strong suit, muscle. He suddenly had to become a major business executive, heading up a workforce of over 1,000 persons and with a payroll running over $300,000 a week. And he had to demonstrate that he could work with other ethnics, including Jews, Irish, Poles and blacks. Here Capone excelled, appreciating any man, provided he was a hustler, crook or killer; and there was never an intimation that he discriminated against any of them because of their religion, race or national origin.

Capone was perhaps the underworld's first equal opportunity employer. Of course, he killed a number of ethnics if they did not bend to his will, but he did the same to many of Chicago's mafiosi, including the Gennas and the Aiellos, for the same reason. Capone did a thorough job of purging his city of Mafia Mustache Petes long before Luciano succeeded in doing so in New York.

Although he was a murderer and continued to order wholesale butchery as head of the outfit, Capone nevertheless changed in public image, mixing well with political, business and even social figures. He took on the character of a "public utility" by limiting his mob's activities mainly to rackets that enjoyed strong public support, such as booze, gambling and prostitution. If you give people what they want, inevitably you gain a certain respectability and popularity; thus Al Capone was cheered when he went to the ballpark. After 1929 Herbert Hoover was not.

Capone surrounded himself with gangsters he could trust, and this trust was, in turn, returned to him by his men. As long as a gangster didn't try to double-deal him, Capone backed him to the limit. Capone was shrewd enough even to hire Galluccio, the hood who had scarred him, as a bodyguard, an act that demonstrated to his men his capacity for magnanimity. It also caused some rival gangs to hook up with Capone, now believing his promises that they would prosper under his wing. He thus gained the loyalty of the Valley Gang under Frankie Lake and Terry Druggan and the machine-gun-happy Saltis-McErlane mob.

Not that Capone could ever relax his guard, as he was constantly under threat of assassination. He was shot at numerous times and once almost had his soup poisoned. In 1926 the O'Banions sent an entire machine-gun motorcade past the Hawthorne Inn, Capone's Cicero headquarters, and poured in 1,000 rounds, but Capone escaped injury when his bodyguard shoved him to the dining room floor and fell on top of him.

One by one Capone did eliminate his enemies, especially the North Siders. His most famous personal killings involved treachery within his own mob. Hop Toad Giunta and two of Capone's most lethal gunners, John Scalise and Albert Anselmi, were not only showing signs of going independent but were cooperating with other Capone enemies to kill him. Capone invited them to a banquet in their honor and, at the climax of the evening, produced a gift-wrapped Indian club with which he bashed their brains out.

This occurred in 1929, a fatal year for Capone, although it hardly seemed so. Just shortly before the Indian-club caper, he committed a monumental blunder in ordering the St. Valentine's Day Massacre in an effort to kill Bugs Moran, the last major leader of the old O'Banion gang. Seven men were lined up against a garage wall and machine-gunned to death by Capone hit men dressed as police officers. The victims thought they were being subjected to a routine bust and had offered no resistance. Unfortunately, Moran was not present at the time. Even worse, the public attitude started to change about the savage bootleg wars. Washington began applying heat. While Capone could not be convicted of murder, he was eventually nailed for income tax evasion and sentenced to 11 years at the federal prison in Atlanta.

In 1934 he was transferred to Alcatraz and within a few years his health started to deteriorate. Released in 1939, he was a helpless paretic, a condition brought on by the ravages of untreated syphilis contracted in his early whorehouse days. In Alcatraz Capone also exhibited signs of going "stir crazy," not uncommon with prisoners on "The Rock."

Capone's family took him to his mansion in Florida where he was to live out the next eight years, alternating between periods of lucidity and mental inertia. His boys from Chicago visited him from time to time but there was no way he could be involved in mob activities. He died on January 25, 1947.

See also "WOP WITH THE MOP, THE"

Further reading: *Capone* by John Kobler; *The Legacy of Al Capone* by George Murray

CAPONE, Frank (1895–1924): Brother of Al Capone

Frank Capone, elder brother of Alphonse "Scarface Al" Capone, was, some experts say, a man who could have written an even bloodier chapter in American crime than his infamous brother. While still in his 20s, he died in a pool of blood, riddled with slugs from a police shotgun. Another great Capone legend was nipped in the bud.

Frank Capone had a dedication to bloodletting and more savage instincts than Al, a man who is conservatively estimated to have ordered the deaths of at least 500 victims. Despite this bloody record, Al always exercised a certain patience. His credo, absorbed from the teachings of Johnny Torrio, was "always try to deal before you have to kill." To Frank Capone, this was an alien philosophy. His favorite observation was, "You never get no back talk from no corpse." And when spoken by Frank, the words, uttered with quiet, almost bankerlike reserve, bore an ominous quality unrivaled by Hollywood-inspired villains.

It was hardly surprising that, when the Chicago-based Torrio-Capone plans shifted from persuasion to force, Frank's labors had their shining moment. In the 1924 city election in Cicero, Illinois, the Democratic Party had the temerity to actually try to unseat the Torrio/Capone puppet regime of Joseph Z. Klenha. On the eve of the April 1 election campaigner Frank Capone took over. He led an assault on the Democratic candidate for town clerk, William K. Pflaum, besieging him in his office, roughing him up and finally ripping his office apart.

During the actual polling the following day, thugs invaded the polling places and screened out voters. They were asked how they were voting and if they gave the incorrect answer, a hoodlum grabbed the ballot from their hand and marked it "properly." They then waited, fingering a revolver, until the voter exercised his or her civic responsibility by dropping the ballot into the box. There were some voters who protested such cavalier treatment, and the thugs stilled their complaints by simply slugging them and carting them from the polling place.

Most honest election officials and poll watchers were frozen into inaction, and those who objected were slugged, kidnapped and held captive until the voting was concluded. The early toll included three men shot dead and another who had his throat slashed. A policeman, operating under the assumption that laws should be enforced, was blackjacked into submission. A Democratic campaign worker, Michael Gavin, was shot in both legs and thoughtfully carried off to imprisonment in the basement of a mob-owned hotel in Chicago. To make sure he was ministered to properly, eight other balky Democrats were sent along with him.

By late afternoon on election day the honest citizenry of Cicero rallied their forces and sought relief from the courts. In answer to their pleas, County Judge Edmund K. Jarecki deputized 70 Chicago police officers who were rushed to Cicero to fight a series of battles with Capone thugs. A police squad under Detective Sergeant William Cusick responded to an emergency call from a polling place near the Hawthorne works of the Western Electric Co. where Al and Frank Capone, their cousin Charles Fischetti and Dave Hedlin were soliciting votes with drawn revolvers.

At that time police rode about in unmarked cars, often long limousines similar in appearance to the vehicles mobsters preferred. Al Capone, Fischetti and Hedlin hesitated for a moment, unsure whether the intruders were rival gangsters or police. Frank Capone suffered no such restraints and immediately opened fire, igniting a general gunfight. Frank moved up on a patrolman and took aim at point-blank range. Whether he missed or the gun misfired is unclear, but before he could press the trigger again, the patrolman and a companion cut loose with both barrels of their shotguns. The elder Capone slumped to the gutter, dead. Al Capone fled the scene, as did Hedlin. Fischetti was seized but soon released by the police.

The boys gave Frank Capone the biggest underworld funeral seen in Chicago up to that time. It was said Al personally selected the silver-plated coffin, festooned with $20,000 worth of flowers. The *Chicago Tribune* noted with some irony that the affair was fitting enough for a "distinguished statesman." It was an understatement. After all, what statesman could bring about the ultimate period of mourning whereby all the gambling joints and whorehouses in Cicero ceased operations for two entire hours in tribute to Frank Capone? And it must be noted, in the final measurement of Frank Capone's contribution to the American dream, that his efforts on behalf of democracy had not been in vain. The Klenha ticket, from top to bottom, was swept back into office in a landslide.

CAPONE, Ralph "Bottles" (1893–1974): Brother of Al Capone

In 1950 the United Press reported: ". . . in his own right [Ralph Capone] is now one of the overlords of the national syndicate which controls gambling, vice and other rackets." It was hardly so. Ralph Capone was never very high on the list of leaders of the Chicago mob, although he did relay orders given by his younger brother, Al.

As much in tribute to his brother as to himself, Ralph was always accorded a position of honor and trust within the syndicate, both before and after Al's death. His nickname, Bottles, came about because of the soft drink bottling plants Al had set him up in. (Al wanted to develop a monopoly on the soda water and ginger ale used in mixed drinks, an activity he figured would continue after the end of Prohibition. As a tactic, it proved very profitable.) During the World's Fair of 1933–1934, Ralph's bottled waters, flavored and plain, were just about the only soft drinks available on the premises except for Coca-Cola, which, thanks to Chicago syndicate tolerance,

Scarface Al's trusted brother "Bottles" Capone later was called "one of the overlords of the national crime syndicate," which he was not.

was permitted entrance. Since Coca-Cola was even then known as the Democratic Party's drink, the mob tolerated this political accommodation to a new national administration.

But Bottles, who received a handsome mob-subsidized income, was responsible for more than soda pop operations. Among other things, he maintained Al's Palm Island estate in Biscayne Bay off Miami Beach while Al was in Alcatraz. Ralph dutifully opened the estate to the mob for meeting purposes and the like while permitting the boys to soak up the sun. Although most of Al Capone's wealth reverted to the Mafia, Al was nonetheless well provided for.

Ralph lived well, so much so that during the Kefauver hearings he was grilled at great length. He really had few facts to contribute on organized crime, never having achieved anywhere near the status of a Lucky Luciano, Meyer Lansky or Al Capone, or the then active leadership of the Chicago Outfit, including Jake Guzik, Tony Accardo, Paul Ricca and Sam Giancana.

Although Bottles Capone prospered because of his Capone relationship, his son, Ralph Jr. did not. Through his school years and college, his marriage and fatherhood, and a depressing series of jobs he abandoned once his true identity was established, young Ralph struggled to escape the Capone name. About a month after his father appeared before the Kefauver Committee in 1950, the son washed down a fatal number of cold tablets with a half quart of scotch.

Ralph Sr. lived until 1974. Although long retired, he was still described in his eighties as a powerhouse in the mob. He wasn't, but he did die rich.

CARDINELLA, Salvatore "Sam" (1880–1921): Black Hand murderer

Within Chicago's Little Italy, Salvatore Cardinella was better known as Il Diavolo, or "the Devil." An obese, violent criminal, Cardinella and his Black Hand gang were so feared by other mafiosi that it was said many paid him Black Hand extortion. The great bootleg gangs that sprang up immediately with the onset of Prohibition also were terrified of Cardinella and made certain not to cross him. It was estimated that the Cardinella mob killed at least 20 people who failed to meet their "pay or die" extortion demands.

Like other Black Handers, Cardinella operated with relative immunity from the Chicago police but, as the federal government began to prosecute extortionists for misuse of the United States mail, Cardinella shifted his operations more to holdups. Bolstering Il Diavolo's effort was his top triggerman, Nicholas Viana, nicknamed "the Choir Boy," a practiced if angelic-looking murderer at the age of 18.

In 1921, after a long reign of terror, Cardinella and Viana along with Frank Campione, another of Il Diavolo's lieutenants, were convicted of murder. Considered a "live cannon" in the underworld, one who attracted too much heat, Cardinella's demise was met with nothing less than joy by the underworld—he was in short, too violent even for deadly Chicago gangsters.

In his death cell, Cardinella plotted ways to survive and came up with an incredible plan for self-resuscitation. He went on a hunger strike, declaring the food at the Cook County Jail was slop. By the date of his execution he had dropped 40 pounds. Just minutes before Cardinella mounted the scaffold, police Lieutenant John Norton, the officer who had apprehended him, got an anonymous telephone call saying that Cardinella's allies "are going to revive him after the execution."

Norton and a squad of detectives rushed to the jail and stopped a hearse which had arrived at a rear entrance to pick up Cardinella's body. Norton opened the black door of the hearse and found a white-clad doctor and nurse. There was also what could only be described as unusual contents for a hearse: a rubber mattress filled with hot water and heated with hot-water bottles; an oxygen tank; and a shelfful of syringes and stimulants.

Norton rushed to the prison where he found Cardinella's corpse laid out on a slab while his relatives were hurriedly signing forms to take possession of the body. The police officer broke off the procedure, declaring the corpse would not be released for 24 hours. Cardinella's relatives broke into wild screaming and curses but could do nothing.

Later, examination of the corpse by doctors indicated Cardinella's hunger strike had had the desired effect. Cardinella's neck had not been broken due to the lightness of his body. He had died of strangulation. The medical men agreed that if the body had received sufficient heat quickly after the execution, it was possible that Cardinella might have been revived.

There was considerable speculation on the source of the tip to Lieutenant Norton. It was almost certain to have come from underworld elements who didn't want Cardinella back in circulation. Those who learned of the bizarre plot evidently did not feel that omerta, the Mafia code of silence, applied.

CARFANO, Anthony   See PISANO, LITTLE AUGIE

CAROLLA, Sylvestro "Sam" (1896–1972): Early New Orleans Mafia boss

New Orleans has been described by crime historians as having the oldest and least harassed Mafia family in the United States. It has also been called the most restrictive, the least hospitable to uninvited incursions. The boss who really established this tradition was Sylvestro "Sam" Carolla, who succeeded the man often described as the first real Mafia boss, Charley Matranga.

Sam Carolla set the pattern for the tough New Orleans mafioso type, a trait well demonstrated when in 1929 Al Capone—unhappy because Carolla would not supply his Chicago operation with imported booze, instead favoring a rival Chicago mafioso named Joey Aiello—sent word he was coming to town to talk to Carolla. Presumably Capone thought Carolla would immediately roll over and play dead. Instead, Carolla gave the "Big Fellow" a lesson in truculence, New Orleans style.

When Capone and his bodyguards stepped from their train at Union Station, Sam was waiting, but he did not return Capone's affable smile. When Capone approached him, hand outstretched, Carolla tucked his own hands behind his back. Just then three uniformed policemen stepped up beside Carolla.

The local Mafia boss said tersely to Capone: "You are not welcome." Then the policemen stepped up, seized Capone's bodyguards and proceeded to break their fingers. Gunmen with broken fingers do not pull triggers. Capone, shocked at this display, turned and walked back to the train.

Bringing in the police was a normal maneuver for Carolla, indicative not only of the boss's influence, but also of what T. Harry Williams described as Louisiana's "tolerance of corruption not found anywhere in America." If, in later years, Sam Carolla's successor, Carlos Marcello, and the mob were to have trouble with the law it was to come almost exclusively from the "feds" rather than local authorities. (This of course all took place after the infamous mass Mafia lynchings of 1891, which, whatever they accomplished, hardly rid New Orleans of organized crime and the Mafia.)

Carolla had arrived from Sicily with his parents in 1904 when he was eight years old. By the time he was 22, Carolla was Matranga's most trusted aide and front man, which explained why Matranga himself never was confronted by the law after the "troubles" of 1891. Carolla handled collections for the old man and passed on his orders.

In 1922 Matranga decided to retire, finding the new criminal world of bootlegging too much trouble at his advanced age. Carolla became head of the New Orleans Mafia and turned it into a gigantic moneymaker. To do so he had to tie up the booze racket, a task he accomplished much more efficiently than Capone did in Chicago. Carolla competitors dropped dead like flies in the ensuing gang wars.

Carolla's most imposing foe was William Bailey, the previously acknowledged bootleg king of New Orleans. Bailey, surrounded by dedicated killers, was a difficult hit. But Carolla's boys clipped Bailey's guards in doorway ambushes and machine-gun traps. Finally Carolla personally took care of Bailey during the 1930 Christmas season. Bailey was leaving his house when two cars pulled up at the curb. Desperately, Bailey sought to retrace his steps, but the front door was locked. As he dug for his keys, Sam Carolla approached him with the traditional Mafia gun—a sawed-off shotgun—and nonchalantly blew Bailey's chest away.

Carolla had it all. He dominated the booze racket and controlled the police (probably far greater than Capone's claim that in Chicago, "I own the police"). Only a small contingent of federal agents troubled him.

When he shot a federal narcotics agent named Cecil Moore in late 1930, it was actually a bit of a mistake; Carolla thought he was being ambushed by some of the late William Bailey's gunmen.

Moore survived and Carolla was charged with the near-fatal shooting. The New Orleans cops tried to help Carolla all they could, presenting evidence that Carolla was in New York at the time of the shooting and that Agent Moore was trying to frame him with a false identification, but the jury had had enough of Carolla and his police allies. He was found guilty. However, Carolla was sentenced to only two years in prison.

Carolla came out of prison in 1934 to find a new deal. Frank Costello and the Luciano-Lansky forces in New York had made a deal with Senator Huey Long to bring in the slot machines that Mayor La Guardia had run out of New York. Carolla and his aide Carlos Marcello made an agreement with the New York mob, the first time the local Mafia had accepted a deal with outside forces. Still, with Prohibition ended, Carolla saw a need for new revenues to beef up the crime family's income now largely dependent on the drug racket. Costello, he understood, offered real know-how on gambling.

The relationship has been a happy one for decades, and despite its generally parochial attitudes the New Orleans family has ever since cooperated with New York.

Once again Carolla's only problem was with the feds. In 1938 he was convicted on narcotics charges and did two years in Atlanta. On his release in 1940 the government started deportation action but matters were delayed until 1945 because of the war.

Carolla's friends tried to save him. Congressman Jimmy Morrison introduced private bills to award Carolla American citizenship, which would stop his deportation. Special privilege bills usually breeze through Congress but these were stopped when they were exposed by columnist Drew Pearson. Morrison didn't give up and interceded in the deportation proceedings, calling Carolla an innocent man. Numerous Louisiana politicians and police officers praised the crime boss's "excellent character and reputation." However, the charges against Carolla were overwhelming and in April 1947 he was deported to Sicily.

In Italy he dealt closely with the deported Lucky Luciano and in 1948 turned up in Acapulco, Mexico, as a liaison between Luciano and the American crime families. The next year Carolla slipped back into the United States. He was not caught until 1950 when he was deported once more.

Back in Sicily Carolla lived lavishly in a villa near Palermo, while long suspected of being involved with Luciano in a number of criminal enterprises. But Carolla's heart was forever in his "old country"—the United States. Finally in 1970 he stole back to New Orleans and the underworld successfully hid the old man out until he died two years later.

CARUSO, Enrico (1873–1921): Black Hand victim

The great Italian opera tenor Enrico Caruso, often cited as a victim of the "Black Hand Mafia" in America, paid extortion money to the mob to avoid being murdered. It was, as far as the Mafia was concerned, probably a "bad rap." There was no such thing as a Black Hand Mafia. There was, in fact, no such thing as an organized Black Hand. Rather, it was a method of extortion employed by many criminals against immigrant Italians who felt unsure, even unsafe, going to the authorities. While some of these criminals were mafioso others were not, being instead mere freelancers who saw an opportunity to make easy money preying on their hapless fellow countrymen. No one, of high or low station, was exempt from Black Hand terrorists, not even a magnificent artist such as Caruso.

Shortly before the outbreak of the Great War Caruso was performing a triumphal engagement at New York's Metropolitan Opera when he received a Black Hand death threat demanding the payment of $2,000. Like most Italians of the day Caruso considered it both foolhardy and useless to report the matter to the police. Instead he paid the money. That however did not end the matter but instead merely whetted the Black Handers' appetites. They hit him with a "pay or die" ultimatum for $15,000.

Realizing that there would be no end to the extortion demands if he kept paying, Caruso had no alternative but to notify the police. The police told him to go ahead and pay the money while they prepared a trap. Following the Black Handers' instructions, Caruso left the extortion money under the steps of a factory. When the Black Handers tried to retrieve the money, the police captured them. The culprits turned out to be two prominent Italian businessmen with no known ties to the Mafia or other criminals. They were convicted and sent to prison.

This did not free Caruso of worry, however. He feared retribution as an informer. Some Black Hand gangs went so far as to kill informers on other practitioners of the racket since they felt it was bad for business to let them live. Caruso became a close friend of Big Jim Colosimo, the great Chicago whoremaster and the man who imported Johnny Torrio and, later, Al Capone. Colosimo, too, had been a victim of Black Handers until he brought in Torrio. That resourceful individual arranged a trap for Big Jim's persecutors, but hardly to turn them over to the law. Instead, Torrio had them slaughtered on the spot and Colosimo was troubled no more.

We can almost see Big Jim leaning across a table at his gilded Colosimo's Cafe—a favorite watering hole between performances for operatic greats like Caruso, Amelita Galli-Curci, Luisa Tetrazzini, and Cleofonte Campanini and other show biz stars such as Al Jolson and Sophie Tucker—to offer the tenor druthers on Torrio's blasting any future Black Hand woes that might develop. Caruso did not accept any such offers, opting for more conventional protection. He was kept under close protection by police and private detectives, both in this country and in Europe, right up to the time of his death.

See also BLACK HAND

CASHING: Counterfeit scam for Mafia juniors

Dealing in counterfeit money is no longer a major activity for the Mafia. Today what few dealings there are involve youngsters who hang around wise guys with high hopes of becoming either a made or connected guy.

Whenever a source of counterfeit money (preferably in $20 denominations) is found, the phony cash is turned over to teenagers who are taught how to soften up the fake bills with cigarette ashes and cold black coffee. The youths are then dispatched to neighborhood stores to buy some small item or two for $1 or $2. They are instructed never to carry more than one phony bill at a time so that if apprehended, they can claim the bill had been passed to them elsewhere. In a real pinch the kids can burst into tears if they face detention and almost always they will be let go. Once a particular neighborhood has been deluged with enough fake bills to put merchants on alert the kids shift to another area.

The kids are also taught how to sell their purchases such as soap and cigarettes as "swag," alleged stolen goods, at half price. They prefer to unload the cigarettes in mob hangouts where they will win recognition for their good works.

CASINO junkets: Mob-sponsored gambling trips

In 1985 the New Jersey State Casino Control Commission launched an investigation of organized crime figures suspected of running casino junkets into Atlantic City. Considering the fact that the casino commission was already eight years old, officials seemed a bit tardy in their exercise.

It was a fact that various crime families around the country were for decades running junkets to Las Vegas, to pre-Castro Cuba, to Antigua, to Haiti, to the Grand Bahamas, to Portugal, to London, to Communist Yugoslavia—to name just some of the spots. The mob, working together with casinos they owned or those they cooperated with, learned of the joys of casino junkets decades ago.

The gimmick involves getting together a group of high rollers who journey to the casino on a cost-free basis. Typical would be a junket from, say, Boston or Pittsburgh to Las Vegas to, say, the Sahara (which at one time paid $50 a head for gamblers so transported). All the gamblers would have to have good credit ratings and also fill out an application stating, besides their source of income, how much credit they had, their banks, their investments and their real estate holdings. The casino ran a credit check and once their credit was approved, they would join a flight to Las Vegas with all food, accommodations and airline tickets paid for by the casino. The only expenses the gamblers had were tip money, telephone calls—and what they spent gambling. Mobs putting together a package of 100 gamblers would make $5,000 a pop—still small potatoes. On many foreign junkets the payoff is enormous, and the junket operators are cut in for a percentage of what each gambler bets.

Since the mob knows it is dealing with genuine "high rollers" on the junkets, all transactions are done on credit. On a trip to the Colony Sports Club—for years the top gambling casino in London, fronted by actor George Raft, but really controlled by top mobster Meyer Lansky—high rollers got for $1,000 free transatlantic transportation, room, board and $820 in chips. These chips are non-negotiable and had to be used for betting purposes. Once the gambler ran through his chips he could order more on credit from the casino. Thus the casino and the junket operators had an exact count on how much each gambler lost. The mob junket operator would get a 25 percent kickback on all monies each high roller lost. It would be unusual for junkets of 20–25 high rollers not to net the operator at least $50,000 and usually much more in commissions.

The casinos for their part know that getting gamblers into their establishments is all that is needed.

Thereafter, greed and compulsion will provide them with a healthy guaranteed margin of profit.

See also COLONY SPORTS CLUB

CASSO, Gas Pipe (1940–), and AMUSO, Vic (1935–): Kill, kill, kill bosses of the Lucchese crime family

The idea may not be totally outrageous that too much credit has been given to prosecutors for having ravaged the Mafia crime families in the prosecutions of the 1990s and, in some cases, into the 21st century. The incredible stupidity of some bosses propelled to power only because of the removal of so many top leaders deserves much credit for bringing the crime families to their knees, from which recovery has been slow and painful.

Longtime mafiosi were particularly shocked by the ascension of Vic Amuso and Gas Pipe Casso to control of the once powerful Luccheses.

"A&C"—as they were called, rose to power in the late 1980s after the former boss Tony Ducks Corallo was imprisoned in 1987. Tony Ducks soon found he could not command the mob from behind bars, and slowly his supporters lost ground to the vicious Amuso and the even more awesome Casso. The pair's power move was more impressive since both were themselves on the run from the law. They operated through others at times but could suddenly turn up in person to do a quick kill, or two or three, which added to their statures and might. Then they would fade away before other family foes or the law could catch them.

The fact that Amuso could stay on the loose for a half decade—while being hunted for a previous 100-year sentence—indicated the chaos within the crime family where doublecrosses abounded, making it all the harder to get an accurate view with so many informers dying if A&C found them first. It was, one wise guy moaned, "just like the damned Civil War." Amuso and Casso were determined to salvage as much of the Luccheses' former cash cows and keep most of that for themselves. In fact, they were determined to take whatever they wanted, killing anybody in the way as well as innocent wise guys who did not oppose them. Casso explained such tactics: "They might do the wrong thing later on."

Just prior to the ascension of the "psycho twins," as some Luccheses have called the duo, Little Al D'Arco, the street boss of the family, was upped to acting boss. He soon learned that his main job was bringing in much of the crime family's revenues to the pair, yet always to the tune of "Are you sure that's all we get?" It was not a refrain that was inspirational to D'Arco. Then they imparted to him plans to knock off Aniello Migliore because of fear that he could lead a revolt against them and take over as boss. D'Arco gingerly inquired what proof they had of this. The boys said they had no proof, just a "feeling." D'Arco grew further alarmed when Migliore was shot, but not killed, inside the glassed atrium of a Long Island restaurant. Casso and Amuso also thought nothing of trying to take down opponents on open streets; witnesses be damned.

In an astounding display, Casso demonstrated how far over the top the pair had gone. He showed a list of 49 names of men slated for the ultimate purging. About half the victims-to-be were charter members of the Luccheses. Asked why they had to go, Casso exhibited his full intellectual logic by saying they were "all creeps." And, Gas Pipe declared, as soon as he was free of all entanglements with government watchdogs, he would invite the creeps to a party and kill them all. Clearly Machiavelli was born much too soon and can be said to have wasted his time concerning himself with the likes of the Borgias and the Medicis. Whatever Gas Pipe Casso's inspiration, it is obvious he could have offered much for Machiavelli to absorb. In the old, relatively orderly days of the American Mafia good reason had to be given to take out an "honored" member. Now under Gas Pipe's rules, "creepery" became a capital offense. It was hardly a wonder that the formerly disciplined crime family was in shambles, legal harassment from without being more than matched by a homicidal craze from within.

Gas Pipe clearly produced more bloodletting within his crime family than there was in any other in America. The Luccheses sported an impressive array of clip artists, but their ranks were thinned out as many of them fell before the Casso-Amuso reign of terror. As a result Casso found he had to rely on sub-par performers; for example, Casso once issued a hit contract that had to be canceled when the assigned killer shot himself in the hand. On another occasion the A&C team sent two hit men to Florida to torture a buddy of a man they were looking for. The boys cornered their quarry and promptly pumped five bullets into him before they remembered they were supposed to ask him something. When the hit men returned to New York, they sheepishly pointed out, "Well, at least we got him." Casso was unimpressed: "Yeah, but even that guy ain't dead." The boys had simply assumed no one could survive five bullets.

Botch-ups like this caused Casso to keep a roster of his killers, and soon many of them had a *u* after their names. When an underling asked Casso why there was a *u* after his name, Casso replied, "That means you're unreliable." Even A&C's star killer, Peter Chiodo, didn't deserve much above a *u*. Once he put a gun to a would-be victim's head and twice pulled the trigger only to have the weapon misfire each time. (He had failed to set the clip properly.) Chiodo tried to laugh it off, saying, "Look how real they make these toy guns nowadays. Scared you, huh?" The proposed target took off and was said not to have stopped running for a couple of thousand miles.

On yet another frustrating occasion, Chiodo and another hit man cornered their victim who pleaded for his life until his bowels gave out. Chiodo was disgusted. "I hate when they do that." Realizing they would have to dispose of a very messy corpse, they walked out on their quivering victim.

Easily, the most efficient A&C hits were those carried out by the pair themselves. Casso found he could use corrupt cops in his murder plots, apparently riding with him to locate a victim, and in another case having the victim picked up by two officers on what seemed to be a routine arrest. However, instead of bringing him in for booking, the rogue cops drove to a warehouse and deposited their cargo at a delivery entrance where Casso was waiting to greet the catch, electric drill in hand. Casso was much devoted to a murder style known as "going up the ladder." It was Casso's performance in the execution of mobster Jimmy Hydell that guaranteed he could never get any deal with the law no matter what mob secrets, true or fanciful, he offered to reveal. Casso had killed many more victims than did Sammy "the Bull" Gravano, but it was, rather, the way he slaughtered that queered any chance of his entering the witness protection program. The autopsy report on Hydell showed he had been shot 16 times, probably starting off with standard "kneecapping" shots to both legs. Then there were shots to the intestines which must have been even more agonizing, then bullets to the groin, the abdomen, and on up to the head, with Hydell undoubtedly constantly begging to be put out of his misery.

Casso insisted he was totally mystified by the autopsy report, all he had done was take out Hydell because the "punk tried to kill me." And he had simply shot his victim in the head. "I don't torture people. I just remember shooting him in the head." That, reasoned Casso, would allow him to enter the witness program since he could tell plenty of mob secrets. The added problem with that was that much of what Casso said was not accurate and in fact insulting to investigators who knew better. His information on many gangland rubouts was patently false although they did always tend to put Casso on the side of the angels. The investigators also had proof that Casso, after he was arrested, tried to work a plot to kill the judge in his case and also the very prosecutor with whom he was later trying to make a leniency deal. Actually Casso was too unwholesome for the law to make any agreement with. Defense lawyers, the prosecution knew, would have a field day on cross examination and, above all, his up-the-ladder extermination of Hydell would have doomed any sympathy with jurors.

After long legal maneuvers, in 1996 Casso and Amuso were sent away for the rest of their lives, with Amuso perhaps a bit more sanguine about it all as it appeared he finally suspected that Casso was determined to take over on his own. Still, into the 21st century Casso kept producing legal briefs condemning the government for not lightening up his life sentence for his "cooperation." Could he help it if he had no recollection of the 15 of 16 bullets that dispatched Jimmy Hydell—even if it meant he had to stop the frightening process in order to reload?

See also LUCCHESE CRIME FAMILY

CASTELLAMMARE del Golfo, Sicily

No Sicilian town has supplied organized crime in America with more important leaders than Castellammare del Golfo, a picturesque town situated deep inside an emerald gulf on the western coast of the island. Most important of these leaders were Salvatore Maranzano, the last man to attempt to place the old-line Sicilian Mafia brand on the American underworld, and Joseph Bonanno (Joe Bananas), the youngest man ever to take control of an American crime family. Others included Joe Profaci, head of a Brooklyn crime family, and Stefano Magaddino, Gaspar Milazzo and Joe Aiello, heads of crime families or *capos,* in Buffalo, Detroit and Chicago,

respectively. Joseph M. Barbara Sr. the host of the notorious mob meeting in Apalachin, New York, in 1957 was another Castellammarese, having come to the United States in 1921 and being at first involved in rackets in Pennsylvania as well as being a suspect in a number of gangland-style murders.

Because so many mobsters were from Castellammare, they naturally aligned themselves with Salvatore Maranzano in the struggle with the older-line mafiosi headed by Joe the Boss Masseria. In fact, the war between the two groups became known as the Castellammarese War, mainly because Maranzano shrewdly built up the myth that his opponents hated all things Castellammarese. The war ended when Joe the Boss was assassinated through the deceit of his aide Lucky Luciano, who switched allegiance to Maranzano. Later on Luciano engineered the murder of Maranzano.

With the death of both old-country leaders, Luciano announced that "knockin' guys off just because they come from a different part of Sicily, that kind of crap," was out. Thereafter, since it "was givin' us a bad name and we couldn't operate until it stopped," Castellammarese as well as other Sicilians got killed not for hometown affiliations, but strictly for business.

See also CASTELLAMMARESE WAR

CASTELLAMMARESE War: Mafia struggle for supremacy

In the 1920s the Mafia in New York gained its most powerful leader to date—a crude, stocky little animal named Giuseppe Masseria, or "Joe the Boss," as he wanted to be called. There had been better, tougher and smarter mafiosi before him but Masseria came to power during Prohibition and accrued his strength from the huge revenues bootlegging brought gangsters. With that and his overwhelming firepower, he could squash most opposition within the Italian underworld, whether the Mafia, the Camorra or freelance.

However, Masseria was considered crude, greedy and short-sighted by the young, sometimes American-born mafiosi around town. They hated his demands for personal power, trappings of "respect" and "dignity" and other old-country virtues which in their view prevented them from growing richer. Masseria sought to prevent the Young Turks from working with the powerful, non-Italian gangs. But the Young Turks watched Jewish and Irish mobsters grow fat while they were fed claptrap about "honor" and "tradition."

Additionally these young rebels objected to the constant struggle for power within the Mafia. Not only were they supposed to battle other ethnics but they had to war among themselves—with Sicilians battling Neapolitans and, even more ridiculously, Sicilians battling Sicilians, depending often on which impoverished village of the impoverished island they came from.

By the late 1920s Masseria became obsessed with the growing power of mafiosi emigrating from the west coast Sicilian town of Castellammare del Golfo. They had achieved important positions in several cities, especially Detroit, Cleveland and Buffalo, but their main power lay in Brooklyn. There the rackets were controlled by a newcomer, Salvatore Maranzano, a mafioso who nurtured his own dream of becoming the boss of bosses. Soon war broke out. In the Masseria organization were such rising talents as Lucky Luciano, Vito Genovese, Joe Adonis, Frank Costello, Willie Moretti, Albert Anastasia and Carlo Gambino. Siding with Maranzano were such future crime leaders as Joe Profaci, Joe Bonanno, Joe Magliocco, and in due course, secret defectors from Masseria, Tommy Gagliano and Tommy Lucchese. However, almost none of these men owed much allegiance to their bosses, wanting only to have the Castellammarese War, as the conflict came to be called, ended.

While Masseria men killed Maranzano supporters and vice versa, a secret underground developed in the two camps, and the war actually became three-sided. The leader of this third force was Luciano who cultivated not only other Young Turks with Masseria but others supporting Maranzano. Tommy Lucchese especially kept him informed of moves being made by Maranzano.

There was considerable debate within the Luciano camp on which leader they should eliminate first. They had for months hoped that attrition would weaken both sides, but finally it was decided first to depose Joe the Boss, a task that was easier since Masseria trusted Luciano. The assassination was carried out in a Coney Island restaurant. Luciano and Joe the Boss had eaten lunch there and then played cards into the afternoon until no other diners were present. Then Luciano went to the toilet just before four of his supporters—Joe Adonis, Bugsy Siegel, Vito Genovese and Albert Anastasia—stormed in and filled Joe the Boss with bullets.

When the police arrived, Joe the Boss was dead. Luciano, who emerged from the men's room, had little to say, except that he'd heard the shooting and "as soon as I finished drying my hands, I walked out to see what it was all about." The press was being delicate when it reported Luciano's statement. His actual words were: "I was in the can taking a leak. I always take a long leak."

With Joe the Boss dead, Luciano and his allies made peace with Maranzano and agreed to accept him as their superior. Technically this marked the end of the Castellammarese War and Salvatore Maranzano crowned himself boss of bosses. A few months later Luciano arranged for Maranzano's execution so that in the end both original contending sides ended up dead losers. The real winner was Luciano and the new national crime syndicate, a conglomeration of varied-ethnic gangs, which became the real "organized crime" in America.

See also LUCIANO, CHARLES "LUCKY"; MARANZANO, SALVATORE; MASSERIA, GIUSEPPE "JOE THE BOSS"; NIGHT OF THE SICILIAN VESPERS

CASTELLANO, Paul (1915–1985): Assassinated crime boss
When Paul Castellano and his driver, Thomas Bilotti, were shot to death in front of a steakhouse on New York's East Side on December 16, 1985, the story made headlines around the country. The reason: "Big Paul," the Mafia's "boss of bosses" (which he was not) was the most feared don in America (which he also was not). Overlooked in virtually all accounts was that the assassinations, as the men stepped from a Lincoln limousine, had been one of the easiest hits on a Mafia don and his bodyguard ever. Neither Castellano nor Bilotti were armed, and neither had taken even the simple precaution of having a backup car of armed gunmen for protection.

Castellano had made a date with three mystery men and had a table reserved for them, Bilotti and himself in Sparks Steak House on bustling East 46th Street. (Probably half the mafiosi in the city could, if they wanted to, have learned where Big Paul would be on 5:30 P.M. on the day of the hit. Why, for safety's sake had he not made a last-minute change of meeting places? Chances are Castellano, if he'd made it into the restaurant, would not even have taken the precaution of having the reserved table switched.) But Bilotti and Castellano barely made it out of the limousine when three men wearing trenchcoats and fur hats approached, pulled out semi-automatic handguns and shot both men repeatedly in the face. One of the assassins paused long enough to fire a *coup de grace* into Castellano's head. The gunmen then fled on foot east to the corner of Second Avenue, one of them speaking into a walkie-talkie as he ran. Then they got into a waiting dark car that sped south and disappeared. It was a piece of cake.

Paul Castellano's death was an indication of his ignorance of the pulse of power in the Mafia. Had he been savvier, Castellano might well have anticipated danger. His doom was settled two weeks before the hit when his underboss Aniello Dellacroce, died of lung cancer. Castellano undoubtedly despised Dellacroce, a feeling that was mutual, but Big Paul did not understand that it was his underboss who had been keeping him alive. But when Carmine Galante was rubbed out in 1979, he at least had operated correctly. He was driven around town, never indicating where he'd be; and on the day of his death he was riding in Brooklyn when "on the spur of the moment" he suggested a small restaurant where he wanted to eat. And still the hit men got him there.

Since becoming boss in 1976, Paul Castellano viewed himself as a different Mafia don—more polished, a businessman far more than a hood. He took the Gambino family more deeply into certain fields, such as the garment trade, trucking industries, construction unions. And he didn't forsake murder. A stolen-car operation he bossed, shipping valuable vehicles as far away as Kuwait, hardly eschewed homicide and apparently carried out 25 murders to get rid of bothersome witnesses and competitors. But Big Paul did object to a murder or two here and there, and in a sense that showed he was forgetting his own roots. That should have told him Mafia power, in the final analysis, belongs to the gunmen. Meyer Lansky always knew that. He too was a businessman, a far better one than Castellano, but he knew that his position had to be backed with muscle, and he had Bugsy Siegel and others around to provide as much firepower as was necessary.

Big Paul probably hated the shooters. He hated his underboss, a man capable of peering into a victim's eyes as he squeezed off a shot, who could watch the impact of instant death. Big Paul probably feared

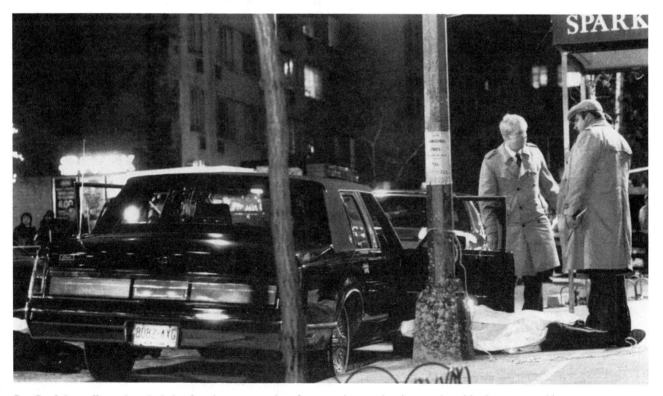

Big Paul Castellano, head of the Gambino crime family, was shot to death outside a Manhattan steakhouse in 1985. Never popular with his men, Castellano got his power in 1976 by edict of his dying brother-in-law, Carlo Gambino. His murder propelled John Gotti into Mafia leadership.

Dellacroce because he knew that the latter as underboss to Carlo Gambino normally would have stepped up to the top spot when Gambino died in 1976. Castellano had one edge on Dellacroce there—he was married to Gambino's sister. Don Carlo was a man who treasured family ties and was determined to make Castellano his successor. Gambino realized it was impossible for Castellano if Dellacroce wanted to fight. At the same time Gambino could hardly have Dellacroce killed. There were too many others in the mob ready to step up and nothing would restrain them, knowing Castellano's limitations. Gambino thus knew he had to deal with Dellacroce. He offered him all of the mob's lucrative Manhattan activities, thus giving his underboss a certain measure of independent power and prestige. Given that, Dellacroce did not want to provoke a war that would ravage the family and probably provoke drastic action by the authorities. He accepted second spot to Castellano.

As Castellano refused to expand the family's activities in certain areas, the Gambinos lost some influence, and the Genovese crime group under Funzi Tieri became the most important organization in the Mafia, as it had been before Gambino had built up his group to primacy through an unremitting mixture of force and cunning. Only with Tieri's death in 1981 and a succession by weaker men were the Gambinos once more to become supreme, just by the sheer weight of their numbers and prestige.

Castellano continued operating the way he felt best, dickering with businessmen and ignoring the hoodlums in his own organization. For example, Frank Perdue, the chicken king known for his "tough man, tender chicken" TV commercials, determined that the retailing strategies of a large supermarket chain in the New York area were not giving him a fair shake. His chickens often didn't make the weekly shopping circulars while his competitors were getting great display. That was when he decided to switch distributors, signing on with Dial Poultry, which happened to be run by two of Castellano's sons. After that, Perdue reportedly had no more complaints about the proper merchandising of his neglected chicks.

While Castellano was smitten with dealing with businessmen, he kept vetoing plans for capo John Gotti, one of the toughest men in the organization, to move into the lush field of airport rackets where a fortune could be made in freight disappearances and union racketeering. Gotti was one of the younger capos straining under the Castellano rule, feeling the don to be so inept that it was costing family members vast profits. All that kept Gotti and others in line was fear of, and a sense of loyalty to, Dellacroce. As Dellacroce's pet, Gotti was rightly feared by Castellano who tried to keep him down by limiting him to goon squad hijackings and other bush-league activities.

Then on December 2, 1985, Dellacroce died. Evidently Castellano didn't fear Gotti much, and he made no attempt to rub him out. Instead, Castellano planned to keep Gotti down by naming Bilotti his underboss. It was incredible. Castellano was acting like he was in some sort of company proxy fight. A smart Mafia boss would have started killing the opposition instantly. Castellano was thinking long-range while the countdown was on.

Gotti or whoever was working against Castellano had cleared things with the other bosses in the city—nobody seemed to mind that Big Paul went. In fact, most of the bosses had reason to be sore at Castellano, who had allowed his fashionable 17-room mansion on Staten Island to be bugged by the FBI. They had been furnished transcripts of some of the tapes since they were, along with Castellano, under indictment for a number of racketeering counts. Castellano had talked disparagingly about all of them, which was bad enough, but the tape also revealed he blabbed about Mafia business with almost anyone who came into his home, even people who did not belong to any crime family. He also told Bilotti things, which violated the Mafia need-to-know code. Castellano's wagging tongue clearly was a menace, and there was the added worry that the 70-year-old Castellano might not be able to take prison. If convicted he could get sentences totaling 170 years and know he was not going to spend his twilight years a free man. Under such circumstances a weak boss like Big Paul might talk.

After the hit at Sparks, much press was devoted to speculation about what the Castellano murder meant. Was it or wasn't it the start of a general gang war, was the hit an inside job, and so on. The only concrete fact to come out of the affair—aside from two corpses on a Manhattan sidewalk—was that additional eavesdropping and informer information confirmed for various investigative agencies a successor to Paul Castellano.

It was John Gotti.

CATALANO, Salvatore "Saca" (1933–1983): Sicilian drug smuggler

The 1970s and 1980s became the heyday of Zips, tough, mean Sicilian gangsters imported into America. They were the prime movers of a massive drug trade operation that became known as the Pizza Connection, a case in which American law enforcement had a hard time sorting out the players. This was especially true of Salvatore Catalano, until investigators finally figured out they were dealing with two drug smuggling cousins with exactly the same name.

In the 1960s Italian and Canadian police experts classified this Salvatore Catalano as an "important international trafficker." He was identified by Italian authorities as an associate of several U.S. and Italian crime chiefs.

At first he seemed the more important of the two Catalanos but eventually law enforcers determined that his younger cousin eclipsed him in more ways than one. To distinguish the pair, the older one was identified as "Saca," The name of a jewelry business he ran in the New York diamond district on West 47th Street, a front for money laundering and drug dealing.

Later the second Catalano came to the fore as a vital cog in the Colombo family and evidenced a penchant for violence and murder that his older cousin may have lacked. Eventually the younger Catalano, or "Toto," a nickname for his given name, ordered the murder of his cousin without a qualm. If other Mafia figures promised the death penalty for those engaged in the drug racket, the traffickers had their own criteria. Death was reserved for those falling victim to the wares they handled. It was evident by 1983 that Saca had freaked out on heroin. For several months he exhibited such erratic behavior that his associates regarded him as a mortal danger to their enterprise.

Saca was shot in the neck and eye by a gunman, possibly Cesare Bonventre, a prime suspect in the murder of Carmine Galante and a close associate of Toto. Government taps indicated that Toto and his closest associates felt no surprise at Saca's demise. One Zip was overheard asking Toto about Saca's funeral: "You're saying the rosary?"

Toto responded, almost apologetically, "What can I do?"

At the funeral Cesare Bonventre showed up in a way that could be construed as a final insult to the victim, driving up in a black Ferrari which he parked ostentatiously outside the chapel. On the sidewalk.

See also CATALANO, SALVATORE "TOTO"

CATALANO, Salvatore "Toto" (1941–): Brutal boss of the Zips

The Zip invasion of the American Mafia hit its zenith under Salvatore "Toto" Catalano, a criminal who exhibited a terrifying penchant for double-dealing. Long a "protégé" of crime boss Carmine Galante, who sponsored many of the Zips coming from Sicily, Toto was regarded by authorities as a prime mover, along with many family bosses in New York and around the country, in the plot to assassinate Galante, an operation accomplished in spectacular fashion in 1979. It was a move that made Catalano and his supporters richer than they had ever been, reaping millions in drug profits from heroin smuggled in from Sicily where it had been processed by Sicilian crime families.

What horrified many American mafiosi was the senseless slaughter and violence Catalano and the other Zips engaged in to further their aims. Toto was considered one of the wildest. Without the slightest qualm he had his own cousin and namesake murdered when he developed a strong heroin addiction. Toto felt his cousin's blabberings might endanger the entire drug operation that later became popularly known as the Pizza Connection.

After the Galante murder, Paul Castellano, the reputed boss of bosses of the American Mafia, decided to fill Galante's position with the Zips. According to assistant U.S. attorney Richard Martin, the lead prosecution in the Pizza Connection trial from 1985 to 1987, Big Paul had a sitdown with Catalano and his leading aides at Martini's Restaurant in Bay Ridge, Brooklyn, to "work out the new terms of payment for the heroin franchise. . . . Carmine Galante was out of the way; now the money would go straight to Castellano himself."

Louis Freeh, another assistant U.S. attorney and later head of the FBI, said: "We know that the Sicilians have been paying off the U.S. bosses on heroin all along. . . . Paul Castellano got paid, in spite of threatening others with death for dealing."

Catalano readily agreed to Castellano's terms, which were more favorable than what the Zips got from Galante. But would the agreement last?

Despite the agreement Castellano continued to have woes with the Zips. They grew stronger in what had been Gambino family strongholds, and they operated rackets without seeking Gambino family approval. Violence broke out and a full-scale war loomed. But the battle never began. The government's Pizza Connection prosecution netted Catalano and all the important Zips, and Castellano fell under the guns of the John Gotti forces that took over the Gambino family.

Even after his arrest Catalano remained a threat, apparently penetrating the secrecy of the witness protection program to learn the whereabouts of some of the witnesses who testified against him. He continued making threats even after the conclusion of the long trial and while appeals were still pending. In the end Catalano's terror campaign was neutralized. He was sentenced to 45 years, meaning that if he served the full time he would be 91 years old when released.

See also BONVENTRE, CESARE; CATALANO, SALVATORE "SACA"; ZIPS

CERONE, John "Jackie the Lackey" (1914–): Day-to-day boss of Chicago Outfit

Captured on tape on a number of occasions bragging about his prowess as a mob executioner, Jackie the Lackey Cerone was a dapper, expensive dresser, a throwback to the Capone era. From the late 1960s he had also functioned as the day-to-day boss of the Chicago Outfit although he took orders from his superior, Joey Aiuppa, and beyond him the ever-present Tough Tony Accardo.

Cerone's was a meteoric rise for a gangster who operated best on the enforcer level, but Jackie the Lackey was highly regarded for his ability to take orders. These orders brought him the bulk of his 20-plus arrests on such charges as bookmaking, robbery, armed robbery, keeper of a gambling house and conspiracy to skim Nevada casino profits. Before the McClellan Committee, he took the Fifth Amendment 45 times.

Cerone served for a time as Tony Accardo's chauffeur, and was called "Accardo's pilot fish." He also served for a considerable period directly under Sam Giancana. Cerone was one of his top men, more than an ordinary soldier, and part of the nucleus of his power. Rather than run a cell of 20 or 30 mobsters as most capos did, Cerone became a master fixer and

political sponsor of applicants to the police force (the mob being much interested in law and order).

Cerone the underling was a notorious namedropper. In 1962, he was overheard on a federal "bug" in Florida bragging to the other gangsters that the hit assignment they were on was awarded by "Moe" (Giancana) to him personally. That particular job was to erase Frankie Esposito, an associate of the syndicate who had fallen into disfavor. The boys discussed various ways to carry out their mission (which at the last minute was cancelled) and Cerone himself came up with the plot that pleased him best. They would approach Esposito when he was alone and, since he knew them all, invite him into their car for a ride. They would then stuff him down on the floor, take him to a boat where they would shoot him, cut his body up in tiny pieces and feed them to the sharks. Cerone said he had brought a special knife along for the purpose.

The boys also took to reminiscing about other hits, especially the horribly gory torture-killing of William "Action" Jackson. The details need not be repeated here, but credit must be given to Cerone's contribution to the festivities—a cattle prod that was put to ghoulish use. Cerone informed the boys he'd gotten the idea from "some coppers who used the same thing on hoods." Some Southern police forces used the prods on civil rights demonstrators, but there is no record of Jackie the Lackey ever being aware of that.

As Cerone moved up the syndicate ladder he proved to be a stickler for Mafia rules and respect and for firm division in the roles played by mere soldiers and capos and higher-ups.

He could wax philosophical about the virtues of the unbigoted organization. On another FBI tape, he told the boys about some of the gang killings he and Johnny Whales, "a Polack" but "a real nice guy," had pulled off in the "old days." Unfortunately, Cerone said, Johnny finally "went off his rocker" and disappeared. He had become afraid of the "Dagos" and told Cerone he feared they might kill him. At this point in the dialogue Cerone turned to Dave Yaras, the Jewish member present, and said, "You see, Dave, he didn't understand that we [the Chicago Outfit] got Jews and Polacks also. I told him this but he was still afraid." When Whales's obsession with fear of Italians became still more intense, Cerone said he brought the matter to Accardo's attention, who obligingly asked if he wished to have

Whales knocked off. Cerone said he assured his boss that he liked Whales too much to have him murdered but that he would have nothing more to do with him.

At the top, after he and Aiuppa replaced Giancana who was drawing too much heat to the organization, Jackie the Lackey did not act so benignly, according to most accounts, exacting a correct code of conduct from Chicago soldiers. It was speculated that if Giancana's 1975 murder was a mob hit (the mob has always insisted it was a CIA job), it had to have Jackie the Lackey's approval—a case of the underling outlasting his mentor.

In 1986, Cerone, aged 71, and his current mentor, Joe Aiuppa, were convicted with three other organized crime figures for conspiring to divert more than $2 million in untaxed winnings from gambling casinos in Las Vegas. Both men were given long prison terms guaranteeing they would spend the rest of their lives behind bars.

CHARITY and the Mafia

Image, especially in recent years, has become a major concern within the Mafia. One of the best ways to polish up their reputations, crime bigwigs have apparently decided, is through charitable giving.

Beneficent gestures are not new to the Mafia, however. Al Capone was big on helping individuals in distress—and seeing to it that the press knew about it. Then, in the Great Depression, Capone got into organized charity in a big way, playing the role of a "socially responsible" gangster, taking care of many of Chicago's unemployed. Capone opened a storefront on State Street to provide food and warmth for the destitute. Puffing on his big cigar, he espoused to reporters his great concern for the jobless. Capone's Loop soup kitchen gave out a total of 120,000 meals at a cost of $12,000. On Thanksgiving Day, Capone said he was personally donating 5,000 turkeys.

Clearly Capone's famous soup kitchen made for great publicity, but, as it turned out, the operation hadn't really cost him very much. City coffee roasters and blenders were leaned on to donate supplies. Various bakeries found their day-old doughnuts and pastries requisitioned by mobsters. Packinghouses saw the wisdom of donating hearty meat dishes, and the South Water Market Commission merchants got into the spirit of things with potatoes and vegetables. Soon everything was on a strict quota basis and

Frank Costello could always be counted on by panhandlers for a touch—especially when photographers were handy. More controversial was Costello's sponsorship of a Salvation Army fund-raiser.

those who felt they were being asked to give too much were informed by mobsters that the Big Fellow

93

was growing concerned that their trucks might be wrecked or their tires slashed.

In fact, there is little doubt Capone actually made a nice profit from his public spiritedness. In December 1930 the price of Capone beer to the speakeasies—produced at about $4 a barrel—was hiked from $55 to $60 a barrel, all to help the poor. Capone salesmen told speakeasy operators: "The Big Fellow says we've all got to tighten our belts a little to help those poor guys who haven't got any jobs."

In more recent years it has become common for crime leaders to attend charity balls and banquets as a method of achieving what has been called innocence by association. In 1949 a famous newspaper flap developed over the vice chairman of the Salvation Army's fund-raising drive. He was the notorious Frank Costello, who promoted a $100-a-plate dinner and entertainment at the Copacabana with tickets that read in part:

Dinner and Entertainment
Sponsored by
Vice-Chairman of Men's Division
Salvation Army Campaign

Costello demonstrated how readily crime figures can move large blocks of tickets. The party was a full house featuring leading politicians, judges and other worthy individuals, including even Dr. Richard Hoffman, Costello's psychiatrist, who wanted his patient to associate with good people, presumably as a form of therapy.

That year Costello presented the Salvation Army with $10,000—$3,500 from the Copa affair and $6,500 of his own. Inquiring journalists also discovered that Costello was active in a number of other charities. He turned up in fact as a member of the Men's Committee of the Legal Aid Society.

New Orleans crime boss Carlos Marcello also is known for his lavish giving, albeit lavish giving with a twist. He once gave $10,000 to the Girl Scouts of America, informing the wealthy society woman soliciting the funds not to reveal his name because he wanted no publicity on the matter. Naturally that ploy had the desired effect as news of Marcello's great philanthropy was all over town in no time.

Ralph Salerno, a former member of the Central Intelligence Bureau of the New York City Police Department, declares in *The Crime Confederation* (which he wrote with John S. Tompkins), that there

is "a general pattern" of many charitable, religious and fraternal groups "knowingly inviting people of questionable reputation to be honored at fund-raising dinners because of their known ability to dispose of large blocks of expensive tickets." At one time three Mafia dons in New York—Tommy Lucchese, Joe Bonanno and Joe Profaci—were all members of the Knights of Columbus, even though that group screens applicants for good moral character.

Many top mafiosi are big donors to churches. It is doubtful they hope for expiation for their sins but rather seek to pay homage to their wives, the piousness of Mafia wives being both legendary and understandable. Chicago don Sam Giancana fit this churchman category. Whenever he was in church the collection box on his side of the aisle would outproduce the other side by at least $500 or $600, that being the amount Sam would drop in.

Joe Profaci was an especially big giver to the church, so big that when a young thief stole a jeweled crown from his local parish, the angry Profaci forced the thief to return the crown and had him murdered anyway. It made sense from Profaci's viewpoint. If he gave a lot to the church and somebody stole from the church, it meant that somebody was stealing Profaci's money. Profaci did not take a charitable view of that.

CHAUFFEURS: Mafia road to success

Chauffeur becomes power broker—a plausible Mafia rags to riches story.

The chauffeur is in a unique position, often knowing more about mob activities than the too highly touted *consigliere*. Mafiosi, it seems, turn loquacious in Cadillacs. Chauffeurs privy to closely held secrets often become a boss's confidant, even his appointment secretary, and, of course, a trusted bodyguard.

Perhaps the best case in point is the Chicago Outfit's John "Jackie the Lackey" Cerone, for years the driver for top boss Tony Accardo. By the 1970s when Accardo was in semi-retirement (although always consulted on important business), Cerone was viewed by law enforcement officials as being the day-to-day head of the mob. Al Capone himself was first recruited to Chicago by Johnny Torrio to act as his trusted driver (although when Torrio did not need him Al went to work as a shill or barker outside one of the mob's whorehouses).

The late informer Joe Valachi would have had far less interesting or informative testimony to provide had he not served as the chauffeur for Salvatore Maranzano. At the conclusion of the Mafia War of 1930–1931, which put Maranzano in position to proclaim himself the boss of bosses, chauffeur Valachi learned Maranzano's intention to go back to war. Maranzano told Valachi he was planning to wipe out such nationwide crime leaders as Capone, Lucky Luciano, Frank Costello, Joe Adonis, Vito Genovese, Willie Moretti, Dutch Schultz and others. Unfortunately for Maranzano his foes got him first. It was also unfortunate for Valachi for he would, as a trusted chauffeur, have moved much higher in crimedom than he did as just an ordinary soldier in Luciano's family. Maranzano had already rewarded a previous driver, Joe Bonanno, with an important position within his own family, and when Maranzano died, Bonanno became the "father" of the Maranzano family.

Not all chauffeurs rise to the top, especially if their boss is marked for extinction. Richard Cain, driver for Sam Giancana, had been a former Chicago police officer, having been assigned to infiltrate law enforcement. He even became chief investigator of the Cook County sheriff's office. Finally discredited by the force, he openly joined the Chicago Outfit and became Giancana's driver and aide. He also served as negotiator, interpreter (Spanish, to help Giancana in his Latin gambling enterprises), as well as keeper of Sam's personal secrets. Giancana trusted him to drive around his problem daughter, Antoinette, who later wrote the best-selling *Mafia Princess*. Cain was shotgunned to death in December 1973, a year and a half before Giancana was murdered. They had both offended the Chicago Outfit, and especially the powerful Joe Aiuppa, by refusing to share the profits they made setting up cruise-ship casino gambling. After Cain's death Dominic "Butch" Blasi took over as Giancana's chauffeur as well as performing Cain's other duties. He was with Giancana the night he was murdered, but neither the FBI nor Giancana's daughter ever believed he was involved in the killing. He was considered too loyal.

Not all of Giancana's drivers were as highly thought of by their boss. Sal Moretti was murdered on Giancana's orders after the driver carried out a hit contract for Sam on Leon Marcus, a banker–land developer. Unfortunately, Moretti had failed to remove from Marcus's body a document that linked Giancana to Marcus in a secret motel deal. On Giancana's orders Moretti did not die easy. He was viciously tortured before he was shot and stuffed in a dry-cleaning bag in the trunk of an abandoned car.

Crime boss Carmine Galante was another chauffeur who made good, but in the end his former boss acquiesced to his murder. In the old days Galante had served as a driver for Joe Bonanno who, it was said, in later years still "felt paternalistic toward him." Galante later went to prison for narcotics violations and when he came out he moved to take over the Bonanno family, with his old patron in a sort of retirement in Arizona. Galante then moved to take over the other New York families, and a nationwide decision was made to eliminate him. It was considered prudent by the other crime bosses to obtain Bonanno's okay to the contract, knowing the esteem in which he had held Galante. Since at the time, despite all indications to the contrary, Bonanno still clung to the idea that his son Bill might be able to take over the crime family or perhaps a portion of it, Bonanno was said to have given his approval—some say with considerable enthusiasm. It would seem blood runs thicker than chauffeurs.

CHICAGO amnesia: Mob intimidation of witnesses

The term *Chicago amnesia*, born more than six decades ago, is still used by police and federal authorities all over the country to describe the reticence of witnesses in testifying against organized crime. In Chicago in the 1920s, law enforcement officials found it virtually impossible to prosecute gangsters because of the fear they instilled in potential witnesses. Even eyewitnesses who eagerly came forward on seeing a crime suddenly developed a startling loss of memory when they learned the identities of the culprits.

Gang leader Dion O'Banion, a practiced expert at witness discouragement, once observed with quaint humor: "We have a new disease in town. It's called Chicago amnesia." And Chicago amnesia was contagious, often contracted through bribes, but quite often through threats or even murder attempts.

The Capone mob and mafiosi all over the country picked up the term, even though they certainly had known and used the tactic previously. Case after case has been lost by the prosecution in court after a crime boss's order went out to "give them amnesia."

CHINESE Mafia: A grab bag of powerful Asian criminals

There is great tendency to refer to a "Chinese Mafia" operating in America. However, scholarly researchers such as Dennis J. Kenney and James O. Finckenauer, say that using such a label shows "the desire for simple answers to complex problems." While there is much Chinese-on-Chinese criminality in this country (as is the case with all ethnic groups), it falls short of true organized crime as defined by the likes of the American Mafia, which has infected so many aspects of national life and business, going far beyond the scope of mere ethnic depredations and affecting the body politic, business life and, in fact, vast segments of national society in a truly corrupting sense.

An additional problem in giving Mafia status to various Chinese criminal or cultural/criminal organizations is that the groups frequently work at cross-purposes. Certainly the Chinese triads are very powerful organizations. They control a vast slice of the worldwide heroin trade, for years working out of Hong Kong. While the triads are also involved in the standard organized rackets such as gambling, extortion, loan-sharking, protection shakedowns and political and civic corruption, the fact remains that basically they are drug traffickers, much of their production coming from the "Golden Triangle" in the mountainous areas of Thailand, Laos and Burma. Overall, the Chinese triads control an estimated 70 percent of the world's opium and heroin supplies, and as such they are a powerful and corrupting influence in much of the world. U.S. supplies of heroin come from Asia, either directly or via Mafia operations in Sicily and elsewhere in Europe.

Thus, some writers, such as Gerald Posner in his book *Warlords of Crime: Chinese Secret Societies— The New Mafia,* claim that the triads are the most powerful criminal syndicates in the world. In such accounts police authorities in Asia are typified by one police superintendent who insists the criminal triads "make the Mafia look like child's play. No one else comes close—not Sicilians, not Corsicans, not Colombians, no one." Posner insists the Chinese triads control the heroin trade in the United States, yet the late Claire Sterling, a recognized authority, took a different tack in her book published about the same time, *Octopus: The Long Reach of the International Sicilian Mafia.* Sterling regarded the Sicilians, not the triads, as the kingpins of the U.S. heroin trade. Both groups obviously had and have great involvement, but what is obvious is that the triads' trade in the United States

tends to involve mostly the Asian populace. It is the Mafia that controls much of the drug "pipeline" with the Sicilians, and after a century of activity in this country it has developed "cultural ties" with vital elements such as corrupt law enforcement connections that the triads have not been able to make.

Other major Chinese players in this country include the tongs, which function as benevolent associations and part business, part cultural societies that are very productive but by their very nature limited in scope. There are also myriad other Chinese organized criminals, including Chinese street gangs. These urban street organizations may eventually become the powerhouse Chinese groups in this country. They have become a sort of para-professional group used originally by the tongs to guard their gambling dens. In time these young criminals became so well armed and thirsty, running their own operations as extortionists, robbers, and murderers for profit, that the tongs could no longer control them. These urban street gangs formed very rigidly controlled memberships who obeyed orders without dissent. They resemble the young mafiosi who, in the past, wrested control of criminality from the Old World–style "Mustache Petes" who tried to emulate fiefdoms in the mother country. These Italian young Turks learned that they had to exert their influence with the power structure of the New World and to cooperate with other ethnics. On the face of it, that seems to be a formidable task, but as younger urban gangsters learned their craft, they seemed to have moved in that direction. For the young Asians this task has been made easier by the respect they have won from the white world, especially as Asian youth prove to be among the most accomplished students. Thus they have become more palatable even to the law enforcement structure. This does not mean the urban Asian-American gangsters have to win over all their opponents, but because they now appear to be more acceptable as business allies, with the ability to bring much money to the table, they are soon likely to achieve status that the young Lucianos, Costellos, and Lanskys reached in the 1920s. The young mafiosi were aided by the great profits achieved in the bootleg era, as they violently edged out their rivals. What can the young urban Chinese gangs do to match that? Their obvious target is the drug trafficking market. Can the other Chinese organized criminals resist, even with centuries of practice behind them? The answer may well be no, since nothing in the world of crime succeeds like money power, however it may be gained.

CIA-MAFIA connection

The link between U.S. intelligence agencies and the Mafia dates to the Lucky Luciano era. It is now generally accepted as fact that, from his prison cell, Luciano aided the U.S. Navy in maintaining security on New York's wartime waterfront—after first victimizing U.S. Intelligence by having the SS *Normandie* burned in its berth on the East River in 1942 while it was being refurbished as a troop transport. Later, Luciano provided intelligence and Mafia operators in Sicily who aided the invasion of the island. And, according to a secret "informal" study by Department of Justice officials some 15 years after World War II, he was also instrumental in getting Vito Genovese in Italy to "turn" in 1944 and work for the Office of Strategic Services, the predecessor of the Central Intelligence Agency. Previously, Genovese, who had fled to Italy with a huge amount of money to avoid prosecution for murder in America, had been close to Mussolini and had contributed mightily to the Fascist effort. However, when the order from Luciano reached him, Genovese dutifully switched sides, goaded on not only by Luciano, but also by the firm belief that it is never right to be on the losing side.

The CIA in later years actively courted the aid of the underworld when needed. They apparently thought there was a genuine need for the Mafia in the infamous Operation Mongoose plot to assassinate Cuba's Fidel Castro. Names that float about in that incredible operation include those of Mafia boss Sam Giancana, Meyer Lansky, flamboyant mobster Johnny Roselli, Tampa crime boss Santo Trafficante, Howard Hughes and Hughes's executive officer Robert Maheu, and a cast of thousands.

In retrospect, it is obvious that only the CIA and Hughes thought there was a real plot to get Castro. Most of the mobsters involved, and Maheu as well, were more interested in ripping off the agency and utilizing it to keep other agencies—such as the FBI—off their backs and out of underworld activities. It has been said that no one but the CIA would have believed such hair-raising tales as boats being shot out from under potential Castro assassins just as they were about to reach the island. The poison the CIA master chemists concocted for mafiosi to plant was simply flushed down mafioso toilets and

never put to use. There is also no evidence that any CIA funds to be paid to Cubans on the island ever left the United States.

The CIA eventually discovered it was duped and there were many observers in and outside the underworld who are still uncertain whether the 1975 murder of Giancana and the 1976 erasure of Roselli was the work of the mob or of a CIA determined at the time to keep the fact that it had been toyed with, robbed and abused by the Mafia a secret.

Other scandals involving the CIA have since surfaced, including charges the agency obstructed efforts to probe the drug trade, that traffickers may have escaped prosecution because of other activities with the CIA. August Bequai, adjunct professor of criminal law at American University, declares in his study, *Organized Crime*: "The agency has also been linked to narcotics deals and prostitution rings within this country. Federal investigators have speculated that some CIA employees may have been running their own narcotics operations for personal gain or even to raise funds for the agency's more clandestine operations."

See also GIANCANA, SAM "MOMO"; OPERATION MONGOOSE; ROSELLI, JOHN; TRAFFICANTE, SANTO, JR.

CICERO, Illinois: Mob-controlled Chicago suburb

During the Capone era of the 1920s, Cicero, Illinois, was a veritable armed camp. An estimated 850 gunmen were there—800 of them Capone men, and 50 of them cops. Mathematics indicate to whom Cicero belonged. Through a process of intimidation and bribery, the Capone forces controlled, it was believed, every official position in the town "from mayor down to dogcatcher."

The situation in Cicero hardly encouraged any ardent police officer even to *think* of standing up to the gangsters. Typical was the policeman posted on the steps of the town hall on a day when Mayor Joseph Z. Klenha offended Capone by some unauthorized act of office. The beefy gang chief knocked His Honor down the steps of the town hall and proceeded to kick him repeatedly in the groin. The officer found the entire procedure rather embarrassing and was able only with difficulty to look the other way.

While it was Capone who consolidated power in Cicero it was Johnny Torrio who first opened it up to syndicate exploitation. His technique was to make

Adolf Hitler's later incursions into Austria and Czechoslovakia seem rather old hat—but strikingly similar.

Torrio realized that the mob needed a safe territory from which to operate without fear of official intrusions; even in Chicago there were some honest political authorities and police officials. He decided Cicero was the perfect base, especially since it was not all that clean to begin with and certain criminal gangs already functioned there. Torrio's opening move included no rough stuff. Without making any arrangements for protection he sent in a troop of prostitutes and opened a bordello on Roosevelt Road. (Cicero had always been clean of prostitution mainly because the West Side O'Donnell Gang disapproved of such low activity, among other reasons feeling that it stirred up too much opposition from the local citizenry.) The Cicero police immediately shut the Torrio brothel. Undeterred, Torrio sent in another score of harlots and opened another joint at Ogden and Fifty-second Avenues. The police demolished the place and clapped the women behind bars. Torrio then pulled out of town, exactly as he had planned.

The honeymoon lasted only two days. Torrio had things sewed up in much of Cook County; suddenly deputies from the Chicago office of Sheriff Peter Hoffman discovered there was slot machine gambling in town. Properly shocked, his men swept in and confiscated every slot machine in Cicero. Then Torrio delivered his ultimatum. If he could not bring prostitutes into Cicero, no one could run slots and bootlegging, and speakeasies would have to go as well. It was not an offer anyone wanted to accept. Then Torrio suggested a compromise. He would not bring prostitution into Cicero (the move having merely been a ploy to force a deal), and the O'Donnells could maintain their beer accounts and, in partnership with a local rogue, Eddie Vogel, continue their profitable slot machine business. In return Torrio wanted the right to maintain his base of operations in Cicero and introduce any form of gambling and vice he wished other than whorehouses. A deal was hammered out. Torrio stuck to his agreement about harlots although the surrounding areas were another matter.

Having got his foot in the door, Torrio then turned the town over to Capone brownshirt-style to lock everything up. Big Al proceeded to extend mob influence by bribe and force. By 1924 Cicero could be called Syndicate City. The only cloud developed when the Democratic Party, harboring some delusion about a two-party system, decided to run candidates against the Klenha slate. Capone brought in hundreds of mobsters to guarantee that no excess of political freedom occurred. On the eve of the election the Democratic candidate for town clerk, William F. Pflaum, was beaten up in his office and the premises demolished. With the dawn of election day, gangsters in seven-passenger black limousines patrolled the streets, terrorizing voters, many of whom decided not to cast their ballots. Those who showed up at the polls were inspected in line by the Capone gangsters who inquired how they intended to vote. If their answer was incorrect, the mobsters confiscated their ballot and marked it for them. Then a Capone hood, massaging a revolver half out of his coat pocket, made sure the voter put the ballot in the box. Honest poll watchers and election officials were cowed into silence and those few who could not be intimidated were simply kidnapped and held prisoner until the voting ended. A Democratic campaign worker, Michael Gavin, was shot through both legs. Policemen were blackjacked.

In early afternoon some Cicero voters found a county judge, Edmund K. Jarecki, who was willing to take action against the Capones. He deputized 70 Chicago police officers, nine squads of motorized police and five squads of detectives and sent them into the town under siege. Throughout the afternoon and evening, police and gangsters fought pitched battles. Among those killed was Al Capone's brother Frank. It was a personal tragedy for Big Al, who a few days later gave his brother the biggest funeral Chicago had seen up to that time, even surpassing that of Big Jim Colosimo in 1920.

Capone consoled himself; his brother had died a winner. The Klenha ticket won in a landslide. Syndicate City was secure.

See also CAPONE, FRANK; HAWTHORNE INN

CIGARETTE bootlegging

Bootlegging became a Mafia fine art during Prohibition when the goods was booze. Now there is a thriving business in bootleg cigarettes. The old Profaci-Colombo family remains very active in this field, importing through syndicate functionaries vast amounts of cigarettes from North Carolina, a tobacco state with no tax on its cigarettes. A great boon to the mob was the U.S. surgeon general's decision in 1964 to start warning the public that smok-

Lawmen with a seized shipment of bootleg cigarettes, a prime mob operation

ing kills. Several states saw in this the ultimate wisdom of saving lives—and handsomely feeding state coffers by jacking up the tax on cigarettes.

The spread between the cigarette prices in many states soon ballooned to 100 to 150 percent more than North Carolina prices and gave the crime families a genuine meal ticket. Individual operatives might also import cigarettes, but they lacked the Mafia's guaranteed distribution method. The mob long controlled much of the cigarette vending machine business and peddled them as well in the hosts of clubs and restaurants it owned directly or indirectly. It also had the muscle to force other businesses to handle the bootleg butts or face other woes.

Despite a steady drumbeat of arrests and seizures of bootleg cigarettes it has been estimated in recent years that as much as 400 million packs sold annually in the New York metropolitan area are bootlegged. The sale of illicit cigarettes in New York has been estimated to cost the state a tax revenue loss of $85 million to $100 million or more annually.

CIRILLO, Dominick V. (1930–): Named boss of Genovese family in 1997

Called "Quiet Dom," he spent four decades maintaining a low profile in the mob. But by late 1997 Dominick V. Cirillo was recognized by federal investigators as the head of the Genovese family, the number one combination—and the wealthiest—in the American Mafia.

It was clear that Quiet Dom represented a new breed of non-flamboyant mob bosses. Cirillo refused to operate as an attention getter eschewing the dapper don quality of a John Gotti, the ostentatious living of a Paul Castellano, or even the bathrobe strolling, "mental case" act of his predecessor as boss, Chin Gigante.

Cirillo lived in an attached house in the Bronx and drove himself around town in inexpensive cars, insisting that he was surviving on little more than $500 a month in Social Security. In an impromptu interview outside the Cirillo home, his son complained the house needed many repairs.

"We don't have money to fix a drain pipe or the roof, and the washing machine in the basement leaks," the son said. "If he had money and was such a big shot, would we be living like this?"

Evidence gathered through informer information and eavesdropping told a very different story, and even more revealing was the way other mafiosi deferred to him in his presence.

By the time Gigante was convicted of murder, conspiracy and racketeering charges, Cirillo was the last surviving member of Chin's inner circle, and he was the obvious candidate for successor. No one else knew as much about the family's far-reaching activities. But it was said that Cirillo took the job of boss with considerable reluctance.

"As boss," said Frederick T. Martens, a Mafia expert who tracked Quiet Dom for 30 years, "he automatically gets more money and a piece of everybody's action in the family, but today there is one major disadvantage. You may be at the pinnacle of power, but the top echelons of law enforcement gear up and turn their sights on you."

Could Quiet Dom's style make him less vulnerable than other bosses? It might and certainly the Genovese mob needed a strong leader. The mob's activities in garbage removal, the Fulton Fish Market, the Jacob K. Javits Convention Center and even the Feast of San Gennaro had been crimped by law enforcement authorities. Cirillo would be under the gun to salvage these operations, while maintaining extremely profitable strangleholds on extortion for labor peace in the construction industry and from businesses on the New Jersey waterfront.

Cirillo already had demonstrated an aptitude for mob politics and infighting by moving up the ladder. In 1953 at age 23 he was convicted of running a heroin ring in East Harlem grossing $20,000 a day. Cirillo did four years for that but since has only been arrested for consorting with known criminals, a misdemeanor used for harassment purposes by detectives. All such charges were dismissed.

What surprised law enforcement was the way Cirillo advanced in the mob—quietly—thereafter. The Genovese family, like most other Mafia groups, generally refuse to advance anyone with a drug record, since convicted narcotics traffickers attract additional law enforcement surveillance. Evidently his know-how made Cirillo an exception to this nearly ironclad rule.

It was clear Quiet Dom would not be an easy target for law enforcement. It was considered unlikely that he would be caught on electronic tape, as he always specialized in "walk talks," whispering to associates on noisy streets rather than on the phone or inside mob social clubs. Investigators also knew Cirillo was a hard man to track with an uncanny knack for shaking tails. Above all he showed "car smarts" when followed by automobile. Frustrated investigators told of suddenly losing their prey, only to discover him now behind them—*trailing them!*

See also SURVEILLANCE TRICKS BY MAFIOSI

CIVELLA, Nicholas (1912–1983): **Kansas City Mafia leader**
The reputed head of the Kansas City crime family for many years, Nick Civella was, though highly trusted, still a lesser among equals within top Mafia circles. Kansas City during Civella's reign was under considerable domination by the Chicago Outfit which exerted important influence over Civella. The Kansas City mobster was utilized in one period, according to federal authorities, as one of three men who crossed the country as couriers for the "grand council of the Cosa Nostra." The McClellan Committee listed Nick and his older brother Carl as criminal associates of important but lesser mafiosi. For some time Civella's role could be described as being a Las Vegas "gofer" for the mob. There are indications that all he received annually from the skim at one leading Nevada casino was a puny $50,000 a year.

Yet Civella did play a valuable role in mob activities. He was the agent through whom Roy L. Williams, later president of the International Brotherhood of Teamsters, was dominated by the mob. At a trial of Midwest crime leaders in 1985, Williams admitted Civella had put him on the pad for $1,500 every month for seven years in return for help in gaining a $62.5 million loan from a union pension fund to finance the acquisition of two casinos; a cynic might note how chintzy the mob could be in their payoffs. The payments lasted until 1981 when Williams was elected president of the union, defeating Cleveland crime family favorite Jackie Presser. Civella alone could hardly have put Williams across—Chicago and St. Louis muscle tipped the scale.

Born the son of Italian immigrants in 1912, Civella was in trouble with juvenile authorities at the age of 10. By the time he was 20 he had been arrested on numerous charges, including car theft, gambling and robbery. He also rose steadily in Mafia circles and, in 1957, despite his denials, attended the Apalachin Conference.

Although he was barred by the Nevada gaming control board from entering casinos in the state, Civella was notoriously active in Las Vegas affairs. He shared in skimming of millions in casino gambling profits, although the theory that he may have been rewarded with only about $50,000 a year may indicate his worth within the entire operation. Quite naturally, Civella always denied the existence of the Mafia and in 1970 said in a newspaper interview, "I even deny, to my knowledge, that organized crime exists in Kansas City."

In 1980 Civella was sent to prison for four years on a bribery conspiracy charge and the following year was indicted on a Las Vegas skimming conspiracy count. His name figured prominently in the 1982 trial of Teamsters boss Williams and four others; ultimately the union leader was convicted of conspiring to bribe Howard W. Cannon, U.S. senator from Nevada. Civella died in custody before he came to trial on the skimming charges.

CLAIMING racket: Payoff for finding new recruits

Called the "claiming racket," it is one of the most lucrative paydays for wise guys. The boys are sent out in search of talent, potential mafiosi wanna-bes who will bring in bundles of money for the mob, enriching a crime family and the higher-ups in the organization. Naturally the wise guy who finds the talent is also handsomely rewarded, getting a large cut of his protégé's take and, perhaps most important, promotion in the mob as a talented money-maker in his own right.

Under the system, a mafioso who latches onto a productive criminal immediately goes to his capo and requests to be allowed to bring his find around. After getting the okay, the mafioso soars in stature as the recruit produces tons of revenues, rewarding the top guys in the mob with considerable loot. The bosses agree the claimant has a right to a big slice of the booty, but there is one catch; he remains responsible for his protégé's behavior. If the latter later betrays the mob, his sponsor faces very serious consequences—usually death.

During the 1980s and 1990s the claiming game lost much of its appeal because so many talented recruits made deals with the law to escape harsh sentences for themselves by throwing other wise guys, and often the top bosses, to the wolves. The ravages to the mob were so extensive, however, that the claiming game had to be resurrected if the Mafia were going to survive. The comeback of the mobs at the turn of the century has been credited by some observers to the rewards of once more bringing in new blood. For the Mafia this is a calculated but necessary risk. Many such recruits can be expected to buckle under the law and turn traitor. The new-breed bosses of the 2000s are reconciled to this and have set up their defenses by dealing retribution faster than ever, even in many cases when no retribution is warranted since the recruit may not have flipped at all. But why take the risk, when the hallmark of the new bosses is to take no chances? The defining case involves a boss who sent out a pair of hit men to do a job. Mission accomplished, and then two other hit men are sent out to erase the first pair. The second pair? Ditto.

With such ground rules now in place, mobsters are willing to go with the claiming game. And now they have a possible survival plan. Somewhere along the line the original sponsor might go to higher-ups and say, "It's funny, but I'm getting vibes. I could be wrong but should we take a chance? We've made a lot of dough out of the guy, but he isn't one of us. Let's write him off." It is a dangerous gambit for the claimer. The bosses might be half convinced with the logic, but they might feel even better if they eliminated both the claimer and the claimed. What the claimer feels he has going for him is that he might say, "Ya know, I have his operations down pat. I can still bring in the loot and his share is now in the pot."

If the selling game goes right, the claimer is safe himself as long as the money flow keeps on gushing. Now the duplicity of the claimer might even impress the new bosses. Here is a guy ready to move up in the new world of the double- and triple-cross rules, the dirtiest version of the game. It's dangerous, but the rewards make it worth the risk.

See also CACACE, JOEL

CLEAN graft: Payoffs to politicians and police

Without clean graft organized crime could not exist in this country. It is the corrupting force that "oils" the police, prosecutor, judges and politicians. The payoff allows the mafioso underworld to run its policy rackets, its bookmaking outfits, its loan-sharking activities, its porno parlors, its prostitution setups.

It should be understood that most police and other members of the criminal justice system will not accept payoffs from narcotics violations—some will but by no means all. When police accept graft it is almost always "on the pad" to all members of a precinct—from the patrolman up through the sergeants, the detectives, the lieutenants, captains and inspectors.

Where to draw the line? Clean graft allows a bookmaker and other gamblers to operate; fixes parking and speeding tickets; lets call girls and hookers operate. It creates an ignorance of liquor violations in still-dry areas of the country. And clean graft affords some politicians and police officers a kickback on the sins that will always be with us. So why shouldn't they have a slice of the pie. Could they otherwise have swimming pools or send the kids to college?

But "dirty graft," offered to cover up the narcotics rackets, or murder, armed robbery or rape, is harder to accept. Some cops do, as do some politicians. Regardless of whether it's accepted or not, the line between clean and dirty graft is illusionary.

In fact, clean graft is what allows the criminal syndicates to operate in the first place. They buy the friendships they need and use the revenues they get from "clean" operations to finance dirty deals. Murder, Inc., was financed almost completely from the revenues of "clean" gambling money. It is the policy revenues, the skimming operations from casinos, the horse and baseball and football bets, that provide the financial backing for huge heroin deals. It was $100,000 in clean money that Frank Costello used to see to it that Murder, Inc., stool pigeon Abe Reles went sailing out a sixth-floor window in a Brooklyn hotel where he was being kept under constant police "guard." The list is seemingly endless.

See also DIRTY GRAFT

CLEVELAND crime family   See LICAVOLI, JAMES T. "BLACKIE"

CLOTHESLINE: Hanging an imprisoned guy out to dry

They call the Mafia the "Honored Society." That doesn't mean that mafiosi cannot cheat or even kill one another if they have good reason and enough power. A mob guy who goes to prison is supposed to be taken care of along with his family. Sometimes, however, the payoff continues for a short time and then stops. There have even been capos who go to prison and find their own crews forget about them, coming through with no money at all. Frequently, the lowly soldiers have been put under another capo and the money may not be there unless they cough it up from their own end. They might even be ordered not to provide support money, thus putting the guy and his needy family "on the clothesline."

Some jailed mafiosi are resourceful enough to set up scams and operations from behind bars to provide for themselves. Some come up with deals to bring in contraband to sell to other prisoners.

When they come out, some may forget about their clothesline treatment. Some may not and blood may flow. Law enforcement officials regard the clothesline tactic as the stupidest thing mobsters do. If a man cannot provide for himself or his family, he grows more resentful and may talk to the law.

The clothesline treatment was part of the reason that Joe Valachi started talking. He was being clotheslined and "put on the shelf" by the big-shot mafiosi. The more resentful he acted the more they suspected him of being a stoolie—and a stoolie he finally became.

COCAINE-HEROIN shuttle scheme

In the aftermath of the Pizza Connection breakup, Mafia forces in the United States and Italy sought to resume narcotics trafficking in a way that cut down heavy shipments of money and the high risks involved. Thus in the late 1980s the so-called cocaine-heroin shuttle was established.

Cocaine purchased in South America was shipped to Italy and there exchanged for heroin. The arrangement was mutually beneficial. Cocaine had become more valuable in Europe than in America as it was adopted by many as their drug of choice. This gave U.S. interests more capital for the purchase of heroin, which commanded top dollar in America. The lack of cash transactions eliminated a considerable amount of money laundering.

Things went smoothly until late March 1988 when eavesdropping techniques revealed the scheme to investigators in both countries. A coordinated assault in the two countries netted some 150 suspected drug traffickers, and there were more arrests over the following year. One of the prize captures was that of Emanuele Adamita who had been furloughed from an Italian prison after serving seven years for a previous drug conviction. He never returned to custody but made his way to New York, where he notified a would-be customer that he could provide heroin and cocaine.

Eleven months later Adamita was in the Parker Meridien hotel in Manhattan with a good customer. Adamita hugged the client and told him he considered him "family." He added they could not be too careful since the police were everywhere. His customer agreed there were rats all around. The customer paid for a pound of heroin, took delivery and kissed Adamita on the cheek. Then the customer announced he was a Drug Enforcement Administration undercover agent and placed Adamita under arrest. The shocked Adamita broke down weeping.

That was one of the final nails in the coffin of the cocaine-heroin shuttle, but no one really believed the crackdown, any more than in the Pizza Connection case, would put the drug traffic out of business permanently. The immensity of the rewards for such criminal activities guaranteed that drug dealing would long remain a problem for law enforcement and continue to fatten the mafiosi, despite all their claims that they stay out of the dirty racket.

COHEN, Mickey (1913–1976): California gangster

Perhaps the most shot-at mobster in American criminal history since Chicago's Bugs Moran, Mickey Cohen became a sort of cult hero on the West Coast in the 1940s and 1950s. Cohen, who rose through the ranks as Bugsy Siegel's bodyguard, had made himself scarce on the day Siegel was shot in Virginia Hill's Beverly Hills mansion. Who had the muscle to make him stay away from his beloved mentor? The general conclusion: Meyer Lansky.

Cohen may have bowed to Lansky, but he wasn't about to cater to Jack Dragna, the top mafioso in Los Angeles. Dragna and his family, forced into a subordinate position by Siegel, were also eclipsed in Cohen's bookmaking operations.

The Los Angeles Family has often been referred to as "the Mickey Mouse Mafia," for its general inef-

fectiveness and its inability to control criminal activities in its bailiwick—a contention given credence in the Mickey Mouse war Dragna waged against Cohen. Cohen escaped at least five attempts on his life. Twice the Dragna hit men tried dynamiting Cohen's home, once with a homemade bangalore torpedo (a military weapon used to destroy barbed wire and blast into machine-gun pill boxes) and another time with a straight dynamite blast. The bangalore job though planted never detonated. The dynamite cache did go off but had been placed directly under a cement floor safe, causing the explosion to travel downward and sideways rather than up. The blast shattered windows throughout the neighborhood but left Mickey, his wife, his dog and his maid unharmed. What upset Mickey the most was the fact that more than 40 suits from his $300-apiece wardrobe were turned into airborne shredded strips by the explosion.

On another occasion a Dragna gunner let go with both barrels of a shotgun as the mobster was driving

West Coast mobster Mickey Cohen, who reformed after doing a long federal prison rap, previously escaped five attempts on his life by Los Angeles Mafiosi, whom he and others dubbed "the Mickey Mouse Mafia."

home late one night. Cohen's Cadillac was peppered with shot but incredibly not a single slug touched him. It was almost as miraculous as the time shotgunners opened up at Cohen as he was leaving a restaurant with a group of friends. Just as the gunmen squeezed off their rounds, Cohen noticed a scratch on his shiny Cadillac and bent down to look at it more closely. The two hit men were still stunned when they reported back to Dragna on how their quarry had lucked out.

Dragna never did get Cohen. Even when he was convicted on a tax rap and sentenced to five years in prison, a major corruption probe cost Dragna the police protection he needed to take over Cohen's operations. Cohen was probably the most-quoted gangster of his day. He once told television interviewer Mike Wallace: "I have killed no man that in the first place didn't deserve killing by the standards of our way of life." When asked to name the California politicians who had once protected his gambling empire, he refused, saying "that is not my way of life."

Cohen was no more communicative in 1950 when he appeared before the Kefauver Committee's hearings on organized crime. Asked by Senator Charles Tobey, "Is it not a fact that you live extravagantly . . . surrounded by violence?" Cohen answered, "Whadda ya mean, 'surrounded by violence'? People are shooting at *me*."

When he was asked to explain why a Hollywood banker had granted him a $35,000 loan without collateral, Mickey quipped, "I guess he just likes me."

Always one to insert himself in the public eye, Cohen in 1958 provided the press with love letters written by actress Lana Turner to Johnny Stompanato. Turner's gangster lover was, in fact, Cohen's bodyguard and had been stabbed to death by Turner's teenage daughter. Cohen also let it be known all around that he—not Turner—paid for Stompanato's funeral.

Cohen was twice convicted of tax violations, serving four years of a five-year sentence on one occasion and 10 years of a 15-year term on the other. When he came out of prison in 1972, Cohen declared his intention to go straight. It was not necessarily a matter of choice. He was partly paralyzed as the result of a head injury he received at the hands of a fellow convict at Atlanta in 1963. Cohen's last major foray in the news occurred in 1974 when he announced he had made contact with certain people who knew the whereabouts of the then-kidnapped Patricia Hearst. Cohen died, some say remarkably, of natural causes in 1976.

COHN, Roy (1927–1986): Mob mouthpiece

In his late years Roy Cohn, a major figure in McCarthy-era anti-communist activities, became a popular lawyer for top mafiosi, including Fat Tony Salerno, Carmine Galante and several members of the Gambino crime family. Among the latter were Carlo's sons Tommy and Joe Gambino, Carmine Fatico, Angelo Ruggiero and John Gotti.

If not for Cohn's counsel, Gotti's career might have ended more than a decade before he catapulted to boss of the Gambinos. In 1973 Gotti was looking at a long prison term for a killing he participated in at the orders of Godfather Gambino. The victim was James McBratney, who had kidnapped for ransom and killed one of the don's nephews. Gotti and two other hoodlums, Ruggiero and Ralph Galione, cornered McBratney in a Staten Island bar. They flashed phony police badges and tried to hustle their quarry away to a more private location where he could be dispatched in the horrible fashion the don wished.

McBratney was not fooled and resisted. Galione produced a gun, which he was forced to turn on menacing bar patrons. A drunk tried to intervene and the gun went off accidentally. Galione panicked and fired three shots into McBratney.

The job had been slightly botched, but Gambino was not displeased. Unfortunately witnesses easily identified the killer trio, and Ruggiero and Gotti were arrested. In the meantime gunner Galione had been shot dead, apparently by McBratney pals.

Gambino decided to get Gotti the best lawyer money could buy, Roy Cohn.

Cohn devised a strategy that satisfied Gambino. Gotti would plea-bargain down to attempted manslaughter, since he had not done the shooting and merely held McBratney. Cohn, the precocious son of a New York judge, was said to have a network of compliant judges, prosecutors and district attorneys and other law enforcement officials who could help things go his way. Carlo bought the idea and ordered Gotti to cop the plea.

Gotti wanted to fight the charge. Aniello Dellacroce, Gotti's mentor in the family, dissuaded him: "Carlo says you take the fall, and that's it."

Gotti remained bitter until he saw the strategy play out. He was sentenced to a mere four years and actually served less than two. Gotti had been certain such a deal was impossible, but everything went smoothly. The district attorney's office didn't even label either Gotti or Ruggiero as "persistent offenders," which both were and which under state law would have earned them very harsh sentences. In *Goombata,* authors John Cummings and Ernest Volkman found Cohn's legal magic "not especially surprising in the history of the Staten Island District Attorney's office, which had a notably lax record in dealing with organized crime defendants."

Still, in his later years the apparently still-smarting Gotti exhibited no desire to utilize Cohn's services.

COLI, Eco James (1922–): Chicago syndicate gangster

Long identified as a mob assassin as well as a muscleman, Eco James Coli sports a record dating back to 1945, with arrests for attempted hijacking, assault and sex offenses. A leading suspect in a number of murders, Coli also was identified as a prize exterminator, working strictly on contracts for the Chicago syndicate bosses. In those labors he was put on an equal performance level with the likes of Fiore Buccieri, Sam DeStefano, Jackie the Lackey Cerone, Willie "Potatoes" Daddano and Marshall Caifano. His conviction for contributing to delinquency resulted in one-year probation; for armed robbery, a sentence of eight to 12 years. On the latter count Coli was released by order of the Illinois Supreme Court in 1955 after having served only three years.

In addition to Coli's alleged hits, he served as secretary-treasurer and business agent for a Teamsters local of funeral drivers, directors, embalmers and others. Coli was the source of considerable political embarrassment when he marched most prominently between Mayor Richard Daley and Governor Richard Ogilvie in Chicago's 1969 Columbus Day Parade. After the parade both officials said they were not aware of his criminal background.

COLL, Vincent "Mad Dog" (1909–1932): Gangster

Vincent "Mad Dog" Coll, the quintessential Irish gangster of the early 1930s, was doomed. He sneered at the organizers of syndicated crime, announcing he would take whatever slice of whichever pie he wished; those who objected could lie down in a gutter and bleed to death, a condition Coll would readily have helped bring about. What's more, Coll enjoyed and indeed reveled in a much bigger press than such more important gangsters as Lucky Luciano, Meyer Lansky, Frank Costello, Vito Genovese, Joey Adonis and others. That alone may have been a contributing factor to his eventual demise.

Coll was known in the New York underworld first as the Mad Mick and later in the press as Mad Dog because of his at least half-demented disregard for human life. Some said he had little concern even for his own life, recalling his abandon in raiding the gangland stronghold of Owney Madden, Legs Diamond and Dutch Schultz. Without a moment's hesitation he accepted a mind-boggling murder contract on Lucky Luciano, Vito Genovese, Frank Costello and Joe Adonis, as though he would not face bloody retribution if he carried out such hits.

Coll was hired for that wholesale slaughter by Salvatore Maranzano, then the self-proclaimed Mafia

Vince "Mad Dog" Coll (left), who bucked the emerging national crime syndicate, was cleared of a murder charge by ace criminal lawyer Sam Leibowitz (right). A few months later mob machine gunners filled Coll with lead.

boss of bosses. Maranzano wished the killings to be carried out by a non-Italian so that suspicion would be diverted from himself and so he could perhaps use the murders as justification for making war on other ethnic gangsters. Coll got a $25,000 advance payment for the killings and was on his way to Maranzano's office to which Luciano and Genovese were being lured for a meeting. Luciano learned of the murder plot and activated a plan he already had in the works so that Maranzano was taken out by killers supplied by Meyer Lansky. When Coll showed up, he discovered his erstwhile employer was dead; he was ahead $25,000 for doing absolutely nothing. He walked off whistling.

Vince Coll came out of the Irish ghetto called Hell's Kitchen in New York determined to make it big in the criminal world. He and his brother Peter became rumrunners for crime kingpin Dutch Schultz, $150 a week each. Vince saw the job as a mere stepping stone. They had to learn the bootlegging craft and then either start their own operation or take over Schultz's. While still working as trusted gunmen for Schultz, the Coll brothers started splitting the Dutchman's operation, convincing some gangsters they would fare better with them.

One who wouldn't go along was Vincent Barelli, a dedicated Schultz hood. The Coll brothers had gone to school with a boy named Carmine Smith, and Carmine's sister, Mary, was Barelli's girlfriend. On that basis Mary agreed to bring Barelli to a meeting with the Coll brothers. When Barelli rejected Coll's offer to defect, Vince shot him. Since she was now a liability rather than an aid, Mary was murdered as well.

Finally, though, Vince Coll decided he was strong enough to move on Schultz, who was at the time busily extending his policy racket in Harlem and devoting less time to the beer business. In the spring of 1931 Vince Coll informed Schultz that he wanted a piece of the beer racket. Schultz's answer was a flat no. The Coll brothers then went on a rampage, hijacking Schultz beer trucks until a full-scale war broke out. On May 30, 1931, Schultz gunners killed 24-year-old Peter Coll on a Harlem street corner. Vince was overwhelmed with grief and over the next few weeks came out of mourning only long enough to mow down four Schultz men. In all at least 20 gunners on both sides were killed. It is difficult to figure out the exact number because the Castellammarese War was in full blaze at the same time; the

police had real difficulty figuring out which corpse should be attributed to which gang war.

Coll had less firepower than Schultz and had to make up for it by paying top dollar for gunmen to join him. Squeezed for cash, he tried to raise it by muscling in on the rackets controlled by Jack "Legs" Diamond and Owney Madden. He also started kidnapping their top aides and holding them for ransom. Even in the underworld the Mad Mick was an outlaw.

On July 28, 1931, Coll picked up his Mad Dog sobriquet when he tried to gun down Schultz aide Joey Rao and several of his men in Spanish Harlem. Coll blazed away with a machine gun but Rao and his men were unscathed. Instead, five children playing in the street were hit and one, five-year-old Michael Vengalli, his stomach virtually shot away, died.

Coll was identified as the gunner and the public demanded that he be brought in dead or alive. Coll realized he would be cornered sooner or later so he kidnapped yet another Owney Madden aide and collected $30,000 ransom. Then he surrendered and with his loot hired the top criminal lawyer of the day, Sam Leibowitz, to defend him. The case against Coll looked airtight—until Leibowitz worked his courtroom magic. Somehow the brilliant defender made it seem the eyewitnesses rather than his client was on trial. In the end Coll went free.

At this point the underworld was said to have put out a $50,000 reward for the trigger-happy Coll. Legs Diamond wanted him, as did Madden and Schultz. Schultz had by this time started to work very closely with Luciano, and Meyer Lansky, who also agreed that Coll had to go, made too many waves and was bad for business. Thus virtually all of the underworld wanted the Mad Dog dead. And the desperate Schultz even walked into the detectives' squad room of the forty-second precinct station in the Bronx and announced that he would reward any officer who bumped off the Mad Mick with a lavish home in Westchester. Clearly, Vince Coll was not very popular—and his days were numbered.

On February 1, 1932, four gunmen entered a home in the North Bronx where a card game was in progress. They had a tip that Coll would be there. Killed were a woman, Mrs. Emily Torrizello, and two Coll henchmen, Fiorio Basile and Patsy del Greco. Basile's brother, Louis, and another female were wounded. Vince Coll showed up 30 minutes after all the shooting.

Eight days later, Coll was in a drugstore telephone booth talking to Owney Madden, threatening to kill him unless he was given money. Madden kept him talking while the call was traced, something the underworld in New York at the time had no trouble doing. Coll was still on the phone when a black limousine with three men pulled up to the curb outside the drug store. One man stood by the car, another just inside the door of the store and the third, with something bulging under his overcoat, strode toward the phone booth. Coll saw the man remove a Thompson submachine gun from under his coat, but in his cramped position the Mad Dog could not react in time. Coll died instantly, his body riddled with bullets.

COLOMBIAN Mafia: Powerful drug trafficking organizations

Who are the deadliest mobsters in America? The American Mafia or the rich and powerful Colombian drug traffickers who have permeated the United States. Many Colombian mobsters have deluded themselves into thinking that they dictate to the American crime families. They like to cite the case of a certain mafioso who masterminded a rip-off of South American traffickers in a huge cocaine deal. The next part is gospel. The Colombians warned the American mobs that unless they righted the matter, there would be open warfare. Nothing less than the verified execution of the offending wise guy would satisfy them, so the Americans could not erase the offender and bury him. The Colombians wanted the dead victim found and wanted to see newspaper articles about the rubout.

This created a bit of a problem for the New York mobs. Less that 20 percent of all homicides make it into print. Leaving a corpse in a car was not always good enough to ensure discovery of the hit. There have been cases of vandals who spot the death car, dump the body where it might not be found for days or weeks, and take the still-operational vehicle. The wise guys solved their problem by putting the body in a luxury car out on a highway where it would be sure to attract attention and ventilating it with machine-gun fire. The hit made headlines and the Colombians were well satisfied that they had made the Mafia knuckle down to them. The wise guy version, told often to lawyers and other interested parties, was that they had framed a wise guy victim due to be hit for other infractions and made him pay with his life in a rubout frame.

It is entirely possible that top Colombian operators suspected they were being hoodwinked, but the fiction was as good as the truth for their men. Business went back to business.

The incident points out the delicate relationship that has developed between mafiosi and the Colombians. The secret behind it all was accommodation, something mobsters generally appreciate. The Colombians started going bigtime in the United States in the early 1970s, supplying the Mafia and various Mexican and Cuban groups. As the cocaine rackets began bringing huge profits to those groups, the Colombians decided to move in directly. Their working agreements with the Cuban Mafia were wiped out in the brutal war for profits. The Colombians had much more money than the Cubans and much more firepower. All the Cubans had going for them was strong profits with the Mafia families. The Cubans were under the illusion that the mafiosi would join the war with them, something the latter considered downright stupid. The mobsters could count and see they could make greater profits with the Colombians and tie up enormous supplies of cocaine, some of which they could ship to Europe where the demand for coke was skyrocketing. In exchange the wise guys bartered much-desired heroin for shipment to America. The Cubans were simply dealt out in bloodletting that took the lives of hundreds.

The Colombians found they could handle business directly with Latino buyers in the States, which they cornered with no objection from the mafiosi because they knew the Colombians would need them more than the mobs needed the Colombians. The Mafia controlled the drug pipeline in the States, and the Colombians needed access to those distribution channels, with all the special deals that were required. The Colombians realized the Mafia could quickly determine when any major shipments were coming in, thanks to their own intelligence systems, one of which were outlaw biker gangs who could blanket the underworld and learn the facts. The Colombians quickly learned they had to accommodate the local crime families, turning over distribution to them or operating on a "tax system," which cut the mobs in for a hefty share of the revenues.

Since that time the cocaine rackets have operated in this arrangement, and the mafiosi gained the fillip of appearing to be uninvolved in much of the cocaine trafficking. The Mafia's main problems have been connected with their heroin operations, which of course were largely financed by its own cocaine revenues. Happily, for the mob, the Colombians can be counted on engaging in much bloodletting with Latino competitors and pursuing their time-honored practice of ruthlessly killing the male offenders and their families, including the women and children. Mafiosi have shaken their heads in disdain at such activities, making sure their attitudes made it back in the public's knowledge. In effect, they ask, why can't these characters behave in the civilized manner in which the Mafia does? That is, of course, utter nonsense, but the mobs have gained considerably by this public relations stunt that has gained favorable mention by some journalists. Ain't P.R. grand, the boys say.

COLOMBO, Joseph, Sr. (1914–1978): Crime family boss

"What experience has he got? He was a bustout guy [petty gambler] all his life. . . . What does he know?" So said New Jersey Mafia boss Simone Rizzo "Sam the Plumber" DeCavalcante in a conversation taped by the FBI. He was talking about Joseph Colombo, who in his day was the youngest Mafia boss in the country and the youngest also to be assassinated. Like DeCavalcante, numerous other mafiosi resented Joe Colombo, who had the reputation of being the Mafia's Sammy Glick, a man who got ahead through sheer opportunism—not by brains or muscle but through being a "fink."

It was in a sense a bum rap. For one thing, Joe Colombo was an accomplished murderer, part of a five-man hit team for Joe Profaci. Two other members of that squad were Larry and Crazy Joe Gallo; when you killed with the Gallo boys you killed with the best. The police attributed at least 15 killings to the team.

In many respects Colombo was also one of the most forward-looking members of the Mafia. He understood the importance of image and tried to change his crime family's way. It was to prove the death of him. But then any crime boss who manages to upset the FBI, other godfathers and his own crime family members is almost certain to go.

When in the early 1960s Joe Bonanno moved to take control of the entire New York Mafia, he planned the murders of several top members of the crime syndicate's ruling board. Bonanno gave the contract to his ally Joe Magliocco, who had fallen heir to Profaci's Brooklyn crime family, and Magliocco in turn ordered his ambitious underboss Colombo to carry out the hits.

It was not a smart move. Joe Colombo was nothing if not a survivor, and he'd always been that way in mob affairs. He survived the assassination of his father, Anthony Colombo, who in 1938 was found dead in his car next to an equally dead lady friend. They had been garroted. Police learned from underworld informers that the elder Colombo had been rubbed out for playing loose with Mafia regulations. A reporter once asked Joe Colombo if he ever tried to find his father's slayers, and he snapped back, "Don't they pay policemen for that?"

Colombo went on to serve boss Profaci far better apparently than his father had. After serving time on the piers as a muscleman, he organized mob-rigged dice games, moved into bigger gambling operations in Brooklyn and Nassau County, loan-sharking, and hijacking at Kennedy airport. And he did hit team duty.

But his survival instinct remained high and it was stratospheric when Magliocco handed him Bonanno's contracts. Colombo figured the odds and decided the chances of Magliocco and Bonanno winning out were low—and zero if he took word of the plan to the intended victims, namely Carlo Gambino and Tommy Lucchese. He figured rightly. Eventually the other side won what in part would be called the Banana War. Bonanno had to retreat. Colombo fared a lot better, being rewarded with leadership of the Profaci family.

Next he had to deal with an insurrection led by the Gallo brothers. But, while fending them off, he still had time for other campaigns. One was disguising his own Mafia family, insisting that all his soldiers hold down a real job. They had to be butchers, bakers or sanitation men—anything just so it was legitimate. "It was almost a fetish with him," an FBI agent once said. Colombo himself worked as a salesman for the Cantalupo Realty Company in Brooklyn. The flaw in Colombo's plan was that his men didn't much like it. One of the prime benefits of a "made" mafioso is that he doesn't have to hold down a 9-to-5 job like "average jerks." Now Colombo was forcing them to do what their way of life was supposed to save them from doing.

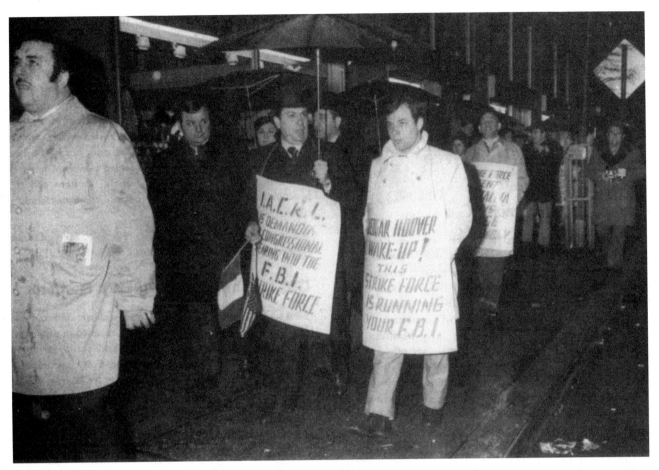

Mafia crime boss Joe Colombo Sr. (holding an umbrella) leads his Italian-American Civil Rights League in picketing FBI headquarters. Godfather Carlo Gambino ordered Colombo to stop all the nonsense, which was producing too much heat. Colombo did not and was assassinated.

Then, Colombo moved on to another ill-conceived program, at least from the mob survival viewpoint. He came up with the idea of improving the image of Italian Americans by forming the Italian-American Civil Rights League. Colombo's idea was that this would make Italian Americans proud of their heritage, and that in unity they would be able to fight the authorities' alleged victimization of them. The league was also intended to fight the Italian gangster stereotype.

Other Mafia leaders looked upon Colombo's effort with varying degrees of distaste and distrust. They had long ago decided that denying the existence of the Mafia simply called more attention to it. Still Colombo was permitted to stage a giant rally on June 29, 1970, at Columbus Circle. Fifty thousand people attended the event, and it was a huge success. Politicians vied for the right to appear at the rally. Even Governor Nelson Rockefeller took honorary membership in the league despite its Colombo imprint.

By his own acknowledgment, Colombo was a hero. He started expanding the league's activities. But meanwhile some of Colombo's lieutenants were alarmed by the declining revenues of the family while their boss was minding everything but crime business. These capos approached other families who were more than annoyed by Colombo's activities, and they agreed that he was going too far. He had to be muzzled.

The chief voice in opposition was the most powerful don in the country, Carlo Gambino, whose life Colombo had saved earlier by finking on Bonanno. But Gambino was more concerned about what Colombo was doing lately. What Colombo had done was greatly annoy the FBI by establishing picket lines at the agency's New York office. By mid-1971 the feds and other law enforcement agencies had 20 percent of the Colombo crime family under indictment for various charges. What if that happened to the other families, Gambino fretted.

According to the most widespread theory, Gambino decided to let the Gallo forces take out Colombo. The second Unity Day rally of the league was set for June 28, 1971. Gallo knew he and his men would never get close enough to Colombo to hit him, but he had other resources. Of all the Italian mafiosi, Joe Gallo had good connections with the black gangsters in Harlem. On the morning of June 28, Colombo showed up early in the rally. Just as the crowd started to form, a black man, Jerome A. Johnson, wearing newspaper photographer's credentials, moved up on Colombo. He was no more than a step away when he pulled a pistol and put three quick shots into the gang leader's head. Instantly, Colombo's bodyguards shot the assassin dead. Colombo did not die on the spot, but he suffered brain damage. He was nothing more than a vegetable for seven years before finally expiring.

There were some troubling aspects to the assassination. Why had Johnson done it when he knew he couldn't get away? Many thought he was simply demented and that there had been no mob plot against Colombo. Carlo Gambino undoubtedly approved that line of thinking, but the police investigation indicated that the assassin had been told others were going to create a disturbance to permit his escape. Johnson was simply double-crossed.

But why kill Colombo so publicly when the mob prefers its rubouts without witnesses? The answer was twofold. Gambino wanted to doom the entire league movement by bathing it in violence. And most of all he wanted to rub Colombo's nose in the gutter, to demean him totally.

The reason for Gambino's venom was not discovered by government agents until 1974, three years after the shooting. According to Pulitzer Prize–winning reporter David Chandler, Gambino had gone to Colombo and ordered him to stop all his nonsense. Colombo, now infatuated by his own importance, spat in Gambino's face. Five weeks later Colombo was paid back, and it must have pleased Gambino to no end that the man who had demeaned the godfather didn't die outright but lingered for years in semi-death.

COLOMBO crime family

The first don of what was later called the Colombo crime family, Joe Profaci, came to power upon the conclusion of the Castellammarese War. Profaci thus served with Lucky Luciano, Vince Mangano, Joe Bonanno and Tom Gagliano as head of one of the five Mafia families in New York that comprised the nucleus of the Mafia force in the national crime syndicate.

Profaci ruled for more than three decades, an amazing feat since he was regarded by other mafiosi and many of his own soldiers as the worst don in New York. Profaci's failing—greed. Alone among the dons Profaci levied a tax of $25 a month from each member, allegedly to build a slush fund to take care of mobsters who got arrested. Of course, he pocketed the funds. And he constantly demanded tribute. Joe Valachi later quoted Carmine "the Snake" Persico as complaining: "Even if we go hijack some trucks he taxes us. I paid up to $1,800."

Eventually Profaci was faced with revolt. A number of his soldiers, including the kill-crazy Gallo brothers, Persico and Jiggs Forlano (a capo and perhaps the biggest loan shark in New York), were rumbling for his demise. Ever cunning, Profaci was not about to cave in to all the rebels and so he divided them, promising rewards that brought Persico, Forlano and others back into the fold, while leaving the Gallos out in the cold. (Persico and Forlano became the staunchest battlers against the Gallos for Profaci.)

Profaci died in 1962 and the power passed to his underboss Joe Magliocco. Like Profaci, Magliocco was upset the way two of the other city crime bosses, Carlo Gambino and Tommy Lucchese, had been interfering in Profaci affairs. Now they tried to undercut Magliocco. Gambino clearly had designs to dominate the Profacis. Only Joe Bonanno stood with Profaci and his successor, while the fifth boss, Vito Genovese, was in prison at the time.

It was now that Bonanno, in his own quest for supremacy, concocted a scheme to kill off Gambino and Lucchese, as well as a few other crime bosses around the country. It may be that Bonanno felt he had no options, that if Magliocco fell, Gambino would turn next on the Bonanno family.

Magliocco agreed to join Bonanno in his plot and gave out the contracts on the two New York City leaders to a dependable hit-man capo for Profaci, Joe Colombo. But Colombo was not dependable this time. Instead of carrying out the hits, he revealed the plot to the intended victims. This lead eventually to the so-called Banana War to dethrone Bonanno; but Magliocco tumbled easier. Summoned to appear before the commission of which he was a member, Magliocco, extremely ill and suddenly very tired, confessed. He was allowed to live (he was to die of a heart ailment in a matter of months) and dethroned.

The grateful Gambino installed the accommodating Joe Colombo as Profaci family chief and thus gained another firm vote in the commission. In time Gambino would rue his choice of Colombo, a man who had ambitious ideas. One idea that Gambino bought at first was that it would be smart to rally Italian Americans into an anti-defamation league to say they were being smeared by all this talk about an Italian Mafia. Actually what Colombo wanted to do was clothe the Mafia with the respectability of the vast majority of Italian Americans. (By contrast the Jewish Anti-Defamation League has never objected to stories about Meyer Lansky, Bugsy Siegel, Gurrah Shapiro, Louis Lepke, Mickey Cohen, Mendy Weiss, Arnold Rothstein or Jake Guzik and other Jewish gangsters.)

After a year of protests by Italian Americans led by Colombo, including picketing of the FBI offices in New York, Gambino had enough and ordered Colombo to cool it. He didn't and he was assassinated.

Unlike other volumes on the Mafia this book will offer no chart listing the various Mafia crime families and their bosses and other leaders. One reason is that any such chart, given the nature of the mob, is subject to abrupt change. But more important, the chart would be inaccurate. Federal listings and those of state and local police agencies frequently vary with one another about who was or is in power when.

The post-Colombo succession was a particular special problem for law enforcement agencies. Despite the fact that hostility between Colombo and the FBI made it the most intensely watched crime family, it took the government three years to discover the new boss was Thomas DiBella. That was with four federal agencies and three local agencies maintaining 24-hour surveillance and eavesdropping on both the Colombo and Gambino families. In 1971 when Colombo was shot (he lingered in a vegetable state for seven years) DiBella was listed as only a low-ranking soldier in the Colombos. Actually DiBella, a retired tractor foreman on the docks, had been in the mob since 1932, but until 1974 no one in official circles ever suspected his importance. He had only one conviction, for bootlegging in 1932.

Because of age, DiBella eventually stepped aside for younger blood although he continued as a top adviser. The leadership passed to former rebel Carmine Persico. There would have been an era of peace for the mob—the Gallo threat had been settled with the death of Larry Gallo and the assassination of Crazy Joe Gallo—except for Persico's constant involvement in criminal prosecutions. He was to spend a total of 10 of the 13 years prior to 1985 in various prisons. The family was in something like chaos until Jerry Langella wrested the leadership to himself, subject to some dispute from Persico at a later date. By late 1986, with both Persico and Langella facing long years in prison, authorities indicated that Victor Orena, a distant Persico relative, had been named boss pro tem.

The family can only boast of about 115 members as well as a few hundred more supporters, making it with today's Lucchese crime family one of the two smallest in New York. But the roster of crimes the family is involved in is impressive: narcotics trafficking, gambling, loan-sharking, cigarette smuggling, pornography, counterfeiting, hijacking and bankruptcy frauds, to name just a few.

Murder is also in the picture, but the boys can be rather understanding about that. According to the police, one potential victim asked that he not be put in cement blocks and tossed into the Gowanus Canal, mob standard procedure. He requested that instead his body be dumped in the streets so that "my family won't have such a hassle getting my life insurance."

The boys agreed, but for various reasons the hit was not carried out. Maybe the Colombos aren't that bad a sort.

COLONY Sports Club: Mob-owned London gambling casino Organized crime discovered that legalized gambling was far more lucrative than the illegal type. The bribery tab was lower and the juicy side rackets, such as skimming and openly promoted casino junkets, added big revenue. In an effort to expand legal operations, mob tentacles soon spread beyond the U.S. borders to Cuba, Haiti, the Bahamas, Portugal and even Communist Yugoslavia. Above all London offered an extremely rich base, one that the mob's financial wizard, Meyer Lansky, did not ignore.

When Castro threw the mob out of Cuba and shut their glittering gambling casinos, Lansky immediately accelerated his efforts in England. The mob opened a considerable number of casinos in that country, some of which were less than totally honest, a situation made possible in part thanks to the British belief in fair play and the misguided notion that everyone abided by high standards. In most of these casinos, especially those backed by Philadelphia godfather Angelo Bruno, the rule provided that smalltime games be kept honest, but whenever a sucker was set up, one good for $30,000 or $40,000 in an hour, the gloves were off and every rig possible was used. Two other mob operators, Joey Napolitano and Richie Castucci, were imprisoned, fined and then kicked out of England after the authorities nailed them for rigging games at the Villa Casino.

None of these operators followed the Meyer Lansky method. Realizing the need for a genuine high-class casino that would attract loads of high rollers, Lansky determined the game had to be legit, with no fast mechanics working the tables, no marked cards or switched decks and no loaded dice. Thus the Colony Sports Club opened.

In theory, the Colony was run by former Hollywood actor George Raft but, according to Mafia informer Vinnie Teresa, he was merely a front for the real owners, Alfie Sulkin, Lansky and longtime Lansky associate Dino Cellini. The Colony was the place to go for English and visiting society. Each day Raft would appear, dressed in a tuxedo, and he would meet people, sign autographs and dance with enthralled women. Raft was later to tell friends, those days in the 1960s were the happiest years of his life, a continuing run of glamour for a star whose movie career had faded.

Raft made millions for the mob at the Colony but the bubble burst when the British government finally became exercised at underworld control of the Colony and deported Raft. Cellini was also booted out but essentially Raft was made the scapegoat in the affair. The British failed to solve the matter of true ownership of the casino and Lansky and Cellini kept up their secret association with it.

See also RAFT, GEORGE

COLOSIMO, Big Jim (1871–1920): Brothel king and Torrio murder victim

Italian-born Jim Colosimo came to Chicago with his father in 1895 and rather quickly achieved the American Dream, underworld style. Having toiled his way up from newsboy and bootblack to street sweeper, Big Jim concluded that hard work was getting him nowhere fast. He turned instead to petty crime, developing fairly good pickpocketing skills. But, after a brush with the law, he decided he needed a safer racket. He got a job working as a collector for two infamous, corrupt aldermen, Michael "Hinky Dink" Kenna and Bath-house John Coughlin. Under the aldermen's tutelage he moved on to poolroom (i.e., betting parlor) manager, saloonkeeper and then the really juicy job as a brothel bagman, collecting tribute for Kenna and Coughlin.

In 1902, while making his appointed rounds, Jim made the acquaintance of a fat, dumpy, middle-aged madam named Victoria Moresco. For both it was love at first sight; Big Jim saw her money and she was taken by his dark Latin virility. To make sure he didn't get away, Victoria made him the manager of her brothel. Two weeks later they married. Under Big Jim's skilled management and with the support of his aldermanic benefactors, the brothel thrived. Big Jim renamed it the Victoria in honor of his bride and raised prices. He also opened up a string of lower-priced bordellos that charged only $1 or $2. Out of every $2 his girls got paid, Big Jim took $1.20. In no time at all he was a millionaire.

But Big Jim had not forgotten his humble streetsweeping days. He organized the street sweepers into a fraternal organization and soon had a lucrative labor shakedown racket going.

In due course Big Jim became the top procurer in Chicago, a city brimming with whorehouse entrepreneurs. His headquarters, Colosimo's Cafe on South Wabash Avenue, became a favorite entertainment and watering hole for a melange of society and entertainment stars, not to mention the cream of the underworld. Many headliners headed for Colosimo's after their own shows, and often included in the late supper crowd were George M. Cohan, Al Jolson, Sophie Tucker and John Barrymore. An opera lover, Big Jim often hosted Enrico Caruso.

Colosimo's Cafe was the one joint Big Jim could be proud of, and although he was hardly about to give up his whorehouses, he was looking for someone to take up their management so he could spend more time being impresario of the finer things in show business.

Colosimo was also looking for protection. His great financial success attracted the attention of

Black Hand extortionists who threatened him with death unless he paid them off. Since their pay-or-die demands were at first rather nominal, Colosimo paid, but as their money bites increased, the great whoremaster saw a pressing need to acquire some muscle to save his assets. Thus in 1909 he sent for one of the few outsiders he knew he could trust, a nephew from Brooklyn named Johnny Torrio. He was known as "Little John" but increased his stature by always proving as tough as the situation required. Torrio was not a man given to personal violence but he saw this was the only way to deal with extortionists. He lured several into traps where they were murdered. The word soon got around that Big Jim was off limits to protection demands.

Colosimo was extremely pleased with his decision to bring in Torrio, not knowing that the decision would eventually prove to be the death of him. Torrio enjoyed no bountiful rewards for good works at first. Colosimo praised him effusively and shunted him off to the Saratoga, his lowest-rung whorehouse where charges were never more than a dollar a trick and often less. Torrio however was a most imaginative male madam and repainted the sleazy joint and ordered all the women to dress in childish clothes so that they looked like young virgins. He raised the Saratoga's prices and business boomed. This more than anything impressed Colosimo who promoted Torrio to his chief aide, the de facto head of the Colosimo vice empire. Big Jim could thus devote more attention to his plush legit cafe and seek romantic attachments other than with his wife whose attractions grew less as he grew richer.

Torrio had only one thought in mind, that to stay on top in crime one had always to take advantage of changing situations, to shift emphasis with the times. It was this perception that would win Torrio recognition by many as "the father of modern American gangsterism." In 1919 Torrio saw the potential offered by the Eighteenth Amendment. Prohibition would turn fast-moving gangsters into multimillionaires. All that stood in the way of expansion of Colosimo's empire was Big Jim Colosimo himself.

Big Jim had by then dumped his wife and planned to marry a beautiful young singer named Dale Winters. Whenever Torrio tried to involve Colosimo in the rich world of bootlegging, Colosimo shrugged

him off, pointed out their vice empire was humming most profitably and turned back to his more gracious pursuits.

Torrio grimly kept on planning and in 1919 imported from New York a 19-year-old youth named Alphonse Capone whom he had known before he left New York a decade earlier and whom he'd seen many times on trips back to Brooklyn. Capone was the perfect foil for Torrio, the thinker. Capone was a man of action who sought to solve problems with the blackjack, the knife and the gun. Capone became Torrio's chauffeur and bodyguard and soon his number two man. Colosimo was still around, but the underworld was already pegging Torrio as the tough in charge.

On May 11, 1920, Colosimo was shot dead in the vestibule of his cafe. Torrio had asked him to be there to receive a large shipment of whiskey. An unknown assailant suddenly sprang from the checkroom and fired two bullets into Big Jim who died in a matter of minutes.

Some careless crime writers have insisted that Colosimo hit was the work of Capone, acting on Torrio's orders. The fact was that Colosimo died according to Torrio's plan but Torrio took care to make sure both he and Capone had solid alibis at the time of the killing. Torrio had already discovered the value of importing outside gunmen to handle important assignments when too much heat would focus on locals.

The killer was Frankie Yale, a top Brooklyn mob leader, who had strongly urged Torrio to import Capone. When Torrio communicated to Yale his need for a good gunner, Yale announced he would handle the matter himself. One eyewitness later identified Yale's photograph as that of the killer, and police discovered he had been stopped at the Chicago train station just after the Colosimo murder. Since the police had had no firm reason to hold Yale, he was allowed to continue to New York. The witness was sent to Brooklyn to confront Yale, but by the time he arrived, he had developed, not unexpectedly, a case of cold feet and could not be sure Yale was the man.

Colosimo's murder remained unsolved, but that mystery is overshadowed by matters of greater significance. Indeed, his death opened the floodgates of crime in America's second city and gave birth to what became known worldwide as the Chicago Gangster.

COMMISSION, the: Mafia "ruling body"

Even with the conviction on November 19, 1986, of three of the so-called Mafia Commission, there is a mistaken impression that the Mafia—or, indeed, organized crime—is entirely governed by this body. But both the Mafia and the national syndicate, two different entities, are far more republican than that. Even in the heyday of the so-called Big Six in the 1940s and 1950s, the commission was not all-powerful—except when its decisions were unanimous.

Confusion is a result of the fact that there are really two commissions. In his autobiography, Joe Bonanno described a national commission that governs the Mafia, speaking only of the commission as a unit representing the five New York families, with a representative from Chicago and at various times from a few additional cities such as Buffalo, Detroit and Philadelphia. Bonanno was exaggerating the importance of that commission.

In the 1930s the syndicate was ruled by a number of leaders headed by Lucky Luciano and Meyer Lansky, some mob leaders in New York and New Jersey with Chicago—still struggling with the loss of Al Capone and trying to win full control of that city—almost unconcerned. In the 1940s the Big Six made the major decisions on syndicate business. Frank Costello and Joe Adonis represented the mafioso interest of the five families in New York. Meyer Lansky represented himself, other Jewish kingpins such as Moe Dalitz, and the jailed or deported Luciano whose standard orders to others were "listen to the Little Man" (Lansky). Longy Zwillman represented the New Jersey mobs and each week two representatives, Tony Accardo and Greasy Thumb Guzik, flew in from Chicago. The ethnic composition of the Big Six was not insignificant, being composed of three Jews and three Italians. So much for the idea that organized crime was virtually all Italian or Mafia.

Throughout the years there was a national commission of the Mafia but it had more limited interests. It was on this commission that the five New York families were represented as well as other crime families drawn from among the 20-odd crime families blanketing the United States. This commission primarily concerned itself with New York–New Jersey–Pennsylvania affairs—not surprising since probably half the mafioso manpower in the country was and is located in this region.

Chicago, especially when represented by Sam Giancana, was at best only a semi-interested member, probably because in recent years not one crime syndicate but two—not just one Mafia, but one plus Chicago—have existed. Chicago at times merely pays lip service to the Commission but nevertheless claims everything west of Chicago as its own. It has not always been able to implement this view but does hold sway over several other crime families.

Organized crime in recent years has seen the growth, rather than the decline in power, of the Italian or Mafia interests. There has been no purge of Jewish mobsters, and to this very day Las Vegas in mob outlook is still regarded as a "Jewish town." But the realities of the calendar have come into play. When Meyer Lansky passed away in 1983 Jewish participation in syndicate matters declined greatly. Many Jewish mobsters remain in lower levels, but the Jewish syndicate leaders never had the slightest interest in nepotism in so far as the structure of organized crime was concerned and thus have been dying away. They were interested in producing great personal wealth for themselves but not in creating dynasties. It would be wrong to say the Italians or mafiosi have been overly interested in nepotism either. Yet there has been some succession of father-to-son in godfather-like situations, but only when the son seemed capable of taking over, as happened with the Trafficantes in Tampa, the Zerillis in Detroit and, according to the FBI, in the mid-1980s with the Patriarcas in New England.

As a result of this, the Mafia form of the commission has become the effective one, not representative of a purge but rather a reflection of a new reality. And this commission remains what it always has been, the central organ of a confederation of crime families. It was the sort of commission that Luciano envisioned early on, one in which various crime groups remained more or less in charge of their own turf, except where such an outfit was too weak to assert its rights. (Had Luciano been a figure in antebellum America, he would have been an ardent states' righter.)

Thus in recent years the commission has not been powerful. It failed to stifle the Profaci-Gallo conflict or to assert its will during the so-called Banana War. None of this indicates that the Mafia is weakening or dying, but rather that the commission remains less than all powerful. That is the nature of the beast.

In the late 1990s much was made in the press that the commission was no longer meeting and had not done so for two years. The last statement was clearly true, but there was little reason for a commission meeting. The less-than-all-powerful unit functions best in aiding to resolve interfamily disputes but is virtually powerless when the disputes are intrafamily. With increased law enforcement prosecutions, the violence within the mob has consisted of leadership struggles among members. The input of outsiders in such warfare has always proved ineffective. While the Mafia was clearly weakening in the 1990s the impotence of the so-called ruling commission is probably of minor moment.

CONCRETE scam: Huge Mafia construction racket

The concrete racket is one of the most lucrative of all construction shakedowns worked by Mafia mobs across the country. FBI tapes showed that in the 1980s Big Paul Castellano, as head of the Gambino crime family until his murder in 1985, got a cut of every gob of concrete poured on the Manhattan skyline. After his demise the money flowed to his successor and murderer, John Gotti. The Gambinos had a rock-solid grip on the necessary construction unions in the greater New York area. As a result construction costs in New York were and are the highest in the country.

The Gambinos did not control the concrete racket alone. It was a cooperative setup run by four New York families, the others being the Genovese, Colombo and Lucchese families. Only the Bonannos were excluded, for being a most troublesome group and at the time removed as a member of the commission.

The racket worked through the establishment of what the mobs called "the club," a network of mafiosi, union officials and contractors in on the scam. If a contractor wanted any kind of work done, he had to clear it with the mob or their crooked union accomplices. A contractor might need cement trucks to deliver cement for a foundation to be poured; he had to pay off. Otherwise the cement mixers just didn't show up and the contractor had a very expensive hole in the ground. If he needed I beams, he didn't get them without paying, or he'd have a crane and crew drawing wages to do nothing. And frequently he had to pay for mob-connected guys on site doing nothing more laborious than drawing a paycheck.

The concrete payoffs could be very big and brilliantly organized by "the club." The mob selected a total of six firms that could do the concrete work. No other contractor could even bid. Even if an outsider won the job the mob would see to it he got no cement, no girders, nothing. The six firms could bid for any job. The mob did not care who won, but the winning contractor had to pay them 2 percent.

As the State Organized Crime Task Force reported, "On all concrete pouring contracts up to two million dollars, the Colombo family extorted a one percent kickback. Contracts from two to fifteen million dollars were reserved for a 'club' of contractors selected by the Commission. These contractors were required to kick back two percent of the contract price to the Commission," whose members would split the revenues four ways. On a $2 million job the four families thus would cut up $200,000 or $50,000 apiece. On juicier jobs of $10 to $15 million the payoff was all the bigger.

Technically the concrete racket belonged to the Colombos, but the bigger outfits muscled in on the major deals. To keep the Colombos from becoming too embittered, the commission decreed they could keep the revenues from all deals less than $2 million, and they could offer the deals to other contractors as well at the bargain price of 1 percent. The commission regarded the arrangement as most magnanimous. The Colombos might not have agreed since they had started the whole scam, but they were not powerful enough to demand honor among thieves.

However, the biggest mob, the Gambinos, could actually hold up the other families when it came to their fair share. Castellano would set up his own deals on some contracts, with the extra "workmen" all from the Gambinos. And Castellano sometimes demanded and grabbed a bigger slice, such as 30 percent rather than the usual 25 percent. He once told his construction bagman: "We do things on our own. We gotta think of our own. Tell it to the fat guy. Tell Chin." Castellano was thus sticking it to the Genovese family. The fat guy was Genovese boss "Fat Tony" Salerno and the Chin was his tough underboss, Vinnie "The Chin" Gigante.

Castellano's bagman, Alphonse "Funzi" Mosca, observed, "It might get a little raw."

Castellano's taped response: "It does, it does. What are they gonna do, sue me?"

There is no indication that the Genovese family did anything to queer the deal. Later, when Gigante became the Genovese boss and Gotti seized control of the Gambinos, Chin tried to rub out Gotti. He feared that Gotti would move into the Genovese construction rackets in New Jersey.

There was always big money in concrete, and partners could be nice, but having no partners was even nicer.

CONNECTED guys See WISE GUYS AND CONNECTED GUYS

CONNOLLY, John J. (1940–): Baddest of the Boston FBI "goodfellas"

He was the star of Boston. John Connolly was the pride of FBI headquarters in Washington, D.C.—and deservedly so if judged by law enforcement results. He was the best informant handler ever for the Boston office. His informants provided the information that sent mafioso after mafioso to prison and in time destroyed that local organization. And Connolly, always dapper in appearance, would haunt the territory of the Italian mob on the North End looking for confrontations with the leaders for face-downs. The mobsters hated Connolly but could do nothing. He was untouchable, and his actions delighted the press. J. Edgar Hoover considered him one who can do no wrong.

In the meantime, one Mafia operation after another faced slow strangulation under assault by the Boston FBI. What Washington failed to notice or at least consider was what was happening to those gambling, shakedown and other rackets. They did not wither away but were taken over by the Irish Winter Hill mob bossed by another notorious gangster, Whitey Bulger. The result was a de facto Bulger-Connolly combination, or as a federal prosecutor later said, "John Connolly became a Winter Hill gang operative masquerading as an FBI agent." Evidence later showed that while Connolly was supposed to be recruiting mobsters to help in the war against the Mafia, he actually co-opted other gangland activities and became part of their "enterprise," as a memorandum produced by the Office of the U.S. Attorney put it later. For years, it turned out, Connolly took bribes from Bulger, tipped him off to investigations being launched and provided information that led to the murders of rival gangsters.

The extent of Connolly's power was viewed with distaste by other law agencies. One who clearly detested Connolly was Frank Dewan, a Boston police officer. Evidence in a later criminal trial showed that in 1998 Connolly forged a letter under Officer Dewan's name to attempt to deceive federal district judge Mark Wolf about the criminal activities of Stephen "the Rifleman" Flemmi, one of his so-called informants and actually a close ally of Whitey Bulger. "In those days," Dewan later recalled, "it was literally a situation where law enforcement was out of control. John Connolly could do anything he wanted in the city of Boston." What Connolly wanted was for Bulger to represent the dominant underworld group with control of the rackets. The FBI in Boston became the willing servant of the Irish gangsters. Connolly had no trouble getting agents to help his endeavors. It is still a matter for investigation how many federal men were on the take. Connolly's former FBI supervisor later admitted on the witness stand that he took money from Bulger and Flemmi.

There was a large measure of trust between Connolly and Bulger. They had been friends since childhood growing up in the same housing project in South Boston. This relationship actually started Connolly's career in the FBI as a man with a special entree, and in the end it was to ruin his career. The Connolly-Bulger alliance came apart in 1995, five years after Connolly left government service but still maintained his powers unofficially. In 1995 as investigators were closing in on Bulger and Flemmi, Connolly was said to have tipped them off that a racketeering indictment was being readied. Bulger went on the run and was still running in the early 2000s. It was known he had tons of loot with him and access to more. Bulger was last seen in London in 2002 shortly before the FBI discovered safe-deposit boxes linked to him there and in Dublin, Ireland. It may not be necessary to view Connolly's apparent aiding of Bulger's escape as anything more than self-interest. It was a given that several members of the Boston FBI wanted Bulger gone out of fear that he might later turn informant against them.

In 2002 Connolly was found guilty of racketeering and obstruction of justice. He was sentenced to 10 years. In a sense Connolly was less ill-treated than William Bulger, Whitey's brother, a former longtime president of the Massachusetts Senate and for 17 years president of the University of Massachusetts. William Bulger, a Democrat, was forced out and then

Governor Mitt Romney, a Republican, was elected. The governor said William Bulger had given evasive testimony about his brother to the House Government Reform Committee under a grant of immunity. In earlier testimony before a grand jury William Bulger made it clear that his loyalty lay with protecting his brother and not helping the government. In the end he was forced to give up his university position. But he was granted a very lucrative pension and the Boston Democrats seemed to rally overwhelmingly to him. Many said South Boston had "lost a good friend." One told the press, "I think very highly of Billy Bulger and very lowly of the guy who gave him the business, the governor, Mitt, whatever you want to call him. Just because Billy is related to Whitey, it ain't his fault."

There was general agreement that the local FBI would need a number of years to regain the public trust.

See also "FBI BADFELLAS"

CONSIGLIERE: Mafia "adviser"

Probably one of the most nonsensical "revelations" made about the Mafia or Cosa Nostra concerns the supposed role of the *consigliere*. We are told this councilor does all sorts of wondrous criminal things for the mob. It is true that many crime families, but not all, do have the post of consigliere, with differing duties and virtually always of a low-order priority. But if there is anyone within a crime family who has the boss's ear, it is probably not the consigliere but rather the underboss, the number two man in the mob. He generally functions as a kind of chief executive officer, supervises many family operations and sees to it that the orders of the family head are carried out.

The consigliere, often misunderstood to be the chief adviser to the don, his super planner, is a figurehead power, a sort of public relations gimmick invented by Lucky Luciano when he came to power in the early 1930s and organized the national crime syndicate. Luciano, in an attempt to establish peace within the organization, knew most trouble started with underlings either trying to get ahead or reacting to real or imaginary mistreatment. He ordered each crime family to establish the post of consigliere, a neutral middleman who would settle disputes within the family and act as a negotiator with the other families in disputes such as over territories.

Luciano also announced that the consigliere would act as a hearing officer, one who would have to clear any plan to knock off a Mafia member. If the consigliere after hearing the evidence decided the would-be victim was getting a bad rap, he could forbid the hit. This was to give the lower-rank members a sense of protection from the unjust acts of a family boss or any of his capos.

Luciano's fairness initiative might well be considered sheer flimflammery. Since Luciano's day to the present, there is no case on record of a consigliere ruling against the edicts of a boss or other superior. To do so would be inviting the death penalty for the consigliere. Even in those cases when a consigliere is allowed to rule on a matter with no interference from above, his decision as often as not ends up either being family-aligned or ignored.

If the consigliere was the brain trust of Mafia legend, it would follow that somewhere along the line a consigliere would have become a boss, perhaps even by the use of cunning force. Yet a run through a roster of consiglieres among the New York families or any other crime family (not always an easy matter since the post is so insignificant that law enforcement agencies often disagree on who holds the post in a particular family) indicates none of the ilk even near top status.

Though more glamorous in books and movies, the consigliere job is most likely dead-end. A better road to advancement lies in doing duty as a chauffeur.

See also CHAUFFEURS

CONSTRUCTION rackets: Still unstoppable in the new Mafia era

In the smashing crackdown on all sorts of Mafia rackets in the 1990s, especially hard hit were the crime families' activities in construction. In the post-2000 era of the rising new Mafia, few criminal activities have come back so quickly as mob control of construction. Shortly thereafter, newspapers in New York were noting the rapid comeback of the mobs there. A typical example was the arrest of 38 individuals, many connected with the Lucchese crime family, once perhaps the top dog in the racket in the East. Police officials concluded the crackdown on mob wise guys and associates indicated mob control of construction in New York remained vibrant than it had been in a decade. Manhattan district attorney, the near-legendary Robert M. Morgenthau, charged that the 38, including union officials, contractors and reputed mobsters, had engaged in bribery, bid-rigging schemes and other ploys that siphoned millions of dollars from construction projects over the previous two years. Among those charged in a 57-count indictment were 11 union officials, some long tainted with mob dealings over the years. One so identified was Michael Forde, head of the District Council of Carpenters as well Local 608. Forde's father headed the local and was convicted of taking bribes in 1990. Morgenthau zeroed in especially on Steven L. Crea, the acting boss of the Lucchese crime family who was said to have played a role in construction schemes for decades.

The setup by the 38 clearly followed standard operating procedures in typical construction rackets. The racketeers siphoned millions from projects throughout the city. Money was diverted to the Luccheses and its partners, corrupt union officials and contractors. Morgenthau said, "Despite law enforcement successes over the years, the indictment demonstrates that the fight against organized crime is far from over" and "still exacts a tremendous cost from the city." Among the victims of such rackets, the district attorney said, were union workers deprived of jobs by their leaders, and nonunion workers who replaced them and were paid far below union wage and received no benefits. Also victimized were honest contractors who were simply frozen out of the bidding by the mob's corrupt alliances, under which their chosen companies underbid other firms. The Luccheses installed what was called a 5 percent "mob tax" on construction jobs. Particularly hard hit were a number of schools and several road and bridge repair projects. Allegedly looted was a fund of $32 million to build modular classrooms.

Construction looting schemes abounded in the past and still do today. For years past the mobs have worked the "concrete racket," which made some of the largest building firms pay out millions in bribes to get concrete for their projects. No payoffs, no concrete, and no concrete meant no structures could stand. A more simplified scheme is the so-called gravel tax levied by the mobs so that builders could avoid a "hole in the ground" scam. The mobs used their mob-connected trucks to deliver the vital gravel as needed and usually at competitive prices, except for one detail. The load on each truck was never quite filled. What can be carried by five trucks, for instance, would be supplied with six. Construction

men know what is going on and do not complain at being billed for six loads of gravel. It's far better than paying nothing for no loads, which can leave the contractor with a dirt road or an unfilled hole in the ground. What happens in some cases is that the contractors themselves get sucked into the racket. The mob cuts them in for a share of the sixth truck's revenues, and the contractors can also list the cost of the loads for the sixth truck as part of their inventory depletion. It is impossible for investigators to go about counting the pieces of gravel in a load, so the scheme just widens and grows. To hear the mobsters tell it, "We ain't doing nothing business itself doesn't do all the time. We just make the job easier all around."

What riled many of the 38 arrestees was that they were arrested in lightning raids rather than simply summoned to report for court appearances. The latter, they said, would have been the businesslike way of doing things, and today in the construction rackets business is business. One thing is certain, construction rackets thrive because of the interlocking interests that can evolve to make business boom and difficult to uproot.

CONTRACT: Murder assignment

It is not accidental that a mob killing is called a contract because murders are, in fact, strictly business matters. And in business, subtlety is often good policy; the use of code words and the method by which the orders are given tend to insulate the man who gives the order.

The mafioso method of contract killing is essentially the same as the formula set forth for Murder, Incorporated, in the 1930s. One of the most knowledgeable reporters on crime, Meyer Berger of the *New York Times,* once explained the technique that came about "when the head men from different cities met and agreed to adopt new rules for the conduct of murder under a loosely formed national syndicate."

He said, "Murder is not the Combination's business. It does no murder for outsiders and no killing for a fee. Indeed, its revised rules sharply restrict the use of homicide to business needs and have probably reduced rather than increased the total number of U.S. murders committed annually. The new handbook sternly forbids murder for personal or romantic reasons, or even for revenge. Executive heads of the Combination debate each murder before causing it to occur, much as a Wall Street syndicate might discuss a maneuver in the stock market." By and large these rules were adhered to (although certainly the murder-happy Vito Genovese had killings done for each of the taboo reasons—for personal reasons, for revenge and even for matters of the heart).

Once a contract is ordered, the wheels are set in motion to guarantee protection for the party ordering the execution. He is isolated from the trigger man, never saying a word to him about the job. First the contract is passed to a second party. This party alone assigns the hit man or killer. In fact, very often even this party will pass the order on to yet another party. Since all negotiations are handled on a one-to-one basis, it does not matter if eventually someone in the line of command talks. What is missing is the vital corroborative witness who knows the complete case.

The actual assassins are simply given the identity of the victim, background on his habits and a place where he can most likely be found. Sometimes they are given a spotter or fingerman who points out the victim. Once the murder is finished, the killers vanish, notifying no one except the person who had given the specific orders. The information could be relayed up the line if necessary but essentially what the police are left with is a killing with no clues and no likely suspects because very often the killers do not even know their victim. Often the conduit between top mob bosses and Murder, Inc., was the organization's chief executioner, Albert Anastasia.

When Anastasia himself was murdered in 1957, the execution followed the same Murder, Inc., rules. Although there were no arrests in the case, it is known that the order originated with Vito Genovese who passed it on to Carlo Gambino who relayed it to Joe Profaci who assigned it to the murderous Gallo brothers, who may have carried out the murder themselves or passed it on one more step to the actual gunners.

Clearly, as some reporters at the time noted, Anastasia himself would have approved of the way his murder was handled. Authorities often eventually learn the details of a great many contract killings through informers, among them such classic characters as Abe Reles, Joe Valachi, Vinnie Teresa and Jimmy Fratianno, but almost never do they get a conviction. As can best be determined the conviction rate in contract murders runs about one-tenth of 1 percent.

COONAN, Jimmy (1946–): Boss of the Westies

Some would say that Jimmy Coonan was a throwback to the old-time Irish hoodlums who once ravaged New York. But wild as he was, Coonan also solidified, by cunning, deception, deceit and sheer effrontery, a renewed tie with the Mafia that had first been forged decades earlier by Owney Madden and Lucky Luciano. This new alliance held until the 1980s when it was shattered by the vicious nature of the Westies themselves, and Coonan in particular.

With a tight hold on the Westies' stronghold of Hell's Kitchen, the west side of Manhattan along the Hudson River, Coonan climbed to the top as the meanest and most brutal Irish hood in recent decades, cementing his power while still in his 20s. A blue-eyed former choirboy, Jimmy could be among the most affable of gangsters, whose ranks he joined at age 17. Unfortunately no one could predict when his explosive temper would lead to an outbreak of violence.

His vicious nature made him a brute among brutes, and with only a couple of dozen supporters he formed the Westies gang and destroyed other mobster groupings in the area. The Westies gained strangleholds on a number of rackets in their domain, including loan-sharking, drug distribution, numbers, counterfeiting, labor racketeering, extortion and murder for hire.

Of course the most important murders involved guaranteeing the sanctity of their turf. It soon became a matter of Hell's Kitchen lore—and fear—how the Westies dismembered their victims and disposed of the grisly remains. Coonan stressed his credo: "No corpus delicti, no crime, no police investigation." Rarely did even the tiniest part of any Westies victim ever turn up.

Under Coonan's supervision the corpses were chopped up. In a seminar on dismemberment, Coonan taught his boys, pointing out for example that severing an elbow was just about the toughest task. The cut-up jobs were done in bathtubs or in old-fashioned kitchen sinks with built-in tubs for laundry. The parts were placed in strong plastic garbage bags and taken to places of disposal. One favorite destination was a sewage plant on Ward's Island in the East River where a confederate working there was tipped handsomely for depositing the grim contents into the sewage being treated that day.

With a few exceptions the mafiosi left the Westies alone, feeling any effort to squash them would result in long bloody warfare since the Westies were incapable of foregoing vengeance for any bloodletting of their ranks.

The Westies, however, did not return the favor. They thought nothing of murdering mob guys who tried to establish themselves in Westie territory. They reverted to an old Irish gangster custom of kidnapping Mafia gangsters for ransom. The victims were released after the money was paid—unless Jimmy Coonan had a whim to kill them anyway.

Actually Jimmy had a master plan. He wanted in to the Gambino family as a special adjunct, a goal achieved not through diplomacy but by demonstrating how much trouble the Westies could be.

Coonan's most daring caper was to murder a big-money mob loan shark named Ruby Stein. Stein did millions of dollars of business lending out money and was totally trusted by the Gambinos who bankrolled him. Ambushing Ruby Stein in a tavern, the Westies appropriated his black book, which listed all outstanding debtors. The Gambinos knew little about who was in the book, expecting Stein to handle all the business and refer them only to defaulters who needed extra pressure to pay up. Without Stein's black book, the Gambinos didn't know who owed them money. Jimmy Coonan did, and he collected from many of them.

The mob men suspected the Westies, but they lacked proof and were unwilling to risk gang warfare by pursuing the matter. Under Paul Castellano, who generally looked for a peaceful way to settle problems, it was decided that overtures should be made to the Westies, exactly what Coonan wanted. The mob would leave the Irish their rackets, taking only a 10 percent cut, and also give the Westies a piece of other Mafia rackets. Coonan looked like a great Irish patriot to his men. And Castellano was not displeased; he now had an extra troop of killers who strengthened his own position within his crime family and with other families as well.

Coonan and his boys handled a number of mob hits, and Jimmy constantly asked for more assignments. "We could use the dough," he explained. In fact, he didn't need the money, having by now accumulated millions, but it provided a cover for the Stein affair. Besides that, Coonan and the Westies truly thrived on hired rubouts, not only for the fee involved, but for the bonus of added cuts in certain enterprises.

The Westies passed from one Gambino handler to another, finally ending up under the supervision of a rising capo, John Gotti. When Coonan first met Gotti, he was much impressed and reported back to his followers: "I just met a greaseball tougher than we are." It was a high compliment indeed and solidified the relationship between the pair for the rest of Coonan's reign.

Eventually, Coonan became more and more restrained in dealing with his own men, and disputes flourished. The Westies reverted to their old custom of pulling unauthorized jobs and killings. And even worse they returned to victimizing one another. Perhaps to accommodate those chaffing at his rule—and to cool off murder plots against himself—Jimmy sought to placate things by purging certain elements. He apparently took part in a plot to frame his No. 2, Mickey Featherstone, for a murder he had no part in. Featherstone could not believe Jimmy had betrayed him, and he finally turned informer to save himself.

That proved to be the end for Jimmy Coonan and was one of the main reasons for Gotti's fall from power as well. Jimmy was convicted under the RICO (1970 Racketeer Influenced and Corrupt Organization Act) statute and sentenced to 75 years. Gotti got life. But the pair's special relationship continued after a fashion. Both were sent into virtual solitary confinement in what mobsters consider a hellhole, Marion Federal Penitentiary, a prison with special space reserved for the toughest and meanest organized crime figures. They were prison mates but were destined never to see each other.

See also WESTIES

COPPOLA, Michael "Trigger Mike" (1904–1966): Syndicate capo

Trigger Mike Coppola earned notoriety in Mafia and popular folklore. A raging sadist and brutal triggerman, his violent nature carried over to his personal life. Allegedly, he arranged to have his first wife murdered in the hospital where she had given birth. Fear of Coppola and his mob's vengeance drove his second wife to suicide. In Florida, after Mike's death, locals for years pointed out the old Coppola house. Haunted, they said. The tale ran that Wife No. 2's ghost was searching for the millions Trigger Mike was known to have squirreled away.

When Lucky Luciano went to prison in the 1930s and Vito Genovese fled to Europe to avoid a murder rap, Coppola had taken over much of the New York crime family's rackets, including the lucrative artichoke racket. He also ran much of the crime family's numbers operation in Harlem. His net was estimated at around $1 million a year—not bad for a man with little on the ball other than a penchant for violence.

Sometimes Coppola had trouble keeping track of all the money coming his way. In 1960 Coppola became one of the first 11 undesirables listed in the Black Book issued by Nevada state officials. All eleven were barred from the casinos; in Coppola's case it was like keeping him from visiting his money. An oft-told underworld story concerns the time he woke up in the middle of the night suddenly recalling that he had forgotten a package in the freezer of one of his favorite night spots. A hurried phone call brought delivery of the package to his door and a sweating Coppola spent the rest of the night thawing out $219,000 of mob money, which he had charge of distributing the following morning.

One need not speculate what Coppola would have done had the money been gone. He would simply have killed off a few employees at the joint and blamed them for taking the money. Coppola was always ready to kill almost anybody to advance his fortunes or protect himself. His first wife, according to the subsequent testimony of his second wife, Ann, happened to be around when her husband and another hood discussed plans for the murder of a New York Republican political worker, Joseph Scottoriggio. The first Mrs. Coppola had been called to testify against her husband in the case, but her appearance was postponed because of her pregnancy. She gave birth to a baby daughter and then conveniently expired in her hospital bed. Coppola's second wife, Ann, later charged that Trigger Mike had bragged about killing Wife No. 1 to keep her from talking.

Ann Coppola was to learn that marriage to Trigger Mike was a living hell and that his first wife was probably better off dead. At their honeymoon party Coppola entertained the guests by taking a shot at Ann. When she became pregnant, Coppola called in a mob doctor to perform an abortion on the kitchen table with Trigger Mike helping out. He was to help out on three more abortions; Ann realized he got kicks out of it. In 1960 Ann discovered her husband was supplying drugs to her teenage daughter by a previous marriage. She filed for divorce and testified in an income tax case against Coppola, who sent strongarm men to kidnap her and administer a harsh Mafia beating. Found severely mauled on an isolated

beach, she recovered and prepared again to testify against him.

Finally, Trigger Mike threw in the towel and pleaded guilty, taking the fall as the mob ordered. The mob had decided they didn't want their racket secret revealed in open court. Trigger Mike served a year in Atlanta Penitentiary and then was put on an additional four years' probation.

Meanwhile, Ann had squirreled away something like a quarter million dollars in underworld money and secretly fled to Europe to escape the mob's hit men. In 1962, in Rome, she would run no more. She wrote a final letter to Internal Revenue, addressing certain portions of it to Attorney General Robert F. Kennedy. Then she wrote a farewell to Trigger Mike, saying: "Mike Coppola, someday, somehow, a person or God or the law shall catch up with you, you yellow-bellied bastard. You are the lowest and biggest coward I have had the misfortune to meet." Then she wrote in lipstick on the wall over her hotel bed: "I have always suffered, I am going to kill

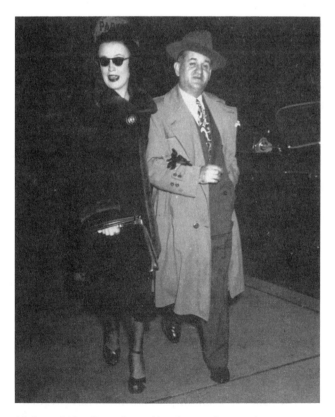

Mafioso Mike Coppola and his first wife together in a happier moment, before he allegedly had her killed in the hospital where she had given birth to a baby daughter. She could, it was said, link Coppola to a murder.

myself. Forget me." She took a dozen sleeping pills and lapsed quietly into death.

Trigger Mike got out of prison in 1963 and he spent his remaining years in disgrace with the mob, both for letting his wife learn his secrets and for being unable to keep her mouth shut. Trigger Mike whiled away his time growing orchids. He might well have been disturbed in even that pursuit had Ann Coppola's last request been honored. She wanted to be cremated and her ashes dropped over his house.

CORALLO, Anthony "Tony Ducks" (1913–2000): Lucchese crime family boss

Admiring mafiosi dubbed Anthony Corallo "Tony Ducks" because he was successful for so many years in ducking convictions. Later, the bloom would come off his sparkling record.

Born in 1913, Corallo grew up in a tough East Harlem neighborhood. His rap sheet dates to 1929 when he was arrested on a grand larceny charge. Early on, as a member of the Gagliano family, the Lucchese predecessor, he got six months in prison after police linked him to a cache of narcotics worth $150,000. After that Corallo shifted more to union activities and gained control of several union locals, the most important of which was Local 239 of the Teamsters in New York City. In 1958 a report of the McClellan Committee stated: "Our study into the New York phony local situation revealed an alarming picture of the extent to which gangsters led by John Dioguardi [Johnny Dio] and Anthony (Tony Ducks) Corallo infiltrated the labor movement in the nation's largest city, using their union positions for purposes of extortion, bribery, and shakedowns. The fact that one of the nation's most powerful labor leaders, James R. Hoffa, the international president of the Teamsters, used Dioguardi and Corallo in his efforts to capture control of the union in New York City only serves to underline the importance of gangster infiltration in the labor movement."

Evidence indicated that Corallo had siphoned off $69,000 from Local 239 funds by listing dummies on the payroll. He invoke the Fifth Amendment 83 times before the committee, and answered no questions about a court-authorized bugging of a New York apartment in which Hoffa was heard giving what appeared to be approval for Corallo to loot union funds provided he didn't get caught.

Anthony Corallo, boss of the Lucchese crime family in the 1970s and 1980s, was nicknamed "Tony Ducks" long before by gangsters for his success in ducking convictions.

In 1962 Corallo was hit with a two-year sentence for paying a bribe of $35,000 to New York Supreme Court Justice James Vincent Keogh and Assistant U.S. Attorney Elliott Kahaner in an effort to get a light sentence for a Corallo associate. Later on in the 1960s Corallo got four and one-half years for conspiring to bribe former New York City Water Commissioner James L. Marcus who was in deep financial trouble and agreed to cash payments from Corallo in exchange for certain emergency cleaning contracts to be awarded to a party named by the mobster. The first such contract was for $835,000.

Also implicated in the case, which later expanded a planned shakedown of the Consolidated Edison utility company was ex-Tammany Hall boss Carmine DeSapio. Marcus as commissioner of the Department of Water Supply, Gas, and Electricity had iron-fisted power over permits Consolidated Edison needed. DeSapio was to act as contact man with certain representatives of the utility. Marcus testified on the Consolidated Edison plot—he got 15 months for the reservoir conspiracy—which the conspirators figured could involve millions of dollars. Marcus said the pressures put on him were so intense that at times he considered suicide. Eventually DeSapio and Corallo were convicted and the former Tammany Hall leader got a two-year prison term.

In the 1980s Corallo was facing charges of bid-rigging schemes concerning garbage disposals on New York's Long Island and involving political figures "on both sides of the aisle." Then there were federal charges that Corallo was a member of the national commission of the Mafia. Part of the government's case came from a sophisticated bug placed in a Jaguar in which Corallo was often driven. It was said that other mafiosi both in the Lucchese and especially in the other crime families were upset not only that Corallo had been so careless as to let the bug go undetected but also by what he had said disparagingly about other Mafia men.

That may or may not have been true. Certainly, he was a counterpoint to the dapper John Gotti who had by then taken over the powerful Gambino crime family. The Lucchese family had always had a penchant for shying away from the limelight—with some exceptions—and certainly Corallo hardly approved of a mob boss outfit that could light up a room. Corallo was dapper enough wearing gray cardigan sweaters. Yet war by other families against the Luccheses was unthinkable. The Luccheses might have been smaller than either the Gambinos or the Genoveses, but they would tolerate no incursions on their territories. Unlike Gotti and some other younger mob leaders, Corallo may not have fit in with the flashier world of the mob that emerged in the 1980s. Before that in Corallo's world bosses were generally rather insulated, prison sentences were rather minimal, and people who had risen to Corallo's level were well tested. The newer ones tended to be untested and untrained. Corallo held them in contempt. But whether Gotti would have ever moved against Corallo is rather doubtful.

Still, because of the successful bugging of his Jaguar, the popular belief that by the late 1980s Corallo would be "ducking" for his life gained currency in the media. The matter of mob vengeance became moot when he was convicted in 1986 for being a member of the Commission, and he was sentenced to 100 years. He died August 23, 2000, in a federal prison hospital in Springfield, Missouri. Without his strong leadership, the Lucchese family had descended to awesome bloodletting throughout the 1990s.

See also LUCCHESE CRIME FAMILY

CORLEONE, Sicily: Mafia spawning ground

It is fitting that the crime family boss in Mario Puzo's *The Godfather* is named Don Corleone, since that town in Sicily has long been regarded as one of the hotbeds of the Mafia and, for many years, one of the main suppliers of Mafia manpower to the United States.

Many of today's mobsters, especially in the New York–New Jersey area, trace their roots back to Corleone. As a matter of historical dispute it might be said that the west coast town of Castellammare del Golfo may have produced more big-time American mafiosi but for sheer numbers Corleone remains unmatched.

A once-prosperous town with a modern population of 18,000, Corleone was virtually denuded of male inhabitants through various Mafia wars. In the period between 1944 and 1948 the town suffered 153 Mafia murders. Estimates at various times placed the number of the town's adult males who had been convicted of crimes and were serving prison sentences or awaiting sentencing at upwards of 80 percent; in recent years working-age males have made up only 10 percent of the population.

Among the Corleonians who transferred to America were such worthies as the murderous Lupo the Wolf (Ignazio Saietta), Ciro Terranova and the Morello family, a huge band of brothers, half-brothers and brothers-in-law who were so numerous that they composed a "crime family" on their own. Antonio Morello, the eldest brother in this nuclear family, was described by police as being responsible for between 30 and 40 murders on his own, and Joe Morello was for a time regarded the Mafia boss of New York City.

COROZZO, Joseph "JoJo" (1943–): Suspected new Gambino boss

By 2003 there was much speculation about who was boss of the Gambino crime family following the reign of the Gottis. Many observers never accepted the idea that John Gotti's brother Peter had been filling the role, and some within the mob snicker at that idea, pointing out that Peter Gotti was never up to snuff for such a role (his nickname was "Retard") and had merely served as a messenger boy for his imprisoned brother until his death. These insiders have maintained that later prosecutions of Peter indicated that prosecutors were only interested in the publicity that any Gotti name could accrue. Prior to Peter's time in the sun, John's son "Junior" had been accepted as the Gambino boss, although like his uncle, he was not regarded as a brilliant boss.

A major suspect as the present top wise guy is Joseph "JoJo" Corozzo, a former driver and lookout for Dapper Don John Gotti. Unlike other Gambino wise guys, Corozzo has been described inside the mob as having a nose for trouble and smelling a rat. In any event federal investigators looking into the family were said to have been unsuccessful in taping Corozzo discussing criminal matters with Mikey Scars DiLeonardo, regarded as a major mob turncoat out to "sink the Gambinos." One thing Scars failed to do was set up Corozzo to talk. It has been said that Scars has sold prosecutors on the intelligence that Corozzo is the big guy in the Gambino family. Corozzo canceled meetings with Scars and, according to some insiders, has come to believe that Scars will try to become the "rat of the 21st century," one who could do perhaps more damage to the top Mafia crime family than even Sammy the Bull Gravano.

The drama of the fencing between Scars and Corozzo has been billed as a battle between, as the mob puts it, "the rat trying to bury us" and "JoJo the rat-sniffer." If Corozzo ends up on top, he will certainly become storied as the new teflon don.

See also DiLEONARDO, MICHAEL "MIKEY SCARS"

COSA Nostra

It is remarkable to consider that, until the appearance of Joe Valachi as an informer in 1963, the public had never heard of the term *Cosa Nostra*. Even the exhaustive Kefauver hearings of about a decade earlier had failed to uncover the term. And though seemingly a household expression today, crime family circles outside New York seemed to have had no knowledge of the term *Cosa Nostra*. In Buffalo the crime family was called "the Arm," in Chicago "the Outfit," in New England "the Office."

When and where, then, Cosa Nostra? Valachi didn't invent the term, but it was carefully nurtured by federal authorities in reviews of his testimony. In a literal sense, it means nothing more than "our thing." But for FBI chief J. Edgar Hoover who insisted for decades that there was no such thing as organized crime or the Mafia, *Cosa Nostra* meant "save face." Says crime historian Richard Hammer, "In order to get Hoover off the hook, a new name had to be created, hence Costa Nostra." This allowed Hoover to say in effect, "Oh, yes, we've always known about that."

Actually the FBI had been aware of the term in the previous year or two when it finally made efforts to probe Mafia business. All they had to go on were passing comments picked up in wiretaps and the like in which various mafiosi made comments in Italian about "cosa nostra," or "this thing of ours."

It was enough for the FBI, which attempted to carry its save-Hoover program even further by adding a *la* to the name so that it could offer the press a convenient new acronym, "LCN," to go along with FBI. Unfortunately, the press was unimpressed and never picked up on it, preferring to stick with *Cosa Nostra* or, to Hoover's continuing discomfort, with *Mafia*. The addition of the *la* to *cosa nostra* just added a note of silliness to the matter; in literal translation it meant "the our thing."

Even Peter Maas, author of *The Valachi Papers*, seems to draw back somewhat from the FBI-inspired formalization of the term, noting in a footnote, "It can be argued that Cosa Nostra is a generic, rather than a proper, name." He goes on: "It is really an academic question, since whatever the term, it adds up to the same thing."

The fact remains that Cosa Nostra is an overblown phenomenon with supposed rituals more often ignored than honored within the mobs. It would be hard indeed to visualize the Chicago Outfit, the descendant of the Capone mob, and probably the most ethnically integrated crime family of all, going in for such nonsense as blood rituals and oaths and formal dogmatic ties to old Sicily. When in recent years the L.A. crime family sought to induct a new member it discovered there was no one around who either knew the words to the oath or could use the Italian dialect.

It is of course too late to purge Cosa Nostra from the crime lexicon, but it must be remembered it is nothing more than an alias for Mafia. And both Cosa Nostra and present-day Mafia are distinctly American, having little to do with the Old World Mafia (other than for business reasons, such as narcotics). In that sense Cosa Nostra represents the new Mafia, one that purged with blood the old Mustache Petes who did not understand the melting pot that is organized crime in America.

It would even be wrong to regard Cosa Nostra as an Italian-American invention. The organization of Cosa Nostra, if not the actual name, which again is no more than "this thing of ours" talk between mobsters, was as much Jewish-made as Italian. It was Meyer Lansky who insisted to Lucky Luciano that there was a need to give a special name to the Italian members of their new national crime syndicate. He said, "There are lots of these guys who ain't able to give up all the old ways so fast. You gotta feed 'em some sugar that they'll understand. You've got to give the new setup a name; after all, what the fuck is any business or company without a name? A guy don't walk into an automobile showroom and say, 'I'll take that car over there, the one without a name.'"

They settled on the name Unione Sicilliano, even though it was the name, with slight variation in spelling, of a long-established Sicilian fraternal organization. Thus while both Luciano and Lansky when talking to other big shots used the terms *outfit* or *syndicate,* the lower-rung Italian mobsters spoke of "Unione" or "arm" or "office" or "mob" or "Mafia"—or even "our thing."

Cosa Nostra has thus matured from its genesis as legend to reality. The Cosa Nostra or Mafia exists. It is not merely, as some writers have put it, "a state of mind." The Cosa Nostra, the Mafia, exists not so much in the eyes of the beholder as in the eyes of the belonger.

See also MAFIA

COSTELLO, Frank (1891–1973): Prime minister of the underworld

A murder mastermind and cunning crime strategist, he was also dapper, a gambler, an ex-bootlegger, an almost very wholesome fellow—that's what Frank Costello was.

The engaging tales about Costello are legion. He told anyone who'd listen that he and Joe Kennedy up in Boston went way back—to bootlegging, in fact. And he was always groomed to staid perfection. There was the time he was on trial and his lawyer asked him to stop wearing $350 suits, which were hurting his case with the jury, and to switch to clothes from the plain pipe rack. Costello was adamant. "I'm sorry, counselor," he said, "I'd rather blow the goddamn case."

A psychiatrist might deduce much from the behavior of a gangster whose obsession with "looking aces" was more important than avoiding a criminal conviction. And yes, Costello did have a psychiatrist, Dr. Richard H. Hoffman, an expert with a Park Avenue clientele. After two years of treatment the newspapers found out about it, and Hoffman admitted he was treating Costello. He said he had advised him to mingle with a better class of people. Angrily, Costello broke off with Hoffman, saying he had introduced Hoffman to a better class of people than Hoffman had introduced him to.

Of course, Costello's "better class of people" were in the political world. He exercised more political pull than any other major executive within organized crime and the national syndicate. Frank Costello stood for the "big fix." He bought favors and thought nothing of spending the mob's money in advance to make sure he could get them when needed. Scores of political leaders and judges were beholden to him. He dangled more of New York's Tammany Hall bosses on a string than any mayor or governor or president. The press described him as "owning" them all, from Christy Sullivan to Mike Kennedy, from Frank Rosetti to Bert Stand, and from Hugo Rogers to Carmine DeSapio. Costello had done them favors, had raised money for them, had delivered votes through political clubs he controlled when such actions really counted. And when it came time for political appointments Costello practically exercised the same sort of duties the U.S. Senate had—to advise and consent. Tammany boss Rogers put the situation in the proper perspective when he said, "If Costello wanted me, he would send for me."

When it came to judges, at various levels, Costello referred to them as "my boys." In 1943 Manhattan District Attorney Frank Hogan obtained a wiretap on Costello's telephone, and his investigators were party to an illuminating conversation on August 23 between Costello and Thomas Aurelio just minutes after Aurelio was informed he was getting the Democratic nomination to a state supreme court judgeship:

Frank Costello, longtime "Prime Minister of the Underworld"—meaning he handled mob dealings with police, judges and politicians—survived an assassination attempt and lived out his years as a Long Island squire.

"How are you, and thanks for everything," Aurelio said.

"Congratulations," Costello answered. "It went over perfect. When I tell you something is in the bag, you can rest assured."

"It was perfect," Aurelio said. "It was fine."

"Well, we will all have to get together and have dinner some night real soon."

"That would be fine," the judge-to-be replied. "But right now I want to assure you of my loyalty for all you have done. It is unwavering."

Despite the revelation of the wiretap, Aurelio won the judgeship after beating off disbarment proceedings.

Clearly, when Costello said something was in the bag, it was, and in a mighty big bag. Indeed, Costello may have been "an almost very wholesome fellow," but he was definitely a corrupter, a character who furnished step stools for slot machines so little kids

could get high enough to plop in their nickels. He was a murderer, not with a garrote or gun, but with upraised hand, voting the death penalty or handling the money payoff for a hit.

Born Francesco Castiglia in Lauropoli, Calabria, in southwest Italy, four-year-old Costello came to New York with his family. The family settled in East Harlem, already turning into a slum area. When Frank was 14 he robbed the landlady of his parents' flat, wearing a black handkerchief over his face as a mask. The landlady nevertheless recognized him and informed the police. Frank made up an alibi that was accepted by the police, and he beat the rap. In 1908 and 1912, he was charged with assault and robbery but was discharged on both occasions. Frank's brother Eddie, 10 years his senior, was engaged in gang activities, and he brought Frank into the fold. At 24, Costello was sentenced to a year in prison for carrying a gun. He was not to return to prison for the next 37 years.

In the early days of Prohibition, his best friends were Lucky Luciano, a Sicilian, and Meyer Lansky, a Polish Jew. Costello never seemed particularly bigoted about crime, possibly because his hatred for his father diminished any bias he may have had about the values of the "old country" Italians. The trio were to become the most important figures in the formation of the national crime syndicate during the 1930s. While Luciano and Lansky took care of organizing criminal outfits, Costello developed contacts and influence among the police and politicians. As the eldest of the trio, Costello had the maturity to impress those to be bribed.

By the mid-1920s the trio's various criminal enterprises were making them very rich. To protect their interests, they were paying, according to statements attributed to Luciano, $10,000 a week in "grease" directly into the police commissioner's office. Later, during the regimes of commissioners Joseph A. Warren and Grover A. Whalen, the amount was said to have doubled. In 1929, just after the stock market crash, Costello told Luciano he had to advance Whalen $30,000 to cover his margin calls in the market. "What could I do?" Costello told Luciano. "I hadda give it to him. We own him." It never occurred to his partners—and later on to other members of the crime syndicate—to question Costello on how he dispensed mob money. Costello was regarded as a man of honor on such matters. Besides, the results were there to see, with cases never brought to court, complaints dropped, sentences fixed, and so on.

Costello became a vital cog in the national crime syndicate, which could not operate successfully without protection. The gangs cooperated and Costello supplied the protection. As part of his reward, Costello got the rights to gambling in the lucrative Louisiana market, where Huey Long was entrenched, hands wide open. And he was hailed by all the crime family heads as the "Prime Minister of the Underworld," the man who dealt with the "foreign dignitaries"—the police, judges and politicos.

Costello is generally credited with neutralizing J. Edgar Hoover and the FBI. For years and years, Hoover maintained that there was no Mafia and no organized crime in America. Costello helped keep it that way, not through bribery, but rather through a simple form of "stroking." The FBI chief was an inveterate horseplayer, a big gambler who claimed never to bet more than $2 a race but used FBI agents to scurry off to make bets for him at the $100 window. Through Frank Erickson, the syndicate's top bookmaker, Costello would learn when a "hot horse" was running (in Mafia parlance, a hot horse does not mean one with a *good* chance of winning, but a *sure thing*) and he would pass the word to columnist Walter Winchell, a mutual friend of both Costello and Hoover. Winchell slipped it to Hoover, and there is considerable evidence from FBI agents about how pleasant Hoover could be after he had a satisfactory day at the track. (There is ample evidence from FBI and Winchell staffers of Hoover's horse betting and of Erickson-Costello-Winchell tips to the FBI head.)

And what was Hoover's attitude toward bookmaking and gambling, which with the repeal of Prohibition became the chief source of income for the national syndicate? "The FBI," Hoover declared, "has much more important functions to accomplish than arresting gamblers all over the country."

In such a cozy arrangement Costello and Hoover lived happily ever after, and the Mafia and organized crime continued to grow.

Costello groupies from the press and admirers have tried to whitewash Costello by noting that he was not a murderer. But he did sit in on all syndicate decisions concerning major hits. If he was at times a moderating force (too much bloodletting complicated his bribery activities), he did join in on murder plots. Within the underworld, Costello is generally credited with being the man who saw to it that Abe "Kid Twist" Reles, the "canary" in the Murder, Inc., exposures, stopped talking, permanently. Among those so stating have been Luciano, Lansky, and another leading Jewish mobster, Doc Stacher. As Stacher put it in an interview with journalists in the 1970s:

> . . . he got to work and found out which room Reles was in at the Half Moon [the Coney Island hotel where Reles was being kept under protective custody]—not so hard because the cops had a round-the clock guard on it. But then Frank really showed his muscle. He knew so many top-ranking cops that he got the names of the detectives who were guarding Reles. He never asked exactly how Costello did it, but one evening he came back with a smile and said, "It's cost us a hundred grand, but Kid Twist Reles is about to join his maker."

Costello's vast influence at so many levels of government was laid bare at the Kefauver Committee hearings of the early 1950s. While Costello insisted that only his hands and not his face be shown on television, that minor nervous finger ballet hardly covered up his anxiety. When he left the stand, Costello knew his days as Prime Minister were rapidly coming to an end. He had become too hot.

In that period—with Luciano deported to Italy and his hopes of being allowed back to the United States shattered, and Joe Adonis being harassed and facing the same fate—Costello faced tax problems that would deliver his second prison term. Meanwhile, the ambitious Vito Genovese moved to take over Costello's position atop the Luciano crime family. Costello needed muscle for support; he depended on mobster Willie Moretti, who bossed an army of at least 50 or 60 gunners, but Moretti, losing his mind from syphilis, was recommended by Genovese for assassination to protect mob secrets. Costello determined he needed a new prop. He decided to build up Albert Anastasia, at the time an underling to Brooklyn Mafia boss Vince Mangano. Anastasia hated Mangano but probably did not have the brains to topple him on his own. Costello rather obviously put him up to murdering Mangano and taking over. Now Anastasia, formerly the chief executioner of Murder, Inc., had the gunners of an entire crime family to come to Costello's assistance. Genovese was countered for a solid half dozen years. Only in 1957 did he finally dare try to have Costello assassinated. Costello survived the murder attempt, the assailant's bullets just grazing his scalp. But later that year Genovese had Anastasia knocked off. It finally looked like Genovese had won. Costello developed a firm desire to retire from mob activities, to battle instead the federal government over taxes and his possible deportation.

Costello still owed Genovese one. Together with Lansky, Luciano and Carlo Gambino, they worked out a cunning plot to have the government take Genovese off their hands. Gambino had connived with Genovese to erase Anastasia and take over the crime family himself, but now he switched sides because he did not want Genovese as an overboss. The four involved Genovese in a narcotics scheme, and when he was deeply involved, they tipped off authorities. In 1959, Genovese was put away for 15 years on a charge the government itself must have sensed odd. During Genovese's imprisonment in Atlanta—where he was to die 10 years later—Costello did a short stretch there as well. The pair had what was said to have been a "sentimental reconciliation." Still, when Costello left the prison he must have had pleasant thoughts about Genovese remaining behind.

During the last decade of his life, Costello shuttled between his Long Island estate and his Manhattan apartment, living the life of a country squire and a retired don—despite the occasional newspaper stories that he was back on top. When he was buried in 1973 his widow, Bobbie, insisted that none of his underworld cronies show up or send flower-bedecked tributes.

One who did show up was a distant cousin who as she turned to leave the gravesite, leaned over to Bobbie's ear and asked: "What are you going to do with Frank's clothes?" The widow walked off without answering, but perhaps dapper Frank would have appreciated the question.

See also GIGANTE, VINCENT "THE CHIN"

Further reading: *Uncle Frank* by Leonard Katz; *Meyer Lansky: Mogul of the Mob* by Dennis Eisenberg, Uri Dan and Eli Landau

COTRONI Gang: Mafia's talent suppliers

Mafia families can get all the new blood they need straight from the Italian underworld, whether it be a hit man for a rubout and a quick return home or permanent gunners for an American mob's operation. The Cotroni Gang operates out of Montreal and is recognized today as the underworld's main importer of bodies. The new blood is mainly Sicilian—Italian-born who are regarded as more dependable than many second- and third-generation recruits.

It was the late crime boss Carlo Gambino who started mass orders for young, tough recruits, having had his fill of locals who eschewed even the most basic Mafia codes and seemed to be chiefly motivated by moving to the suburbs. A report by Canadian authorities a few years ago indicated the Cotronis charge between $2,000 and $3,000 per recruit. They are brought into Canada without a visa and for a three-month stay by showing merely $300 in cash and a Canadian address where they can be reached. The Cotronis, expert smugglers, also trade in narcotics, not only in Canada but also in Florida through certain other ethnic gangs.

These new recruits have increased the problems of American law enforcement officers enormously. New arrivals can be put out on mob street duty but not be identified as mafiosi for a considerable length of time.

CRAMMING: Mafia's $200 million telephone scam

Not without a hint of admiration, the *New York Times* described the mob's foray into new crime rackets in the early 21st century, in particular an audacious money grab of millions from consumers via their phone bills. Stated the *Times,* "Forget gambling, loan-sharking and labor racketeering. New York organized crime figures bilked millions of unsuspecting consumers out of more than $200 million over five years by piggybacking bogus charges on their telephone bills." It represented one of the mob's most sophisticated operations and indicated the resurgent Mafia was ready for the most advanced new rackets of the new century. The Mafia has discovered the Internet.

The wise guys developed a scheme that was brilliant in its simplicity. It involved a network of dummy companies stretching from the East Coast to Kansas that utilized a billing fraud called "cramming," which provided the mob with huge new revenues. And the $200 million is only the estimate of the take by some members of the Gambino crime family. Other Gambinos and other crime families are believed to have gotten involved and added as a new wrinkle an Internet Web site that shook down thousands of consumers in this country, Europe and Asia with offers of free tours of adult entertainment sites. One official has said, "We think this is just the tip of the iceberg."

Even when federal authorities crack down on such crammers and force their operations off the billings of major phone companies that in turn pay the crooks, the Mafia, unlike other operations of this type that would simply fade away, keeps on coming. The mob prints up its own bills similar to those of the major phone companies and mails the charges directly to victims, who are informed that if the consumers fail to pay, they will face "cancellation of all services." While several wise guy crammers have been indicted on charges of racketeering, racketeering conspiracy, money laundering and other charges, it is believed that many victims are still paying off the mob.

"CUBAN Mafia": Fast-rising, fast-declining organized crime group

There was a time in the 1980s that the so-called Cuban Mafia was being touted as the new and fast-growing successor to the American Mafia. On paper, at least to some enterprising journalists, there seemed to be a good argument to support the claim. These Cuban gangsters were the heirs to the pre-Castro era in Cuba when they operated as allies to the Mafia's stranglehold on the lucrative casino business on the island. After the collapse of Bay of Pigs efforts, many of the Cuban gangsters, like their former mob masters, fled to the United States. They resumed their activities with the approval of the American mobs—after paying appropriately for the right to operate.

The "godfather" of this new Mafia was a former Cuban vice cop, Jose Miguel Battle, who ran what the Cubans dubbed "the Corporation." The President's Commission on Organized Crime heard reports that the Corporation had at least 2,500 people working for it in the New York City area. The group was estimated to take in about $45 million a year in illegal gambling in New York and New Jersey. Through its Miami section, this mob took in millions more from drug trafficking, especially in cocaine. The Corporation had a vicious set of enforcers who kept competition within the Cuban communities at a minimum and killed any number of scatterbrained interests trying to move in on it. The Cuban mob also victimized the business community by killing some who would not join it or convincing some to join by burning down their business properties and homes. As their profits soared, especially from the drug trade, the Cubans grew in power and sported a reputation for wiping out not only the competition but their wives and children as well. So great was the group's need for money laundering that it bought up winning tickets in the Puerto Rican lottery, paying the winners more than their prizes, just to establish a source for "legitimate" income.

In the main, of course, cocaine was the Cubans' golden goose, and as they grew more prosperous, the mystique around them grew. Hollywood showed them as brutal killers who gave no quarter, but the speculation that the Cubans would take over organized crime in America was about to dim. The Cubans, like other crime groups, drew their supplies from the Colombian Mafia, perhaps a bit more deserving of that title. As demand for coke in the United States boomed, the Colombians, true to their pattern of not sharing, started up their own distribution channels, especially in Miami, New York, Los Angeles and Chicago. The Cubans were about to be declared out.

That was not something that came easily to the Cuban mobsters. Apparently they were starting to believe their own press clippings, but the Colombians were not to be matched for bloodletting. Corpses began to pile up, and in Florida the Dade County morgue was dubbed by the Colombians as the Dead County morgue. Miami and metropolitan Dade County resembled a war zone, with mall parking lots being sprayed with bullets in gang battles of a type not seen since the Capone days in Chicago. The Cubans did not have the muscle to resist but undoubtedly thought the mafiosi would come to their aid, since their partnership with them had always been so lucrative. The Italian mobs, however, fully believed in a form of Darwinian thought in the survival of the fittest among their allies. The Colombians won out, and it was deal time for the two new partners.

See also BATTLE, JOSE MIGUEL, SR.; COLOMBIAN MAFIA

D

DADDANO, William "Willie Potatoes" (1925–1975): Chicago Outfit assassin and torturer

A top-echelon syndicate hood, Willie Potatoes Daddano was one of Boss Sam Giancana's favorite assassins. He was so refined at torture, whether with ice pick or blow torch, that he could keep a victim alive for hours of pain and torment. However, like quite a few psychopaths who have always distinguished the Chicago Outfit from the comparatively run-of-the-mill butchers in some other crime families, Daddano had his more human side. Doing time in prison, he broke down in tears when he learned that his mentor Giancana had been murdered. At home and with friends, he was, according to Antoinette Giancana, Sam's daughter (*Mafia Princess*), "a pussy cat" who would nod with approval at a child reciting the Ten Commandments.

While details of his tortures might best be left to the medical texts or lovers of sadism, Willie Potatoes was described as a ruthless and pitiless killer by FBI investigators, the Chicago Crime Commission and the press. His record included more than 10 arrests, charges that included bank robbery, burglary, hijacking and larceny. He was also a prime suspect in at least seven murders. Daddano ran gambling and vice activities for the organization in DuPage, Will and Kane Counties, Illinois. He was also the muscle behind the infiltration of much of Chicago's "scavenger," or garbage, industry.

Active in loan-sharking as well, he once informed a debtor who fell behind $1,000 in his "juice" payments: "If you don't pay the thousand, I'm not going to shout; I'm not going to holler. I'm going to hit you in the head [kill]."

The debtor was subsequently so frightened of Daddano's wrath that he borrowed from other loan sharks, sold a diamond wristwatch, his car, his house and cashed more than $27,000 in bum checks just to keep up his payments. When you faced a collector like Daddano, you didn't worry about having the law come after you.

Other members of the mob were equally frightened of Daddano. Sometimes assuming the identity of a deaf-mute, he would converse in perfect sign language, demonstrating the various means of murder in sign language—a rather more sinister communication than a loud vocal threat.

Mob law, according to Willie Potatoes, meant a low-level mobster had no recourse from his judgment. If he suspected treachery, he might order the suspects to submit to a lie detector test. Facing the criminal justice system, a criminal can stand on his rights and refuse to take such a test. Not with Willie Potatoes. On at least two occasions he ordered gunmen to submit to such tests even though they knew that if they flunked they faced instant extermination. In one known case, a gunman failed the test and got the fatal Daddano torture treatment. Likely a fulfilling experience for the sadistic Willie Potatoes, perhaps the most satisfying aspect of the murder was the fact that the hoodlum coughed up the $25 in advance for the polygraph.

Daddano would not have appreciated being stuck for the tab.

Daddano died in prison a short time after his mentor and hero figure, Giancana, was shot to death. Naturally some writers could not resist observing Willie Potatoes's demise was probably due to a broken heart.

DADILLACS: Getting a car just like dear old murderous dad's
The "Dadillac" typifies the subculture of children of crime family members, in which it is not uncommon for many of the boys to emulate their fathers. Thus, they whine and pine for a big car of their own and, lacking this, the occasional driving rights to their wise guy fathers' Cadillacs. One Mafia child, Dominick Montiglio, who entered the witness protection program in the 1980s, reminisced about times when "guys drove around in their fathers' Cadillacs, left hand draped out the window, pinkie ring twinkling, a *cugette* [female companion] leaning into their laps. We called the cars Dadillacs."

DALITZ, Moe (1899–1989): Head of Cleveland and Desert Inn syndicates
In a conversation taped by the FBI, New Jersey Mafia bigwig Angelo "Gyp" De Carlo was talking about Jewish mobsters: "There's only two Jews recognized in the whole country today. That's Meyer [Lansky] and . . . Moe Dalitz."

Ever since the 1920s Moe Dalitz was considered one of the top men in the syndicate. Even Lansky himself had much to learn from Dalitz's operation. He studied Dalitz's maneuvers closely, applied them to New York and later refined them and raised organized crime to a most professional level throughout the country.

Dalitz started out in crime in Detroit with the old Jewish Purple Gang and later shifted his operations to Cleveland. There he and three others—Morris Kleinman, Sam Tucker and Louis Rothkopf—set up the Cleveland syndicate, which dominated the bootleg booze racket to Ohio from Canada. The Cleveland syndicate was also the top dog in Cleveland crime, having learned the deft use of the bribe rather than the bullet. Dalitz also formed friendly relations with the "young Americans" of the Mafia—Al and Chuck Polizzi, Tony and Frank Milano and the three Angersola broth-

ers—and backed them until they achieved primacy among the mafiosi in Cleveland. Relations between the two groups would remain cordial for the ensuing decades; just as Lansky aided Lucky Luciano's rise in New York, so did the Dalitz group help out the Young Turks who became known as the Mayfield Road Mob. Just as Luciano-Lansky would triumph over the two contending forces of Masseria and Maranzano in New York, so too would Polizzi-Dalitz win out over competing mafiosi, the Porello brothers and the Lonardo family.

With the end of Prohibition the Cleveland syndicate and their Mafia allies operated gambling casinos in and around Cleveland and then spread out to the surrounding states of Kentucky, West Virginia and Indiana. Eventually the Cleveland syndicate pulled out of the area in favor of Las Vegas where they took over the Desert Inn and so became known as the Desert Inn syndicate. The four partners always shared everything equally. Called the Big Four, they quickly gained control of other casinos and for many years dominated the Vegas gambling industry.

Dalitz cemented relations with gang leaders of various ethnic origins from all around the nation. "However," notes Virgil Peterson, former longtime head of the Chicago Crime Commission, the group "maintained its identity as a predominantly Jewish underworld organization and there is no evidence to indicate it ever fell under the control of the Italian Cosa Nostra."

When Dalitz got his back up, no one could rattle him. There is the oft-told tale of Dalitz sitting in the dining room of the Beverly Rodeo Hotel in Hollywood. Heavyweight champion Sonny Liston, in an ugly mood from drink, approached the old bootlegger. Words were exchanged and the angry Liston drew back a powerful fist. Dalitz did not move and his voice was not loud but crisp. "If you hit me, nigger, you'd better kill me, because if you don't, I'll make one telephone call and you'll be dead in twenty-four hours."

The racial slur was Dalitz's way of demonstrating that he feared nothing in provoking a man officially crowned the toughest fighter in the world. The room itself was electric in its silence, even police intelligence officers who had overheard the exchange sat bolted in their chairs nearby. Liston stared at the then 64-year-old gambler, fist still poised. Dalitz, a man proud of his self-proclaimed fine tastes in art and his recognition in the social and philanthropic worlds, now bared the instincts of the hoodlum. Seconds ticked by. Then suddenly Liston dropped his arm, wheeled about and left without another word. The champ checked out of the hotel immediately.

In the late 1960s Dalitz sold the Desert Inn to Howard Hughes. Tax men were closing in on him and skimming appeared a dying art in the casinos. It could not be determined if Dalitz stripped himself of other concealed ownings. Later on, skimming was back and apparently so was Dalitz. In later years Moe continued to use his clout with the political establishment, making contributions to both parties and was involved in a luxury retreat in California for the super-rich—that is, people like him.

In his last few decades, Dalitz placed dozens of offspring of mobsters from the old days in legitimate positions that guaranteed their futures. In that sense, like the passing of Meyer Lansky, Dalitz's death reflected a similar retreat of Jewish influence in organized crime. And, like Lansky, Dalitz was mourned by the mafiosi.

DEAD Man's Eyes: Mob superstition

There is an old belief, said by some to go back to the Old World, that when a person dies, the last scene he sees is forever imprinted on the retina of his eyes. In the case of an underworld hit, that often means the mob killers. Thus it is logical for hit men to shoot out victims' eyes and so remove damaging evidence.

The superstition was evidently heeded widely in New York City around 1900, a period coinciding with a number of Black Hand and Mafia murders. The origin of the belief, thought by some to be particularly strong in Sicily from where the mafiosi and numerous Black Handers emigrated, is most difficult to determine. But it affected non-Mafia killers as well. Dead Man's Eyes was explained to Monk Eastman, the infamous Jewish gang leader, after he noted that some murder victims were getting their eyes shot out. After his next murder, he recalled the custom, and, whether or not he believed it, decided to err on the side of caution. He trudged back up three flights of stairs to blast out the eyes of his latest corpse.

Some observers of criminal behavior attribute the increase in eye shootouts around 1900 with the criminals' growing awareness of the miracles of scientific detection. Fingerprinting and other advances had proved effective, so it seemed possible a retina-picture development method might be found.

For many years, doctors at the New York medical examiner's office explained to the press they had studied and studied the eyes of corpses and found no such image. Evidently the underworld acknowledges the lessons of medical research—eye shootouts have decreased in recent years.

DEAD Man's Tree: Chicago "murder notice" site

Even before Prohibition Chicago's 19th Ward was known as the Bloody Ward. As the Italian population exploded in size and encroached on the old Irish neighborhoods, armed political warfare ensued.

Shut out of political influence by the old Irish power structure, the Italians rallied around Tony D'Andrea, a defrocked priest who concealed his criminal past as a whoremaster and counterfeiter. Eventually president of the powerful Unione Siciliane, D'Andrea ran for office in the 19th on several occasions against John "Johnny de Pow" Powers, the Irish boss of the ward, but continually lost the elections.

With the onset of Prohibition, the mafiosi who moved into bootlegging in Little Italy, the heart of the 19th, felt they had to have their own men in power to guarantee the safety of their operations. The Genna brothers, the top Sicilian gangsters of Little Italy, backed D'Andrea in yet another assault on Powers for alderman of the ward.

The Gennas—as, indeed, the Powers forces—believed they could influence the balloting and so they reinforced their campaign with the murders of their foes' supporters. The militant arm of the Powers group countered in kind. A bizarre landmark of this political and criminal competition was a certain poplar tree on Loomis Street in Little Italy. It became known as "the Dead Man's Tree." Both sides took to announcing their intent to murder a certain enemy by posting his name on the tree. The postings served two purposes: often shattering the man's nerve and thus making him an easier victim, or, if nothing else, at least magnanimously according him the opportunity of getting his affairs in order. Virtually all the 30 men murdered in the D'Andrea-Powers war had their names posted on the Dead Man's Tree. That included Tony D'Andrea himself, who in 1921 was one of the last killed in the conflict.

In the end, the Genna brothers discovered all the murders had been in vain. They found that all the men they could not vote out of office or otherwise murder could be bought. Not a single conviction was obtained in any of the slayings, but at least Little Italy gained a tourist attraction in the poplar.

DEATH Corner: Chicago murder site

In the early days of the 20th century, Black Hand terror groups held sway in all the large Italian ghettos in the United States. The Black Handers, some mafiosi, some Camorristas and others freelance criminals, were extortionists who extracted money from fearful Italians under the threat of death for themselves or their families. Such terror tactics worked only if backed up by some actual murders. The Black Handers in Chicago recognized this truth and, to reinforce their intentions, made one location a regular murder site. "Death Corner," as the press called it, was surely an added factor in Black Hand terrorism.

Death Corner was located at what was then the intersection of Milton and Oak Streets in the Little Italy section of the city. Over one 15-month period alone, from January 1910 through March 1911, 38 Black Hand murders occurred there. In this period—and for a considerable period of time thereafter—a great many residents of Little Italy went blocks out of their way to avoid traversing the Death Corner. They also made excruciating efforts to pay up on the Black Handers' demands.

See also BLACK HAND; SHOTGUN MAN; WHITE HAND SOCIETY

DEATH penalty for godfathers: New raging debate

There is no stranger debate about the death penalty than a current one raging in legal circles, where much previous opinion has been turned on its head. The argument is about whether the Mafia dons should be executed for their crimes. The most remarkable aspect in the dispute is the position of the various parties. Yes, some say, the dons must die, but oddly, the leading exponents are opponents of the death penalty. And conversely, prosecutors are immovably opposed.

The record since the new federal death penalty laws went on the books beginning in the late 1980s frames the question perfectly. But critics, some even in Congress, have become enraged that while the law has often sought the death penalty against young blacks and Hispanics who are guilty of street crimes and gang violence, there has never been a case of a

don facing the threat of execution. Even death penalty opponents sneer that the apparent popular fascination with the mob gives these worst-of-all criminals immunity from capital punishment.

Says Elizabeth Semel of the law school of the University of California at Berkeley, a longtime capital punishment critic, "We have demonized young black men and young Hispanic men who engage in violent gang activity in a way that we have not demonized—and arguably have romanticized—white men who engage in the same conduct."

The numbers involved can be staggering. While the average occupant on death row may have killed one or two people, Mafia dons, almost without exception, have ordered, approved and meticulously plotted the killing of dozens or even hundreds during their reign. John Gotti, for example, gave the official order or okay for the murders of all 19 of Sammy the Bull Gravano's victims, as well as countless other hits by other members of the crime family. Yet Gotti was not regarded by the law as fodder for the death penalty.

From the prosecution's viewpoint the reluctance of going for the death sentence is for varied reasons, with one major drawback being the quality of the case brought against the don. All witnesses would have to be members of the mob and then turn informer, and while juries might convict the don of "conspiracy" and the like, they could very well draw back from a conviction that resulted in the death sentence. As one attorney puts it, "It would be a public relations nightmare if the jury found the don guilty of conspiracy to commit murder, but then clear him of the main charge. Court cases would also tend to be more dragged out and subject to many more appeals that would leave cases in limbo for years."

In 2004, however, the government appeared to have bent to pressure and announced a procedure to determine if Joseph C. Massino, the boss of the Colombo crime family, could be tried under federal statutes for murder. Since the conviction of Gotti and the heads of the other three crime families in New York by 1992, Massino has become known as the "Last Don" and in time an embarrassment to the government because of his ability to stay out of the reach of prosecutors despite massive efforts to nail him by breaking down his often-ingenious safety measures to prevent penetration by investigators. Finally, the investigators broke through Massino's defenses and with the aid of mob defectors gathered evidence against him. However, the announcement that studies were under way on the feasibility of going for the death sentence failed to have the expected result. Some court observers saw the ploy as simply an act of vengeance for a dozen years of frustration trying to corner Massino. Other defense lawyers told the press they saw the move as nothing more than a negotiating ploy to pressure Massino to plead guilty to charges in a conspiracy case, which is how other dons basically have been trapped, with or without trial.

It could take years, if ever, for Massino to go to the death chamber but would at least take some pressure off the government to explain why supreme efforts for so long have been limited only to the lessers in crime.

A complication in reaching the death penalty in the Massino case developed in November 2004 when the judge in charge announced he would order the next U.S. attorney general to reconsider John Ashcroft's decision to seek the death penalty, saying he found it "deeply troubling."

"Mr. Ashcroft's choice," Judge Nicholas G. Garaufis said, "to make such a sobering and potentially life-ending decision now, after several delays, and only after tendering his resignation to the president and announcing to the country that he no longer wishes to preside over the Department of Justice is deeply troubling to this court."

The judge did not question the attorney general's right to make the death penalty decision but pointed out that Massino already faced a life term after he had been convicted recently in seven murders. The judge did not say he was holding off on the death penalty but declared he would not bring the case to trial until fall 2005—or later. But it was clear any death penalty case would be a long time in coming.

See also MASSINO, JOSEPH C.; SCIASCIA, GERLANDO "GERRY"

DeCARLO, Angelo "Gyp" (1902–1973): New Jersey racket boss

A longtime New Jersey boss of Mafia loan-sharking, gambling activities, and stolen securities operations, Angelo "Gyp" DeCarlo was maudlin about the Mafia. Based on FBI tapes made from illegal bugging of DeCarlo's office from 1961 to 1965, some startling sentiments were revealed. Released under court order, portions of the transcripts appeared in the press. As reporter Fred Graham noted, "reputations collapsed throughout New Jersey as racketeers were quoted as swapping favors with police chiefs, prosecutors, judges, and political chieftains."

Among those who saw their political fortunes wrecked were Hudson County political boss John J. Kenny and Newark mayor Hugh Addonizio. Congressman Peter Rodino escaped censure by the public by explaining away satisfactorily the kind of things said about him. Singer Frank Sinatra got another heavy dose of the constant linking of him with mob figures.

Equally important was the picture painted of DeCarlo himself, especially in view of the kindly treatment he was to receive later from a national administration. DeCarlo spoke glowingly of the old days in the "combination" and his self-approval of his role as a thug and murderous brute. At one point Harold "Kayo" Konigsberg, a notorious mob enforcer, asked him: "Will you tell me why everybody loves you so?"

DeCarlo's reply was honest if perhaps not totally responsive. "I'm a hoodlum," he announced proudly. "I don't want to be a legitimate guy. All these other racket guys who get a few bucks want to become legitimate."

The tapes, typical of many mob conversations, turned to discussions of past murders, which, whatever embellishments or contradiction with known facts, were reflective of the characters involved. DeCarlo had to observe rather philosophically to other mobsters that victims "as little as they are, they struggle."

He seemed most happy reminiscing about one victim to whom he said,

"Let me hit you clean." . . . So the guy went for it . . . we took the guy out in the woods, and I said, "Now listen . . . You gotta go. Why not let me hit you right in the heart, and you won't feel a thing?" He said, "I'm innocent . . . but if you've gotta do it . . ." So I hit him in the heart, and it went right through him.

DeCarlo almost certainly had a financial mystery man named Louis Saperstein poisoned with arsenic, but when DeCarlo and an aide were sent to prison in 1970 for 12 years, it was for extortion, not murder, in the Saperstein case.

DeCarlo was back on the front pages just 19 months later when President Nixon mysteriously commuted his sentence and let him out of prison, only one of four acts of clemency Nixon granted that year out of hundreds of applications.

What made the clemency so unusual was the odd way it came about. DeCarlo petitioned for his release, claiming he was suffering from cancer; he had made that claim for years. Normally such a request would automatically be routed to the Newark prosecutor's office and then through Criminal Division in Washington for recommendations, before reaching the attorney general. This particular petition simply zipped straight to Attorney General Richard Kleindienst who approved it and shot it on

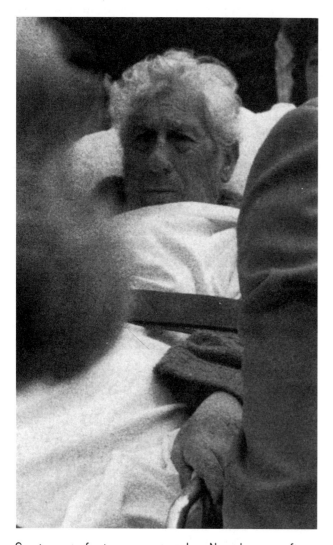

Coming out of prison on a stretcher, New Jersey mafioso "Gyp" DeCarlo was said to have enjoyed special pull when he won a lightning-fast presidential pardon in 1970. Although suffering from cancer, he was well enough to carry on mob rule for a time.

to White House Special Counsel John Dean. President Nixon's signature came through so that DeCarlo could be released two days before Christmas, 1972, a touching reward for a kindly hit man who popped a victim straight through the heart to save him pain, especially from an outspoken remember-the-crime-victim administration.

Naturally the tale churned through the Washington gossip mill. There were reports that, through Vice President Spiro Agnew, the clemency had been arranged by singer Sinatra—whose smiling picture graced DeCarlo's office wall and whom DeCarlo, on tape, praised lavishly. There was also talk that DeCarlo had contributed handsomely to Nixon's reelection campaign, which would be a stirring example of citizenship for a man behind bars. Denials and no-comments filled the air and Special Watergate Prosecutor Archibald Cox even conducted an investigation into the irregular events. Nothing came of the probe.

DeCarlo had returned home on a stretcher and then seemed well enough to pick up his mob rule. But 10 months later he succumbed to cancer. His death revealed an added bit of irony. DeCarlo had been hit with a $20,000 fine when he was sentenced, and he was told that if he did not pay the fine by October 25, 1973, he would be returned to prison. DeCarlo died on October 20, his debt still unpaid. To the very end DeCarlo managed to live by his stated credo: "I don't want to be a legitimate guy."

See also LAUNDERING

DeCAVALCANTE Tapes: FBI eavesdropping

Some of the most enlightening and, happily for some tabloids, the juiciest reading about the Mafia was released in 1969 in the 2,300-page FBI eavesdropping log of the DeCavalcante Tapes. The text, based on recordings made in a plumbing supply shop run by Samuel Rizzo "the Plumber" DeCavalcante, the boss of a 60-man Mafia family in New Jersey, was transcribed in newspapers, magazines and two paperback books. The *New York Times* for days allocated as much or more space to the DeCavalcante conversations as to the Ecumenical Council in Rome. While the tapes revealed much of DeCavalcante's romantic interests, they did serve a greater purpose.

The tapes, covering a period from 1961 to 1965, confirmed much of what informer Joe Valachi had

Sam "the Plumber" DeCavalcante, boss of a 60-man crime family in New Jersey, had his office bugged for four years by the FBI, an operation that confirmed much of Joe Valachi's revelations about the Mafia, or Cosa Nostra.

Some felt the tapes had value in explaining the social organization of the Mafia as DeCavalcante arranged for his crime family to pick up the tab for the wedding of his underboss's daughter or sought to help resolve the affairs of the son of his organization whose marriage was on the rocks. Sam the Plumber considered failed marriage a blot on his crime family's good name. It was intriguing to hear a man deeply involved in nefarious practices just as deeply concerned with the intricacies of the seating arrangements at a mob wedding.

DeCavalcante's own behavior might have left something to be desired. The recordings revealed he was having an affair with his secretary, Harriet, the sister of Sam's partner in the plumbing supply business and with whom DeCavalcante could converse in passable Yiddish. Married man DeCavalcante was not only cheating with Harriet but also cheating on her with a number of other women. Some readers of the tape transcripts got their biggest kick out of Sam talking to Harriet's husband on one telephone while whispering words of endearment to Harriet on another.

DeCavalcante was hardly an important Mafia godfather, although he played his role to the hilt. Really a sort of gofer for the commission in its efforts to tame Bonanno, DeCavalcante was noted to feel frustrated by his status. He also felt nothing could be done about resolving the Bonanno crisis, which he felt could explode into "World War III."

The release of the tapes did DeCavalcante no good. He was convicted on an extortion-conspiracy charge and sentenced to 15 years. After serving his term in Atlanta, DeCavalcante retired to Florida and, in the 1980s, was linked to a secret plan to invest in three casinos in Miami if the voters approved legal gambling. The voters rejected the move by a two-to-one margin. It may have been a bigger disappointment to DeCavalcante than the revelations of the tapes.

DELLACROCE, Aniello "Mr. Neil" (1914–1985): Gambino crime family underboss

In many respects, Aniello "Mr. Neil" Dellacroce was the model of the mythic Mafia don. His name in Italian meant "little lamb of the cross," and the underworld is rife with tales of the pleasure he took in killing people. A federal agent once said of him, "He likes to peer into a victim's face, like some kind of

revealed. They effectively demonstrated that, in the New York Mafia's five families, there existed the same formalized structure of the boss, underboss, consigliere, capos and soldiers. The tapes also confirmed that there was an organ called the commission supposedly designed to monitor crime family activities around the country. What the recorded conversations did not do is establish that the commission was an effective body; in fact many of its own members paid it little attention.

The DeCavalcante Tapes revealed much of the struggle the New York families were having controlling the ambitious Brooklyn boss Joe Bonanno as well as much of the intrigues leading up to the Banana War. They indicated that the commission and many mafiosi regarded Bonanno's son, whom the father was trying to position as his successor, "a bedbug."

dark angel, at the moment of death." Sometimes he even traveled about the country on mob business done up as Father O'Neill, a play on his first name. On other occasions he was Timothy O'Neil. He also sought to confuse his enemies on both sides of the law by occasionally having a lookalike pose as him in public.

Dellacroce spent decades in the Mafia and was a faithful follower of the murderous Albert Anastasia and, later, Carlo Gambino. Gambino had conspired in Anastasia's 1957 assassination but there is no accurate information on whether Dellacroce was involved or whether he believed a boss ever should be deposed. When Gambino took over the Anastasia crime family, Dellacroce stepped up to the position of underboss and seemed to be in line eventually to succeed Gambino. He had all the prerequisites, including the cool toughness and mercilessness the job required.

However, when Gambino was dying in 1976, he tapped his brother-in-law Paul Castellano as his successor. Gambino was smart enough to realize that if the tough Dellacroce wanted to fight, he could probably crush the less-than-imposing Castellano. To placate Dellacroce he offered him essential control of all

Gambino crime family underboss Aniello "Mr. Neil" Dellacroce was said to take extreme pleasure in killing: "He likes to peer into a victim's face, like some kind of dark angel, at the moment of death."

the family's lucrative Manhattan activities. It was not an offer Dellacroce could refuse, and for a time it defused the harsh feelings by the Dellacroce and Castellano factions.

Compromises seldom stay glued in the Mafia; it figured that power would sooner or later shift to the stronger side of the Gambino family. Except for the fact that Dellacroce was in ill health, it seemed he would eventually take over. Certainly the Young Turks aligned with Dellacroce favored expansion into more violent types of crime, such as armored car robberies and hijackings as well as narcotics. Castellano laid greater emphasis on loan-sharking, union construction shakedowns and relatively easy crimes, such as car theft on a wholesale level.

Police experts indicated that only Dellacroce could hold the Young Turks back, especially John Gotti, a dapper though deadly capo in the organization, described as having patterned himself after his idol, Albert Anastasia. Gotti held back striking at Castellano, it was said, out of fear and respect for Dellacroce.

Then on December 2, 1985, Dellacroce, who was suffering from cancer, died in a New York hospital. Two weeks to the day later Paul Castellano and one of his trusted capos, Thomas Bilotti, were gunned down outside a mid-Manhattan steak house.

There was speculation that Dellacroce's death made certain Castellano's demise. Castellano, who was likely to go to prison for a number of federal offenses, was planning to name Bilotti as underboss to take over as acting boss if need be. A police source was quoted, "When Dellacroce died, it left Gotti without a rabbi." It was a situation that forced Gotti to move with more than deliberate speed against Castellano. If he didn't, Gotti knew that Big Paul would tighten a death noose on him.

A curious story in *Time* magazine, datelined on the day of Castellano's murder but printed earlier, declared that Dellacroce had been an informer for the FBI for some two decades. Among other things, it claimed Dellacroce had tipped off the FBI when Carmine Galante, a would-be boss of bosses, was marked for death. He also was said to have given the FBI leads on the long-unsolved murder of Teamsters boss Jimmy Hoffa and that he helped to break some major narcotics cases. Perhaps the most stunning, or the most unbelievable, part of the story was that Dellacroce never asked for some kind of a payoff—most Mafia informers want legal clearance for themselves or money or both.

Not unsurprisingly the New York media seemed underwhelmed by *Time*'s disclosures, ignoring the story pending some additional proof. It can be speculated whether the story would have appeared if Castellano's murder had become known first. Some observers looked on the story as a form of FBI disinformation. It was possible that the FBI—clearly the source of *Time*'s account—was seeking to rattle the boys in general or quite possibly was intent on using the story as a ploy to cover up its real informers. There had been for many weeks some feeling in the underworld that Castellano might break or indeed might have already broken, that he was not tough enough to take a long prison term at the twilight of his life. Maybe the FBI was carrying out a "dirty trick" operation to plant suspicions on all the elderly dons it was bringing to trial? That could make them hit candidates and perhaps more interested in accepting a deal with the government.

The one thing that was certain was that Aniello Dellacroce, alias Father O'Neill, remained as enigmatic a figure in death as he had been in life—the quintessential Mafia don.

DeMEO, Roy (1941–1983): Assembly-line hit man

In the 1970s and 1980s hit man Roy DeMeo was the most feared man in the New York Mafia. It was not hard to understand why. According to some estimates he killed somewhere between 25 and 37 people. A leading FBI authority indicated the victim toll may have reached 200. That would make him a true competitor of Pittsburgh Phil Strauss, the fabled Murder, Inc., killer in the 1930s. In a sense DeMeo was the most inventive of serial hit men since he did his killing on an assembly-line basis.

A lot of DeMeo's income came from the stolen-car and stolen-parts racket, but Roy had another kind of chop shop, this one for dismembering bodies. In a special "horror clubhouse," fronted by a bar with a separate entrance at the side rear, victims could walk in and never come out, at least not in one piece, and often not even in 10 or 15 pieces.

One defecting member of DeMeo's crew of young punks explained what happened: "When the person would walk in, somebody would shoot him in the head with a silencer, somebody would wrap a towel around his head to stop the blood, and somebody would stab him in the heart to stop the blood from pumping.

"They would then drag him into the bathroom, put him in the shower, bleed him, pull him out, put him on a pool liner in the living room, take him apart, and package him."

DeMeo, a former butcher's apprentice showed his men how to take a body apart, limb by bloody limb and how to put the head through a compacting machine. It could be tiring work and sometimes the boys took a break for hot dogs and pizza, the gory job only half done. Some of the guys who could do the killings had trouble with the dismemberment work and paused to throw up, which made DeMeo giggle. He'd point out the work was like dismembering a deer.

DeMeo was a wise guy in the Gambino family, working under capo Nino Gaggi, who was said to be the only man DeMeo feared. At the same time, DeMeo was the only man Gaggi feared. It was truly a partnership made in hell. DeMeo's first hit for Gaggi was in 1972, killing a pornographer who could finger both of them as extortionists. From there on, there was no stopping DeMeo. He and his crew were said to murder for profit, or for revenge, and very often for the sheer fun of it.

Soon all the crime families in New York knew what an accommodating soul DeMeo was. Once some of his confederates entered the murder clubhouse to find three naked bodies hanging upside down in the bathroom. DeMeo told them to pay it no mind, that it was "something special" he was doing for another family who wanted the victims to disappear for good.

Whenever the death chamber was not slated for murder or dismemberment, the crew brought in lady friends for all-night dates. To keep the place presentable, the flooring had to be redone repeatedly.

Most of DeMeo's victims were errant mobsters, including at times even members of his own crew. But there were also some innocent bystanders, such as a young vacuum-cleaner salesman, mistaken by a paranoid DeMeo for an assassin out to kill him. If a person was even suspected of being an informer, DeMeo had him clipped. A 19-year-old girl named Cherie Golden fell into that category. She was a new girlfriend of a criminal tied to DeMeo who might decide to turn snitch to save himself from a long prison term.

When Nino Gaggi was tried on racketeering charges, DeMeo and his boys whacked out three

Roy DeMeo (left), the most feared hit man in the Mafia in recent times, was a virtual assembly-line murder machine, having killed somewhere between 25 and 200 victims. The only man he ever feared was Nino Gaggi (right), his immediate superior in the mob. Actually, DeMeo was the only man Gaggi ever feared. Gaggi finally gathered up his courage and killed DeMeo after family boss Paul Castellano ordered him eliminated.

government witnesses, including a New York housing police officer.

DeMeo carried out personal killings at the behest of godfather Paul Castellano, including that of Big Paul's son-in-law. The son-in-law had been fooling around with other women and beating his pregnant wife, who suffered a miscarriage as a result. The son-in-law was never seen again after that.

By the early 1980s Castellano had become disenchanted with his brutal hit man. He knew that federal agents were investigating DeMeo's murder crew. The trial would lead to Gaggi, and from Gaggi to Castellano himself. But no one could slow down DeMeo. He became erratic, doing kills that did not seem necessary. DeMeo took to expounding on the great joy of killing people. "It is like having the power of God," he told an associate. "Deciding who lives, who dies."

In late 1982 Castellano ordered the stone killer to report to his Staten Island mansion. DeMeo didn't show. Perhaps it was arrogance, or perhaps he felt Castellano planned to dispose of him.

Shortly thereafter a bug in Castellano's home revealed indications that Castellano was talking to John Gotti about rubbing out DeMeo. Another bug in Gotti headquarters indicated that John and his brother Gene discussed the fact that DeMeo had killed 37 people—all the victims they knew about. Apparently Gotti demurred on the contract.

Big Paul then turned to Nino Gaggi. "Take care of him, Nino," the crime boss was heard saying on the tape. Gaggi could get close to DeMeo, who still trusted him, and that was it. On January 10, 1983, DeMeo was no longer a problem to the Gambino family. His body was found in the trunk of his own car.

Ironically, after DeMeo's death, Gaggi was arrested and would have faced prosecution, but he suffered a fatal heart attack while being held in jail.

Still, the noose was tightening on Castellano, and he faced almost sure conviction. Gotti and his crew saved the boss from that fate by whacking him out.

See also DRACULA; WOMEN AS MAFIA VICTIMS

DEMOTIONS in the Mafia

As in big business, promotions in the Mafia are normal operations based on a prescribed ladder, from buttonman or soldier to capo to underboss. New openings are created through retirement, illness, jailings, natural death or violent death. And a successor to a syndicate post is held to exceptionally high standards of performance. Mafiosi who can't cut the mustard are quickly replaced, whether willingly or unwillingly.

Within the Honored Society, certain behavior (although, as in many other organizations, the rules tend to be applied selectively) automatically leads to demotion in rank—if not more serious retribution. Carmine Lombardozzi, a high-ranking member of the Gambino family, fell into disfavor for all sorts of misdeeds, including bringing dishonor on the organization when, although a married man, he took up with the daughter of another member of the crime family; for punching a policeman and above all failing to prevent his brothers and other relatives from assaulting an FBI man at the funeral of his father. This last misdeed, it was ruled, brought the organization too much bad publicity at a time when the mob was going all out to prove there was no such thing as the Mafia. Eventually Lombardozzi won his way back into mob good graces by purging himself of his bad habits (for instance, divorcing his wife and marrying the young lady in question), and demonstrating his "class" by making the mob millions in shady Wall Street operations. Being a moneymaker remains the most convincing way to expiate one's sins within the Mafia.

Sometimes a man is put in a certain job to obtain certain results, and failure means dismissal. Gaspar DiGregorio was installed by the national commission—or at least the four other New York crime families—to replace Joe Bonanno as head of that family. This followed Bonanno's promise to quit following his aborted attempt to dispose of a number of other leaders, including Carlo Gambino and Tommy Lucchese. Bonanno sought to have leadership passed to his brother-in-law Frank Labruzzo and his own son, Salvatore "Bill" Bonanno, but the other families refused to buy that, realizing the pair would just be fronts for the elder Bonanno. DiGregorio was assigned to eradicate Bonanno influence, and he tried to do so in what became known as the Troutman Street Shootout in Brooklyn in December 1966. A great number of DiGregorio gunners sought to ambush Bill Bonanno. Apparently 100 or more bullets were fired, but there were no casualties and not a single wound was inflicted, not even on an innocent victim. Naturally the commission was infuriated by the fiasco, evidently feeling somebody should at least have been scratched. DiGregorio was consigned to the doghouse, and the commission installed Paul Sciacca in his place. Sciacca himself was demoted back to the ranks in 1970.

A mafioso held in awe by the public if not by his fellow gangsters, Ciro Terranova was likewise demoted in the 1930s by Lucky Luciano. Terranova was assigned to drive the murder car in 1931 when Joe the Boss Masseria was murdered under Luciano's plans. The four killers marched calmly out of the Coney Island restaurant where they had dispatched Masseria, but the trembling Terranova was so shaken he could not get the car in gear. Contemptuously, Bugsy Siegel shoved him away, took the wheel himself, and sped off. Later Luciano had Dutch Schultz killed, and Terranova, who had been Schultz's No. 2 in the Harlem numbers racket, moved to take over. Luciano and Vito Genovese then informed Terranova he was now in retirement, replaced by Trigger Mike Coppola. Generally, such displaced crime leaders are assassinated for fear they will go to war to retain their rights. Luciano correctly judged that Terranova would do nothing.

A recently demoted top Mafia boss, according to an FBI report, was Jerry Angiulo, the top man in Boston, who with the death in 1984 of New England boss Raymond Patriarca, moved to take over the entire area. However, Angiulo was never held in very high esteem by New England mafiosi, and a full-scale revolt developed. Even his underboss, Ilario Zannino, opted, the FBI said, for Patriarca's son, Raymond J. Patriarca, who then took over. Angiulo was removed as boss in Boston, and reduced to the rank of a mere soldier. In theory Angiulo did not have to take it, but as he faced massive federal racketeering prosecutions that could put him away for 170 years if convicted, chances were excellent that Angiulo would simply take being cut down.

Of course the streets of many big cities have been littered with corpses of mafiosi who did not take their demotions with the good grace Mafia rules require.

DENTISTS: Latest in mob musclemen

There was a time when mob musclemen were noted for being "legbreakers," as a result of their efforts on behalf of bookmakers and loan sharks who had clients slow in paying their debts. The muscleman art has since become a bit more sophisticated. Mayhem, beyond the mere threat of such action, has come to be regarded as self-defeating since a hobbled victim can hardly hustle up money. Punching has come into vogue with good hitters being known as "dentists" for their ability to always knock out teeth. Debtors, or as the mob prefers to view them, "welchers," who lose some teeth develop an urgent fondness for keeping the others still in their mouth. As a result underworld dentists are now considered the debt collectors of choice.

DEPORTATION of mafiosi

Over the years scores of mafiosi and other members of organized crime have been deported, but very few deportations have been successful against top-ranking criminals who put up a fight. The government struggled to deport such syndicate leaders as Frank Costello, Meyer Lansky and Paul Ricca, the longtime head of the Chicago Outfit. None were deported.

In the case of Lansky a bizarre situation developed after he voluntarily left this country to live in Israel, claiming his rights as a Jew to immigrate there under that nation's Law of Return. Up until then the United States had failed to have Lansky deported; in a reversal, it now pressured Israel to deport him so that he could be brought back to America for criminal prosecution. Eventually Lansky gave up the battle to stay in Israel, tried to find refuge in a number of Latin American countries but finally was returned to the United States. Ironically, the government lost its criminal case against Lansky. He lived out his 10 remaining years in retirement in Florida.

The government proved less than a match for the wily Paul Ricca as well. In 1957 Ricca was stripped of his citizenship and in 1959 he was ordered deported. A minor gangster would not have been able to fight, but Ricca had the resources to put up

all sorts of legal appeals and delaying actions. He obtained a court stay on the deportation to Italy by bringing an action before an Italian court, insisting that his Italian citizenship be dropped. In turn, the Italian government said it did not want such an unwholesome character in the country, one who had behaved in such terrible fashion in America, even though there was an old murder sentence outstanding in Italy. Apparently, journalists observed, the Italians were afraid Ricca would contaminate their prisons.

Frustrated immigration authorities then told Ricca he would have to find a country to which he could be deported. Ricca promptly obeyed instructions and sent applications to no fewer than 60 countries. Apparently he was so overwhelmed with a desire for full personal disclosure to potential host countries that he included in each application a packet of news clippings that made clear why the U.S. government found him so undesirable. Somehow no country developed any interest in accepting him. When Ricca died in 1972 at the age of 74 he was despite fits of senility still successfully fending off the government's deportation efforts.

When the United States sought to ship Frank Costello back to Italy in 1961, the Italian government again balked. They pointed out that Costello had been brought to America at the age of four, two years after his father had gone across and saved up the $8-a-person fare for Costello's mother and sister (Costello was young enough to go free and slept in the huge iron pot his mother had used for cooking in Calabria). A spokesman for the Italian government said, "Italy should not be expected to carry the burden of a man who was born in Italy, lived here only a short time, and then spent most of his life in the United States. It's not blood that makes a man a criminal; it's society, and we definitely do not want to pay for such men."

There is much to be said for the Italian government's position that what we are really doing is trying to export our American criminals by merely citing their places of birth.

The U.S. government had stripped Costello of his citizenship for concealing his bootlegging activities when he was naturalized in 1925. At first the Costello deportation was upheld by the Supreme Court but Costello's lawyer, Edward Bennett Williams, took note in a minority opinion by Justice William O. Douglas that bootlegging itself was not a ground for denying naturalization to an alien in the 1920s. Eventually, on further appeals the Supreme Court by a six-to-two vote overturned the deportation order. After eight years of legal battling, the government threw in the towel.

Carlos Marcello, the Mafia boss of New Orleans, arrived in this country as a babe in arms in 1910. Eventually the government tried to get rid of him. Marcello was born of Italian parents in Tunisia, which was at the time under French rule. The United States was singularly unsuccessful in getting Italy, France or Tunisia to take back a criminal who had spent virtually all his living days in America. According to leaks from federal authorities, Marcello had guaranteed he would get the reaction he wanted in Italy by paying bribes of an average of $10,000 apiece to key members of Parliament. At the time Marcello wasn't sure how France and Tunisia would act so to be on the safe side he arranged, the story went, for forged documents to indicate he was born in Guatemala. Even though the U.S. government had plenty of cause to believe the claim was based on forgery and bribery, it virtually shanghaied Marcello out of the country in 1961 and deposited him in Guatemala "where you have citizenship."

Marcello smuggled himself into El Salvador and then trekked through the jungle to Honduras. Then, in as whacky a conclusion as any American deportation case, Marcello simply got on a commercial airliner to Miami and passed right through customs and immigration without even being checked. He remained in the United States thereafter.

Actually the best, and sometimes the only way, to get rid of important mobsters is by convincing them to go voluntarily to avoid prosecution. The government might have put Joe Adonis away for a few years on criminal charges but instead an agreement was worked out that stayed prosecution if he left. Adonis, with several million dollars in two Swiss banks, opted for exile in Milan in 1956, living out 16 years in lavish comfort.

The most famous deportee of all was Lucky Luciano who was released from a New York prison, where he was doing 30 to 50 years, because of what was said to have been his great aid to the war effort. His release by Governor Thomas E. Dewey, the man who originally prosecuted him, did not free him from being deported in 1946. Luciano was under the illusion that if and when Dewey was elected president he would be allowed to return to the United States. The

"if" never happened so Luciano's grasp on reality cannot now be measured. He remained in exile and as such became the leader of numerous lesser mafiosi who were deported before and after him. Later on Luciano petitioned President Dwight D. Eisenhower on his own behalf and those of other deportees to be readmitted, but the plea was rejected. It was not too tough on Luciano who for almost the rest of his life received something like $25,000 a month from the syndicate. The lesser deportees did not fare too well. Many were impoverished and many of those banished to Sicily were cheated and robbed of what little funds they had by native mafiosi. The rules of the Honored Society simply did not apply to a bunch of damned foreigners.

DESIMONE, Frank (?–1968): Los Angeles Mafia boss

The impotence of the Los Angeles Mafia has been an embarrassment—not only to the Mafia, but also to the zealous L.A. press. Even under Jack Dragna, journalistically dubbed the "Al Capone of California" and considered the toughest of all the Mafia chiefs in that city, the crime family already qualified as the "Mickey Mouse Mafia."

When Bugsy Siegel came to town in the late 1930s as the representative of the New York mobs, he rather officiously reduced Dragna to junior partner. Chicago moved into the movie rackets in Hollywood without even consulting Dragna. Worst of all, even after the national board of the syndicate eliminated Siegel, Dragna was unable to wrest control of Siegel's rackets from Bugsy's bodyguard, Mickey Cohen. Bookmakers who should have paid tribute to the mob simply did not, with impunity.

By comparison Dragna's successor, Frank DeSimone was a creampuff. He ruled from 1957 to 1968, and it was not a happy period for the mob there or for DeSimone in particular. Right at the start of his reign he was netted in his first inter-family act, attending the ill-fated Apalachin Conference.

Later on DeSimone was undoubtedly very shook up to discover that Mafia boss Joe Bonanno had added him as a victim in a plot to knock off several crime family leaders, including Carlo Gambino and Tommy Lucchese in New York and Stefano Magaddino in Buffalo. Why little DeSimone? Bonanno had moved much of his interests west and operated part-time out of his "vacation territory" in Arizona. This gave him access to Nevada and southern

California rackets. Apparently Bonanno was as prepared to take out DeSimone as he would to swat a fly. By the last few years of his rule, informer Jimmy "the Weasel" Fratianno reported that "DeSimone's scared of his shadow, never goes out nights. The guy's gone bananas."

When DeSimone died in 1968, the L.A. mantle passed to his underboss, Nick Licata, a debatable improvement if any improvement at all.

DeSTEFANO, Sam (1909–1973): Chicago Outfit enforcer and sadist

Sam DeStefano was answering to a higher authority when he killed his brother. Whenever Sam Giancana said kill, he killed. Whenever Paul "the Waiter" Ricca said "make-a him go away," DeStefano saw to it that the man went away—permanently.

The number one madhatter of the Chicago Outfit, Sam DeStefano was considered the most demented of all the mob's killers—and thus a particular favorite of Giancana and Ricca. An extortionist, rapist, loan shark, hijacker, counterfeiter, narcotics trafficker and sexual psychopath, he insisted on torturing his victims before the kill. When he got the contract to hit Leo Foreman, a sometime mob associate, he had three of the boys lure Foreman to a suburban home, take him into a basement sauna-bomb shelter, and shoot but not kill him. They then used a butcher knife on him a couple of times, but still did not kill him. They were waiting for Sam. Then Sam walked in, dressed in pajamas. "You thought you'd get away from me," one of the three, Charles Crimaldi, who turned state's witness, quoted Sam as screaming. "I told you I'd get you. Greed got you killed."

Foreman begged Sam to spare him, "Please, unk, oh my God," Foreman cried. (In better days he'd always referred to DeStefano as "unk.") Then, Crimaldi related, Sam grabbed a gun and shot him in the buttocks. They watched him writhe in pain for a while, then one of the others stabbed him several more times and Foreman lay still. They took turns cutting chunks of flesh from the corpse's arms and then DeStefano looked upset. He observed Foreman's face was frozen in what looked like an unmoving smile. "Look at him," Sam said. "He's laughing at us. Like he's glad he died."

Victims of Sam's torture, police and even fellow hoods conceded he was mentally deranged. That may be what made him so valuable to Ricca and Giancana. As a "juice collector" he had no equal. Loan shark victims would do almost anything to find money to pay their debts to the mob. One of DeStefano's favorite ploys was to shove a debtor into a telephone booth and jam an ice pick in his stomach. "I'll pull your eyeballs out. I'll put ice picks in you." He meant it.

Another time he took a loan shark debtor into a jeweler's and bought him a wristwatch. He told the jeweler to engrave it "From Sam to Bob," explaining to the juice victim "so when they find you in a trunk they'll know I was your friend."

Once six juice victims worked out a desperate plot to kill DeStefano. They planned to darken their faces, arm themselves with hand grenades and army rifles, and attack Sam's house, rolling the grenades down his breezeway. Unfortunately, they chickened out.

DeStefano was very useful to the mob at eliminating competing loan sharks. One Peter Cappelletti tried it for a while until DeStefano came after him. He abducted him, chained him to a radiator, tortured him and in full view of his wife urinated on him. Then Sam and his men unchained him and threw him to his wife's feet. "I'm giving back his life to you," DeStefano announced magnanimously.

DeStefano had contempt for almost everybody, including the law. He ranted in courtrooms and sometimes wanted to testify with a bullhorn. On one occasion he became outraged when the name of a fellow mobster was used at his trial. DeStefano jumped to his feet shouting: "I'll not have the names of any gangsters mentioned during my trial." He demanded the right to cross-examine a detective. "I want to know his background. Joe Stalin may have sent him."

In 1969 author Ovid Demaris profiled DeStefano in his book *Captive City* and dubbed him "the gangster police elect as the most likely to be discovered in a car trunk." He proved close, but it was an event that could not be considered until Ricca's death in 1972. Ricca's opinion always received a hearing and was even revered as if from a deity.

Equally obedient to Giancana, DeStefano didn't balk at the contract in 1955 on his younger brother Michael. Because he was a drug addict, it was Sam's way of curing him. For the same reason, he stripped the body clean and washed it to remove the stain of narcotics. When questioned about how he had killed his brother and then handled the body, DeStefano was reduced to wild giggling and making his interrogators repeat their questions over and over. Instead of answers, he just giggled on.

In 1971, DeStefano was sentenced to three and a half years for threatening a government witness. That was on appeal when the authorities broke the Leo Foreman murder. Indicted were Sam, his brother Mario and a rising hoodlum named Tony Spilotro. Sam was by this time talking even more wildly than before. He was diagnosed as having cancer but there were those, especially Spilotro, who feared his antics in the upcoming murder trial. There were others in a burglary ring that Sam bossed who also worried about his unpredictability. Not even Sam Giancana, shorn of some of the power he had previously enjoyed, could save him, much as he wanted to. DeStefano was excellent life insurance for Giancana.

The trouble was that DeStefano had no life insurance of his own anymore. In 1973, the 64-year-old hoodlum was doing some chores in his garage in a nice residential section on Chicago's Far West Side. He was sweeping with a new broom when he saw the barrel of a shotgun aimed at him. The double blast knocked him flat, severing his left arm at the elbow while the lead bored into his heart. The killer or killers had let Sam die quick and easy, a charity he hardly ever granted his victims.

DETROIT crime family See ZERILLI, JOSEPH

DEWEY, Thomas E. (1902–1971): Gangbuster and near assassination victim
Thomas E. Dewey was a knight in shining armor, the fearless gangbuster who almost took up residence in the White House. In the underworld, Dewey had a different reputation.

In *The Last Testament of Lucky Luciano*, Luciano portrays Dewey as a man on the take, who demanded and got big bucks as "campaign contributions" to commute Luciano's 30- to 50-year prison term. (Coauthor Richard Hammer, in his introduction, explains that much in the book "is angry, scurrilous, even defamatory.")

Although the same charge was raised by Democrats at election time, no hard proof was ever offered to back up Luciano's claim. However, a thorough analysis of Dewey's record on crime has never been made and his dedicated biographers have had little

interest in doing so. This does not mean that the Dewey record is not somewhat troublesome.

It was Dewey's crimefighting prowess that moved him along politically—to the governorship of New York and the Republican candidacy for president in 1944 and 1948. Dewey's career began as a Wall Street lawyer. As a prosecutor of errant industrialists, businessmen and financiers, he showed limited effectiveness. It was against gangsters that Dewey shone. In various enforcement positions—U.S. attorney, special prosecutor, district attorney—he clapped in prison or sent to the electric chair such gangsters as Luciano, Waxey Gordon, Gurrah Shapiro and Louis Lepke.

Before he nailed Luciano, Dewey had targeted Dutch Schultz, the king of Harlem policy rackets and many other illicit enterprises. The Dutchman combined a brilliant criminal mind with the off-the-wall acts of a flake, always fond of solving dilemmas with a gun. When Dewey's men were closing in on his operations, an angry Schultz went before the national board of the crime syndicate to demand that Dewey be knocked off. This was counter to one of the founding rules of the organization, which Luciano later restated, "We wouldn't hit newspaper guys or cops or DA's. We don't want the kind of trouble everybody'd get." Led by the forces of Luciano and Lansky, the crime board voted Schultz down. "I still say he ought to be hit," the mad Dutchman raged in defiance, "and if nobody else is gonna do it, I'm gonna hit him myself."

If at first the mobsters thought Schultz was just letting off steam, they changed their minds in October

As a young prosecutor Tom Dewey (here being sworn) built a racket-buster image that turned him into a presidential candidate. Some found his anti-mob record rather spotty.

1935 when they learned Schultz had an actual murder plan in place. Dewey's Fifth Avenue apartment was staked out by a man who posed each morning as the father of a child pedaling a velocipede. That man watched as Dewey and two bodyguards walked by to a neighborhood drugstore, from where the prosecutor called his office each morning from one of several booths. Dewey feared the mob might tap his home phone.

As the Schultz plan was supposed to work, the "caser" with the child would one morning be in the drugstore with a gun and silencer awaiting Dewey's arrival. He would shoot Dewey as he entered a telephone booth and then walk out past the bodyguards waiting unsuspecting outside.

Hurriedly the national board of the syndicate passed a death sentence on Schultz and he was murdered in a chop house in Newark, New Jersey, before he gave final okay to the Dewey rubout.

Dewey did not learn of his "almost assassination" until 1940 when it was revealed to him by Murder, Inc., prosecutor Burton Turkus. His eyes widened when mention was made of the proud papa with the child on the velocipede. After five years he apparently still remembered them.

By that time Dewey had had Luciano sent to prison for 30 to 50 years for compulsory prostitution, the longest sentence ever handed out for such an offense. After World War II, Dewey backed a parole board's recommendation that Luciano be freed, an action for which Dewey was roundly attacked by political opponents. The move, Dewey insisted, was made because of Luciano's aid to the war effort. It may well have been influenced by Luciano's intercession in the Schultz plot. To his dying day Luciano insisted there was another reason—that after considerable negotiations, the mob had contributed $90,000 in small bills to Dewey's campaign fund.

Although it would be unacceptable to give credence to such a source as Luciano without independent evidence to confirm the charge, there were in later years reasons enough to find Dewey's actions unfortunate and troublesome. Luciano's claims that, for instance, a New York police commissioner being on the take can be supported when it is shown that his acts were precisely what the mob wanted. In Dewey's case this was not clear, although some in the underworld view his sending Louis Lepke to the electric chair in 1944 as having a link with the alleged

payoff from the mob. At the time the right wing press, especially the Hearst *New York Daily Mirror*, speculated that Lepke, one of the top-ranking members of the national crime syndicate, tried to save his own life by offering Dewey "material . . . that would make him an unbeatable presidential candidate." The thinly veiled reports inferred that Lepke could deliver to Dewey Sidney Hillman, president of the Amalgamated Clothing Workers and President Franklin Roosevelt's most important labor adviser, as the instigator of several crimes including one of murder. In any event, Dewey, after granting Lepke a 48-hour reprieve, did not deal with Lepke and let him go to his death.

Many Dewey sycophants lionized him for that act. Prosecutor Turkus said, "To the credit of Dewey, he did resist and he did reject. He would not do business with Lepke, even with the greatest prize on earth at stake—the presidency of the United States." But had Dewey granted clemency to Lepke, it more than likely would have guaranteed his defeat. If he had gotten Hillman—assuming Lepke could deliver him—the price essentially would have been letting such men as Luciano, Shapiro, Adonis, Costello, Lansky and Anastasia off the hook on murder charges. Indeed, Lepke indicated he would leak no mob information. To let Lepke live for the price of Hillman alone (although Hillman was never directly named) would appear a politically motivated effort to dethrone FDR by nailing his chief labor adviser.

There are other explanations to the incident, especially that Lepke might not have been able to hand Dewey the labor leader because he had no evidence. When Lepke was strapped into the electric chair, it was likely that the biggest sighs of relief came not from Hillman or the White House, but from the ruling board of the crime syndicate. They inherited Lepke's racket empire and none of the headaches he might have given them.

By the early 1950s, Dewey, disappointed at the end of his White House hopes, also exhibited considerable disinterest with his racket-busting past. His actions regarding the Kefauver crime investigation hearings in 1950 and 1951 were disturbing even to Republicans on the committee and in Congress. Dewey refused to appear at the New York City sessions although he said that if given enough advance notice he might offer the senators a few minutes of his valuable time in his private office. The offer made no allowances for the committee's staff or counsel, investigators, court stenographers and so on, and under these circumstances, they declined leaving New York City for Albany. In refusing to appear—a remarkable position for a racketbuster who had constantly hauled witnesses in for questioning and declared an innocent man would want to help official inquiries—Dewey's behavior differed little, many held, from the actions of mobsters thumbing their noses at the U.S. Senate.

The committee wanted to question Dewey about the facts surrounding Luciano's pardon, an action he had never been obliged to answer in an official forum, and also about the wide-open gambling in Saratoga in upstate New York, where evidence indicated the rackets and the fix were operated by Meyer Lansky. From the evidence the committee did hear, Governor Dewey was just about the most uninformed man in the state on gambling in Saratoga. His superintendent of the state police, John A. Gaffney, said it was not his responsibility to do anything about gambling there or pass along information about it to Dewey. However, even deprived of police intelligence, Dewey undoubtedly had to know what was going on in Saratoga, a watering hole for the social set in which Dewey mixed. Yet Dewey's ignorance about gambling was not repeated concerning bailiwicks other than in his own state, if the words of gambling expert John Scarne are to be accepted. Scarne related he once asked Dewey at a Republican rally in the Waldorf Astoria why he had cold-shouldered the committee. Dewey responded, according to Scarne, more or less in the following words: "Scarne, I knew that when I issued that invitation to Kefauver and his four Senate stooges, they would never show up in Albany. They knew that I knew that the Committee members' five states had more political corruption, gambling, casinos, bookies and houses of prostitution than any other five states in the country."

Thus we are left with a governor of New York knowing more about crime and corruption in such states as Tennessee, Maryland, Wisconsin, Wyoming and New Hampshire (of all places) than in his own.

Had the Dewey misadventures ended with Kefauver, his acts still might be construed as nothing more than political competitiveness, even though a number of other governors from both parties—Stevenson of Illinois, Lausche of Ohio and Youngdahl of Minnesota—had eagerly cooperated. By the early 1960s, however, Dewey had become more accommodating than ever about mob gangsters and the way they operated in the new gambling scene. The former racketbuster became a major stockholder in Mary Carter Paints, which somehow just seemed to have an interest in gambling in the Bahamas. And on Grand Bahama the man pulling the strings for Mary Carter Paints (later renamed Resorts International) was none other than Meyer Lansky, who had long before learned how to invest secretly in companies through the wonders of Swiss bank accounts. While this did not disturb Dewey, it appears to have upset reporters for the *Wall Street Journal* who uncovered the seamy story of political payoffs on the islands and won a Pulitzer Prize for their efforts.

Despite considerable turmoil Mary Carter still went ahead. The casinos that opened were filled with familiar racket faces behind the tables and in the management offices, and the manager of one of the clubs was Lansky's man Eddie Cellini (brother of Dino Cellini who ran Lansky's interests in England).

It was a rather sorry finale for Tom Dewey. "From racketbuster to racketbacker," someone said. It may have been a harsh verdict, but in a field where some behavior is required to match that of Caesar's wife, Dewey could not be said to have won a cigar.

See also "Kefauveritis"

DIAMOND, Jack "Legs" (1896–1931): Lone wolf racketeer

Jack "Legs" Diamond was often called the "clay pigeon of the underworld" because he survived so many attempts on his life. Nobody liked Legs. The police hated him, Dutch Schultz hated him and so did a varied group of mobsters, including Owney Madden, Vince Coll, Meyer Lansky, Waxey Gordon, Louis Lepke, Gurrah Shapiro and Lucky Luciano to name just a few. It was said in the end that gunners for Schultz put Diamond to sleep permanently after catching him snoozing in his bed. But it would only have been a matter of time before one of the above, or one of several others, knocked him off. Legs Diamond was a double-dealer and a chiseler, and he was never known to keep his word to anyone, except maybe to his brother Eddie.

Some said the nickname of "Legs" came about because in Diamond's early days as a package thief his long limbs never failed to carry him beyond the law's reach. But other underworld cynics said he was so named due to his habit of "running out on his friends." Typical was the case of Diamond's henchman-bodyguard John Scaccio who did the dirty work for the Diamond mob when they sought to take over a number of rackets in Greene County, New York. When Diamond himself escaped prosecution in the case, he put up no money for Scaccio's defense, withdrew his attorneys from the case and let Scaccio face the music alone. Scaccio drew a long prison term. Diamond was equally infamous for promising his boys who went to prison that he would pull some strings to get them freed early. Naturally, as soon as they were gone, he forgot about them.

After his early heisting days Diamond showed up slugging and killing for Little Augie Orgen, the top labor racketeer in the early 1920s. Diamond is credited with masterminding the killing of Kid Dropper which made Little Augie number one in the field. Little Augie turned over to Diamond some of his bootlegging enterprises. It turned out that Little Augie was the last man Diamond was loyal to. He served as his bodyguard and even took some bullets in his arm and leg when Little Augie was gunned down on a Lower East Side street in 1927. Diamond's loyalty, however, did not extend to seeking revenge against his boss's killers—Louis Lepke and Gurrah Shapiro—whom he had recognized. When he was released from the hospital, he made peace with them. Lepke and Gurrah took over Little Augie's labor rackets while Diamond took over the rest of the deceased's bootleg business and his narcotics operations. From there on Legs understood the rewards of disloyalty.

Diamond was catapulted into the big time. He became a Broadway sport, even opening through fronts his own joint, the Hotsy Totsy Club on Broadway in the 50s. Diamond often invited underworld rivals to peace meetings there. Many of them ended up murdered in a back room.

In 1929 Diamond and his lieutenant, Charles Entratta, killed a hoodlum named Red Cassidy right at the bar in full view of a number of Hotsy Totsy employees and patrons. Diamond and Entratta fled certain arrest and conviction. From hiding they decided to clear themselves and did so by killing the club bartender and three customers. Four others, including the hat-check girl, disappeared. Diamond and Entratta were clairvoyant enough to suspect the witnesses would not reappear. With no one left to testify against them they resurfaced and said blandly

Bucking the national crime syndicate, "Legs" Diamond (foreground, left) became known as the "clay pigeon of the underworld" because of the many attempts on his life. He was called "unkillable" until three bullets in the head, while he was sleeping, gave the lie to that label.

they understood the police wanted to talk to them about something. Naturally, they were not prosecuted.

However, Legs's absence had created some complications. Dutch Schultz had moved in on Diamond's rackets while he was gone. What the Dutchman took, he was seldom known to return. A full-scale war began.

War had almost broken out between them in 1928 when Legs suspected Schultz of sending an expeditionary force out to Denver to kill Eddie Diamond, his brother, who was battling tuberculosis. Later Diamond determined that the great brain of the underworld, fixer Arnold Rothstein, was behind the attempt. After Little Augie's death in 1927 Diamond had worked for Rothstein and served him as a high-priced bodyguard. Rothstein, Broadway's leading gambler, paid Diamond $1,000 a week to protect him from poor losers at cards, to escort heavy winners to their homes and to persuade debtors to pay up. Meanwhile Rothstein helped Diamond expand his bootleg and drug operations, but the pair quarreled just before Rothstein's murder and split up. As an object lesson to Legs, Rothstein sent the hit squad to get Eddie. Eddie survived and lived to come East and die in bed of his affliction, but Diamond exacted full vengeance on the five hit men, killing them all.

Now in the war with Schultz the rest of the underworld cheered Schultz on, supplying him with any information they got on Diamond's doings. Schultz was himself a rogue elephant within the emerging national crime syndicate but compared to Diamond he could be regarded as a solid team player.

There were those who were convinced that Diamond would never be killed, that he in fact couldn't be killed. In the past it had been that way. In October 1924 rival gunmen peppered his head with shot and put a bullet in his heel in an ambush. Diamond drove himself to the hospital and got his wounds tended. The second near miss on his life came when Little Augie was assassinated. Diamond lost so much blood from wounds that doctors said he could not survive. He did.

The war with Schultz added to his battle injuries and his reputation for being murder-proof. Shortly after he personally knocked off a pair of Schultz enforcers in October 1930, Legs was curled up in a cozy suite with his mistress, showgirl Kiki Roberts. Suddenly gunmen stormed in and pumped him full of lead. Kiki escaped injury and called for an ambulance. Legs was sped to the hospital where, confounding the doctors, he survived. The following April, Diamond was ambushed coming out of a roadside inn. He took a bullet in the back, another in the lung, a third in the liver and a fourth in the arm. Again, the surgeons said he had no chance. Again, Diamond recovered.

By now Legs himself was convinced he was unkillable. When a gangster informed him that a couple of Brooklyn mugs had been sent to get him, he replied, "What the hell do I care?"

Meanwhile Diamond was terrorizing a great many mobsters. He let it be known that when he was fully recovered from his wounds he was taking a bigger piece of the action in Manhattan. He served notice on Joey Fay that he was taking over more of the nightclub rackets and Waxey Gordon that he was getting more of the bootlegging and moonshining

business. Lansky and Luciano realized they were going to be next on Legs's "want list."

Thus, it was never determined with certainty exactly who were the hitters who put Legs away in December 1931. Diamond was hiding out in a room in Albany, New York, a location known only to a few of his confederates. He was sound asleep when the two hit men slipped into the room. One held him by the ears while the other shot him three times in the head. Diamond this time was absolutely, positively dead.

See also HOTSY TOTSY CLUB

DICKEY, Orange C. (1920–): Army captor of Vito Genovese

The experiences of a 24-year-old sergeant in the army's Criminal Investigation Division, Orange C. Dickey, demonstrated the difficulty that has always existed in prosecuting Mafia-connected members of organized crime. A former campus cop at Pennsylvania State College, Dickey broke the case of a lifetime when he arrested American mafioso Vito Genovese in Italy in 1944 on black-marketing charges.

Genovese had fled to Italy in 1937 to escape a murder rap. He became a fervent supporter of Benito Mussolini, even to the extent of having a political opponent of the Italian dictator hit in the United States. When by 1944 it was obvious which side was going to win the war, Genovese switched his allegiance once again. He turned up at the headquarters of the Allied military governor, Colonel Charles Poletti, formerly New York lieutenant governor under Thomas E. Dewey, and ended up becoming an official interpreter on Poletti's staff, assigned to the huge supply base at Nola.

It was a case of putting the fox in charge of the hen house, and Genovese soon parleyed his position into that of the biggest black-market operator in occupied Italy. He hustled huge stocks of cigarettes, liquor, wheat, food and medicines on the black market; it was as though the crime kingpin had never left New York.

Genovese carried passes that gave him free access to supply bases throughout Italy and he bore testimonials of his great devotion to the United States. Military officers, who later demonstrated no inclination to prosecute Genovese after he was exposed, attested to his "invaluable" contributions to the war effort. He was, they said, "honest . . . trustworthy, loyal and dependable . . . worked day and night . . . exposed several cases of bribery and black-market operations among so-called civilian personnel . . . is devoted to his adopted home, the U.S.A. . . . served without any compensation whatever."

Compensation or no, Genovese had made and salted away millions. His testimony, which was so valuable in breaking up operations of other black marketeers, was nothing more than a move to get rid of competitors. Dickey tracked Genovese down and arrested him. He found Genovese's apartment in Naples; the young sergeant said later he had never been inside such a lavishly furnished place or seen so extensive a wardrobe for one man. This was in a time of wartime misery for most civilians.

At first Dickey did not know who Genovese was, not even having heard the name before. However, Genovese had made underworld enemies in his criminal operations and a tipster supplied Dickey with a publication from the 1930s which bore Genovese's photograph and identified him as a notorious member of the American underworld.

In August Dickey forwarded a communication to the FBI in Washington advising the agency of Genovese's apprehension and inquiring about any outstanding charges against him. He got no answer until the end of November when he was told a warrant would arrive from Brooklyn shortly on a murder charge.

In the meantime Dickey faced enormous pressure to release Genovese. When he reported his findings to the provisional U.S. officer at Nola, he was ordered to drop the investigation. Instead Dickey went to Rome where he saw Colonel Poletti who refused to discuss the case. Dickey then turned to Brigadier General William O'Dwyer, in Italy on leave from his post as Brooklyn district attorney. It was a waste of time. Incredibly, O'Dwyer, who had overseen the prosecution of Murder, Inc., blandly told Dickey that Genovese was of no "concern" to him.

When a crestfallen Dickey returned to Naples he was ordered by superiors to take Genovese out of a military prison and have him either put under bond or transferred to a civilian jail. Stubbornly, Dickey chose the second alternative, tucking him away in the most secure Italian jail he could find and constantly checking up personally on his prisoner.

Finally in December confirmation came from Brooklyn that a warrant would be sent. By this time

Genovese realized all his powerful supporters had been unable to pressure Dickey, and so he offered the $210-a-month non-commissioned officer a quarter of a million dollars in cash simply to "forget" about him.

"There are things you don't understand," Genovese said. "This is the way it works. Take the money. You are set for the rest of your life. Nobody cares what you do. Why should you?"

When finally Dickey was not going to go for the bribe offer, Genovese turned vicious. He threatened to have Dickey and his family killed.

Nothing worked, and Dickey and his prisoner boarded a troop ship bound for home. Aboard ship, Genovese's tone changed again. He was very relaxed. "Kid," he told Dickey, "you are doing me the biggest favor anyone has ever done to me. You are taking me home. You are taking me back to the U.S.A."

It was almost as though Genovese knew something. He probably did. The murder charge against him required the testimony of two witnesses, Ernest Rupolo and Peter LaTempa, both hoodlums who had talked. If one was silenced, the murder case against Genovese would collapse.

Genovese landed on January 8, 1945. Immediately when the news broke, a frightened Peter LaTempa rushed to Brooklyn authorities and begged to be held in protective custody. He was placed in what was reported to be a secure cell. A week later LaTempa died there. He had been poisoned.

Genovese went free, and Sergeant Dickey was still a young but certainly a wiser man. Ironically, Genovese probably would not have returned to the United States on his own. His return, with Lucky Luciano removed from the scene, would greatly affect the development of the Mafia and organized crime in America.

See also LATEMPA, PETER; RUPOLO, ERNEST "THE HAWK"

DiLEONARDO, Michael "Mikey Scars" (1955–): "Most-feared rat" of the comeback mob

By 2003 the "resurrection" of the Mafia in America, especially of the Gambino crime family, was becoming clearer to many crime watchers, although the wise guys were getting shock vibes of another "rat attack" on the mob. This may seem odd as the FBI appeared to have a large backlog of potential informers, but most informers can only give small measures of Mafia activities. The rest of their claims have to be weighed and balanced against other sources, and their credibility tested. Over the years it has been informers or mob defectors who stunted the Mafia outfits. "Rats" such as Abe Reles, Joe Valachi, Jimmy "the Weasel" Fratianno, Sammy "the Bull" Gravano, and other biggies were credited with hammering the final nails in the Mafia coffin. That did not quite happen, however. The mob survived, bloodied no doubt but still able to function. Now with the bellweather Gambinos clearly on a murderous upgrade, the mob was worried about another rat in the ointment—a fresh Sammy the Bull—wrecking their newfound activities: Their obvious suspect was Mikey Scars DiLeonardo. That fear became ominously apparent in early 2003 when a June 2002 indictment was stripped of the Mikey Scars name and replaced with that of Peter Gotti, the brother of the late dynamic family boss, John Gotti.

The defection of DiLeonardo was a shocker to the wise guys. He had long been a bosom buddy of John Gotti Jr. and was trusted with many Gotti secrets and activities. Even when DiLeonardo was indicted for murder and racketeering, the mob take was that he would beat the raps, especially since he had beat federal extortion charges in a sensational strip-club trial in Atlanta in 2001. But apparently the feds had plenty of evidence against him, and soon DiLeonardo was doing some fancy flipping. He suddenly needed to reveal some alleged mob secrets he was privy to. What he offered to the feds, it was said, implicated Junior Gotti (godfather to Scars's teenage son) in three criminal acts: the 1983 fatal stabbing of 24-year-old Danny Silva; giving the order for the murder in 1992 of a "Bonnie and Clyde" stickup couple who had robbed a string of mob-connected social clubs (the couple was found dead in their maroon Mercury Topaz, each with three bullets in the head); and the attempted murder of Guardian Angels founder and radio talk show host Curtis Sliwa who was shot in the back and legs as he scrambled to flee from a taxi his would-be killers had stolen.

There were sundry charges against Peter Gotti and some of the most deadly Gambino soldiers, but the main charge certainly was that against JoJo Corozzo, a former driver and lookout for Dapper Don John Gotti. DiLeonardo fingered Corozzo as the new Gambino boss rather than figurehead Peter Gotti. It was said that Scars was all wired up to tape Corozzo in a discussion of current criminal doings, but the meet was canceled when Corozzo learned that DiLeonardo had flipped.

DiLeonardo's story of why he had defected was the standard canary song. He claimed he had been betrayed by the Gambino brass when they ignored his plea to provide for his lady, the usual treatment for an important wise guy on his arrest. That was not done for DiLeonardo or his mistress, 33-year-old Madelina Fischetti. According to Fischetti, the bosses told Scars "to tell me to go on welfare." The mob also suddenly stopped the flow of money routinely kicked up to Scars at the same time that feds had frozen his legitimate assets. The irate Fischetti was quoted by newsmen as saying, "They just left him hanging like a piece of garbage."

If the story was accurate, the mob would have been made up of clowns and idiots, who were tempting fate. It was dandy for the mob to claim Scars had offended the "rules" by going though with a messy divorce from his older mob-connected wife of 17 years, Toni Marie Fappiano, the sister of highly regarded Gotti soldier, Frankie Fap. The Mafia tradition was that while *goumatas* (mistresses) are for fun, wives are for keeps. Tradition or no tradition, the mob would not have moved against Scars if it meant imperiling the mob. It did so because Scars was warbling, and the mob suspected a deal had been worked that would in due course put him in the witness protection program. Fischetti started identifying herself as Scars's wife even though the feds denied a secret marriage was part of any cooperation deal.

None of this was terribly significant in the brutal cops-and-robbers game being played out. It was clear the government had a lot on Mikey Scars, who now was volunteering other wise guys to take his place in the law's crosshairs. Time will tell how much of Mikey's claims will stand up. Certainly the material on Peter and Junior Gotti have to be most appetizing to the law, prosecutors never being able to pass up any Gotti stories. For Junior Gotti, the Scars testimony could be devastating and extend his prison time considerably. Meanwhile in late 2003 Fischetti insisted she was living in terror of mob retribution: "My husband has helped a lot of people. He's saved lots of peoples' lives." Mikey's people-saving activities were one thing, but his cooperating with the authorities was arguably less likely to save his own life.

See also COROZZO, JOSEPH "JOJO"

DIO, Johnny (1915–1979): Labor racketeer

Under crime family boss Tommy "Three-Finger Brown" Lucchese, Johnny Dio, real name John Dioguardi, was one of organized crime's top "labor relations experts"—that is, labor racketeer. Dio was vital to Teamsters boss Jimmy Hoffa, who used him in his efforts to capture control of the union in New York City. Authorities also said Dio was the man who ordered the acid blinding of labor columnist Victor Riesel in 1956. At the time Riesel was causing Hoffa a good deal of grief with his hard-hitting columns. The law had conspirators ready to testify to Dio's role in the case but because of threats that reached them behind bars, these witnesses refused to speak in court and Dio went free.

Dio's standard labor relations method was to frighten everyone who might talk; it worked in the Riesel case as it did so often in the garment industry where the Lucchese family established any number of shops with no labor difficulties of any sort. If other manufacturers wanted the same consideration, they had to pay for Dio's assent. The underworld looked upon Dio as a master of his craft and other crime families invited him into their area to show them how to engage in the same rackets.

The Dragna family in Los Angeles brought Dio in as a consultant to advise on how to open factories by controlling the unions. Dio's blueprint for financial success showed the Dragna forces how to use terror against the International Ladies Garment Workers Union so that mob businesses could run without worrying about union pay scales and rules. By getting waivers on just about every contractual stipulation, the mob businesses got the edge on competitors who had to run under strict union conditions. The Dragna plan worked to perfection; profits, using what amounted to Mexican slave labor, were enormous.

Dio, who started out in crime as a protégé of Louis Lepke and Gurrah Shapiro, worked as a soldier in the Brooklyn Murder, Inc., troop. In the 1930s, New York racketbuster Thomas E. Dewey described Dio as "a young gorilla who began his career at the age of 15." By the age of 20, Dio was already an important mobster and a gang chieftain at 24. In the 1950s Senate investigators named Hoffa and Dio as the masterminds behind paper locals of the union that eventually got control of the highly remunerative airport trucking business in New York City. "It cannot be said, using the widest possible latitude," the McClellan Committee declared, "that John Dioguardi was ever interested in bettering the lot of the workingman."

Informer Joe Valachi was able to add some additional illuminating details about Dio. For about 12

Labor racketeer Johnny Dio (center, being booked) allegedly ordered the acid blinding of labor columnist Victor Riesel to score points with Teamsters boss Jimmy Hoffa.

years Valachi had a dress shop on Prospect Avenue in the Bronx, operated completely by non-union Puerto Rican women. "I never belonged to any union [sic]," Valachi testified. "If I got in trouble, any union organizer came around, all I had to do was call up John Dio or Tommy Dio and all my troubles were straightened out."

Dio was finally convicted when he branched out into stock fraud and he was sentenced to 15 years in prison in 1973. He died in a hospital in Pennsylvania where he was moved from a penitentiary by federal authorities. Dio's death attracted no newspaper attention for several days, even though a paid death notice appeared in the *New York Daily News*. It was as if the name Dioguardi had not meant anything.

See also RIESEL, VICTOR; TELVI, ABRAHAM

DIRTY graft: Payoffs to police and courts

Corrupt police officers frequently make a distinction between "clean graft" and "dirty graft." There are many who will accept so-called clean money but reject so-called dirty money. Clean graft is paid for overlooking such violations as gambling rackets, loan-sharking, liquor violations, prostitution and other activities described as vices natural to man. But police officers who accept clean graft turn down payoffs from mobsters engaged in narcotics violations. Drug money is considered dirty and not to be touched—usually.

As the Knapp Commission, which studied police corruption in New York City, noted, many officers who would take nothing but clean graft considered robbing narcotics dealers "clean," since "the City is going to get it [the money] anyway and why shouldn't they." As one witness explained at the commission hearings on stealing from arrested drug dealers: "The general feeling was that the man was going to jail, was going to get what was coming to him, so why should you give him back his money and let him bail himself out. In a way we felt that he was a narcotics pusher, we knew he was a narcotics pusher, we kind of felt he didn't deserve no rights since he was selling narcotics." In one typical arrest $127,000 was turned in to the Department while three officers split an additional $80,000. In another case $150,000 was confiscated and only $50,000 turned in while the arresting officers took $100,000 for themselves.

The corrupting influence of money can become overwhelming for most cops. Jack Newfield of the

Village Voice told of a black officer in the ghetto who locked up a heroin dealer. The dealer had on his person $5,000 more than the cop's annual salary and offered the entire sum to the officer to let him loose. The cop turned it down, and the dealer said, "Don't be a fool. If you don't take it, the judge will."

It was, unfortunately, a statement with considerable accuracy to it. There seem to be plenty of judges who will accept the mob's dirty graft. The record of the courts in New York City has been singularly disheartening. In the 1970s the State's Joint Legislative Committee on Crime, chaired by Republican Senator John Hughes of Syracuse, showed that major heroin dealers systematically received more lenient treatment than other defendants. Over a 10-year period 44.7 percent of indictments against organized crime figures were dismissed by State Supreme Court justices, compared to only 11.5 percent for all defendants. In 193 cases where mafiosi were convicted by a jury, the judge let the defendants off with no prison sentence 46 percent of the time. In Brooklyn, a staff report indicated that only 6 percent of heroin dealers charged with felonies got more than one year in prison. In the Bronx by contrast the comparable figure was 31.6 percent. Tolerant Brooklyn judges dismissed 42 percent of the felony cases against heroin dealers compared to only 15 percent of such cases thrown out by Bronx judges. (Three of the city's five Mafia crime families—the Gambinos, the Colombos and the Bonannos—have been centered in the hospitable borough of Brooklyn.)

Judges with records of coddling Mafia narcotics men cannot be ferreted out by simple analysis of their total narcotics sentencing figures. Most tend to be "tough judges" in run-of-the-mill cases involving minor characters against whom they throw the book. In some cases even the district attorney's offices have criticized cases of "oversentencing," allowing such judges to denounce the prosecutors as being "soft on criminals."

Unfortunately, there has never been the equivalent of a Knapp Commission for the investigation of the judiciary that can compare with the unit's work on police corruption. Consequently, we know more of the mob-connected activities of the police than those of the courts.

The Knapp Commission concluded that a "sizeable majority" of the city's 30,000 policemen took some form of graft. More sickening perhaps is the fact that the number of cops willing, able and eager to take dirty graft was obviously increasing. The commission noted, "[M]ore relaxed attitudes toward drugs, particularly among young people, and the enormous profits to be derived from drug traffic have combined to make narcotics-related payoffs more acceptable to more and more policemen." Graft from drug rackets puts young policemen in more direct crime contact with the Mafia and organized crime, which constitutes, as the saying goes, "the General Motors of the narcotics racket."

The taking of clean graft from the mob legitimizes the acceptance of dirty drug money as well, eventually; once cops are on the take they are willing to do ever more to keep the money flowing. The following, in the Knapp Commission's words, are some of the typical patterns or "numerous-instant" conduct exhibited by dirty graft takers:

- Purporting to guarantee freedom from police wiretaps for a monthly service charge.

- Accepting money or narcotics from suspected narcotics law violators as payment for the disclosure of official information.

- Accepting money for registering as police informants persons who were in fact giving no information and falsely attributing leads and arrests to them, so that their "cooperation" with the police may win them amnesty for prior misconduct.

- Introducing potential customers to narcotics pushers.

- Revealing the identity of a government informant to narcotics criminals.

- Kidnapping critical witnesses at the time of trial to prevent them from testifying.

- Providing armed protection for narcotics dealers.

- Offering to obtain "hit men" to kill potential witnesses.

Organized crime in short has turned dirty graft from an activity of a few "rotten apples" into a police cottage industry.

See also CLEAN GRAFT

DOCK Rackets: New Mafia's return to the waterfront

In 2002 it was like a return to the time of the classic movie *On the Waterfront* of a half-century ago. The mobs were back plundering the docks and the dockworkers' union. In twin cases being developed in Brooklyn and Staten Island, New York and in New Jersey, indictments alleged that the top two of the so-called Five Families—the Genovese and the Gambino—were back in business looting the docks. The two crime families, the government alleged, shared control of the waterfront, with the Genoveses running things in New Jersey while the Gambinos handled Brooklyn and Staten Island. Both crime clans used "threats of force, violence and fear" to control the docks. As one official said, "When it comes to the waterfront, the greedy grip of organized crime knows no bounds."

Just as in the 1940s, the wise guys rigged union elections. They guided the selection of a managed-care system so that they reaped fat kickbacks—$400,000 in one case. Dockworkers were forced to pay for their own jobs, and in one case mobsters extorted thousands of dollars from an injured longshoreman's disability settlement. So great were the mobsters' powers that they were said to control much of the doings of the local union and indeed the international union. One observer said, "It was just like the old days in the 40s even though these guys were too young to remember that."

Although the imprisoned John Gotti was at the time gravely ill in federal custody, the name still permeated the charges. John's brother Peter, the purported boss of the Gambino crime family, was indicted, as was another brother, Richard V., and Richard Jr. "So many Gottis were involved," said one journalist, "that the case took on a very sexy flavor." But the waterfront rackets could hardly be regarded as a family matter. The pie was so great that major crime families who clearly hated one another still had to cooperate on the docks. There simply were too many heads to bang, too much private and public money to be looted, that the boys seemingly had no time to worry about crossing one another—at least for now.

DONS: Mafia big shots

Some newsmen have traced the rise of a particular mobster upward in importance with a crime family until they finally announce he has been made a don. In that sense the don is the most capable leader of a group. Within the divisions of a crime family the soldiers following a particular capo or underboss might refer to him as "Don."

The title of don derives from Italy; it is a title of respect and honor all over southern Italy and Sicily and, for that matter, Spain. Although comments in the press and by law enforcement officials posit the title of "Don" as a specific position in the Mafia hierarchy, it has nothing to do with the structural makeup of the mob.

As a matter of personal vanity some mobsters want to be addressed by the title. Thus Vito Genovese was referred to as Don Vito. Joseph Barbara Sr. the host of the notorious Apalachin crime conference, was often called Don Giuseppe, a recognition of the fact that he was for many years an important member of the Buffalo Magaddino family.

The title don was sometimes cynically applied. In the early years of the syndicate, for instance, Genovese bridled at the increasing number and power of Jewish chieftains, and when Frank Costello suggested the Luciano-Lansky forces bring in the powerful Dutch Schultz, Genovese screamed, "What the hell is this? What're you tryin' to do, load us up with a bunch of Hebes?" Before Luciano, Meyer Lansky and Bugsy Siegel, Costello wheeled on Genovese and said very quietly, "Take it easy, Don Vitone, you nothin' but a fuckin' foreigner yourself." It was the custom thereafter of both Costello and Luciano and occasionally some other important boss, to call Genovese Don Vitone when they wanted to rub his nose in the dirt. Genovese never forgot this and his personal vendetta against Costello would extend over some three decades, always obsessed by the Don Vitone affront, until he masterminded the attempt on Costello's life.

Costello himself was often referred to as Don Francesco by mobsters and even by columnist Walter Winchell. Costello was a very tight-lipped gambler and often had information on a good thing, and when he did, other mobsters found the one way to get him to share the information was to ask, "Have any good tips, Don Francesco?" Costello could seldom resist such flattery and would share his hot information—although it inevitably cut into the odds he would receive.

Unlike "Mustache Pete," used disparagingly against some old-line mafiosi who could not alter their ways and adapt to the new methods of syndicate crime in America, the term *don* usually indicates a much respected oldster, of which there were and are many today in the American Mafia. In the New England crime family under the late Raymond Patriarca there was even a mob advisory council made up of the "old Dons," respected by the current leaders

as the men who had made the mob decades previously. Informer Vinnie Teresa said of them: "They got the town [Boston] in the bag, and it's been in the bag ever since. They were the ones who made the connections with the police departments. They'd had connections in the district attorney's office for thirty or forty years. They made the mob."

In their twilight years these men were accorded the title of don and although they no longer did anything except sit around in lounge chairs, Patriarca saw they got their cut from some kind of racket. And when they were needed in a crisis they were called to a meeting, just to get their thinking since they knew the nuances of mob mentality around the country. In this sense the concept of don has remained uncorrupted within the Mafia from its meaning in the old country.

DOUBLE-DECKER coffin   See MAFIA COFFIN

DRACULA: Keeper of DeMeo's murder clubhouse

His name was Joseph Guglielmo, and he was said to have been some sort of cousin of Roy DeMeo, the assembly-line hit man for Paul Castellano and the Gambino family. To others in the vicious murder crew, he was known simply as Dracula, or Drac for short. Dracula actually lived in the murder clubhouse where dozens of killings and dismemberments took place. It was his job to tidy things up and to make sure the bathroom was locked when unexpected visitors arrived or when the murder crew on a non-lethal night might have lady friends in for some affairs of the heart. After all a naked body or two might be hanging there to let the blood drip out. Drac also cleaned the floors, no easy task since despite all precautions blood inevitably stained them.

Dracula had to scrub and scrub and scrub and eventually, when the stains got too deep, repaint the floor. Just after one paint job, Dracula told a confederate with a certain pride in his voice, "There's a lot of history in that floor."

Dracula himself probably could not determine exactly how many killings and dismemberments took place in the clubhouse, but the most conservative estimates place the figure in the dozens.

No one ever quite knew how old Dracula was, though apparently he was somewhere in his 50s, and he was more or less regarded as a sort of mascot. However, when the feds started nearing the truth about the slaughter setup, Castellano felt the heat and decided it would be best if his prize killer, DeMeo, ceased his activities permanently. DeMeo was whacked.

This left Dracula in a peculiar position. He was indicted but never located. Authorities assumed that the murder mascot had lost his value to the mob, and that he too had been murdered and cut up in little pieces.

See also DeMeo, Roy

DRAGNA, Jack (1891–1957): Los Angeles crime boss

He was called by officials and the press "the Al Capone of Los Angeles"—something of an overstatement.

Boss of the "Mickey Mouse Mafia," Dragna was never strong enough to control crime in California or in nearby Las Vegas. L.A. became known within the national syndicate as an outfit incapable of organizing the diverse criminal elements of California in any effective manner. Independent bookmakers saw little reason to seek Dragna's "protection," and refused to pay him tribute.

When the eastern mobs decided to move the racing wire business into California, no serious thought was given to having Dragna handle it—even though California was his territory and syndicate rules required it. Instead, Bugsy Siegel was sent in. Similarly, the Chicago Outfit paid Dragna no mind when they moved in with their Hollywood rackets. If the L.A. Mafia and Dragna had been powerful, it would have been interesting to see Chicago stake its claim to everything west of the Windy City. As it was, Dragna could do little but acquiesce to the outsiders.

Dragna was particularly galled when Siegel moved in, but a firm warning from Lucky Luciano (from behind bars in New York) was enough to warn Dragna off. Siegel's presence involved more than the gambling wire. He was also the advance man for the eastern mobs seeking to establish a gambling empire in Las Vegas, a big-time operation for which Dragna was also deemed unsuited. Essentially, Dragna became little more than Siegel's hired gun, and inwardly he seethed and wished for the demise of the handsome, blue-eyed intruder.

Dragna was a man who thought small. The limit of his successful capers involved such matters as providing protection to certain illegal operatives and then sending in a confederate to shake them down. They would come crying to Dragna for protection and he would agree to do so, demanding, however, an extra payment. In at least one case the would-be victim kept insisting his tormentor, Dragna's secret ally, had to be killed, and when Dragna saw the victim could not be "cooled," he ordered the victim murdered. Dragna was a cheat, often victimizing not only outsiders but his own men as well.

When Siegel was assassinated, the story made the rounds that Dragna himself had eagerly handled the assignment, but this was very unlikely. Despite his denials, Meyer Lansky pushed for Siegel's execution and would hardly have trusted Dragna to carry it off successfully. As near as can be determined, the Siegel assassination was carried out by a longtime Lansky hit man, Frankie Carbo, who had previously committed a number of murders in league with Siegel. Naturally Lansky's people spread the gospel that Dragna had done the job.

Dragna rose to the top among the "home-grown" California mobsters only because he was the best of a poor lot—although practiced murderers, they simply lacked the abilities of their eastern compatriots. He was born in Corleone, Sicily, in 1891, and first immigrated to this country in 1898 with his parents. They returned to the old country 10 years later, but Dragna came back to the United States for good in 1914. Within a year he was convicted of extortion and did three years in San Quentin. After that Dragna was arrested many times but was never convicted—at least, in escaping punishment, he exhibited a true godfatherly trait.

After Siegel's demise it might have been expected that Dragna would at last establish his power in California, but he proved incapable of curbing Chicago and New York's intrusion into California, and, more significantly, into Las Vegas. Dragna never was able to get in on any major action in Vegas, and his incompetent dealing with Mickey Cohen, Siegel's top aide, who refused to cut Dragna and other mafiosi in on any of Bugsy's old L.A. gambling revenues, probably sealed his reputation as a blunderer. The Dragna family tried to kill Cohen any number of times and failed every time to the point, it was said, that it became a Hollywood comedy epic. As a result, Dragna simply never rated highly in the national councils of the underworld and was allowed in only on low-level action.

In his biography, *The Last Mafioso*, Jimmy "the Weasel" Fratianno tells of an alleged shakedown effort he and Dragna put on kingpin Lansky to get a cut of the Vegas action. According to Fratianno, he personally whacked around Lansky's tough underlings, Doc Stacher and Moe Sedway, until Lansky got the message that Los Angeles would have to be taken care of. Even if Fratianno's word is accepted on those claims, nothing came of it. Dragna later told Fratianno that Lansky sent word they could get a piece of the Flamingo (a Las Vegas casino hotel) for $125,000, a princely sum in the early 1950s. Dragna didn't have it and Los Angeles wound up with nothing. Fratianno functioned best on a lowly hit man level despite his ambitions and simply could not grasp the significance of a situation in which the alleged shakedown victim sets the terms. Lansky was actually rubbing their noses in the dirt, making them an offer they had to refuse, and demonstrating the full extent of his power.

Dragna's influence continued to wane. After he died in 1957, he was followed by a number of bosses and acting bosses—Frank DeSimone, Nick Licata, Dominic Brooklier, Louie Tom Dragna and Fratianno—all save Fratianno, at least by Fratianno's estimation, inferior even to Jack Dragna. The word on the West Coast mob remained—Mickey Mouse Mafia.

See also COHEN, MICKEY

DRAGNA, Louis Tom (1920–): Syndicate gangster

Louis Tom Dragna, identified by some journalists as the boss of the Mafia in southern California, was described by a federal judge in 1983 as "genteel"—even after he was convicted in the judge's court of racketeering, conspiracy and extortion. Informer Jimmy "the Weasel" Fratianno would probably describe him as "yellow."

Louie Dragna served as acting boss of the Los Angeles family in the 1970s when then-reigning boss, Dominic Brooklier, was off doing a stint in prison. Brooklier knew what he was doing; Dragna would never have had the nerve or the inclination to take over the mob permanently. At the same time, Brooklier realized that Dragna needed more spine. He named hit man Fratianno as co-leader with Dragna.

Louie Dragna was the nephew of the longtime boss of the family, Jack Dragna, who had died in 1957. Louie's father, a capable killer, served as Jack's consigliere until that same year.

After Fratianno turned federal informer, he described how Louie Dragna, sitting in a room with several other mobsters, watched when Fratianno and another expert killer, Frank "Bomp" Bompensiero, garroted one Russian Louie Strauss as he entered the room. Years later Dragna, according to Fratianno, was still ecstatic about how that killing had gone and told him: "I've never forgotten how quickly it happened to Russian Louie. The fucking guy walked in Gaspare's house and you and Bomp moved so fast he was a goner in ten seconds." The ingracious Fratianno said he put Louie Dragna down by telling him he "ought to try" killing someone himself sometime.

Louie was also in the dressmaking business. According to Fratianno, he was schooled by racketeer Johnny Dio who flew in special from New York to offer advice in the violent ways of slugging and intimidation so that it wouldn't be necessary to worry about union pay scales or rules. Eventually, the business Dragna started, Roberta Manufacturing, was doing $10 million a year and was perhaps the most profitable plant in its field in California, paying its Mexican women help, Fratianno estimated, an average of 85 cents an hour. Dragna is also believed to have been involved as an investor in the Las Vegas casino field; he was one of 11 "undesirables" banned by Nevada gambling authorities in their first "Black Book" issued in 1960.

In 1980 Louie Dragna was convicted along with four others—Brooklier, Jack LoCicero, Mike Rizzitello and Sam Sciortino—on conspiracy charges involving extortion of bookmakers and pornography dealers. The Justice Department's Organized Strike Force viewed the case as the most significant Mafia prosecution ever in Los Angeles. Of the five, U.S. District Judge Terry J. Hatter Jr. imposed the mildest sentence on Louie: two years with a recommendation that he be confined in a minimum-security honor camp. When he imposed sentence, Judge Hatter said he was taking into consideration Dragna's lack of prior convictions, the only one being a 25-year-old case involving extortion which was overturned on appeal. Hatter said he thought Dragna was on the "genteel" side and that he'd been drawn into the mob's conspiracy to extort pornographers and gamblers through a sense of loyalty to the deceased members of his family who had been leaders of the L.A. Mafia in the 1950s.

The Federal Bureau of Prisons refused to go along with Hatter's recommendations and slated Dragna to be sent to a medium-security prison. A federal attorney called Dragna a man "tied to La Cosa Nostra for

32 years." In a most unusual move the judge then tossed out the original sentence and resentenced Dragna to spend a year in a local community treatment center, placed him on five years' probation and fined him $50,000. At the treatment center Dragna was to be allowed out during the day to work at Roberta Manufacturing and return at night to the treatment center. Thus if Dragna was merely to be regarded as a reputed mafioso, he was subjected to a punishment federal authorities regarded as more reputed than real.

DRUCCI, Vincent "Schemer" (1895–1927): Chicago gang leader

The story may well be apocryphal except that Vincent "Schemer" Drucci was involved. It concerned the time the Schemer almost got Al Capone. He cornered him alone in a Turkish bath and almost strangled the notorious gangster to death before Capone's bodyguards showed up. The Schemer ran away—stark naked—jumped in his car and drove off.

Al Capone considered Vincent "Schemer" Drucci his toughest rival. The Schemer was capable of almost anything, no matter how insane, and Capone often referred to him as "the bedbug."

Drucci, one of the chief lieutenants in Dion O'Banion's North Side mob during the 1920s, was virtually the only Italian gangster in the predominantly Irish gang and certainly the only one O'Banion ever felt at ease with. Drucci took control of the gang after O'Banion and his successor, Hymie Weiss, were assassinated by the Capone forces.

The underworld tagged him "Schemer" because of his bizarre and totally off-the-wall plots for robbing banks and kidnapping millionaires. He was the object of several murder attempts by Capone gangsters and others, but he survived all underworld onslaughts. While trading shots in a gun battle with Capone gangsters, he roared with laughter and danced a jig to avoid the bullets pockmarking the pavement around him. When the ambushers gave up and drove off as the police arrived, Drucci was not about to stop the fight. Despite a slight leg wound, he tried to commandeer a passing automobile, hopping on the running board. He stuck his gun at the driver's head and shouted, "Follow that goddamn car." Police had to wrestle him off the auto.

When Drucci took over the O'Banion Gang, Capone beefed up his personal protection—the Schemer was capable of the wildest plot to get at him. When Capone was in a building, his machine gunners were stationed in the hallways. When he slept, his most trusted bodyguard slept on a cot placed flush with Capone's bedroom door.

Drucci tried several times to get Capone and is known to have once tracked him to Hot Springs, Arkansas, in hopes of getting him. Frustrated when all his schemes went awry, Drucci decided on some monstrous second-best strategy. He had his boys kidnap Theodore "the Greek" Anton, who owned a popular restaurant over Capone's headquarters at the Hawthorne Smoke Shop. Capone had a genuinely warm regard for the Greek, who, in turn, idolized Capone for his tenderheartedness, such as buying all a newsboy's papers for a large denomination greenback and sending him home. Capone was dining in the restaurant when lurking O'Banionites grabbed Anton, and Capone immediately realized the inevitable consequences. Big Al remained in a booth the entire evening crying inconsolably. Anton's tortured and bullet-riddled corpse was later found in quicklime. Raging, Capone swore he would kill Drucci, but it so happened that the next several moves were all made by the Schemer—against Capone and his men.

The Capones never, in fact, got Drucci. The duty—and what many Chicagoans called the honor—went to a police detective named Dan Healy, long noted for being rough on big gangsters. Whether he was too rough with Drucci was a matter of considerable speculation. In April 1927 Drucci was arrested while perpetrating some election violence against reformers trying to supplant the William Hale Thompson machine. The unarmed Drucci was put in a police squad car. In some accounts Drucci became violent, but this has been disputed. The fact is that he was in a police car surrounded by armed officers when suddenly, in broad daylight, at the corner of Wacker Drive and Clark Street—"for no reason that anyone could ever adduce," one journalist put it—Healy simply turned his revolver on him and pumped four bullets into him. The O'Banionites wanted Healy brought up on murder charges. "Murder?" asked Chief of Detectives William Schoemaker. "We're having a medal struck for Healy."

The North Side O'Banions did Drucci up fine at his funeral. There was a $10,000 casket of aluminum and silver, and the body lay in state for a day and a night at the undertaking establishment of John A. Sbarbaro, who moonlighted as an assistant state's attorney. There were so many flowers that the walls in the place were not visible. The chief floral design was a throne of purple and white blooms with the inscription, "Our Pal." Drucci's blonde widow said proudly after the burial, "A cop bumped him off like a dog, but we gave him a king's funeral."

(A postscript must be added about Dan Healy. When he killed Drucci, the Schemer was in deep disfavor with the Capone Gang. After Healy retired from the police force he turned up as chief of police of Stone Park. Stone Park was a West Side suburb noted for investment by syndicate gangsters in cocktail lounges, motels and Vegas-type gambling setups.)

See also STANDARD OIL BUILDING, BATTLES OF THE

DUKE'S Restaurant: Mob headquarters

Some newsmen called it the Mafia White House, but it was more the mob's Cabinet Headquarters. The address was 73 Palisades Avenue, Cliffside Park, New Jersey. The name of the place was Duke's Restaurant and it was, in the 1940s and 1950s, the meeting place and safe sanctuary for the leaders of the national crime syndicate. Presiding over Duke's which was situated directly across the street from the Palisades Amusement Park, was Joey Adonis, one of the leading mafiosi not only in New York and New Jersey, but also across the country.

Duke's appeared to be little different from thousands of other Italian restaurants, with a long bar and booths and serving typically tasty meals. However, at the rear of the public dining area there was an "ice box door," nearly indestructible and totally soundproof, that led to a large hidden room—often called the control room—from which the Mafia and much of organized crime planned and directed their operations.

Here on various days Adonis or Albert Anastasia marshaled their criminal activity, collecting the proceeds from various rackets, handling "table matters"—trials of syndicate mobsters for various alleged offenses—and deciding on hits. But on Tuesday, the most important day of the week, the top leaders of American crime converged on Duke's for their cabinet meetings. Generally these leaders were the so-called Big Six, the men who dominated the national commission. Winging in from the Midwest were Tony Accardo and Greasy Thumb Guzik, the representatives of the Chicago Outfit; Adonis; Frank Costello, running matters for the imprisoned and later deported Lucky Luciano; Meyer Lansky, who came from almost anywhere since he handled mob activities from Saratoga, New York, to Florida, the Caribbean and Las Vegas; and Longy Zwillman, the boss of New Jersey, noted as being a power in naming that state's governors and—of supreme interest to the mob—its attorneys general.

Duke's attracted considerable interest during the historic Kefauver Committee's hearings of the early 1950s, but probers came away with little hard evidence. Gangster Willie Moretti assured the committee the only reason he went to Duke's was for the cuisine and the ambiance, which, he said with a delightfully straight face, was "like Lindy's on Broadway." Mobster Tony Bender took the Fifth Amendment rather than say if he'd ever been in Duke's, insisting that even a visit to a restaurant could be incriminating.

A lot of law enforcement agencies kept an eye on Duke's, some trying to learn its secrets, others trying to protect them. Surveillance was carried out by the Internal Revenue Service, the Bureau of Narcotics and Manhattan District Attorney Frank Hogan's investigators. It was never easy. Law enforcement agents found that once they had crossed the George Washington Bridge into New Jersey, they were shadowed, hounded, badgered and sometimes even arrested by various local police departments. Investigators parked in a car outside of Duke's to log the various alleged diners entering Duke's were ordered to move by police, even after they displayed their credentials. Duke's was virtually in foreign territory.

After the Kefauver hearings, Duke's lost its value to the mob and the crime leaders abandoned it. It closed shortly thereafter—a menu of pasta minus the Mafia was not enough to keep it going.

E

EBOLI, Thomas "Thomas Ryan" (1911–1972): Genovese aide

Although he rose extremely high in organized crime circles, including sitting on the so-called commission as Vito Genovese's proxy when the latter went to prison, Tommy Eboli was clearly over his head. After Genovese's death in 1969, Eboli proved incapable of holding the crime family together. It was basically a case of a muscleman trying to do a brain's work.

Actually, it is often a myth that a crime family boss can long continue to hold control of his family's affairs from behind bars. But in the case of Genovese it was true. He knew how to pick subordinates he could cow so that they would never dream of trying to dethrone him. Eboli, a volatile and violent man, was always in awe of Genovese, considering Vito to be even more fearsome than himself. With such a personality, Eboli was extremely valuable to Genovese, a faithful retainer always eager to do his master's bidding.

But, despite fealty to Genovese, Eboli was too hotheaded to rule successfully. Under his own name and the alias of Tommy Ryan, Eboli made numerous forays into the sporting world as a sometime prizefight manager. He was eventually barred from boxing, not because of his underworld connections, but rather for jumping into the ring to deck a referee over a decision against his fighter. With his temperament he was always eager to do mayhem himself when he should have assigned it to underlings, thus qualifying as another underworld "cowboy," like Bugsy Siegel.

When Genovese, from his jail cell, ordered Eboli to have another top aide, Tony Bender, erased, Eboli, underworld whispers had it, did the job himself. Even in an affair as hot as the attempted assassination of Frank Costello, Eboli, according to a police theory, insisted on personally driving the escape car.

Eboli was not the only Genovese lieutenant put in charge when the boss went to prison. Control of the old New York Luciano-Costello family was left to a two-man regency of Eboli and Gerry Catena. Neither of them, in spite of whatever personal ambitions they had, were capable of running the family, placating the organization and still kowtowing to Genovese, who raged and spat orders from his Atlanta jail cell.

Eboli demonstrated little tact in dealing with other mafiosi. As a member of the commission he sometimes spoke mindlessly, insulting other members with comments Genovese had given him privately. As a result, even after Genovese's death in 1969 and Catena's imprisonment in 1970, Eboli had few allies to prop him up in power.

But Eboli did manage to build himself a private racket empire—nightclubs, music and records, vending machines, jukeboxes and Greenwich Village bars catering to homosexuals. He showed a pronounced disinclination to cut any of his troops in on the gravy and did little to lead them in other ventures or even supply them with financing in drug deals.

Not that Eboli wasn't deeply involved in drug trafficking himself. In 1972, Eboli helped finance a major deal with Louis Cirillo, tabbed by federal authorities as the largest wholesaler in the nation. Because he could not swing the required $4 million up front himself, he cut in Carlo Gambino and the leaders of other crime families. Possibly, he was seeking to ingratiate himself with them, but authorities cracked the plot. Cirillo got 25 years in prison. At that he was luckier than Eboli. The crime families' $4 million had gone down the drain. Gambino and the others blamed Eboli for the loss and suggested he make good. Eboli refused, under the illusion that the mob operated on some sort of luck-of-the-draw philosophy.

Intense discussions were held on replacing Eboli, the somewhat errant boss of the Genovese family. Gambino saw that his drug-money losses would be insignificant if he could get a cut of what the Genovese family should net from their rackets. Gambino had by this time gained varying degrees of control over the three other New York families, and, with his own man heading the Genovese family, his position as de facto boss of bosses would be virtually secure. Gambino decided on Funzi Tieri as Eboli's successor.

Eboli was not bright enough to gauge how perilous his situation was. In the early morning hours of July 1, 1972, the 61-year-old Eboli left the apartment of one of his many mistresses, in the Crown Heights section of Brooklyn. His bodyguard-chauffeur, Joseph Sternfeld, was opening the rear door of his Cadillac when a gunman in a red and yellow van put five shots in Eboli's face and neck at a range of about five feet. Eboli had not even time to grab the gold crucifix he wore around his neck. Eboli's bodyguard insisted he had hit the pavement at the sound of the first shot and had not seen who had done the shooting, a line that led to a perjury indictment. It eventually was dropped.

The saying in the underworld was that Eboli was granted the full "respect" of a boss in his hit. After all, it was said, he could have been popped on his way in to see his lady friend, but it was decided to let him have his joy before dying.

EGAN'S Rats: St. Louis gang

An independent criminal gang given a "new life" with the onset of Prohibition, Egan's Rats became the most powerful mob in St. Louis in the 1920s, working closely with the Capone gang in Chicago and the Purple Gang of Detroit.

Egan's Rats was founded around 1900 by Jellyroll Egan, who specialized in offering his army of hood-

lums as "legbreakers" to anti-union businessmen. As with other criminal gangs around the country, these activities sharply decreased just before World War I and remained only a minor activity in the immediate postwar period. Had it not been for Prohibition, it is highly unlikely that Dinty Colbeck, who took over on the death of Jellyroll Egan, could have held the organization together. Bootlegging meant enormous profits, more than the Rats had ever made before, and Colbeck emerged as the most important crime figure in the city.

Like criminals elsewhere who had once operated on the benevolence of politicians, Colbeck now became the dispenser of enormous bribes to crooked politicians and police so that his enterprises could operate without harassment. Dinty operated much like the cock-of-the-walk, approaching a policeman on the street, pulling out a huge wad of bills, and asking, "Want a bribe, officer?"

Dinty remained all his life a multi-purpose thief. He took his gang into safecracking and jewelry thefts, using Red Rudensky, a gang member who was the best safecracker of the 1920s. Colbeck also loaned out his men to other criminal gangs when they needed "out of town talent." There is considerable speculation that the Rats supplied some of the killers in the infamous St. Valentine's Day Massacre. Another Rat, Leo Brothers, may have been the murderer of Chicago newsman Jake Lingle or may simply have been loaned out to Capone who felt he needed a "fall guy" to take the heat off the case.

Just as Prohibition gave Egan's Rats a second crime life, Repeal took it away. The gang lost its importance when it could not adjust to the postbootlegging era. It was left to others to organize gambling in St. Louis, and Mafia elements, greatly factionalized in the city previously, came together in narcotics activities. Dinty Colbeck himself was assassinated in the late 1930s by rival mobsters, and the last of the Rats scurried off to join other criminal combinations in other cities.

EGG, break an   See WHACK

EIGHTH of the Eighth: Crime spawning area

In the early part of the 20th century, there was probably no more fertile breeding ground in America for the overlords of organized crime than a tiny waterfront district in Brooklyn. Called the "eighth of the eighth," a phrase for the Eighth Election District of the Eighth Assembly District, the area was overstocked in saloons, vile brothels, dreary tenements and other unsavory dens, and was labeled by one crime historian "a depraved, crime-ridden Barbary Coast of the East." More important, it was a veritable institution of higher education for a cadre of teenagers who emerged as top leaders of organized crime. The roster from just this single district included:

Johnny Torrio, the mastermind who first brought a high degree of unity to the warring mobs of Chicago in the 1920s.

Al Capone, Torrio's successor and certainly the most successful crime boss to rule a major American city.

Frankie Yale, the national head of Unione Siciliane and, for a time until his assassination in 1927, the most powerful gangster in Brooklyn.

Charles "Lucky" Luciano, the architect, together with Meyer Lansky, of the criminal syndicate that controlled much of the illegal activities in the United States.

Joe Adonis (Joseph Doto), who by the 1930s was the gangster political boss of Brooklyn and valued ally of Frank Costello.

Albert Anastasia, one of the most powerful crime family leaders in America and Lord High Executioner of Murder, Inc., who for years directed the activities of the hit men enforcers who carried out the deadly edicts of organized crime.

ENGLISH, Charles Carmen "Chuckie" (1914–1985): Chicago Outfit capo

Extremely close to Chicago crime boss Sam Giancana, Chuckie English (né Inglese) had dinner at the Giancana house the night of Sam's murder but is dismissed as a murder suspect by the late don's daughter, Antoinette Giancana. She said that since childhood she regarded him as "family." In fact, in the period after Giancana's death there was some speculation that a bloody purge of his most loyal followers would ensue and that English would be a likely victim. That did not happen.

With a record dating back to 1933, English has been charged over the years with such sundry crimes as murder, robbery, extortion, hijacking, loan-shark-ing and counterfeiting phonograph records—the last, a major Mafia industry. He was identified in both the Valachi hearings and the 1983 U.S. Senate subcommittee hearings, and took the Fifth Amendment 56 times before the McClellan labor rackets committee.

Giancana used English as the point man for Chicago's crime penetration of Arizona. English was his constant golf companion, it being said they felt it safest to discuss crime strategy on the fairway. English stood by while Giancana was the subject of an FBI lockstep surveillance, a technique described to force the subject to react in illogical ways and perhaps betray himself in some fashion. An exasperated Giancana did slip once, sending an irate English after two FBI agents to relay his message: "If Bobby Kennedy wants to talk to me I'll be glad to talk to him and he knows who to go through." The clear inference to the FBI agents was that the party indicated was singer Frank Sinatra. Sinatra was known to be very tight with Giancana—and for a time at least with the Kennedys.

Actually this scene was cited by some members of the Chicago crime family as proof that Giancana was starting to go "goofy" and that the senior powers, Paul Ricca and Anthony Accardo, should take control of the outfit from Giancana. English appears to have been criticized for not talking Giancana out of such injudicious conduct. It appears to have started Giancana on a slow road down from power, to his later removal and ultimately to his murder in 1975.

Chuckie English suffered no retribution—at least, of a fatal nature—with Giancana's departure, but he clearly lost his muscle within the organization. Long a high-ranking lieutenant, English was demoted to mere soldier status, serving under Joey "the Clown" Lombardo. English continued to bewail his reduced status and to bad-mouth the Outfit's leadership, which he felt was inferior to that during his good old days with Giancana. Finally, Accardo had enough and ordered English put to sleep.

See also PASS

ENVELOPE: Mob gift custom

It is the Mafia custom at gangland weddings, baptisms and funerals to donate an "envelope" to those involved, to the bride and groom, to the proud parents and to the grieving widow, respectively. When Chicago crime boss Sam Giancana's daughter (of

Mafia Princess fame) was married, wedding guests from New York to California contributed envelopes totaling more than $130,000, and this was in addition to more than $40,000 given previously at the bridal shower.

The most important envelopes are those given to widows of mobsters who have come to a bad end. When Chicago mafioso Sal Moretti was murdered, the largest envelope was presented to the widow by Giancana who offered his words of regret. Never mind that it was Giancana who had ordered the Moretti hit.

But for sheer tenderheartedness after a hit, honors must go to Sammy "the Bull" Gravano. He was in on the killing of Louie Milito, whose body was never found. Milito's daughter came to the Bull for help since her father and he were longtime business partners. "Don't worry, princess, I'll get back to you," Gravano told her. He did, but offered no trace of Milito. Instead, he gave her an envelope with enough cash to aid the widow and family. As he said in *Underboss,* "I felt bad for her and the kids."

Gravano had gotten an earlier contract on Milito canceled, but finally he agreed he had to be hit. The widow and kids "were why I had fought to keep him alive, even though her and Louie were getting close to a divorce." The Bull claimed it had cost him $20,000 to finish construction the victim had been doing on his house. He also told the widow to check with him if anyone gave her any problems "because sometimes there are assholes who will get their little brave pills because a guy is dead."

In Gravano's view he was carrying the envelope custom to a higher moral plane.

ETHNIC succession in the Mafia See BLACK MAFIA

EYES in the sky: Crooked gambling technique

Once organized crime moved into gambling in a big way, it was only logical that its operatives would set up cheating operations. A common method used in both crooked casinos and private games was called "eyes in the sky," concealed peepholes in the ceiling through which silent watchers could stare at card players. Meyer Lansky, a leading proponent of such peeping methods in casinos, gave them something of a legitimate explanation—they were needed to watch dealers and players to make sure there was no collusion between them. However, the likely purpose was to cheat big bettors in key games.

Mob leader Vito Genovese was involved in a number of eyes-in-the-sky swindles. In one private game, Genovese and one of his lieutenants, Mike Miranda, bilked a gullible merchant out of $160,000, in part by getting signals from a spy in the room above as to what cards the merchant had in his hand.

But cheating is not merely a case of Mafia vs. dupe. Following the eyes-in-the-sky scam described above, Genovese and Miranda, promised another mobster, Ferdinand "the Shadow" Boccia, $35,000 to set up the victim. Instead they hired two hoodlums, William Gallo and Ernest "the Hawk" Rupulo, to assassinate Boccia. They hired Rupulo to dispatch Gallo. Later still, Rupulo was killed. It appears the guiding principle in Mafia gambling scams is: Cheat everybody.

F

"FBI Badfellas": Worst alliance between feds and mobsters

For decades the late FBI director J. Edgar Hoover was accused of failing to permit his agents to go after organized crime and the Mafia in particular. Knowledgeable sources, not illogically, declared Hoover was fearful that if his men got too involved with organized crime they would inevitably be mired in corruption because so much money was around for the taking. Later facts proved this worry well founded. (Hoover was dead by the time of the massive involvement between the FBI and Boston Irish mobsters to frame a number of mafiosi for crimes, including murders, for which they were not guilty, but that did not preclude censure for him.)

For decades, it emerged, FBI agents in the Boston office had provided tips to organized crime leaders to help them eliminate witnesses against them, sent innocent men to prison for life, lied to other law enforcement agencies and covered up crimes committed by their informers. Later court testimony showed that many agents, besides the worst offender, John J. Connolly Jr., got into bed with mobsters and took money as rewards for their help in rooting out informers. Investigations undertaken internally by the FBI found that the agency heads in Boston covered up misconduct by agents.

The House Government Reform Committee after the turn of the 21st century, decades after Hoover's death, came up with what investigators called a "smoking gun" memo from 1965 that showed Hoover was informed that four innocent men with links to Boston mafiosi had been sent to prison for life for a murder the FBI knew was committed by one of its Boston informers. In 2002 a congressional investigator declared that the actions of the Boston bureau revealed "a culture of concealment, where the FBI got itself into a protective mentality and cared less about justice being done than about protecting itself when agents made mistakes." Covered up for years was the fact that agent Connolly had helped a powerful organized crime outfit in Boston headed by James "Whitey" Bulger, who was allegedly an FBI informer. The evidence adduced more logically that Bulger appeared to have the local FBI "in his hip pocket." Later agent Connolly tipped off Bulger that a secret indictment order was out against him, and Bulger fled. Whitey Bulger was still in hiding in 2004 and on the FBI's 10 most-wanted list with a $1 million reward for his capture.

It can be said that the FBI was perhaps more successful in breaking the power of the Italian Patriarca and Angiulo mobs, which controlled organized crime in New England, than any other Mafia group in the United States. Bulger's Irish Winter Hill Gang then proceeded to take over rackets in Boston, in gambling, loan-sharking, selling drugs and committing murders when they served their interests. The FBI simply looked the other way.

There was much to look away from. Typical findings by the House Government Reform Committee included that two mobsters, Joe Barboza and Vincent Flemmi, killed a small-time hoodlum named Edward Deegan, as shown in memorandums from the Boston office to headquarters in Washington, D.C. Shortly thereafter Hoover's office demanded to know what progress was being made to turn Vincent Flemmi into an informer. The Boston office replied five days later that he was in a hospital recovering from gunshot wounds but because of his connections with the Mafia he "potentially could be an excellent informant." Hoover was also informed that Vincent Flemmi (not to be confused with his brother, Stephen, another mobster) was known to have killed seven people, "and, from all indications, he is going to continue to commit murder." But the agent added, in words that apparently soothed Hoover, "the informant's potential outweighs the risk involved." One congressional investigator called the exchange chilling: "The most frightening part is that after being warned about Flemmi's murders, the director does not even respond. There is no message not to use a murderer as a government informant."

Later, Stephen Flemmi became an informant. Many cases were solved, but others were not, including the murders of two girlfriends of Stephen whose bodies were later found in sandy graves in Boston Harbor. There were strong indications that the women were about to talk to authorities. What was amazing was how long the so-called FBI badfellas functioned, especially since other law agencies began to see that the Boston FBI had been "penetrated," leading to bad relations with all other law enforcement agencies.

Eventually, there were too many loose strings and Connolly was indicted and finally sentenced to 10 years imprisonment, the maximum under federal sentencing guidelines. Connolly did far better than four men wrongfully tried, convicted and sentenced either to life imprisonment or the electric chair. At that Connolly might be said to have gotten off very lightly. By the time the four victims of a frameup for murder were "cleared," almost three decades had passed. Two of the four had died in prison. Another, Peter Limone had been sentenced to death but was spared when Massachusetts outlawed the death penalty in 1974. The fourth man, Joseph Salvati, spent 30 years in prison (his wife visited him every week during those 30 years) and later took up residence in a modest apartment on Boston's North End. Recently Limone and the survivors of the two men

who had died behind bars filed a $375 million lawsuit against the Justice Department. Salvati sued the FBI for $300 million. In all, suits against the government have been estimated to have passed the $2 billion mark. Meanwhile very few on the government side have had to pay any penalty since the statutes of limitations in most cases had passed. Besides the monies being contested, as a strict count from a law and order viewpoint it was stated that the FBI's New England operation had been "one of the greatest failures in the history of federal law enforcement." It was estimated that more than 20 people had been killed by informants in Boston, frequently with the assistance from the bureau's agents.

See also CONNOLLY, JOHN J.

FERRO, Don Vito Cascio (1862–1932): Sicilian Mafia leader

Don Vito Cascio Ferro is often called the "greatest" of all the Mafia leaders of Sicily. He was certainly the most charismatic—physically impressive, tall, lean, elegantly attired in frock coat, pleated shirt, flowered cravat and wide-brimmed fedora. In his later years he also adorned himself with a wide, flowing beard. Today, more than a half century after his death, many Sicilians still speak of him in awe and cite him as an example of the manly virtues of dignity and strength. He was virtually illiterate but he bore himself with the manner of royalty. When he ventured forth from Palermo, he was greeted by mayors at their town gates; they kissed his hand in homage.

Don Vito carried the Honored Society to the apogee of its power on the island, developing the practice of *pizzu*, which translates as "wetting the beak," a system under which the Mafia collects a small tribute or tax on virtually every business in Sicily. Under Don Vito every sort of businessman and shopkeeper had to pay regularly for protection. If they refused, their businesses were ruined, shops and homes destroyed and crops burned.

Some historians attribute to Don Vito the development of the system of protection payoffs in the United States as well, but such methods of extortion flourished in New York City long before Don Vito visited there in 1900. In fact, Virgil W. Peterson, longtime head of the Chicago Crime Commission, feels ". . . his later operations in Sicily may have been influenced somewhat by what he had observed in New York City."

Don Vito was born in 1862 to tenants of an aristocratic landowner, Baron Inglese, at Bisaquino. His criminal career started early with arrests for assault in 1884; threatening public officials, extortion and arson and assault by 1893; and, in 1899, he was accused of taking part in the kidnapping of a baroness. Don Vito fled to New York City where he found refuge with a sister who operated a small shop on 103rd Street.

Don Vito's activities in this country are hazy, but police suspected him of killing at least one man. The victim was stabbed to death, chopped to pieces and stuffed in a barrel. Before the New York police could locate Don Vito, he fled to New Orleans where it was said he cemented relations with certain criminals to print counterfeit dollars in Sicily and smuggle them into the United States.

When Don Vito returned to Sicily he expanded his criminal activities, formed his key Mafia band in Palermo and organized much of the crime on the island. He was known to send counterfeit money as well as other contraband to mafiosi in both New York and New Orleans, and he dispatched many Sicilian criminals to the United States as part of his criminal network.

In 1909, the legendary New York police detective Joseph Petrosino came to Sicily to gather evidence for the deportation of Italian criminals from the United States. Petrosino was murdered almost certainly at Don Vito Cascio Ferro's instigation. A popular theory, one fostered by Don Vito himself, was that the Mafia chieftain did the job himself.

Petrosino was walking in the deserted Piazza Marina one night when two men jumped out from behind a tree and shot him three times in the back and head. Blood flowing down him, Petrosino held himself erect by grabbing the iron grating of a window. Then a third man appeared and fired the coup de grace, a bullet directly in the detective's face.

Don Vito, according to this version, had been dining that evening in the house of a deputy to the Italian Parliament. Midway through the cheese serving he had excused himself, taken his host's carriage and driven to the Piazza Marina. After killing Petrosino, he took the carriage back to his host's home and continued dining. The host later swore Don Vito had never left his company the entire evening.

There is little doubt that the killing of Petrosino added much prestige and power to Don Vito, both in Sicily and with grateful gangsters in America. Don

Vito concentrated for several years on building his power in Sicily, but he had long-range plans for becoming the head of the Mafia in America as well. In 1927, Don Vito sent his agent, the cunning Salvatore Maranzano, to New York to organize the Mafia forces there under one leadership. It is not clear whether he intended to install Maranzano in power there or follow himself. Chances are he had the latter course in mind since Benito Mussolini, jealous of Mafia power, was seeking to destroy the criminal society in Sicily.

In 1929 Don Vito was arrested by the Italian government. Because he could not find real evidence against Don Vito, Mussolini's chief agent in his anti-Mafia campaign, Cesare Mori, manufactured a frame-up charge of smuggling. Don Vito contemptuously refused to speak at his trial until its conclusion when he said, "Gentlemen, since you have been unable to find any evidence for the numerous crimes I did commit, you are reduced to condemning me for the only one I have not." Don Vito was confined in Ucciardone Prison where he died in 1932, and for many years other criminals took it as a high honor to be confined in the cell where the greatest Mafia chieftain spent his final years.

Meanwhile, in America Maranzano was on his own once Don Vito was imprisoned. He decided he could fill the void as the boss of bosses of the American Mafia. He fought the Castellammarese War to a successful conclusion with the death of his arch-foe Joe the Boss Masseria. Maranzano organized the New York Mafia into five families with himself above them all.

However, Maranzano's and Don Vito's dream of a Sicilian boss of bosses in America lasted less than five months. Maranzano was murdered by the Luciano-Lansky combination that would instead put in place a multi-ethnic national crime syndicate.

FIVE Iron Men: Kansas City crime rulers

It has been said there were few cities in America west of Chicago that could match the corruption that gripped Kansas City, Missouri. Yet numerically the number of actual mafiosi in the city was rather small. This may be explained in part by the presence of the Chicago Outfit which, from the time of the establishment of the national crime syndicate by Lucky Luciano and Meyer Lansky, laid claim to everything to its west. (Chicago's claim was recognized basically everywhere but in Nevada and California and, to a limited extent, in Arizona.)

The other mobs had little interest in going into Kansas City; they recognized it as being an empire to itself under the powerful administration of political boss Tom Pendergast. As a matter of fact, in the deliberations started in the late 1920s and early 1930s that culminated in the formation of the national syndicate, Pendergast was the only political boss invited to take part. When Pendergast found it inopportune to attend himself, he sent Johnny Lazia, the king of the North Side wards, as his spokesman.

Pendergast, who controlled the Mafia in Kansas City far better than did other political machines, made it obvious to the mobsters that he was as ready to use violence and murder as they were. When Lazia was hit with a tax evasion conviction in 1934, he showed signs of turning informer against the machine; his lips were sealed by a machine gun assassination almost certainly decreed by the Pendergast forces.

According to a report of the Federal Narcotics Bureau, the Kansas City Mafia entered into the narcotics trade in 1933 with the end of Prohibition. Among the main personnel in the operations were such important mafiosi as Joseph De Luca, Nicole Impostato and James De Simone.

With the death of Lazia, Charley Binaggio, the fastest rising criminal light in Kansas City, eventually took over the North Side wards and delivered votes for the Pendergast machine. When Tom Pendergast and his machine got in deeper legal troubles, Binaggio continued to advance. As an apparent Mafia member himself (to others he insisted there was no such thing as a Mafia, past, present or future), he became one of the "Five Iron Men" who ruled much of Kansas City criminal activities. Others of the five were Binaggio's enforcer, Charley Gargotta (of whom Senator Estes Kefauver, following the crime hearings of the 1950s, would say, "If ever a human being deserved the title of 'mad dog' it was Gargotta") and three other mafiosi, Tano Lococo, fat Tony Gizzo and grizzled old Jim Balestrere, the reputed Mafia boss in the city.

Balestrere, an ancient Sicilian-born mobster, had a public line of playing dumb and representing himself as a poor old jobless fellow who lived on a little income from a piece of business property (which turned out to be used for a gambling enterprise) and on a few dollars given him by his children. He used

the same ploy before the Kefauver committee. He told the senators that after Prohibition he "needed a job" as he could no longer sell sugar to bootleggers, and he went to Tom Pendergast for assistance. He said Pendergast fixed it up so he got a cut of a keno gambling game run by some local racketeers. With a straight face, Balestrere said he had not put up any money. "I just went up there every month and checked up there and they give me a check, and I walk right out."

"In other words, Tom Pendergast simply gave you a sort of gift?" he was asked.

"Give me something to live."

Then, amazingly, Charley Binaggio did the same sort of thing, just sort of giving him a piece of a gambling joint known as Green Hills. It happened, Balestrere said, one day as he was just walking to the movies. He ran into Binaggio who asked, "What are you doing?"

The old mafioso told the Kefauver committee: "I said, 'Ain't doing nothing. I am trying to do some, to open me a little business or something like that.' He said, 'You know, I am getting a piece out at the Green Hills. Do you want any?' 'Oh,' I said, 'I am not much in the gambling business. I don't know much about it.'

"He said, 'Well, that is all right.' I didn't see him no more. About thirty days later he came in and brought me some money. I said, 'What is this?' He said, 'We win, and here is your end.' Okay, I took the money."

In all he got $5,000, he said.

Tongue in cheek, committee chief counsel Rudolph Halley asked what would have happened if Binaggio had told Balestrere he had lost $500. Balestrere became very earnest and said, "With the kid, I used to know him so well, I don't think he would tell me anything out of the way."

Binaggio eventually told someone something out of the way, and he and Gargotta were subjected to underworld execution in 1950. Their deaths together with Lococo's imprisonment for income tax fraud spelled the end of the Five Iron Men, although the Mafia influence did not die in Kansas City. By the 1970s, Mafia power had passed to Nick Civella who became a power in Las Vegas gambling and, in partnership with the Chicago family, instrumental in putting the later-discredited Roy Williams in as head of the Teamsters. When Civella went to prison in the 1970s, it was said he still ran his crime family from behind bars despite the power struggle that ensued between Carlo De Luna and Carlo Civella for position.

See also BINAGGIO, CHARLES

FIVE Points Gang: Pre-Prohibition gang

Probably more modern-day gang leaders came out of the turn-of-the-century Five Points Gang and its allied organizations than from any other outfit in America. The Five Pointers were the last great pre-Prohibition gang in New York, composed of an army of about 1,500 eye-gouging terrorists, virtually all Italian. They represented the transition between the 19th-century cutthroat Irish street gangs—such as the Dead Rabbits, the Plug Uglies and the Whyos—and the outfits of the 1920s, which formed the nucleus of what became organized crime in America.

The only chieftain the Five Points Gang ever had was an ex-bantamweight prizefighter of some skill named Paolo Antonini Vaccarelli, better known as Paul Kelly. In the pre–World War I era of union organizing and union busting, Kelly leased out his troops to businessmen as strikebreakers, to other mobs as hit men for hire and to politicians to control voting.

Kelly was an efficient organizer, and members of youth gangs that flocked to him for recognition hoped for nothing more than eventually to gain admission to the Five Pointers proper. One of Kelly's most ardent admirers was Johnny Torrio, then a young man in his early 20s, who ran a youth gang called the James Street Gang under Kelly's tutelage. Thus, through Torrio, Kelly became in future years the sponsor and spiritual godfather of such very young gangsters as Al Capone, Lucky Luciano and Frankie Yale. While the Five Pointers were virtually all Italian and fought many a battle with Monk Eastman and his equally large and powerful collection of Jewish gangsters, Kelly recruited some other ethnics. Among them were the likes of the Jewish Kid Dropper who was, before his murder in 1923, the biggest labor slugger-extortionist in the postwar era. Kelly was probably the first to indicate to Torrio—and certainly to Luciano—that Italians could cooperate with gangsters of other nationalities in the quest for money. It was a lesson that Luciano never forgot.

Kelly maintained his headquarters in the New Brighton Dance Hall on Great Jones Street. He owned the place, which was one of Manhattan's fleshpots and a magnet for slumming socialites eager to rub shoulders with a real live gang leader like Kelly. Kelly could play the role because he was dapper and urbane, with a certain amount of self-education and a touch of cultural tastes. For many he became Society's naughty darling.

However, it was criminality that kept Kelly and the Five Pointers going. By 1915 the gang was rapidly deteriorating. With reform movements, labor slugging faded as an activity, and late that year Kelly found a permanent little niche for himself in a little labor fiefdom—organizing the Garbage Scow Trimmers Union, the ragpickers on the dumps at the East River and several other small but later influential harbor unions. Kelly left his bailiwick on the Lower East Side and moved into a house at 352 East 116th Street, owned by his gangland friends, the Morello family and Ciro Terranova.

All that remained of the Five Pointers were their heritage and their successful graduates—Torrio, Capone, Luciano, Yale and others, who went on to raise the heights of criminal power during the Prohibition era.

FLAMINGO Hotel: Las Vegas's first plush casino

It started with the Flamingo, the first of Las Vegas's glittering casinos. It was built with mob money under the supervision of violent and colorful Bugsy Siegel.

Siegel, a longtime associate of Meyer Lansky—with Lucky Luciano one of the top two powers in organized crime in America—had come west in the late 1930s to handle the mob's betting empire. In time, he became a fervent shill for turning Las Vegas, then a dusty stop in the middle of the desert, into a glittering gambling paradise.

Actually, Lansky had pioneered the idea and sent an aide, Moe Sedway, there in 1941. At the end of World War II, Siegel, Sedway, Gus Greenbaum and Israel "Ice Pick Willie" Alderman—all close Lansky associates—bought a small nightclub there. They later sold the place and invested the revenues in the Nevada Project Corporation, the vehicle that financed the building of the Flamingo. Lansky was exercising a tactic he had learned by studying the ways of big business, having underlings go out front on an idea and then step forward to take the credit if things worked out right.

But Siegel appeared to be doing nothing right in building the hotel, which he named the Flamingo, the nickname of his mistress, Virginia Hill, the former bedmate of numerous high mafiosi from coast to coast. From the beginning, construction was beset by troubles that led to inflation of the costs. Anxious mobsters saw their investments being gobbled up—$2 million became $4 million which became $6 million—and started worrying that Bugsy was doing more than wasting their money. Virginia, a practiced bagwoman taking mob money to Switzerland to be stashed in numbered accounts, started going there regularly on Bugsy's behalf. When asked why she was flying off to Zurich so often, she got rather vague, mumbling that she was shopping for furnishings and curtains for the hotel. The mob had a different theory, that Siegel was skimming off the construction money and had tucked away more than a half million dollars in his personal account.

The building contractor, Del E. Webb, got pretty concerned about a sudden influx of mobsters on the site and complained to Siegel about it. The handsome gangster laughed and assured Webb not to worry. He used a line that was to become a classic, "We only kill each other."

At the time Siegel probably still thought he could survive. The mob, from Lansky on down, had advised him they wanted their money back. Bugsy undoubtedly thought he could pay them back by skimming off the profits once the Flamingo opened. Unfortunately, the opening was a disaster. Siegel, a man about Hollywood, had assembled a top-flight cast to attract an expected horde of guests—George Jessel was master of ceremonies and featured stars included Jimmy Durante, Baby Rose Marie, the Turn Toppers, Eddie Jackson, and Xavier Cugat and his band. Among the guests were some of Siegel's Hollywood friends, George Raft, George Sanders, Charles Coburn; but many more did not show up. Among other errors, Siegel had staged his opening between Christmas and New Year's, a period considered deadly in the entertainment business.

Siegel's fate was then sealed, and a death sentence was passed on him at a famous meeting in Havana presided over by the deported Lucky Luciano. Lansky, who actually called the meeting, did little or nothing to save Siegel. Bugsy was assassinated the following June. By the end of the year new management inserted by Lansky had turned the Flamingo around and it made a $4 million profit—and that

was nothing compared to the unreported profits that were skimmed off.

The Flamingo was a huge success, even if it killed Bugsy Siegel. The mob began pouring millions into Las Vegas, building casino after casino. The Flamingo had a checkered history thereafter, always involving Lansky, although he did not appear as an owner of record. In the mid-1950s, the Flamingo was bought by the Parvin-Dohrman Company which was headed by Albert B. Parvin, a one-time interior decorator whose chief claim to fame previously was having laid the carpets in many of the big hotels. In 1960, Parvin sold the place to a syndicate headed by Miami Beach hotel man Morris Landsburgh (of the Eden Roc) who was coincidentally an old buddy of Lansky's. Lansky collected a $200,000 finder's fee from Parvin in the transaction. Landsburgh and his associates tired of the Flamingo when the government started digging into allegations of skimming in Las Vegas. In 1967 they sold out to Kirk Kerkorian, a former non-scheduled airline operator. And Lansky collected a fee when that sale was made. Lansky (along with five others) was indicted for skimming $30 million from the Flamingo from 1960 to 1967; he was accused of having hidden interests in the Flamingo during those years.

Lansky was not convicted on any of the charges.

See also GREENBAUM, GUS; LAS VEGAS; SIEGEL, BENJAMIN "BUGSY"

FORTY Thieves: Harlem's black rivals of the Mafia

Black ghettos have long been prime looting ground for the Mafia's gambling operations. While there is much talk about the blacks taking over numbers operations, the fact remains that most numbers banks run by ghetto residents are required to pay franchise fees to the Mafia. Recently and for years for example, a top Harlem operator, Raymond Marquez, paid Fat Tony Salerno of the Genovese family 5 percent of his take just to operate. That figure was extremely low because Marquez had always been a favorite of top mafiosi, his father having worked for Vito Genovese.

The belief that blacks own and operate their own rackets—as much an example of black pride as anything else—is nothing new in the black ghettos. In Harlem in the late 1930s, an extremely tough gang of blacks, the Forty Thieves, came along. According to ghetto folklore, they effectively battled the East

Harlem mobsters for a piece of the numbers business and did not make payoffs to the Italians.

If there is truth to this legend, the truth is odd. It certainly would represent an abrupt change in organized crime's tactics in Harlem. Dutch Schultz had moved in during the early 1930s to take over the Harlem numbers from black independents who had run it when the organized criminals failed to appreciate the racket's potential. Once Schultz did so, he moved with savage efficiency to take over. His enforcers used guns, knives, blackjacks, brass knuckles and, more imaginatively, wet cement (to blind a victim). A legendary black woman operator, Madame St. Clair, had to hide in a cellar under a pile of coal to keep from being murdered by some of Schultz's hit men. Schultz used Ciro Terranova's gunners to keep Harlem under control and when the empire passed after the Dutchman's death to the supervision of the brutal Trigger Mike Coppola, the enforcement tactics did not ease.

Despite these obvious facts, a mystique built up around the Forty Thieves. These undoubtedly tough gangsters started out as an extortion ring, operating from 140th Street and Seventh Avenue. In 1939, they established what they described as their own policy setup. Harlemites fully believed that the Forty Thieves bankers ran their banks without paying a cent to the East Harlem syndicate. The Forty Thieves claimed as much to other blacks and said they maintained their own hit men who kept Mafia mobsters away. The perception was that Italian criminals had no stomach for battling tough blacks; but the argument still seems specious. The full force of the Italian underworld would have come into play.

In fact, the mob probably could have tamed the Forty Thieves without using force. Other black operatives functioned only by paying off Coppola, who saw to it that they operated with minimal police interference. Recalcitrant Forty Thieves would have faced not only gangland violence but also official harassment. Most likely the Forty Thieves paid, like other blacks, but found their posture of supposed deadly independence very valuable in "selling" their extortion shakedowns. After all, there was not much hope for a small black businessman standing up to black racketeers who supposedly took the measure of the Mafia.

See also BLACK MAFIA

FORTY-TWO Gang: Chicago juvenile gangsters

The worst juvenile gang produced in the United States, the 42 Gang was certainly the best "farm team" Chicago's Capone Mob ever had. It would be hard to find a bigger collection of crazies than the notorious 42 Gang—even the Jewish and Italian cliques of Brownsville and Ocean Hill, Brooklyn, gangs feeding Murder, Inc., did not supply anywhere nearly the number of soldiers for the national crime syndicate. And surely no juvenile gang gave Chicago police nearly as much trouble as the 42ers.

More is known about the 42ers than other criminal gangs because they were the specific subjects of many scholarly analyses. In 1931, an in-depth study by sociologists of the University of Chicago revealed some incredible statistics. Of members considered to be in the original 42, more than 30 had been maimed, killed or were serving time for such crimes as murder, armed robbery, rape (a prime gang pastime) or other felonies. Ready to commit any act for a quick buck, they stripped cars; robbed cigar stores; marched into nightclubs and staged holdups; slipped into peddlers' stables and stole their carts or killed their horses, hacking off the hind legs to supply certain outlets with horse meat. In their home—the "Patch," or the Little Italy section of Chicago's West Side—they were idolized by many neighborhood girls, who became both their sexual playthings and valuable accessories in criminal activities. The girls acted as lookouts and, more important, as "gun girls," carrying the gangsters' weapons under their skirts so the boys were "clean" if intercepted and searched by the police.

The gang's name was taken from the story of Ali Baba and the Forty Thieves. They called themselves the 42 Gang because they figured they were one better than the thieves plus Ali Baba. Actually, when they were founded in 1925, the gang totaled no more than 24, some as young as nine years old, but over the years they actually did total about 42. They suffered considerable attrition through violence and arrest, but so did their enemies. The gang killed a number of robbery victims, stool pigeons and policemen.

The boys' reformatory at St. Charles seemed like the home away from home for the 42ers. Back in 1928 Major William J. Butler, the institution's head, got a long-distance warning from a gang member. He was told, "Unless you let our pals go, we'll come down there and kill everybody we see. We've got plenty of men and some machine guns." Butler reported the threat routinely to the Chicago police, who, rather hysterical about it, warned him to take the call seriously. Butler armed himself, and had the state militia called out to guard the school. Within a few days, a 42er scouting party of three showed up headed by Crazy Patsy Steffanelli. They were grabbed outside the reformatory walls and freely admitted they were scouting ways to have machine gunners bust into the joint. The episode brought considerable press coverage to the 42 Gang, and calls for tougher treatment for hardened juvenile criminals. The *Chicago Tribune* declared the real decision lay between sending 42ers to Joliet penitentiary or to the electric chair.

The press coverage pleased the 42ers to no end. Their ultimate ambition was to turn the heads of the big bootlegging gangs—especially the Capones. They staged robberies just to have a lot of cash to spend freely in Capone mob hangouts. Occasionally the big mobsters were impressed enough to use some of them as beer runners or drivers, but for a number of years they considered "these crazy boys" too dangerous to have around.

Finally the Capone men accepted one 42er. Ironically, it was Sam "Mooney" Giancana, and his nickname fit; he was one of the "mooniest" of the gang. Still, he was an excellent wheelman who never got flustered under pressure. Tony Accardo took him on as his driver. Later, as Giancana learned to curb his wild behavior, he moved up the syndicate ladder under the patronage of Accardo and Paul Ricca, the latter especially seeing executive material in this cunning savage. As Giancana moved upward, he brought a number of 42ers after him. Among those who went on to make a considerable mark in the Chicago syndicate were: Sam Battaglia, Milwaukee Phil Alderisio, Sam DeStefano, Leonard and Marshall Caifano, Charles Nicoletti, Fifi Buccieri, Albert Frabotta, William Aloisio, Frank Caruso, Willie Daddano, Joe Caesar DiVarco, Rocco Potenza, Leonard Gianola and Vincent Inserro.

Another 42er didn't last long among the Capones. He was Paul Battaglia, Sam's older brother, and one of the first leaders of the 42 Gang. Paul got careless about whom he robbed; he was a fingerman for gunners who specialized in sticking up horse betting rooms and handbooks. Since such operations by the mid-1930s had come under the Capone Syndicate, information could be swapped around about the

holdup men. Pretty soon Paul was the known common denominator in the holdups. That earned him a mob assassination—a couple of bullets in the head.

This left Sam Battaglia with two options, frequently faced in the Mafia and organized crime. He could seek revenge or he could accept a loved one's murder as "just business." Sam opted for the second way and later achieved the level of underboss under Giancana when the latter reached don status.

See also GIANCANA, SAM "MOMO"; YOUNGBLOODS

FOUR Deuces: Capone mob headquarters and vice den

The address, 2222 South Wabash Avenue, gave the place its name—the Four Deuces. Standing out front late in 1919 was a chubby, round-faced character, shilling. The journalist Courtney Ryley Cooper later recalled: "I saw him there a dozen times, coat collar turned up on winter nights, hands deep in his pockets as he fell in step with a passer-by and mumbled: 'Got some nice-looking girls inside.'"

He was young Al Capone, newly summoned to Chicago by Johnny Torrio, at first for the most humble of chores, including that of capper for a brothel.

Capone would mature, and so would the Four Deuces. For a time the mob's headquarters, it was also one of the most notorious pleasure joints operated by Torrio and Capone. A four-story structure, it gave over the first floor to a saloon, with a steel-barred gate setting off a large office area. No one but members of the mob passed this barrier. Solid steel doors led to gambling rooms on the second and third floors while the fourth housed what became by Capone standards, a very lavish bordello.

The cellar at Four Deuces was also the scene of a number of murders. A famed, incorruptible Chicago judge, John H. Lyle, wrote:

I got some first-hand information on the resort from Mike de Pike Heitler who bitterly resented the mob's invasion of his field [prostitution]. Shuffling into my chambers one afternoon, he told me: "They snatch guys they want information from and take them to the cellar. They're tortured until they talk. Then they're rubbed out. The bodies are hauled through a tunnel into a trap door opening in the back of the building. Capone and his boys put the bodies in cars and then they're dumped out on a country road, or maybe in a clay hole or rock quarry."

Years later Lyle and a retired police lieutenant took a tour of the then-abandoned building and discovered the tunnel and trap door. Police were reasonably certain that at least a dozen gangsters had been slaughtered in the Four Deuces.

Other mobs gave the Four Deuces considerable competition, especially the nearby Frolics Club. Frolics offered women and booze of Four Deuces quality at lesser prices. Rather than file unfair business practice charges, the Capone mob dealt with the problem more ingeniously. One night when the boys had a corpse on their hands, they transported the body over to the Frolics Club and jammed it into the furnace. One of the Capone men then placed an indignant telephone call to the police to complain about the illegal crematorium being run at the Frolics Club. In moments sirens signaled the arrival of the police who, with flailing axes, burst into the club and hurried to the cellar. Sure enough, there was a partially burned corpse in the furnace. The authorities padlocked the joint and had the police virtually tear down the entire structure looking for more corpses.

They found none but the Frolics Club never reopened. Over at the Four Deuces the booze flowed like water in celebration.

FRANSE, Steven (1895–1953): Mobster and Genovese murder victim

A rather inventive journalist once labeled Steve Franse's murder the "Dear Abby Murder Case." Franse, a longtime trusted associate and racket partner of Vito Genovese, was innocent of any misdoing. But he died because of the ugly spectre of sex in a form hairychested mafiosi could not abide.

Franse went back to Prohibition with Lucky Luciano and Genovese, and he was about the only person the ever-suspicious Genovese would completely trust. When Genovese had to flee the United States for Italy in the late 1930s, he took a fortune in cash with him. He also left plenty behind, from various secret investments to a quarter of a million dollars in cash in a vault of a Manufacturers Trust Company bank on Fifth Avenue. Genovese left two keys, one with his wife Anna, whom he adored and, in fact, for whom he had murdered her previous husband just so he could have her. The other key was with Franse.

Genovese remained out of the country until the conclusion of World War II. When he returned, he was shocked to hear tongues wagging. Franse had been Anna Genovese's constant companion and, while looking after Vito's business investments, had also looked after Anna's, which she said had "nothing to do with syndicate money." But this was not what bothered Genovese. Franse had not kept a close eye on Vito's wife, and she had simply used Franse as a convenient cover for her dalliances with lovers of both sexes, at least so Vito believed.

His wife had clearly fallen out of love with Genovese. She was to sue him for separate maintenance, revealing in the process much about his underworld activities and income, such as getting between $20,000 and $30,000 a week from the Italian lottery alone. The underworld fully expected Genovese to deal with her in the manner always accorded stool pigeons, but Genovese could not bear to do so. Action, however, was required for Genovese to save face, and Franse was the logical victim.

According to Joe Valachi, the kill contract was passed to him, Pat Pagano and Fiore Siano. Since Franse was a longtime friend of Valachi's, it was a simple matter for his partners to lure him to Valachi's restaurant to show him the joint. Franse got the grand tour ending abruptly in the kitchen where one of the killers got him in an armlock from behind and Siano began slugging him in the belly and mouth. "He gives it to him good," Valachi said. "It's what we call 'buckwheats,' meaning spitework." Obviously, this murder was a matter of honor to Genovese and he wanted Franse to die hard. He did, finally being strangled with a chain around his neck.

FRANTIZIUS, Peter von (?–1968)

Founder of an establishment called Sports, Inc., Chicago gun dealer Peter von Frantizius came to be dubbed by the press "The Armorer of Gangland." Regarded as the regular supplier for the Capone gang, he furnished the machine guns and other firearms that figured in many of the most spectacular gang killings of the 1920s. Once pressed to explain the sale of six machine guns to underworld mobsters he told a coroner's jury with a perfectly straight face that he had assumed they were for the Mexican government to put down revolutionaries. The machine gun involved in the murder of big-time gangster Frankie Yale in Brooklyn in 1928 was traced back to Frantizius.

Frantizius lived a charmed life as far as the law was concerned, never being the subject of prosecution, and Sports, Inc., continued to thrive even after Frantizius died in 1968. The company's letterhead continued to list "P. von Frantizius, Pres. & Gen. Mgr."

FRATIANNO, Jimmy (1913–1993): Informer

Among the recent criminal informers, including Joe Valachi and Vinnie Teresa, Jimmy "the Weasel" Fratianno was by far the highest-ranking mob figure ever to "turn" and testify against important crime leaders until Sammy "the Bull" Gravano. His nickname harkened back to his youthful fruit-stealing days in Cleveland's Little Italy, when he demonstrated, to the admiration of onlookers, how he could outrun pursuing policemen fast as a weasel. If that won him the admiration of the underworld, it was nothing compared to the high esteem he enjoyed among mob leaders due to his willingness to kill even good friends if so ordered from above. He was involved in 11 murders by his own count.

Only after he was the object of a death plot himself did Fratianno turn on the mob and begin telling all. His testimony helped convict Mafia bosses in California and New York, but perhaps his more important contribution was in detailing the mob's best-kept secrets. Unlike Joe Valachi, whose information was almost totally limited to New York City, Fratianno was a high-ranking capo-regime, or lieutenant, and, for a time, acting boss of the Los Angeles family. He could offer a more authoritative overview of the workings of organized crime, including eye-opening facts about the CIA's attempt to kill Castro while at the same time Florida crime boss Santo Trafficante, a key mafioso involved in the plotting, may well have been cooperating with the Cuban leader, in effect collecting from both sides of the street.

Fratianno's story was told in a best-selling book, *The Last Mafioso,* in which the Weasel is shown to develop a way common to most informers. He turned informer much earlier than the public believed, a situation probably true of Joe Valachi as well. Fratianno found it worthwhile to get the law on his side by feeding it certain information and gaining a special measure of freedom thereafter, since the FBI does not keep too close tabs on its informers. While he was spilling minor facts to the FBI, Jimmy the Weasel kept maneuvering himself all the way up to becoming an acting boss of the Los Angeles crime family.

After his testimony in a number of cases, Fratianno entered the witness protection program. Some

years later he was bounced from it, apparently for some infraction or infractions. He died in 1993 of natural causes.

See also OPERATION MONGOOSE

FRENCH Connection   See PALERMO CONNECTION

FRIDAY and Saturday nights

"Friday night" and "Saturday night" have very special connotations in the wise guy vocabulary. Friday night is the time for wise guys to howl. As far as mob wives are concerned, that night is a husband's time to play cards with the guys. The wives need not expect their husbands to get home until Saturday morning or even midafternoon. Actually Friday nights are when mob guys take out their girlfriends. It is not unusual on Friday nights on New York's Mulberry Street in Little Italy to see a stretch limo pull up in front of a restaurant and spew out a number of sexy young women and their mob lovers. Things are different on Saturday night when all the mob guys go out with their spouses. This arrangement eliminates the chances of a wise guy running into other mafiosi's wives while out with his girlfriend, and the news—be it helpful or catty—getting back to the injured wife.

"FRIEND of ours" and "friend of mine": Code introductions

When a mafioso introduces a colleague to another mafioso who does not happen to know him, he uses the coded message: "Meet Tommy, he's a friend of mine," or "he's a friend of ours." If the person is presented to other mafiosi as a "friend of ours," it indicates that he is a made man and can be trusted. But if that person is "a friend of mine," he is not a made man, and the phrase gives due warning to the other wise guy to say only what he feels safe to say. Nevertheless, by using the phrase "a friend of mine," the wise guy making the introduction is vouching for his "friend," so if that friend turns out to be an informer or an undercover law enforcement agent, the wise guy faces a certain fate—a fatal one.

When Sammy "the Bull" Gravano was made, he was ecstatic the first time he was introduced to other made men with the comment "Sammy is now a friend of ours." As Sammy recollected, "Chills went up and down my spine." Presumably being accorded the "friend of ours" accolade was mobdom's equivalent of receiving the Order of the Garter.

FUNERALS of gangsters

Frankie Yale, the powerful Brooklyn mafioso, took an avid interest in the lavish funeral given Dion O'Banion, Chicago's vicious North Side Irish gang leader. Yale had a vested interest in the matter; he was one of the three assassins who had blasted O'Banion away in his flower shop in 1924. In a sense, Yale was entirely responsible for the funeral.

Of the O'Banion rites one Chicago newspaper commented with a mixture of awe and annoyance, "Presidents are buried with less to-do." The bronze and silver casket for the deceased had been made to order in Philadelphia for $10,000, then rushed to Chicago by express car. Before the funeral, 40,000 persons passed through the undertaker's chapel to view the body as it "lay in state," as the *Chicago Tribune* termed it. At the funeral, the Chicago Symphony Orchestra performed the "Dead March" from *Saul*, while the pallbearers—labor racketeer Maxie Eisen, president of the Kosher Meat Peddlers' Association, and five distinguished triggermen, Hymie Weiss, Bugs Moran, Schemer Drucci, Frank Gusenberg and Two Gun Alterie—bore the casket to the hearse. Behind them trooped solemn-faced Johnny Torrio and Al Capone, and then henchmen as well as criminals from many other gangs. Outside the funeral parlor was a wreath, so enormous that it could not be carried inside, bearing that classic, touching message, "From His Pals."

The funeral procession was a mile long with 26 cars and trucks loaded with flowers, including rather garish arrangements sent by Torrio, Capone and the Genna brothers, perhaps fittingly since all of them were involved in the execution of O'Banion. Ten thousand people followed the hearse, jamming every trolley car to the area of the Mount Carmel cemetery. At the gravesite another 5,000 to 10,000 spectators waited. An honest judge of the era, some say a rarity for the age, John H. Lyle, called the funeral "one of the most nauseating things I've ever seen happen in Chicago." Back in New York Frankie Yale was more impressed. In fact, he told friends he certainly hoped that when his time came, he would get a more impressive funeral than O'Banion had enjoyed.

Yale went to his reward in a hail of lead in 1928, and the boys tried to do right by him. Fifty thousand dollars was lavished on his send-off. The coffin was nickel and silver, and flower stores in Brooklyn were denuded to the tune of 38 carloads of flowers. Flags flew at half-staff. About 250 autos in a funeral cortege followed the hearse through the streets of Brooklyn to Frankie's resting place in Holy Cross Cemetery. Among the 10,000 mourners were two widows, each insisting she was the genuine Mrs. Yale. It was left to a rather prideful *New York Daily News* to claim that Yale's funeral "was a better one than that given Dion O'Banion by Chicago racketeers in 1924."

In the 1920s and 1930s big gangster funerals were considered only proper and fitting. As one mobster informed the press, "That's what buddies are for."

Before O'Banion's death the biggest funeral held by the North Side gang involved Nails Morton who had a 20-car flower procession. O'Banion had a 26-car procession. When O'Banion's successor, Hymie Weiss, was assassinated, he had only 18 cars with flowers, a fact that upset his widow. Patiently, Bugs Moran of the North Siders had to explain that, since the deaths of Morton and O'Banion some 30 others in the gang had died, which played hob with the number of donors. Weiss's successor, Schemer Drucci, had a touch less impressive a funeral than Weiss's, but his wife was satisfied; he was buried under a blanket of 3,500 blooms. She said: "A cop bumped him off like a dog, but we gave him a king's funeral."

By the 1940s more simple funerals became the style. When Al Capone was laid to rest in 1947, Chicago boss Tony Accardo strictly limited mob attendance, deciding who was "too hot" and might cause a disruption. As Accardo said, "We gotta draw the line someplace. If we let'em, everybody in Chicago will crowd into the cemetery. Al had no enemies." (Presumably Tough Tony could not resist that last humorous comment; after all, it did have an element of truth. Accardo knew Capone's enemies were mostly dead by then, very few having departed this world from natural causes.)

Still later, mob big shots were no longer honor bound to attend funerals at all because of the disruptions that might occur. However, when longtime crime boss Tommy Lucchese died in 1967 and his family let it be known they "understood" if no one attended, many top mafiosi did attend, including Carlo Gambino, Aniello Dellacroce, and Joe and Vincent Rao, insisting they had to come in person to show the great esteem they had for Lucchese. Perhaps what they respected most about him was that for the last 44 years he had never been convicted of a thing.

When Frank Costello passed away in 1973, his widow was firm. She wanted none of his unsavory friends to attend the funeral. Her wishes were respected.

When Gambino godfather Paul Castellano was murdered in December 1985, he was buried in a secret rite after John Cardinal O'Connor barred a funeral mass for him—"after a great deal of prayer," according to a spokesman for the Archdiocese of New York. Castellano suffered the same fate as Carmine Galante and Albert Anastasia, who were also denied funeral masses. Faring better were Crazy Joey Gallo, Carlo Gambino and Joe Colombo. Canon law 1184 stipulates that funeral masses will be denied to "manifest sinners" who have not shown some sign of repentance before death. In many cases, mobsters get the benefit of a doubt, especially if they die in bed. One Catholic expert explained, "The assumption is that they had time to reflect and to repent in some fashion before death. But the way he [Castellano] went out, it's very difficult to see how anybody could say that he had time to reflect and repent."

Cardinal O'Connor in his official statement said that both church law and possible negative reaction by the faithful guided his decision to forbid a funeral mass for Castellano. In 1979 Terence Cardinal Cooke denied the mass for Carmine Galante, also a rubout victim, but as an "act of charity" he permitted a priest to recite prayers at a service in a funeral home. O'Connor did the same for Castellano, and added in condolence, "We extend deepest sympathy to the family."

The O'Connor decision did not meet with total approval within the church. The Reverend Louis Gigante, pastor of St. Athanasius in the Bronx and brother of two reputed mobsters, criticized it. He said he would have celebrated a funeral mass for Castellano. "If he was not a Catholic in life, we should have told him, 'You're no good,'" Gigante said. "Don't say it now, when the family is going to get hurt."

G

GALANTE, Carmine (1910–1979): Would-be "boss of bosses"

Everyone was afraid of him whether he was on the street or behind bars. By the late 1970s, Carmine Galante, the boss of the Bonanno family even from prison, was dreaded by the Mafia underworld. He would be getting out shortly and there would be all-out war. Galante was, after Carlo Gambino's death in 1976, considered to be the toughest mobster among the New York crime families. No one boss was considered mean, cunning or ruthless enough to stand up to the Cigar, as he was called because of the ever-present cigar clenched between his teeth.

No one ever came up with an accurate estimate of how many murders Galante committed or how many more he later ordered in a life of crime that dated back to when he was 11 years old. Galante was the button man in a number of murders ordered by Vito Genovese, including the "clipping" of radical journalist Carlo Tresca in New York in 1943. At the time, Genovese was in Italy actively currying favor with Benito Mussolini, who wanted Tresca's antifascist activities stopped.

Galante was already in the Joe Bonanno family and would in time become Bonanno's driver and eventually his underboss. As such he was a willing confederate in Bonanno's grand plan to expand the crime family's interest south to Florida and the Caribbean and north into Canada. Galante won a reputation with other mobsters as being "as greedy as Joe Bananas."

It was a relief to most other mobs, if not to Bonanno, when Galante was sent to prison for 20 years in the early 1960s for a narcotics violation. In 1964 Bonanno further enraged the other mobs by plotting to eliminate most of the governing leadership of the rival families, which led to the famous Banana War that ended in the ruination of Bonanno's plans and his hopes to install his son as his successor as head of the crime family. Meanwhile, Galante plotted his strategy behind bars. He regarded no one in the Bonanno family as his equal and looked forward to accomplishing what his old boss had failed to do. Mainly, as he told others in the federal penitentiary at Lewisburg, Pennsylvania, he would "make Carlo Gambino shit in the middle of Times Square."

Galante got out on parole in 1974 after doing 12 years. Suddenly he said nothing. In time of war Galante believed one should not talk but rather kill, kill, kill. Yet he had to move slowly because the ailing but shrewd Gambino was ready for his forays. Then in 1978 Galante was grabbed by federal agents again and returned to prison for violating parole by associating with known criminals—other Mafia figures.

The government tried to keep him behind bars, claiming a contract had been issued against Galante. Using lawyer Roy Cohn, who labeled the story a trick by the government, Galante won his release.

Over the next several months at least eight Genovese family gangsters were cut down by Galante gunmen in a war for control of a multimillion-dollar

Carmine Galante, a power in the Bonanno crime family, tried to gain control of the New York Mafia until "the Cigar problem," as other mafiosi called him, died in a restaurant assassination, cigar still in mouth.

drug operation. With Gambino dead, Galante leaned on the other crime families to fall in behind him—or else. The word he sent out was, "Who among you is going to stand up to me?"

The fact was there was no one. There was, however, according to later reports via the underworld grapevine, a meeting in Boca Raton, Florida, to decide what was to be done about the Cigar. From there messengers were sent out to mob leaders asking approval for a contract on Galante. Among the big shots in on the original planning were Jerry Catena, Santo Trafficante, Frank Tieri and Paul Castellano. Phil Rastelli, then in jail, was consulted as was even the semi-retired Joe Bonanno who it was felt might retain some paternal feeling for his former close associate. Bonanno was said to approve.

On July 12, 1979, Galante made a "spur of the moment" decision to drop into Joe and Mary's Restaurant in the Bushwick section of Brooklyn. The owner, Joseph Turano, Galante's cousin, was leaving on a vacation trip to Italy soon, so it was an educated guess that Galante would drop in some time.

Galante did not trust many men but he trusted those with him that day. It was a mistake. One left the restaurant early, complaining of not feeling well. A couple of others made phone calls during the meal.

Just as Galante finished the main course in the restaurant's rear outdoor area and stuck a cigar in his mouth, three masked men suddenly came through the indoor section into the courtyard. "Get him, Sal!" one of the masked men yelled. One of the executioners stepped forward and cut loose with both barrels of a shotgun. Galante died with his cigar still in his mouth.

The Cigar problem had been solved.

See also GENOVESE, VITO; TRESCA, CARLO

GALLO, Crazy Joe (1929–1972): Brooklyn Mafia rebel

Crazy Joey Gallo like Joe Colombo was one of the most maligned Mafia leaders of recent years. Many rival Mafia men considered him "flaky" and hard to deal with—a reputation that Gallo himself nurtured. First and foremost a shakedown artist, Gallo figured a harassed victim had to be more impressed, and frightened, by a man with the reputation of being a touch mad.

Like Meyer Lansky in the 1930s, Crazy Joe in the 1960s recognized changes in the underworld, realized that as the ghetto composition altered that portion of organized crime that was ghetto-oriented had to change as well. Gallo understood that more and more "street action" would be taken over by blacks because of sheer mathematics. He also understood that the mob men who first figured this out and acted on it would grow in power compared to those old-line Italian and Jewish gangsters who continued to sneer about "niggers." Above all, Crazy Joe realized nothing in crime is carved in stone. Situations and power structures change. Years before, he had questioned the stranglehold the older underworld elements had on various activities. "Who gave Louisiana to Frank Costello?" he once demanded in a conversation taped by law enforcement officials.

While in prison for extortion in the 1960s, Crazy Joe befriended black criminals. He sought to break down convict color lines by having a black barber cut his hair; he became friends with Leroy "Nicky" Barnes and tutored him on taking over control of the drug racket in New York's Harlem and elsewhere. He sent released black prisoners to work in crime operations controlled by his family.

Crazy Joe Gallo (in cuffs) was maligned as an underworld flake but actually was one of the more forward-looking mobsters of the day.

Crazy Joe's first arrest occurred at age 17, and in his criminal babyhood, he was charged with burglary, assault and kidnapping. Within the Brooklyn Mafia, he gained a reputation as an effective enforcer and moved up rapidly. When the plot on the life of Albert Anastasia was worked out in 1957, Carlo Gambino gave the assignment to crime family boss Joe Profaci, who, in turn, passed it on to Gallo and his brothers Larry and Albert. Some theories say that Crazy Joe himself was the chief gunner in the rubout, but others hold he merely planned the job and assigned the actual shooting to others. Some recent informer information credits Carmine "the Snake" Persico as being the gunman.

Later Gallo went to war with the Profacis because he felt the Gallos had not gotten their fair share of the rackets in Brooklyn. The conflict took more than a dozen lives. After Profaci died of natural causes in 1962, and Joe Colombo Sr. became head of the Profaci family, the war continued. When Colombo was shot and "vegetabled," to use Gallo's quaint description, the murderer turned out to be a black man—Jerome A. Johnson. Gallo was instantly hauled in for questioning because of his known ability to recruit black troops when he needed them. Nothing, however, could tie him to the crime, and he was released.

Meanwhile, almost magically, a "new" Gallo developed. He had been released from prison in 1971. There he had not been the typical Mafia prisoner, and not simply because of his relationships with blacks. He also read the two newspapers he was allowed a day from front to back. And he had books sent in several times a week. They were not simple tomes, the lightest reading being Hemingway. Gallo got so he could fluently discourse on Camus, Flaubert, Kafka, Balzac, Sartre and Celine. He had taken up painting in Green Haven Prison and won from the administration an extra-bright bulb in his cell so that he could master his palette better. Today Gallo originals still hang in the homes of administrators and guards at Green Haven.

When he got out Gallo was soon moving in different circles. A movie made from Jimmy Breslin's novel *The Gang That Couldn't Shoot Straight,* in which Gallo was portrayed in a comic light, annoyed him somewhat, but he invited the actor who played him, Jerry Orbach, and his wife, Marta, to dinner. The Orbachs were surprised and impressed by his knowledge of literary matters. There was talk of Marta doing a book with him on his prison experiences.

And Gallo moved regularly in theater circles. He became quite a unique celebrity, a sort of "house mobster" in the homes of various show business people.

In theory, Gallo still made his headquarters in his old mob stomping ground of President Street in Brooklyn. Actually, he lived in a lavish apartment on 12th Street in Greenwich Village, near many of his new-found friends. His Colombo foes were unaware of this.

On April 7, 1972, Gallo was in the Copacabana nightclub celebrating his 43rd birthday at a party that included as guests the Orbachs, comedian David Steinberg and his date, and columnist Earl Wilson and his secretary. About 4 A.M. the party broke up and Gallo, his bodyguard "Pete the Greek" Diapoulas, and four female friends and relatives adjourned to the Chinatown–Little Italy area in search of food. They ended up in Umberto's Clam House where they sat at a table, both Gallo and his bodyguard with their backs to the door.

Gallo probably felt secure; there is a Mafia code that bars any rubouts in New York's Little Italy. However, in Crazy Joe's case, an exception was made. A man walked in with a .38-caliber pistol in his hand. Women screamed and customers fell to the floor as the gunman opened up on Gallo and his bodyguard. When the shooting started, Gallo deserted the table in a headlong rush along the bar for the front door. That move may have saved the lives of others at the table. The gunman kept firing at Gallo, who staggered to the street a few feet from his Cadillac before he collapsed, dying.

His sister was to scream Crazy Joe Gallo's epitaph: "He was a good man, a kind man. He changed his image; that's why they did this to him!"

See also GANG THAT COULDN'T SHOOT STRAIGHT, THE; PROFACI, JOE

GAMBINO, Carlo (1902–1976): Crime family leader

After Lucky Luciano left the American crime scene—first by his imprisonment and later by his deportation to Italy—only one mob leader exhibited the cunning and brains to become what may be described as the de facto "boss of bosses" in the Mafia. That man was not Vito Genovese, Joe Bonanno or Carmine Galante—all of whom undoubtedly pictured themselves as worthy of such a role. Rather it was the retiring Carlo Gambino.

Gambino was a study in contrasts. Short and bulbnosed, he was considered a coward by many in the underworld. Joe Bonanno called him "a squirrel of a man, a servile and cringing individual. When Anastasia was alive, Albert used to use him as his gopher, to go on errands for him. I once saw Albert get so angry at Carlo for bungling a simple assignment that Albert raised his hand and almost slapped him. . . . Another man would not have tolerated such public humiliation. Carlo responded with a fawning grin."

Gambino was a man who preferred being misunderstood. He enjoyed playing the humble corner-fruit-market shopper on expeditions to the old neighborhood (from a fashionable Long Island retreat), much as Mario Puzo's *Godfather* who was modeled after Gambino. He always appeared ready to turn the other cheek. "Gambino was like the hog snake, which rolls over and plays dead until trouble passes," said Albert Seedman, chief of detectives of the New York Police Department. But within the

Easily the most cunning Mafia leader since Lucky Luciano, Carlo Gambino (in cuffs) was the model for *The Godfather*. He propelled the then-small Anastasia crime family to the foremost position in organized crime.

closed circles of the mob, Gambino was the firm traditionalist, demanding every sign of respect due a godfather. He even exercised the secret fine points of honor among mafiosi. When Gambino shook hands with a person, he turned his palm under the other's, indicating he was merely going through a formality. If however he accepted the man, he would shake hands by putting his own palm on top.

Gambino had been an ever-ambitious youthful associate of Luciano and Meyer Lansky, the twin architects of organized crime in America. He rose through the ranks to become underboss to the brutal Albert Anastasia in the 1950s, aiding him in deposing their crime family's first boss, Vince Mangano, whose body was never found.

When in the late 1950s Vito Genovese made his move for the prime position in the Mafia, he approached Carlo Gambino about deposing Anastasia. Then he, Gambino, would inherit Anastasia's family—and obviously, in Genovese's mind at least, become the latter's vassal. Gambino had no intention of letting that happen, and while he agreed and handled much of the arrangements for Anastasia's assassination, he immediately began plotting Genovese's end as well.

Anastasia was murdered in a New York barbershop in 1957 shortly after an assassination attempt on Frank Costello was botched. This was to place Genovese in a dominant position, but one that Gambino was determined would be short-lived.

Despite his double-dealing about Anastasia, Gambino quickly made peace with Costello and the exiled Luciano, both of whom had been close to Anastasia. Together with Meyer Lansky, the four of them plotted to remove Genovese from the scene by having the federal government take care of him. Genovese, within just a few months of reaching the pinnacle, was set up in a narcotics case (actually a second one, since federal agents bungled a first frame arranged by Gambino and allowed Genovese to get away) and was sentenced to 15 years in prison. He died there, and Carlo Gambino inherited the position as the strongest family leader in New York.

He kept solidifying his position by judicious alliances and killings until few save Joe Bonanno even thought to challenge him. When he died in October 1976 of a heart attack, Gambino went out in true *Godfather* style. Reporters and onlookers were cordoned off from the hundreds of mourners at his funeral. Hard-faced guards needed only a few threatening words to discourage any would-be intruder. Things were handled with the decorum that Carlo Gambino would have demanded.

See also ANASTASIA, ALBERT; APALACHIN CONFERENCE; COLOMBO, JOSEPH, SR.; GENOVESE, VITO

GAMBINO, Michael: Bogus mafioso

When *The Honored Society* hit bookstores in November 2001, it created quite a stir in publishing circles, but perhaps somewhat less within Mafia society. Simon & Schuster signed a contract for a half million dollars for the book authored by Michael Pellegrino, who claimed it was based on his experiences as the illegitimate grandson of crime family boss Carlo Gambino, who died in 1976. In the book Pellegrino was given the name of Michael Gambino and recounted what purported to be the inside dope on much of the organized crime group's workings. Shortly after the book appeared, the embarrassed publisher was forced to withdraw it from circulation after it determined that Pellegrino was not related to the Gambinos in any form. The publisher sued Pellegrino for fraud and filed a federal lawsuit against the agency that had represented Pellegrino in the matter. There was some speculation the mob had "ratted" on the deal.

GAMBINO crime family

Although it is difficult to put a dollar value on criminal interests, the Gambino crime family is certainly the richest and most powerful criminal organization in the United States today. Worth hundreds of millions of dollars, the family has a criminal workforce of at least 800 men, and its empire ranges from every borough of New York City to the green felt of Atlantic City and Las Vegas, to the heroin plants of Sicily and Asia, to stolen car outlets in Kuwait. Small wonder it has been labeled by one newspaper as Gambino, Inc. In his reign from 1957 to 1976 Carlo Gambino took a second-string crime family and built it into the Mafia's jewel in the crown, far more wealthy than even the family originally ruled by Lucky Luciano, far more powerful than the Capone-descended Chicago Outfit.

The original family dates to the pre-national syndicate days of Alfred Mineo and Steve Ferrigno in the 1920s when Joe the Boss Masseria controlled the Mafia. They were murdered in 1930 in a bloody ambush carried out by Joe Profaci, Nick Capuzzi, Joe Valachi and a gunman known now only as Buster from Chicago. Taking over were Vince and Phil Mangano, who became part of the modern American Mafia as constituted by Luciano. They ran an outfit limited largely to rackets in Brooklyn, the waterfront and gambling—horse betting, the numbers, the Italian lottery. The Manganos lasted until 1951 when Phil Mangano, the less important brother, was murdered by orders of underling Albert Anastasia, already infamous as the chief executioner of Murder, Inc. Vince disappeared at the same time and Anastasia simply took over. No one dared object.

Anastasia, unofficially aided and advised by Frank Costello (who belonged to another family), expanded the organization greatly into new rackets, especially gambling, loan-sharking and narcotics trafficking, through the piers the mob controlled. Anastasia could only go so far, being a mad hatter who was distracted into meaningless and dangerous activities. (He'd order a citizen knocked off who recognized bank robber Willie Sutton, a criminal with no ties to the mob, simply because he hated "stoolies.")

Anastasia was also caught up in the intrigue between his friend Costello and Vito Genovese for control of the largest family, Lucky Luciano's own organization. In 1957, Genovese deposed Costello and succeeded in having Anastasia killed with the connivance of Anastasia's aide, Carlo Gambino. Once Gambino achieved his goal of control of the Anastasia crime family, he had no further need for Genovese, a mobster with delusions of becoming the new boss of bosses. In machinations involving the deposed Costello, the deported Luciano and Meyer Lansky, and probably others, Gambino arranged to have Genovese set up and delivered into the hands of the federal narcotics people on a framed case.

Over the succeeding years, Gambino extended the power and influence of his crime family. The relatively small Mangano operation became the biggest in New York and the nation. Gambino, with the departure of Costello from the active scene, became Meyer Lansky's most important partner in national syndicate enterprises and became recognized, as Luciano was in the 1930s, as the de facto boss of bosses. Gambino foiled the plots of Joe Bonanno to assassinate him and other crime leaders and so to become the most powerful don in the United States.

In the 1970s, ill health forced Gambino's gradual withdrawal from the public eye, although he remained the cunning kingpin right up to his death in 1976. Before he died, Gambino settled on his succession. Logically it should have been his underboss, Aniello Dellacroce, a tough killer who could prevent incursions into the family's rights. (Indeed, Dellacroce proved to be a key man in the assassination of Carmine Galante in 1979 when the latter moved to take over the New York families.) However, Gambino believed strongly in family ties and tapped Paul Castellano, his brother-in-law, as his successor.

Some dons would have so decreed and left their decision to the fates. Gambino realized that if Dellacroce went to war, he would destroy Castellano. The cunning Gambino realized too that murdering Dellacroce would solve nothing. Another would replace him and the less than-imposing Castellano would still be in the same boat. Gambino had to make Dellacroce Castellano's life insurance policy. He accomplished that by offering Dellacroce essential control of all the family's lucrative Manhattan activities, a sort of crime family within a crime family arrangement that Dellacroce could not refuse.

To further his plans, Gambino counted on the support of Frank "Funzi" Tieri, who he had installed as the head of the old Genovese family after he arranged to have boss Tommy Eboli "clipped." Tieri was Dellacroce's match and could be counted on to remain loyal to Gambino after death and to be supportive of Castellano. He was, but his natural abilities inevitably overshadowed Castellano's; without even trying, Tieri emerged as New York's most powerful don.

In a sense, then, Paul Castellano presided over a decline of the Gambinos, but in 1981 Tieri died. Weaker leadership, or perhaps a divided one, in the Genovese family righted the Gambino fortunes, and under Castellano and Dellacroce primacy was restored. Dellacroce, suffering from cancer, made no move to depose Castellano, even though a Young Turk element, epitomized by a violent capo named John Gotti (who modeled himself after his idol, the murderous Albert Anastasia), grew constantly more dissatisfied with Castellano's rule. However the Young Turks, out of a combination of fear and genuine affection for the old boss, dared not strike as long as Dellacroce lived. Dellacroce, like the Turks,

felt that the family should get into the lucrative fields of armored car robberies, hijackings and expanded narcotics activities, while Castellano laid great stock in loan-sharking, union construction shakedowns and such relatively easy crimes as car theft. With those activities fully manned, Castellano tried to starve the Young Turks.

On December 2, 1985, Dellacroce died. Paul Castellano lasted just two weeks, being assassinated along with an aide obviously being groomed as a counter to John Gotti. Within days of Castellano's assassination, it was obvious to law enforcement people that John Gotti had officially become the new boss of the richest and most powerful crime family in America.

See also GOTTI, JOHN

GANG That Couldn't Shoot Straight, The: Book and movie parody of Crazy Joe Gallo Gang

While *The Godfather* was rather well received by most mafiosi, Jimmy Breslin's *The Gang That Couldn't Shoot Straight*, based on the Gallo Gang and its war with the Profaci crime family, was not. As Peter "Pete the Greek" Diapoulas, Joey Gallo's grade-school chum and later bodyguard, explains in his book *The Sixth Family*, "The writer our crew would have loved giving a beating to was Jimmy Breslin."

In the Breslin opus, the Gallos and Profacis—clothed in fictional names, but closely paralleling their real-life situations—were all rather inept, often comically so. Rather caustically Pete the Greek declared:

The whole thing was funny. The Profaci war was just a bunch of laughs. Well, Breslin should have spent one night with us, found out what it would feel like if some Profaci clipped him in the ass. Even with a small Baretta, he wouldn't be fucking laughing.

Joey Gallo served as the model for Kid Sally Palumbo, a characterization that angered Gallo, either because the Brooklyn gangster was made to look silly or because the name Palumbo sounded like Gallo's hated enemy "Colombo." The Gallos were also upset that the movie was filmed in their Brooklyn backyard around President Street. Quite naturally the mobsters had asked what was going on but were only informed some kind of comedy was being filmed. The fact that there were a dwarf and a lion in the cast should have alerted the mobsters; Armando the Dwarf was a real-life hanger-on with the gang, and the gang did have a lion as mascot.

After the film's Broadway premiere, Joey Gallo was incensed. But he was also curious and thus invited actor Jerry Orbach and his wife Marta to dinner (Orbach had played the Gallo role in the film). Though Orbach played the fictional Gallo for a laugh, he was truly taken by the real Gallo. He and his wife learned Gallo was a man who could converse knowledgeably about such writers as Sartre, Camus, Kafka and Hemingway. And they learned that the gang actually did keep a three-quarter-grown lion in a cellar; Crazy Joe said they did so to send poor-paying loan shark victims down for a visit. After that, Gallo said, with a straight face, everyone paid up.

The movie did not really hurt the Gallos' image, even if they were portrayed as ineptly boobytrapping an enemy's car so that it exploded with much smoke and noise but did no real harm at all. On the other hand, the movie proved in a way the death of Crazy Joey. His friendship with the Orbachs had flourished. If it had not, Gallo might not have become big on the entertainment social circuit. He might not have decided to celebrate his 43rd birthday in a party at the Copacabana nightclub with the Orbachs, comedian David Steinberg and his date, and columnist Earl Wilson and his secretary. About 4 A.M. Gallo, Pete the Greek and four female friends and relatives adjourned to the Chinatown–Little Italy area in search of food and ended up in Umberto's Clam House, where Gallo was shot to death and Pete the Greek ended up as he so liked to term it, "clipped . . . in the ass." Without his new showbiz orientation, Gallo's birthday festivities would have been entirely different—he might not have ended up in Umberto's, where he was cornered by a gangster who could shoot straight.

GARMENT industry rackets

The underworld's involvement in the garment industry dates to the beginning of the 20th century. Today, it remains a lush field for organized crime.

Labor sluggers, mostly Jews (as were most of the workers), were hired by employers to crush union activity. Labor soon retaliated by hiring its own criminal sluggers, sometimes simply outbidding the employers' gangsters with higher pay. This led to the Labor Sluggers War just prior to World War I between rival gangs seeking dominance. As a result, no real cohesive criminal leadership was established until the 1920s when criminal mastermind Arnold Rothstein took an active interest in the field. Rothstein provided financial aid and know-how for the two gangsters who would dominate the field after his murder in 1928—Louis Lepke and Gurrah Shapiro.

Unlike the other labor racketeers in the field, the pair followed the Rothstein blueprint and lifted labor extortion in the garment industry to new heights. Instead of simply using their sluggers and gunmen to terrorize labor unions during strike periods, Lepke worked them directly into the unions, and by threat, violence and murder took control of one local after another. At the same time manufacturers who hired Lepke and Shapiro to handle their union problems "soon found themselves," in the words of crime reporter Meyer Berger of the *New York Times*, "wriggling helplessly in the grip of Lepke's smooth but deadly organization. He moved in on them as he had on the unions." In the process the pair personally took out of the garment industry rackets anywhere from $5 million to $10 million a year.

To back their will, the pair employed an army of 250 enforcers and collectors. In the whole field only the fur trade escaped domination. The left-wing Needle Trade Workers Industrial Union made no bones about hiring gangsters in the 1920s, but they were able to fend off racketeer domination probably because of the long socialist tradition of its members. That, combined with a readiness to keep their own internal squads of enforcers and even to outbid the Lepke forces in bribes to the police so that they instead arrested the strike-breakers, kept them apart.

When Lepke and Shapiro were convicted of labor racketeering and conspiracy in the mid-1930s (with Lepke later going to the electric chair on murder charges), most of the crime syndicate's interests in the garment field fell under the control of Tommy Lucchese, known to many as Three-Finger Brown. Within the Lucchese family gangster Johnny Dio was a prime operative, continuing to play off both the employees and the employers. Mob figures could set up manufacturing businesses and obtain racketeer-dictated exemptions to union contracts on pay scales and rules so that they could hold down costs and thus gain an important advantage over the competition. Dio's blueprint for financial success extended to the West Coast where his expertise put the Los Angeles Dragna family in the garment manufacturing business while utilizing what amounted to Mexican slave labor.

In recent decades both the Lucchese and Gambino families operated garment industry rackets that according to estimates added 3.5 percent to the retail costs of all garments produced. The Gambino interests were savaged when in the early 1990s Tommy and Joseph Gambino, the late Carlo's sons, plea-bargained out of jail time by giving up some of their trucking firms and paying a $12 million fine. (Tommy later went to prison.) In 1998 major indictments were made against the Lucchese family's acting bosses due mainly to the efforts of ex-police commissioner Robert McGuire, who was a court-appointed "special master" for the garment industry. It seemed likely the mob's hold on the industry would be enormously reduced.

See also DIO, JOHNNY; LEPKE, LOUIS; SHAPIRO, JACOB "GURRAH"

GENNA brothers: Mafia foes of Capone

They were called the Terrible Gennas, and for good reason. Devotees of violence—some more vicious, others more cunning, but all murderous—the Gennas are part of the reason that today the Chicago Outfit, the heir of the old Capone Mob, is the least mafioso-oriented crime family in the country, with a far bigger ethnic mix than others.

From the first, Johnny Torrio and Al Capone had to battle some of the most backward Mafia families to move into American crime. One group was the Aiello crime family, another the Gennas who recruited many of their soldiers from mafiosi emigrating from the same Sicilian village as themselves. The Genna brothers had been among the premier Black Hand extortionists in Chicago, but they quickly forgot such bush league stuff with the advent of Prohibition. Dominating Chicago's Little Italy, they turned that entire area into one large cottage moonshining industry.

There were six Genna brothers who came to this country in 1900—Bloody Angelo, Mike the Devil, Pete, Sam, Jim, and Tony the Gentleman. The first five fit the classic mold of many Sicilian killers of the day—arrogant, treacherous, devious, bloodthirsty and devoutly religious. All of them carried crucifixes in their gun pockets. Only Tony the Gentleman was different. He studied architecture, constructed model tenements for poor Italian immigrants and was noted as a patron of the opera. He eschewed living in Little Italy and resided in elegant style in a leading downtown hotel.

Tony the Gentleman was personally opposed to killing—not that he objected to his brothers doing so. He sat in on family councils when murders of opponents were planned, but he simply did not wish to soil his aristocratic hands on so vulgar a task. Besides, the Gennas had some of the most savage hit men in Chicago in their ranks. There was Sam "Samoots" Amatuna, a gangster dandy who loved music and opera almost as much as he loved filling a victim full of lead; Giuseppe "the Cavalier" Nerone, a university graduate and mathematics instructor turned gunman; and the infamous murder duo of Albert Anselmi and John Scalise, who brought to the American underworld the practice of rubbing bullets with garlic in the hope of producing gangrene in any victim who survived an immediate gunshot wound.

Combined with the Gennas' constant application of deadly force was their ability to corrupt the police. As one newsman put it, "if a cop will take money from the Gennas, he'll take it from anybody." The Gennas had no trouble at all getting cops to take their money. In 1925 their office manager confessed that the Gennas had on their pad five police captains, some 400 uniformed officers, many headquarters plainclothesmen, as well as others from the state attorney's office.

Most of the police officers were attached to the Maxwell Street precinct in Little Italy. The cops were paid $10 to $125 a month, depending on their importance and length of service. All day on monthly bribe day, police officers trooped in and out of the Gennas' alcohol plant at 1022 Taylor Street, openly counting their graft on the street. The Gennas found they had to contend with a particularly venal form of police dishonesty, with "imposters" turning up from other precincts, pretending to be from the Maxwell Street station. The local police brass aided in solving that dilemma for the Gennas by furnishing the mob with a checklist of badge numbers.

The Gennas had many families in Little Italy producing raw alcohol at home. Since the average home still could produce 350 gallons of raw alcohol a week, for much less than $1 a gallon, and further processing by the Gennas did not cost too much, they made a handsome profit selling their booze at $6 a gallon wholesale.

As part of their graft-bound duties, the police were required by the Gennas to crack down on those alky cookers in Little Italy not working for the Gennas but selling independently. The Gennas, therefore, supplied the police with a complete list of their own stills, and whenever a private operation was uncovered, the police moved in with axes swinging. Naturally the newspapers were alerted in advance so that they could run stories and pictures of the precinct's ever-alert fight against crime.

Overall the Genna operation grossed $350,000 a month. After expenses, the six brothers netted a clear profit of $150,000 per month, or almost $2 million a year. They always sought to extend these profits, which put them in conflict with the efforts of Johnny Torrio to bring the bootleg gangs under one umbrella. The Gennas agreed to Torrio's arrangement, but proved hard to control as they constantly flooded other gangs' territories with their cheap booze at prices the other gangs couldn't match. A three-way competition soon developed among the Gennas, the Torrio-Capone forces, and the North Side's O'Banion gang.

The Gennas proved to be the first losers in the ensuing bootlegger battles. Bloody Angelo Genna was assassinated on May 25, 1925. He was driving in his roadster when he became aware of North Side gangsters tailing him. He picked up speed but, in his desperate effort to elude the enemy, ran into a lamppost and was pinned behind the wheel. All he could do was watch helplessly as a shotgunner stepped out of the pursuing car and blasted him to death.

Mike Genna swore vengeance on the O'Banions, and the following month he, Anselmi and Scalise went out hunting for North Siders. What Mike didn't know was that Anselmi and Scalise had switched their allegiance to Capone and were actually taking him for a ride. As it developed the police saved them the trouble. The three got caught in a gun battle. Anselmi and Scalise killed two officers, wounded another and fled, leaving the wounded Genna to be captured. As Mike Genna was being put on a stretcher, he used his good leg to cut loose with a mighty kick and knock out one of the attendants. "Take that, you dirty son of a bitch," he snarled. He died two hours later.

Tony the Gentleman, the mastermind of the Gennas, figured that Anselmi and Scalise had defected and decided to go into hiding. Before he left, he notified his supporter Nerone to meet him on a darkened street corner. Tony the Gentleman didn't know that Nerone also had deserted the Genna cause. When Tony Genna approached Nerone, the latter seized him in a vise-like handshake. Just then one or two gunmen stepped out of the darkness and pumped Tony full of lead.

That broke the Gennas. The three remaining brothers fled, Jim all the way back to Sicily, where he was soon caught and imprisoned for two years for stealing the jewels from the statue of the Madonna di Trapani. Eventually all three Gennas returned to Chicago on a pledge to stay out of the rackets. They ran an importing business in cheese and olive oil and lived out their days in relative obscurity.

GENOVESE, Vito (1897–1969): Mafia boss

Despite all the hype about the American Mafia being ruled by a "boss of bosses," the last man to lay claim to the title was Salvatore Maranzano in 1931, and he lasted only a few months before being assassinated. Since then, the press has assigned the mantle to various mafiosi, but none have really deserved it. Carlo Gambino did achieve a sort of de facto status, but he knew the value of humility and made no effort to grab the title.

In 1957 Vito Genovese made an overt effort to seize overall mob leadership. He was to fail almost as ignominiously as Maranzano did, although he ended up being "taken out" by the feds rather than by bullets.

In many respects Genovese, who preferred being called "Don Vito," had all the qualifications for being the boss of bosses. He was one of the most feared of the Mafia dons, killing as readily as Albert Anastasia, but possessing the cunning to plot his foes' downfall—a quality the slow-witted Anastasia did not possess. As much as any single person, he can be credited with keeping the Mafia in the narcotics business, a move that some other mafiosi, such as Frank Costello and, despite the contentions of federal narcotics authorities, Lucky Luciano, at times strongly opposed.

Genovese started out in Luciano's shadow in the 1920s and in the course of knocking off many rivals rose to the top with Lucky. After World War II he started a murder campaign to gain new status for himself, with Luciano in exile in Italy. He is known to have ordered the deaths of Willie Moretti in 1951, Steve Franse in 1953, and Albert Anastasia in 1957. And he was the obvious mastermind behind the attempt on the life of Frank Costello, which eventually led to Costello's retirement.

Facing a murder charge in 1937, Genovese was forced to flee to Italy, where he succeeded in ingratiating himself with Benito Mussolini, despite the Fascist leader's ruthless campaign to destroy the Italian Mafia. He became the chief drug source for Mussolini's foreign minister and son-in-law, Count Ciano. During the war, to further gain Mussolini's approval, Genovese ordered the execution in New York of Il Duce's longtime nemesis, radical editor Carlo Tresca, a mob hit that was performed by a rising mafioso named Carmine Galante. By 1944 Mussolini's regime was crumbling, and the opportunistic Genovese surfaced suddenly as an interpreter for the U.S. Army's intelligence service. Due to his energetic and diligent labors for the U.S. Army, a number of black market operatives were arrested in southern Italy. However, the military's pleasure with Genovese soured when it was discovered that he himself had simply taken over the operations.

Genovese was returned to the United States after the war, but all the witnesses to the murder charge against him were silenced. He won his freedom. He then sought control of the Luciano family and the dominant role in the American Mafia. To succeed, he had to eliminate acting family chief Frank Costello and diminish the outside influence of Meyer Lansky, while continuing to pay lip service to Luciano. Not being fools, Costello and Luciano from afar continually set up roadblocks against him, and it took Genovese almost a decade to move in earnest, building a war chest out of a secret narcotics racket.

Costello was Genovese's first target, but the murder plot backfired. Costello was only slightly wounded. A few months later, however, Genovese had Anastasia murdered, an advantageous move for Genovese since Anastasia was Costello's main muscle. Without him, Costello, the "Prime Minister of the Underworld," was helpless.

Next, Genovese sought to tighten his new stranglehold on the Luciano crime family. He was a prime mover in the famed Apalachin Conference in upstate New York. Genovese probably even expected to be anointed boss of bosses at the meeting, but it ended in a total fiasco when authorities raided the affair and scooped up dozens of Mafia figures. Genovese had been set up beautifully by Costello/Luciano/Lansky, none of whom were present, and by Carlo Gambino who was. (Gambino and Lansky had cooperated with Genovese in the killing of Anastasia for their own motives. Gambino wanted to take over the Anastasia crime family, and Lansky was angered by Anastasia's moves to invade the Cuban casino scene, which Lansky deemed his domain. Now, with Costello, they tipped off the authorities about the meeting.) Instead of emerging the foremost mafioso in the nation, Genovese succeeded in angering the nation's bosses, who blamed him for the Apalachin disaster.

Genovese knew that sooner or later he had to eliminate Costello, Lansky and even Luciano. He probably did not yet suspect Gambino's role. Don Vito's mistake was in assuming he had time to act; he knew his enemies would not risk open gang warfare. But warfare was not necessary. Just as their cunning stopped Apalachin, so it stopped Genovese. Costello, Lansky and Luciano concocted a major narcotics smuggling deal. There is reason to suspect that they even induced Chicago don Sam Giancana to join the conspiracy. (All that would have taken was Lansky's offering Chicago a bigger cut in Cuba.) Then, having dropped the deal in Genovese's lap, the four conspirators pitched in $100,000 for a minor Puerto Rican drug pusher named Nelson Cantellops to implicate him. Although it was hardly credible that a low-level figure like Cantellops could have the information to trap a big shot like Genovese, the federal government chose not to be too inquisitive. Genovese and 24 of his supporters were nailed, and, in 1959, Genovese was sentenced to 15 years in prison.

According to informer Joe Valachi, Genovese continued to direct the activities of his crime family from behind bars. Genovese became paranoid about the frameup and suspected almost everybody. He had his top aide on the outside, Tony Bender, assassinated, suspecting him of being involved. Later he also suspected Joe Valachi of being an informer and ordered him killed in prison. Desperately Valachi opted for government protection and turned stool pigeon, becoming one of the prize informers of all time, revealing many Mafia, or as he preferred calling it, "Cosa Nostra," secrets.

In 1969 Genovese died in prison, proof that mere brawn was insufficient to take over organized crime in America. In the 1970s statements attributed to Luciano, and later confirmed by Meyer Lansky and others, revealed how they made the government their partner in getting rid of Don Vito.

GENOVESE crime family

Lucky Luciano, who triumphed as a result of the Mafia wars of the early 1930s, reconstituted the five crime families that had been apportioned by the late, deposed Salvatore Maranzano. Maintaining control of the crime group previously headed by Joe the Boss Masseria, Luciano had inherited that family when he arranged the murder of Masseria. Within the New York Mafia, it remained for several decades the largest and most powerful of the crime families.

In this family, soldier-cum-informer Joe Valachi served under a succession of bosses—first Luciano, followed by Frank Costello, then Vito Genovese. Costello took over when Luciano, convicted on a prostitution count in 1936, was sent to prison. By rights Genovese, as Luciano's underboss, should have succeeded, but he had his own problems with the law. Fearing prosecution on a murder rap, he fled to Italy, where he was to ingratiate himself with Italian dictator Benito Mussolini.

Costello was not an ordinary godfather. He had little time for family affairs, being too involved in his own private criminal enterprises with Meyer Lansky and others—activities that stretched from New York to New Orleans, and later to Las Vegas and Havana, Cuba. As a result, Costello allowed his various capos considerable independence in running the rackets. Either because of this or despite it, more members of the family became millionaires than in any other Mafia group. Joe Valachi later said he knew of 40 or 50 members of the family who were millionaires. This and Costello's expertise at arranging the political fix—for which he was nicknamed "the Prime Minister"—made him very popular with his capos and soldiers.

After World War II, Genovese was returned to the United States for trial on that old murder charge, but nothing came of it; a couple of well-timed murders eliminated the key witnesses against him. A tug of war developed between Costello and Genovese, with Costello yielding slowly. Little by little Genovese eroded Costello's power, and when Willie Moretti was murdered, Costello lost a lot of armed muscle that would have stood up for him. Costello shrewdly countered by goading the murderous Albert Anastasia into killing his own bosses in the Mangano family—Vince and Phil Mangano—and taking over. Anastasia now controlled more firepower than ever before and, being totally loyal to Costello, was the perfect foil for Genovese.

Six years elapsed before Genovese felt powerful enough to take on Costello once again. In 1957, he plotted an unsuccessful attempt on Costello's life. Later the same year, he was the key man behind the barbershop rubout of Anastasia. Genovese was assisted by Anastasia underling Carlo Gambino, who seized control of the Anastasia crime family, but then maneuvered against Genovese. Gambino conspired with Costello, Meyer Lansky and the exiled Luciano, all of whom had come to hate and fear Genovese's ambitions to become a new "boss of bosses."

Before their plans were implemented, Costello won approval from all the crime families to have the right to retire and keep his income. In exchange, Genovese won control of the old Luciano family. He didn't reign long. The Apalachin fiasco caused Genovese to lose face. Then the Gambino-Costello-Luciano-Lansky alliance finished him off by setting him up in a phony drug deal. Genovese was railroaded to prison for 15 years, where he died in 1969.

Although Genovese continued to rule his outfit from behind bars—using Jerry Catena or Tony Bender as his outside men—his power was waning. He used Bender to arrange a number of hits, but later, suspecting Bender had been in on the plot against him, ordered his elimination. After Catena retired to Florida with a heart condition, Genovese relied on Tommy Eboli as his outside man. Eboli was a man of action and not particularly adept at thinking independently. Slowly, the Genovese family lost its muscle, and the shrewd Gambino, up till then head of a relatively small crime group, gained in power and prestige until he had the foremost organization in the country—far mightier than the outfit he had forcibly inherited from Anastasia.

From his cell Genovese cursed this turn of events, but could do nothing about it. Further weakened by the testimony given by Valachi—which hurt him more than any other mafioso—Genovese was alternately criticized by mobsters for forcing Valachi to "rat" and for failing to eradicate him.

Gambino, much like Luciano in the 1930s, became the de facto boss of bosses. He decided he had to do something about the Genovese family, which was floundering under the inane rule of Eboli—a man who was described by one mafioso as "not giving a damn if his boys were making out or starving."

Gambino arranged for Eboli's elimination in 1972. He replaced him with Frank "Funzi" Tieri, a close personal friend in the Genovese group and highly popular. Tieri brought the Genoveses back strong, while remaining a firm Gambino loyalist. With Gambino's death in 1976, Tieri reached his primacy and regained much of the esteem and power the crime family had enjoyed earlier. Tieri's name could invoke fear in mafiosi all around the country if there was an indication that he was in any way unhappy.

Overall, Tieri was happy except about the situation in Atlantic City, where casino gambling was legalized in 1976. Angelo Bruno, the longtime boss in Philadelphia, refused to give up control of the area. Allegedly, Tieri posted a $250,000 bounty on Bruno. In 1980, someone must have collected; Bruno was assassinated. Tieri's family and the Gambino crime group moved in.

When Tieri died in 1981, the fortunes of the family declined once again. Law enforcement officials weren't quite sure who ruled the Genoveses. Some said it was elderly Philip "Cockeyed Phil" Lombardo, while others named Fat Tony Salerno. The federal government, during the national commission prosecution in the mid-1980s, singled out Salerno.

Whoever held the reins, the Genovese crime family remained the second most powerful in the nation, with major muscle in gambling, narcotics, loansharking, and extortion rackets. The family also maintained considerable interest in waterfront activities in Brooklyn and New Jersey, New York's Times Square pornography business, labor unions, the carting industry, restaurants, seafood distributors and vending machines. Genovese membership was estimated at 200 in the late 1980s, with perhaps three times as many supporters who were not "made" mafiosi. In 1987 with Salerno under a 100-year sentence the active leadership of the family passed to Vinnie "the Chin" Gigante, who became famous for his ploy of walking the street in a bathrobe and mumbling to himself in an effort to appear mentally defective and unable to face prosecution. That act finally collapsed in 1997 when Gigante was imprisoned. The leadership of the family then passed to Dominick "Quiet Dom" Cirillo.

After Cirillo was forced into the background because of ill health, the leadership situation became more of a blur, but the numbers of members convinced some observers that the family was still a viable force in the new Mafia. While prosecutors celebrated having the Genoveses "on the run," others were impressed that one sweep alone took in 73 "leaders and associates" of the crime family. The group simply turned up new members by the dozens, hardly the sign of an organization withering away. Since the arrests of the 73 represented probably a third of the wise guy membership of the family at about 200–250 at most, it had to be a considerable haul, especially since 45 others had been netted about a half year earlier for other offenses. In the latest case, the indicted individuals were hit for a number of allegations including racketeering charges bringing in millions, including $1 million in the embezzlement of a carpenters' union based in Tuckahoe, New York. Other charges included labor racketeering, loan-sharking, illegal gambling operations, gun trafficking and distributing counterfeit money.

The most spectacular charge was one involving a number of the defendants in a plot to steal $6 million in payroll money from a printing plant owned by the *New York Times*. The plan was foiled by an undercover detective who had "risked his safety on almost a daily basis" in an investigation that lasted more than three years. The detective later moved outside the city to avoid being recognized by a Genovese crew charged with uprooting undercover agents. The mob efforts were fruitless; the plot cracked, and arrests were made. According to prosecutors and spokesmen for some news publications, the mob planted a member of the gang inside among newspaper company production people to learn about big money shipments. One of the main plotters was said to be Anthony Capanelli, who worked as a fill-in pressman from time to time for the *New York Post*. He worked with a former police officer known as Joe Dingha to set up the aborted caper. As a top member of the investigative team put it, "We will permit no such return to 'business as usual' for members of organized crime and criminal element in New York."

As a result it became obvious that government claims of having "wiped out" or even "crippling" the Mafia crime families were far from accurate. The truth was that the Mafia was not down and out but rather showed the ability to climb back on the canvas to keep up the criminal fight.

GIACALONE, Diane (1950–): Federal prosecutor and Gotti's pet hate

An assistant U.S. attorney in Brooklyn, Diane Giacalone was the first to pursue John Gotti on RICO (1970 Racketeer Influenced and Corrupt Organization Act) charges. It earned her the hatred of Gotti, but also the enmity of the FBI and the "Gambino squad," which had set their sights on the newly crowned head of the Gambino crime family.

Born in a middle-class Italian community in Ozone Park, Queens, the future domain of Gotti, Giacalone attended Our Lady of Wisdom, a Catholic parochial school for girls. On her way to school each day she passed several "social clubs" where men sat outside, seemingly with nothing to do and no job to go to. It was said that one of those clubs was the Bergin Hunt and Fish Club (where Gotti would later rule) and that there she suffered barrages of wise guy taunts that later inspired her to seek revenge by attacking Gotti.

The story may well be apocryphal, but regardless Giacalone went on to law school and became a federal prosecutor. To bring her case against Gotti, Giacalone battled the FBI whose agents had their own investigation going and felt they could do a better job. Some felt the FBI had "sandbagged" Giacalone and even that they "double-crossed" her. FBI men denied this, but the agency did pull its agents off her task force. Jules Bonavolonta, head of the FBI's Gambino squad, bitterly opposed Giacalone, later stating, "Diane Giacalone was an extraordinarily talented lawyer, but when it came to street smarts, even though she came from John Gotti's old neighborhood, she didn't have any—none."

The FBI task force objected to Giacalone on two main points: One, her case against Gotti was exceedingly weak, and two, she learned independently that one Willie Boy Johnson, a close pal and murder accomplice of Gotti, had been an FBI informer for many years (although he never implicated Gotti in anything). Giacalone figured that if she revealed his informer role, he would be forced to testify against Gotti. The FBI said he would never testify, but that the revelation would put his life at risk unnecessarily. (Later, after the trial in which Willie Boy refused to aid the prosecution, Gotti did indeed have him killed.)

At the time Giacalone remained adamant, even accusing the FBI of letting Willie Boy get away with murder and of being a virtual partner-in-crime with him.

Such comments were more than some agents could take. One irately said: "You know, if you were a man, I'd knock you on your ass."

It was the wrong thing to say to the female prosecutor. She bounded from behind her desk and put up her fists, saying, "Okay, let's go at it right now. C'mon!" There were no fisticuffs but Giacalone refused to back off the Gotti case.

As much trouble as the FBI gave her, the Gotti defense team gave her more. When she first brought the case, Gotti was outraged that his prosecutor was a woman. "I guarantee you no girl is ever gonna put us in jail," he snarled to associates. "We'll make her cry, we'll buy her jury. Whatever the fuck it takes, but, guaranteed, she'll never put us in jail."

It is doubtful if any prosecutor, male or female, was ever subjected to as much abuse as Giacalone was. Opposing counsel baited her throughout the trial, referring to her as the "Dragon Lady" and the "Lady in Red" because of her red attire. Gotti groupies in the spectator section sneered at her as "Little Red Riding Hood."

During a dispute with one lawyer, she pointed her finger at him and called him a liar. He responded, "Take your finger out of my face and stick it up your ass." Chief Gotti lawyer Bruce Cutler disparaged her with such comments as, "See if the tramp will give us an offer of proof." The judge simply could not control the outbursts.

As the FBI predicted, Giacalone could not successfully prove her case that Gotti had accepted as tribute a share in the loot some freelance crooks had taken in an armored car robbery. Without proof of that, the entire RICO charge collapsed.

During the trial Giacalone called no less than 78 witnesses, warning the jury that they were "horrible people." Unfortunately, many of these witnesses proved so horrible that the defense made mincemeat out of them by pointing out their own criminality. This was hardly surprising since the one person who knew everything they'd done was John Gotti. One witness even admitted he was there, as he declared, "to save his own ass" from prosecution. And he wasn't alone.

One admitted to pistol-whipping a priest and murdering three Florida drug dealers after making an agreement to testify against Gotti. After the defense was finished with him, he was asked what he thought of Gotti. "He is," he replied, "the finest man I ever met." Naturally, the jurors did not put much stock in his testimony—save perhaps for his final evaluation of the mob boss. Another admitted to two murders and drug trafficking and claimed he'd been allowed to keep illicit money upon his last arrest in return for testifying against Gotti.

Giacalone was even forced to drop one witness she had planned to call. He was Matthew Traynor, a longtime friend of Gotti, a drug dealer, bank robber, and convicted perjurer. He was doing time for a bank robbery and sought to reduce sentence by testifying against Gotti. After preparing him to testify, Giacalone caught him in a lie and dropped him from the case.

Traynor then contacted the defense and offered to tell things about Giacalone. What he said shocked the courtroom. He testified that Giacalone had given him drugs so that he would lie about Gotti. He said he had often been stoned when they prepared his testimony. Once, Traynor said, he told Giacalone that he needed "to get laid," and she "gave me her panties out of her bottom drawer and told me to facilitate myself. . . . She said, 'Make do with these.'"

The angered prosecutor objected vehemently and brought 17 witnesses to rebut Traynor's testimony. However, it was clear the jury did not buy all the testimony meant to buttress Giacalone's reputation.

The verdict was a foregone conclusion. The discredited witnesses were a dream for the defense. Gotti and all his associates, even Willie Boy Johnson, were found not guilty on all counts. Amid the back-slapping on the Gotti side, the crime boss, called out, "Shame on them," pointing at Giacalone and her co-prosecutor. "I'd like to see what the jury's verdict would be on those two."

Gotti strode out in triumph. It was the beginning of his sobriquet as the "Teflon Don," one against whom charges could not stick. Much later it was learned that one juror had been "reached" before the trial so that no verdict would have been possible in any case.

Certain memoirs by FBI people and others made it clear they were not unhappy with Giacalone's defeat. However, some prosecutors vowed to make Traynor pay for his lies, on the theory that, "Maybe Diane is a bitch, but she's *our* bitch." They confronted Traynor, and he admitted to perjury in exchange for a limited additional sentence of five years to be added to his bank robbery time.

Diane Giacalone kept whatever bitterness she felt to herself. Some time later she quit her prosecutor's post and moved on to a legal position with the local transit authority.

GIANCANA, Sam "Momo" (1908–1975): Syndicate leader

He was, a police report stated, "a snarling, sarcastic, ill-tempered, sadistic psychopath." That was a young Sam "Momo" Giancana, a man who would become for a time the most powerful Mafia boss west of the Mississippi. If he never was truly the most powerful (he was kept in check by the two most powerful "elders" in the Chicago Outfit, Paul "the Waiter" Ricca and Tough Tony Accardo), Giancana qualified nonetheless as the most ruthless of the top bosses in organized crime. He was also perhaps the screwiest, originally nicknamed "Mooney" because he was considered as nutty as a "mooner." (Giancana himself corrupted that into "Momo," which was a much safer moniker to use around him.)

Some observers saw Giancana's involvement in various CIA plots to assassinate Cuban Premier Fidel Castro as a sign of Giancana at his mooniest. There is considerable evidence that certain other leading mafiosi in that CIA madness were in it solely to milk funds out of the U.S. government, but Giancana was a firm believer in the viability of the caper. In another of his unstable moments Giancana was said to have put out a "contract" on Desi Arnaz because he produced the television show called *The Untouchables,* which glorified federal agent Eliot Ness and vilified, from Giancana's viewpoint, the Italian gangsters of the Capone mob. If a murder order was given to hit men to get Arnaz, it apparently was withdrawn. It is known that quite a few Giancana-ordered murder assignments were canceled by Ricca and Accardo.

Yet there is no doubt that Giancana brought about the deaths of scores of men; considering he bossed the Chicago Outfit, the most dog-eat-dog crime family in the country, the total could be in the hundreds. A graduate of the juvenile 42 Gang, probably the worst of its ilk in the Chicago of the 1920s, Giancana started his arrest record in 1925 and, through the years, was arrested more than 70 times. The charges included: contributing to delinquency, burglary, larceny, assault and battery, fugitive, damage by violence, assault to kill, conspiracy to operate a "book," possession of concealed weapons, suspicion of bombing, gambling, possession of a fictitious driver's license, and murder. The prime suspect in three murders before he was 20, he was indicted for one of these when he was 18, released on bail and then never tried when the key witness somehow got himself murdered. He did three prison terms early on, for auto theft, operation of an illegal still, and burglary.

Like other members of the 42 Gang, Giancana's greatest wish was to be noticed by the Capone mobsters, who used some of the 42 boys for minor chores such as stealing a car when one was needed for a job. Giancana captured the most attention because he was an excellent "wheel man" who considered no obstruction too large when he was driving, especially in making an escape from the scene of a crime. Eventually, Giancana came under the wing of Tony Accardo and Paul Ricca, serving both at times as chauffeur. Ricca especially was impressed by Giancana's bearing—that of a mindless twerp eager to kill when ordered. Ricca had, at the time, catapulted to the heights within the mob and had learned the best possible life insurance was to have a bunch of maniacal killers backing him up. Giancana was that in time and, more important, would have a bunch of ruthless young 42ers ready to do his bidding. Under Ricca's tutelage, Giancana moved upward in the Chicago Outfit, and, as he did, brought other 42ers in with him, men like Sam Battaglia, Milwaukee Phil Alderiso, Marshall Caifano, Sam DeStefano, Fifi Buccieri, Willie Daddano, Frank Caruso, Rocco Pentenza and Charles Nicoletti.

By the 1950s the ravages of age had downed many of the old Capone hands, operatives and enforcers—Terry Druggan, Golf Bag Hunt, Greasy Thumb Guzik, Phil D'Andrea, Little New York Campagna, Claude Maddox and Frank Diamond. Accardo and Ricca promoted Giancana to operating head of the mob. It represented in a sense the changing of the guard, and Giancana promoted up the ladder his old 42er buddies and other young men. As these gangsters took over, they became known as the Youngbloods.

The mob took over more rackets than ever before. In the early 1950s, Giancana had masterminded the move to take over from the black numbers kings. A few judicious murders in this field upped the income of the Chicago Outfit by millions of dollars a year.

Sam's star rose higher and higher. He was no godfather whose hand was to be kissed, who was to be hugged by hulking enforcers. The name of the game in Giancana's crime family was money, and he who produced wealth for the mob earned its respect, provided the cash flow continued unabated. Sam moved in entertainment circles, and his friends included Frank Sinatra, Joe E. Lewis, Phyllis McGuire and Keeley Smith. His relationship with the Kennedy family can only be called complex, and there is little doubt that for a time he shared a mistress with the president of the United States.

Giancana's interests ranged from Las Vegas to Mexico to Cuba and elsewhere, no one knowing them all. And there was the CIA connection that haunted Giancana the last 15 years of his life. Somewhere in all these activities were the seeds of Giancana's doom.

In 1975, the details of the Giancana-CIA relationship were still coming out, and Sam was slated to go before a Senate investigating committee to testify. For several years he had been in decline with the mob because of his excesses. His murders, his love affairs, his battles with the FBI attracted too much heat. Before his death, Ricca reluctantly decided Giancana had to cool it. He was replaced in his boss role by Joey Aiuppa, a selection that Giancana did not like.

Giancana busied himself with gambling enterprises in Mexico. Now he was a source of considerable irritation to Accardo and Aiuppa, who pointed out to Giancana that he was living on mob money. Giancana saw it as his money. He had become a much-hated man—by the mob, by the CIA, by the FBI, perhaps by the other mafiosi involved in the Castro caper.

On June 19, 1975, Giancana was in the basement kitchen of his Oak Park, Illinois, home cooking a little snack before bedtime. Someone was with him: his murderer, but Giancana never suspected. As Giancana had his back turned, minding his sausages, a gun, a .22-caliber automatic with a silencer, was placed inches from the back of Giancana's head. There was a slight plop and Giancana crashed to the floor. Professionals know that a single shot to the head does not always kill. The murderer rolled Giancana over and placed the gun under Giancana's chin and shot bullet after bullet, six more in all, into his jaw and brain.

When the news broke of the assassination, CIA Director William Colby announced, "We had nothing to do with it." Newsmen checked with syndicate figures and got the same response from that quarter. Someone was lying. One of Giancana's daughters said it was all very unfair to her father, that he deserved a medal for the good works he had done for the government.

See also FORTY-TWO GANG; YOUNGBLOODS

GIANNINI, Eugenio (1910–1952): Informer and Joe Valachi murder victim

The life expectancy of a Mafia informer tends to be rather short, but the remarkable Eugenio (Gene) Giannini served 10 years as a stool pigeon for the Federal Bureau of Narcotics while chumming with many top American mafiosi. He was at the same time, in a practice not uncommon among informers, double-crossing the narcotics bureau and doing his own drug deals.

Unfortunately for Giannini he went too far when he approached the exiled Lucky Luciano in Italy and offered to supply him with considerable counterfeit dollars if he could find a buyer. Apparently instinctively, Luciano did not trust Giannini and left the deal hanging.

In the meantime Giannini was arrested by the Italian police on another matter. Finding himself confined in a rather unwholesome jail, he desperately smuggled out some letters to Charles Siragusa, the narcotics bureau man in Rome, reminding him of the services he had done the bureau in revealing narcotics violators as well as his burgeoning contact with Luciano.

It was a most injudicious thing to write. Letters smuggled out of Italian prisons tend to be read by unknown eyes. In some unknown way information about what was in the Giannini letters soon filtered back to Luciano.

The word soon got from Luciano to Vito Genovese in New York and then to Genovese's man, Tony Bender, who passed the word to the later-informer Joe Valachi. Giannini had to be killed.

Valachi shook his head sadly, saying, "There goes my couple of thousand he owes me. . . ." About a month later Bender sent for Valachi a second time and told him the mob had been unsuccessful in locating Giannini. From the drift of the conversation, Valachi said later he was afraid it might be thought he was sheltering Giannini to protect his $2,000. Out of self-defense, Valachi later testified to a U.S. Senate subcommittee, he volunteered to take the contract on Giannini. On September 20, 1952, Giannini was found shot to death. The job had been done by three young punks assigned by Valachi to do the actual killing, following his detailed script.

However, some crime experts have felt that Valachi lied, or as Virgil W. Peterson, for 27 years head of the Chicago Crime Commission, put it, "was considerably less than forthright" with the Senate subcommittee. It may have been that Valachi was not at all concerned about $2,000, if indeed Giannini owed that to him.

When Giannini had been arrested in Italy, Dominick "the Gap" Petrelli, Valachi's best friend, was taken with him. Giannini, although the subcommittee was never so informed, had bragged to Italian authorities in Petrelli's presence that he was an informer for the Federal Bureau of Narcotics. There was no way Petrelli would not have informed Valachi, his dearest friend, of this. Not long after this Petrelli, like Giannini, was murdered for being an informer, which leaves one to speculate about Valachi as well. Giannini, with whom Valachi was involved, was an informer. His best friend, Petrelli, was an informer. It could well have been that Vito Genovese was not wrong when he gave Valachi the "kiss of death," maintaining Valachi too was a stool pigeon and that his informing days had begun before he went to Atlanta.

Valachi took on the Giannini hit for no compensation—perhaps he enjoyed the very valuable bonus of protecting himself.

GIGANTE, Vincent "the Chin" (1926–): Mob enforcer

From the public's point of view, Vincent "the Chin" Gigante's claim to fame springs from the attempted slaying of Frank Costello in 1957. Even though Gigante, who went on trial for that crime, walked out of court a free man, he remains in popular theory linked to it.

According to this version, Vito Genovese ordered Costello killed so that he could seize the leadership of organized crime in New York. The then-300-pound Gigante reportedly took shooting practice daily in a Greenwich Village basement in preparation for the rubout. On May 2, 1957, Costello entered his apartment building on Central Park West. At that moment a large black Cadillac pulled up to the curb, a huge man got out, rushed past Costello, and entered the building. When Costello entered the lobby, the big man, from behind a pillar, appeared behind Costello. "This is for you, Frank," he called.

Vinnie "the Chin" Gigante, alleged gunman in the attempt on Frank Costello's life, was by the 1970s regarded as the no. 3 man in the Genovese crime family.

Costello turned, a movement that probably saved his life. The bullet grazed the right side of his scalp just above the ear. The fat man turned and hurried from the lobby, convinced he had delivered a killing shot.

But Costello was not seriously hurt, although he required hospitalization. Following the code of omerta, he insisted he did not know his assailant. However, the building's doorman had gotten a good look at the gunman, and, based on his evidence, an arrest order went out for the Chin. He didn't turn up. Informer Joe Valachi later reported, "The Chin was just taken somewhere up in the country to lose some weight." When fat camp adjourned, Gigante came in and surrendered, claiming he'd just heard the cops were looking for him.

It was a slim, trim Gigante who sat in the courtroom on trial for attempted murder. There wasn't much of a case against him. The doorman now wouldn't or couldn't identify him as the gunman. When Costello was put on the stand, Gigante's lawyer, Maurice Edelbaum, a noted and high-priced criminal attorney, conducted his interrogation on the absolute assumption that Costello would refuse to identify his client.

Edelbaum treated Costello harshly, reviewing all the Kefauver Committee's revelations about him and inferring that anyone who tried to kill Costello would be doing the community a favor. The lawyer then had Costello put on his glasses and study Gigante carefully. Costello did so and then swore that he had never seen Gigante in his life. Next Edelbaum leaned toward the witness and thundered, "You know who shot you. You know who pulled the trigger that night. Why don't you tell the jury who it was?"

Costello said nothing. Later Edelbaum informed a friend, "I would have dropped dead if he answered."

The jury acquitted Gigante.

Gigante rejoined the Genovese forces while the powerful New York Mafia split into two camps. On the one side stood Genovese and his supporters seeking control of the city's most powerful crime family, and on the other side, the aging Costello, who was also being harassed by federal officials, the deported Lucky Luciano and the crafty Meyer Lansky. On the surface, an agreement was reached that brought peace. Genovese agreed that Costello would retire, but be allowed to maintain his racket revenues. Costello and his friends agreed to the arrangement, and, apparently to show good will, the Chin was even invited to a number of Costello parties.

However, behind the scenes the double-dealing continued. Carlo Gambino, who had joined forces with Genovese to kill off Costello supporter Albert Anastasia, now secretly switched sides, having achieved his goal of leadership of the Anastasia crime family. The Costello-Luciano-Lansky-Gambino forces concocted a frame that would deliver Genovese to federal authorities on a narcotics rap. Part of the deal called for each of the four to contribute $25,000 apiece to a fund to bribe a minor dope pusher, Nelson Cantellops, to implicate Genovese. Costello, for his $25,000, insisted that the Chin had to be included among those caught in the net. It was a favor the others willingly granted. The plot worked to perfection, and, in 1959, Genovese got 15 years imprisonment, and 24 of his aides also drew long terms. The Chin got seven years.

In the 1970s the Chin was back in the fold. Later, according to some printed accounts, he suffered from

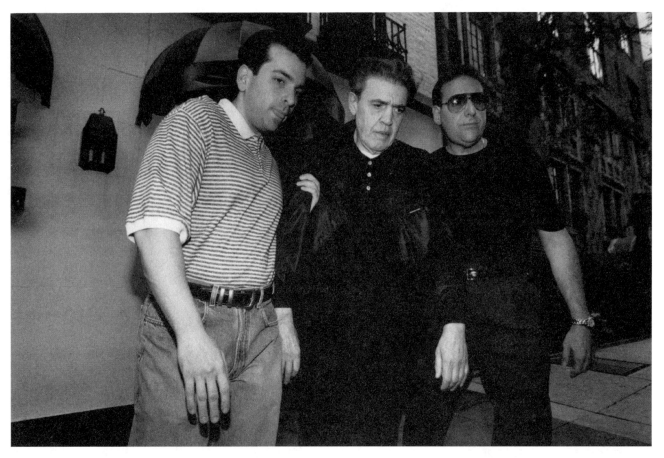

Two unidentified men escort the Chin to court. The court discounted his "dummy act" and sent him to prison on racketeering charges for 12 years.

a mental ailment and frequently regressed to childhood. Other reports claimed that he had actually risen to the rank of consigliere in the crime family under Frank Tieri (all of which tells volumes about the overall intelligence frequently available about the Mafia). In fact in 1987 with the conviction of Fat Tony Salerno, Gigante was named acting boss, this despite the fact that he sometimes walked on the street in Little Italy in his bathrobe, mumbling incoherently. Both the family soldiers and the police saw this behavior as a dodge to avoid possible future prosecution. Under Gigante the Genovese family became once more the most powerful of all, eclipsing the Gambino family under John Gotti, with whom he had a running battle for power. Eventually Gigante's "dummy act," collapsed under attack by federal prosecutors, and in December 1997 he was sent to prison for 12 years, making it unlikely at his age that he would resume control of his family, presuming of course that he survived his term.

In 2003, after years of his "dummy act," Gigante finally confessed he had long faked symptoms of mental illness. This followed an extended campaign by prosecutors to demonstrate how Gigante had conned judges and mental experts with his slobbering, muttering, and wandering about Manhattan in his bedclothes. In the process Gigante had fooled some of the most respected minds in forensic psychiatry and neuropsychology—in one case alone a prominent Harvard psychiatrist, five past presidents of the American Academy of Psychiatry and Law, and the man who invented the standard test for malingering. What apparently threw off some experts, as one put it, was that Gigante could be both mentally ill and a malingerer. In all, no less than 34 experts were convinced Gigante was not faking and was not capable of taking part in various legal hearings. The broad assessment was that in the matter of mental illness versus malingering doctors were convinced by Gigante's act. The evidence was not supportive of any other diagnosis. Besides dementia, additional diagnoses included various forms of schizophrenia and other serious mental disorders.

Gigante finally gave up his pose when prosecutors threatened to go after relatives who supported his claim of incompetence. For many years prosecutors indicated that they believed and said they could prove that Gigante's brother, the Reverend Louis Gigante, a noted worker with the poor, who had long championed his brother's condition, was himself a made member of the Mafia. It was a sort of charge that the government was hardly likely to pursue, with the headlines and public outcry that might ensue. It was now said that the Chin wanted that stopped for sure. There could be yet another reason for Gigante to throw in the towel. As it was he was not likely to get out until 2007, so he might as well take a short additional sentence to wipe the slate clean. In a deal with prosecutors Gigante pleaded guilty to obstruction of justice with the concurrence of the judge so that he would be eligible for release in 2010.

Most Mafia watchers thought it rather silly that Gigante might come out and try to pick up his rule of the Genovese family when he would be in his mid-80s and other leaders would not be likely to cede power back to him. It would be a unique situation with mobsters referring to scientific findings and declaring the Chin was "crazy as a bedbug" and not to be trusted to keep mob secrets. It would be the same situation that had occurred decades earlier when the mentally impaired Al Capone was released and never considered likely to return to power. As Greasy Thumb Guzik put it, not unkindly, "Al is nutty as a fruitcake." Capone never was capable of even trying to come back. Would an aging Gigante try? As one law official said, "We'd have a genuine case of the 'bedbug wars.'"

GIVE-UP guys: Hijacking scam

A large portion of truck hijackings, especially at such popular stealing grounds as New York's Kennedy airport, are not genuine hijackings or stickups, but rather arranged affairs involving "give-up guys." These are truckdrivers who have come under mob influence, perhaps by getting in debt to bookmakers or loan sharks or by being bribed.

These give-up drivers let their trucks and loads get hijacked either in staged stickups or while leaving their trucks along their route to get a bite to eat with the key "accidentally" left in the ignition. When the driver returns, his truck and its valuable load is gone. The mob protects such give-up guys, since they can be used again in a similar caper. Naturally the trucking firms may desire to fire these men, but the mob, through its control of certain unions, can bring the firm's activities to a complete halt through a driver walkout, forcing management to accept give-ups as a part of normal business.

GODFATHER, The: Novel and movie

Although it may be called a romantic novel (author Mario Puzo's own description of it), *The Godfather* and its later movie adaptations did much to form the public conception of the Mafia today. It may also be said to have molded the mafiosi's own concepts of themselves and their world.

Robert Delaney, a New Jersey State police detective, penetrated that state's mob organizations and was able to provide firsthand intelligence on organized crime and its members for a U.S. Senate subcommittee in 1981. He testified, "The movies *Godfather I* and *Godfather II* have had an impact on these crime families." He told of members who saw it three, four or as many as 10 times. He said once, while part of a group dining at a restaurant with Joseph Doto (the son of Joe Adonis), "Joe Adonis Jr. gave the waiter a pocketful of quarters and told him to play the jukebox continuously and to play the same song, the theme music from *The Godfather*. All through dinner, we listened to the same song, over and over."

Senator Sam Nunn asked, "You are saying sometimes they go to the movie to see how they themselves are supposed to behave, is that right?"

"That is true," Delaney said. "They had a lot of things taught to them through the movie. They try to live up to it. The movie was telling them how."

Longtime crime boss Joseph Bonanno (Joe Bananas) has his own evaluation of *The Godfather*. In his autobiography, *A Man of Honor*, he explains the extraordinary response to the work:

This work of fiction is not really about organized crime or about gangsterism. The true theme has to do with family pride and personal honor. That's what made The Godfather *so popular. It portrayed people with a strong sense of kinship to survive in a cruel world.*

Bonanno, however, does not offer us any star rating for the film.

GORDON, Waxey (1888–1952): Prohibition bootleg king

He was as prosperous and resourceful as any bootlegger during Prohibition, and for a time it seemed ridiculous—nearly impossible—to think of forming a national crime syndicate without including Irving Wexler, better known as Waxey Gordon.

Waxey was a master of the payoff and the fix and could solve almost any problem. When New Jersey reformers became upset by the noise created by the steady flow of Gordon trucks rumbling out of his illegal breweries, Waxey's inspired solution came in the form of big payoffs to politicians. And they proved worth it. Thereafter, Waxey's beer was pumped through pressure hoses laid in the sewer systems of Elizabeth, Paterson and Union City.

A youthful Waxey started out in crime as a rather efficient pickpocket on New York's Lower East Side, and picked up his nickname because he could slide a victim's wallet out of his pocket as though it were coated with wax. As he perfected his criminal talents, Gordon graduated to labor slugging, joining the Dopey Benny Fein Gang, which included such other eager bashers as Louis Lepke and Gurrah Shapiro.

As with so many criminals of the era, it was Prohibition that made Waxey. He became a protégé and junior partner of Arnold Rothstein—Mr. Big—in rumrunning, and became one of the leading illicit liquor importers on the East Coast. By the mid-1920s, Gordon was raking in between $1 million and $2 million a year in personal profits. He boasted a plush suite of offices on 42nd Street, owned nightclubs, speakeasies, illegal gambling joints, and a fleet of oceangoing rumrunners. He owned a brewery in New Jersey and a large distillery in upstate New York. His distilleries in Philadelphia cut, reblended and rebottled booze for scores of leading bootleggers around the country. In his personal life, Waxey maintained an expensive apartment on New York's Central Park West, and lived in a castle, complete with moat, in southern New Jersey. For conveyance, he collected a fleet of fast and glossy automobiles.

Gordon was powerful enough even to force his way into a "shotgun partnership" with the Luciano-Costello-Lansky-Siegel forces in New York, although hostility between himself and Lansky grew so intense that it became impossible for them to sit at the same

Prohibition bootleg king Waxey Gordon, Meyer Lansky's arch foe in the so-called underworld war of the Jews, was eliminated by a Lansky-Luciano double-cross that fed evidence to prosecutor Tom Dewey.

table together. The ill-feeling between them became known within the underworld as "the War of the Jews," and that meant actual warfare. Each suspected the other, rightly, of double-dealing. Lansky hijacked many of Gordon's liquor shipments, while Lansky correctly suspected Gordon of dealing with the mafiosi who opposed Luciano. Several gunmen in each camp were killed by their opposite numbers.

In the 1930s Gordon also warred with Dutch Schultz, each anticipating the end of Prohibition, and each jockeying for control of the future legit beer distribution rights in New York. By that time Gordon had been dubbed New York's Public Enemy No. 1. Neither Schultz nor Lansky could knock Gordon off because he enjoyed the fierce loyalty of his men, who would not be lured into any betrayal plot.

Finally the Lansky-Luciano forces figured out how to get rid of Gordon—let Uncle Sam do it. Gordon was tossed to the income tax wolves. Jake Lansky, Meyer's brother, fed information to the tax men about Gordon's operations and income, and a young, ambitious federal prosecutor named Thomas E. Dewey showed that the bootleg king took in $2 million a year while reporting an average net income of a mere $8,125 annually. In December 1933 Gordon was convicted, never suspecting the role in his downfall played by Lansky and Luciano; he was sent to Leavenworth under a 10-year sentence.

When he got out in 1940, Gordon was flat broke. All his property and wealth was seized or gone. He jauntily told reporters: "Waxey Gordon is dead. From now on it's Irving Wexler, salesman." But Gordon's downfall was not yet complete. Desperate for a stake, Waxey tried very minor-league crime capers; in 1951, he switched to some small-time narcotics dealing. He was caught as he was passing a $6,300 package of heroin to a federal narcotics informer.

Weeping to arresting officers, Waxey cried: "Shoot me. Don't take me in for junk. Let me run, and then shoot me!" One of the aging gangster's confederates pulled $2,500 from his pockets and slipped two diamond rings off his fingers. "Take this," he pleaded. "Take me. Take the whole business. Just let Pop go."

To the end, Waxey Gordon had the full loyalty of his men. At the age of 63, he was given 25 years to life, and shipped off to Alcatraz. It was a cruel punishment; Alcatraz was for dangerous prisoners, which Waxey was not. It didn't much matter. He only lived six months, dying of a heart attack on June 24, 1952.

See also WAR OF THE JEWS

GOTTI, John (1940–2002): Godfather with cult following

Both the Mafia and prosecutors agreed that the most important "godfather" in American crime through the 1990s would be John Gotti, subject of course to the vagaries and uncertainties of mob longevity and legal prosecutions. As one observer has stated, "There's no doubt in my mind the press will be labeling him the new 'Boss of Bosses'—if he lives that long."

Gotti was cut from the old mold, a type some law enforcement officials say hasn't been matched around New York Mafia circles since the demise of Albert Anastasia, the chief executioner of Murder, Inc., and reportedly Gotti's underworld idol.

By 1985, Gotti was considered the top capo in the Gambino crime family, the most powerful Mafia organization in the nation. At the time, he was running rackets—at JFK airport as well as other Gambino operations throughout the New York metropolitan area—and was a particular favorite of underboss of the group Aniello Dellacroce, an aging but still brutal mafioso. As much as Dellacroce liked Gotti, boss Paul Castellano hated him, or more accurately feared him, which in the Mafia automatically breeds hatred.

In 1985, both Castellano and Dellacroce were indicted on a number of charges. Both in their late 60s, long prison terms would effectively end their reigns in the mob. It looked like just a simple waiting period for Gotti.

He waited in style, brutal perhaps, but suave. "Gotti looks like a movie star," said a detective who knew him quite well. "He wears hand-tailored clothes, drives a big black Lincoln and likes good restaurants."

One of five brothers, Gotti worked his way up through the Mafia ranks. He became a capo as a reward for "good works" he did for the late family chief, Carlo Gambino. In 1972 Gambino's nephew, Manny Gambino, was kidnapped by other underworld characters who demanded a $350,000 ransom. After part of the ransom was paid, the kidnappers murdered Manny and buried the corpse in a New Jersey dump. The FBI arrested two suspects while Carlo Gambino put out a contract on a third, James McBratney. McBratney was later dispatched in a Staten Island bar by a three-man execution squad. Gotti, convicted as one of the death squad, served a portion of a seven-year sentence in Green Haven prison. He was no stranger to iron bars, having previously done time for hijacking.

On his release, Gotti was welcomed back by Gambino who saw to it that he moved up rapidly for services rendered. In 1978 or 1979 Gotti was named a capo and became a top associate of Dellacroce. Gotti was known to feel that Dellacroce deserved to be the head of the family instead of Castellano, as thought many other mafiosi. But Dellacroce kept Gotti in line.

Dellacroce knew he was dying of cancer. He told Gotti to be patient, a characteristic that was not Gotti's long suit. Nor was gentility. Toughness was the key. He was once overheard telling another mafioso: "Can you beat this—they're telling me I'm too tough for the job. Can you imagine what our thing [Cosa Nostra] is coming to?"

Subject only to the uncertainties of mob longevity and legal prosecution, dapper John Gotti was regarded by many experts as the certain "Godfather of the 1990s," combining the traits of ruthlessness and cunning to a degree that could match that of Al Capone. It was not to be, although it took seven years for the law to depose him.

On another occasion he was overheard chastising an underling for not returning his phone calls. "Follow orders," he was reported to have said, "or I'll blow up your house." The underling, obviously cowed, apologized and swore it wouldn't happen again. "You bet it won't," Gotti was quoted as saying. "I got to make an example of somebody. Don't let it be you." Seasoned officers swore that if they had shut their eyes and just heard words, they would have been sure it was the ghost of Albert Anastasia talking.

All the law could do was watch Gotti, around whom odd things had a way of happening. Something or other happened to 51-year-old John Favara,

a friend and neighbor of Gotti living in the Howard Beach section of Queens. In 1980 Favara ran over and killed Gotti's 12-year-old son, Frank, in a traffic mishap officially declared accidental. Four months later Favara was shoved into a car by some men as he left his job in a furniture plant and was never seen again.

According to police, after the death of young Frank, the Favara family was deluged with anonymous threatening letters and phone calls and their car was spray-painted with the word "murderer." From informers police got reports that Favara had been chainsawed to death and then dumped in a car that was put through a demolition machine and reduced to a one-square-foot block. There was no word on who the chain-sawer could have been.

But there were more important things than a simple murder to worry about. Trouble was brewing in the Gambino family. Dellacroce was so ill he might never stand trial, but many of the young mafiosi worried about Paul Castellano standing up to the prospect of living out the rest of his life behind bars. There was worry that he might start thinking of swapping mob secrets for his freedom.

Gotti didn't seem worried. Then Castellano named a mobster close to him, Thomas Bilotti, to the position of capo, the equal of Gotti. If Dellacroce died, the story went, Castellano was going to name Bilotti underboss, and if he, Castellano, went to prison, Bilotti would take over as godfather. Gotti would be out in the cold.

Dellacroce died on December 2, 1985. Two weeks later Paul Castellano and his protégé Bilotti were shot to death outside a Manhattan steakhouse. Gotti was in.

Within eight days it seemed Gotti was in charge of the biggest Mafia family in the nation. He was the center of attention at a party in a reputed meeting place of the Gambino family, the Ravenite Social Club at 247 Mulberry Street in Little Italy.

"All the big shots from the family were there," an investigator was quoted, "and Gotti walked in like he owned the joint. He obviously had no fear of anyone."

In 1986, Gotti faced federal prosecution on racketeering charges that could take him out of action for some time. But Gotti probably marked a new trend in the Mafia—back to younger bosses, as was the case in the 1920s and 1930s—because with the government hitting the mobs hard and going after the leaders, the Mafia worried whether the old dons could take the heat. If even one talked, the damage would be enormous. Younger bosses would have a different outlook. A 20-year sentence could mean getting out in six or seven years with good behavior. They could do such time standing on their heads; they could hang tough. Toughness was John Gotti's middle name.

And Gotti was adding a touch of coolness. Heading for an appearance in a federal courtroom, he insisted a female radio reporter enter before him. "I was brought up to hold doors open for ladies," he said.

It was the same sort of elegance that Al Capone, up until then a firm believer in violence, developed after becoming top boss when Johnny Torrio bowed out in 1925.

Gotti faced intensive federal prosecutions in the late 1980s, and it seemed highly likely that the young mob boss would almost certainly be convicted and would have to be replaced, if only temporarily, by a new leader of the Gambino family. But it was soon evident that even from behind bars Gotti was not about to hold still for being replaced. Given Gotti and his supporters' propensity for violence, it remained doubtful as well that the other New York crime families would dare to interfere with the powerful Gambinos. As one insider is reputed to have said, "When the Gambinos spit, the other families drown."

That meant any real opposition would have to come from within the family, and no one seemed capable of moving on Gotti, or his handpicked caretakers—his brother Peter and a childhood buddy, Angelo Ruggerio—while he was imprisoned for his trial. Then in early 1987, shocking government attorneys, Gotti beat the rap.

Next an effort was made to convict Gotti on RICO (1970 Racketeer Influenced and Corrupt Organization Act) charges. The lead prosecutor was Diane Giacalone, but her case was ill prepared and promised little chance of success, partially due to backbiting between the prosecutors and the FBI team investigating Gotti, members of which felt they could eventually produce a stronger case. Gotti and his cohorts were acquitted, and the mob leader's reputation was truly made. He became known as the "Teflon Don" against whom criminal charges simply could not be made to stick. It made grand press for Gotti, but his days were numbered.

The FBI produced a solid RICO case against him based on 100 hours of incriminating tapes. And they convinced Gotti's underboss, Sammy "the Bull" Gravano, to flip and testify against his chief. Gravano, who confessed to 19 murders, was out to save his own neck, and some criticized the government for granting him almost complete immunity, since Gotti was doomed on the tape evidence alone. However, it was obvious that the prosecution could not dare risk losing its case. A loss would probably leave Gotti free of any future prosecutions under RICO. Gravano's testimony thus was vital.

Gotti was convicted in 1992 and sentenced to life without parole. By the late 1990s it was unclear if Gotti would or even could continue to head the Gambino family from behind bars through his son. John Gotti Jr. was listed as acting boss of the family, but it was apparent that real power was gravitating to John J. D'Amico, a top Gambino capo and close friend of Gotti. Whether he remained a friend was open to question.

The doubts rose from the fact that cold-blooded analysis of the Gotti record proved disturbing to a number of Gambino family wise guys. In the short time before Gotti was tucked away in prison, the membership in the family had dropped from something over 250 to around 150. With Gotti at the head, the family had gained a reputation for dapperness, but Gotti's imposing presence on the TV nightly news exposed many of the capos and soldiers to discerning scrutiny by law enforcement officials. Gotti constantly ordered his men to come to the mob's Ravenite headquarters on Mulberry Street, even though the area was blanketed by FBI cameras. Many of the wise guys knew that quiet discretion and the shadows should have been the call; however, they dared not voice their fears to the boss and knew better than not to show up, since Gotti decreed and carried out the death sentence in such cases.

While all the mobsters hated Sammy "the Bull" Gravano for his ratting, they privately acknowledged the Bull's charge that Gotti's arrogance had done much to bring down the boss and their organization.

Law enforcement circles generally felt that Gotti and his son would become less major factors in the Gambino family. Indeed, crime would probably march on without the Gotti influence, and that is what happened.

Confined in maximum security from the time of his imprisonment, Gotti was in virtual isolation, allowed only a few visits from family members and his attorneys. He was kept in an eight-by-seven feet underground cell for 22 to 23 hours a day in Marion Penitentiary, a highly regimented federal facility, where he knew a great many other inmates there such as "Nicky" Scarfo, the homicidal former boss of the Philadelphia crime family, and Jimmy Coonan, the equally homicidal ex-head of the Westies, New York's Irish mob with ties to the Mafia. But he never saw them or heard their voices; each one's isolation was complete.

There is no doubt the conditions in Marion started to crack Gotti, although for a time he maintained control in some Mafia matters by issuing orders to his son, John Jr., or his brother Peter when his son was also imprisoned. But with the passage of time the full impact of his punishment hit Gotti. Prison-made videotapes viewed by *New York Daily News* reporters Jerry Capeci and Gene Mustain caught the heavy toll taken on the once powerful crime boss. He felt doomed and forgotten by his relatives. In one video Gotti said, "Right now I'm cursed. I'm stuck in this joint here and that's the end of it. This is my realm, right here. That's the end of it." When relatives did visit him, not too common an occurrence, he raged to them about the indifference of some of them as well as his steadily declining influence on the mob.

On a philosophical note, he said, "My life dictated that I take each course it took. I didn't have any multiple choice." Next then he might turn defiant, however, saying, "Listen to me carefully, you'll never see another guy like me if you live to be 5,000." Then the self-pity would take over: "I take credit for my, my, my bad deeds. Maybe I flatter myself. Maybe me and a lot of other people think I am more important than I really am."

Reports of cancer ailments depressed him further. He was assigned no work, no communal recreation. For a time he beat off the worst symptoms of his cancer and declared himself victorious. "Cosa Nostra forever!" he rejoiced for a time. Finally the cancer returned, and Gotti thought about being allowed to go home to die. There was also some suggestion that he might be shifted to a lower-security facility, but there was fear Gotti would face physical attacks from lesser criminals looking to gain a "rep." Most likely, officials wanted Gotti kept as an object lesson to other mafiosi of what could happen to them if they refused to cooperate.

Gotti made his final escape when he finally lost out to his cancer in June 2002.

See also MARION PENITENTIARY

GOTTI, John, Jr. (1964–): Stand-in boss for his imprisoned father

Prior to his 1992 conviction for murder and racketeering, John Gotti, boss of the Gambino family, made his son a capo. Gotti realized that the "big pinch" was coming, and he prepared to run his crime family from behind bars. When he went to prison, he named his son acting boss, which gave John Jr. the authority to convey his father's orders to the family.

As a relative, Junior was permitted to visit his father in the federal prison in Marion, Illinois, and he did so twice a month. They were separated by a thick Plexiglas partition, and no exchange of notes was permitted and could only talk over a phone monitored by guards; yet it was said that Junior had little trouble deciphering his father's orders on mob affairs. It was believed Gotti made himself clear through eye movements and voice inflections so that sometimes the opposite of what was said was the real message.

There was considerable doubt that Gotti would be able to continue as boss from behind bars, partly because of his son's arrogant style, which at times alienated Gambino associates. (The press capitalized on his arrogance and labeled him the "baby monster" after he was arrested for his role in two youthful brawls.) Even though the elder Gotti could be extremely vicious, he could also turn on considerable charm. While Gotti was famed for his finely tailored suits, his son dressed like a slob in jogging clothes. And while the elder Gotti lived in a nondescript house in middle-class Howard Beach, his son moved into a $700,000 home in exclusive Oyster Bay on Long Island. Everything about the younger Gotti irritated certain mobsters.

In January 1998 Junior was arrested and indicted along with 139 others. The charges included telecommunications and construction fraud, labor racketeering, loan-sharking and extorting money from a topless nightclub on Manhattan's Upper East Side named Scores, a favorite of celebrities and tourists. The mob reportedly extorted everyone from the owners to the coat-check girls, parking attendants and topless dancers, and the take was said to be in the millions.

John Gotti Jr., accompanied by one of his lawyers after a brush with the law. In 1998 Junior Gotti was charged with extorting money from a topless nightclub called Scores, which had little to do with the scores of sporting events. A lawyer informed the press that young Gotti had never been to Scores and "detests those places. He thinks they are degrading to women and disgusting."

Junior's lawyer called the indictment weak and "a bit silly." The only reason Junior was being charged, the lawyer insisted, "is his name." He said young Gotti had never even been to Scores. "He has nothing to do with Scores. He absolutely detests those places. He thinks they are degrading to women and disgusting."

Obviously the authorities hoped the indictments would cause chaos within the crime family. Lewis D. Schiliro, acting director of the New York office of the FBI, declared, "Yet another generation at the top of the Gambino family chart will soon be gone." And he added about Junior's situation, "It doesn't pay to be No. 1."

Junior did not remain No. 1 for long. Surprising most observers he suddenly copped a plea, not emulating his father by toughing it out in great style. It became known that Junior conferred with his father, who okayed his son making a deal, one that represented closure, assurance that prosecutors would bring no other charges and that his sentence would run between 70 and 87 months. Would this finally break the Gotti hold on the crime family? The betting was that the senior Gotti would try to continue using a pipeline to the mob via his brother Peter.

GOTTI, Peter (1939–): Alleged Gambino crime family boss
When a 2002 federal indictment named Peter Gotti, an older brother of the more famous John Gotti, as the current Gambino family boss, he became the third Gotti to be so named. Previously, John's son, Junior, held the title until he followed his father to prison. Actually, some argue that John sought to keep control of the crime family by using his son and later his brother as surrogates or, according to some, "gofers," carrying out his orders.

By the time John was dead, there was considerable thought, outside the circle of federal persecutors, that Peter was little more than a front man for the mob. One of Peter's lawyers, Gerard Shargel, raged in court, "Forgive me for stating the obvious: John Gotti is dead." According to the attorney, "in a certain twisted and perverted way, the government mourns his death," because they had lost a defendant who would pack the crowds into a courtroom. Thus, according to some defense lawyers, the feds just had to go wild whenever any Gotti name came up—that it was like wonderful old times.

Some mob observers insist the Gambino family was delighted not to have a strong leader so that capos could run their own show and "kick up less upstairs" to Peter Gotti, who was only a front. This has indeed happened in the mob before. In the Chicago Outfit, post–Al Capone, the popular belief was that Frank "the Enforcer" Nitti was in charge but was little more than a front man for Tony Accardo and Paul Ricca. When the pair told Nitti he had to cop a plea to get the rest of the mob off the hook with the law and do the time for all of them "or else," he knew what they meant. Terrified at doing prison time, Nitti shot himself.

This thesis, applied to Peter Gotti, did not have to go that far. He was a convenient scapegoat in any

Gambino operation since it could all be blamed on the Gotti breed. Many inside the mob insist Peter never could cut it in the mob and was dubbed with the nickname "Retard" to indicate that fact. He was "celebrated" cautiously in the crime family for a level of incompetence that even John, according to one description, found "breathless." Trying to explain to Peter Gotti that he was involved in a conspiracy was a monumental task and not always convincing. In a conference with a federal prosecutor and his attorney, the renowned Bruce Cutler, the official tried to explain to Gotti why he was being charged as taking part in a conspiracy. If he knew what was going down, he was in on it, the prosecutor told Gotti, but the latter responded, "But I never got a dime out of it." Didn't matter, the prosecutor responded, if he knew what was happening, he was in on the conspiracy. Gotti kept saying, "But I got no money out of it."

Finally, the prosecutor desperately appealed to Cutler to explain the facts to his client. "Can you help me out on this?" Cutler, not trying to be uncooperative, simply responded he could not do any better getting his client to understand what constituted conspiracy.

The government does not buy the "retard" claim, the prosecutors more likely feeling that Peter Gotti was simply "pulling a Gigante," the mob boss of the Genovese family who walked around Greenwich Village in a bathrobe mumbling to himself, pretending to be weak minded. They see Peter as far smarter than he talks. The government claimed before Peter was being brought to trial that it would prove that Gotti received money from Jerome Brancato, allegedly for illegal activities. These payments, prosecutors claimed, were required by the mob code that gives the boss control over captains and a financial cut in their dealings. Other observers see Peter as a pawn in mob operations and certainly no powerhouse. Defense attorneys say that even if it is shown that Peter got some money from criminals who had been closely tied to John Gotti, it does not imply guilt. As is typical of their claims, they would be sure to remind jurors that the prosecutors must prove guilt, not just guilt by association. "At bottom," one lawyer involved in the case in which Peter Gotti was one of many players, said, "there is nothing illegal about associating with somebody, even somebody the government calls the mob, as long as you do not commit the crime."

Some claim that even though Peter Gotti may be far less important than anyone, including himself, may think, it is inevitable that he will end up being sent away for 50 to 70 years or so. Almost every crime caper pulled by Gambino mobsters (and even those by others) in recent years was invariably linked to Peter Gotti as the family boss. If it was on the waterfront or in gambling operations or in shakedowns of Hollywood people or others, Peter Gotti was generally named the overall boss. Fifty to 70 years would be hard time for a man who will undoubtedly come to feel he was much better off in 1979 when he retired as a sanitation worker on a disability pension. Far more than for most involved in organized crime, it will be no easy matter to figure out if Peter Gotti was a genuine mob insider or merely an outsider looking in.

The ambiguity of the justice system's view of Peter Gotti was readily apparent after he was found guilty of money laundering and racketeering. Defense attorney Shargel asked that his client get less than the maximum sentence since he was in poor health and was at most a mob boss in name only. Gotti could have been given 15 years (and mob bosses usually get the "max"), but the judge imposed a sentence of only nine years. The judge said that the record "strongly suggests that Peter Gotti did not exhibit leadership characteristics."

This is an artist's sketch of Peter Gotti during a hearing at the Brooklyn, New York, federal court Friday, March 26, 2004. A judge delayed the sentencing of the brother of late mob boss John Gotti after a three-hour hearing failed to settle how much time he should get for a racketeering conviction.

The judge noted, however, that he was "still a leader," which meant he deserved a stiff sentence.

Attorney Shargel told the judge that Gotti was blind in one eye and suffered from thyroid goiter, sciatica, emphysema, rheumatoid arthritis, post concussion syndrome and depression, and that a long prison stay could further damage his health. Shargel further pleaded for leniency by stating: "Peter Gotti may have had the title of acting boss, but I don't think there's anyone who thinks he has managerial capacity, if you will. I don't think there's anyone who knows Peter Gotti who thinks he was making important decisions, if you will."

Gotti still faced a possible additional 70 years in imprisonment for taking part in an unsuccessful 1999 plot to kill Mafia turncoat Sammy "the Bull" Gravano. That matter went to trial in November 2004. However, many legal opinions held that Gotti wouldn't get a major sentence in the matter and that he might well get off with a sentence concurrent to his nine-year term.

Perhaps the major import of Gotti's prosecution was not that it would destroy the Gambino crime family, but recognition that at last the Gotti influence within the mob was fading. This would not make the real bosses of the Gambinos happy. As long as Peter Gotti was handy, he could be kicked around.

Some observers find the prosecution to be very cynical for sitting on "Mikey Scars" DiLeonardo, apparently expected to be the law's turncoat of the early 2000s while they prosecuted Peter Gotti. Scars has informed federal investigators that rather than Peter Gotti, the true boss of the Gambino family was JoJo Corozzo, who has been described as sublimely happy with Gotti being out there as a sitting duck. From the feds' viewpoint, it has been said, there would be plenty of time to unmask Corozzo after the last of the Gottis was taken care of. In the meantime the claim can be made that once again a fatal blow has been struck against the Gambinos. The downside to this, some observers warn, was that the Corozzo influence can continue to solidify. This theory can be argued on either side. From a more personal view, Peter Gotti will get his, as the *New York Times* has noted, "Gambino Crime Boss or Not."

See also COROZZO, JOSEPH "JOJO"; DI-LEONARDO, MICHAEL "MIKEY SCARS"; DOCK RACKETS; LOVEFELLAS

GOTTI "Fan Club": Imprisoned Mafia boss's loyal supporters

After the second attempt by the government to imprison him, John Gotti was transformed by some into a hero, especially in his home territory of Ozone Park and Howard Beach in Queens. And the support continued even after his conviction in 1992, when his fans staged perhaps the wildest protests ever made on behalf of a mob boss. On Gotti's sentencing day in federal court, about 1,000 people arrived on chartered buses outside the court; marchers surrounded the building, chanting "Free John Gotti" and "Freedom for John."

As word of the life sentence for Gotti spread from the courtroom down to the lobby and out to the street, the angry crowd charged forward, egged on by members of John Gotti Jr.'s crew shouting into bullhorns. The demonstrators tried to storm the building, fighting an outmanned squad of cops and federal guards. The police department rushed in an additional 100 officers to hold back the protesters, but a number of policemen were injured and required first aid in the lobby. Frustrated, the crowd vented their rage on cars parked outside, turning three completely over. Police arrested a dozen Gotti supporters, including one of Gotti's nephews, 22-year-old Joseph Gotti.

Federal officials insisted the entire demonstration had been orchestrated by the Gotti forces. James Fox, director of the FBI's New York office, told the press: "That was an orchestrated and planned event, not spontaneous. It was directed by the crew of John Gotti Jr."

While that may be true, the riot left little doubt that some still maintained a near-mythic adulation of John Gotti despite his crimes. According to his lawyers, Gotti still gets as many as 100 letters a week in prison. Many come from crackpots, but others are from strangers wishing him well, some even ask for advice on coping with crises in their own lives. Occasionally, Gotti deigns to respond.

Dear Mr. Gotti,

I am writing this letter to you to see if you would write a letter of encouragement to my aunt who is terminally ill with cancer. She and I both are great admirers of yours and if anyone knows about courage it's you.

I know in my heart a note of best wishes from you would mean so much. God bless you and your family. I pray you'll be reunited with your family in the very near future.

Whenever Gotti faced court action, he could mount support from demonstrations, such as this one led by his usual lead attorney Bruce Cutler (with bullhorn in hand), with up to 1,000 participants charter-bused from his home neighborhood of Ozone Park and Howard Beach in Queens, New York.

Gotti was touched enough to have a lawyer write the sick woman and pass on his best wishes, advising her to "stay strong."

One cynic noted that Gotti did not respond in writing himself. That could be because many fans want nothing better than a personal letter from him, something that might become a valuable collector's item in the future.

John Gotti was not the sort to give out freebies.

GRAVANO, Sammy "the Bull" (1945–): Turncoat underboss for John Gotti

The headline in the *New York Post* blared "KING RAT!"

The *Daily News*, the city's other main tabloid was a bit more inventive on its front page: "DON'S NUMBER TWO WILL SING THE HITS."

They were talking about Sammy "the Bull" Gravano, John Gotti's underboss in the Gambino crime family. He had decided to "flip," the first time ever

that an underboss facing trial with his boss had turned against him. "This defection is unprecedented in the annals of New York organized crime," said Edward McDonald, former head of the Eastern District's Organized Crime Strike Force.

Prosecutors were confident in November 1991 that they were about to destroy the image of "the Teflon Don," the best-known mobster since Al Capone and one who had beaten all past charges against him and created a persona of invincibility that infuriated law authorities.

But this time was different. The prosecution had over 100 hours of taped conversations that doomed Gotti with his own words. The Bull—so named for his compact muscular body and thick bovine neck— had actually witnessed the damning situations recorded on tape and could provide personal corroboration the authorities had never had before against Gotti.

It could be said that what made Gravano so fascinating to the authorities, the press and the public was his very unwholesomeness. Gravano confessed his guilt to a mere 19 murders.

One newspaper splashed its front page with a tombstone labeled "R.I.P." and listing all 19 Gravano murder victims from Joseph Colucci in 1970 to Louie DiBono and Edward Garafalo two decades later.

Despite this, the prosecution was ready to trade immunity for information about Gotti, including facts tying him to the scene of the curbside murder of Paul Castellano outside a fashionable New York steakhouse. The damage the Bull did the Gambino family was staggering. Besides Gotti, Gravano was directly responsible for dozens of convictions, guilty pleas or added prison terms for Gambino family members.

Top aide Frank Locascio (Frankie Loc) went down, along with seven capos, for counts varying from murder to racketeering. That group included Tommy Gambino, the son of Carlo Gambino and operator of the family's empire in the garment industry. High-up figures in the Colombo family and New Jersey's DeCavalcante family fell, as did the underboss in the Genovese family and a consigliere and three capos from other New York families. The Bull also caused eight union officials to plead guilty to charges of labor racketeering. Others who fell under the Bull's tell-all were a city criminal intelligence cop who was feeding information to Gotti and a corrupt juror from one of Gotti's previous prosecutions.

It remained stunning to many observers that the Bull had flipped; however, it was obvious that he had

Sammy the Bull (left) and John Gotti, during the best of times before the worst of times.

no choice, since otherwise, he concluded in conference with his lawyer, he faced a sure sentence of 50 years to life. The tapes had doomed him, and Gravano was bitter about that. Gotti's words on the tapes tied the Bull to two or three murders for certain. He blamed Gotti's "big mouth" for dooming him.

Some observers noted that if the case against Gravano had been that strong, and it obviously was, it was doubly true about Gotti himself. Why then, they wondered, was it necessary to make a deal with Gravano? The only explanation was that the prosecution suffered from "teflon don syndrome," a fear that if the case against Gotti somehow fell through, the government would never be able to prosecute him again. Under that theory Gravano was a godsend.

In 1995, in exchange for his testimony in the Gotti case and some others, the prosecution agreed to no more than a five-year sentence for Gravano. As he had been imprisoned since 1990, he was free.

After that the Bull was out there somewhere. The new Gravano was described as a man with a legit job, determined to start a new life. It didn't happen.

Sammy the Bull's saga turned out to be a continuing one, well past 2000. The reason was simple. Sammy the Bull could not cut it in a normal life after his ghoulishly happy days of robbery, extortion, and murder. At first he followed the standard witness protection drill: plastic surgery, sticking to a newly furnished identity, keeping a low profile. It took all of nine months for Gravano to tire of that. He had to bust loose. How could he be expected to "live 20 years in a cabin and be scared to death?" He left the witness protection program. His wife divorced him, selling their home and some building property in her name and left New York with their children. That was the official version, but some people in the media predicted there would someday be a family reunion for the Bull.

Gravano's was a plight that confounded many criminals who entered the protection program. The need to return to crime is overwhelming. Dominick Costa, a mob-connected safecracker, had it made in the witness program safely buried in a small Minnesota town but felt sat on by his keepers. He eventually found a way to get back in the swing—the small bank across the street from his quarters. He cracked the safe and got $40,000, but the law soon figured out who had done it, and Costa lost his safe spot and went to jail.

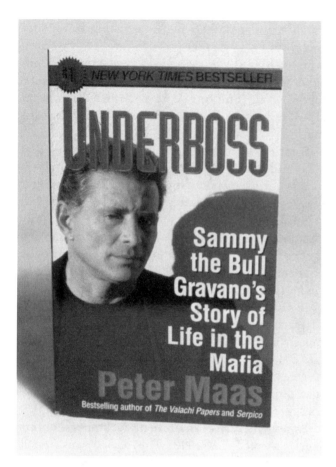

Underboss, the story of Sammy the Bull's life in the Mafia by Peter Maas, became a national best-seller. Afterward the kin of several of Gravano's murder victims started a legal campaign to deprive the mobster of any financial rewards from the book, but Gravano has proved a tough nut and has given up nothing.

Sammy the Bull was not that kind of small-timer. He operated on a bigger scale and, after living rather openly plugging his book, went into business in a racket he knew well—drugs. He set up his new life in Arizona operating there and on the East Coast with his own multimillion-dollar Ecstasy combine, which authorities charged included his wife, his daughter, his son, and 32 others. Caught dead to rights seeking to return to his "glory days," Gravano pleaded guilty to federal drug charges in May 2001 and was sentenced to 20 years in prison and fined $100,000.

Already, before his sentencing, Gravano had other travails. The fact that he had been fined $100,000 was not uninteresting to some observers, especially since he traveled to Brooklyn, home base of the Gambino crime family, to set up his operations.

There had long been speculation that Sammy had squared things with John Gotti's family by paying off regularly for dispensation for his past treacheries. The Mafia has long been known to be forgiving of almost anything as long as the money flowed in. According to this thesis, Gravano's Ecstasy revenues took over as his take from his biography and his legitimate businesses in Arizona was fading. The problem here was that Gravano may well have welched on his payments; after all that was part of the game.

Even before the feds nailed Gravano on the Ecstasy rap, the Gambinos had once more had it with Sammy. Apparently the mob had decided that turncoat Gravano just couldn't be trusted. The feds claimed that John Gotti's brother, Peter, acting boss of the crime family, had plotted with Gravano's brother-in-law Edward Garafola and Gambino soldier Thomas Carbonaro to arrange Gravano's demise in Arizona. According to prosecutors, Carbonaro and one Fat Sal Mangiavillano found that a hit in Phoenix was not so easily done. Gravano had his house surrounded with a chain-link fence, off which bullets could well ricochet. The spot across the street was too open to wait around to do some shooting; they had to worry that Sammy would spot them. In addition, the FBI was at the time holding a convention in Phoenix, forcing the plotters to wear hoop earrings and leather bikers' caps to keep from being spotted. By then the boys felt they could not wait out the end of the convention because some of the agents were taking vacation time once the meetings ended. Whey they got back to New York, Carbonaro and Fat Sal heard about Gravano's bust in the Ecstasy case, which gave Fat Sal another idea: Maybe they could send Sammy a letter bomb. Carbonaro, he later told prosecutors when he was arrested, was not impressed. Fat Sal had forgotten that prisons use X-ray machines.

That may have provided a comic topper to any possible hit but perhaps more of interest on conceivably why the plot never came off was the fact that Sammy the Bull announced in 2003 he would testify for Carbonaro whom he doubted had taken part in any hit plot. Gravano's line apparently would be that Carbonaro had been part of his crew before he ratted on Gotti and that he and his wife had stayed in contact with Carbonaro and his spouse when the Bull entered the witness protection program. In all his informing, Gravano had steadfastly refused to inform on his own crew members. That may well have given him an entree to a peace deal for a time with the Gambinos. Gravano apparently always gave himself an out.

Deals, deals, deals, that was all Sammy knew. And while in the witness program and later, he merrily, according to court papers filed in Arizona, went on plotting crimes, revenge, and what have you. Noted attorney Ron Kuby, protégé of the late famed civil rights attorney William Kunstler, was one of Gravano's targets after Kuby roused the Bull's ire by representing the families of 12 of the 19 people Gravano admitted killing in his days within the Gambino family.

The plan, according to court papers, called for Kuby to be lured to Texas where there was more evidence against Gravano available. There, it was alleged, Sammy himself would take Kuby out or have some associate drug dealers do it for him. Kuby did not fall for the lure. But Sammy also had other things to worry about then. He got his 20-year federal sentence and faced trial in Arizona on state charges. There were other headaches for Sammy. In New Jersey charges were readied claiming Gravano had hired a hit man to take out a New York police detective, Peter Calabro, near his home in New Jersey in 1980. This was not a murder Gravano had confessed to, and, if true, it would be a charge hard to admit since police are adamant that no cop killer gets a deal. On the other hand, some legal observers felt it was an old case and tying it to Sammy might be difficult.

It was all problematic, but many thought Gravano was at the end of his rope and would never outlive his prison sentences. Then there were those who thought Sammy might make a deal. The Arizona charges meant nothing because they would be served concurrent with his federal sentence, and journalists in the Southwest thought they saw the elements for a bargain. Sammy knew a lot about drug deals and dealers in Arizona, Texas and elsewhere. He could, some journalists felt, offer the law so much in busting up drug rackets that he could get chunks of his jail time rescinded once again.

On the other hand this could be all fantasy. But there is no doubt Sammy would go on scheming, looking for an arrangement. Sammy was an unrepentant criminal and a practiced turncoat. Sammy the Bull's career may or may not be at a dead end. Stay tuned.

See also GOTTI, JOHN; *MALLIOCCHIA*

GREED of crime bosses: Top of the mob shakedown artists

Near the end of his life, Carlo Gambino, the de facto boss of bosses, became enraptured by money—other mobsters' money. He might receive a cut of $25,000 from a capo and then a few days later, confront the same capo and snarl: "Where the hell is my 25 grand?"

This was Carlo Gambino, and normally he would never have acted that way, except that he was, as the wise guys knew and whispered, losing it, going senile. Had that happened with most other bosses, the wise guy assumption would have been that it was a boss shakedown. Carlo by his reputation got a bye on that. In the mob, men turn "green-eyed," and as one moves up the ladder the greed of the players becomes more intense. Most crime bosses view the whole world as their victim, but their top choice is their own men. Bosses call this "showing them respect," but it really means "show me the money." And even if there is no money, they still want it.

Many of the family civil wars revolve around a boss's insatiable greed.

Ten years after the death of Carlo Gambino, two tough wise guys who had clawed their way to the top of their families, John Gotti and Philadelphia boss Little Nicky Scarfo, were debating their old bosses' greed. According to Philadelphia informer Phil Leonetti, who took part in the discussions, said of Angelo Bruno, the old family boss, "If we would go to him to ask a favor to try to get into a business, he would say, 'No, it's a bad idea,' and then behind our back, he would send his son-in-law or his cousin to get the deal." That rankled Scarfo and Leonetti, since "if he wanted to kill somebody, he would know who to come to; he would come to us."

"Jesus," John Gotti commiserated, "Paul [Castellano] was the same way, the same type of guy. He did the same thing with us. He wouldn't let us make a living and on top of everything else, he wanted to kill me."

Not surprisingly both Bruno and Castellano ended up murdered. Other bosses over the years faced similar problems. Joe Profaci, one of the founding fathers of the five families in New York, was a notorious "miser thief," as many of his men called him. He grabbed such a huge cut of revenues for himself that he finally provoked the Profaci-Gallo war. That conflict was still unresolved when Profaci died from natural causes—and undoubtedly, said the Gallo people, tried to take his loot with him.

Carlo Gambino's heir, his cousin Paul Castellano, stood out in the 1980s as the most practiced boss when it came to parsimonious behavior. His sticky fingers simply never let loose of any of his soldiers' money that came his way by mistake. Once Sammy "the Bull" Gravano made a score for $120,000 and was to cut it up in three equal shares of $40,000 for Castellano, for corrupt union people and for himself. Being magnanimous the Bull paid off Castellano and the union boys as the dough rolled in and figured he'd take his share last. Unfortunately, an associate who collected the last $40,000 gave it to Castellano.

Figuring he was dealing with a man of honor, the Bull went to Paul and explained what happened. "So," he said, "that money's mine."

Then, Castellano made a big show of jumping out of his skin and pointed in wild panic toward the ceiling, as though he suspected FBI bugs all over the place. He told Sammy, "Don't bring it up to me anymore. I'll bring it up to you."

He never did. At the time Sammy hadn't been concerned since Paul was "worth a trillion." It turned out that a trillion, forty thousand was even better in Paul's mind.

That caper was equaled or exceeded by Castellano's other dirty dealings within the mob. Castellano set up an outfit called Metro Concrete for his son-in-law and himself, and they simply grabbed away millions of dollars worth of crooked business from various family companies. At the same time Castellano short-circuited many construction union kickbacks directly and cut his own soldiers out of the loop, taking a monstrous chunk out of revenues due his people.

Perhaps his greatest sin was selling out Frank Piccolo, the family capo in Connecticut, to the Genovese family. The Genovese people wanted exclusive control of the gambling and loan shark revenues in the state, but Piccolo was grabbing some of the loot for the Gambinos. This should have delighted Castellano, but the Genoveses kept pushing, asking for the right to kill Piccolo. Castellano finally agreed, in part to solidify his position with the rival group and have allies in case he faced an insurrection from within. Also as part of the deal the Genoveses would cut Paul in personally for a share of the state's profits. So, Piccolo died, and the Gambino family was hurt, except for Castellano himself.

In that sense, Castellano's greed added a link to the chain of events leading to his destruction. When Gotti decided to make his move against his family boss, he sought approval from the other New York families. The Genoveses had no objection. If Castellano departed the planet, they would have Connecticut for themselves and face no obligation to continue the payoffs to Paul's murderers, especially since Gotti would have his hands full getting a handle on all the other revenues coming in.

Of course, Gotti as boss meant just another greedy boss, despite his insistence he was making everybody richer. Gotti needed the money. He had an expensive wardrobe and lifestyle and during the pro-football season he might lose as much as a quarter million dollars a weekend to gambling.

Right after taking over, Gotti lectured his capos about not overpaying their soldiers. He particularly went after Sammy "the Bull" Gravano, complaining he was giving too much of their scores to their men. It was not good, he said, to let them make "too much money." He spoke of the virtues of keeping the men down, broke and hungry. He pointed out he paid his chauffeur $600 a week, this to a man who might be in a situation of having to save the boss's life. The Bull was shocked, pointing out that if the driver had to pick up one fair-sized tab during the week, he'd have nothing left to take care of his family.

Gotti could not be persuaded; he just didn't want the guys getting "too fat."

There was some prudence in Gotti's orders to the Bull. Gravano was cutting up scores more than the other capos, and thus getting more loyalty from the men. Some day the Bull could command such loyalty that his crew would do anything for him—including getting rid of John Gotti.

Some experts have no doubt that sooner or later, had not the government gone after the mob, there would have been a Gotti-Gravano war. But that is the dilemma for Gotti and all other bosses: to "overpay" the boys or stiff them. Greed usually provides the course of action.

GREEK Mafia

Although it operates on a fairly modest scale, the Greek mob is generally considered a good money proposition for the Mafia, "provided them Greeks don't get too greedy." For years the Greek mob operated under the command of Spiros Velentzas in Greek immigrant communities in Queens, New York. The Velentzas empire ran a number of horse parlors using satellite dishes to pick up transmissions of races around the country. Perhaps even more lucrative for the operation was "barbut," a dice game that escalated into very high stakes. The traditional crime families made no effort to take over such gambling, feeling those "rotten Greeks know the damn game so good they'd cheat us blind." Thus Valentzas was able to arrange tribute to the Lucchese family for rights to operate. That solved the problem with the mob, but Valentzas had other woes, as other legal and illegal Greek immigrant groups looked to muscle in on the gambling empire. The word was that Valentzas went to the Luccheses to complain about this incursion by "foreigners." The Luccheses, though harassed then by federal investigators, were not going to lose their Greek meal ticket. As usual the intruders were summoned to a sitdown from which they only left quite dead.

Only occasionally did the Greek Mafia overstep the bounds themselves, trying to extend the operations in areas that put a chink in the revenues of the Gambino family. That matter was solved readily by mere threats, which did include a description of the dire punishments to come. One thing was certain, the Greek Mafia was not going to regain in Queens the glories that were Greece.

GREENBAUM, Gus (1894–1958): Mob bookmaker and murder victim

Referred to by some contemporaries as "the second toughest Jewish mobster in Vegas" (Moe Dalitz was number one), Gus Greenbaum, besides managing a number of casinos in Las Vegas, was the mob's principal Arizona bookmaker. Greenbaum went all the way back to New York's Lower East Side with Meyer Lansky, being involved in bootlegging as well as handling a number of gambling assignments.

When Bugsy Seigel was shot dead in Virginia Hill's plush Beverly Hills mansion, his blood had not even dried when in far-off Las Vegas three men—Morris Rosen, Moe Sedway and Greenbaum—marched into the lobby of the Flamingo, Siegel's newly opened casino hotel, and announced they were taking over. It was apparently clairvoyance

that prompted them to do so before Siegel's murder became generally known.

Lansky put Greenbaum in charge of the business end of the Flamingo and within a year the losses Siegel had incurred were transformed into a $4 million profit. There was no way of guessing how much money was "skimmed" off before tax forms were filled out, although an educated rue of thumb puts it around three times the reported profits.

Greenbaum was sitting pretty. The Flamingo and Vegas flourished, and Greenbaum kept it that way. He exhibited the toughness that made his word law. When two Kansas City hoodlums, Tony Broncato and Tony Tombino, heisted $3,500 in the only successful armed robbery in Vegas since the opening of the Flamingo, Greenbaum took it as a personal affront. He passed the death sentence on them, and although the two Tonys went into hiding, they were located in Los Angeles and murdered. The job was done by hit man Jimmy Fratianno.

With the passing years, Greenbaum became a problem for the mob. An inveterate gambler and womanizer, he became an alcoholic and turned to drugs. Still, he did have a way of turning casinos into gold mines. When Chicago—specifically Tony Accardo, Sam Giancana and the Fischettis—took over the Riviera in Las Vegas, they borrowed Greenbaum to do his thing. The Riviera prospered, but perhaps not as well as might have been expected. Greenbaum, to finance his personal habits, was skimming the skim. In December 1958 Greenbaum and his wife were found dead in their home in Phoenix, their throats cut.

The gory murders were said to have upset Lansky. Not that he had not authorized the Greenbaums' assassination, but he had undoubtedly let the contract go to the Chicago Outfit, known to prefer brutal murders to simple kills. The dispatching of Mrs. Greenbaum, Chicago felt, would be an added inducement to other employees to play fair with the mob.

See also SKIMMING

"GREEN eyes": The Mafia's greediest

Paul Castellano had "green eyes." Angelo Bruno, the longtime boss of the Philadelphia mob had green eyes. Sammy "the Bull" Gravano had green eyes. The term within the Mafia is used for any mobster, high or low, who is deemed too greedy. It applies especially to a boss or other chieftain far up the crime family ladder who appears to be hogging everything for himself. It is a trait that certainly plays a role in their ultimate fate—getting whacked out by those under them.

Sammy the Bull, who rose to be John Gotti's underboss before he turned informer to save himself, showed such green eyes in his new position under Gotti that his superior was driven to distraction.

Gotti understood the perils of obsessive greed and ruthlessness, and he felt it would in time split the Gambino family and plague it with constant intrafamily warfare. In addition Gotti felt he was being victimized by the Bull and being left out in the cold. Gravano was building a business empire of companies tied into construction and feeding off the mob's controlled rackets.

FBI tapes caught Gotti complaining to Frankie Loc, another top aide, "Where are we going here? Every fucking time I turn around there's a new company popping up. Building, consulting, concrete. And every time we got a partner that don't agree with us, we kill him. You go to the Boss, and your Boss kills him. He okays it. Says it's all right, good. Where are we going here, Frankie? Who the fuck are we? What do I get out of this here?"

Working up to a full head of steam, Gotti continued, ". . . Sammy, slow it down. Slow it down. You come up with fifteen companies. For Christ sakes you got . . . concrete pouring. You got tiled floor now. You got construction. You got asbestos. You got rugs. What the fuck next? The other day . . . Sammy says, 'And I got the paint, and I got—'

"'You got a paint company?' I told him.

"He said, 'Well, six weeks ago we started a paint company. Don't you remember I told you?'

"'I don't fuckin' remember you told me. What am I, fuckin' nuts? Now you got me thinking that I'm fuckin' nuts! When did you tell me you got a paint company? When I was looking over there?'"

Then Gotti complained angrily, "Four fuckin' years, I got no companies!"

Gotti remembered some of the hits Gravano had pulled off after convincing Gotti that certain mafiosi had been disrespectful of him and "talking behind his back." After they were killed their businesses, a construction company and a steel outfit, fell under the Bull's control.

Gotti now knew the Bull was playing him for a sucker.

In another world, with no FBI or other cops, just Gotti and Sammy, it would have been interesting to see how it played out. The green eyes syndrome certainly would have been the death of one of them.

GUARANTEE: Mafia's "protection" plan

There is no honor among thieves, that is, among thieves *outside* the Mafia. A Mafia boss can make a "guarantee" to disparate criminal elements that a deal will be lived up to by all the conspirators. If there is any backsliding, the boss will invoke godfather-like and fatal vengeance.

In fact, this theory of guarantees is as credible as the Tooth Fairy. A case in point concerned a Mafia guarantee involving three fast-money operators in New Jersey. In contact with gangsters attached to mob circles in New England who had millions in hot stock on their hands, the three New Jersey operatives—Gil Beckley, Joseph Green and Gerald Zelmanowitz—were prepared to pay a small fraction of the stocks' market value and sell them at a huge profit. The key man in this was Zelmanowitz, who was known both nationally and internationally as a master at "moving paper." The deal presented all sorts of problems concerning personal trust, and it required a number of meetings with much incriminating talk. There would have to be transfers of cash in neutral surroundings and assurances had to be given that none of the financial paper had already been put on the market, where it would be likely to attract very strong law enforcement heat. There had to be guarantees that neither side would be cheated, conned or ripped off, sold bad goods or for that matter be held up at gunpoint or even set up for the police to "square" some previous charge.

Under the circumstances, the parties sought a traditional guarantee that all was well and requested the intervention of a Mafia figure respected—or feared—by both parties. This Mafia figure was to guarantee the deal for all and for this service would be paid 6 percent of all transactions. This was important money and a plenty high rate since the mafioso boss would probably do nothing more than oversee the agreements. However, it was understood that if anything went wrong, he would step in and promptly see that the offending party or parties were "hit in the head."

In this Beckley-Green-Zelmanowitz caper the man brought in was Fat Tony Salerno, then high up in the Genovese family and in later years the top boss. Within this arrangement Salerno became the "rabbi" of the deal, giving the transactions his "blessing" but ready to deal out damnation if it was required. At a number of meetings Salerno just sat there nodding sternly and collecting 6 percent. He would never do any more than that. Meanwhile the Zelmanowitz group handed over $60,000 for $305,000 in Indiana Toll Road bonds, and in another transaction some $20,000 as an advance for $2 million in stock that Zelmanowitz was to sell on consignment.

Then the roof fell in. Zelmanowitz dumped some of the Indiana bonds to a Newark brokerage house, but was later arrested when they turned out to be distressingly counterfeit.

This was of course a gross violation of the guarantees in the conspiracy and Zelmanowitz, out on bail, rushed to Salerno to complain. The Mafia bigwig was suitably outraged and ordered two offenders brought in for a meeting forthwith or their legs would be broken.

The confident Zelmanowitz was astonished by the offenders' lack of fear. Then they informed Salerno that the bonds had come to them from an associate of Salerno's in Connecticut. If the bonds were phony, they said, Fat Tony should deal with his man. Zelmanowitz was stunned by Salerno's rather quiet reaction. He had visualized an awesome mafioso arising in righteous wrath and having the offenders killed. Instead all Salerno said was that he would see that Zelmanowitz got his money back. He never got in contact with Zelmanowitz about the matter again.

Zelmanowitz was simply left twisting in the wind. Needless to say, when the paper expert tried to sell some of the stolen stock he was again arrested. Some of the stock had unfortunately been sold earlier and the law was on the lookout for the rest of it. This was of course, a further violation of the guarantee offered by Salerno.

This time Zelmanowitz realized the futility of contacting Fat Tony. Instead, he accepted a better guarantee offered by federal authorities and entered the witness protection program. Zelmanowitz testified against a prominent mafioso, Angelo "Gyp" DeCarlo, and in the course of that trial mentioned the activities of Fat Tony Salerno.

After that strange things happened. Gil Beckley and Joe Green, Zelmanowitz's partners who could have tied Salerno to any alleged conspiracy, passed into the world of the permanently missing. Salerno was brought to trial but eventually the charges had to be dropped. The guarantee seemed to have worked better for him than for the others.

Another gullible buyer of a guarantee was a West Coast racketeer named Frank Borgia who enjoyed "protection" from Los Angeles boss Jack Dragna. Then Borgia found himself being crossed by racketeer Gaspar Matranga who was shaking him down. Borgia came back to Dragna, demanding exercise of his guarantee. What he didn't realized was that Matranga and Dragna were in it together. Dragna was not satisfied with a paltry 6 percent and he and his partner planned to split whatever they got in the shakedown. When Dragna saw that Borgia was so steamed up that he couldn't be cooled, he had no choice but to have him killed, a mission carried out by Frank Bompensiero and Jimmy "the Weasel" Fratianno.

A Mafia guarantee never comes in writing, and thus, the saying goes, "is not even worth the paper it isn't written on."

GUGLIELMO, Joseph See DRACULA

GUZIK, Jake "Greasy Thumb" (1887–1956): Capone financial brain

The loyalty between Al Capone and Moscow-born Jake "Greasy Thumb" Guzik was one they still talk about in mob circles.

Starting under Capone, Guzik was the trusted treasurer and financial wizard of the mob, and in the years after Capone's fall, he was considered the real brains of the organization, along with Paul "the Waiter" Ricca and to a slightly lesser degree Tony Accardo. Because Guzik was incapable of using a gun or killing anyone, Capone protected Guzik, and once killed a man for him out of pure friendship. Such friendship was not forgotten, and Jake Guzik to his dying day a quarter century after Capone's removal from the scene, continued to be one of the most honored chiefs of the Chicago Outfit, and some say virtually its boss.

During the 1940s and 1950s, when the national syndicate was dominated by what was called the Big Six, it was Guzik and Tony Accardo who flew east weekly to meet with the other heads of the organization: Joe Adonis, Frank Costello, Meyer Lansky and Longy Zwillman. It was an interesting ethnic division of three Italians and three Jews and told precisely what the Mafia's role in organized crime was at the time.

Guzik, a childhood pimp, had come into the Capone organization early on when, without even knowing the Big Fellow, he had saved Capone from an ambush, having overheard two gunmen from a rival gang planning the hit. Once a man did him a good turn, Capone embraced him and would never turn on him—unless that man later first betrayed that trust.

In May 1924, Guzik got into an argument with a freelance hijacker named Joe Howard, who slapped and kicked him around. Incapable of physical resistance, the rotund little Guzik waddled back to Capone to tell him what had happened. Capone charged out in search of Howard and ran him down in Heinie Jacobs's saloon on South Wabash Avenue, bragging about the way he had "made the little Jew whine." When Howard saw Capone, he held out his hand and chimed, "Hello, Al." Capone instead grabbed his shoulders and shook him violently,

demanding to know why Howard had mistreated his friend. "Go back to your girls, you dago pimp," Howard replied. Capone wordlessly drew a revolver and jammed it against Howard's head. The bully hoodlum started to snivel. Capone waited several seconds and then emptied the revolver into Howard's head.

After the Howard killing—which required a certain amount of fixing—Guzik was Capone's faithful dog, ready to do anything for him. Years later when Capone was in fading health, it was Guzik who saw to it that Capone and his family never wanted for anything.

Capone quickly came to depend on Guzik's advice in the various gang wars that developed as he tried to organize Chicago. Jake also served as the mob's principal bagman in payoffs to police and politicos, hence the origin of the nickname Greasy Thumb. Actually, the name was applied years earlier to Jake's older brother Harry, a procurer of whom it was said "his fingers are always greasy from the money he counts out for protection." Later, the title was transferred to Jake, whose thumb was much more greasy sine he handled much more money. One of his chores

"Greasy Thumb" Guzik (turned toward his attorney) was called in the 1920s Al Capone's brains. He remained the honored financial brains of the Chicago Outfit until his death in 1956.

was to sit several nights a week at a table in St. Huberts Old English Grill and Chop House, where district police captains and sergeants who collected graft for themselves and their superiors could pick up their payoffs. Also calling at Guzik's table were bagmen sent over from City Hall.

The only serious legal problems that Guzik ever had were with tax men, and he eventually did a few years behind bars. He handled incarceration with aplomb and afterward returned to mob money duties. At the Kefauver Committee hearings, he made an interesting if uncommunicative witness, pleading the Fifth Amendment on the ground that any response to the questions might "discriminate against me."

Never once was Guzik's position in the mob questioned, even though the Outfit was in many ways a dog-eat-dog crime family. All the big bosses—Nitti, Ricca, Accardo, Giancana, Battaglia—gave Jake complete authority on legal matters. They were not Capone, but they knew Guzik's loyalty was firm to the gang that Capone built. When Al Capone was released from prison in 1939, reporters asked Guzik if the Big Fellow was likely to return and take up command of the organization. "Al," Jake said, "is nutty as a fruitcake." From anyone else the remark might have been taken as a disparagement, but it was Guzik merely being honest; all the other gang members knew his devotion to Capone was unwavering.

Guzik died on February 21, 1956, fittingly, at his post at St. Hubert's, partaking of a meal of lamb chops and a glass of Moselle, and making his usual payoffs. He keeled over of a heart attack. At his services more Italians were in the temple than ever before in its history.

HAMS: Smuggling technique

The use of "hams," a gimmick very popular during Prohibition with rumrunners seeking to evade federal agents and the Coast Guard, is popular even today with narcotics smugglers.

Under pursuit, the smugglers simply jettisoned gunny sacks, or "hams," containing several bottles of liquor—or several pounds of dope—wrapped in straw. Attached to each ham was a bag of salt and a red marker. The ham, weighted down by the salt, would sink to the bottom. In time, the salt melted and the marker would float to the surface. When the marker emerged, the danger usually had passed. The smugglers then returned to the scene and reclaimed the treasured hams.

Some overly enthusiastic writers on the Mafia have claimed this method of smuggling is of Sicilian origin. In fact, there is probably not a waterfront area in Europe or Asia where the ploy is and has not been familiar for centuries.

HAVANA Convention: 1946 underworld meeting

The most important underworld meeting since the 1929 Atlantic City Conference, the Havana convention in December 1946 was the last at which Lucky Luciano was able to exercise his full authority. Luciano had been exiled to Italy in 1946, but in no time at all got himself two dummy passports. He slipped back to Latin America and by October had

gotten into Cuba—considered a safe haven because of the mob's activities there.

Meyer Lansky had been put in charge of bringing in crime leaders from all over the country for the meeting. Among those present were such men as Frank Costello, Tommy Lucchese, Joe Profaci, Vito Genovese, Joe Bonanno, Willie Moretti, Joe Adonis, Augie Pisano, Joe Magliocco, Mike Miranda, all from New York and New Jersey; Steve Magaddino from Buffalo; Santo Trafficante from Tampa; Carlos Marcello from New Orleans; and Tony Accardo, and the Fischetti brothers, Charlie, Joseph and Rocco, from Chicago. Among Jewish mobsters present were, besides Lansky, Dandy Phil Kastel, Doc Stacher, Longy Zwillman and Moe Dalitz.

Much of the meeting concerned strictly Italian Mafia business. The rest, specifically the problem of Bugsy Siegel—who pointedly was not invited to attend—had to do with syndicate problems.

Much has been made of the appearance of Frank Sinatra, a popular young Italian-American singer from New Jersey, as an attendee. There was even talk that Sinatra, who flew in with Joe and Rocco Fischetti, the cousins of Al Capone, had been carrying a bag with $2 million for Luciano. Actually, if anyone was bearing cash it would have been Rocco Fischetti, even leaving aside the problem of fitting $2 million in a single bag. Not that Sinatra apparently arrived empty-handed. He was also said to have brought Luciano a gold cigarette case. Later, during one of

Luciano's absences from his Naples home, Italian police searched the place and found a gold cigarette case with the inscription: "To my dear pal Lucky, from his friend, Frank Sinatra."

However, Sinatra was not there to take part in the deliberations. Luciano later described him as just "a good kid and we was all proud of him." Sinatra had come with the Fischetti brothers to be the guest of honor at a gala party. As such, he provided a cover story for the many Italian mobsters in attendance, providing a reason for them to be in Havana. Why, they hadn't even been aware that Lucky Luciano was in town. They had come because Sinatra had a singing engagement there.

Besides honoring Sinatra the boys worked long and hard at their sessions. When Luciano left the United States in 1946, he put Costello in charge of his crime family, just as he had done earlier during the years of his imprisonment. Now, however, Vito Genovese, who had recently been returned to the United States from his self-imposed exile in Italy to face a murder charge (which he beat), was trying to fill the Luciano vacuum. The Luciano-Lansky alliance had called the convention to reassert Lucky's former position of control. Luciano harbored the hope he could bide his time in Havana for a few years while he waited for the proper political strings to be pulled so he could return to the United States.

The conference was not a total success for Luciano. Genovese actually suggested to him privately that he ought to retire. Undoubtedly Genovese approached some of the other conferees with the same suggestion. In any event, Luciano easily handled Genovese's effrontery and set up roadblocks against Genovese's ambitions. He stopped Genovese from seizing more power and blunted Genovese-inspired complaints that Albert Anastasia, the chief executioner of the mob was becoming "kill crazy." Apparently Anastasia was pushing for the assassination of Bureau of Narcotics Director Harry Anslinger. Luciano squashed that, but he did not "defang" Anastasia, knowing he would make a potent weapon in any future war with Genovese.

However, Luciano lost out on other fronts, such as narcotics. Like Lansky and Costello, and possibly Magaddino and a few others, Luciano wanted the syndicate to withdraw from the narcotics business, but the absence of a vote of confidence on the subject proved deafening. Many of the crime chiefs would not or, perhaps on account of opposition from their own underlings, dared not give up the trade. Luciano was forced to accept a compromise whereby each crime family decided individually what to do about drugs. Personally, Luciano figured abandonment of the narcotics trade by all the mobs would aid his try to get back into the United States, but he now saw his word was no longer law.

Another serious matter for decision was the passing of the death sentence on Benjamin "Bugsy" Siegel, longtime underworld partner of Luciano and Lansky. Siegel had squandered huge sums of mob money building what by then looked like a sure lemon, a plush Las Vegas gambling casino-hotel named the Flamingo. In addition to being a bad businessman, Siegel was a crook, skimming off much of the construction money, and shipping it off to Switzerland. It was Lansky's motion that sealed Siegel's doom: "There's only one thing to do with a thief who steals from his friends. Benny's got to be hit."

Later Lansky would do a lot of posturing and insist he tried to save Siegel. It is true he got the hit postponed for a while both to see if Siegel could make a go of the Flamingo and so the syndicate could recover its money. In due course, however, Siegel was assassinated.

After the convention, Luciano thought he could stay on in Cuba. His presence, though, was revealed to the U.S. government which put pressure on Cuba to kick him out. The Cuban government, which held the mob and the mob's bribe money in very high regard, resisted for a period of time, but finally was forced to give in. Luciano had to return to Italy, convinced that it had been the double-dealing Genovese who had tipped off the Federal Bureau of Narcotics of his location, just 90 miles from the U.S. shore. Luciano's dream of getting back to America was shattered after the Havana conference. Slowly over the years his influence in the syndicate waned, although he remained an important power as long as Lansky backed him.

HAWTHORNE Inn: *Capone headquarters and shootout scene*
The Hawthorne Inn in Cicero, Illinois, was for almost 50 years a headquarters for the Capone mob and its modern successor, the Chicago Outfit. Located at 4833 22nd Street, it was a two-story structure of brick and tiles which on Capone's orders was made into a fortress. Bulletproof steel shutters

protected every window and armed guards stood at the ready at every entrance. The entire second floor, lavishly furnished, was reserved for Capone's personal use. The press labeled the place Capone's Castle.

On September 20, 1926, Capone was almost killed in his castle. A stream of automobiles packed with gangsters bossed by Hymie Weiss, the successor to the murdered Dion O'Banion, roared past the place and poured well over 1,000 bullets into the hotel in an effort to assassinate Capone. Capone was sitting with bodyguard Frankie Rio in the hotel's restaurant when the first tommy gun started rattling. Rio threw himself on top of Capone on the floor while a hail of bullets ripped up the dining room around them. While much woodwork, plaster, mirrors, glassware and crockery splintered, Capone and Rio were unscathed. Only another gangster, Louis Barko, rushing in to aid Capone, went down with a shoulder wound.

The street had been filled with pedestrians during the lunch hour and all scattered when the shooting started. In all, 35 automobiles parked near the hotel were sprayed with bullets, but only one person was hit, Mrs. Clyde Freeman, sitting with her baby son in an automobile that was struck 30 times. Miraculously, the child was unhurt although the mother was creased across the forehead, the bullet injuring both her eyes. Capone paid $5,000 for medical treatment that saved her vision.

Later, newsmen asked Capone who had done the shooting. He answered, "Watch the morgue. They'll show up there." About three weeks later Hymie Weiss's bullet-riddled corpse was wheeled in.

Thereafter bus tours made mandatory sightseeing trips past Capone's Castle, which later was renamed the Towne Hotel, remaining for years a meeting place for the Chicago syndicate. Officially it was owned by Rossmar Realty, Inc., of which Joe "Ha Ha" Aiuppa was president. Aiuppa was an early Capone triggerman, later the boss of Cicero and eventually head of the entire Chicago Outfit.

On May 24, 1964, the *Chicago Sun-Times* ran the following story:

STATE POLICE BREAK UP DICE GAME IN CICERO GAMING FORT:

State police battered down steel doors to raid a barboot [Greek dice] game in a basement of a Cicero coffee house and arrested 15 men fleeing through a network of catacombs.

The raiders, armed with crowbars, sledge-hammers, axes and an FBI warrant, said it was the most impregnable gambling fortress they had ever broken into.

When the officers, led by State Chief of Detectives John Newhold, entered the one-story coffee house at 2208 South Cicero (which runs at right angles to 22nd Street) in the suburb, it was empty.

By tapping and pounding on the walls, the detectives turned up a secret door in a panel. This led to an empty back room. Here in the floor was a trapdoor encased in steel straps that was bolted shut from below.

After several minutes of sledge-swinging, the raiders broke through and found themselves in an underground passage that led to another steel door.

This door took another several minutes of similar ax and crowbar work before it yielded. Crashing through, the police found an elaborate barboot dice game layout. They arrested four men as keepers. . . .

Spilling into the catacombs were 11 other men who were arrested as players. . . .

It was the third time in slightly more than a year that the big barboot game had been knocked over.

The raiders found an underground passageway leading to the Towne Hotel. . . .

On February 17, 1970, the mob had had enough of the Towne. A fire totally destroyed the hotel. When state officials questioned Aiuppa about the ownership of the place, he pleaded the Fifth Amendment 60 times.

HEITLER, Mike "de Pike" (?–1931): Whoremaster and mob victim

Probably few criminal setups lent themselves better to syndicate control than whorehouses. But first, the major syndicate mobs had to take over or squeeze out independents in the field. Many, if they were valuable enough, were absorbed into the syndicate operations and paid well for their services. Others were simply discarded.

In Chicago in the 1920s, Mike "de Pike" Heitler was a special case. If ever there was what could be called a "grand old man" of flesh peddling, it was de Pike, whose career spanned more than half a century.

Heitler's nickname of de Pike derived from his operation of the cheapest fancy house in Illinois (he was a piker). De Pike's price was 50¢ and in his joint at Peoria and West Madison, he was believed to have been the first to offer sex on an assembly-line system.

De Pike sat by a cash register and had the customers lined up waiting their turn. As a girl came downstairs with a satisfied customer, the next man in line handed de Pike 50¢. He gave the girl a brass check that she could later redeem for 25¢.

The idea was to keep the traffic moving at high speed. De Pike employed another picturesque character, Charlie "Monkey Face" Genker, who, as his nickname indicates, was not a natural beauty. In contemporary accounts, he was said to resemble a Surinam toad. Monkey Face's duty at de Pike's joints was to chin up the door and poke his ugly face through the transom to urge the prostitute and her client to speed things up. Monkey Face was very effective. His sudden appearance was not something customers enjoyed; even his possible appearance encouraged some to carry through on their chores rapidly to beat Genker to the punch.

Heitler operated with relative freedom from the law for decades, and, for the most part, his bribes were generally limited to no more than passing out some brass checks to the police. He did have to take a few busts and convictions for white slavery now and then, but the punishments were of little consequence. However, when Johnny Torrio and then Al Capone enveloped the entire prostitution racket in Chicago and its environs, de Pike lost his influence with the police. Heitler's choice was either to become a paid Capone employee or simply be declared "out." De Pike opted to stay in, but his situation continued to deteriorate through the 1920s. Capone relied more and more on Harry Guzik to look after his whorehouse affairs, and de Pike felt slighted over the lack of respect for a man of his years in the field.

Itching for vengeance, Heitler began "ratting" on the mob and many of Capone's affairs. He informed Judge John H. Lyle about the doings in a Capone resort called the Four Deuces. As Lyle recounted in his book *The Dry and Lawless Years,* de Pike related: "They snatch guys they want information from and taken them to the cellar. They're tortured until they talk. Then they're rubbed out. The bodies are hauled through a tunnel into a trap door opening in the back of the building. Capone and his boys put the bodies in cars and then they're dumped out on a country road, or maybe in a clay hole or rock quarry."

Heitler was not being imprudent informing Judge Lyle, who was a Capone hater and an honest judge, a rather rare breed for the era. However, Heitler was a little less selective at other times. He wrote an anonymous letter to the state attorney's office, outlining many facets of the Capone brothel operations. De Pike's anger had clearly got the best of him if he believed that affairs in the state attorney's office were secret from Capone. Within a short time, Capone ordered de Pike to appear before him at his office in the Lexington Hotel. The letter Heitler had written was on Capone's desk. Capone correctly deduced that the information in it could only have come from Heitler. He told him, "You're through."

Undoubtedly de Pike was marked right then for execution, but a certain etiquette was followed by the mob when they received information from their own informers inside official agencies. These sources generally emphasized they would not be a party to homicide, and thus it was not done—at least not for months.

Heitler might even have lasted a half year longer than he did had he not continued his troublesome letterwriting. In one, he named eight Capone figures as having been involved in the plot to murder *Chicago Tribune* reporter Jake Lingle. He gave a copy of that letter to his daughter. Unfortunately, he passed another copy to the wrong parties. On April 30, 1931, two boys found de Pike's charred torso in the smoldering wreckage of a house in a Chicago suburb.

HELLS Angels: No. 1 biker gang and mob allies

The Hells Angels is the richest and most powerful of the biker gangs in the United States, and its tentacles extend to Canada, Australia, New Zealand, Brazil, Colombia, and a number of western European countries. The Angels has become an amazingly sophisticated network of criminal gangs and from time to time has been a valuable asset to the mob. It has been quite a rise from the bikers' early rowdy (and worse) days as the POBOB—"the Pissed Off Bastards of Bloomington." They picked that monicker after a California motorcycle gang riot in 1946. That action came to a head when one of their members was arrested in a melee after a number of bike races over the Fourth of July weekend. Gang members stormed the local jail to free him. Over the next couple of decades they evolved into the Hells Angels and came to be looked upon by some mafiosi as interesting talent useful for special situations. The Angels aped the structure of the Mafia and were used by the latter to

Hundreds of bikers head to the cemetery on Saturday, May 4, 2002, in Stockton, California, for the burial of Stockton motorcycle owner and Hells Angels member Robert Emmett "Festes" Tumelty, 50, who was killed during a fight with a rival gang.

carry out such chores as murder, arson, assault, and loan shark collections, the mob noting that wild and wooly bikers seemed to have a wholesome effect on deadbeats.

While mafiosi can get the shakes about some Angels' continuing penchant for needless violence and confrontation with the law, they do like the fact that Angels can be uncompromising in their determination to exterminate informers. In recent years biker homicides have decreased. According to Margaret DiCanio in the *Encyclopedia of Violence,* "The gangs started developing outside criminal contacts. Accountants, real estate developers, lawyers and businesspeople who were not afraid to take a few criminal risks became gang associates. Money laundering became more sophisticated. Recruitment became increasingly selective and included only those who could bring a needed skill. Drug distribution increased and criminal activities became more hidden. New chapters were started overseas." Individuals in the media viewed with humor that some biker gangs operated in big cities sans motorcycles, as though the members were more taken with the mystique of the biker world. It is not a view held by law enforcement, who see the new Angels as a sign of the group's "professionalization," as operations go further underground and members are less involved in overt criminal activity. Says DiCanio, "With professional help, they have engaged in public relations (and even political lobbying) to improve their public image. They launder money through overseas property development. In short,

they have come to resemble a good many other business enterprises."

Actually the Hells Angels more resembles a Mafia crime family and has extensive and sophisticated counterintelligence tactics to shield it from prosecution. The President's Commission on Organized Crime declared some clubhouses "are fortified with elaborate electronic and physical security systems. Gang members do extensive background checks on prospective members, often using female associates who have been placed in positions with public utilities, government services and law enforcement agencies to assist them." The tactic is right out of the Gambino crime family bible.

Much of the Hells Angels' corruption of police and other public officials became public after Senate hearings chaired by Senator Charles Grassley interviewed a former Angel named "Butch." Butch acknowledged that he knew of public officials who made information available to the gang. He said, ". . . police officers in a couple of towns . . . provide a lot of information, movements of clubs. . . ." Butch told of a telephone installed in a clubhouse, and one police official had the number and his calls were forwarded. "This phone was installed in the closet upstairs," Butch explained. "No one was to touch it. It was for specific phone calls from this one police official that he would call in case there was any word that he had to us on indictments or anything that pertained to any club member. It was a call forwarding type thing, that you called it, and then it went on out to someone else's house, to the president's house. He had the number and another policeman had the number."

The Hells Angels and some other outlaw biker gangs fit the definition of organized crime groups, but the fact is they chose to be submissive to the mob in their relationships. Some hysterical writers have tried to make the case that the Hells Angels and others of its ilk have numbers to overwhelm the Mafia and take over, but this is regarded by virtually all observers and the bikers themselves to be a pipe dream. The Hells Angels has found the most productive ploy is being a partner—and a reliable one—with the mob.

See also OUTLAW BIKERS AND THE MAFIA

HIJACKING

Ever since the advent of Prohibition, hijacking has been a regular activity of organized crime. Hijacking existed before Prohibition, but the lure of a liquor-laden truck attracted gangster activity at a level never before witnessed in the United States. The crime continued almost as a force of habit after Prohibition ended and today still constitutes an important source of revenue for organized crime. Crime families remain especially active in hijacking cigarette shipments, especially because they have the wherewithal to dispose of such loot through gangland enterprises of various sorts.

Syndicate hijacking is not haphazard. Even if the actual hijackers are freelancers, the crime family functions as their patron, guaranteeing to handle the merchandise, as well as providing protection and "squaring" an arrest if operations go awry. The organized crime functionary tells the hijackers the specific items to be stolen—such as color television sets, electronic equipment, clothing. Usually the hijackers do not pick a truck to loot at random, but intelligence is supplied them by the mob when particularly valuable shipment can be hit. Often such information comes from "inside men," sometimes planted in key jobs or else recruited through other mob activities. For instance, through the mob's gambling and loan shark operations, the gangsters can put pressure on men owing them money and order them to supply information on shipments. If the victim happens to own the business, it makes matters all the more simple as the mobsters inform the businessman that insurance will cover his losses. Under such circumstances, the businessman can become an eager accomplice and is induced to make a targeted shipment all the more valuable.

Equally important to major syndicate hijackings is the fact that they tend to be perpetrated with police protection in one form or another. Because of good rapport with many police officers who accept "clean-graft"—payoffs for allowing such activities as gambling to operate—organized crime has little trouble inducing police officers to stay away from certain areas when a hijacking is scheduled. The Knapp Commission, which investigated police corruption in New York City, reported that this was standard operating procedure.

Generally recognized as the foremost hijacking mob in American history is Detroit's fabled Purple Gang, probably the most feared bootleg hijackers of Prohibition days. Many members kept on hijacking other types of goods after the dry era. In fact, it is stated by law enforcement officials that some Purple Gang oldtimers, now in their 70s and 80s, still mastermind a large number of hijackings in Michigan and surrounding states.

HILL, Virginia (1918–1966): Syndicate bagwoman

There have been many women in American criminal history, but none quite like Virginia Hill. The newspapers insisted on calling her the Queen of the Mob. It wasn't that accurate. Mistress of the Mob, perhaps. She paraded around with money to burn—with $100 bills that filled her purse and her pockets—paying for a champagne party in a nightclub or for barefoot rumba dancing. In 1951 in executive session before the Kefauver Committee Virginia Hill was asked by that self-proclaimed moralist of the panel, Senator Charles W. Tobey of New Hampshire: "Young lady, what makes you the favorite of the underworld?" "Senator," a much-sanitized version of her reply went, "I'm the best goddamned lay in the world."

Virginia Hill's salty testimony was a highlight of the Kefauver hearings. She was both the "bagwoman" and "mistress of the mob," having been the lover of numerous top mobsters around the country.

That nearly told it all about Virginia Hill, a trusted bedmate of many of the syndicate's top gangsters and a bagwoman for the mob, hauling funds to secret Swiss bank accounts and wherever else her masters ordered.

Hill had come a long way since she'd hit Chicago in 1934 to do a turn as a cooch dancer at the World's Fair. She ran through a series of husbands and lovers. First and last was the bookmaking king and tax expert for the Capone boys, Joe Epstein, who felt responsible for her many years after she left him and kept supplying her with money on a monthly basis. Epstein told Lansky in 1946, "Once that girl is under your skin, it's like a cancer. It's incurable." After Epstein came the deluge. There were the brothers Fischetti, Tony Accardo, Murray Humphreys, Frank Nitti, Joe Adonis, Frank Costello, and last, her true love, Benjamin "Bugsy" Siegel. When Lucky Luciano was released from prison and subjected to deportation, the mobsters gave him a lavish send-off aboard ship. Both Siegel and Adonis were present, and the nervousness and hostility exhibited by Adonis toward Siegel was clearly attributable to jealousy over Virginia.

Hill was truly in love with Siegel; yet she was conveniently away in Europe when Bugsy was shot to death in her living room by a syndicate assassin in 1947. When Siegel was shot, Joe Epstein in Chicago got in touch with Hill in Paris and sent her money so that she could stay there until the dust settled. Siegel was suspected by the mob of skimming off the syndicate's funds while building the Flamingo Hotel and Casino in Las Vegas. The boys all suspected he used Hill to get the money to Switzerland for him. Lansky went to see Virginia after the assassination and told her the money had to be returned. She returned it. Still after his death Hill spoke lovingly of Siegel (he had named the Flamingo in honor of her nickname) without being critical of the syndicate.

She provided the Kefauver hearings with several of its high points in her saucy testimony. She also added some off-the-stand drama by socking reporter Marjorie Farnsworth of the *New York Journal American* with a right cross to the jaw and shouting at other reporters: "You goddamn bastards! I hope an atom bomb falls on all of you."

After that dramatic peak in her life, Virginia took a new husband and wandered the pleasure centers of Europe. The government still suspected she oversaw the Swiss bank accounts of several mobsters. She was said to supply funds steadily from Switzerland to the exiled Luciano in Italy.

But Virginia missed the action and she was growing old. She no longer possessed the charms that would permit her to return to the good old mob days. She tried suicide a number of times. Finally in March 1966 she swallowed a large number of sleeping pills and lay down on the pure-white snow slopes outside Salzburg, Austria, probably remembering the great high times as the mists of death closed in on her.

See also BAGMAN

HINES, James J. (1877–1957): Mob-controlled Tammany leader

Known as the last powerful Irishman in Tammany Hall, Jimmy Hines spanned the two eras of crime in America—the period when the politicians dominated the criminals and when the criminals dominated the politicians. Hines, a blacksmith's son, came up in the rough-and-tumble of New York politics when the old Irish gangsters quaked in fear of Tammany and did the bosses' bidding. When things changed with the onset of Prohibition—which made the criminals so rich they could buy politicians by the pound—Hines changed with the system. He saw the Tammany world of precinct patronage being undermined by the successors to Irish power—Jews, Italians and middle-class white professionals as well as blue-blood reformers. Hines saw he needed new allies. He found them in organized crime but would find he could not call the tune.

Most payoffs from the underworld to Hines were funneled through Dutch Schultz, the maverick numbers boss of Harlem, and Frank Costello, already known as the Prime Minister, the Mafia's emissary to the political machines. When Hines attended the 1932 Democratic convention in Chicago, Costello shared a suite with him. On the Schultz payroll alone, Hines received from $500 to $1,000 a week. Payoffs from Costello were believed to be higher and overall it has been estimated that Hines garnered for himself something like $5,000 a week.

One of Hines's principal duties was protecting the numbers rackets for Schultz and, after the latter's murder in 1935, for the Luciano-Costello elements that took over. As Dixie Davis, a flamboyant corrupt lawyer who worked for Schultz, later confessed:

"Hines . . . could and did have cops transferred when they bothered the numbers. He had magistrates throw out good cases that honest cops had made against George Weinberg and Lulu Rosenkrantz. He gave his support to a district attorney who didn't bother us much."

The district attorney was William C. Dodge who preceded Thomas E. Dewey as Manhattan D.A. Hines called Dodge "stupid, respectable and my man." His man did all he could for Hines and organized crime. Dodge steered a 1935 grand jury away from important mob rackets, but his efforts failed when the grand jury, incensed at his actions, "ran away."

It was through Schultz and Costello that the mob controlled the police. John F. Curry, boss of Tammany Hall until 1934 when he was deposed, testified Hines frequently called him to get "recalcitrant" cops demoted or transferred. Curry would call the commissioner of police and invariably Hines's wishes were complied with. A former chief inspector, John O'Brien, confirmed Curry's testimony.

When Dewey moved from special prosecutor to district attorney, he went after Hines while at the same time getting a conviction against Lucky Luciano. On May 25, 1938, Hines, once the most powerful Democrat in New York State and President Franklin Roosevelt's primary patronage dispenser in New York City, was officially charged as "a coconspirator and part of the Dutch Schultz mob." Dewey trotted out proof that Hines was the bagman for the mob and paid off police, judges and even the district attorney. Hines's first prosecution ended in a mistrial, but he was convicted in a second trial on February 25, 1939. After appeals were exhausted Hines went to Sing Sing in 1940, served four years and was paroled. He died in 1957 at the age of 80, the last of his kind.

True, bribery remained a hallmark of the relationship between politicians and organized crime. But Hines's free-wheeling methods had to give way in most areas, and especially in New York, to more discreet and sophisticated methods.

"HITMOBILE": Mob car for assassination missions

Mafia executions frequently involve the traditional black car. Either stationary or in motion, hit men within the vehicle—the "hitmobile"—can cut down victims and rapidly flee the scene.

Designing and equipping hitmobiles requires considerable ingenuity. A typical car, allegedly designed by one of the Chicago Outfit's most creative killers, Milwaukee Phil Alderisio, included quite a few options unavailable at the Ford plant. According to a report issued by Chicago authorities:

On May 2, 1962, the Chicago police received a call that a suspicious automobile was parked in front of 1750 Superior Street, in Chicago. Upon investigation, police officers discovered a 1962 Ford sedan parked at the specified location. Crouched on the floor of the car to avoid detection were two notorious Capone syndicate hoodlums, Phillip Alderisio, of 515 Longcommon Avenue, Riverside, Ill., and Charles Nicoletti, of 1638 North 19th Road, Riverside, Ill. Alderisio and Nicoletti informed the investigating officers that the car did not belong to them, and they had no idea as to the identity of its owner.

They insisted that they were merely sitting on the floor of the automobile waiting for some unidentified person when the police arrived at 1 a.m. on May 2, 1962.

Alderisio and Nicoletti were taken into custody and subsequently released on a $1,000 bond.

The automobile in which Alderisio and Nicoletti were riding at the time of their arrest was registered in the name of Walter Getz, of 9340 South New England Avenue in Oak Lawn, Ill. This address turned out to be a vacant lot and the Walter Getz nonexistent.

Under the dashboard of this automobile were concealed three switches. Two of these switches enabled the operators of the car to disconnect the taillights. Without taillights, the police would have difficulty in following the car at night.

The third switch turned on an electric motor which opened a hidden compartment in the back rest of the front seat. This compartment was fitted with brackets to hold shotguns and rifles. And by demonstrating this particular opening in the back rest, we found that a machine gun could be secreted in the compartment also.

Newsmen labeled the car a "hitmobile" and gave it considerable play, although nothing much happened to Alderisio and Nicoletti. They could not be linked legally to the car or convicted on any charge. They were released, but the car was seized by the Chicago police for their official use thereafter.

It is believed that special hitmobiles used from time to time for specific murders are promptly run through a demolition machine and reduced to a square foot of scrap.

HOFFA, James R. (1913–1975): Labor leader and obvious murder victim

Up until the time he disappeared in 1975, longtime Teamsters boss Jimmy Hoffa had a lot of enemies. In the 1950s and early 1960s, none was more potent than Robert F. Kennedy, the president's brother, attorney general from 1961 to 1964, who succeeded in putting Hoffa in prison for a few years. But when the Mafia later turned on Hoffa, after years of cooperation and manipulation, that was, as one organization crime figure put it, "all she wrote." Hoffa disappeared—permanently.

There is little doubt that Hoffa was murdered. The FBI constructed a scenario that they concluded told the story pretty well. It may or may not be correct in all details, but one thing seems sure: Jimmy Hoffa's not coming back.

Hoffa was for decades a controversial Teamsters union leader, one with strong connections to organized crime. However, despite his underworld connections and a long list of shady dealings, he remained immune to prosecution until he became the target of Robert F. Kennedy, chief counsel to the Senate Select Committee on Improper Activities in the Labor or Management Field (more popularly called the McClellan Committee), and later attorney general.

As attorney general Kennedy made the "Get Hoffa" campaign a top priority of his administration. Kennedy's efforts resulted in the labor leader's trial in 1962 for extorting illegal payments from a firm employment Teamsters. The case ended in a hung jury, but Hoffa was then nabbed for attempting to bribe one of the jurors. He was sentenced to eight years in prison. In 1964 Hoffa was convicted of misappropriating $1.7 million in union pension funds. He fought off entering prison until 1967 and ended up doing 58 months, having his term commuted in 1971 by President Richard Nixon with the proviso that he stay out of union politics for 10 years.

Hoffa did not take that proviso seriously and started legal action against the stipulation. In the meantime he went ahead with his efforts to regain control of the union from his former protégé, Frank Fitzsimmons. The Mafia was particularly cozy with Fitzsimmons, finding him easier to manipulate than the strong-willed Hoffa. True, there was a recording heard by the McClellan Committee in 1961 in which Hoffa seemed to be offering his permission for Anthony "Tony Ducks" Corallo to steal from union funds so long as he was not caught at it. But Hoffa

actually was a tough bargainer and his assistance did not come cheap. Fitzsimmons was regarded by organized crime as a man who could be counted on always to be looking the other way. In addition, Fitzsimmons was welcome at the White House and Hoffa was not. A return to power by Hoffa would lead inevitably to further FBI surveillance of union activities—which was hardly conducive to tranquil mob operation. Time after time the mob told Hoffa to cool it, but in mob language he proved "hard of hearing and kept coming on."

On July 30, 1975, the 62-year-old Hoffa went to a restaurant in suburban Detroit, Manchus Red Fox, supposedly to meet three men, one a Detroit labor leader, another an important Detroit mob member and the third a power in New Jersey Teamsters activities. Hoffa arrived first, at 2 P.M. A half hour later the trio had not shown up, and Hoffa called up his wife to say he was waiting somewhat longer—the last documented conversation Hoffa had. At 2:45 he was seen getting into a car in the restaurant parking lot with several other men. Investigators later were satisfied that Hoffa never got out of that car alive, that he was garroted and his body run through a mob-controlled fat-rendering plant that was later destroyed by fire.

The government's list of suspects was large and included, after intensive probing of underworld sources and convicts seeking reductions in their sentences, Russell Bufalino, Anthony "Tony Pro" Provenzano and two Hoffa "cronies," Thomas Andretta and Gabriel Briguglio. Another suspect, Gabriel's brother Salvatore Briguglio, was believed to be talking to the FBI and was shot to death in New York in March 1978.

According to the FBI reconstruction of the Hoffa murder, Tony Pro had called the so-called peace parley with the union leader and then ordered him killed. Provenzano denied even being in Detroit at the time and, indeed, seemed to go out of his way to seal an airtight alibi; at the time of Hoffa's disappearance, Tony was touring a number of Teamster locals in and around Hoboken, New Jersey.

There are many loose ends in the Hoffa case. For instance, why, if he were going to order Hoffa's execution, had Tony Pro linked himself to a meeting with Hoffa when he had to know that Hoffa would and did mention he was to meet with him. Then there was the odd fact that the men who took care of Hoffa showed up 45 minutes late, hardly the norm for mob hit men for whom promptness is not only a virtue but also a necessity for staying alive themselves. The answer could be that the decision to hit Hoffa was a last-minute thing, with the Mafia hot line buzzing all around the country to get approval. In any event, the FBI's theory that Hoffa was murdered, and by a particular method, was backed up from traces of his hair and blood found later in the abduction car.

There were other theories. One Teamsters official, subjected to considerable questioning by the FBI, stuck to his own inside version, that Hoffa had "run off to Brazil with a black go-go dancer."

In the years since 1975, Hoffa has been declared legally dead and most of the suspects in the case have gone to prison for other crimes, some of the convicting evidence having been uncovered during the Hoffa probe. Any murder convictions in the Hoffa case per se are strictly on hold and probably depend on some member or members of organized crime talking to get out of prison. As one unidentified Teamsters vice president has been quoted, "We all know who did it. It was Tony and those guys of his from New Jersey. It's common knowledge. But the cops need a corroborating witness, and it doesn't look like they're about to get one, does it?"

Jimmy "the Weasel" Fratianno offers an alternative theory in *The Last Mafioso*. He tells of an important Cleveland mobster with close links to the Detroit family, saying it was nonsense about Tony Pro and Bufalino, that Detroit was not an organization that needed outside help. He linked local mafiosi big shots to the case: "Tony Giacalone was in tight with Hoffa and he's the one that set him up. Tony Zerilli and Mike Polizzi gave the order and that was all she wrote." Certainly there was no way Hoffa could be killed in their area without Detroit giving the okay, but in a sense we are merely talking mechanics. The fact is the Mafia held its own private union election, and Hoffa was voted a dead loser.

A definitive break in the Hoffa case finally came in 2001. DNA testing revealed that a hair found in a car that Hoffa's longtime friend, Charles (Chuckie) O'Brien, was driving on the day the ex-teamster boss vanished belonged to Hoffa. O'Brien who was expelled from the Teamsters in 1990 for association with organized crime had always been regarded as a suspect in the Hoffa disappearance, but investigators were never able to disprove his contention that Hoffa

had never been in the car. The car O'Brien was driving was owned by Mafia enforcer Anthony Giacalone's son. While this was solid enough evidence, most experts said it would never be enough to break the quarter-century-old case. DNA evidence or not, the Hoffa murder was still a perfect enough crime.

See also PROVENZANO, ANTHONY "TONY PRO"; ZERILLI, JOSEPH

HOOVER, Herbert (1874–1964): Al Capone nemesis

Al Capone called him "that bastard Hoover" and blamed him for his going to prison. Capone should have been talking about J. Edgar Hoover, the head of the Federal Bureau of Investigation, but he was not. J. Edgar, as early as 1930, demonstrated that he most certainly was not going to have anything to do with any form of organized crime, and certainly not with the Capone mob in Chicago. There were considerable grounds for J. Edgar Hoover, despite his later denials, to enter the fight against Capone. Yet the definitive biography *Capone* by John Kobler astonishingly finds it necessary to mention J. Edgar Hoover only once, when the head G-man innocuously visited the federal penitentiary at Atlanta while Capone was doing time there.

Capone's real enemy on the national level was "that bastard" President Herbert Hoover. He held the president responsible for getting him convicted on income tax charges, preventing a later "deal" to settle the claims and giving him a long sentence compared to the short ones handed to other gangsters, including his own brother Ralph Capone.

It was now a matter of folklore inside the underworld that the president railroaded Scarface Al to prison because of a personal vendetta. Legend has it that Hoover hated the Chicago kingpin for one or both of two reasons. One allegedly dates to shortly after Hoover won the 1928 contest against Al Smith and vacationed at the J. C. Penney estate on Belle Isle in Florida, not far from the Capone compound on Palm Island. The tale goes that there was so much shouting, females crying, and shooting during the night from the Capone retreat that Hoover could not sleep. His puritanical ire aroused, Hoover decided then and there to destroy the famous gangster when he took office. The second reason describes an enraged Herbert Hoover. The president-elect watched in dismay as a drove of reporters suddenly abandoned him in a Miami lobby when a more important personage—Al Capone—strolled in.

There probably is little truth to either story. But Hoover was determined to crush Capone who he viewed as a disgrace to the national honor. When he came into office, he found the presidential aim thwarted. It was obvious that Capone had local and state authorities in his hip pocket and had nothing to fear at that level. On the federal level were only corrupt Prohibition agents and J. Edgar Hoover.

It was Colonel Frank Knox, the publisher of the *Chicago Daily News,* who finally came forward with a solution. Like the president, Knox despaired of law enforcement's inability to nail Capone and told President Hoover the only hope was to go after him on two federal offenses—bootlegging and income tax evasion.

Hoover turned to his Treasury Department for action, and Andrew Mellon, the secretary of the treasury at the time, later recounted the events that occurred daily at "meetings" of the president's so-called Medicine Cabinet, a group of high officials he had in to the White House each morning to toss around a medicine ball. "Every morning when the exercising started, Mr. Hoover would bring up the subject," Mellon said. "He'd ask me, 'Have you got that fellow Al Capone yet?' And at the end of the session, he'd tell me, 'Remember now, I want that Capone in jail.'"

In due course Hoover succeeded. Some observers consider Hoover one of this nation's most inept chief executives, but had other presidents followed in Hoover's footsteps, the outlook for the Mafia and organized crime would have been bleak indeed.

HOOVER, J. Edgar (1895–1972): FBI director

Organized crime, the American Mafia and the national crime syndicate were chartered in the 1920s, concurrent with the establishment of J. Edgar Hoover's Federal Bureau of Investigation. Both groups—according to former FBI agent Neil J. Welch and ex-U.S. attorney David W. Marston, in their book *Inside Hoover's FBI*—matured in the 1930s. "Although they were presumptive enemies," the authors suggest, "during their first four decades they competed primarily for newspaper space."

J. Edgar Hoover was the best FBI director organized crime could ever have wanted; it was difficult for syndicate members to be antagonized by a law enforcement official who claimed neither organized crime nor a Mafia existed in the United States. Without a man like Hoover heading the FBI it is inconceivable that organized crime and the Mafia could ever have reached the heights of power, wealth and administrative organization.

Prohibition gave new life to the criminal gangs of an earlier era that had started to collapse just prior to World War I. Bootlegging brought about the reconstruction of the gangs; suddenly they became so wealthy and powerful that, instead of being the puppets of the political machines, they pulled the strings. Illiterate punks became the great robber barons of the 20th century, and it was these men who provided the muscle to create organized crime in America (in its truest meaning of a syndicate with interlocking relationships with other mobs around the country).

To establish a national syndicate, various levels of government officials, politicians and law enforcement groups were subverted. Aiding in this task was Hoover, who refused to stalk syndicate gangsters, denying the existence of such groups as a crime syndicate or Mafia.

Many theories have been offered for Hoover's bizarre behavior, and in each there is probably at least partial truth. Hoover probably was fearful that, like other law enforcement agencies that came in contact with organized crime and the Mafia, the FBI would be tarred with the brush of corruption, since syndicate criminals had huge funds available for the fix. He preferred his agents move against such perils to the republic as teenage car thieves. These were readily apprehended, and he could cite endless if meaningless statistics to the Senate Appropriations Committee that XXX numbers of cars worth XXX numbers of dollars were recovered, thus justifying further expansion of the FBI budget.

One-time number three man in the FBI, William C. Sullivan, stated in his book, *The Bureau: My Thirty Years in Hoover's FBI* (published just after his accidental death): ". . . the Mafia is powerful, so powerful that entire police forces or even a mayor's office can be under Mafia control. That's why Hoover was afraid to let us tackle it. He was afraid that we'd show up poorly. Why take the risk, he reasoned, until we were forced to by public exposure of our shortcomings." Sullivan, more or less regarded as Nixon's man in the agency, was most likely to succeed Hoover if Nixon had carried out his wish to fire

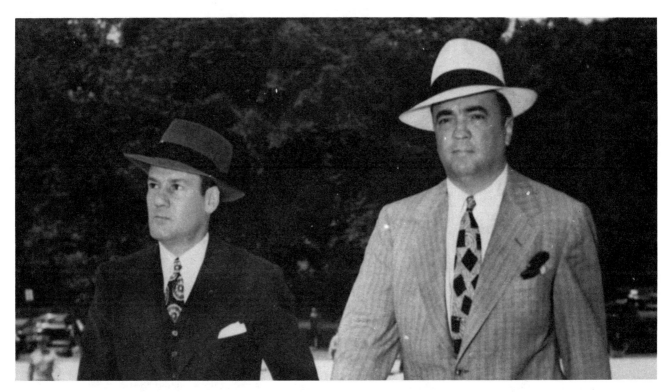

J. Edgar Hoover (right), the "Mafia-blind" head of the FBI, with his top aide, Clyde Tolson (in what photographers called Tolson's traditional half-step-behind position).

Hoover, a step that Nixon drew back from. ("Christ almighty," Assistant Attorney General Robert Mardian once reported to Sullivan of an aborted attempt, "Nixon lost his guts.")

In place of fighting organized crime, Hoover lay special emphasis on relatively easy targets, with a highly publicized war on so-called public enemies—Dillinger, Ma Barker (who never was charged with any crime), Pretty Boy Floyd, Machine Gun Kelly (who never fired his gun at anyone in anger) and other targets more easily hit than the Mafia. "The whole of the FBI's main thrust," said Sullivan, "was not investigation but public relations and propaganda to glorify its director."

Historian Albert Fried has written that "Hoover paid so little attention to organized crime, indeed, so little that one could accuse him of dereliction of duty." In *The Rise and Fall of the Jewish Gangster in America,* Fried contends that Hoover thought organized crime "constituted no immediate danger to established order. Or, as some have argued, he assumed that the gang/syndicate members . . . were in fact pillars of the status quo. They at least had a vested interest in the health of the free enterprise sys-

tem, in America's triumph over communism and for that matter over Socialism and liberalism too—over anything that might remotely threaten their specific opportunities." Thus, Fried concluded, the more intelligent mobsters, à la Al Capone, Moe Dalitz and Meyer Lansky, were valuable defenders of capitalism and thus to a certain extent "J. Edgar Hoover's ideological kinsmen."

A Hoover biographer, investigative reporter Hank Messick, carries the idea even further, declaring, "John Edgar Hoover has received support, as well as more tangible rewards, from right-wing businessmen who, in turn, have dealt directly and indirectly with organized crime figures who have not been disturbed by John Edgar Hoover."

However, the Fried-Messick theses may be granting a depth to Hoover's motivations that was not really there. The more standard view is that Hoover simply was too afraid to go after the Mafia and organized crime and rationalized this fear by claiming: 1) the problem didn't exist and 2) (falsely) that his agency lacked the authorization to do anything anyway. This so the argument goes, suffices to explain his reluctance to war on the syndicate.

Additionally, Hoover regarded some members of organized crime as "ideological kinsmen" for reasons other than what Fried states. He once told Frank Costello in the Stork Club, "Just stay out of my bailiwick" and that he in turn would stay out of his. Costello's bailiwick was gambling. Hoover, an inveterate horseplayer, was very tolerant of that activity and said, "The FBI has much more important functions to accomplish than arresting gamblers all over the country." Only to Hoover was it not apparent that with the end of Prohibition, gambling became the chief source of revenue to organized crime, the grease that kept the mob's other rackets functioning—everything from buying protection from the law to financing enormous narcotics enterprises—and murder.

Hoover's morning-noon-and-night devotion to duty has always been a bit exaggerated; within the FBI his disappearances in the afternoon were legendary. He and his lifelong sidekick Clyde Tolson would head for a bulletproof car in the courtyard of the Department of Justice after announcing they were off to work on a case. Actually, they would be on their way to make the first race at Bowie, Pimlico, Charleston, Laurel, Havre de Grace—wherever the bangtails were running. Hoover's preoccupation with the races became so pronounced that he was frequently photographed at the $2 window and had a form letter that was sent out to irate citizens objecting to his wagering. (He said he was really only interested in the improvement of the breed and only bet $2 now and then so as not to embarrass his hosts.)

In truth, Hoover played the role of decoy at the $2 window. As Sullivan stated, and others have confirmed, "He had agents assigned to accompany him to the track place his real bets at the hundred-dollar window, and when he won he was a pleasure to work with for days."

But nobody seemed more determined to keep Hoover happy than the boys in the mob. A happy Hoover was not likely to destroy gamblers and syndicate criminals, and so the mob developed a technique to stroke the FBI kingpin. The key in this operation was Costello and a mutual friend, gossip columnist Walter Winchell. Hoover got horse tips from Winchell who got them from Costello who, in turn, got them from Frank Erickson, the nation's leading bookmaker. The tips were on "sure things," a term that does not connote in mob vernacular the

Frank Erickson, the mob's top gambler, was the first player in the hot-horse-tip pipeline that went from Erickson to Frank Costello to Walter Winchell to J. Edgar Hoover, who then rushed to the track.

best horse in a race as much as the one who was going to win. Erickson and Costello spelled sure thing: "F-I-X."

This cozy arrangement, corroborated by Winchell staffers, had the desired effect from Costello's viewpoint. He was a man whom Hoover could not dislike, one whom he invited for coffee at the Waldorf Astoria. "I got to be careful of my associates," Costello told him. "They'll accuse me of consortin' with questionable characters." But as long as Costello provided Hoover with solid tips—and didn't run with a youth gang heisting cars or join the Communist Party—he was relatively safe from retribution.

Some may object to the idea of Hoover being influenced so simply by the mob, through a few race winners, but only a true horseplayer can really comprehend the warm feelings a gambler has for the man giving him a tip that stands up.

Whatever the reason, from malfeasance to nonfeasance, to laziness, to fear, to stroking by the mob, J. Edgar Hoover kept right on denying the existence of organized crime. The charade ended by what FBI agent Welch called "an accident." The accident was the discovery of the underworld conference at Apalachin, New York, in 1957. As Welch stated:

"The victims of this accident came in through crime figure Joe Barbara's front door. The lucky ones made it out into the woods . . . Sixty others left in state police cars. It was the biggest roundup of organized crime bosses in national history, and it was an accident."

And another casualty was Hoover. The *New York Herald Tribune* wondered in an editorial where Hoover and his FBI were while organized crime was growing in America. Not even Hoover had the nerve to go on with the line that it didn't exist. He threw the FBI into a turmoil, demanding his agents now get him off the hook and prove there was a Mafia and that the bureau had known about it all the time.

The hot potato was thrown to the research and analysis section and the FBI was off on an incredible three-decade game of catch-up, learning everything about the previously invisible forces of organized crime and the Mafia. Several agents were put on the research, and one agent, Charles Peck, stayed in the office every night until 11 or 12, reading no fewer than 200 books on the Mafia and checking through the *New York Times* coverage of "organized crime" for the previous 100 years. The conclusion was inevitable: The Mafia existed and had operated in America for many decades.

While many FBI agents now felt free to launch investigations against the mobs, Hoover soon tired of the chase and probably would have eased back on FBI crackdowns as the heat dissipated. But the appointment in 1961 of Robert Kennedy as attorney general kept Hoover on his toes. Unlike his predecessors, who had been fearful of tangling with Hoover, Robert Kennedy pushed the FBI chief hard; he had to go after the "Cosa Nostra."

When Kennedy resigned office, Hoover saw to it, as Sullivan put it, that "the whole Mafia effort slacked off again." In fact, the FBI war against the Mafia remained slack until Hoover's death in 1972. Since then the Mafia and the FBI have been in a persistent confrontation.

On the day of Hoover's death in 1972 three men, identified to an onlooker as "Gambino guys from Brooklyn," were leaving Aqueduct Racetrack in New York. One picked up a copy of the *New York Post* headlining the FBI chief's demise and rushed back excitedly to the other two. One of them, clearly the highest-ranking of the three, kept up a brisk pace and announced with a shrug of the shoulders: "You

know what I feel about this—absolutely nothing. This guy meant nothing to us one way or the other."

See also COSA NOSTRA; KENNEDY, ROBERT F.

HORSE killings and mobsters

In Mario Puzo's *The Godfather*, one of the most darkly humorous scenes involves the killing of a horse by the Corleone forces to win their way in a Hollywood matter. The incident is not based on specific reality, but it does reflect a long tradition of horse killing by mobsters.

At one time in the primitive days of organized crime, horse poisoning was big business. In New York in the period immediately before World War I, three organized gangs operated as horse killers for pay. They would steal or poison horses to order. At the time the horse was the lifeline of many businesses, especially the produce, ice cream, beer and seltzer trades. Businessmen or lowly hucksters, faced with stiff competition, would often hire gangsters to destroy a rival's trade. The simplest way to accomplish this was to poison the competitor's horse, thus destroying his distribution system. It was common on the Lower East Side to see a produce seller with two dead horses in the street trying to get rid of his stock at half price to clamoring housewives before all his wares were spoiled.

The New York horse poisoning racket was controlled by Jewish gangsters, but in many Little Italys around the country, the practice abounded. Black Handers often poisoned a horse as the first attempt to coerce a businessman into making extortion payments. The practice fell into disuse by 1920 because of legal actions by authorities and because Black Hand gangsters moved into the more profitable field of bootlegging.

Since then horse killings have become more or less extracurricular activities. A psychopathic mafioso in Chicago, Samoots Amatuna, once chased after a Chinese laundry wagon driver, determined to shoot him for returning one of his silk shirts scorched. At the last moment Samoots was overwhelmed by what some writers considered a most unusual outburst of humanity whereby he spared the Chinese's life. He shot his horse instead.

When the celebrated Nails Morton was thrown while riding a horse and then killed in Lincoln Park, Chicago, in 1924, his pals in Dion O'Banion's North Side gang, abducted the animal from its stable at gunpoint and took it to the spot where Nails had been killed. There the poor beast was executed for its "crime." Each gangster solemnly shot it in the head. However, before shooting, the zany Two Gun Alterie first socked the hapless horse in the snout.

See also ALTERIE, LOUIS "TWO GUN"; MORTON, SAMUEL J. "NAILS"

HOTSY Totsy Club: Mob nightclub

It was said that Lucky Luciano once warned his gangsters to stay away from New York's Hotsy Totsy Club on Broadway between 54th and 55th Streets. They could, Luciano felt with considerable justification, end up being killed there. Technically the joint was owned and operated by little Hymie Cohen, but he was really just fronting for Jack "Legs" Diamond, the pathological mobster and killer.

Diamond liked to drink there and fool around with the girls there, but most of all he liked to commit homicide there. Many gangsters with whom Diamond was on the outs were lured into the nightclub for a boisterous reconciliation. And if any reconciliation was to be made, it was on Diamond's terms. Otherwise, the gangsters were led into a back room and slaughtered, later to be lugged out of the place as "drunk."

One night in 1929 Diamond and his top sidekick Charley Entratta got into an argument with a couple of tough waterfront characters. Pretty soon it looked like mayhem was about to break loose. Hymie Cohen yelled to the orchestra to play louder, and the boys struck up a deafening rendition of "Alexander's Ragtime Band"—as though trying to wake the dead. Rather than drown the shooting, the band offered a weak accompaniment for the percussive blasts. Diamond shot one character, Red Cassidy, and as he slumped to the floor Diamond leaned over and put two more slugs in Cassidy's head. Entratta joined in by gunning one Simon Walker to death. It was an injudicious act on Diamond and Entratta's part since there were a number of witnesses to the murders. The pair fled.

Then from hiding Diamond directed a rash of murders to clear his name from the taint of a homicide charge. That meant the bartender had to be knocked off as well as three customers who clearly had seen what had happened. Diamond's partnership with Hymie Cohen was also liquidated, with the front man joining the suddenly dead. In addition the

cashier, a waiter, the hatcheck girl and another club regular disappeared, never to be heard from again.

After this minor purge the police were embarassingly free of any witnesses to the original murders, and Diamond and Entratta came forward, saying they had just heard they were wanted for questioning about something or other. The charges against them were dropped.

HUGHES, Howard (1905–1976): Mafia victim

In the mid-1950s outside investors started buying into the Las Vegas hotel-casino scene. In the mid-1960s, under most unlikely circumstances, billionaire Howard Hughes showed up. Hughes was a big gambler, and a lousy one at that. One night he lost a huge amount at Moe Dalitz's Desert Inn where he had already rented the entire ninth floor. Reacting in typical Howard Hughes fashion when his ego was bruised, he offered to buy the place for $30 million. Since he offered cold cash in full, the owners of the D.I. sold out on the spot.

Actually, it was a good deal for the mob at the moment; the federal government was all over town, looking for evidence on skimming operations. To some it looked like the day of the skim was passing. Hughes provided the mob with a perfect escape hatch. In almost no time at all Hughes began buying up casino after casino in Vegas and Reno—the New Frontier, the Sands, the Silver Slipper, the Landmark, the Castaways. Within a few years his acquisitions were providing 17 percent of Nevada's gambling tax revenues.

The motive for Hughes's Las Vegas fever was ascribed to various reasons, everything from wanting to get back into a form of show business, to a personal belief that he could make the casinos more profitable, to the simple desire just to have a state all his own. Perhaps more to the point was the fact that his move into Nevada gambling was a vital multimillion-dollar dodge to avoid the undistributed profits tax. It was a matter of either spending the money or giving it to the government. Hughes inadvertently decided it was better to give the money to the underworld for something tangible in return.

Unfortunately the record shows Hughes didn't get much of anything. His investment in Vegas turned into a disaster. He gullibly kept many mob employees in their casino positions. It's no wonder a large undercover owner in the Desert Inn, Johnny Roselli, bragged to informer Jimmy Fratianno: "Right now we've got the D.I. in good hands." Hughes fully expected to up the 20 percent legally admitted profit most casinos earned on investment, but at best he never made more than 6 percent. By 1970 Hughes was millions of dollars in the hole. It was all too bruising to Hughes's ego and probably put him to bed far more than his travails with Clifford Irving's bogus biography.

Finally Hughes bowed out of Vegas and slowly the mob's influence returned. The full measure could not be gauged, however, because the money the criminals took from Hughes undoubtedly went to a new army of fronts who became the owners of record of some of the casinos.

See also LAS VEGAS

HUMPHREYS, Murray Llewellyn "the Camel"
(1899–1965): Chicago mob's Mr. Fixit

By underworld standards, Al Capone's opinion of Murray Llewellyn Humphreys was sterling: "Anybody can use a gun. The Hump uses his head. He can shoot if he has to, but he likes to negotiate with cash when he can. I like that in a man."

Throughout his criminal career Humphreys lived up to Capone's opinion. A Welshman (sometimes called "the only Welshman in the Mafia"), he was noted as the mob's Mr. Fixit, providing the underworld with strong ties to public officials, judges, police, businessmen and labor leaders. Together with Gus Alex, he succeeded Jake "Greasy Thumb" Guzik in the top fixer position after Jake's demise in 1956.

Dapper, with loads of class (he adopted his middle name because he figured that gave him more tone), he was nicknamed Murray the Camel because of his fondness for camel hair coats. To be sure, it was his sophistication—sartorial and intellectual—that made him so valuable to the mob. A rarity among the Capone gangsters, Murray was a high school graduate, a fact that even impressed Capone. As such an obvious brain, his aphorisms made deep impressions on his fellow mobsters. Some of his enlightened contributions to criminal knowledge were:

The difference between guilt and innocence in any court is who gets to the judge first with the most.

Go out of your way to make a friend instead of an enemy.

If you ever have to cock a gun in a man's face, kill him. If you walk away without killing him after doing that, he'll kill you the next day.

No good citizen will ever testify to anything if he is absolutely convinced that to do so will result in his quick and certain death.

Humphreys demonstrated considerable originality in his capers. He is the only Mafia associate who ever paid federal taxes on ransom money received in a kidnapping. The ransom—$50,000—was paid for the release of Robert G. Fitchie, president of the Milk Wagon Drivers Union, who was grabbed from his home in December 1931. After his release, Fitchie would not identify the men who snatched him, but Steve Sumner, the union secretary, later informed Internal Revenue agents that Murray the Camel had collected the money in person. It wasn't until 1952, 21 years later, that the IRS got around to forcing Humphreys to pay taxes of $25,000.

Within the mob the Camel got primary credit for neatly incapacitating gang leader Roger Touhy, who had for years resisted Capone's takeover in Chicago. At the very same time the Camel was able to do a favor for a good friend, John "Jake the Barber" Factor, an international stock swindler who at the time was fighting extradition to England where he was wanted for a $7 million fraud. Factor conveniently disappeared from sight and Touhy, framed on a Factor kidnapping charge, was sent to prison for 99 years. Naturally, because he had been vital to the legal case against Touhy, Jake the Barber remained in this country, and afterward the English matter cooled off.

Touhy remained imprisoned for a quarter of a century until freed when a federal court reviewed the case and found him innocent, ruling there had never been any kidnapping of Factor at all. Touhy lived less than a month. He was murdered in 1959; the story was that Murray the Camel declared no one was more entitled to the $40,000 contract on Touhy than he himself. After the Touhy murder, the Camel was questioned but no direct evidence could tie him to the crime.

A half year after Touhy was rubbed out, the Camel bought 400 shares of stock in an insurance company at $20 a share. The seller turned out to be Jake Factor, then eager to establish a clean slate for himself as a good citizen since he was trying to operate on the Las Vegas scene. (Touhy had clearly been an embarrassment to him.) Eight months after the Camel bought the stock, he sold it back to Factor for $125 a share, coming up with a neat profit of $42,000.

The IRS, long nurturing special thoughts about the Camel and his money transactions, looked at the deal and declared that the $42,000 was clearly payment for services rendered and was subject to full income taxes rather than the capital gains the Camel wished to pay. For his part, Factor said he owed Humphreys a favor for the aid he had given in the 1933 kidnapping.

In 1965, the aging Camel was in trouble with federal authorities once more. FBI agents came to his elegant apartment on the 51st floor of the Marina Tower in Chicago. He was charged with lying to a federal grand jury investigating the Chicago crime syndicate. Humphreys did not react in his normal cool manner. He pulled a loaded .38 revolver on the astonished G-men. One of the agents yelled: "Murray, for Christ's sake, don't you know we're FBI agents. Put down the gun." The Camel had to be overpowered, shackled and brought in for arraignment. He posted bail and returned to the apartment.

The word circulated quickly that Murray the Camel had acted off his rocker. It was the first intimation anyone had that Humphreys might be going softheaded. Within a few hours the Camel was dead. Heart attack, a coronary thrombosis, the medical examiner said. The examiner also spotted a small laceration just below the deceased's right ear. Some noted that persons unknown, with a hypodermic needle could have caused the puncture and injected the Camel with air which would have produced the blood clot to the heart.

See also TOUHY, ROGER "TERRIBLE"

HUNT, Sam "Golf Bag" (?–1956): Capone torpedo

Among the most creative and most deadly of the Capone gunmen, Samuel McPherson Hunt also had the distinction of being an accomplished golfer. And he managed to combine his two favorite pastimes, golfing and murder. Hunt made it a habit to carry his weapon, a semi-automatic shotgun, in his golf bag while stalking his prey. Once he was stopped by a detective who opened the bag. Hunt's innocent explanation: "I'm going to shoot some pheasants."

It happened that the first man he ever shotgunned didn't die, and his fellow gunmates on Tony Accardo's enforcement squad always referred to the lucky target as "Hunt's hole in one."

He gained his nickname of "Golf Bag" following one of his more colorful assassinations, the victim of which was destined to remain anonymous. It happened on a peaceful morning in 1927 when a Chicagoan was taking a stroll along Lake Michigan's South Shore. Suddenly there were loud explosions. The stroller knew shotgun blasts when he heard them. He hurried in the direction of the shots, and on the grass found a corpse, so recently shot that the blood still flowed.

The stroller hurried to a telephone and called the police. A police car responding to the call came across two well-known suspicious characters less than a half-mile away. They were Hunt and another very accomplished torpedo, Machine Gun Jack McGurn. McGurn was carrying no machine gun, and all Hunt had was a golf bag. Hunt's explanation: "Jack and I were going out to play a little golf." Unimpressed, the officers peeked into the bag and among the golf clubs found a semi-automatic shotgun. The odor and warmth of the barrel indicated the weapon had just been fired. It looked like the police had lucked into a perfect case, but when the stroller ushered the officers to the spot where he had found the body, it was no longer there. Either the dead man had got up and walked off, or the other Capone hoodlums had a car nearby and had packed off the corpse for a quiet burial elsewhere. All the police had was a pool of blood on the dewy grass.

There remained no case against Hunt, who escaped with nothing worse than a permanent nickname tagged on him by the press, "Golf Bag" Hunt. All in all, it is believed that Golf Bag killed at least 20 men. When he wasn't busy at that sport or putting around the greens, he proved to be a mean enforcer in the mob's union rackets. He outlived most of the old-time Capone torpedos until, in his late 50s, he was carried away by a heart ailment.

I

IANNIELLO, Matthew "Matty the Horse" (1920–   ):
Mafia sex czar

Long the reputed kingpin of New York sex bars, massage and porno parlors, and a number of gay transvestite hangouts—not to mention some of Manhattan's well-known eateries—Matty the Horse Ianniello was often targeted in official investigations. He almost always beat the rap, even when accused on narcotics and extortion charges.

Matty the Horse, so nicknamed in his youth for his hulking 5-foot-11-inch, 220-pound frame, ran a number of sex businesses for the old Genovese crime family. His only conviction came in 1971 when he was charged with criminal contempt for failing to answer questions before a Manhattan grand jury probing police corruption. He got off with a $1,500 fine and a one-year suspended sentence. Yet he remained the undisputed boss of a wide network of midtown sex establishments—topless, gay and transvestite bars. According to additional federal inquiries, he was pegged as head of porno and massage parlors in the Times Square area and at one time was thought to have controlled at least 80 midtown bars.

Matty the Horse ran his operations to the letter of organized crime law, milking them in every conceivable way, according to officials. Matty the Horse was said to control all "services" to these establishments, such as providing them with topless and go-go dancers, vending machines and garbage collection.

Although he was never listed as the owner, he was also said to control a number of well-known restaurants, including a posh Little Italy spot, S.P.Q.R. He was also linked to Umberto's Clam Bar, although his brothers were officially listed as owner and manager (the restaurant where Crazy Joe Gallo was gunned down in 1972). Matty the Horse was there at the time and cowered in fear in a corner of the kitchen when slightly wounded Pete the Greek, Gallo's bodyguard, confronted him and snarled, "If you had anything to do with this, it's gonna be real bad."

"You think I'm crazy, to let this happen in this place?" police quoted the frightened Matty the Horse replying. "I don't know nothing."

Neither the remnants of the Gallo forces nor the police were able to prove that he knew anything, and Matty the Horse went back to his charmed-life sex businesses. In 1985, however, he was arrested in Florida on charges of racketeering and organized crime. Among other things, the 65-year-old crime kingpin was accused with his aides of skimming off several million dollars in profits from the New York sex business and restaurants under his control. By late 1986 he was convicted on a number of charges and faced others.

The federal government seized a number of Ianniello businesses, including Umberto's and four New Jersey garbage collection firms. According to a federal spokesman, standard procedure dictates government operation of enterprises seized through forfeiture. He allowed, however, that the Mardi

Gras, a near-landmark Broadway topless bar, would be sold off.

ICE pick murders: Efficient execution method

Long a favorite rubout method of organized crime hit men, the so-called ice pick kill is employed to make a murder victim's death appear to be the result of natural causes. Generally, the victim is cornered in some out-of-the-way place, and while two or three hit men hold him, the executioner jams the ice pick through the eardrum into the brain. The pick produces only a tiny hole in the ear and a minute amount of bleeding, which can be carefully wiped away. After examining the corpse, doctors generally conclude that the cause of death was a cerebral hemorrhage. It takes expert medical examination to discover the true cause, and, unfortunately, few localities can or do provide such expertise.

The ice pick murder technique has long been ascribed to the Italian Mafia by some writers as a direct import from Sicily. But the technique was most likely perfected into art by Israel "Ice Pick Willie" Alderman, a Minnesota mobster who was close to Meyer Lansky in bootlegging days and later was one of the first investors—along with Lansky, Bugsy Siegel, Moe Sedway and Gus Greenbaum—in Las Vegas gambling. Ice Pick Willie ran a second-story speakeasy in Minneapolis where he proudly claimed to have committed 11 murders with a quick and trusty ice pick. It always looked like the dead man had simply slumped in a drunken heap on the bar, and Alderman would laughingly lecture the "drunk" as he dragged him into a back room. The corpse was dumped down a coal chute to a truck in the alley and carted away. (Alderman was arrested many times for robbery and murder, but was never convicted.)

Undoubtedly, the ice pick kill is still used. But the mob, when preferring a murder to be obvious, will add 70 or 80 stab wounds to deliver the gory message.

INDEPENDENT criminals and the Mafia

There is a rule among independent criminals: Never cross the local crime family.

One very prominent burglar who was making big heists around Washington, D.C., decided when the heat was on to switch his turf. He moved on to Philadelphia, but, before pulling any capers, he cleared his presence with Angelo Bruno, the head of the Philadelphia family. It was an act of respect, and Bruno not only accepted the burglar's application, he also waived the mob's claim to a cut of the burglar's loot.

Usually, independents are expected to "wet the beak" of a mob leader, that is, give him a taste of his profits; depending on whether he shares his loot or not, the independent will receive grief or a lot of grief. The Profaci family's area of Brooklyn was generally a closed shop. Former New York City Chief of Detectives Albert Seedman once learned the details, partially based on taped conversations between an independent named "Woody" and Carmine "the Snake" Persico, of a half-million-dollar swindle against a May's Department Store in Profaci territory. Persico insisted that the swindler pay a hefty share of his take. Woody was reluctant to hand over so much and wanted to know why. Persico responded in part:

"When you get a job with the telephone company or maybe even May's Department Store, they take something out of every paycheck for taxes, right? . . . And every year, it gets to be a little more. Now, people gripe, but they pay those taxes, Woody. They pay it, because if they don't, the government is going to tromp down on them. It's fact of life. Now why, you may ask, does the government have a right to make you pay taxes? Well, it's a fair question. The answer to that question, Woody, is that you pay taxes for the right to live and work and make money at a legit business. Does that make sense? . . . Well, it's the exact same situation. You did a crooked job in Brooklyn. You worked hard and you earned a lot of money. Now you got to pay your taxes on it just like in the straight world. Because we let you do it. *We're* the government. That's why I say we're always in the picture."

There was no appeal for the tariff rates in Profaci territory. For years the streets of Brooklyn were littered with corpses of those who did not play according to the rules.

In New Jersey, a Gambino capo Joe Paterno was described as having crooks "wet his beak" for 10 percent of what they got from their scams. Part of the understanding was that, if they got caught, they would have the benefit of Paterno's connections. One donor in such an arrangement later explained, "I didn't have to furnish him with an accounting; if at the end of the week I gave him $200, that meant that I had taken in $2,000 for myself. He didn't ever question my word; I was beating him and he probably knew it, but as long as he was getting something for doing absolutely nothing, there were no complaints."

When there was a complaint about an independent's action, mob justice was swift and sure. A young thief once committed the cardinal sin of robbing a church in Profaci territory, taking a jeweled crown from St. Bernadette's, an act that was in the eyes of kingpin Joe Profaci, an ardent churchgoer, not only sacrilege against the church but also against the mob itself. The word was sent out that the crown was to be returned immediately or death sentences would follow. That meant no fence would dare touch it, and the thief returned it.

However, a few diamonds were missing. As far as Profaci was concerned, the matter remained a capital offense. The thief was strangled to death—with a rosary. Vinnie Teresa, the informer, later observed: "If Profaci hadn't had the kid put to sleep, Profaci would have lost a lot of prestige in the community. After all, he owned Brooklyn, he was the boss."

Sometimes Mafia bosses required more of their local independents than a cut of the financial action. For instance, Blackie Audett, a leading professional stickup man during Prohibition, was allowed to practice in Chicago provided he handled an occasional assignment from the mob. And when Audett was positively identified in a bank robbery, Capone ordered him out of town immediately. Audie left. Although independents can be useful to the syndicate, they are also expendable. For instance, the mob may need more than just bribe money to keep a "bought" police officer happy. They feed him some independent so that the officer makes some merit points back at the station and solidifies his own position with the Mafia.

Perhaps even more important, it should be understood that all crime family bosses immediately assure that if a major crime occurs in another family's area, that mob gave its approval. If it turns out that the other family did not, and does nothing about it, it is an invitation for other criminals—independents and rival Mafia men alike—to move in.

See also STREET TAX

INITIATION rites of the Mafia

In 1964 informer Joe Valachi described his induction into the "Cosa Nostra":

I sit down at the table. There is wine. Someone put a gun and a knife in front of me. The gun was a .38 and the knife was what we call a dagger. Maranzano [the boss] motions us up and we say some words in Italian. Then Joe Bonanno pricks my finger with a pin and squeezes until the blood comes out. What then happens, Mr. Maranzano says, "This blood means that we are now one Family. You live by the gun and the knife and you die by the gun and the knife."

Although some crime observers have described Valachi's testimony on initiation rites as "amateur-night material," the ritual is clearly derived from the practice of Old World Italian criminals. Nineteenth-century historian Charles William Heckethorn in his *The Secret Societies of All Ages and Countries* described a contemporary Camorra initiation:

On the reception of a picciotto [beginning member] into the degree of camorrist, the sectaries assembled around a table on which were placed a dagger, a loaded pistol, a glass of water or wine, and a lancet. The picciotto was introduced, accompanied by a barber who opened one of the candidate's veins. He dipped his hand in the blood and, extending it towards the camorristi, he swore for ever to keep the secrets of the society and faithfully to carry out its orders.

The American underworld in the 19th century practiced the same sort of rituals. Jonathan F. Green, a Valachi of the 1840s, revealed the details of the operations of the "Secret Band of Brothers" which, according to him, offered the same idealized criminal society with the same sort of dagger and fire blood oaths and rituals. Green said the Secret Brothers had an organization command that included grand masters and vice-grand masters; above them all a "worthy grand." These were the equivalent of bosses and capos, above them all a boss of bosses, the structure Valachi attributed to the Cosa Nostra. Non-believers of Valachi's testimony insist the informer had simply been briefed on the Heckethorn and Green disclosures and that he gave them a Sicilian veneer. This can be countered with the claim that secret criminal groups worldwide instinctively develop in similar ways, and so it was inevitable that Valachi produced the same sort of picture as Green.

Basically Jimmy "the Weasel" Fratianno corroborated Valachi's story 15 years later. He said that in the 1940s, Jack Dragna, with gun and dagger, presided over the Weasel's initiation as a made man in the Los Angeles crime family.

Not all Mafia families followed the blood and fire ritual for inductees. The Capone Mob, for instance, did not go in for it, instead having recruits swear fealty to Al Capone with their hand on a Bible (actually a parchment manuscript of biblical excerpts written in Greek). Apparently that seemed very holy to the boys.

Informer Vinnie Teresa said of the blood-and-fire routine: "That may have happened in the old days, but I never heard of it happening in New England." There matters were handled in a businesslike manner. A would-be member had to be sponsored by a top boss, and, Teresa said, "before you were picked you had to have your notches for the organization, you had to have proved yourself by killing a guy you were ordered to hit." It so happened, if we are to believe Teresa, he never became a "made man" himself—which in itself makes his description somewhat suspect.

In addition to the blood and fire ceremony, Valachi said that he was informed of two traitorous acts which, if performed, brought death without trial: 1) revealing the secret of the organization and 2) violating another member's wife.

Fratianno added a third taboo, punishable by death: dealing in dope.

For some mafiosi, the induction rituals were clearly silly. Lucky Luciano, for example, tolerated the rituals because they gave hoodlums a sense of "belonging." They also added an element of fear by reinforcing the fatal consequences of betrayal. Certainly when Vito Genovese and Frank "Don Cheech" Scalise opened their family to new "made" members and charged them $40,000 or $50,000 under the table for the privilege, they undoubtedly gave them a scare ritual with the price of admission. After all, that kind of tab certainly entitled the applicants to some bit of entertainment.

See also ARGOS LECTIONARY

IN-YOUR-FACE: High honor for an esteemed murder victim
In common usage the term *in-your-face* is used to describe someone lacking respect, offensive. Oddly, in the mob world an in-your-face act is literal and is

a mark of respect. Mob custom dictates that a murder victim is not to be shot in the back but rather is to be permitted to face death. This is especially true if the victim is a wise guy or boss previously held in high esteem.

Thus when a young Vinnie "the Chin" Gigante was ordered to hit Frank Costello, he waylaid him in the lobby of his swank apartment house on New York's Central Park West. As the crime boss came through the lobby, the Chin stepped out from behind a pillar behind Costello and called out, "This is for you, Frank." The greeting was a show of respect that allowed Costello to turn and face his would-be killer, and it unintentionally saved his life. The bullet creased the right side of his scalp just above the ear. Gigante hurried off, convinced he had shown Costello the respect due by shooting him fatally from the front.

On the other hand when Chicago crime boss Sam Giancana was rubbed out in 1975, he was shot in the back of the head while cooking sausages for himself and his lethal guest. Newsmen later interviewed syndicate figures who said the mob would never have carried out a hit in such a disrespectful fashion. It was proof, said these underworld sources, that the killing was the work of the CIA seeking to silence Giancana about government-Mafia efforts to assassinate Fidel Castro. The fact was that by mob standards Giancana got the treatment they believed he deserved. He had already been stripped of his authority and thus was just a "bum" to be taken care of as easily as possible.

The in-your-face concept may be losing its meaning among the modern mob killers. Neither Roy DeMeo nor Sammy "the Bull" Gravano showed any inclination to let a victim get it up front, reasoning that anyone ordered killed was a bum.

Perhaps the last important in-your-face hit was that of the much-feared Carmine Galante, the would-be boss of bosses. (The assassination of Paul Castellano hardly measures up although he was hit from the front only because in that case the hit tactic was determined by the need for expedience on a crowded New York street rather than niceties such as honor and respect.) Galante was shot as he sat in an outdoor restaurant with a cigar in his mouth. A bit of dark humor developed in Mafia circles. Some of the boys allowed that while the front shooting represented a show of respect, the fact that he was not allowed to have dessert seemed "disrespectful."

ITALIAN rope trick: Murder method

In what may have been an effort to ethnicize a common method of murder into an Italian mold, Jimmy "the Weasel" Fratianno in his memoir-confession, *The Last Mafioso* by Ovid Demaris, introduced what he called the "Italian rope trick" and confessed to taking part in more than one such gang execution.

Typical was the time he invited a California gangster named Frank Niccoli, an ally of Jewish mobster and gambler Mickey Cohen, to his home for a friendly conversation. Actually, Fratianno had a murder contract on Niccoli—if he could not induce him to leave Cohen and join or rejoin the Cosa Nostra elements. Over a bottle of beer Niccoli made it evident that he would side with Cohen in any underworld gang war. Just then the doorbell rang and Fratianno answered it. If he had succeeded in "turning" Niccoli, the execution would have been called off; otherwise reinforcements were at hand. Fratianno feigned surprise at his guests, Joseph Dippolito (Joe Dip) and Sam Bruno, but welcomed them into the house. "You guys know Frankie Niccoli?" he asked.

Niccoli rose. "I don't think I've had the pleasure," he said, extending his hand to Joe Dip. Just as Joe Dip's grip fastened on Niccoli's hand, two more men, Nick Licata and Carmen Carpinelli came charging into the house. That raised the odds against Niccoli to five to one.

Joe Dip flipped the victim around and bear-hugged him from behind. Licata drew a rope from his pocket and handed it to Jimmy the Weasel, who announced, "Frankie, your time's up," and looped the rope around Niccoli's neck. Fratianno handed one end to Bruno and the two men pulled hard, literally squeezing the life out of Niccoli who died with a surprised look on his face. Even when Dippolito released his hug on the victim, the two garrotters kept pulling, even going down with Niccoli as his body slumped to the floor.

It was an efficient if not neat killing. Fratianno complained that the hapless victim had urinated on his new rug. One of the others informed him, "They always piss. Sometimes they shit. Count yourself lucky." (Never again did the Weasel allow such a rope murder to be performed in his hallowed home.)

To accord such garroting the title of the Italian rope trick was rather misleading, since the homicide method had long been favored by Irish gangsters in 19th-century America, long before the arrival of the mafiosi. And within organized crime such rope tricks were perennially in vogue with the equal-opportunity Jewish and Italian killers of Murder, Inc.

Indeed, the Weasel's method was little more than a mercy killing compared to the finesse of such Murder, Inc., experts as Pittsburgh Phil Strauss, Abe Reles and Buggsy Goldstein. A case in point in true mastery of rope murder was the execution of one Puggy Feinstein in Brooklyn. As Reles later confessed:

"I give Phil one end of the rope, and I hold the other end. Puggy is kicking and fighting. He is forcing his head down, so we can't get the rope under his throat. Buggsy [Buggsy Goldstein] holds his head up, so we can put the rope under. Then me and Phil exchange ends . . . cross them, so we make a knot . . . a twist. Then we cross them once more. Then we rope around his throat again, to make two loops.

"Buggsy gets Puggy by the feet, and me and Phil get him by the head. We put him down on the floor. He is kicking. Phil starts finishing tying him up . . . [and] gets his feet tied up with the back of his neck. He ties him up like a little ball. His head is pushed down on his chest. His knees are folded up against his chest. His hands are in between. The rope is around his neck and under his feet. If he moves the rope will tighten up around his throat more." That was how Puggy died slowly, a favorite variation by some rope trick specialists.

J

JAMAICAN posses: Going further the fastest

The Jamaican posses are among the youngest and most violent of the new organized crime groups. It may be an indication of their sophistication that they have tended to adopt the names and terminology of western films, one of the few youthful joys found in the poverty and political unrest of Kingston, Jamaica. By 1970 these various posses had moved into the United States, where, as best can be determined, they are something in excess, perhaps huge excess, of 25,000 members, in possibly 30 or 40 different posses. Originally the posses looked upon the United States as a cash cow and simply sent their illicit gains back to their homeland. However, as their revenues soared, they found it necessary to keep the money invested in the States. They advanced with unabated violence, engaging in murder, torture, maiming and kneecapping. While cocaine and crack are the gangs' main sources of funds, they are also big in money laundering, robberies, kidnappings, and firearms trafficking. They service the illegal immigration racket with fraudulent passports and visas and falsified documents. They are big in insurance frauds and bank kiting. With money pouring in they have invested in commercial properties, restaurants, travel agencies and trucking companies. While law experts say the posses have moved "farther faster" than any of the newer organized crime groups, the posses have a singular inability to widen their activities to the full range of Mafia enterprises. The main reason is that they prefer force to get their way and show no ability to accommodate corrupt political or law enforcement elements. This is unlike in Jamaica, where the posses are said to exercise considerable influence on the government. While they have worked to some extent with the Colombian drug cartels and some street gangs, such as the Crips, they only further distance themselves from corrupt elements of authority in the United States. Their constant mass shootouts on city streets have not really been in vogue since the days of Al Capone. As the Mafia no longer seeks to have confrontation with legal authorities, this shuts the Jamaican posses out of the main illegal actions such as gambling, loansharking and other lucrative rackets that may often involve payoffs to the legal powers. Overall, the Mafia appreciates the Jamaican posses for keeping so much of the heat off real organized crime.

JEWISH Mafia

Organized crime in America was born of the amalgamation of the two most powerful ethnic crime groups in the underworld of the early 1930s—the Italian mafiosi and the Jewish gangsters. The prime architect of the so-called Jewish or Kosher Mafia, as some journalists referred to it, was Meyer Lansky, who judiciously pulled the strings that brought many powerful Jewish gangsters around the country under the umbrella of the emerging national crime syndicate.

Lansky worked closely with Lucky Luciano and aided him in his fight against the old-line mafiosi then under the competing leaderships of Joe the Boss Masseria and Salvatore Maranzano. These old-world Sicilians, especially Masseria, hated gangsters of other ethnic derivation, cooperated with them only when absolutely necessary and looked forward to the day they could get rid of them. Luciano and Lansky realized there was no room in the underworld for such counterproductive bigotry, and they plotted to get rid of both Masseria and Maranzano.

After a bloody war and much intrigue that ended in 1931, both Masseria and Maranzano had been eradicated. Now it became necessary for Lansky and Luciano to "sell" their program of "brotherhood" to their Jewish and Italian followers.

Lansky set about the task of uniting the Jewish gangs across the country. His missionary work brought in the Purple Gang from Detroit and the Moe Dalitz forces operating in Cleveland. He followed this up with a momentous convention of East Coast forces at the Franconia Hotel in New York City on November 11, 1931. Those attending included Bugsy Siegel, a longtime partner of Lansky and Luciano; Louis "Lepke" Buchalter; Joseph "Doc" Stacher; Jacob "Gurrah" Shapiro; Hyman "Curly" Holtz; Louis "Shadows" Kravits; Harry Tietlebaum; Philip "Little Farvel" Kovalick; and Harry "Big Greenie" Greenberg.

Lansky explained to the participants that Luciano had successfully united the Italian mafiosi, and that the Lansky-Luciano "combination" or national crime syndicate was the wave of the future. All the participants agreed, and the Franconia conference established a firm platform: "The yids and dagos would no longer fight each other," the quotation attributed to the loquacious Siegel.

Jewish gangsters who were thought to be constitutionally unsuited to the new "interfaith" combination of shared spoils with other ethnics, such as the "unsuited" Waxey Gordon, bootleg king of Philadelphia, were eliminated. The combination did this by continuing its business dealings with Gordon and then feeding information to Internal Revenue so that he could be put away on income tax charges. He was then replaced by the far more compliant Nig Rosen and Boo Boo Hoff.

The fact that some in attendance at the Franconia meeting—Big Greenie and Bugsy Siegel—were eventually murdered did not alter the interfaith feelings of the combination. Bugsy might well have appreciated the fact that his murder was approved by a combined vote of, to use his words, "yids and dagos."

Jack Dragna, the late boss of the Los Angeles Mafia, gave a fairly succinct description of the Jewish Mafia to Jimmy Fratianno, the hit man who later turned informer: "Meyer's got a Jewish family built along the same lines as our thing. But his family's all over the country. He's got guys like Lou Rhody and Dalitz, Doc Stacher, Gus Greenbaum, sharp fucking guys, good businessmen, and they know better than try to fuck us."

Only on the last statement was Dragna suffering a delusion—or perhaps he was trying to impress Fratianno. The fact is that whenever Lansky gave an order Dragna jumped.

See also WAR OF THE JEWS

JOHNSON, Ellsworth "Bumpy" (1906–1968): Black "mafioso"

It has become the vogue in recent years to speak of a "Black Mafia," a group emerging with a Cuban or Latin look, eventually to supplant the 50-year reign of the Italian-Jewish syndicate. But black criminals who advance the furthest today are those who cooperate with rather than oppose the Mafia. Harlem's Ellsworth "Bumpy" Johnson, a black millionaire, was very cooperative.

A virtual folk hero for four decades, Bumpy was famous for flashing his "wad" as he strode through hordes of his Harlem admirers. His status was acknowledged by the New York crime families, too. When a black in Harlem objected to white control of the rackets, Bumpy got the enforcement contract to handle the problem.

In that sense Bumpy Johnson was, as cited by Nicholas Gage in *The Mafia Is Not an Equal Opportunity Employer*, an exception to the title of the book. Like a true member of organized crime, Johnson paid his dues, serving three prison terms for selling narcotics and facing a fourth conviction when he dropped dead of a heart attack at the age of 62. In prison, Bumpy had become a scholar in philosophy and history. He wrote poetry and saw several of his poems published in a review dedicated to the black freedom movement.

Black freedom or no, Bumpy Johnson, as Gage noted, "took the only safe road open for a black gangster—exploitation of fellow blacks—and he still managed to die of natural causes."

See also BLACK MAFIA

JUKEBOX racket

The jukebox industry is legitimate, but it has long been attractive to organized crime, which picks its interests by the nature of the business rather than by its legality or illegality. The mob is especially lured to businesses where the skim makes it possible to siphon off profits before any taxes are paid. This makes nightclubs, bars, restaurants—and jukeboxes—so inviting. And the Mafia has been in jukes since the early rule of Lucky Luciano.

The racket is simple and unvarying. The mobsters move in on the jukebox operators' association as well as on the local unions whose members service the jukes. Then territories are sliced up among mob operators, and full monopolies are established. No one is permitted to invade the areas, and any rival jukes are sabotaged. Restaurant or tavern proprietors are forced to accept only mob jukes or be threatened or actually physically attacked. They are further warned that picket lines will be set up around the establishment until the owner is driven out of business. (The same techniques are used in related enterprises, such as cigarette vending operations.)

The juke business is popular with the mob because it can at times allow the gangsters to make certain special types of payoffs and push careers of singers and musicians they favor. In *Brothers in Blood* Pulitzer Prize winner David Leon Chandler tells how in the 1940s Jimmy Davis, the outgoing governor of Louisiana, was helpful in working out a compromise between New Orleans crime figure Carlos Marcello and old-style political boss Sheriff Frank Clancy so that three gambling casinos could open on the New Orleans side of the river while not competing with locally owned gambling joints on the more populous western side. Chandler states, "Governor Davis's compensation, if any, is unknown." However he noted that in the 1960s the FBI hit on a possible theory. Close to 100,000 old phonograph records were dredged out of New York's East River, most of them copies of "You Are My Sunshine" sung by Jimmy Davis, who had been a country music singer before becoming governor.

Subsequent FBI investigation indicated that Governor Davis "had done a favor for Cosa Nostra, and in return the mob-owned jukebox companies of America had bought the Davis recordings and placed them in tens of thousands of jukeboxes." After a time, the story went, the owners—and presumably the customers—had their fill of "You Are My Sunshine," and the mob had to pull out the records. Having no further use for them, the mob deep-sixed the disks in the East River.

238

KANSAS City crime family See FIVE IRON MEN

KARPIS, Alvin "Creepy" (1907–1979): Public enemy wooed by Mafia

By and large the members of the Mafia regard independent criminals and public enemies as far beneath them. An exception to this exclusion was public enemy Alvin "Creepy" Karpis. Al Capone held him in high regard, and on numerous occasions he tried to recruit Karpis as a gunner for the outfit. Karpis turned down all offers.

It was not that Karpis disliked Capone. He once told a writer that Capone was "a wonderful person . . . a real man." Karpis pointed out that free-lance gangsters often upset members of organized crime. They felt a fugitive bank robber and the like would generate heat that could affect their rackets, and so they frequently informed on them. And informing on independents allowed mob-ally cops to play hero. "That just wasn't in Al's nature," Karpis told Capone biographer John Kobler. "He always knew when we hit town and where we stayed, but he never tipped off the cops."

Karpis often espoused his reasons for refusing to join the Capones. He pointed out, "I'm a thief; I'm no hood." Capone, for one, understood Karpis's pride. The FBI's J. Edgar Hoover did not. When Karpis was finally apprehended in 1936 in New Orleans with Hoover on hand to personally take

credit, the FBI boss constantly referred to him as a hood. Karpis lectured back:

You don't understand. I was offered a job as a hoodlum and I turned it down cold. A thief is anybody who gets out and works for his living, like robbing a bank or breaking into a place and stealing stuff, or kidnapping somebody. He really gives some effort to it. A hoodlum is a pretty lousy sort of scum. He works for gangsters and bumps guys off after they have been put on the spot. Why, after I'd made my rep, some of the Chicago Syndicate wanted me to work for them as a hood—you know, handle a machine gun. They offered me $250 a week and all the protection I needed. I was on the lam at the time and not able to work at my regular line. But I couldn't consider it. "I'm a thief," I said. "I'm no lousy hoodlum."

Karpis was sent to Alcatraz, where he was to have a joyful reunion with Capone. Capone learned from him the latest about his own mob, particularly that one of Capone's favorite enforcers, Machine Gun Jack McGurn, had been murdered in what very much looked like a mob rubout. But Karpis noticed a vacant look on Capone's face. Sometimes when he was talking to him, Capone seemed neither to hear nor recognize him. It was the late stages of Capone's advanced syphilis playing hob with his central nervous system.

Karpis remained in Alcatraz long after Capone had been released from prison and died. Transferred from Alcatraz to McNeil Island Penitentiary in Washington in 1962, he was released on parole in 1969 and deported to Canada. He lived out his last years in retirement in Spain.

KEFAUVER Committee hearings: Senate organized crime investigation

Back in 1950 and 1951, for week after week, the Kefauver Committee hearings were the hottest show on television. Many Americans did not then own TV sets, but accommodating retailers put sets in their windows and piped the sound outside so that crowds of pedestrians could view the media phenomenon.

The Senate Special Committee to Investigate Crime in Interstate Commerce—more simply known as the Kefauver Committee—was the first of many probes into crime to command such public attention. Thanks to television it became probably the most important probe ever of organized crime in America. Scores of crime figures and politicians came under the camera's scrutiny as the hearings went on the road, hitting one city after another.

The committee, headed by Democrat Estes Kefauver of Tennessee, included fellow Democrats Lester C. Hunt of Wyoming and Herbert O'Conor of Maryland and Republicans Alexander Wiley of Wisconsin and Charles W. Tobey of New Hampshire. Paraded before them by chief counsel Rudolph Halley were more than 600 witnesses, from minor hoodlums to major racketeers to public servants, from policemen

The most famous television scenes of the Kefauver hearings were shots of Frank Costello's hands. The underworld's "prime minister" refused to have his face appear on camera.

to mayors and governors. The hearings made the phrase "taking the Fifth" part of the American vernacular, as dozens of witnesses invoked the constitutional right against self-incrimination, not always in the most eloquent of ways. Gambler Frank Erickson took the Fifth "on the grounds it might intend to criminate me" and Jake "Greasy Thumb" Guzik of the Chicago Outfit didn't want his replies to "discriminate against me." (Guzik appeared without a lawyer and said he'd learned all about the Fifth by watching television.) Probably no congressional prober effectively frustrated the "I Refuse to Answer" legions as well as Kefauver. In his soft-spoken way he just kept asking questions without browbeating witnesses until they usually became so mesmerized that they started giving answers, often despite coaching they had received from high-priced lawyers.

The committee's televised sessions were hypnotic. In Chicago, viewers were treated to the confession of Captain Dan Gilbert, chief investigator for the state's attorney's office in Cook County and often described as "the world's richest cop," that his office had not raided a single Chicago bookie joint in over a decade. He ascribed his personal wealth to playing the stock market and betting on sports events and elections. He assured the committee he won $10,500 in 1948 betting that Truman would beat Dewey. In New Jersey the committee ferreted out millionaire mobster and fixer Longy Zwillman, from whom former Republican Governor Harold G. Hoffman had personally solicited support in 1946. In 1949, in the interests apparently of good government, Zwillman offered the Democratic candidate for governor, Elmer Wene, $300,000, and all he asked in return was the right to pick the state's attorney general. Wene rejected the offer and lost.

In Louisiana, which Kefauver described as "Fantasia in law enforcement," the probe turned up county sheriffs and other lawmen who said they had not cracked down on gambling on the grounds of a fair employment practices rule. They said thousands of people, many old and underprivileged, would lose their jobs in the illegal casinos. It was probably only fair that these officers would concern themselves about the income of others considering how well they were doing themselves. The New Orleans chief of detectives, laboring at $186 a month in salary, managed to build a safe-deposit nest egg of about $150,000.

In Detroit, the committee dug up information that mob figures like Joe Adonis and Anthony D'Anna had hold of important business concessions with the Ford Motor Company in spite of their well-known crime backgrounds. The panel determined that a meeting was held between D'Anna and Harry Bennett, at the time Henry Ford's chief aide, at Bennett's request "to instruct him [D'Anna] not to murder Joseph Tocco, who had a food concession at a Ford plant. . . . Bennett entered into an agreement that D'Anna would refrain from murdering Tocco for five years in return for the Ford agency at Wyandotte. As a matter of record, Tocco was not murdered until seven years after this meeting. Also as a matter of record, D'Anna did become a 50 percent owner in the Ford agency at Wyandotte within a matter of weeks after the meeting."

In New York City, Virginia Hill, the lady friend of a number of top mobsters and reputed bagwoman for the mob, provided comic relief by denying any knowledge of the mobsters' business. They just all pushed money on her. Hill also provided the action highlight of the hearings when, on leaving a session, she threw a right cross to the jaw of *New York Journal American* reporter Marjorie Farnsworth. Turning on the remaining horde of reporters and photographers, she shouted: "You goddamn bastards. I hope an atom bomb falls on all of you."

Frank Costello added to the drama in New York when he refused to be shown on television and threatened to walk out of the hearings. He finally testified under an agreement that his face would not be shown. Instead, the cameras focused in on his hands in what became known as the "hand ballet." Costello was examined on his wide criminal interests—his activities in casinos, slot machines and other forms of gambling in Lousiana; his connection with a harness racing track in which he received an annual fee for seeing that bookmakers did not do business on the premises; his power in New York politics, including the power to name a great many judges to the bench. He was asked why Tammany boss Hugo Rogers had once said, "If Costello wanted me, he would send for me," and said he was as baffled by the remark as the committee seemed to be.

Unfortunately for Costello the questions got sharper and tougher and finally he staged a famous walkout. Costello had lost his muscle as the Prime Minister of the Underworld under the committee's hammering. As much as politicians were noted for their love of mob money, they would be hesitant thereafter to deal with Costello. He faced a future of legal battles, including 18 months for contempt of Congress. And he later did another term for income tax evasion.

Costello was not, however, the chief casualty before the committee. Former New York City Mayor William O'Dwyer came out of the hearings as a national symbol of civic corruption. It became clear that during O'Dwyer's reign—both as mayor and earlier as district attorney in Brooklyn—"Bill O" made regular accommodation with organized crime. The national Democratic organization became so embarrassed by O'Dwyer that he was forced to resign his mayoralty for the relative sanctuary of the ambassadorship to Mexico.

The committee produced overwhelming evidence of O'Dwyer's friendship with Joe Adonis and that he was a frequent visitor at Frank Costello's home. There was also sworn testimony that envelopes of money passed to O'Dwyer from leaders of city unions. O'Dwyer had only a hazy recollection of such matters. In its report the committee blasted O'Dwyer:

> *A single pattern of conduct emerges from O'Dwyer's official activities in regard to the gambling and waterfront rackets, murders and police corruption, from his days as district attorney through his term as mayor. No matter what the motivation of his choice, action or inaction, it often seemed to result favorably for men suspected of being high up in the rackets. . . . His actions impeded promising investigations. . . . His defense of public officials who were derelict in their duties and his actions in investigations of corruption, and his failure to follow up concrete evidence of organized crime . . . have contributed to the growth of organized crime, racketeering and gangsterism in New York City.*

When the Kefauver investigation ended, the committee made a number of suggestions to tighten the law against the Mafia and other racketeers and crooked politicians. Although many of these suggestions were implemented, cynics held that after a few months it would be back to business as usual for the mob. But that did not happen—at least not completely. Costello's power was broken. Adonis later agreed to deportation to avoid going to prison. Gambler Willie Moretti, who had supplied considerable comic relief at the hearings, was later executed by his associates who feared the loose tongue he exhibited would eventually entrap them.

The underworld was not destroyed. FBI chief J. Edgar Hoover was forced to take some face-saving steps to compensate for his stubborn inattention to organized crime, and, by the end of the decade, the publicity storm the Kefauver Committee had started had engulfed Hoover. He was forced to pit his agency in an all-out war against the Mafia and organized crime—the crime bodies he had for decades assured everyone did not even exist.

Kefauver himself was catapulted into national political prominence and the mail the senator and the committee received was copious and laudatory. "I was deeply moved by the quietly eloquent, almost Lincolnesque quality of your words," a New Orleans housewife wrote. A "lifelong Republican" from San Francisco decided "I'd like the privilege and pleasure of voting for you for the next President of the United States." A wire from St. Louis read: "I am a small time racketeer. . . . Don't know nothing but think you are a swell guy."

Kefauver's fame won him a vice presidential nomination, but he lost out in the Eisenhower landslide.

See also "KEFAUVERITIS"

"KEFAUVERITIS": Mystery "ailment" of mobsters under probe

During the Kefauver Committee hearings—officially, the Special Committee to Investigate Crime in Interstate Commerce—running from May 10, 1950, to May 1, 1951, a strange malady suddenly struck crooks and politicians as they were subpoenaed. It was called "Kefauveritis," after Estes Kefauver, the soft-spoken but hardnosed Democratic senator from Tennessee who chaired the committee and became America's first television-promoted crimebuster.

When it became known that the traveling Kefauver Committee was coming to town, organized crime figures in many cities developed unexpected heart attacks, laryngitis, appendicitis, nervous breakdowns and an almost paranoid desire for privacy. Travel fever was another symptom as Mafia types were consumed with a bug to see the country, the world—if possible, the moon—so long as it was far away from Kefauver.

As mobster after mobster either evaded appearing or refused to answer questions, "Kefauveritis" apparently struck other witnesses as well. Governor

Thomas E. Dewey of New York likewise did not appear to testify although urged by both Democratic and Republican members of the committee and despite the fact that many other governors, of both parties, did appear. Former racketbuster Dewey would do no more than have his counsel present formal statements. However, he did allow that if he was given enough advance notice, he might give the senators a few minutes of his valuable time in his private office. He said the senators could even stay at the Executive Mansion. Exactly how the committee's large staff of counsel, investigators, court stenographers and so on would fit into Dewey's office was a problem not tackled. Under the circumstances the committee decided not to leave New York City for Albany, and the committee and the nation were deprived of hearing Dewey's explanation for his pardon of Lucky Luciano and for wide-open gambling conditions, run by organized crime and by Meyer Lansky in particular, in Saratoga Springs—just 33 miles from Albany.

In refusing to appear—a remarkable attitude for a racketbuster who constantly had hauled witnesses in for questioning and always held an innocent man would want to help official inquiries—Dewey behaved little differently than the mobsters who tried to thumb their noses at the U.S. Senate. In the process, of course, he demonstrated that contagious "Kefauveritis" afflicted the upperworld as much as the underworld.

KENNEDY, Robert F. (1925–1968): U.S. attorney general

Robert F. Kennedy was the first attorney general of the United States to make a serious attack on the Mafia and organized crime. Many hold he was also the last one. As Harry J. Anslinger, former U.S. Commissioner of Narcotics, put it:

"Many former attorneys general . . . would let loose a blast against the underworld and then settle back in their chairs and let it go at that. They seemed to think they had performed their duty merely by calling attention to the problem. Not so with Bob. He followed through. He knew the identity of all the big racketeers in any given district, and in private conference with enforcement officials throughout the country he would go down the line, name by name, and ask what progress had been made."

Quite naturally Anslinger's opinion differed from J. Edgar Hoover's, with whom he had a less than cordial relationship. For years, Hoover had asserted there was no such thing as a Mafia or organized crime. Because of the Apalachin Conference bust of 1957, Hoover finally had to alter his line, and when Bobby Kennedy became attorney general in 1961, Hoover was further forced to expand the FBI fight against the Mafia.

On John Kennedy's assassination, Hoover slacked off on the Mafia investigation. Neil J. Welch, a retired special agent in charge of several top FBI offices, and David W. Marston, former United States attorney from Philadelphia, note in their book *Inside Hoover's FBI:* "When Kennedy stepped down as attorney general, Hoover moved immediately to undo all that he had done and perhaps never realized that one Kennedy accomplishment was indelible: When the FBI finally penetrated organized crime, agents gave the credit not to J. Edgar Hoover, but to his nemesis, Robert F. Kennedy."

See also HOOVER, J. EDGAR

KID Dropper (1891 or 1895–1923): Labor racketeer king

At the beginning of the 1920s Nathan Kaplan, better known as Kid Dropper, was considered the top gangster in New York City. He had been a lowly member of the Five Pointers Gang prior to World War I (a bit of an oddity as a Jewish mobster in what was virtually entirely an Italian outfit), but he learned the criminal craft well and murdered his way to the top of the labor slugger-extortionist field.

Kaplan picked up the Kid Dropper moniker in his youth. His scam, dropping a wallet filled with counterfeit money on the street, "finding" it and selling it to a gullible victim since he "didn't have time to locate the owner and collect a reward." Naturally, the marks would agree to return the wallet, paying the Kid what they agreed the likely reward would be. Whether or not the marks intended to return the wallet, they each ended up with nothing but some worthless counterfeit money.

As late as 1911, when Kid drew a seven-year prison term for robbery, he was not considered an important criminal. When he was set free, however, he filled a void in the labor slugging field left by the passage of Joe the Greaser Rosensweig and Dopey Benny Fein. In partnership with another vicious thug, Johnny Spanish, Kid Dropper formed a new gang of labor sluggers. It was not a partnership made in heaven since the pair had a long history of hating

one another. Years earlier they had had a falling out over a woman, and Spanish taught the Kid a lesson by shooting her, for which he drew a seven-year sentence.

Obviously the boys were not going to maintain their new relationship for long, especially since each viewed himself as the logical leader of the gang. Soon open warfare broke out between the pair and each turned loose a troop of killers against the other. Bullet-ridden corpses soon became a common sight in the garment district where both sides sought to dominate the rackets. The war came to an abrupt end on July 29, 1919, when the Dropper's forces learned that Spanish was dining in a Second Avenue restaurant without his usual collection of bodyguards. When Spanish stepped into the street, three gunmen, one said to be Kid Dropper himself, pumped him full of bullets.

Thereafter the Kid dominated all the labor slugging rackets in the city, working at times for the employers or the unions and sometimes for both at the same time. Between 1920 and 1923 Kid Dropper was said to have been responsible for at least 20 murders. He became a popinjay on Broadway and appeared, said one writer, "in a belted check suit of extreme cut, narrow, pointed shoes, and shirts and neckties of weird designs and color combinations, while his pudgy face, pasty-grey from long imprisonment, was surmounted by a stylish derby pulled rakishly over one eye." He did not make Johnny Spanish's mistake and was always surrounded by a bevy of gunmen.

There was good reason for this. The Dropper now faced newer and more deadly opponents than Johnny Spanish had been. They were led by Jacob "Little Augie" Orgen, a pitiless killer with such supporters and "comers" in his ranks as Jack "Legs" Diamond, Louis "Lepke" Buchalter and Gurrah Shapiro. Soon the two sides were slaughtering each other, especially for control over the wet wash laundry workers. From 1922 to mid-1923 their bloody warfare resulted in 23 murders. Once Lepke and Shapiro almost got Kid Dropper just outside his Lower East Side headquarters, but, barely missing him, they killed one of his men and an innocent bystander.

In August 1923, Kid Dropper was seized on a concealed weapon charge and hauled into the Essex Market Court. While he was being transferred to another court, he was led to the street by a phalanx of policemen past a swarm of newsmen and onlookers. As the Kid was entering the police car, a minor and dim-witted hoodlum named Louis Kushner jumped forward and shot him through the windshield. Kushner had been "stroked" by the Little Augies into believing that if he knocked off the Dropper he would come into their gang in a top position.

Dropper collapsed inside the car, while his tearful wife fought through the police to reach her husband. "Nate! Nate!" she cried. "Tell me that you were not what they say you were!" Instead, the Kid came back with a typical underworld line. "They got me!" he gasped and died.

Kushner heard the Dropper's last words and declared triumphantly, "I got him. I'd like a cigarette."

In a curious finale to the murder, Kushner got as his lawyer James "Dandy Jim" Walker, the darling of Tammany and soon to be mayor of New York. The district attorney, another Tammany man, agreed with Walker that what Kushner had done was naughty manslaughter rather than cold-blooded murder and Kushner in the end only had to serve a few years for a crime that could have sent him to the electric chair.

Meanwhile Little Augie swallowed up the Dropper's illegal enterprises, to keep them only until 1927 when Lepke and Shapiro rubbed him out and took over the bulk of the union rackets in the city.

KIDNAPPING of mafiosi

In recent years, only a handful of criminal cases have concerned kidnap for ransom—that is, cases reported to the authorities. But contrary to official records, kidnapping for ransom is prevalent, and it involves the most dangerous victims in the world—Mafia members.

The idea of seizing and holding organized crime figures for ransom is not a brand new one. It was exploited for considerable reward in the 1930s by Chicago's so-called College Kidnappers. Named for the fact that their leader, Theodore "Handsome Jack" Klutas, was an alumnus of the University of Illinois and that most of their members were college graduates, the group specialized in snatching underworld characters who not only could afford to pay ransom but also were least likely to go to the police. Very often the victims of the College Kidnappers were members of the Capone Mob. In response to

the kidnappings, the group was added to the Chicago Outfit's death list. Klutas or his men didn't seem too worried, though; between 1930 and 1933, they took in an estimated half million dollars, mostly from the mob.

In 1933, Capone gangsters cornered a minor member of the College Kidnappers, Babe Jones, and forced him to offer Klutas a payoff to cease kidnapping mob members. Klutas indicated he liked the deal, but as soon as Jones left, he ordered Jones's assassination, figuring him to be a weak character who would in time leak too many gang secrets to the Caponeites.

Jones's car was stolen. Then he received a phone call, allegedly from police in Joliet, that the vehicle had been found and could be picked up at a certain garage. Jones, knowing how the College Kidnappers worked, took the precaution of driving past the garage dressed as a woman. He spotted two assassins known to him in a car outside the garage.

Now Jones was trapped between the College Kidnappers and the Capone gang, who had no further use for him since Klutas had rejected the bribe. In desperation, Jones turned to the police. He revealed the addresses of various gang hideouts, and Klutas was machinegunned to death from a police ambush at one of the locations. No doubt when word of Klutas's death reached the then-imprisoned Al Capone, he was thrilled by the triumph of law and order.

Gangster Vincent "the Mad Mick" Coll made a career out of kidnapping for ransom New York mobster kingpins attached to the Legs Diamond and Owney Madden gangs. In June 1931, Madden had to pay $35,000 to get back his right-hand man, Big Frenchy Demange, whom Coll had snatched off a street corner.

Charged in 1932 with killing a five-year-old boy in a street shootout with other gangsters, Coll figured he needed the best legal brains in the business. Once more he kidnapped a Madden man and collected $30,000. The funds went to ace criminal lawyer Sam Leibowitz, who got Coll off on the murder rap. Coll's kidnapping days ended later that same year when he was cut down in a public phone booth as he was engaged in a long telephone conversation with Madden, threatening to snatch him and kill him.

The notorious Gallo brothers of Brooklyn masterminded the most audacious mob kidnapping in recent years. In early 1960, they snatched four or perhaps five members of the Joe Profaci family. The victims included Joseph "the Fat Man" Magliocco, Profaci's brother-in-law and underboss; Frank Profaci, the boss's brother; and two powerful aides, Salvatore "Sally the Sheik" Mussachia and John Scimone, Profaci's trusted bodyguard and chauffeur. Some were snatched from their homes, others on the street or from a social club. Joe Profaci was himself a target, but he was tipped off in time, boarded a plane to Florida, and checked himself into a hospital. The Gallos, angry that Profaci was not cutting them in for enough of the family crime income, warned they would kill their hostages unless their demands for more equitable treatment were met.

Surprisingly, Profaci seemed to agree. He said if the hostages were released, a sitdown would be held on the Gallo complaints and the situation would be rectified. The kidnappers were inclined to accept the offer, especially Larry Gallo and Joe Jelly, the gang's top assassin. Only Joe Gallo objected violently. "You kill one," he said, "you tell them you want one hundred G's in cash as a good faith token, then we sit down and talk."

The argument ended with Larry slapping his hotheaded brother and insisting the hostages go free. They were released except for Scimone, who was held an extra week. In captivity, Scimone expressed sympathy for the Gallos' position and asked how he could help them. Before Scimone was freed, he was badly beaten to make it appear that he had gotten the extra-tough treatment because he had refused to renounce his boss.

The kidnapping did not have a happy ending for the Gallos. Profaci stalled on their demands, and, after an armed truce of about six months, the old don went to war on the upstarts. Using some Gallo defectors, he had Joe Jelly taken for a fishing expedition in which he ended up as fishfood. Larry Gallo was almost strangled to death in a famous ambush in a Brooklyn bar where he had been lured by Scimone, Profaci's bodyguard, who had expressed a willingness to aid the Gallo cause. In Old Man Profaci's book, kidnappers got no deals, just Mafia vengeance.

Carlo Gambino, the most powerful Mafia leader of the 1960s and 1970s likewise gave kidnappers no quarter, especially in a 1972 case in which three free-lance kidnappers grabbed the don's nephew, Manny Gambino, and demanded a $350,000 ransom. After part of the money had been paid, the kidnappers went ahead and killed Manny and buried his body in a New Jersey swamp.

The FBI learned of the kidnapping and arrested two suspects, much to Gambino's annoyance. He preferred taking revenge personally. A third suspect, James McBratney, evaded arrest and Gambino put out a contract on him. He was caught in a Staten Island, New York, bar and executed by a three-man hit squad, headed by mafioso John Gotti, who was later convicted of the killing and drew a seven-year sentence. When Gotti got out, Gambino advanced him far up the crime family ladder to the trusted position of capo.

Kidnapper exterminators are much esteemed in the mob.

KING'S man: Mafioso with direct access to the godfather

A truly powerful mafioso is one called a "king's man" with the authority to go directly to the boss or godfather of a crime family without having to deal with any buffers. Shortly after the death of Neil Dellacroce, John Gotti's sponsor within the mob, godfather Paul Castellano cut Gotti down to size. From then on Gotti was not to have direct access to Castellano but would have to go through Tommy Bilotti, a mob guy regarded by most as weak in the thought department and particularly annoying to Gotti.

This stripping of Gotti's position indicated further degradations or "knockdowns" to be meted out later by Castellano. It was enough for Gotti to decide that he would have to strike at Castellano quickly.

KISS of death: Mafia murder signal

The "kiss of death"—an opponent informed by a kiss on the lips that his days are numbered. Contrary to standard mob m.o.—catch the victim unaware—the kiss is an indication of danger, or a warning. When an errant debtor is cornered by several toughs and so kissed, he will suddenly find the inspiration to come up somehow with the money he owes. Occasionally it has been used on relatively hapless victims who cannot fight back, such as frightened targets of Black Hand extortionists or "debt collectors" for shylock operators.

Vito Genovese, not one of the smartest although one of the most brutal mob leaders, gave Joe Valachi a kiss for "old times' sake" while they were both imprisoned in the federal penitentiary in Atlanta. It backfired and turned Valachi into one of the most important informers in underworld history Genovese clearly did so because he wanted to demonstrate to others—both in the prison and outside—how potent his power remained. What it did in the final analysis was prove that his power was limited.

Probably no Italian crime leader was as contemptuous of the Mafia custom of kissing as Lucky Luciano. Upon his ascent to power in 1931, he ordered the act stopped even as a form of greeting when mafiosi met. Such public acts, Luciano understood, might strike terror in the hearts of Sicilian peasants but were counterproductive in the United States.

"After all," he said, "we would stick out kissing each other in restaurants and places like that."

KNOCKDOWN: Demotion, Mafia style

A "knockdown" is the most desirable type of demotion in the Mafia, since it has the merit of saving the mobster from being hit. A prerequisite is that the mobster's offense did not cost the mob money, which is a capital offense. For instance, if a capo (or lieutenant) fails to support his wife and family according to mob standards, he might simply be reduced to the rank of a mere soldier.

This has happened to a number of former big-timers. One was Marshall Caifano, a longtime member of the Capone mob and later Chicago's representative in Las Vegas overseeing the mob's casino interests. He was terrible at the job and attracted too much attention to himself by getting arrested in brawls. Eventually the true Chicago godfather, Tony Accardo, demoted him to the status of a common soldier and gave him only menial tasks as punishment for his incompetence. Caifano was smart enough to take it and in his 60s got permission to relocate to Florida. Accardo spoke disparagingly of him, urging he be given very little, "but don't let him starve."

One who was not about to take a knockdown was John Gotti. It was obvious in 1985 that Paul Castellano was planning to knock Gotti down. First, he took away Gotti's "king's man" status, that is a capo with the right to direct contact with the boss whenever he wanted. Then Gotti and his supporters learned that Castellano was getting ready to break up the Ravenites, Gotti's crew. Gotti would be reduced to the status of a common soldier, and both he and his crew would be cut off from the prime sources of income. Most likely Castellano planned to have Gotti killed later for rebelling against the boss's

will. In this case the knockdown never happened. Gotti and his supporters assassinated Castellano and took over the crime family.

See also KING'S MAN

KORSHAK, Sidney (1907–1996): Fabled fixer for the mob

Until his death in January 1996 at age 88, Sidney Korshak was known as a master fixer beyond compare and the mob's man in Hollywood and other points in the West. Despite or because of this, Korshak moved easily in Tinseltown, proving himself an indispensable ally for movie producers, top business executives and politicians.

Korshak always carried out the instructions of the Chicago Outfit, which nursed him with great skill, warning lower level mobsters never to approach him lest they bring down his reputation for integrity and trust. As Chicago mob boss Joey Aiuppa once told a minor mobster: "Don't put any heat on Sid. He can't be seen in public with guys like us. We have our own ways of contacting him." It was apparent the warning came with penalties up to and including death for disobeying. Korshak himself knew where his power came from. As Chicago capo Murray Humphreys once reamed him out, he reminded Korshak that he was "our man, we raised you, you drop everything when we call."

Korshak exercised his power, and that power reached around the globe even for rather mundane tasks. One time comedian Alan King, long a performer in Vegas, was coldly informed by a desk clerk at a plush European hotel that there were no rooms available. King went to a lobby phone booth and placed a call to Korshak in Los Angeles. Before he even hung up, the desk clerk was knocking on the phone booth door to inform King his suite was ready.

Others held Korshak's demonstrations of power in considerable awe. An admiring Robert Evans, the former head of Paramount, related in his 1994 book *The Kid Stays in the Picture* what the master fixer could accomplish with single phone calls, especially to take care of "labor problems": "Let's just say that a nod from Korshak, and teamsters change management. A nod from Korshak and Santa Anita and Vegas shut down. A nod from Korshak, and the Dodgers can suddenly play night baseball."

Evans had special reason to be both admiring and grateful to Korshak. When the producer wanted Al

Pacino for the top role in *The Godfather,* Sid rather quickly got the actor released from his exclusive contract at MGM.

Korshak was the son of a wealthy Chicago family and got his law degree from DePaul University in 1930. Almost immediately he was handling the defense for members of the Capone crime syndicate. As such, Korshak, who often boasted that he paid off judges, was shunned by the city's business elite. That was until it was found that he could squash demands from legitimate unions by arranging instant sweetheart contracts with other, very pliable unions, often the Teamsters.

By the late 1940s Hollywood beckoned him, as moviemakers were likewise entranced with his ability to bring labor peace. Korshak became a close buddy of many moguls, including Lew Wasserman, Kirk Kerkorian and the late Charlie Bludhorn who had taken over Paramount Pictures.

One of the most ardent fans of Korshak was the onetime president of the Teamsters, Jackie Presser, who later described him as "the smoothest sonovabitch in the business. There's nothing he can't fix . . . and he don't even have an office. This guy don't even have a briefcase. Keeps everything in his head."

Korshak conducted his business from the Bistro in Beverly Hills, ensconced at a corner table, flanked by two telephones that kept ringing, and in between calls he had private chats with friends and beautiful women who came by to give him a friendly kiss. His business calls were said to come from such clients as Schenley, Diners' Club, the Chargers, the Dodgers, the Knicks, the Rangers, Seeburg, National General, racetracks around the country, hotel chains such as Hyatt and Hilton and probably another hundred top companies. Whenever he got a call relating to the affairs of his Chicago clients, he would leave his table with a bagful of coins to conduct business from one of scores of telephone booths.

If a union cooked up a strike, reliable Sid would "arbitrate" it, but there would be no under-the-table payoff. Instead Korshak would have a big legal bill mailed to his Chicago office; he never attempted to get a law license in California, which made his activities much harder to trace. Sid would pay the full taxes on the sum and cut up the balance with his mob allies through his "handler," Gus Alex—all nice and clean.

Korshak's main activities for the mob were most appealing to a number of legitimate enterprises, in particular his ability to tap millions of dollars from the Teamsters' notorious Central States Pension Fund, which did much to finance the growth of the Las Vegas casino industry.

Personally, Sid lived the good life. His wife played tennis with Dinah Shore and other important women, and Korshak himself never seemed to be without female friends. Back in his Chicago days, he was known for giving wild late-night parties at which were always the most beautiful and accommodating showgirls. A former Chicago judge told the *New York Times* in 1987, "Sidney always had contact with high-class girls. Not your $50 girl, but girls costing $250 or more."

Mobsters often talked enviously among themselves about Korshak's private life. John Roselli, the Chicago mob's longtime overseer in Vegas, observed that Sid had "been shacking up with Stella Stevens for years." It was said that Sid was also responsible for seeing that other female friends got anchor spots on some leading Hollywood gossip TV shows.

In an era when mob figures were constantly coming to violent ends, Sid Korshak was too valuable to face any danger.

L

LA: Dirty word for new-century mafiosi

La, as a new word for the mob, was declared verboten by the late John Gotti in the early 1990s. Gotti had previously decreed no mob guy was permitted to use the phrase *La Cosa Nostra* for Mafia. The fact that Gotti himself frequently broke his own rules is of no consequence: He was often caught on the Gotti Tapes, a record of the government's electronic bugging of Gotti, pontificating, "I'm Cosa Nostra" and "La Cosa Nostra now and forever!" Gotti rules never applied to John Gotti.

On the tapes Gotti proclaimed, "And from now on, I'm telling you if a guy just so mentions 'La,' or if he wants to say 'La, la, la, la.' He just says 'La,' the guy I'm gonna strangle the cocksucker. You know what I mean? He don't have to say, 'Cosa Nostra,' just 'La,' and they go. . . ." After that Gotti really waxed obscene, more than is necessary to quote here. With Gotti later convicted, the emerging leaders can be said to have truly hated Gotti for his big mouth on tape, but they did like his La edict, and the boys from the dawn of the new century were forbidden from even uttering a "La."

Insiders say two crime bosses in the recent rebirth of the Mafia—the security-conscious Joe Massino, the boss of the Bonanno crime family, and Joel Cacace, acting boss of the Colombo family—rigidly enforced the no-La rule. Whether there were any executions for simply saying "La" is difficult to ascertain, since motivations behind mob killings are often part of a web that is challenging to untangle. But *La* may have played a role in some mob purges. In any event saying "La" is hardly the way to get ahead in the murderous society.

LABOR leasing: Trucking racket

A mark of organized crime's hold on the Teamsters Union is its ability to work rackets that allow it to get rich while union truckers are thrown out of work. In the 1970s Anthony "Tony Pro" Provenzano, later imprisoned for murder, came up with the "labor leasing" racket. Tony Pro was a vice president of the Teamsters, a union which was expelled from the AFL-CIO for corruption. He was also a capo in the Genovese family.

Under the Provenzano setup, firms that used a high volume of trucking, such as furniture manufacturers and retail chain stores, would be guided to "labor-leasing" companies, which were connected with Tony Pro, to provide drivers for their trucks. These labor-leasing companies, controlled by mafiosi, took the work on a fee basis and then paid drivers at a scale far below that paid union members under the Teamsters' National Master Freight Agreement. This meant the union drivers who had previously worked directly for the firms needing truckers were thrown out of work while nonunion, lower paid drivers working directly for the leasing company essentially took over their jobs.

The fact that so many mafiosi or members of their families have gone into running such leasing outfits or into the trucking business in general is often cited as proof that with the passage of time the Mafia is "going legit." Other observers see it as nothing more than the Mafia's supreme ability at innovation in racketeering.

LANGELLA, Gennaro "Jerry Lang" (1939–): Colombo crime family leader

There was some dispute as to Jerry Langella's position in the Colombo crime family in the mid-1980s. According to some he was merely the acting boss while Carmine "the Snake" Persico was doing time. Others maintained Langella had wrested control from Persico and had no intention of letting the violence-prone Snake get back into power. It was going to be an interesting confrontation if and when Persico, who had done 10 years in prison out of the last 13 and was facing more charges, got out.

Langella, who started in the Brooklyn mob family when he was 20, quickly gained a reputation as a man who could scare almost anyone when he wanted to—and he did a stint as Persico's bodyguard. Langella, in a sense, epitomized a Young Turk in the New York Mafia and feuded with a number of older bosses of other Mafia families, claiming, for example, they were cutting the Colombo family, not considered to be in the same class with the Gambinos or Genoveses, out of a fair share of return on revenues for certain construction shakedowns.

Langella was known to have befriended certain other youthful elements in those families and is reputed to have warned allies of John Gotti (of the Gambinos), another Young Turk, that the elderly boss Paul Castellano feared him and would seek to kill him shortly after Christmas 1985. Gotti's patron in the crime family, underboss Aniello Dellacroce, had died on December 2. Nine days before Christmas Castellano was assassinated. Gotti was suspected of ordering the rubout and Langella was suspected of not being even a wee bit sorry about it.

Under Langella the Colombos have allegedly been greatly involved in narcotics trafficking, loansharking, gambling, hijacking, criminal receiving,

A youthful Jerry Langella, before he became head of the Colombo crime family while Carmine Persico was behind bars, had by age 24 been picked up as a "prime suspect" in a number of rubouts.

bankruptcy frauds, counterfeiting, cigarette smuggling and pornography. On this last count it is said that two mafiosi, believed to be Colombos, showed up one morning at the offices of two of the most successful pornographic filmmakers in the East and asked if they had any personal belongings in their desks. The filmmakers asked why and the boys were very patient. "Because this is now ours," one said, "but we're letting you take your personal stuff. So hurry up and get out."

The men got out. It was your average everyday Mafia mob takeover. However, Langella's reign would prove short. He was hit with a mass of criminal charges that resulted in a 100-year sentence, and Persico's return was unhampered, save in due course by federal prosecution once again.

See also MacIntosh, Hugh "Apples"

LANSKY, Meyer (1902–1983): National crime syndicate founder

There was a godfather of the national crime syndicate, the parent organization of what became the American Mafia—and thus a real godfather of the American Mafia. He was called with total respect the "little man," and Lucky Luciano's advice to his followers was always "listen to him." He himself would brag with typical quiet elation: "We're bigger than U.S. Steel." And an agent of the FBI would say of him with grudging admiration: "He would have been chairman of the board of General Motors if he'd gone into legitimate business."

He was Maier Suchowljansky, better known as Meyer Lansky, a Jew from Grodno, Poland. While many mafiosi speak of "our thing" which excludes all but Italians, it is a matter of record that none of the top mafiosi ever excluded Meyer Lansky from anything. Only among the lower-rung levels of the Mafia was there any belief that Lansky, because he was not Italian, was just a money man to be respected and trusted, one who lacked real power to "vote" in the top councils.

Lansky truly had the first and last word in organized crime. When the Big Six dominated the syndicate in the 1940s and 1950s, Lansky voted and all the others followed. Greasy Thumb Guzik from Chicago thought Lansky the genius of the age. Tony Accardo marveled at the money Lansky brought in. Longy Zwillman, head of the New Jersey rackets, followed Lansky's lead at all time. Ditto Frank

Costello, who was Lansky's partner in New Orleans, Las Vegas and elsewhere. And Joey Adonis was under strict orders from the deported Lucky Luciano to "listen to Meyer." The voting usually went six-zip Lansky.

Everybody listened to Meyer because it paid. If they listened well, he might, for instance, give them a slice of the pre-Castro Cuban action. Lansky cut in Chicago, Detroit, New Jersey and New York. When the Trafficantes of Tampa tried to go in big on their own in Cuba, Lansky used his Batista connection to squash the move. Then he gave them a slice, smaller than what many other mafiosi got. That was Lansky's way. Jack Dragna, the Los Angeles Mafia boss, once tried to use muscle on Lansky to get a piece in Las Vegas. Lansky talked him in circles, got him up on tiptoes, and then not only didn't kiss him but gave him nothing. It was Lansky's way.

Despite a rash of publicity during the last decade of his life, Lansky remained the most shadowy of the organized crime leaders. Although Luciano technically held the title, Lansky was regarded as equal and perhaps superior to Luciano as the godfather of organized crime as it emerged in the 1930s. Together, they were the successors of the warring Prohibition gangs as well as of the old-line Mafia, headed by the so-called Mustache Petes (particularly, Joe the Boss Masseria and Salvatore Maranzano). And the Mafia as it exists today, owes as much to the Jewish Lansky as to the Sicilian Luciano for its shape and prosperity.

They were the perfect match: the well-read, even studious Lansky, who could survey all the angles of a given situation, and the less-than-erudite Luciano (he could make out the *New York Daily News* or *Daily Mirror* but he freely admitted the *New York Times* threw him), who made up for his limitations with a brilliant flair for organization and the brutal character to set any plan in motion.

Through the years Lansky built an image of being alien to violence, but it was a myth. In the 1920s he and Bugsy Siegel organized the Bug and Meyer Gang, which some described as the most violent of the Prohibition mobs in the East. They worked alternately as liquor hijackers and protectors of booze shipments for bootleggers willing to meet their prices, which were so exorbitant that it amounted to extortion.

Bug and Meyer muscle was also available for "slammings" and rubouts for a fee and was the fore-

The aging "Jewish godfather of the Mafia," Meyer Lansky (holding hat) was much harassed by the law but seldom convicted. His death in 1983 left a gaping hole in the competent leadership of the national syndicate.

runner of Murder, Inc., the enforcement troop of the national syndicate. Many Bug and Meyer graduates, in fact, moved into Murder, Inc., in the 1930s; Lansky had as much to do with the forming of that outfit as anyone. He proposed the enforcers be put under the command of a triumvirate composed of Louis Lepke, Albert Anastasia and Bugsy Siegel. Other leaders of the emerging national crime syndicate objected to the kill-happy Siegel, feeling he would be too loyal to Lansky and would give Lansky too powerful a hold on the apparatus of the extermination crew should the confederation fall apart in a war of extermination. Lansky agreed to drop Siegel from the murder troop, but his influence was not dented. It was said that no major assignment for Murder, Inc., ever went forward without Lansky being consulted. That was true even in the elimination of Siegel in 1947 for spending or stealing too much of the syndi-

cate's money in his Las Vegas hotel operation. "I had no choice," Lansky was quoted as telling friends, but others insisted he had pushed hard for the vote to kill his close friend. He did suggest the mob hold off execution for a time, though, while pressure was exerted on Siegel to produce profits from his Las Vegas ventures. It was Lansky's way.

Both Luciano and Lansky independently said that they had planned the formation of a new syndicate as early as 1920, when Luciano was in his early 20s and Lansky was only 18. They were greatly influenced in this by the older Arnold Rothstein, the great gambler, criminal "brain" and mentor who, acting on his own plan for a national syndicate, nurtured Lansky's and Luciano's development. Rothstein's murder in 1928 shortened what the pair may have considered too long an apprenticeship. Lansky and Luciano together survived the crime wars of the

1920s by cunning alliances, eliminating one foe after another, even though they lacked the manpower and firepower of other gangs. When they effected the assassinations first of Masseria and then Maranzano, they stood at the pinnacle of power in the underworld. Even Al Capone realized they were more powerful than he.

In remarks attributed to Luciano, he once explained, "I learned a long time before that Meyer Lansky understood the Italian brain almost better than I did. . . . I used to tell Lansky that he may've had a Jewish mother, but someplace he must've been wet-nursed by a Sicilian." Luciano often said Lansky "could look around corners," or anticipate what would happen next in underworld intrigues, and that "the barrel of his gun was curved," meaning he knew how to keep himself out of the line of fire. Through the years that was Lansky's way.

Lansky never begrudged Luciano his top role, realizing that the title brought the clear dangers of notoriety and, no matter how many payoffs were made, the hazard of being the target of the law. It was also necessary to sell Luciano as the top man in order to win the support of the Italian mobsters. Lansky had fewer difficulties selling Jewish mobsters like Zwillman or Moe Dalitz, or even the often unpredictable Dutch Schultz, on the value of syndication; they understood the profits involved. The Italian mafiosi were different, many cut adrift by the war of survival that had just been concluded. Lansky told Luciano: "A lot of these guys need something to believe in." He urged Luciano to keep some of the old-style Mafia trappings used by the Mustache Petes. Luciano had no patience for the nonsense of "made men" and blood oaths but agreed to let those who wanted such rituals have them. He did eliminate the position of "boss of bosses"—and immediately, as Lansky anticipated, gained that position de facto. At Lansky's suggestion the organization took the name of Unione Siciliano, a corruption in spelling of the old fraternal organization. Eventually Luciano just called it the "outfit" or the "combination." Luciano imbued in his men that all the traditions really meant little, that the important thing was money-making. (In time, though, Luciano saw the merits of the structure of the Italian wing; it gave him a power base and cemented that power. Even when imprisoned for a decade, his support never eroded and he could issue orders and have his revenues set aside for him.)

As late as 1951, when his name surfaced during the investigation of bookmaking czar Frank Erickson, the *New York Times,* with one of the most reliable news libraries in the world, did not know exactly who Meyer Lansky was. The newspaper identified him as "Meyer (Socks) Lansky," evidently mistaking him for Joseph (Socks) Lanza, the waterfront racketeer. During the Kefauver investigation (1950–1951) into crime, Lansky was considered so unimportant that he was not even called as a witness to testify. The committee did not even mention him in its first two interim reports. Only in the final report did the investigators correct their oversight and announce: "Evidence of the Costello-Adonis-Lansky operations was found in New York City, Saratoga, Bergen County, N.J., New Orleans, Miami, Las Vegas, the west coast, and Havana, Cuba."

Lansky was revealed as "the brains of the combination." The "little man" became acknowledged as the one who held together Luciano's crime empire while he was behind bars. Lansky was the money man trusted to hide or invest millions for the syndicate, and he saw to it that Luciano got his share of the profits even after he was deported to Italy. It was Lansky who opened up what was for a time the syndicate's greatest source of income, gambling in Havana. He alone handled negotiations with dictator Fulgencio Batista for a complete monopoly of gambling in Cuba. Lansky was said to have personally deposited $3 million in a Zurich, Switzerland, bank for Batista and arranged to pay the ruling military junta, namely Batista, 50 percent of the profits thereafter.

In the rise and fall of underworld fortunes, Lansky was immune to replacement because he was too valuable to lose. Thus, he could agree with Vito Genovese that Albert Anastasia should die and then later he could take part in a fantastic conspiracy that delivered Genovese himself to the feds. Despite this duplicity, Lansky faced no retribution.

Lansky's arrest record over the years was bush-league stuff and it was not until 1970 that the federal government made a concerted effort to get him on income tax charges. Lansky had skimmed untold millions out of Las Vegas casinos which the syndicate secretly owned. The government also sought to deport him as an undesirable alien. In 1970, Lansky fled to Israel where so many of his Jewish underworld associates had retired. Lansky claimed Israeli citizenship under the Law of Return, which accorded citizenship to anyone born of a Jewish mother. Lansky poured millions of dollars into the country to win public support, but he proved an embarrassment to the Israeli government. Law enforcement officials warned that Lansky was not retiring from organized crime but would use Israel as a base of operations. After a long battle in the courts and bitter debate by the public, Lansky was forced to leave Israel in 1972.

In 1973, after undergoing open-heart surgery, Lansky was put on trial in Miami on the income tax charges that had worked so well against many crime bigwigs since Al Capone. It was a disaster for the government; Lansky was acquitted. In December 1974, the federal government gave up its efforts to put the then 72-year-old organized crime legend behind bars.

Lansky maintained his position in the syndicate right to the very end. In the early 1970s his personal wealth was estimated at around $300 million and by 1980 it must have grown to at least $400 million. Some profilers have tried to explain Lansky's continuing to make money as an indication of his inner need for power and the ability to exercise it. They tend to overlook the more simple explanation: Lansky felt a man could never have too much. His drive was always for more.

However, in 1991 a British writer, Robert Lacey, published *Little Man* in which he insisted Lansky died hard up. The theory gained few supporters. A *New York Times* reviewer found the book "banal" and dismissed Lacey's claim that criminal investigators never pinned anything substantial on Lansky. "But such evidence proves exactly the opposite point, argue those who insist Meyer Lansky was a criminal mastermind who left behind a vast secret fortune. No one ever laid a finger on Lansky precisely because he left no fingerprints anywhere. The more you argue there was no fortune, the more you prove there has to have been," continued the article.

Similarly, Lacey's theory would mean that Lansky, who had shown such men as Huey Long and Fulgencio Batista of Cuba the joys of foreign numbered accounts, neglected to set up anything for himself out of the millions he admittedly accumulated.

Lansky had created organized crime in its syndicate form, but he was never interested in creating any dynasty. His children and wife were kept totally away from mob business. And he looked for no successor. In that sense Lansky was the quintessential Jewish-American mobster. They either stayed until they died or else they sold out their positions in the rackets and went into retirement.

Meyer Lansky had outlived Lucky Luciano by 20 years but, in the end, Luciano's handiwork in the national crime syndicate—the American Mafia—was the portion that survived, simply because it was a structure, an apparatus that needed running, that automatically filled all vacancies because it remained a money-making machine. Yet Lansky in large measure created the American Mafia and was its real godfather.

See also JEWISH MAFIA; LAS VEGAS

LANSKYLAND: Florida Jewish community

The area around Hallandale and Gulfstream Park Racetrack in Florida is still referred to by many residents as "Lanskyland," after Meyer Lansky. It cannot be denied that the Jewish retirees of the area still recall Lansky (who died in 1983) with a certain warmth, an attitude that is interesting when compared with the Italian-American attitude, which is often anger at the mere mention of the Mafia as a real entity. American Jews, having escaped the ghettos that made their ethnic group one of the main reservoirs of manpower during the foundation of the crime syndicate, are assured enough not to feel tarnished by Lansky, and indeed are unconcerned by his later-life claims that he was being persecuted as a Jew and, worse still, that "anti-Semites have used my name to attack Jews."

The Lansky folklore remains potent in the area. They talk of his Colonial Inn where so many members of the respectable world came to gamble illegally in Florida—judges, senators, big businessmen and, according to Lansky himself, such individuals as Joseph Kennedy (four or five times a week) and Secretary of Defense James V. Forrestal. In the very heart of Lanskyland, there is now a shopping mall off Hallandale Beach Avenue, erected on the site of another Lansky casino, the old Plantation Club. In the shopping mall there is a bookstore where, as author Hank Messick notes with some pride, literally thousands of copies of his biography, *Lansky*, sold. After Lansky was returned from Israel in 1972, the bookstore had another run on the book and sold out all over again.

The attitudes of Lanskyland inhabitants offer a significant insight into the theory of ethnic succession in organized crime (a theory that in the main is far off the mark). The Jews no longer feel their ethnic group plays an important role in organized crime, and when the last few activists departed—men like Moe Dalitz, for example—they left no successors. Thus Lanskyland and its memories merely harken back to another day in Jewish-American history—bitter perhaps in the experience of some—but one of fading impact.

There can be no Lanskylands for Italian Americans while the Mafia thrives. And it continues to thrive and, indeed, continues to expand its hold over organized crime—despite the claims of a few writers about the aging of the mafiosi.

LANZA, Joseph "Socks" (1904–1968): Racket boss of fish industry

Joe Lanza, one of the most powerful mobsters in New York—but to whom tribute was paid by almost every family in the country that ate fish—was not called "Socks" because he wore colorful footwear. He got his nickname because of his socking ability. He was so tough that even Teamsters' locals quaked at his power and paid him extortion money rather than risk his wrath at the Fulton Fish Market, which supplied the city with seafood and influenced the price around the entire nation.

Lanza, who started working as a fish handler at the age of 14, was semiliterate but very powerful. Many journalists insisted on calling his Fulton Street domain Lanza's Fish Market; Lanza made it a firm rule that everyone paid tribute—"every dealer, big and small, retailer or wholesaler," said one investigative report. Lanza collected $10 from every boat that came in the harbor, $50 from every truck that went out, and $2,000 from every trucking firm in the fish business. And no stall could operate without a Lanza okay and levy. A member of the Luciano family and very close to Frank Costello, he ran this tariff up to a $20-million-a-year racket and his personal income never fell below $1 million annually.

Lanza achieved his power through brute force. At the age of 14 he tipped the scales at 200 pounds and even hardened thugs steered wide of this youthful desperado with the cocky grin. As a teenager he was arrested on suspicion of murder, burglary and carrying concealed weapons but there were no convictions. From 1917 to 1919 he worked as a fish handler at the Fulton Market for $12 a week. By the time he was 19 he was ready to make his big move.

He organized his own union, called the United States Sea Food Workers Union, and tied up the market so that everyone had to meet his extortion demands.

Lanza worked with impunity until the 1930s when he finally got sent to federal prison for two years for violation of the Sherman Anti-Trust Act. Going behind bars did not crimp Lanza's style. His aides kept up the pressure for payments and from prison Lanza started extorting Teamsters Local 1202, warning that unless tribute was paid the union could not operate at the market and all the top officials of the local would be killed. Since there had been a number of murders at the market already, it was obvious Lanza was not kidding. After his release, Lanza really put the screws on the Teamsters. The local president, Sol Shuster, had to juggle his books in order to make the huge payoffs Lanza demanded.

In 1943 Lanza was caught on extortion charges and sentenced to 7½ to 15 years. He was released in 1950 to come back to a steadily thriving racket at the market. In February 1957 he was arrested as a parole violator for consorting with criminals, gambling and living way beyond his means. Held for a hearing, Lanza, who was very powerful in political circles, pulled strings to get a favorable hearing before a parole trial commissioner who, despite staff recommendations, ordered him released on parole.

Writing in *The Nation* shortly after the decision, prizewinning reporter Fred J. Cook declared:

Joseph (Socks) Lanza, the racket boss of New York's huge Fulton Fish Market, is living proof that muscle builds millions, defies laws and prison, and rules vast segments of the American economy. His case demonstrates once again that the power of the underworld reaches to the seats of the mighty and that, even when sad mischance brings about the imprisonment of a gangster, his empire goes on and on.

The decision caused such a furor that the parole commissioner, James R. Stone, a relative of Charles A. Buckley, Democratic leader of the Bronx, was forced to resign. Tammany boss Carmine DeSapio was linked in testimony to the Lanza case, and it was viewed later as the first sign of a decline in DeSapio's prestige as a national political leader.

Lanza was ordered back to prison, did a bit more time and returned to the fish market to take up a hold that would remain unassailable to his death.

Needless to say, Lanza's empire survived him as the Genovese crime family moved to solidify its hold on New York's fish supplies.

LAROCCA, John Sebastian (1902–1984): Pittsburgh mafioso

A much-overrated mobster, John Larocca was often described as the Mafia boss of southwestern Pennsylvania and Pittsburgh. Some knowledgeable observers, however, have tended to regard him as the leader of the Mickey Mouse Mafia-East, a play on the description of several West Coast crime families because of their general ineffectiveness and their inability to protect their own turf from incursions by the New York and Chicago mobs. Larocca's empire was just as ineffective, although probably for more understandable sociopolitical reasons.

In those areas where the political forces have the will they can readily triumph over so-called organized crime. From the early 1900s, vice in Pittsburgh was controlled directly by the ward political machines. "Ward syndicates" kept tight control of the numbers rackets, slot machines, houses of prostitution and unlicensed saloons. Madams could only rent houses from syndicate-approved real estate agents who charged exorbitant rents. All illegal businesses had to pay protection money to police and other city officials and the funds were handled directly by the ward chairmen or other representatives of the political machine.

A prizewinning newspaper reporter, Ray Sprigle, once wrote a series of articles that pointed out the firm control the ward chairmen held over the numbers racket. It was pointed out no one syndicate could take over the East Liberty section of Pittsburgh because too many wards were involved and the chairmen guarded their interests well. The chairmen also held sway over the police whom they could appoint and promote, and thus used the police to raid and perform "protection and enforcement" services. In other words the police were charged with keeping both the operators of various illegal enterprises toeing the mark and at the same time seeing to it that no competition moved in.

Under such circumstances mafioso activities could only, at best, be superimposed on this locally controlled racket setup. As a result neither the early mob leader, Frank Amato of Braddock, Pennsylvania, nor his successor in 1956, John Larocca, amounted to much in the national councils of organized crime. Even informer Vinnie Teresa, not a top-rung mobster himself, could sneer about Larocca and describe him simply as "a mob guy from Pittsburgh who some people say is a boss but he isn't."

Larocca—whose police record began in 1922 when he was sentenced to three to five years in prison for assault with intent to kill and maim—was not among those arrested at the notorious Apalachin Conference in 1957 when it would have been logical to have introduced him to mob leaders from around the country. Either Larocca was not considered important enough, the most likely conclusion, or he proved to be so speedy afoot that he outlegged police pursuers through the woods.

Whether or not he held the reins, Larocca did run a profitable operation. Certainly he became a millionaire and was very effective in bossing a group of gambling junket operators who supplied "high roller" victims for various mob casinos both inside and outside the country.

When Larocca died in 1984 at the age of 82, the impact of his death was virtually unfelt by organized crime elsewhere. It was perhaps a tribute to a political system that long ago established the principle of taking care of its own. Larocca was succeeded by Michael James Genovese who was only acknowledged as "acting boss"—clearly an indication by other Mafia families that the Pittsburgh Mafia is in the minor leagues.

LAS Vegas: Organized crime's Promised Land

The first men to gamble in Las Vegas were the Paiute Indians who peopled the area before the town existed. When the Mormons ventured down from Utah in the 19th century to try to convert these Indians to Christianity, they were ignored by the Paiutes who had far more interest in playing a kind of roulette in the sand with bones and colored sticks. The Paiutes and the mobsters of organized crime were to enjoy a similar association with Las Vegas. Conceived as a gambling mecca, modern Las Vegas was built almost exclusively by mob money.

During World War II Las Vegas was little more than a dusty jerkwater town in the middle of the desert, with a few gas stations, greasy-spoon diners and some slot machine emporiums. It was popularly said that Bugsy Siegel was the first to visualize the town as a glittering gambling mecca, but the fact is he was pushed at first by Meyer Lansky who in 1941 ordered Bugsy to send a trusted aide, Moe Sedway, to work in Las Vegas. For a time Bugsy thought it was a zany idea that he had little time for—he was far happier being a Hollywood playboy—but Lansky kept pushing, realizing that an area with legalized gambling offered far more profits and less crooked overhead than illegal casinos elsewhere.

When World War II ended, Bugsy warmed to the idea of Las Vegas with glitter. His enthusiasm convinced mob figures to invest big money to develop the town. Lansky now was able to hang back. If the idea fell through Siegel could take the rap; if it succeeded, Lansky would step forward to take credit.

With a bankroll of something like $6 million in mob funds, Siegel built the Flamingo, which turned out to be a monumental bust because he was forced to open early, before public interest could be built up. Bugsy had other woes. He had skimmed off huge sums of construction money, and when the mob discovered this, they gave him a deadline for its return. Siegel's only hope was to get the Flamingo to succeed. When it didn't, he was summarily murdered.

Nevertheless, Las Vegas grew. With Lansky now overseeing the Flamingo it turned profitable by the end of its first year. Now the mob really piled in. State officials set up strict rules aimed at keeping the Mafia out, but to little avail. With appropriate fronts, the syndicate simply took over. The Thunderbird became Lansky's baby although he had slices of many other places. The Desert Inn was largely owned by Moe Dalitz and others of the Cleveland mob.

The Sands was controlled behind the scenes by Lansky, Joe Adonis, Frank Costello and Doc Stacher. Actor George Raft was brought into the deal, and singer Frank Sinatra was sold a 9 percent stake. Sinatra was said to have been extremely flattered, but as Stacher later stated, "The object was to get him to perform there, because there's no bigger draw in Las Vegas. When Frankie was performing, the hotel really filled up."

The Sahara and the Riviera were controlled mainly by the Fischetti brothers, Tony Accardo and Sam Giancana, the rulers of the Chicago Outfit. The Dunes was a goldmine for Raymond Patriarca, the top mafioso in New England.

When the Stardust was being built, Dalitz started complaining that it would drain funds away from his Desert Inn. Dalitz looked like he was ready to solve the problem the way a problem was handled during the bootleg wars of Prohibition, but Lansky suggested a meeting to try to iron out the problems. Representing the Stardust interest was mobster Tony Cornero, one of California's pre-war gambling-boat operators, while Dalitz and his right-hand man, Morris Kleinman, were present for the D.I. Winging in from New Jersey was Longy Zwillman. A deal was hammered out so that each group ended up with an interlocking interest in each other's hotels, and when the lawyers got through with it, nobody could really tell who owned what where.

When Frank Costello was shot in 1957, police found a tally in his coat pocket that matched the revenues of the Tropicana for a 24-day period. It was apparently a revelation to the Nevada Gaming Control Board that Costello and his longtime partner, Dandy Phil Kastel, were the chief owners of the Trop.

Caesar's Palace was a case unto itself. Its decor and architecture certainly evoked images of ancient Rome, or as comedian Alan King put it: "I wouldn't say it was exactly Roman—more kind of early Sicilian." In any event it had a Roman legion of Mafia investors, among them Accardo, Giancana, Patriarca, Jerry Catena (one of Vito Genovese's top aides), and Vincent "Jimmy Blue Eyes" Alo (a longtime buddy of Lansky's). The biggest investor of all may well have been Jimmy Hoffa and the Teamsters Union's pension fund, with at least $10 million sunk into the Palace (and another $40 million sprinkled around town). The money was in the form of "permanent" loans and undoubtedly contributed to the retirement of more aging mafiosi than over-the-highway truckers.

In the 1960s billionaire Howard Hughes started buying up hotels, collecting 17 Nevada casinos in all. The big mobsters got out, but most of their underlings remained in place; it was a matter of maintaining required "expertise." Things however went wrong for Hughes. He had expected to make more than 20 percent on investments from the lavish joints but never did better than 6 percent, and by 1970 his holdings were several million dollars in the red. After Hughes bailed out of Vegas, the mobsters returned to the scene.

Although the boys suffered some convictions in the late 1970s, the FBI launched the real assault on the Mafia's hold on Las Vegas casinos in the following decade. As a result numerous casinos that had previously been "mobbed up" were sanitized and taken over by legitimate owners. Among those establishments were the Tropicana, the Stardust, Desert Inn, Circus-Circus, Caesar's Palace, the Fremont, the Aladdin, the Sands, the Riviera and the Sundance. Two others, the Dunes and the Marina, were torn down.

The biggest loss of all to the mob was the Stardust, which was a gold mine to the Chicago Outfit, the skim being absolutely fabulous. It was taken over by the reputable Boyd family, who were surprised by its huge profits, with every penny of income recorded. Ex-FBI agent William F. Roemer Jr., longtime senior agent of the FBI's organized-crime squad in Chicago and an expert in Las Vegas doings, said, "The amount of skim had been so heavy that the profit and loss statement did not present a true picture of the gold mine that the Stardust was."

The FBI investigations into Las Vegas skimming took a decimating toll on the mob. Organized crime control of the Tropicana Hotel was broken with the convictions of several Kansas City mob chiefs. A second more sweeping probe uncovered control of a number of casinos by Chicago, Kansas City, Milwaukee and Cleveland mobs. Among those netted in the investigation were Joey Aiuppa, the top boss in Chicago; John Cerone, the Chicago underboss; two other Chicago capos; Frank Balistrieri, the boss in Milwaukee, and the top leaders in Kansas City, along with a top figure in Cleveland. All drew huge sentences and probably faced the rest of their lives behind bars.

In 1994 Roemer declared organized crime presence in Vegas was nowhere what it had been, although he said "concerns remain" regarding three other hotels.

See also FLAMINGO HOTEL; GREENBAUM, GUS; HUGHES, HOWARD; SIEGEL, BENJAMIN "BUGSY"; SPILOTRO, TONY "THE ANT"

LAST Chance Tavern: Kansas City gambling den

The most controversial gambling den in the 1940s and 1950s probably couldn't have existed anywhere but in Kansas City, often considered the most crime-ridden city in the Midwest, surpassing even Chicago.

The Last Chance Tavern was situated in a building on Southwest Boulevard right on the Missouri-Kansas state line. In Kansas City—where the blatant was the ordinary in the operation of the old Pender-

gast Machine, and the one run later by Charley Binaggio—it was hardly surprising that Binnagio himself was a partner in the ownership of the building.

After Binaggio's murder in 1950, the Kefauver crime hearings came to Kansas City to probe the almost limitless corruption in the town. The senator found the Last Chance a typical example of conditions in Kansas City. He later observed with wry humor:

The Last Chance was an intriguing establishment located on the border between Kansas and Missouri with a thin wall right on the state line. When the cops from one state would come to "raid" it the gamblers with great hilarity would shift their equipment over to the other side and carry on without interruption. Cops from both states never seemed to arrive at the same time, so everybody had a lot of fun and Binaggio's gang made a lot of money. Senator [Charles W.] Tobey did not think much of this operation. After we pried from Eddie Osadchey how the racket worked, Tobey exploded: "You know, Mr. Chairman, if I had been one of those cops, I would have gone across and brought them back and knocked them cold and said, 'Here they are in Kansas territory.'"

Senator Tobey, considered the innocent among the probers, failed to understand the depth of corruption the Last Chance represented, and the fact that Charles Binaggio may well have been an actual member of the Mafia (with other Kansas City mafiosi such as reputed boss Jim Balestrere and Tano Lococo said "to own a piece of him"). Binaggio was the only mafioso in American history to achieve the highest quasi-official status of a political boss.

See also BINAGGIO, CHARLES

LaTEMPA, Peter (1904–1945): Genovese murder victim

According to a mob adage, it was as well for a stool pigeon to wind up dead as it was to be under protection in Brooklyn. Surely canary Abe Rele's "flight" out the window of a Brooklyn hotel is a case in point. Surely, too, was Peter LaTempa's death a demonstration of the long reach of the mob in Brooklyn.

Mobster leader Vito Genovese had fled from New York to Italy in 1937 to avoid prosecution for the murder of Ferdinand Boccia. The case against the boss was based primarily on the evidence of Ernest "the Hawk" Rupolo, who was doing a nine-to-20-year sentence for attempted murder in a job assigned him by Genovese. To earn his release, Rupolo revealed details of the Boccia kill. Rupolo's word was not enough by itself to convict Genovese, and there was no supporting circumstantial evidence. There was, however, another witness to the murder, a hoodlum named Peter LaTempa. Pressure was put on LaTempa to talk, and, by the time Genovese had fled the country, LaTempa did, feeling his squealing no violation of omerta because Genovese would never be prosecuted anyway.

Later, near the end of World War II, Genovese was taken into custody by the U.S. Army and was returned from Italy on January 8, 1945. Like a shot from a cannon, LaTempa turned up at the Brooklyn district attorney's office, demanding to be put in protective custody. He was lodged in the Raymond Street jail. On January 15, one week after Genovese's return and long before the court case against him could get started, LaTempa died behind bars. He had taken his regular medication for gallstones and gone to sleep. He never woke up. An autopsy showed he had taken enough poison "to kill eight horses."

How LaTempa's medication had been tampered with was, of course, never determined. With LaTempa's death, the case against Genovese went out the window. When he beat the murder raps—as he had to since only Rupolo testified against him— the presiding judge railed at Genovese: "By devious means, among which were the terrorizing of witnesses, kidnapping them, yes, even murdering those who could give evidence against you, you have thwarted justice time and again."

Some justice was served though. Rupolo eventually was murdered as well.

See also RUPOLO, ERNEST "THE HAWK"

LA Tuna, Texas, Federal Correctional Institution:
"Stool pigeon haven"

Called "Stool pigeon haven," the La Tuna Federal Correctional Institution has been home to the three most valuable and notorious informers in recent history—Joe Valachi, Vinnie Teresa and Jimmy "the Weasel" Fratianno—as well as a number of lesser informers.

La Tuna, 21 miles from El Paso, Texas, looks much like a Spanish adobe church. Dry, hot and miserable, it is not exactly a country club. In fact there

are many other institutions where informers might better be kept, and probably with better physical security.

But many of the informers themselves felt the explanation for the choice of La Tuna was the fact that the guards there were probably the most reliable in the federal prison system. Almost all the guards are of Mexican descent. Teresa was at first very leary of them. He reasoned that all of them came from impoverished circumstances, and he feared the mob would dangle a huge amount of money in front of them, and he would quickly be a dead man. Teresa soon learned his apprehensions were unfounded. The guards proved friendly, understanding and above all, not on the take—a fact that impressed him very much.

Joe Valachi was equally as frightened at first on being in La Tuna and, in fact, when Teresa arrived, he was certain that Vinnie was a hit man commissioned by the mob to kill him. This upset Teresa, for a very good reason. Valachi had killed one federal prisoner in Atlanta whom he thought was out to kill him. Teresa worried that Valachi would try to whack him out. Finally, the pair had a "sit-down" and after the earnest discussion decided they could trust each other.

Valachi still suspected Mafia treachery and when a small plane circled overhead while he and Teresa were taking the sun on a patio reserved for trusties or honored prisoners, he became convinced it was a Cosa Nostra plane with a hit man who was going to blast the two of them. The FBI checked out the mysterious plane and later advised guards to fire some shots if it ever flew over too low thereafter. The plane never reappeared.

Teresa and Valachi became close friends, a situation important to the latter because he never received any visitors. His wife and family had forsaken him, a situation about which he said, "I don't blame them."

Valachi still harbored illusions that some day he would be released from La Tuna, and he became embittered when it never happened. But he had killed a federal prisoner; there was no way the government could ever let him go free. And he was a dying man, suffering from cancer. When Valachi was on his deathbed, Teresa was allowed access to his cell to help nurse and care for him.

Later Jimmy Fratianno occupied the "Valachi suite" at La Tuna, and it was here that most of the interviews for his memoir, *The Last Mafioso* by Ovid Demaris, were conducted.

La Tuna is now a byword in the criminal world, a symbol of the fact that the federal government can protect informers, that as a stool pigeon haven it is completely safe—though not, perhaps, the country club that many of the Watergate offenders occupied.

LAUNDERING: Circulating underworld illegal money

Money comes easy to the mob. Using the funds can be somewhat tougher.

The Mafia and its allies have developed the methods of laundering money to a fine art. A literal flood of money is obtained from the Mafia's casino skimming rackets as well as from narcotics and the like. The amount of cash is so great that the mob would have trouble spending it without "laundering," mainly by gaining control of businesses that have a huge cash flow. Amazingly, mafiosi all over the country are heavily involved in car washes and report the income. Not only that, but they overreport the number of cars they wash simply to justify a larger inflow of funds. IRS agents once staked out a car wash suspected of being a Mafia front—an operation washing more than cars. During a blizzard that dumped 18 inches of snow in a brief period, management reported washing 120 cars although not a single car was seen going into the car wash.

Banks play an important role in laundering the Mafia's huge flow of cash, and the mob is known to have set up a number of banking institutions, especially in Florida, some run by men with very close friends in Washington. More recently, the mob transferred many of its laundering operations to Puerto Rico because a government crackdown in Miami, called Operation Greenback, created too much heat. Drug smugglers are particularly active in Puerto Rico, and even buy up winning lottery tickets at a premium on the black market as yet another supposed justification for their large incomes.

Of far greater importance are Swiss banks. The mob ships in huge amounts of money that only such bigtime operators as the "gnomes of Zurich" can absorb. There are many ways funds are laundered through Swiss banks. One is investing, tax free, in blue-chip American firms, as well as playing anonymous and rather dirty tricks in the stock market, such as rigging prices. Another way is the loan-back. In their book, *Dirty Money,* Thurston Clarke and John Tigue Jr., who investigated and prosecuted a wide range of international swindlers and rogues, describe the loan-back thusly:

A New Jersey gambler has a half million dollars in profits salted away in a numbered Swiss bank account. He buys a string of car washes for $1 million, financing it with $50,000 down and $450,000 with a legitimate first mortgage. Then he "borrows" the other half million from his Swiss bank. Actually he is borrowing his own money and repays the half million as though it too is a legitimate loan. That means he has interest charges. This charade allows him to pay himself interest and deduct the interest at the same time from his taxes. Thus, he brings his money back into the country. True, it eventually goes back out of the country. But that is no problem; once he pays off the loan to himself, he can relend it again to himself. The Swiss bank does not necessarily know it is involved with a mobster because the loans go through a number of layers of insulation through dummy foreign companies.

One New Jersey mobster, Angelo "the Gyp" DeCarlo, was known to have laundered $600,000 through Swiss bank accounts established for him by Gerald Zelmanowitz, a confessed dirty-money business consultant to organized crime. (DeCarlo eventually went to prison for 12 years, but was pardoned in 1972 after doing only 33 months by President Richard M. Nixon. Nixon about that time was himself becoming acutely aware of the problems of laundering money, which as John Dean informed him, "is the sort of thing Mafia people can do," and the president replied thoughtfully, "maybe it takes a gang to do that [launder money].")

The fact that Swiss banks maintain what are known as "omnibus accounts" at American brokerage houses makes it easy for the Mafia to buy into U.S. business by purchasing anonymously the shares of blue-chip companies. Naturally, if they make a profit they pay no capital gains tax because there are no records of their names in the United States tying them to the stock purchases, and the Swiss banks are bound by their country's laws never to reveal their identities to the American government. The mob can also play hob with margin rules and disguise insider trading simply by buying blocks of stock through different Swiss banks. Then by exercising their proxies, they can determine how a company will be run.

Laundering is a sophisticated business, and the mafiosi involved in it have come a long way from the crude Black Hand rackets and bootleg wars which got them started. But cash has no name. It is anonymous and it can move around the world without a trace if the person who owns it wants it that way. The mob wants it that way and will pay the operating costs.

LEPKE, Louis (1897–1944): Syndicate leader

In the 1930s, Louis Buchalter, better known as Louis Lepke, was the foremost labor racket czar in the United States. He was also the only top-echelon leader of the national crime syndicate to be executed, dying the richest man in American history ever to go to the electric chair.

Only 5 feet 7 inches and of slender build, Lepke usually dressed conservatively, and looked entirely the part of a dignified successful businessman rather than the greatest high-level exponent of violence in the rackets. As a Lepke associate once put it, "Lep loves to hurt people." His behavior was in counterpoint to his very nickname; "Lepke" derived from "Lepkeleh," an affectionate Yiddish diminutive meaning Little Louis (which his mother used). In the real world, the name Lepke was not held in affection but rather in unadulterated fear.

In the early 1920s, while most underworld characters were attracted to the fast, easy money available through bootlegging, Lepke, as a protégé of criminal mastermind Arnold Rothstein, opted for a field with more permanence. Realizing that if he worked fast and ruthlessly he could have the labor racketeering field in New York sewed up tight, he moved quickly into the lush garment industry. Eventually, through control of the tailors and cutters unions, he milked millions from the field. It was little wonder Thomas E. Dewey referred to him as the worst industrial racketeer in America, and J. Edgar Hoover, belatedly and ever-hopeful of being number one with the press, labeled him "the most dangerous criminal in the United States."

In the early 1920s, Lepke and another thug, Jacob "Gurrah" Shapiro, with whom he had worked since their teenage days, linked up with Little Augie Orgen, the top labor racketeer of the period. Little Augie concentrated on offering strikebreaking services to garment industry employers and unions, which Lepke realized was merely scratching the surface of the opportunities in the field. Little Augie stood in the way of Lepke's success, and in 1927,

Lepke and Shapiro and a couple of accomplices ambushed and killed him.

Lepke and Shapiro began concentrating on the union side of the business, eventually taking control of a number of locals, gaining them real leverage at blackmailing employers while at the same time hiking and skimming the membership's dues.

They moved into the bakery drivers union. Thereafter if the bakers wanted to ensure that their products got to market fresh, they had to cough up a penny-a-loaf "tax." This was followed by extension of operations into other industries, often in league with Tommy Lucchese, a mobster with close links to Lucky Luciano. Soon levies were extracted from such businesses as poultry, cleaning and dyeing, handbags, shoes, millinery, leather and restaurants, until payments to Lepke amounted to an estimated $10 million annually just for "protection."

A very close associate of Meyer Lansky, Frank Costello, Joe Adonis, Dutch Schultz and Luciano, Lepke was part of the leadership that formed the new crime syndicate. All the founders recognized the necessity for having an enforcement arm within the setup, and Lepke was given charge of what would

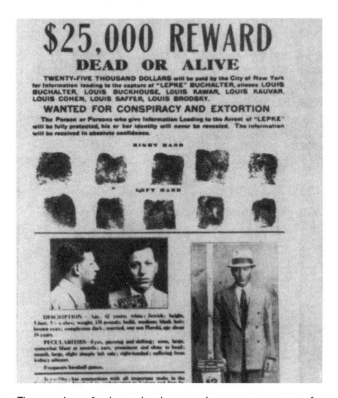

The manhunt for Louis Lepke was the most intensive of the 1930s, ending only when other crime leaders tricked him into surrendering.

later be dubbed by the press, "Murder, Inc.," which ultimately carried out hundreds of hits. As his top aides, Lepke chose the brutal Shapiro and the even more kill-crazy Albert Anastasia.

With the money rolling in through his 250-man army of sluggers and gunmen, Lepke rose to multi-millionaire class and lived life accordingly. He resided in a plush apartment in mid-Manhattan and maintained chauffeur-driven cars for trips to race-tracks and nightclubs. He wintered often in Florida and California or sojourned in Hot Springs, Arkansas, where Owney Madden controlled the town as a safe haven for important gangsters. Once Lepke traveled there with Luciano, Lansky, Adonis and Tammany Hall leader Jimmy Hines.

Courting the spotlight was not wise, but the arrogant Lepke was sure he had the power to square his legal problems. Real trouble developed when Thomas E. Dewey, then an ambitious special prosecutor, took after him. While Dewey concentrated on bakery extortion, the federal government stalked Lepke for restraint of trade. Then the Federal Bureau of Narcotics picked up on hints that Lepke headed a massive narcotics smuggling operation that included extensive bribing of U.S. customs agents. Arrested and put out on bail, Lepke decided to go into hiding. While he was hunted nationwide, he was secreted away in various Brooklyn hideouts by Anastasia, and he continued active control of his union rackets.

The manhunt put extreme pressure on the entire syndicate and hamstrung their rackets. The heat was really on. In New York, Mayor Fiorello La Guardia supplied still more heat, ordering police commissioner Lewis J. Valentine to start a war on hoodlums. Soon all the crime families were being badly hurt. Word was sent to Luciano, convicted by Dewey and confined in Dannemora Prison, but still the number one voice in the mob.

Luciano readily decided that Lepke had to surrender for the good of all. However, he knew as well as Lepke that the authorities had enough to put him away for life. Luciano decided Lepke had to be conned into coming in. Through Longy Zwillman, the New Jersey crime boss, it was arranged for a hoodlum Lepke trusted, Moe "Dimples" Wolensky, to carry a message that a deal had been worked out with J. Edgar Hoover. If Lepke surrendered directly to the FBI chief, he would be tried on federal narcotics charges and let off with five years. State charges would be dropped.

Lepke believed the fairy tale and surrendered on a Manhattan street on August 24, 1939, to gossip columnist Walter Winchell and Hoover. Almost from the second he entered Hoover's car, Lepke knew he had been doublecrossed. Hoover had not consented to any kind of deal. Lepke got 14 years on the narcotics charge but was also turned over to Dewey, who pinned a 39-years-to-life sentence on him.

That did not end Lepke's problems, although he maintained enough power from behind bars to have Dimples Wolensky murdered for his part in the treachery. The Murder, Inc., investigation broke. Through the evidence offered by the famed "canary" of the murder troop, Abe Reles, and others, Lepke was linked to the 1936 murder of a candy store owner named Joe Rosen, a former trucker in the garment industry forced out of business by Lepke. Rosen kept talking of going to the district attorney's office. Lepke, in turn, ordered three of his top aides—Mendy Weiss, Louis Capone and Pittsburgh Phil Strauss—to silence him permanently. Seventeen bullets did the job.

Even though Reles "went out the window" on November 12, 1941, in a mysterious fall from a hotel where he was under constant guard by a police detail, there was more than enough evidence to convict and sentence to death Lepke, Weiss and Capone, Strauss in the meantime was sentenced to the same fate for other murders.

With various legal moves Lepke stalled off his execution until March 1944, a presidential election year. Shortly before his execution was slated, the newspapers were filled with accounts that Lepke was talking and there was speculation that if he really "opened up," he could blow the lid off politics right up to the White House. Lepke could identify, said the press, "a prominent labor leader, powerful in national politics, as a man who had inspired several crimes." The FDR White House in 1944 was known for its "clear it with Sidney" motto, referring to Sidney Hillman, president of the Amalgamated Clothing Workers and Roosevelt's most intimate labor advisor. It was an open secret that Hillman was the labor leader referred to in the Lepke stories. Lepke himself was quoted as saying: "If I would talk, a lot of big people would get hurt. When I say big, I mean big. The names would surprise you."

On the day of Lepke's execution the labor rackets czar requested a meeting with Manhattan District Attorney Frank Hogan. After a 90-minute conference, Hogan communicated with Dewey, who was now governor and an active candidate for the presidency in that year's election. At 9:50 P.M. Dewey suddenly granted a 48-hour stay of execution. Newspaper speculation was rife. The *New York Mirror* declared the stay was granted because "Lepke offered material to Governor Dewey that would make him an unbeatable presidential candidate."

That was what Lepke himself clearly believed, but by two days later nothing more had happened. That afternoon Lepke released a statement through his wife who visited his death cell. It said, "I am anxious to have it clearly understood that I did not offer to talk and give information in exchange for any promise of commutation of my death sentence. I did not ask for that! . . . The one and only thing I have asked for is to have a commission appointed to examine the facts. If that examination does not show that I am not guilty, I am willing to go to the chair, regardless of what information I have given or can give."

Obviously, Lepke had done some talking, from his point of view offering a deal that the ambitious Dewey could not refuse. At the same time Lepke's public statement was clearly intended to inform the syndicate he had not and would not talk about other top crime bosses. By having his wife read the statement he was also telling the mob he understood that his life and hers and the rest of his family's would be worth nothing if he revealed syndicate secrets.

Lepke still thought his revelations about Hillman and "other political figures," quoted the newspapers, were enough to save him. They did not. It was possible that Lepke had very little on Hillman, no more than that he had agreed to violence in certain union strike situations. There was newspaper speculation that one man had been murdered as a result of this violence. Other leaks indicated that it was a case of mistaken identity and no killing had been ordered. But even if some truly explosive information had been offered against Hillman, Dewey could not have accepted it on Lepke's terms and disregard the rest of organized crime.

Lepke did not understand the politics of the situation. Neither did Burton B. Turkus, the Murder, Inc., prosecutor, who would later write, "To the credit of Dewey, he did resist and he did reject. He would not do business with Lepke, even with the greatest prize on earth at stake—the presidency of the United States!" Dewey had not accepted Lepke's offer because he could not. Far from winning the presidency if he had, it would have certainly guaranteed his defeat. If he had gotten Hillman—if Lepke could have delivered him—the price would be essentially to let such men as Luciano, Shapiro, Adonis, Lansky and Anastasia off the hook. Dewey would have stood as a political opportunist had he made a deal that had not included such gangsters. Lepke had sat in on murder votes with all of them. Dewey would have been passing up murder charges on such ilk to get Hillman and through him FDR and so achieve the White House.

Lepke's statement was followed by silence.

The rest of that afternoon and into the early evening Lepke kept up a jaunty appearance, clearly expecting to win a further delay. "Only late in the evening," Turkus wrote, "with the final minutes of his life ticking away, did he slowly begin to realize that maybe he had relied on the wrong miracle-maker."

At 11:05 P.M. the executions commenced. Louis Capone first, then Mendy Weiss and finally Louis Lepke. He walked across the execution chamber and virtually threw himself into the squat electric chair.

See also DEWEY, THOMAS E.; GARMENT INDUSTRY RACKETS; JEWISH MAFIA; MANTON, MARTIN T.; ORGEN, JACOB "LITTLE AUGIE"; ROTHSTEIN, ARNOLD; SHAPIRO, JACOB "GURRAH"; STAND-UP GUY; WINCHELL, WALTER

LEWISBURG Federal Penitentiary See "MAFIA MANOR"

LICATA, Nick (1897–1974): Los Angeles crime family boss

Nick Licata may have been the only man to become a crime family boss after a hit contract had been issued on his life.

Licata immigrated to the United States from Italy when he was 16 and joined the Detroit Mafia family under Joe Zerilli. He later fell in disfavor for an offense—the details of which law enforcement agencies never determined—and he fled to California. Zerilli issued a contract on Licata and, since he was in Los Angeles' territory, the Mafia boss there, Jack Dragna, was responsible for the execution.

Instead, Dragna talked Zerilli out of the contract and then took Licata under wing. Some say Dragna was bought off. More likely, Dragna recruited

Licata, a capable killer or "worker" to elevate the quality of the Los Angeles outfit. Licata proved to be very good at the art of murder and an asset for Dragna, who later had the further pleasure of teaming the star killer with Jimmy "the Weasel" Fratianno. The pair once took out a Dragna contract victim, Frank Niccoli, by strangling him with a rope in 10 seconds flat. (To hear Jimmy the Weasel tell it, Licata was not really all that good at killing and once stalled on a contract for 18 months until Dragna reassigned it to Fratianno.)

After Dragna died in 1957, while Fratianno was doing a prison bit, Licata was promoted to underboss to Frank DeSimone, Dragna's successor. Now a Los Angeles crime power, Licata was reinstated in Detroit, with the marriage of his son to the daughter of Black Bill Tocco, the most respected capo in the Detroit family.

When DeSimone died in 1968, Licata took over, but the L.A. family had become and would remain known as the "Mickey Mouse Mafia." Licata had been unable to curb the many independent criminals and gamblers working Southern California; his sphere of influence was eroding rapidly. The Chicago and East Coast crime families, who saw L.A.'s weaknesses, moved in on a number of rackets—even though that was supposed to be against Mafia rules.

When Licata died, one newspaper account declared he had been "a true 'Godfather' in every respect." The only possible excuse for such a silly statement was that *The Godfather* movies were so hot right then and one did have to say something topical about Licata. Licata as godfather was more fictional than Don Corleone.

LICAVOLI, James T. "Blackie" (1904–1985): Cleveland crime family boss

James T. "Blackie" Licavoli is perhaps best remembered as one of the first organized crime figures to be convicted under RICO, the federal Racketeer Influenced and Corrupt Organization statute.

One of the large number of Licavoli family members prominent in organized crime in St. Louis, Detroit and Cleveland, Licavoli became boss of Cleveland organized crime after the death of John Scalish in 1976. Licavoli, alias Jack White, had come to Cleveland in 1938 and quickly established himself in the vending and gambling rackets there, in Youngstown and in Warren. Frequently on the defen-

sive, he was subpoenaed to testify at the Kefauver hearings in 1951, but refused to answer questions. Later, he fought rival mobsters for control of Cleveland crime.

Important organized crime came to Cleveland during Prohibition when the smuggling racket there was controlled by Jewish mobsters Moe Dalitz, Sam Tucker, Morris Kleinman and Lou Rothkopf. Dalitz was also well connected with Detroit's Jewish Purple Gang. It was to Detroit that the Licavolis, under Yonnie and Peter Licavoli, came as hired guns from St. Louis.

Dalitz formed a close association with the Licavoli mafiosi and with the Cleveland-based Mayfield Road Mob, a mafia group including Frank and Tony Milano, and Al and Chuck Polizzi. Eventually Dalitz and his closest colleagues moved on to more rewarding climes such as Miami, Las Vegas and Havana, and the Mafia was left to hold the northern cities of Detroit and Cleveland. In a sense the Cleveland Mafia, especially the Milanos, could be said to have been creations of Moe Dalitz.

Through the ravages of age and violence, Cleveland leadership eventually passed to John Scalish, but when he died in 1976, a war erupted between rival factions. One of the chief prizes involved was influence over the Teamsters Union. Whoever controlled the Mafia in Cleveland held powerful sway on the future of Jackie Presser, than a rising power nationally in the union. Control of the Teamsters meant many sources of revenue, not the least of which would be access to vast "loans" from the union pension fund.

By logical mafioso succession, leadership of the Cleveland family after Scalish's death belonged to James "Blackie" Licavoli. But Licavoli's succession was challenged by another ambitious mafioso, John Nardi. Already ensconced in a position of leverage as an officer within the Teamsters local, Nardi moved to edge out Licavoli with the aid of Danny Greene's Irish Gang. One after another, Licavoli supporters were rubbed out, and Licavoli appeared to be in most serious trouble when perhaps his toughest ally, mobster Leo "Lips" Moceri, disappeared permanently, leaving behind his bloodstained car in a hotel parking lot outside Akron.

Other important crime families soon expressed impatience and/or interest in events in Cleveland. Funzi Tieri, the boss of the Genovese family in New York, offered Licavoli help, which was declined.

Blackie understood that when a big family comes in with an offer of aid, it has a bad habit of "staying for dinner," cutting itself in for a piece of the pie. (Los Angeles was a prime example of such a situation.) Licavoli also had to worry about interference from Chicago, especially after that crime family's chief, Joey Aiuppa, declared the Second City neutral and ordered no Chicago soldiers, even those with close ties with Cleveland, to help Licavoli in any fashion. To Licavoli, this meant Chicago was being guided by its own Teamsters policy, and no rules of succession of the "Honored Society" would apply.

To whatever extent Licavoli may have been intimidated by outside crime families, he still managed to fight an effective war. The Nardi foe parked an automobile loaded with dynamite next to his auto outside his union office. When Nardi came out to his automobile, the dynamite car was detonated by remote control, and Nardi killed. A short time later, Danny Greene also went to his reward. Blackie Licavoli had won out; he even enjoyed a measure of independence of both the Chicago and New York mobs.

Licavoli proved to be a cunning boss. He penetrated the Cleveland FBI office and bribed a female clerk to feed him information about organized crime investigations, including the identities of a number of informers. Licavoli was later to tell Jimmy Fratianno, as is recorded in *The Last Mafioso,* "Jimmy, sometimes, you know, I think this fucking outfit of ours is like the old Communist party in this country. It's getting so there's more fucking spies in it than members."

Fratianno, a lifelong friend of Licavoli, was at the time a secret FBI informer, and fear that the Cleveland FBI office leak might reveal his activities undoubtedly was a convincer that he go into the witness protection program.

It was one thing for Licavoli to be philosophical about leaks, but the embarrassed federal government was hardly amused. Not surprisingly, Licavoli became a prime target for a RICO conviction, especially after he beat murder charges in the Nardi and Greene rubouts, as well as state charges of bribery. Licavoli, however, was convicted of federal RICO charges in 1982 and sentenced to 17 years in prison. He died three years later at the Oxford Federal Correctional Institute. It will take a number of years to determine if such RICO prosecutions can kill the Mafia in Cleveland or whether the Mafia structure is more important than whatever leadership is chopped down. Already there is evidence that other organized crime elements have moved in to fill the vacuum.

See also NARDI, JOHN

LINGLE, Alfred "Jake" (1892–1930): "World's richest reporter" and mob victim

Jake Lingle made $65 a week as a police reporter-legman for the *Chicago Tribune.* Yet he owned a house in Chicago and a summer place in Indiana. He wintered in Florida or Cuba and maintained a residence at the Stevens Hotel on Michigan Avenue. An inveterate gambler, often betting as much as $1,000 on a single horse race, Lingle traveled in a Lincoln, complete with chauffeur—certainly the only $65-a-week Chicago newsman ever to do so.

On June 9, 1930, Jake Lingle was shot to death. At first the Chicago newspapers lionized him as a gallant member of the profession, but the facade soon collapsed. The double life of Jake Lingle soon became apparent as the public read that the diamond-studded belt buckle he wore was a gift from Al Capone. Lingle was exposed as being the funnel between the Capone mob and his boyhood pal, Chicago police commissioner William F. Russell. (Russell himself was given a furlough from his post and later forced to resign.) It would later be learned that Lingle held a joint $100,000 stock market account with Commissioner Russell ("Jake's like a son to me," Russell often said) and had had enough resources on his own to lose $180,000 in Simmons Bed in 1929.

Lingle himself was in debt to Capone for at least $100,000 and had been extorting funds from Capone's mobsters as well as those of the rival Bugs Moran gang. Playing both ends against the middle, Lingle used his muscle with the police commissioner to barter gambling and liquor licenses. "I fix the price of beer in this town," Lingle had bragged, and in a sense it was a fact since obviously the cost of protection was a major item in determining what the mobsters had to charge for their suds.

Lingle had explained away his free-spending lifestyle by saying he had inherited anywhere from $50,000 to $160,000—Lingle's story was never quite the same—and that he had sold a lot of stock at huge profits just before the market crash.

Lingle had been a valued asset to the *Chicago Tribune* because he had friends on both sides of the law. He was able to get stories from the Capones, from

Bugs Moran's North Siders and from the police. Indeed, he was considered so close to Russell that he became known as "Chicago's unofficial chief of police."

On the day of his murder, Lingle informed his editor he was going to try to contact Bugs Moran about a gang war story. He didn't try very hard, instead heading down Randolph to catch a train to Washington Park racetrack. With a racing form under his arm, Lingle was puffing a cigar as he headed through the pedestrian street tunnel. A snappily dressed young man worked his way through the crowd behind Lingle. Without a word the young man leveled a revolver to the reporter's head and squeezed the trigger. Lingle pitched forward dead, his cigar still in his mouth, the racing form still under his arm.

Lingle became an instant national folk hero. Rewards for collaring his murderer totaling $55,725 were posted by Chicago newspapers and other civic groups. Harry Chandler of the *Los Angeles Times,* president of the American Newspaper Publishers' Association, eulogized Lingle as a "first line soldier."

Unfortunately, Lingle's image could not hold up to even the most cursory investigation. Lingle's role as a master fixer was soon evident, and it also developed he had secret partnerships with some of the local brothel keepers who cut him in on their business to silence him. There was considerable evidence he had doublecrossed Capone in various illegal deals and was shaking down a number of Capone's followers. Lingle had also promised favors to many political leaders, apparently for hefty payoffs, and then failed to come through for them.

When the facts about him started surfacing, *Tribune* publisher Colonel Robert McCormick alternated between shock and anger as competitor newspapers crucified the late star reporter. In a counterattack, he editorialized, "There are weak men on other newspapers." He set out to prove it by running a 10-part series by a St. Louis reporter, Harry T. Brundige, that named some other errant scribes. One was Julius Rosenheim, a legman for the *Chicago Daily News,* who had been shot to death by gangsters a few months earlier. He had blackmailed bootleggers, brothel keepers and gamblers by threatening to write stories about them in his paper.

There were many others; some worked with Capone, others with the North Side Gang and still others immunely operated their own rackets.

McCormick didn't give up hope of removing some of the taint to his man Lingle; he assigned reporters to dig through probate court records to prove that Lingle had, indeed, inherited much of his wealth. Sadly, it turned out that Lingle did not get $50,000 or $160,000 from his father's estate, but a piddling $500.

Four months later the *Tribune* could report, no doubt with considerable relief, that the police had charged one Leo V. Brothers with the murder. Brothers, alias Leo Bader and "Buster," an accomplished arsonist, bomber, robber and murderer, was imported, the story went, from St. Louis to handle the Lingle hit. Brothers was convicted on the basis of eyewitness identification and drew a 14-year sentence, which was denounced by most newspapers as a ludicrously light punishment and indicative of powerful forces working in Brothers's behalf. Brothers, penniless, had managed to enlist a high-pressure, high-priced defense team of five legal experts, a fact that spurred considerable speculation that Brothers had been recruited to "take the fall" and so defuse public concern about the case. When Brothers heard his sentence, he smirked, "I can do that standing on my head."

As it turned out, he only had to stand on his head for eight years, whereupon he faded away. Until his death in 1951, Brothers remained silent about who had covered the bill for his legal defense. And to his grave he took the secret of who killed Jake Lingle, the "world's richest reporter."

See also BROTHERS, LEO VINCENT

LITTLE Joe: Mafia execution signature

Four bullets in the head, each in two straight rows, or two deuces—in dice game parlance, this is called "Little Joe." In the Mafia world of murders, this is the execution method for welshers, loan shark debtors, and others who have failed to deliver. (When a loan shark victim is so dispatched, the mob enforcers make sure that all other debtors to the mob know the meaning of Little Joe. The system works more effectively than methods devised by collection agencies.)

Perhaps the best-known Little Joe victims were Charley Binaggio and his number-one aide and muscleman Charley Gargotta. In the late 1940s Binaggio was the political and crime boss of Kansas City, Missouri, having effectively wrested power from Jim

Pendergast, the rather ineffective nephew and successor of the deceased and infamous political boss, Tom Pendergast.

A man of limitless ambition, Binaggio looked to achieve complete power in the state by getting his own man into the governorship. That required money and Binaggio got $200,000 from "mobsters in the east," meaning primarily the Chicago Outfit. For that sum Binaggio promised he would see to it that both Kansas City and St. Louis were thrown "wide open" to syndicate operations, especially gambling.

After the election, won by his candidate Forrest Smith, Binaggio found he couldn't deliver on his promises. He begged for more time. The crime families agreed to a short extension, but warned him either to keep his promises or repay their investments. Binaggio could do neither and in April 1950 both he and Gargotta were found murdered in Binaggio's offices at the First Democratic Club. Both men had been shot four times in the head, in two neat rows of two bullet holes each. Little Joe.

LOAN-SHARKING

Aside from gambling, loan-sharking is believed to be the prime source of steady income to the Mafia. Its popularity with the underworld lies in its simplicity—no heavy equipment is needed to operate, merely money, brass knuckles, an ice pick, a knife or gun. And its practice is widespread. The New York State Commission of Investigation established that "one hundred twenty-one of the high echelon members of the five recognized criminal syndicates operating in great New York were engaged in loansharking."

Also called shylocking or six-for-five, the loan shark racket can generally produce a profit of up to 20 percent *per week* and sometimes even higher. Under six-for-five, for every $5 a borrower gets he must return $6 the end of the week. Magnanimously, the loan shark will allow his victim merely to pay back $1 and keep the $5 loan in force another week.

Loan-sharking is especially lucrative with compulsive gamblers. Sometimes the gamblers score big and pay back the loan the same day or overnight. (It is customary to allow such debtors off the hook for a mere five-and-one-half for five for overnight use.) But most face paying at the weekly rate. In one New York investigation, it was found that the syndicate

was netting 3,000 percent interest. In Dallas, a less expensive mob shylock let lenders off for a mere 585 percent annual rate. A man borrowed $20 to pay a doctor and was charged interest of $2.25 weekly. After nine years he had paid back $1,053 and still had the $20 debt to take care of. These represent loan-sharking rates in the ghettos. In the corporate white-collar world, syndicate loan sharks can be a bit more competitive, offering businessmen and the like, hard up for large amounts of cash, loans at a mere 5 percent per week interest.

Crime-family loan-sharking operates on three levels. At the top is the family boss, who generally finances the operations himself, making money available to his capos (lieutenants) for about 1 percent weekly interest. The boss's net comes to 52 percent a year, not bad considering it is loaned risk-free. As far as the boss is concerned, his capos have accepted full responsibility for his money. If they fail to keep up his interest payments or fail to return the entire capital if required, they know they will be "hit in the head."

The capos, as the second echelon, relend the money to lower-rank members of the mob at anywhere from 1.5 to 2.5 percent a week. These soldiers then make their money by collecting interest at 5 percent or more a week, depending on what the traffic will bear.

As collateral, the borrower puts up no security at all—other than his body and those of his family. Loan sharks typically employ "leg breakers" to see that the "vigorish," or interest, is paid on time. The idea that debtors who fail to make their payments always end up dead is an exaggeration. A corpse cannot repay a loan, whereas a debtor with a few broken limbs can. Occasionally, though, it is good business to kill off a welsher as an example, and generally the victim owes very little.

Sometimes limb-breaking is unnecessary. In a well-documented case of a corporate executive with considerable assets, the mob thought better of using violence to get its money back and then some. The businessman fell behind on vigorish payments of $1,425 weekly to the First National Service and Discount Corporation, 475 Fifth Avenue, New York, a Mafia front. Underworld conferences were held between the backers of First National, the Genovese family, and Santo Trafficante, the Florida crime leader. It was decided that the mob would place its own man in charge of the businessman's plant to aid in recovering the debt. Before long the firm's assets were drained off so that the full loan and considerably more went into Mafia coffers and the company then was tossed into bankruptcy.

In the 1960s the New York State Commission of Investigation heard testimony that Nicholas "Jiggs" Forlano was the biggest loan shark in the city. Forlano was referred to generally as a "shylock's shylock"—a mass wholesaler with a reputation for moving money efficiently and quickly. Forlano was technically a member of the Profaci family but had become so big that he serviced several crime family bosses, who in turn gave him money at the rate of 1 percent a week. Together with his partner, Charles "Ruby" Stein, he was identified by the commission as holding "key positions in the intricate network of criminal usury operations in the New York area."

Forlano gained a reputation of being a tough not to be trifled with. For a time he employed the violence-happy Gallo brothers as his collectors, but he could also handle matters himself. Once he stormed into the offices of another leading loan shark, Julio Gazia, who was in hock to Stein for $150,000. The fact that Gazia was related by marriage to Vito, and his brother Michael, Genovese meant nothing to Jiggs, who announced very menacingly that Ruby Stein wanted his money. Gazia, whose debtors lived in mortal fear of his wrath, was equally as frightened of Forlano and subsequently went into hiding, seeking the protection of Michael Genovese. Eventually, Genovese worked out a settlement that got Forlano and Stein their money.

Forlano's forte was intimidation, a style well demonstrated in an incident related by former Chief Inspector Albert A. Seedman of the New York police. The object of Forlano's terror tactics was Sidney Slater whom Forlano and two other Profaci mobsters came across at the Copacabana. Slater's lady friend left the table on request and the foursome engaged in not unfriendly discussion for a short time.

Suddenly Forlano asked, "What are you doing in a fancy place like this anyway?" Before Slater could answer, Forlano took a swing at him. Something flashed on Forlano's fist. Slater thought it was a ring on his finger, but it turned out to be a steel hook, the kind used by newspaper delivery men to cut the cord around newspaper bundles. It sliced Slater just under his eye.

Slater jammed his napkin to his bleeding eye as a waiter approached and explained it was 4 A.M., closing time, and would they like a last drink.

"No thanks," Jiggs Forlano said, and he and his companions left while Slater sat there, the napkin now deep crimson.

In this particular case the intimidation style backfired, and Slater instantly turned police informant. Among Forlano's loan shark victims that hardly ever happened. They followed the underworld rule of paying the vigorish and keeping their lips buttoned tight.

Loan-sharking thrives today because it is accepted by too many forces in society—the criminals, many police, businessmen who have exhausted their ability to get loans from more traditional and reputable sources. It has also been established that organized crime loan sharks have even been able to subvert portions of the banking community. Through the payment of bribes to bank officers and employees the mobsters have gotten hold of bank funds for shylock purposes, often by getting loans with patently weak collateral. One bank in New York's garment center actually was used as a base of operations by loan sharks.

It takes a certain moral blindness to regard loan-sharking as a minor crime, as indeed many police do, considering bribes from such sources to be "clean graft" compared to narcotics money or payoffs to square homicides.

The pressure exerted by loan sharks is seldom restricted to beatings or leg breakings—and it can be far more demeaning. In Chicago, for instance, the syndicate leaves business cards at certain employment agencies, which are handed out to applicants who don't get jobs. The loan sharks are eager to lend such men money. It is not a high-risk operation; the mobsters know with the right pressure, anyone can be made to sweat until money comes out through their pores. Jam an ice pick next to a victim's eyes and threaten not to miss the next time. Most will repay—even if they have to steal the money from their mothers or put their wives or daughters on the street to turn tricks.

Victimizing the wives of debtors is a Mafia custom, despite the alleged rules about not molesting womankind. A particularly effective collection method is the threat and even the carrying out of the threat to bite off a wife's or daughter's nipples unless the debtor squares his payments.

See also LOAN SHARK SCAMS

LOAN shark scams

The average mob loan shark usually gets his funds from within his own crime family, where the family boss lets out money at 1 percent per week to his capos, who in turn lend it to the street loan sharks at 1.5 to 2.5 percent. Clearly, if the loan shark can produce his own sources of money, he can cut his costs for funds in half. There is little doubt that doctors, dentists and countless other professionals maintain safe deposit boxes jammed with $100 bills, all secreted away from the prying eyes of the Internal Revenue Service. Many of these professional people lend their money to organized crime figures for use in loan-sharking rackets. For this the doctor or dentist is paid 1 percent per week for the use of the money, while the loan shark puts it on the street for anywhere from 5 to 20 percent a week. Still, it is a good deal for the tax dodger. Instead of having hidden money produce nothing, it gets put to work at 52 percent a year—far more than the professional person could hope to achieve if the money were invested openly.

It is common for organized crime figures to insist they are upright citizens and to point to the hosts of professional people, upstanding doctors, dentists and the like they proudly number among their friends. Friends indeed.

Unfortunately, too many so-called respectables have learned that dealing with organized crime is not all sweetness. There are many more of these respectables eager to rent out more money than even the loan sharks need. Thus ripoffs have become common. A professional or business person with a money hoard will approach a loan shark and in due course he will be offered a chance to "invest" his funds. He might start off advancing $25,000 or so. When each week he gets back $250, his appetite is whetted, and he will double, triple, quadruple his investment, depending on his greed quotient. Meanwhile the mobsters are simply returning the sucker a small portion of his own money, inducing him to put up still more. Suddenly the money flow stops. The lender calls the loan shark. His calls go unanswered. There is nothing the sucker can do. He can hardly go to the police and tell them he has been financing a loan shark with contraband money. He would himself face criminal prosecution for tax dodging. Additionally, as a pillar of the community and highly regarded by friends, neighbors and associates, he cannot risk the embarrassment and loss of reputation a disclosure of the facts would cause.

Criminal informer Vinnie Teresa worked this loan shark scam to perfection, victimizing so-called honest businessmen. In one case Teresa took a man with a desire to play the supposedly profitable role of a "silent loan shark" for $30,000, and worked him up to $100,000 within a couple of weeks without even giving him a dime back. When the man started calling him, Teresa snarled in his best underworld tones, "You don't want to wind up in a box, you better not call again. You're a sucker . . . you been taken. Now shut up."

Teresa was never bothered again.

See also LOAN-SHARKING

LOCKSTEP surveillance: Law enforcement harassment

Lockstep surveillance, or "rough shadowing," is a technique of harassment employed by law enforcement agencies, especially against organized crime figures. Designed to make a target crack from the pressure of constant exposure, the surveillance is both obvious and constant.

Probably the most famous target of a lockstep surveillance was Sam Giancana, then boss of the Chicago crime family. In 1963 the FBI conducted a 24-hour watch of his every move as well as that of everyone in his household. The agency, in an effort to gather tip-offs on his criminal activities, had already used illegal bugs in homes, hotels and motels around the country to eavesdrop on his active love life.

Giancana was followed wherever he went and FBI cars maintained a constant vigil outside his house. FBI agents, as many as six at a time, shadowed him, even on the golf course, often playing right behind him and driving balls so close that his game was upset. Once on the sixth green he was so shook up by the FBI agents that he took 18 putts. The surveillance also fouled up Giancana's efforts to run his organization—he liked to issue crime orders on the fairway to underlings playing with him.

Once, seeking to shake off his followers, Giancana took sanctuary in a church, but the FBI men followed him and verbally baited him for his ignorance of the mass ritual. He took his cue from other worshippers on when to stand, kneel and sit. The agents sat behind him and whispered: "Kneel, asshole . . . Sit down, asshole." When such harassment continued at church Giancana had movies made of the FBI following him to St. Bernadine Catholic Church and to Mt. Carmel Catholic Cemetery where he claimed FBI vehicles blocked off both exits, trapping him and other visitors against their will.

In thwarted efforts to lose his shadows, Giancana often only managed to upset himself more. Once he pretended to retire for the night and then suddenly charged out of the back door of his house, threw open the garage door and roared off in his car. Two minutes later, after circling the block to shake the tail, he tried to back his car into the garage at high speed. He managed to hit the garage door casing, crushing a fender. Then, as he got out to assess the damage, he forgot to put on the brake and the car rolled down the street. Cursing, Giancana caught up to it and finally made a successful pass at the garage at more ordinary speed. By the time Giancana crawled into bed, he was more in need of rest than the FBI men.

Finally, Giancana brought a court action to get the FBI to cease lockstepping him. Remarkably, he won, and the agency was enjoined from continuing the practice. The decision was vacated for technical reasons and in the meantime local police agencies took up the chore.

Important gang figures, unlike Giancana, usually don't go to court to challenge possible lockstep surveillance since they will be forced to get on the stand to claim that none of their activities is a cause for law enforcement surveillance. They would then be subject to cross-examination about their activities and thus open themselves to a perjury charge.

The practice of lockstep surveillance is not limited to the FBI and police. It has been alleged that corrupt local authorities have used lockstepping against criminals as a way of getting leverage for bribes. Private detectives have been targeted in personal vendettas as well.

The courts are very much inclined to find for a private citizen who has been subjected to rough shadowing. Perhaps the classic example of this concerned the late author Iles Brody, who was jostled in crowds and awakened by late hour phone calls by private detectives. The lockstepping had been arranged by rich friends of the Duke and Duchess of Windsor in an effort to stop publication of Brody's breezy book *Gone With the Windsors*.

Brody won his case. The results for Sam Giancana were rather different. There are those observers who insist his hauling the FBI into court and loosing a flood of publicity proved upsetting to crime family senior bosses Paul Ricca and Tony Accardo and started the procedure whereby they clipped his leadership role within a couple of years. And some years later Giancana ended up murdered.

LOESCH, Frank J. (1853–1944): Chicago Crime Commission founder

A venerable corporation counsel, a founding member of the Chicago Crime Commission and five times its head, Frank J. Loesch coined the term *public enemy* in the 1920s. Referring to the syndicate gangsters who plagued Chicago, Loesch sought to dispel the romantic aura the yellow press of the city and nation had given gangsters.

In the 1930s the FBI director recoined the term for such armed stickup men as John Dillinger, the Barker Brothers, Baby Face Nelson, Pretty Boy Floyd, Clyde Barrow and Bonnie Parker, and Machine Gun Kelly. Experienced crime observers have snickered at Hoover's description of public enemies, which never included the real enemies whose depredations looted the pockets of every person in the country—the syndicate gangsters like Luciano, Costello, Lansky, Lepke, Schultz, Anastasia and others. Some said Hoover, who in the early 1930s and indeed for decades thereafter denied there was any such thing as organized crime, shifted the emphasis to distract public opinion from syndicate to freelance crime—and in all but a few cases, relatively trivial and overrated gangsters, stumblebums of crime, like Machine Gun Kelly. Machine Gun never fired his weapon at anyone, ever, in his career.

Loesch saw the syndicate mobsters as the prime opponents of law and order, and combatted them with direct action. He was one of the few citizens Capone, number one on Loesch's list, either feared or respected. It was Loesch who went to Capone following the bomb-throwing, April 1928 Republican primary in which professional terrorists on both sides, most Capone mobsters, murdered party workers, bombed the houses of candidates and intimidated voters. The police did nothing and appeared ready to do nothing again in the November elections.

"Now look here, Capone," Loesch demanded, "will you help me by keeping your damned cutthroats and hoodlums from interfering with the polling booths?"

"Sure," Capone announced benignly. "I'll give them the word because they're all dagos up there, but what about the Saltis gang of micks on the West Side? They'll have to be handled different. Do you want me to give them the works, too?"

Loesch, not to be outdone, said he would be delighted.

"All right," Capone said. "I'll have the cops send over squad cars the night before the election and jug all the hoodlums and keep 'em in the cooler until the polls close."

Capone kept his word and the police dutifully followed orders, sweeping the streets in an election day dragnet.

"It turned out to be the squarest and most successful election day in forty years," Loesch was to say later. "There was not one complaint, not one election fraud and no threat of trouble all day."

It was of course an awesome display of raw power by the greatest mob leader in America—but also a tribute to the ability of Frank Loesch to exert a considerable measure of influence.

See also PINEAPPLE PRIMARY; PUBLIC ENEMIES

LOMBARDO, Antonio "the Scourge" (?–1928): Capone consigliere

Nicknamed "the Scourge," Antonio Lombardo concealed a Machiavellian bent behind an urbane exterior as a wholesale grocer.

While Johnny Torrio is credited with teaching Al Capone everything he knew, Lombardo, after Torrio's departure from Chicago in 1925, took up the role of mentor. In return, Capone made Lombardo his consigliere and utilized him as his prime adviser.

The Scourge urged Capone to make accommodation with the Irish North Side Gang, even after Capone killers had dispatched their colorfully murderous chief, Dion O'Banion. Since the surviving O'Banions were upset about Dion's passing, Lombardo, with his noted pragmatism, told the North Siders he would arrange to have O'Banion's killers, the hit team of Albert Anselmi and John Scalise, delivered to them. Such double-dealing and treachery was justified on Lombardo's part as being for the greater good of the mob. Capone by his own standards considered himself too honorable to accept such terms. As for handing over the hit men for execution he said, "I wouldn't do that to a yellow dog." It was one case where even a barbarian like Capone would not accept Lombardo's deviousness. Yet the Scourge managed to turn the entire episode into a major underworld public relations coup, declaring it proved that "Big Al's the best buddy any of his boys could ever hope to have."

Capone got to appreciate Lombardo almost as much as he did Torrio. He adopted court tasters to sample his food before eating—a custom Lombardo himself practiced. Ultimately, Capone installed him as president of Chicago's large branch of the Unione Siciliane, a fraternal organization which during Prohibition became a front for bootlegging and other criminal activities in Chicago. Despite his association with Capone and the fact that he fingered many men for death, Lombardo received a rather favorable press, even succeeding in getting published a glowing testimonial he wrote for himself:

> Chicago owes much of its progress and its hope of future greatness to the intelligence and industry of its 200,000 Italians, whose rise in prestige and importance is one of the modern miracles of a great city.
>
> No people have achieved so much from such small beginnings, or given so much for what they received in the land of promise to which many of them came penniless. Each life story is a romance, an epic of human accomplishment.
>
> Antonio Lombardo is one of the most outstanding of these modern conquerors. . . . He was one of hundreds who cheered joyously, when, from the deck of the steamer, they saw the Statue of Liberty, and the skyline of New York, their first sight of the fabled land, America. With his fellow countrymen he suffered the hardships and indignities to which the United States subjects its prospective citizens at Ellis Island without complaint, for in his heart was a great hope and a great ambition.
>
> Mr. Lombardo . . . accepted the hardships as part of the game, and with confidence in his own ability and assurance of unlimited opportunities, began his career. . . .

Such glowing testimony undoubtedly swelled the Capone gangsters with pride at having such a man of words in their ranks. But words were hardly enough to shield Lombardo from attack by Big Al's enemies. On September 7, 1928, Lombardo was killed in a rush-hour crowd at State and Madison Streets, one of the busiest intersections in the world. Two dumdum bullets tore away half his skull. An angry Capone vowed that "the dirty rats who did the job"—the Aiello Mafia mob—would pay for the crime. Capone kept his promise.

LOMBARDOZZI, Carmine "the Doctor" (1910–1992):
Dollar-wise capo

When crime boss Paul Castellano, the reigning head of the Gambino family, was gunned down on a New York street in December 1985, journalists instantly speculated on the most likely masterminds for the hit within the crime family. Speculation was also made on which capos within the organization became likely targets on account of the hit. Generally exempted on both counts was 75-year-old Carmine Lombardozzi, known as the financial wizard of the Gambinos.

A genuine moneymaker, Lombardozzi has earned such nicknames as "the Doctor," "the King of Wall Street" and "the Italian Meyer Lansky." More important, although listed as a capo in the family, Lombardozzi was said to run all the family's lucrative loan-sharking and stock operations, and, as such, was too valuable to be caught up in any power-struggle warfare. One of the conferees at the notorious Apalachin conclave in November 1957, he later was described by Federal Judge Irving R. Kaufman as "an important member of loan-shark and gambling rackets in Brooklyn, and an associate of premier criminals for most of his life."

In the early 1960s Lombardozzi and his partner, Arthur Tortorello, alias Artie Todd, and Joey Grasso, were charged with operating several stock swindles. They went to federal prison in 1963 for parole violation. Through usurious loans to securities business back-office staffs, Tortorello had mounted operations that permitted him to gain control of a number of stock brokerage houses. Through one firm, Carlton Securities, almost $1 million in unregistered worthless oil stock was sold. Also issued was a million shares of worthless stock in an electronics firm.

In 1962 $1.3 million in negotiable securities were stolen from the brokerage firm of Bache & Company. A stock record clerk had been prevailed upon to tuck the stolen stocks under his shirt. (The later Wall Street joke was: "When the Mafia talks, stock clerks listen.") John Lombardozzi, Carmine's brother, was arrested for attempting to dispose of the securities; and what was described as solid information was unearthed disclosing that Carmine had distributed some of the securities which eventually turned up in banks in Switzerland.

Edward H. Wuensche, an ex-convict fence turned informer, told a U.S. Senate subcommittee he was aware of or handled $40 to $50 million in stolen securities between 1958 and 1963, and that on one occasion "I received stolen securities . . . from Carmine Lombardozzi. These securities, I believe, were part of a theft in 1962 from Bache & Co. They included shares of AT&T, General Motors, and Union Oil Co. I believe, in total, there were about 25,000 shares of stock which we got from Lombardozzi."

Wuensche also told the senators: "In the early sixties . . . Mr. Carmine Lombardozzi used to bear the title of 'The King of Wall Street.' . . . Carmine had more young clerks under his thumb who were either trapped because of indebtedness, gambling and otherwise, and if he said, 'Go get me XYZ,' they darn well went in and got it, because they were afraid of losing their lives."

Lombardozzi, according to officials, handled all the loan-sharking operations for the Gambino family and was considered quite facile at rolling over the funds so received and in infiltrating the securities industry. His criminal sophistication gained him respect as an elder of the crime family. Even mafiosi know the wisdom of the tale of the goose that laid the golden egg. It was observed by some journalists that there was no greater show of sadness over a fellow mobster's death than at the fabulous moneymaker's lavish funeral.

See also DEMOTIONS IN THE MAFIA; SEX AND THE MAFIA

LONG, Huey (1893–1935): Syndicate partner and assassination victim

He was the Kingfish of Louisiana politics, serving first as governor and later as U.S. senator. As far as the national crime syndicate was concerned, Huey Long was the best political friend the mob ever had. Long controlled the state—whatever he said went—and he invited New York mobsters under Frank Costello and Meyer Lansky to "come on down, y'all."

When New York City mayor Fiorello La Guardia started busting up the syndicate's slot machines, a desperate Costello had to find a new haven for his one-armed money makers. The mob cultivated Long—or perhaps it was vice versa. In any event, the mob shipped one-armed bandits and other slots by the thousands to Louisiana, soon making New Orleans the illegal slot machine capital of the United States.

And that was only the beginning of the Long-syndicate joint venture. The slots were for the poor folks who could only part with nickels and dimes. Lansky worried about the big spenders, those who could afford to part with big bucks. There was a need to offer them luxuriously equipped casinos so they could play for high stakes. Long was interested, but still a mite hesitant. It meant a lot of payoffs all around, and he was very worried what to do about his own graft payments which Lansky said would equal $3 or $4 million a year.

Huey was already in hot water with the tax people. He railed to Lansky and a top aide, Doc Stacher, that the new president, Franklin Roosevelt, reneged on a promise to call off the tax sleuths. How was Long supposed to conceal $3 million or $4 million a year from the government snoops? Patiently Lansky and Stacher explained to him the wonders of Swiss bank accounts and numbered accounts in particular. Stacher added:

> You have nothing to worry about. We'll take the money there for you with our special couriers and nobody but you and us will know your number. And only you will be able to draw on the account. Your signature and secret code which you give the bank—you don't even have to tell us—will be your protection. To put money in, all we need is the number. To draw it out, you need the code that only you will know. You must never write it down. Keep it in your head.

Long was entranced with this sophisticated fillip to the art of graft and gave the syndicate carte blanche to set up casinos. There were several choice locales—the famous Blue Room at the Roosevelt Hotel and the fabulous Beverly Country Club, both in New Orleans, as well as numerous others. Moe Dalitz had already been opening joints in Ohio and Kentucky, but Louisiana represented the break into the big time, the beginning of countrywide development of casinos by the syndicate—in Hot Springs, Arkansas, on Florida's lush East Coast and elsewhere. The mob had much for which to be thankful to the Kingfish.

Then, in 1935, Long was shot to death by a demented assassin—or perhaps by overzealous bodyguards who shot Long while trying to protect him. If the syndicate thought it at first to be a disaster, the boys soon discovered otherwise. There were plenty of other politicians eager to take payoffs, and they didn't even think as big as ole Huey. Lansky and Costello could count. The payoffs decreased and the

profits soared. They were, indeed, very thankful to Huey Long—for everything.

LOOSE mouth disease: Deadly ailment

Up until recently, before a number of disciplines had been reinstated by the crime families, it was common for mafiosi to talk about other mob guys in ways that incriminated the entire mob. Feds always listened to gossip and the complaints of one wise guy about another. It led to a number of arrests and the crimping of a number of mob activities. By the late 1990s the new family bosses were cracking down on so-called loose mouth disease.

One loose mouth gossip who came to a bad end was Gerlando Sciascia, a 65-year-old Bonanno capo who resented the upward movement of another capo, Tony Grazino. Sciascia groused that Grazino had a "cocaine problem" that was endangering everyone. The trouble was he told too many people about it, and it got back to Bonanno boss Joe Massino, who, the government alleged, solved the problem by disciplining not Grazino but Sciascia for having a loose mouth and in the process for questioning Massino's authority. The gossipy Sciascia was soon found on a Bronx street with three bullet holes in his head. While Massino came under fire in 2004 for the rubout, it was said most mob guys felt it had been wise to remove Sciascia from the scene and prove once again that gossip can kill.

LOS Angeles crime family See MICKEY MOUSE MAFIA

LOVEFELLAS: Mafiosi's woes with cheating affairs

In many respects it struck New Yorkers that they were being treated to the most bizarre Mafia love affair in years. In the clink awaiting sentencing on racketeering charges, the brother of the late John Gotti and the reputed boss of the Gambino crime family, Peter Gotti, found himself enmeshed in torrid accounts of his private love affair with a busty female 20 years his junior. If there was something Gotti did not need at the time, it was a love scandal. Certainly it made him the new Mafia "lovefella." If Gotti struck some as a less-than-imposing mob boss, his role as an aging lothario probably was even more stunning.

It became a tabloid soap opera seldom seen in Mafia love matters. In the old days the mob bosses would call a halt to such embarrassments as forcefully as necessary. Basically, that meant telling the wise guy to break it off. Gotti was the weakest of the new mob bosses (if he really was one). Apparently, unknown to his wife, Gotti had had a 15-year or so relationship with the young Marjorie Alexander and kept his wife from knowing or at least interfering. During his long trials with the law, Alexander, together with two sons, was a fixture in the courtroom, clearly wishing Gotti well and making weekly visits to his jail cell. Some thought she might be an aide to Gotti's defense team. That all went by the wayside when Gotti was convicted and faced a likely 15-year sentence for his transgressions on criminal matters.

Alexander went to pieces and publicly declared what a wonderful guy he was. She told the press, "What does a little Jewish girl from Long Island have in common with Mr. Gotti? I can't begin to tell you how much we have in common. He's my 'bud' and I'm his." There is little doubt that the possibility of losing Gotti panicked Alexander, and she did something mob mistresses should never do, petitioning the sentencing judge for leniency for her lover. The following are two excerpts from her letters to the judge.

While Peter was not a boy scout, he was not, and is not a mob boss. . . . If ever a man doesn't belong in a family with such an infamous name and reputation, it is Peter. He is not his brother, John. Nor did he ever aspire to be. I know Peter for 14 years, now. No one on this earth is closer to him, than I.

Your honor, in plain English, Peter was no more the mob boss of the "et als." than Fredo was the boss of the Corleones in the Godfather.

And while Alexander called him her "soul mate," the real Mrs. Gotti, engaged in a divorce action, penned what one newspaper called a "poison letter asking the judge for the max." She wrote, "His self-serving greed and philandering has put him where he is and deserves to be. . . . I hope you can see through his pitiful act of innocence and weigh all the facts. Only then will you serve justice, and I feel you will."

In March 2004, Alexander, clearly under stress, checked into a Long Island motel. A few days before, she had told a tabloid that Gotti was not happy about seeing his paramour splashed all over the front pages. She had publicly implored Gotti that he shouldn't be mad at her: "I just want people to know who you are." On March 30, Alexander was found dead on the motel bed. She had swallowed a bottle of sleeping pills and tied a plastic bag around her head. In a note to the maid, she apologized for any trouble she caused her and left her a tip.

A mournful Gotti said, "I feel an angel has been taken from me." There was little speculation that the mob had done away with Alexander and, according to one lawyer, little anger by wise guys toward Gotti. As the attorney said, "They seem to feel the whole thing puts a human face on them all"—about as happy a spin the mob has ever put on anything.

In the old days such lovefella sagas or soap operas would have brought strong rebukes from the mob's ruling commission. The idea that wise guys had such messy marriages or personal relationships would produce a "cease and desist" order of sorts, backed up with the threat of violence. Under the new Mafia structures the bosses generally have had to let matters slide. Even one of the new powerhouse bosses, Joel Cacace, acting boss of the Colombo family, might have had problems pulling what prosecutors allege he did. For family business he had two hit men carry out a hit, then had two other hit men take care of the first set of hit men. After that he had another two hit men take out the second pair of hit men. Somewhere along the line the love bug hit Cacace, and he married the widow of one of the first pair of hit men. And in an interesting subplot, Cacace's bride later left him and married an ex-police officer who was then mysteriously murdered. The police list that crime as unsolved.

Mob rules allow any wise guy to carry on an affair of the heart, but the old bosses did not permit mobsters' actions to get out of hand to the detriment of the organization. Paul Vario, a powerful capo in the Lucchese family, expected to be Tommy Lucchese's choice as his successor. Lucchese, however, expected certain decorum from a boss. Vario got into one wild sexual escapade after another, and finally one incident completely teed off Lucchese. Vario paid too much attention to a young beauty in a Brooklyn nightclub, and this set off Mrs. Vario who promptly stripped herself naked and paraded through the club until her husband knocked her out for showing such disrespect for him. The result was that Lucchese wondered how a top leader who could lose such control of his wife could manage a crime family. Vario was scratched from the running.

For all his power even John Gotti was fearful of the wrath of other mobsters when shortly after the death of his sponsor, underboss Neil Dellacroce, and the murder of Paul Castellano that allowed Gotti to become boss of the family, Gotti took the first opportunity to score with his old sponsor's beautiful daughter, who was considered untouchable on the pain of death by her father. That caused nothing but admiration for Gotti among other mobsters, but then some writers reported the affair, which upset relatives of Gotti, and thus peeved the boys tremendously. They had no objection to the writers' reporting on some of Gotti's brutal murders, but letting it be known that he was unfaithful to his wife was just too vicious. The word was Gotti did a lot of sweating to avoid marital problems.

Dino Rastelli, at the time a leading capo in the Bonanno family and later the boss, had nothing but trouble with his wife, Connie, for years. She could not abide his playing around. Once hiding out in Canada, Rastelli took up with a young thing until Connie, back in Brooklyn, heard about it and shot up north, clobbered her rival and warned Rastelli she'd shoot him if he ever did anything like that again. Being from the old school, Rastelli felt that his wife would never really mess around with a made mafioso. He kept on playing with another female in Brooklyn, and an angry Connie emptied a gun at him on a street, hitting him twice. Rastelli now felt it was time to leave his wife, but Connie proved most vindictive. She turned over information she knew about mob drug trafficking and also that the wise guys had found out where some witnesses were held under wraps. The mob had had enough and decided to violate its own rules about wives and put her to sleep.

A recent lovefella to get in trouble is Mikey Scars DiLeonardo who was allegedly hung out to dry after he bounced his mob-related wife of 17 years for a younger mistress. The way Mikey Scars tells it, while he was held in custody by the law, he asked the Gambino family to take care of his mistress and their three-year-old son. Instead, the boys told him to have his mistress, Madelina Fischetti, go on welfare. Talking to the press, Fischetti raged, "They just left him hanging like a piece of garbage. It shows they have no loyalty. I hope they think twice next time somebody gets arrested and help him out."

Mikey Scars is expected to be the most important of the turncoats of the 2000s, and it is silly to think the treatment of his self-proclaimed wife caused him to turn on the mob. It is known he faced a whole series of charges and made a deal. Meanwhile, the mob continued to say it was not supporting any mistress over a wife who has a brother in the crime family and is outraged by Mikey's treatment of his sister. The fact that he was naming names of mobsters alleged to have committed crimes up to murder is the real sin of this lovefella, as far as the Mafia was concerned.

But the lovefellas keep circling the candle and often get burned. For three days in 1999, Dorothy Fiorenza enthralled a Brooklyn courtroom testifying about her affair with Colombo chief Andrew Russo. Russo ended up going to prison, and Fiorenza went into the witness protection program. Some lovefellas just never do get it.

LOVETT, William "Wild Bill" (1892–1923): Irish waterfront racketeer

Under Wild Bill Lovett, the White Hand Gang—the last organized-crime hold by Irish gangsters on the New York waterfront—reached its pinnacle of power. The gang was made up of diverse Irish gangsters who around the turn of the century combined on the waterfront to repel the Italian gangsters seeking to move in on dock rackets. To counter these upstarts, considered part of La Mano Nera, or Black Hand, the Irish organized under the name of the White Hand.

Shortly after the end of World War I, Wild Bill Lovett took control. His slight 5-foot-7-inch, 145-pound frame belied the terror he inspired in the Brooklyn Bridge and Red Hook sections of Brooklyn. He demonstrated his viciousness in the way he achieved leadership of the gang.

The previous leader, Dinny Meehan, had been assassinated in his sleep. Contending for his crown were Wild Bill and a pier rowdy named Timmy Quilty. In the interests of peace and gang unity, the pair agreed on a most democratic method of choosing a new boss. They would engage in a dice contest, and the first man to throw a seven would become the undisputed leader.

The contest was held in a Furman Street bar and was attended by a number of gang members and curious dock hands, much impressed with this new experiment in democracy. Quilty rolled first and came up with a seven. "I'm the boss!" he crowed, flushed at the abrupt end of the "election." Wild Bill

Wild Bill Lovett (handcuffed prisoner on right) was a bloodthirsty if innocent-looking killer who headed the Irish gangsters battling the mafiosi invading the waterfront.

glared sour-faced and liquor-glazed at the ivories. It was clear he was seeking grounds for a recount. Suddenly he pulled an automatic pistol from his waistband and emptied the clip into the still-smiling Quilty. "Now I'm boss," Lovett said and left the bar. No one disputed his election.

Lovett was never charged in the Quilty murder but in all he was arrested 19 times for charges ranging from disorderly conduct to several other murders. However, he spent only a total of seven months in jail for all his capers.

Wild Bill extended the White Hand's power to all the docks from Red Hook to Greenpoint, forcibly ejecting mafiosi who had gotten a foothold. As a first warning to vamoose, he shot foes in a limb. If they came back, he shot to kill. His tactics in extortion were also straightforward. Any dock owner or shipper who didn't pay tribute was beaten, stabbed or shot and his goods and property looted or burned.

White Hand mistreatment of both the dock owners and the mafiosi guaranteed further violence. Wild Bill was the subject of several assassination attempts and he carried seven bullets in his body from such tries. In one instance, it was suspected that the dock owners hired gunmen to kill him. In other cases, it was known the attempts were made by the Mafia.

It seemed Wild Bill Lovett was invincible. Wounded while a machine gunner with the 11th Infantry Division in France during the war (he was awarded the Distinguished Service Cross), the Germans had been unable to kill him. Now the Black Hand Italians—and even the Irish—were having similar difficulty. On January 3, 1923, in a shack on Front Street, two slugs penetrated Wild Bill's chest just above the heart and another just below it. He was given up for dead, but refused to name his assailant. Remarkably, Lovett recovered. Shortly thereafter an Irish gangster named Eddie Hughes was bumped off. There was considerable speculation as to who had put Hughes up to the murder try but Hughes died without telling. When Lovett was asked his opinion, he gave a logical answer: "My enemies."

About this time Wild Bill fell in love. He proposed to Anna Lonergan, touchingly known as "the Irish Rose of the Brooklyn Waterfront." Anna was the sister of Pegleg Lonergan, Lovett's second in command. At first Anna spurned Wild Bill because, she said, she didn't want to be a young widow, but finally in August Lovett got her to consent to marriage by promising to give up his gang activity. The couple went on a Catskills honeymoon and Pegleg Lonergan stepped into control of the White Hands.

Wild Bill and his bride settled down in Little Ferry, New Jersey, living under the name of Brady to mislead any old grudge-bearers. Lovett kept his promise to his wife until October when there were rumors on the docks that he was coming back. This did not please the Mafia who regarded the erratic Lonergan as an easier target than the crafty Lovett. It may also have been that Pegleg resented Wild Bill's rumored resumption of power.

On October 31, 1923, Halloween, Lovett headed for the city, telling his wife he had some business to take care of. He wound up drinking at the Loader Club with an old longshoreman buddy. After they had polished off a bottle of bootleg rye, Lovett passed out at the table while his buddy staggered off elsewhere in search of more filled cups. Five hours later the club was empty save for Lovett stretched out on a bench snoring. Suddenly two armed men charged into the club. Lovett opened his eyes and grinned at them sleepily as they opened fire. Lovett was hit three times. Then a third assassin charged in, waving a cleaver. He brought it down into Lovett's skull. Naturally, the newspapers could not resist reporting that the cleaver man had said, "Trick or treat, Bill."

The Mafia spread the word that Lovett had been done in on the orders of Pegleg Lonergan so he could maintain his hold on the White Hands, but the cleaver killer was in fact an assassin known by the alias of Dui Cuteddi (Two Knives). Afterwards, he was shipped back to Sicily and pensioned off richly for his good works as mafiosi moved to take over the waterfront, a task they completed in only a few years.

See also WHITE HAND GANG

LUCCHESE, Thomas "Three-Finger Brown" (c. 1900–1967): Crime family boss

Considered one of the "classiest" mafiosi in the United States, Thomas "Three-Finger Brown" Lucchese was an ex-con who maintained long and close relationships with many of the nation's top criminals. He also mingled socially with many influential figures of the upperworld—businesspeople, prosecutors, judges, members of Congress—in the guise of a respectable businessman.

Mobsters liked serving under the thin, 5-feet-2-inch Lucchese. His New York crime family was considered to be the fairest and most peaceful, especially when Lucchese stepped into the top position following the death from natural causes of Tom Gagliano, whom he has served faithfully for years.

The mix of peacefulness and Lucchese could be viewed as an odd one considering his early years, ones marked by frequent bloodletting. Born around 1900 in Palermo, Sicily, he came to America in 1911. He picked up the nickname "Three-Finger Brown" (after a famed baseball pitcher of that name), following an accident in 1915 that cost him a digit. His criminal record was replete with arrests for grand larceny, car theft, receiving stolen goods and homicide, but his only conviction came in the early 1920s for grand larceny. In the 1920s, he served for a time as bodyguard for Lucky Luciano when both were working under Joe the Boss Masseria. He may have been Luciano's favorite killer, high recommendation indeed, since the bloodthirsty Albert Anastasia was always eager to please Lucky. Lucchese hit several Maranzano men during the war to win control of the New York Mafia, and may well have been involved in as many as 30 murders.

After Luciano arranged Masseria's assassination, he then used Lucchese as the fingerman in Maranzano's murder on September 10, 1931. That started

Lucchese's rise to the highest levels in the councils of the modern American Mafia.

An extremely popular boss, he exerted great power in the garment industry rackets and ran smooth operations in gambling, loan-sharking, narcotics and the construction rackets. As a corrupter, he was the equal of Frank Costello and had friends and connections at all levels of local government. He was also a close friend of Armand Chankalian, administrative assistant to the United States attorney for the Southern District of New York. It was probably through Chankalian that Lucchese developed a friendly relationship with U.S. Attorney Myles Lane. When Lucchese applied for a certificate of good conduct in 1945, Chankalian served as a character witness. Lucchese's application was granted by the New York State Parole Board.

Through Chankalian, Lucchese also met Assistant U.S. Attorney Thomas Murphy, who gained fame as Alger Hiss's prosecutor. As Virgil Peterson, the longtime head of the Chicago Crime Commission, notes in his 1983 book *The Mob:* "The welcome mat was out for Lucchese at the Murphy residence and Murphy and his wife were entertained as dinner guests at the Lucchese home."

After Mayor Bill O'Dwyer quit to become ambassador to Mexico, Lucchese became an important supporter of the new mayor, Vincent Impellitteri, backing him in his race for reelection in November 1950. Previously, Impellitteri had named Murphy police commissioner, and Lucchese, apparently because of his high interest in law and order, made a personal call at the Murphy home to offer his congratulations. Later when the Murphy-Lucchese friendship became well known, Murphy declared he had been totally unaware of Lucchese's criminal history until 1950.

It was often said that Lucchese support for Impellitteri had been a calculated move to take over the top political connection spot in the Mafia from Frank Costello, who had aligned himself with Tammany boss Carmine DeSapio. There were others, however, who saw in it a typical mob ploy of covering all bets.

Lucchese died on July 13, 1967. He had undergone surgery for a brain tumor a few months earlier and was also suffering from heart disease. His funeral was one of the biggest in underworld history with well over 1,000 mourners. There were judges and businessmen and politicians, and also hit men,

An extremely popular boss, Tommy Lucchese headed a crime family that dominated the New York garment industry rackets as well as the city's gambling, loan-sharking, narcotics and construction rackets. As a corrupter, he was the equal of Frank Costello.

narcotics peddlers, loan sharks and Mafia bosses attending. It was known that the FBI and the New York police would be filming the crowd, and the Lucchese family let the word out that they would understand if big shot Mafia men felt they should not appear. Many did not show up, but they sent emissaries to deliver envelopes of money in condolence. Other important mafiosi refused to be put off, among them Carlo Gambino, by then the most powerful of the New York bosses and a longtime friend of Lucchese, and Aniello Dellacroce and Joe and Vincent Rao. It was for them a sign of respect, perhaps as much as anything for Lucchese's ability, despite his activities, of avoiding conviction for some 44 years.

LUCCHESE crime family

The Lucchese crime family grew out of Joe the Boss Masseria's outfit of the 1920s.

Tom Reina headed up a sub-group that controlled many Bronx rackets as well as the lucrative ice distri-bution business in all of New York City. Reina chafed under Masseria's rule because Joe the Boss demanded such a heavy tribute from him for the rights to operate. When Salvatore Maranzano came on the scene to compete with Masseria for top power, Reina expressed secret sympathy for his cause. Lucky Luciano—then a subchief to Masseria, but secretly working to see that Masseria and Maranzano both continued to weaken each other—became fearful that Reina's switching sides would throw too much power to Maranzano. Also, Luciano had secret allies serving under Reina, Tom Gagliano and Tommy Lucchese, also known as Three-Finger Brown. If a switch took place, Gagliano and Lucchese might be killed by Masseria. The only solution, Luciano and his followers agreed, was to hit Reina before he could switch. Vito Genovese carried out the execution on a Bronx sidewalk.

Masseria was easily convinced that Maranzano had been behind the hit, while Maranzano figured Masseria had discovered Reina's duplicity. Masseria, to the anger of Gagliano and Lucchese, brought in his own man to fill Reina's job, an uncouth mafioso named Joe Pinzolo. Lucchese and another ally murdered Pinzolo, and again Masseria was led to believe it was the work of Maranzano. Now the Luciano forces figured it would be a good thing for Gagliano and Lucchese to switch to Maranzano's side, but secretly so that Masseria wouldn't suspect. This gave Luciano extremely valuable spies in the Maranzano camp.

Shortly after the defection, Luciano's people murdered Masseria and left Maranzano the victor in what was called the Castellammarese War. Luciano was awarded Masseria's old crime family, and Gagliano took over the Reina group with Lucchese as his underboss, a relationship that continued harmoniously long after the murder of Maranzano (in which Lucchese served as the fingerman, Maranzano never suspecting the close relationship between Luciano and Lucchese) and through the establishment of the new national crime syndicate.

Lucchese in tandem with Louis Lepke handled much of the crime family's activities in gambling and in the garment district unions. Lucchese took over the crime family on Gagliano's death from natural causes in 1953 and extended the influence of the family in the political arena. He was a prime backer of Mayor Vincent Impellitteri, the victor in a special mayoral election to replace Mayor William O'Dwyer who had resigned. This victory gave him primacy over Frank Costello and his Tammany Hall ally, Carmine DeSapio, who had backed the losing side. After the election, Lucchese also disclosed his close personal friendship with former federal prosecutor Thomas Murphy (of Alger Hiss fame) whom Impellitteri had named police commissioner. Lucchese died of natural causes in 1967. Leadership passed to Carmine Trumunti, who had had an unspectacular but highly successful career in the rackets in East Harlem. Even Lucchese had not thought highly of him, and he was soon replaced by the much more resourceful Anthony "Tony Ducks" Corallo, described by police as "in gambling, labor racketeering, extortion, strongarm, and murder." Corallo was involved in a graft scandal during the mayoralty of John Lindsay, which involved as coconspirators DeSapio, the ex-boss of Tammany Hall, and James Marcus, a man intimately involved with the Lindsay administration.

Still under Corallo, the estimated 110 "made" member crime group, with a support force of at least five times that many, was allegedly involved in such criminal activities as narcotics, gambling and loan-sharking, with additional dubious dealings in garbage removal, construction and the garment industry. With Corallo facing a 100-year sentence in 1987, he was said by authorities to have named a longtime confidant, Aniello Migliore, as his stand-in. The Corallo-Migliore era did not last long, and the Luccheses slipped into a decade of murderous disputes, turncoat troubles and wholesale convictions.

The low point for the Luccheses came in the 1990s when the organization fell under the sway of boss Vic Amuso and underboss Gas Pipe Casso, who became known in journalistic and legal circles as the "Kill, kill, kill boys." They were determined to salvage all the riches of the family for themselves despite the relentless onslaught by law enforcement. They removed more Luccheses than the authorities could with a reign of terror that appalled even the most cold-blooded members of the crime group. More than any other of the New York families, the Luccheses stayed in disarray, jailed by the feds if lucky or murdered by the the Amuso-Casso combine. By the time Amuso was run to earth and taken into custody, he may well have been rather relieved, probably speculating that Gas Pipe was going to eliminate him as well. With both of the A&C boys sent off for

life sentences, the theory was that the once powerful Luccheses were ticketed to sure extinction.

That did not quite happen. Despite a continuing period of internal disputes, turncoat woes, and wholesale convictions, the family held together by concentrating on the pockets of racket strengths, at times in the garment industry and especially the construction field, in the process sharing the loot in certain situations with either the Gambino or Genovese crime groups.

In 1998 the latest acting boss, Joseph A. DeFede, faced prosecution for garment industry rackets, auguring more intrafamily violence, although the family still was potent with an estimated 120 wise guys and some relatively safe rackets.

In the post-2000 era the mantle of acting boss had passed to Steven L. Crea who was known to his followers as a "genius at construction"—in rackets, that is. When Crea was busted by New York authorities, the spectre arose again of the Luccheses once more slipping back into murderous chaos. That might not happen since both the Gambinos and the Genoveses may need them in reestablishing their powers in certain fields. As one observer put it, the Mafia families are the true nine-live cats of the underworld.

See also CASSO, GAS PIPE, AND AMUSO, VIC; CONSTRUCTION RACKETS

LUCIANO, Charles "Lucky" (1897–1962): National crime syndicate founder

Charles "Lucky" Luciano, without doubt the most important Italian-American gangster this country ever produced, left a far greater impact on the underworld than even the illustrious Al Capone. In 1931, Luciano created what can be called the American Mafia by wiping out the last important exponents of the Sicilian-style Mafia in this country. Together with Meyer Lansky, Luciano was also a founder of the Mafia's "parent" organization, the national crime syndicate, a network of multi-ethnic criminal gangs that has ruled organized crime for more than half a century, a criminal cartel which has bled Americans of incalculable billions over the years.

Luciano was born Salvatore Lucania near Palermo in Sicily and was brought to this country in 1906. In 1907, he logged his first arrest for shoplifting. During the same year, he started his first racket. For a penny or two a day, Luciano offered younger and smaller Jewish kids his personal protection against beatings on the way to school; if they didn't pay, he beat them up. One runty kid refused to pay, a thin little youngster from Poland, Meyer Lansky. Luciano attacked him and was amazed when Lansky gave as good as he got. They became bosom buddies after that, a relationship that would continue long after Luciano was deported back to Italy.

By 1916, Luciano was a leading member of the Five Points Gang and named by police as the prime suspect in a number of murders. His notoriety grew through his teen years, as did his circle of under-world friends. By 1920, Luciano was a power in bootlegging rackets (in cooperation with Lansky and his erstwhile partner Bugsy Siegel) and had become familiar with Joe Adonis, Vito Genovese and, most important among Italian gangsters, Frank Costello.

Luciano was amazed by the old-line mafiosi who counseled him to stay away from Costello, "the dirty Calabrian." But Costello led Luciano astray—by rit-ual mafioso standards—by introducing him to other ethnic gangsters like Big Bill Dwyer and Jews like Arnold Rothstein, Dutch Schultz and Dandy Phil Kastel. Luciano was much impressed by the way Costello bought protection from city officials and the police, which Lansky had already been telling Luciano was the most important ingredient in any big-time criminal setup. Rather than heed the admo-nitions of Mustache Petes, Luciano believed instead the old line mafiosi were the problem and should be eliminated.

Although he maintained separate ties with Lansky, Luciano by the late 1920s had become the chief aide in the largest Mafia family in the city, that belonging to Giuseppe "Joe the Boss" Masseria. Luciano had nothing but contempt for Joe the Boss's Old World ways, with its mumbo-jumbo of the Sicilian Mafia that stressed "respect" and "honor" for the boss and distrust and hatred of all non-Sicilians. In Luciano's opinion, Masseria's prejudice against other gang-sters, Sicilian as well as non-Sicilian, created an unconscionable obstacle to making real profits. Joe the Boss passed up extremely lucrative deals by fight-ing gangsters with whom he could have cooperated for their joint benefit. And Joe the Boss was more intent on waging otherwise long-forgotten feuds with fellow Sicilians based on which town or village they had come from than he was on making money.

In 1928 the Castellammarese War erupted between the numerous forces of Joe the Boss and

Lucky Luciano, one of the founders of the national crime syndicate, in exile in Italy talks to an interviewer. He wiped out the old-line Italian mafiosi and replaced them with what may be called the American Mafia.

those of a fast-rising mafioso in New York, Salvatore Maranzano. Over the next two years, dozens of gangsters were killed. Luciano avoided the conflict as much as possible and instead cemented relationships with the young, second-line leadership in the Maran-zano outfit. It soon became clear that younger mob-sters in both camps were waiting for one boss to kill off the other. Then the second line could dethrone the remaining boss. Luciano soon emerged as the leader of this clique.

The war moved into 1931 with Maranzano win-ning, but Masseria was still powerful. Luciano finally felt he could wait no longer without imperiling his supporters in both camps. Three of his men and Bugsy Siegel, lent by the cooperative Lansky, shot Joe the Boss to death in a Coney Island restaurant. Luciano had guided him there and stepped into the men's room just before the execution squad marched in.

The assassination made Maranzano the victor in the Castellammarese War and, in supposed gratitude to Luciano, Maranzano made Luciano the number two man in his new Mafia empire. Maranzano pro-claimed himself the "boss of bosses" in New York and set up five crime families under him. That was only the beginning of Maranzano's plans. He was determined to become the supreme boss of the entire

Mafia in the United States. To achieve that end, Maranzano compiled a list of two gangsters who had to be eliminated: In Chicago, Al Capone; in New York, Lucky Luciano. Maranzano understood Luciano had his own ambitions and figured to crush him quickly.

But Maranzano was not quick enough. Luciano and Lansky learned of Maranzano's plans in advance. Maranzano was going to summon Luciano and Vito Genovese to his office for a conference. He had lined up a murderous Irish gunman, Mad Dog Coll, to assassinate the pair either in his office or shortly after they left. Instead, moments before Coll arrived to set up the ambush, four of Lansky's gunners, pretending to be government agents, entered Maranzano's office and shot and stabbed him to death.

In a very real sense, Maranzano's death finished the "old Mafia" in the United States. It has long been rumored that Luciano followed up that day with 40 or 60 or 90 other assassinations in an operation given the vivid name of "The Night of the Sicilian Vespers," but this was utter nonsense. No list of victims was ever compiled and actually no deluge of killings was necessary. During the late 1920s, many of the oldtimers had either died naturally or been assassinated by Young Turks of the same persuasion as Luciano. And, since about half of all Mafia strength was centered in the New York–New Jersey area, the key killings to oust the old line were simply those of Joe the Boss and Maranzano.

The remnants of the old Mafia were incorporated in a new national crime syndicate, a more open society that combined all the ethnic elements of organized crime. The new syndicate included such important mobsters among its governing directors as Lansky, Joe Adonis, Dutch Schultz, Louis Lepke and Frank Costello. There is no way the organization could have been Mafia-dominated; it is actually possible that Jewish gangsters may have outnumbered the Italians.

The boss of bosses position was eliminated in the syndicate, although in fact Luciano became the boss in everything but name in the Mafia division. Luciano's original idea was to drop the whole Mafia setup, but Lansky prevailed upon him to keep it, as much to keep the peace as to recognize the substantial Italian subculture in crime. Luciano agreed and in time discovered that maintaining an American-brand Mafia gave him a power base that protected him from any wars among other ethnic elements. Similarly, Lansky could not be seriously threatened by Jewish or other mobsters because they knew he had Mafia troops he could call on.

The syndicate moved to control bootlegging, prostitution, narcotics, gambling, loan-sharking and labor rackets. Independent gangsters could have the rest, which in profit meant practically nothing.

Luciano was now at the top, a dandy dresser and well-known sport on Broadway. He looked menacing, however, thanks to a famous scarring he had received in 1929, when knife-wielding kidnappers severed the muscles in his right cheek, leaving him with an evil droop in his right eye. Through the years, Luciano told many stories of the incident. He once claimed he was kidnapped by drug smugglers who, eager to hijack it, wanted intelligence about a big shipment that was coming in. Or he was nabbed by rival gangsters, including Maranzano himself, and rogue cops who tortured him to get information. Or he was kidnapped by a policeman and his sons because he had taken advantage of the cop's daughter. Whatever the tale, he had survived a "ride"— something few gangsters had; there was a great popularization of his nickname of "Lucky."

In 1936, Luciano's doom year as a free power in the American underworld, special prosecutor Thomas E. Dewey convicted him on compulsory prostitution charges. The underworld insisted it was a "bad rap," claiming Dewey framed the case with perjured testimony of pimps and whores who would say anything to avoid going to jail themselves.

The conviction, from Luciano's viewpoint, was somewhat ironic. In 1936, Dewey was making life miserable for Dutch Schultz and his operations. The Dutchman went before a board meeting of the syndicate calling for Dewey's execution. Luciano opposed the insane idea, which would obviously only produce more heat. When the adamant Schultz stormed out, saying he would go ahead on his own, Luciano obtained a contract on Schultz. It was carried out.

Luciano, Dewey's benefactor, got 30 to 50 years on the prostitution charge, far tougher than any other such sentence in legal history. Nevertheless he continued to maintain active leadership of the syndicate from behind bars. In 1946 Luciano was paroled for what was described by Governor Dewey as his wartime services to the country. It was evident that Luciano did order the mob to help in tightening wartime security on the New York docks. Additional later claims that Luciano was instrumental in enlisting the Mafia in Sicily to aid the Allied invasion of the island are more debatable.

When he was released in 1946, Luciano was deported to Italy. He sneaked back to Cuba later that year to run the American syndicate from that offshore island. From Cuba, Luciano approved the execution of Bugsy Siegel for looting the syndicate's money in building the Flamingo Hotel in Las Vegas. But government agents soon discovered Luciano's presence in Cuba, and he was forced to return to Italy where he continued to issue orders to the states and got his monthly cut of syndicate revenues delivered by special couriers, including Virginia Hill.

With the assassination of Albert Anastasia (1957) and the forced retirement of Frank Costello shortly thereafter, Luciano's influence started to wane. Vito Genovese even plotted to have him assassinated, but Luciano was still powerful enough to form a plot with Lansky, Costello and Carlo Gambino by which Genovese was delivered into the hands of U.S. narcotics agents in a rigged drug deal.

Near the end of his life relations between Luciano and Lansky started to sour. Luciano felt he was not getting a fair cut of mob income, but having suffered a number of heart attacks was in no shape to mount a serious protest. Gradually, he began to reveal to journalists his version of many of the past criminal events in the United States and, obviously, some of his revelations were self-serving. In 1962, he died of a heart attack at the Naples airport. Only after his death was Lucky Luciano allowed to come back to the United States, the country he considered his only true home. He was allowed burial in St. John's Cemetery in New York City.

See also ATLANTIC CITY CONFERENCE; BROADWAY MOB; HAVANA CONFERENCE; *NORMANDIE, SS;* SEVEN GROUP

LUCIANO-COSTELLO crime family   See GENOVESE CRIME FAMILY

LUMPING: Construction racket for skimming federal dollars

In recent decades, federal contracts that mandate the use of union labor have been easy prey for the mob. The scam, known as "lumping," calls for substituting union workers with cheaper non-union labor and backing them up with mob muscle to guarantee the cooperation of union workers on the job. For example, suppose a drywall company gets a multimillion-dollar contract for a housing rehabilitation project. Although the contract calls for union laborers, the company hires an outside firm (which may or may not be mob-connected) to do the actual drywall work.

A major scam outfit of this kind was owned by Sammy "the Bull" Gravano, the later mob turncoat. Using the mob's influence on certain construction unions, Sammy paid off the top union officials and then used cheaper, inferior labor. Sammy and the major contractor holding the contract would split the profit. Most of the other jobs were manned by union workers, and they did not protest, having been warned by their union officers, usually in an effective handwringing act, that the mob was muscling in on the job and that dire things could happen if anyone interfered. Undoubtedly few union workers believed their officers were not involved, but they knew better than to say anything about the scam.

LUPO the Wolf (1877–1944): Black Hander and murderer

While it would be useless to name any particular mafioso in America as the most fearsome of all, Ignazio Saietta would certainly rank as a contender. Better known to the Italian immigrants of New York as Lupo and to the press as Lupo the Wolf, he was the most proficient and deadliest of the Black Hand racketeers victimizing the Italian community with extortion demands.

The Black Hand was not an organized society but was various gangs and freelancers. Lupo the Wolf, however, was a leader of the Morellos, the foremost Mafia crime family in the city in 1900. Lupo the Wolf refined the techniques of the Black Hand extortion method, promoting himself into the very embodiment of evil in the Italian community.

Lupo came from Sicily in 1899 and gained his awesome reputation within the next two years. It was common for Italians to cross themselves at the mere mention of his name. His underlings knew they had to obey him implicitly, never debating an order. Lupo was known to have murdered a young relative on mere *suspicion* that he had betrayed him.

Many of Lupo's victims—at least 60, according to many estimates—were Lupo's Black Hand targets who refused to pay and others were gangsters in competition with Lupo and the Morellos. They were dragged to and tortured in what became known as the Murder Stable at 323 East 107th Street in Italian Harlem. Screams in the night, common in the area, filled neighbors with fear but seldom brought police investigation; the screamers were murdered and buried on the premises.

Lupo attracted police attention fairly often for various murders and kidnappings, but firm evidence was not found. He was finally nailed by the Secret Service for a counterfeiting operation he ran in the Catskill Mountains. He was sentenced to 30 years and after serving 10 was paroled in June 1920. The following year Attorney General Harry M. Daugherty gave him permission to make a trip to Italy. This was not viewed as any sort of favoritism, the hope being he would not return. Lupo did return in 1922 and entered the wholesale fruit and bakery business with his son.

Over the next decade the crime scene changed in America and Lupo clearly did not fit in. His methods, based so completely on terror and murder, were becoming obsolete. The emerging national crime syndicate always tried first to operate through bribery. Lupo was informed he was out, and he retired to Brooklyn where he was permitted to run a small Italian lottery. On his own he formed a protection racket involving bakers. In 1936 Governor Herbert Lehman petitioned President Franklin D. Roosevelt to have Lupo returned to prison for racketeering on a broad scale. Lupo went back to Atlanta to serve out another few years on his original sentence. When he returned to Brooklyn he had no remaining power and died a few years later.

See also BLACK HAND; MURDER STABLE; PETROSINO, JOSEPH

MCGURN, Machine Gun Jack (1904–1936): Capone enforcer

No Hollywood scriptwriter could create a more fitting gangster character than the real life Machine Gun Jack McGurn. In fact, he served as a model for so many movie characters, he—or at least, his estate—should have been able to sue for infringement of copyright. McGurn had it all: the good boy turned bad to avenge his father's murder; the boxer; the high-life sport who dolled himself up like Rudolph Valentino, with his normally curly black hair parted in the middle and pomaded straight; the lady's man, slick with women, preferably blondes, draped all over him; the sheik of the jazz age, a ukelele-strumming snaky dancer. And, in criminal action, he was also dramatic, mowing down foes with the tommy gun—his favorite weapon—and, for the perfect movie touch, often pressing a nickel into the hand of a victim.

Born James DeMora, McGurn was still a teenager when his father was murdered in Chicago's Little Italy by the Genna gang which controlled alcohol production in the area. His father made the mistake of selling his homemade stuff elsewhere for a higher price, and that earned him fatal retribution. Legend has it that the son soaked his hands in his father's blood and vowed revenge. He started preparing for his vengeance by perfecting his shooting aim, popping birds off telephone wires with a Daisy Repeating Rifle.

For a time he tried boxing and became a reasonably efficient welterweight under the name of Battling Jack McGurn, but it soon became apparent he didn't have the stuff to make it to the top, and his manager dropped him. McGurn went back to hunting his father's killers. Since he knew they were Genna men, he finally hooked up with the Capone mob since he knew sooner or later he'd be shooting at Gennas that way.

McGurn became one of Capone's most reliable hit men, especially adept with a newfangled instrument of death, the tommy gun. Thus Battling Jack McGurn was transformed into Machine Gun Jack McGurn. The police at various times credited him with from 25 to 28 known kills, including five or six from the Genna Gang, presumably those whom he decided had taken part in the murder of his father. In the hand of each Genna man, McGurn placed a nickel to indicate his contempt for the dead men—lousy nickel-and-dimers.

Capone relied on McGurn more and more, and in time hardly went anywhere without Machine Gun Jack somewhere nearby. When Capone personally beat the brains out of three gangsters who had betrayed him—Albert Anselmi, John Scalise and Hop Toad Giunta—McGurn did the holding. He was also suspected of being a principal and perhaps the planner of the St. Valentine Day's Massacre.

He was arrested, but charges against him had to be dropped when showgirl Louise Rolfe insisted he'd been with her at the time of the massacre, winning for herself eternal fame as what the newspapers called "the Blonde Alibi." Later that alibi was proved to be false, and McGurn was charged with perjury. The Blonde Alibi was going to be forced to testify against him, but he solved that dilemma by marrying her; she could then legally refuse to do so.

McGurn spent so much money in nightclubs that he decided it would be cheaper to own them, and he eventually had pieces of six or seven of them. One of them was the Green Mill which had done terrific business for an entire year with a young comic named Joe E. Lewis. At contract renewal time, Lewis was offered a hefty raise to $650 a week, but a rival joint, the New Rendezvous Cafe, topped that with a $1,000 offer, plus a piece of the cover charge. Lewis gave notice.

McGurn was irate. "You'll never live to open," he warned Lewis. Lewis did open on November 2, 1927, but eight days later McGurn's promise bore bitter fruit. Lewis answered a knock at his bedroom door and let three men in. Two carried pistols with which they proceeded to beat him, fracturing his skull. The third man had a knife and with it carved up Lewis's face, throat and tongue. Somehow Lewis survived. He had to learn to talk all over again, and it was 10 years before he made it all the way back to the top of his profession.

After Capone went to prison for income tax evasion, McGurn's star started to set. He may have been a Capone favorite, but he was not necessarily the pal of other gang members. He was iced out of a number of rackets and left with little besides his nightclubs. They folded because of the Depression, and Louise Rolfe dumped him as well. He apparently was reduced to getting by in some small narcotics deals.

On February 13, 1936, the eve of the anniversary of the St. Valentine's Day Massacre, McGurn was in a bowling alley with two men when three gunmen walked in. The trio drew guns, so did the pair with McGurn. All five guns turned on McGurn. In McGurn's right hand they left a nickel, and beside the body they left a comic valentine, which read:

> You've lost your job,
> You've lost your dough,
> Your jewels and handsome houses.
> But things could be worse, you know.
> You haven't lost your trousers.

All that gave the newspaper plenty to speculate about. The nickel could indicate the slaying was the work of some remaining Genna men or relatives of those he'd killed. On the other hand, since the shooting happened on the night before the anniversary of the St. Valentine's Day Massacre, that meant Bugs Moran or some remaining North Siders were involved. More likely it was the work of Capone gangsters who wanted him out of the way and knew how to leave some false leads. It was all worth thinking about, but hardly worth doing anything about. Nobody seemed too concerned about finding the killers—and nobody ever did.

MACINTOSH, Hugh "Apples" (1927–): Colombo crime family enforcer

Hugh "Apples" MacIntosh couldn't help but make a big impression. A size-52 suit, but not the least bit fat (he did not like being called fat), this dreaded enforcer was considered, with Carmine "the Snake" Persico, the toughest and roughest at his calling.

Apples started out as an associate of the Gallo brothers, but switched allegiance with Persico back to Profaci, where the pair ultimately sided with Joe Colombo against the Gallos. In the Gallo wars he was charged in the murder of a Gallo gunner, Alfred Mondello, but the indictment was later dismissed.

MacIntosh was with Persico during the 1960s mob war for control of the Colombo crime family. A government-taped conversation of Apples with an IRS agent, Richard Annicharico, posing as a bribetaker, and Victor Puglisi, the Colombos' alleged go-between with Annicharico, illustrates his casualness toward violence:

> *MacIntosh: "I was there when he [Persico] got shot."*
> *Puglisi: "I hear they didn't use pistols; they used carbines. . . . How far were they? Close?"*
> *MacIntosh: "They were close, Vic. They pulled up alongside."*
> *Annicharico: "They were good shots."*
> *MacIntosh: "They didn't have no balls."*
> *Puglisi: "They didn't take their time?"*
> *MacIntosh: "That's right, no balls—they didn't finish the job. . . . They shot through the car. They shot through the . . ."*
> *Annicharico: "Through the door, through the car?"*
> *MacIntosh: "Through the door, through the motor. [Persico] got hit in the mouth."*
> *Annicharico: "Yeah?"*
> *MacIntosh: "He spit the bullet out . . ."*

While there were many capos outranking him, MacIntosh was considered to be Persico's most important ally in the Colombo family. If the Snake was released from prison and MacIntosh avoided a long jail term it was probably Apples who was determine if his erstwhile buddy got back his boss position. As it turned out the Snake did get out of prison for a time and resumed his boss role. He did so despite the fact that Apples himself had indeed gone to prison for a long sentence.

MADDEN, Owney "the Killer" (1892–1965): Bootlegger and murderer

A brutal killer in his youth, Owney Madden was living proof that there was a place even for WASPs (white Anglo-Saxon Protestants) in the upper regions of organized crime. Enjoying a firm relationship and friendship with Lucky Luciano, Meyer Lansky, Frank Costello, Tommy Lucchese, Carlos Marcello, Al Capone and others, Madden transformed himself from a mindless youthful bloodletter, "that little banty rooster out of hell," into a sleek, dapper sophisticate of crime.

After his father's death, Owney Madden came to New York in 1903 from his native Liverpool, England, to live with an aunt in the already notorious Hell's Kitchen. Owney soon joined the Gophers, one of the major gangs of the day, and was arrested 44 times for illegal escapades but managed to stay out of jail. He had mastered the mugger's art and was accomplished with all the weapons of the craft, the slung shot, blackjack, brass knuckles and his favorite, a lead pipe wrapped in newspaper. Because of his proficiency at mayhem Owney progressed to head of the gang. In that esteemed position he was raking in an estimated $200 a day for the robberies, labor beatings, killings and intergang attacks he planned for his young punks. He committed his first murder at 17 and could tote up five by age 23. By the time he was 20, Owney was also in what he called "the insurance business." He sold "bomb insurance" to scores of merchants who were worried about having their storefronts blown out.

The police charged, but were unable to prove, that Madden had killed his first man, an Italian, for no other reason than to celebrate his election to leadership of the Gophers. Some of his other homicides were affairs of the heart. When he discovered in 1910 that an innocuous clerk named William Hen-

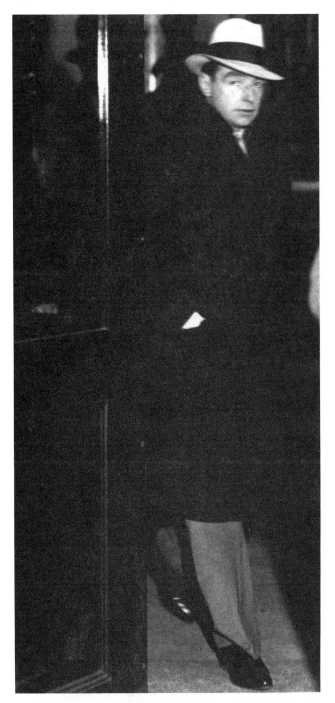

A stone killer in his youth, Owney Madden left the New York rackets to become the crime king and good ole boy of Hot Springs, Arkansas, which he ran as a sort of cooling-off spot for organized crime big shots.

shaw had tried to date one of his girls, Madden pursued him aboard a trolley car at Ninth Avenue and West 16th Street and shot him to death before a dozen passengers. Before getting off the trolley,

285

Owney paused to toll the bell for his victim. Henshaw stayed alive long enough to name Madden as his killer. A dramatic rooftop chase across Hell's Kitchen ensued. But, once caught, Madden was cleared; the trolley passengers were nowhere to be found.

In November 1912 Owney took on 11 gunners from the rival Hudson Dusters. He tried to outdraw and outshoot the whole bunch and ended up ventilated with five bullets himself. In the hospital Madden refused to name his assailants. "It's nobody's business but mine," he told the police.

By the time he was released from the hospital, Madden's boys had knocked off six of his attackers. However, Owney the Killer had a new problem. Little Patsy Doyle was trying to take over the Gophers and had killed some Madden loyalists in the process. Little Patsy passed the word everyone should follow him because Madden was crippled for life. In due course Owney set him up for an ambush in a saloon at Eighth Avenue and 41st Street and dispatched Little Patsy with a bullet in the lung and two more in the body. For this offense Madden did eight years in Sing Sing.

When he was released in 1923, Owney the Killer had undergone a sort of metamorphosis. He had gained a measure of finesse and underworld respectability because he talked more of using his brains to get ahead. He formed a new gang and went into rumrunning and rackets involving laundry services and coal deliveries. He was such a steady producer that Tammany's Jimmy Hines provided him protection. Madden now moved as an equal among such criminals as Luciano, Costello, Waxey Gordon, Longy Zwillman, Louis Lepke, and the Bug and Meyer team of Bugsy Siegel and Meyer Lansky.

When in the early 1930s Vince "Mad Dog" Coll was running around Manhattan kidnapping and murdering top criminals, it was Owney who kept him talking on the telephone until gunmen showed up to cut off the Mad Dog's connection. Also in the 1930s Madden moved into the boxing world, catapulting a hapless Primo Carnera into the heavyweight boxing championship. Carnera ended up without a penny but Owney made a million dollars out of the deal.

In 1932 Owney had to go back to prison for a short stint as a parole violator, and when he got out he was subjected to various harassment arrests. With Prohibition over and mobsters scrambling for new rackets, Madden, having accumulated several million dollars, decided to retire. He moved to Hot Springs, Arkansas, a town he saw to be very ready for corruption. Hot Springs already had a reputation as a "cooling off" spot for criminals on the run and Madden opened several casinos for Lansky there, consulting often with Carlos Marcello in New Orleans.

It was a nice quiet existence, and from time to time some of the boys would come down to Hot Springs when on the lam. Bugsy Siegel came, so did Luciano before he gave up on the prostitution charge that would send him to prison. Owney was the king of Hot Springs with the local cops performing heroic works keeping him from being annoyed by pesky journalists. They had better had since if he was dissatisfied with their performances he'd have them transferred or broken.

Owney achieved a considerable measure of respectability. He married the postmaster's daughter and in 1943 became an American citizen. It was his wife who pleaded his case at his naturalization hearings. "We are fighting a World War to do away with intolerance and persecution," she said. "I believe Mr. Madden is entitled to some consideration."

By the time he died in 1965 he had achieved a status somewhere between a good ole boy and a Southern gentleman.

MAFIA

It is useful in a historical sense to trace the origin of the Mafia back to Sicily. In many respects, however, the history is confusing because the Mafia today is not the same one that emerged at the end of the last century.

The American Mafia is really only a little over a half century old, and it came into being when Lucky Luciano and his allies—including Jewish gangsters in large numbers—wiped out the last important Old World Mafia leaders: Joe the Boss Masseria and Salvatore Maranzano. This new Mafia had no tolerance for the old ideas of the Sicilian mafiosi. The old "Mustache Petes" felt that "honor" had to be maintained either by avoiding or by warring against other ethnics and indeed other Italians. Settling old vendettas was more important than making money. These ideas were preposterous to the new mafiosi, who moved with other ethnics to organize the underworld in the most efficient methods. This new Mafia cooperated with others to increase crime profits, and they killed only those who stood in the way of profits.

In order to secure profit as the primary Mafia objective, many of the old Mustache Petes were eliminated and mobsters did this almost by instinct from about the middle of Prohibition on. Luciano was not the first to rebel against the old guard, but since he converted the East Coast Mafia—which composed probably more than half the numbers of the mafiosi nationally—his action was the most significant.

For many years our understanding of the Mafia has been limited by argument on whether there even was a Mafia. In the recent decades that argument has been more or less settled, and the principal argument remaining is whether or not organized crime and the Mafia are one and the same thing.

In part the confusion revolves around an understanding of the real nature of organized crime. Some observers argue that organized crime has existed since the earliest days of the nation and, indeed, earlier. This is true if the mere acting in concert of a number of criminals means that crime is "organized." But organized crime achieves its status not only by the fact of groups of practitioners, but also by a network of agreement between such groups. Organized crime is syndicate crime in which certain activities are apportioned out to the various gangs and honored in the main by these gangs. For instance, New York mobs accept the primacy of New England mobs in New England, and if they have to come into New England territory, permission is required. Gangs in one area may be asked to carry out a killing for a gang from another area, and it has the right and duty to carry out such a killing. No rewards are paid in matters of territorial rights. This was never the case in pre-Prohibition crime. The Bloody Tubs gang in Baltimore in the 19th century, for instance, had no such obligation to take care of the needs of the Dead Rabbits or the Daybreakers or other criminal organizations in New York.

Prohibition and the nature of the crime business it engendered required intercourse between mobs in different cities. Al Capone in Chicago was dependent on booze supplies from Canada coming through Detroit where the Jewish Purple Gang dominated. A rapport developed between these groups. If the Purples needed a killing of a recalcitrant member who had fled to Illinois, it fell to the Capones to see that their problem was resolved. Similarly, Capone could

not send his own killers to Detroit to handle a job. The Purples would not permit this and would probably have killed such intruders for the insult. Instead, Chicago would request Detroit to take on the hit assignment.

It was a new form of cooperation in the underworld, and although it hardly worked to perfection at all times, mobsters came to appreciate the concept. Thus disparate Jewish mobs, Italian mafiosi and non-mafiosi, some Irish, Polish and even WASP criminal organizations, joined together in a de facto union. In 1931 the gangs organized a national crime syndicate on a permanent and efficient basis, largely through the handiwork of Lucky Luciano and Jewish mobster Meyer Lansky.

At the time the Mafia forces, extended to include Italian gangsters from any part of Italy rather than just Sicilians, were hardly the most dominant. No census exists of the composition of the syndicate at the time, but if one judges by cities involved, it is possible that Jewish mobsters actually outnumbered mafiosi. It is not a matter of great moment since cooperation between Italian and Jewish criminals had long become a matter of course. The Italians had felt the poverty of the homeland and the Jews their ghettos of Europe. Both arrived at the same time and both felt the same lash of discrimination in America.

Typical of this Jewish-Italian cooperation was the composition of the national syndicate's infamous enforcement arm, Murder, Incorporated—about half Jewish and half Italian. A rapport developed between the two groups that did not develop in the main with Irish gangsters, who throughout the 19th century had dominated American crime and who found themselves being threatened by the expanding activities of both the Italians and Jews. As a result, probably more Irish criminals were wiped out in the establishment of organized crime in America than any other national grouping.

But a fundamental difference ultimately emerged to separate what may be called the Jewish and Italian Mafias. The Italians united in a structured organization with crime families, an order based on a leader or boss, an underboss or two (the second sometimes called a consigliere, although such duties had different meanings with different crime families), a number of capos or lieutenants, and then a group of soldiers. This hardly composed the entire crime family, but was probably only a minority composition of the group. Some clamored and hoped and even bribed to become "made" members of the family, while others had little such interest. Luciano had sanctioned this order within the new American Mafia. Although he personally had little interest in such trappings, he came to realize that after the brutal New York wars of 1928 to 1931, many of the survivors still clung to their upbringing of mafioso organization with the need to render fealty to a leader.

The Jewish mobsters showed no need for such a structure and indeed felt little loyalty to their own areas of operation. When the Dalitz forces of Cleveland and the Purples of Detroit saw criminal revenues in their areas decreasing and new and greater opportunities developing in Florida and Nevada gambling, for instance, they dissolved their operations (or turned them over to local mafiosi) and moved on. The Mafia could hardly transfer its entire operation in such a manner. The very structure of the organization kept them tied to a geographical sphere of operation.

Yet, its structure gave the Mafia its very lifeblood. By the 1960s or 1970s a fundamental change was taking place in organized crime. The Mafia, rather than withering away, as many experts had predicted, actually was gaining in strength while the Jews declined. This was hardly the result of any purge or falling out between the groups, but rather the result of the different organizations among them. The Jewish mobsters were empire builders, not dynasty builders. Nepotism among Jewish gangsters was virtually non-existent and their removal from ghetto life produced a decreasing supply of fresh young punks eager to step into crime. Among the mafiosi the situation was different. When the Jewish mobsters of the 1920s and 1930s died off, more often than not they were replaced by Italians. The switch from Longy Zwillman to Jerry Catena in New Jersey serves as an example. As the ravages of age hit the longtime syndicate mobsters, the structure of the Mafia filled the void.

We understand very little about the Mafia and are misled by a great number of myths—that there is nothing unique about mafiosi (and their Jewish counterparts); that the Mafia is dying; that there is any such thing as ethnic succession in organized crime. But the Mafia is an exploitive society, not only of its victims but also of its practitioners, a quality from which it derives much of its strength and ability to renew itself.

Organized crime developed in America as a pure aberration, something new on the world scene—not even seen in Sicily, the birthplace of the Mafia. There were three fundamental reasons for the genesis of organized crime in the 1920s and its continuing growth—Prohibition, the Great Depression and J. Edgar Hoover.

Previously the country was plagued by the great criminal gangs of *un*organized crime, criminal groups that found allies and protectors among the aspiring politicians of the day. For the aid rendered them by the gangs, the politicians overlooked their minor peccadilloes of bashing open a few heads among the honest citizenry now and then, of looting the waterfront and banks, of fielding armies of prostitutes. The important thing was that the gangs could win elections and maintain the politicians in power by intimidating voters at election time.

There were gangs such as the Dead Rabbits, the Bowery Boys, the Whyos and many more. The last important such gangs were the 1,500-member primarily Jewish Monk Eastman Gang and the equal-numbered Italian Five Points Gang under Paul Kelly. But shortly before the First World War these organizations had turned into liabilities for the political power structure. Reform movements were spreading and the politicians could no longer allow the gangs to rob and kill (often to order with detailed price lists) and expect Tammany or its local equivalent in other cities to offer protection. The politicians, concerned with their own survival, turned their backs on the gangsters and allowed frequent arrests and imprisonments, and the great gangs started to fall apart.

There were no rackets that could support such a criminal establishment and splinters of the gangs fought each other for control of what rackets were available, such as unionbusting, strikebreaking and the like. None of this meant that crime as an institution was finished or that citizens could walk the streets in total safety, but rather that the die was cast and criminality as a way of life rather than merely as a youthful, generally ghettoized activity was waning. The Great War took many gangsters away from home and further fractionalized their organizations and many returned home in 1919 to face a most unusual prospect—actually seeking work to survive.

Then the first major break occurred for the future of criminality. The nation, unlike other advanced Western nations, embarked on a fatal but "noble experiment" of social legislation, the outlawing of demon rum by the Prohibition amendment. Instantly, the great criminal gangs coalesced again. As Prohibition was doomed to fail and criminals gained a popular image as bootleggers, the seeds of organized crime were planted. The criminals became far richer than they had ever been before. It was no longer necessary for them to curry favor with the politicians. They were the great source of wealth in the country and they bought the politicians and the police in wholesale lots. The politicians of the 1920s could not dictate to criminals as their predecessors had done; they had to come to them hat in hand and palms open.

At the coming of Prohibition, the main occupants of the ghettos were predominantly recent immigrants, the Italians and Jews. Criminality within these ghetto ethnic groups was exactly the same as it had been when the Irish were there and would remain the same later on when blacks and Hispanics moved into the ghettos. But the Jews and Italians achieved their primacy in crime at the time when crime really paid. Although this alone was inducement to remain in crime, still with Repeal many of the bootlegging criminals dropped out of crime to live off their acquired wealth.

But a second development further institutionalized crime—the Great Depression. Ethnic progression should have moved many of these ethnic groups out of the ghettos but they were frozen there by the economic climate. Ghetto youths, progressing beyond the usual mindless ghetto crime, saw no salvation save in crime. They flocked to the new criminal syndicates and provided a glue that held the Jews and Italians to their criminal organizations.

The Great Depression coincided with the Luciano-Lansky plan to take syndicate crime national, a program that met practically no federal resistance. This third development, or non-development, saw J. Edgar Hoover spending all his time fighting communists and what he perceived to be the deadliest peril of all to the nation—juvenile car thieves. He would not fight organized crime, declaring it and the Mafia to be myth, a position he would hold for more than three decades until he was carried, figuratively screaming and kicking, into battle against organized crime and the "Cosa Nostra" (a term invented to give him an out for his years of insisting there was no Mafia). In fact, Hoover paid so little attention to organized crime that, as historian Albert Fried noted,

"one could accuse him of dereliction of duty." And a strong case could be made that the leaders of organized crime had their own special ways for "stroking" Hoover to keep him most docile.

In any event organized crime thrived in the Depression and beyond, and the Mafia perhaps most of all, if not in revenues (Lansky alone probably ended up with a personal fortune in the $300 to $400 million range) certainly as the surviving structure. Helping that development was the aforementioned exploitive nature of the Mafia.

In the Mafia, the boss soaks and exploits his underboss, the underboss the capos, the capos the soldiers and the soldiers the "non-made" hangers on. This may best be illustrated in the loan-sharking racket. The crime boss in a typical operation finances much of the action by advancing money to his underboss and/or capos for about 1 percent weekly interest. This is not what you would call a risk loan. The boss's underlings are fully responsible for the principal and interest and no excuses are accepted if the money is lost. The money must be repaid. This second-echelon group then relends the money to lower-ranking members of the mob at anywhere from 1.5 to 2.5 percent a week. These soldiers then make their money by collecting interest at 5 percent or more a week, depending on what the loan traffic will bear. A capo or soldier might end up in an especially lucrative situation that nets him a bonanza. If so, he can expect his superiors to move in on him for a larger cut.

The Mafia does not put its members on any payroll but merely affords them the right to operate and the right to be gouged by their superiors. Oddly though, this underworld version of the Peter Principle gives the Mafia its very vitality. The mafioso accepts the gouging because he hopes to ascend the ladder at least in a small enough way so that he can become a little more of a gouger and a little less a gougee. The Mafia in reality is a ladder of troughs.

It seems unlikely that the Mafia is doomed to wither because of what is called "ethnic succession in organized crime." The exponents of this theory seem to overlook the difference between ghetto crime and organized crime. There has been an upward mobility from the ghetto that has led all ethnics to better positions in society, but the Jews and Italians stayed in organized crime after their profits from crime had raised them far beyond the ghettos. The similarities between the Italian Mafia and such new menaces as the "Black Mafia," the "Cuban Mafia" (or Latin Mafia), the "Chinese Mafia," and the Pakistanis, Vietnamese and Japanese are difficult to draw. Except for humble beginnings, the Mafia as a crime group has no real equal.

There is no doubt that the Mafia overall is reducing its stake in narcotics, not so much because of the growth of competition from other ethnics but rather because of the heavy penalties involved. However the process is a slow one, and the Mafia often funds much of the operations of non-Mafia groups. Chinese gangsters probably control 20 percent of this country's heroin traffic from bases in Hong Kong and Taiwan and many of this country's Chinatowns. In almost all cases these groups have formed working alliances with the traditional Mafia families. In black and Hispanic ghettos gambling operations fees are generally paid to the Mafia for the "franchise" to operate and because the Mafia maintains the key to political and police protection. The abandonment of street-level activities, the high-visibility part of many rackets, has always been a hallmark of organized crime and should not be overemphasized as a sign of transition.

The fact remains the Mafia thrives and moves into more sophisticated areas of racketeering because of its members long learning period in organized crime. The crude mafiosi of the 1920s who fought the booze wars with garlic-coated bullets were not capable of the sophisticated crimes of stock manipulation, computer theft and other financial flimflams that the Mafia engages in today. Today the new ethnics are, with some exceptions, about 50 years behind the times.

Proof positive that the Mafia is a growing concern comes from the fact that an endless supply of young gangsters are panting for admission. They wait impatiently on the periphery, doing the odd jobs for the mob, or as one New York police official put it, "fencing stolen goods for family members with only a small cut for himself, or even dirty work like burying bodies." They seek membership to win the "right to do the hijackings rather than the peddling, the rubouts instead of the shoveling. He might even be allotted a loan-sharking or numbers territory, franchises with a steady income and, because of the family protection, little fear of competition."

One aspirant in New York was so eager for membership that he flipped for joy when told he was to be "made." He got all dressed up on the big night and drove off with some of the boys, never to be seen again. He was not to be made, but unmade, having fallen into disfavor and slated for execution.

Whither the Mafia? In the late 1980s it appeared that profound changes were taking place because of heat from the federal government's crackdown on the leadership of the various crime families. The government obviously hoped that pressuring the bosses, traditionally men in their 70s, might produce some who would crack under the strain of convictions and the anticipation of dying in jail. Previously, the famed informers—Reles, Valachi, Teresa, Fratianno—despite all the hype from their promoters, were not top-drawer operatives. The revelations of some of these informers hurt the Mafia and organized crime more than others, but if a boss would talk, the rewards could be electrifying.

Would such men, in contradiction of their entire career philosophy, talk? The motivation of most informers originally is that they were "screwed" by other mafiosi, robbed of their money while in prison. The bosses do not have such justification. However, there seemed good reason to suspect that the government was only provoking lower-echelon mafiosi to kill their bosses, for fear that they might talk. That could have been an added reason for the assassination of Paul Castellano, head of the Gambino family, on December 16, 1985. At the age of 70 he was facing a whole series of indictments. Conviction would doom him to spend the rest of his life behind bars. Would Big Paulie talk?

A very suspicious story appeared in *Time* magazine just a short time before Castellano's murder (actually datelined the day of the killing but printed earlier). It claimed that Aniello Dellacroce, the number two man in the Gambino family directly under Castellano, and who had died of lung cancer on December 2, had been an FBI informer. *Time*, it seems, may have been fed FBI disinformation. That Dellacroce, known as a very tough mafiosi, had talked seemed highly dubious to many observers. Many crime observers believe that the agency used Dellacroce as a scapegoat to protect other very real informers. It is also argued that the Mafia, nervous that a man like Dellacroce would defect, would think, how about Castellano, who was considered personally far weaker than Dellacroce?

The true efficacy of the FBI efforts to nab bosses cannot yet be measured. Yet, the Mafia can counter the threat by returning to the ways of the Mafia during the early syndicate days. Then the leaders of most crime families were in their 30s or 40s. The benefits were obvious. If a boss of 75 were hit with a 20- or 30-year sentence, he could crack, knowing he was at the end of the line. A boss aged 40 could do such a term "standing on his head," getting out in as little as six or seven years, allowing for good behavior. The older boss might talk, the younger would not. And a shift to younger bosses might not weaken the Mafia at all, but rather strengthen it in the long run. One thing remains certain, bloodied or not, as one young mafioso told a reporter defiantly, "We ain't dead, that's for damned sure."

The American Mafia is still a rather young creature, only in its 60s. Rather than learning from the Sicilian Mafia, today it is more aptly described as Sicily's tutor. The 1985 testimony of Tommaso Buscetta—the high-rank Sicilian mafioso, whose defection led to the arrests of hundreds of alleged mafiosi in Italy—described the structures of the two Mafias on each side of the Atlantic as similar, but added that only the American version had an organization called "The Commission." Buscetta said the idea of a commission was pressed on the Sicilian Mafia by two members of the American Mafia—Lucky Luciano and "a gentleman named Bonanno coming from the United States in 1957." Buscetta said Luciano and Joe Bonanno had told their Italian counterparts that such a commission was valuable to resolve disputes between the crime families, 20 in Palermo alone, throughout the island.

U.S. law enforcement agencies had no problem figuring why Luciano and Bonanno were so interested in having a commission established in Italy. By reducing the disputes, the arguments over spoils, they would guarantee that the heroin pipeline from Sicily to the United States functioned smoothly. It was the hallmark of the American Mafia—exporting good old American know-how.

MAFIA, origin of

Historians disagree as to the age of the Mafia. Some trace its origin to 1812, others to 1860. Still others say it goes back to the 13th century to the society that was founded in Italy to fight the oppression of the French Angevins. Its slogan then was *Morte alla Francia Italia anela!* ("Death to the French is Italy's cry!") The word *mafia* was taken from the first letters of each word of the slogan.

In the 19th century, the Mafia emerged as a criminal culture, sometimes victimizing wealthy landowners but more commonly renting themselves out as hired guns to oppress the peasants.

So much for the historical views. Ask the American mafiosi—those who'll tell you "there ain't no Mafia"—and they'll give a different version, one that crime family boss Joe Bonanno repeats in his recent autobiography, *A Man of Honor.* The term *mafia* was coined in the revolt that developed after a French soldier raped a Palermo maiden on her wedding day on Easter Monday 1282. A band of Sicilians angrily struck back by slaughtering a French troop, and as news of the retaliation spread, other Sicilians arose in town after town, killing the French. Thousands of French died, and the slogan of Mafia became their battle cry, arising from the hysterical cries of the raped girl's mother who ran through the streets shouting *ma fia, ma fia,* "my daughter, my daughter."

Bonanno and other more romantically inclined mafiosi much prefer this version, which puts the Mafia on the side of the angels.

MAFIA Coffin: Corpse disposal method

When it comes to disposing of corpses, the Mafia is certainly creative. Indeed, only those victims the mob wants to be found are ever discovered.

The Mafia Coffin is perhaps the most ingenious method of disposing of corpses. A body is delivered to a mob undertaker—either a voluntary plotter or one being forced to cooperate, perhaps because of heavy loan-sharking—who alters a coffin and adds a false bottom, the result sometimes called a Double-Decker Coffin. The victim is placed beneath the false bottom of the Mafia Coffin. Another soon-to-be-buried legit corpse goes on top. The mourning family of the deceased is not even aware that their beloved one is sharing his final burial place with a hit victim, and the pallbearers are simply impressed with the apparent weight of quality wood used for the coffin.

The Mafia Coffin is not used much anymore. It would be too easy for the law to one day have the coffin opened and find the extra body. In theory of course the undertaker can simply deny having put in the extra panel and insist some unknown killers must have dug up the coffin and stuck in the extra corpse, though this alibi fails to account for the extra panel. The New York City police credit Joseph Bonanno

(Joe Bananas) with perfecting the method at his own funeral parlor in lower Manhattan. But the crime family leader takes no credit for the custom in his recent autobiography, *A Man of Honor.*

MAFIA gun

The *New Orleans Times* in 1869 first reported the presence of a group of "notorious Sicilian murderers, counterfeiters and burglars, who, in the last month, have formed a sort of general co-partnership or stock company for the plunder and disturbance of the city." They were armed with typical Italian shotguns. These weapons at times featured barrels sawed off to about 18 inches and the stocks sawed through and hollowed out very near the trigger. The stock was then fitted with hinges, so that the gun became a sort of "jackknife" and could be carried on a hook sewn inside a coat. Such weapons were messy but brutally effective.

As corpses turned up, heads or entrails blown away, the New Orleans papers dubbed the murder weapons "Mafia guns," especially imported from Italy. It is doubtful that mafiosi brought many such weapons with them from the old country; there was little need for that. Although a weapon typical in Sicily and indeed in many parts of Europe, such guns were also rather popular in much of the American South. Western outlaws had already started sawing down shotguns to conceal them.

Sample "Mafia guns," typical murder weapons used in early gangland killings. These were identified as three of the weapons used in the assassination of New Orleans police chief David Hennessey.

In 1890 the celebrated murder of Chief of Police David Hennessey convinced the New Orleans populace that it was the work of the Mafia when several weapons said to have been used in the crime proved to be such shortened Mafia guns. One particularly was labeled of Italian make, having a hinged stock which allowed it to be folded into a compact carrying size. Actually it was an American gun produced by the W. Richards Company.

Eventually 11 mafiosi were lynched for the Hennessey murder and from this the brotherhood learned a lesson. They abandoned all use of such weapons in favor of more traditional ones. Despite that, whenever a sawed-off shotgun was used in a shooting the press for years afterward immediately reported it as a "Mafia job."

"MAFIA Manor": Special prison accommodation for wise guys

In decades not long past the federal prison of choice for Mafia men was Lewisburg Federal Penitentiary located within the dark hills and abandoned coal mines of central Pennsylvania. The institution's proximity to New York, the heartland of about half the Mafia membership in the United States, and the scores of mob guys sent there earned it the name "Mafia Manor" one generally regarded as not totally discarded. It was not an extreme exaggeration to say the boys confined there found it as close to a home away from home as a prison could be.

In that sense they are following an old mob tradition. When Al Capone was confined in Pennsylvania's Eastern Penitentiary on a gun charge, the helpful warden, Herbert B. Smith, supplied him with considerable creature comforts. Big Al had a large one-man cell, which he furnished with rugs, pictures, a desk, a bookshelf, a dresser, lamps and a $500 radio console—tops for the era. While other prisoners received visitors only on Sundays, Capone had such privileges seven days a week. Capone did not have a private telephone in his cell, but he made do using the one in the warden's office, with the required privacy, whenever he so desired.

The same was true of Lucky Luciano when he was incarcerated at New York's Clinton State Prison. Lucky's private cell had curtains over the cell door and an electric stove. He was not the Birdman of Alcatraz, but he doted over a pet canary. His prison uniform was rather unique as he wore a silk shirt and highly polished shoes. He was always surrounded by a phalanx of paid inmate guards while he held court for inmate visitors, dispensing advice and orders, and if he was so inclined, special favors.

By the 1960s Lewisburg prison held hundreds of Mafia or Mafia-connected inmates, all carving out more enjoyable confinement conditions. They had protection from black prison gangs, a generous supply of candy and cigarettes and less than onerous work assignments. Especially well accommodated over recent years were the likes of John Gotti, Paul Vario, the notorious Johnny Dio, Joe Pine—a Connecticut crime boss—Carmine Galante and Henry Hill (of *Wiseguy* fame).

These men were assigned to an honor dorm in a separate three-story building, which Hill described as looking more like a Holiday Inn than a prison. There were four inmates to a room with comfortable beds and private baths. The establishment, which prisoners gratefully dubbed "Mafia Manor," boasted an unlimited supply of wine and liquor, kept in bath oil or aftershave jars. The boys, contrary to the rules, cooked in their rooms. Most rooms had a stove and pots and pans and silverware. Hill related, "We had glasses and an ice-water cooler where we kept the fresh meats and cheeses. When there was an inspection, we stored the stuff in the false ceiling."

Some of the guys in Mafia Manor ate in the regular mess hall no more than a half dozen times or so throughout their entire terms. During his confinement Carmine Galante, an underboss and killer under Joe Bonanno and a convicted narcotics mastermind, roamed the prison with immunity, fearless even of the toughest black leaders. Whenever he approached a pay phone with a long line of inmates waiting to use it, he would bull his way to the front of the line and shout, "Get off the fucking phone, nigger!" It was something that would not have been tolerated from any other white prisoner.

After Galante's release, he tried to take over most of the crime family operations in New York, and he was murdered. There was, it was said, great joy in Lewisburg.

But the bribery of guards continued as usual. Certainly there were guards who were not on the take, but they would, said Hill, never inform on those that were.

MAFIA social clubs

Almost all Mafia chapters have one or more "social clubs" where the boys meet. It is generally understood that the premises are likely bugged by law enforcement agencies and signs abound advising the boys, "THE WALLS HAVE EARS." Theoretically nothing

The Ravenite Social Club, the Little Italy headquarters of John Gotti, became in the 1980s and 1990s the most famous mob hangout in America. At first it sported a store front facade, as shown in this surveillance film, but later Gotti had the front bricked over to prevent government peeping and to lessen the danger of rival mob bombings.

incriminating is supposed to be said there, with activities restricted to card playing and sports betting, but inevitably possible scams, some amazingly weird, are discussed. This is quite understandable since the main preoccupation of mafiosi is making money, and the more dishonest the method, the better.

Since the boys do a lot of killing, investigators frequently hear mobsters discussing the latest underworld hit and speculating on who did what to whom. This is a charade since very often those doing the speculating are the ones who did the deed. John Gotti was heard many times wondering who had popped off Paul Castellano, a matter he certainly did not have to speculate on.

There is of course a general rule that no killings ever take place on the premises, but sometimes the restrictions are pressed to the limits, especially during periods of mob tensions or warfare. Such was the case when it appeared major bloodletting was about to break out between the Gambinos under Gotti and the Genoveses under Chin Gigante.

Gotti's men at their Queen's headquarters, the so-called Bergin Hunt and Fish Club, greatly feared an assault by the Gigante people, and into the midst of it all stepped a tragic figure, one William Ciccone, a somewhat retarded young man from the neighborhood. Ciccone took to standing across the street and gaping at the Bergin. Gotti's men immediately concluded that whoever he was, he was up to no good and could well be the advance man in an attack by foes. The men stormed out of the club armed with baseball bats and beat the squealing Ciccone senseless, caring little who might be watching. Ciccone's shattered body was dumped into the back seat of a car. Later he was shot to death and his body placed in the basement of what was described as a mob-owned Staten Island candy store. It was found there by a uniformed policeman before it could be buried the next day. As Howard Blum noted in *Gangland*, "His murder was never solved. But nobody stared into the Bergin anymore."

After John Gotti took command of the Gambino family's headquarters, the Ravenite, on Manhattan's Mulberry Street, he was determined to discourage snooping by the public or law enforcement. The Ravenite's storefront windows were bricked over leaving only two very small windows and a single door. If the Ravenite, with garbage cans lining the front, lacked the splendor Gotti liked for his personal appearance, the new design cut down on surveillance

camera work and perhaps more importantly offered more protection from rival mob bombers.

Still the Ravenite proved to be a sieve for evidence gathered by the FBI, especially in an upper floor flat the mob thought the agents could not penetrate, and perhaps it was also a fount on the cultural attitudes of mafiosi. As Gene Mustain and Jerry Capeci observed in *Murder Machine*, the mob's most prolific killer, Roy DeMeo, once brought his 12-year-old son to the social club and the boy was asked what he would do if a bully picked on him. "I'd shoot him and cut his fucking head off!" the kid responded.

"That's my boy!" the elder DeMeo roared, and the rest of the men very nearly rolled on the floor in laughter.

MAGADDINO, Stefano (1891–1974): Buffalo crime family boss

When Stefano (Steve) Magaddino, the longtime godfather of the Buffalo–Niagara Falls crime family, died in July 1974 at the age of 82, one journalist described him as "the grand old man of Cosa Nostra." In many ways Magaddino started much of the aura that clothes Mafia godfathers, at least in the public's perception. An illiterate, Magaddino was by no means a stupid man, instead affecting a rustic simplicity. Even his cousin, Joe Bonanno, who came to hate him and was said to have actively plotted his murder, said "his instinct for self-preservation was uncanny."

There is some confusion as to when Magaddino came to this country—some say in 1903 and others not until the 1920s. Magaddino settled in Brooklyn in a large Castellammare community and was regarded as one of the leaders. The main enemies of the Magaddino family in Sicily had been the Buccellatos, also by then well represented in Brooklyn. One day Magaddino and a friend, Gaspar Milazzo, were shot at as they left a store. Two innocent bystanders were killed. A short time thereafter several Buccellato men were shot to death, and Magaddino and Milazzo thought it wise to leave Brooklyn. Stefano headed for Buffalo and Gaspar to Detroit where each were to remain and found crime families.

As the *Niagara Falls Gazette* put it, Magaddino was "associated with a string of beverage distributorships here, beginning in 1927." Through bootlegging revenues—Niagara Falls and Buffalo became major illicit gateways for Prohibition liquor from

Canada—Magaddino made his family one of the most profitable crime units in the country, heavy into loan-sharking, shakedowns, gambling and labor rackets.

He also demonstrated his "instinct for selfpreservation" over the years by surviving several attacks on his life. In 1936 his sister was killed in a bomb attack clearly intended for him. The killers had hit the wrong house, Stefano and his sister being next-door neighbors. In 1958 a hand grenade was hurled through his kitchen window but failed to explode. In the early 1960s his cousin, Bonanno, put him on a death list in a push to become the main mafioso in the nation, but Magaddino turned the tables on Joe Bananas by having his men kidnap him off New York's Park Avenue. Magaddino held Bonanno prisoner for a time and after a two-year "disappearance" Bonanno finally opted for retirement in Arizona, a refuge dictated by his health in more ways than one.

If Bonanno could marvel at his older cousin's instinct for survival, the FBI was entitled to the same view. As FBI agent Neil J. Welch, once considered the likely head of the FBI during the Carter administration, has noted, "Magaddino had peacefully coexisted with the FBI for more than three decades." This of course was mainly during the period that J. Edgar Hoover was denying the existence of the Mafia. Magaddino on the other hand knew the FBI existed. In fact when FBI surveillance of mafiosi in the Buffalo area finally escalated, Welch, for a time special agent in charge there, reported, "Magaddino boldly countered by putting the FBI under surveillance, ordering his men to record agent names and license numbers and carefully monitoring FBI comings and goings at the Buffalo office." Naturally Hoover's enforced dress code and punctuality requirements for agents made it simple for Magaddino's soldiers to spot the FBI agents. Not only did the Mafia know who was watching them, but they also undoubtedly knew which agents were involved with Communist Party surveillance as well. These they could simply ignore.

While Magaddino was modern enough to invade non-Italian areas—the family's influence extended into Ohio and Canada—he never lost the old-fashioned Mafia emphasis of victimizing one's own. Italian immigrants were imposed on not only to buy alcohol from the Magaddino forces but also, during Prohibition and after, to buy a nonalcoholic concoc-tion called Home Juice which was peddled door-to-door. The immigrants soon learned that buying the brew might not improve their health but refusing to could have the contrary effect. Even in death, grieving families could turn to the Magaddino Funeral Home for the ultimate service.

Construction projects frequently were required to stay on the good side of the godfather. He would, for example, assign a lesser mobster to monitor activities on the construction site to make sure the family got its agreed-upon "tax" per cement truck delivery. In one case a mobster accused of turning in an underestimated number was immediately snatched up by a pair of brawny enforcers and brought to the godfather. Magaddino explained he expected his *soldati* to be honorable men and he was now disappointed. Did the soldier have any explanation? Anxiously, the mobster said and proved to Magaddino's satisfaction that he had turned in the right count to a higher rank soldier named Tony. Magaddino pursed his lips and told the soldier to look at the sun. "Today, you see the sun," the godfather declared softly. "Tomorrow, Tony, he no see the sun."

It was because of such tight-fisted control of the family that Magaddino maintained his power almost into his 80s. Only then did the family start coming apart, when the mobsters learned that Magaddino was keeping so much of the family's revenues for himself. Magaddino's take came to $530,000 in one year in which he informed the family that profits were insufficient to allow for the usual cash distributions.

This embarrassing revelation led to all kinds of tribulations for the godfather, with his son's wife raging of her mate: "That dirty son of a bitch. Until today I never thought there was a Mafia—I asked him to take me to Florida this winter and he told me we were broke!"

By the time Magaddino died in 1974 the family had become splintered because of old-fashioned Mafia greed. In the power vacuum, the Russ Bufalino family from Pittston, Pennsylvania, expanded into Buffalo's crime area.

See also BONNANO, JOSEPH

MAGLIOCCO, Joseph (1898–1963): Joe Profaci successor

Known as an indecisive Mafia leader, Joe Magliocco nevertheless moved among the elite of crime family leaders. The right-hand man of Joe Profaci, the longtime Brooklyn crime boss, he was present at both the 1928 mob meeting in Cleveland and the Apalachin Conference in 1957. Magliocco's sister was married to Profaci who named him his heir apparent; after all, Magliocco made an excellent underboss. Over the years as corpses piled up on Brooklyn streets under Profaci's firm rule of obedience, Magliocco was known as the man who got things done.

Magliocco was one of several Profaci men kidnapped by the Gallo brothers and their associates in the early 1960s in a demand for more financial opportunities in the family's criminal enterprises. After his release on a promise that the kidnappers' demands would be considered, Magliocco was firmly against giving them a thing. He often traveled thereafter in his limousine with a loaded shotgun on his lap.

When Joe Profaci died of cancer in 1962, the power passed to Magliocco who now found himself in a position that was beyond his abilities. Under the circumstances, he fell under the influence of another crime family boss, the tough and cunning Joe Bonanno who had long been close to Profaci. With Vito Genovese behind bars, Bonanno had come to the conclusion that he could dominate the Mafia and become the most powerful crime boss in the country. To achieve this aim he concocted a plan to assassinate two other New York City family heads, Tommy Lucchese and Carlo Gambino, as well as his own cousin, Stefano Magaddino, boss of the Buffalo family. To solidify his position with Magliocco, he brought him into the plot. Magliocco came willingly because both Gambino and Lucchese were trying to undercut his leadership claims in the Profaci family. Magliocco passed the contract on Gambino and Lucchese to a rising young capo named Joe Colombo. It was a mistake.

Colombo knew his Mafia war history. Such assassinations would provoke a major conflict and he would be a prime target. Colombo, known to some observers as "the Mafia's Sammy Glick," figured out that Magliocco would never pull off such a power play—chances were he hadn't figured out Bonanno's total involvement—and that he, Colombo, could probably do better dealing with his would-be victims. He informed them of the plot on their lives. Gambino could appreciate such treachery within a crime family. He had himself achieved control of the Albert Anastasia family by conspiring in the murder of that leader in 1957.

Gambino called an emergency meeting of the Commission, the so-called ruling body of the Mafia. Actually its powers were limited in general because any interference with any particular family would do nothing but provoke a shooting war. Still, all the crime leaders were appalled at the murder plot which promised to revive the violence of the early 1930s as well as the power struggle of the late 1950s when Vito Genovese ascended to a position of top power after the elimination of Anastasia.

The commission ordered Magliocco and Bonanno to appear for questioning, Gambino being shrewd enough to realize that Magliocco lacked the guts to have come up with the coup idea on his own. Bonanno ignored the summons, but a frightened Magliocco appeared. He pleaded guilty to the plot and was let off with a $50,000 fine and forced to resign as a family boss.

It may seem remarkable that Gambino and Lucchese didn't have him killed, but they realized Magliocco was a sick man destined not to live long and executing him would back most of the Profacis and the Bonanno forces into a corner, provoking the shooting war they were trying to avoid. Additionally they were probably trying to send a message to Bonanno that he would get off with relatively mild treatment himself. The quaking Magliocco retired to his Long Island home and died of a heart attack a few months later.

The authorities learned most of the story of the plot through the celebrated taped conversations of a New Jersey Mafia leader, Sam "the Plumber" DeCavalcante. The conversations became public knowledge about five years after Magliocco's death, revealing that the commission knew Bonanno had masterminded the plot and that when it failed, the commission was convinced Bonanno arranged for Magliocco to be murdered.

"They feel that he poisoned Magliocco," DeCavalcante said. "Magliocco didn't die a natural death. . . . See, Magliocco confessed to it. But this Joe [Bonanno] didn't know how far he went. Understand? So they suspect he used a pill on him—that he's noted for it. So he knows the truth of all the damage he done. . . ."

On the basis of DeCavalcante's statement, Magliocco's body was taken from the vault where it lay for five years and subjected to a second autopsy. No trace of poison was found.

MALLIOCCHIA: Attempt to rattle witnesses

It was the *malliocchia,* the attempt to shake up a witness, to disrupt or even stop his testimony. The prosecution in the 1992 John Gotti trial spotted it early and complained to the judge that sitting with the Gotti spectators in the first row was a young man named Joseph D'Angelo. The prosecution's main witness, Sammy "the Bull" Gravano, had long had D'Angelo under his wing. D'Angelo's father had been one of the Bull's best friends and when the father was murdered, Sammy took care of the son with attention and money. Now the young man was sitting in court with the Gotti contingent.

The prosecution complained to the judge that the only reason D'Angelo was present was "to intimidate and try to make Mr. Gravano clam up." The judge agreed and ordered D'Angelo into the second row.

When Gravano took the stand he could barely see D'Angelo, who was short and blocked out by bulky federal agents lining the wall of the courtroom. The ploy, however, was not completely successful as D'Angelo stood up when the Bull was about to start his testimony, slowly working his way to the aisle while staring at Gravano. The Bull, clearly tense, watched the young man leave the courtroom. Then a few moments later D'Angelo returned to the room, this time clearly rattling the informer so that he stumbled in reply to a question.

Later on, Gravano settled down, but he was still nettled during a recess, complaining to government lawyers about the D'Angelo caper. "What is this, a movie?" he said angrily.

In a manner of speaking, it was. The routine had been played out in *The Godfather,* when Michael Corelone imported a witness's relative from Sicily to shake him up before a congressional committee. In the movie the witness reneged on his testimony.

Malliocchia failed in the Gotti case, especially after the Gotti forces were unable to convince the Bull's wife to attend the trial when her husband was testifying. She told both Sammy and the Gotti people that she wasn't going to be part of anything, that she was finished with Sammy's life and everything attached to it.

The *malliocchia* stunt is used at many mob trials, but it has proved less than successful when the informer witness is looking at 20 or 30 years or even a life sentence if he does not testify.

MANGANO, Vincent (c. 1888–1951?): Mafia boss and Anastasia victim

When Lucky Luciano and his allies purged the Mafia of its Mustache Petes in the early 1930s, Vince Mangano survived. Although only in his mid-40s he was still much older than the remaining Young Turks. He became clearly a partner in the Luciano plottings, but he retained a little too much of the Old World traditions that doomed others and would eventually doom him as well.

Mangano came to America with his father and young Joe Profaci, another future crime family boss, in 1922. Mangano became part of the Al Mineo crime family, which was particularly strong in Brooklyn waterfront rackets. (Other early members of the Mineo family were Albert Anastasia and Frank Scalise.) Mineo was murdered during the Castellammarese War, and Mangano assumed the leadership of the crime family, crossing sides with Luciano and others to the Salvatore Maranzano camp after the murder of Joe the Boss Masseria. As entitled by his position, Mangano became a high-ranking member of the board of directors of the new national crime syndicate, although not what was then the top six.

Mangano concentrated on waterfront rackets, working closely with Emil Camarda, a vice president of the International Longshoremen's Association. Mangano and Camarda started the City Democratic Club, among whose charter members were such devotees of the principles of democracy as Anastasia and Mangano's lethal brother, Philip Mangano. Investigators later learned that many of the crimes committed by Murder, Inc., were plotted in the City Democratic Club.

Anastasia became the chief executioner of Murder, Inc., and although Mangano remained technically his boss, Albert moved closer to crime chieftains like Louis Lepke, Frank Costello and Lucky Luciano, with whom he had closer personal ties than with Mangano. This led over the years to increasing conflict between Mangano and Anastasia; they often had to be separated by other crime bosses to prevent fisticuffs.

Matters came to a head in 1951 when on April 19 the body of Philip Mangano was found in the tall grass of a marshland near the Sheepshead Bay section of Brooklyn. He was dressed only in a white shirt, white shorts, white undershirt, black socks and black tie. He had been shot three times in the back of the neck, in the right cheek and in the left cheek. The police could not inquire of Vince Mangano about the fate of his brother because Vince was missing, and he has remained missing to this day. Clearly he too had been murdered.

Anastasia was obviously a prime suspect in the murder and disappearance of the two Manganos, but authorities seem to have concentrated more on the likes of Frank Costello and Joe Adonis, neither of whom had apparently anything of substance to offer. Adonis did, with a perfectly straight face, express the callous opinion that Phil Mangano must have been involved in an affair of the heart since he had no pants on when he was found.

A meeting of the other New York crime bosses was called to inquire into the matter of Vince Mangano's disappearance—Phil's murder was not of major consequence—and without admitting anything, Anastasia accused Vince Mangano of plotting to kill him. In that thesis Anastasia got confirmation from Costello. Faced with a fait accompli, the bosses acknowledged Anastasia as the new boss of the Mangano crime family.

Actually there had been considerable politicking prior to the Mangano murders. Vince had realized he was becoming increasingly isolated, and appealed to his old friend, crime boss Joe Profaci, for aid. All he seemed to get was neutrality. He then hinted to Joe Bonanno that he wanted support. Instead, in what authorities have long noted to be a Joe Bananas trait, Bonanno left town on vacation, returning only after the Mangano affair had been concluded.

Anastasia had clearly had ambitions to take over the Mangano crime family, but he was also goaded into it by Costello. At the time, 1951, Costello was himself facing strong pressure from Vito Genovese and needed protection. Until then, Costello had relied on the muscle of New Jersey mobster Willie Moretti, who maintained a powerful army of 50 or 60 gunners. However, Moretti was, at the time, going out of his mind due to the ravages of untreated syphilis, and Genovese was lobbying earnestly with other crime leaders that Moretti be "put to sleep" for his and the organization's good. With Moretti out of the way, Costello knew he needed another source of support, and Anastasia, with the full might of a crime family behind him, would make a powerful counter to Genovese. Thus undoubtedly Costello revved up Anastasia to make his bid for power when he did.

MANGANO crime family See GAMBINO CRIME FAMILY

MANTON, Martin T. (1880–1946): Corrupt federal judge

When Woodrow Wilson made him a federal district court judge, Martin T. Manton at the age of 36 was the youngest federal jurist in the country. In time, he became the most crooked—something the crime syndicate was quick to discover.

Early on, Manton lived up to his wunderkind reputation, moving further up, to the appellate court, within a year and a half. In 1922 he was almost named by President Harding to the Supreme Court. In one 10-year period Manton produced 650 opinions, something few other jurists have ever equalled. It turned out, however, that the underworld concurred with many of his decisions. Maintaining a special bagman to negotiate the sale of his verdicts, he dispensed his decisions, according to a later description, "on an over-the-counter basis."

Soliciting a bribe once, Manton said, "While I'm sitting on the bench I have my right hand and my left hand." He used both hands when it came to taking mob money.

In 1933 a federal grand jury indicted 158 persons, including crime syndicate bigwigs Louis Lepke and Gurrah Shapiro, for violation of the antitrust laws in racketeering in the fur industry. In 1935 both men were convicted, sentenced to two years in prison and fined $10,000. Federal Judge John C. Knox refused bail pending appeal, but then Manton, as senior judge of the U.S. Circuit Court of Appeals, freed them on bond. Later, with Manton presiding, Lepke's conviction was reversed.

In 1939 Manhattan District Attorney Thomas E. Dewey, acting on a plethora of evidence, accused Judge Manton of taking underworld bribes. Manton resigned his post, announcing he would fight to clear his name. He was brought to trial. To many the charges seemed so unbelievable that Manton readily obtained character-witness testimony for his defense from Judge Learned Hand and two former presidential candidates, Al Smith and John W. Davis. He was convicted, and in a personal, bizarre appeal of his own case before the Supreme Court, he argued: "From a broad viewpoint, it serves no public policy for a high judicial officer to be convicted of a judicial crime. It tends to destroy the confidence of the people in courts." This "judicial robes defense" got nowhere with the High Court.

Manton, the highest-ranking judicial friend of the mob, served 19 months of a two-year sentence and died in 1946 in disgrace.

MARANZANO, Salvatore (1868–1931): First and only "boss of bosses"

Was there really a Mafia boss of bosses in America? A man more powerful than Al Capone, Lucky Luciano or Meyer Lansky?

Salvatore Maranzano was so powerful he could compose an execution list that included the names of Luciano, Frank Costello, Vito Genovese, Joe Adonis, Willie Moretti, Dutch Schultz and the "fat guy" in Chicago, Capone. Maranzano could do all this because he was the boss of bosses. He said so himself.

Unfortunately, Maranzano's reign came to a violent end after only four months. After that, despite the earnest efforts of enterprising journalists, the Mafia boss of bosses title was relegated to the scrap heap. Organized crime was more powerful than any so-called superboss. In that sense Maranzano died a fraud; still, he was one of the most important personalities in American crime. He founded, if we are to completely trust informer Joe Valachi, what was to be known as the Cosa Nostra.

Maranzano was an old-line mafioso, holding to the crime society's tradition of "respect" and "honor" for the family boss and continuing the blood feuds with enemies of decades past. But he did have modern ideas about crime and wanted to institutionalize it in America—with himself on top. If he had survived the bloodletting of the early 1930s, organized crime may well have had a different look today.

When Maranzano initially came to the United States is not certain. It appears he was here in 1918, again in 1925, and once more in 1927, and it's possible he moved in and out of the country several times before settling here in 1927. At that time Maranzano was sent by the most powerful Mafia leader in Sicily, Don Vito Cascio Ferro, specifically to organize the American crime families, even non-Italian ones, under one leadership. Don Vito, who had been in America in earlier decades, apparently saw himself heading such an organization, and apparently Maranzano was content to be his most favored fol-

lower. However, shortly after dispatching Maranzano, Don Vito was arrested by the Fascists and put in prison for the rest of his life. That left Maranzano on his own.

Maranzano surrounded himself with gangsters who had emigrated from his hometown in Sicily, Castellammare del Golfo. By 1928 he had attracted so many supporters that the foremost Mafia boss of New York, Giuseppe "Joe the Boss" Masseria realized he was a danger. A cunning adversary, Maranzano—college educated and originally a candidate for the priesthood—indeed intended to depose Joe the Boss and so exploited the idea that Masseria hated all Castellammarese.

Joe the Boss was a glutton in personal habits as well as in his administration of criminal activities. He demanded that other mafiosi pay him enormous tribute. Maranzano cultivated the resentment this stirred up in Masseria's subchiefs and he worked on winning defections by promising a fair division of loot. Maranzano particularly tried to lure away Lucky Luciano who had by that time become one of Masseria's most valuable aides and had reorganized gang activities for maximized profits. Luciano, however, resisted Maranzano's overtures, having plans of his own.

To check Maranzano's growing strength, Joe the Boss finally declared war. Masseria could field a few hundred more gunners than Maranzano and was confident he could crush him. From 1928 to 1930 the death toll between the two camps probably exceeded 50. The police were handicapped in trying to get a count; it was hard to tell which corpse belonged to the Castellammarese War (as the conflict was known) and which to the ordinary booze wars raging in the underworld.

As the Castellammarese War continued, it took on a third dimension. Luciano was cultivating younger gangsters on both sides with his ideas for an entirely different crime setup. His would ally the Italian criminals with powerful Jewish mobsters into a syndicate that would slice up the crime pie fairly and would even make the pie bigger. What impressed many young mafiosi was that Luciano, through Frank Costello enjoyed excellent relationships with important elements in the police and in politics. He offered far better protection than either Joe the Boss or Maranzano. Luciano soon was in a position to know what each chief was up to, having secret supporters spying for him in both camps.

For years Luciano had been close to Jewish mobster Meyer Lansky who he regarded as the most brilliant criminal mind in the country; their original plan was for Lansky to line up the Jewish mobsters around the country and Luciano the various Italian elements. Lansky had the easier chore, all but a few important Jewish mobsters saw the virtues of a national crime syndicate. Among the Italian crime families, Luciano had to proceed more cautiously. The pair decided the safest course was to let Masseria and Maranzano weaken each other with continual bloodletting until one or the other perished. Then as the Luciano/Lansky team gained strength, they would strike the remaining old don.

However, by 1931 Masseria and Maranzano were still at it. Maranzano gave far better than he got, but he was not yet the victor. Fearful that Maranzano would accumulate too many supporters as the conflict continued, Luciano and his cohorts decided to eliminate Joe the Boss. On April 15, 1931, Luciano lured Masseria to lunch at a restaurant in Coney Island. After the meal the pair played cards while all the other patrons cleared out. Then Luciano went to the men's room. While he was gone, four assassins rushed into the establishment and laid down a fusillade of 20 bullets. Masseria was struck six times and was dead when Luciano strolled out of the men's room.

Luciano then declared peace with Maranzano. Maranzano was pleased and, in supposed gratitude, made Luciano his number one man in his new organization. In a remarkable conclave, he summoned 500 gangsters to a meeting in the Bronx and outlined his grandiose scheme for crime. The New York Mafia would be divided into five major crime families, each with a boss, a sub-boss, lieutenants and soldiers. Above all the five families would be a "boss of bosses." That was Salvatore Maranzano. Maranzano dubbed this new organization Cosa Nostra, which really meant nothing more than "our thing."

All would be peaceful and profitable, he asserted. Secretly though, Maranzano did not believe that. He rightly gauged Luciano's great ambition, and realized that by dealing with non-Italian mobsters, Luciano was creating his own power base, one that would soon threaten Maranzano. He also knew that Luciano still commanded the loyalty of many important men within this new Cosa Nostra. He composed a death list of top mobsters who had to be eliminated. The list included Luciano, Costello, Genovese, Adonis, Moretti, Schultz and Chicago's Capone, who had been friendly with Luciano for years.

Maranzano knew it would not be easy to kill all these men and he decided not to risk all-out war before at least some were eliminated. Otherwise, he could not be sure who was on whose side and who might betray him to Luciano. Maranzano decided to have the job handled by non-Italians so that he could pose as innocent. He recruited the notorious young Irish killer Vince "Mad Dog" Coll and arranged for him to come to his office in the Grand Central building at a time when Luciano and Genovese would be present. Apparently Coll was to kill the pair that day and "lose" their bodies so that he could knock off as many of the others as possible before the murders became known. Maranzano gave Coll $25,000 as a down payment and promised him $25,000 more on the elimination of the first two victims.

However, Luciano got wind of the assassination plan and knew the murder operation would start when he got a phone call summoning him to Maranzano's office. Luciano, through Lansky, already had his own murder team in training with a plot to kill Maranzano. He ordered that training speeded up. On September 10, 1931, Maranzano telephoned.

Shortly before Luciano and Genovese were slated to arrive at Maranzano's headquarters, Tommy Lucchese walked in. Maranzano was unaware of Lucchese's link to Luciano. (In fact, Lucchese was Luciano's main spy inside the Maranzano organization even before Masseria's murder.)

Shortly after Lucchese arrived, four men walked in flashing badges and announcing they had questions to ask Maranzano. The four were Jewish gangsters Luciano had borrowed for his counterplot since Maranzano did not know them. They also did not know Maranzano which was why Lucchese was present—to make sure they got the right man.

The bogus officers lined up Maranzano's bodyguards against the wall and disarmed them. Then two went into Maranzano's office and stabbed and shot him to death. The assassins and Lucchese charged out. So did the bodyguards when they found that their boss had been executed. On the way down the emergency stairs, one of them ran into Mad Dog Coll coming to keep his own murder date. Informed of the new situation, Coll turned and left whistling. He was $25,000 to the good.

Maranzano's death had far-reaching effects on organized crime in America. Essentially, it marked the end of the Italian Mafia in America. What remained was a new American Mafia that would become part of a national syndicate with other ethnics, something the old Mafia was too rigid to allow. Luciano immediately eliminated the post of "boss of bosses" and called the new organization the "combination" or "outfit" or as a sop to the traditionalists among the mafiosi the "Unione Siciliano," a corruption in spelling of the longtime Sicilian fraternal organization. The concept of "Cosa Nostra" died as well with Maranzano, not to be revived by federal authorities and a cooperative Joe Valachi until the early 1960s, as a way to get J. Edgar Hoover out of a deep hole. For decades he had denied the existence of the Mafia and organized crime, but now he could announce with a straight face that the FBI had been studying the "Cosa Nostra" for a long time. Thus even when he was partially right he was 30 years behind the times.

See also MUSTACHE PETES; NIGHT OF THE SICILIAN VESPERS

Carlos Marcello was an enduring ruler of the New Orleans Mafia, an organization that allows no other mafioso to enter the area without special permission.

MARCELLO, Carlos (1910–1993): Mafia boss of New Orleans

One of the most stolid, hardline crime family bosses in the country, Carlos Marcello ran New Orleans and Louisiana like a closed shop—a tradition in that Mafia chapter since its creation in the last century.

Nobody from any crime family "insulted" Marcello by coming to New Orleans without permission. Informer Joe Valachi once told Vito Genovese, his New York boss, he wished to go to New Orleans for Mardi Gras. Genovese's reply, Valachi testified, was, "'Don't go.' No explanations, just 'Don't go.' They didn't want anybody there. And I was told if I ever had to go to Louisiana, Genovese would call ahead and get permission. Genovese himself had to get permission. It was an absolute rule."

Carlos Marcello was born Calorso Minicari, in Tunis, North Africa, in 1910, of Sicilian parents. He was brought to America at the age of eight months. His first arrest occurred when he was 20 for bank robbery. The case was dismissed, a not unusual beginning for the future bigs of crime. His police record includes such charges as dope peddling, gambling, income tax evasion, robbery and aggravated assault. Marcello won a full pardon from Louisiana's governor for the assault conviction; the New Orleans family has always enjoyed a cozy relationship with many local and state officials.

By the mid-1930s, the young Marcello had become one of the most trusted aides of Mafia boss Sam Carolla, and while the latter sojourned for a brief period in federal prison, Marcello took charge of discussions with the Luciano-Lansky-Costello clique from New York. The trio had won rights from the Kingfish, Senator Huey Long, to bring their gambling operations and slot machines into the state. In a sense, this violated the New Orleans crime family's rule excluding outsiders, but the offer was too good for Marcello to refuse. The New Yorkers supplied all the capital, Long provided the political protection, and the New Orleans family took a hefty share of the profits. Years later, an irate Crazy Joe Gallo demanded "Who gave Louisiana to Frank Costello?" It would have been interesting to see how long the Gallos might have lasted had they come down to New Orleans and asked that of Marcello directly.

Over the years Marcello was subjected to a number of deportation attempts, none of them successful. Once, when efforts were being pressed to have him sent to Italy, it was said Marcello responded by sending off a lawyer to Rome with a bagful of money. The going rate for key figures in the Italian Parliament was put at $10,000 each, and, in due course, the Italian foreign ministry informed the U.S. government that Marcello was not an Italian citizen and would not be accepted for deportation. Remarkably, the U.S. government had not made until then a formal deportation request. It was said payments continued for another three years while further unsolicited decisions emanated from Rome. The U.S. government did try to interest France and Tunisia to take Marcello, but these efforts came to naught. Finally, in a bizarre episode, the United States virtually kidnapped Marcello and deposited him in Guatemala, claiming he was a citizen of that country.

Finally, facing popular outrage, Guatemala demanded the United States take him back. Washington refused and Marcello was virtually smuggled into El Salvador. From there Marcello and his lawyer trekked through the jungle into Honduras. Then, in a zany conclusion to the affair, Marcello simply got on a commercial airliner to Miami and walked right through customs and immigration without even being checked. He was back in the United States to stay.

In December 1960, Attorney General–designate Robert Kennedy announced he had two priority targets on taking office: Teamsters president Jimmy Hoffa and Carlos Marcello. Bobby Kennedy's ability to go after Marcello disappeared with the assassination of President John F. Kennedy.

In the meantime, Marcello had grown in stature within the Mafia. He was consulted on all major syndicate actions and appears to have made friends within the CIA, having been involved in the supposed plots to kill Fidel Castro of Cuba. Ever since the assassination of President Kennedy, theories contrary to the findings of the Warren Commission have often pointed to the Mafia as the real killers, especially toward Santo Trafficante Jr. of the Tampa, Florida, crime family and Marcello, both of whom were quoted as making threats against the Kennedys because of the administration's pressure on organized crime. According to this thesis, the mob's real target was Bobby Kennedy. The best way to tame the attorney general's office was to eliminate the president.

Marcello throughout the years denied the charges. He was subjected to considerable legal problems near the end of his life but persisted in his claim that he was no more than a "legitimate businessman" being harassed by the government. Essentially, Marcello's rule over his family—out of the country, in prison or

on the loose—was ironclad. Also beyond dispute is that Marcello was a multimillionaire, his wealth in 1975 estimated at more than $60 million. In failing health, he died in 1993.

See also BOURG, FRANK; CAROLLA, SYLVESTRO "SAM"; CHARITY AND THE MAFIA; DEPORTATION OF MAFIOSI

MARION Penitentiary: For the Mafia's most dangerous

It became home for Mafia boss John Gotti after his conviction in 1992. It was also labeled inhumane by Amnesty International. It is the United States Penitentiary at Marion, Illinois, the most restrictive of all federal penal institutions for its time. When Gotti was delivered to the Marion warden, there were at least two mob men he knew (but never got to see) in the prison—Nicodemo "Nicky" Scarfo, the brutal ex-boss of the Philadelphia family, and Jimmy Coonan, the top honcho of the Westies, the New York Irish mob affiliated with the Mafia, and some of the crime cartel's most ardent killers.

Other notorious prisoners included John Walker, the Navy man who sold classified information to the former Soviet Union; Edwin Wilson, a U.S. government employee who sold weapons to Libya's Muammar al-Qaddafi and conspired to kill eight witnesses to his crime and Jonathan Jay Pollard who spied for the Israelis. It was an open question whether these prisoners were there because they constituted a continuing menace to the nation and society or because they were incarcerated in such a way to inflict great mental punishment on them.

Kept in the most restrictive level of confinement in prison, an 8-by-7-feet underground cell for 22 to 23 hours a day, Gotti had no work, no communal recreation, no communal education classes. Food was delivered through a slot in the cell door. All that he was allowed in his cell was a single cot, a basin, a toilet, a radio and a black-and-white TV. There was not even a chair to sit on. Rather than spend all his hours prone on his cot, Gotti folded his mattress into an L shape, which he propped against the wall to simulate a chair. It was said he read, watched television (mostly talk shows) and exercised by doing probably 1,000 pushups a day. He was taken to his shower shackled in chains inside a movable cage. His contact with the outside was limited to five monthly visiting periods, mostly with his lawyers or his son Junior. The FBI admitted Gotti continued to rule the Gambino family through his son, who served as acting boss of the family, passing along his father's instructions.

Most lifers sent to Marion are kept there 30 months and then transferred to a regular maximum-security prison elsewhere. Gotti's time on that basis was completed in 1995, but he remained in Marion. It was said that his lawyers did not press the issue of his long confinement for fear it would prolong the situation or possibly cause his transfer to an even harsher federal prison that had since opened in Colorado.

Some speculated that authorities still harbored hopes that Gotti would "break" and finally turn informer against the mob in exchange for some form of leniency. Some members of the media insisted they had indications that there had even been an attempt on Gotti's life, most remarkable considering his isolation.

Other observers saw Gotti being used as a "horror example" for other mafiosi who get arrested on what could await them if uncooperative.

MASSERIA, Giuseppe "Joe the Boss" (c. 1880–1931): Mafia leader

By the mid-1920s Joe the Boss Masseria was the undisputed boss of the New York Mafia, a tribute to treachery, extreme good luck and a willingness, even an eagerness, to kill. A stocky, 5-feet-2-inch gunman with cold, beady eyes, Masseria had fled a murder charge in Sicily in 1903. Within a few years in New York he was arrested for extortion and burglary and became a member of the notorious Morello Gang, the city's first important Mafia crime family.

While the Morellos' top killers, Lupo the Wolf and Ciro Terranova, dominated the gang, Masseria considered himself more than their equal. In 1913, with Morello and Lupo the Wolf in prison, he led a faction seeking to take over much of the Morello rackets. Masseria brazenly led attacks directly on the Morello headquarters at 116th Street, once killing a cousin, Charles Lamonti, right on the doorstep. Six months later he knocked off Lamonti's brother on the same spot.

Then Masseria hit a run of luck. Nick Morello, the acting head and the most far-sighted of the family, was killed by rival Camorristas in Brooklyn. The Camorra leaders themselves went to prison for the murder, leaving Masseria an open field. And, by the

Joe the Boss Masseria, treacherous head of the New York Mafia, was a Mustache Pete who had to die before Lucky Luciano could form the national crime syndicate.

time Joe Morello and Lupo the Wolf came out of prison in the early 1920s, the rotund but deadly Masseria had locked up much of the bootlegging racket in the Italian sections of New York.

After his release, Lupo retired from the crime scene, but the Morellos tried to rally under Peter Morello. Peter allied himself with another rising mafioso, Rocco Valenti, who was regarded by Masseria as a major threat. Once Valenti caught up with Masseria and a couple of bodyguards on Second Avenue. He cut down the unarmed Masseria's protectors, and then calmly reloaded and followed the fleeing Masseria into a millinery shop. Valenti fired several times at Masseria at fairly close range and in what must have looked like a grim Keystone

Kops comedy sequence, his rotund target ducked and weaved and all the bullets whizzed by him. It was amazing since Valenti had committed at least 20 murders and was regarded as a cool, accurate shooter. Frustrated and fearing the arrival of the police, Valenti retreated, and thereafter Masseria gained a reputation as "the man who could dodge bullets."

Finally, Joe the Boss let Valenti know he was willing to make peace and a meeting was arranged in a restaurant on East 12th Street. When Valenti showed up with three cohorts, Masseria was not present, but three of his men were. Suspecting a doublecross, he raced for the street. The Masseria gunmen wounded two of Valenti's men and chased after Valenti, who hopped on the running board of a passing taxi and was shooting back, when he was shot dead by one of the gunmen. Valenti's assailant: Charles Luciano, a man destined for big things.

The Morellos shortly thereafter sued for peace. Some were retired while others were absorbed into Masseria's operations. Masseria was now the top Mafia power, and five crime families in Manhattan, Brooklyn and the Bronx were subservient to him. For a time his only problem was the rising Luciano, a valuable crime organizer, but an upstart who was too chummy with Jewish gangsters like Meyer Lansky and the young and homicidal Bugsy Siegel. Masseria hated Jews and told Luciano to break off with them and to put his operations with them in the Masseria pot. He was wasting his breath. Luciano wasn't the only headstrong lieutenant. Frank Costello bridled under Masseria's criticism for paying off the politicians. Joe the Boss allowed it was all right to bribe an official once in a while when necessary but his boys should not "sleep with them" all the time because the politicians would eventually corrupt them. Costello marveled at anyone so stupid as not to understand it was the other way around.

By 1927, Masseria faced a new threat. A newly arrived Sicilian mafioso named Salvatore Maranzano sought to push him aside. It was generally believed that Maranzano was the advance representative of Don Vito Cascio Ferro, the most important Mafia leader in Sicily, who was looking to move into American crime. But Don Vito would never come; Mussolini's fascists imprisoned him. Nevertheless, Maranzano decided to advance on Masseria and become the American boss of bosses on his own.

Masseria at first was not worried by the Maranzano threat. He had more gunners and better men. One was his old foe, Peter "the Clutching Hand" Morello. And he had brilliant youngsters headed by Luciano, and including such stalwarts as Joe Adonis, Frank Costello, Willie Moretti, Albert Anastasia and Carlo Gambino. However, these Young Turks were not as loyal as he thought. All of them were working with Lansky and Siegel and with Dutch Schultz whom Masseria particularly disliked.

However, the Young Turks stayed in line for a time. They couldn't switch gangs; they hated Maranzano as much as they hated Masseria. They were waiting instead for a time when they would be able to operate without any of the so-called Mustache Petes and their outmoded, old-country, Mafia-style codes. The only code these young gangsters were interested in was making money. Fighting Mafia wars was a hindrance to that goal, and the Castellammarese War between Maranzano and Masseria was just such a hindrance.

Luciano organized the Young Turks. Their plan: bide their time until Masseria killed Maranzano or vice versa. But by 1931 both were still around and the Castellammarese War was taking a bloody toll. Luciano decided it was time to act. He had thought Maranzano would perish first, but, as the war continued, Maranzano got stronger and Masseria weaker. Since it was easier to murder someone who trusted you than someone who did not, Luciano and his supporters—including outsiders like Lansky and Siegel—decided to take out Masseria.

On April 15, 1931, Luciano suggested to Masseria that they drive out to Coney Island for lunch. They dined at Nuova Villa Tammaro, owned by Gerardo Scarpato, a friend of a number of mobsters. Joe the Boss stuffed himself and after all the other diners left, he and Luciano played cards while Scarpato went down to the beach for a walk.

About 3:30 P.M. four men came charging through the door to Masseria's table. They were Bugsy Siegel, Joe Adonis, Vito Genovese and Albert Anastasia. All produced guns and blazed away at Masseria. Six bullets struck Joe the Boss and the Castellammarese War was over.

Newspaper accounts of the sensational murder focused on Luciano's statement to the police that he had gone to the bathroom and when he heard the shooting, he dried his hands and came out to see what was happening. It was a bit of self-censorship by the press. Actually Luciano told the police, "I was in the can taking a leak. I always take a long leak."

After the assassination Luciano negotiated a peace with Maranzano and pledged support to him. However, both Maranzano and Luciano were aware that sooner or later one or the other would have to go.

See also CASTELLAMMARESE WAR; MUSTACHE PETES

MASSINO, Joseph C. (1943–): The "Last Don"

To all outward appearances, Joe Massino is hardly a charismatic Mafia don. By looks he could be said to resemble the murderous Luca Brasi, the dull-witted enforcer of *The Godfather,* but Massino is by no means a dullard. By the turn of the 21st century, Massino was regarded by both federal investigators and Mafia wise guys of the five New York families as

Joseph Massino, reputed boss of the Bonanno crime family, in an undated file photo. More than 70 years after a bloody mob war ended with a peace producing New York City's five Mafia families, the heads of each crime syndicate are simultaneously behind bars for the first time.

the toughest, meanest and most resourceful of the mafiosi still at large after the far-flung prosecutions by federal authorities. By then the leaders of the other four families, from John Gotti on down, were safely incarcerated and hardly likely ever to return to their positions of power on the outside. But Massino seemed to be untouchable. The head of the long-dormant Bonanno crime family, he took over the leadership in the late 1980s and seemed to function as little more than a vassal under Gotti's control of the powerful Gambino family.

There is no record of Massino ever contradicting any of the acts of Gotti, although he undoubtedly felt Gotti frequently went off on birdbrain tangents. Certainly Massino must have bridled under Gotti's insane policy of constantly ordering his wise guys to show up at Gambino headquarters on Mulberry Street in Little Italy. The FBI's cameras grinded away nonstop, and thanks to Gotti the agency built up a fabulous rogues gallery to identify wise guys. Massino could not offend Gotti by not showing up himself and was therefore present as government bugs picked up an overblown Gotti assuring him that if "they would leave us alone for another year, we will be so set up they can never take us apart." All Massino could do was listen silently and contribute nothing to the conversation. Gotti of course would be proved wrong, and his empire would soon destruct—even self-destruct.

From early on in his career Massino moved up steadily because of his penchant for secrecy and guarding himself and his allies from surveillance by the law. Now as the head of a fairly ineffective crime group, Massino needed Gotti's sponsorship, and Gotti in turn needed Massino. By rehabilitating the Bonannos from the purgatory of nonrecognition by the other three families, Gotti worked to restore them to membership in the Commission so that he always would have a second vote and be that much closer to actual control of the entire Commission.

By 1992 Gotti was put away by the feds, something which was close to a godsend for Massino. He turned the Bonannos into the powerhouse it had not been since the early part of the reign of the legendary Joe Bananas. Massino set up a wall of secrecy that challenged the FBI. Meetings by the family's top brass often involved the renting of five or so trucks from various legitimate rental outfits, and the boys would be picked up with, say, four of the trucks and all transferred to the fifth, which would go on to the final destination. Since all the vehicle outlets were clean, there was no way the feds could bug them in advance. Massino also came up with the idea of holding mob meetings far outside New York, as far away as Mexico, France or England. Then a few of the boys would sojourn on to Sicily to check out possible talent for import to the States.

Massino also became "king of the 'uh,'" never saying anything on the phone for fear of wiretaps. If the speaker always simply said "uh," in response to other mobsters, it would be much harder to convict him of involvement in a criminal enterprise. Other mafiosi tried that as well but seldom with the same success. The late crime boss, Carmine Galante, was one of the most prudent phone users in the Mafia, and the FBI seldom got more than a simple "uh" out of him. His legal defenders claimed he was simply expressing his disinterest in the entire subject. Once in a while Galante might slip, but it does not appear that Massino ever did.

The transformation of the Bonannos under Massino was stunning. When he took over in 1986, the Bonannos were in total disrepair. Their activities seemed to be home video pornography, pizza parlors (with a fillip as an ideal way to hide illegal aliens), espresso cafés, restaurants and a major narcotics trade over which the bosses had by then started to lose control to rogue members. Massino led a determined operation to bring the outfit to bay. Jockeying with the approval of Gotti, Massino built up a force of about 100 active wise guys and while crackdowns were going on elsewhere, no major figure in the Bonanno family was under indictment. By 1998 the family had grown so much in stature that it was rivaling the Gambinos and was close to being the second most powerful outfit in the East. Chagrined law officials shifted the main efforts to getting Massino and the Bonannos. Further sticking in the craw of the law was the fact that Bonanno wise guys had become so enamored with Massino that they started calling the family the Massino crime family—although the law and the Mafia itself have long sought to restrict the naming of crime families to the leadership power in force in the early 1960s.

By 2004 the prosecutors were ready to bring Massino up on a number of murder charges, the cases all built around defecting members facing prosecution. For Massino to be convicted it was clear a strong case against him would have to be made by independent evidence, especially since federal prose-

cutors revealed they were considering seeking the death penalty—a first for any godfather. Part of the reason for this move obviously was pressure about death sentences handed down to blacks and Hispanics for committing relatively few murders while ignoring the Mafia godfathers who ordered the murders of foes by the scores if not hundreds. Even so, the approval was less than enthusiastic, and the suspicion would not die down that the law was going after Massino simply because he had been such an embarrassment for so long.

The outcome of the death sentence strategy was unclear by 2004, and some legal observers insisted the government would drop execution for a guilty plea from Massino, also not considered a sure thing. Massino in any event represented a part of a wiser, tougher and, above all, meaner new leadership for the American Mafia. Whatever his own fate, it seemed obvious that others will adopt his tactics in rebuilding a stronger era of mobdom.

Massino was convicted of ordering seven murders. Witnesses included six inducted Bonanno wise guys, the first ever to testify against the family. Massino was due to get life without parole. However, one charge remained, and the government said it would seek the death penalty in that case.

Within legal circles, there was a strong objection to the ploy. Detractors said the charge should have been linked to the other seven. Even the judge on the case offered strong criticism of outgoing attorney general John Ashcroft. Judge Nicholas G. Garaufis said, "Mr. Ashcroft's choice to make such a sobering and potentially life-ending decision now, after several delays, and only after tendering his resignation to the president and announcing to the country that he no longer wishes to preside over the Department of Justice, is deeply troubling to this court."

The judge agreed that Ashcroft was within his rights but urged Ashcroft's successor to reach an "independent assessment." The judge clearly indicated it might be a year or longer before the case would come before his court.

Some suspected that the actual motive behind the decision was simply to get Massino "to rat out," something no top Mafia boss had ever done. Then came another bombshell: Joe M. was singing about family secrets and offering even more. Within and without the mob the revelation was doubted as an effort to sow panic. Leaks of this sort are not at all unusual. There were leaks that big shots in the Gambino crime family, including tough and mean Aniello Dellacroce, John Gotti's mentor, had spied for the FBI and that Gotti himself was about to go for a deal. Clearly, again here the ploy was meant to cause the Gambinos to self-destruct. It never happened. The mobsters wouldn't buy it. In Massino's case, his fate may be of little consequence. The accepted theory is that the main thrust was an attempt to get the mobsters suspicious of one another until finally "the wheels would come off."

Early reports were that the plan, if there was one, was not working. The mob still held Massino in high regard. Mafia beliefs die hard. Time will tell if such respect is viable in the mob.

See also BURIAL GROUND OF THE MAFIA; DEATH PENALTY FOR GODFATHERS; SCIASCIA, GERLANDO

MATRANGA, Charles (1857–1943): Early New Orleans Mafia boss

After the infamous mass lynching of mafioso criminals in New Orleans in 1891—an incident clearly accompanied by strong, general anti-Italian bias—Charles Matranga remained as the sole Mafia chieftain in power in the city. He was in parish prison when the lynch mob of many thousands stormed the establishment, in response to the murder of Chief of Police David Hennessey, and hanged a number of Italians being held there. Matranga evaded the mob. Later he was set free because the case against him was too weak, based on the testimony of only one informer.

The early history of the Mafia in America is rather hazy. Indeed, even the firm statements of crime historians are contradictory. Yet without dispute is the fact that New York and New Orleans were the most common ports of entry for Italian immigrants in the 19th century and that among these immigrants were a number of Italian criminals with some ties to such organizations as the Mafia in Sicily and the Camorra in Naples.

The members of these societies tended to band together in the new country, not necessarily with the same loyalties as previously. In New Orleans, the mafiosi element clearly won out over the Camorristas. By 1891, the main contenders were two rival groups of mafiosi, one headed by the Provenzano brothers and the other by the Matranga brothers—Antonio and Carlo or Charley.

Some historians insist the real leader of the Matranga mafiosi was Joseph Macheca, a prosperous fruit importer and shipping company owner who was among those lynched. In any event, after the lynchings Charley Matranga continued his crime rule. One observer who disputes this is Humbert S. Nelli, who, in *The Business of Crime*, insists "if indeed he had ever headed a *mafia* group, he lost this prominent position. Nothing occurring in the remaining fifty-two years of his life connected him with criminal activities . . . he led a quiet life as a stevedore for the Standard Fruit Company . . . until his retirement after fifty years of service in 1918. . . ."

Actually nothing in Matranga's remaining "life connected him with criminal activities" because the 1891 lynching not surprisingly left a profound impression on him. Matranga was one of the first mafiosi to appreciate the value of using a buffer between him and public awareness of his role. For some years before his retirement from active leadership of the New Orleans Mafia in 1922, Matranga used young Sam Carolla as his front man, issuing all orders through him.

Until Matranga died on October 28, 1943, at the age of 86, he continued to receive tribute from the longshoremen's associations and steamship lines which benefited from his benign approval. He was given a lavish funeral, attended by executives of Lykes, United Fruit, Standard Fruit, and large steamship companies—a remarkable tribute for a lowly stevedore, one who had been arrested for murder and almost lynched. The fact was Charles Matranga was a Man of Tradition and his big-business victims had to honor that tradition right up to the end.

See also CAROLLA, SYLVESTRO "SAM"; NEW ORLEANS MAFIA MASS LYNCHINGS

MATTRESSES, hitting the: Gang war tactic

A long-established custom among mobsters going to war against rival gangs, "hitting the mattresses" means being under seige away from home in bare rooms containing only mattresses on the floor. The mattresses are thrown up at the doors and windows for protection should a shoot-out occur. In recent years a great many mobsters hit the mattresses during the Banana War and the Gallo-Profaci conflict. For some, hitting the mattresses is a terrifying period of tension and boredom; others tend to thrive at it. It was said from the time of the Castellammarese War of 1930–1931 that Joseph Bonanno (Joe Bananas), as if he had ice water in his veins, could take the mattress life in so-called safe houses much better than most other mobsters. On the other hand, Crazy Joe Gallo went nuts in such an environment, and instead of remaining in the sanctuary of the mattresses, he ventured forth in 1972 and was promptly assassinated.

MICKEY Mouse Mafia: California crime families

The Los Angeles, San Diego, San Jose and San Francisco crime families are known to criminal groups and crimefighters alike as the Mickey Mouse Mafia. When in 1984 police in southern California launched an all-out drive to stop an attempt by organized crime to take over some $50-million-a-year book-making operations, they labeled the campaign "Operation Lightweight." Los Angeles Police Chief Daryl Gates explained: "We feel the name is appropriate because organized crime is such a lightweight in Southern California."

All the California crime families have been considered second rate—even Los Angeles when it was bossed by Jack Dragna, considered to have been California's toughest mafioso. The Chicago mob, for instance, extended its influence in Hollywood, especially in movie rackets, regardless of the Los Angeles family's feelings. The New York mobs did the same, sending in Bugsy Siegel and others to extend their gambling empire into the West. This extension was Meyer Lansky's idea and he got Lucky Luciano to warn Dragna not to interfere. Dragna acquiesced to Luciano's orders even though Lucky was at the time in Dannemora prison. Clearly, a Luciano behind bars was more awesome than a Dragna on the loose.

Another who showed contempt for the West Coast Mafia mobs was Jimmy "the Weasel" Fratianno, as near to an efficient killer as ever flourished in those climes. Of James Lanza, boss of the San Francisco family, Fratianno once told an underworld associate: "What has he ever done besides sell olive oil and insurance? Them guys in San Francisco and San Jose wouldn't last two minutes if some real workers moved into their towns. Maybe we ought to move in and take over both towns. Knock off a couple of guys, scare the rest shitless."

Fratianno considered doing just that but instead moved into a power vacuum in Los Angeles where the imprisonment of the then boss and underboss left Louie Tom Dragna, the deceased Jack's nephew, in charge. Dragna was a weakling and Fratianno, brought in as acting boss, tried to put some backbone into L.A., pointing out that the other crime families had no respect for them and the more they failed to resist incursions, the more incursions would follow.

Fratianno's plan never reached fruition. He aroused hostility among several important mobsters, especially in Chicago, and came under suspicion of being an informer. (He started feeding federal investigators bits of information, mainly because that allowed him to operate more freely without FBI interference since the agency did not maintain strict surveillance over those whom they thought were serving them.)

To this day, even though they represent one of the lushest areas of the country, the California mobs remain the weak sister of organized crime, truly the Mickey Mouse Mafia.

MIDNIGHT arrests of mobsters

A great many arrests of organized crime figures are called "midnight arrests," or more likely those made between 2 and 4 A.M. Mobsters so arrested have been zeroed in as potential informers who would be ready to make a deal with authorities to avoid their own prosecution. By taking such a suspect into custody in the wee hours of the morning, authorities are letting them have more time to think about making a deal since it is unlikely his criminal confederates will know immediately that he is in custody.

Realistically, some observers regard these post-midnight arrests as a cunning method to put added pressure on a possible informer. He knows that his criminal associates understand the tactic. Thus the arrestee understands the rest of the mob will figure that the authorities regard him as a weak link. They will wonder why that is so. Additionally the arrestee has to wonder what the mob will do about it when he later turns up and claims he has said nothing. The mob seldom operates on the honor system and the more the man thinks about it, the more logical it seems that he should flip.

MIDNIGHT Rose's: Candy store "office" of Murder, Inc.

Under the elevated subway tracks at the corner of Saratoga and Livonia Avenues in the Brownsville section of Brooklyn there was in the 1930s a tacky little candy store where two topics of conversation dominated: 1) how many runs the Brooklyn Dodgers would lose by that day and 2) murder.

It was said that more individual murders were planned in the candy store than at any other spot on Earth. The store, owned by a woman who kept it open 24 hours a day, was thus called Midnight Rose's. Here the professional killers of Murder, Inc.—the Jewish and Italian gangsters who made up the enforcement arm of the national syndicate in the 1930s—congregated. Midnight Rose's was the "war room" of the mob where, over egg creams and other savory refreshments, homicide specialists were briefed and dispatched on "hits."

The gunners, knifers and garroters from Midnight Rose's knocked off some 300 to 500 victims, although there were those enthusiasts who called such figures absurdly low.

See also MURDER, INCORPORATED

MIRABELLA, John (1905–1955): Mafia hit man

Because he plied his trade in such out-of-the-way spots as Detroit, Toledo, Youngstown and the like, John Mirabella never garnered the national press like the big-city mob hit men. It was, a cynic might observe, an outrage. Mirabella was a true master of murder.

His memoirs would make those of Jimmy "the Weasel" Fratianno read like Sunday school texts. Mirabella was tough, and he knew where so many bodies were buried that he had to be pensioned off for years of retirement while on the lam from the law. The normal laws of practicality, for which the Mafia is noted, might suggest the mob could save a small fortune as well as gain peace of mind by the simple expedient of knocking him off. The problem that arose was where could someone tough enough be found to take Mirabella out. The consistent answer was nowhere. Ever.

Mirabella labored originally for the Licavoli family, who moved into Detroit to provide added muscle for the notorious Purple Gang. The Purples were vicious Jewish mobsters who could kill with the worst of them, but even they came to respect Mirabella. He killed with finesse, wiping out some of the toughest enemy bootleggers with deadly efficiency.

In 1930, Mirabella handled what is still regarded by many as Detroit's most shocking murder, that of pioneer radio newscaster and muckraker Jerry Buckley.

Buckley made war on the mobs, which in one period of 14 days gifted the city with 11 killings, and on a city hall that seemed totally unconcerned with cleaning up the gangster element. At 1 A.M.—shortly after he had broadcast a recall election special declaring that the rascals were thrown out—Buckley was sitting in a hotel lobby in a happy mood when three gunmen entered. One stood guard by the door while the other two approached Buckley and pumped six shots apiece at him. Only one slug missed; Jerry Buckley crashed to the floor dead. In time, Mirabella was identified as the lead gunner, the craftsman who planned the operation, but, by that time, Mirabella had vanished.

The Licavoli forces were chased out of Detroit by the ensuing heat and settled for a time in Toledo where beer baron Jackie Kennedy held sway. There Mirabella proved a vital hit man, who demonstrated his value by putting many Kennedy enforcers on a slab in the morgue.

Getting the hoods was one thing, but Kennedy was another. When boss Yonnie Licavoli gave Mirabella the contract on Kennedy, the previously murder-proof booze baron was as good as stone cold dead. Love had come to Kennedy in the form of a beautiful brunette who, after many weeks of romance, accompanied him on a walk through a quiet Toledo suburb. As they strolled a dark street, the woman had hold of Kennedy's gun arm. He never had a chance when Mirabella stepped out of a black car and shot him dead at close range, close enough that his female accomplice did not get in the way of any bullets.

By early 1934, murder warrants were out on Mirabella for the Kennedy and Buckley rubouts, as well as for a half-dozen others. Yonnie Licavoli went to prison for conspiracy to commit murder, and many other top mafiosi faced serious legal problems. If John Mirabella could be found, he might spill the secrets of many Mafia murders and could send many a member of the Honored Society to prison—probably even to the electric chair.

The general rule of thumb is that a hit man with that much knowledge is better off dead. But Mirabella did not face that fate. No one would take him on, and he disappeared into the grimy, steeltown surroundings of Youngstown. In 1945, Mirabella, long carrying the name of Paul Magine, married a local woman. Mirabella appeared to be the owner of a produce business, but he was never on the premises. Instead he was a constant habitue of gambling joints and bookie parlors. He was never short of money and was seldom without a bottle of Scotch in his hand.

Once a week, Mirabella, the FBI was later to discover through informers, had a visit from Cadillac Charley Cavallaro, a top Youngstown mafioso. Author Hank Messick in *The Private Lives of Public Enemies* relates the testimony given the FBI by Cavallaro's chauffeur-bodyguard: "They always embraced and kissed each other on the cheek, each cheek, and had a helluva reunion, as if they hadn't seen each other for years. Then Charley would hand over a wad of dough. All the way home he would curse and rave about having to give money to 'short coats and leeches,' but the next week he'd go back and the same thing would happen all over again."

Nobody could figure out anything to do with Mirabella but pay him off. Even in a perpetual alcoholic haze, he inspired nothing but fear.

In the end, Mother Nature did the Mafia a favor. At the age of 48 Mirabella died of cirrhosis of the liver. Killer Scotch had taken the Detroit-Cleveland-Toledo-Youngstown mobs off the hook.

MORAN, George "Bugs" (1893–1957): Gangster foe of Capone

By the late 1920s, Al Capone was the rising star of organized crime in Chicago. Left in his way were only a few potent foes, chief of whom were the Aiello family of mafiosi and the depleted ranks of Dion O'Banion's North Side Gang. The latter was bossed by George "Bugs" Moran. Although he gained his nickname from his often bizarre and flaky behavior, Bugs was known, especially to Capone, as a brutal and efficient killer.

Bugs Moran ascended in the O'Banion Gang largely due to Capone's machinations. In 1924, Capone had engineered O'Banion's murder, and in 1926, he got the successor, Hymie Weiss. The leadership of the North Siders next fell to Schemer Drucci who was killed by a policeman in 1927. That elevated Moran to the top spot.

Capone realized with Moran in charge, the shooting war with the O'Banion gang would escalate. That was the Bugs's way. Through the years it would have been impossible to dredge up an O'Banion mob shooting caper in which Moran was not involved. He was said to be the first to put a bullet in the head of a riding academy horse the O'Banions snatched and "executed" after it had thrown and kicked to death

their celebrated compatriot Nails Morton. He was the gunman who charged across the street to finish off Johnny Torrio after he had been hit four times by shots fired at his limousine (Moran's gun misfired and Torrio lived.) Moran was also in the lead car in the famous machine-gun motorcade that sprayed Capone's Hawthorne Inn with over 1,000 slugs.

Moran's hatred for Capone bordered on the pathological; he often referred to him, in or out of his presence, as "the Beast" or "the Behemoth." To vex him, Moran would frequently make peace with Capone and then break the agreement within a matter of hours.

Bugs considered Capone a lowly human, especially since he'd deal in prostitution. A regular churchgoer, Moran, like his predecessors, refused to let whorehouses operate in the gang's North Side territory. Capone kept trying to set up shops, sending offers to split the profits evenly with Moran. Irate, Bugs once thundered, "We don't deal in flesh. We think anyone who does is lower than a snake's belly. Can't Capone get that through his thick skull?"

Moran, born of Irish and Polish immigrant parents in Minnesota in 1893, grew up in the predominantly Irish North Side of Chicago. He grew up with street gangs, committing 26 known robberies and serving three incarcerations before he was 21. He was soon running with Dion O'Banion, who loved him like a brother. A natural pair, both possessed the same sort of homicidal "wit." Once Moran ran into Judge John H. Lyle, one of the city's few honest and courageous jurists of the era, at a baseball game and said, "Judge, that's a beautiful diamond ring you're wearing. If it's snatched some night, promise me you won't go hunting me. I'm telling you now I'm innocent."

Moran's sense of humor made him rather a darling of newspapermen. Portrayed as something of a jolly good murderer, he was made out to be a likeable fellow. This good press probably put more Chicagoans on Moran's side with hopes that he would win the war of survival with Big Al.

But the war ended in a draw. The closest Capone got to getting Moran was in the St. Valentine's Day Massacre in 1929. The Capones suckered Moran into believing he was about to buy a load of hijacked booze from some Detroit racketeers and Bugs arranged to have the loot delivered to the gang's headquarters, a garage, on the morning of February 14. Moran was late for the appointment, having overslept. Accompanied by two aides, Bugs rushed to the garage just in time to spot three men dressed as policemen and two others in plainclothes enter the garage.

Believing it to be a police shakedown, Moran decided to wait until they left. Minutes later, machine-gun fire was heard from inside the garage, leaving six Moran men and an innocent bystander dead. Moran took off. He announced, "Only Capone kills like that," and promised vengeance. In order to get Capone, Moran allied himself with the Aiellos and some disgruntled Jewish mobsters under Jack Zuta in a plot to get some of Capone's men to defect and kill Big Al. All their plots failed, and both Joe Aiello and Zuta died from Capone bullets.

Throughout the 1930s, Moran's power waned even though Capone himself had gone to prison on income tax charges. In 1936 Moran may have enjoyed a measure of retaliation when Machine Gun Jack McGurn, a Capone enforcer generally held to have been one of the planners or perpetrators of the St. Valentine's Day Massacre, was murdered. The press speculated that Bugs Moran had finally got his revenge; but McGurn, at that time on the outs with the mob, was more than likely killed by Capone adherents.

After that it was all downhill for Moran. His crimes turned petty compared to what they had been in the bad old days. Eventually he moved to Ohio and in July 1946 he was seized by the FBI along with two others for robbing a bank messenger of $10,000. During Prohibition Moran would have tossed around such a sum as if it were confetti. Moran got 10 years for the crime; when he was released he was rearrested for an earlier bank robbery and sent to Leavenworth for another 10-year stretch. He died there of cancer in 1957.

All his underworld chums—O'Banion, Weiss, Drucci—had lavish gangster burials. Bugs Moran outlived them all but his funeral was a quick burial in a wooden casket in a potter's field outside the prison's walls.

MORANO, Don Pelligrino See CAMORRA; MORELLO, NICHOLAS

MORELLI Gang: New England holdup mob

In 1927 two anarchists, Nicola Sacco and Bartolomeo Vanzetti, were executed for a 1920 Massachusetts robbery in which two victims were killed.

The Sacco-Vanzetti case remains to this day a cause célèbre, with many feeling they were innocent of the charge and had been convicted in an era of superpatriotism and hysteria about foreign radicals. Within mob circles there was never any doubt as to the pair's innocence, a fact confirmed in the 1970s by underworld informer Vinnie Teresa (whose testimony has probably been of greater value to authorities than that of another renowned informer, Joe Valachi).

According to Teresa, the $15,776.51 payroll robbery of the Slater and Morrill Shoe Company of South Braintree, Massachusetts, on April 15, 1920, was the work of the notorious Morelli gang. The Morellis were five brothers who moved to the New England area from Brooklyn during World War I. Two of them, Frank "Butsey" Morelli and Joseph Morelli, were the leaders of a terrorist mob that ran roughshod over several states, pulling all sorts of robberies and burglaries. Much speculation by civil libertarians has tied the Morellis to the robbery for which Sacco and Vanzetti were electrocuted. Newspapers from time to time revived the case, and mentions were often made of Joseph, who died in 1950, and Butsey, who in the 1950s went so far as to sue the *Boston Globe* for printing a story linking him to the crime.

Butsey was at the time dying of cancer and his motive in this, says Teresa in his book *My Life in the*

Murders attributed to Sacco (right) and Vanzetti (left) were, according to recent trusted criminal informers, actually committed by New England's Morelli Gang.

Mafia, had nothing to do with trying to clear his name—he was generally identified as the first Mafia boss of Rhode Island—but rather to shield his adopted son from the unwanted publicity. Butsey insisted to the boy he had nothing to do with the Sacco-Vanzetti case. Teresa said he asked Butsey, "What the hell are you suing them for? You can't beat a newspaper."

Butsey replied, "What they said was true, but it's going to hurt my kid. I don't give a damn about myself. I'm ready to die anyway. But look what it's doing to my boy. He's a legitimate kid. He never knew what was going on before."

As to the murders, Butsey told Teresa: "We whacked them out, we killed those guys in the robbery. These two greaseballs took it on the chin. . . . That shows you how much justice there really is."

The fact that Teresa's testimony has been considered reliable enough to lead to the indictment or conviction of more than 50 mob figures certainly lends his disclosure about Sacco and Vanzetti a considerable measure of credibility.

Further reading: *My Life in the Mafia* by Vincent Teresa, with Thomas C. Renner.

MORELLO, Nicholas (1866–1916): Mafia leader

Great men are creations of their times. When Lucky Luciano and Meyer Lansky formed the national crime syndicate in the early 1930s, they succeeded because the underworld could at that time be logically organized. But Luciano was not the first to dream of a national crime syndicate. Nicholas Morello, of the notorious Morello family, rose far above his relations to realize that the Americanization of the gangs would have to give birth to a great criminal network, each of its components at peace with the others and in concert controlling all the rackets in the country.

Morello probably saw less need to cooperate with other ethnics than Luciano would later, mainly because during World War I the great ethnic Irish and Jewish criminal gangs were disintegrating. This was even true to some extent of the Italian gangs, but the mafiosi and Camorristas maintained their cohesion. (With the later advent of Prohibition the Irish and Jewish mobs would reorganize.)

In fact, Morello should have had an easier time organizing crime in America than Luciano and Lansky would later, but he found himself too mired

down by old-country conflicts. While Morello's Sicilian gangs controlled the rackets of East Harlem and Greenwich Village in Manhattan, the Brooklyn Camorristas, immigrant criminals from the Camorra gangs of Naples, extended their power in Brooklyn, collecting protection money from Italian storekeepers, coal and ice dealers and other businessmen, as well as operating rackets on the Brooklyn docks.

The Camorristas were under the leadership of Don Pelligrino Morano, a man who had his own dreams of expansion—all aimed solely at eliminating the Manhattan mafiosi. When Morano ordered his men to move in on the East Harlem rackets, money considerations were probably secondary. He really looked to demean his Old World rivals.

The more forward-looking Morello thought it foolish to continue such old battles and offered to make a peaceful settlement. Morano took such a move as a sign of weakness and spurned the offer. By 1916 the warfare was so intense that only the most hardy mafioso or Camorrista dared cross the East River into the other's domain. They usually returned home in a hearse.

Then, surprisingly, that same year Morano announced he was in favor of Morello's call for an armistice. He invited Morello to come to Brooklyn to discuss terms, of course guaranteeing him safe conduct.

Morello proved wisely cautious and for six months did no more than dicker about holding such a peace meeting, though he realized he would have to go if he hoped to advance his master plan. The meeting was arranged in a café on Navy Street, and Morello showed up accompanied only by his personal bodyguard. Morano was deeply disappointed. He had hoped Morello would bring his top lieutenants with him. Still, Morello was the main prize, and as soon as the mafioso and his bodyguard stepped from their car, a five-man execution squad opened up on them, killing them in broad daylight.

Morano was greatly surprised when he was arrested for murder. He had been under the assumption that the payoffs he had made to a New York police detective, Michael Mealli, had "cleared the operation with the cops." Some of the killers cooperated with the law for lighter sentences and Morano and his top aides were sent to prison for life. When the sentence was pronounced, the *Brooklyn Eagle* reported: "Morano was surrounded by a dozen Italians who showered kisses on his face and forehead.

On the way to the jail other Italians braved the guard and kissed Morano's hands, cheeks and forehead."

With Morello dead and Morano imprisoned, what the newspapers called the first Mafia War came to an end. So too did the dreams of Nick Morello for a "great combination" of the gangs. At the time Salvatore Luciana was only a teenage thug, but already he appreciated what Morello had tried to do. When he grew older he would Americanize his name to Charles "Lucky" Luciano and he would Americanize the Mafia as well.

See also MORELLO FAMILY

MORELLO, Peter "the Clutching Hand" (1880–1930): Early mafioso

One of the most important members of the notorious Morello family, Peter "the Clutching Hand," Morello was a devious killer whose tactics terrified his enemies. During the 1920s he was the body-guard-adviser to Joe the Boss Masseria, regarded at the time as the most important mafioso in New York. Joseph Bonnano (Joe Bananas), shortly thereafter a boss of one of New York's five crime families, made it clear why Morello was also called "the old fox"—he did Masseria's thinking for him.

The Clutching Hand was cut down in August 1930 during the Castellammarese War. By whom is a matter of some dispute. Informer Joe Valachi insisted the job was done by Buster of Chicago, a mysterious hit man imported by Salvatore Maranzano, the leader of the anti-Masseria forces. This, like much of Valachi's testimony, has been viewed with considerable doubt by Mafia watchers. Morello was cut down in his East Harlem business office, and it is doubtful that a stranger like Buster could have gotten to him, especially since at the moment he was handling a huge amount of cash, receipts from his loan-sharking racket.

Far more believable is Lucky Luciano's version. The ambitious Luciano, like Morello, was allied with Joe the Boss, but he had decided by then that the time was ripe to get rid of Masseria. That being the case it was decided that Morello had to die first. As long as Morello lived, Masseria was considered impregnable, and even if the Boss were killed, Morello would undoubtedly go underground to carry on a fierce war with Luciano.

Luciano assigned Albert Anastasia and Frank Scalise to the job and they were able to penetrate Morello's headquarters. They found Morello with a collector in his operation, Giuseppe Pariano, and, as Luciano put it, "he hadda get it too." As a bonus, Anastasia and Scalise appropriated the $30,000 in cash lying on Morello's desk.

See also MORELLO FAMILY; SCALISE, FRANK "DON CHEECH"

MORELLO family: Early American mafiosi

The first Mafia family firmly established in this country was literally a family of criminals. The Morellos settled in New York in the latter part of the 19th century, after emigrating over the years from the Sicilian town of Corleone, a community credited with supplying more Mafia members to America than any other place on the island.

The American head of the huge clan of brothers, half-brothers and brothers-in-law was Antonio Morello, a brutal and cunning criminal credited with personally committing between 30 and 40 murders in the 1890s. His two younger brothers, Joe and Nick, succeeded him to leadership. Joe was noted as even more vicious, and with his brother-in-law, the notorious Lupo the Wolf, operated the so-called Murder Stable in East Harlem where enemies or victims of the gang were taken and either convinced to give in or tortured and killed. The screams in the night from the Murder Stable were an awesome yet frequent sound in East Harlem. But Joe lacked the vision to be a great crime leader and he was soon superseded by his brother Nicholas. Not illogically, Nick Morello was described later as an early version of Lucky Luciano in that he also dreamed about forming a great criminal syndicate to run all major rackets in the country. However, he was assassinated by Brooklyn Camorristas in 1916, and the superstructure that was to become national organized crime remained unbuilt for another decade and a half.

Nick was the last Morello to achieve leadership of the clan, which later passed on to Ciro Terranova, who maintained, despite personal weakness, a measure of authority in the Mafia until the 1930s. Peter "the Clutching Hand" Morello rose to near top power as the number one adviser to Joe the Boss Masseria, but he was killed during the Castellammarese War in 1930. His demise, since he was clearly the brains of the Masseria loyalists, assured the doom of Joe the Boss.

This hardly spelled the end of the Morellos in organized crime. Today a great many Morello descendants remain entrenched in various New York–New Jersey Mafia rackets.

See also MORELLO, NICHOLAS; MORELLO, PETER "THE CLUTCHING HAND"; MURDER STABLE; TERRANOVA, CIRO

MORETTI, Willie (1894–1951): Syndicate boss

In his day, Willie Moretti was a tough enforcer and syndicate boss, a power in New Jersey rackets to whom extortion, dope pushing and murder were part of the normal way of doing business. By the time he died in what the mob regarded as a "mercy killing," he was a clown, the comic relief at the Kefauver hearings, and a real threat to the mob with his loose lip. That was to prove to be the end of tough Willie Moore, as he was sometimes known.

A boyhood friend of Frank Costello, Moretti was in his younger days as rough and ready as any gangster. In New Jersey, he bossed an enforcer troop of about 60 gunmen, who protected his longtime partner, Longy Zwillman, and his own racket interests. The racket interests were extensive, often intermingled with the New York interests of Lucky Luciano, Frank Costello, Joe Adonis and others. *New York Times* crime reporter Meyer Berger once observed, "the Morettis had their bookmaking agents among workers in the major factories in Bergen, they shared the bookmaking profits pouring into the New York mob's astonishingly widespread New Jersey wire system, and they were partners in plush casinos and so-called 'sawdust,' or dice barns deep into Pennsylvania."

Their top casino in Bergen was the Marine Room in the famed Riviera nightclub, located just north of the George Washington Bridge on the Palisades. The Riviera was a nightclub with top entertainers. The floor show was open to the public; getting into the gambling room was another matter. All the players had to be known or they had to stay in the dining rooms and watch the show.

Moretti was known within the underworld as singer Frank Sinatra's original godfather. They had become fast friends when the singer from Hoboken was performing for peanuts in local roadhouses and clubs. In 1939, Sinatra, while singing with Harry James's orchestra, made his first hit recording, "All or Nothing at All." Band leader Tommy Dorsey signed him for what Sinatra must have regarded as a

Willie Moretti ran off at the mouth at the Kefauver hearings, providing much entertainment for senators and the television audience. The mob was much less amused. Moretti met with the inevitable bloody consequences.

princely sum, $125 a week. Sinatra's popularity was soaring thanks to the bobbysoxers who followed him everywhere. But he was locked in by his contract to Tommy Dorsey. The much-repeated underworld tale of what happened is this: One night Willie Moretti showed up at Dorsey's dressing room and stuck a gun into the band leader's mouth. Moretti then suggested that Dorsey might sell Sinatra's contract. The price agreed on was one dollar.

A few years after that Moretti started acting funny at times, showing the first signs of mental illness brought on by the ravages of untreated syphilis. Moretti loved to gamble and claimed to be winning bets on horses for millions of dollars. He tried to place bets on horses and races that didn't exist. He even started at times to talk about syndicate affairs, matters that were not to be mentioned in public. Eventually quite a few capos loyal to Costello began saying Willie was a threat to everyone.

Costello had been best man at Willie's wedding and held him in high affection. Costello decided the best thing to do with Moretti was to get him out of the line of fire, sending him for a long vacation out West with a male nurse. Moretti frequently telephoned Costello, in conversations wiretapped by the police, begging to be allowed to come back. Costello refused and went on protecting Willie from himself. Only when Moretti became less voluble was he allowed to return.

When Moretti was called before the Kefauver committee, many mobsters wanted him knocked off, even though he had been behaving better. Costello again prevented it, and after much stalling Moretti finally appeared before the Senate committee. He proceeded to talk and talk and talk, though he said very little. No, he explained, he was not a member of the Mafia because he didn't have a membership card. And he offered such pearls of wisdom as "They call anybody a mob who makes six percent more on money"; and concerning gangsters he knew: "well-charactered people don't need introductions." When Moretti left the stand, the committee members seemed satisfied. Senator Estes Kefauver thanked him for his forthrightness, and Senator Charles Tobey found his frankness "rather refreshing."

"Thank you very much," Willie replied to the praise. "Don't forget my house in Deal if you are down on the shore. You are invited."

The mob was quite pleased with how Moretti had handled himself on the witness stand, but Willie started to deteriorate in late 1951. He talked regularly to New Jersey newspapermen and made noise about holding a press conference to review gambling in New Jersey. Vito Genovese, a Costello enemy, began strong lobbying for Moretti's execution. Genovese knew that if he could get rid of Moretti he could move his own men into Willie's operations and further erode the power of Costello. Moretti, Genovese said, was losing his mind, and the entire organization could be in trouble. "If tomorrow I go wrong, I want you to hit me in the head too," Genovese said. Finally even such a staunch ally as Albert Anastasia was convinced that a "mercy killing" was necessary for the sake of both Willie and the syndicate.

The mobsters felt they'd done right by Moretti by shooting him up front. He was due the respect of seeing what was happening to him, especially, so the saying went, as everyone genuinely liked Willie.

On October 4, 1951, Willie sat down in a New Jersey restaurant with three or four men (the testimony varies on this). When the waitress stepped into the kitchen, they were chatting amiably in Italian. Suddenly there were several gunshots and when the waitress peered through the kitchen door, all the customers except one were gone.

Fifty-seven-year-old Willie Moretti lay dead on the floor, his left hand on his chest. It was a typical mob rubout, and there would be no convictions. Willie had been shot up front, supposedly a mark of "respect" accorded to bosses. They had a right to see what was happening.

In this case it could well have been a sign of respect since, after all, everybody genuinely liked Willie. They just happened to like him better dead.

MORI, Cesare (1880–1942): Mussolini's Mafia fighter

Probably no individual was more responsible for the mass exodus of mafiosi from Sicily to the United States than Cesare Mori, one of Benito Mussolini's most devoted agents of suppression. Mussolini had used Mori earlier to wipe out socialist unrest during his political campaign in Bologna, and Mori was one of the chief architects of Mussolini's 1922 march on Rome when he seized complete power. As a reward for fascist labors, Mussolini appointed Mori prefect of Palermo, the most powerful position on the island. Mori's principal task in Sicily was to unseat the lazy and corrupt administrators and replace them with ardent Fascists. Since the administrators in most of the towns were allied with the Mafia, the "Honored Society" fell into conflict with the Fascists. The Mafia used the same tactics of terrorism in fighting the government that it used against its many victims. Many of Mori's new appointees were assassinated as soon as they took office. The Mafia even carried its vengeance into downtown Palermo, murdering leading Fascists in the streets before hundreds of witnesses.

In 1924 Mussolini himself visited Sicily and was embarrassed by the Mafia in Piana dei Greci, where the mayor, Don Ciccio Cuccia, who was also the Mafia boss of the area, bawled Mussolini out for coming with so many police motorcyclists to guard him. He said, "Your Excellency has nothing to fear when you are by my side." Then he turned to his men and announced, "Let no one dare touch a hair of Mussolini's head. He is my friend and the best man in the world!"

Inwardly, Mussolini seethed, understanding full well Don Ciccio's message that he, not the leader from Rome, was the true power. Don Ciccio made the point all the more clear when Mussolini was slated to make an address from a balcony to the local populace. The only audience the Mafia leader permitted to show up, one account states, was "twenty village idiots, one-legged beggars, bootblacks and lottery-ticket sellers."

The enraged Mussolini afterward ordered Mori to wage all-out war against the Mafia. Two months later Cuccia vanished into a Fascist prison, and the drive to stamp out the Mafia went into high gear. Mori's methods were, if anything, more ruthless and barbarous than those used against the socialists. Rights of those arrested were wantonly abused. Confessions were extracted by torture. One of the most common methods involved stretching a suspect on his back over a wooden box with his hands and feet wired to the sides of the box. The victim was then drenched with brine and whipped. The brine made the lashes more painful but left no marks. Other tortures involved administering electric shock to the genitals, one of the earliest known uses of this brutal method, and forcing prisoners to swallow saltwater through a funnel until their stomachs swelled painfully.

Fascist judges paid no attention to such minor details and convicted accused mafiosi by the hundreds. An estimated 600 innocent persons were also convicted through such tortures and the lying testimony of jealous neighbors or Fascist Party members. In some cases members of separate Mafia gangs were convicted of the same crimes in different courts, and others were convicted of crimes that had never occurred. From the American point of view, the worst aspect of Mori's campaign was that it caused at least 500 young mafiosi to seek refuge in the United States.

Mori terrorized the citizenry in the Mafia-infested Western provinces and paraded about as a conquering Roman of old. It was common for towns he visited to decorate triumphal arches with the welcoming words, "Ave Caesar."

Mori's campaign ended in 1929 following the conviction of Don Vito Cascio Ferro, the most charismatic of all the Mafia leaders, on a framed-up charge of smuggling. Don Vito, who died in prison in 1932, denounced his judges in court, saying, "Gentlemen, since you have been unable to find any evidence for the numerous crimes I did commit, you are reduced to condemning me for the only one I have not."

In any event, by the time of Ferro's death, Mori had crushed most Mafia organizations. Those that survived pledged fealty to Mussolini, a position they maintained until the Allied invasion of Sicily during World War II.

Whatever is thought of Mori's methods, there was little doubt that he offered the world the most authentic description of the Mafia, one that applies still today both in Italy and in the United States— even if it conflicts with the versions offered by American governmental agencies and such controversial informers as Joe Valachi. In a book he later wrote, *The Last Struggle with the Mafia,* Mori noted it was not an "association in the sense of being a vast aggregate organized and incorporated on regular principles." The Mafia, he observed, functions with statutes, rules of admission, and election of chiefs. The chief attained power simply by imposing his will on others. Members were accepted automatically if they had the proper qualifications and were automatically expelled or permanently eliminated when they no longer met these qualifications. Profits were not divided by any set measure but went proportionally to the strongest. Only in a few cases, Mori said, were there any Mafia groups that held regular meetings, had secret laws and used concealed marks of recognition, but they were clearly the exception to the rule. Most important, Mori found the Mafia to be a "potential state which normally takes concrete form in a system of local oligarchies, closely interwoven, but each autonomous in its own district."

This description is true of organized crime in the United States today. A crime family in New York would not dream of going into Detroit to kill an individual without clearing it first with the local powers and indeed would most likely request the local organization to take care of the matter for them. It would then be up to the local organization to comply if it so wished. If however it preferred to grant the proposed victim sanctuary, there is little the outside crime family can do. The organization of such crime fiefdoms clearly is not based on tradition, but rather on raw power. It is this tradition of Mafia power and regional autonomy that keeps organized crime in America somewhat disorganized.

The disorganized nature of the Mafia kept Mori from achieving total victory and left him with many adversaries in Sicily. Mori died in 1942, probably a

pity from the mafioso point of view since Mafia vengeance on him under protection of the Allies would certainly have been as brutal as the justice accorded Mussolini by the partisans.

See also FERRO, DON VITO CASCIO; MUSSOLINI SHUTTLE; TWENTIES GROUP

MORTON, Samuel J. "Nails" (?–1924): Chicago mobster and "horse rubout victim"

Within the madcap underworld of 1920s Chicago, Nails (so called because he was as tough as nails) Morton was always believed to have died because of treachery, and a treachery most despicable because it was carried out by a dumb animal.

Nails was a top enforcer for the Dion O'Banion Gang, virtually the only Jew among the North Side Irish mobsters. As much as any single gunner, Morton was responsible for holding the Italian gangsters under Torrio and Capone—as well as the Genna brothers and others—at bay on the North Side from 1920 to 1924. Morton, known by the police to have committed several murders, enjoyed respect bordering on terror from other mobsters mainly because he had won the Croix de Guerre in France in the Great War and been promoted on the battlefield to a first lieutenancy. That, and the fact that he concocted very inventive death traps for foes, made rival gangsters avoid confrontations with him. Often he would try to lure an enemy into combat by accusing him of making anti-Semitic slurs.

However, as celebrated as Morton could be for his killing ways, he was to become most noteworthy for the way he died and the gangland vengeance that followed.

Nails, who developed a yen to circulate in finer circles, took to horseback riding in Lincoln Park "where the society swells ride." One day in 1924, a riding stable horse threw Nails and kicked him to death. It was an act that could not be overlooked or forgiven. Four leading O'Banions—Bugs Moran, Little Hymie Weiss, Two Gun Alterie and Schemer Drucci—descended on the riding stable and at gunpoint kidnapped the offending horse. The creature was led to the spot where it had dispatched Morton, and there, after the very angry Alterie punched the horse in the snout, was shot in the head, once by each gangster, in worthy underworld fashion. Gang boss O'Banion bewailed the fact he had not been around when Nails was killed and vengeance exacted; such moronic behavior fit O'Banion as well as his men.

Yet despite his unsavory record, Nails was accorded an elaborate funeral with considerable military, fraternal and religious honors. City, county, state and federal officials were prominent in attendance, and the *Chicago Daily News* reported: "Five thousand Jews paid tribute to Morton as the man who had made the West Side safe for his race. As a young man he had organized a defense society to drive 'Jew-baiters' from the West side."

A year after Morton's death ill-fated plans were laid for a memorial tribute to him. The printed announcement of the service bore the names of Rabbi Felix A. Levi, General Abel Davis, Captain Ed Maher and the Reverend John L. O'Donnell. The principal address was to be made by a leading attorney, Frank Comerford. Perhaps what sent matters awry was the added announcement that also participating in the tribute would be Johnny Torrio, Terry Druggan and Hymie Weiss (the new leader of the North Siders, Dion O'Banion having by then been assassinated). General Davis backed out of the arrangements, saying it would be an error to flaunt such gangsters and Morton's record "in the faces of decent citizens." The whole affair then fell apart. It was, said one writer, "another kick in the head for poor Nails."

MOTORCADE murders: Automobile procession assassinations
During the inception of organized crime in the 1920s, the motorcade system of killing came into vogue. Whether Hymie Weiss or Bugs Moran—both subsequent leaders of the Irish O'Banion Gang, the prime opposition in Chicago to the Torrio-Capone forces—invented the system is unclear. Bugs Moran, a cunning if rather pathological killer, was always attracted to spectacular killings and probably deserves the credit. Certainly he headed up more such murder convoys than any other gangster.

Moran and a dozen gangsters, each armed with a fully loaded tommy gun and riding in a half-dozen limousines, swept past the victim's home, place of business or hangout. As the motorcade slowed, each gunner spattered a thousand or so .45-caliber cartridges in the general direction of the target. Such overkill was generally effective, even if a few innocent bystanders occasionally got caught in the deadly hail of bullets. That was merely an unfortunate sidebar to otherwise spectacular success.

The most publicized murder motorcade of all was one that failed, an attempt to rub out Al Capone at the Hawthorne Inn in Cicero, Illinois, in 1926. A two-story brick structure, the inn had been converted to Capone's specification into a fortress. Bulletproof steel shutters protected every window, while armed guards were stationed at every entrance. The second floor was reserved for Capone's private use.

The building, dubbed Capone's castle, almost became Capone's deathtrap. On September 20, Capone and bodyguard Frankie Rio were dining in the rear of the Hawthorne's restaurant when a single car drove past and opened fire with a machine gun. When the shooting stopped, the pair, with the other diners, rushed to the windows and doors to see what had happened. There were no bullet marks. The gunners had been firing blanks.

Frankie Rio understood instantly and knocked Capone to the floor, falling on top of him. Just then a convoy of 10 cars passed slowly in front of the inn, and a seemingly endless number of guns protruding from every one of the curbside windows let loose a deadly hail of fire. Directly above Rio and Capone, woodwork, mirrors, glassware and crockery splintered. A Capone gunman, Louis Barko, who had rushed into the restaurant when the blank shots were fired, went down with a bullet through his shoulder.

In all 1,000 bullets were fired, and the inn, restaurant, lobby and offices were literally ripped asunder. Thirty-five cars parked at the curb were riddled with bullet holes. Remarkably, no one was killed, although Mrs. Clyde Freeman, sitting in a car with her infant son on her lap, was struck by a bullet that creased her forehead and injured her eyes. Capone footed $5,000 in medical bills to save the woman's eyesight.

MOVIE racketeering
The mobs moved in on Hollywood moviemakers during the reign of Al Capone, when the industry was still silent. Movie executives tended to be silent, too, when faced with Capone threats.

The Capones made their first move through George Browne and his associate Willie Bioff, a longtime pimp. Together, they ran Local 2 of the International Alliance of Theatrical and Stage Employees (IATSE). To show what fine fellows they were, Browne and Bioff had the union ladle out free soup for unemployed actors. And the two proceeded to ladle more than soup. That same year they pressured a large financially pressed Chicago movie chain to cancel 20 percent paycuts on its employees. As an alternative, Bioff said they would take $20,000 under the table.

By the time Capone went to prison for income tax evasion, his titular successor, Frank Nitti, had decided to move heavily into movie extortion. He slated Browne to run for the IATSE presidency in the 1934 election. Browne predictably had the Chicago votes sewn up; Lucky Luciano and Louis Lepke saw that he got support in New York; and Al Polizzi took care of the campaign in Cleveland. Browne won in a walk. And Willie Bioff went along to watch over Browne.

For delivering unto Browne the union presidency the Chicago Outfit took 50 percent of all illegal money that was taken in. Later, the fee was raised to 75 percent. This did not represent a squeeze on Browne and Bioff. There was so much money coming in they had no complaint.

The fee for avoiding a strike by projectionists in New York was set at $150,000 (a fabulous sum for Depression days), in Chicago $100,000. Refusal resulted in stink-bombings of the theaters. In 1936 Bioff told the head of Loew's, Inc.: "Now your industry is a prosperous industry and I must get two million dollars out of it."

Bioff and Browne then worked out a settlement that called for the four big distributors—MGM, Loew's, Paramount and Twentieth Century-Fox—to cough up $50,000 a year each, and a smaller company to pay $25,000. In addition, the two leaders got a number of concessions that pleased the union membership, and they were hailed at the 1938 convention. Browne and Bioff then turned around and levied a 2 percent tax on all their members' earnings, which brought in $60,000 a month. This did not please the membership; it led to a revolt. That, combined with exposures by columnist Westbrook Pegler, led finally to the duo's conviction on racketeering charges in 1941.

Facing long prison terms, Bioff and Browne started talking. As a result of their testimony most of the Chicago Outfit's leadership were convicted— Nitti, Phil D'Andrea, Paul Ricca, Charlie Gioe, Lou Kaufman and Johnny Roselli—and given 10-year prison terms.

They served the minimum sentence and were paroled in a little over three years, a development that provoked a national political scandal. When they got out, the mob influence in Hollywood had hardly deteriorated. Roselli continued to be a power in the movie capital and even turned movie producer himself, turning out a number of law-triumphs-over-crime epics such as *He Walked by Night*. Roselli had no trouble getting to make these projects. He made the movie moguls an offer they couldn't refuse. And when the mob wanted to promote the career of some worthy or unworthy actor or actress it had little trouble getting the proper results.

Since the movie shakedown convictions of Browne and Bioff, the mob has become much more sophisticated in its operations. A union threatens a strike and a lawyer-labor relations expert arbitrates it. He draws a colossal fee for his services on which, minus expenses, he pays the taxes. The balance is then cut up with Chicago.

See also BIOFF WILLIE MORRIS

MURDER, Incorporated: Enforcement arm of national syndicate

When the national crime syndicate was being set up in the early 1930s, they realized that "muscle" would always be necessary for the maintenance of order. Since the mob never had any of society's misgivings about the justification of the death penalty, they decided it would be very businesslike to set up a special troop of killers that all the crime groups around the country could call on for rubouts. The most attractive feature about such a troop was that the killer could come in from out of town, knock off a victim he wouldn't even know, and disappear, leaving the authorities without even a suspect or motive. Police investigations are based on looking for motivation and when a stranger kills a stranger, they seldom can get a handle on the matter. They might suspect the local crime figures of instigating the rubout but they can't prove a thing.

Many forerunners to the syndicate murder troop existed in American criminal history, including killer gangs in the 19th century who committed murders for pay, with prices generally ranging from a low of $2 to a king's ransom of as much as $100. However, the syndicate bosses set up something new, Murder, Incorporated, a very elite group of killers, based in Brooklyn. Unlike the bloodletters who preceded them, they were not available for hire by outsiders, but were reserved strictly for mob business.

The purpose of the new crime syndicate, composed of an ethnic conglomerate of Young Turk mafiosi,

Abe Reles (left) and Buggsy Goldstein (center) after their arrest in the Murder, Inc., investigation. The pair personally may have killed at least 60 men. Reles eventually provided information on more than 200 murders of which he had knowledge.

Jewish, to a lesser extent Irish, and Polish and Wasp gangs—that blossomed in Prohibition—was to cut up the rackets in orderly fashion. These included gambling, loan-sharking, labor racketeering, narcotics and prostitution. Syndicate founders sagely figured there would be some opposition to their plans, hence the need for an enforcement arm to back up the national board's decisions. (It was probably little different than in the corporate world where every powerhouse executive has his hatchetmen.)

Under the rules, Murder, Inc., killed only for pressing business reasons and was never to be brought into action against political figures, prosecutors or reporters. Lansky and Moe Dalitz, then the most potent criminal power in Cleveland, were most adamant on these rules. The other big shots concurred, feeling that rubouts of such "civilians" would stir the public too much and produce "heat" that would be bad for the syndicate. Bloodletting of good guys, they agreed, would complicate their ability to bribe politicians and the police, a vital ingredient in any crime syndicate operation.

A whole new vocabulary was introduced by the members of Murder, Inc. The killers accepted "contracts" to "hit" "bums." Many psychologists have pointed out the significance of the term *bum*. It was a rationalization that allowed the killers to regard their victims as being of a lower species and deserving to die. It was little different than Nazi death camp executioners speaking of the victims as "scum" and "subhumans."

Albert Anastasia is often described as the Lord High Executioner, or operating commander of the troop, but he took orders from Louis Lepke, the country's number one labor racketeer and a member of the syndicate's ruling circle. At times, Joey Adonis also issued orders. However, none of the estimated 400 to 500 murders believed to have been committed by Murder, Inc., ever went ahead without the concurrence, or at least the absence of any negative vote, of other crime bigs, notably Lansky, Luciano and Frank Costello. Bugsy Siegel probably best summarized the top gangsters' attitudes toward Murder, Inc., when he informed construction executive Del Webb, rather philosophically, that he had nothing to fear from the mob because "we only kill each other."

Directly below Anastasia, Lepke and Adonis were a number of lieutenants, including Louis Capone (no relation to the Chicago Capones), Mendy Weiss and Abe "Kid Twist" Reles. Instructions for specific murder assignments were generally passed from on high to just one underling who in turn passed the word on so that it could not be proved in any criminal prosecution that the men at the top were involved. Some of the more celebrated killers of the mob included Pittsburgh Phil Strauss, the man who easily held the top score in kills; Vito "Chicken Head" Gurino, who honed his shooting skill by blasting off the heads of chickens; Happy Maione, the wearer of a perpetual scowl; Buggsy Goldstein; Blue Jaw Magoon; and Frank "the Dasher" Abbandando.

The Dasher could lay claim to having obtained the quaintest nickname of the troop. It was the result of one of his earliest hits, one that he almost bungled. Assigned to take out a big, lumbering longshoreman, he aimed his gun at point-blank range, only to have the weapon misfire. Thoroughly embarrassed, Abbandando dashed off with his angry would-be victim thundering after him. Abbandando raced around the block so fast he actually came up behind his target again, and this time succeeded in pumping three bullets into the man. Thereafter Abbandando was known to his cohorts as the Dasher.

Overall, the Dasher was said to have been involved in about 50 murders. Pittsburgh Phil was named in 58 murder investigations and authorities agreed his total of kills was probably about twice that number.

The boys, headquartered at a 24-hour candy store in the Brownsville section of Brooklyn called Midnight Rose's, awaited assignments and swapped intelligence of effective murder techniques. When an assignment came in, the designated killer hit the road to wherever the victim lived. He didn't come back until the job was done.

The principal that "we only kill each other" was never better illustrated than in the rubout of crime lord Dutch Schultz, himself a founding ruler of the crime syndicate. In 1935, Schultz had become the prime target of special prosecutor Thomas E. Dewey, and he demanded that Murder, Inc., hit Dewey. This was in direct violation of the founding rules of the organization, and Schultz was voted down. Only Albert Anastasia thought the idea had merit, but he backed off under the withering opposition of his superiors, Luciano, Lansky, Costello and Adonis. Schultz stormed out of the meeting, insisting he was not bound by such a decision and that he would handle the job himself. Immediately, a new vote was taken, and the principle of law and order prevailed. Schultz got the death penalty. The job was carried out shortly thereafter in a Newark chop house. Two of the three Murder, Inc., gunmen involved were Charlie "the Bug" Workman and Mendy Weiss.

In 1940 Murder, Inc., unraveled when a number of lesser mob members were picked up on suspicion of various murders. Also picked up was Abe Reles,

not a smalltimer. Reles got the idea that someone might talk and doom him, so he decided to talk first. He became known as "the canary of Murder, Inc.," and eventually gave details on some 200 killings in which he personally participated or had intimate knowledge of. Several top killers went to the electric chair, including Pittsburgh Phil, Louis Capone, Mendy Weiss, Buggsy Goldstein, Happy Maione and Dasher Abbandando. Also executed was Louis Lepke, the first and only top chief of the syndicate ever to suffer that fate.

In November 1941, Reles was still doing his canary act, and it was believed his testimony would eventually doom Albert Anastasia, Bugsy Siegel and quite possibly others. However, before he could testify in what were described as "perfect cases," Reles "went out the window" of a Coney Island hotel where he was supposed to be under ironclad police protection. Whether Reles's death was suicide, accident or murder has never been established, but later Luciano, Lansky and Doc Stacher told friends and interviewers that through the good political offices of Frank Costello (and a sum believed to be $100,000, a king's ransom in that period) it was arranged to see to it that "the canary who could sing couldn't fly."

Of course, all this meant was the end of Murder, Inc., I. Other troops of killers were started up, one known to be centered in New Jersey. Murder, Inc., remained in business.

See also MIDNIGHT ROSE'S; PITTSBURGH PHIL; RELES, ABE; STATE STREET CRAP GAME

MURDERS of dons: "Respectful" assassinations

When Sam Giancana was murdered in 1975, a theory immediately developed that it could not have been a Mafia job. He had not been shown the "respect" due a don in death. Giancana was shot in the back of the head as he grilled some Italian food for himself and whomever murdered him. Then the killer had rolled him over and fired bullets from beneath his chin up into his jaw and brain. If the mob had had Giancana murdered, the theory went, it would have been respectful; he would have been shot in the face because a don is entitled to see the shot that kills him. Ergo, the Giancana rubout had been a CIA job.

This notion is about as nonsensical as the idea that big bosses are entitled to a last meal, hence they are often shot at a restaurant table, facing their killers. True, Joe the Boss Masseria and Carmine Galante, to name just two, really were killed after they had partaken of their main courses—and they were shot from in front. The fact is that dining table murders are popular with the mob because the victim never has a chance to reach for a weapon. Of course, he is shot in front. A genuine custom for Mafia men is to sit with their backs to the wall.

Mob killers would much prefer shooting a boss or any victim from behind since it is obviously safer. But, when Frank Costello was almost assassinated, he was rushing for the elevator in the lobby of his Manhattan apartment building. He passed a fat man standing there who called out after him, "This is for you, Frank!" As he turned, he saw his would-be assassin's right arm extended and a gun pointing directly at his face at a distance of no more than 10 feet. The man fired. The fact that Costello saw the shot gave him just enough time to jerk his head to the side so that he wound up with no more than a bloody flesh wound.

Later the newspapers would say the gunman's tactics were a mark of respect for Don Francesco, that he was only to get it up front. That was not so. His assailant, Vincent Gigante, had called to him to freeze him into a stationary target rather than a moving one.

Albert Anastasia got it sitting in a barbershop chair. He managed to jump from the chair and dive for the floor but 11 bullets tore into his body. Then one of the murderers stepped forward and applied the *coup de grace,* a shot to the back of the head. Anastasia got about as much respect as he ever gave his victims as the chief executioner for Murder, Inc.

Anastasia had succeeded to the head of the Mangano family by killing the boss, Vince Mangano, and his brother Phil. It has always been accepted that the kill-crazy Anastasia did it personally. How he got rid of Vince Mangano was never determined since the body was never found. Phil Mangano was found. The details of his death can only be speculated upon since he was found immaculately dressed but pantsless. Questioned by police, Anastasia said the absence of Phil's pants made him think he had been the victim of a crime of passion. Surely, he wasn't the victim of a respectful hit man.

About the only major crime leader who was dispatched with a genuine show of respect was Willie Moretti, gunned down in a restaurant in New Jersey where he had been sitting with four men. When the waitress stepped into the kitchen, he and his assailants were chatting amiably in Italian. Suddenly, she heard several gunshots. When she came out,

Moretti lay on the floor dead, shot in the face. Actually the Moretti slaying was a Mafia "mercy killing," made necessary because a mental illness brought on by syphilis was causing him to babble more than the mob could allow. It was decided he had to go.

However, no one had anything against poor Willie, and everyone felt he was entitled not to be shot in the back like a dog. And they gave him a wonderful funeral. Some bosses do get to go in style.

MURDER Stable: Mafia extermination site

In 1901, the Mafia presence in New York was considered by many citizens to be less than certain. But the disclosure of the infamous Murder Stable site convinced even the most skeptical that there was a "Mafia" or a "Black Hand" or some organized concern of Italian criminals. Oddly, the discovery came while the New York police and the U.S. Secret Service were more concerned about the presence of foreign anarchists.

Early in 1901, the Secret Service got wind of rumors that there was an anarchist plot to assassinate President William McKinley. The service enlisted the aid of New York police detective Joseph Petrosino, who would later become the first genuine police menace to the American Mafia and various groups of Black Handers. Petrosino infiltrated anarchist circles in New Jersey and found there to be no organized plan to kill the president. His investigations, however, revealed that a number of individuals were all capable of trying the assassination.

More important, within the context of discovering the Mafia in action, Petrosino and the Secret Service stumbled across the "Murder Stable," a property located at 323 East 107th Street in the heart of Italian Harlem. A gang of Italian criminals, headed by some brothers named Morello and a particularly fearful individual named Lupo the Wolf, were the terrors of the area; screams through the night struck dread in neighbors living in the stable area. The authorities dug up the premises, unearthing the remains of about 60 murder victims. The property belonged to one Ignazio Saietta, a.k.a. Lupo the Wolf. It was determined that Lupo the Wolf and the Morellos used the place to torture their enemies into compliance or to death. Among the murder victims was a teenage Morello whom Lupo the Wolf decreed had too loose a lip about gang affairs. He executed him slowly and savagely, striking fear in other gang members and discouraging them from straying in any fashion.

Remarkably, nobody was convicted for the wholesale killings in the Murder Stable. Lupo insisted he was no more than the landlord of the place and could hardly be held responsible for what his tenants did. The "tenants" turned out to be no more than Italian names that could not be traced.

Even more remarkably, the Murder Stable apparently continued to be used as a murder site until about 1917 by Lupo the Wolf (until he was imprisoned on unrelated charges), the Morellos and another relative through marriage, gangster Ciro Terranova.

See also LUPO THE WOLF; MORELLO FAMILY; PETROSINO, JOSEPH; TERRANOVA, CIRO

MUSSOLINI Shuttle: Mafiosi exodus from Sicily

Shortly after his rise to power in Italy in 1922, Benito Mussolini launched an all-out war against the Mafia in Sicily. As a result, somewhere between 500 and 1,000 young mafiosi fled for America, where they provided fresh manpower for the old-line Mafia gangs. Many were happy to go, attracted by the huge monies that could be obtained in the bootlegging rackets.

Sicily's most important Mafia leader, called by some observers "the boss of bosses," Don Vito Cascio Ferro, masterminded the escape routes on what became known as "the Mussolini Shuttle." The northern route called for smuggling the emigrant fugitives into Marseilles from where they were booked passage either directly to New York or to Canada, from where they slipped into the United States via Buffalo or Detroit. A southern route meant slipping out of Sicily to Tunis, thence to Cuba and on to Miami, Tampa, Norfolk or New Orleans.

Most of these emigrants owed allegiance to Don Vito and were expected to aid his obvious push to take over much of the Italian criminal activities in the United States. However, Don Vito himself was imprisoned by Mussolini in 1929 and died in 1932, leaving these erstwhile gangsters free to join various contending factions. Most joined the Young Turks under the more Americanized gangsters such as Lucky Luciano and Frank Costello and would in time take part in the destruction of the old-line mafiosi or Mustache Pete elements, who had tried to rule the U.S. underworld according to the traditions of the Sicilian Mafia.

In that sense Mussolini did much to foster organized crime in America, a result Il Duce probably saw as rather amusing. However, Mussolini's campaign against gangsters cost him much support among Americans of Italian descent who viewed the new criminal migrations as producing more crime in their communities and so stirring fresh anti-Italian feelings among the general population.

See also FERRO, DON VITO CASCIO; MORI, CESARE; TWENTIES GROUP

MUSTACHE Petes: Older-generation mafiosi

The early Mafia leaders in this country tried to maintain Sicilian criminal traditions in a new country and society. Younger Italian gangsters considered this impossible, preferring instead to cooperate not only with Italian criminals, but also with other ethnics—especially the highly organized Jewish gangsters. In time, the Mustache Petes—as the young mafiosi not-so-lovingly dubbed the old Sicilians—were considered an obstacle in "Americanizing" crime.

In New York and other cities, the Mustache Petes were eliminated from power, usually through assassination. But often, the younger generation of criminals, fattened by huge bootlegging profits, used political force and the police to isolate and so take the Mustache Petes out of circulation. Among the younger gangsters were Lucky Luciano (always much more comfortable working with Jewish gangsters than with many of his own kind), Frank Costello, Joe Adonis, Vito Genovese, Albert Anastasia, Tommy Lucchese and others. Even Joe Bonanno, a young mobster perhaps more steeped in "tradition," "honor" and "respect," saw the need to modernize and so opposed the Mustache Petes. After the bloody Castellammarese War—which eliminated the old Mafia as a force in the United States—a far wealthier, healthier and more powerful "Mafia" emerged in organized crime.

Luciano and his cohorts found they could work well with such Jewish gangsters as Meyer Lansky, Bugsy Siegel, Louis Lepke, Cleveland's Mayfield Road Gang (later Nevada's Desert Inn Syndicate) and Detroit's Purple Gang. The Mustache Petes, they felt, were too set in their ways to see the true riches and power a crime syndicate could bring. Besides, the old guard—the Morellos, Lupo the Wolf, Joe the Boss Masseria and Salvatore Maranzano—were interested primarily in exploiting fellow Italians and not the public at large.

N

NARCOTICS racket

It is difficult to estimate exactly how much wealth narcotics trafficking adds to the coffers of the American Mafia. But narcotics profits, alone, guarantee the organization's enduring wealth and power. And these profits are regarded as the real source of funds for buying the Mafia's political and police protection.

J. Edgar Hoover can legitimately be faulted for failing to go after the Mafia and organized crime, but his dogged efforts to keep the FBI out of narcotics investigations is strangely logical. He wanted to keep the reputation of the FBI simon-pure, something he knew would be impossible because corruption and bribery was virtually inevitable in policing the narcotics field.

According to a recent government estimate, the average heroin junkie needs about 50 milligrams of the drug each day to satisfy his cravings. Figuring the average cost at $65 a day, a habit costs $24,000 a year. Many experts consider such figures as much too conservative. But using those figures for a minimum 100,000 hardcore addicts, also a conservative figure, the heroin racket adds up to at least a $2.5 billion business. Add to this the massive trade in marijuana (with at least 10 million regular pot users) and cocaine (considered "safer" than heroin by most users) and the total dollar figure in the narcotics business is clearly staggering.

Of course, the cost to the narcotics dealers is penny ante compared to the rewards. By the 1970s, it was said that the return on capital invested made drug smuggling the most prosperous industry in the world. In 1960, a kilo of heroin was obtainable in Marseilles, France, where it was manufactured from morphine base, for about $2,500. In New York, it brought $6,000 a kilo wholesale—and over $600,000 on the street. By 1980, a kilo of grade four heroin cost about $12,000 from the supplier and brought a quarter of a million dollars in New York at wholesale prices. Cut with quinine and milk sugar, the heroin sold for several million dollars at street prices. No legitimate business, even Arab cartel oil, could come close to that.

This bottom-line figure made it obvious that the Mafia's so-called No Narcotics Rule was sheer nonsense. No criminal organization that accepts the murder of human beings as a routine part of business could pass up such profits on the grounds of "honor" and "morality." Mafia leaders who attempted to proscribe narcotics dealing were either lying or deluding themselves. There was and is no way to keep their criminals out of crime's most lucrative business.

See also CATALANO, SALVATORE "TOTO"; GALANTE, CARMINE; NO NARCOTIC RULE; PALERMO CONNECTION; ZIPS

NARDI, John (1916–1977): Murdered Cleveland mobster

One of the few criminals in recent years to attempt to dislodge a Mafia family from power with the aid of "outsiders," John Nardi was a power in the Cleveland Mafia and high up in local Teamsters affairs. For years he had felt that he never got the recognition he deserved under the mob reign of John Scalish, and when the latter died in 1976, he made a bid for power in alliance with Danny Greene, head of the so-called Irish Gang.

Syndicate crime in Cleveland had always been ethnically mixed, with a strong representation of Italian mafiosi, Jewish gangsters headed by the resourceful Moe Dalitz, and various Irish criminals. By the 1970s, the Jewish elements had long since departed for the lush legal gambling climes of Las Vegas and illegal action in Florida. But under various Italian leaders, and finally Scalish, the Mafia had become fairly dominant. However, Danny Greene and the Irish gangsters in alliance with Nardi moved to take over the Cleveland rackets as well as the important mob influence within the Teamsters.

War broke out between the Nardi-Greene forces and those of the mafiosi under James T. "Blackie" Licavoli, also known as Jack White. The Nardi-Greene gangsters scored first, knocking off a number of their enemies with bombs planted in their cars. The Licavoli forces for a time seemed incapable of striking back. They did come up with a plot to lure Nardi and Greene to New York where they could be hustled to a large meat-packing plant in New Jersey controlled by Paul Castellano, then taking over as boss of the Gambino crime family. It would be possible, as one plotter put it, "to kill them right there, freeze and bury them."

As quaint a murder plan as it would have been, it never came to pass. Meanwhile, crime families in Chicago and New York grew impatient with the failure of the Licavoli forces to win out. Finally, the Licavolis built a better bomb trap than their foes had built earlier. They loaded a car with dynamite and parked it right next to where Nardi parked his automobile at his Teamsters office. When Nardi came out to his car, an assassin pushed a remote-control switch which blew up the dynamite car and killed Nardi in the process. Later that same year, Danny Greene was murdered as well. Frank "Funzi" Tieri, head of New York's former Genovese family, sent congratulations to Licavoli, having greatly admired the way Nardi had been dispatched.

See also LICAVOLI, JAMES T. "BLACKIE"

NEIGHBORS of mafiosi

When in December 1985 Paul Castellano was shot to death on a New York City street, television and newspaper reporters scurried immediately to the exclusive Todt Hill section of Staten Island where the former head of the Gambino crime family had resided. They failed to find any neighbors with an ill word to say about Castellano. "Great neighbors," one was quoted, "and a credit to the neighborhood."

The local residents were particularly proud of the 17-room white-porticoed mansion at 177 Benedict Road which they referred to as "the White House." Many felt the Castellano family added class to the neighborhood and certainly helped property values.

Such attitudes toward mafiosi by neighbors are hardly unusual. There have never been any major complaints from respectable citizens in fashionable Sands Point, Long Island, where there has long been a considerable Mafia colony. When Tommy "Three-Finger Brown" Lucchese died, he was considered in his Long Island, New York, suburb a "wonderful neighbor." One told the press: "If he's a gangster, I wish all of them were."

Even in Brooklyn in what was the turf of Crazy Joe Gallo a reporter asked a neighbor if he thought the Gallo men were gangsters. "That's only what the papers say," was the response.

The general rule of thumb among members of the Mafia and their allies is that they merge with their neighborhoods. Home for many years for top syndicate criminal Meyer Lansky was a three-bedroom ranch-style house in Hallandale, outside Miami. He walked his dog, described rather uncharitably by some newsmen as "the ugliest dog in the world," and drove rented Chevrolets. Mrs. Lansky helped out image-wise by selling her used clothing in the garage of the house in a typical display of middle-class frugality.

Frank Tieri, the boss of the old Genovese crime family, was also the epitome of neighborly kinship. Around his modest two-family house in the Bath Beach section of Brooklyn, he could be counted on to guide an untended kindergartner out of the street if the child raced out after a ball.

Tony Accardo, the longtime Chicago big shot, a believer in living lavishly, might not have been quite as fondly thought of by neighbors. Often at Christmas time he would install a carillon that would send Christmas carols thundering through the otherwise placid and reserved River Forest area. Other residents probably did not appreciate the noise, but there is no record of any objection made by them. Such complaints would be un-Christian, un-Christmasy—and perhaps unhealthy.

"The White House," murdered mafioso Paul Castellano's white-porticoed mansion on Staten Island, New York.

While most neighbors think kindly of mafiosi, these neighbors can rest assured that they have had to pass muster with the mobsters. Most big mobsters have their boys run checks on all the neighbors to learn all about their habits and lifestyles. According to his daughter, Sam Giancana could inform Mrs. Giancana on all the goings-on of various neighbors. When daughter Antoinette brought other children to the house, Sam immediately checked out their families. If he objected to something in their parents' backgrounds—ethnicity or other faults—the children were not permitted in the Giancana household again.

It's smart to stay on the good side of Mafia neighbors. One who did not was 51-year-old John Favara, a friend of John Gotti—known to police at the time as a capo in the Gambino family and called by the law one of the most violent mafiosi. In 1980, Favara ran over and killed Gotti's 12-year-old son, Frank, in a traffic mishap officially declared accidental. Four

months later, Favara was kidnapped as he left his job in a furniture plant; he was never seen again.

According to police, after the death of young Frank, the Favara family had received unsigned threat letters at their Howard Beach, Queens, home, and their car had been spray-painted with the word *murderer*. Police got reports that Favara had been chain-sawed to death, and then placed in a car that was run through a demolition machine and reduced to a one-square-foot block. Meanwhile, Favara's wife sold their house and with her son and daughter moved far away from Howard Beach.

NEPOTISM and the Mafia: Do the kids go straight?
It happened at a meeting of the commission in 1988. Although there was great friction between John Gotti of the Gambino family and Chin Gigante of the Genovese family, and indeed the latter had even attempted to have the former whacked, there was an

effort at friendly relations. In a moment of pride, Gotti said that his son, John Junior, was now a made mafiosi. Undoubtedly Gotti expected a round of congratulations. He did not get any from the Chin. Instead, Gigante's face dropped, and he looked grayer than usual through a five-day growth of beard (his usual composure), "Jeez," he said, "I'm sorry to hear that."

It was not sentiment stemming from fear. He was truly sad, his voice tinged with genuine sympathy. No one said anything. Sammy "the Bull" Gravano who was present reflected later, "So here was Chin, who's supposed to be crazy," in effect saying that no mob guy should want his son to become a made member of the Mafia. As Gravano noted, "And there was John boasting about it. Who was really crazy?"

Actually most mafiosi claim they do not want their sons following in their footsteps. Most are not successful at preventing it. Their sons see their stature grow because of the fathers' activities and men with limited education making big money, and their drive to follow in their footsteps often becomes irresistible. Mobsters who succeed in setting their sons on a straight path usually swell with pride. Tommy "Three-Finger Brown" Lucchese never stopped boasting about his eldest son who went to West Point to lead a successful military career and life that avoided all connection with his father's "business."

Chin Gigante never permitted any of his sons to be made. Neither did Paul Castellano nor Sammy the Bull, the latter vowing he would see to it that his son never followed in his footsteps.

Carlo Gambino, at least according to mob dogma, always said he would have his sons stay legit or he would kill them. The fact remains, however, he set them up in the mob-contaminated trucking business in New York's garment district. If that was an effort to keep them clean, it was a rather unique approach.

There have been many instances of high Mafia bosses moving up as their father's successor. That was true of the Trafficante father and son in Tampa, the Patriarcas in New England, the Zerillis in Detroit and so on. It remains difficult to determine if the fathers in these cases really wanted that kind of succession.

There is no doubt that Joe Colombo Sr. was following family tradition. His grandfather was in the mob and strangled for some breach of mob etiquette. Similarly, Colombo's father Anthony was rubbed out in the same fashion in 1938, and it was well known he had broken mob rules. None of this disillusioned Joe Colombo. Once asked by a reporter if he had ever tried to find his father's killers, Colombo gave him a withering look and snapped, "Don't they pay policemen for that?" There was no rescuing the third Colombo from the forces of nepotism.

Today the most prominent Mafia son of course is John Gotti Jr. It was said that Gotti originally wanted both his sons, Junior and Frank, to be successful in legitimate fields. The effort to set them straight was wasted in Junior's case. Years of training at a military academy did little good, and he gravitated to the fringes of the mob, soon being dubbed the "baby monster" by the press (and by other mafiosi out of hearing range of his father).

The elder Gotti had no choice but to accept his son into the Gambino family. It might have been different in the case of young Frank, who unlike his brother, showed a great aptitude for learning. Gotti sent Frank to an expensive private school and beamed about his son's academic abilities. He would corner mob associates (some of whom could barely read) with his report card. "Look at that, four fucking A's! Did you ever hear of a kid who was so smart in school, huh?" And Gotti was even more impressed by the teachers' many comments of praise added on the back of the report card.

Gotti intended to send his son to a top Ivy League university and probably would have made sure he became a leader in some honest profession.

Then 12-year-old Frank was killed while riding his bike when a car driven by a neighbor, John Favara, struck him. Favara would die for his no-fault driving. That probably placated John Gotti to some extent and perhaps weakened his resolve to save Junior from the life. After John Gotti went to prison for life, he had to name his son "acting boss" of the crime family because under prison regulations he could visit his father and through various codes get orders to pass along to the mob. With John Jr.'s subsequent imprisonment for 77 months, during which time the elder Gotti died, the son could entertain the possibility he might get out and perhaps be free of his underworld problems. But by 2003 it was apparent that that probably would not come to pass. It was said testimony by a highly prized turncoat could be the vehicle for numerous other charges against the younger Gotti. "Mikey Scars" DiLeonardo would probably implicate Junior in a number of violent crimes. One would be the stabbing death in 1983 of 24-year-old Danny Silva in a dispute in a Queens bar. Then there would be

Mikey Scars' testimony in the 1992 "Bonnie and Clyde" ordered hit of Thomas and Rosemarie Uva who had robbed a string of mob-tied social clubs. The pair ended up each with three bullets in the head. Then there was the informer's expected testimony concerning Junior's alleged knowledge of the 1992 attempted killing of Guardian Angels founder and talk radio host Curtis Sliwa after he made disparaging on-air remarks about the Dapper Don. Sliwa took lead in the back and in his legs as he desperately departed a taxi his assailants had stolen.

It is really only a fine point whether some mafiosi manage to keep their offspring from becoming made men. Among those who follow in their father's footsteps there is no likelihood they will move up the management ladder. In fact, often the comparison with the father makes it most difficult for them. Joe Bonanno tried to make either of his sons fit for leadership but failed miserably. By the time of his death in 2002, the elder Bonanno had given up that hope, finally realizing neither could, would or perhaps even wanted to cut the mustard.

Both Chin Gigante and Sammy the Bull insisted they would never allow their offspring to take Mafia vows, but they were far less successful keeping them on the straight and narrow. In 2002 the Chin's son, Andrew Gigante, pleaded guilty to conspiracy to commit extortion and accepted a two-year prison term. When Sammy the Bull was convicted in his "rehabilitation" days for a major Ecstasy racket, his wife and daughter were caught in the net, as well as his son, no matter the Bull's vow. Whatever Sammy was, he was hardly a lovable dad.

In the Gigante, Gravano and Gotti cases nepotism apparently was a disaster for the offspring. Most mob guys fail at this, but at least one mob boss apparently did a good job of shielding his son from any criminal activities. Anthony "Tony Ducks" Corallo was one major godfather who shielded his family, whom he called "the dearest thing in the world," and insisted their privacy not be tampered with. Carolla never provided any information about his survivors, a son and daughter, and his orders were still strong enough on his death in 2000 that friends and allies would not provide any information about them.

NESS, Eliot (1902–1957): Head of the "Untouchables"

In 1928, a University of Chicago graduate, 26-year-old Eliot Ness, was put in charge of a special Prohibi-

tion detail set up to harass the Capone gang. The local police and regular Prohibition agents were incapable of doing so since most, if not all, were on one or another of Capone's bribe payrolls.

Ness set about assembling a squad of nine agents who would be "untouchable," or unbribable. Meticulously, he went through hundreds of files until he came up with nine agents—all in their 20s—who had "no Achilles' heel in their make-ups." Incorruptible, they also were experts in varied activities helpful in fighting bootleggers—wiretapping, truck driving and, above all, marksmanship. When the detectives moved into action, the underworld soon found them to be dedicated to their task, defiant of all threats and violence and unresponsive to cash payments. It was the underworld, stunned to find lawmen of the period who could neither be bought nor frightened, that dubbed Ness's men the "Untouchables."

The Untouchables are now a part of American criminal folklore. Latter-day television, in a show called *The Untouchables*, attributed much more credit and impact to them than they deserved, insisting they practically brought the Capone organization to its knees. Actually, their frequent raids of mob stills and distribution centers did cost the Capones a considerable amount of money but hardly caused Chicago to dry up—despite the claims of Ness at the time and his enthusiastic biographers then and now.

Ness thrived on personal publicity and always informed the press whenever a major raid on a brewery was in the works. The army of photographers who descended on the site frequently got in the way and sometimes even caused a raid to be bungled, but Ness's superiors were pleased. The publicity he produced proved that the Capone gang was not invulnerable. And Ness did provide a sort of smokescreen, distracting Capone while other federal agents infiltrated his organization to come up with tax evasion facts that eventually sent America's greatest gangster to prison.

After the fall of Capone, Ness continued warring on Prohibition violations in Chicago and, later, in the "moonshine mountains" of Tennessee, Kentucky and Ohio.

Although his Chicago exploits are best remembered, Ness's most impressive work against organized crime took place in Cleveland, Ohio, where he was named public safety director in 1935 by a reform city administration. Cleveland at the time was as corrupt a big city as any in the nation, its police force notorious for being "on the pad," taking underworld graft. Builders couldn't operate in the city without paying off labor racketeers. A vicious gang called the Mayfield Road Mob, Jewish and Italian criminals working in profitable harmony, strangled and blighted virtually every neighborhood with gambling, bootlegging and prostitution rackets. Violence was common on the streets, and gang killings and the one-way rides were about as prevalent as they were in Chicago. Given a free hand, Ness knew that if he was to create a new environment in the city he would have to reform the police department. He ordered mass transfers and fired officers for taking bribes or being drunk on duty.

During his six years on the job, Ness himself was the object of shootings, beatings, threats and even an attempted police frame-up. But in the end, Ness was able to carry out what was called his "Midwest Mop-up," transforming Cleveland, in the words of one crime historian, "from the deadliest metropolis to 'the safest big city in the U.S.A.'" The Mayfield Road Mob was crushed, and such syndicate leaders as Moe Dalitz were forced to move their gambling operations to outlying counties, and, eventually, because of continuing pressure, into northern Kentucky.

During World War II, Ness served as federal director of the Division of Social Protection for the Office of Defense, cracking down on prostitution and venereal disease around military establishments and vital production areas throughout the country. After the war, he worked in private business until his death at 54 in 1957.

NEW Orleans Mafia mass lynchings

There are two theories about the infamous mass lynchings of (alleged) mafiosi in New Orleans in 1891: One, an enraged populace rose up against Mafia criminality, which was real and running roughshod over the law; two, the attack was triggered by the most heinous, bigoted feelings and actually encouraged by the power structure of the day. Just a week after the lynching the *Saturday Review* stated, "it is at least possible that some hatred of very industrious and successful competitors in business mingled with the more respectable zeal of the lynching party." Neither theory is airtight. Although there was some desire to undermine the growing economic power of local Italian Americans, only the most rabid of the "there-ain't-no-mafia-school" could deny the criminal society's presence in New Orleans.

New Orleans probably was the most anti-Italian city of the era, and its mayor, Joseph A. Shakespeare, was one of the most anti-Italian politicians of his time. A letter from his office castigated Southern Italians and Sicilians as " . . . the most idle, vicious and worthless people among us. . . . Except the Poles we know of no other nationality which is [as] objectionable as a people."

But turn-of-the-century New Orleans was filled not only with venal politicians and police on-the-take, but also with many Italian criminals. It was the Italian immigrants who jammed the New Orleans ghettos, which, like any other ghetto, spewed out criminals. Undoubtedly, many Italian criminals of the period were not mafiosi, but it must be conceded that New Orleans represented one of the main ports of entry for mafiosi into the United States, probably rivaling New York.

It is difficult to pinpoint the first appearance of the Mafia in America but it was probably in New Orleans during the late 1800s. Between 1888 and

Slain New Orleans chief-of-police David Hennessey

1890 the New Orleans Mafia (made up of disparate groups as was the case in Sicily) committed an estimated 40 murders without serious opposition. During this period, Antonio and Carlo (or Charley) Matranga, two Honored Society members from Palermo, Sicily, took control of the Mississippi River docks. Tribute had to be paid to them before a freighter could be unloaded. However, the Matranga operations were challenged by the Provenzano brothers, leaders of another Mafia group. War broke out between the two groups, and killing along the docks became a regular occurrence.

The police failed to stop the battling until the flamboyant chief of police, David Peter Hennessey, personally took over. Soon the Matrangas found themselves hassled at every turn while the Provenzanos were left virtually unbothered. The Matrangas sent warning to the chief but the pressure continued. So they tried to bribe him, only to have him reject their offer. This convinced the Matrangas that the Provenzanos had offered him more and that Hennessey was determined to have a piece of the riverfront rackets for himself. So they fell back to an old Sicilian custom of killing the government official who got in their way. They did not understand the ramifications that would follow the killing of an American police chief.

Hennessey wrote his epitaph when police, conducting a routine murder investigation, charged two Provenzano brothers with complicity in the murder of a Matranga gangster whose head had been sliced off and stuffed in a fireplace. The Matrangas, determined to kill off the Provenzanos, hired some of the city's foremost lawyers to aid the prosecution. Then Chief Hennessey came to the rescue. He told the press he had uncovered the existence of a criminal society, the Mafia, in the city and would offer proof during the Provenzanos' trial. On October 15, 1890, Hennessey left his office for home. He was cut down by a shotgun blast a half-block from his house. Hennessey managed to direct some shots at a number of his fleeing assailants and when asked who had shot him, he whispered "Dagoes" and collapsed.

The murder outraged the citizens of New Orleans who liked Hennessey, despite many unsavory elements in his police record with the city and despite the likelihood that he might be on the take. A grand jury was convened and announced that "the existence of a secret organization known as the Mafia has been established beyond doubt." Nineteen men

One of two men strung up by a mob determined to destroy what was perceived to be the Mafia in New Orleans.

described as Mafia members were indicted as principals and conspirators in the Hennessey murder, but the trial was perceived by most people as a farce. A large number of the 60 potential witnesses were threatened, intimidated or bribed, and several members of the jury were later found to have taken bribes as well. Despite what was regarded as overwhelming

The lynchers cornered and executed seven of the alleged mafiosi in firing-squad fashion.

evidence against at least 11 of the defendants, all but three were acquitted, and the jury could not reach a verdict on these three.

All the defendants were returned to the parish prison to await final disposition of their case and then released. There can be little doubt there was considerable elation and celebration of the jury verdict in the Italian section of the city, which inflamed public opinion. (Some observers maintain that the celebrations in the Italian quarter were solely festivities for the birthday of King Umberto I of Italy, but it is ludicrous to believe that a people as discriminated against as the Italians would not celebrate the acquittal of their countrymen. If they had not, the Italians would have been strikingly different from any other national or racial group under similar circumstances.)

What followed was a blot on New Orleans. Two days after the trial's surprise ending, a great number of mass meetings and other protests fanned by outright bigotry were held. Ultimately, a mob of several thousands, headed by 60 leading citizens, marched on the jail. They had a death list composed of the 11 defendants against whom the evidence was the strongest. Left off the list were those defendants against whom the evidence was weakest, including the Matranga brothers.

Two of the mafiosi were pulled screaming to the street and hanged from lampposts. Seven others were executed by firing squads in the jail yard, and two more were riddled with bullets as they hid in a doghouse built for the jail's guard dog. Prominent in the lynch mob were a goodly number of blacks, giving the lynching a unique dimension in the American South.

While some newspapers denounced the hangings, the citizens and especially the business community seemed rather pleased by what had been done. A new song, "Hennessey Avenged," by a popular poet named Fred Bessel became a best-seller.

For a time the lynchings threatened international complications. Italy recalled its ambassador, severed diplomatic relations with the United States and demanded reparations and punishment for the lynchers. Eventually, the affair was settled with Washington paying $25,000 to the dead men's relatives in Italy.

The lynchings did not kill the Mafia in New Orleans, although newspapers announced, "The Mafia Exterminated." However, the affair did make an impression on mafiosi. Charley Matranga, who was to pick up the leadership of the mafiosi in New Orleans and rule until the early 1920s, managed to stay in the background thereafter and issue orders that were carried out by front men. And when Lucky Luciano formed the national crime syndicate, a basic rule was enunciated that under no circumstances was a police officer to be murdered.

NIGHT of the Sicilian Vespers: Mafia folklore

According to a former U.S. attorney general, "forty members of La Cosa Nostra died by gunfire" on September 10, 1931—the same day the Luciano-Lansky forces eradicated the last obstacle to their power, Salvatore Maranzano. Many criminal accounts hold these murders took place all around the country as old Mustache Petes were assassinated to make way for the new order of organized crime. Yet, no one has ever been able to compile a list of the 40 supposed victims on the Night of the Sicilian Vespers.

A number of murders in the New York area were tied to Maranzano's fate, but these were more or less predictable rubouts of the crime leader's more ardent supporters. Such underlings included Jimmy Marino, gunned down as he stood in the doorway of a Bronx barbershop, and Louis Russo and Sam Monaco, who were reported missing and not found for three days when their bodies, throats slit and skulls smashed, washed ashore in Newark Bay. (Informer Joe Valachi recollected, "Sam had an iron pipe hammered up his ass.") The Luciano-Lansky final touch was obvious: Maranzano faithful were admonished to eschew revenge and join the new setup.

But what of the alleged murders glorified in the press as the Night of the Sicilian Vespers? Luciano maintained that mass slayings were unnecessary, and he was right. Younger mafiosi around the country had been knocking off older Mustache Petes in the past few years for the same reason Luciano had killed Maranzano and before him Joe the Boss Masseria: They stood in the way of new ways to make money. And Luciano said, "The real and only reason Maranzano got his was so that we could stop the killin'. That it was all over."

There was one other killing that fatal night, however. Gerardo Scarpato, the owner of the Nuova Villa Tammaro, the Coney Island restaurant where Joe the Boss was murdered, was killed. Scarpato had conveniently disappeared from the restaurant to go for a walk along the beach before Luciano went to the bathroom and four killers walked in and gunned down Joe the Boss. It may be presumed that Luciano felt killing off Scarpato would be a nice gesture to the Masseria faithful.

See also CASTELLAMMARESE WAR; LUCIANO, CHARLES "LUCKY"; MARANZANO, SALVATORE; MUSTACHE PETES

NITTI, Frank (1884–1943): Capone mob lieutenant

Probably no gangster in American history should be more indebted to television than Frank Nitti. He was introduced to the video-watching public as the great Chicago underworld brain, the foe of the intrepid Eliot Ness and *The Untouchables*.

The post-Capone Outfit has always proved a bit confusing to the law and mob watchers alike. Using "front men" to a far greater extent than other crime families—the conviction of Capone had been a sobering lesson—the boys made it difficult for outsiders to determine the exact power structure. No wonder in later years other syndicate criminals looked at Chicago with unconcealed horror. Informer Vinnie Teresa said, "Chicago is an eat-'em-up-alive outfit . . . everyone is struggling to get on top, and they don't give a damn who gets it in the back."

In this context Nitti was valuable as a man to take the heat and, for that matter, even assassins' bullets. In that gem of prairie corruption, even Chicago mayor, Anton Cermak, could dispatch his own police "hit men" to try to knock off Nitti so he could replace him and other Caponeites with his own more subservient gangsters. Yet other mobsters, including Lucky Luciano and Meyer Lansky, when establishing the national crime syndicate in the early 1930s, dealt with Paul "the Waiter" Ricca as the leader of the Capones. They gave no thought to Nitti; he didn't even know what was going on.

Born in 1884, Nitti started out as a barber with a goodly clientele of petty crooks who came to him to fence their stolen goods. This underworld work put him in touch with the Capones at the start of Prohibition; he had ways of peddling some hijacked booze, no questions asked. Within a few years, Capone tabbed him as an efficient organizer and relied on him to see that his orders were carried out.

After Capone went to prison, the newspapers had to have a new Mr. Big. Nitti was very visible. They hailed him as the new head of the Capone mob, and Nitti probably even believed it himself. But it was ludicrous to expect the likes of the Fischetti brothers, Jake Guzik, Tony Accardo, Paul Ricca, Murray Humphreys and others to follow his orders. Only his front-man role made Nitti important.

In 1932 two police officers invaded Nitti's headquarters and shot and severely wounded him. They were acting, later testimony indicated, under orders of the new mayor, Cermak, who was determined to take over from the Capone mob and redistribute its territories to more favored criminals, especially those bossed by Cermak's favorite gangster, Teddy Newberry. Nitti lingered near death for a time but finally recovered, a feat that added to his legend.

When the mob under Willie Bioff and George Browne got into its shakedown rackets against the movie industry, Nitti's name was used as a terror tactic against the film moguls, who were threatened with his personal vengeance. However, federal investigators succeeded in getting evidence against the Chicago gangsters and with Bioff and Browne both talking, Nitti and Ricca were indicted along with several others. Ricca had by this time more obviously taken charge of the mob, often countermanding a Nitti order by saying, "We'll do it this way. Now let's hear no more about it."

Ricca decided the movie indictments made the time perfect to call in Nitti's cards as a front man. At a meeting of the top leaders of the mob he ordered Nitti to plead guilty and take the rap for all of them. The thought terrified Nitti who had served 18 months in the early 1930s on an income tax charge. He got the "shakes" at the idea of returning behind bars. That sort of reaction made Nitti a logical candidate to seek mercy from the prosecution by confessing and naming all the others.

"Frank, you're asking for it," Ricca raged at him, still demanding he be a "standup guy" and take the rap for all. Nitti recognized Ricca's words as a death sentence. The next day, March 19, 1943, Nitti was seen walking along some railroad tracks. He drew a pistol from his pocket and put a bullet in his brain.

NO hands rule: Mob code of conduct

Adopted by various mafioso leaders since about 1930, the "no hands rule" forbids any mob member from physically attacking another. The purpose of the rule—apparently first propounded by Salvatore Maranzano and later insisted upon by Lucky Luciano—was to prevent needless outbreaks of gang warfare.

The rule was especially important in New York where five crime families operated in the city. Inevitably there was friction between family members about racket rights in certain spots or the exclusivity of a certain shakedown, gambling or loan shark victim. Crime family leaders reserved to themselves the right to decide such matters and did not approve the actions of a hit-happy low echelon hoodlum in provoking a situation in which "honor" would require all-out warfare.

Thus the rule was set. The mere laying of one's hands on another gangster was cause enough for even the death penalty to be imposed on the offender. While such a "Cosa Nostra code" would seem to guarantee civilized behavior, such was seldom the case. The late Joe Valachi was noted for using violence to keep other Cosa Nostra members from treading on his financial interests, and, on one occasion, he knocked out fellow racketeer Frank Luciano (no relation to Lucky) when he caught him appropriating some of their joint monies.

Taken to the "table"—a Mafia trial—Valachi was tried by Murder, Inc., boss Albert Anastasia, noted for his unpredictable actions. He could have ordered Valachi's death with a snap of the finger. However, Anastasia went the other way, declaring Valachi to be more in the right than his victim and giving what amounted to an award of damages to Valachi.

In actual practice, the no hands rule does not seem to have been rigidly enforced. When it was, most likely it represented a family boss's method of achieving some end of his own.

NO narcotics rule: Alleged Mafia code

There has long been a myth that most or all organized crime bosses eschewed the "dirty business" of drug trafficking. Giving added credibility to such nonsense was the famous, if not always lucid, testimony of informer Joe Valachi. He told one tale that, as former Chicago Crime Commission head Virgil Peterson has noted, "was viewed with skepticism by many knowledgeable law-enforcement officers."

Valachi declared that under Tony Accardo the Chicago Cosa Nostra paid its soldiers $200 a week to stop dealing in narcotics. Later, apparently in light of inflation, this weekly stipend was increased to $250. According to Valachi, this caused considerable problems in New York City where mobsters were ordered out of the racket with no compensation whatsoever.

In fact many New York mobsters in various of the five crime families were deeply involved in drug trafficking with and without approval from above. Many members of the Lucchese and Bonanno family engaged in narcotics dealings. Joe Bonanno insisted in his autobiography, *A Man of Honor,* that "My Tradition outlaws narcotics. It had always been understood that 'men of honor' don't deal in narcotics. However, the lure of high profits had tempted some underlings to freelance in the narcotics trade." In point of fact, Bonanno's underboss, Carmine Galante, was convicted on a narcotics charge.

In 1948 Frank Costello, the caretaker-head of the Luciano family after Charlie Lucky was deported, ordered the family to stay out of drugs. Of all the bosses, probably Costello was the most genuinely opposed to dealing in dope. Since he operated mainly through cooperation with the political power structure on such matters as gambling, he understood that narcotics was the one activity he often could not square—the politicians would be too frightened of public outrage. However, Costello's edict applied only to the Luciano family while others ignored it or paid it no more than lip service. Vito Genovese, who finally wrested control of the family from Costello, issued the same edict while actually keeping up a lifelong activity in dope. Genovese did have a few underlings murdered for violating the no drugs rule, but took a different attitude if he himself was cut in for a major portion of the profits. Indeed, Genovese died in jail for narcotics dealing.

It was estimated by informers and law enforcement officials in the 1970s that of the 450-some members of the Genovese crime family at least 100 remained, many to this day, involved in the dope racket. The statistics are probably similar in other crime families—with or without a no narcotics rule.

See also NARCOTICS RACKET

NORMANDIE, SS: Mafia wartime sabotage

On February 11, 1942, not long after the United States entered World War II, the night skies over New York's Hudson River piers turned crimson in a spectacular fire. Ablaze was the former French liner *Normandie,* renamed the *Lafayette,* which was being converted to a troop carrier. It would have made a most efficient troopship since its high speed would have made it an extremely difficult target for German wolfpack submarines then decimating Atlantic shipping.

The fire gutted the *Normandie*. Flames burned fiercely all over the ship, and it was clearly arson. Officially, the government inferred it was not sure what had happened. It might have been Nazi sabotage or it might simply have been due to worker carelessness. At U.S. Navy headquarters in Washington, "carelessness" was not taken seriously; that possibility had been raised simply to prevent civilian panic. But what had happened to the *Normandie*?

The truth was not revealed for almost three decades until the posthumous memoirs of Lucky Luciano explained that the ship had been sabotaged by the Mafia. That explanation was later confirmed by the usually tight-lipped Meyer Lansky who, still later, revealed the same basic facts to his Israeli biographers.

It was the Mafia that struck the match to the *Normandie*. The purpose was to light a fire under the military authorities so that they could be panicked into enlisting the imprisoned Lucky Luciano into efforts to stop sabotage on the docks. Even before the *Normandie* fire, naval intelligence was convinced that German- or Italian-speaking dock workers were signaling information to off-shore enemy subs. It was clear to these intelligence operatives that they did not have the power to prevent this and neither did the New York police. The only force capable of doing so was the underworld.

The first man to see the opening this gave the Mafia was Albert Anastasia, a longtime Luciano loyalist. Albert conferred with his brother, Tough Tony Anastasio, who then took a plan to Frank Costello, acting head of Luciano's crime family. Costello journeyed to Dannemora Prison to present the idea of burning the *Normandie* to Luciano who saw it would give him tremendous leverage with the government. Officials would have to deal with him to keep the docks safe.

With a nod from Luciano, the *Normandie* burned. Later, Luciano would gloat: "That god-damn Anastasia—he really done a job. Later on, Albert told me not to feel too bad about what happened to the ship. He said that as a sergeant in the Army he hated the fuckin' Navy anyway."

The burning of the SS *Normandie* in 1942—sabotage or a Mafia act of war?

The *Normandie*'s fate galvanized official Washington to action. Almost instantly an emergency plan called Operation Underworld came into being, calling for utilizing the Mafia to help the war effort. The Navy approached Joseph "Socks" Lanza, the racket boss of the Fulton Fish Market, with the idea. Lanza explained he was a small fish in the matter and passed the Navy on to Costello and Meyer Lansky. They let it be known that only Luciano could give the okay.

The mob had won their war. Officials fell all over themselves trying to please Charley Lucky. Costello said he was unhappy being in Dannemora, the "Siberia" of the New York penal system, and maybe he should be transferred to Sing Sing. Officials went one better and moved him to Great Meadow Prison, the most pleasant institution in the system.

Luciano passed the word that the mob had to do all possible on the docks to aid the war effort. Lansky personally lectured Anastasia, telling him that he and his brother mustn't burn any more ships. "He was sorry," Lansky recalled, "not sorry he'd had the *Normandie* burned but sorry he couldn't get at the Navy again."

From Great Meadow Luciano issued many orders, ostensibly concerning the war effort, but in conversations with Costello and Lansky he spent most of his time exerting active control once more over the national crime syndicate. And after the war of course Governor Thomas E. Dewey, who had put Luciano in prison for 30 to 50 years on a charge of compulsory prostitution, agreed to his release because of his patriotic services to the government.

See also ANASTACIO, ANTHONY "TOUGH TONY"; LUCIANO, CHARLES "LUCKY"

NOSE jobs: Punishment for wise guy addicts

In the newly assertive Mafia it cannot be said that mob guys are punished for dealing in drugs. The money is too inviting. But the new Mafia bosses appear to be enforcing a "nose job" under special circumstances. New recruits are warned that mob guys who are hooked on drugs are a danger to the entire mob, as bitter experience has proven. They can give away mob secrets while under the influence, and under the new emphasis on security, this cannot be tolerated, and offenders may well suffer a nose job, which means blown away with a gun stuffed up the nose.

NO slander rule   See SCIASCIA, GERLANDO

NUMBERS racket

The numbers racket in various forms has been known to the world since at least 1530 when the Italian national lottery started (well before the political unification of Italy, indicating perhaps that gambling may have been more of a driving force than nationalism). Through the centuries—and certainly in our time under Mafia rule in the United States—the numbers game has been without doubt the biggest and most profitable gambling racket of all. According to recent estimates, at least 20 million people a day engage in this illegal pastime, and the total annual take is in the billions, with organized crime reaping a quarter billion in profits in New York City alone. Even state lotteries have not crippled the illegal racket; numbers players don't have to make the IRS their partners in big scores.

So-called policy shops, where people go to play the numbers, showed up in America in the 1880s. Al Adams, a New York operator, had about 1,000 policy shops in the city, and was one of the biggest bribe donors to Boss Tweed's Tammany Hall. Adams became known as "the meanest gambler in New York" because he rigged the numbers results not only to cheat his clients but also so that he could then bet heavily on the correct numbers with other operators so that he could drive *them* out of business and take over their shops. Eventually Adams went to prison after Tweed was dethroned. To reassure numbers players that everything thereafter would be legit, operators switched to taking the numbers from Treasury Department figures, released daily by telegraph, and obviously not to be fixed.

While numbers had been played in the United States since 1880, the game has changed many times, and, although long popular in Harlem, penny-ante numbers, which was to prove the most lucrative of all, came into being only in the 1920s. Before that even black operators in Harlem sold only 50¢ and $1 numbers tickets. Later they experimented with a 10¢ ticket. Over the years both Lucky Luciano and Meyer Lansky told various interviewers that Lansky was the true inventor of numbers, meaning the game, which could be played for as little as a penny by inhabitants of the poorest ghettos. Certainly among the players on the Jewish Lower East Side the opinion was that numbers was Lansky's game.

Interestingly the Chicago Outfit did not discover numbers until the 1940s when Sam Giancana was doing time in the federal prison at Terre Haute. Black racketeer Edward Jones bragged to him how much profit he was making out of the numbers racket, with most of his customers making bets as little as one cent to a nickel. The Chicago Outfit then slaughtered the black operators and took over. Even though there was a national crime syndicate and the New York mobs under Luciano and Lansky had made millions out of the racket, they had never informed Chicago how profitable the business was. Within organized crime the fact remains that things operate the same as in legitimate business.

The term *policy* applied to the numbers game has its derivation in the penny insurance that was highly popular in the poor ghettos; both were a cheap gamble on the future. The winning number, one in a thousand ranging from 000 to 999, paid off at 600 to one. Meaning that for 1¢ a winner would get back $6 (or less in certain localities). Since mathematical odds against the player were actually 1,000 to one the profit potential in numbers is far greater than in any other form of gambling. Numbers operations thus could support a whole bureaucracy from the "banker" on top down through operators, distributors, agents and runners. Basically, only the agents and runners face much risk of arrest, and it is the duty of those above them immediately to bail them out and put in a fix to prevent a conviction, or, at worst, to support the families of those sent to prison.

Whether or not Lansky was the inventor of penny-ante numbers or not, it was hardly a copyrightable idea, and it soon was embraced by armies of independent operators. A Madam St. Clair, a Harlem operator, became a millionaire from numbers and would have done so even if she hadn't thrown in an extra fillip—her policy wheel was credited with providing a magical potency to the players.

The mobsters were not about to let independents like St. Clair clean up in numbers. Prohibition beer czar Dutch Schultz pioneered the forcible takeover of the numbers racket in Harlem, terrorizing individual bankers into buying his protection and then simply announcing he was assuming control of their businesses. Madam St. Clair once avoided mob execu-

tioners by hiding in a pile of coal in a Harlem cellar. Schultz reintroduced the old Adams method of cheating on the numbers results which had been switched by then to the wagering totals of various racetracks. Schultz's "mathematical brain," Otto "Abbadabba" Berman, worked out a system to rig the numbers so that only low-played numbers won.

After Schultz was murdered by the syndicate the numbers racket in Harlem was effectively taken over by Luciano and Lansky, with operations under the supervision of Vito Genovese, Luciano's right-hand man.

Over the years probably as many murders have been committed to gain control of and hold onto the numbers racket as were done during the old mob bootleg wars. Certainly, numbers money remains in many areas the prime source of illegal payoffs to politicians and police for protection. It is often said that the Mafia has been losing control of the numbers racket as the ghettos turn increasingly black and Hispanic. It is a theory nurtured by the Mafia. The fact remains that the mobs in some places have simply granted "franchises" to certain ethnics (as in the past to Poles and Jews, among others, in their ghettos) and for their pay guarantee full protection to the numbers operators.

See also BERMAN, OTTO "ABBADABBA"

NUT: Backing for a mob enterprise

The nut is the start-up money needed to pull off a caper. Individuals or crew divisions within a crime family are expected to raise their own funds for the activities they wish to promote. Of course, they can tap funds from higher-ups, but that nut is not a diminishing asset. Should the funds be advanced for a drug shipment, for instance, the borrower must be good for the debt since the bosses tolerate no loss of their money even if the drugs are seized by authorities. In such a case the bosses can be magnanimous and merely demand their initial investment be returned. Offering excuses in such situations can have a direct bearing on the borrower's life expectancy.

O

OAKES, Sir Harry (1873–1943): Murder victim

In 1943, U.S.-born Sir Harry Oakes, a tough old examiner who became, according to some, the world's richest man, was murdered. The Bahamas's number one citizen, Sir Harry was catered to by the duke of Windsor, the former king of England and then-governor of the islands.

In the aftermath of Sir Harry's death in 1943, kept secret by the duke for some hours, ensued one of the most inept police investigations, and probably the most celebrated murder trial, of the war years. The duke of Windsor, after the discovery of the body, called in American lawmen to investigate, informing them that Sir Harry had committed suicide—a remarkable observation since Sir Harry had died of massive head wounds made by some kind of pronged instrument. What's more, the bed where Sir Harry lay had been set ablaze and the dead man's body incinerated. In a macabre touch, feathers were spread over the burned corpse. Clearly this was no run-of-the-mill suicide!

But if it wasn't suicide, that meant the investigation run by imported Miami police captain Otto Barker and Edward Walter Melchen was aptly described by one authority as "one of the most lackadaisical criminal investigations of modern times." There was considerable evidence that the murder was committed by American gangsters seeking to infiltrate the island for gambling purposes. Harry Oakes had the prestige and power to get the official okay for such activities, but the former gold hunter who hit the second largest gold strike in history was a contrary individual who could give his word one moment and break it the next. It appeared he had taken $1 million as a downpayment from a leading American mobster operating out of Miami, Meyer Lansky, and then refused to push for the establishment of a casino in Nassau. The Florida investigators developed no interest in their fellow Miamian and instead came up with "evidence" that pinned the murder on Sir Harry's unwanted son-in-law Alfred de Marigny, an aristocratic Frenchman from Mauritius, who though handsome and charming, was suspected by Bahamian society of being a bad sort.

The trial proved to be a sensation and the social event of the year on the islands. Wealthy landowners had their servants queue up for seats at the trial long before dawn. De Marigny was tied to the murder by tainted evidence, particularly a fingerprint of very dubious origin and worth. The prosecution's case was built on innuendo. De Marigny had a bad reputation and wanted his father-in-law's money. Sir Harry disliked him intensely and was not about to give him any money. His son-in-law murdered him.

The defense's case was aided by the highly professional work of a famed American private detective, Raymond Schindler, who had to contend with all sorts of roadblocks set up by the local authorities. He was denied access to many matters, was followed and his telephone tapped. Yet he easily destroyed the prosecution's case—a conclusion approved by Erle Stanley Gardner, one of the many writers assigned to cover the 13-week trial. It took the jury only two and a half hours to clear de Marigny.

But who killed Sir Harry Oakes? The royal government was decidedly uninterested in finding out thereafter. There are law enforcement agencies in the United States whose investigators have been convinced by a number of underworld informers that they have discovered the true story. The thesis, presented in a number of recent books on the case, has Lansky more than a little upset by Sir Harry's refusal to go through with his agreement. Lansky insisted that a local mild-mannered Bahamian real estate man named Harold Christie (who no one at the time knew had a Boston police record) was in on the deal to get Sir Harry to see the light. Christie knew what the underworld did to men who crossed them, knew that Sir Harry's high position would offer him no protection.

Finally, the story goes, Lansky said he was sending a special emissary to settle matters once and for all. He was accompanied by four button men who arrived aboard a fast power cruiser on the afternoon of July 7, 1943. Christie and Sir Harry drove down to the docks and went aboard the craft. Sir Harry, rather than Lansky's emissary, did most of the talking and yelling. He said he had no intention of letting gangsters get a foothold on the islands. Lansky's emissary said nothing, but he nodded slightly to one of the enforcers. Sir Harry went down hard when hit in the head with a four-pronged winch handle.

Christie was terrified by the sudden violence, but Lansky's man assured him Sir Harry was only stunned. He had the real estate man and one of the button men pack the millionaire into the car and take him back to his mansion. There it was obvious that Sir Harry was never going to wake up again. Christie was frozen with fear, but Lansky's operative went about the grisly task of undressing the dead man and getting him into pajamas. Then the bed was set on fire, followed by the corpse. The feathers were a last-minute detail, intended apparently to give the killing a bizarre touch. Christie was left to say whatever he wanted, but he could not mention Lansky or his enforcers at all.

Of course, the Oakes case was never officially solved and Lansky had not been tied to it in any firm way by 1963, when, 20 years after the murder, Lansky got his gambling monopoly in the Bahamas. According to later investigation, the cost to Lansky to get the fix in was approximately $1 million—the same amount offered Sir Harry Oakes.

O'BANION, Charles Dion "Deanie" (1892–1924): Gang leader and Capone rival

He was Al Capone's toughest competitor in the latter's struggle for power in Chicago, the gangster capital of the world. Even after he was assassinated in 1924 in a Capone–Johnny Torrio coup, O'Banion's ghost continued to haunt Capone. O'Banion supporters, enraged by his murder, refused to give in and for the balance of the decade the carnage on Chicago streets reached unparalleled levels.

O'Banion had a kind of perverse charisma; he was as charming a psychopath as one could find. And he would do anything for a laugh. His sense of humor was legendary, although best appreciated by the criminal mind. Among his more innocent practical jokes was giving a friend Ex Lax and telling him it was sweet chocolate. Really thigh-slapping fun was his shotgun challenge. He would surreptitiously fill both barrels of a shotgun with hard-packed clay and then bet some friend or acquaintance that he could not hit the side of a barn some 30 feet away. With the money down, O'Banion made a ritual out of loading both barrels and handing the shotgun to the sucker. He moved back out of the way of the inevitable recoil as the patsy pulled the trigger. The backfire would cause him to lose an arm or an eye or even three-fourths of his face. Dear Deanie would still be howling about it the following day.

Chicago chief of police Morgan Collins labeled O'Banion "Chicago's archcriminal" and said he killed at least 25 men. Others said Collins was less than half right, that O'Banion had at least 60 murders to his credit as he cheerfully made his appointed murder rounds, always with a rosary in his pocket and a carnation in his buttonhole. He also had three pistols tucked away in special pockets of his expensive made-to-order suits. For years O'Banion had been the darling of the Democrats for his skill at getting out the vote, until he switched to the Republicans at higher pay. The oftquoted joke of the time was: "Who'll carry the Forty-second and Forty-third wards?" The answer was, "O'Banion, in his pistol pocket."

O'Banion grew up in the Little Hell district on Chicago's North Side. He lived a double life as an acolyte and choir boy at Holy Name Cathedral and as a street punk in a tenement jungle jammed with saloons and whorehouses. Thanks to his training in the church choir Deanie became a singing waiter in the tough dives on Clark and Erie. He brought tears to the customers' eyes with sentimental Irish ballads, and when they were deep in their cups, he'd pick their pockets.

After-hours, O'Banion labored as a street mugger, becoming partners with a young Lou Greenberg, destined to become the multimillionaire owner of the Seneca Hotel on the city's Gold Coast. One midnight, each without knowing the other was present, they had pounced on the same victim in an alley, and then over his prostrate body contemplated bashing the other for the loot. Instead, wisdom prevailed. They split the take and became partners. The arrangement continued for several months until in 1909 Deanie was imprisoned three months for robbery. In 1911 he did another three months for carrying concealed weapons. Although he was arrested many times thereafter, it was the last prison time O'Banion did in his life. He quickly learned that Chicago was the city of the fix and always spent the money required to cool the ardor of policemen, prosecutors and judges.

He graduated from street mugging to a form of journalism as a slugger for Maxie Annenberg, Moe Annenberg's brother. Maxie at the time was in charge of promoting sales of the Chicago *Tribune,* and O'Banion was used mainly to bop newsdealers to convince them that the *Trib* was not only the world's greatest newspaper but for their purposes Chicago's *only* newspaper. Later on O'Banion transferred his loyalties to the newer Hearst papers in town. At the same time O'Banion learned the safe-cracking art under one of the racket's foremost practitioners, Charlie "the Ox" Reiser. From Reiser he learned the theory that convictions were impossible without witnesses and dead witnesses made for terrible testimony. It didn't always come to that. On one occasion an executive of Hearst's *American* put up $5,000 bail to secure his release on a safecracking charge. There were newspapers to sell, after all.

By the time Prohibition came, and with it the enormous new opportunities for criminals, O'Banion was the leader of a mighty gang on the North Side. Among the senior members were Bugs Moran, Hymie Weiss, Schemer Drucci (the only Italian O'Banion ever trusted and vice versa), Dapper Dan McCarthy, Two-Gun Alterie and Frank Gusenberg. The O'Banions, almost completely Irish in lower-level manpower, formed an alliance with many Jewish gangsters of the old 20th Ward, especially those working with Nails Morton, and the gangs more or less merged. When Morton was killed in a horseback riding accident, the grief-stricken O'Banions exacted the proper underworld revenge by executing the horse.

O'Banion's approach to Prohibition, even before it went into effect, was to stockpile supplies by hijacking booze from legitimate sources. He tried to continue the same method when the 18th Amendment became effective. "Let Johnny Torrio make the stuff," he was quoted. "I'll steal what I want of it." However, even a consummate thief like O'Banion could not steal enough to meet the needs on the North Side, and he started taking over some of the area's top breweries and distilleries.

This switch in tactics removed a major source of conflict between the Torrio-Capone mob and the North Siders, although Torrio and Capone were deeply upset that O'Banion would not let them operate whorehouses in the North Side, which would have added millions to their income. Deanie's religious inclinations simply would not allow dealing in bodies—although he seemed totally untroubled about filling bodies with lead. Still, if they won O'Banion's forbearance about hijacking, Torrio was

Dion O'Banion was a doting bridegroom and husband who spent his evenings at home when not out committing homicide.

more than content to let the Irish keep the North Side.

Torrio was more concerned with syndicating the booze and other rackets in the city so that the various elements could function without harassment from other gangs. Given the makeup of the various gangs, the concept in at least some cases bordered on the utopian. In the first place O'Banion couldn't give up hijacking booze forever; the principles of stealing were too strongly ingrained in him. Then too the Terrible Gennas could not be controlled. A murderous Sicilian family, they had organized moonshining in Little Italy into a veritable cottage industry, with the manufacturing of bathtub booze the chief source of income for many families. Since such rotgut was produced so cheaply, the Gennas could and did invade other areas and undersell other bootleg gangs.

O'Banion for one was not going to stand for that. Neither would Torrio. The O'Banions and the Gennas believed in direct action and warred on each other. Torrio, more cunning than either of them, solved his problems by secretly helping Gennas knock off O'Banions and O'Banions knock off Gennas.

Then O'Banion pulled a swindle that victimized Torrio and caused him to lose face in the underworld. He informed Torrio he was quitting the rackets and was heading West as soon as he could sell off an illegal brewery for a half-million dollars. Torrio jumped at this opportunity to be rid of the unpredictable O'Banion and eagerly put up the money. Almost instantly after the deal was closed and Torrio took possession, federal agents swooped down and seized the brewery and charged Torrio with violation of the Prohibition law. Torrio discovered O'Banion had learned in advance of the upcoming raid and dumped off the property on Torrio. Even when Hymie Weiss, O'Banion's loyal lieutenant, urged him to make amends to Torrio, the gang chief rejoiced contemptuously, "Oh, to hell with them Sicilians."

Now all-out war was inevitable although Mike Merlo, a power in politics and the head of Unione Sicilana, the now bootlegger-corrupted fraternal organization, kept the peace for a time. Then in November Merlo died of natural causes and Torrio was free to act. O'Banion knew an attack was coming but figured his enemies would wait until Merlo was in the ground. He was wrong.

Deanie ran a florist shop on North State Street, directly opposite the church where he had once been a choir boy. The place was partly a dodge to provide him with a legitimate front, but it also satisfied his love for flowers. And O'Banion got a perverse joy out of making a small fortune from selling his blooms for the many gangland funerals. He did a land-office business for the Merlo affair, some of his creations selling for thousands of dollars. On the evening of November 9, he got a special order by telephone for a custom wreath to be picked up the following morning. At the appointed time three men appeared. "Hello, boys," O'Banion greeted them. "You from Mike Merlo's?"

The man in the middle nodded and grabbed O'Banion in a firm handshake. It was an old trick but O'Banion, given the solemnity of the occasion, fell for it. He could not escape the handshake and reach the guns he had on him at the time. The other two men pulled out guns and started firing. O'Banion took a bullet in each cheek, two through the throat at the larynx, and two in the right breast.

They gave O'Banion one of the most flowerbedecked funerals Chicago had ever seen. Naturally the murder was never officially solved, although the killers were later identified as Albert Anselmi and John Scalise. The handshaker was Frankie Yale, a big-shot gangster imported from New York especially for the job by Torrio and Capone.

The death of Deanie did not end the war, as the remaining O'Banions sought savage revenge for their chief's death. Weiss and Drucci who in turn succeeded to leadership met lead-filled ends, and Johnny Torrio as well was nearly assassinated. Recovering from his nearfatal wounds, Torrio decided he'd had enough of Chicago and retired back to Brooklyn, taking $30 million with him in consolation. In the meantime Capone took charge and continued the war to win control of Chicago, masterminding the infamous St. Valentine's Day Massacre which wiped out all the top North Siders except for Bugs Moran.

The importance of the fight with the O'Banions was that it kept Capone off-balance for years. He too thought of organizing crime nationally, but, unable to do what had to be done in Chicago, he was forced to leave that promising field open for the New York mobs under Lucky Luciano and Meyer Lansky.

O'BRIEN, John Patrick (1873–1951): **New York mayor**
Following the resignation of the corrupt if charming Jimmy Walker, John P. O'Brien was elected to serve

out the remaining year of the mayoral term. It was a stunning victory for organized crime.

O'Brien, known for his mediocre talents as a surrogate court judge and his unswerving loyalty to Tammany Hall, was clearly under the thumb of two Tammany leaders, James J. Hines (then controlled by mobster Dutch Schultz, a member of the new Luciano-Lansky national crime syndicate) and Albert C. Marinelli (then directly dominated by Lucky Luciano). When reporters inquired if the mayor was going to name a new police commissioner, he said, "I haven't had any word on that yet."

In 1933, O'Brien was succeeded by Fiorello La Guardia, and underworld payoffs to the police commissioner's office—during the reign of the supposedly reputable Grover Whalen it came to $20,000 a week delivered in a plain brown bag—ceased. Under La Guardia's first police commissioner, Major General John J. O'Ryan, who served briefly, and the incorruptible Lewis J. Valentine, who held the post for almost 11 years, the police department was to have its longest run of honesty in the city's history.

O'CONNOR'S Gunners: Chicago police machine-gunning unit

In 1927, William O'Connor, the new chief of detectives in Chicago, went out on a limb. Gang wars were terrorizing the city, but the press and his constituents were unconvinced that O'Connor could stop the shooting. What the situation called for, Chief O'Connor decided—and convinced corrupt Mayor Big Bill Thompson was necessary—was an elite unit, an armored car force that could match the gangsters bullet for bullet.

O'Connor picked volunteers from the police force who had fought in the war in Europe and could handle a machine gun. To this squad of super-armed men, he issued an order of almost unparalleled irresponsibility:

Men, the war is on. We've got to show that society and the police department, and not a bunch of dirty rats, are running this town. It is the wish of the people of Chicago that you hunt these criminals down and kill them without mercy. Your cars are equipped with machine guns and you will meet the enemies of society on equal terms. See to it that they don't have you pushing up daisies. Make them push up daisies. Shoot first and shoot to kill. If you kill a notorious feudist, you will get a handsome reward and win promotion. If you

meet a car containing bandits, pursue them and fire. When I arrive on the scene, my hopes will be fulfilled if you have shot off the top of their car and killed every criminal inside it.

There was considerable hesitation by many persons to accept such a shoot-first-think-afterward program; they worried about innocent bystanders being cut down in the crossfire. However, such worries by members of the public—and, perhaps, by the gangsters themselves—proved unnecessary. O'Connor's Gunners turned out to be regular johnnies-come-lately to crime scenes, hardly ever turning up in the right place at the right time.

ODESSA by the Sea: Brighton Beach, Brooklyn, as center of Russian Mafia activities

While there is real doubt that a true "Russian Mafia" exists in America, popular belief is that the Brighton Beach section of Brooklyn is the capital of the most important "other Mafia" now functioning in the United States. There is no doubt that the area is the center of much violence and brutality, at times said to rival the worst activities of the Mafia in Brighton Beach and Coney Island in its earlier days. It has been estimated that many thousands of illegal immigrants have entered the United States in recent years from the former Soviet Union under a grant of refugee status as politically oppressed people. Many Brighton Beach inhabitants have come from Odessa and surrounding areas. The Black Sea port of Odessa has a long history of criminality, dating back to the days of the early czars and the pirates who ravaged the waters. Thus Odessa was long a thriving black market and developed a centuries-old criminal subculture. Although most residents of Brighton Beach are clearly law-abiding, they have been tarred as the Odessukuya, or Odessa Thieves, often described in the motherland as the worst of all Russian criminals. According to federal authorities, many of these illegals have come out of Soviet prisons, obtained identifications of dead or imprisoned Soviet Jews and used them to reach the United States, often muddying their trails by first immigrating to Israel. This "shuttle plan" is similar to one used by Italian mafiosi early in the 20th century, who traveled first to North Africa and then on to the American land of opportunity, their criminal backgrounds lost in the shuffle.

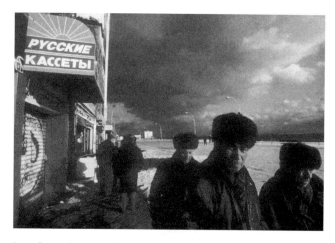

Local residents walk along the boardwalk in the Brighton Beach section of Brooklyn, New York. Populated by over 60,000 Russian immigrants, "Little Odessa" hosts numerous nightclubs and restaurants, some of which serve as headquarters for the newly established mobsters of the Russian mafia in New York.

OMERTÀ: Mafia rule of silence

Translated simply *omertà* means "manliness." It is not manly to be an informer, to tattle to the law or outsiders.

Omertà is often thought to apply only to the upper echelon of organized crime. Yet these ranks inform regularly—when it suits their purpose. However, the code of silence is enforced with regard to underlings. A man who sings or squeals is a rat. Rats get killed. Thus many a bullet-riddled hood dies coughing up blood but refusing to tell the law who has gunned him down. Underworld underlings are required to go like "men" and rely on their colleagues to avenge their deaths.

There is a reason besides self-preservation that causes Mafia leaders to enforce omertà. When hoods refuse to talk, it is a way of telling victims and witnesses that they too are bound by omertà. If they talk, they can expect the same end.

Omertà goes back to the birth of the Mafia in Sicily in the 13th century when the Mafia was organized to drive out the Spanish invaders. As the Mafia turned criminal, it did precisely what the Spanish had done—terrorize the people, hire out to large landowners who wanted to cow the farmers. The Mafia was ready to kill and it was protected by the code of omertà.

The rule of silence, the real power of omertà that the Mafia brought to America, sealed the lips of victims and witnesses. Going to the police was the cardinal sin. Hapless immigrants could do nothing but silently accept the terror of the Mafia and various Black Hand extortionists. A minor violation of omertà could result in a slit tongue; a major violation, a slit throat of either the offender or a member of his family.

Omertà is strictly for victims, witnesses or lower-level mafiosi. The higher-ups think nothing of "ratting" to police to get rid of competition. The cops would take care of the competition and the cunning mafiosi stepped in to fill the void. Lower-grade drug dealers involved with the Mafia are stupid if they believe omertà protects them. The Mafia often operates with police protection but realizes it must reward corrupt officers with more than mere money. The police must be allowed to look brave and efficient, so mafiosi feed them a dealer, allowing them to make a spectacular pinch now and then to placate public opinion. And omertà be damned.

Because higher-up mafiosi make a mockery of omertà, the code has virtually collapsed within the Mafia. Because of that the federal government now has close to 1,000 informers, including scores of Mafia men of the Valachi stripe, under its wing. As Vinnie Teresa, one of the most productive informers of all, put it: "But looking back on my life with the Mafia members, I realize now that omerta—the code—was just a lot of bullshit."

ONORTA: Southern Italian criminal society

It would be a mistake to believe that only the Mafia of Sicily and the Camorra of Naples supplied America with all its Italian criminals. The Onorta Societa (or Society of Honor) did so as well. The Onorta was centered in Calabria in southern Italy, a mountainous and remote province that prior to the 20th century was almost totally insulated from the vitality, revolutionary fervor and dynamism of the northern Italy.

In outlook and organization the Onorta had much in common with the Mafia and Camorra. It relied on extortion and banditry for funds and honored secret rituals and passwords. Calabria remained feudal and agrarian into the 20th century, and the society was family oriented; when one had troubles one called on one's family and friends for aid. There was no concept of loyalty to any state, rather authority was gauged by the family's standing in its community. The dominant families in a Calabrian community ran the local Onorta.

Calabria was an impoverished area. So, despite the power of the Onorta; many of the young banditry followed the immigrant stream to America. Criminals of Calabrian background were hardly less prevalent in America than were the early mafiosi. Onorta brigands settled especially in the southern United States, principally in New Orleans, and then moved north to St. Louis, Kansas City and Chicago. Others settled in New York. But Onorta bonds weakened quickly here, and society members tended instead to merge readily into whichever Mafia or Camorra gangs held supremacy. By about 1918 when the Mafia-Camorra wars in the United States had petered out, the Onorta was already integrated into the new, combined underworld.

Oddly, the Onorta appears to have disappeared at the same time in Calabria. Calabria still has secret societies, but they are better described as a network of Mafia crime families with close working relationships to Sicily.

OPEN hit: Free-for-all murder order

In the old days of rigid Mafia discipline, a boss might order an "open hit," meaning any member of the mob could take out the unwanted man at the first chance anyone got. It was particularly useful when a victim was suspicious he might be on a death list and took special precautions that made him a slippery target. In later years the ploy was much harder to pull off as law enforcement used enough bugging and surveillance to frequently hear of the hit order. The FBI could readily pick up conversations between a couple of wise guys talking about making a try themselves or describing the tries of other mobsters. One can imagine how many mobsters were turned by the law when such conversations were played for the would-be victim. As a result, in the new, more cautious mob world, open hits are rarely used, and bosses rely almost completely on specific hit assignments. If the proposed hit is later botched or not even attempted, the bosses know who to blame and those hit men may find themselves put under "contract" themselves.

A recent exception were co-bosses Vic Amuso and Gas Pipe Casso who inherited control of the Lucchese family and sought to maintain control by wholesale killings, often bordering on the screwball if not outright insane, to wipe out their enemies. Under those circumstances they issued open hit orders almost willy-nilly and then might also put out open hits on the gunners they were relying on to make earlier open hit orders. As a result, there were more desertions from the crime family than any other as the mobsters tried to survive. Also the bosses themselves came closer to implications in the hits than they would in more secretive ploys. Thus the open hit method is used to a lesser extent. If a crime bigwig wants to engage in a cover-up, the current modus operandi is to assign a couple of killers to take out a victim then have a couple of hit men take care of the first set of hit men, and then the second pair is taken out by a third set of killers. Joel Cacace has been singled out by investigators for going this devious route.

OPEN territories: Organized crime's apportionment plan

While the public argument may go on about whether the Mafia exists or if organized crime has divvied up the country, the question of territory is always settled firmly and forcibly when outsiders try to muscle in on a crime family's domain. In some two dozen–odd cities around the country, certain crime families are, by common consent, recognized as being preeminent. As such they must police their own areas and guarantee, with violence if necessary, to repel invaders. All the national syndicate or the ruling commission will do is, perhaps, order the intruder out to prevent a bloody war over what is regarded as a "closed territory."

However, certain areas—too lush and profitable to be controlled by a single family and thus constantly subjected to incursions—have had to be declared "open territories," available for plucking by any family with the know-how and the will to mine its riches. If Las Vegas had not been declared open territory, it would doubtlessly look today like Dresden after World War II. No single family would ever have the strength and, equally important, the financial and political muscle needed to fight off the other crime families angling for a stake in legal gambling.

There are today at least two other open territories. One is the Miami area of Florida, partly under the influence of the new "Cuban Mafia," but really still a syndicate stronghold. In the 1930s, the mobs declared Miami and its surroundings "open" when an overly ambitious New York mobster, Little Augie Pisano, fostered the illusion he could take over the town and start his own crime family there. Unfortunately for Pisano, an oldtime Lower East Side gunman, crime genius Meyer Lansky, was already ensconced in Hallandale, where he operated the fantastically profitable Colonial Inn, invested in dog racing and gained control of a bookmaker wire. For a time, Lansky tolerated Pisano's presence, and they shared Florida's East Coast gambling rackets. But finally Lansky demanded that the commission declare Miami and Miami Beach open territories. Pisano screamed, but Lansky, predictably, won out. Efficient exploitation of the Miami market required more finesse than Pisano could hope to possess. Even the Trafficante family of Tampa did not try to swallow Miami whole, realizing the task of fighting Lansky, Chicago, Detroit, Cleveland and several other families from points north would be impossible.

The other notable open territory is California. While the police in that state often speak disparagingly of the local crime families and call them the "Mickey Mouse Mafia," the state is hardly free of important organized crime forces. Chicago has always been involved in Hollywood, everything from shakedown rackets and labor extortion, to promoting an acting career now and then, to even producing some B-movies. And Meyer Lansky sent in Bugsy Siegel to mine what he knew to be enormous, unexplored gambling opportunities. When Siegel got there, he rumpled the feathers of L.A. crime boss Jack Dragna, one of the few toughs on the local scene. Anticipating complications, Lansky visited Lucky Luciano, then incarcerated in Dannemora prison, and got him to agree that California was so big and wide open that everybody had to be allowed in. Luciano sent an edict to Dragna "requesting" his "full cooperation" with Siegel, who was "coming West for the good of his health and the health of all of us." In such diplomatic language are open territories made.

One crime area that never became open territory was Havana, Cuba, during the reign of Cuban dictator Fulgencio Batista. Lansky had its vice operations especially its casino trade, sewed up tight. When the Trafficante forces from Florida tried to muscle in, he had Batista inform them: "You have to get approval from the 'Little Man' [Lansky] before you can get a license on this island." Of course, Lansky did not try to swallow all the profits himself, knowing he too would then have to battle all the crime families, and he set about putting several underworld powers in his debt. He turned around and gave Trafficante a piece, and he cut in the Chicago people as well and Moe Dalitz and certain other Cleveland mafiosi.

One he refused to allow in, probably as much for personal reasons as any other, was Albert Anastasia who in the late 1950s moved aggressively, trying to get in after Lansky turned him down. Anastasia kept pressing, trying to work through some local Cuban businessmen and with Trafficante, who must have informed Lansky. Lansky, in the meantime, learned of a Vito Genovese–Carlo Gambino plot to kill Anastasia, and he immediately sent word he would support the hit, even though on a personal level he hated the anti-Semitic Genovese far more than Anastasia. But Genovese had no designs on Cuba, and the shining principle of territorial integrity won out yet again when Anastasia was killed.

Atlantic City, the newest legalized casino city in America, is yet to be determined a truly open territory. When gambling was first legalized there, Angelo Bruno, the Philadelphia crime boss, felt it should remain part of his domain. The other crime families had had little interest in impoverished Atlantic City and its numbers rackets, but casino gambling was a new ballgame. Bruno proved stubborn and was promptly assassinated. According to knowledgeable sources, the Gambino family from New York moved in. Others followed. Over the next decade or so Atlantic City will become totally open or it will, as one investigator put it, become known as "the city of corpses by the seashore."

OPERATION Mongoose: CIA-Mafia plan to kill Fidel Castro

Few plots to kill a government leader have received more publicity than Operation Mongoose, a "super secret" CIA initiative to use the Mafia to assassinate Cuba's Fidel Castro. In time the CIA admitted all—or so the agency said. CIA heads later acknowledged that the plot should never have involved organized crime, but the fact is that the CIA's confession was itself a form of cover-up.

While the CIA has been advocating the "elimination of Fidel Castro" as early as 1959, it was the mobsters themselves who volunteered to come aboard for such good works. Actually, the mobsters were more interested in getting the intelligence agency in their hip pockets for their own reasons. Most important of all, most mafiosi involved in the plotting actually engaged in a scam, never really trying to kill Castro and instead robbing the CIA of untold sums of money.

There are to this day strong underworld claims that a number of later alleged gangland slayings were actually CIA hits aimed at covering up the agency's embarrassment at being so easily suckered.

The first mobster to propose underworld participation in a Castro hit appears to have been Meyer Lansky, who felt Castro's assassination was the only way to get the mob back in the casino business in Cuba—despite the fact that Castro indicated a willingness to let Lansky back in to run things provided the government shared in the profits, presumably on a 50-50 basis. Lansky was not overly interested, even though he sent his brother Jake to carry on negotiations, because he doubted that skimming the profits would be possible under Castro's watch. On a more philosophical, if not dominant, level, Lansky was very anti-communist. It was Lansky who contacted the CIA and explained that some of his people still on the island could carry out the assassination.

Meanwhile, via Moe Dalitz, a syndicate power in the Las Vegas casino business, Howard Hughes learned of this proposal, and as one of the grand exponents of "the Communist threat to America" he ordered Robert Maheu, his chief of staff, to find suitable "Mafia killers" to carry out the operation. Maheu recruited Johnny Roselli and his boss, Chicago syndicate leader Sam Giancana, into the operation. Apparently through them, although possibly independently, Tampa, Florida, crime boss Santo Trafficante Jr. also signed up.

It was then that the grand mafioso scam began. The CIA was involved in all sorts of ludicrous plots, including such bizarre ploys as blowing the Cuban leader off the ocean floor while he was satisfying his passion for skin diving, injecting deadly poison into him with a specially prepared "pen," letting him puff on some poisoned cigars, or contaminating his clothes with tubercle bacilli and fungus spores. Other zany plots were also abandoned, including one to infect Castro so that his beard would fall out, ruining his macho image.

The first scheme the CIA suggested to Roselli was a nice, simple, Capone-style ambush with machine guns blazing. Greatly amused but maintaining a straight face, Roselli said he doubted such Chicago tactics would work in Cuba, and it would present recruitment difficulties because chances of the machine gunners getting away would be virtually nil. (The survival instinct for hit men has always been a bit higher than that of political assassins.) Then the

CIA was taken down the garden path as the mobsters fed them one phony story after another. Whatever wild plots the CIA came up with, Trafficante sat on, in the meantime conning the intelligence agents with thrilling tales of his men risking their lives—slipping into Cuba and having their boats shot out from under them. The stories, Roselli was later to tell informer Jimmy "the Weasel" Fratianno, were "all bullshit."

The CIA scientists came up with a liquid poison that would kill in two or three days and turned it over to Trafficante for transmittal to his phantom Cuban rebels. The stuff was simply flushed down a toilet. There is certainly no record that any of the CIA money and equipment—all kinds of guns, detonators, explosives, poison, boat radar and radios—ever got to Cuba. Some government aides even developed the theory that Trafficante had sold out to Castro and was feeding him all sorts of information about the anti-Castro movement in Florida, as well as the scoop on CIA plots. It should be remembered that Trafficante had always jockeyed for a more important slice of the Cuban gambling business but that Lansky had cut him short. If Castro ever allowed the mob back in, Trafficante, it was said, would be in a better position to get a major portion of the take.

In time, the CIA agents involved in the plotting became rather discouraged about the chances of Mongoose succeeding. There must have been a flurry of joy when Giancana reported to them—conversations by Giancana were monitored by the FBI who at the time knew nothing of the CIA's activities—that, as an FBI report said, "Castro is in advanced stages of syphilis and is not completely rational." That joy must have given way to severe depression when Castro did not go the blithering way of Al Capone.

Perhaps the only mobster who thought the assassination of Castro was a viable option was Giancana, the mooner of the underworld as his nickname "Mooney" indicated. According to Roselli, Giancana was angry about Trafficante's foot-dragging. Giancana felt if the mob pulled it off it would have the U.S. government by "the short hairs," and there would have been little the underworld could not do thereafter with impunity. Whether his guess was right or not, Giancana soon involved the CIA in some very "X-rated" activities. In the midst of all the anti-Castro plots, Giancana put the CIA's indebtedness to the underworld to the test. He had, he informed the agency, a little problem requiring CIA assistance. The agency was in no position to refuse the small favor.

However, the favor went wrong when sheriff's deputies in Las Vegas arrested two men, supposedly in the act of burglarizing the rooms of comedian Dan Rowan. Actually they were planting CIA bugging devices. It turned out that Rowan was going around with singer Phyllis McGuire of the McGuire Sisters, and Giancana wanted a bug placed in Rowan's room just to see how cozy matters were between the comedian and the woman Giancana considered his private property. The CIA had okayed the venture and then had to engage in a massive coverup, not to mention feeling the heat of embarrassment when the rival FBI learned the details of the caper.

The lid was kept on Operation Mongoose for a few years, but it was a plot that wouldn't disappear even after it was officially abandoned. In the 1970s there were congressional inquiries, and in 1975 Giancana was slated to go before a Senate committee headed by Senator Frank Church of Idaho. Instead he was murdered. In *Mafia Princess* Antoinette Giancana, Sam's daughter, declares, "I've always felt very strongly that the subpoena requiring Sam to appear before the committee was the death warrant that led to his murder."

John Roselli did testify shortly after Giancana's death. He told of some CIA plots, but led congressional investigators on a merry-go-round by insisting he had no recollection of the key events. Unfortunately, Roselli talked differently in private with gangland friends. He told them of Giancana's words to him when he had gotten his subpoena: "Santo's shitting in his pants, but you can't keep his name out of it. I introduced the guy to the CIA. . . . This Santo's crazy to think we can stop his name from surfacing." Roselli was also known to be dropping around the office of columnist Jack Anderson, sometimes having lunch or dinner with him. It was not an activity to inspire confidence in Tampa (Trafficante's bailiwick), in Chicago, or for that matter in Langley, Virginia, CIA headquarters. The old and sickly Roselli's severed body ended up floating ashore inside a 55-gallon oil drum in Florida's Biscayne Bay.

To the day he died Roselli firmly held that the CIA had not had Giancana murdered, that it was done on orders of Chicago crime boss Tony Accardo and Joey "Ha Ha" Aiuppa. There is some evidence that Gian-

cana and Aiuppa had had a major falling out over the division of family gambling revenues. It is not known whom Roselli would have blamed for his own murder.

One thing was apparent after Operation Mongoose and the CIA's forays with the underworld. In a showdown, the Mafia could get the better of America's top intelligence brains.

See also CIA-MAFIA CONNECTION; GIANCANA, SAM; ROSELLI, JOHN; TRAFFICANTE, SANTO, JR.

ORGEN, Jacob "Little Augie" (1894–1927): Labor racketeer and syndicate victim

Much is made of the elimination of the Mustache Petes, the old-line mafiosi, by Lucky Luciano as a vital prelude to the establishment of the national crime syndicate. But the same sort of purge had to be carried out against Jewish gangsters who would not fit the emerging scheme of things.

Jacob "Little Augie" Orgen, one of the last bigtime, pre-syndicate Jewish mobsters, had no place in organized crime. When Little Augie was murdered in 1927, his garment industry rackets fell logically to the notorious Louis Lepke, a protégé of Arnold Rothstein, considered to be the greatest criminal mastermind of his day and the spiritual godfather to Meyer Lansky and Lucky Luciano's national crime syndicate. Rothstein viewed Little Augie as a mindless criminal who only thought of extracting the biggest profit at the moment, not of what was best in the long run. Such a failing proved the death of Little Augie.

Orgen had been schooled as a labor slugger in the years before the outbreak of World War I in the organization of Dopey Benny Fein, the foremost labor racketeer of that period. Fein worked both sides of the street, carrying out sluggings and murders for employers seeking to stop the unions or introduce strikebreakers, or for the unions seeking to recruit new members or terrorize strikebreakers. Sometimes Dopey Benny worked for both sides in the same dispute, an arrangement that impressed Little Augie.

By 1915, police action put Dopey Benny out of business, and labor slugging was virtually nonexistent over the next four years. But in 1919, Little Augie made a comeback in the labor slugging racket, and union activities picked up. He organized his own gang, called the Little Augies, and contended with the forces of the much larger Kid Dropper organization, then in control of most of the slugging rackets. By 1923, Little Augie numbered among his troops the young Louis Lepke, Lepke's gorilla-like sidekick, Jacob "Gurrah" Shapiro, and another rising gangster, Jack "Legs" Diamond.

When Little Augie masterminded Kid Dropper's murder, he became top dog in the labor slugging field. Unfortunately, the field became less lucrative because of police enforcement and because many more sophisticated labor leaders switched away from violence to achieve their ends. Lepke, advised by Rothstein, explained to Little Augie that they should drop the slugging tactics and instead penetrate the local unions and take control of them. Then, besides skimming the local treasuries, they could extort money from employers who wanted labor peace.

The take from such a setup would be much greater than what they got out of simple slugging assignments, but Little Augie was not convinced. He wanted an immediate return for his criminal time. He insisted on sticking with the old ways and switching part of the operations to bootlegging. Taking the long view, Lepke realized Prohibition could not last forever, and he was interested in building a permanent empire. Little Augie now stood in his way.

In October 1927 Little Augie was walking along a street on the Lower East Side with Legs Diamond, his personal bodyguard. A black touring car pulled up. There were four men inside. Gurrah Shapiro jumped out, firing a gun. Louis Lepke from behind the wheel also opened up. Diamond was shot several times but survived. Little Augie fell dead with a bullet in the head.

Little Augie was buried by his father, a highly religious Jew, who ordered that the coffin nameplate read:

JACOB ORGEN
Age 25 Years

Little Augie was really 33, but his family had considered him dead since 1919 when he had returned to a life of crime and organized the Little Augies.

Lepke and Shapiro went on to organize the labor extortion field.

See also DIAMOND, JACK "LEGS"; LEPKE, LOUIS; SHAPIRO, JACOB "GURRAH"

OTHER Mafias: Supposed inheritors of the Mafia's power

It has proven to be a fairy tale: a slew of other Mafia-style ethnic gangs and organizations primed to succeed the Mafia as the new bosses of organized crime in America. The fairy tale falls apart for two reasons: 1) The Mafia is far from dead and 2) except in isolated sections where law enforcement agencies have a particularly vexing problem with certain limited crime activity, most investigative forces tend to shrug off the idea of so-called new Mafias. In 2003 the The New York Times, some might say belatedly, came to the conclusion that the old Mafia persists while at the same time "other bands of ethnic criminals come and go."

Many examples of the decline and fall of "other Mafias" are offered in the preface, highlighting the rise and decline of so many of these supposedly "comer" crime families. Suffice it to note here merely a couple: the Cuban Mafia, as offered by Hollywood in the resurrected version of Scarface pointing implicitly to the seeds of that element's destruction; or to the Russian Mafia, a.k.a. the Russian-Jewish Mafia, which has forever "got no respect" by law enforcement, contrary to the hype these groups of thugs have enjoyed especially in the eastern media. For more than a decade and a half the Russian Mafia has been disdained by the Justice Department as less than organized crime, never rising among the activities of thugs, blackmailers, extortionists, and murderers. True, their activities might be said to have it all for the required brutality, but these groups have found it wise to render to the American Mafia what is theirs and be satisfied with the scraps of illegality. To their credit they have indeed found some rewarding activities that invite competition from their own ilk and finally one side will appeal to the mob for aid in solving the conflict. The boys readily agree and call for a peace meeting of the competing forces. The solution is offered with brutal swiftness and one side is summarily executed on the spot. The "victors" quickly see the wisdom of agreeing with the mob that they are entitled to say 25 percent of the action thereafter, with no further mafiosi convincing required. Such sects of the Russian Mafia continue to operate with mob approval until such time when the mob finds a better, more rewarding approach for itself.

Thus it is hardly surprising that law enforcement agencies have done little to deal with the Russian Mafias, or others, and indeed while some "other Mafias" are accorded much attention by the media many such groupings are found to have their investigative files limited to little more than news clippings about them from the trusty *Times*.

The main failing of all other Mafias is their inability to impose themselves on the body economy or body politic in general. The Mafia, even in a weakened state, still can gain trust of important elements in the business world and corruption-prone forces of law enforcement or the political world. Hispanic forces or Asian elements can operate in their own community with ease but cannot readily move beyond that. It is hard for Asian forces, for example, to win great trust with authorities. Simply put, the forces of corruption can trust the Mafia but no other criminal groupings. The Mafia, despite any claims by enthusiastic prosecutors, have successfully insinuated its members in the public's awareness and won support where it really counts whenever "the heat" lessens ever so slightly. Bluntly but not inaccurately put, the American Mafia continues to survive because of the residues of its power and the fact that it has become, like the fictional TV family, the Sopranos, as American as apple pie.

See also Agron, Evsei; Black Mafia; Barnes, Leroy "Nicky"; Chinese Mafia; "Cuban Mafia"; Forty Thieves; Greek Mafia; Jamaican posses; Johnson, Ellsworth "Bumpy"; Odessa by the Sea; Russian Mafia; Vietnamese Mafia; Yakuza

OTTUMVO, Vincenzo (?–1889): Early Mafia victim

Although his personal history is mostly a mystery, Vincenzo Ottumvo has the distinction of being regarded as the first recorded Mafia victim in the United States. (He almost certainly was not.) A Neapolitan, Ottumvo was killed by Sicilian criminals in New Orleans on January 24, 1889, during a card game. The crime resulted not from a gambling dispute, but rather from the first shot in an Italian gang war that was to be waged in the city between Neapolitan and Sicilian gangsters.

Apparently, Ottumvo was a member of a Neapolitan "Camorra" faction vying with the Sicilian Mafia for control of the lucrative New Orleans waterfront rackets—at least, that seems to have been the case. However, it is not inconceivable he was a Sicilian mafioso. An almost total lack of knowledge of the ins-and-outs of Italian criminality, together with a high degree of venality, on the part of the New Orleans police guaranteed that the Ottumvo murder,

along with several others that followed in ensuing months, would remain forever in the unsolved file.

There is little reason to believe that Ottumvo was truly the first victim of the American Mafia. The Sicilian underworld had existed in New Orleans since the time of the Civil War, and, indeed, the first Black Hand extortion murder may have occurred as early as 1855. (Not all Black Hand murders were the work of mafiosi, but it would be more remarkable if none were.)

See also Camorra

OUTLAW bikers and the Mafia

There has long been a history of cooperation between outlaw biker gangs and the Mafia. In fact, it can be safely said that no group of outlaw bikers would pass up an opportunity to work for or with the mob. And valuable work they appear to have done. Testifying before a U.S. Senate committee, a high official of the Bureau of Alcohol, Tobacco, and Firearms stated, "We know for a fact that outlaw motorcyclists have performed bombings and arsons for the more traditional organized crime groups. Additionally, at the time of the death of Phil Testa up in the Philadelphia area and when Nicodemo Scarfo took over the organized crime family there, there was certainly evidence that the Pagans were involved in the death of Phil Testa."

Even though some mafiosi bridle at the suggestion, the bikers started off with the same philosophy in recruiting for the mob. Neither group ever strove to live lives anywhere like those of normal citizens. Both groups developed their own standards of morals, ethics, and boundaries of behavior. Bikers may sport symbols and mottos like "FTW" (Fuck the World), beliefs hardly at variance of the guiding principles of the Mafia.

Outlaw bikers clearly adopt the principles that embrace the attributes of the mob, discipline and violence. And they have punishments for gang members who stray from their rules. Those can range from penalties such as burning off club tattoos to assassination. Just as it can take years for a mob associate to work up to wise guy status, biker recruits do gofer duties for a long time, and they are expected to show their violent traits. Once in, they have to "roll their bones," or kill somebody. If they flop at this, they themselves can be killed, as one defector has asserted, "because by this time they know too much."

Outlaw bikers are ready to take on any chore for money. If the mob is big in stolen cars and chop shop activities, the biker outlaws do the same with motorcycle thefts and sell whole or by the parts through gang-run repair shops. They have a jump on the mob when it comes to prostitution services, as female associate members frequently are required to perform in club-owned nightclubs, bars, and massage parlors. And along with sundry burglaries, forgery, counterfeiting, fraud, loan-sharking and assaults, several gangs do a land-office business in stolen weapons, not simply handguns, known as "kid's stuff," but on up to explosives and on-order antitank weapons. They are ever ready to "ride shotgun" for other criminal elements needing help in transporting drug shipments and international sex slaves. A recent estimate proposed that outlaw bikers control at least 40 percent of the U.S. methamphetamine traffic, and they have a considerable stake in handling cocaine, heroin and marijuana. Since they manufacture a good amount of their own products, they end up with a higher profit margin than many other dealers.

As a result some of the gang members have moved into the millionaire class. The President's Commission on Organized Crime has pointed to reports that gang members were "abandoning their outlaw image, wearing business suits and driving luxury cars: in essence, becoming an outlaw motorcycle gang without motorcycles."

Of course much of the manpower in outlaw gangs remains on two wheels, which still constitutes appeal to new members. Above all, the outlaw bikers are determined to maintain security in their ranks and to provide similar services for organized crime for a fee. Bikers maintain photo galleries of their members and of their enemies. The mob finds such services valuable as well. They provide the outlaws photos of defectors or witnesses they are interested in. Since bikers circulate around the country, they have a good chance of locating a hidden quarry, especially in small-town areas where few mafiosi ever venture. In such duties outlaw bikers are better suited to solving some mob problems quickly. Bikers frequently disregard their own safety or even perils to bystanders when on such a mob chore. There have been instances when they have gunned their bikes up the stairs of courthouses and jails to get to a witness.

During recent periods when many of the Mafia families were in disarray, law enforcement experts feared the cyclists could move big-time into all elements of organized crime. But as the mobs righted themselves, it became evident the outlaw bikers lacked the expertise in too many areas. Bikers were not about to invade the financial world as the mobs do on Wall Street, for instance. And there is no need for them to go to war with the mobs for such control. Biker outlaws are not known to go up against stronger opposition, concentrating more on hapless individuals. Thus, under the circumstances the status quo has continued in the mob–outlaw biker world.

See also BANDIDOS; HELLS ANGELS; OUTLAWS, THE; PAGANS

OUTLAWS, the: Biker gang more violent than the Hells Angels
There is no doubt that the Hells Angels is the biggest, most powerful biker gang in the country (and

James Lee Wheeler, president of the International Outlaws motorcycle gang, is shown in this undated Hillsborough County, Florida, sheriff's office booking photograph. Wheeler is currently facing charges that he oversaw a highly organized drug operation that used murder to intimidate rival gangs and expand the Outlaws' network.

elsewhere), but the Outlaws gang often is more awesome. Authorities say Angels do not match up with Outlaws, either in violence or a disdain for sophistication. They are easily more daring, and like members of their bigger rival, they are ready to stage spectacular escape raids to free members in custody, especially in smaller, less-manned areas. They have been known to sweep up courthouse steps to get to their members or more likely to get at witnesses about to testify against them. While mafiosi consider the Outlaws "real crazies," they can make good use of them. Like the Angels, the Outlaws are supplied with photos of defectors now in the witness protection program. The Outlaws, in their normal activities cover huge chunks of territory in the United States and Canada, as well as in Australia. When they spot a possible suspect, they report the intelligence back to the mob for a nice reward.

Less imaginative than the Angels, the Outlaws' forays into the "legit" world are more or less limited to businesses such as massage parlors, pornographic bookstores and similar outlets. The main activity of many of the gang's 1,500 or so members is production and distribution of methamphetamines, and they offer back-up for Mafia supplies.

P

PAGANS: Outlaw biker gang most allied with the Mafia

The Pagans is next to the Hells Angels in its criminal sophistication and internal discipline and organization, according to the President's Commission on Organized Crime. The gang enjoys the closest ties to traditional organized crimes, and many sheriffs say the Pagans is most used both as hit man and enforcer by mobsters to take the sting off the Mafia's own activities. Although smaller in size than the Hells Angels, the Pagans outfit is regarded as more trustworthy by the mob in carrying out its contracts than other "crazy bikers." When it serves the Mafia's purpose, members of the Pagans have handled mob purges within a crime family. According to Stephen E. Higgins, acting director of the Bureau of Alcohol, Tobacco, and Firearms, there was "certainly evidence" that the Pagans was involved in the murder of Phil Testa, who took over control of the Philadelphia crime family after the murder of Angelo Bruno.

PALERMO Connection: Mafia's heroin pipeline

Since the early 1960s, the central pipeline for heroin shipments to the United States has shifted away from Marseilles, France, following the New York Narcotics Bureau breakup of the so-called French Connection. The Marseilles shipments were thereafter replaced by the Palermo Connection—giving the Mafia, both Sicilian and American, a firm hold on heroin. From 1973 to 1983 at least 60 percent of all heroin brought into the United States came through Palermo; as a result, that city, in impoverished Sicily, is one of the richest in Italy. Also as a direct consequence of the Palermo Connection, an average of two gang murders per week occur in the island capitol.

No one in Palermo has been safe. In 1982 alone, among the victims of Mafia violence were two judges, two police chiefs and a leading Christian Democrat political leader. The Sicilian Mafia's power has remained undented despite unified political opposition. Pio La Torre, the leader of the Sicilian Communist Party, and a member of the Parliamentary Anti-Mafia Commission, became a forceful opponent against the secret society. He proposed the "La Torre law," which would provide access to private bank accounts as well as legalize telephone taps on Mafia suspects. On April 30, 1982, La Torre was shot and killed in an ambush.

The same fate befell General Alberto Dalla Chiesa, the police official who had crippled the Red Brigades. Appointed prefect of Palermo, he demanded that the La Torre law be passed despite the death of the communist leader; instead, four months after La Torre's murder, Alberto Dalla Chiesa was shot dead, along with his young wife and his police escort. This at last led to a vigorous campaign against the Mafia by the Catholic Church, with the pope visiting Palermo to denounce the society. The La Torre law was passed, and mass arrests and trials of alleged Mafia figures, including those in "white collar" professions, followed.

The international press was filled with reports of the inevitable decline of the Mafia, both in Sicily and, because of information gained through the investigation and testimony of high-ranking defectors, in the United States.

However, throughout the crackdown, at least 20 heroin refineries remained active in Sicily, with the capability of turning out a half billion dollars worth of heroin a week. As one expert stated in 1984, "It seems doubtful whether even the anti-Mafia law can get to the root of the problem."

The Palermo Connection remains alive and well.

See also NARCOTICS RACKET

PARSLEY racket: Restaurant extortion

In a mid-Manhattan restaurant not long ago, four Happy Hour customers were served mixed drinks decorated with what they dubbed "green garbage."

"What's all this?" they protested to the waiter.

He shrugged, "Mafia parsley."

According to Jimmy Breslin, a columnist for the *New York Daily News,* steakhouses and other midtown Manhattan restaurants were serving "meals that appeared to be growing lawns."

The proliferation of "green garbage" in New York restaurants is the result of the mob's parsley shakedown. Restaurants are required to buy underworld supplied parsley with which to garnish their dishes. It is not enough that they heap the greenery on meats and salads, but they are under pressure to add them to mixed drinks. If confirmed martini drinkers find that parsley alters the lemon-peel tinge to their drinks, they are taken care of. The parsley is put at the side of the glass.

As the mob jacked up the price of parsley from 5¢ to 40¢ a bunch, some restaurateurs found their parsley bill running even with the cost of a waiter's salary.

Mobsters from East Harlem checked to make sure the restaurants were not stinting in the greening of their customers. In the 1980s some restaurants tried to cut parsley orders by saying business was off. Since most customers simply pushed the parsley aside, the restaurants tried to recycle the parsley by washing it off and reusing it. True, a check showed the mob the restaurants were not stinting on putting out the parsley, but the suppliers were not fooled. A count of tablecloths and napkins given to mob-connected laundries proved that the restaurants were not ordering enough greenery.

Confronted by such a scientific survey, one steakhouse owner nervously ordered an extra 150 bunches of parsley on the spot.

In recent years, New York diners' incredible appetite for parsley seems to have spread around the country. At about the same time the mob effectively put down the Great Parsley Rebellion in New York, it moved into Montana to spread the green. The Montana State Crime Control Commission reported investigating some restaurant bombings in Butte (called Apache Indian jobs because, done right, nothing is left but a few flaming timbers and a chimney). The commission tied the bombings to the parsley-selling activities of New York mobsters. Further investigation revealed that one crime family had taken control of vast acreages in Ventura County, California, where parsley could be cut five times a year, enough eventually for the total greening of America.

See also APACHE INDIAN JOBS

PASS: Forgiveness, Mafia style

A pass is an act of forgiveness by the higher-ups in the mob. It may or may not be more apparent than real. A classic case involved Chuckie English, a long-time lieutenant under Chicago boss Sam Giancana. When Giancana was hit, some of his most ardent followers were also eliminated, both before and after the murder. It is standard mob procedure to eliminate those figures more likely to form a protective web around the target before he is killed or in other cases to eliminate those most likely to attempt vengeance. Some supporters however are left alone, an indication after a period of time that they have been granted a "pass" from the bloodletting. They are usually allowed to retain their posts in the family, although sometimes they suffer a demotion in rank.

English was allowed to live, but he was busted from lieutenant to common soldier and assigned to the Joe Lombardo crew, a division of at least 40 soldiers. In time English got a few bones tossed his way, a situation that should have contented him. That was not Chuckie's style unfortunately, and for years he often whispered to others that the regime under his old buddy Giancana had been so much better than the current one. Amazingly it took a full decade for English to outwear his pass. Eventually Chuckie's bleating got more vocal and the boss of bosses of the Chicago outfit, Tony Accardo, had enough. English was taken out in the parking lot of his favorite hang-out, Howarth's. His example made it obvious that a pass demands a certain code of behavior. Of course, those granting the pass are also supposed to follow a code of behavior—unless the pass is granted with fingers crossed. A case in point was Willie Boy Johnson, a mob associate of John Gotti's, going back to their kindergarten days. In later years Willie Boy got very upset about how the mob was treating him, and when he got in trouble with the law, he bargained his way out by agreeing to inform on gang activities. In a monumental screw-up by authorities Gotti found out about Willie Boy's longtime snitching, which appeared to have been fairly selective. In any event both he and Gotti were brought up in a case of attempted murder, and if Willie Boy had talked more Gotti would have lost his "teflon don" image early on. According to Sammy "the Bull" Gravano in *Underboss,* Gotti told Willie Boy: "You did a bad thing all them years. But I'll forgive you. It's not the first time it happened. You can never be with us after this case. But nothing will happen to you."

According to Gravano, Johnson wanted more assurance and asked Gotti to swear on his dead son's head. Gotti did, and Willie Boy stayed with the defense. Gravano recalled that Willie Boy swallowed Gotti's promise completely.

After Gotti beat the rap, he waited until Willie Boy really believed he'd gotten a pass. One day Willie left his house and his pass expired as he went down with 13 bullets to the head.

A pass that has apparently held up was one for Joe Bilotti, the brother of Tommy Bilotti who went down with Paul Castellano in 1985. In the aftermath of the double murder, Gotti took over the family and he was inclined to take out Joe Bilotti as a matter of prudence. According to Sammy the Bull, he intervened and told Gotti that Joe was a good soldier and would live by the rules. Another Gotti supporter agreed with the Bull, and the dubious Gotti permitted Gravano to meet with the surviving Bilotti.

Gravano claimed he reassured Joe all was well, that the killing of his brother was simply business. He reminded Joe that he had a tough job with 18 kids to take care of (Joe and Tommy each had nine kids). Rather proudly the Bull bragged in his book: "And Joe's still alive today."

It may be Joe Bilotti did not care for those words in *Underboss,* since it essentially pegged him as a Gravano man, something that might not sit well

since Gravano became the greatest mob stoolie of the 1990s.

It could become another example that a pass is not necessarily forever.

PATRIARCA, Raymond L. S. (1908–1984): Mafia boss of New England

Some Mafia observers contend that New England's Raymond Patriarca was the most double-dealing Mafia boss in the country. The head of the Massachusetts state police once told a legislative committee that Patriarca was so ruthless and devious that he regularly hijacked liquor shipments he was hired to protect.

Despite this, or perhaps because of it, Patriarca, until his death in 1984, was much respected by other Mafia bosses, and he was frequently called in to serve as a mediator in gang wars. While doing time in the early 1970s for his part in a double murder conspiracy, Patriarca was, much like Vito Genovese, able to run his mob from behind bars. And whether imprisoned or free, he often warned other Mafia bosses to stay out of his territory—all of New England—and they did.

Patriarca ran his organization with an iron fist. He once ordered an old mafioso to murder his own son because the son had cost Patriarca some money in a crime arrangement that went awry. When the old mafioso fell to his knees, crying he could not kill his own son, Patriarca threw the man out of the organization. The only reason he did not have the old man killed was that Henry Tameleo, his underboss managed to cool Patriarca off and get him to relent on the murder order.

Patriarca's ruthlessness extended to his men in other ways. Once Patriarca put up $22,000 for his men to handle a load of stolen cigarettes. Unfortunately, the FBI seized the load. That did not interest Patriarca in the least; he wanted his money back—Patriarca was always a partner in profits, but never in losses. His men had to scrounge up the $22,000 to pacify their boss.

Patriarca also tolerated no upstart trying to start up criminal activities in his area. He demonstrated his thoroughness in the Irish wars in Boston when a young gangster named Bernard McLaughlin tried to muscle in on the mob's loan-sharking rackets. McLaughlin and his supporters were virtually exterminated to the last man. In another explosion of his infamous temper, Patriarca for a time put a death sentence on his own brother because, while in charge of mob security, he had failed to spot a FBI bug placed in Patriarca's office.

Born to Italian immigrant parents in 1908 in Worcester, Massachusetts, Patriarca moved to Providence when he was four. He left school at eight to shine shoes and work as a bellhop. Eventually he discovered that armed robberies and working for liquor smugglers during Prohibition were more rewarding. In the 1930s the Providence Board of Public Safety branded him "Public Enemy No. 1" and ordered the police to arrest him on sight.

Yet in all Patriarca went to jail only once in that period, for armed robbery in 1938. He got five years but only served a few months, which brought legislative calls in Massachusetts for an inquiry into the pardon granted him by then-Governor Charles F. Hurley. It turned out that a prime factor behind the pardon was a heartrending plea from one Father Fagin, who turned out to be a nonexistent priest. It developed the petition had been drawn up and guided past government officials by the governor's right-hand man, Executive Councilor Daniel Coakley. Coakley was later impeached and barred thereafter from ever holding public office in the state.

The scandal marked Patriarca as a man with political connections, and by the early 1940s he had assumed a major Mafia leadership role. In the 1950s, he became the top boss, his influence extending from Providence to cover Boston and the rest of New England.

For a quarter of a century, as Patriarca built his base, he enjoyed relatively little public exposure. Finally though, because of Joseph Barboza, a Patriarca enforcer and hit man who turned informer, he was convicted of conspiracy to commit murder, specifically having a mob member, Rocco DiSiglio, eliminated for being the fingerman for a stickup gang victimizing mob crap games.

He did six years for that, and when he came out he resumed leadership of the organization. Yet Patriarca enjoyed a spirit of loyalty where it might not be expected. Another mob informer, Vinnie Teresa, who effectively crippled much of the mob with his testimony in a number of trials, refused to testify against Patriarca. Raymond, he said, had always treated him fairly, and he would not cross him. There were few men who would have said that about Patriarca.

See also ANGIULO, GENNARO J.

PENSION bandwagon for wise guys: Security for the insecure

For years Genovese crime boss Vincent "the Chin" Gigante walked the streets of New York's Greenwich Village in pajamas or bathrobe mumbling to himself and passing himself off as nothing short of feeble-minded. It was revealed in 2003 that the Chin, from 1990 until his racketeering conviction and jailing in 1997, was on the dole from the government for his "disability," while at the same time the government was trying to prove in court that he was faking. In all, the "Oddfather" was being awarded $900 a month for his alleged disabilities. In 2003 the Social Security Administration announced it was demanding that he return the money since he was "not entitled" to the benefits. It was a matter of conjecture if the government would be able to get the money back. At least, however, the septuagenarian Chin had been cut off from his Social Security awards after he was incarcerated, the agency explained, because "the government's already paying food, clothing and shelter" for him.

As it was, the Chin was a piker among big league mafiosi at putting fingers in the public till. Peter Gotti, the reputed successor of his brother John as head of the Gambino crime family, as of 2003 had raked in something like $5,000 a month in disability from Social Security and New York City for 14 years. The exact amount was never revealed because of privacy laws. Gotti was listed as working as a "sanitation man" until he was injured after claiming he'd fallen off a sanitation truck and wrenched his back. City pensions may be paid to inmates and apparently have never been stopped to Gotti.

Many wise guys learn how to get on the pension bandwagon. Primo Cassarino, who was convicted along with Peter Gotti in March 2003 for shaking down action film star Steven Seagal, worked as a city garbage collector for 10 years, became fully vested in 1992 at $36,877 and then also claimed to have fallen off a truck and filed for disability. Wise guys just seem to have real trouble staying on trucks. In this case Cassarino ended up with egg and whatever on his face when an FBI wiretap caught him discussing how he needed phony documents to renew the disability benefits.

All these disclosures had the potential of perhaps salvaging some of the public's tax dollars. With Gotti in jail after his conviction but still not sentenced, a gimmick in the law might take away his loot if he—

and other wise guys—were not only given prison time but fined as well. The fine would allow the city to garnish Gotti's pension. It remained possible that many wise guys will find that unsympathetic judges might very well slap on a fine to plug the pension loophole.

PERSICO, Carmine (1937–): Boss of Colombo crime family

One of the most violent enforcers and collectors for Brooklyn Mafia don Joe Profaci, Carmine Persico was introduced to Profaci's rackets by Larry Gallo. Eventually Persico joined Larry and his two brothers, Crazy Joe and Kid Blast Gallo, in an open revolt against the Profaci rule. Profaci, perhaps the most grasping Mafia boss in decades, extracted tribute constantly from his soldiers. Persico once complained to later-informer Joe Valachi: "Even if we go hijack some trucks he taxes us. I paid up to $1,800."

With the Gallos and Persico there was a lot of nasty firepower standing up to Profaci, who relied on all his deviousness to resolve his dilemma. He promised to do right for a few of the rebels, including Jiggs Forlano and Carmine Persico, if they would return to the fold and show their fealty by going after the Gallos. Persico jumped at the chance and did all he could. In fact, New York police would later say it was Persico who tightened the garrote on Larry Gallo when he was lured to a bar in Brooklyn, allegedly for an anti-Profaci plotting session. Gallo narrowly survived; a police officer walked in at the critical moment. It was a scene that was to be replayed in fictional form in *The Godfather*. The Gallos called Persico "the Snake" after that. So did the police. Persico advised his friends to call him "Junior."

After Profaci's successor, Joe Colombo, was shot in 1971, Persico became a capo under the almost secret rule of elderly Thomas DiBella who was boss of the family for three years before the FBI and other investigative agencies discovered the fact. Eventually DiBella stepped aside because of his years and functioned as consigliere, or adviser, while Persico, the former rebel, took over as boss. Bizarre events dominated his reign, most of which was spent in prison (although this didn't stop the federal government from indicting him in the mid-1980s on racketeering charges for crimes they said he masterminded behind

bars). Persico became one of the very few mafiosi to ever make it on the FBI's Most Wanted list after he fled the indictment and eluded capture for several months.

Persico was also a unique would-be hit victim who ended up with a spent bullet in his mouth after enemy mobsters pumped several carbine shots into a car in which he was riding. Persico spat out the bullet.

An avid reader about himself in the newspapers, Persico took deep offense in December 1985 when writer Pete Hamill, covering his racketeering trial for the *Village Voice*, recalled Persico's younger days (Hamill had grown up in the same Brooklyn neighborhood). "Man to man," Hamill wrote, "Junior wasn't very good with his hands . . . But if Junior caught you while three others were holding you, he was devastating."

Ignoring the advice of his lawyers, Persico penned an angry letter to the *Voice*, calling Hamill's story "biased, degrading, angry, perverse, and unprofessional."

Hamill's response in part was:

> Mr. Persico's many years behind bars obviously have refined his prose style beyond the narrow limits he had attained 35 years ago in our old neighborhood. . . . In those days, his usual reply to criticism was to mutter, "Your sister's box!" before creasing your skull with a length of pipe. Who now can dispute the possibilities for rehabilitation afforded by the joint?

However, Persico had more than a war of words to wage or a legal battle to engage of with the government. He had spent almost 10 years of the previous 13 behind bars, a fact that left his godfatherly role a bit frazzled, despite the government's claims about what he could manage from prison. Another capo, Jerry Langella ran the family on the outside.

Persico had the misfortune of being out of prison and back in control of the Colombos when the government in 1986 polished its RICO approach in the Mafia Commission case against the top bosses of several families. Persico may have been the most outraged of the defendants about the use of membership in the Mafia as enough, or close to it, to win a conspiracy conviction. Persico, in his usual pride in his own abilities, acted as his own attorney.

His most memorable comment to the court was an anguished outcry: "Without the Mafia, there wouldn't even be no case here!"

The Snake got it absolutely right. He also got a 100-year sentence for murder and conspiracy.

See also MACINTOSH, HUGH "APPLES"

PETROSINO, Joseph (1860–1909): Police detective

The first police officer in America to battle the Mafia effectively, Joe Petrosino was named head of the newly formed Italian Squad of the New York City police in 1905. The need for the Italian Squad was overwhelming. At the turn of the century, more than 500,000 of New York City's 3 million residents were Italian. But most of the cops were Irish with a lesser number Jewish. With nary an Italian on the force, the mafiosi gangsters enjoyed the particular advantage of a police force that could not understand them.

Petrosino had first been recruited to be a policeman in 1883 by Police Inspector Alexander "Clubber" Williams precisely because of his ethnic background. By 1895, Petrosino had risen to the rank of detective and was assigned to the Lower East Side. He took time to learn the various dialects of the Italian immigrants squashed into the ghetto and to gain their confidence; soon he was gathering information that enabled him to solve many murders and extortions of the Black Hand. He reported to superiors that the Black Hand was not a distinct organization but various freelance criminals who threatened victims with death unless they paid protection money.

Petrosino nailed many Black Handers, including one who had tried to victimize opera star Enrico Caruso. (The singer and the detective became fast friends.) In 1901, Petrosino uncovered the infamous Murder Stable in Italian Harlem where some brutal mafiosi killed and buried at least 60 victims who operated in competition with their rackets or would not pay them protection money. It was for many the first proof of the Mafia's existence in New York.

In 1905, Police Commissioner William McAdoo authorized the Italian Squad and put Petrosino in charge of the 27-man unit. In the four years Petrosino ran the squad, Black Hand crimes dropped by half. Several thousand arrests were made, and 500 men were sent to prison. In 1908, there were 44 bombings with 70 arrests, 424 Black Hand extortion complaints with 215 arrests. Also, numerous mafiosi were deported on Petrosino's evidence.

Petrosino appeared before congressional committees, urging modification of the immigration laws to forbid the entry of known criminals. He warned that Italian authorities were phonying the passports of some immigrants to rid their jails of undesirables, a sort of pre-Castro boatlift.

Early in 1909 Police Commissioner Theodore Bingham sent Petrosino to Palermo, Sicily, to gather information about deportable criminals. The assignment was so secret that fellow officers were told he was home ill. Yet inexplicably a story appeared in the *New York Herald* attributing to Bingham the fact that Petrosino had gone to Sicily. On the rainy night of March 12, 1909, Petrosino was standing in the piazza of the Garibaldi Garden when four shots rang out. Petrosino was hit three times, in the shoulder, throat and right cheek. His murderer got away. Later a strong case was made that the New York detective had been gunned down personally by Don Vito Cascio Ferro, the most important Mafia leader in Sicily. Don Vito claimed to have spent the evening at dinner at the home of a Sicilian member of the Italian parliament, and his host backed up the story. However, many believe that Don Vito slipped away long enough to do the killing and then return to cement his alibi. Don Vito had the motivation to do the killing personally. A few years earlier Don Vito had come to America to expand his criminal empire, but had been run out by Petrosino.

The death of the legendary Italian detective sent shockwaves through New York City. He was brought back for a martyr's funeral. A quarter million people jammed the streets of Little Italy as a procession of 7,000 escorted the body to the grave. A short time thereafter, Bingham was fired as police commissioner because of the news story that revealed Petrosino's whereabouts. Petrosino's death had saved literally hundreds of mafiosi from deportation, a bitter fact that would plague the United States in later decades.

See also BLACK HAND; MURDER STABLE

PIGEON coop tip-off: Is a wise guy gone for good?

For some reason a fair number of mafiosi keep pigeons. Whatever lies behind the practice, it is sometimes helpful to authorities. Every once in a while a pigeonkeeper will vanish, and the police will be in the dark about what happened to him. However, if a short time later the pigeon coops are taken down, it is a sure sign that the mobster is no longer among the living.

That was the case of Sonny Black, a high capo and for a time acting boss of the Bonanno family. Black had been conned by undercover operative "Donnie Brasco"—FBI agent Joe Pistone—to whom he trustingly gave entrée into mob activities. When Brasco emerged from his cover, Black, who refused to seek refuge as an informer, went to a mob meeting where damage and guilt was being assessed. A week later two men were seen taking down Black's pigeon coops, and the FBI concluded Sonny Black was dead. His body was discovered about a year later.

PILLOW Gang: St. Louis Mafia family

Carmelo Fresina was, in his own fashion, the most colorful mafioso in St. Louis, heading up what was certainly the most colorfully named criminal group, the Pillow Gang. Fresina would arrive at a sit-down of the gang, put on his chair the trusty pillow he always carried and, easing himself down, discuss such sundry criminal activities as extortion and murder. Then when the meeting was over, he would pick up his pillow and leave.

The Pillow Gang added a bizarre touch to Prohibition-era St. Louis criminality, in the early part of this century marked by curiously ineffectual bands of mafiosi. This is surprising since St. Louis was one of the early settling spots of the Mafia in this country. Some of the first mafiosi to arrive in New Orleans in the 19th century soon headed north to avoid police trouble and nested in St. Louis. The city boasted its first Black Hand activity in 1876. Yet, perhaps due to the quality of the mafiosi involved, the Italian criminals failed to achieve dominance for a long time. During the Prohibition era five gangs of major importance operated in St. Louis: Egan's Rats, perhaps the most important; the Hogan Gang; the Cuckoo Gang, mostly hoodlums of Syrian descent; the so-called Green Dagoes, composed mostly of Sicilians; and a gang of Americans of Italian descent, who could be described as Young Turks, in the same sense as Lucky Luciano played that role in New York.

The Cuckoos cooperated with the American-born Italians in waging war against the Sicilians, of which Fresina and his Pillow Gang were an important branch. Fresina had once been shot in the buttocks and thereafter he carried a pillow with him to use when sitting. Somehow, Fresina's pillow tended to detract from the dangerous image the mob tried to project. It did not promote a feeling of terror in others.

It remained for that illustrious senatorial prober, Estes Kefauver, to sum up Fresina's career with a humor he seldom seemed to possess: "Eventually Fresina, an extortionist and bootlegger, was dispatched with two bullets in the head and no longer needed his pillow."

It would be many years after the fall of the Pillow Gang before the Mafia would become a powerhouse in St. Louis crime. The impetus came around World War II, from Kansas City, which dispatched Thomas Buffa and Tony Lopiparo to set up a branch of the K.C. family there and build up an organization primarily on the narcotics trade. Buffa eventually was assassinated, in 1946, and over a period of time the St. Louis crime family was to pass to the control of Anthony Giordano. While he was in prison in the 1970s James Giammanco became acting boss.

PINEAPPLE Primary: Violent 1928 Chicago election

Probably no U.S. election in the 20th century can match the violence or social disregard of the April 1928 Republican primary in Chicago. Referred to by the press as the "Pineapple Primary," the event was characterized by the bombs, nicknamed pineapples, used in wholesale lots by gangsters seeking to have their ticket succeed. Both sides employed professional terrorists and the Capone ranks provided most of the bomb throwers. The police seemed singularly unable to stop any of the violence.

In the primary, a rebel faction headed by Republican senator Charles S. Deneen challenged the ruling faction headed by Mayor Big Bill Thompson and State's Attorney Robert E. Crowe. Thompson and Crowe were aligned with Governor Len Small, who, like the former pair, was a friend of mobsters. Deneen, carrying the banner of reform, was backed by racketeer Diamond Joe Esposito, who clearly desired to seize the Capone mantle for himself.

Violence erupted on both sides at the primary. The first attack victims were the Thompson-Crowe men. The homes of Charles C. Fitzmorris, Thompson's city controller, and Dr. William H. Reid, the commissioner of public service, were bombed. Further bombings of Thompson-men homes followed when the mayor announced, "When the fight is over, the challengers will be sorry."

In due course, the homes of Judge John A. Swanson, Deneen's candidate for Crowe's seat as state's attorney, and Deneen's own home were blasted, and

Esposito, having ignored death threats from the Capones, was assassinated. A black-humored couplet, written by a Chicago newsman, probably best summed up the terror of the Pineapple Primary:

The rockets' red glare, the bombs bursting in air
 Gave proof through the night that Chicago's still there.

Two days before the primary, on Easter Sunday, the united clergy of Chicago—Protestant, Catholic and Jewish—denounced the Thompson-Crowe-Small forces: "We have a governor who ought to be in the penitentiary. . . . Ours is a government of bombs and bums. . . . O Lord! May there be a reawakening of public spirit and consciousness. Grant that we may be awakened to a sense of public shame. . . ."

The appeal was not enough against the muscle, guns and bombs of the Capone forces, who supported the Thompson machine. And Cook County chicanery and fraud never reached a higher state of perfection than in this primary; ballot-box stuffing, voting under fictitious names, and harassment of voters numbered among the less violent crimes. Ultimately the Capone forces carried the day.

In the general election, however, the result was stunningly different. Capone was astute enough to realize that the national and international outcry against the Pineapple Primary was the death knell for the Thompson machine. When 75-year-old civic leader Frank J. Loesch, the founding member of the Chicago Crime Commission, called on him and insisted that he allow a peaceful general election vote, Capone did so.

"All right," Capone, who was famed for bragging that he owned the police, said, "I'll have the cops send over squad cars the night before the election and jug all the hoodlums and keep 'em in the cooler until the polls close."

Capone's word became the police's duty. A dragnet swept the streets clean.

"It turned out to be the squarest and the most successful election day in forty years," Loesch later related in a lecture at the Southern California Academy of Criminology. "There was not one complaint, not one election fraud and no threat of trouble all day."

In the election, Chicago's voters turned out in unprecedented numbers to vote against gangsterism. Governor Small and State's Attorney Crowe were

swamped, and every Thompson candidate went down to defeat in the backlash of the Pineapple Primary.

However, Capone remained sanguine. His criminal machine had flourished during a previous reform regime, and he was confident it would survive another campaign of virtue. His power was too deeply intermeshed with the police, the courts and the ward politicians for him to be alarmed. His reasoning did not prove faulty.

See also LOESCH, FRANK S.

PISANO, Little Augie (?–1959): Leading New York mafioso

Little Augie Pisano was perhaps the quintessential mafioso. Born Anthony Carfano, Little Augie took his nickname from a deceased East Side gangster. He came up the hard way as a gunman and sported a huge scar on his left cheek which he wore as a badge of honor, much in the style of an aristocratic Prussian duelist.

A longtime friend of Frank Costello and Joe Adonis (and for a time running Brooklyn rackets for the latter) Little Augie Pisano exhibited only one real sign of overwhelming ambition—he moved to Miami with plans to make it his private fiefdom. Miami represented an enormous rackets potential and required a fine touch with political circles. But Meyer Lansky saw its potential too and that it would require a huge amount of underworld manpower and brains. Lansky urged that the cities of Miami and Miami Beach be declared "open territory" (as would be done later with Las Vegas) so that various crime families could skim their grand potential.

Despite Costello's closeness to Pisano he ordered him to curb his ambition and understand he had to work with Lansky. A dutiful soldier, Pisano did, and his loyalty thereafter to both Costello and Lansky never diminished. In the end, his loyalty was to prove the death of him.

In 1957 Vito Genovese, seeking to take control of the Lucky Luciano crime family, under the local direction of Costello since Luciano's deportation in 1946, ordered Costello assassinated. The job was botched and Costello survived.

Costello refused to tell the police who had tried to kill him, but Genovese, fearing all-out war, ordered all the important members of the crime family to report to his Atlantic Highlands, New Jersey, mansion—now an armed camp surrounded by

40 gunners, as a demonstration of unity with his cause. Little Augie was the sole capo—at the time he ran the family's rackets in the upper Bronx—who refused to show. It was a sin Genovese would not forget, but he had more pressing matters, dealing with Costello and the murderous Albert Anastasia who had vowed to stop Genovese. Although Anastasia was eliminated, Genovese was forced to let Costello retire from the rackets, and it was apparently part of the deal that Little Augie was accepted back in good grace.

The peace lasted until 1959 when Genovese ordered Little Augie hit. The would-be assassins had considerable trouble getting Little Augie alone. He was often with his good friend Tony Bender, chief operator of the crime family's rackets in Greenwich Village, and the killers asked if it was all right to blow away Bender at the same time. Genovese had a strong need for Bender at the time and vetoed the suggestion. Finally Bender discovered his good friend was being set up and he cheerfully agreed to put Little Augie on the spot.

On September 29 Little Augie was partying at the Copacabana with a friend, Mrs. Janice Drake, a former beauty queen, with whom, the cutting underworld comment went, he was having a platonic relationship. She was the wife of comedian Alan Drake, whose career Little Augie had helped. (Mrs. Drake's relationship with Little Augie was never clear. She was grateful to him and called him "Uncle Gus." It was possible she was merely a flamboyant symbol that the mobster liked having around as flattering to his image.) They were joined, apparently by chance, by Bender who invited them and a few others to dine with him at Marino's restaurant, not far from the Copa. During dinner a phone call caused Little Augie to leave hurriedly, Mrs. Drake on his arm.

At 10:30 P.M., about 45 minutes later, they were found in Little Augie's black Cadillac on a dark street near La Guardia Airport in Queens. Both were sitting in the front seat, heads tilted toward each other like young lovers. Both had been shot in the back of the head.

Police later theorized that the killers had been hiding in the back seat of Little Augie's car and forced him to drive to his place of execution. Mrs. Drake, they said, had died just because she happened to be along for the ride.

See also BENDER, TONY

PITTSBURGH crime family See LAROCCA, JOHN SEBASTIAN

PITTSBURGH Phil (1908–1941): Murder, Inc.'s premier hit man

Pittsburgh Phil Strauss was once philosophizing with a friend early in his career as a murderer. "Like a ballplayer, that's me," Pittsburgh Phil mused. "I figure I get seasoning doing these jobs. Somebody from one of the big mobs spots me. Then, up to the big leagues." Pittsburgh Phil had it right. He was spotted by some very discriminating experts, men named Louis Lepke, Lucky Luciano, Joe Adonis, and Albert Anastasia. And he achieved great success in his chosen field—murder. In time he became the most prolific killer Murder, Inc.,—and all of syndicated crime—ever produced.

Killing didn't seem to bother Phil, although he worried greatly for his own health. The contract murder of one Puggy Feinstein offers an example. Phil and a few of the boys lured him into a Brooklyn home and there Phil shoved Feinstein down on a

Unshaven Pittsburgh Phil on his way to the Sing Sing death house. The Murder, Inc., premier killer had at least 100 victims.

couch and went to work on him with an ice pick. Puggy, fighting for his life, sunk his teeth into Pittsburgh Phil's finger. Irate over such foul play, Phil yelled, "Give me the rope. I'll fix this dirty bum." Phil, with the aid of a confederate, put a loop around his neck and another around his feet and effectively trussed him up. As Puggy kicked he merely tightened the rope around his neck and in time strangled himself to death while the boys watched. Then they took Puggy's body to a vacant lot and set it ablaze. The boys then adjourned to Sheepshead Bay for a seafood dinner. Phil, however, was not happy. "Maybe I am getting lockjaw from being bit," he worried. Phil was so upset about his finger that he barely managed to finish his lobster.

Born Harry Strauss—he adopted the name of Pittsburgh Phil, although he had never been to the smoky city—the Brooklyn-bred thug became so popular that when an out-of-town mob or crime family needed an outsider for a contract, they almost always requested Phil. He packed his briefcase with a shirt, a change of socks, underwear, a gun, a knife, a length of rope and an ice pick, hopped a train or plane to his destination, pulled the job and caught the next connection back to New York. Often Phil did not even know the name of the person he had killed, and generally he didn't care to find out.

When investigators cracked Murder, Inc., in 1940, the office of Brooklyn district attorney William O'Dwyer developed solid evidence tying Phil to 28 killings. Law enforcement officers from Connecticut to California came up with a like number in which Phil was positively identified. That of course represented merely the known homicides attributable to him. A present-day crime historian seriously suggests that Phil bumped off at least 500, but this seems nonsensical. However, there is little doubt that his murder toll well exceeded 100. This is an impressive figure, even by Murder, Inc., standards; the three next active killers in the mob, Dasher Abbandando, Kid Twist Reles and Happy Maione, in combination probably no more than matched Phil.

Pittsburgh Phil was also the dandy of the troop, noted for wearing $60 suits, in Depression times a princely sum. New York's incorruptible police commissioner, Lewis Valentine, once said of Phil in a police lineup: "Look at him! He's the best dressed man in the room and he's never worked a day in his life!"

Quite naturally the tall, lean, handsome Pittsburgh Phil was much-pursued by the young ladies of Brownsville. His love affair with Evelyn Mittleman, a Brooklyn beauty dubbed the Kiss of Death Girl, was one of the underworld's more touching, climaxed by Phil's eradication of a rival for her affection.

It is almost amazing that, between his Beau Brummel and Don Juan activities, Phil had the time for mass murder, yet he always seemed to complete his contracts. Once, at the very moment Commissioner Valentine had Phil in his office for an interrogation, his homicide detectives were slaving unbeknownst over one of Phil's labors. The corpse in question was one George Rudnick, suspected by labor extortionist Louis Lepke of being an informer.

Rudnick had been taking the sun one afternoon along Livonia Avenue when Phil and some of his colleagues snatched him up in a car. It was a short drive to the execution chamber, a garage at Eastern Parkway and Atlantic Avenue. Some hours later Rudnick's body was found in a stolen car at the other end of Brooklyn. The medical examiner gives some indication of Phil's savagery:

This was a male adult, somewhat undernourished; approximate weight 140 pounds; six feet in height. There were 63 stab wounds on the body. On the neck, I counted 13 stab wounds, between the jaw and collar bone. On the right chest, there were 50 separate circular wounds. He had a laceration on the frontal region of the head. The wound gaped, and disclosed the bone underneath. His face was intensely cyanic, or blue. The tongue protruded. At the level of the larynx was a grooving, white and depressed, about the width of ordinary clothesline. When the heart was laid open, the entire wall was found to be penetrated by stab wounds. My conclusion was the cause of death was multiple stab wounds, and also . . . asphyxia due to strangulation.

When the Purple Gang in Detroit marked a cunning mobster named Harry Millman for execution, they found they couldn't handle the job themselves. One try failed and Millman was on the alert. A hurried call brought Phil to Detroit. Millman moved in crowds and ate in congested restaurants to frustrate would-be assassins, but he could not figure on Phil's daring. Millman was in a packed restaurant one evening when Phil strode in with an assistant. They emptied two revolvers, killing Millman and wounding five other diners in the process, and calmly paraded out.

Phil always said he could learn more about murder. When he executed Walter Sage, a New York mobster who was knocking down on the syndicate's slot machine profits, he lashed Sage's body to a pinball machine after ice-picking him 32 times and then dumped him in a Catskills lake. Seven days later, the grisly package floated to the surface due to the buoyancy caused by gases in the decomposing body. "How about that," Phil observed sagely. "With this bum, you gotta be a doctor or he floats."

There seems to have been only one contract that Phil failed to carry out. He was sent to Florida and followed the intended victim about until the man went into a movie theater and sat down in the last row. Armed only with a gun, Phil felt it would make too much noise. Then his eyes fell on a fire axe in a glass emergency case. This, he reasoned, was an emergency. Phil took the axe, but by the time he was poised to kill, the target had moved up several rows. In anger Phil tossed down the axe, walked out of the theater and headed back to Brooklyn, declaring the job was jinxed. As he told the troop back home: "Just when I get him set up, the bum turns out to be a goddamn chair hopper."

Usually, though, Phil could adapt to any situation. On another Florida job, he was to put away an old mafioso who spoke not a word of English. Phil went to him and by sign language showed him a suitcase full of weapons and made him believe he was out to kill someone else. The mafioso, eager to be helpful, picked up a rope and led Phil to a dark street where he indicated the deed could be done. Phil nodded, promptly strangled the man and went home.

Phil's murder career lasted a decade and had not Abe Reles—probably the most important stool pigeon ever to come out of organized crime—started talking he could conceivably still be at his chores, a very lethal senior citizen. Reles turned informer because he saw the law was closing in and was afraid that if someone else in Murder, Inc., informed first, he himself would go to the chair. Actually, no one important in Murder, Inc., was ratting, only some minor hoods who could really prove nothing. However, there was enough for Phil, Reles, Happy Maione and Buggsy Goldstein to be brought in on suspicion. Then Reles started talking. Before he was finished, Murder, Inc., was out of business. Big-timers like Lepke, Mendy Weiss and Louis Capone were sentenced to the chair. Reles's canary act came to an abrupt end when he "went out the window" of

a Brooklyn hotel while under what can only be described as remarkably inefficient police guard. Meanwhile, Pittsburgh Phil was also doomed. He was indicted along with Goldstein for the Puggy Feinstein slaying. To be on the safe side the prosecution lined up five more homicide indictments against Phil if they proved necessary. They didn't. The case against him was overwhelming so Phil did the next best thing; he did an insane act. He refused to wash, shave or change his clothes. When asked at his trial to give his name, he merely licked his lips. Returned to the defendant's chair, he spent most of the rest of his trial trying to chew off the leather strap on a lawyer's briefcase. Newspaper readers reveled over Phil's bizarre acts, but the jury was not impressed. They found him guilty of murder in the first degree.

Even in his death cell Phil kept up his insane act, hoping for a commuted sentence. On the last day of his life, he figured out the ploy wasn't going to work and he cleaned himself up and became his dapper old self. He bade farewell to Evelyn, the Kiss of Death Girl. And he further set the record straight by admitting that before his trial he'd offered to turn state's evidence if he was allowed to talk to Reles first. The authorities knew better than to let Phil get into the same room with Reles. As Phil now admitted, he did not intend to turn informer. "I just wanted to sink my tooth into his jugular vein. I didn't worry about the chair, if I could just tear his throat out first." None of Phil's listeners doubted he would have done so if he could.

On June 12, 1941, Goldstein went to the chair, and a few minutes later, at 11:06 P.M., Pittsburgh Phil followed him. The syndicate had lost its best hitter.

PLANTS: Secret Mafia members

"Plants" are one of the Mafia's major long-term investments. Intelligence agencies rely on "sleepers" or "deep agents"—plants who lead normal lives and are only called upon when the situation warrants. Crime families do the same thing. With more astuteness than some so-called experts who insist the Mafia is dying, they recognize they are making a major investment in time, and in doing so they reveal their own view of their longevity and viability.

Crime family plants are noncriminal characters usually recruited in youth and are deliberately kept free of criminal activity so they can move into high places in business, labor or the political world. The

Chicago Outfit also developed plants to function within law enforcement agencies. Whether for law enforcement or crime, the main asset of these plants is their anonymity.

One crime historian, David Leon Chandler in *Brothers in Blood,* offers Anthony Scotto as an example of a labor plant. Hailed as a "new breed" labor leader—college educated, articulate, bright— he was the president of Local 1818, International Longshoremen's Association, long a stronghold for the Anastasia-Gambino crime family. In fact, Scotto was related by marriage to the late Tough Tony Anastasio. Despite his background, Scotto was named American delegate to the International Labor Organization by two presidents, Lyndon Johnson and Richard Nixon. More important for the mob, in his local post, Scotto could offer jobs to, and influence, any firm doing business involving the New York wharves, and he was in a position to provide intelligence on import and export shipments.

But one can quarrel with Chandler's description of Scotto as a plant since the FBI had accumulated a large file on him and identified him as far back as 1969 as a capodecina (captain) in the Gambino family.

Probably a better example of a Mafia plant was John C. Montana, a prominent Buffalo, New York, businessman. By the late 1950s, he had a virtual monopoly of the city's taxicab business and was named Man of the Year by the Erie Club, the official social organization of the Buffalo Police Department. Yet he had been a capo in the Magaddino family since 1931, under wraps except when Don Stefano Magaddino could not resist trotting him out in 1931 for a number of top hoodlums who were traveling by train through Buffalo to Chicago for a major underworld meeting. (One hood got off in Buffalo to make a 30-minute phone call. Montana showed his muscle by postponing the train's departure until all the boys were ready to go.)

Montana was nailed with about 60 other hoodlums attending the notorious Apalachin Conference in 1957. Unlike the other mobsters, he insisted he did not know Joseph Barbara, the conference host, and had only stopped at the house when his car brakes failed and he looked for help. Before Apalachin, Montana had often told other mafiosi, as Joe Valachi put it, "he didn't want to be seen with any of us other members." After Apalachin, Montana tried to keep Magaddino mobsters away all the more because

they were keeping him "hot." However, his usefulness as a crime family plant was shot, and Magaddino dropped him as a secret capo.

As the children of many mafiosi are moving into honest professions, it is hard to tell if they are legit or are actually sleepers. Without doubt, the most valued plants are those in Las Vegas and now Atlantic City. They perform vital functions for the mobs and can be trotted out when needed as front men.

See also SCOTTO, ANTHONY M.

POLITICAL contributions and the Mafia

The mob long ago learned the value of making political campaign contributions to advance the interests of organized crime. Moe Dalitz, the syndicate's number one man in Las Vegas since the 1950s, contributed to candidates of both the Republican and Democratic parties. In this, Moe was simply following a long mob tradition. According to an estimate by Virgil Peterson, for 27 years head of the Chicago Crime Commission, Al Capone contributed a total of a quarter of a million dollars to the Chicago mayoralty campaign of Big Bill Thompson in 1927. It is also a matter of record that Tommy "Three-Finger Brown" Lucchese in 1949 made a large campaign contribution to the re-election campaign of Bill O'Dwyer for mayor of New York, a contribution made in cash, in small bills, two months after the election.

Richard M. Nixon also was reported to have received mob contributions early in his political career. Meyer Lansky had met Nixon on one of Nixon's numerous visits to Miami. Earlier, when Nixon was practicing law in Whittier, California, Nixon also met Bugsy Siegel, Lansky's close friend, and according to columnist Drew Pearson, Siegel's right-hand man, Mickey Cohen, collected and then donated $26,000 in contributions to Nixon's campaigns for Congress.

Although Nixon would thereafter be linked fairly often to Lansky, especially in forays to the plush Lansky gambling casinos on Grand Bahama and Paradise Island (the latter financed in part by a corporation called Mary Carter Paints—later Resorts International—in which Nixon's close friend and mentor, Thomas Dewey, was a heavy investor), any quid pro quo may well have been an exaggeration. Lansky was always a virulent anti-communist. Nixon's politics always appealed to him, especially because they represented the idea of firmness in the world, a firmness against radicalism that might have prevented Castro's rise in Cuba and the loss for Lansky of a multimillion-dollar gambling empire.

Still, when the mob donates, it generally expects a payoff. The syndicate contributed $200,000 to elect Forrest Smith governor of Missouri in 1948; Kansas City crime boss Charley Binaggio claimed Smith would throw both Kansas City and St. Louis to syndicate gambling enterprises. Smith was elected, but Binaggio could not deliver. Binaggio was promptly assassinated.

New Jersey was for years considered to be dominated by the organized crime political money dispensed in the 1940s and 1950s by syndicate boss Longy Zwillman. In 1946 Republican governor Harold G. Hoffman personally solicited financial support from Zwillman, and, in 1949, Zwillman offered Democratic gubernatorial candidate Elmer Wene $300,000 in campaign funds with only the small proviso that he, Zwillman, be allowed to name the state's attorney general. Wene declined the offer and lost the election.

Oddly, while most mafiosi tend to contribute to the Democratic Party machines in political control in mob centers of operations, they often tend personally to lean to Republican politics. As informer Vinnie Teresa put it: "We vote whatever is the best way to make money. If it's going to be one of these guys who is going to be on the reform kick all the time, we'll all band together and vote against him. I'm a registered Democrat but I voted for Nixon in 1968, and I bet the mob really turned out for Nixon in 1972."

It has been said that in recent years the mob went the same way Teamsters Union money went in national campaigns.

See also BINAGGIO, CHARLES

PRE-HITS: Preludes to a major mob assassination

Generally, before Mafia elements get rid of a major mob figure, an effort is made to eliminate some of the target's major supporters. The tactic eases the big hit and also removes forces likely to launch a vengeful counterattack.

This was true of the Castellammarese War in New York in 1930–1931 when those seeking to depose Giuseppe "Joe the Boss" Masseria, first sought to take out his most important aides such as Steve Ferrigno and Al Mineo. Only after they were out of the way was the successful direct strike made on Joe the

Boss. This left Salvatore Maranzano on top, but to get there he had to absorbed a number of rising mobsters loyal to Lucky Luciano who clearly planned to unseat Maranzano, fatally. Maranzano decided Luciano had to go, but he noted with growing unease that Luciano controlled an army of murderous talents, men like Joe Adonis, Frank Costello, Vito Genovese, Willie Moretti, Albert Anastasia and Carlo Gambino.

Before he could move against Luciano, Maranzano felt he had to eliminate a goodly number of these men, as well as some of Lucky's non-Italian allies, such as Dutch Schultz and Meyer Lansky. Maranzano never got the chance. Luciano got wind of Maranzano's plans and struck first. Pre-hits are fine when one has the luxury of time and opportunity.

Sam Giancana was one Mafia man who understood the pre-hit concept. Or at last he should have. The pre-hit program preceding his murder, which at the time was not a guarantee that he would be hit but prudent preparation by the Chicago mob, spanned about a year and a half. Among his staunchest supporters who were rubbed out were Richard Cain and Mad Sam DeStefano, one of the outfit's most demented killers, who could be counted on to kill anyone going after his master. Either Giancana couldn't read the signs or he didn't know how to avoid the inevitable. Possibly he conned himself into believing that he was immune to mob murder. He was wrong.

There was no pre-hit maneuver when John Gotti masterminded the assassination of Gambino family boss Paul Castellano. Time was of the essence. Gotti had to move quickly since Castellano could call on a vast reserve of killers that would outlast him in a prolonged war. Gotti struck quickly and eliminated Castellano.

Afterward Gotti and his forces expected a war to break out within the Gambino crime family between themselves and the Castellano allies. For four months nothing happened. Then came the first pre-hit. One of Gotti's most important aides and his underboss, Frank DeCicco, was killed by a bomb blast in his car. The newspapers saw this as a declaration of war by the Castellano forces, but Gotti knew better. He knew this pre-hit was a masterstroke by Genovese boss Chin Gigante. DeCicco would have been dangerous to deal with, and getting rid of him would weaken the Gotti team. Undoubtedly, Gigante had more pre-hits in mind, but both sides became very wary in their movements. As it turned out, the most important pre-hit of all came not from either side but from the law, which ended up sending both Gotti and Gigante to prison on various charges for what figured to be the rest of their lives.

PRIO, Ross (1900–1972): Chicago Syndicate leader

Short, portly Sicilian-born Ross Prio was, according to informer Joe Valachi, one of the seven "top power brokers" within the Chicago Outfit. Considering the fact that Valachi's knowledge of mob affairs beyond New York was rather limited, that made Prio very big. He was indeed one of the strongest and richest hoods in the outfit, with power that rivaled any in the organization—except at various stages that of Paul Ricca, Tony Accardo and Sam Giancana. Pretty much a "don" in his own right, Prio was overlord of the lush North Side, the area Al Capone tried for so many years to wrest from the O'Banions, and boss of the old multimillion-dollar Cadillac policy game.

Brought to the United States by his adoptive parents when he was nine years old, Prio collected an impressive police record, although everything on it before 1929 was destroyed by court order. He was regarded by the mob as an expert in the political fix and a corrupter of the police. He was known to have been a "money lender" to a Chicago police captain who just happened to serve as head of the department's intelligence unit. Prio was also regarded as one of the mob's top torturers and murder specialists. His reputation was so fearsome that in one case he "persuaded" a plaintiff to drop a million-dollar lawsuit against a leading Chicago politician.

He was a murder suspect on several occasions and was questioned about a number of bombings. Among Prio's "honest" occupations was operation of a milk company. By the sheerest of coincidences a number of rival dairy firms ended up being wrecked by bombs. Prio ended up owning several dairies, presumably by making the owners an offer they couldn't refuse.

Prio took the Fifth Amendment 90 times before the McClellan Committee. He insisted he was just a little old businessman, taking his lead from his old-time mentor Al Capone (just an antique dealer). Prio had a number of "legit" lines. Besides the milk business, he was in cheese and canned whipped topping, and he owned several currency exchanges, office buildings, hotels, motels, nightclubs, restaurants, finance companies, vending machine outfits and attendant services for clubs and hotels. He also had extensive holdings in oil wells, resort real estate and Las Vegas casinos. He was a regular visitor at the Chicago Playboy Club, both for pleasure and to visit some of his money. Prio's various enterprises parked playboy cars, checked playboy coats and handed out playboy and playgirl towels in the restrooms.

Prio was consulted on all syndicate murders. One exception appeared to be a hit ordered by mob boss Giancana to be carried out in Hollywood, Florida. Federal agents bugged a mob headquarters there and recorded the discussion. One of Chicago's premier hitters, John "Jackie the Lackey" Cerone, was overheard advising several gangsters in on the projected killing to make sure they not be seen by Prio, who was taking the sun in the area at the time.

The plan was that the victim would be lured into a car by Cerone and the killers would then force him to the floor, take him to a boat, shoot him, and cut up his body in small bite-sized pieces for the sharks. At the last minute the contract was canceled. Presumably Prio heard about it and voted no. When Prio said a man died, he died, but if he said he lived, the man continued breathing as long as Prio desired.

In the jungle law of the Chicago Outfit nobody ever wanted to cross Ross Prio, and there is no record that even his superior, Sam Giancana, ever did. When Prio died of natural causes in 1972, he could have toted up his wealth and stood miles ahead of his first boss, Al Capone.

PRISON gangs and the Mafia

There has long been a tie, at times tenuous and in other cases fairly durable, connecting some prison gangs and the Mafia. Prison gangs meet some of the criteria of being a form of organized crime, although in a very structured environment. Some of these gangs engage in typical Mafia activity, which includes corruption of officials, in this case limited largely to guards, but sometimes including other personnel within and without the institution. Mafiosi sometimes find it useful to utilize prison gangs to carry out certain violent chores for them, especially for hit assignments, so they are free of suspicion. Because the gangs maintain a discipline on the outside, their members are also available there to the mob as needed. As a major outside activity is drug trafficking, the mob integrates with them and thus has a supply pipeline available for use by other crime groups. The Colombians find it useful to make use of such supply routes for their merchandise and pay the mobs for their cooperation. It is a matter of some conjecture how much mafiosi pay the outside prison mobsters out of this, but apparently it is enough to keep the career criminals happy.

The Mafia is also very happy because these gangs more than other outsiders can be counted on to keep secrets. They enforce their silence rules as well as or perhaps better than the Mafia itself does, since treachery is often a key ingredient within the so-called Honored Society. Many mafioso leaders have to overcome a strong antipathy to using outside criminals. Carlo Gambino, for instance, did not like rackets that required the use of too many organized noncareer criminals. Chop shop and stolen car rackets require the use of outside mechanic experts, who Gambino feared would crack under police investigation and turn on the mob to save themselves. That is a peril ever present for the crime families, and thus dealing with firm career crooks becomes a pleasure. Outside prison gangs maintain a stern code in their membership and will react violently when they judge such actions to be required. Typical among these is the so-called Dixie Mafia, drawn in large measure from tough southern prisons. The Dixie Mafia may be largely a journalistic invention in that its "organization" is rather loose, more operating on a unorganized networking basis. Still, there are members of this loose group always ready to carry out missions for the mob, ranging from extortion to contraband trafficking of all types to homicides to order.

Some of the other prison gangs known to cooperate at times with the mob still take care of their own businesses. Even those gangs noted in prison for following strict racial or religious lines generally make an exception in dealing with the Mafia. It is, as one mobster has been described as explaining such acts, "sort of professional courtesy." This would apply to the Texas Syndicate, made up of Mexican-American inmates from El Paso and San Antonio, and to the Mexican Mafia, composed of Mexican Americans from southern California in several of the state's institutions and seven other states. Its leadership structure can be said to closely mirror the Cosa Nostra organization, which gives mafiosi confidence in dealing with them. Any outfit that mimics the mob can't be all bad.

PROFACI, Joseph (1896–1962): Crime family boss

If the average crime family "godfather" is supposed to inspire respect, Joe Profaci, the longtime boss of the Brooklyn crime family, missed the boat.

There probably was not a boss hated by more of his own men than Profaci, precisely because he ran his outfit in the "approved" old Sicilian manner, requiring every member of the family to pay him monthly dues of $25. By contrast, in Buffalo old Stefano Magaddino dispensed family funds every Christmas until he got too penurious to do so in his old age, but Joe Profaci never had suffered any such failing of giving. He simply took and took. Carmine Persico Jr., who later became a successor to the leadership of the family, once complained about Profaci to Joe Valachi: "Even if we go hijack some trucks he taxes us. I paid up to $1,800."

In theory, the $25 monthly payments were to establish a slush fund to take care of legal fees, bribes and support payments to a soldier's family if he was imprisoned, but it was a custom long abolished in other crime families. Profaci, although a multimillionaire who lived in a huge mansion on a 328-acre estate on Long Island, which boasted a hunting lodge and its own private airport, just was not going to miss any stray penny. Crime paid for Joe Profaci even if it did not pay as well as it should have for his soldiers. While it was true that all crime family bosses required their men to pay tribute to them in the form of a slice of whatever rackets they ran, it was supposed to be given with "affection" or as a "token of respect." Profaci leaned very hard on his men to get his, and he ruled with an iron hand, ordering the execution of anyone objecting to his methods. For years the streets of Brooklyn were dotted with the corpses of those not following Profaci's rules of the game.

The personal life of Profaci presented an entirely different picture of the crime boss. He has often been described as the most devout Catholic of the Mafia leaders, although there were those in the underworld, among them the Gallos and their followers, who said Profaci embraced religion most fervently after he developed cancer. Profaci attended St. Bernadette's Catholic Church in Brooklyn and even had a private altar constructed in his basement so that mass could be celebrated at family gatherings by a priest who was a close friend of the Profacis. In 1949 a group of leading Italian Americans, including some priests, petitioned Pope Pius XII to confer a knighthood on Profaci, a "son of Sicily" who, they said, had become a benefactor to the Italian-American community. Profaci was the leading importer of tomato paste and olive oil in the country, owned more than 20 other businesses and was known as the kindly employer of hundreds of fellow countrymen. These citizens also pointed out that Profaci was a most generous donor to many Catholic charities.

Profaci's dream of papal approval was shattered however when the Brooklyn district attorney, Miles McDonald, protested to the Vatican that Profaci was a leading racketeer, extortionist, murderer and Mafia leader.

But the rebuff did not dampen Profaci's desire to demonstrate his religious zeal—if in a somewhat murderous fashion. A young independent thief had the effrontery to steal a jeweled crown from St. Bernadette's. Profaci took it as an insult not only to the Lord but also to the godfather himself. He passed the word that the crown was to be returned forthwith or blood would flow. The thief had no choice but to return the crown—no fence would dare handle it without the sure punishment of the mob. It was restored to the church, with a few of the jewels missing, and Profaci still ordered the death sentence. The thief was strangled with a rosary. Whatever Profaci's judgment would be in the hereafter, the incident did much to solidify his exalted position on earth, in the mob world, demonstrating how mighty his wrath could be.

Despite Profaci's ironfisted rule, he faced strong opposition within his family. The most determined opposition came from the Gallo brothers, who waged war against Profaci from 1960 until 1962 when Profaci died of cancer. The cause of the Gallo revolt was money—and the lack of it dispensed to their group by Profaci. The Gallos were willing and eager to be loyal to Profaci, a matter which they demonstrated when they killed a leading Brooklyn policy banker, Frank "Frankie Shots" Abbatemarco. The Gallos and their top gunner, Joe Kelly, had worked for Frankie Shots for several years, but when Profaci ordered him killed, they eagerly complied. Frankie Shots's offense was to deny Profaci a $50,000 tribute, and the Gallos were promised a good portion of his racket for dispatching him. However, after the rubout, Profaci sort of forgot his promise and divided up the Shots's empire among his family and friends.

The Gallos joined forces with other dissidents, including Jiggs Forlano, a high-powered loan shark operator, and Carmine Persico Jr., originally a Gallo trainee. The anti-Profaci forces kidnapped several of the enemy and barely missed snatching Profaci himself, who was tipped off and fled to Florida where he checked into a hospital for safekeeping. The kidnappers figured to hold the Profaci men until the crime boss agreed to deal with them fairly. Profaci secured the release of his men by making such promises and then split the enemy by promises of rewards to Forlano and Persico and some others if they would turn on the Gallos. The result was the bloody "mattress war" between the Profacis and the Gallos. The contest was still unresolved at Profaci's death.

If Profaci died hating the Gallos, that was nothing compared to his hatred for two fellow crime family godfathers, Carlo Gambino and Tommy "Three-Finger Brown" Lucchese. They like Profaci were members of the national commission and, noting the troubles in the Profaci family, "suggested" that Profaci "retire." Profaci, not unjustifiably, saw the Gambino-Lucchese ploy as an attempt to take over the Profaci empire and refused. All-out war threatened until the leader of another Brooklyn crime family, Joe Bonanno, threatened to take up arms on Profaci's side if outsiders tried to depose him. Bonanno realized that if Profaci fell, Gambino and Lucchese would next turn on him.

Despite his many woes, Joe Profaci managed to die still in command of the crime family he had ruled for over three decades.

See also GALLO, JOSEPH; INDEPENDENT CRIMINALS AND THE MAFIA

PROFACI crime family See COLOMBO CRIME FAMILY

PROFILING, mob style

A custom today that has reinvigorated the mob is the mafioso ability to win support in the "right circles." For decades, starting with Prohibition and continuing thereafter, the mobsters learned the art and values of the payoff. The mobs always collected "right cops" in their rosters, ones who could do their bidding. This "networking" of bribe takers has helped the resurgence of the mobs because of the trust inherent in the relationship between rogue officers and mobsters. With the flowering of "other Mafias" popularly thought to be determined to take over the weakened mobs, it created a dilemma for on-the-take officials. The code between wise guys and rogue officers was based on mutual trust, both parties needing the other. Even as the mob came under severe pressure from law enforcement, the residue of goodwill between mobsters and rogues could not be eliminated. With ethnic bigotry coming into play, dishonest officers still felt comfortable only with the devils they previously knew. A dirty cop could trust a wise guy but never a member of the Russian Mafia, the Cuban or Colombian Mafias, Chinese Mafias or, indeed, any other ethnic group speaking languages they could not comprehend. Any deals would have to be handled by longtime mob allies. This dynamic offered the traditional mafiosi the road to salvation, while dooming the emerging new mobsters to mere second-string roles. This mob-style "profiling" has become an important practice in the world of crime.

One of the more striking forms of criminal profiling involves the so-called Black Mafia. Rogue cops have long dealt with black racketeers for whom protection could be available at a price—a rather stiff price. Blacks today rant about what they call "Jim Crow racketeers." They can pay the cops directly or through the mob. The latter method on a dollar and cents basis is superior because the protection comes cheaper through the Mafia. Of course, there is a markup for the mob, but still the price is less for black racketeers. The blacks take the deal but still are resentful that they are victims of this special form of racial profiling. Profiling thus has become a lucrative source of profit for the real Mafia.

PROHIBITION

The greatest day for organized crime in America was January 16, 1920, the day the Eighteenth Amendment went into effect. Prohibition descended on the land and so did a new criminal influence that was to fester, thrive and corrupt long after Repeal in 1933. The proponents of Prohibition saw in their legislation the cure for all the social ills in America. Instead it produced new ills without getting rid of the old. Law enforcement agencies, hardly pristine over the preceding 70 or 80 years since they first were established, were seduced by bribes as never before. In the end, Prohibition was the mother of organized crime.

The great street gangs of America—born in the 1820s and 1830s and operated up to World War I—functioned in two chief fields: committing various forms of violent crime; and acting as bully boys or enforcers for the political machines of the big cities.

But by 1914 the gangs were in turmoil. In New York, the 1,500-member Eastman Gang was falling apart, their leader out of action behind bars. The Eastmans' arch rivals, the mostly Italian Five Pointers, were scattering. Their leader, Paul Kelly, reading the new morality of reform correctly, understood that an enlightened public would not much longer tolerate gang violence in elections, and he deserted his cohorts, moving into relatively minor labor racketeering activities. Even that old reliable, prostitution, a leading gang activity, was hitting hard times. Reformers were everywhere. Then, during World War I, the federal government shuttered many of the country's most infamous vice centers—especially those in Chicago, New Orleans and San Francisco.

Immediately after the close of the Great War it happily appeared that the era of the great gangs was over. But Prohibition in one fervent swoop threw society's natural social development into chaos. Across the country 200,000 speakeasies sprang up and large bootlegging organizations were required to supply their needs. Gang criminals, having gone straight out of sheer necessity, returned to their organizations. In New York alone, 15,000 saloons were closed by Prohibition, and 32,000 speakeasies came into existence. The owners of every one of these joints was breaking the law and paying bribes to remain in business. New York became a city on the take, the United States a country doing the same. Bootleggers and rumrunners brought in booze from outside the borders, using brawn and bullets if bribes didn't work. The production of alcohol became a cottage industry in many towns, especially in the Little Italies of major cities, producing foul odors that lay heavy over entire neighborhoods. Since these odors were readily identifiable and the police did nothing to intervene, the police were branded, as never before, as obviously corrupt.

The Jewish Purple Gang of Detroit, till then more dedicated to spectacular robberies and murders, became one of the most important and deadly Prohibition gangs, controlling much of the liquor supply smuggled in from Canada. In Cleveland, the violent Mayfield Road Gang emerged as an extremely potent force, and of course, Chicago's Al Capone gained recognition as the country's most infamous gangster. It was estimated that Capone himself made some $60 million from bootlegging and rumrunning.

In New York, the Broadway Mob—controlled by Lucky Luciano, Meyer Lansky, Frank Costello, Joe

Adonis and Bugsy Siegel—was taking in about $12 million a year just from booze. In their operation they had about 100 men on the payroll—drivers, bookkeepers, enforcers, guards, messengers and even fingermen (to look for liquor shipments by other gangsters that they could hijack). In an era when a department store clerk made perhaps $25 a week, most of Luciano's men were drawing a base salary of at least $200 a week. This gave the operation a payroll overhead somewhere over $1 million annually and left $11 million out of which they had to cover all expenses—mainly supplies and graft. "Grease" alone exceeded $100,000 a week. Ten thousand of this, according to Luciano, went to top police brass, but that represented only a small part of the payoffs. All the precincts had to be taken care of—their captains, lieutenants and sergeants, all the way down to cops on the beat. After all costs, the combination still came out with $4 million or so in pure profits.

These Prohibition criminals had all begun as mere ghetto criminals, fresh from the source of most violent crime in any metropolis. In the 19th century an Irish ghetto criminal might call it a good day if he cracked a citizen's skull and walked off with $10 for his efforts. But these later ghetto criminals struck it rich thanks to the accident of Prohibition. They were mostly Jews and Italians—those were the ethnic groups that had taken over the ghettos—but their great wealth was to raise them above the level of mindless street marauders as their ghetto predecessors had been and their ghetto successors would be. They had gone beyond organized ghetto crime to organized syndicate crime. Unlike earlier criminals who were bought by the politicians, they accumulated so much wealth that they reversed things and bought the politicians.

Disrespect for law grew as it became fashionable for even the most respectable citizens to serve bootleg liquor in their homes and visit lavish speakeasies. In the White House, President Warren G. Harding paid lip service to the dry movement and turned the nation's first residence into a private saloon. Most Prohibition agents themselves violated the law and took enormous bribes. Many ran their own bootleg operations. The Treasury Department between 1920 and 1928 fired 706 agents and prosecuted another 257 for taking bribes. Nobody claimed they got all the crooks. Top T-man Elmer L. Irey described the agents as a "most extraordinary collection of political hacks, hangers-on and passing highwaymen." In

New York, an angry and frustrated Captain Daniel Chapin ordered a lineup of all agents and declared, "Now everyone of you sons of bitches with a diamond ring is fired." Half were.

Finally, when the Democrats won the White House and the Congress in 1932, Prohibition was doomed. The Twenty-First Amendment killed it off in 1933. It did not kill off the great Prohibition gangs; they and various Mafia crime families rich with loot remained in business. The national crime syndicate was formed. The mobsters, now well connected with the political and police world, were a group that wanted to continue to feed at the trough themselves.

In the end, Prohibition gave birth to and nurtured organized crime and did such a brilliant job that today we still can't get rid of syndicated gangsters.

See also BOOTLEGGING

PROSTITUTION, new Mafia rackets in

By and large, since the conviction of Lucky Luciano for compulsory prostitution in 1936, the East Coast Mafia has managed to stay clear of convictions for such charges. Luciano was convicted by then–racket buster Thomas E. Dewey for 30 to 50 years, which was a far tougher sentence than had ever been handed out for such a charge. The eastern mobs howled it was a "bum rap," one handed to Dewey in a frameup with the perjured testimony of pimps and prostitutes who would say anything to avoid going to jail. To some it was doubtful that Luciano, with the money pouring in from many other rackets, would bother with such "small potatoes" as commercial sex.

This was not a racket ignored in Mafia strongholds such as Capone's Chicago and Ohio, West Virginia and western Pennsylvania, but the New York godfathers kept their men out of such rackets, mainly on the basis that some political elements, in the pocket for the mob, did not want to provoke reform elements against them. Again, it was a case of more important financial fish to fry. Furthermore, practitioners of the sex racket were likely to crack under the pressure and be eager to surrender bigger mafiosi for a way out for themselves.

During the height of the so-called sexual revolution, the New York mobsters insisted they had followed the right course, since "too many broads were giving it away for free and you can't make money out of that." But the attitudes of the eastern mobs changed as law enforcement cracked down hard on Mafia activities. During this period the other ethnic organized crime gangs pushed hard into new territories, with the Vietnamese, the Chinese and to a lesser extent the Russians and Koreans branching into first massage parlors and then lap dancing clubs and so on. The wise guys saw promise here and got in as well. But the big money in prostitution remained the independent hooker rings that handled outcall services to customer's homes or hotel rooms. The payoff was much greater, anywhere from $100 to $250, or more. In their need for more revenues the Mafia went into the upscale outcall, or "escort," services.

A breakthrough in this end of the business may have come in April 2004 when a joint New York Organized Crime Task Force, the police department, and the FBI looked into the illegal gambling activities of the Gambino crime family on Staten Island. They wiretapped a social club on Fingerboard Road and noticed some known leaders in the sex racket visiting there. Trailing these individuals they uncovered a series of corporate fronts and escort services with such names as Gentlemen's Delight, Day Dreams and Personal Touch that charged customers $250 for sex. The outfits were said to send out 15 to 20 limousine drivers to dispatch 30 to 40 prostitutes each day. Billings were done by merchant accounts held by escort services or limousine companies and in one case by a company that hired musical bands for weddings. The task forces arrested 16 people on charges of enterprise corruption and two others for falsifying business records and promoting prostitution and money laundering, activities of interest especially to the mobs. The media saw this as more than a simple sex business but an important field for the mobs, their gambling and other activities. The new Mafia saw the broad field of paid sex as becoming a major profit center in the 21st century.

PROVENZANO, Anthony "Tony Pro" (1917–1988): Mafia union racketeer

A prime suspect in the disappearance and almost certain murder of former Teamsters union president Jimmy Hoffa, Anthony Provenzano, often referred to as Tony Pro, had strong organized crime support from the start of his career in labor. One of Tony Pro's early sponsors was Tony Bender, a longtime associate of Vito Genovese who controlled much of the rackets along the New York and New Jersey waterfronts and, in connection with these, ran a number of Teamsters locals as well.

Provenzano was installed as a shop steward in a trucking company in 1945, and, by 1950, Bender had moved him along to become organizer for Teamsters local 560 in Union City, New Jersey. Bender was known to have used longshoremen to smuggle heroin into the country, and federal authorities long believed that Provenzano was deeply involved in narcotics trafficking.

Over the next several years Provenzano's rise continued in the Teamsters; he became president of Local 560 and a vice president of the International. Even when Tony Bender disappeared permanently—undoubtedly killed by order of Vito Genovese, behind bars at Atlanta penitentiary—Tony Pro had a clear run. He had become very important both to the mob and his local; others he controlled became the hubs of various organized crime activities. Tony Pro oversaw bookmaking, numbers and loan shark activities run by his business agents and shop stewards. Even more lucrative was the widespread, often blatant pilferage of cargoes being trucked through New Jersey. Without a pass from Tony Pro no shipment could be considered "safe," and the price was not cheap. This was demonstrated by the successful prosecution and 1966 conviction of Provenzano for extorting $17,000 from a trucking company. One of the witnesses slated to testify against Tony Pro had been Walter Glockner but he was gunned down and killed. Still, there was enough evidence against Tony Pro; he was sent to Lewisburg federal penitentiary in Pennsylvania where he did four and a half years.

In the prison he served as a prison capo under the boss of that institution, mob leader Carmine Galante. It cannot be said that Provenzano had a hard time there, being more or less in charge of assigning cons to some of the prison jobs. Informer Vinnie Teresa, upset at the 15 minutes of daily backbreaking labor spent cleaning a yard area about 10 by 20 feet, told Provenzano he wanted something easier. Provenzano assigned him to radio duty. His work each morning before breakfast consisted of pressing a button that turned on the radios in the cells throughout the prison. That finished the work for the day. Tony Pro assigned someone else to turn the radios off at night.

When Provenzano finished his term he returned to his union duties, where no major opposition now existed. Back in the late 1950s and early 1960s there had been some opposition, but the rebels were seriously injured on two occasions, and several were targets of bombings and shotgun blasts.

The last important opposition to Tony Pro was Anthony Castellito, secretary-treasurer of Local 560, who announced plans in 1961 to compete against the mob leader for the presidency. That June after a union meeting, Castellito, like Jimmy Hoffa later, was seen getting into an automobile—and seen no more. In 1975 Hoffa disappeared. After his release from prison in 1971 Hoffa announced plans to recapture the Teamsters union presidency from Frank Fitzsimmons, a leader with whom the underworld had become most comfortable. The mob had little interest in Hoffa's return since he would probably be more demanding in dealing with them. Provenzano, as *the* man in the East Coast Teamsters, was said to have warned Hoffa to go away on a number of occasions. It has been a police theory since Hoffa's disappearance that it was Tony Pro who ordered his abduction and secret execution. The charge has never been proved.

In the meantime, charges were brought against Provenzano that he had ordered Harold Konigsberg, a longtime enforcer in the Genovese crime family, and Salvatore Briguglio to kill the long-missing Anthony Castellito. (Briguglio was also a prime suspect in the Hoffa case.) On March 21, 1978, Briguglio, suspected of being a talker to the FBI, was shot on a New York street. Tony Pro was convicted after trial in Kingston, New York, in the Castellito matter. Both he and Konigsberg were sentenced to life imprisonment. Tony Pro died in prison of a heart attack at the age of 71.

See also HOFFA, JAMES R.

PUBLIC enemies: Organized crime mobsters

When the average person is asked to name the most famous "public enemies" in the world of crime, the names he mentions are Dillinger, Bonnie and Clyde, Machine Gun Kelly, Ma Barker and the like. Among this group, despite the constant raging against them by the FBI's J. Edgar Hoover, Machine Gun Kelly never fired his weapon at anyone and Ma Barker was never so much as charged with a crime.

The press-conscious Hoover stole the idea from others and launched a publicity campaign in the early 1930s to dub a group of criminals, mostly little more than armed stickup men, the Public Enemies. At the time, Prohibition was ending and the old bootleg mobs were forming the new nationwide criminal syndicate. Apparently fearful and certainly uninterested in tangling with such major mobsters, Hoover concentrated his wrath on minor criminals, cloaking them in the mantle of master criminal. For instance, while John Dillinger killed at most one person and his gang about nine others, Al Capone in Chicago was responsible for no less than 500 to as many as 1,000 murders. Had the full energies of Hoover's agency been turned on the major menace of the Capone-Luciano-Lansky organizations, it has been argued by many crime experts, organized crime today would be far less effective and pervasive, if not totally eliminated.

The first use of the term *public enemies*, before it was appropriated by Hoover, was made by Frank J. Loesch, a venerable corporation counsel and civic leader in Chicago and a founding member and longtime head of the Chicago Crime Commission. He compiled a first list of 28 Chicago public enemies—"persons who are constantly in conflict with the law"—in an effort to counter the romantic aura with which certain elements of the most sensational press of the city and nation had endowed gangsters. Loesch's list included

1. Al Capone
2. Tony "Mops" Volpe
3. Ralph Capone
4. Frankie Rio
5. Jack "Machine Gun" McGurn
6. James Belcastro
7. Rocco Fanelli
8. Lawrence "Dago Lawrence" Mangano
9. Jack Zuta
10. Jake Guzik
11. Frank Diamond
12. George "Bugs" Moran
13. Joe Aiello
14. Edward "Spike" O'Donnell
15. Joe "Polock Joe" Saltis
16. Frank McErlane
17. Vincent McErlane
18. William Neimoth
19. Danny Stanton
20. Myles O'Donnell
21. Frank Lake
22. Terry Druggan

23. William "Klondike" O'Donnell
24. George "Red" Barker
25. William "Three-Fingered Jack" White
26. Joseph "Peppy" Genero
27. Lee Mongoven
28. James "Fur" Sammons

Almost any member of this list would make Hoover's "public enemies" look like boy scouts.
See also LOESCH, FRANK J.

PURPLE Gang: Infamous Detroit mob

One of the most feared bootlegging mobs during Prohibition, the Detroit Purple Gang was basically an all-Jewish outfit. The gang dominated the city's criminal activities and was responsible for at least 500 killings—a record that, proportionally speaking, exceeded the tally of the Capone mob in Chicago. Its leaders, Benny and Joe Bernstein and Harry and Louis Fleisher, maintained close ties to the Cleveland Syndicate and such stalwarts as Moe Dalitz and Chuck Polizzi. Detroit was a pivotal importance during Prohibition because it served as a funnel for illegal booze shipped across the border from Canada.

The Purples engaged in competition with another mob, the Little Jewish Navy, and to aid them in their killings, they imported Yonnie Licavoli and his gunners from St. Louis. Licavoli and his brothers, cousins and friends in time formed what would be called the Licavoli family of the Mafia in Detroit. Licavoli did not ever challenge the authority of the Purples, whose other gunmen were considered so proficient that, according to a leading theory, three of them—George Lewis and brothers Phil and Harry Keywell—were borrowed by Al Capone to help carry out the St. Valentine's Day Massacre in 1929. The Purples did not limit themselves to booze running, but accumulated additional millions in jewelry robberies, hijacking and extortion. They were also involved in drugs and were one of the prime suppliers to jazz musicians of the 1920s.

When the national crime syndicate was formed in the 1930s under the aegis of Lucky Luciano and Meyer Lansky, the Purples were invited to join. No coercion was used—the gang was considered too bloody and powerful to be subjected to force. However, the Purples accepted, disbanded their own organization and took an important role in the crime cartel's far-flung gambling activities, often providing any "muscle" that was needed.

The name of the Purple Gang was too colorful to be allowed to die, and years later any really tough character from Detroit was quickly labeled by the press as being a member of the Purple Gang.
See also PURPLE GANG, MODERN

PURPLE Gang, modern

A new Purple Gang evolved in New York City in the late 1970s, taking its name from the legendary Detroit Purple Gang of Prohibition infamy. It would take quite a collection of deadly mobsters to live up to such a fabled moniker, but the newer-look Purples, say authorities, justify the accolade. In fact, the new Purples have often been called New York's sixth crime family, deserving of all the angry attention of the five established mafioso outfits.

All quite young—in their 20s or 30s—the new Purples graduated from "gofer" positions for established narcotics traffickers to become, says the Drug Enforcement Administration, a criminal organization with an "enormous capacity for violence" and a "lack of respect for other members of organized crime." Small by comparison to the established families, the new Purples number somewhat more than 100. Membership is restricted to young Italian Americans who were raised on Pleasant Avenue between 110th and 117th Streets in East Harlem—still an underworld stronghold where deals are constantly struck between mafioso narcotics traffickers and the new black gangs that have taken over the street operations in the drug racket.

Money-hungry, these youths, almost all graduates from youth gangs, are feared by the underworld and police authorities as well. There is considerable worry that the Purple Gang will eventually start a shooting war against both the Mafia families and the blacks. Members of the gang talk openly of having control of all drug trafficking on the East Coast. Indeed, as long as the Purples remain on the scene, it is presumptuous, and in fact laughable, to talk of an emerging "Black Mafia." The Purples seem also to be establishing ties with the Latino drug traffickers, and they may also prove the masters of the so-called Latin, or Cuban, Mafia as well.

In the late 1970s the *New York Times* traced the activities of the gang and found it was dominant in the large-scale distribution of drugs in the South

Bronx and Harlem. The Purples were also pulling muscle jobs for two crime families' extortion activities, as well as carrying out the murders of at least 17 victims, including two police plants. Supplementing their drug activities, the Purples are deeply involved in international gunrunning and are alleged to have direct ties to certain Latin American terrorists.

PUSHCART rackets: Enduring scams for the mob

A century ago pushcart rackets were a big deal for the emerging American Mafia. They shook down dealers and demanded tribute for allowing small-time vendors to operate and to keep out competitors. Today, the pushcart rackets appear to outsiders to have faded away. Surprisingly, that is far from the truth. The new Mafia has learned how to milk an old-time racket and in fact add considerable profitable scams. The offshoot revenues justify keeping their eye on pushcarts. Today a vendor cannot simply open up wherever he or she wishes without expecting some unhealthy consequences. And equally unhealthy is a vendor's trying to get supplies on his or her own. Vendors are required to deal with suppliers who are either mob dominated or ones who have made an accommodation with the mobsters. Included are beverage and butane suppliers. Once when Joe Bonanno's son Bill was attempting to make it big in the mob, he received an education when he took part in a jurisdictional dispute between vendors of the Bonanno and Lucchese families. The Luccheses demanded the rights to two spots held in the Wall Street area, big money-making enterprises despite the prosaic appearances. Bill couldn't see the dispute as worth fighting over, but there was a real possibility that it might come to that. As it was, the Bonannos won out. There was a mess of money involved. The stands each did hundreds of sales in sodas each day, and the mob held the loyalty of the vendors by underselling other beverage suppliers. Key to this was the fact that under bottle and can deposit rules the vendors paid 3.5¢ for each deposit item, so if cans were returned, vendors could collect the standard 5¢ deposit and net an extra profit of 1.5¢. In practice, however, no one returns cans to the pushcart for a refund. But the mob, meanwhile, has made an extra profit simply by importing cans and bottles from a deposit-free state such as Pennsylvania. For the privilege of engaging in this scam the vendors gladly allow the mob to store their carts after hours for a fee the competition cannot or dares not match. Add to this the price of weiners, rolls, napkins and the like, and the mob is really cutting the mustard. The big money the mob has learned is the deposit money, and they have expanded it in other outlets, especially in Chinese takeout, with the savings considerable since the custom in many Chinese food outlets is to award one or more free cans of soda depending on the amount purchased by a customer. In recent years the mob has used their "expertise" at this to supply street fairs with all the drinks at bargain prices.

Far from being a penny-ante operation, the racket in all its variables, is a multimillion-dollar business that can warrant a pushcart war if necessary.

R

RAFT, George (1895–1980): Movie actor and gangster pal

Whether George Raft or Frank Sinatra was more often linked with the Mafia is a tough call.

A small-time hood turned successful movie gangster, Raft's first association with a big-time hoodlum was with the charismatic Bugsy Siegel. Bugsy had been sent to Los Angeles in the late 1930s by the East Coast crime families to develop their national gambling empire and to lay the groundwork for their eventual colonization of Las Vegas. Siegel was taken with Raft's portrayal of the coin-tossing gangster in *Scarface*, a character Siegel viewed as the mirror image of himself. The pair became inseparable, seducing starlets by night and betting the horses heavily at Santa Anita racetrack by day.

When Siegel opened the glittering Flamingo Hotel in Las Vegas in December 1946, Raft was an honored guest and reciprocated by greeting other movietown figures. But the Flamingo was an instant flop, showing no sign of its future glory. Siegel, who had skimmed off hundreds of thousands of dollars of mob money advanced for construction purposes, was murdered.

Raft took the demise of his favorite gangster very hard, so hard, in fact, that a tenderhearted Meyer Lansky, who rather obviously had had to give his okay for the Siegel hit, felt he had to do something to ease the actor's grief. He soothed Raft with a job as a sort of superior toastmaster at his Capri Hotel in Cuba. It was the beginning of Raft's career as a super shill for the mob, an occupation that grew as his movie career faded.

Raft proved enormously important to the mob, far more than his compensation reflected. When the mob built the Sands in Las Vegas, Joseph "Doc" Stacher, one of Lansky's closest associates, saw the importance of the Hollywood connection. As he later explained in retirement in Israel: "To make sure we'd get enough top-level investors, we brought George Raft into the deal and sold Frank Sinatra a nine percent stake in the hotel."

Inevitably, Raft was marked as an associate of underworld characters. Accordingly, the authorities began to create some domestic problems. Even the Communist authorities made it hot when, in the case of Havana, Raft lost out as Castro came to power and routed the Lansky-Batista combination that ran the casinos. In the 1960s, the elderly Raft became a star of the London scene, playing the operator of the Colony Sports Club, a sort of Rick in a real-life *Casablanca*. (Raft ironically was the pre-Bogart choice for the part).

The Colony was a plush place, controlled by Lansky and his frequent associate in casino operations, Dino Cellini. It quickly became the "in" place to go for English and visiting society. Raft was always in the limelight, appearing each evening in a tuxedo, meeting people, signing autographs, and dancing with awed women.

Later Raft would confide to friends that his days at the Colony were the happiest of his life. As he put it to informer Vinnie Teresa, "Vinnie, those were the best days I've had in years. I had a chauffeured Rolls-

Royce, beautiful women with me every night, a beautiful penthouse apartment in the Mayfair area, and five hundred dollars a week. Who lived better than I did? What did I care about what was going on in the casino every night or who was involved? I never did anything wrong." Whether Raft did anything wrong or not finally meant little to British authorities, who decided he was fronting for mobsters. Making him the scapegoat, they deported him from the country.

After that Raft tried for shill jobs both at home and abroad, but in due course he was subjected to the same sort of official disapproval. Raft in time became poison to the mob, and eventually he was finished as both an actor and a casino shill.

Raft had made millions for the mob, and Teresa was later to call him "the best investment Lansky and Cellini made" in England. With a recommendation like that, it was perhaps inevitable that Raft died broke.

See also COLONY SPORTS CLUB

RAGEN, James M. (1881–1946): Gambling kingpin and mob murder victim

After Prohibition, gambling was embraced by the national crime syndicate as a principal source of revenue. But from 1940 to 1946, after the conviction and imprisonment of publisher Moe Annenberg, the mob lost control of the horse-racing wire business. Annenberg had been essentially a creation of the Chicago Al Capone/New York Luciano-Lansky-Costello axis, as organized crime switched from booze to gambling as the prime source of revenue.

The mobsters were in disarray, outmaneuvered by James Ragen, who skillfully converted himself into the most powerful figure in gambling in the country.

Ragen had come up the hard way in the Chicago underworld, having started out as a circulation slugger for the *Chicago Tribune* during the era of the great newspaper circulation wars, when Max Annenberg, Moe's older brother, was circulation manager. Ragen learned the art of violence with a host of future big criminals, including Dion O'Banion, Walter Stevens, Frankie and Vince McErlane, Mossy Enright and Tommy Maloy, men who later turned Chicago into a bloody murderground. Ragen had the distinction of outliving most of his fellow students of mayhem while at the same time maintaining a certain independence from the Capone mobsters.

The federal government had mistakenly thought that the imprisonment of Annenberg in 1940 and the dismantling of his Nation-Wide News Service would be a crippling blow to illegal gambling around the nation. However, Ragen moved quickly to take advantage of the syndicate's plan to lay low for a time. His Continental Press Service met the urgent need of bookmakers and became the dominant racing wire in the nation, providing the latest results from dozens of tracks directly to thousands of bookie joints.

Finally the mob started pressuring Ragen to come in with them, even dangling a handsome buy-out price for his business. Ragen had been in the Chicago underworld too long not to know the score. He told friends he knew how the mob worked and that if he sold out, there was no way he would be allowed to live to collect his payoff. Faced with Ragen's intransigence, the mob set up Trans-American Publishing under the murderous Bugsy Siegel and forcibly took over the lush California market, charging bookies $100 a day for the necessary racing information. Ragen, however, maintained a tight grip on the rest of the country, and it soon was obvious things could never change as long as Ragen lived. Such details were no problem to the mob. In June 1946 Ragen was cut down by a fusillade of bullets from a passing car. Remarkably, he survived and was taken to a hospital where he was put under 24-hour police guard.

From his hospital bed, Ragen, no believer in omerta, charged the mob with trying to kill him off. It was not the smart thing to do in 1946 Chicago. In September Ragen died, supposedly of his wounds; however, an autopsy showed death resulted from mercury poisoning. The mob had had no trouble penetrating Ragen's police protection, and his death was officially listed as a gang murder. Several mob big shots were quizzed in the case, including Greasy Thumb Guzik, but the final results were the usual ones for Chicago: no arrests, no convictions, one body. And the way was open for the mob to grow fat on ever-increasing gambling profits.

See also ANNENBERG, MOSES L.

RAGEN'S Colts: Chicago Irish gang

The recalcitrant Irish gangsters were the most reluctant to join with other ethnic gangs in what was to become organized crime in America. Many important Irish gangsters, unable to conform to the syndicate mold, had to die. There were Mad Dog Coll in New York and Dion O'Banion in Chicago, to name two. But some Irish gangsters were finally tamed and joined up, their descendants today important allies of mafiosi in many cities.

In Chicago Al Capone's toughest chore was making peace with Irish gangsters. He was far more successful with the Jews, the Poles and even the blacks. There were times when he must have felt sure that Ragen's Colts were a lost cause.

The Colts were at the pinnacle of their power in the first two decades of the century, dominating the South Side of Chicago around the stockyards. Described as racists, jingoists, political sluggers, bootleggers and murderers, they, like many other gangs in early Chicago, started out as a baseball team. Frank Ragen, the star pitcher, was also the star political operator of the outfit which was officially called Ragen's Athletic and Benevolent Association.

Ragen soon proved invaluable to the Democratic Party in the city, offering Colts' firepower and muscle in campaigns. Many members of the city council and state legislature owned their election to the gang. "When we dropped into a polling place," one Colt bragged, "everybody else dropped out."

By 1902 the gang numbered 160, and just six years later it adopted a motto, "Hit Me and You Hit 2,000," which was probably only a slight exaggeration. Over the years the list grew of aldermen, sheriffs, police brass, country treasurers and numerous other officeholders beholden to the gang. Even Ragen himself took a job as a city commissioner. But, as always, the most notable members of the gang were accomplished criminals. Among such worthies were Gunner McPadden with a list of homicides to his credit so large that no one, McPadden included, could make an accurate count; Dynamite Brooks, a saloon keeper with the reputation of killing when he got drunk; Harry Madigan, another saloonman and owner of the Pony Inn in Cicero, who was charged with several kidnappings and assaults during various elections; Stubby McGovern, a deadly hit man who bragged he never failed in an assignment; Danny McFall, who despite murdering two business competitors was named a deputy sheriff; Yiddles Miller, a boxing referee and notorious racist, who denounced the Ku Klux Klan as a bunch of "nigger lovers"; and Ralph Sheldon, a fearless bootlegger and hijacker said to "take no prisoners."

Besides providing political muscle duty and operating a number of rackets, the Colts were always ready to provoke a race riot, starting one in 1919 that nearly destroyed the city. A black youth swimming off a South Side beach strayed into white, segregated waters. Bathing Colts promptly stoned and drowned him. The Colts then took to the streets baiting blacks. After nightfall they roared into the Black Belt, shooting blacks on sight, dynamiting, and looting shops and homes and setting others on fire. Black veterans of the war seized up their service weapons and fired back. Rampaging blacks in turn overturned streetcars and automobiles carrying whites and destroyed property. The rioting continued for four days before finally wearing itself out, leaving 20 whites and 14 blacks dead, with another 1,000 burned, injured and maimed.

With the onset of Prohibition even the Ragen Colts had no time for organized bigotry. They shifted into bootlegging. Ralph Sheldon formed a splinter group which had little interest in making or importing booze, much preferring to hijack the wares of other gangs, a habit not conducive to peaceful racketeering.

Still, Capone showed extreme tenderness dealing with the Colts although he was forced to do battle with them, seeing the possibility of winning their cooperation, something he had consistently failed to do with the forces of other Irish mobsters like Dion O'Banion and Spike O'Donnell. Eventually most of the Colts, even Sheldon who for a time had shifted alliances from one group to another and would do so again, joined the combination. Today the descendants of the original wild Colts remain important figures with organized crime.

RASTELLI, Philip (1918–1991): Boss of Bonanno family

A mafioso famed for having one of the more involved marriages in the underworld, Phil "Rusty" Rastelli was the boss of the Bonanno family in the early 1970s, then stepped down when the violent Carmine Galante was released from federal prison. After Galante was murdered—police have often linked Rastelli with the 1979 assassination—he resumed the top spot. After his return to power there were steady reports of rumbles against his rule, but then there have been rumbles in the Bonanno family ever since Joe Bonanno was forced into retirement in the late 1960s.

Rastelli probably found Mafia activities tame compared to his married life. His wife Connie was gunned down in 1962 after she'd informed federal agents that Rastelli was a drug trafficker. Before that, federal law enforcement sources have indicated, Connie had been a big help in her husband's activities, very unusual for a Mafia wife. She was described as driving getaway cars during heists, keeping books for her husband on gambling operations and even running abortion mill rackets set up by Rastelli.

Rastelli was not always entranced with his wife. Once, on the lam in Canada, he took up with a young woman. On finding out, Connie shot right up to Canada and proceeded to clobber her young rival senseless. She also informed Rastelli that if he fooled around any more she'd kill him.

Rastelli apparently operated under the assumption that no wife would really mess with a "made" mafioso and continued his straying ways after he got back to New York. Connie promptly cornered him on a Brooklyn street and emptied a gun at him, hitting him twice, but not wounding him seriously. After that, Rastelli thought it best if he didn't go back to his wife at all, but Connie was not the sort to be neglected. She warned him she'd talk to the law about his activities.

As far as the mob was concerned, Mrs. Rastelli had overstepped her bounds. She was visited by Big John Ormento, a sinister crime leader, and warned to stop making such threats. But Connie's threats weren't idle. She went to the feds and started talking—at the very time the government was investigating Ormento and several other important mafiosi about narcotics activities. Connie was able to supply the government with information that the mob was planning to kill the key witness against them. The federal agents doubted her claim until she supplied them with the address in New Jersey where the government had the witness under wraps.

The witness was shifted to another secret location and eventually the government won its case against Ormento and a number of other big shots. However, before a case could be built against Rastelli, Mrs. Rastelli was blown away by a mob gunman.

From 1976 Rastelli was in and out of prison on an extortion charge and then for parole violation for meeting with other mobsters. In the mid-1980s he was under numerous federal indictments. After the mob rubout of Gambino boss Paul Castellano in December 1985, there was considerable speculation that Young Turks in the Bonanno family would seek to take out Rastelli because all the charges were making Rastelli ineffective as a leader or, more important, might be inspiring him to start talking. Immediately after the Castellano shooting, U.S. marshals put Rastelli "under protection" at a secret hideaway.

To the aging don it might well have seemed like Connie Rastelli all over again.

Late in 1986 Rastelli was convicted of taking part in a massive labor racketeering conspiracy. The charges were made under the federal Racketeer Influenced and Corrupt Organizations (RICO) Act. Under a 12-year sentence he died of liver cancer at 73.

RAT Pack and the Mafia, the: Sinatra's Hollywood followers
The connection between Frank Sinatra and the mob can hardly be classified as late-breaking news. But he was not the only celebrity in the mob's barn. As the acknowledged leader of the Rat Pack, Sinatra was one among other members, including such Hollywood stars and showbiz people as Peter Lawford, Dean Martin, Sammy Davis Jr., Joey Bishop, Tony Curtis, Janet Leigh, Robert Wagner, Natalie Wood, Shirley MacLaine, Jimmy Van Heusen and others.

Rat Pack members performed regularly in Las Vegas, and their circle attracted many admirers and hangers-on, including mobsters like Johnny Roselli, the Hollywood–Las Vegas honcho for Chicago's Sam Giancana. Much has been made of Sinatra's closeness to mob figures and his alleged desire to "run" with gangsters, but the idea that he sometimes cooperated out of fear—as did many of the Rat Packers—should not be dismissed.

It was said that Sinatra talked to Giancana about the value of the Chicago Outfit aiding the 1960 presidential campaign of John F. Kennedy. Giancana, as his biographer, William Brashler, has stated, "made no commitment without expecting something in exchange." Clearly, what Giancana expected—and informed his mob associates he expected—were connections in the White House through Sinatra to get the federal government off his back. (Giancana had also tried to achieve that goal by cooperating with the CIA in the ill-fated plots to assassinate Fidel Castro.) It turned out Giancana expected too much from Sinatra, whose influence on John Kennedy was less than generally believed and virtually nil with Bobby Kennedy, attorney general. (Bobby Kennedy forced J. Edgar Hoover, that less-than-zealous Mafia fighter, to have the FBI get tougher with the mob.) Giancana was furious—with Bobby Kennedy, Sinatra and the whole Rat Pack. It turned out the only Kennedy whom Sinatra had any "in" with was old Joseph, and by that time the elder Kennedy's influence on his sons was itself rather limited.

The boys from Chicago grew more angry as under the Kennedys the heat intensified, as we can hear in a famed conversation between Giancana and a tough outfit hoodlum named Johnny Formosa, recorded for posterity. Formosa told his boss: "Let's show 'em. Let's show those fuckin' Hollywood fruitcakes that they can't get away with it as if nothing's happened." Formosa's solution on Sinatra: "Let's hit him." And of the Rat Packers: "I could whack out a couple of those guys. Lawford, that Martin prick, and I could take the nigger and put his other eye out."

The offer was undoubtedly attractive to Giancana's psychopathic heart-of-hearts, but even Giancana could temper his natural inclinations when money was concerned. "No," he said. "I've got other plans for them."

Thus it was that a short time later Sinatra and a number of the Rat Packers were appearing at the Villa Venice, a former sleazy clip joint turned plush nightclub outside Wheeling, Illinois. Whoever the owners of record, there was firm knowledge that Giancana and the mob were the real operators. Among those performing before big-spending crowds were Sinatra, Eddie Fisher, Dean Martin and Sammy Davis Jr. Outside, a bus shuttled customers to a plushly furnished quonset casino a mere two blocks away.

The FBI descended on the Rat Packers and learned that all of them were performing gratis as a personal favor to Sinatra. Fisher rambled in his talks with the FBI but said very little. Davis was more outgoing, informing agents he had cut short some lucrative Las Vegas dates to work the Villa Venice gratis "for my man Francis." The FBI wanted to know if he was also doing it for friends of Sinatra. "By all means," Davis said. Sam Giancana? "By all means." Davis added only one other thought: "Baby, let me say this. I got one eye, and that one eye sees a lot of things that my brain tells me I shouldn't talk about. Because my brain says that, if I do, my one eye might not be seeing *anything* after a while."

The *Chicago Daily News* reported, "During the past 20 days since singer Eddie Fisher started off the new star policy at the Villa, a heavy toll has been levied at the hut on the [Villa] patrons. Individual losses of as much as $25,000 have been reported."

Basing an estimate on overheard conversations, the FBI determined that the one-month operation of the Villa Venice and its shuttle service had brought Giancana and the boys a cool $3 million.

Giancana's "other plans" for the Rat Pack had been taken care of. The mob leader was still unhappy about the Kennedy problem, but consoled himself counting the net. And the Rat Pack was alive and well.

See also SINATRA, FRANK

Further reading: *The Don* by William Brashler; *The Mafia Is Not an Equal Opportunity Employer* by Nicholas Gage; *Mafia Princess* by Antoinette Giancana and Thomas C. Renner.

READING, Pennsylvania: Mafia's East Coast "Cicero"

Cicero, Illinois, the longtime captive city of the Capone mob, was thought unique; a situation like Cicero could never happen again. But, it could and it did. Called the "Pretzel Capital of the World," Reading, Pennsylvania, was turned into a pretzel by the Angelo Bruno crime family of Philadelphia in an operation described as the outright rape of an American city.

Working together with local underworld figures, the Bruno operatives in the 1950s and early 1960s corrupted most of the Reading city administration from the mayor on down. In the heart of peaceful Pennsylvania Dutch country the Bruno hoodlums set up an illegal Las Vegas of the East, boasting what has been described as the biggest crap game east of the Mississippi and perhaps in the entire country. The "Reading Game," as it was called, operated out of Philadelphia from the 1950s to 1962, when the FBI finally smothered it. Each night big gamblers from all over the East gathered in a restaurant in the heart of Philadelphia. They would be picked up by "luggers" and hauled 50 miles to Reading where the million-dollar dice game was played on high-rolling "California tables."

A hoodlum for a time involved in the operation later explained: "Everybody made a buck on the game. They rented their limousines from a funeral director, because they only used them from ten at night until seven in the morning." He indicated how much freedom organized crime enjoyed in the Quaker City at the time, declaring: "They even had a cop out in front of the restaurant—he'd blow a whistle like a hotel doorman to signal a limo when he had a full load coming in for the game. It looked like opening night on Broadway. The cops never touched them."

Naturally, the game enjoyed official protection in Reading as well, and the gambling represented merely one symptom of the rape of Reading. In conjunction with the gambling, for the edification of the players, the largest East Coast red-light district flourished. Reading was also saddled with the biggest illegal still since Prohibition, and the operation was tied right into the city water supply.

Meanwhile Reading went down the drain. Industry started pulling out, and the downtown area turned into a near wasteland, with revenues diverted away from such frivolities as civic improvements. As citizens became restive, the mob even brought in some "reformer" puppets to try to maintain the mob status quo. Finally a Justice Department task force moved in. Federal agents found only one civic improvement made in recent years—the installation of new parking meters. It was an investigation into this situation and the fact that the company installing the meters had a history of paying off municipal governments to win such contracts that broke the Reading mess wide open. By 1962 the FBI had crushed the Reading Game and the Bruno crime family faced deportation back to Philadelphia.

The lesson of Reading however was more meaningful than the mere battle against a single Mafia family. The year 1962 was significant. Attorney General Robert Kennedy had been lighting fires under a reluctant FBI Director J. Edgar Hoover to at last recognize the organized crime menace and the Mafia.

Reading was cleaned up rather quickly and one must wonder what conditions might have been in Reading in the 1960s had Hoover been forced to act against the emerging national crime syndicate in the early 1930s. For three decades Hoover had denied the existence of the Mafia and organized crime, instead concentrating on the most bumbling, incompetent, independent criminals he labeled "public enemies." He refused to involve himself against crime syndicates which he insisted weren't there or to take assignments fighting Prohibition rackets or the narcotics trade. And he said his men had more important things to do than chasing after gamblers. Thus Hoover ignored the main sources of wealth for organized crime, which provided mobs the power and influence to seduce politicians, judges, police officials and other important figures both in and out of government. Reading provides a symbol of how Hoover's intransigence and inaction became one of the three main reasons organized crime and the Mafia festered and flourished in the United States to an extent not seen anywhere else in the industrialized world.

RED dye murders: Mafia extortion hoax

The Mafia did not originate red dye murders. The trusty confidence swindle actually went back many decades. But several crime groups, including the Genovese family and the Gallo brothers, often used the gimmick in their extortion plots. It works as follows.

A victim is picked out, often a bookmaker or some other money man, and pressure is put on him and another *supposed* victim at the same time. There is a general sitdown meeting involving the mobsters, the victim and the phony victim. The mobsters become upset when both their victims are reluctant to pay the protection money demanded. Suddenly things turn violent, and the mobsters pull guns and force the two victims into a car. There the phony victim keeps arguing with the mobsters and suddenly some shots are fired. They are really blanks. The phony victim, however, has been fitted with small explosive caps that discharge blood—really, red dye. The phony victim is pronounced dead before the startled eyes of the real victim. The car is pulled off the road and the "body" dumped in some bushes. Then the mobsters turn to the real victim to determine if he now sees the wisdom of purchasing protection. He generally does. (In one case, the Genoveses got a sucker to agree to pay protection of $100 a week, plus a new Cadillac every Christmas for one of the mafiosi.)

The red dye hoax seems to be rather sparingly used. Perhaps this is because it requires the utmost faith by the phony victim in his confederates. In the twisty world of Mafia contract plots, all that is necessary to rub out a mobster is to sell him on acting the ruse in a red dye murder. In such a case, the murder is real.

REINA, Tom (1889–1930): Early New York crime family leader

Few killings illustrate the sinister twists that are possible in Mafia intrigues as well as the case of Tom Reina, whose murder on February 26, 1930, is considered by most crime historians to be the start of the bloody Castellammarese War.

It is a simplification to call the Castellammarese War a two-sided affair. True, the battle was primarily between the New York Mafia factions of Joe the Boss Masseria and Salvatore Maranzano. But a third, and ultimately decisive force was Lucky Luciano and the Young Turks (aided by the important Jewish mobsters under Meyer Lansky and Bugsy Siegel), who conspired to defeat both sides. They danced back and forth in cunning maneuvers to weaken both foes.

Reina was an important Masseria partner, albeit not an enthusiastic one. He was casting friendly eyes toward Maranzano—especially after Masseria began pressuring him for a cut of his rackets. Through allies serving under Reina, especially Tom Gagliano and Tommy Lucchese, Luciano, himself also allied with Masseria, learned of the Masseria plans to assassinate Maranzano supporters Joe Profaci and young Joe Bonanno. Since Luciano was counting on Profaci and Bonanno in his future national crime syndicate, he wanted to prevent their deaths, and equally he did not want Reina to defect to Maranzano since that might tilt the contest too much in the latter's favor. Therefore the Luciano forces decided Reina had to be killed.

In his so-called *Last Testament* Luciano claims, "I really hated to knock off Tom Reina, and none of my guys really wanted to either. Reina was a man of his word, he had culture, and he was a very honorable Italian." This need not be taken as pure gospel. Luciano gained the allegiance of Gagliano and Lucchese by promising them the Reina empire.

On the Wednesday night of his murder, Reina, as he did once every week, had dinner at his aunt's home on Sheridan Avenue in the Bronx. When Reina left the house, Vito Genovese, a Luciano underling, was waiting. Reina was surprised to see him but started to wave his hand at Genovese. As he did, Vito blew his head off with a shotgun.

Joe Valachi would later marry the dead Reina's daughter, but his information on the Reina assassination, as on a number of other matters, was of only limited value.

RELES, Abe "Kid Twist" (1907–1941): Murder, Inc., killer and informer

When Abe Reles, a Brooklyn gangster, was picked up by police in 1940, he sported a rap sheet with 42 arrests accumulated over a 16-year period. Hauled in on charges of assault, robbery, burglary, possession of narcotics, disorderly conduct and six charges involving murder, he nevertheless had done only six minor stretches, with never a single major conviction.

Reles might well have eluded conviction again. The law didn't know the *real* Abe "Kid Twist" Reles, a man who had personally taken part in at least 30 murders. The law also did not know there was such a thing as an organization later to be dubbed Murder, Incorporated, the enforcement arm of the new national crime syndicate. Some cops knew about something called "the combination," which linked up a great many Jewish and Italian mobsters, but that such an organization had a special troop to handle assassinations was something they had not even guessed. Murder, Inc., did exist and had by then handled something like 400 to 500 murders in the 1930s.

But once Reles started singing in what was called the most remarkable "canary act in underworld history," goggle-eyed investigators cleared up 49 murders in the borough of Brooklyn alone, many of which they hadn't even known had happened. Reles knew; he had been in on the ground floor when Murder, Inc., was created. He qualified as a second-rung leader in Murder, Inc., standing just below such top leaders of the extermination "troop" as Louis Lepke and Albert Anastasia. As an underworld stool pigeon, he was much more highly placed than Joe Valachi, for instance, and his information was much more accurate.

When Reles was picked up in 1940 along with other major and minor members of Murder, Inc., on suspicion of homicide, Kid Twist started worrying that someone else of importance might start talking. He opted to save his own skin by talking first. His deal with prosecutors: He would not be prosecuted for any murder he participated in provided he revealed it, divulged all the details and named all his accomplices.

Then Reles started talking. He said that such troop members as Pittsburgh Phil, Happy Maione, Dasher Abbandando, Charlie Workman, Mendy Weiss, Louis Capone, Chicken Head Gurino and Buggsy Goldstein, to name some, were sent on murder assignments not just in New York but all around the nation, at times to knock off characters whose identities they didn't even know. Reles (like Pittsburgh Phil) was proud of his handiwork and often trekked down to Times Square after a job to pick up

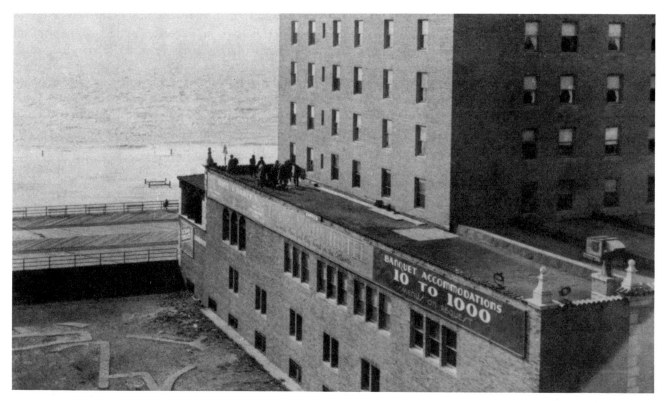

Murder, Inc., "canary" Abe Reles flew out a window of a Coney Island hotel while in police custody. Was it a jump, fall or heave?

an out-of-town paper to find out just who some of his victims were.

One murder Reles "read about in the *Times*" was that of a loan shark named Whitey Rudnick. Working as a team Pittsburgh Phil, Dasher Abbandando and Happy Maione had stabbed him more than 60 times, smashed open his skull and, just to be on the safe side, strangled him. Reles was not exactly contrite about the Rudnick killing, announcing that Rudnick deserved what he got since "he was a stool pigeon."

Abbandando and Maione were to go to the chair for that one. Pittsburgh Phil was not prosecuted for the crime, but only because the prosecution had so many others to choose from. (Phil committed somewhere in excess of 100 Murder, Inc., rubouts.) Reles doomed Phil and Buggsy Goldstein for the vicious garroting of a gambler named Puggy Feinstein. Reles provided so much information on the rubout of crime kingpin Dutch Schultz that one of the hit men, Charlie Workman, after reviewing the mounting evidence against him, switched to a plea of guilty to settle for a life sentence instead of the electric chair.

Kid Twist's grand jury testimony helped build a successful case against the great crime boss Louis Lepke as well as two important Lepke aides, Louis Capone and Mendy Weiss. They were convicted for the assassination of a garment industry foe named Joseph Rosen, but Reles was not around to testify at the trial.

He had taken part in several trials for more than a year, during which time he was kept under close protective custody on the sixth floor of a wing of the Half Moon Hotel in the Coney Island section of Brooklyn. Sometime during the early morning hours of November 12, 1941, Reles jumped, fell or was picked up and heaved out a window to his death— this despite the fact that he was always guarded by six officers and was never supposed to be left alone in a room, even while he slept. In Reles's room, police found several sheets tied together and proceeded to develop a variety of theories, some rather amusing. They said he was trying to escape, or climb down one floor so that he could then romp back upstairs and scare the daylights out of his guards in a malicious prank, or commit suicide. If it were a suicide attempt Reles apparently wanted to climb down the sheets part way so that he wouldn't have to fall too far. The hitch in all the police theories was that the Kid's body had landed a good 20 feet away from the wall of the building, which would have made him a gymnast of near-Olympic abilities.

Twenty years later, an ailing Lucky Luciano, one of the chief founders of the national crime syndicate in the early 1930s, insisted that Frank Costello had set up Reles' demise and that $50,000 had been distributed within the police department to have Reles flipped out the window. Years after that, interviews in Israel with Meyer Lansky and Doc Stacher confirmed Luciano's story, but the fee was $100,000 in all—evidently the wealth was not enjoyed only by members of the police department.

The syndicate at the time had not been averse to sacrificing all those who were electric chair–bound but wanted Reles's evidence halted before he doomed more, including Albert Anastasia and Bugsy Siegel. In later inquiries, William O'Dwyer, then the Brooklyn district attorney and later mayor of New York, was subjected to intense criticism for failing to prosecute Anastasia in what was described as a "perfect case" based on Kid Twist's testimony. O'Dwyer insisted the case "went out the window" along with Reles.

In the 1945 prosecution of Anastasia, O'Dwyer's performance was denounced by a grand jury as one of "negligence, incompetence and flagrant irresponsibility." In the words of the grand jury O'Dwyer was

> . . . in possession of competent legal evidence that Anastasia was guilty of first degree murder and other vicious crimes. The proof admittedly was sufficient to warrant Anastasia's indictment and conviction, but Anastasia was neither prosecuted, indicted nor convicted. . . . The consistent and complete failure to prosecute the overlord of organized crime . . . is so revolting that we cannot permit these disclosures to be filed away in the same manner the evidence against Anastasia was heretofore "put in the files."

There were worse innuendoes swirling around Reles's death. Ed Reid, the prize-winning reporter for the *Brooklyn Eagle*, charged that "Reles served several purposes besides being a fount of information about gang activities. Some of the information he gave out was used by unscrupulous persons connected with law enforcement in Brooklyn—to shake down gangsters."

Had Reles remained alive, other important members of the syndicate, beyond even Anastasia and Siegel, might have been nailed, and a far more lethal blow would have been dealt the crime syndicate. As it was, Murder, Inc., was smashed—as it existed in Brooklyn—but the syndicate continued to grow.

As for Abe Reles's epitaph, he was "the canary who could sing but couldn't fly."

See also MURDER, INCORPORATED

"RESPECT" in the Mafia

There has probably been more nonsense written about *rispetto*, or "respect," among mafiosi than about any aspect of the organization. For example, important dons are shown "respect" when assassinated; it is required that they be shot from in front, that they have the right to know they are being killed with the proper decorum.

Actually Mafia hits, regardless of the target, are made as quickly and efficiently as possible. Often the rubout occurs while victims are dining. Since they are usually sitting with their back to a wall, a shot in the face is more practical than polite. And a shot from the front also eliminates errors of victim identification and, ultimately, is more likely fatal.

Possibly one of the few truly respectful Mafia killings was that of mobster chieftain Willie Moretti. Very popular with most of the Mafia, he was erased in a "mercy killing" because he was "going off his rocker" and babbling too much. He was shot in front. In 1985 Gambino crime family boss Paul Castellano was shot from in front as he got out of his limousine, but then few people get out of automobiles backwards.

In major Mafia rubouts, such dons as Salvatore Maranzano, Albert Anastasia and Sam Giancana got absolutely no respect in the way they were killed. A longtime boss, Vince Mangano, ended up permanently missing and thus allowed not even a funeral, hardly a sign of respect. When the would-be assassin of Frank Costello called out to him, "This is for you, Frank," before firing, he probably was not trying to make Costello turn and take the bullet in the face. He was more likely trying to freeze a moving target.

Regardless of assassination modus operandi, Mafia bosses are treated with deference. They demand it and they get it, not out of respect but out of plain fear. In Sicily the *gabelloti* (loosely, tax-men), mafiosi who kept order on great estates and then came to own them, earned respect for their capacity for violence. A corporation executive earns "respect" from his underlings because he can sever them. A Mafia boss severs his inferiors; only the method varies slightly.

It is hardly surprising that mobsters scrape and bow before their boss, speak in hushed tones, hold doors, offer seats and speak only when spoken to. According to one son of a New York family boss: "My father would light a cigarette and five people would jump to push the ashtray close to him. At dinner, people would wait to speak until he spoke to them. If he put down his fork, you stopped eating, even if you weren't finished. My father was god to everybody."

Respect has come to have an entirely different meaning in the modern American Mafia. It is a quality dominated by the dollar sign. Top mafiosi demand their underlings show respect by turning over a portion of their illegal earnings. A mobster who bows and scrapes but gives no money is a candidate for a car trunk. Similarly, when members of a crime family move on to the turf of another don, he takes offense because this is not showing respect—and appropriate revenues that should be his. As informer Vinnie Teresa has pointed out, New England Mafia boss Raymond Patriarca demanded respect by getting a piece of the action on everything that went on in his domain. He always took a piece of the profits but never a piece of any losses. Once Patriarca joined a conspiracy to handle a load of stolen cigarettes. He put up $22,000 but after the loot was obtained, the FBI seized it. Patriarca wanted to know from nothing. He was only a partner in profits, not losses, and the other conspirators had to scrape up $22,000 to pay him back.

Still Patriarca could himself exhibit respect toward older dons, even though they were retired and played no more role in crime and could do no more than sit around on chairs on the sidewalk. Patriarca saw that they got their cut and an envelope out of some kind of mob racket. If there was a serious mob problem, he also called them in for consultation. He knew they were familiar with the members of organized crime all around the country and their characteristics. Teresa said that Patriarca felt gratitude toward them: "They got the town [Boston] in the bag, and it's been in the bag ever since. They were the ones who made the connections with the police departments. They'd

had connections in the district attorney's office for thirty or forty years. They made the mob."

One Mafia boss who always demanded the trappings of respect was Carlo Gambino. In that sense his mob presence was far different than his public image of a mild, turn-the-other-cheek, vulnerable little man. But he was transformed in mob contracts. He followed all the demands of honor his position commanded and exercised the little-known points of honor among mafiosi. If he shook hands with a person he did not accept, he turned his palm under the other's, making it clear he was merely going through the motions. If he accepted the man, he shook hands by putting his own palm on top.

Again, though, Gambino's main interest in honor lay in the requirement of payment as a sign of respect. He granted a subordinate, Joe Paterno, supervisory rights for the crime family's affairs in much of New Jersey. Paterno was expected to hand over a certain percentage of the take. If the amount stipulated was 25 percent, Paterno turned over that amount religiously. Similarly, criminals operating under Paterno had to do the same. One criminal engaged in long-term looting of a manufacturer's warehouse had to get Paterno's approval to operate. He also had to show respect by paying Paterno 10 percent of what he stole each week. Paterno was rather easygoing about it. As the criminal later related, when he gave Paterno $200 at the end of the week it meant he had taken in $2,000 in total. Paterno never questioned the mobster's word. Actually, he was cheating Paterno and Paterno probably knew it. But on the other hand Paterno was getting 10 percent of something for doing zero percent. That was respect.

RESTAURANTS and the Mafia

The day after Paul Castellano was rubbed out along with a top aide outside the Sparks Steak House in December 1985, the crowds were out in force. Some of the people had come to eat at the East 46th Street, Manhattan, restaurant, others merely to gawk, take pictures, and try to find bloodstains amid the drippings of oil and anti-freeze at the spot where Castellano had fallen.

In the crowd was a somber-faced restaurateur. He told reporters he would have "dragged the body around the corner to my place" if he had realized how much publicity the killing would generate.

Inside Sparks, regular patrons of the restaurant bewailed the fact that the establishment would now be so popular that they would have a hard time getting a table thereafter. Only in New York, ran the consensus of opinion both inside and outside the steakhouse, would people step over bodies lying in the street to get into a popular eatery.

Mafia watchers over the years have had to become restaurant watchers. One Sparks street groupie suggested that New York restaurant guidebooks add a category of those eating places where Mafia hits occur. A diner inside Sparks observed: "I always eat at these places. Would Mafia dons eat at crummy Italian restaurants?"

The point was well taken. When police raided a Forest Hills, Queens, restaurant named La Stella in 1966 and arrested 13 important mobsters from around the country at what was dubbed a "Little Apalachin" meeting, the New York Times made a notable contribution to investigative reporting by dispatching its food critic, Craig Claiborne, to the restaurant. He gave La Stella an impressive two-star rating.

The fact that so many Mafia hits have occurred in restaurant settings has been cited as a sign of respect to a marked Mafia don—he should be accorded a last meal. More likely, the reason there are so many kills in restaurants is that they are one of the easiest places to catch victims off-guard. When Joey Gallo was assassinated and his bodyguard shot at Umberto's Clam House in New York's Little Italy, they were sitting with their backs to the entrance when gunmen came in and started shooting.

There is a myth that mafiosi sit with their backs to the wall at all times. An old Mafia custom of drilling

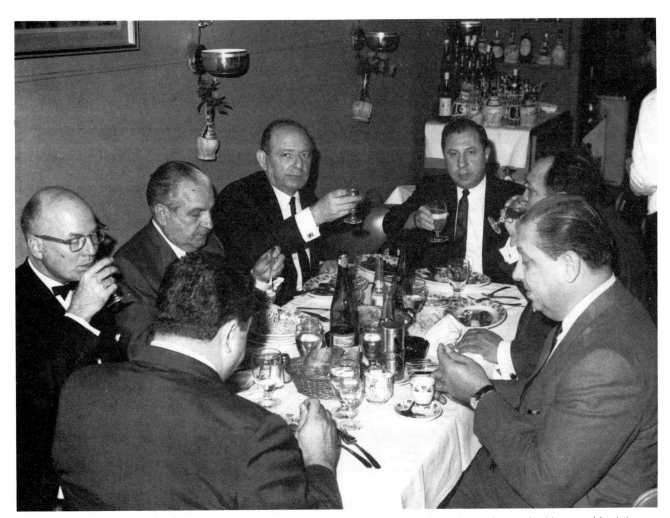

Several mafiosi and their lawyers return to New York's La Stella Restaurant where the mobsters had been nabbed during a "Little Apalachin" meeting. Santo Trafficante (third from left) toasts the news photographer. The New York Times promptly dispatched food critic Craig Claiborne to the restaurant, and he accorded it an impressive two-star rating.

a hole in a wall, shotgun-size, long ago discouraged such safety tactics. More commonly, mafiosi will make reservations at a restaurant and on entering ask that their table be changed—as a safety precaution to throw off any well-laid assassination plans.

Carmine Galante, the head of the Bonanno family, was making a move to gain dominance over the other crime families in 1979 when he made the mistake of taking lunch on the rear patio of the Joe and Mary Italian-American Restaurant in Brooklyn. Three men in ski masks appeared suddenly, taking Galante and his bodyguard by surprise and cutting them down. The restaurant, it might be noted, did not enjoy a big pickup in business—the owner was also slaughtered in the attack.

Joe the Boss Masseria was shot to death in a Coney Island restaurant where he had gorged on a ton of Italian food with his aide, Lucky Luciano, who had masterminded the plan to knock off Masseria. Luciano stepped into the washroom seconds before four gunmen came in and executed Masseria. The restaurant, Nuova Villa Tammaro, did a stunning business after the slaying, a situation pleasing for owner Gerard Scarpato, a friend of Luciano. Scarpato's joy did not last long. He was himself murdered a few months later when Luciano's other major rival, Salvatore Maranzano, was hit, completing Luciano's task of wiping out the old-line Mafia leaders in New York and permitting him to take part in building the new national crime syndicate. There is a theory that Scarpato was eliminated as a gesture by Luciano to remaining Masseria partisans that the past was no more and that everyone should start with a clean slate. On the other hand Luciano could simply have been tidying up. Murder charges enjoyed no statute of limitations, and Scarpato might simply have been viewed as a bit of a threat.

Another mobster to exit in a restaurant was Dutch Schultz, cut down with three aides in a Newark chop house on orders of the new ruling body of the syndicate in 1935.

Little Augie Pisano was set up in a restaurant named Marino's in New York in 1959. His killer or killers apparently hid in the back of his car and forced Pisano to drive to his and a lady friend's place of execution on a dark Queens street.

In actual restaurant killings it is remarkable how few innocent bystanders get hurt. Perhaps this reflects a Mafia tradition to reduce public anger. Occasionally, however, there are slipups. In August 1972 four businessmen were dining in the Neapolitan Noodle Restaurant on New York's East 79th Street when they were all summarily executed by a hit man said to have been imported from Las Vegas. His target had been four members of the Colombo family. He simply shot the wrong diners.

RICCA, Paul "the Waiter" (1897–1972): Chicago mob leader

Known for his elegant manners and dress, Paul Ricca was probably as traditional—and stereotypical—a mafioso as the Chicago Outfit ever sported. Paul "the Waiter" Ricca, both soft-spoken and mean, issued his fearsome murder instructions with a simple phrase, "Make'a him go away." The object of such orders was of course as good as dead.

Ever since Al Capone's departure from the scene in the early 1930s, controversy has raged among journalists as to who has been the boss of the Chicago Outfit. Among those held to be in command were Greasy Thumb Guzik, Frank "the Enforcer" Nitti, Tony Accardo, Sam "Momo" Giancana, Joey Aiuppa and Paul Ricca. In fact, for 40 years Ricca was the top man. He frequently delegated duties to others but no important move was made without his permission. He was always consulted. Ricca's death in 1972 was regarded by the mob as the passing of the Patriarch.

Ricca came to America in 1920 from Sicily. When he was 17 he had killed one Emilio Parrillo for which he eventually served two years in an Italian prison. He was also questioned about scores of other murders, including 14 in a family feud, but nothing came of that. Upon release from prison for the Parillo killing, Ricca went right out and slaughtered Vincenzo Capasso who had been the chief witness against him in the Parrillo trial. Ricca then fled Italy and ended up in Chicago, where he worked first as a theater usher and later as a waiter, a job which not only earned him his nickname, but also provided him with an answer when asked by police about his occupation. Ricca wrangled an introduction to Al Capone and since they had mutual friends among certain gangsters who had returned to the old country, he was quickly accepted into the Torrio-Capone mob.

Ricca became a power in the Capone days, known to Big Al as a man who could figure the angles in any sort of racket. It was a mark of Ricca's prestige when

Capone stood up as best man for him at his wedding in 1927. Through the 1930s Ricca continued to grow in stature, and by 1939 he was well in command of the organization. Within the Chicago syndicate power gravitated to the man strong enough and cunning enough to seize it, and the only ones regarded as even close to him in cunning and strength were Guzik and Accardo, but in each trait respectively.

Ricca understood that real power in the mob was determined by the street mobsters, and he knew how to rally force to his side. He had a long string of syndicate killers allied with him, many of them psychotics who would do anything to curry his favor. Ricca gave them plenty of orders.

However, as much as Ricca was dedicated to the bullet, he had great admiration for the bribe as well. A firm devotee of the fix, he paid off politicians at almost every level of government. Although he was arrested often and went to prison several times, he always seemed to get off with surprisingly short sentences. Together with much of the mob leadership, Ricca was caught in the enormous shakedown of the motion picture industry in the early 1940s. Along with most of the others he was sentenced to 10 years in 1943 but was released in August 1947 supposedly due to the intercession of Attorney General Tom Clark. The early paroles in the case enraged the Chicago press, which published Ricca's claims that his influence extended into the White House. Printed accounts had Ricca instructing his lawyers to find out who had the final say in granting him a speedy release, saying: "That man must want something: money, favors, a seat in the Supreme Court. Find out what he wants and get it for him."

While it must be noted that several of the Chicago newspapers were bitter enemies of President Harry Truman, the facts were that Attorney General Clark did allow the early parole of Ricca and the others to go through, and Clark was appointed to the next opening on the Supreme Court. In 1952 the conservative *Chicago Tribune* called for Clark's impeachment because of his "utter unfitness for any position of public responsibility and especially for a position on the Supreme Court bench." Its vitriolic editorial raged: "We have been sure of [his] unfitness ever since he played his considerable role in releasing the four Capone gangsters after they had served the bare minimum of their terms."

From the mob's viewpoint, the important thing was having the masterful Ricca back in circulation and once more the real power in the Chicago underworld. Tough Tony Accardo, who had visited Ricca in his cell by masquerading as his attorney, had kept Ricca informed of syndicate activities. Within a few years, Ricca, when he was so inclined, permitted Sam Giancana to give syndicate orders. But he and Accardo remained in the background, well insulated from official investigations. In the Kefauver Committee hearings on organized crime in the early 1950s, Ricca was dubbed "the national head of the Crime Syndicate." The McClellan Committee in 1958 referred to him as America's "most important" criminal. Ricca's testimony on the witness stand before each committee was punctuated by frequent pleas of the Fifth Amendment.

In 1957 Ricca was stripped of his citizenship and two years later was deported. Ricca resorted to a myriad of appeals and delaying actions, even getting a court stay on deportation to Italy by bringing an action before an Italian court, demanding that his Italian citizenship be dropped. In a remarkable action, the Italian government would not take Ricca back, even to serve out his old murder term, presumably because he might adversely influence Italian prisons and criminals.

Frustrated American immigration officials ordered Ricca to apply to other countries to grant him refuge. Following instructions, Ricca sent letters to some 60 countries, supposedly seeking asylum. But apparently, in an idealistic desire for full disclosure, he also included a packet of news clippings to explain why the United States wanted him to emigrate elsewhere. No nation expressed the slightest interest in accepting him. The government was still trying to deport Ricca when he died in 1972.

By then Ricca might well have accepted deportation to Italy. He spent many hours at the Alitalia terminal at O'Hare Airport listening to Italian tourists speaking the native tongue. The consensus was that Ricca had turned a bit senile, spending so much time at the airport, but federal agents suspected he was arranging meetings with smugglers of contraband or drugs.

Ricca died in bed in October 1972, an event that would cause shockwaves in the outfit. He had been Giancana's staunchest supporter, there being no accurate count on the number of victims Giancana had made "go away" as Ricca wished. Giancana had acted too irrationally for Chicago's liking through the 1960s, and Ricca agreed with Accardo that he had to be trimmed back in power. However, as long as Ricca lived Sam was safe, as were some of Giancana's more erratic backers like Mad Sam DeStefano. Within months of Ricca's death DeStefano was murdered by the mob. A couple of years later Giancana was assassinated as well. Ricca's hand was all-powerful, but not from the grave.

RICCOBENE, Harry (1910–): Philadelphia Mafia war combatant

He looked, a prospective juror in a murder case once said, like "a little Santa Claus." At 74, Harry Riccobene, short and with a flowing white beard, resembled St. Nick only in appearance. One of the leading mafiosi struggling for power in the Philadelphia crime family during the brutal gang war of the early 1980s, Harry Riccobene was better known for hot lead slugs than holiday toys.

The Philadelphia conflict started after the rubout of the longtime don of the Philly Mafia, Angelo Bruno, in 1980. Bruno had been murdered by New York Mafia elements who decided to terminate Philadelphia's traditional right to the rackets in Atlantic City. The New York mobs, especially the Genoveses and the Gambinos, felt it had been all right for Philadelphia to enjoy such primacy when the seashore city was in a state of decline, but the coming of the lavish and legal casinos altered that view. Atlantic City was now bigtime and the New York mobs moved in quickly and swatted Bruno away. Bruno's successor, Chicken Man Testa, apparently also tried to resist New York; he was assassinated in 1981 by a remote-control bomb placed under his porch.

Leadership now fell to Little Nicky Scarfo who had two worries—New York and the elderly, but murderously spry, Riccobene. As near as could be determined, Little Nicky reached an agreement with the New Yorkers in which rackets in Atlantic City were to be shared, if not on a 50-50 basis at least on one that gave Philadelphia something other than hot lead. Riccobene was another matter. There were going to be no compromises between the two sides. And Riccobene also wanted Atlantic City.

The warfare that followed was byzantine. Riccobene gunners took out Scarfo capo Frank Monte, the number three man in the faction, with six bullets from a telescope-equipped rifle at a range of 100 feet. After several tries they also killed Salva-

tore Testa, the wild 28-year-old son of the late Chicken Man, snatching him, clad in tennis whites, as he was off for a match. (Young Testa had such a fearsome reputation that when he and two other Scarfo men took up posts outside the Philadelphia jewelry store of Riccobene's nephew, Enrico, the jeweler opted to commit suicide rather than come out to face them.) Riccobene lost his half-brother Robert who was cut down by a Scarfo gunner loping by in a jogging suit.

However, the Monte killing easily constituted the most bizarre incident of all. It started out when Monte declared his faction was taking over Riccobene's lucrative loan-sharking and gambling business, said to be worth more than $550,000 a year. Monte approached Harry's half-brother Mario and demanded he set up his older half-brother for execution. Mario, in a temporary outburst of fraternal devotion, informed Harry of the plot. It was then that Harry Riccobene ordered Mario, and two dedicated hit men in his outfit, Joseph Pedulla and Victor DeLuca, "to get them before they get us."

The killers waited for several hours in a camping van for Monte to appear and approach his Cadillac on a Philadelphia street. When he did, Pedulla later admitted he "poked the barrel of a gun out the van's back window" and pumped bullet after bullet into Monte. Unfortunately, Mario Riccobene, DeLuca and Pedulla were all arrested, for a non-fatal shooting of Salvatore Testa; other information linked them to the Monte killing. All three finally turned state's evidence in the Monte case when the prosecution agreed they would have to serve no more time than what they got for the Testa shooting. All three thus served up Harry Riccobene for sure conviction on first-degree murder charges.

Harry took the witness stand to deny he sanctioned any murders. "I'm not a boss of anything," he said innocently. Why, he testified, he had advised restraint by his panicked associates when they expressed concern about death threats from the Scarfo side, which he characterized as nothing more than unfounded rumors. It was not an argument that impressed the jury very much.

Perhaps the most intriguing testimony came from Mario Riccobene, who said he had decided, in part, to testify against his half-brother because that way he could hope to get free some day and be able "to get back at the people who did what they did to my family."

It was evident that fraternal devotion was not dead in the Mafia although it could at times become somewhat murky in its application.

See also SCARFO, NICODEMO "LITTLE NICKY"

RICO: 1970 Racketeer Influenced and Corrupt Organization Act

It had been a steady parade over the years: aging Mafia mobsters making court appearances and putting up bail. They were flanked by lawyers and bodyguards and quickstepped their way past a gauntlet of reporters, photographers and television cameramen, snarling and cursing and fending off cameras with coats and umbrellas. Occasionally a top mafioso or two was forced to do a short prison stretch, terms, as they said, they could "do sitting on their heads." But Mafia prosecutions consistently amounted to little due to lack of evidence.

In the mid-1980s, the federal government tried a new tactic, belatedly utilizing RICO, the 1970 Racketeer Influenced and Corrupt Organization Act. RICO allowed for long prison terms if the government could prove Mafioso connection to a criminal "enterprise" or to a criminal "commission" that functioned as a criminal enterprise.

Why did it take 15 years for the U.S. Justice Department to go all out with RICO? In the 1970s juries simply were not convicting RICO cases, and appeals courts differed on the statute's proper use. Finally, in 1981 the Supreme Court resolved the disputes with a generous interpretation of federal power. Suddenly, long prison terms hit mob leaders in Los Angeles, New Orleans and Cleveland. These efforts were carried out in some cases by FBI forces and prosecutors who weren't at all sure the tactic would really work. In 1985 the biggest case of all was launched against the five New York crime families. The top echelon gangsters of these groups were still astonished and outraged that they could be convicted under RICO by their very membership in the Mafia or the National Commission. When Frankie "the Beast" Falanga was brought in a federal prosecutor's office and informed he would be indicted on RICO charges, he flew into a rage and bounced out of his chair, screaming, "RICO? I don't even know any fucking RICO!" Some said he took the whole thing so seriously that he dropped dead just before going to trial.

In late 1986 the commission case concluded with the conviction of Fat Tony Salerno, Carmine "Junior" Persico and Tony Ducks Corallo. Even though John Gotti was acquitted in 1987 on 69 counts of federal racketeering and conspiracy charges and six of his aides were also cleared, Gotti would be nailed under RICO five years later. By then RICO had gained the stature of the atomic bomb of criminal law.

But even an activated RICO was not viewed as sufficient to stop organized crime. Sending crime leaders to prison for 30 or 40 years or longer didn't really interrupt the Mafia as long as its machinery remained intact. Some bosses continued running their organizations from prison. Legal experts agreed that the big test for RICO was the fact that it authorized seizure of illicitly obtained wealth and its proceeds. If RICO could crack that nut—take away their bars, their restaurants, their carting companies, even their casinos—the Mafia would collapse. By the late 1990s that matter was still in dispute by some who found the evidence at best anecdotal on the financial accomplishments of the law.

The catch was that RICO was being used in ways never intended by its framers, but this reflected the difficulty of fashioning a law against one group of people while immunizing most other citizens. Business spokespeople have become highly critical of RICO. Many critics had noted that in the 1980s the law was used by non-governmental forces, since it allowed for triple damages for extortion. Thus Greyhound bus lines sued the Amalgamated Transit Union for trying "to extort wages and benefits from Greyhound," even though the union was engaged in a lawful strike.

By late 1989, the Justice Department revised its RICO guidelines so that homes and businesses would not be confiscated in all cases and innocent third parties ruined by zealous enforcement. Critics agreed this helped but there were other concerns, such as the law being applied to political situations. Not surprisingly, when a federal jury in 1998 in Illinois found that people picketing abortion clinics were guilty of extortion, the anti-abortion forces claimed RICO was being used to deny free speech and equating their protest with racketeering.

Among those upset was G. Robert Blakey of the Notre Dame Law School, considered to be the father of the RICO law. He insisted that in the Illinois case, "The judge and jury are succeeding in morphing coercion into extortion." Others did not necessarily agree.

It all represented the contradictions within RICO. Such conservative voices as *Investor's Business Daily* denounced the Illinois decision. It did not criticize the jurors but simply called the decision "a defeat for free speech. And RICO is to blame."

It seems clear that more challenges to RICO are in the offing, but whether they ever aid the cause of mobsters remains to be seen.

RICO, H. Paul (1925–2004): Ex-FBI agent charged with helping arrange a mob killing

When in 2003 H. Paul Rico, a 78-year-old former FBI agent, was indicted on a murder charge for aiding mobsters in the killing of a wealthy Oklahoma businessman, it was yet another black eye for the FBI in the Boston office whose members had been convicted of working with a section of the Boston underworld. Rico was a longtime player in the Boston scandals that ripped the federal agency in that state with charges of aiding and protecting members of the notorious Winter Hill Gang run by James Bulger in his war with Mafia elements.

In 1981 55-year-old Roger Wheeler, president of the Telex Corporation and owner of World Jai Alai, a major player in the gambling business, was murdered in Tulsa, Oklahoma. At the time Rico was chief of security of World Jai Alai. The hit man was John Martorano of the Winter Hillers, who would later testify against the biggest fish of the rogue FBI agents in Boston, John Connolly Jr., in an arrangement in which Connolly became in essence a member of Bulger's gang and helped gang members who were his informants. Connolly was convicted in 2002 and went to prison for 10 years.

A key witness against Connolly was hit man Martorano who also implicated Rico in an alleged homicide, the murder of Roger Wheeler. Martorano admitted the hit and told the court in the Connolly case that Rico approached him about taking out Wheeler because the gang figured the World Jai Alai executive had discovered that the mob was skimming $1 million a year in jai alai profits. According to the hit man informer, Rico had provided him with a physical description of the intended victim, along with the make and license number of his car and his home address. After that, Martorano testified, he shot Wheeler point blank in the head as he got in his car after a round of golf. The record seemed to indicate that although the Tulsa police had tried earlier

Former FBI agent H. Paul Rico, 78, is shown in this October 10, 2003, Dade County, Florida, Detention Center photo. Rico was arrested at his home near Miami and was charged with conspiring with his old informants in the 1981 murder of Oklahoma businessman Roger Wheeler.

to charge Rico for the murder, no case came to pass until in 2003 when he was indicted by a grand jury. A lawyer for Martorano insisted the FBI had not acted in the Oklahoma charge and that the indictment had been caused by a runaway grand jury. The office of the Tulsa County district attorney issued a statement that it had "no comment at this time on the ongoing criminal investigation into the murder of Roger Wheeler." Needless to say the news media, the public and law enforcement showed keen, even explosive, interest in the indictment both in Tulsa and Boston.

Rico died on January 17, 2004, at a Tulsa hospital while awaiting trial.

See also FBI BADFELLAS

RIDE, take for a: Underworld murder method

"Take for a ride" has long been a standard in the underworld lexicon, coined in the bootleg wars in Chicago in the early 1920s by Hymie Weiss, one of the leaders of the North Side O'Banion Gang. When Steve Wisniewski hijacked one of the mob's loaded beer trucks, Weiss was accorded the duty of exacting the proper retribution. He invited the unsuspecting Wisniewski for a drive along Lake Michigan, from which he never returned. As Weiss later explained, "We took Stevie for a ride, a one-way ride."

Weiss set the standard for other mob killers, instigating a technique identifiable to the press as "a professional job." Weiss decreed that from the back seat a hit man put a .45 to the back of the victim's neck as he sat in the front seat of the car. At the proper moment the gun was fired. As Weiss explained to fledgling hit men, it was important to make sure the bullet did not "take a course"—that is, be deflected by a bone so that in an outlandish quirk the victim might survive. Even more embarrassing would be an instance in which the bullet might be deflected by the skull and slant off into the driver of the car instead.

RIESEL, Victor (1914–1995): Journalist and Mafia victim

A nationally acclaimed journalist specializing in labor affairs, Victor Reisel, at the peak of his popularity in 1956, had his syndicated column published in 193 newspapers. In a post-midnight radio broadcast in New York on April 5, 1956, Riesel attacked the abuses of racketeering in Local 138 of the International Union of Operating Engineers on Long Island. He particularly went after William C. DeKoning Jr., the head of the local, and his father William C. DeKoning Sr., fresh out of prison after doing time for extortion. Riesel had also attacked Teamsters leader Jimmy Hoffa, who was known in a moment of rage to have said that something had to be done about Riesel's probing columns.

After the broadcast the labor columnist dropped into Lindy's, a landmark Broadway restaurant at 51st Street. About 3 A.M. Riesel left the restaurant. As he reached the sidewalk a young man approached him and hurled a liquid into his face and eyes. The liquid was sulfuric acid; Riesel was left permanently blind.

A federal investigation determined that the assailant was 22-year-old Abraham Telvi, who had been hired by two ex-convicts long active in garment industry rackets. Most important, authorities arrested John Dioguardi, better known as Johnny Dio—a leading labor racketeer who traced back to Murder, Inc.—as the mastermind of the blinding plot. A few minor associates of Dio's were convicted. Two others were prepared to testify against Dio, but

Labor reporter Victor Riesel gets emergency treatment after his acid blinding.

after receiving death threats, they refused and Dio went free.

Some three and a half months after the acid attack on Riesel, Telvi was shot to death on the Lower East Side. After he had seen how much heat was generated by the crime, he had been demanding more pay for his role in the matter.

See also DIO, JOHNNY; TELVI, ABRAHAM

ROBERTS, Johnny (1904–1958): Hit-man murderer of Willie Moretti

Johnny Roberts, one of the murderers of New Jersey mob leader Willie Moretti, became a "made" member of the Mafia the hard way. He was also taken out the hard way.

Roberts, whose real name was Robilotto, was originally sponsored for membership in the Mafia by Tony Bender but was rejected because his brother was a policeman. Albert Anastasia had more muscle than Bender, and he succeeded in getting him admitted to membership. After that Roberts became a trusted Anastasia capo and expert killer.

The police came up with sufficient information, if not legal proof, that Roberts was the gangster who in 1951 brought Willie Moretti into a New Jersey restaurant. When the waitress went into the kitchen, Moretti was shot to death by Roberts and two or three other men who then fled, leaving only a couple of hats behind. One of the hats was traced by a cleaning mark to a place right across from a building where Roberts's brother lived. Waitresses tentatively—but only tentatively—identified Roberts from a picture as the man who came in with Moretti. However, neither hat fit Roberts. Informer Joe Valachi, a close friend and frequent loan-sharking and rackets partner of Roberts, said when he asked Roberts about the hats, the latter replied, "Don't worry . . . it ain't my hat . . . it belonged to the other guys."

There seems little doubt that the Moretti murder was carried out on Anastasia's orders. A Mafia consensus had been reached that Moretti was talking too much because of illness, and had to be eliminated in a "mercy killing." Roberts was arrested for the murder, but later the charges were dropped for insufficient evidence.

Roberts stood in good mob graces as long as he served Anastasia, but when Anastasia was murdered in 1957, his situation altered. Carlo Gam-

bino, a partner in the conspiracy to erase Anastasia, moved to take over the crime family but faced strong opposition from others who remained fiercely loyal to the memory of their departed boss. The clique was headed by Armand "Tommy" Rava, and for a time Roberts agreed to join his group. Joe Valachi went to visit Roberts to advise him not to join in *any* conspiracy, but Roberts shrugged him off, saying, "Don't worry about it, Tony [Bender] and Vito [Genovese] already spoke to me." He was staying out of it.

Roberts was caught in the shifting currents of mob loyalties. It appears, contrary to what he told Valachi, that he did join the conspiracy for a while. Later, according to Valachi, Roberts told Rava "he wanted to be counted out of it" and "they killed him because he was trying to declare himself out."

The 54-year-old Roberts turned up dead on a Brooklyn street corner with multiple gunshot wounds in the face and head. In an episode not reported in *The Valachi Papers* but occurring after Roberts's murder, Carlo Gambino's brother, Paul, visited Valachi and, according to Valachi, said, "I have a lot of respect for your opinion regardless of how other people feel. What should we do [about the conspirators]?" Valachi said he told Gambino: "Go right ahead before they pounce on you."

Chances are Valachi was coloring what really happened. Probably the Gambinos had pumped Valachi on who Roberts may have told him were in the conspiracy against them. Chances are Valachi revealed plenty to them. In *The Valachi Papers* he appears less than sanguine, saying simply, "I heard later it was true [that Roberts had been in the conspiracy], him and some other boys—fifteen or twenty—were going to pounce on Carlo, but he beat them to it. Well, no matter what, everyone mourned Johnny Roberts." It may well be that Valachi actually informed on Roberts and almost certainly on Rava and others. A few days after the Paul Gambino visit, Rava and his pals were located in a club in Brooklyn. A large number of shots were fired, and Rava and others were killed. It was said Rava was secretly buried. Although Rava was never found, the New York police presumed he was very much deceased.

Valachi was always considered a small-timer within the Mafia, but he showed a more finely honed instinct for survival than his pal Johnny Roberts.

See also MORETTI, WILLIE

ROBILOTTO, John   See ROBERTS, JOHNNY

RONSISVALLE, Luigi (1940–   ): "Hit man of honor" and informer

Before Sammy "the Bull" Gravano turned informer, one of the most important mob turncoats was Luigi Ronsisvalle, a slit-eyes mob hit man who boasted of 13 killings—five in Sicily and eight in the United States. He was characterized as a "diabolically funny mob hit man." In a field where murderers were a dime a dozen, he cut out a unique niche for himself.

Ronsisvalle insisted to investigators that he was a "hit man of honor," one who considered himself as more moral than other killer imported by the Bonanno crime family and certainly more upstanding than his new bosses.

He always claimed to have the finest motives for his killings, such as loyalty to the family and so on. Indeed, he could have been a model for some of the mob killers fashioned by Mario Puzo in *The Godfather*. Since that book appeared just about the time of Ronsisvalle's arrival in America in 1966, it might well have been that Ronsisvalle copied his persona from the novel.

At first Ronsisvalle never dreamed of violating omerta, the code of silence. When he first came to America at the age of 26, his father gave him some sage advice: "When you see something, shut your mouth. If you see something you don't like, run around. If you hear things that don't belong to you, don't hear them. Mind your business. That's most of the rules."

Ronsisvalle honed the persona of an honorable hit man and considered many of his killings most ethical. Some examples include

- A gambler who could not cover his last bet in a poker game and desperately put up his wife. He lost the hand and took the other two card players home to enjoy the sexual favors of his wife. Later she tearfully complained to her brother, who took up a collection to buy a murder contract on the husband for $2,000. Ronsisvalle thought it a most moral endeavor and waited outside the man's house until he emerged early one morning to go fishing. He whacked him out with several shots. Ronsisvalle was annoyed when asked the name of the victim. "I don't know his name," he said simply.

- In a hit that would have done the fictional Don Corleone proud, a man came to the Mafia to complain that a cook who worked in a Brooklyn restaurant had raped his 14-year-old niece. Ronsisvalle cornered the cook in his kitchen and put him down permanently with five shots.

Ronsisvalle considered himself blameless in any of his killings. "In a sense, the way I believe it," he explained, "you give me thirty thousand dollars, and I am sent to kill a person. You kill him, not me."

It saddened him that the rest of the mob did not match his highmindedness. There was no honor among them, he found. Once Ronsisvalle helped a fence and three associates from the Gambino family rob a diamond dealer on New York's West 47th Street. The associates stiffed Ronsisvalle out of most of his share. When he complained, the fence tried to set him up with a woman in a hotel room and murder him. Ronsisvalle threatened violence and the loot was divided at a high-level sit-down involving the Bonanno and Gambino families. Ronsisvalle still felt he had not gotten all he was entitled to. Gambino boss Castellano walked away from the meeting with a $10,000 diamond in tribute for himself.

The high-minded hit man was further disillusioned about the honor in the mob. Michele Sindona, a notorious Italian banker with close ties to the Mafia in both Italy and the United States, tried to recruit Ronsisvalle to murder the government attorney in New York who was prosecuting him. Sindona offered $100,000 for the job. The offer frightened the hit man because he knew that unlike the custom in Sicily, the mobs in America never killed law enforcement people.

Sindona's plot fell through. Shortly thereafter Ronsisvalle was arrested for a petty crime and contacted Sindona for bail money. The rogue banker felt Ronsisvalle was seeking to extort blackmail and would simply keep the bond money, so he refused the demand. Ronsisvalle, however, was not bluffing and was consumed by a feeling that the bail money refusal was an "affront" to old country Mafia rules. Thus the incident became the catalyst for him to flip and admit all to the authorities, including his record of 13 murders. Ronsisvalle was simply done with the Mafia's so-called ethics.

He said he was tired of the rackets, especially of drug dealing. He proved a key government witness, one of the most valued underworld turncoats since

Joe Valachi about two decades earlier. Ronsisvalle eventually went into the witness protection program.

See also SINDONA, MICHELE

ROOM of death: Palermo torture and murder chamber

The Mafia, both in the United States and Italy, has traditionally established "murder houses" where wholesale killings could take place without the troublesome need to keep moving around. One such place in Brooklyn was bossed by the notorious Roy DeMeo, butcher for Paul Castellano and the Gambino family. An even more brutal operation was run in a decrepit storehouse near Brancaccio, a rundown section of Palermo, Sicily. Some of the Brancaccio victims died for their knowledge about Italian Mafia matters, but perhaps an equal number were silenced to stop leaks about the "Sicilian connection," the heroin pipeline from the island to the United States. Victims were seldom dispatched quickly but tortured to ascertain what smuggling secrets they might have revealed to authorities. Undoubtedly, some of the victims cleared themselves under the tortures but were too far gone to survive. Still the local mafiosi were not unhappy about such miscalculations since the horrors of the Palermo "room of death" remained a valuable lesson to cohorts considering defecting.

New inductees to the Mafia were sometimes taken to the room of death to witness the slow, painful killing of a suspected informer. As the victim, finally, gratefully, expired before an inductee's eyes, he was informed, "That's how you could die."

During the massive arrests against the Italian Mafia in the 1980s, the bosses of the Cupola—the ruling Sicilian Commission—found it wise to shut down the murder room. The boss or bosses overseeing the deadly acts there were assassinated. This spirit of mob tidiness is hardly unusual. The same fate awaited Roy DeMeo when his operation got too hot. Undoubtedly, his erasure was approved by Gambino boss Castellano, even though DeMeo had always been one of Big Paul's most ardent supporters and a most willing executioner.

See also DEMEO, ROY

ROPE trick   See ITALIAN ROPE TRICK

ROSELLI, John (1905–1976): Chicago Outfit figure and Las Vegas power

Although technically Johnny Roselli was a mere soldier in the Chicago Outfit, he was one of its most potent powerhouses, serving as the mob's—and Sam Giancana's—representative in Las Vegas. All the family's business there had to be coordinated by Roselli. It was he who looked after Chicago's portion of the skim and decided when a Las Vegas offense required a "hit." This was true even though Roselli always followed the Chicago (and other mobs') doctrine: Kills had to take place outside Nevada or, at the very least, a corpse had to be dumped beyond state lines so there would be no heat.

Roselli was born Filippo Sacco in Esteria, Italy, and came to America in 1911 with his mother. They settled in East Boston where his father, who had gone ahead, was working. His father died suddenly, and Johnny's mother remarried. His stepfather, Roselli maintained, turned him to a life of crime by talking him into burning down the family home. The stepfather then decamped with the insurance money. Because the insurance company was suspicious of young Sacco, he quit school in the seventh grade and ran away from home, never again contacting his family, although he did arrange through the years to have money sent to them.

Using the name of Johnny Roselli, he hooked up with the Capone Mob and continued to grow within the mob after Capone's fall. In the late 1930s Roselli represented Chicago's interests in Hollywood and extorted $1 million from movie companies by threatening to have unions under his control slow production, causing studio costs to soar. Sentenced along with a number of Chicago crime figures, Roselli did three years for the caper but returned to Hollywood still a powerhouse. He even produced a number of crime films, including *He Walked By Night,* in which the law always triumphed—not over organized crime but rather over lone-wolf-type criminals. If he'd had his druthers, Roselli would have given up his life of crime to become a maker of Hollywood B-movies. His idea of the top man in Hollywood was Brynie Foy, known at Warners as the "Keeper of the B's."

Roselli clearly loved the Hollywood life and even made it into the fabled Friars Club. It was an event to remembered by other Friars. In 1968 Roselli and four confederates swindled a number of Hollywood personalities—including singer Tony Martin and comedians Phil Silvers and Zeppo Marx—out of

$400,000 in a crooked card game. It was a typical Chicago Outfit caper, involving peepholes in the ceiling so that observers could see the players' cards and signal a confederate in the game via equipment he wore in a girdle under his clothes. That Roselli could take Zeppo Marx in such a scam was a tribute to his ability, since Zeppo was one of Hollywood's shrewdest crooked gamblers.

None of this altered Roselli's role in Las Vegas as Chicago's rep, and it was a credit to his efforts that such major operators as Moe Dalitz and Meyer Lansky never shorted the outfit.

Roselli was linked along with his superior, Chicago boss Sam Giancana, with Operation Mongoose, the so-called CIA-Mafia plot to assassinate Cuba's Fidel Castro. Castro had tossed the underworld out of Cuba, and the Lansky-Chicago forces were out a fortune from their shuttered Havana casinos. Giancana figured that killing Castro would open up Cuba once more. Roselli was perhaps a bit more sanguine. He realized the plot would get nowhere and like certain other Mafia leaders, such as Tampa's Santo Trafficante Jr., used Mongoose as a scam to swindle the CIA.

In 1975 Roselli testified at a special hearing of the Senate Intelligence Committee five days after Giancana had been murdered in his Oak Park, Illinois, home. Giancana had also been subpoenaed, but his death prevented his testimony. There was considerable speculation that Giancana was killed because certain elements, either in the underworld or in the CIA, did not want the scamming of the intelligence agency known. Roselli solved his testimony problem by talking much and saying little. He disclosed some details of Mongoose, and said he looked upon his efforts as a "patriotic" expression of his love for his country. He said that plots involving poison pills and poisoned cigars had failed. He did not tell the senators that no poison ever went to Cuba, that instead the mobsters had simply flushed it down the toilet. They did not do the same with CIA funds given them to organize the various plots with their supposed Cuban allies.

After his CIA testimony, Roselli's lawyer urged him to hire a bodyguard, but Roselli laughed it off. He had done long service to the mob and felt he was safe going into retirement in Plantation, Florida. "Who would want to kill an old man like me?" he asked. Privately, however, Roselli was talking about the way the CIA had been conned. He was known to

have become friendly with columnist Jack Anderson. What he might have been saying was probably discomforting to some people.

In late July Roselli was asphyxiated, and his body sealed in a 55-gallon oil drum. Holes were punched in the drum and heavy chains coiled around it to weigh it down, and the drum was dumped into Florida waters. The idea was to make the drum stay down indefinitely, but gases caused by the decomposing body brought the drum to the surface.

"Deep Six for Johnny," *Time* magazine headlined its full-page story on Roselli. The magazine noted: "Roselli was one of a breed that is dying off—usually by murder."

See also BARREL MURDER; CIA-MAFIA CONNECTION; GIANCANA, SAM; OPERATION MONGOOSE

ROTHSTEIN, Arnold (1882–1928): Criminal mastermind

Today Arnold Rothstein is remembered by students of crime as the so-called mastermind of baseball's worst gambling disgrace, the Black Sox scandal of 1919 when the World Series was fixed. Rothstein was a multimillionaire gambler, but he was much more than that. Indeed, he stands as the spiritual father of American organized crime.

He was known by many nicknames—Mr. Big, the Big Bankroll, the Brain, the Man Uptown, the Fixer. All were accolades to his importance in the world of crime, to his connections with the underworld and the upperworld of police, judges and politicians. Although he operated strictly in the background, Rothstein may well have been the most important criminal of his era. At various times he financed the criminal activities—in fact, usually masterminded them—of the likes of Waxey Gordon, Dutch Schultz and Legs Diamond. He was the early tutor of Lucky Luciano, Meyer Lansky, Frank Costello and Johnny Torrio. (Torrio never returned on a visit to New York from Chicago without having discussions with Rothstein.) It is generally acknowledged that Torrio, and later Lansky and Luciano, learned from Rothstein the joys of forming alliances, regardless of ethnic considerations, not only with underworld confederates, but also, above all, with those who could perform the political fix. The dollar, Rothstein pointed out, had only one nationality, one religion—profit.

Rothstein became known to all as the man who had influence everywhere and could fix anything. He could clear virtually any illegitimate activity through his political and police contacts. During Prohibition, a later study showed, Rothstein intervened in literally thousands of bootlegging cases that went to court. Of a total of 6,902 liquor-related Rothstein-era cases, 400 never even came to trial while another 6,074 ended in dismissal. Most of the credit had to go to Rothstein whose credentials with Tammany leader Charles Murphy were impeccable. Rothstein's record in prostitution and gambling cases was equally as impressive.

Rothstein and Murphy altered the way graft was collected in New York. Up until their time the standard procedure was to use police as major graft collectors, allowing the politicians to remain somewhat aloof from the process. This was possible when the politicians, the hub of all illegal activities, bought the criminals and used them as they wished. With the new wealth of Prohibition, the central power shifted to the criminals—and above all, Rothstein. He could buy the political leaders, and insisted on direct payoffs to eliminate possible police defections. The police got separate graft but they now became secondary to the power of the criminals and the politicians. When the criminals wanted changes in police procedures, the politicians saw that those changes were made. Is it any wonder that Rothstein in 1925 served as the inspiration for Meyer Wolfsheim in *The Great Gatsby* and later on for Nathan Detroit in the musical *Guys and Dolls?*

The Rothstein style was to hang back, to remain in the background while still seizing a major portion of all loot. Prohibition, he realized, was too immense a field to be dominated by one man or even one gang, so he moved himself into the safest part of the racket, importation, the area most insulated from arrest. Through aides, he made agreements with European distilleries for supplies. In that fashion he made himself immune to gangland assassination—if he was killed, the flow of good liquor would slow. He was simply too valuable to be allowed to die. (This was a lesson Meyer Lansky learned well, especially in gambling and the movement of money. The Mafia's later dependence on Lansky allowed him to move freely among the various gangs, indeed to be recognized as the ultimate power. That "Meyer is a Jew and has no vote" was a fiction maintained in the lower ranks of crime. The fact was that when the "Little Man" spoke, all the mobsters listened.)

Rothstein learned how to keep the various gangs content by apportioning supplies among them. By

Arnold Rothstein's importance in criminal history is frequently underestimated. Remembered as a gambler and fixer in baseball's Black Sox scandal of 1919, he was actually the bankroller and spiritual father of American organized crime.

the mid-1920s, he had already started tapering off his interest in the booze racket, realizing Prohibition had to end some day. He was already laying the groundwork for a number of criminal empires—gambling, labor racketeering, diamond and drug smuggling. In fact, Rothstein was thinking in terms of a national syndicate. Lansky and Luciano, who instinctively leaned that way, heard his message clearly.

But Rothstein, the Brain, self-destructed. Gambling obsessed him and he bet compulsively. He made huge bets, won some and lost more. In 1928, Rothstein played in one of Broadway's most fabulous poker games, one that lasted nonstop from September 8 to 10. At the end, Rothstein was out $320,000. That Rothstein could lose shocked the wise guys of Broadway, but not nearly as much as the fact that Rothstein welshed on the debt. He declared the game had been fixed.

On November 4, Rothstein was murdered at the Park Central Hotel. The prime suspects were the two California gamblers who had beat him in the game, Nigger Nate Raymond and Titanic Thompson. The case was never solved, and there have long been

394

reports that the debt was merely a cover for the real motive of the murder, that an ambitious Dutch Schultz saw a chance to increase his own empire vastly by knocking off Rothstein.

Ironically, no suspicion ever rubbed off on Lansky and Luciano who profited most by Rothstein's demise. It was they who moved on his ideas for a new syndicate. They developed close ties with labor racketeers Louis Lepke and Gurrah Shapiro, who in turn reached understandings with Schultz and other Jewish gangsters. And they gained the support of the young mafiosi and other Italian criminals who eventually purged the old-line Mafia leaders Joe the Boss Masseria and Salvatore Maranzano.

Lansky and Luciano became the fathers of the national crime syndicate, and in many respects Rothstein's pivotal role was forgotten. Instead, his name is more widely recalled in constant retellings of the Black Sox scandal, and how he was alleged to have planned the fix by bribing several players of the Chicago White Sox to throw the World Series to the underdog Cincinnati Reds. Supposedly, Rothstein financed the great baseball betting coup through ex-featherweight boxing champion Abe Atell, although no firm evidence supports this. It is known that he was approached for financial backing, and it is also known that, at least at first, he withheld agreement. Rothstein probably didn't put up any money, realizing the deal was so good it would go through with or without him. So why should he pay out bribe money? Instead, Rothstein remained aloof, simply bet $60,000 on his own on Cincinnati, and won $270,000. That version surely reflects the real Arnold Rothstein.

See also GARMENT INDUSTRY RACKETS; LEPKE, LOUIS; LUCIANO, CHARLES "LUCKY"; ORGEN, JACOB "LITTLE AUGIE"; SEVEN GROUP; SHAPIRO, JACOB "GURRAH"

RUM Row: Bootleg fleet

Within months of the onset of Prohibition on January 16, 1920, organized crime had set up floating liquor markets, or "Rum Rows," all the way down the Atlantic coast and along the Gulf of Mexico. Flotillas of rumrunners rode the swells just beyond the three-mile limit, where they were safe from Coast Guard interference, and awaited the arrival of small speedboats belonging to bootleggers who figured they could load up with booze and outrace a government cutter to shore.

Eventually these fleets stood off Boston, New York, Norfolk, Savannah, Tampa, Mobile, New Orleans and Galveston, but the most important Rum Row stretched from Maine down to New Jersey. European goods, especially Scotch, were unloaded here, as well as huge quantities of liquor from Canada.

Easily the most famous rumrunner of the day was the founder of the New England/Mid-Atlantic Rum Row, Captain William McCoy, whose goods were always first-rate and unadulterated—thus both he and his contraband liquor became known as "The Real McCoy." McCoy preferred serving the New York area because that was where the money was. One of his prime customers was Joe Adonis, who handled the imports for the Broadway Mob headed by himself, Lucky Luciano, Frank Costello and Meyer Lansky. The Broadway Mob supplied good whiskey to all the speakeasies in Manhattan, and while it was common for some importers to duel with the government gunboats known as rum-chasers, the Adonis fleet seemed for some reason to have less trouble than others. Part of this good fortune appears attributable to Frank Costello who was already functioning as a fixer for the mob.

Rum Rows, which included every type of vessel afloat from old fishing boats to luxury cruisers and yachts, remained an embarrassment to law enforcment

The U.S. Coast Guard ambushes a small boat trying to bring booze ashore from "Rum Row."

for the life of Prohibition, strikingly visible confirmation that Prohibition was too profitable and served too many customers to ever be enforceable.

RUPOLO, Ernest "the Hawk" (1908–1964): Stool pigeon and Genovese hit victim

The violation of omerta, the mafia code of silence, generally means quick and fatal retribution, but in the case of Ernest "the Hawk" Rupolo, a low-level mafioso, the punishment was slow mental torture.

Rupolo, like many another hoodlum, made it on Vito Genovese's death list. Rupolo's offense was rather daring; he was one of only a few men who had ever testified against Genovese, whose temperament and reputation for ruthlessness generally discouraged such informers.

The gang leader had given Rupolo a contract to kill another mobster, Ferdinand Boccia, in 1934. Nailed by the authorities for several other offenses, Rupolo sought leniency by ratting on Genovese, who avoided prosecution by fleeing the country in 1937. Genovese was brought back from Italy in 1945 to stand trial for the Boccia murder, but he beat the rap after the only corroborative witness, Peter LaTempa, conveniently was slipped some poison while he was being held in jail in protective custody.

This left Rupolo in a very embarrassing position. His testimony had proved useless, and he faced Genovese's vengeance. Still the government felt honor-bound to free Rupolo, although agents strongly advised him to remain in prison. Knowing well that Genovese's power reached behind bars—LaTempa's demise proved that—Rupolo felt he had no choice but freedom.

Remarkably, nothing happened. This did nothing to alleviate Rupolo's fear of murder, and finally he realized that Genovese was taking a full measure of vengeance by making him squirm. Over the years Rupolo lived a terror-filled existence, running in fright whenever he saw a Mafia hoodlum. Was this the one, his hit man?

When Genovese was sent to prison in 1959, Rupolo must have experienced the long-forgotten feeling of elation. But he knew and the underworld knew Genovese still enjoyed his suffering. But by 1964 Joe Valachi had talked, and Genovese's bloodlust needed fulfilling. He could not get Valachi, but someone had to die. Rupolo's squirming no longer pacified Genovese. In August, Rupolo disappeared from his usual haunts, and on August 27, his mutilated corpse was fished out of Jamaica Bay. It was pockmarked with dozens of ice pick wounds, and the back of his head had been blasted away.

There was no one to testify to Genovese's involvement in the murder.

RUSSIAN Mafia: Disorganized crime

Does the so-called Russian Mafia constitute genuine "organized crime"? This is more than an esoteric question. It involves an understanding of what has happened in organized crime in the last decade or so. Is the Russian Mafia really a threat to the American Mafia? Or is it a prop that has aided the traditional Mafia to make a strong comeback, which has become more apparent in the beginning of the 21st century? In the 1990s it was clear that the Department of Justice, while proclaiming its triumphs over the Mafia at the time, had no interest in pursuing this "other Mafia." As the *Washington Post* reported, ". . . since the Justice Department does not consider the Russian mob to be organized crime, it doesn't treat it with the seriousness that it reserves for more VIP criminals." It was noted neither the FBI nor the New York City police was doing much about the Russian "Mafia." The *New York Times* declared the Russians were not a major enforcement problem since they were tiny in size. In the assessment of the Russian Mafia in the early 1990s it was found that the findings of the Immigration and Naturalization Service consisted of little more than material taken from the *Times*.

Less knowledgeable investigators have insisted that the Russians perpetrate many of the crimes practiced by mafiosi, going so far as attributing the word *Malina* as the Russian term for "Mafia." Actually, however, *Malina* is used by Odessa criminals both in Russia and in the United States as a generic term for the underworld; it literally means "raspberry." It is very difficult for law enforcement to get a handle on Russian crime groups because they are disparate in numbers and loyalties. The government has not been able to put a number on the gang members, and even the name of "Russian Mafia" is somewhat of a misnomer, since a great number of the criminals are of Soviet-Jewish background.

Many members are in this country legally as political refugees, but it is known that within this group are considerable numbers of Soviet criminals who are not Jewish at all but had acquired their identities from dead or incarcerated Jews in the Soviet Union. Some, it has been alleged, further launder their identities by first immigrating to Israel before moving onto the United States. Still others are suspected to have been long time "sleepers" planted in the United States with fake identities by the KGB. Left on their own with the fall of the Soviet Union, these former agents gravitated toward the crime groups. Most criminal groups come from various geographical locations, such as the Odessa Gang—historically the most violent of criminals in the country—the Kiev Gang, the Moscow Gang, the Leningrad Gang and smaller scattered groups called "gypsy gangs."

From time to time some of these groups have attempted to unite or at least cooperate with one another, but such arrangements are very fluid and are marked by such great treachery in the divisions of spoils that they simply degenerate into warfare far greater than that seen in the American Mafia in its brutal organizing years. The various Russian Mafia groups have tried to move into such areas as Philadelphia, Los Angeles, and as far away as Toronto, Canada. They may pull singularly brutal crimes but operate without any trust within their own ranks and with corrupt elements on the outside. Thus the Russian Mafia apparently will never achieve full maturity but will operate simply as junior partners with various mafiosi who at the turn of the century were demonstrating that their power has ceased to diminish. Rather, they frighten the Russian Mafia and other ethnic groups into subservience to the elements who still control within the American power structure.

See also AGRON, EVSEI; ODESSA BY THE SEA; OTHER MAFIAS

S

ST. LOUIS crime family   See PILLOW GANG

ST. VALENTINE'S Day Massacre: Capone mass killings

At first Al Capone probably regarded the St. Valentine's Day Massacre of February 14, 1929, a monumental success, although the main target, his archenemy Bugs Moran, avoided the slaughter. After all, knocking off six rival members of the Irish North Side Gang in one fell swoop was a noteworthy coup. However, Capone soon learned a massacre of St. Valentine's proportions really riled up the citizenry; for the first time, all the people of Chicago looked upon him not as their vital bootlegger, but as a savage, coldblooded murderer.

Of course, Capone denied having anything to do with the crime, but there is no doubt it was a Capone operation from start to finish. Capone gunners, dressed up as policemen, carried out the executions not only of the gangsters but also of an innocent man who happened to be around at the time.

The massacre had been part of the long-raging war between the Capone mob and the heirs of the North Side gang headed by Dion O'Banion in the early 1920s. By 1929, a series of leaders, starting with O'Banion, had been shot to death, and only George "Bugs" Moran remained capable of running the North Siders, frustrating Capone's efforts to take over their lucrative racket area.

Capone set up the North Siders by having a Detroit gangster offer Moran a load of hijacked booze. Bugs jumped at the proposition, and agreed to take delivery of the goods at the gang's headquarters, a garage at 2122 North Clark Street. What followed was to shock not only Chicagoans but people throughout the civilized world; no other gangland rubouts ever received the publicity given the St. Valentine's Day Massacre. Several Capone gangsters, dressed in policemen's uniforms, rushed into the garage at the appointed time. They lined up the Moran henchmen—Adam Meyer, Al Weinshank, James Clark, John May and brothers Frank and Pete Gusenberg against the wall, along with Dr. Reinhardt H. Schwimmer, an optometrist and gangster groupie, who just happened to be around. The gangsters offered no resistance, figuring it was nothing other than a routine police bust. Then two of the raiders cut loose with Thompson submachine guns, mowing the seven victims down like rats.

Only one thing was amiss—Moran was not one of the victims. Having overslept, he and two others, Willie Marks and Teddy Newbury, had just rounded a corner near the garage when they saw what appeared to be police officers going inside. Moran figured the raid was a mere police shakedown and decided to remain out of sight until the officers left. When the machine-gunning started, the trio took off. Brought in during the ensuing investigation, Moran moaned, "Only Capone kills like that."

But at first the massacre was not regarded as a Capone hit. Many people actually believed the killers had been real police officers. The Chicago police were held in such low esteem that it seemed entirely possible. Frederick Silloway, the local Prohibition administrator, told reporters:

The murderers were not gangsters. They were Chicago policemen. I believe the killing was the aftermath to the hijacking of 500 cases of whiskey belonging to the Moran gang by five policemen six weeks ago on Indianapolis Boulevard. I expect to have the names of these five policemen in a short time. It is my theory that in trying to recover the liquor the Moran gang threatened to expose the policemen and the massacre was to prevent the exposure.

The next day Silloway was singing a different tune, saying his statements were taken out of context and that he was misquoted. If that were true it was one of the most monumental misquotations there has ever been. Silloway's Washington superiors ordered him transferred from Chicago, in the way of placating local authorities, but a cloud of suspicion continued to hang over the police. More and more, though, public opinion turned against Capone, as people started agreeing only Capone could kill like that.

Major Calvin H. Goddard, a leading expert on forensic ballistics, was imported from New York. After he tested the bullets, he declared that they had not come from any machine gun owned by the Chicago police—or at least all those he examined. About a year after the murders, the police came up with the death weapons. They were found in the home of a professional killer, Fred Burke, who was known to have done jobs for the Capone organization.

In April 1930, Burke was caught in Michigan but was never brought to Illinois to be tried for the

The brutal St. Valentine's Day Massacre held such morbid fascination with the public that some newspapers actually ran inserts of closeups upside-down so that victims could be more readily identified by readers. More important, it marked a turning point in the public's tolerance of the Capone mob.

massacre. Instead, he was convicted in Michigan for the slaying of a policeman and sentenced to life imprisonment—there was no death penalty in the state. The underworld started whispering that Illinois was afraid to try him because his testimony would prove the guns had been planted in his home. Despite a flood of accusations over the years, the culprits in the St. Valentine's Day Massacre were never identified. The cast of characters kept changing, and the only one known to a moral certainty to have taken part was Burke. Aiding him, according to one theory, were Shotgun Ziegler, Gus Winkler, Crane Neck Nugent and Claude Maddox. It was generally held that the planning for the job was in the hands of Capone enforcer Machine Gun Jack McGurn.

Capone was severely criticized at the 1929 underworld conference in Atlantic City for the massacre, and he finally agreed that he would go to jail for a brief period on some kind of charge to defuse public opinion. A bust on a gun charge was arranged for in Philadelphia, and the Chicago gang leader did a short stint under rather comfortable surroundings in Pennsylvania. That was the limit of justice exacted for the St. Valentine's Day Massacre.

SALERNO, Anthony "Fat Tony" (1911–1992): Alleged boss of Genovese crime family

In October 1986 *Fortune* magazine rated Anthony "Fat Tony" Salerno, the 75-year-old head of New York's Genovese crime family, as America's top gangster for power, wealth and influence. Not all experts would agree with that assessment or indeed, despite federal prosecution of Salerno on racketeering charges, that he ever became the boss of the Genovese clan (since the death of Funzi Tieri in 1981). They hold the theory that elderly Philip "Cockeyed Phil" Lombardo really reigned.

What is not in dispute is the fact that Fat Tony through the years was able to strike terror in others, at least outside the Mafia, if not quite as thoroughly within it.

Under Genovese boss Tieri, Salerno functioned at times as consigliere while at the same time allegedly bossing a $50-million-a-year numbers racket in Harlem, as well as a major loan-sharking operation. While there is much talk about the Mafia being pushed out of the ghettos by the emerging black and Hispanic gangsters, Salerno has long given the lie to

that line. For years one of Harlem's biggest operators, Spanish Raymond Marquez, reportedly paid Salerno 5 percent of his income for the rights to operate. Of course, it has always been alleged that everyone doing business in Harlem—be they black, brown, white or yellow—had to give Fat Tony something.

The reason: The wrath of Fat Tony was considered awesome. Fear of Salerno has even extended to informers placed under the federal witness protection program. One such witness who uninhibitedly identified a New Jersey Mafia boss, Gyp DeCarlo, balked when asked to identify Fat Tony. The witness had already testified that Fat Tony Salerno had been involved in certain wrongdoings, but on the stand he got cold feet and declared he had meant another Fat Tony Salerno.

In the 1970s and 1980s Salerno divided his time among Miami Beach, a 100-acre estate in upstate Rhinebeck, New York, and his apartment on posh Gramercy Park in Manhattan. He provided an indoor riding arena and private schooling for his children, and spent $27,000 on new cars—all on a declared income of $40,000. Salerno was sentenced to a six-month jail term in 1978—for the first time—on gambling and tax evasion charges.

Under him the Genovese crime family was said to operate in numerous fields and rackets, including narcotics, gambling, loan-sharking, extortion, waterfront activities, pornography, union rackets, carting rackets and vending machines.

Fortune started its hit parade of the nation's top 50 mob bosses in 1986 as a list somewhat akin to its annual list of America's top 500 companies. It said organized crime is a $50 billion a year industry and "mirrors the management structure of a corporation."

Impressed by Salerno's trappings of wealth, common to many top mobsters, the magazine declared him to be the top "earner" of the underworld. Lost in their description is an authoritative picture of the shifting tides of Mafia power. From the late 1950s until his death in 1976, Carlo Gambino became the top mafioso in New York and the nation, in the process raising the smaller, former Anastasia family to preeminence over the larger Luciano-Costello-Genovese group. Gambino was instrumental in the deposing of Genovese and slowly asserted his authority over the Genovese family, eventually installing Tieri, an old and loyal friend, as boss.

Before his own death, Gambino ordered control of his crime family passed to Paul Castellano, his

Cigar-chewing Fat Tony Salerno, surrounded by newsmen, was alleged to be the head of the Genovese crime family after the death of the powerful Funzi Tieri.

brother-in-law. Castellano, although he headed the most powerful crime family, did not get that much respect in the underworld; Tieri pushed his family back to the top rung, although, ever-loyal to Gambino, he never sought to depose Castellano. When Tieri died in 1981, Castellano and the Gambino family reasserted their old powers: Salerno and the Genoveses' efforts to expand through Philadelphia into Atlantic City were stunted, and the Gambinos took over more of the activities in the New Jersey gambling city.

Fat Tony maintained his tough-guy form right up to his indictment on RICO charges, when he realized his time had passed. Of all the defendants in the so-called Mafia Commission trial, Salerno seemed oblivious to any strategies to fight. During the trial, he spent his free time during recesses munching away on Baby Ruth and Mars bars and the like. Once while awaiting the return of the jury from lunch, he pulled out an Almond Joy.

A member of the prosecution's team, in a friendly moment, approached Fat Tony and offered him a granola bar, saying, "They're really much better for you, Mr. Salerno. Better than all that chocolate."

Fat Tony waved the granola bar away and said, "Who the fuck cares. I'm gonna die in the fucking can, anyway."

Fat Tony was right—he did die in the can five years into his 100-year sentence.

SALERNO, Ralph (1925–2003): Police expert on the Mafia

When Detective Sergeant Ralph Salerno retired from the New York City Police Department in 1967 he was regarded as knowing more about the American Mafia than any other person not sworn into the criminal society. He was reviled by the mob as an Italian who had "betrayed his own people" by turning in wise guys to the law. Recriminations and threats meant nothing to Salerno. One time he was confronted in court after a guilty verdict in a murder charge against the defendant's brother. The brother wanted to know how he could do such a "low-life" thing as hurting his own kind.

Salerno bristled, "I'm not your kind, and you're not my kind. My manner, morals and mores are not yours. The only thing we have in common is that we both spring from an Italian heritage and culture—

and you are the traitor to that heritage and culture, which I am proud to be part of." It was a lecture that undoubtedly soared way above the mobster's comprehension level.

What the mob came to recognize in Salerno is a policeman without fear and without temptation and a "master bugger." Salerno was considered the no. 1 expert on court-authorized wiretaps. He could determine by the nuances in an eavesdropped conversation if, for example, a wanted mobster was simply making himself scarce or had ended up "swimming with the fishes" or some similar sealed fate. Salerno's conviction total of Mafia types made him much sought after as an expert witness on loan-sharking and other criminal activities, and he appeared before both houses of Congress and in federal and state courts. He also lectured frequently at universities in the United States and Canada. When Salerno retired in 1967 he had put in more than 20 years in the police department's intelligence branch and as a supervisor of detectives in the central investigations division. He later served as a consultant in the Department of Justice and the National Council on Crime and Delinquency. His 1969 book, *The Crime Confederation,* is regarded a classic of the field.

SANCTIONED stoolie: Inter–crime family spy

The mob has frequently used informers as double agents to infiltrate other crime families and groups, including the police, in hope of discovering useful intelligence. In the assassination of Paul Castellano, head of the Gambino crime family and reputed boss of bosses, Frank DeCicco was a sanctioned stoolie for the Gotti group inside Castellano's inner circle and was the key man in setting up the godfather's rubout. (Four months later DeCicco was blown up in a car bombing).

A much honored sanctioned stoolie was Tommy Lucchese, also known as Three-Finger Brown, who was Lucky Luciano's favorite killer in the Mafia wars of the 1920s and 1930s. Later in the war between Joe the Boss Masseria and Salvatore Maranzano, Lucchese sided with Maranzano while Luciano was with Joe the Boss. Actually Lucchese was the inside spy for Luciano, who was determined to depose both bosses. Luciano accomplished half his goal by having Masseria murdered and then made a temporary peace with Maranzano, waiting his moment to strike. That came when Lucchese informed him of

Maranzano's plan to have Luciano assassinated by non-mob gangsters.

Luciano struck first as four men pretending to be police officers entered Maranzano's headquarters just as Lucchese "happened" to enter. Lucchese's presence was necessary because the hit men did not know their intended victim by sight. Maranzano was dispatched and the new de facto boss of bosses, Luciano, named Lucchese the head of one of New York's five crime families, which even after the latter's death in 1967 continued to bear his name.

SAN Francisco crime family   See MICKEY MOUSE MAFIA

SAN Jose, California, crime family   See MICKEY MOUSE MAFIA

SAUPP, John Joseph (1910–1962): Murdered convict

The prison murder of John Joseph Saupp, an inconsequential forger and mail robber, was, according to U.S. Attorney General Robert F. Kennedy, the "biggest single intelligence breakthrough yet in combating organized crime and racketeering in the United States."

Saupp's fatal misfortune was his striking resemblance to Joseph (Joe Beck) DiPalermo, a syndicate hoodlum and Atlanta prison associate of crime leader Vito Genovese. Genovese had decided that another prisoner, minor crime figure Joseph Valachi (who was doing time for a narcotics offense), had turned stool pigeon. He passed the death sentence on Valachi, and only by luck did Valachi survive three attempts on his life. Then Genovese, who was Valachi's cellmate, gave him the "kiss of death," indicating to Valachi that the campaign to kill him would continue and that he was doomed.

Valachi tried to be extra careful, waiting for the fourth attempt. He strongly suspected that among those out to execute the murder assignment was Joe Beck. On June 22, 1962, Valachi found himself surrounded by a group of prisoners, three of whom he suspected of being would-be killers. Just then another prisoner walked by him. Valachi, thinking it was Joe Beck trying to get behind him, seized a length of pipe from some nearby construction work and attacked his nemesis, banging him over the head.

Only after Valachi was taken to the associate warden's office did he discover he had fatally wounded the wrong man, that the victim was Saupp, a man he didn't even know. Saupp died about 48 hours later.

Valachi was now doubly on the spot. Mob leader Genovese still wanted him dead, and the authorities now had him on a murder charge. The only way out for Valachi was to turn federal informer. He did, and in his celebrated public testimony before Senator John McClellan's Permanent Subcommittee on Investigations, he revealed more secrets about organized crime than any witness up until that time.

John Joseph Saupp is chiefly remembered as the hapless catalyst who brought about Valachi's testimony. On his murder, Valachi, a longtime mob hit man, said, "You can imagine my embarrassment when I killed the wrong guy."

See also VALACHI, JOSEPH

SCALISE, Frank "Don Cheech" (1894–1957): crime family underboss

The murder of Frank "Don Cheech" Scalise remains, like many other Mafia murders, unsolved. But even more than most, the hit is tangled in a web of mob intrigue that almost certainly can never be unraveled.

A close ally of Lucky Luciano since Prohibition days, Scalise was part of the Mangano family and aided Albert Anastasia in wiping out the Mangano brothers so that Anastasia could take over the crime family. In fact, Scalise and Anastasia had long been partners in murder. According to Luciano, in August 1930 they had killed Peter "the Clutching Hand" Morello on his orders. (It was perhaps the most important killing of the Castellammarese War, since Morello was the adviser of Joe the Boss Masseria and, as Joe Bonanno put it, "the brains of his outfit." Luciano felt the same way about it and knew that once he had Morello killed, Joe the Boss would be relatively easy.)

Anastasia and his underboss Don Cheech were inseparable through the years and were constantly involved in all sorts of deals, shady even by Mafia standards. It was certain that in 1954 Scalise and Anastasia started selling memberships in the Mafia to eager applicants for $40,000 to $50,000 when the "books" or membership rosters, were opened for the first time since the early 1930s. It was said that Scalise collected about 200 of these kingsized kickbacks.

Frank Scalise's body lies covered up in a Bronx, New York, fruit store, a murder scene appropriated for *The Godfather*. His brother was to suffer a more grisly fate.

Now the guessing game begins. One theory has it that when Anastasia heard the accusations against his underboss, he angrily ordered his murder, and Scalise was cut down by four bullets in the neck and head as he was buying fruit at a favorite Bronx fruit stand (this was the model for the attempted assassination of Don Corleone in the *The Godfather*). Another theory was that the murder was ordered by Anastasia not out of anger, but to prevent further speculation that he, Albert A., was getting a cut of the membership kickbacks.

Another theory holds Scalise innocent of the charge, claiming that Vito Genovese, as part of a campaign to discredit Anastasia with whom he was involved in a struggle for control of Mafia affairs in New York, had cooked up the plot. Anastasia, the theory goes, simply outmaneuvered Genovese by having Scalise killed, a bit of double-dealing not beyond the Anastasia character. Still another theory maintains that Genovese had Scalise killed and then spread the word that Albert had done it. Since one of the gunmen was almost certainly Jimmy "Jerome" Squillante, a very close associate of Genovese, the Genovese theory looks best.

However, none of the Scalise murder theories is conclusive. Scalise was also known to be involved in drug smuggling, and it was said that he had welshed on his responsibility to reimburse his underworld partners when the government grabbed a heroin shipment. For that reason, Scalise was marked for death.

In any event, Genovese profited most from Scalise's demise, it being a fairly common tactic in the Mafia to knock off an enemy's most powerful supporter before going after the main target. It had been done in the case of Joe the Boss Masseria and in 1957 was shortly to be the case with Anastasia.

Confusion or no, the death of Frank Scalise was not without its touch of "honor." His brother Joe quickly vowed vengeance, but then noticed that Anastasia was staying rather quiet about matters. Joe Scalise dropped his vow and disappeared for a number of weeks, reappearing only when the word went out that all was forgiven, that it was understood he was merely expressing normal filial devotion.

Shortly after he came out of hiding, Joe Scalise was invited to a party at Squillante's home. Joe unwisely accepted and was barely inside the door when the boys fell on him with sharp knives. His corpse was butchered down to smaller pieces and carried outside to a waiting garbage truck. (Squillante bossed the New York garbage-collection racket at the time.)

See also SQUILLANTE, JIMMY "JEROME"

SCARFACE: Gangster movie

The Godfather was *the* Mafia movie of the 1970s, and one that has done much to form the public conception of organized crime today. But it was not the first popular film to do so.

Scarface was made in 1932. Preceded by two noteworthy crime movies, *Little Caesar* and *Public Enemy*—the former patterned after the exploits of Chicago's Cardinelli gang and the latter after that city's O'Banion Gang—*Scarface* enjoyed the greatest impact because of a notorious curiosity about and fear of Al Capone. Accurate about the scar, there remained questions about its authenticity—especially from Al Capone himself. At least Capone saw few

similarities—and sent a couple of torpedoes to check out the facts.

The screenplay had been written by Ben Hecht for Howard Hughes's studio. One night there was a knock on the door of Hecht's Los Angeles hotel room, and two sinister-looking hoods confronted him with a copy of the screenplay.

"You the guy who wrote this?" one demanded.

Hecht had to admit he was.

"Is this stuff about Al Capone?"

"God, no!" Hecht assured them. "I don't even know Al." He rattled off the names of Chicago underworld characters he had known in his reporter days—Big Jim Colosimo, Dion O'Banion, Hymie Weiss.

The Capone emissaries were appeased, one announcing: "O.K. then. We'll tell Al this stuff you wrote is about them other guys." As they started to leave, however, the other one had a thought. "If this stuff isn't about Al Capone, why are you calling it Scarface? Everybody'll think it's him."

"That's the reason," Hecht replied. "Al is one of the most famous and fascinating men of our time. If you call the movie *Scarface*, everybody will want to see it, figuring it's about Al. That's part of the racket we call showmanship."

This was a readily accepted explanation. If there was anything the Capones appreciated it was a scam. "I'll tell Al. Who's this fella Howard Hughes?"

"He's got nothing to do with it. He's the sucker with the money."

"O.K. The hell with him." Placated Capone's hoods departed.

The power structure of Chicago was not nearly as placated about *Scarface* however. As Ralph Salerno and John S. Tompkins have noted in *The Crime Confederation*, "The movie was so explicit in its exposure of municipal corruption that the city of Chicago banned it until World War II."

SCARFO, Nicodemo "Little Nicky" (1929–): Philadelphia crime family boss

He was described by one law enforcement official as Philadelphia's answer to Crazy Joe Gallo. That was one of the more favorable comments made about Nicodemo "Little Nicky" Scarfo, who after four years of unrelieved bloodletting, emerged in the mid-1980s as the undisputed leader of Philadelphia's crime family.

Lt. Col. Justin Dintino, head of New Jersey's State Police Intelligence Bureau, told a U.S. Senate committee Scarfo was "an imbecile." How then by 1984 had this "imbecile" jockeyed his way to the top of the Philadelphia Mafia underworld when in the last four years some 20-odd mobsters had been rubbed out? Frank Booth, director of intelligence for the Pennsylvania Crime Commission, said it was because "there is nobody left to challenge him." But Little Nicky Scarfo, with fierce instincts for survival, is a lot smarter than he is given credit for. Always on guard, he was confined in prison during part of the Philadelphia bloodletting and officials noted he actually patted down a son when he came to visit.

During the gang war, the 5-feet-5-inch Scarfo was sent away for 17 months to a federal penitentiary on a gun charge, perhaps a fortuitous sentence since it kept him out of the line of fire during the height of the killings. And Little Nicky, renowned for his hot temper and penchant for violence, turned his incarceration into a bona fide plus, maintaining and even enhancing control of his organization while in a prison 2,000 miles from his home. Probably realizing he was on top of the heap, Scarfo did nothing to upset his chances while behind bars, and showed the unusual forebearance actually to request he spend the last two weeks of his 17-month stay on a two-year sentence in solitary confinement. The reason: He had been feuding with another inmate and didn't want the dispute to get out of hand and in any way endanger his upcoming release.

There had been considerable speculation that Scarfo had succeeded where predecessors like Angelo Bruno and Phil "Chicken Man" Testa had failed. He cut deals that they had not been able to do, so that gunners from the much larger Genovese and Gambino crime families in New York stopped invading the City of Brotherly Love and knocking off the native mafiosi. Scarfo must be given credit for knowing how to count. There was no way he could match the soldiers the Genoveses and Gambinos could trot out from New York to back up their claims to the illicit business flowing from the Atlantic City casino industry.

Angelo Bruno, the "Gentle Don," who had ruled the Philadelphia mafiosi for two decades in relative peace, died because he could not count as well as Little Nicky. He thought he had the answer to the New York mobs' superior numbers in the rules of the Mafia. Atlantic City was long recognized as part of Philadelphia's territory, so Bruno, at times a member of the national Mafia commission, informed New York he stood by his rights under the bylaws of the Honored Society. No outside family could come in without being invited by the host Mafia and Bruno wasn't inviting.

However, there were megamillions involved in controlling restaurants, bars, beer distributorships, laundry, vending machines and other businesses, to say nothing of rights to run gambling junkets and more direct connections with the casinos. The only one interested in Mafia rules was Bruno, and when a gunshot tore a gaping hole in his head in March 1980, his objections became moot. His successor, Chicken Man Testa, was blasted away by a remote-control bomb. Then Scarfo took over and he cut his deal. If you can't beat your foes in a Mafia war, he reasoned, the next best thing is to join them. The pie was enormous in Atlantic City and Little Nicky settled for a healthy slice instead of trying the impossible and the suicidal by attempting to keep the whole bag.

Ironically, it was Angelo Bruno who set Scarfo up to take control in Philadelphia. He had been displeased with Little Nicky's violent ways way back in 1963 when the hoodlum got a prison term for manslaughter after stabbing a longshoreman to death in an argument about a seat in a restaurant. Bruno looked for the worst place to send Scarfo when he got out and decided on Atlantic City, which, in the mid-1960s, was a stagnant, depressed area. Ten years later the plush casinos were licensed and Little Nicky, in mob vernacular, "had really stepped in it." He was on the scene, had the connections with the power structure and suddenly was a big man in the mob—under Bruno and Testa, but coming on.

There were those seeking to unseat Little Nicky even after he apparently solved the New York rampage. The forces of Harry Riccobene, a diminutive man with a flowing white beard and a mean disposition, put up a stiff battle against Little Nicky. However, they did not give as good as they got (although they did kill Salvatore Testa, the 28-year-old son of the slain Chicken Man Testa, regarded as a real comer in the mob). Still the Scarfo men, sharing their leader's reputation for ruthlessness, drew more blood. Riccobene's nephew, Enrico, actually committed suicide when he learned that three of Little Nicky's boys were laying for him outside his Sansom Street jewelry store. And one of Riccobene's half

Little Nicky Scarfo (right) and his nephew Phil Leonetti raise their hands in thankful prayer after they and a third defendant are acquitted of murder. Later Leonetti avoided further charges by turning on his uncle as a federal witness, dooming Scarfo to spend the rest of his days behind bars.

brothers, Robert, was shot dead about the same time by a Scarfo supporter in a jogging suit. By the end of 1984 the 74-year-old Riccobene was almost certainly permanently removed from the crime picture when he was convicted in the murder of Frank Monte, a Scarfo loyalist.

Scarfo was definitely on top. Some called it dumb and murderous luck and predicted he would fall. They were right. Scarfo had too suspicious a nature and he soon turned to ordering the deaths of loyal followers, starting with Salvatore Testa, his most competent hit man, because he feared he would make a play for his position as family boss. For a time Scarfo wanted to kill two of his own cousins out of the same fear, but others talked him out of it. According to informer Phil Leonetti, Little Nicky even considered having his wife murdered because he felt she had "little by little" robbed him of "around $400,000." She was gambling at the Trump Plaza in Atlantic City.

As the body count mounted, many younger wise guys realized they could be the next victim of the mad boss's wrath, and they started defecting to the FBI. Scarfo, Leonetti and 15 others were convicted in 1988 on murder and racketeering charges. While they waited sentencing, there were further defections from among those convicted, the most important being Leonetti, who was Scarfo's "beloved"—to use Little Nicky's word—nephew and recently appointed underboss. Leonetti became a very important federal witness and guaranteed enough evidence against Scarfo that he would never be a free man again.

Scarfo ended up in Marion Penitentiary doing life in a maximum security cell where later John Gotti would also be lodged. Scarfo was known to refer to Phil as "my faggot nephew."

See also RICCOBENE, HARRY; TESTA, SALVATORE

SCARNE, John (1903–1985): Gambling expert and mob consultant

An internationally recognized authority on gambling, John Scarne was perhaps closer than he ever admitted to the forces in the national crime syndicate. That he met many of them in the capacity of gambling expert and helped them set up casinos that were cheat-proof—by the customers—was readily understandable. Scarne had great value to the gambling interests. His oft-proclaimed statement—that because of his skills he was barred from gambling in Las Vegas—made him the perfect shill, inferring to the public that the casinos could be beaten. But above all, Scarne clearly was himself fascinated by his contacts with mobsters—a fascination that has befallen many others.

Through the years, Scarne was acquainted with the likes of Arnold Rothstein, Frank Costello, Meyer Lansky, Joe Adonis, Bugsy Siegel, Frank Erickson, Albert Anastasia, Willie Moretti, Jake Lansky, Abe Reles, Santo Trafficante and countless others. And he was forever denying there was anything called the Mafia and the national crime syndicate. In a curious book he wrote in 1976, *The Mafia Conspiracy*, Scarne expounded his thesis that attacks on any Italian organized crime figure were nothing more than anti–Italian-American Mafia frameups by the federal government, determined to deprive the ethnic group of its civil rights.

Despite his track record as a best-selling author with some 18 books to his credit, Scarne could get no publisher to handle *The Mafia Conspiracy*, in which crime family boss Joseph Colombo was characterized as "the great Italian-American Civil Rights leader." Scarne claimed he had put up $50,000 of his own money to publish the book, but there were those who saw it as a mob apology, something the mob would gladly have financed.

The book is a bizarre document, clearly demonstrating Scarne's respect for—or awe of—Meyer Lansky, yet at the same time revealing a certain ethnic frustration, recognition of the fact that the Jewish elements within organized crime constituted the dominant factor in bigtime gambling, whether in Las Vegas, Cuba, Florida or upstate New York. Scarne noted that Tampa, Florida, crime boss Santo Trafficante was merely a part owner in some gambling enterprises in Cuba and that the Hotel Capri Casino was "the only one of the nineteen Havana casinos operated by an Italian-American group." In his desire to clear the Mafia of importance in Cuba, Scarne ignored the fact that Meyer Lansky allowed many Mafia families to have pieces of his many enterprises.

In his book Scarne defended Lansky from charges made by the government, especially those made by informer Vinnie Teresa that Lansky was involved in gambling casinos in England and the paymaster to various mafiosi running lucrative gambling junkets. A cynic might suspect that Lansky may well have aided in the book's publication. Lansky was a realist who understood the value of denouncing harassment of the mobs in terms of bigotry. Men like Lansky and Moe Dalitz could claim they were victims of anti-Semitism, so why not offer the Mafia the same sort of defense? And Lansky would have been shrewd enough to tolerate even an outburst or two from Scarne.

Thus Scarne identified Ohio's ruling gambling syndicate as the "Jewish Mob," headed by the likes of "Morris Kleinman, Moe Dalitz, Louis Rothkopf, Samuel Tucker and Thomas J. McGinty—all non-Italians." Scarne carried his conspiracy theory further, declaring: "It's my judgment that Senator McClellan and Senator Lausche introduced the Senate bill to outlaw the mythical Mafia simply as a diversionary tactic to protect the non-Italian mobsters operating in their home states of Arkansas and Ohio."

Scarne's book is not without value as a sociological document. Scarne would not have written it in the 1940s or 1950s or even the 1960s; by the mid-1970s he could because of the ethnic succession taking place in organized crime (although it is not the ethnic succession spoken of by such observers as Daniel Bell). When the national crime syndicate was formed in the early 1930s it was predominantly a mixture of two ethnic groups (and of course remains so to some extent today), the Italians and Jews, and the Jewish gangsters may have been more dominant than the Mafia. The ethnic succession that arose was simply an aging process, as the Jewish gangsters accumulated wealth but saw no need for establishing a succession to their empire. Of Moe Dalitz it was said by crime expert Hank Messick, "Moe thinks you can never get enough." Lansky also believed in the "more" philosophy, actively raking in crime profits into his late 70s.

However, the Jewish mobsters neither established nor wanted a structured empire. As Jewish ranks thinned—by the ravages of age rather than bullets—the Mafia, with its structured organization, with positions to be filled, simply moved into the vacuum, so that the Mafia influence in organized crime expanded. As the mafioso influence grew, Scarne was even safer expounding his "there ain't no Mafia" line and citing what was now rapidly becoming the ghost of Jewish gansterism.

SCHULTZ, Dutch (1902–1935): Underworld leader

It happened at an important meet of mob leaders in the mid-1920s before the syndicate was formed. In the midst of serious discussions of criminal matters, Dutch Schultz, one of the flakiest of the big gang leaders, couldn't resist sticking it to Joe Adonis, a gangster always vain and proud of his good looks and star quality. Schultz, at the time, had the flu and had been ordered by his doctor to stay in bed, but he showed up at the meet. When Adonis dropped a cute remark in the discussion, Schultz, looking to top him, suddenly pounced on him with a hammerlock and breathed right in his face, saying, "Now, you fucking star, you have my germs." As it happened Adonis did indeed catch Dutch's flu, and for a week, his voice hoarse, he kept telephoning Lucky Luciano to see that Schultz stayed out of his way. It was hardly a matter of epic import, but it illustrates the problems the world of organized crime would face with the unpredictable, "unorganizable" Dutchman.

If organized crime connotes anything it is that the rackets have to operate by some universally accepted rules. For Schultz there were no rules—other than those he liked or made. Those who broke *his* rules ended up dead; not only was he the flakiest of the bosses, he was also the most cold-blooded. In the end, he had to be "blown away" himself because he threatened the delicate balance between the syndicate and the authorities, and organized crime demands a certain respect for law and order.

Schultz, whose real name was Arthur Flegenheimer, was born in the Bronx, New York City. He had a minor record until the 1920s when he blossomed out as one of the many protégés of early criminal mastermind Arnold Rothstein. Schultz soon ran a gang that took over much of the beer trade in the Bronx. He was already flaky but also tough and mean, and he actually may have had a keener sense for potential sources of new racket revenues than even Meyer Lansky and Lucky Luciano. It is difficult now to determine whether it was Lansky or Schultz who first saw the enormous potential offered by penny-ante numbers in Harlem. In any event it was Schultz who moved in aggressively on the independent black operators there and with unremitting violence turned them into his agents in a new multimillion-dollar racket. Through a mathematical genius named Otto "Abbadabba" Berman, he figured out a way to doctor the results of the numbers game so that the smallest possible payout was made.

Not even his own gangsters liked or respected Schultz, but they did fear him. His payroll for torpedoes and the like was probably the lowest in the city, and he flew into a rage whenever a gunman asked him for a raise. Only Abbadabba got really big bucks, $10,000 a week. Berman had to threaten to take his mathematical skills to other mobsters unless he got the money. If he had left, Schultz doubtlessly would have exterminated him, but that would hardly have solved the problem of a huge drop in income, so the Dutchman turned magnanimous and paid him.

Mobsters looked down on Schultz. A dapper dan Schultz was not. Luciano once told an interviewer in disdain, "The guy had a couple of million bucks and he dressed like a pig." Schultz himself told an interviewer, "I think only queers wear silk shirts. I never bought one in my life. A guy's a sucker to spend fifteen or twenty dollars on a shirt. Hell, a guy can get a good one for two bucks!"

Luciano also said of Schultz: ". . . he worried about spending two cents for a newspaper. That was his big spending, buying the papers so's he could read about himself."

Schultz actually was an avid newspaper reader. He allowed he had taken the name of Dutch Schultz because "it was short enough to fit in the headlines. If I'd kept the name of Flegenheimer, nobody would have heard of me." Schultz could as well go bananas over what was written about him. He once verbally laced into *New York Times* crime reporter Meyer Berger because he had described him in a story as a "pushover for a blonde."

"What kind of language," the gangster raged, "is that to use in the *New York Times?*"

Actually, Schultz wasn't all that offended. There was only one way to do that. His notorious "mouthpiece," Dixie Davis, later said of him: "You can insult Arthur's girl, spit in his face, push him around—and he'll laugh. But don't steal a dollar from his accounts. If you do, you're dead."

Among those who are most popularly thought to have done so (and died for it) was the homicidal Legs Diamond. Having survived several murder attempts by Schultz and other mobsters, he became known as the clay pigeon of the underworld. When he was finally put to sleep permanently, in a bed in an upstate hotel room, Schultz commented: "Just another punk caught with his hands in my pockets."

Schultz fought a no-quarters war with Vincent "Mad Dog" Coll, a former underling who sought to feed his ambitions by taking over part of Schultz's

Dutch Schultz lingered two days after being shot in a Newark, New Jersey, chop house; the death sentence is believed to have been carried out to keep the underworld leader from having prosecutor Tom Dewey assassinated.

empire. On February 8, 1932, Coll found himself trapped in a telephone booth by men generally held to have been Schultz machine gunners.

Wiping out Coll gave Schultz an added measure of prestige in the syndicate, and no one else gave serious thought to knocking him off, although certainly Lucky Luciano and Meyer Lansky wanted to take over his beer and policy rackets. In addition, they knew Schultz was too erratic and sooner or later would jeopardize them all. But Uncle Sam seemed to come to the rescue by indicting Schultz for income tax evasion.

While Schultz was out of circulation awaiting trial, the other syndicate members moved to take over his rackets, with Lansky and Longy Zwillman in New Jersey getting cooperation from Schultz's right-hand man, Bo Weinberg. Then in a shattering development, Schultz beat the rap and came back to claim his empire. All the syndicate men could do was claim they were minding the store. Schultz squinted at them, indicating that sooner or later he'd settle that score, but his immediate attention fell on Bo Weinberg, who he suspected as being the traitor within his ranks. Weinberg disappeared. One story holds that Schultz killed him with his bare hands, another that he put a bullet in his head, and still a third that he had Bo fitted with a "cement overcoat" and heaved into the Hudson River while still alive. Schultz was capable of any of the above.

There is an excellent chance that war would have broken out shortly between Schultz and Luciano, Lansky, Zwillman and others, but again the law interfered, this time in the form of special prosecutor Thomas E. Dewey, who in his war on vice and racketeering had turned his main focus on Schultz in 1935. All around, Schultz saw his operations stunted and his revenues decreased. He knew only one answer to that: Kill Dewey. Schultz went to the national board of the syndicate with his demand that Dewey be assassinated. The mobsters were all shocked except for the kill-crazy Albert Anastasia who saw merit in Schultz's idea, totally unmindful of the heat to be generated in the murder of a prosecutor. Even Anastasia backed off when he realized the implications. Schultz's request was dismissed.

He stormed out of the meeting, warning defiantly: "I still say he ought to be hit. And if nobody else is gonna do it, I'm gonna hit him myself."

His attitude sealed his fate. The boys voted a quick contract on him, with Anastasia backing the idea.

On October 23, 1935, Schultz, Abbadabba Berman and two enforcers, Lulu Rosenkrantz and Abe Landau, were having a business meeting and meal at one of Schultz's favorite hangouts, the Palace Chop House and Tavern in Newark, New Jersey. Schultz got up from the table and went to the men's room. While he was there, two gunmen entered the Palace. Their technique was picture perfect. One of them checked the men's room on the way in, and seeing a man at a urinal, shot him. This was to prevent the killers from later being surprised from behind. Then they shot the three Schultz men at the table.

It was then that the hit men discovered that Schultz was not at the table. Remembering the man in the john, they found it was Schultz. The gunman who had done all the shooting, Charles "the Bug" Workman, paused long enough to clean out the money from Schultz's pockets and fled. Amazingly Schultz was able to stagger to a table where he fell unconscious.

Schultz lived a couple more days in the hospital but did not name his killers, instead talking mostly gibberish with considerable mysterious mumblings about all the money he had hidden.

Eventually Workman was convicted in the Schultz rubout and did 23 years in prison. He never said who had ordered the Dutchman killed. The Bug probably didn't even know such details.

SCHUSTER, Arnold   See TENUTO, FREDERICK J.

SCIASCIA, Gerlando (1934–1999): Victim of the Mafia's no slander rule

One of the newer rules passed by the new Mafia leaders during the recent resurgence of the mob was "thou shalt not speak ill of other wise guys." In the old days there were no hit, no killing, and no drugs rules in action, under the pain of death. Now a no slander rule also applies. It is the bosses' way of offering no additional openings for crime busters to find out inner secrets of the mob. Of course, there always was a no slander rule against lower-ranking minions for bad-mouthing the godfather or other high-ranking mob figures, but now the edict was extended to others. The reason was the same, to keep

This surveillance photo of reputed organized crime figures (from left to right) Gerlando Sciascia, Vito Rizzuto, Giovanni Liggamari and Joseph Massino, taken on May 6, 1981, outside the Capri Motor Lodge in the Bronx borough of New York, was released by the Justice Department on January 20, 2004. Law enforcement officials unsealed a 20-count indictment that charged 27 members and associates of the Bonanno crime family with murder, conspiracy and other crimes.

the bad-mouthing from rebounding on the new bosses. The new bosses know their new setups are fragile indeed and under constant pressure by the law. Silence therefore is imperative.

This is the reason that Gerry Sciascia had to die. Sciascia, a capo in the Bonanno crime family, openly criticized another capo in the same outfit, one Anthony Graziano, for having a cocaine problem. There was a time when such criticism might have been tolerated, but not under the new order. The family boss, Joe Massino, would not tolerate Sciascia's blabbing. Massino had recently elevated Graziano in the leadership and now Sciascia was tearing down not only Graziano but the boss as well. For this offense, it was said, Massino told underlings that Sciascia "had to go." The victim went under the boss's careful ministrations, according to the law, as Massino sent out the order for the job, assigned the killers, and arranged for the untraceable murder weapon. Next, say informants, Massino and his wife went on an extended Mexican trip. In March 1999 Sciascia was invited to meet with another capo. The meeting resulted in Sciascia having three bullet holes in his head and three others in sundry places. When Massino returned from

Mexico he told others, "It served him right for telling me how to run the family."

The new Mafia may be changed, but like its predecessors, it is not a democratic society and allows no strings for the law to work back to the all-powerful boss.

SCOTTO, Anthony M. (1934–): Longshoremen's union leader

He was for a time hailed a "new breed labor leader," one who could bring respectability and honesty to the New York waterfront. Anthony M. Scotto came to the fore in New York longshoremen's union affairs after the death in 1963 of Anthony "Tough Tony" Anastasio, to whom he was related by marriage. His father-in-law, also named Anthony Anastasio, was Tough Tony's nephew.

Scotto moved in high-echelon political and business circles. But, in 1979, federal investigators found that labor racketeering was still the order of the day on the waterfront. Scotto was then general organizer of the AFL-CIO International Longshoremen's Association and president of the union's Local 1814 in Brooklyn, Tough Tony's old fiefdom and one of the top three posts in the 100,000-member union, representing workers from Maine to Texas. Scotto was arrested.

Scotto's father-in-law was tried along with him, and both were convicted despite such character witnesses for Scotto as New York governor Hugh L. Carey, (who called him trustworthy, energetic, intelligent, effective and dedicated) and two former New York mayors, Robert Wagner and John V. Lindsay. Scotto was convicted of taking more than $200,000 in cash payoffs from waterfront businesses despite his claim that he had "never taken a cent" for himself from anyone. He did allow he had accepted a number of "political contributions," not payoffs, totaling $75,000, which he claimed he gave to New York lieutenant governor Mario M. Cuomo in his unsuccessful bid for the mayoralty in 1977 and to Carey for his successful 1978 reelection try.

Scotto could have been sentenced to 20 years imprisonment, but U.S. District Judge Charles E. Steward Jr. gave him only five years and fined him $75,000, explaining he had been "extremely impressed" by letters from numerous business, labor and political leaders pleading for leniency.

See also PLANTS

SEAGAL, Steven (1952–): Action film tough guy and Mafia victim

It wasn't just like in the movies. It was a Mafia reality show. In films, Steven Seagal handled the bad guys with splattery aplomb. But in real life he was up against the Mafia, whose credo, no matter the situation, was always the same: turn fear into money. In Seagal's case it was some $700,000 for starters and more to come later. How did it happen that Seagal came to be in a real-life shakedown script with him as the intended victim who allegedly was determined not to reveal any payoffs were made? Seagal's woes began in the summer of 2001 when the actor split with his business partner of 15 years, producer and accused mob associate Jules Nasso. The latter responded by hitting the star with a $60 million lawsuit.

As the dispute raged, neither participant knew that the FBI was deep into an investigation of the Gambino crime family and taped a conversation allegedly between Nasso and a reputed hard-eyed New York capo named Sonny Ciccone in which the pair discussed extorting money from an "entertainment figure" later identified as Seagal. Nasso and Ciccone were charged with extortion.

It must be said that getting information out of Seagal was like pulling teeth. But the truth came out after a court ordered the actor to overcome his reluctance and appear for testimony. Finally Seagal apparently had no recourse but to testify, and while it had the elements of a scene straight out of a bad Hollywood movie, he was picked up by "guides" who took him by car to Brooklyn with an obligatory switch of vehicles to prevent pursuit. In the end he was deposited in the darkened upstairs dining room of Gage & Tollner, a landmark Brooklyn restaurant, where the specific mob threat was made that Seagal would have to pay $700,000 for severing his business ties with Nasso, an associate of the Gambinos and the brother of a genuine soldier in the mob. Among other matters besides the shakedown for money, Sonny Ciccone lectured the actor on the matter of eye contact, something highly practiced in film art, after Seagal let his gaze wander as the capo was speaking. As Seagal later put it, "Sonny explained to me that it would be better if I looked at him when I spoke."

The experience so intimidated the screen tough guy that he agreed to pay the $700,000 as a down payment on $3 million. (It was to be left for later

that Ciccone also would demand $150,000 for every future Seagal film.) Later, after the shakedown meeting, Nasso informed Seagal that if he had balked, he would have been killed. That too had certain comic overtones. It turned out neither Ciccone or his underling nor the Nassos were armed, and the FBI bugged a conversation between Ciccone and another mobster chortling how scared Seagal was, adding it was right out of the movies and "if we only had guns in our belts, it would be really good." By contrast Seagal told jurors he had a licensed weapon on him for the meeting, saying, "In New York, I always carry a gun."

In the ensuing investigation Seagal seemed to shift in and out of his film persona, insisting at the later trial he never was frightened but was "uncomfortable" and "increasingly uncomfortable." And he was prepared to fight back. Under prosecution questioning, Seagal said he went to see an imprisoned mobster of another crime family whom he knew for help in the matter. Seagal said he could not turn to the government because, in part, he was too well known. "I can't go in the witness protection program. They can't help me." If sometimes on the stand Seagal held

Actor Steven Seagal testifies as U.S. District Court judge Frederic Block looks on, in this Brooklyn, New York, court drawing on February 11, 2003. The defendant are (from left) Jerome Brancato, Richard Bondi, Anthony "Sammy" Ciccone, Primo Casarino, Peter Gotti in the front row and Richard V. Gotti and Richard G. Gotti in the back.

to his tough guy image and bellowed his answers to defense attorneys, there were other signs of a more tame attitude. He had to put on reading glasses to study court exhibits and carefully arranged two shawls over his lap, apparently to warm his chilly knees.

Careerwise, Seagal's moviemaking had veered toward a more placid approach, which apparently may have led to the dispute between Seagal and Nasso. He apparently was eschewing extreme violence because of his adoption of Buddhism. In interviews the Nasso camp insisted Seagal had walked out on movie commitments because his Buddhist advisers had warned him that his violent movies could stand in the way of "felicitous reincarnation." Seagal gave a very worldly response to this by declaring in court, "That's the dumbest lie I've ever heard in my life." He said he broke up his partnership with Nasso because the latter was an abusive person who was on mood-elevating drugs and "going into psychotic rages."

While the Seagal case drew the most media coverage, the government concentrated more on convicting Ciccone and Nasso's brother Vincent on waterfront racket charges. Julius R. Nasso was sentenced in the Seagal matter after a guilty plea, drawing a prison term of a year and a day. Under a plea agreement, Nasso agreed to pay a $75,000 fine and receive mental health counseling after his release. It seemed clear enough the mob had had their fill of Seagal. As to whether the actor's future films will be on the tamer side in his apparent pursuit of felicitous reincarnation, will have to be left to Seagal enthusiasts as they monitor the splats, whacks and bams to be offered to an adoring public.

SEVEN Group: Predecessor of the national crime syndicate

The bloodletting that accompanied the onset of Prohibition has never been accurately measured, but it was inevitable when suddenly the prospect of enormous profit was dangled before basically not-too-well-to-do criminals.

With the end of World War I, there weren't all that many opportunities available for organized criminals. The political bosses did use them to control elections, but unfortunately elections did not come around every month. In the old days the political bosses accepted the responsibility of seeing after their criminal cohorts in "slow periods," putting them to

work as bouncers, as shills for gambling joints and whorehouses, and so on. However, this too was changing as reformers—bluebloods, businessmen, the middle class, leaders of various ethnic groups—were demanding a cleanup. In more and more parts of the country political leaders could not operate in such blatant style any more. They had no more use for the criminals and no reason to support them.

The Volstead Act of 1919 dramatically altered everything. For criminals, there was a new opportunity for making millions. Gangsters slaughtered old buddies to take over bootlegging rackets, and explosions of gunshots and bombs filled the air of almost every American community of almost every size.

Yet with exceptions here and there, by the late 1920s peace had settled on the bootleg world. It came through the Seven Group.

Forward-thinking gangsters had decided all the warfare was interfering with making money. There had to be peace in obtaining liquor and there had to be an end to gangs hijacking each other's supplies. The answer lay in some sort of organization that could constitute a central liquor buying office to handle all orders for booze and give everyone a fair share. This system would reduce the deadly competition for supplies and the inordinate protection costs for shipments. This would leave the individual bootleg gangs with more than ample time and resources to take care of any freelance hijackers who might be foolish enough to continue to carry out raids.

Who deserves credit for originating the idea is difficult to tell, but it was probably either Arnold Rothstein, often called the Brain, or Johnny Torrio, also called the Brain. Certainly both of them—and Meyer Lansky and Lucky Luciano—were all boosting the idea by 1927.

The organization known as the Seven Group, since it was originally comprised of seven separate power groups, included Luciano and Frank Costello from Manhattan; Joe Adonis from Brooklyn and parts of Manhattan; Longy Zwillman from New Jersey and Long Island, New York; Waxey Gordon and the rising Nig Rosen from Philadelphia; Nucky Johnson from Atlantic City; Meyer Lansky and Bugsy Siegel, the protection "enforcers"; and Torrio who came out of his Brooklyn retirement to offer organizational advice.

When peace suddenly broke out in the mid-Atlantic area as the Seven Group established its authority, other gangs around the country clamored to join, among them those bossed by Moe Dalitz in Cleveland, King Solomon in Boston and Danny Walsh in Providence. Even Al Capone was attracted but the Chicago gang wars had gone on too long to be simply switched off by an appeal to reason. By the end of 1928 there were at least 22 gangs in the Seven Group.

By that time Rothstein had been murdered, apparently not because of a gangland plot against him, but over a huge gambling debt that he had welshed on to professional gamblers. That did not stop the momentum of the Seven Group and it led to the next logical step in the solidifying nationwide criminal link—mafioso, Italian, Jewish, Irish, Polish or whatever.

In 1929 the underworld held a vital conference at Atlantic City where plans for new criminal enterprises and cooperation after the end of Prohibition were discussed. Had it not been for the success of the Seven Group such a conference would not have been held and the confederation of the gangs around the country might never have come to fruition nor created the national crime syndicate.

See also ATLANTIC CITY CONFERENCE

SEX and the Mafia

A sort of mystique has built up around the members of the Mafia and organized crime on the matter of sex—licit or illicit. Mafiosi have three advantages most men do not enjoy: 1) they have considerable money to lure women with; 2) if married, their work keeps them out to all hours of the night or even away from home for days at a time, with alibis; 3) they rarely need alibis anyway since their wives are expected to ask no questions.

Much of the conversations picked up by police wiretaps concern sexual matters. Mafiosi are accomplished sexual gossips. Longy Zwillman may well have been properly labeled by the press as "the Al Capone of New Jersey," but whatever his accomplishments in organized crime, and they were many, he was regarded as quite the stud. His romance with budding actress Jean Harlow made him much celebrated within the mob and it was said the high point of a gathering of the boys would come when Longy fished out of his wallet what he claimed was a lock of Harlow's pubic hair.

Although there are rules in the Honored Society that prevent a mafioso from violating another member's wife, the imposition of the death penalty for sexual offenses is rather unheard of. The real purpose of the rule on sexual behavior is to cut down on "matters of honor" that could inhibit the orderly activities of the crime family.

Still, sexual charges are sometimes brought. One involved a highly ranked member of the Gambino family, Carmine Lombardozzi, who was brought up on charges by a lower-ranking member, Sabato Muro. Lombardozzi was ordered to put things right after he became involved with Muro's daughter. Carmine did what was required of him by divorcing his wife of 27 years and marrying the younger woman.

Prudery within Mafia circles is common when it applies to the female members of a mafioso's family. Walter Stevens, one of the most dependable hit men employed by Johnny Torrio and Al Capone, was a terror on the matter of sex. He censored his children's reading material, ripping out pages of books that he considered immoral. His daughters were not allowed to wear short skirts or use lipstick or rouge, and he screened what movies they could attend. In fact, Torrio was himself probably the greatest mob prude of all. After a quarter of a century dealing with the mob's prostitution and other sex rackets, he could rightfully claim to have never touched even one of the women.

Torrio had a morbid fear of venereal disease and maintained a strict loyalty to his wife. His protégé Capone had no such compulsion and so developed the syphilitic affliction that would eventually end his life. The same was true of top New Jersey mobster Willie Moretti who finally had to be shot in what other mafiosi considered to be a "mercy killing" because they feared his mental health, affected by advanced syphilis, would cause him to blab mob secrets.

Moretti, also known as Willie Moore, tended to hold others to a higher standard than himself. Thus when gossip columns started to report that singer Frank Sinatra was going to divorce his wife Nancy to marry actress Ava Gardner, he shot off a telegram to Sinatra to whom he had long been a patron: "I AM VERY MUCH SURPRISED WHAT I HAVE BEEN READING IN THE NEWSPAPERS BETWEEN YOU AND YOUR DARLING WIFE. REMEMBER YOU HAVE A DECENT WIFE AND CHILDREN. YOU SHOULD BE VERY HAPPY. REGARDS TO ALL. WILLIE MOORE."

Another don operating on the double standard was Chicago boss Sam Giancana. As a reading of

Mafia Princess by Antoinette Giancana and Thomas Renner makes obvious, Giancana was capable of jumping out of the bed of his mistress if necessary to commit murder, if he suspected any man of trifling with his daughters.

Sex for gangsters is looked upon as normal recreation, and, despite the rules, almost any peccadillo is permitted if the women are "outsiders." Thus it really was quite all right for Vito Genovese to have a man killed because he wanted his wife for himself. There is a mob rule against killing for personal reasons but affairs of the heart can at times be excused. Similarly, sex capers that produce no heat are acceptable. No one seriously objected when some of the boys in Detroit's Purple Gang got a little too involved in fun and games at the LaSalle Hotel one hot summer night and the body of a beautiful girl came hurtling down some 10 stories to the street. Since the Purples at the time enjoyed considerable official cooperation, police took one look at the victim, who was bound and gagged, and decided it was a classic case of suicide.

Mobsters are expected to pamper their wives and take them away for trips, cruises and the like. However, it is not at all uncommon for the boys to stash their old ladies in Deck A and their broads a deck below. The custom is known as "bringing both sets."

An exception to this rule is Christmas time when tradition dictates fidelity to the wives. For years when the Copacabana flourished as a secret Frank Costello operation, the Christmas rule at the Copa was mob wives only—no girlfriends allowed.

Promiscuity is regarded in Mafia circles as an expression of manliness. Thus it was never clear whether Lucky Luciano was more angry that Thomas E. Dewey convicted him on prostitution charges or that the prosecutor brought on a parade of hookers who indicated Luciano was impotent.

Sex also represents a condemned man's last wish, even though he may not know it. When Tommy Eboli was violently removed from his post of acting boss in the Genovese crime family, the assassins knew he was on his way to see a lady friend in Brooklyn. He could have been popped on his way into her apartment building but it was apparently decided that Eboli was entitled to the "respect" shown a boss. They let him have his evening of joy even though that meant hanging around for hours. Then they shot him to death as he came out.

SHAPIRO, Jacob "Gurrah" (1899–1947): Labor racketeer

By the late 1920s the foremost industrial racketeers in New York City and very likely the nation were Louis Lepke and Jacob "Gurrah" Shapiro. Of the two, Lepke had the brains, attired conservatively with the look of a respectable businessman, while Shapiro, squat, heavyset and gravel-voiced, a gorilla in man's clothes, provided the fearsome brawn.

His nickname of Gurrah said it all. Whenever he told someone to "get out of here"—which was often—it came out in a snarling "Gurra dahere." His underworld associates dubbed him "Gurrah" for his contributions to underworld English.

Teenagers, Gurrah met Lepke in 1914 on the Lower East Side while both were attempting to rob the same pushcart. It marked the beginning of a rewarding partnership. Lepke realized even then he would have a need for Shapiro's muscle—and Shapiro *must* have seen the need for a brain.

As a matter of fact, Shapiro was lucky eventually to have two brains working for him. Lepke—together with some other aspiring criminals, Lucky Luciano and Meyer Lansky—had come under the tutelage of the greatest criminal mastermind of the day, Arnold Rothstein, who, if he had lived, would have left a powerful imprint on organized crime as it developed in the 1930s. Rothstein saw a great potential in labor racketeering, far beyond just beating up strikers for pay.

Learning from him, Lepke and Shapiro moved into the union field in the garment industry and terrorized certain locals through a mixture of beatings and murders. Once they gained control of a local, they were set up to take kickbacks and skim on the dues from union members while at the same time extorting huge payoffs from garment manufacturers who wanted to avoid strike troubles.

They began working with Jacob "Little Augie" Orgen, the top labor racketeer of the day, to provide strikebreaking crews for employers. Lepke and even Shapiro soon discovered Little Augie was years behind the times, only looking for the biggest immediate payoff and not trying to build a good thing. Lepke and Shapiro realized they did not need Little Augie, who must have sensed their attitudes since he formed a new alliance with the Diamond brothers, Legs and Eddie, to provide him with extra muscle and protection. It did Little Augie no good. On the night of October 15, 1927, Little Augie and Legs Diamond were at the corner of Norfolk and

Delancey Streets on the Lower East Side when Louis Lepke drove up. Shapiro jumped out, gun in hand, while Lepke started firing from inside the car. In the hail of bullets, Diamond went down, severely wounded. Diamond recovered. Little Augie was not as lucky; he was dead on the spot.

The field belonged now to Lepke and Shapiro, and they put the squeeze on both the unions and the employers. Many employers who tried to hire their muscle soon found themselves under the gangsters' domination.

Gurrah was happiest when he could use force. He always firmly believed that a bust in the teeth was better than a harsh word, and that a bullet or a bottle of acid was more fun than a bust in the teeth.

When Lepke led his organization into Lansky and Luciano's emerging national crime syndicate, he was put in charge of Murder, Inc., the execution arm of the organization, probably because it was felt that he would need it most in his labor extortion field. Lepke's chief aides in Murder, Inc., were Albert Anastasia and Gurrah Shapiro, two natural killers who truly enjoyed the work. Gurrah handled a number of hits personally and devoted much of his spare time seeking out young talent for the murder troop.

In 1935 racketeer Dutch Schultz came before the ruling board of the crime syndicate with a proposal that special prosecutor Thomas E. Dewey, who was after him, be assassinated. Not surprisingly Shapiro and Anastasia favored the idea. Everyone else paled at such a suggestion, realizing that such a murder would simply generate more heat for everyone. When Luciano and Lepke voted against the idea, Anastasia and Shapiro, each regarding their boss as mentor, fell into line. Only Schultz continued to demand the Dewey murder, and when it was clear he would get no support in his insane plot, he announced he would go it alone. As a result, Schultz was murdered before he could carry out his plot.

Later Gurrah came to feel that his initial instinct to support Schultz had been right. With Schultz out of the way, Dewey went after the Lepke-Shapiro labor rackets. In 1936, Gurrah was sentenced to life for labor rackets. Lepke was also sent to prison and later went to the chair on an old murder he had commissioned.

During Lepke's murder trial Gurrah managed to smuggle a message out of the penitentiary to his mentor. He reminded him of Schultz's murder plot and concluded triumphantly: "I told you so."

Before Shapiro died in prison in 1947, he bitterly told other convicts that he had been a fool to follow Luciano, Lansky and Lepke, that if he had stuck to his own code of violence he would have been a free man.

See also GARMENT INDUSTRY RACKETS; LEPKE, LOUIS; MANTON, MARTIN T.

SHOTGUN Man (?–?): Unidentified Black Hand hit man

No mafioso hit man was more identifiable to more people and yet enjoyed greater immunity from arrest than an early Chicago killer dubbed by the press "the Shotgun Man." Little was ever known about him, save that he was believed to be Sicilian and that for years before appearing in Chicago's Little Italy he had served as an assassin for various Mafia chieftains in the old country.

In Chicago as in Sicily, the Shotgun Man took up chores for various Black Hand extortionists who threatened victims with death if they failed to pay their blackmail demands. Some Black Handers were from the Mafia, others from the Camorra, the Naples-based criminal society, and still others were mere freelancers capitalizing on the immigrants' fear of the Black Hands. The Black Handers did kill some recalcitrant would-be victims, thus advertising their serious intentions.

The Shotgun Man specifically personified the Black Hand evil. One can well imagine the icy terror that gripped recipients of Black Hand extortion demands if they were asked if they wished to share the fate of some Italian businessman who was really not yet dead. Then the Shotgun Man would dispatch the businessman. As a rule, the threatened victims immediately paid up.

Annually for several years, anywhere from 12 to as many as 50 victims of Black Handers were killed, and the Shotgun Man was acknowledged to be the hit man in perhaps one-third of the cases. Between January 1, 1910, and March 26, 1911, the Shotgun Man shot 15 Italians on orders from various Black Handers. In all, the total number of Black Hand killings in that time frame was 38. In March of 1911, the Shotgun Man cut down four victims within a 72-hour period, all at the intersection of Milton and Oak Streets, a spot that became known as "Death Corner."

The Shotgun Man blithely walked the streets of Little Italy with no fear of exposure, even immediately after a killing. Many witnesses could have identified him, but it was said throughout the community that the Black Handers who purchased his services enjoyed political protection. If the Shotgun Man was arrested, he would be turned loose in a short time with an excellent memory of his accusers.

The Shotgun Man was reportedly paid handsomely for his lethal labors, and it was said he remained at his duties only until he acquired enough wealth to retire to Sicily. Indeed, after a period of eight or nine years, the Shotgun Man left Little Italy. To take up a tranquil life in Sicily? No one will ever know.

See also BLACK HAND; DEATH CORNER; WHITE HAND SOCIETY

SIANO, Fiore "Fury" (1930–1964?): Mobster and Joe Valachi relative

In the traditional old-line mafioso state of things, a crime family was exactly that—a family. Brothers, brothers-in-law, sons, cousins, uncles, nephews—when they were all together it was believed that omerta, the code of silence, would be kept. Even in the most perfect of worlds there might be weaklings who could not stick with blood, and they would be exterminated within the family. At the same time, it was the duty of mafiosi to protect other relatives at all costs.

It was his family that doomed Fiore Siano. Siano was the nephew of informer Joe Valachi. Valachi had brought Siano, his sister's son, into the mob, or what he called the Cosa Nostra. Valachi was proud of the "kid," as he called him. Siano was a very good murderer. He fully deserved his nickname "Fury."

Twice Valachi used him as a hit man, both in very important murders. One was at the behest of Vito Genovese, who ordered the death of Steve Franse, a once-trusted associate, whom the gang boss blamed for his wife, Anna Genovese, "falling out of love with him." Siano followed instructions meticulously, seeing to it that Franse suffered before he died. The victim was badly beaten before he was finally strangled with a chain. Siano pummeled his victim, leaving his with contusions and abrasions of the face and body as well as a fractured rib.

An even more important hit was that of Eugenio Giannini, a mobster heavily involved in narcotics dealings, and, at the same time, an informer for the Federal Bureau of Narcotics. Lucky Luciano, in exile

in Italy, learned of Giannini's duplicity and ordered his extermination. Siano was one of an efficient three-man hit team that handled the job.

Fury Siano's future in the mob looked and was secure. Then Joe Valachi turned informer. Siano started walking around with a haunted look on his face. About nine months after it was learned Valachi was telling all, Siano suddenly vanished.

A New York City police intelligence report stated: "Siano disappeared about the end of April or the beginning of May, 1964. He has not been seen since three unknown males took him out of Patsy's Pizzeria, 2287 First Avenue, during the aforementioned period. Siano is believed dead. The rumor is that his body was disposed of in such a manner as to prevent it from being discovered."

The old mafioso belief that blood was a litmus test in criminal organization held true in Siano's case, in this case that "bad blood" infected the family.

Valachi spent his last years in federal custody, protected from underworld retribution. His family, he reported, would have nothing to do with him. "And I don't blame them," he said.

See also FRANSE, STEVEN; GIANNINI, EUGENIO

SICILIAN flu: Imaginary and real mafioso ailments

Mafiosi, when arrested or facing investigative committees or court appearances, develop a gamut of medical maladies ranging from heart trouble to common colds.

It is common for FBI agents derisively to diagnose such ploys as "Sicilian flu," a term coined when the late Buffalo boss Stefano Magaddino promptly took to bed when agents came to arrest him. He claimed to have the flu and was much too ill to be fingerprinted. As Special Agent Neil Welch put it, "It won't hurt. We just want to hold his hand." Subjected to a bedside arraignment, Don Stefano sucked on an oxygen tube and gasped, "Take-a the gun. Take-a the gun and shoot me, that's what you want!" At the time, Don Stefano was 77, and some five years from his final reward.

Claims of ill health do seem to have some validity however, in the cases of the older dons. Ascribing heart conditions to "Sicilian flu" may in fact be a bit uncharitable. Carlo Gambino claimed his heart condition kept him abed most of the time in his tightly guarded home on Long Island. More likely he stayed in bed because, stripped of his citizenship, his "bum ticker" protected him from deportation. He still schemed, issued orders and, indeed, seemed to have little trouble venturing forth when crime family business beckoned. Yet in the end it was a heart attack that put him down for good.

Scientific study is elusive on the subject, but it is obvious to any reporter on the Mafia beat that members of organized crime suffer more from heart attacks and heart disease than the population as a whole. Perhaps the high incidence of stress-related diseases is an indication of the pressures on Mafia Dons. Is a heart disease a condition that goes with the territory?

SIEGEL, Benjamin "Bugsy" (1905–1947): Syndicate leader and victim

In superlatives about members of organized crime Benjamin "Bugsy" Siegel certainly stands out in the most precocious category. When he was 14 years old he was running his own criminal gang and soon became a power on the Lower East Side. He teamed up with Meyer Lansky and the two formed the Bug and Meyer Mob, which handled contracts for the various bootleg gangs operating in New York and New Jersey—doing so almost a decade before Murder, Inc., was formed to handle such matters. The Bug and Meyers also kept themselves busy hijacking the booze cargoes of rival outfits. While Lansky clearly was the brains of the operation, Siegel was no flunky and stood on equal footing with him. Siegel frequently bowed to Lansky's wishes out of a genuine affection and high regard in which he held Lansky.

By the time Siegel was 21 it would have been hard for him to mention any heinous crimes he had not committed. He was guilty of hijacking, mayhem, bootlegging, narcotics trafficking, white slavery, rape, burglary, bookmaking, robbery, numbers racket, extortion and numerous murders.

Along with Lansky he hooked up with some rising Italian mobsters—Lucky Luciano, Frank Costello, Joe Adonis, Albert Anastasia, Tommy Lucchese, Vito Genovese and others—and with them would become one of the founding members of the national crime syndicate. Along the way, Siegel carried out a number of murders for the new combination to bring it to fruition. (Siegel was one of the gunmen who cut down Joe the Boss Masseria in a Coney Island restaurant in 1931.)

Siegel was always a man of the gun, feeling that a few homicides could clear up most any problem. And he was a "cowboy." Years later a deputy district attorney in California explained why Siegel almost always had to lend a hand personally in mob murders: "In gangster parlance Siegel is what is known as a 'cowboy.' This is the way the boys have of describing a man who is not satisfied to frame a murder but actually has to be in on the kill in person."

In the 1930s Siegel was sent from New York to California to run the syndicate's West Coast operations, including the lucrative racing wire to service bookmakers. The Los Angeles Mafia was bossed by Jack Dragna. Siegel soon made it clear who was in charge. Considering Siegel's reputation for violence and the fact that he had the backing of Lansky and Luciano who, from prison, sent word to Dragna that he had best cooperate, Dragna had to accept a second fiddle role.

Just because Siegel was a bit of a psychopath didn't mean he wasn't a charmer. As the saying went, he charmed the pants—and panties—off Hollywood, while at the same time he functioned as a mob killer. He was so enthused about killing, he was called "Bugsy," but not in his presence. Face to face, he was just plain Ben. A suave, entertaining sort, Siegel hobnobbed with Hollywood celebrities, including Jean Harlow, George Raft, Clark Gable, Gary Cooper, Cary Grant, Wendy Barrie (who once announced her engagement to Bugsy and never gave up hoping) and many others, some of whom put money into his enterprises. Siegel could be at a party with his "high class friends" and then slip away for a quick murder mission with a longtime murder mate of his, Frankie Carbo (who later became the underworld's boss of boxing). Siegel played his cowboy role in 1939 when he knocked off an errant mobster named Harry Greenberg on orders from New York.

While a busy man about Hollywood, running the mob rackets and committing murder, Siegel still had time for some truly bizarre stunts. There was the time he and one of his mistresses, Countess Dorothy diFrasso, traveled to Italy to peddle a revolutionary explosive device to Benito Mussolini. While staying on the diFrasso estate, Siegel, the wild little Jew from New York's Lower East Side, met top Nazis Hermann Goering and Joseph Goebbels. Underworld legend has it that the Bug took an instant dislike to the pair, for personal rather than political reasons, and planned to bump them off. He only relented because of the countess's anxious pleas. The explosive device proved a failure and Bugs and his lady returned to Hollywood where he took on the added mob chore of setting up a narcotics smuggling operation out of Mexico.

In the early 1940s Lansky had Siegel scout out Las Vegas as the possible site for a lavish gambling casino and plush hotel. At first Siegel thought the idea was loony, regarding Las Vegas as little more than a comfort station in the desert for passing travelers. However, the more Siegel looked at the possibilities the more he liked the idea, and he became the enthusiastic booster for a legal gambling paradise. He talked the syndicate into putting up a couple of million dollars to build a place, and the figure soon escalated to $6 million.

Siegel dubbed the place the Flamingo, the nickname of another Siegel mistress, Virginia Hill. At one brief time after the Flamingo opened Siegel had four of his favorite women lodged in separate plush suites. They were Virginia Hill, Countess diFrasso and actresses Wendy Barrie and Marie McDonald. Whenever she saw Wendy, Virginia went wild and once at the Flamingo punched the English actress, nearly dislocating her jaw.

However, woman trouble was not Bugsy's main worry. The syndicate was upset about its $6 million.

Bugsy Siegel, shot to death in the home of mob mistress, Virginia Hill. The hit almost certainly was carried out on orders of Meyer Lansky, the Bug's lifelong friend, and Lucky Luciano, although both denied responsibility.

When the Flamingo first opened, it proved a financial disaster. Reportedly, the mobs from around the country demanded their money back. What really upset them was the accurate suspicion that Bugsy had been skimming off the construction funds, as well as some of the gambling revenues, and having Hill park it in Switzerland for him.

The syndicate passed the death sentence on Siegel at the famous Havana conference in December 1946. Despite his later denials, the key vote was cast by Meyer Lansky and affirmed by Luciano. Siegel knew he was in deep trouble but got what he thought was an extension of time to turn the Flamingo around. By May 1947, it was making a profit and Bugsy started to relax.

On June 20, Bugsy was sitting in the living room of Virginia Hill's $500,000 mansion in Beverly Hills. Virginia was in Europe at the time. Siegel was reading the *Los Angeles Times* when two steel-jacketed slugs from an army carbine tore through a window and smashed into his face. One crashed the bridge of his nose and drove into his left eye. The other entered his right cheek and went through the back of his neck, shattering a vertebra. Authorities later found his right eye on the dining room floor some 15 feet from the body.

Some thought Jack Dragna, nursing his longtime hatred for Bugsy, had carried out the hit personally, but this was almost certainly not true. The most informed guess was that Frankie Carbo handled the chore on direct orders from Lansky, who doubtless grieved that such an old and dear friend had to go.

In the grim months before Siegel's murder, construction tycoon Del Webb had expressed nervousness about his personal safety with so many menacing types around the Flamingo. In a philosophical mood, Bugsy told him not to worry. He noted he himself had carried out 12 murders, all of which had been strictly for business reasons. Webb, Bugsy said, had nothing to fear because "we only kill each other."

That was certainly true in the Bug's case.

SILVER Street: Capone Mob vice area

Probably no family in organized crime organized vice to quite the extent of the Capone Mob. A typical Capone area in the 1920s was Silver Street in Hurley, Wisconsin. Sometimes referred to as B-girl U., it was the site of a mob-run crime school that functioned as long as B-girl bars and brothels were a major portion of mob operations. Much of Silver Street was composed of honkytonks where teenage girls, brought there from Canada and around the Midwest, were taught the gentle arts of "mooching and dipping." When they were fully schooled, they were shipped from Hurley to underworld dives all over the country.

Many of the girls lured from Canada thought they were getting dancing jobs, but when they arrived, they were informed the jobs were gone. Since most didn't even have money enough to return home, they were ripe for propositions claiming they could make some money simply by drinking with honky-tonk customers; if they got the customers drunk they could steal money from their wallets. The girls were taught the art of the "swift dip," which involved taking a wallet, removing the money, and slipping the wallet quickly back into the drunk's pocket. Particularly proficient girls were taught the dosages and administration of the Mickey Finn, while those not up to such deceptions were forced into prostitution.

Runaway girls were especially victimized, many ending up as virtual slaves. Some were turned into strippers on the underworld's burlesque lounge route. Girls who tried to get away were subjected to violence, beatings (that did not affect their market value), knifings or acid in the face (if they were to be made an example of for the other girls). Eventually, most girls were turned into narcotic addicts to make them more cooperative.

The Capone Mob's business in vice and in Silver Street died a natural death after a couple of decades, but not because of reformers or the mobsters' own regeneration. The nature of vice changed after World War II, swinging away from whorehouses to independent call-girl setups that the mobs found much more difficult to control.

SINATRA, Frank (1915–1998): Mafia's favorite singer

Sinatra and the mob—it's an old and long, long story and perhaps less significant than one might think. Some feel there is much to be made of it. Sinatra himself felt too much was made of it. He was in showbiz, he said, and there is no way to avoid gangsters all of the time.

Still, it's closer to the truth to say that Sinatra went out of his way to be with them than to avoid them. He flew to Havana in 1946 to attend a big under-world bash for Lucky Luciano (who had only months before been deported back to Italy after being paroled from his organized prostitution conviction). Later, when Luciano was away from his home in Naples, Italian police found a gold cigarette case with the inscription: "To my dear pal Lucky, from his friend, Frank Sinatra."

During the Kefauver investigation, Sinatra was questioned in advance by committee counsel Joseph L. Nellis to determine if he should be called to testify. At a 4 A.M. meeting held in an office atop Rockefeller Center, Sinatra was asked about mobsters he knew, and he acknowledged "knowing" or "seeing" or saying "hello" and "goodby" to an impressive—but possibly incomplete—list of them: Lucky Luciano; the brothers Fischetti, Joe, Rocco and Charles, cousins of Al Capone and powers in the Chicago Outfit; Meyer Lansky; Frank Costello; Joe Adonis; Longy Zwillman; Willie Moretti; Jerry Catena and Bugsy Siegel. Ultimately the Kefauver Committee did not call Sinatra. With Sinatra's career then in decline, the committee felt no real purpose would be served by lambasting him in public and perhaps finishing off his career. Implicit in that decision was the fact that Sinatra, even if the senators didn't know it at the time, was little more than a Mafia groupie. Joe E. Lewis and Jimmy Durante would qualify just as readily.

After the hearings Sinatra's career revitalized, and he continued to be linked with mafiosi, but it would be hard to tell whether Sinatra was more entranced with mobsters or they with him. Each at various times may have gained something from the other. Ralph Salerno, a specialist on organized crime formerly with the New York Police Department, quoted by Nicholas Gage in *The Mafia Is Not an Equal Opportunity Employer,* was upset that people, knowing Sinatra was an acquaintance of presidents and kings, would figure his other pals were okay. "That's the service Sinatra renders his gangster friends," says Salerno. "You'd think a guy like Sinatra would care about that. But he doesn't. He doesn't give a damn."

Actually the mob was able to use Sinatra and his P.R. clout many times. When Doc Stacher, Meyer Lansky's close associate, was building the Sands in Las Vegas, he told interviewers years later, "we . . . sold Frank Sinatra a nine percent stake in the hotel. Frank was flattered to be invited, but the object was to get him to perform there, because there's no bigger draw in Las Vegas. When Frankie was performing, the hotel really filled up."

Sinatra's first gangster friend appears to have been Willie Moretti, the New Jersey extortionist, narcotics trafficker and murderer. Moretti, also known as Willie Moore, took a liking to the young fellow New Jerseyan and helped him get some band dates when he was struggling in local clubs and roadhouses for peanuts.

Then Sinatra recorded his first hit song with Harry James in 1939, "All or Nothing at All," and eventually went to work for Tommy Dorsey for what seemed an astronomical salary of $125 a week. A myth built up after Sinatra and Dorsey had parted that they remained warm friends. "Hot enemies" would have been a better description. Sinatra's popularity had soared. Bobbysoxers followed him everywhere. He desperately wanted to dump Dorsey, and the underworld story has long circulated that Willie

Young Frank Sinatra's career, according to many accounts, was fostered by mobsters, and he was described as being close to many top maifosi, charges which the singer persistently denied.

Moretti came to the rescue. Moretti was said to have obtained Sinatra's release from the band leader in convincing Mafia style, jamming a gun in Dorsey's mouth. The hard bargaining that followed called for Dorsey to get $1 in compensation for selling him Sinatra's contract.

Not that Moretti didn't also chastise the singer at times. When Sinatra's marriage to his first wife, Nancy, was busting up and he was planning to marry Ava Gardner, the mobster wired Sinatra: "I AM VERY MUCH SURPRISED WHAT I HAVE BEEN READING IN THE NEWSPAPERS BETWEEN YOU AND YOUR DARLING WIFE. REMEMBER YOU HAVE A DECENT WIFE AND CHILDREN. YOU SHOULD BE VERY HAPPY. REGARDS TO ALL. WILLIE MOORE."

As it turned out, Sinatra had little more time in which to offend Moretti. The mafioso was executed by the mob. His advanced syphilis affected his brain, and it was feared he was revealing too much about Mafia operations.

In later years Sinatra was frequently linked with a number of other top mafiosi, especially Sam Giancana and Johnny Roselli, the Chicago mob honchos. Sinatra was embarrassed with a news photograph showing him with an arm around Luciano at the time of the infamous Havana gathering. In more recent years another widely published photograph, taken in Sinatra's dressing room at the Westchester, New York, Premier Theater, shows the star grinning widely in the company of such mafiosi as the late Carlo Gambino, hit man-cum-informer Jimmy "the Weasel" Fratianno, and three others later convicted and sentenced for fraud and skimming the theater's box office.

In 1985, cartoonist Garry Trudeau depicted a tribute to Sinatra by President Ronald Reagan and followed it in the next panel with the Westchester theater photo. Outraged, Sinatra issued a statement through his personal public relations firm: "Garry Trudeau makes his living by his attempts at humor without regard to fairness or decency. I don't know if he has made any effort on behalf of others or done anything to help the less fortunate in this country or elsewhere. I am happy to have the President and the people of the United States judge us by our respective track records."

Over the years Sinatra was as thick with presidents and presidential candidates as with mafiosi. He had close ties with John Kennedy (until barred from the White House by Robert Kennedy after he checked Sinatra's background), Hubert Humphrey (who scheduled him for a series of fund-raising concerts but quietly dropped him from the campaign in 1968 after a *Wall Street Journal* piece listed some of his underworld relationships), Richard Nixon, Spiro Agnew, Gerald Ford and, of course, President Reagan.

Jimmy the Weasel, after he turned informer, was apparently quite upset when the Federal Strike Force didn't go ahead with a case that had what he clearly regarded as Sinatra star quality. According to Fratianno, Sinatra "gofer" Jilly Rizzo approached him and complained about a former Sinatra security guard the singer had fired; he was supposedly supplying the weekly tabloids with material about Sinatra. The word was that the man, Andy "Banjo" Celentano, was about to write a book about Sinatra. The Weasel quoted Rizzo as saying: "We want this guy stopped once and for all," meaning that Celantano should have his legs broken and be put in the hospital. "Let's see if he gets the message." Fratianno accepted the assignment to watch Celentano, but neither he nor other California mafiosi could locate their target. Celentano solved their problem altogether by suffering a fatal heart attack on October 8, 1977.

Clearly, the Weasel saw a delightful show trial in his revelations and was disappointed when the Federal Strike Force showed little interest in the matter. There was no evidence tying in Sinatra, and certainly federal lawyers weren't wild about pursuing Jilly Rizzo. Not when, as one told Fratianno, "you've got a chance to put bosses in prison. Those are one-in-a-lifetime chances. With an informant-type witness, overexposure is a terminal disease." Politely, the government was telling Fratianno that there was no legal case and they were not going to let him grab headlines for scandal purposes.

Unlike with cartoonist Trudeau, Sinatra expressed no outrage when deadly hit man Fratianno recounted the details of the alleged incident in his book *The Last Mafioso*.

See also RAT PACK AND THE MAFIA, THE

SINDONA, Michele (1920–1986): Criminal financier

At one time banker Michele Sindona served as a financial adviser to the Vatican and was hailed by Italian government officials as the "savior of the lira." When it became clear he worked hand in glove with both the Italian and American Mafia, an Italian state prosecutor denounced him as one of "the most dangerous criminal elements in Italian society."

As Sindona's true character was bared, he faced fraud charges in the United States, as well as fraud and later murder conspiracy charges in Italy. He fought back by recruiting his Mafia cohorts to eliminate anyone who threatened him. Sindona recruited hit men to kill a government-appointed liquidator of his bank in Milan. The man was murdered.

A murder plot in the United States proved less successful. Sindona sought a "Zip" hit man to murder Assistant U.S. Attorney John Kenney who was prosecuting a case against him. The hit man, Luigi Ronsisvalle, had previously handled some "rough-up work" for the financier. Sindona wanted him to plant heroin or cocaine on Kenney's body to make the murder seem drug related. While he was an accomplished contract killer, Ronsisvalle balked, saying, "You talking about something heavy." Ronsisvalle was not considered a smart man, but he knew the American mobs frowned at killing prosecutors; in fact the mob made it a practice, such as in the case of Dutch Schultz's plot to have prosecutor Tom Dewey assassinated, to whack out anyone daring to upset the status quo in that fashion.

Sindona continued the plot with others but finally backed off when one of the intermediaries arranging the would-be murder carelessly mentioned Sindona's name on a telephone that the banker feared might have been tapped. Sindona was convicted for his American crimes and sentenced to 25 years. U.S. authorities then shipped him to Italy where he was convicted on charges there and sentenced to life imprisonment.

Shortly after his conviction the 65-year-old Sindona drank a fatal cup of poisoned coffee in his prison cell. The coffee in his cup had been laced with cyanide. He keeled over and shouted, "They have poisoned me."

Nevertheless authorities decided Sindona had committed suicide.

SKIMMING: "Tax-free" gambling profits

The Mafia would like to see gambling legalized—they are the greatest proponents of such a system. Whereas hundreds or thousands patronize illegal gambling houses, millions a year would visit legitimate operations. The "take" in legal gambling is all the bigger—even if everything is run on the level.

The fact that profits are supposed to be reported to the government is of trivial concern to the mob. The reason is "skimming," stripping away profits before figures are given to tax authorities, and even before the money gets to the iron-barred casino counting rooms where tax-agent observers are present. Lou "Rhondy" Rothkopf, for years one of the secret owners of the Desert Inn in Las Vegas, once bragged to underworld associates that the casino in its first year of operation declared a profit of $12 million, but the mob had skimmed off an additional $36 million.

There are many ways to skim off huge amounts of money even in the casino's heavily guarded cages where the accountants and bookkeepers labor. It is also possible to do it out on the floor, with "high rollers" getting a run of "luck" and walking away with a bundle before IRS agents can swoop down on them for identification. The virtue of such big pay-offs is not just in the skim. It is great advertising for the casino and lures in more customers hopeful of a big win.

The skim, as perfected by Meyer Lansky, is a work of criminal art, and it is virtually untraceable. Moe Dalitz, for years the big man at the Desert Inn, was unsuccessfully charged with income tax evasion in 1968. And a few years later, Lansky and five others who had interests in the Flamingo were accused of skimming off $30 million—very likely a massive understatement—but none of the charges ever resulted in conviction for Lansky.

According to the best estimates obtained from informers, skimming either runs about triple the reported profits or about 20 percent of the handle (the total amount of money bet). This adds up to a monumental problem for organized crime because all those funds have to be "moved"—"laundered" or "washed"—and stashed some place where they can be used in a way that does not invite federal scrutiny. Again, it was principally Meyer Lansky who showed the mob how to manage skimmed funds, providing one more reason why he was called "the Genius" and why he also ended up at the time of his death with a personal fortune estimated at between $300 and $400 million—all untouchable by the U.S. government.

See also LAUNDERING

SLOT machines

The importance of slot machines to the growth of organized crime can hardly be exaggerated. With the end of Prohibition, it was the gem in the crime crown of the great bootleg gangs.

While the slot machine or one-armed bandit goes back to the 1880s, when the first such device turned up in the saloons of San Francisco, the real pioneer of slots in Mafia circles was Frank Costello. Costello, with by far the best political connections of any mobster in New York, saturated the city with slots in the early 1930s. In all, he placed about 5,000 around town—in lunchrooms, drug stores, speakeasies, candy stores and other locations. In establishments that catered to schoolchildren, Costello had his machines equipped with wooden chairs so that the little kiddies could play such a delightful grown-up game. Even in depression days, a low figure of $10 a day per machine produced a daily gross of $50,000, or about $18 million a year. Actually, experts believe Costello and his mob took in at least twice that much.

Of course, not all the income was profit. Expenses were heavy. The police and politicians had to be paid off. (According to one expert this meant "half the police force and all of Tammany Hall.") Costello equipped his machines with a special sticker which informed an inquisitive policeman if he was dealing with a legit mob slot. If it did not have the sticker, the officer was expected to sabotage the apparatus. The color of the sticker might change without notice so that any cheating independents using counterfeit stickers could be weeded out. Occasionally a misguided policeman would think it his duty to bust a protected machine, a shocking misdeed that inevitably resulted in his transfer to the wilds of Brooklyn or Queens.

During the regime of Mayor Jimmy Walker, the Costello-organized racket worked to perfection. Mafiosi in the Luciano family (Costello a chief lieutenant) were given no pay for their various racket chores but were accorded a given number of slots. Actually all they got were the stickers, giving them the right to set up the slots, which they had to buy and locate without infringing on the territories of others. Informer Joe Valachi testified that during this period permission to run 20 slots produced a weekly take for himself and a partner of $2,500.

Things took a decided turn for the worse for the New York mob when reform mayor Fiorello H. La

Guardia came into office, and appointed Lewis J. Valentine, an honest cop, police commissioner. Valentine set about filling the upper ranks of the department with more honest officers than ever before in the city's history. Honesty in both city hall and police headquarters was more than even Costello could endure, and the gang leader was on the defensive when the mayor launched a war against slot machines. Costello pulled wires in the courts to get an injunction restraining La Guardia from interfering with the operation of the machines, but the feisty mayor simply ignored the order and dispatched special squads of flying police around town to smash the machines. Costello was appalled at such rank disobedience of the law, but eventually conceded that the slots would have to be moved to safer territory.

Happily for Costello, he found a helping hand in the form of Governor Huey Long of Louisiana, who issued a "Y'all come on down" invitation at, of course, an appropriate commission rate $20,000 a month (to be left in a tin box in New Orleans' Roosevelt Hotel). Even with Long's untimely assassination in 1935, Costello did not have too much trouble maintaining his machines in Louisiana or even in anti-Long New Orleans. The appropriate officials were approached by Costello's number one agent, Dandy Phil Kastel, and a suitable business arrangement was achieved. The income from slots to Costello, Kastel and Meyer Lansky, who got a slice of almost all gambling enterprises in the country, came to at least $800,000 a year. This was after business expenses were deducted, including payoffs to political figures and police officials and a gift of 250 machines to the local Mafia chief, Carlos Marcello, to install in the Algiers section of the city, located on the west bank of the Mississippi. Marcello got two-thirds of the take and turned back one-third. In return, Marcello made sure no other racketeers gave the slot syndicate any trouble. Costello always understood that one does not look to the police to control members of the underworld.

For a while, the slots racket operated without additional trouble until reform reared its ugly head. Despite the payoffs, the slots were endangered. To solve the problem, the Louisiana Mint Company was formed, and the slots were converted to dispense mint candy. A test case was hurried to the Louisiana Supreme Court for a decision as to whether the candy vending by the machines took away the gambling stain to them. It was long rumored that

Costello-Kastel-Lansky ensured a favorable decision by buying four judges. In any event, the slots were found to be legal.

Finally though, in another reform wave in the mid-1940s, the Louisiana Supreme Court ruling was overturned, and the candy-dispensing machines were held to be gambling devices. The slots were tossed out of New Orleans. The ever-vigilant Costello had, by this time, made arrangements to move the machines just beyond the city line in gambling casinos in Jefferson Parish. Then, with the growth of legitimate casinos in Nevada, the slots were shipped into those establishments, almost all of which were controlled by the mob through various fronts.

Today, slot machines are legal in Nevada and Atlantic City, New Jersey, and smaller legal establishments elsewhere. The profits are enormous, far greater percentagewise than the dice, blackjack or roulette tables. The sales pitch is generally made, and is said to have originated with Costello, that since the machines have operated without payment of graft, they now pay off at 95 percent. Actually, it is believed that the true payment rate is about 75 percent. The slots remain as they were under Costello—genuine bandits.

SMALL, Len (1862–1936): Illinois's "pardoning governor"

Organized crime functions best where it can put the fix in on all three levels of local government—city, county, state. Illinois, in the heyday of Al Capone in the 1920s, met mob needs with flying colors. It would probably be impossible to find any other state with corruption more rampant. At the top of the heap was Governor Len Small, who carried his obvious collaboration with organized crime to the blatant limit. There is no known instance of Small ever turning his back on a bundle of currency.

Small was a Kankakee farmer and obedient follower of Chicago mayor Big Bill Thompson. Small entered the executive mansion in 1921 and shortly thereafter was indicted for embezzling $600,000 during his previous tenure as state treasurer. The governor promptly announced he had immense faith in the jury system in Illinois, and clearly he knew what he was talking about. While his lawyers defended him in court on the supposed merits of the case, Small enlisted some more professional assistants in special behind-the-scenes activities.

Among these exponents of the justice system were Walter Stevens, already dubbed the dean of Chicago's gunmen; Umbrella Mike Boyle, a corrupt labor union official; and Ben Newmark, formerly chief investigator for the state's attorney, but by then a leading thief, counterfeiter and extortionist. This trio did a far better job of getting the jurors to come to an acceptable verdict through bribes; where a touch of the green did not work, threats against the lives not only of the jury but also of their families seemed to do the trick. Illinois justice found Small innocent. A man of considerable gratitude, the governor was happily able to repay the boys shortly thereafter for their good works by granting all of them pardons for sundry bad works they had committed—Boyle and Newmark for jury tampering, and Stevens for his major vocation, murder.

Now Small built a real head of steam under his infamous pardoning machine. During his first three years in office, he pardoned no less than 1,000 felons. If that might seem like something of a national record, it was nothing compared to what he did over the next five years when he turned loose another 7,000 on a strictly cash basis. Longtime Chicago journalist George Murray in *The Legacy of Al Capone* explained the technique thusly:

> The Republican party machinery of the state was then in the hands of Len Small as governor, Robert E. Crowe as state's attorney of Cook County, and William Hale Thompson as mayor of Chicago. . . . When Crowe would convict a wrongdoer the man could buy a pardon from Small. Then Small and Crowe would split the take and Crowe would go into court for more convictions. The voters returned this team to office year after year.

Quite naturally the most reliable campaign workers for the party machine were the Capone Gang, and it was not until 1928 that the string ran out in the infamous Pineapple Primary. Incensed at the very idea of such wonderful political leaders facing serious political opposition, the Capone gang came out shooting and heaving grenades. Despite such ardent aid from the racketeers, the Small-Crowe ticket went down to an overwhelming defeat as enraged voters went to the polls in record numbers. "It was purely a revolt," declared the Illinois Crime Survey, "an uprising of the people, expressing themselves through the ballot. The birth of 'Moral Chicago' was hailed throughout the world."

That conclusion was to turn out rather too rosy. Still, the citizens of Chicago and Illinois probably felt it was quite an improvement to have convicted felons show up at prison and put in a bit of time.

See also PINEAPPLE PRIMARY

SNEAKERS: Drug-dealing mafiosi

One of the reasons for the comeback of the mob around the turn of the 21st century was a failing of the new Mafia leadership to bar mafiosi from the drug trade. The no narcotics rule, even though not too rigidly enforced, was a wise move by the old mob leadership, but it was consistently undermined by lower-standing wise guys. With increasing pressure put on the mobs on all criminal activities, the mobs found they couldn't recruit new, dependable members without the promises of huge profits—far more than the rewards to each individual from gambling or loan-sharking. The boys were therefore allowed to "sneak."

The dangers from dealing in junk remain for mafiosi: Monumental prison sentences can force newer members to crack under pressure and name other mob guys. The answer by the new ruthless mob bosses is quick death sentences for likely squealers. It may be that the unofficial policy of turning a blind eye to sneakers will prove to be a deadly Achilles' heel in coming years for the mobs. For now they have little choice. Perhaps further cooperation with non-Mafia gangsters by extending an okay for them to operate for an increased Mafia tax might work. It is a dangerous gamble, but the mobs can live with these kinds of risks.

See also NO NARCOTICS RULE

THE Sopranos: Making the mob a smash on television

Everybody loves *The Sopranos*—the television audience, the critics, and even the mob. Actor Vincent Pastore portrayed the cuddly cat burglar, hit man, and mob informer "Big Pussy," who went to sleep with the fishes after his friend Tony Soprano exposed him—and effectively wrote Pastore out of a juicy acting job. It doesn't matter. Although he is now permanently departed from the lucrative gig, Pastore still enjoys his fame. New York pedestrians wave to him on the street and pay their respects: "Hey, Puss!" Even members of the five families who bump into him in public, give greeting. As Pastore says, "They, uh, always want to meet you if you've played somebody they know."

The Sopranos owe it all to Mario Puzo's *The Godfather,* which burst onto America's conscience in the 1970s. *The Sopranos* had an easy time succeeding compared to the hostilities Puzo's epic endured in a day when mentioning the Mafia was politically incorrect.

A quarter century of undying popularity of *The Godfather* made *The Sopranos* as acceptable as the red, white and blue. The tale of the Sopranos makes them seem part of a romantic novel, and Puzo thought the same of his creations as well.

Only occasionally does some minor wise guy insist the mobsters are not as tough as in real life, where they rule by inducing fright in everyone, especially among their own supporters. Of course, the ex-mobsters reaping rewards as consultants find the show picture perfect. Compared to Puzo's characters, the Sopranos are relative marshmallows, frequently pushed around by their wives and their kids.

The real mafiosi kill women as well as men, including their wives, and they are nothing if not nasty, mean and brutal. If their relatives have to go according to mob rules, so be it. But *The Sopranos* and *The Godfather* characters are all really selling Mafia pipedreams. Everybody loves them, although it must be noted that some in the jaded audience show disappointment in closing episodes in which there is no sweeping final bloodbath. Puzo never let his fans down on that.

What next in the Mafia pipedream world? Maybe real-life mobsters playing roles similar to themselves. Some old Mafia hands will whine, "What have we become?"

But if it sells. . . .

SPENDING habits of mafiosi

They talk big, they act big and above all they spend big. When it comes to spending nobody can match mafiosi.

The stories are legion about Al Capone buying all of a newsboy's papers and sending him home with a $20, or $50 bill, or tipping a waitress $100 for a cup of coffee. Since then, mafiosi big and small have tried to live up to Capone's standards.

It is a matter not merely of imitation, but rather of behavior that goes with the territory. Mafiosi live a life that demands "respect," but such respect often can only be measured in money, and thus it is natural for them to live high and spend big. To them it means having "class." Once Carmine "the Snake" Persico, a power in Brooklyn, handed a waiter $50 in payment for a check that came to something like $5.

"I'll have to get your change, sir," the waiter, looking at the denomination, said.

"Did I ask for change?" Persico asked, in a tone somewhere between magnanimity and annoyance.

Mobsters are notorious overtippers. As a rule, informer Vinnie Teresa said, mobsters give at least 25 or 30 percent as a tip. Henry Tamelo, the underboss of the New England mob, who later went to the death house on murder charges, gave 50 percent. "When he walked into a club, the waiters were busy throwing customers out of a booth to find him a seat."

Teresa explained why mobsters liked to dress up in $500 silk suits, $100-plus shoes, travel in luxurious cars, and parade into fancy places with beautiful women on their arms. "Ninety percent of all mob guys come from poverty. They grew up with holes in their pants, no shoes on their feet. They had rats in their rooms and they had to fight for a scrap of bread to eat. Now they made it."

Some mobsters would wonder what their lives were all about if they could not be ostentatious. No one could convince Chicago crime boss Tony Accardo to live in anything less than a 22-room mansion that sported an indoor pool, two bowling alleys and a pipe organ. The bathroom fixtures, all gold-plated, were valued at a half million dollars.

On the other hand crime boss Joe Colombo's platinum-blonde wife never overdressed. As a sympathetic friend once remarked: "Poor Lucille has to walk around in rags because of those IRS jerks." Colombo learned that bit of personal restraint from his predecessor, Joe Profaci, who was known to his underlings as a man of exceedingly "short arms"— not the sort to part easily with a buck. Waiters were lucky to get 10 percent from Profaci, but, on the other hand, he gave a fortune to the collection plate of the Catholic Church.

So too did Chicago's psychopathic Sam Giancana, who was never known to put less than several hundred dollars in the envelope at mass. Giancana was not so stupid as to think he was buying himself absolution. He did it for his very devout wife. When his wife died, he donated a communion rail for St.

Bernardine Church in Forest Park, Illinois, in her memory. It cost, the FBI reported, $13,000.

One reason mobsters spend so much, Teresa reported, was that they figure the money will keep coming. Teresa himself made something like $10 million in a 28-year crime career, but also spent "all I made like there was no tomorrow."

At the top of the crime ladder a surprising number of bigwigs feel no compulsion to spend big, feeling they have no need to prove themselves to others or even to themselves any more. Lucky Luciano dropped the loud dress, which marked, for example, members of Chicago's Capone Mob, in favor of the refined attire of a gentleman. It was no easy task. His mentor Arnold Rothstein once told him, "I want you to wear something conservative and elegant, made by a genteel tailor."

Luciano was taken aback. "What the hell are you talkin' about?" he replied. "My tailor's a Catholic."

Rothstein curbed Luciano's extravagant spending habits as well, explaining to him that the very rich don't overspend and overtip to get respect. A wage-earner group ever after disappointed with Luciano's spending style was Polly Adler's hookers. If a prostitute thought her sojourn to the Waldorf Towers for a session with Luciano was going to pay her much more than the then going rate of $20, she was sadly disappointed. At most Lucky would slip a $5 bonus in her brassiere as she dressed. "I didn't want to do nothin' different," he said. "What do you think I was gonna do—spoil it for everybody?"

Meyer Lansky would have been hard to spot as an organized crime big spender. Before his flight to Israel, home for Lansky was a modest three-bedroom ranchstyle house in Hallandale, Florida. He walked the family dog (described by some biographers as the ugliest dog in captivity), rented Chevrolets and spent most nights at home with his wife. He never flaunted his wealth, estimated to be as much as $400 million, because he always thought back to his associates who did—Luciano, Frank Costello, Vito Genovese, Louis Lepke, Joey Adonis, Bugsy Siegel, Mickey Cohen and Albert Anastasia—and observed they all wound up imprisoned, deposed, deported, executed or assassinated. Lansky could be a handsome tipper however, at least when dining alone or with friends. Whenever he dined with his wife, he was careful to keep his tipping moderate.

Probably the greatest joy for a mob spender occurs on a visit back to the old country, generally to an impoverished village. In 1927, Frank Costello, already a racket millionaire, returned to the village of Lauropoli, an obscure hill town in Calabria, Italy. Following obligatory services in the village church, the entire populace, man, woman and child, formed a line on the church steps to greet Don Francesco Castiglia. Costello's biographer Leonard Katz tells the story in *Uncle Frank:*

> One by one Frank's sister introduced them, and for each she had a tale of woe.
> "His wife needs an operation."
> "Five thousand lire. Next."
> "He wishes to send his son to school to learn a trade."
> "Three thousand lire. Next."
> "A landslide destroyed his crops."
> "Two thousand lire. Next."
> "Her husband died suddenly and left her with two small children."
> "Eight thousand lire. Next."
> And so it went until the line was exhausted.

It was in Lauropoli that Costello made his grandest buy of all. A mousy little man approached and handed him a piece of paper, explaining it was an IOU signed by his mother. He had given her two sacks of flour on account, and she had left for America without paying him. Costello recognized his mother's handwriting and not only redeemed the IOU but paid handsomely in interest for the intervening 35 years.

"I never wanted a piece of paper so bad in my life," he told a friend years later. "The old bat nagged me to death all my life. It was always: 'Frank, why don't you get out of the rackets?' or 'Frank, why don't you go straight?' She always swore she never did anything wrong in her life. I wanted that piece of paper to show her how she had beat this poor old guy out of two sacks of flour.

SPILOTRO, Tony "the Ant" (1938–1986): Chicago Outfit's Las Vegas enforcer

He was from 1971 to 1986 "the man"—the most feared hoodlum in Las Vegas, and hoodlum was perhaps the most polite name for Tony Spilotro. He really lacked the finesse to do his job, a role previously played by representatives like Johnny Roselli. Spilotro was more at home as a hit man, squeezing a victim's head in a vise until his eye popped out to get him to talk.

Spilotro learned his killer craft under Mad Sam DeStefano, perhaps the most sadistic of all the Chicago Outfit's enforcers. DeStefano was a master at torturing and killing with an ice pick, among other pathological methods, and Spilotro proved an apt student. He killed with precision and without failure (he even took care of DeStefano when it was decided he had to go), and he attracted enthusiastic attention from the top masters of the organization, such as Tony Accardo, Joey Aiuppa and Jackie Cerone.

The position of enforcer in Las Vegas opened up when Marshall Caifano was withdrawn for having attracted too much attention to himself, and Spilotro took over. Unfortunately he chose to ignore many edicts from the mob (save that of carrying out hits, which was a matter of pure joy to Spilotro).

At the helm Spilotro set up burglary rings to take the tourists, something the outfit opposed. It wanted the gamblers to come to Vegas because it was crime free, or as crime free as the mob wanted it.

Killings, which the mob also didn't want, were done in Vegas. The preferred method was to take victims out to the desert in Arizona, slaughter them and hide their bodies. Spilotro also began dealing in dope. This was a capital offense in Chicago, but Spilotro figured he was safe so far away from the Windy City.

Then there was the messy love triangle involving Spilotro and Lefty Rosenthal—the mob's "inside man" in the casinos—and his beautiful wife Geri (a tale portrayed in the book *Casino* by Nick Pillegi and the movie by the same name). Spilotro could have had far more beautiful and younger willing showgirls than ex-showgirl Geri, and the affair complicated matters since he and Lefty were supposed to run things for Chicago together. But scoring with Geri was the ultimate aphrodisiac for Tony, or as former FBI agent William F. Roemer Jr. put it, "Now he had a chance to screw his pal!"

Chicago viewed it as a messy and violent soap opera, a minor matter that should not have set off major repercussions. But there were far more serious problems caused, the mob felt, by Spilotro. His inattention and headline grabbing sparked a tremendous crackdown in Vegas. Nevada authorities, working with undercover FBI agents, seized control of the Stardust—the biggest cash cow of all the casinos, with a skim running into the millions. It was the first step in the complete uncovering of the skimming done at many casinos.

Meanwhile as the law closed in on Spilotro, some of his closest associates whom he had brought to Vegas turned informer to save themselves. Their information led to the arrest and conviction of the top mafiosi in Milwaukee, Kansas City and Chicago.

Spilotro could not have done anything more wrong. Yet, amazingly, the press speculated that with the outfit's leadership going to prison, most for the rest of their lives, it remained for Tony Spilotro to take over as the new head. This was sheer nonsense.

Joe Ferriola was anointed the new boss. In his induction speech to the capos of the outfit, as spies within the mob reported, he had only one item of business to discuss. He announced, "We wouldn't be in the mess we are now in if it weren't for one thing. The way that asshole out there in Las Vegas has ruined us."

Rather than being promoted to boss, Spilotro was slated for execution. Tony was recalled from Vegas supposedly for an important meeting. He and his brother Michael were taken at gunpoint to a cornfield and a pre-dug hole. Both were batted unconscious and buried, still alive. That touch probably had been sanctioned by the outfit.

The FBI learned the details of the brothers' gruesome end from the wife of one of the mob diggers who had prepared the hole. No one was ever convicted for the murders. Probably no one cared that much anyway.

See also DeStefano, Sam

SQUILLANTE, Jimmy "Jerome" (?–1960): Garbage collection racketeer

The boss of the New York garbage collection racket—picking up trash at exorbitant rates or not at all—Jimmy "Jerome" Squillante, was considered a vicious killer.

Informer Joe Valachi named Squillante as one of the gunners who murdered Frank "Don Cheech" Scalise, underboss to Albert Anastasia, on June 17, 1957. Scalise, one of the most important allies of Lucky Luciano since bootlegging days, was picking out some fruit at a favorite fruit stand in the Bronx. Squillante and another gunman walked up behind him and put four bullets into his neck and the back of his head. Ironically, according to Valachi, Squillante had been sponsored some years earlier for Mafia or Cosa Nostra membership by Scalise.

After Cheech's death, his brother Joe Scalise publicly vowed vengeance. Joe undoubtedly thought Albert Anastasia would back him, but the latter remained oddly quiet, and Joe, nowhere near the menace that his brother had been, lapsed into silence and disappeared from sight. After a couple of months, however, Joe Scalise got word that all was forgiven, and he returned to his favorite haunts.

According to Valachi, Joe made the mistake of accepting an invitation to a party at Squillante's home on September 7 where he was fallen upon by celebrants armed with butcher knives. Squillante personally cut Joe's throat. The body was cut up into disposable sections and hauled off by one of Squillante's trash trucks.

Squillante himself only survived the Scalises by three years. He was indicted on extortion charges and vanished. Apparently, the word went, it was decided that Squillante was not the sort who could stand the pressure of trial and prison. He was "put out of his misery."

Squillante's corpse was not carted away in one of his own vehicles. Instead, after he had been dispatched with a bullet in the brain, he was loaded into the trunk of a car, and the car was put through a crusher that brought it down to a compact scrap cube ready for melting in a blast furnace.

See also SCALISE, FRANK "DON CHEECH"

STACHER, Joseph "Doc" (1902–1977): Meyer Lansky ally

When a trio of Israeli journalists were engaged in the late 1970s in writing a biography of Meyer Lansky, their prime source of material was a former top syndicate mobster and longtime intimate of Lansky, Bugsy Siegel, Lucky Luciano and Frank Costello. Joseph "Doc" Stacher, who emigrated to Israel in 1965, revealed considerable information about organized crime in America, almost as much as the better-publicized informers. But, unlike the stool pigeons, Stacher wasn't tattling. Said the Lansky biographers: "He was so proud of Meyer that he felt we should know the truth about his old friend's exploits."

Stacher had reason to be grateful to Lansky, who made him a millionaire several times over, and Stacher was typical of many young gangsters—Jewish and Italian—who remained loyal to Lansky all their lives. Brought to Newark, New Jersey at the age of 10, Stacher quickly moved from juvenile thief to important member of the Bug and Meyer gang, headed by Lansky and Bugsy Siegel. In the 1920s he was running truckloads of bootleg liquor with the gang as well as aiding emerging New Jersey syndicate leader Longy Zwillman run many of his gambling enterprises.

In 1931 Stacher was the chief organizer, on Lansky's orders, of a meeting of all the top New York–area Jewish mobsters at the Franconia Hotel. At the conference, it was decided that the "Jewish Mafia" would merge with the Italian Mafia into a new national crime syndicate—what eventually became organized crime in America.

Lansky made Stacher his man in Las Vegas, representing the mob's interest there, especially as a payoff man. He also operated as the official bribe paymaster to Cuban dictator Fulgencio Batista, who "allowed" the syndicate to build and operate lavish casinos on the island.

Jimmy "Jerome" Squillante's position as boss of the New York garbage collection racket afforded the boys numerous opportunities to chop up bodies and have the remains trashed. Squillante himself is said to have suffered a different fate when his turn came, being tucked in a car put through a crusher.

STANDARD Oil Building, Battles of the

It was not until the 1960s that the U.S. government finally nailed Stacher for any meaningful charge, that of income tax evasion. Facing a five-year rap, Stacher could not be deported to his native Poland which would not accept him. Instead he made a settlement with Internal Revenue and immigrated to Israel, a right he had as a Jew under that country's "Law of Return."

Stacher worried if he would get Israeli citizenship and reputedly had his longtime close friend, singer Frank Sinatra, intervene through friends for an Orthodox member of parliament to come to his assistance. The M.P. owed Sinatra because the singer had contributed heavily to the American fund-raising done for religious educational institutes in Israel. To further aid the M.P.'s cause Stacher donated $100,000 for an Orthodox charity. Instead, the M.P. used the money to build a kosher hotel in Jerusalem. Outraged at being ripped off, Stacher sued in a court case that drew headlines and laughs throughout the country. Israelis were amused that such a giant figure in American crime could be so taken by a meek-looking rabbi. Stacher was regularly referred to in the Israeli press as one of the leaders of the "Kosher Nostra," as distinguished from the Cosa Nostra. In the end Stacher got his money back.

After Stacher demonstrated to other Jewish mobsters that they could find a haven in Israel, scores followed his example. Lansky himself tried to immigrate in 1971, but public uproar as well as heavy pressure on the government by American officials made him too notorious and he was kicked out of the country.

When Stacher died of cancer in 1977, Lansky, back in the United States, sent an enormous bunch of red roses, the inscription on the ribbon reading: "To Doc from Meyer." Stacher's funeral was rather impressive by Israeli standards but was small potatoes compared to the gangland send-off he would have gotten in the States.

See also BAGMAN; JEWISH MAFIA

STANDARD Oil Building, Battles of the

The so-called Battles of the Standard Oil Building in 1926 caused Lucky Luciano to dub Chicago, "A real goddam crazy place. Nobody's safe in the streets." The fact that the remarks were made by a visiting New York businessman, gangster Lucky Luciano, goes far to explain why and how the term *Chicago gangster* became world famous.

In the first battle of Standard Oil, Hymie Weiss and Schemer Drucci, successors to the assassinated Dion O'Banion as leaders of the Irish North Side gang, were ambushed as they were about to enter the new 19-story building on South Michigan Avenue. They were on their way to a bribe-paying meeting with Morris Eller, the political boss of the 20th Ward, who took care of protection for the mob's North Side speakeasies. Weiss and Drucci had just made it to the bronze Renaissance-style entrance when four gunners of the rival Capone Gang stormed out of a car and rushed them, guns drawn. Spotting the enemy, Weiss and Drucci dove for the safety of a parked car, and, drawing their guns from their shoulder holsters, started returning fire. The area was choked at the moment with morning rush hour pedestrians. One bystander went down in the first volley, while scores of other citizens either ducked for cover or else stood frozen in horror.

Weiss wisely started to fall back, car to car, but Schemer Drucci, often referred to by Capone as "the bedbug," lived up to that sobriquet by charging right at his attackers. The frightened Capone gunmen backed off to a sedan parked on the other side of the avenue and then drove off, with a cursing Drucci firing after them. Drucci jumped on the running board of a passing car, jammed his weapon to the driver's temple and ordered, "Follow that goddam car." Just then a police flivver arrived, and officers wrestled the crazed Drucci to the pavement.

Questioned by police, Drucci denied there was any gang battle at all, just a case of some punks "trying for my roll"; he flashed a roll of $13,500. The cops brought in Louis Barko, a Capone hood, who had been recognized as one of the gunners, but Drucci followed the underworld code and said, "I never seen him before." Barko and several other suspects were released.

None of the ensuing publicity convinced either gang that they did not have more right to the area than the citizens of Chicago. On August 15, five days after the first battle, Weiss and Drucci were again attacked at virtually the same spot. They were driving in a sedan when gangsters in another car blazed away at them. The North Sider's car was riddled with bullets, but miraculously neither Weiss nor Drucci was hit. They jumped from their car and made it to the sanctuary of the Standard Oil Building, firing back over their shoulders.

On September 20, the O'Banion Gang made a famous counterattack by striking at the Capone headquarters at the Hawthorne Inn in Cicero. A convoy of eight cars filled with gunmen drove slowly past the establishment, and unloaded an estimated 1,000 slugs in an unsuccessful effort to kill Al Capone. All they managed to do was nick a few pedestrians and hit Louis Barko in the shoulder inside the Hawthorne Inn. Later, the police arrested Drucci on suspicion that he had fired the shots that downed Barko. Barko, commenting on Drucci, said, "Never saw him before." Apparently he didn't even remember being brought before Drucci after the first Standard Oil shootout.

The outrage about the shootings was enormous, but nothing much came of it all. One sage said that *somebody* should have at least been saddled with a good stiff fine. But then again this was Chicago, "a goddam crazy place."

STAND-IN: Mafia substitute

The mob has often used "front men" and "stand-ins" to take the rap for crimes committed by more important bigwigs. For example, it is considered necessary—and even proper—that Mafia rackets, such as gambling operations, take a hit once in a while to give the police, who may be providing protection, some credibility. But few important mafiosi relish the idea of going into a lockup and being mixed with common riff-raff.

A solution is offered by the "stand-in." Mafiosi bosses or capos enlist a "stand-in" to take the bust. He goes to the lock-up, is accused of being the racketeer involved and so on. If need be, the stand-in takes the rap and goes to jail in a conviction. In return, the stand-in receives payment in cash, or the promise of a more important place in the mob afterward, or both. Occasionally, when an important mobster is grabbed before arrangements can be made, the fix is put on later. The stand-in takes over for the real criminal immediately after the first arraignment, even standing trial, and if found guilty, doing the time.

STAND-UP guy: Mobster who won't "talk"

In the argot of the Mafia, it is a great compliment to be called a "stand-up guy," one who stands up to considerable pressure and threats from law enforcement officials and refuses to turn stool pigeon.

The witness protection program is and has been loaded with fugitives who fall short of "stand-up guy": Joe Valachi, Vinnie Teresa and Jimmy Fratianno, for example. In fact, almost all mafiosi doing time can win leniency if they talk, but many have refused. This does not always reflect strength of character but, as in Peter Joseph Salerno's case, the fear of mob retribution against themselves or members of their family.

Peter Joseph Salerno had every intention of being a stand-up guy. A professional jewel thief, he came to have close contacts with the Genovese crime family. However, Salerno began to believe that when in doubt the mob will kill a potential stool pigeon. He was in Atlanta (like Joe Valachi) when he learned there was a contract out on him, and he decided to turn, becoming one of the federal government's most reliable witnesses against the Mafia and on whose head is posted $100,000.

Probably the highest-ranking stand-up guy in syndicate history was Louis Lepke, the labor racketeer and boss of Murder, Inc., who became in 1944 the only top-level crime executive before or since to be executed. Lepke was known to have information concerning high political and union officials, and his revelations would probably have put Governor Thomas E. Dewey in the White House. The speculation is that Dewey wanted not only a labor official (allegedly Sidney Hillman who was very close to President Franklin D. Roosevelt), but also the crime bosses as well. On the day of his execution, Lepke had his wife read a statement he had dictated in his death cell:

I am anxious to have it clearly understood that I did not offer to talk and give information in exchange for any promise of commutation of my death sentence. I did not ask for that! [Lepke himself inserted the exclamation point.] . . . The one and only thing I have asked for is to have a commission appointed to examine the facts. If that examination does not show that I am not guilty, I am willing to go to the chair, regardless of what information I have given or can give.

Obviously the phrase "information I have given" meant Lepke had talked some, but, by using his wife to make the announcement, it was clear he was signaling the syndicate that he was not talking about the crime cartel. He was talking only about politicians and labor people, which the syndicate would tolerate so long as he did not reveal information about the mob. By using his wife as a spokesperson, he was telling the boys he realized no member of his family would be safe if the crime leaders thought he was talking about the organization.

What Lepke couldn't grasp was that Dewey, whatever his desires and ambitions, could not possibly accept a deal that delivered political figures, his electoral enemies, but let every important crime leader in the country—Luciano, Lansky, Anastasia, Siegel, Costello, Adonis, Lucchese and many others—off the hook.

As a result, Louis Lepke went to the chair—a stand-up guy.

STATE Street Crap Game

The importance of gambling to the Mafia cannot be overestimated. It provides the mob with the money and power to set up other operations that the public finds less wholesome such as narcotics dealing and murder.

A case in point, Brooklyn's State Street Crap Game, operated by the mob in the 1930s, financed Murder, Inc., the official mob extermination branch. The game was run in a building just off the busy corner of State and Court Streets in downtown Brooklyn. It was for high rollers, attracting wealthy businessmen, and, at times, even police brass and politicians—who suffered big losses and ended up beholden to the gangsters.

Abe Reles, together with Pittsburgh Phil Strauss, one of the two most important hit men of Murder, Inc., was designated by crime bosses Louis Lepke and Albert Anastasia to be the official shylock of the game. Reles's underlings would move among the players, wads of money at the ready, making loans at a trifling 20 percent interest—per week. (Mob hit men are seldom if ever paid for any particular murder, but are usually put on a sort of retainer, often consisting of exclusive rights to a certain racket, such as gambling.)

The play per night at the State Street game was usually in excess of $100,000, and Reles's nightly profit from the shylock operation was, by his own estimate, anywhere from $1,000 to $2,000. And the businessmen—compulsive gamblers who ended up paying huge amounts of "or else" interest—never realized they were footing the bill for murder.

When Reles turned stool pigeon concerning Murder, Inc., operations, the authorities cracked down on the State Street game with a subsequent big loss to the mob. However, gambling is the easiest racket to get started anew and with the public, the politicians, the police—up to and including J. Edgar Hoover—claiming gambling was at most a "minor" crime, the mob's loss was hardly irretrievable.

STEVENS, Walter (1867–1939): Hit man

The press was to call him the Dean of Chicago Gunmen, and Al Capone used him for dozens of murders, with never a complaint. In fact, Walter Stevens probably killed more members of the Spike O'Donnell Gang for Capone than any other gunner.

Stevens started his career as a professional killer some time around the turn of the century. He once did a killing as a favor for a mere $50, and on another occasion a "half a killing" for just $25. Stevens became an honored slugger and killer for Mossy Enright in his union-busting operations. When Enright was murdered in 1920, Stevens started renting out his guns to other mob leaders, and he soon became a favorite of Johnny Torrio and Capone.

In all, Stevens is believed to have committed at least 60 murders. Direct evidence linked him to at least a dozen murders, but since his activities were centered in Chicago and Illinois, it went without saying most of the evidence never led to any prosecutions. In fact, Stevens only went to prison for one murder, that of a policeman in Aurora, Illinois. But the conviction didn't amount to much. Len Small, then the governor of the state, was himself indebted to Stevens for some past mayhem. Having some years earlier been charged with embezzling more than a half-million dollars while state treasurer, Small remembered Stevens's part in bribing jurors and threatening others to achieve an acquittal. Now Small pardoned Stevens.

As mean and deadly as Stevens was in his professional life, he was a bit of a pussycat at home. Very well educated and read, he was fully conversant on the works of Robert Burns, Robert Louis Stevenson and Jack London. This was very highbrow among the Capones. He neither smoked nor drank, and for 20 years took loving care of an invalid wife. Stevens adopted three children and saw that all received excellent educations. He was very prudish as a father and censored the children's reading material, ripping out pages of books he thought immoral. The children could only attend stage plays and movies that met his puritanical standards. His daughters were not to travel down the road to degradation by wearing short skirts or lipstick and rouge.

Stevens got out of the killing business in the late 1920s when, for the first time, an attempt was made on his life. After that, members of the underworld would say of him—although never to his face—that he was like Johnny Torrio: "He could dish it out, but he couldn't take it."

Stevens would more realistically put it that he had beat the odds longer than most hit men, and it was time to hang up his guns.

STOCKADE, the: Torrio-Capone syndicate brothel

The Maple Inn, popularly known in the Chicago area as the Stockade, was the largest brothel run by the Torrio-Capone syndicate in the 1920s. But flesh peddling was not the Stockade's claim to fame. Rather, the whorehouse was one of the very few 20th-century Mafia operations ever to be the target of vigilante action.

It was Capone's technique to take over communities just beyond the Chicago city line and engage in excesses far beyond those carried out within the city itself. The suburban village of Forest View soon came to be referred to by Chicagoans as "Caponeville." Booze wars, murder, gambling dens, physical intimidation of public officials and above all prostitution greatly upset the decent citizens of Forest View. Law enforcement officials remained doggedly unable or unwilling to meet this gangster invasion and rape of what had previously been a quiet community.

The symbol of the Capone blight on Forest View was the Stockade, an immense old stone-and-wood structure that housed gaming rooms and a bar, as well as a 60-girl whorehouse. However, the Stockade was more than just that. It was a hideout for wanted Capone gangsters and an arsenal with secret chambers hidden behind false walls, floors and ceilings.

Within this labyrinth was an extra-large chamber to which the whores could retreat in case of a raid. For the gangster on the run, there was a particularly lavish room beneath the eaves soundproofed with cork lining. The fugitive in residence enjoyed a most comfortable living area with deep pile rugs, comfortable couches and easy chairs. There was also a

speaking tube to place orders for food and drink which was conveyed to the hideaway by dumbwaiter. The puncture eyes of female figures painted on the ceiling gave the secreted criminal an overview of the rooms below, including the saloon and gambling hall. The secret compartment contained a number of steel-lined panels built into the walls in which were stored dynamite, grenades, shotguns, rifles, automatic pistols, machine guns and ammunition.

The residents of Forest View felt helpless against this Capone invasion stronghold—until 1926, when State's Attorney Robert E. Crowe, taking considerable heat at the time for a scandal involving his aides cooperating with gangsters, ordered an attack on Capone's suburban empire. Among the joints hit was the Stockade, and axe-wielding raiders smashed slot machines, crap tables, roulette wheels, beer barrels and cases of whiskey, and hauled away the prostitutes as well as the ledgers and a safe jammed with cash receipts.

Capone accepted this for what it was meant to be—a short-lived inconvenience—and he planned to keep the resort closed for a short period before a gala reopening. Since there appeared to be little to protect, the mob kept only a skeleton crew of guard over the Stockade.

The following night Forest View vigilantes struck, attacking in a convoy of automobiles. The Stockade was set ablaze in a half-dozen places. Frantic Caponeites sounded fire alarms and several nearby fire brigades arrived. However, they made no effort to stop the fire, only seeking to prevent its spreading to neighboring homes.

"Why don't you do something?" an irate gangster demanded of a firefighter.

"Can't spare the water," was the laconic reply.

Ironically, the Capone forces were angered by such a departure from the standards of law and order and demanded an investigation. "Investigate?" Chicago deputy chief John Stege, a determined Capone enemy, said. "I should say not. No doubt the flames were started by some good people of the community." And the Reverend William H. Tuttle said, "I appreciate the wonderful news. I am sure no decent person will be sorry."

Faced with such citizen opposition, the Capones backed down. Indeed, over the next few years Capone began backing away from blatant prostitution activities, especially in stiff-necked suburban areas, because of the hostility it aroused and the vigilante passions it nurtured. It was a learning experience for organized crime.

See also VIGILANTISM AND THE MAFIA

STOCK "geniuses": Financial wizards, Mafia style

Wanna make it big in the stock market? Follow the mob financial experts. Bull market, bear market, the wise guys always make out. They get hold of stocks that are bound to go up, just as certain stock analysts predict. They pick a stock at $5 and sell out quickly at, say, $8, for an impressive 60 percent profit. The mob guys may not know how to read a balance sheet or a stock report, but they do know numbers. Predicting a stock's profits will soar is easy to do when they can pick their own numbers—or have rogue analysts do it for them. The incentive for such educated numbers people may be as simple as one of the mob's standard ways of influencing people—holding people out of a high window headfirst.

Actually, it is not difficult to get so-called experts to play the numbers game with their forecasts. In a February 2003 letter to Berkshire Hathaway shareholders, legendary investor Warren E. Buffett wrote, "Managers that always promise to 'make the numbers' will at some point be tempted to make up the numbers."

It was a lush field the Mafia couldn't miss out on. The fact that the feds were driving the mobs out of some of their traditional rackets, actually opened up the joys of Wall Street for the boys. As one expert put it, "They used to have the number racket in Harlem. They used to have the Fulton Fish Market. They used to have garbage. They went seamlessly into Wall Street."

It must be admitted that the Mafia needed to be hit with a ton of bricks before they fully appreciated the potential. (It was the same thing at first about stolen jeans. The older mafiosi did not see the sense in stealing such "junk" as dungarees until they saw what younger customers were willing to pay for the stuff. That convinced them—and even got them to wearing jeans themselves.) They finally noticed that the so-called Russian mob and certain other eastern European gangsters were getting into stock scams. They tended to concentrate on lower-priced securities not listed on major stock exchanges. The stocks were pushed by corrupt stock sellers who could find enough suckers to push up a stock to a point where the crooks could then pull out leaving the victims

with huge losses. These mobsters kept their salesmen allies in line with the threat of force. But it was only a matter of time until major Mafia families came on the scene, often having been approached by the corrupt stock people looking to get the East European gangsters off their backs when they began taking the lion's share of the profits. It was of course too naive to think the Mafia in the long run would be fairer partners, but for a time the corrupt stock promoters usually considered themselves the major partners in the arrangement. They could indicate to the mobsters when certain operators would not join in the schemes, and the mob would apply their usual convincers, the threat of violence and when needed very harsh violence.

Quickly, the mobs saw far greater potential in stock frauds, and in the 1990s the six Mafia families in New York and Philadelphia were enlarging their toeholds on Wall Street. They may not have understood the theories behind junk bonds and derivatives, but a market for derivatives exceeded $100 trillion. To the mobsters, especially the Colombos, Wall Street was an easily penetrated area with tons of money for the taking. They found it easy to take advantage of the kind of people who could be recruited in so-called chop houses, pushing worthless stocks. The time had passed when M.B.A.s and Ivy League credentials were vital to achieve success on Wall Street as far as unscrupulous brokerage houses were concerned. Even a young punk with a moxie for fraud could become a stock hustling genius. Such was the case of 20-year-old Louis Pasciuto, who at the time was pumping gasoline in his native Staten Island, New York. He was found to be a genius at pushing stocks on unsuspecting buyers, mainly because he showed no compunction about stealing. Young Pasciuto became very rich, especially since he had his "Mafia guy"—one Charlie Ricottone—who babysat him with protection that also extended to the management of the houses using Pasciuto. The "guys" also settled disputes between various chop houses, which meant eventually that they controlled many of the houses.

It was a wonderful world for Pasciuto. The mob took care of everything. An imposter was hired to take Pasciuto's National Association of Security Dealers exam for him. Pasciuto just lived the good life with a yacht, a Ferrari, and an impeccable wardrobe. Unfortunately, his relationship with his

"Mafia guy" got messier and messier: The mobster wanted more and more money. It was, of course, the standard never-ending Mafia shakedown. Unfortunately, Pasciuto was spending and gambling away money faster than he could steal it from his fat cat stock-buying victims. Ricottone, a veteran of the Colombo wars, was not pleased, so he just tightened the screws on Pasciuto. He suggested he would have to have Pasciuto's wife gang-raped.

As a result Louis grew more desperate and careless. He was charged with cashing bad checks and committing securities fraud. And his Guy was after him. Pasciuto decided to cooperate in 1999 and over the next few years helped the FBI and prosecutors make dozens of arrests of Mafia-affiliated brokers and extortionists in the next few years.

But it was doubtful that Pasciuto was little more than a drop in an ocean of stock thievery. Gary Weiss, a senior staff writer at *Business Week*, told Pasciuto's tale in a 2003 book, *Born to Steal: When the Mafia Hit Wall Street*, but he disputes the idea that the mob is or even can be gotten out of Wall Street. He argues that organized crime may have played a major role in the spectacular rise—and then fall—of the financial markets. He sees organized crime still having a corrosive influence in the financial world. The honey in part is that mere $100 trillion floating around in the derivatives market alone. Clearly, the Mafia ain't leaving that.

STOCK theft and manipulation

There are bulls and bears on Wall Street. There are also mafiosi. The bulls and bears sometimes make money and sometimes lose money. The mafiosi *always* make money.

Organized crime has long played the market, and they have carried it far past the old-time crude bucket shops that operated early in the century. Officials of the Securities and Exchange Commission once estimated that 90 percent of all stock frauds in the country are the work of about 150 operators, almost all pinstriped Anglo-Saxons but with strong financial backing of the Mafia crime families. There is no way to estimate the Mafia's take in stolen securities. Known thefts in the 1970s ran at about $45 million annually, but investigators in a report to Senator McClellan estimated there was $25 billion in stolen and counterfeit stock floating around.

Stock fraud and theft is considered an "open territory" by organized crime, and the various crime families operate such schemes anywhere in the country. It is not considered an impingement of New York territory, for instance, for the Marcello family in New Orleans to work a swindle on Wall Street, or in Chicago or on the West Coast.

Securities used by racketeers may be stolen, inflated or even counterfeited; the Mafia can call on the best engravers, printers and suppliers of excellent paper as needed. The mobs had plenty of training in counterfeiting, producing funny ration stamps during World War II. It is simpler, however, to steal the certificates. This can be done in several ways, one through the theft of registered mail at airports (which is one indication of the importance of mob control of rackets at major airports) or by pilfering them from banks and brokerage houses.

The mob finds it easy to subvert low-paid employees at brokerage houses to do their dirty work. First they involve these clerks in gambling and get them in hock to gang loan sharks. Then the loan sharks threaten the clerks with beatings or death, finally offering them a way out by pinching some certificates. The clerks are instructed how to steal the securities, but, more important, to destroy the microfilm records of such stocks and bonds. In one case the mob got a million dollars worth of securities from Merrill Lynch, Pierce, Fenner and Smith, the country's largest brokerage. Even though the company finally discovered the theft, it was unable to determine which certificates were taken because the microfilms were also gone. The stolen securities were good as gold.

A congressional committee investigating the activities of syndicate mobsters in stock thefts found that such certificates were readily moved "through confidence men, stockbrokers and attorneys of shady reputation, fences, and other persons who have the ability, technical knowledge, skill, and contacts to sell the securities or to place them advantageously as collateral in financial transactions."

Not even Charles "Bebe" Rebozo's close relationship with President Richard M. Nixon exempted his Key Biscayne Bank from falling victim to a loan of $195,000 obtained by one Charles L. Lewis of Atlanta, Georgia, who put up 900 shares of IBM stock as collateral. Eventually Rebozo attempted to sell the stock only to discover it was stolen. Indictments in the case later linked the theft to two close

Meyer Lansky gambling accomplices, Gil Beckley and Fat Tony Salerno, who later became head of a New York crime family.

STREET tax: Payment to mob to okay non-member criminal operation

The Mafia "street tax" is one imposed on any number of illegal or "fringe" enterprises for the right to operate in Mafia-controlled areas. Burglars, thieves, hijackers, X-rated movie houses, pornographers, chop shop operators, pimps and prostitutes are required to pay tribute to the mob. For many years Harlem's top numbers racketeer, Spanish Raymond Marquez, paid a street tax of 5 percent of his take to a leading Mafia boss, Fat Tony Salerno, and thus was free of any mob headaches.

Freelance crooks operating within a crime family's territory can face very high taxes. For instance, an independent thief or hijacker working New York's JFK airport may be subjected to a 25 percent tax by the Gambino crime family. Some families demand as much as 50 percent of the take when a crook fails to clear his caper in advance. However, many sharp crooks do not feel it safe to clear things in advance because a crime family may have plans of their own and can make points by turning the independent in to the law so that the authorities then owe them one. Clearly the no snitching rule does not apply to outsiders if it serves mob purposes.

SUCKERS: Expendable wise guy wanna-bes

Contrary to common belief and the claims of prosecutors, the mob has little trouble recruiting new recruits. This is more true than ever in the new Mafia that emerged by the turn of the 21st century. These newcomers may not be the most dependable sort and likely to "spill their guts" if arrested, but contrary to common belief, this does not worry the mob too much. These adherents are not likely to be around too long. They are there because the mob needs them. Many operations require a lot of bodies and not necessarily too much upstairs. Gambling needs all kinds of "laborers" to get the operations to go. They have to tote up slips, and for illicit gambling joints or floating games they have to supply transportation for the players. The mob will take almost anyone. The Bonanno crime family in New York recently used a 93-year-old grandmother in one of the outfit's wire rooms. Her job was to tidy up the place, which included flushing betting slips down the toilet in case of a raid. Another man worked for the New York finance department by day and then did gambling chores, hoping to make it up to the level of a wise guy wanna-be.

These recruits have true value; they are "suckers." Most mobs use them in a number of rackets, and if they are caught they usually don't have much information to offer the law. In the 1990s the Boston mob grabbed these recruits wholesale as what Boston reporters Gerard O'Neill and Dick Lehr call quasi–wise guys. Young suckers were integrated into gambling operations, then into other activities if they seemed dependable and might even hold their tongues a bit. This made them even more expendable. The suckers were offered a lot of meaningless camaraderie so that they could take the fall for the mob if necessary. Many were promised several hundreds of dollars if they had to do time, with the further guarantee that they would move way up when they got out. Generally, the money stipend vanished after a few months, and the suckers were on their own. Amazingly, most of those who came out had not been disenchanted, their eyes still set on the prize—full membership in the mob. As a result Boston had plenty of dirty workers handy for dangerous tasks. Some even were assigned roles in mob hits. If anyone got caught in such a job, it was almost invariably the throwaway suckers.

In the long run some of these victims get unhappy, but they could be held in line by making them think they were being regarded by seasoned wise guys as new "big shots." Of course, some of the brighter ones realize they are going nowhere, and they come to regard the FBI as a savior for them. This means the tactic can turn very hairy for the mob. The usual solution: have them taken out before they start talking to the law. And the new Mafia leaders are so petrified of informers that they quickly give the okay when someone, perhaps even another sucker, wants the suspect sucker taken out for his own reasons. As a result some suckers are wiped out on a mistaken belief that they might start talking to the law. Miscarriages of justice do not worry the current mob bosses. A murder now and then will keep other suckers in line until they are needed. In today's Mafia a sucker's lot is not a happy one.

SURVEILLANCE tricks by mafiosi: Mob counterploys

While much is made of law enforcement surveillance techniques, it must be said that some mafiosi are quite adept at avoiding detection. Acknowledged by a number of investigators as among the more talented is Dominick V. Cirillo, known as Quiet Dom, and said to have taken command of the Genovese crime family after the arrest and conviction of Vinnie Gigante. According to John S. Pritchard III, supervisor of the FBI's Genovese squad in the 1980s, Cirillo was an elusive target who relied on "walktalks"—whispering to associates on noisy streets, rather than using the telephone or meeting inside social clubs where federal investigators could record their conversations. "He would leave his home in the Bronx," the retired FBI expert said, "make a stop in East Harlem to visit relatives and then drive downtown and park his car on the East Side or midtown. On foot, he usually had an escape hatch, going into a building or restaurant that had more than one entrance and try to lose us."

Cirillo had an excellent antenna for spotting surveillance cars and "would drive onto a highway and abruptly pull over to the side. If we stopped or slowed down, he had us made and was behind us—on *our* tail."

In that, Cirillo was carrying on a tradition long practiced by the Buffalo crime family under the late Stefano Magaddino, who insisted his men not only spot FBI surveillance men but counter their operations. Thus the FBI was kept under surveillance as mafiosi recorded their license plate numbers and the agents names. This occurred during the period when J. Edgar Hoover's good grooming and dress code for agents was more important than tracking mob guys, and the latter had little trouble spotting their adversaries. In time they could even separate those men assigned to anti-Mafia duties and those keeping tabs on the Communist Party. Being good patriots, the mobsters did not share their intelligence with the "rotten Reds."

See also CIRILLO, DOMINICK V.

T

TALENT hunters: Spanning the globe for recruits

By the 21st century the Mafia families had given top-drawer attention to security. It supplemented the Mafia's desperate need to recruit safe new members. Easily the crime boss most determined to carry out such a process was Joe Massino, the last of the bosses of New York's five families to be indicted in 2003. Massino held his men to strict adherence to security, and he followed the lead of the late Carmine Galante to limit his comments on the telephone to mere grunts. He is credited with calling safer intra-gang meetings by having the wise guys picked up at various points in rented trucks, then all being transferred to a different rented truck chosen at the last moment, and finally the boys being taken to the meeting place.

Massino, along with some other top mafiosi, inaugurated the practice of calling some meets in Mexico or even European nations, such as France or England, where generally U.S. investigators could not react quickly enough to arrange any bugging. After such a meeting the boys would frequently head for Italy and Sicily for a talent hunt for new recruits. The boys learned from bitter past experience that the screening had to be done well to avoid those who might turn informers or, just as dangerously, switch sides in later intrigues in the United States. It has been said that they tended to recruit from large family groupings who guaranteed their later loyalty with a promise of swift vengeance for any offender. Like any system, the tactic could not be regarded as foolproof, but the crime families recognized Massino as an innovator worth listening to. It has been said that the loss of Massino to the feds would be a deadly blow to the emerging leaner, meaner Mafia in America.

See also MASSINO, JOE

TANGORRA, Joseph "Joey Flowers" (1950–): Mobster going "shrink"

Lucchese mobster Joseph "Joey Flowers" Tangorra can in the wise guy world be viewed as playing a dangerous game, following in the footsteps of Tony Soprano of the acclaimed hit television series. Flowers had been talking to a shrink, which is what the fictional Tony Soprano does in the popular series. The fact is Soprano has a lot of leeway in his performance; Joey Flowers did not. If nothing else Flowers is a man overwhelmed by bad luck, which might make him a logical candidate for the couch, but not in the Mafia world. In fact, the word goes that the boys are eager to put him out of his mental difficulties.

Joey, in federal custody since 2001, apparently had not committed the unforgivable sin of talking to the FBI or government prosecutors. The trouble is he started talking, and talking and talking, to himself, to prison psychiatrists and other medical people about his steady depressions, followed by severe panic attacks. An impartial observer might say Tangorra had enough reasons to talk to the shrinks. Back in 1992 he and another mobster were putting the squeeze on a debtor when Joey's partner accidentally shot Joey in the back. After that Joey suffered a number of resultant ailments. More recently Joey was hit by state prosecutors on racketeering charges, and this was followed by federal prosecutors on similar charges.

After that Tangorra flipped, in the psychiatric meaning of the word. He was seen a block away from his Brooklyn home waving a copy of a recent indictment. This was not considered the proper behavior of a made guy, a capo at that. Afterward Tangorra was described by his lawyers as suffering a deteriorating mental condition, being an emotional wreck, and in need of a thorough evaluation. When he was returned to the Metropolitan Detention Center in New York, other inmates taunted him as being a "rat." This apparently gave Tangorra even more reason to panic and act out his frustrations with a particular nasty antagonist. Both Joey Flowers and his foe went into isolation. Tangorra then grew fearful of returning to the general population.

He picked up some additional woes when federal prosecutors denied he needed psychiatric attention, that what had him depressed was the fact that he could be facing life imprisonment for his crimes, in short that he was faking. The courts for the time being felt Joey needed more treatment. Then Tangorra had insult added to his injury when one Lester Ellis was ready to testify against him. Ellis was the companion who had shot him in the back by accident. As the months dragged on it appeared unsure whether Joey Flowers would ever exchange a standard prison cell for what some of his fellow inmates called the loony bin.

"TAP game": Moves and countermoves in use of wiretaps

The meeting to work out plans for the would-be assassination of John Gotti took place in Cassella's Restaurant in Hoboken, New Jersey, owned by a Genovese soldier. It was a logical location since the hit was ordered by Vinnie "the Chin" Gigante, the head of the Genovese crime family.

The one catch was that the FBI knew about the place and at times had previously bugged it. Naturally the Genovese men were suspicious, so they were careful about where they held their meeting. It took place in the ladies' bathroom. To get access the boys banged impatiently on the door to rouse the females inside.

A woman's voice called out, "Just a minute, OK?"

"Go piss in the street, lady," snarled Louie Manna, the capo in charge of the projected hit. "We got to have a fuckin' business meeting."

The toilet flushed and out came the woman.

Four plotters, Manna, restaurant owner Motts Cassella, Frankie Danello and Bocci DeSiscio, piled into the pink-tiled room and devised a plot in which Gotti and his brother Gene would be ambushed as they left the Gambino's Bergin clubhouse in Queens.

As it happened, the projected hit never took place. The FBI warned the Gottis of the plan.

Yes, the restaurant's men's room had been bugged, but the FBI had the foresight to plant a tap in the ladies' room as well. Such was one of the continuous cat-and-mouse episodes of the "tap game" between the FBI and its Mafia prey.

Sometimes all does not go well. Mafiosi like to have huge guard dogs for their homes or hangouts. Such was the case with Colombo soldier Donnie Shacks who kept two very mean Rottweilers posted at his social club, The Maniac Club. To get in to plant their tapes agents fed the dogs meatballs laced with thorazine. The idea was that the drug would discourage the animals from bothering the agent or even leave them out cold in the courtyard. Instead the dogs gobbled down all the meatballs and dashed straight for the club. There the dogs erupted all over the premises with, as one agent described, "the force of what appeared to be several fire hoses." Then the dogs passed out cold. Agents who entered the club had to tread carefully around the swamp of fecal material to install the hidden microphones.

No one ever accused Donnie Shacks of being long in the thought department, but he suspected something had made the dogs produce the terrible mess. He had the club swept by an electronics expert and uncovered the bugs. Score one for the mob.

Fortunately for the FBI, mafiosi are incessant talkers and even when they suspect their phones are tapped they will use it to call in an expert to check it out. That was what Gotti sidekick Angelo Ruggiero did when he feared his home might have been bugged. A former New York City detective named Conroy was brought in, and he swept the residence. Conroy found the place clean, and a grateful Ruggerio paid him $1,000 in cash. Conroy's analysis had been on target, but only because the FBI had overheard his hiring, entered the house and removed the bugs. As soon as the search was completed, agents reentered the house and restored the bugs. Mean-

Surveillance photo of Angelo Ruggiero, or "Quack-Quack" as the FBI dubbed him, who was outfoxed in a tap game ploy and whose words did much to cause the downfall of John Gotti.

while Ruggiero, believing his phone was clean, talked so much that agents nicknamed him Quack-Quack. Ruggiero's chatter played a huge role in the downfall of Gotti and numerous other mafiosi.

Perhaps the most celebrated tap game was that played on Tommy DiBella when he was acting boss of the Colombos. The FBI had set up a sting operation with an informant utilizing bugs on his business premises. One day a Colombo soldier spotted what he thought was a security system meant to protect the premises. Actually it was a sophisticated bugging set-up.

The mob guy wanted to know where the man had gotten it. Thinking fast, the informant said he had gotten it free from a buddy who had ripped it off and given it to him.

"Gee," said the gullible soldier, "Mr. DiBella would love to have such a system."

"No problem," the informant assured him, "I'll get them to boost another security system and install it for Mr. DiBella for free."

For that price, Mr. DiBella certainly wanted the system.

When a workclothed FBI man came to DiBella's Staten Island house and identified himself as the man with the security system, DiBella said sternly, "Yeah? Well, you look like a fucking FBI agent to me."

"No shit, Mr. DiBella," the agent replied. "What does one look like?"

Now the 75-year-old boss laughed. "Ah, I'm just busting your balls. Come on in, guy."

The subsequent busts made law enforcement history.

TELVI, Abraham (1933–1956): Hit man

A 22-year-old hood, Abraham Telvi was recruited by labor racketeer Johnny Dio to acid-blind crusading labor columnist Victor Riesel in 1956. Eager to get ahead in organized crime, Telvi agreed to the proposition, according to a federal investigation, by Joseph Peter Carlino.

Fingered by Gondolfo Miranti, Riesel found himself confronted by Telvi at about 3 A.M. as Riesel was leaving Lindy's, a famous New York Broadway restaurant. Telvi hurled sulphuric acid in Riesel's eyes and face, blinding him permanently.

Eventually, Miranti and another man involved in the plot were all set to identify Dio as the mastermind of the attack, but in the end refused to testify because of underworld threats. Charges against Dio and three others had to be dropped.

Telvi did not fare nearly as well. He had been paid a meager $1,175 for doing the job, and when he saw the heat being generated in the investigation, he angrily started dunning Dio and the other conspirators for a more equitable reward. In mid-July, Telvi was told he would get his bigger payoff in two weeks. The promise was not broken. On July 28, exactly two weeks later, Telvi was murdered in gangland style on the Lower East Side.

See also DIO, JOHNNY; RIESEL, VICTOR

TENUTO, Frederick J. (1915–1952?): Hit man and Mafia victim

In February 1952 Arnold Schuster, a 24-year-old Brooklyn clothing salesman, became a short-lived hero after he spotted the highly publicized, wanted criminal Willie "the Actor" Sutton, while riding on a New York City subway train. He followed Sutton, notified the police and Sutton was captured. On March 9, 1952, Schuster was found dead on the street where he lived. He had been shot four times, twice in the groin and once in each eye—all the markings of a Mafia murder.

Although Sutton had no connection with the Mafia or organized crime, Schuster's death had been decreed by Albert Anastasia, the brutal crime family boss. Watching the new celebrity, Schuster, being interviewed on television following Sutton's capture,

Anastasia flew into a screaming rage, not unusual for him. "I can't stand squealers!" he shouted. "Hit that guy!"

The murder was carried out by Frederick J. Tenuto, at the time on the FBI's list of 10 most-wanted criminals. Tenuto had a police record dating back to the age of 16 and had been in prison several times in the 1930s and 1940s. He was doing a term of 10 to 20 years for the hired killing of a Philadelphia man when he escaped from prison, only to be quickly recaptured. In 1945 he escaped again and was retaken. In 1947 he escaped a third time with four other men, including Sutton.

Shortly thereafter Tenuto turned up in Brooklyn underworld haunts where he came under the protection of Anastasia, a man of violence who always appreciated another cut of the same cloth. (If Tenuto had been around when Anastasia was issuing orders to his by then defunct Murder, Inc., troop, Tenuto would doubtless have been one of his star hitters.) Anastasia ordered Tenuto to take care of Schuster. Unfortunately, Tenuto was identified by a witness as he fled the scene of the crime.

This made not only Tenuto but also Anastasia vulnerable. Ordering Schuster's murder was a stupid thing for Anastasia to do. Anastasia made amends by

Career criminal Frederick Tenuto demonstrates the perils of operating on the fringes of the Mafia. He carried out a murder assignment for Albert Anastasia, only to be himself eliminated as a threat to the Mafia boss.

ordering Tenuto murdered. Tenuto's body was never discovered although, according to some police informants, he had been given a "double-decker funeral"—being placed in the paneled false bottom of a coffin with an about-to-be buried corpse.

The brutal Anastasia had solved his immediate problem, but the Schuster murder was later used by Vito Genovese as a justification for having Anastasia assassinated as a "Mad Hatter," whose irrational deeds were a threat to the entire organization of the Mafia.

See also ANASTASIA, ALBERT

TERESA, Vincent Charles "Fat Vinnie" (1930–1990): Mob informer

When Joe Valachi started singing, the mob price on his head was set at $100,000. On Vincent Teresa it was a half-million.

In the public mind Joe Valachi was the most important criminal informer in recent decades, a tribute more to the draw of television than to the gravity of his revelations. But many crime experts find Valachi's testimony limited in scope and not always consistent. Experts agree that Jimmy "the Weasel" Fratianno and Teresa—who follow Valachi by about a decade—were both far more productive "pigeons" for the law, and a strong case is made that Teresa, or Fat Vinnie, ranks as the number one informer.

Teresa had been the number three man in the mafioso crime family in New England—by his own count, which may have been somewhat inflated—when he started to talk, not out of any great moral reformation but because his own mob stole his money, failed to aid his wife while he was in prison and menaced one of his children.

While Valachi knew very little of import outside of New York crime circles, Teresa's knowledge ranged from Massachusetts to the Bahamas and Europe. He provided hard information that could stand up in court, testimony about mob infiltration of business, about crooked casinos and gamblers, fixed horse races, gang wars and stock thefts. He also cleared up several murders that authorities had shunted off to the unsolved file. His evidence led to the indictment or conviction of 50 mob figures and provided valuable leads on hundreds of others. And he did something no other mob informer ever dared do—he testified in open court about the "Little Guy," the much-feared Meyer Lansky.

In a book he wrote with Thomas C. Renner, *My Life in the Mafia,* Teresa traced the way $150 million poured into underworld coffers through his own efforts. In a 28-year crime career Teresa had himself netted $10 million which went almost as fast as he stole it.

Upon completion of his testimony Fat Vinnie was "buried" under the federal witness protection program with a new identity as Charles Cantino. In 1984, the Cantino address was Maple Valley, Washington. The federal government itself blew Fat Vinnie's cover in December 1984 when a grand jury indicted him and five members of his family on charges of smuggling hundreds of exotic and expensive birds and reptiles into the country. Most of the animals were listed as endangered species. There was talk in the underworld that Fat Vinnie had himself once more become an endangered species.

See also MORELLI GANG

TERRANOVA, Ciro (1881?–1938): Mafia leader

Although Ciro Terranova often gained a "good press"—from the underworld's point of view—as a brutish killer, the fact remains he was one of the most overrated mafiosi ever to be called a boss. Terranova came to the fore during the heyday of New York's Morello family and Lupo the Wolf; as long as he had them to lean on, he too was a dynamic crime figure. He could and did order a number of murders but gained a reputation as a man who could not do the dirty work himself.

Actually he operated quite well as a number two man and was to thrive as a junior partner to Dutch Schultz in the Harlem numbers racket. He was also called "the Artichoke King" by the newspapers for running an efficient racket with Morello muscle behind him. As informer Joe Valachi explained: "He tied up all the artichokes in the city. The way I understand it he would buy all the artichokes that came into New York. I didn't know where they all came from, but I know he was buying them out. Being artichokes, they hold; they can keep. Then Ciro would make his own price, and as you know, Italians got to have artichokes to eat."

With the passing from the active roster of most of the leading Morellos and Lupo the Wolf by the 1920s, Terranova was in position to claim the leadership of mafioso elements in New York. He proved incapable of that and had to settle as an underboss to Joe the Boss Masseria. During the Maranzano-Masseria war of 1930–1931, he had another opportunity to assert his leadership but could only watch as Lucky Luciano took up the reins. Luciano and his assistant Vito Genovese tabbed Terranova a weakling and one who could be, according to Valachi, "stripped [of power] . . . a little at a time."

Luciano's disdain for Terranova was rooted in the cowardly role the latter had played in the murder of Joe the Boss. Luciano arranged the killing by luring Masseria to a meal in a Coney Island restaurant. While Luciano went to the men's room, four killers—Genovese, Albert Anastasia, Joe Adonis and Bugsy Siegel—marched in and ventilated Masseria. The quartet marched rapidly out of the restaurant to a waiting black limousine where Terranova sat at the wheel. The four killers were cool and relaxed, but Terranova was trembling, so much so that he was unable to put the car in gear. Contemptuously, Siegel shoved him away, took the wheel himself and sped off.

When, in the new order in the underworld, Luciano ordered Dutch Schultz's murder, Terranova moved to take control of the Harlem numbers racket. Luciano and Genovese informed Terranova he was now in retirement, replaced by Trigger Mike Coppola. Usually, such displaced crime leaders are assassinated for fear they will go to war to retain their rights. Luciano correctly figured that Terranova would do nothing.

Three years later, according to a gloating Valachi who hated Terranova for personal reasons, "he died from a broken heart." Generally speaking the death of Terranova was considered the final demise of the old Morello Gang, the first Mafia family established in New York. Many descendants of the Morellos are still active but have been absorbed by the other crime families.

See also LUPO THE WOLF; MORELLO FAMILY

TESTA, Philip "Chicken Man" (1924–1981): Philadelphia Mafia boss

Few American cities acknowledge their mafiosi as freely as Philadelphia, the City of Mafia Love. Mafioso watching has long been considered a fine spectator sport. A restaurant in the city noted as a feeding place for the Mafia, Cous' Little Italy, even sported a hamburger called the Testa Burger, named after a godfather of the early 1980s, Philip "Chicken Man" Testa. The *Wall Street Journal,* a publication much impressed with effective methods of salesmanship, cited the pitch for the Testa Burger, "If you didn't eat it, you'd get your fingers broken."

It was a gag, but Phil Testa, in his criminal activities, was no laughing matter. Classified by the FBI as one of the most violent members of the Angelo Bruno crime family, Testa was also its underboss. Bruno, known as "the Gentle Don," was assassinated in 1980, almost certainly by New York Mafia crime families seeking to take over Atlantic City's new and enormously valuable crime concessions (flowing from now-legal casino gambling). The consensus among crime specialists was that Testa would be a tougher man to down than Bruno and that he would fight for what the Philadelphia mafiosi regarded as their turf.

Testa, in fact, was considered a man who would fight almost anybody over almost anything. Testa operated from the cover of a chicken shop on Christian Street. One time a rookie FBI agent, doing a routine check on a federal job applicant, wandered into the place to question the proprietor. Testa had four of his brawny enforcers heave him out into the street.

With Testa running the mob, a local newspaper thought it would be wise, considering the great public interest in local mafiosi, to have its resident astrologer study the Testa future in the stars. "With Neptune in exact conjunction with his retrograde Jupiter," the horoscope proclaimed, "no matter what's going on, Testa will come out in a better position than he started."

It was at best a short-term forecast. In March 1981, almost a year after Bruno's rubout, Chicken Man Testa got his. He was blown to bits when a shrapnel-filled remote control bomb tore up his house and porch as he returned there in the middle of the night. Most theories lent themselves to the likelihood that the New York mobs had struck again. But the once-homogenous Philly mob was indeed coming apart. Rivals within his own organization had eliminated Testa, and the two decades of peace in Angelo Bruno's Philadelphia Mafia was over. Bruno's and Testa's deaths demonstrated that with bloody certainty.

(The night after Testa was blown up, Cous' Little Italy stopped serving the Testa Burger.)

TESTA, Salvatore (1956–1984): Mafia mobster

An FBI agent once said of young Philadelphia mafioso Salvatore Testa, "He wants to be a bad guy in the worst way—and Lord knows he's got the breeding." He certainly did, being the son of the late, violence-prone Philadelphia Mafia bigwig, Philip "Chicken Man" Testa.

Young Testa most assuredly looked forward to the day when he would be the Philadelphia godfather, an attitude that undoubtedly dismayed some other criminals, both within and without the crime family. As a result, Sal Testa became the clay pigeon of the Philadelphia underworld.

The elder Testa, who had succeeded the murdered, longtime Mafia boss Angelo Bruno, was himself blown to bits by a remote-control bomb planted under the porch of his home in March 1981. A little over a year later, Sal Testa, now a capo under the new boss Nicodemo "Little Nicky" Scarfo, made his most amazing escape from death. He was eating clams outside a South Philadelphia pizza parlor when two would-be executioners blew him out of his chair with shotgun blasts. Testa took eight slugs in his body but recovered.

The gunmen, who were caught when their car crashed into a utility pole as they were fleeing, turned out to be soldiers for a rival mob leader, Harry Riccobene, a gentle-looking but murderous septuagenarian mafioso.

After young Testa made an unsuccessful try at Riccobene's life, he was almost cornered again when he and three bodyguards were driving through a warehouse district in South Philadelphia. Their car was cut off by another one loaded with four Riccobene gunmen. Several shots were exchanged but Testa was unscathed. Still in his 20s, the hood was labeled by mob associates "unkillable."

Sal Testa was said to regard his foes as foul-ups. Then he turned careless. One day in September 1984, Testa, clad in tennis whites, left home for an afternoon of sport. At 10:23 P.M. on September 14, police in southern New Jersey received an anonymous call from a man who reported finding a body alongside a country road 20 miles southeast of Philadelphia. Testa had been shot twice in the back of the head at close range with a small-caliber gun. He was the 23rd victim in the Philadelphia underworld since Bruno's murder had shattered the longtime peace that prevailed in the mob. Sal Testa had turned out to be no more unkillable than any of the others.

In fact, he had been eliminated by members of his own murder crew on orders of Little Nicky Scarfo, who had originally promoted young Testa to capo. The problem, from Scarfo's view, was that Testa had worked hard at the killing game and had distinguished himself as the real rising star of the Philly crime family. Scarfo began seeing every expression by Testa as a show of disrespect and ordered him hit before he made a direct move for the boss job.

TIERI, Frank "Funzi" (1904–1981): Crime family boss

Although dubbed by some segments of the press as the "new boss of bosses"—that mythical title many journalists and some law officials show a consuming interest for having filled—Frank "Funzi" Tieri was no such animal. But, in the era after the demise of Carlo Gambino in 1976, Tieri may well have been more equal than the others among the New York crime family godfathers.

Tieri was perceived by many mobsters as the nearest reincarnation of Lucky Luciano. Luciano's great power within the Mafia, or what he liked to refer to as the "outfit" or "combination," derived from his gifts as a "moneymaker." Indeed when the Luciano-Lansky group made its move in the early 1930s to take over from the old Mustache Petes, the dreaded Albert Anastasia embraced Luciano in a bear hug and said, "You're gonna be on top if I have to kill everybody for you. With you there, that's the only way we can have any peace and make the real money." Meyer Lansky also had the Midas touch, and in later years so did Tieri.

Before Tieri came to power in 1972, the Luciano-Genovese crime family had fallen on hard times, relatively speaking, at least as far as the low-level soldiers were concerned. After Vito Genovese's imprisonment in 1950, operating control passed successively to a number of Genovese yes-men who seemed more concerned with their own financial wealth than that of the soldiers. This situation, in fact, made the rubout of Tieri's predecessor, Tommy Eboli, highly popular with the soldiers; Eboli showed a suicidal disinclination to share much of his personal racket empire with the troops.

It is generally acknowledged that the death of Eboli was engineered by the Mafia's then leading godfather Carlo Gambino, in part over a dispute about mob millions and also to extend Gambino's influence over yet another crime family. Tieri was Gambino's handpicked successor to the old Luciano throne. A close personal friend of Gambino's, Tieri proved a popular choice with the soldiers. Even federal agents had to admit Funzi Tieri was a good pick. One said, "He's a real class guy, a real moneymaker, one of the classiest gangsters in the New York City area." An underworld source had a similar accolade for him: "He's an earner. He always was and he always will be. And he keeps the boys happy. Under him everybody earns. That's the key. You got to keep the boys happy or else they'll turn on you."

Tieri was born in 1904 in Castel Gandolfo, the small Italian village about 15 miles south of Rome that is best known as the papal summer residence. Tieri immigrated to the United States in 1911, and, aside from an armed robbery conviction in 1922, he was not successfully prosecuted again until his twilight years, despite running one of the most widespread crime family operations in the eastern United States. Under him were such syndicate noteworthies as James Napoli (Jimmy Nap), Fat Tony Salerno, Philip "Cockeyed Ben" Lombardo, Nicholas "Cockeyed Nick" Ratteni, Gentleman John Masiello, Fat Larry Paladino, Matthew "Matty the Horse" Ianniello and Vincent "the Chin" Gigante. In addition to controlling most gambling and loan-sharking in New York City, Westchester, Long Island, and New Jersey, Tieri oversaw operations in Florida, Puerto Rico, Las Vegas and California. For several years he covered himself in so many layers of distance from criminal activities that he seemed immune from prosecution.

Tieri ran his empire with none, or at least less, of the mindless violence that marks many crime-family operations. He showed his men how to milk loan shark victims and then ease up when needed. In one case a Tieri underling made a $4,000 loan to a businessman at 3 percent a week interest, so that the annual "juice" came to $6,240. After three years the businessman was falling behind in his payments, and Tieri ordered: "Look, we've made thousands on him since he took the loan. Even if he dies tomorrow, we're way ahead." The victim was not to be killed but coddled, and, under an eased-up treatment, was taken for whatever more could be extracted from him. Tieri issued a similar decree in the case of a victim described as a "degenerate gambler." He told his capos: "Go easy. The guy's a sickie and we've made a fortune off him. Give him an easy payment schedule.

Whatever we get from him, even if it's ten bucks a week, will be gravy."

None of this indicated to his men that Tieri was a softie. He believed in violence in getting the average loan shark debtor to pay up and "not try to cheat us." He ordered many a broken leg and decreed any number of executions—especially against mob members caught skimming profits. The Mafia, more so than even prominent law-and-order types, is a firm believer in the death penalty.

When Pasquale "Paddy Mac" Maccriole, a mob loan shark, turned up as a corpse in the trunk of his own car in 1978, it was a foregone conclusion that Tieri had ordered the slaying. Then there was the disappearance of Eli Zeccardi, Tieri's reputed underboss. There was a story that an Irish gang had kidnapped him and demanded a $200,000 ransom, which was not paid. After that Tieri claimed that the four or five Irishmen involved in the plot had been hit. But the word on the underworld grapevine was that Tieri had invented the kidnap tale and had Zeccardi executed for certain infractions. The Irish tale was thus just a cunning cover story; Tieri was always known for the treachery that his position required.

Tieri could however be most diplomatic in handling important mob murders. Eavesdropping investigations indicated that Tieri was the key figure in the Mafia's decision to eliminate Carmine Galante, who had designs on control of much of the mobs' criminal activities. Tieri had emissaries sent around the country to seek approval for the hit from various crime bosses, including, allegedly, even the much-hated Joe Bonanno in Arizona. Tieri had abided with the general mob decision that Bonanno was poison and not to be dealt with, but he made an exception in this matter. It was reported that Bonanno approved the murder of Galante, who was then head of the former Bonanno family. (Of course, if Bonanno was impressed by Tieri's interest in his views, he most certainly also understood that Tieri's interest in "peace" among the New York families also meant that Bonanno was not to try another comeback, for himself or for his son whom the elder Bonanno had once envisioned as his successor.)

Tieri lived in a modest two-family house in Bath Beach, Brooklyn, with his wife and two granddaughters whose mother had died in 1978. And each day he left his home for the house of his mistress, about a mile away. She was a former opera singer who met Tieri when she first arrived from Italy many years ago. Tieri's influence was enough to give her a start in opera. By the 1970s she no longer sang, but Tieri remained an ardent opera fan. He often did the food shopping on the way to his mistress's home (from which he ran much of the mob's business) and liked to quibble with the local butcher or grocer about prices—liver prices were outrageous, flounder was up too much. Tieri was a multimillionaire but to his dying day never liked to be taken and never paid a food bill until checking the storeman's addition.

From 1922 to 1980, Tieri was arrested nine times but beat the charge every time. The score was, as the underworld said, nine-zip Funzi. Through the late 1970s Tieri flourished in his role as wisest of the godfathers, an excellent measure of his ability being the fact that many mobsters defected from other crime families to join his ranks. In 1980, however, Tieri became the first man ever convicted under new federal statutes of heading an organized crime family. According to the government, he was "the boss of a family of La Cosa Nostra" and he was connected to a "pattern of racketeering" as well as the murder of three of his associates in the last three years.

In January 1981 Tieri came into federal court for sentencing in a wheelchair. With the aid of a lawyer and a nurse, he approached the bench and told the judge in a hoarse whisper, "I'm a very sick man, very sick." He unbuttoned his shirt to show Judge Thomas P. Griesa a scar from an operation. Among the ailments with which Tieri was afflicted were gallbladder problems and throat cancer. "I'm in your hands, judge."

The judge gave him 10 years. Tieri remained free on bail pending appeal of his conviction. He died two months later. In the sense of not serving any time, the final score was 10-zip Funzi.

See also GENOVESE CRIME FAMILY

TOMMY gun: Mobster weapon

The Thompson submachine gun—nicknamed the "tommy gun," "Chicago Piano," "chopper" and "typewriter"—was described by a Collier's magazine crime reporter: "the greatest aid to bigger and better business the criminal has discovered in this generation . . . a diabolical machine of death . . . the highest powered instrument of destruction that has yet been placed at the convenience of the criminal element . . . an infernal machine . . . the diabolical acme of human ingenuity in man's effort to devise a mechanical contrivance with which to murder his neighbor." With accolades like that, the American Mafia quite naturally became the weapon's best customer.

The weapon was named the Thompson (inevitably shortened to the affectionate "tommy") after its coinventor, Brigadier General John T. Thompson, director of arsenals during World War I. Thompson had tried to get the weapon ready for use in trench warfare (he called the weapon "a trench broom"), but it was not perfected until 1920. Weighing less than 9 pounds and firing .45 caliber bullets from a circular magazine, the Thompson was effective up to 600 yards and could spew out 1,500 rounds a minute.

To Thompson's disappointment the army had no interest in the weapon which at $175 seemed expensive. Ironically, its prodigious rate of fire also worked against it. The army felt it used too much ammunition.

The underworld had a more positive attitude about the gun. Organized bootlegging gangs found it a spectacular aid as an intimidator weapon during hijackings, and the way it could turn an automobile into a sieve in a half-minute made it very attractive for assassination purposes. Best of all, it was completely legal. While many states and cities had passed laws similar to New York's 1911 Sullivan Law, prohibiting the possession of easily concealed weapons without a permit, there were no restrictions on tommy guns, which could even be ordered through the mail. When stricter federal and state laws finally were enacted, the underworld was still supplied, although the illegal price jumped into the thousands of dollars.

According to some crime historians, the first victims of the tommy gun were William H. McSwiggin, an assistant state's attorney, and Jim Doherty and Tom Duffy, two hoodlums from the O'Donnell Gang who were taken out in front of the Pony Inn in Cicero, Illinois. It was said by some that Al Capone handled the weapon personally.

Capone was a true devotee of the tommy gun, but he was hardly the first. Tommy guns were first used by the Saltis-McErlane Gang of Chicago's Southwest Side. Both Joe Saltis and Frank McErlane were a bit dimwitted, and they had murderous instincts. They took gleefully to a killing weapon on which all one had to do was squeeze the trigger and hold on. After them, every mob in Chicago and every Mafia family around the country had to have its supply of tommies.

After the underworld demonstrated the value of the tommy gun, the U.S. Army and its allies took a more positive view of the weapon, supplying their troops with almost 2 million of them in World War II.

TORRIO, John (1882–1957): Syndicate "brain" and Capone sponsor

His contributions to the fathering of syndicate crime were enormous. Johnny Torrio taught Al Capone all he ever knew. Yet that hardly measures Torrio's impact on organized crime. He was nicknamed "the Brain," a sobriquet borne, significantly, by two other men—Arnold Rothstein and Meyer Lansky. Crime historians agree that this trio, often working in tandem and certainly conferring frequently, laid out the basic strategy for organizing crime in America. Lucky Luciano, similarly, is recognized as the "doer" who ultimately carried out the plan.

If there is any knock on Torrio it is that he failed to develop a doer to carry out his plans to the fullest. His protégé, Capone, did not organize crime in America and, in fact, never completed the chore of organizing Chicago although he was nearing that goal when he went to prison in the early 1930s. Experts agree Chicago was the toughest place of all to bring under organized control; by comparison Luciano, with strong assistance from Jewish mobsters, had a relative breeze in New York.

Even after Luciano and Lansky succeeded in genuinely organizing crime, they frequently sought out the advice of the then-retired Torrio. (By that time Rothstein had been murdered.)

Born in Italy in 1882 and brought to New York at the age of two, Torrio grew up in the ghetto of the Lower East Side. He was still in his teens when he rose to the positions of subchief in Paul Kelly's huge Five Points Gang, one of the city's two most powerful (the other being the Eastmans), and of head of his own subgang, the James Streeters. Torrio managed in this period to avoid ever being arrested although his reputation as a tough young gangster grew. Known as Terrible Johnny, he took part in a number of gang battles and was adept with fists, boots and knives. As an opponent, he was regarded as cold, cruel and above all calculating. He was extremely short but his natural meanness qualified him as a bouncer at Nigger Mike's on Pell Street, regarded as one of the roughest and wildest joints in Manhattan, where, incidentally, Irving Berlin got his start as a singing waiter.

By 1912 the Bowery was no longer a big-money center, and Torrio shifted his personal interests to a bar and brothel for seamen in an even tougher section near the Brooklyn Navy Yard. Now and then he offered strong-arm employment to one of his James Street gang, a big, bullying teenage hoodlum named Al Capone.

Torrio felt the rewards of the whoring business were limited; he got into hijacking and narcotics. He expounded on how crime could be made into a big business. Those who listened to him, including Capone started calling him "the Brain."

As early as 1909 Torrio was trekking west to Chicago from time to time to do mob chores for his uncle by marriage, Big Jim Colosimo, the biggest whoremaster in that city. Around 1915, when Torrio was 33, Big Jim offered Torrio a full-time job with him. Torrio turned over most of his Brooklyn racket operations to his partner, Frankie Yale. In Chicago Torrio took over running most of Big Jim's whore joints, everything from such landmarks as the House of All Nations to the low-cost joints on what was known as Bedbug Row. Under Torrio all of these places upped their revenues handsomely.

Late in 1919 Torrio brought Capone out to Chicago, after he was informed Capone was having some troubles concerning a couple of murders. Technically, Capone was to help out in the whorehouses, but actually Torrio wanted Capone as his link for Prohibition and the bootlegging that would follow, knowing the racket would be worth a mint. The only trouble was that Torrio couldn't interest Big Jim in the booze business. He had made the mistake of making Colosimo so rich that he was lazy and couldn't see the need for more money. Torrio understood that Big Jim was a hindrance to his own ambitions and to the operation in general. He resolved that he had to go. By this time Capone was Torrio's number one aide, but he knew neither of them could assassinate Big Jim without coming under immediate suspicion. Frankie Yale came west to handle the job.

Once Colosimo was erased, Torrio simply moved in and took over the entire organization. Anybody objecting had to deal with Capone. However, Torrio didn't see himself merely as the head of Big Jim's old empire. He wanted to build a new kind of empire in Chicago, one that brought all the gangs under a single confederation. Each gang would have its own area to milk without any competition. He called all

Like Arnold Rothstein and Meyer Lansky, Johnny Torrio was nicknamed "the Brain." Also like the other two, Torrio, as Al Capone's boss and mentor, played a key role in organizing crime in America.

the gangs together—the Italian gangs, many of whom were mafioso, the North Side Irish, the South Side Poles, etc. He promised them that they'd all make millions and, what was more important, actually live to enjoy their wealth. Torrio did not believe in the veiled threat; the alternative, he said softly, was war and he would win that. It was join the new syndicate setup or, sooner or later, die.

The various gang leaders were tough men who'd made it to the top because they could shove better than others, but most of them were persuaded, by Torrio's logic and perhaps as well by his threats. Some of the others, especially among the Irish gangs, said they would join up but didn't. War soon raged, with the tough North Siders headed by the murderous and erratic Dion O'Banion. The Italian Genna gang joined but never stopped double-dealing, continuing to invade other territories with its lower-priced rotgut. The wars that raged often were multisided and marked by double crosses, with henchmen bribed to kill their own leaders.

Several Genna men fell, but O'Banion remained a thorn. Then suddenly O'Banion sent word to Torrio that he wanted to quit the rackets and get out. If he could sell his Seiben Brewery for a half-million dollars, he would be through. Torrio jumped at the offer. It was a cheap price to pay to have O'Banion go away. A week after the deal was finalized and O'Banion got his money, federal agents raided the brewery and confiscated everything. Torrio realized O'Banion had suckered him. He discovered O'Banion had been tipped off that the federal action was in the works and had cunningly let Torrio take the loss.

Torrio stormed about his office, brandishing a gun and screaming he'd have vengeance on the Irish mobster. It was an uncommon reaction from Torrio who seldom let his emotions show. Torrio made good on his threats. Frankie Yale, Colosimo's assassin, was sent for again. Yale and two hoods, Albert Anselmi and John Scalise, murdered O'Banion in the flower shop he ran.

Capone was overjoyed by O'Banion's murder, but Torrio knew it would only produce more gang conflict. O'Banion's gang, now bossed by Hymie Weiss, would fight and the longer it took Torrio to subdue them, the greater the chances other gangs would start revolting. As expected, Weiss and some of his boys tried to ambush Torrio as he was riding in his limousine. The chauffeur and Torrio's dog were shot to death, but Johnny escaped with just two bullet holes in his gray fedora. Torrio had Capone and his gunners out looking for Weiss but Hymie stayed undercover. Then on January 24, 1925, Torrio was ambushed in front of his apartment building. He was cut down with a shotgun blast and then a second gunman pumped four slugs into him. Hit in the chest, arm and stomach, Torrio hovered near death for a week and a half while Capone kept a troop of 30 hoods stationed around the hospital to ward off any further tries at him.

After Torrio recovered, he did a lot of thinking. His dream for a syndicate setup in Chicago was far from realized and any hope for a national syndicate was still far in the future. And there was an excellent chance he'd be killed. He'd survived five years at the top in Chicago gangland, no easy task. He was 43 years old and had $30 million. Torrio's pioneering was done. He told Capone: "It's all yours, Al. I've retired."

Torrio walked away from what was up until then the greatest setup ever established. It was he rather than Capone who had first said, "I own the police force." Now he was going to retire in Brooklyn after lazing around for a year or two in the Mediterranean sun.

The law and the press often expressed doubts that he really retired, but basically he did except for occasionally playing elder statesman. Luciano and the emerging national crime syndicate often sought his advice, as did Capone. Torrio attended the underworld's landmark 1929 Atlantic City Conference, and it is known that his counsel was sought before the decision was voted to hit Dutch Schultz because of his dangerous plan to assassinate prosecutor Thomas E. Dewey. It was said that several Murder, Inc., hits also required his approval. Torrio said it wasn't so at all, that he was a has-been who just wanted to die in bed.

In April 1957 Johnny Torrio sat down in a Brooklyn barbershop chair and suffered a heart attack. He lingered long enough to die in bed. He was 75.

Ironically, a few months later, Albert Anastasia was assassinated in a barber chair in Manhattan. Anastasia had been relaxing with his eyes closed when the assassins struck. Torrio, on the other hand, had not been an assassination victim and hadn't expected to be. But in the barber chair, he had been sitting Chicago-style—with his eyes wide open and the chair facing the door so that he could see who was coming. Johnny Torrio was the cautious one right to the very end.

TOUHY, Roger "Terrible" (1898–1959): Bootleg kingpin

It has been said by some observers of the syndicate crime scene in America that FBI chief J. Edgar Hoover may have done the wise thing to pretend for decades that organized crime and the Mafia did not exist. The case of Roger "Terrible" Touhy demonstrated that the FBI did not fully comprehend the nature of such criminals and that the agency was used and abused by organized crime in framing Touhy.

The FBI may be said to have never understood poor Roger the Terrible. When they went after him in lieu of dozens of other more terrifying gangsters, they picked on a man whom the Chicago Crime Commission never had on its roster of public enemies, and, as a federal judge would later note in a major finding, had never even been associated in any way with a capital offense.

Yet amazingly, just as Touhy proved a thorn to the FBI, he was equally regarded as a true terror by Al Capone, who regarded Touhy as one of the stumbling blocks to his plans to organize all crime in Chicago.

Roger "Terrible" Touhy was pretty much a creation of sharp public relations, his own. As far as the entire underworld had it figured, the Terrible Touhys—Roger, the boss, and his five brothers—controlled all booze operations in the Chicago suburban area of Des Plaines and had their empire backed with such firepower that they were impregnable.

Press coverage indicated the Touhy Gang to be about the most vicious in the Midwest. Yet Touhy was a middle-class bootlegger, one who employed no more muscle than necessary to convince all the speakeasies and saloons in his area to handle Touhy beer and booze exclusively. Indeed, firepower was less a reason for Touhy's success than his ability to handle the fix as well as any figure in the underworld. Not only was Touhy the master of the fix, but he knew how to supplement cash payoffs with fringe benefits that meant so much. He rewarded the local politicians and police brass with bottled beer brewed especially for them and often bearing their own personal labels.

Perhaps Touhy's reputation as a ferocious gangster was sealed by his looks—kinky-haired, beady-eyed, with a hawklike face, clearly a man to be feared. And Touhy knew how to act the part, forcing even Al Capone to back down to him. Touhy had once sold the Capone boys 800 barrels of his superior beer for $37.50 a barrel (his cost of production was $5.50 at most), and Capone then tried to short Touhy with $1,900 in the payoff, claiming that some of the barrels had leaks. (Capone always pressured people that way.) Touhy came back with his regular routine. He assumed his famed hard stare, and said softly, "Don't chisel me, Al." Capone paid the $1,900.

Roger and his five brothers had not started out as criminals. They grew up in respectable circumstances, the sons of a policeman. In the early 1920s, the Touhys went into the trucking business, "strictly legit," at least by Touhys word. Business, however, did not boom until they started filling the trucks with beer. The Terrible Touhys raked in a fortune.

Roger Touhy took control of the Des Plaines area in the northwest section of Cook County. In those days a bootlegger was hardly an unpopular figure, and Touhy found ways to increase the esteem in which he was held. He kept out lowlife criminals and especially clamped down on brothels. Whenever a group of mobsters tried to open a roadside whorehouse, Touhy would relieve the local police of the need to take action. He sent in his own enforcers to wreck the joint. Even when Capone personally noted that Des Plaines was, as he charmingly put it, "virgin territory for whorehouses," Touhy's response was his hard-eyed stare, which convinced Capone to drop his plans.

Whenever rivals made noise about wanting to move in, Touhy would invite them to his headquarters for a visit, where they were greeted by what appeared to be an armed camp, the walls lined with submachine guns. What the visiting hoods didn't know was that the weapons had been made available by cooperative local cops just for a good show. While the gangsters were conferring with Touhy, underlings would come rushing in for weapons, mumbling something about having a great chance to rub out some party. Touhy would nod his head slightly in assent and return to the dialogue as though the matter was of minor importance. When Touhy's visitors left, they were fully convinced they would be the loser in any war with the Terrible Touhys. At various times such Capone gunners as Murray "the Camel" Humphreys and Frank Nitti were so shaken that they reported back that Capone would be facing a terrible bloodletting if he tried to move in.

Still the Capone gang tried to get Touhy—even after Big Al went to prison. Deciding violence was out, they resolved to use another method, helping the law get something on him. Suddenly Touhy found himself in big trouble with the FBI. It is unclear if the Chicago Outfit had anything to do with the first incident, but it is not beyond the realm of possibility. Touhy and several of his henchmen were arrested for the kidnapping of William Hamm Jr. The FBI announced it had a strong case against Touhy, but a jury thought differently, finding him not guilty. Later, the FBI switched the charge to the real culprits, the Barker-Karpis gang. By coincidence Alvin "Creepy" Karpis had long been close to the Capone Gang.

Next the FBI arrested Touhy for the alleged 1933 kidnapping of Jake "the Barber" Factor, an international confidence man with ties to the Capones. This was despite underworld grapevine information that indicated the abduction was a fake masterminded by

Factor and the Capones. Special agent Melvin Purvis announced that his arrest of Touhy in the Factor snatch was a landmark in the art of detection. "This case," he said, "holds a particular interest for me because it represents a triumph of deductive detective work. We assumed from the start, with no material evidence, that the Touhy gang was responsible for the crime."

Touhy's first trial ended in a hung jury. He was convicted the second time around and was sentenced to 99 years. Touhy went to prison screaming frame-up while the Capones swarmed into Des Plaines.

In 1942, Touhy escaped from prison but was recaptured soon and saddled with an additional sentence of 199 years. Still, there were many persons, including several journalists, who considered him innocent of the Factor kidnapping, and took up the fight to clear him. In the 1950s Touhy at last won a rehearing on his original conviction. After a searching inquiry lasting 36 days, Federal Judge John H. Barnes ruled that Factor had not been kidnapped at all but had disappeared "of his own connivance." Judge Barnes had plenty of criticism to hand out to several quarters, especially to the FBI, the Chicago police, the state's attorney and the Capone Gang. It took a few more years of legal jockeying before Touhy was released. He collaborated on a book, *The Stolen Years*, about his ordeal. Just 23 days after Touhy won his freedom, he was gunned down as he was entering his sister's house in Chicago. As he lay dying, the former gangster muttered: "I've been expecting it. The bastards never forget."

The underworld had no doubts about who had knocked off Touhy—the word was the price on his head was $40,000—that it was the handiwork of longtime Capone mobster Murray "the Camel" Humphreys. Six months after the Touhy rubout, Humphreys bought 400 shares of First National Life Insurance Co. stock at $20 a share from John Factor, Touhy's old nemesis, and a man at the time eager to have an unsullied slate as he was attempting to operate in Las Vegas. Eight months later, Humphreys sold the shares back to Factor for $125 a share, turning a profit of $42,000 in capital gains. The IRS looked at the transaction and related details and declared that the $42,000 was clearly payment for services rendered and that it was subject to full income taxes.

The Humphreys-Factor financial dealings were not the only noteworthy matter occurring after

"Terrible" Touhy lies dying after being shot. Released from prison after doing 25 years on a mob frame-up, he said, "I've been expecting it. The bastards never forget."

Touhy's death. Early in 1960, a few months after the murder, retired FBI man Purvis committed suicide.

TRAFFICANTE, Santo (1886–1954): Tampa crime family boss

Like his predecessor, Ignacio Antinori, Florida Mafia chief Santo Trafficante Sr. was a shadowy force. Born in Sicily in 1886, he had lived in Tampa since the age of 18. By the 1920s, Trafficante had emerged at or near the top of the Tampa family. While he apparently shared power with old-liner Antinori, Trafficante cemented his relations with New York gangsters, including the rising star Lucky Luciano. Antinori instead allied himself with mafiosi in Kansas City and St. Louis—not exactly true power bases while the national crime syndicate, under Luciano and Jewish gangster Meyer Lansky, was aborning in the early 1930s.

Trafficante deftly maneuvered himself into a position of authority and was probably the godfather of the Tampa family before Antinori was conveniently murdered in 1940. Trafficante did not alter Antinori's operations, which were primarily in the narcotics trade, especially with the French underworld of Corsica and Marseilles. But he greatly extended the family activities in gambling, bit by bit wresting away the major wagering empire of an independent West Florida operator, Charles Wall. Only when the ambitious Trafficante tried to move to Florida's lush east coast did he stumble, there facing Lansky, a man at the top of the syndicate and one who tolerated no competition in his own domain. Lansky could operate on any level, exercising control through the bribe or the bullet as needed. Musclewise, he commanded the gunners of his own old Bug and Meyer Gang, and the forces of the South Detroit Purple Gang, which had relocated, and had the aid of Moe Dalitz and the rest of the Cleveland Syndicate. Wisely, Trafficante headed back to the Gulf Coast.

Trafficante always wanted to make it big in Cuban casinos and dispatched his son, Santo Jr., to Havana in 1946 to operate mob casinos. However, even in Cuba, Lansky was top dog, maintaining top-echelon influence with the government so that Trafficante never was more than a junior partner on the island. With a careful eye to mob alliances, Lansky cut many other gangsters in on the Cuban action—the New York mobs, the Chicago Outfit, the Dalitz Jewish mob, etc. Tampa made a lot of money in Cuba, but never achieved its ambition of making the island part of its own territory.

Still, Trafficante remained the power in his own bailiwick, especially after 1945 when he forced Wall to enter into a number of partnerships with the crime family. The fact that Wall suffered three attempts on his life seems to have been a potent convincer. Wall sought to ensure his own safety by keeping a sort of "insurance" document that revealed his dealings with Trafficante. The document kept him alive through his retirement in 1952, and, indeed, until 1954 when the elder Trafficante died. The following April Wall was found murdered in his home, savagely beaten and his throat slashed. With the elder Trafficante dead, Wall's insurance simply lapsed. The police got hold of the document in 1960 but by then there was nothing in it that could harm anyone living.

Santo Trafficante Jr. succeeded his father as boss of Tampa, one of the few times in the American Mafia when a son succeeded his father as godfather. It was a tribute to both Trafficantes and their ability to exercise power and terror to achieve their ends. For half a century Tampa was Trafficante country.

See also TRAFFICANTE, SANTO, JR.

TRAFFICANTE, Santo, Jr. (1914–1987): Second generation Tampa godfather

Despite numerous stunted ambitions, Santo Trafficante Jr. was regarded as one of the most powerful of the Mafia bosses in the United States. He ruled the Tampa, Florida, family with an iron hand and, following a long Mafia tradition in that city, has kept it profitably involved in many standard organized crime activities, such as gambling, loan-sharking and, above all, narcotics dealing. Florida is regarded as the top entry point for drugs into this country.

Born in this country, he is one of the few sons of a Mafia don to succeed to the godfather position in a crime family. His father, Santo Trafficante Sr., was boss for many years until his death in 1954. The elder Trafficante bequeathed his crown to his son, and his offspring had the required cunning, forcefulness and determination to take it.

Through the years it has been difficult for law enforcement officials and other observers to gauge Trafficante's activities, although it has been well known that he, as much as his father, initiated the crime family's move into the gambling casino world of pre-Castro Cuba. Trafficante took up Cuban residence in 1946 and remained there until Fidel Castro ejected the mobs in 1959. After that Trafficante

Santo Trafficante Jr. inherited his father's mantle as godfather. He was wooed by the CIA in its anti-Castro assassination debacle.

returned to Tampa and maintained the family's international ties in other fields. It has been alleged that in 1969 he journeyed to Saigon to make arrangements with the Corsicans there to ship Indochinese heroin unto the United States.

Trafficante was known to have been deeply involved in the CIA efforts to involve the underworld assassination attempts on Castro. Under pressure of a court order granting him immunity from prosecution, but threatening him with contempt if he refused to talk, Trafficante admitted to a congressional committee in 1975 that he had in the early 1960s recruited other mobsters, such as Johnny Roselli, to assassinate Castro. "It was like in World War II," he told the committee. "They tell you to go to the draft board and sign up. Well, I signed up." According to Trafficante, he and his fellow underworld conspirators considered "poison, planes, tanks. I'm telling you, they talk about everything." Eventually, he said, the plots all failed.

Others give a different interpretation of the facts, that Trafficante above all others took the CIA for a ride. This version, backed by Roselli's statements, holds that Trafficante had no intention of trying to get Castro, that poisons prepared by CIA master chemists were simply flushed down Florida toilets, and moneys from the CIA to be siphoned to Cubans on the island never left the United States. Some lawmen, and Roselli and his superior, Chicago boss Sam Giancana, ended up believing that Trafficante had even sold out to Castro. When Castro took power, he jailed Trafficante for a time, then suddenly released him and allowed him to leave with all his money. The theory holds that Trafficante became Castro's agent in Florida, and when the CIA plots developed, he probably reported everything to Cuban agents in the state. There has long been a theory among many researchers that the assassination of John F. Kennedy was actually a Castro retaliation for the CIA-Mafia plots against him. In 1978 Trafficante testified once again before a House assassination committee on the Kennedy murder. This time the committee was especially interested in a sworn statement made to committee investigators by Cuban exile leader José Alemán that months before the Kennedy assassination, Trafficante had told him, "Kennedy's gonna get hit."

However, in public testimony, Alemán, clearly fearful of Trafficante's wrath, gave the comment a different interpretation. What the mob boss probably meant, Alemán said, was that Kennedy would be hit by Republican votes in 1964—not bullets. It was the first and only time Trafficante was granted status with George Gallup as an expert on voter opinion, and for that matter it was virgin use of the term *hit* in mob lingo as being synonymous with "landslide."

Trafficante glided through the probe. He was one of the most successful Mafia bosses in that respect—suspected of much but convicted of little until his death in 1987 of a heart ailment.

See also BAY OF PIGS INVASION; CIA-MAFIA CONNECTION; ROSELLI, JOHN

TRAPMAN: Mob security specialist

As important to organized crime as hit men or respectable business fronts, the trapman provides rich mobsters with psychological well-being—via readily accessible hiding places for funds. This security specialist builds traps or secret panels or hidden safes. Very few top mob leaders do not make use of such traps in either their homes and/or their offices.

Many years after Bugsy Siegel was murdered in Beverly Hills and his Flamingo Hotel in Las Vegas sold to other interests, a hidden safe was found in the hotel floor. Siegel had undoubtedly used the safe to hide much of the operating and building funds he'd skimmed off and indeed hidden from his underworld partners. It was empty when discovered and since Bugsy had expired too suddenly to have emptied it himself, someone who knew about the trap must have done it—or a trapman had talked to the mob.

Mobsters have a passionate dislike for safety deposit boxes—at least, in this country—and not all of them truly trust the Swiss or Bahamian banks with all their wealth. They like to keep their funds close at hand, often in concealed safes which also hold vital records and arms caches. Their houses often contain phony walls or even panels in swimming pools. One important mobster who maintained a close financial arrangement with Meyer Lansky, the late Trigger Mike Coppola, was said to have kept at least $300,000 stashed in various traps in his Alton Road home in Miami Beach.

Mobsters demand very sophisticated traps, such as a trap built behind a trap, a fireproof trap inside a stove or furnace, or one with an opening mechanism that can only be triggered in another room located often on another floor than the actual trap.

The trapman tends to be a non-crime person, pledged to secrecy. Since only the trapman and his client know of the trap, the security specialist has two vital reasons to maintain his silence: He likes the high pay he gets for his work and, even more important, he wants to stay alive. If a trap is busted, the trapman is the logical suspect.

Top trapmen do work for non-syndicate clients as well. Doctors and dentists, notorious for saving their "non-taxable" $100 bills, also feel unsafe with bank safe deposit boxes—which can be opened by tax authorities. Thus they prefer to keep traps in their homes.

Ethically, the only time a trapman is allowed to break his silence is if his client suddenly dies. Then, the trapman is allowed to come forward and reveal the trap to the dead man's associates—even to associates who may have conspired in the victim's death. If the trap is found to contain money, the trapman, under the mob's special code, is entitled to a percentage of the find.

TRESCA, Carlo (1875–1943): Anti-Fascist and Mafia murder victim

Officially the 1943 murder of anti-Fascist, anti-Communist editor Carlo Tresca on New York's Fifth Avenue remains unsolved. Yet everyone in the Mafia and New York police knew who ordered the murder and who pulled the trigger. It was a Mafia operation all the way.

Tresca was the editor of *Il Martello* and had known Benito Mussolini since 1904 when the latter was in his short-lived leftist youth. Now in exile in America Tresca was an implacable foe and caustic critic of Mussolini. In 1943, in wartime New York City, Tresca had little to fear from the Fascist dictator. Unfortunately for the 68-year-old syndicalist, Vito Genovese, who had fled to Italy before the war to avoid a murder charge, was now close to Mussolini. He was a big-money contributor to the Fascist cause and further ingratiated himself with Il Duce's son-in-law and foreign minister, Count Galeazzo Ciano, by keeping him supplied with narcotics.

When Mussolini raged about Tresca, "Genovese's countryman," for constantly attacking him, the gangster sought to ingratiate himself all the more by promising to have Tresca taken care of. Genovese got the contract back to New York to his aides Mike Miranda and Tony Bender who passed it on to a then

Anti-Fascist, anti-Communist editor Carlo Tresca was shot down on New York City's Fifth Avenue in 1943, a hit ordered by fugitive Vito Genovese as a favor to Benito Mussolini.

minor Brooklyn hoodlum named Carmine Galante, who would in the 1970s rise to become the boss of the Bonanno Family.

On the evening of January 11, 1943, Tresca was walking on Fifth Avenue near 15th Street with a friend, attorney Giuseppe Calabi, also a political exile from Italy. As they crossed 15th Street on the west side of the avenue, it was quite dark since the wartime dimout was in effect. The men paid no particular attention to a figure standing on the corner. As they approached him, the loiterer reached in his pocket. He came up with a .38-caliber pistol and started shooting. One bullet crashed through Tresca's right cheek and lodged at the base of his skull. Another hit him in the back and lodged in his left lung. Tresca died in the gutter where he fell. The killer escaped by car.

Calabi and other witnesses were able to record the license number: 1C-9272. That number meant something to the law. About two hours before the killing, Galante, out of prison on parole, had made his weekly report to his parole officer in downtown Manhattan. It was standard procedure for parole officers to trail parolees out of the office in the hope of seeing them consorting with other criminals, a violation of the terms of their release. Galante had entered a car and driven off. A parole officer had not tried to follow Galante but had recorded the license number of the car: 1C-9272.

Picked up as a suspect in the Tresca assassination, Galante denied all. He had not gotten in any car. He'd gone uptown by subway and seen a Broadway movie, *Casablanca,* with Humphrey Bogart. Questioned about the plot of the film, Galante was remarkably and suspiciously vague. He did not appear to even remember the phrase, "You must remember this. . . ." It was suspicious but hardly an indictable offense, especially since none of the witnesses to the murder could identify the killer because of the dimout.

Galante had to be released, and when Genovese returned to the United States after the war, he had nothing to fear from any further investigation of the Tresca assassination.

Police kept Galante under a phone tap for four and a half years, hoping he would make some slip about the case. A police detective who worked on the investigation later recalled, "He was real cagey, that guy. Someone would call him and say, 'Hello,' and all he'd say back was 'Humm' and the other guy would say 'Meet you at 1 P.M.,' and he would say 'Humm.' That's all he ever said on the phone."

See also GALANTE, CARMINE; GENOVESE, VITO

TWENTIES Group: Mafioso leadership migration

In the 1920s, shortly after his rise to power in Italy, Benito Mussolini declared war on the Sicilian Mafia, ordering his number one enforcer, Cesare Mori, prefect of Palermo, to wipe out the criminal gangs. Mori conducted a brutal campaign of terror and torture and forced many mafiosi to flee. Many of these headed for the United States in what came to be known as the "Mussolini Shuttle."

The mafiosi so forced to come to America became powers in the underworld and did much to mold the forces of organized crime. Known as the "Twenties Group," they included Carlo Gambino, who passed through customs on December 23, 1921, a pre-Mussolini refugee but one already feeling official heat in Sicily. Within the next several years, Gambino was followed by Joe Bonanno, Antonio Magaddino and Stefano Magaddino in 1924; Joe Profaci, Mike Coppola and Joe Magliocco in 1926; and Salvatore Maranzano in 1927. All these men would rise to be the bosses or underbosses in various crime families. All came more or less as representatives of Don Vito Cascio Ferro—if not the so-called boss of bosses of the Mafia in Sicily, then certainly the most powerful and colorful chieftain.

Ferro clearly had designs on expanding his influence in America, and so great was his power and influence that all his protégés moved into positions of power in America with startling speed. The Twenties Group found a great many allies already in the United States, mafiosi like Joe Aiello, the leading Mafia leader in Chicago who would eventually fall under the guns of non-mafioso Al Capone; Joe Zerilli, a power in the Detroit family; and Gaetano Reina, Tommy Lucchese and Tom Gagliano in Brooklyn.

With the imprisonment of Don Vito Cascio Ferro in 1929, the Twenties Group splintered, although for a time Don Vito's top representative in the United States, Maranzano, tried to establish himself as the boss of bosses. The Twenties Group proved to have no more lasting allegiance to the Sicilian traditions than other opportunistic gangsters had had, and soon the Twenties members formed alliances with other non-Mafia gangs in the quest for a more tangible tradition—the American dollar.

See also FERRO, DON VITO CASCIO; MORI, CESARE; MUSSOLINI SHUTTLE

UNDERTAKER'S Friend, the: Underworld "Green Chair Curse"

An ordinary green leather chair in the office of William "Shoes" Schoemaker, Chicago's chief of detectives in 1924, became known as "the Undertaker's Friend" or the "Green Chair Curse." Many apprehended mafiosi were grilled by Schoemaker as they sat in the green chair, and Schoemaker and journalists soon noted that many of the criminals so grilled died in gangland slayings shortly thereafter.

Considering the high mortality rate during Prohibition's booze wars, the death toll was a rather underwhelming discovery but the newspapers, always alert for a new angle on the bloodletting, seized upon the story of a "curse" and started calling the chair "the Undertaker's Friend." Shoes, realizing he was on to a good thing, began keeping a record of the criminals who sat in the chair and later died violently. When the "preordained" occurred, Shoes marked an X next to the gangster's name. On the X list were such noteworthies as the bloody Genna brothers (Angelo, Tony and Mike), Mop Head Russo, Porky Lavenuto, John Scalise, Albert Anselmi, Samoots Amatuna, Antonio "the Scourge" Lombardo, Schemer Drucci, Pickle Puss DePro, Zippy Zion and Antonio "the Cavalier" Spano. Some of them plopped down in the chair with bravado; others trembled with fear. It made no difference. The results were inevitable. Stories related how many mafiosi adamantly refused to sit in the chair (Sicilians were said to be the most superstitious of all criminals). An almost certainly apochryphal tale relates that Al Capone himself declined an offer from Shoes to take a seat.

Shoes retired in 1934 at which time there were 35 names in his notebook, 34 X-ed out. Only one criminal, Red Holden, was still among the breathing, and he was doing that in Alcatraz for train robbery. "My prediction still stands," Shoes said in his parting shot. "He'll die a violent death. Maybe it'll happen in prison. Maybe we'll have to wait until he gets out. But mark my words, it'll happen."

Shoes died four years later. The chair had passed to Captain John Warren, Shoes's aide, who also kept track of the green chair's death toll. Warren died in September 1953, and the score stood at 56 out of 57—Red Holden was still alive. Released from Alcatraz in 1948, he promptly got involved in a number of shootouts, all of which he survived. Then he was sent up for 25 years on a murder charge. On December 18, 1953, Holden died in the infirmary of Illinois's Statesville Penitentiary. Predictably various publications assured their readers that Holden went out bragging. He had beaten the curse of the Undertaker's Friend.

Holden's demise also sparked a newspaper hunt for the green chair. It was traced to the Chicago Avenue police station, where it had been consigned to the cellar after Captain Warren's death. When a maintenance man discovered it had become infested with cockroaches, he chopped it up and disposed of it in the furnace.

It was of course the end of the curse, and in fact, some argued the green chair had ended up with a perfect record, since it had been destroyed before Holden died of natural causes.

UNTOUCHABLES, The   See NESS, ELIOT

VALACHI, Joseph M. (1903–1971): Informer

Despite its notoriety, Joe Valachi's testimony before a Senate committee never led—directly—to the jailing of any criminal. That was not the importance of Valachi's testimony about organized crime, what he called "Cosa Nostra." A barely literate, low-ranking member of the Mafia whose first-hand experiences were frankly limited to less-important events, Valachi was obviously talking beyond his personal experience. Additionally, Valachi was not the most discerning observer. In the underworld the telling of false tales between mobsters, the claims of credit not deserved for important incidents, are common. When another criminal bragged to Valachi that he did this or shot so-and-so, Valachi tended to believe it. As a result some of his information is false and some strains credulity.

Yet Joe Valachi remains one of only a few Mafia members who violated omerta, the code of silence. In September and October 1963 the gravel-voiced, chain-smoking killer enthralled much of the national television audience as he told Senator John L. McClellan and the Senate Permanent Investigations Subcommittee about the inner structure of the Mafia and organized crime.

"Not since Frank Costello's fingers drummed the table during the Kefauver hearings," the *New York Times* editorialized, "has there been so fascinating a show."

The Valachi revelations were often chilling, including the details of a number of murders in which he took part. Even though he functioned mainly on the street level, he still offered an inside view of the struggle for power within the Mafia and of the double-dealing that is part of the Honored Society. While it is true that many of the incidents and facts that Valachi described were known to police, he still filled in some gaps and provided a rationale linking one development to another and added to an understanding of the dimensions of syndicated crime.

Valachi joined Salvatore Maranzano's organization in the late 1920s and was indoctrinated officially into the organization in 1930. He served Maranzano until his assassination in 1931 and thereafter spent most of his time under Vito Genovese in the Luciano family. His criminal record dated back to his teens. As a "soldier," or "button man," in the mob his duties included that of a hit man, enforcer, numbers operator and drug pusher until 1959, when he was sentenced to 15 to 20 years on drug trafficking charges.

Confined to the federal penitentiary in Atlanta, Georgia, Valachi was a cellmate of Genovese, who had become head of the Luciano crime family and, after Luciano's deportation to Italy, according to Valachi, the "boss of bosses" within the Mafia. Clearly, Valachi was in no position to comprehend the workings of the national crime syndicate or gauge the vital importance to organized crime of men like Meyer Lansky, Longy Zwillman, Moe Dalitz and others. He saw only the Italian end of the racket, which was typical among lower-echelon Mafia soldiers. (The lower one goes in the Mafia structure, the more one finds the will to believe in the all-powerfulness of the Italian society.)

In 1962, Valachi later revealed, Genovese wrongfully came to suspect Valachi of being an informer and gave him the "kiss of death," a sign to Valachi that Genovese had ordered his assassination. Valachi was terrified and in his terror later mistook a prisoner named Joe Saupp for Joe Beck (Joe DiPalermo), whom he identified as the man assigned to kill him. Valachi killed Saupp with an iron pipe and after he got a life sentence for that killing, he decided to turn informer and get federal protection.

By the time he sang for the McClellan Committee, he was guarded by some 200 U.S. marshals, which at least indicated how highly the federal agents regarded his revelations. The Mafia itself thought highly of them too, putting a $100,000 price tag on Valachi's head. Valachi himself was not surprised by that. "You live by the gun and the knife," he said, "and you die by the gun and the knife."

In all it was said that Valachi helped to identify 317 members of the Mafia, and Attorney General Robert F. Kennedy called Valachi's testimony "a significant addition to the broad picture" of organized crime. "It gives meaning to much that we already know and brings the picture into sharper focus."

This did not prevent disparagement of many of Valachi's claims. Quite a few law enforcement officials found much of Valachi's testimony little more than good theater, much of it erroneous and even ludicrous. Many considered the idea of Genovese as the boss of bosses from 1946 on as absolutely silly. The most important voice within the American Mafia in 1946, at the Havana conference in December of that year and for many years thereafter, remained Luciano, even in exile. Otherwise the most important voice was the "little man," Meyer Lansky. As Luciano himself put it to his Italian associates, "listen to the little man" or "listen to Meyer." But poor Valachi could never have comprehended a Jew telling mafiosi what to do. There is no doubt Genovese wanted to become Boss of Bosses, but he never made the grade, even after he had Albert Anastasia murdered in 1957. More powerful hands than his doomed him after that.

Although the underworld sought to disparage Valachi, he was never considered very highly. Another Mafia informer, Vincent Teresa, later confined with Valachi, came to like him but said he was a small-timer and a mob gofer. "To the mob, Joe was a *facci-due*—two-faced in Italian. No one trusted him in the mob long before he talked." There is ample suspicion in the case of Eugenio Giannini, whose murder Valachi arranged, to indicate that Valachi may well have been an informer long before he went to Atlanta.

Quite naturally the mob itself sought to discredit Valachi, and his nickname may be a case in point. In *The Valachi Papers*, Valachi explained that in his youth, he built makeshift scooters out of wooden crates. "This earned him the nickname Joe Cargo, which later in his criminal career was corrupted to Cago." However, the mob told it different, pointing

Although some of informer Joe Valachi's direct testimony strained credulity and none of it ever led to the jailing of any criminal, he did offer a new view of the struggle for power within the Mafia and the double-dealing that is part of the Honored Society.

out jocularly that "Cago" was an Italian word for excrement. Perhaps a better illustration of the fact that Valachi was not highly thought of in the Mafia was revealed by some of his own testimony which was not reported in *The Valachi Papers*. It turned out that the highly placed Paul Gambino, Carlo's brother, came to see Valachi shortly after the Anastasia murder when it looked like war could break out in the crime family. Paul Gambino said, "I have a lot of respect for your opinion regardless of how other people feel. What should we do?" It was obvious that Gambino really was not seeking Valachi's advice but rather was pumping him if he knew of any plot against the Gambinos. The key words of course were "regardless of how other people feel."

There is need, in a historical sense, to compare, Valachi's many disclosures to the later revelations in the memoirs or reminiscences of such syndicate higher-ups as Luciano, Lansky and Doc Stacher, among others. Certainly these throw considerable doubt on Valachi's versions of who killed such victims as Peter "the Clutching Hand" Morello, a job he credited to "Buster from Chicago." Luciano credits the murder to Anastasia and Frank Scalise, a claim that also fits far more logically. Apparently Buster was pulling Valachi's leg. Similarly, Valachi really had no inside information on who was in on Joe the Boss Masseria's murder and had the names in several cases wrong.

Then too there was a feeling that Valachi had been coached to refer to "Cosa Nostra" as a proper name rather than as merely a generic term meaning "our thing" used by mafiosi in casual conversations. The Cosa Nostra label proved very important to the FBI's J. Edgar Hoover, who for decades insisted there was no such thing as a Mafia or organized crime—the better not to have to fight them. With disclosure of a "new" crime group, suddenly, with a straight face, Hoover could assert the FBI knew all about the Cosa Nostra and that "agents have penetrated its workings and its leadership" for "several years."

On balance, there can be no doubt that Valachi's testimony, supplemented by *The Valachi Papers*, had a devastating effect on the Mafia. At the end of 1966 a survey by the New York City Police Department showed that in the three years since Valachi talked more members of the syndicate in the New York–New Jersey–Connecticut metropolitan area had been jailed than in the previous 30 years.

The Valachi revelations sank Vito Genovese as well. Up till then he had ruled the Luciano-Genovese family from behind bars, but now his influence started to collapse. Indeed the family, long the most important in the country, lost influence, and the previously much smaller Anastasia family under the shrewd Carlo Gambino grew in numbers and power and became the foremost outfit.

VALENTI, Rocco (?–1922): Mafia shooter and Luciano victim

In the early 1920s, the Mafia in New York and New Jersey was splintered into contending groups, all seeking supremacy. Remnants of the Morello family tried to reassert their authority under Peter Morello, while others followed Valenti, Salvatore Mauro and Joe the Boss Masseria. Masseria made it plain he intended to take over the entire Italian underworld in New York. Morello, more concerned with Mauro at the time, finally succeeded in knocking him off. Then Morello turned to an alliance of convenience with Valenti. Morello considered himself the boss of this partnership; Valenti thought otherwise.

A seasoned killer, Rocco Valenti was known to have committed 20 murders and was regarded as the most accurate shot in gangland—a claim which proved to be embarrassingly exaggerated on two occasions.

On August 9, 1922, Valenti, unbeknownst to Morello, went after Masseria alone. He caught up with the quarry and his two bodyguards on Second Avenue. Calmly and accurately, Valenti cut down Masseria's protectors. Unarmed, Masseria was totally helpless. Valenti calmly reloaded, while the rotund Masseria charged into a millinery shop at 82 Second Avenue. The proprietor, Fritz Heiney, later told police what happened: "The man with the revolver came close to the other fellow and aimed. Just as he fired, the little fellow jumped to one side. The bullet smashed the window of my store. Then the man fired the gun again. Again the other man ducked his head forward. The third shot made a second hole in my window." In all, the windows were broken, several mirrors smashed, some hats destroyed—and Masseria ended up with two bullet holes in the crown of his new straw boater. Frustrated and fearing the arrival of the police, Valenti fled, leaving Masseria unscathed and, until his assassination, known as "the man who can dodge bullets."

Disheartened, both Valenti and Morello agreed to make peace with Masseria, and a sit-down was scheduled at a restaurant on Twelfth Street off Second Avenue. Valenti and three others from the anti-Masseria side showed up; and three Masseria men showed. For a while, the men talked peacefully outside the restaurant when suddenly Valenti realized that neither Morello nor Masseria were there. Valenti must have realized that the two had struck some sort of deal and he was odd man out.

Valenti turned and ran as guns were pulled. A couple of the Valenti men were wounded, and the three Masseria men followed Valenti into the street and fired as he fired back. Two of the assassins shot wildly and wounded a street cleaner and an eight-year-old girl, two of the hundreds of spectators on the street. The third gunman, the one who had plugged the two Valenti men, was cool. Planting himself in the middle of the street, he fired at Valenti who, still shooting, had hopped on the running board of a passing taxi. The calm assassin brought him down with a well-aimed bullet. Valenti hit the street dead.

He had been outgunned and outaimed by an icy-nerved foe, a young hoodlum named Salvatore Lucania, later to become better known as Lucky Luciano. It may have been a consolation for Valenti to know that nine years later Luciano saw to it that a trusting Masseria would also exit in a hail of bullets.

VALENTINE, Lewis J. (1882–1946): New York police commissioner

When Lewis J. Valentine was promoted to chief inspector of the New York Police Department in January 1934, he assembled his commanding officers and announced: "Be good or begone. This department has no room for crooks. . . . The day of influence is over. . . . I'll stand up for my men, but I'll crucify a thief. I'll be more quick to punish a thief in a police uniform than any ordinary thief. The thief in uniform is ten times more dangerous."

Fiorello La Guardia was in the mayoral office only a matter of months when he promoted Valentine to police commissioner. Known then and throughout his career as an honest cop, he became the worst police enemy of organized crime in that era. But Valentine had already been frequently harassed by the likes of Frank Costello and Lucky Luciano, the latter probably the top Valentine hater of the period.

During his 42 years on the force Valentine was known by only one description: honest cop. His mere appointment was a bad sign to the mob, since it had long been the habit of police watchers to measure a New York police administration's honesty and devotion to duty by how it treated Valentine, a rigidly straight cop, who attacked the mobs and crooked cops with equal vigor.

Valentine joined the force in 1903, was made sergeant after 10 years and later became a lieutenant on the "confidential squad," charged with rooting out graft-takers on the force. But Valentine fell from grace under Commissioner Richard E. Enright. He was continually passed over for promotion to captain, although he achieved the highest score in the force on civil service examinations. To satisfy Tammany Hall and the mobs, upset by his constant raids on politically protected gambling operations, Enright ultimately transferred Valentine to the wilds of Brooklyn, a tactic designed specifically to either tame do-gooders or drive them off the force. Later, under Commissioner George V. McLaughlin, Valentine was back in favor and promoted to captain, deputy inspector, inspector and deputy chief inspector all within one year's time. He became even more famous for his gambling raids and his incorruptibility.

When the corrupt mayor Jimmy Walker named Grover Whalen police commissioner in 1928, Valentine was again on the outs. Whalen, during his first six hours in office, abolished the police confidential squad, charged with unearthing police corruption and related political malfeasance, and busted its commander, Valentine, back to captain. (Later, Luciano was to brag that during the Whalen reign $20,000 a week was delivered to the commissioner's office.)

Under La Guardia, Valentine finally found a boss he could depend on. They paired perfectly in the mayor's efforts to "run out the bums and rats," which, while it did occasionally shake up civil rights advocates, also imbued the department with a genuine spirit of reform. "I'll promote the men who kick these gorillas around and bring them in," Valentine said, "and I'll demote any policemen who are friendly with gangsters." In his first six years as commissioner, Valentine fired 300 policemen, officially rebuked 3,000 and fined 8,000.

He was credited with getting more honest men into the higher ranks of the department than ever

As an ax swinger against mob gambling devices, New York police commissioner Lewis J. Valentine was a comparatively rare cop in his day—high brass not on the take.

before in its long-tarnished history. For the first time, the syndicate and the mafiosi faced a tough department, and by the 1940s several top mobsters, such as Joe Adonis, transferred their bases of operation to the safer confines of New Jersey.

Valentine deserved most of the credit for forcing Murder, Inc.'s, Louis Lepke to surrender, although J. Edgar Hoover grabbed the limelight. It was Valentine who squeezed the underworld so tight that crime bigwig Lepke barely had space to breathe, and Valentine warned he would keep up the pressure until the mobs realized all their operations would be crippled unless Lepke surrendered. The syndicate finally suckered Lepke, convincing him a deal had been made with Hoover; he would face only federal charges, and be free within a few years. Lepke bought it, but insisted he surrender to Hoover. He was terrified that Valentine's men would shoot him down on sight.

La Guardia decided not to run for reelection in 1945, and it was a tribute to Valentine that all three contenders for the post pledged to retain him. When William O'Dwyer won, Valentine decided to retire. Better than others he knew successful suppression of organized crime demanded honesty both within the department and in the political sphere. If either sector failed, the job of the other was adversely affected. (Still true today. Organized crime can flourish where either the political administration or the criminal justice system in its broadest sense—police, prosecution, courts—is corrupt.)

Valentine signed a lucrative contract as a narrator-adviser for the *Gang Busters* radio show but soon tired of that and went to Japan for General Douglas MacArthur to reorganize the Japanese police. He died in December 1946 after returning to this country.

Further reading: *Night Stick* by Lewis J. Valentine

VALLEY Gang: Irish allies of Al Capone

The most ostentatious of all the Chicago gangs of the 1920s, even the lowliest member of the Valley Gang of rumrunners and bootleggers rode about in Rolls-Royces.

An Irish street gang formed in the 1890s the gang for decades was a group of mindless sluggers and killers. But, perhaps rather remarkably, great wealth gave them a certain maturity. They moved willingly into the ranks of organized crime and became one of Al Capone's most stalwart legions. In that, they differed from many other Irish bands of criminals in many cities who, sneering at the concept of organizing crime and sharing rackets, had to be dealt with violently by those mobsters determined to syndicate crime on a rational basis.

In the 1890s the Valleys were no more than a neighborhood band centered on 15th Street in the Bloody Maxwell section of the city. Around 1900, the Valley Gang graduated to such pastimes as burglaries, picking pockets and, somewhat later, hired murders. About the time World War I broke out, the gang was under the leadership of Paddy Ryan, a.k.a. Paddy the Bear. Possessed of a huge physique, he unfortunately hadn't a brain to match. Through sheer bully and terror tactics, Paddy the Bear controlled much of the crime in Bloody Maxwell from a saloon he ran on South Halsted Street. In 1920, Paddy was murdered by a rival gangster, Walter Quinlan, also known as the Runt. (Later Paddy the Bear was avenged by his son, Paddy the Fox.)

Leadership of the Valleys passed from Paddy the Bear to Frankie Lake and Terry Druggan, who led the gang to great prosperity. Under Lake and Druggan, the gang concentrated on bootlegging and rumrunning and eventually owned a string of breweries. The boys went quite overboard in enjoying the finer things in life—rewards not exactly common for former street rowdies—but they all maintained a level-headedness about protecting their newfound riches. In the past the Valleys might have been noted for cracking a copper over the head with a blackjack, but they quickly discovered that a wad of bills made a more efficient weapon. The Valleys suddenly became the darlings of the police and politicians.

In 1924, Lake and Druggan got a year in jail from a judge for contempt in disobeying an injunction against one of their bootlegging fronts. But the politicians were determined that their meal tickets not suffer any inconvenience in prison. Morris Eller, boss of the 20th Ward, told Sheriff Peter Hoffman, "Treat the boys right." The boys themselves distributed bribes totaling $20,000 to Warden Wesley Westbrook and other officials at the Cook County Jail. For this they enjoyed a unique imprisonment even by Chicago standards.

A newspaper reporter who went to the jail to interview the pair was informed, "Mr. Druggan is not in today."

Well, how about Frankie Lake, the reporter suggested. The response: "Mr. Lake also had an appointment downtown. They'll be back after dinner."

As a result of this dialog, the *Chicago American* launched a major exposé about the treatment of the Valley Gang chieftains. It turned out the pair came and went as they pleased. Druggan's chauffeur-driven limousine picked him up so he could spend most of his evenings with his wife in their plush duplex apartment on the Gold Coast. Lake invariably visited his mistress in her North State Parkway home. The pair also dined in the best Loop restaurants, shopped, attended nightclubs and theaters, played golf and, when feeling the need, visited their doctor or dentist. For taking part in this miscarriage of justice Sheriff Hoffman was fined $2,500 and got 30 days in jail, and Warden Westbrook got four months.

Al Capone liked the Valley Gang chieftains' style, and a mutual respect developed on both sides. Eventually the Valley Gang was absorbed en masse in the Capone organization. Capone supporters often claimed the treatment the Valley Gang received showed that Big Al took good care of those gangsters of any ethnic background who joined him willingly. By the time Terry Druggan, one of the last of the Valleys, died in the 1950s, he was a millionaire many times over, as were many of his cohorts.

"VIETNAMESE Mafia": A fading threat

Early on, following their appearance on the organized crime scene, the Vietnamese crime gangs were labeled "the most vicious and ruthless of the Asian criminal groups." The New Jersey State Commission in 1989 found them to be even more violent than the Chinese gangs and that their violence made them "a matter of special national concern."

After the Vietnam War, Nguyen Cao Ky, a former leader in South Vietnam, set up an anti-Communist organization in exile manned by former generals in the defeated South Vietnamese army. But rather than focusing on the battle against communism, Ky built up a force of recruits among fellow immigrants to rob, kill, sell drugs and shake down Asian businesses and gambling operations. It was not an easy task because, unlike other Asian groups, the Vietnamese immigrants did not come out of a tradition of organized crime. As a result the Vietnamese tended to disperse over a wide area, thus keeping their organizations loose and local. These immigrants did learn the ways of organized crime quickly, however, and some were allowed to cooperate with other Asian ethnic groups, hiring out as hit men and enforcers. On their own they were active in many fields, including extortion, robbery, auto theft, arson, gambling, prostitution, narcotics trafficking and so on. The Vietnamese could stage spectacular shootouts, such as one that occurred at a burial service in New Jersey for a gang member who had been assassinated. Automatic weapons suddenly blazed away leaving seven badly wounded.

Yet despite the Vietnamese gangsters' depredations, they were slowly eliminated. The explanation, not generally appreciated fully by the law, is that upward mobility doomed the Viet gangsters. The Vietnamese are exceedingly hard-working people and, being in small enclaves around the country, they were better assimilated into society. As Dennis J. Kenney and James O. Finckenauer observed in *Organized Crime in America,* "As the Vietnam War generation of immigrants dies off or at least ages out of criminal behavior and other Vietnamese find legitimate means of upward mobility, these gangs may disappear and never become a full-blown form of organized crime."

Some observers see the same thing happening to some other ethnic "Mafias," that being the case because a true Mafia requires a long cultural identity, both in its country of origin and in the United States. Admittedly some of these other Mafias will produce a huge amount of criminal activity, but having real staying power in an alien environment is no simple accomplishment.

VIGILANTISM and the Mafia

In the mid-1850s Californians went on a lynching spree against the Sydney Ducks, former inmates of the penal colony in Australia who established themselves as a large organized band of criminals. The

same thing happened in New Orleans where citizens, terrorized by an indistinct population of Mafia, Camorra and other Italian criminals, raided a prison and murdered 11 alleged gangsters. Vigilantism, it seems, was part of the American way.

The New Orleans incident was triggered by the shooting death of Chief of Police David Hennessey. The cop lived long enough to identify his murderers as "dagos." On the basis of this rather sketchy evidence, 19 Italian Americans were rounded up; when the first of these were brought to trial, no convictions followed. Shortly thereafter an inflamed citizen group well-organized by certain political and business leaders stormed the jail and brutalized and lynched 11 of the men.

There are those who saw the prisoners as innocent and believed that the true motive for the lynching was not revenge for an officer's death but a determined ploy to undercut the growing economic power of local Italian Americans. However, there is little doubt that the average citizen was convinced he was doing battle with the vile Mafia and reacted according to 19th century American standards.

Yet while vigilantism continued well into the 20th century, such extralegal tactics against what by then had become the very visible threat of the Mafia and its like virtually ceased. Amazingly, the only place where it maintained any momentum was in the most fearsome precinct of American crime, the Chicago-area domain of the Capone mob.

The cause of the birth of the West Suburban Citizens' Association was a Capone whorehouse opened in 1925 on the southern boundary of Cicero, Illinois. The brothel was near Hawthorne Race Track, where the Capones thought it a civic service to offer a haven of respite for both winners and losers leaving the track. A local newspaper published a huge story on the brothel that infuriated respectable citizens and led to a meeting of clergymen from Cicero and the surrounding Capone-infested communities. The guiding spirit, the young Reverend Henry C. Hoover of Berwyn, insisted on pressuring Cicero's chief executive and chief of police as well as the county sheriff and the state's attorney. A delegation from the newly formed association was received courteously on all its calls and got promises that action would be taken. None was.

The Citizens' Association decided that it therefore had no choice but to take the law into its own hands. An action committee appropriated a large some of money that was to be expended with no questions asked. The money ended up in the hands of Hymie Weiss, the leader of the O'Banion gang and a mortal enemy of Capone. The whorehouse shortly thereafter burned to the ground one night. Emboldened by their success, the leaders of the Citizens' Association forced the reluctant sheriff to furnish a token force of deputy sheriffs to make a raid on the Hawthorne Smoke Shop, an innocuous name for the major Capone vice center. Accompanying the lawmen was the Reverend Hoover—actually he was the the de facto leader of the raid—and scores of the association's most militant members. Much to the chagrin of the deputies, the raiders started ripping the place apart, dismantling roulette wheels, chuck-a-luck cages and crap tables, which they prepared to carry off in three trucks.

A pajama-clad Capone charged over from the Hawthorne Inn next door where he had been sleeping, and screamed at the minister, "This is the last raid you'll ever pull!"

The young minister stared at Capone through his pince-nez and said, "Who is this man?"

Capone identified himself, and Hoover replied, "I thought it was someone like that, more powerful than the president of the United States."

To another raider Capone screamed in frustration: "I own the place!" It turned out to be a most injudicious remark.

Capone goons then struck back. They broke the nose of a raider, a real estate man, with a black jack. Another man was thrown to the ground and beaten, all without interference by the sheriff's men. A few days later a member of the Citizens' Association was shot in his garage and left for dead. He needed a month in the hospital to recover.

Capone's terror-tactic response did not discourage further vigilante attacks on his organization, and taking heart from the Citizens' Association, residents of Forest View set fire to the Stockade, a 60-girl brothel, the largest Capone vice operation in the county. Frantic Capone gangsters sounded fire alarms and several nearby fire brigades responded. However, instead of stopping the fire, they merely prevented the flames from reaching neighboring homes. An irate gangster demanded that a firefighter turn his hose to the main fire and was told dryly: "Can't spare the water."

After the raid, amused citizens read the angry comments of the Capone forces condemning the lack of law and order in Forest View and demanding an investigation.

The vigilante raids were successful. Although many mob operations were back in place within 24 hours and with appropriate police protection, Capone nevertheless learned that he was better advised to back away from blatant prostitution activities in stiffnecked suburban areas. It was a lesson the crime syndicate learned well in later years.

Ironically, the illegal vigilante activities against Capone were to cause him great legal problems later when the government moved against him on income tax evasion charges. The government not only proved that the Hawthorne Smoke Shop was a huge moneymaker, but also produced members of the West Suburban Citizens' Association who had heard Capone utter those incriminating words during the raid: "I own the place!"

See also STOCKADE, THE

WALK/TALK: Mob effort to avoid eavesdropping

For years before his conviction, it was a common sight on New York television to see John Gotti and some of his cohorts "going for a walk" for several blocks from his headquarters at the Ravenite club on Mulberry Street in Little Italy. The technique, dubbed "walk/talk" by the boys, had them talking in true gangster style with lips barely moving. All this was to avoid being overheard and also to frustrate lip-reading experts from picking up their conversations. The Gotti forces understood their headquarters itself was assuredly bugged, so they opted for walk/talks to solve their dilemma. It was wasted effort. The FBI had not simply bugged the club but had stationed cameras on surrounding streets with bugs and zoom lenses. And that was only the beginning of the woes for the Gotti forces.

One time after the Gotti parade had gone on its usual walk/talk route, going perhaps two blocks, turning left for another two or more blocks, then right a bit further, they felt they were now safely away from the Ravenite area bugging. But they were not. Sammy "the Bull" Gravano happened to peer into a partially opened van parked on a street. The Bull noticed the man inside was looking at a television screen. And there was the Gotti parade—live! Gravano rushed to inform Gotti and the information even rattled the dapper don. "How could that be?" he said.

A couple of Gotti's musclemen hustled over to harass the snoop, demanding to know who he was.

The man turned off the screen and said tersely, "You know who I am."

Sammy joined in the needling, asking if they would be shown on TV. The law enforcement man needled back, "All I can tell you is we have very sophisticated equipment," and he drove off.

Back at the Ravenite, Gotti announced a counter-plot. From then on they would get into a car and drive some 20 blocks away and get out (they assumed their vehicle was bugged as well). Then, said Gotti, "We'll just get out and start walking and go to different spots every day."

It was not known if the tactic frustrated the FBI, but Gotti dropped the routine after only a few times. It was too much trouble, apparently. Undoubtedly it also reflected the level of concentration of the mobsters compared to that of the FBI. There was another factor: It was a blow to Gotti's vanity when suddenly he was not shown on TV that much, something the crime boss was very unhappy about. As Gravano explained, he "was falling in love with himself."

WAR of the Jews

Before modern organized crime could be established in America, it was necessary to bump off those Italian and Jewish gangsters who were not responsive to the notion of a national syndicate. In the case of the Italians, Lucky Luciano solved the problem, exterminating the leading Mustache Petes, old-line mafiosi who were set in their ways and incapable of cooperating

464

with other ethnics, and often loathe even to ally themselves with mafiosi from other Sicilian villages. The Jews were the responsibility of Meyer Lansky, who not only brought Jewish gangsters into the fold, but also achieved for himself supremacy among his coreligionists. (Most already accepted his primacy, due to his obvious intellectual superiority and the muscle effectively supplied by his chief aide, Bugsy Siegel.)

Lansky's plan was opposed principally by Waxey Gordon, the bootleg king of Philadelphia. Both he and Lansky had been "brought up" by Arnold Rothstein, perhaps the finest criminal organizer of the 1920s, not illogically nicknamed "the Brain." After Rothstein's murder in 1928, ill feelings between Lansky and Gordon erupted. Gordon suspected, rightly, that Lansky (and Luciano) had frequently hijacked his liquor shipments while Lansky suspected, rightly, that Gordon sought to make deals with Luciano's enemies within the Mafia.

The feud turned bitter and violent and each side suspected the other, undoubtedly rightly, of several gang murders. Luciano for a time tried to act as peacemaker, but, by 1931, Lansky and Gordon had come to blows in what became known as the "War of the Jews."

Luciano realized that one or the other of the Jewish mob leaders would have to go, and that leader would not be Lansky. Just as Lansky had helped solve Luciano's Mustache Pete problems, Charley Lucky now took care of Lansky's. It was Luciano who decided the solution lay with the government. Internal Revenue was, at the time (1931), trying to levy tax evasion charges against Gordon, but their case was weak and sketchy. Luciano saw to it that all sorts of incriminating documents reached officials. Gordon was sent to prison, never realizing the true cause of his woes.

Lansky saw that, with the end of Prohibition, the future in booze lay in controlling legitimate trafficking of imports. His natural rival would undoubtedly prove to be Charles "King" Solomon of Boston who handled much of the scotch whiskey entering the country. Solomon's murder took care of that detail, and shortly after that, Lansky's ethnic creation, the Jewish Mafia, finely honed by him in the early 1930s, became the dominant element in syndicate crime along with the Luciano forces.

The "War of the Jews" had ended in a momentous victory for organized crime.

See also JEWISH MAFIA

WATERFRONT rackets

General corruption long proliferated along the waterfronts of most major American ports. Mafia gangsters, first successful in the rackets in New Orleans, ultimately made their biggest push on the New York–New Jersey docks, the country's largest and richest port area. Throughout the 19th century the docks had been the domain of Irish gangsters, but early in the 20th century warfare was almost constant between Irish and Italian gangs for dominance. The flood of Italian immigrants had altered the situation and forced the Irish to battle what they called the "dago invasion." But no matter which ethnic group maintained control of the waterfront, "service" was the same for customers trying to do business—they always had to pay.

Slowly the Italians, under Paul Kelly (Paolo Vacarelli) and later under Albert Anastasia, Joe Adonis and Vince Mangano, gained dominance over the Irish. By 1925 with the murder of Pegleg Lonergan, the last important leader of the Irish White Hand Gang (hit in person, by no less a personage than a visiting Al Capone from Chicago), the Italian gangsters won the docks.

Joseph Ryan, president of the International Longshoremen's Association and with important connections in Tammany Hall, put the union's shakedown operations on an organized basis. Anastasia, Mangano, his crime family head, and Adonis, the payoff man for Brooklyn politicians and police, solidified the underworld's lock on the docks.

Shippers had to pay if they wished to guarantee their goods would be loaded or unloaded. Thefts of cargo ran into six figures monthly. Workers were bled for kickbacks to "hiring bosses" who decided who would work each day at dock "shape-ups." They were even billed monthly at a set fee for using a mob barber for haircuts, whether they got the cutting there or elsewhere. Loan-sharking became a way of life on the waterfront, and new workers were guided to syndicate agents working inside the union. Since the dockworker's occupation was seasonal, shylocking thrived. The loan sharks demanded a dockworker turn over his pay card as security. The worker had to present his pay card to collect his wages. In such cases the shylocks collected the wages and took out their interest before giving the hand the rest of his money. In a typical case a longshoreman borrowed $100 and for the next 36 weeks had $10 a week taken from his pay. "You," he was advised, "have only paid the interest up to now. You still owe the hundred." Hundreds of New York dockworkers were in the same boat.

By the late 1930s Anastasia and his brother Tough Tony Anastasio directly controlled six ILA locals in Brooklyn. One insurgent who dared to challenge their hold disappeared, his body turning up a year later in an Ohio lime pit. Another, Peter Panto, was taken for a ride, strangled and his body buried in a mob chicken-yard graveyard in New Jersey.

The mob was frightened by no one in attempting to extract tribute. The *New York Daily News* in 1948 was harassed by a picket line set up around a ship from Canada bringing in newsprint. The pickets demanded $100,000 in tribute, and failing that, one dollar a ton on all newsprint shipped in. Since the newspaper at the time used 300,000 tons, the cost would have been significant. The newspaper broke the scheme by sending the ship to Philadelphia and then having the cargo shipped by freight to New York.

Vigorous prosecutions and reform and finally the death of Albert Anastasia in 1957 and his brother Tough Tony in 1963 brought some improvement to the docks. The eventual rise to power of Anthony M. Scotto, a young college-educated relative by marriage to Tony Anastasio, was said to represent the dawning of a new era on the waterfront under a "new breed labor leader."

However, in 1979 it was found that conditions had not changed all that much on the waterfront. Scotto, despite character-witness testimony from the governor and two New York City ex-mayors, was convicted on labor racketeering charges.

See also ANASTASIO, ANTHONY "TOUGH TONY"; LOVETT, WILLIAM "WILD BILL"; SCOTTO, ANTHONY M.; WHITE HAND GANG

WEISS, Hymie (1898–1926): O'Banion Gang boss

There are those who have said that little Hymie Weiss—rather than the jolly Irish psychopath Dion O'Banion—was the toughest foe Al Capone ever faced in his battle to take over Chicago crime. The Polish-American Weiss, O'Banion's successor as leader of the intractable Irish North Side gang, stood up to the encroachments of the Johnny Torrio–Al Capone combination for several bloodstained years.

Hymie was a most devout cold-blooded murderer who hardly ever missed Mass. He would never dream of venturing forth without crucifix and rosary in his pocket. And he always carried a gun or two. With the latter, a cynical newsman observed, he "could perform his own version of the last rites on an enemy."

Crime experts credited Weiss with being the one responsible for building O'Banion's bootlegging empire. He was more thoughtful, forward-looking and resourceful than the often explosive O'Banion and relied far more on reason and bribery than "Deanie" ever did. He also left his mark in the criminal dictionary, having originated and christened the "one-way ride." In 1921, a gangster named Steve Wisniewski offended the O'Banions by hijacking one of their loaded beer trucks. O'Banion assigned Weiss to exact the proper vengeance. He invited Wisniewski for a drive along Lake Michigan, from which the hijacker never returned. As Weiss quaintly stated to friends, "We took Stevie for a ride, a one-way ride."

Weiss was born Earl Wajciechowski, which the family changed to Weiss shortly after they arrived in the United States from Poland. Befriending O'Banion in his teens, he became an accomplished burglar, car thief, safecracker and hired slugger in the newspaper wars and for labor unions. O'Banion's passion in that period for jewel theft and other safecrackings was swelled by Hymie, whom O'Banion called the "best soup artist in Chicago." With Prohibition, the boys moved into bootlegging, and Weiss, as O'Banion's right-hand man, showed saloon keepers the superiority of O'Banion's merchandise, explaining that there was not a bit of lead in the booze barrels, but there would be if they bought elsewhere.

Weiss wept openly and honestly at O'Banion's grave after the latter was murdered in November 1924. There was no doubt at all that Torrio and Capone had engineered Deanie's murder, even though Capone boldly showed up at the services, albeit with six bodyguards. Weiss kept the O'Banion gunners in check at the cemetery, having promised the Irishman's grieving widow there would be no further violence until after their beloved Deanie was planted. The Chicago police had 100 officers at the gravesite to ensure peace. Asked by a reporter if he held Capone responsible for O'Banion's assassination, Weiss threw up his hands in mock horror for the merest suggestion of that. "Blame Capone? Why Al's a real pal. He was Dion's best friend, too."

Then Weiss went back to plotting revenge.

For two months, Weiss maintained a cover of peace. (He even banished Two Gun Alterie from the gang because he kept publicly stating the gang was going to get Capone.) Finally on January 12, 1925, Weiss, Schemer Drucci and Bugs Moran tailed Capone's black limousine to a restaurant at State and 55th Streets. They drove slowly by and pumped 26 slugs into the vehicle. The chauffeur was wounded but two bodyguards in the back seat were unhurt. Capone, who had stepped into the restaurant seconds earlier, was unscathed. Then Hymie tried to get Johnny Torrio as he was riding in his limousine. The chauffeur and Torrio's dog were killed, but Torrio escaped with just two bullet holes in his gray fedora.

Torrio and Capone raced to knock off Weiss before he could strike again, but Weiss stayed out of sight. Then on January 24, 1925, Torrio was ambushed in front of his apartment house as he and his wife, Anna, returned from a Loop shopping trip. As Mrs. Torrio entered the apartment house lobby, Torrio followed with an armload of packages. Weiss and Bugs Moran jumped out of a passing blue Cadillac. Weiss downed Torrio with a sawed-off shotgun. Then Moran, wielding an army .45 automatic pistol, squeezed off two shots. Poised to apply the coup de grace—a shot pointblank through the head—Moran and Weiss instead fled at the sound of an approaching vehicle (which turned out to be a laundry truck). Torrio hovered near death in the hospital for more than two weeks. When he was discharged, he retired from Chicago crime and turned the whole operation over to Capone.

Weiss's attempts to rub out Capone continued. Perhaps the most famous occurred in Cicero on September 20, 1926, when a fleet of automobiles filled with his gangsters drove past the Hawthorne Inn and ventilated the building with 1,000 bullets and slugs from shotguns, handguns and machine guns. A Capone bodyguard and a woman bystander were shot, but again Capone was not hit.

Three weeks later, on October 11, 1926, Weiss bought it himself. Capone assassins machine-gunned him to death as he crossed the street to his headquarters above O'Banion's old flower shop. A bodyguard, Paddy Murphy, was killed in the same blaze of bullets, and three others with them were wounded. The shooting came from a second-floor room across the street, a room rented the day following the Cicero raid.

Weiss, aged 28, left an estate believed to be worth well in excess of $1.3 million. His widow seems to have been most upset by the fact that there were only 18 carloads of flowers for Hymie's funeral while earlier funerals for O'Banion and Nails Morton of the North Siders had rated 26 and 20 loads each. Bugs Moran patiently explained to the widow that since the murder of O'Banion, 30 other members of the gang had fallen, mostly to Capone guns. This had considerably reduced the number of available flower donors.

WESTIES: New York Irish mob allied with the Mafia

An argument could be made on both sides whether the most kill-crazy mobsters in New York in recent years were the brutal hit men of the Gambinos under Roy DeMeo, who maintained what can only be called a slaughterhouse flat in Brooklyn, or the Westies, who terrorized Manhattan's Hell's Kitchen neighborhood and the surrounding West Side (the original setting for *West Side Story*).

Those aficionados who favored the Westies (many of whom were former choirboys) could cite as an example the fate of one of the gang's own members, Patrick "Paddy" Dugan. From the Westies viewpoint Dugan's transgressions were many and clearly called for the death penalty. Dugan was in the habit of making money on the side by shaking down loan sharks, even after the Westies had decided to align themselves with the Gambinos and cease such unseemly behavior. Dugan was warned many times to stop all non-sanctioned operations but simply did not obey. Then Dugan murdered one of Westies leader Jimmy Coonan's close buddies and his fate was sealed.

Dugan was murdered, and in typical Westies style his body was sliced up into little pieces for disposal. Coonan retained the severed fingers, which he added to a bag full of the fingers of other victims. Coonan showed the bag to others to encourage them to be more cooperative.

This hardly meant the Westies were not a sentimental bunch. They decided Dugan still was a reasonably good lad, so they took his severed head to a local ginmill, propped it up on the bar and for several hours Coonan, other Westies and friends of Dugan sentimentally toasted the deceased's memory. They even lit a cigarette of Dugan's brand and placed it between the dead man's lips.

The Westies never comprised more than a couple dozen men, but they were so kill-crazy their foes must have thought they were up against a Roman legion. The mob became a fearsome operative in narcotics, extortion, loan-sharking, labor racketeering and kidnapping. The Westies kidnapped several Mafia men for ransom and in some cases even after collecting the money consigned their victim to the depths of the Hudson River. The mafiosi knew that if they tried to invade Westie turf they faced certain death.

Then Coonan pulled his greatest coup, murdering a big-money mob loan shark named Ruby Stein. Coonan had a special motive in disposing of Ruby since he was in to the loan shark for $70,000, and other Westies were in for similar sums. More important the Westies came into the possession of Ruby's "black book," which recorded the millions of Mafia dollars that were out in loans. The Westies simply went out and took over many of the loans.

After the death of Carlo Gambino, his successor Paul Castellano decided he had to tame the Westies, but he feared killing them, realizing the gang was monstrous about retribution. Instead, he took them into the Gambino family fold, using them in a number of rackets and for a number of hits. The matter of the Stein murder and his missing book was ignored, the mob taking an estimated $4 million hit, as the Westies swore they knew nothing about the matter. By the early 1980s many of the Westies were very rich; Coonan himself was worth millions.

Together with the Gambinos, the gang operated many juicy rackets. They infiltrated the union representing personnel working on the U.S.S. *Intrepid,* the aircraft carrier museum anchored in the Hudson River. That gallant ship had survived kamikaze attacks in World War II but was almost sunk into bankruptcy by the skimming of ticket receipts and the padding of payroll with no-show jobs. The Westies also dominated certain backstage unions at Broadway theaters and were said to be a partial cause of rising ticket prices.

Despite the wealth heaped on the gang, the fact remained once a Westie always a Westie. Some of them continued unauthorized stealing from other mobsters as well as from their own associates. Many were constantly drugged up and followed an old custom of playing Russian roulette for $1,000 a bullet.

Disaffection spread in the ranks, some of the boys faulting Coonan for "trying to be more Italian than Irish." Coonan himself left for the comforts of New Jersey and only came to the West Side when absolutely necessary. Several Westies determined it was time to kill Coonan, but their plans never worked out. To relieve some of the pressure on himself, Coonan with some other Westies framed the gang's number two man, Mickey Featherstone, for murder. Featherstone was convicted and then decided to turn informer, something that shocked the denizens of Hell's Kitchen because Mickey had been regarded as the most stand-up guy in the mob.

Featherstone's evidence landed a number of Westies in prison on RICO (Racketeer Influenced and Corrupt Organization) Act charges. Jimmy Coonan got 75 years. Some others got 40- or 50-year terms. The Westies were decimated, while Featherstone and a few others went into the witness protection program, and the alliance between the Irish and Italian gangsters was finished.

Some said the Westies destroyed themselves or that law enforcement did them in. Others however noted yet another irresistible force. Gentrification drove many of the working-class elements out of the neighborhood. They had been the primary victims of the Westies, and without the main victims, the ravagers were likewise ravaged.

(It might be noted that even with the Westies hold on the Broadway unions broken, no one noticed any reduction in theater ticket prices.)

See also COONAN, JIMMY

WEST Suburban Citizens' Association   See VIGILANTISM AND THE MAFIA

WHACK: Term for murder

Originally *whack* was the criminals' word for beating up or injuring a victim, but in the Mafia lexicon it now means murder. The term continues to be used by the mob on the theory that the courts will not accept its mention as indicating a killing. That has turned out to be a vain hope as prosecutors have been able to prove to jurors that when the whackees mentioned in mob conversations end up dead, it is obvious that the word has no "benign" meaning.

Thus it has become more common for mobsters to use such phrases as "break an egg" to replace whacking. Jurors seem to be amused by the new vocabulary—but still convict.

WHALEN, Grover A. (1886–1962): New York police commissioner

One of the most ineffective police commissioners in New York City's history, to take a most charitable view, was Grover Whalen, remembered today as "the Official Greeter of New York City" and originator of the city's celebrated ticker-tape parades. In fact, Whalen presided over the most corrupt years of the police department since before the Great War.

From the very first day in his police post, Whalen started acting in the mob's best interest. In later years, neither Lucky Luciano nor Frank Costello made much of a secret that Whalen had always been in their hip pocket. In fact, $20,000 a week was said to have been delivered in a trusty, plain paper bag to the commissioner's office at police headquarters. The charge was never proven, but the amount does seem in line with any measure of compensation for value received.

In 1928, Whalen, general manager of New York's John Wanamaker department store, was tapped by the corrupt Jimmy Walker as police commissioner. Whalen was reluctant at first to accept, but John Wanamaker officials, urged by the mayor, promised Whalen that if he took the post, his $100,000-a-year salary from the store would continue as a supplement to his city pay.

Within six hours of taking office, Whalen started serving the underworld. First, he abolished the police confidential squad, which unearthed police corruption and political malfeasance. Next, he busted its commander, Lewis J. Valentine, back to his civil-service rank of lieutenant and transferred him to the wilds of Long Island City. It had long been the habit of police watchers to gauge a New York police administration's honesty and devotion to duty by how it treated Valentine, a rigidly honest cop who attacked the mobs and crooked police with equal fervor.

Commissioner Whalen had made it clear which way he was taking the department that first day. During the ensuing period the mob operated with more impunity than at any other time until the reign of William O'Dwyer after World War II.

Whalen's administration represented, for instance, the heyday of the slot machine racket with special "police stickers." Under the aegis of Costello, the mob set up slot machines all over the city (some with special stools so that little schoolchildren could get high enough to feed in coins), all with colored stickers that informed the local police that the machine was a legitimate graft payer. If a machine failed to have a sticker, it was subject to police seizure, and the sticker colors were changed frequently to prevent freelance operators from counterfeiting them. A police officer who made the mistake of interfering with a mob machine could expect to be transferred to the outer edges of the city, inevitably far away from his home. The system was extremely well known to policemen in the city as well as to every journalist, and there was no way it could continue without an okay from the commissioner's office.

With Whalen's record of doing right with the mob there is little reason to doubt the story of Costello, who handled police payoffs for the syndicate, informing Luciano once: "Yesterday, around noon, Whalen called me. He was desperate for thirty grand to cover his margin [on the stock market]. What could I do? I hadda give it to him. We own him."

Whalen's administration permitted the Luciano-Lansky-Costello combination to accumulate the money and power needed to wipe out the old-line mafiosi and create a modern underworld of organized crime. During his tenure, Whalen diverted public attention away from serious crime by organizing traffic campaigns, encouraging anti-communist demonstrations, and providing showmanship—with the omnipresent gardenia in his lapel—as chairman of the mayor's reception committee for distinguished visitors.

See also BAGMAN; VALENTINE, LEWIS J.

WHITE Hand Gang: Irish waterfront gangsters

Around 1900, the various powerful Irish gangs on the Brooklyn waterfront combined into the White Hand Gang, so named because they said they were battling the "Black Hand dagoes." Indeed, from about 1900 to 1925, a grim war was waged along the New York waterfront between Irish and Italian gangsters for control of the lush rackets there. Slowly the Italian mafiosi gained, but at a tremendous loss of blood and manpower.

After World War I, the White Handers retained a firm grip on the Brooklyn Bridge–Red Hook sections and collected tribute from barge and wharf owners. Those who declined to pay saw their wharves and vessels looted, burned or wrecked. All longshoremen had to pay a daily commission for the right to work. Some paid willingly because they were Irish and saw their salvation in the vows of the White Handers to keep the docks clear of Italians.

Following the pattern of the Irish-American gangsters of the 19th century, the White Handers were a violent lot and could be counted on to kill one of their own if there was a quick profit in so doing. It was never determined who murdered White Hand leader Dinny Meehan shortly after the war, but the power thereafter passed, after some obligatory bloodletting, to Wild Bill Lovett, a pinched-faced little man who looked too weak to harm a fly. He could, however, shoot a lot of people. Wild Bill was considered the greatest worthy ever to head the White Handers, and he actually had the Mafia-Camorra elements on the run as he extended White Hand influence.

Lovett was assassinated in 1923 by a mafioso murder expert nicknamed Dui Cuteddi (Two Knives), using no such namesake weapons, but rather a cleaver. Dui Cuteddi was shipped back to Sicily with a handsome pension for his fine services, and the Mafia elements came on strong under a triumvirate of Vince Mangano, Albert Anastasia and Joey Adonis. Adonis was heavily involved in bootlegging at the time, partners with the likes of Lucky Luciano and Frank Costello, but Prohibition, it was realized, was a short-term situation, while the waterfront rackets were forever.

The White Hand power passed to Richard "Pegleg" Lonergan, a zany killer who had lost a leg in an argument with a train during a railway looting expedition. He was a pock-faced killer, with, according to the police, at least 20 murders to his credit. He would maim any Mafia terrorists trying to move in on his docks. Then he would turn around and demand double tribute from the hapless victim who had the effrontery ever to pay off Italians.

However, if the Mafia had been cunning enough to murder a crafty opponent like Wild Bill Lovett, a mad hatter like Lonergan could not survive for long. On the day of Christmas 1925, Lonergan led a contingent of his men into the Adonis Social Club, a South Brooklyn speakeasy owned by the Mafia. Although the Irish hoodlums were greatly outnumbered, Lonergan was contemptuous of the foe, including a rather fat-faced one with a long scar on his face. Seeing two Irish girls dancing with Italian gangsters, Lonergan kicked them out of the place, ordering them to "get back with the white men."

Suddenly all the lights went out and guns blazed in the darkness. When vision was restored, Lonergan and his top aides, Needles Ferry and Aaron Harms, lay dead in a pool of blood. The rest of the White Handers had fled.

Eventually the police investigation identified the man with the scar as none other than Al Capone, then back from Chicago for a sentimental visit to his old home ground. The police could not substantiate reports that Capone had personally plugged Lonergan and had to drop any prosecution of him. Capone himself insisted he had had nothing to do with the killings, declaring, "I never met an Irishman I didn't like." On his return to Chicago, Capone continued his extermination campaign against the Irish O'Banion Gang.

The New York mafiosi were grateful for Capone's caper in Brooklyn, and it was said that if Capone hadn't triggered the violence, Lonergan and his cohorts might have walked out safely. As it was, the White Handers had been stripped of their last important leader. The gang disintegrated within three years and the New York waterfront became secure Mafia country.

See also LOVETT, WILLIAM "WILD BILL"

WHITE Hand Society: Anti–Black Hand Italian citizens' group

In 1907, an odd exercise in law and order was attempted in Chicago by an organization of Italian business and professional men, the Italian Chamber of Commerce, Italian newspapers and several Italian fraternal orders. For one of the rare times in American history, an ethnic group, the White Hand Society, was organized to fight criminals of the same ethnic background. (The more common tendency among all ethnics is to belittle such criminal activity as a slur upon the entire group, something Italian Americans started doing a half-century later.)

At the time, the Chicago Italian community was being terrorized by Black Hand gangsters. Black Hand extortionists were rampant in every big-city "Little Italy" in the country, but nowhere as active as in Chicago. The Black Handers threatened people with maiming or death—for the victim or members of their families—unless tribute was paid. Murder victims of the Black Hand—many of these extortionists were mafiosi although others were not or only pretended to be Mafia (or Camorra) members—

ranged anywhere from a dozen to as many as 50 a year in Chicago.

Hiring attorneys and private detectives, the White Handers, virtually every one of whom was threatened with death, sought to cooperate with the police to exterminate the Black Hand by providing them with the evidence needed for convictions. It was a vital function since the police, having little knowledge of the various Italian dialects or of Italian customs, had done little on their own—and some said had little interest in doing so.

The White Handers brought about the conviction of several Black Handers and drove from the city what were described as the 10 most dangerous of the terrorist gangsters. Unfortunately, many of the Black Handers convicted were quickly released on parole through the efforts of fellow conspirators who put up cash to suborn officials. These Black Handers returned to their extortion activities with a vengeance.

What had started out as a most impressive citizens' effort to fight crime sputtered to a stop. In 1912, Dr. Joseph Damiani, the president of the White Hand Society, said in an interview with the *Chicago Record-Herald* that the members of the group "were so discouraged by the lax administration of justice they were refusing to advance further money to prosecute men arrested on their complaints." They were further disheartened by the fact that they were unable to bring to justice the notorious Shotgun Man, a known assassin who carried out many murder assignments for the Black Handers. Witnesses viewed the failure of the society to keep convicted terrorists in prison as sufficient reason to consider only their own personal peril if they testified. Another woe for the society was the fact that many rank-and-file Italians had come to feel that the White Hand effort to expose crime in the Italian community was leading to a backlash against all Italians by other Chicagoans, a viewpoint unfortunately well founded. By 1913, the White Hand disbanded; the Black Handers extended their reign of terror for the next several years.

See also BLACK HAND; SHOTGUN MAN

WHITE spot: Mafioso operating in black areas

In underground scenes a white person associating only with blacks might be referred to as a "white spot." In mob circles the term refers to a mob collec-

tor who oversees activities, such as numbers, in black neighborhoods or who collects tribute for many enterprises. There are occasional reports of resistance to paying off the mob in some areas but such noncompliance seldom lasts, mainly because the mob controls much of the official reaction to such criminal activities.

In short, the mob enjoys better relations with some local authorities and thus can provide protection cheaper to black racketeers than the latter can negotiate on their own. No doubt black racketeers look upon this as a form of white-black discrimination. From a practical outlook therefore "white spots" become the blacks' exploiters of choice.

See also STREET TAX

WILLIAMS, Edward Bennett (1920–1988): Defense lawyer

Maliciously called "the mob's best legal friend" and "the Burglar's Lobby in Washington," Edward Bennett Williams through the years defended mob figures like Frank Costello and mob-connected individuals like Jimmy Hoffa. Yet attorney Williams was never deterred. As he once put it, "I'm called the Burglar's Lobby in Washington because I defend people like Frank Costello. The Sixth Amendment of the Constitution guarantees the right of legal counsel to *everyone*. It does not say to everyone *except* people like Frank Costello."

Williams was responsible for a number of landmark decisions concerning organized crime, one being a 6-2 decision of the U.S. Supreme Court overturning an order to deport Costello. In another famous case Williams took on police investigators engaged in illegal eavesdropping. The case involved three gamblers who ran a $40,000-a-day mob-connected sports betting parlor in a row house on 21st Street, N.W., in Washington, D.C. Police entered the house next door and drove a spike into the common wall between the houses. The spike, part of an electronic listening setup, was inserted into a duct, turning the entire heating system into a sort of microphone. The police gathered records of scores of conversations involving betting transactions. The gamblers were convicted and sentenced to long terms in prison. Williams took over their appeal and argued before the Supreme Court that the eavesdropping had been "more subtle and more scientifically advanced than wiretapping," and constituted gross violation of the rights of the defendants against unreasonable searches and seizures. Williams insisted the tactic differed little from the police crashing into a house in the middle of the night without a search warrant. The Supreme Court agreed and threw out the convictions.

Williams long spoke out against the extension of congressional investigative committees' powers, to what he considered "the legislative lynch." He said, "When Estes Kefauver first ran roughshod over the rights of hoodlums in 1950, the country was amused. Then the leftist intellectuals, who didn't spring to the defense of the hoodlums, found that their turn was next. While this was going on, labor thought it was funny, but they soon discovered that they were being clobbered."

Once, after Robert Kennedy, a longtime friend of Williams, became attorney general, Kennedy went after Teamsters boss Jimmy Hoffa. He was so confident that he said he'd "jump off the Capitol dome" if he lost the case. After Williams got Hoffa acquitted, Williams offered to provide Kennedy with a parachute. It marked the end of a beautiful friendship.

Many federal prosecutors despised Williams for thwarting their attempts to jail organized-crime figures. Williams's supporters see his role as being the defense attorney who is vital not so much to his client, but to the entire criminal justice system—a defendant without the best possible protection weakens the entire structure of justice.

This view was countered by Rudolph Giuliani, who as a federal prosecutor for Manhattan in the 1980s spearheaded the general federal assault on the Mafia. He said in a newspaper interview: "I don't socialize with mob lawyers. When I was in private practice, I wouldn't represent mob people. I didn't mind representing businessmen who might be charged with something. That's someone who has a largely legitimate aspect to their lives, and if they get in trouble, whether innocent or guilty, there's still some good to them. Organized crime figures are illegitimate people who would go on being illegitimate people if I got them off."

Williams's position—all defendants deserve equal opportunity of legal representation—and Giuliani's—the defense lawyer serves as a sort of judge of his clients—are the philosophies between which all students and practitioners of the law must make a choice.

WILSON, Frank J. (1887–1970): Secret Service Capone nemesis

In the late 1920s, neither the local police nor the FBI under the nervous leadership of J. Edgar Hoover could think of any reason to put America's most infamous gangster, Al Capone—who masterminded bootleggings, hijackings, gambling and scores of murders across state lines—behind bars. The task remained instead for Frank J. Wilson, a treasury agent.

Elmer I. Irey, chief of the Internal Revenue's enforcement branch, came up with the idea for convicting Capone under a 1927 Supreme Court decision upholding the right of the government to collect income tax even on illegal income. It was an idea not easily implemented. First it was necessary to determine that Capone's gross income exceeded the standard exemption of $5,000 for each of the several years he had filed no return. Capone had no bank accounts, signed no checks. He never signed a receipt for anything and had no property in his own name. Thus Wilson, assigned to the case by Irey, had to analyze the Big Fellow's "net worth" and "net expenditure."

Wilson managed to plant agents on the periphery of the mob's activities and, finally, within it. Soon Capone, who sneered at any number of lawmen, began to quake whenever Wilson's name was mentioned. By comparison, he regarded the activities of the much-publicized Eliot Ness and his Untouchables as petty annoyances. Finally the heat became so intense on Capone that an informer reported: "The Big Fellow's eating aspirin like it was peanuts so's he can get some sleep."

Against the advice of his top lieutenants, Capone ordered five gunmen be brought in from New York to hit Wilson. Government agents got wind of the plan and tried to pressure Capone to call off his killers, but Capone vanished from sight with the contract in effect. Capone had been tipped off by corrupt local police officials that the feds were looking for him. Stalled in their efforts to seize Capone, the agents turned to Johnny Torrio, Capone's old mentor, who was in Chicago at the time. Torrio was informed that if the hit men were not pulled out within 24 hours, federal agents would start stalking them, and there would be warfare in the streets. Torrio explained to Capone that with the assassination plot exposed it could not be put into effect. Capone had no choice but to cancel the rubout order. Torrio then got on the telephone with a federal agent and announced, "They left an hour ago."

This proved to be Capone's last hurrah at beating the tax case. Now it moved into the courts with ledgers in the hands of bookkeepers and accountants. Wilson was in his element. In the end, Capone went to prison, a fate that was to remove him permanently from organized crime.

In 1936 Wilson went on to become head of the Secret Service, and in that position did much to wipe out another crime which from time to time had been popular with syndicate criminals—counterfeiting. For the first time in history the amount of counterfeit money fell to insignificant levels.

Further reading: *Special Agent* by Frank J. Wilson and Beth Day.

WINCHELL, Walter (1897–1972): Gossip columnist

Known as the King of Broadway, gossip columnist Walter Winchell was also an important, but not always well informed, reporter on crime matters. Because of his journalistic power—1,000 newspapers carried his column at his zenith, and his radio news show was usually among the top-10 and frequently No. 1 in the ratings—he was used, and sometimes abused, by the police, J. Edgar Hoover and organized crime. In fact, Hoover and the mob both used Winchell's column to expound their identical, favorite theme—there was no such thing as organized crime in America. "Mafiasco," Winchell called it.

There was little doubt that Winchell scored a number of crime scoops, some through Hoover, probably many more through mob chief Frank Costello, with whom he was very chummy. Winchell was the first newsman to report that Albert Anastasia, the former head of Murder, Inc., had ordered Arnold Schuster, a private citizen, murdered because Schuster had spotted wanted bank robber Slick Willie Sutton and tipped off the police. Sutton had no connections with the mob—Anastasia just couldn't stand "stoolies."

Trusted by the underworld, Winchell was chosen to handle the surrender of Louis Lepke to Hoover in 1939. Lepke wanted Winchell involved in the surrender because he feared that otherwise he might be shot down by the law.

Winchell was attracted to certain underworld types such as Costello. (Costello associate Phil Kastel once told a columnist, "There isn't a newspaperman around who wouldn't sell his grandmother for a paragraph, except Walter Winchell.") Winchell could be counted on by the mob to offer them self-serving whitewash interviews. An infamous one with Costello created an uproar both from subscribing newspapers and irate readers. Many attacked Winchell as shilling for the mob.

Costello pooh-poohed the idea of organized crime and organized gambling. Winchell asked him: "Do you think organized gambling can be legislated out of existence?"

Costello replied, "Not in a million years . . . The quickest way to wipe out big shots in the underworld is to make gambling legal. . . . Legalize it and you do three things. Get rid of corruption, raise tax money and knock off the underworld."

Winchell was hardly sophisticated enough to wonder why mobsters favor legalized gambling. The answer was of course that the underworld makes more out of legalized gambling than the illegal kind. Las Vegas proved that point. Crime families in New York, Chicago, Detroit, Cleveland and Los Angeles—and certainly Costello personally—made more out of Vegas than they ever did out of all their illicit operations in New York, Louisiana and Florida combined. Legal gambling eliminates the need for payoffs to police, the army of armed thugs necessary for protection. The payment of taxes is a minor matter considering what can be "skimmed" off the income from the top. And above all the "pot" is much greater. Legal casinos attract millions of bettors a year, far more than any underground setup could.

At times Winchell's gullibility on criminal matters knew no bounds. He saved one of his major "exclusives" for his autobiography which appeared after he died. In it he gave his readers the "lowdown" on the unsolved murder of Bugsy Siegel. Winchell insisted the killing was carried out by two gunners of Brooklyn's Murder, Inc., Happy Maione and Dasher Abbandando, assigned to do the job because Siegel had squandered $4 million of the mob's money building the first elegant hotel in Vegas, the Flamingo. Winchell's ultimate sources, via other journalists, he proudly proclaimed were "Thomas E. Dewey (when he was still district attorney) and Frank Hogan (when he was Mr. Dewey's chief aide)."

Siegel was murdered in 1947, by which time Dewey had long been governor of New York State and Hogan district attorney. In any event neither Dewey nor Hogan would have imparted such a ludicrous theory since by 1947 both Happy Maione and Dasher Abbandando were five years dead, having gone to the electric chair in 1942 for sundry other murders but hardly that of the still healthy Bugsy Siegel.

Winchell's "exclusive" was typical of many of his statements on crime. Indeed, his prime importance may have been as a helpmate to both G-man Hoover and crime czar Costello. Hoover was a compulsive horseplayer and Winchell passed on to him tips from Costello on "sure things," a rather specific and hardly innocent term in underworld parlance. This hardly meant that Hoover was thereby in Costello's pocket but it was perhaps a contributing factor of some importance in what may be called an "era of good feeling" between the FBI and organized crime that kept federal agents effectively out of the mob's business for some three and a half decades.

This hardly indicates that Winchell himself was less than honest. As the quintessential Broadwayite Winchell would have to have considered gambling among the more minor vices, and while he was always tender to Costello and some others of his ilk, he carried on a long feud with Lucky Luciano whom he considered a procurer, a drug peddler and a murderer. This took a bit of personal courage from Winchell who did not have such qualities in high supply. On one occasion he was afraid to leave his office at the *New York Daily Mirror* because he had offended underworld figures and finally did so only when gangster Owney Madden promised him safe escort.

Actually he was safe from Luciano's vengeance since the latter had established the credo among the new crime syndicate mobsters that under no circumstances was a newspaperman to be killed.

For a time Luciano resided at the Barbizon Plaza Hotel while Winchell had an apartment across the street at the St. Moritz. Luciano once said, "He found out I was movin' into his neighborhood and I heard he didn't like it too much. I said to myself, 'Fuck him.'" Frequently walking along Central Park South, Luciano would see Winchell and he'd wave to him and call, "Hi, neighbor." Luciano recalled, "It burnt him to a crisp."

Later, Luciano heard that a penthouse apartment was available at the St. Moritz and he decided to rent it. When Winchell heard the rumors, he advised the

hotel's management that if it took in Luciano, Winchell would vacate and use his column to attack the hotel as a gangster hangout. The St. Moritz rejected Luciano.

Luciano was irate, especially since Winchell paid no rent there himself. "He got his apartment on the cuff for mentionin' the St. Moritz in his column once in a while," Luciano recalled later. "And he talked about *me* being a racketeer."

In the twilight of his journalistic career Winchell lost his contacts with the mob as the older gangsters he knew ended up dead or retired. At the same time his relationship with J. Edgar Hoover grew more distant. Hoover at the time was under pressure from Attorney General Robert Kennedy to start battling organized crime. Under those circumstances Walter Winchell probably became an embarrassment.

WISE guys and connected guys

In a large crime family in which there are 250 or so "made" men, or "wise guys"—official Mafia members—there would be at least 10 times as many "connected guys"—men associated with wise guys and taking orders from them. Most of these connected guys hope to become wiseguys, provided they meet the ethnic qualifications.

The made man or wise guy is a "soldier," the lowest rank among Mafia members, but this hardly indicates he is not a man of substantial means. Most soldiers in both the Gambino and Genovese families are believed to be millionaires in their own right. Actually, many connected guys are also as rich, or in some cases richer, than the wise guys.

The average connected guy must adhere to the same rules as the made guys. They take orders from their soldier sponsor, or if they are excellent producers, more likely they take them from the captain, or "capo," over that soldier. The connected guys must report on everything they do. They give "respect" to their superior, and they share the profits with him. (Despite all the talk in the mob about "respect," it is always measured more by the profits brought in than by anything else.) But the connected guy must behave with a certain decorum. The connected guy is not to argue or talk back to a wise guy or to raise a hand to one. "When you are not a wiseguy," mobster Lefty Ruggiero told Joe Pistone, an FBI undercover agent who penetrated the mob as the fabled "Donnie Brasco," "the wiseguy is always right and you're always wrong. It don't matter what. Don't forget that, Donnie. Because no other wiseguy is gonna side with you against another wiseguy."

Some wise guys delude themselves about the reliability of this so-called rule. There is an exception—and it is spelled m-o-n-e-y. As related by Henry Hill in *Wiseguy*, when Tommy DeSimone, connected to the Vario crew inside the Lucchese crime family, murdered Billy Bates in a private dispute, it was an imprudent act. Helping Tommy in the act was Jimmy Burke, the infamous Irish gangster and mastermind of the Lufthansa robbery, and Hill. Burke restrained Bates while DeSimone killed him. The three of them disposed of the victim's body. The catch was that Bates was a made guy with the Gambinos, but none of the trio was made.

Hill later stated, "If the Gambino people ever found out that Tommy had killed Billy, we were all dead."

In due course the Gambinos did find out. They went to Paul Vario, the head of the crew, and demanded the appropriate punishment. It was arranged with ingenious mob cunning. DeSimone was given the good news that he was to be made. Tommy was overjoyed and went off happily with two Vario boys to what was not an initiation, however, but an execution.

Although Hill did not address the matter, undoubtedly Tommy was tortured to reveal the events of the murder, and he most certainly revealed the roles of Burke and Hill. Yet nothing ever happened to the pair. The reason was obvious. Hill and especially Burke were huge money makers for the mob, and that was enough to save them. The avenging of the late, made Billy Bates had to be limited to DeSimone. The surviving pair had the best of all possible connections—that old reliable, m-o-n-e-y.

WOMEN, mafiosi's attitude toward

Do Mafia men beat their wives, their daughters, their girlfriends? Of course they do, but probably less than one might expect of men in such a violent profession. This is not too hard to understand. Though they are men of violence, their violence is part of their "business" activities. To carry that behavior over to non-business situations strikes them as unnecessary, stupid and, toward women, most unmanly.

It is rare for a Mafia man, especially one on the lower echelons to beat a woman because such behav-

ior could mark him as intemperate. And it is somewhat rare to hear a mob guy use foul language in front of a woman, his wife or otherwise. That might not be true during moments of "recreational rape," but in most situations swearing at women would not be proper in personal relationships. By contrast a strongarm guy seeking to pressure a loan shark victim might speak very coarsely to that man's wife, daughter or lady friend. This qualifies as legit behavior because it is business. Likewise it's perfectly acceptable to "put a woman to sleep" if she becomes a threat to mob business, as was the case of mob boss Rusty Rastelli's woman.

Virtually all wise guys hold their women to a very high standard. One mobster told undercover FBI operative "Donnie Brasco" that "if a female swears, she's a *puttana*—a whore" and that if his girl ever "said 'fuck,' I'd throw her out the window." This was from an accomplished hit man.

WOMEN as Mafia victims: Mob gallantry myth

Part of John Gotti's self-portrait was that he brooked no mistreatment of women, and the same has been said of other mob leaders. Gotti was famous for holding doors open for women reporters and making comments about how he was brought up to be nice to the weaker sex. In the first of his three important trials in the 1980s and 1990s, James Sanetore, a turncoat witness against Gotti, was asked by the defense during cross-examination: "Mr. Sanetore, didn't you burn a woman's breasts with cigarettes?" The criminal witness was irate: "Absolutely not. All we did was tie her on the bed and throw burning matches on her breasts. That's all we did."

Left unanswered was how the Gotti side knew about the witness's transgressions.

The mistreatment of women is a staple of forcing loan shark victims to cough up the money they owe at exorbitant interest charges. One common method is to threaten violent punishment of the wife.

Clearly, the mob tolerates the murder of women, many of whom are innocently under the gun in gangland affairs. All it takes is the feeling that she knows too much about criminal activities and is likely to cave in under scrutiny by prosecutors.

Such was the fate of Cherie Golden, a 19-year-old brown-haired beauty with brown eyes and a cherubic smile who had won a Twiggy look-alike contest. She was wooed by John Quinn, a married mobster with six kids on Long Island, who showed Cherie off in Little Italy restaurants. Unfortunately, he also took Cherie along while negotiating the purchase of hot cars and to a number of chop shops he ran. His superiors in the mob did not like that and warned Quinn to dump Cherie. He refused and then got in severe legal trouble. Suddenly he looked like a prime candidate for becoming a turncoat, and that made Quinn an obvious hit candidate.

Quinn was invited to a mob meeting in a Brooklyn tavern with Roy DeMeo, his boss in the car racket and the Gambino family's ace killer. Quinn brought Cherie along and left her outside in his car. He went inside and was promptly put to sleep with a silencer-equipped gun.

Cherie did not hear the shot. Two of the mob's members came to the car and started flirting with her, one on each side of the vehicle. As one of the men distracted the young girl, she turned her head toward him and the other one drew a gun and shot her in the brain. As her head whipped around, she took another bullet in the face. The killers disposed of her body, removing her halter top just to give the police a possible sexual angle to investigate.

DeMeo made the hit on his own without getting higher approval, which upset the recently installed new boss, Paul Castellano. Big Paul recognized the murder as one that could produce very bad press. He wanted to know why the girl was killed. DeMeo's direct superior, capo Nino Gaggi, was also angered but had to put the best face on the situation and explained she knew too much about the stolen car operations. Castellano was not convinced but could do nothing. He ordered that DeMeo not do any hits without prior approval. "Just talk to Roy," Castellano said. "Make sure people just don't start going who don't have to go."

No punishment was exacted for Cherie's murder, and none seemed to have ever been meted out for other Mafia killings of women. Often a woman is killed simply as an object lesson to her husband or boyfriend to keep his silence.

While Hollywood extortionist Nick Circella was doing time, the Chicago mob worried he might flip to gain his freedom. A mob enforcer visited Circella's lady friend, Estelle Carey, a Chicago cocktail waitress. The mob also feared Estelle might talk to help her man, an action that could inspire other women to talk. They decided Estelle had to die and that she had to be killed in grisly fashion to make a vivid point.

They tied her to a chair, tortured her, broke her nose, battered her face, stabbed her several times and cut her throat. Weapons used on her included a flat-iron, a blackjack and a rolling pin. Then she was doused with gasoline and set on fire. The only witness to the horrid homicide was Estelle's pet poodle cowering in a corner. But when her body was found, the torture hit had a most salutary effect. Nick's lips—and those of several females who were thought likely to gab—stayed very zipped.

When Gus Greenbaum, a leading casino operator in Las Vegas, was marked for execution for skimming the mob's skim money, it was decided his wife should die with him. Meyer Lansky ordered the killings and handed the contract to the Chicago mob, an outfit known, as in the case of Estelle Carey, for a passion for brutality. Greenbaum and his wife were found dead in their home in Phoenix, their throats cut. After the killings Lansky supposedly spread word that he had merely ordered straight hits. But this was doubtful since the killings were meant to encourage other Vegas employees to see the wisdom of playing fair with the mob.

See also COPPOLA, MICHAEL "TRIGGER MIKE"; RASTELLI, PHILIP

"WOP with the Mop, the": Alcatraz disparagement of Al Capone

Al Capone's sphere of influence was large, indeed, but not large enough to matter at Alcatraz, "The Rock." The convicts operated under a different "social order" on who was a supercriminal and who was not. Capone's term in the federal prison was hard, not so much because of the sternness of the penal system and its employees, but rather on account of his fellow inmates.

One day Capone and a number of other convicts were lined up at the barber shop for their monthly haircut. The mighty Capone saw no reason to wait and stepped to the front of the line, making the error of cutting ahead of James Lucas, a mean Texas bank robber doing 30 years.

Lucas knew who Capone was but was not impressed. He snarled, "Hey, lard ass, get back at the end of the line." Capone turned and gave Lucas a withering look that would have chilled many a mobster—on the outside.

"You know who I am, punk?" Capone asked.

Lucas reddened in rage. He grabbed the scissors from the convict doing the haircutting and stuck the point into Capone's fat neck. "Yeah," he said, "I know who you are, greaseball. And if you don't get back to the end of that fucking line, I'm gonna know who you *were*."

Capone went to the rear of the line and never again tried to pull rank in Alcatraz. Not that this prevented him from further hostility. Capone suffered his first real violent treatment when he failed to join a prisoner strike after the death of a convict to whom the warden had denied medical treatment because he said he was malingering.

Capone ignored the protest and stayed on his prison laundry job. Other prisoners started calling him "scab" and "rat," and finally Capone was allowed to go to his cell until the strike was crushed. When he returned to work, an unknown convict threw a sash weight at his head. Shoved aside by another convict, train robber Roy Gardner, the weight missed, hitting Capone's arm and causing a deep cut. Capone was transferred to new work mopping up the bathhouse, whereupon the convicts promptly nicknamed him "the wop with the mop." His nemesis, Lucas, one day crept up behind him and stabbed him in the back. Capone was hospitalized for a week, and Lucas was sent to the Hole (solitary confinement). There were other efforts to maim or kill Capone, but friendly convicts, attracted by Capone's payment of money on the outside, protected him. They frustrated a plot to spike his breakfast coffee with lye. On another occasion Capone was on his way to the dentist when a con jumped him from behind and almost strangled him before Capone broke loose and floored him with a single blow.

Such stories reached the press, which informed its eager readers how far the once powerful King of Chicago had fallen. Capone's wife unsuccessfully petitioned the attorney general to have Capone transferred to another institution, so the persecution of "the wop with the mop" continued.

Later on in his confinement Capone began slipping in and out of lucidity. His paresis, caused by an advanced stage of syphilis, prompted most prisoners to let up on him, extending him the sympathy due any convict going "stir crazy."

In January 1939, Capone was shipped out of Alcatraz for the Federal Correctional Institution on Terminal Island near Los Angeles. He was too sick for the rigors of the Rock. Capone was released from custody in November, destined to become increasingly less coherent during the last eight years of his life. When he was released, reporters in Chicago asked his longtime faithful aide Jake "Greasy Thumb" Guzik if Capone was returning to control of the mob. Guzik replied, "Al is nutty as a fruitcake." There can be little doubt that the harassment he endured as "the wop with the mop" had not helped Capone's overall condition.

477

Y

YAKUZA: Japanese organized crime units

Probably no combination of outside forces with the Mafia conjures up more fear among investigators than a possible full-time alliance between the American mob and the Japanese yakuza. The yakuza have in the past been allied with criminal activities in Hawaii, where there is an enormous Japanese population, and later intrusion by the yakuza in the West Coast of the United States has been obvious.

In many respects the yakuza organized activities have been the mirror image of the American Mafia. The yakuza consist of a number of crime families, and its actual criminal activity is very Mafia-like. They are very involved in prostitution, gambling, pornography, loan-sharking, smuggling, extortion and various trucking rackets. Just like the Mafia, they break strikes and other dissenters for corporations especially at stockholders meetings. They are deeply involved in entertainment, where they shake down movie studios, nightclubs and professional sporting clubs. And it has been estimated that half the yakuza profits come from drug trafficking. Like the American mobs the yakuza are heavy into money laundering and of course infiltrate legitimate business. In this last activity they have little trouble with the authorities as the organizations are frequently accepting in Japanese society. Many wear lapel pins that identify them as yakuza, much like fraternal and business organizations such as the Rotarians.

One group that seems to give the yakuza no trouble is the police—to such an extent that American mefiosi are startled. Bribery is much less needed in Japan since the yakuza and most police are of the same conservative persuasion. The police and the mobsters seem to be frequently on a first-name basis. Researchers declare that the Japanese police frequently give warnings to the yakuza gangs before major raids. To allow the police to save face, the mobsters will leave behind a few guns to be confis-

A Japanese tattoo artist works on a yakuza gang member. Members typically sport elaborate body art.

478

cated. It is a tactic mafiosi fully understand. In Hawaii the yakuza and the American mobs worked well together, and the mafiosi thrived on providing the yakuza guns and pornography to ship back to Japan. U.S. handguns worth $100 to $200 in the States easily bring $1,000 in Japan. The main cooperation between the two gangs in Hawaii involved gambling and drug trafficking, and for a while it greatly flourished until the early 1980s when several federal task forces of American investigators struck at the yakuza for fear of further encroachment in California and elsewhere stateside. The crackdowns petered out by 1985 because of budgetary cutbacks.

Still, the arrangements between the two ethnic groups continued for a while, but the mafiosi were not happy about the growth of yakuza power in California and Nevada. Japanese mobsters operated on trust with the Americans since huge sums of money had to be exchanged on trust. To build that trust Japanese gangsters visited the mafiosi in Las Vegas and the two groups ate, drank, gambled and had access to sex. That did not prevent a cultural divide from developing, or as one mafioso allegedly said to an investigator, "They just don't-a talk good like-a us." More important the mob learned that the corrupt law enforcement community was still wary of the "yellow peril." Rather than try to argue about it, they cut off working with the yakuza. Of course the yakuza still maintain a presence in the United States, but the seemingly most dangerous combination of criminals internationally has simply not jelled. Will that change in the future?

YALE, Frankie (1885–1928): New York mob leader

Brooklyn gangster Frankie Yale had in the past performed yeoman service for Johnny Torrio and Al Capone. When they both ended up in Chicago and needed on two occasions a positively trustworthy killer—first to take out Big Jim Colosimo and later, Irish mob leader Dion O'Banion—they contacted Yale for possible hit men. Yale on both occasions decided to handle the very sensitive murders himself. After all, what else were buddies for. Undoubtedly when Al Capone decided to have Yale himself put away in 1928, he probably did feel a mite badly about it, just for old time's sake.

As a teenager Yale was a partner with Torrio in the old Five Points Gang and had probably killed a dozen men before he reached voting age. Around

1908 he and Torrio worked a profitable Black Hand extortion racket among Italian immigrants in Brooklyn, threatening to kill them unless they paid protection money. They also became partners in the Harvard Inn, a bar and brothel near the Brooklyn Navy Yard. Torrio later moved to Chicago and Yale maintained the Harvard, eventually employing Al Capone as a bouncer. When Capone drew heat for a couple of murders, Yale got in touch with Torrio, and Capone went to the Windy City to work in the Jim Colosimo vice empire.

In the early 1920s Yale improved his own position tremendously, building up an important bootlegging and rumrunning operation and taking over control of the national Unione Siciliane, an important Sicilian fraternal organization that had become in part a criminal-front organization. He also ran protection rackets in several fields and invaded the New York tobacconist trade by forcing dealers to order at very high prices some very cheap cigars he manufactured. Thus in Brooklynese "a Frankie Yale" came to mean any sort of product that was overpriced and no good. When police zeroed in on Yale and demanded to know his livelihood, he announced blandly, "I'm an undertaker." In a very broad sense, Yale was telling no lie.

There is little doubt that Yale was imported by Torrio and Capone to murder Colosimo so that Torrio could take over and expand on the lazy Colosimo's crime empire. Torrio and Capone also brought in Yale to take care of O'Banion because the victim did not know him and Yale could approach O'Banion in his flower shop without arousing suspicion. As Yale shook O'Banion's hand, he held on tight so the Irish mobster could not reach his guns. Then two of Capone's favorite gunners, John Scalise and Albert Anselmi, pulled their own guns and shot O'Banion.

By 1928 the relationship between Capone and Yale had soured. First, Yale was trying to take over the huge Chicago chapter of Unione Siciliane, whose members' alcohol-cooking operations Capone needed for his booze operations. Yale was trying to get such moonshining profits sent to the national office which he controlled. In addition, Capone had been depending on Yale to see to landing imported liquor on Long Island and shipping it on to Chicago. Suddenly, truckloads of Capone booze were being hijacked before they ever got through Brooklyn. Suspecting a doublecross, Capone sent one of his men,

James "Finesy" De Amato, to Brooklyn to spy on Yale. De Amato was discovered and gunned down on a Brooklyn street, but not until he had notified Capone that Yale was indeed heisting his liquor and then reselling to him.

In June 1928 Capone held a meeting in Florida with a number of Chicago henchmen, including Dan Serritella, Jake Guzik and Charles Fishetti. He also sent out a henchman to buy two .45-caliber revolvers and several other guns from a Miami pawnshop. On

Assassinated mob leader Frankie Yale received the most garish New York underworld funeral in history, and the *New York Daily News* noted with considerable local pride that it "was a better one than that given Dion O'Banion by Chicago racketeers in 1924."

June 28, 1928, six Chicago mobsters who had been visiting Capone in Florida took the Southland Express back for Chicago. Instead, four got off the train in Knoxville, Tennessee, bought a used black sedan from a Nash agency and drove to New York City.

On July 1, 1928, Yale was driving along 44th Street in Brooklyn when a black sedan crowded him to the curb. Yale and his car were ventilated with a hail of bullets. The assassins abandoned the black Nash a few blocks away and vanished, leaving behind several weapons, including two .45-caliber revolvers traced back to Miami and a Thompson submachine gun that proved to have come from a Chicago gun dealer named Peter von Frantizius known to be a supplier of weapons to the Capone mob. It was the first time in New York that a machine gun, popular in Chicago, had been present during a killing.

They gave Frankie Yale a spectacular funeral, the biggest and best any gangster had gotten in New York. It was in line with Yale's wishes. He had been very impressed with the funeral Dion O'Banion had gotten in Chicago, and he had always said he wanted one that would surpass it. That was no easy task; after all, music for O'Banion's funeral was provided by the Chicago Symphony Orchestra. Still they did Yale up proud. The funeral cost more than $50,000 in 1928 dollars. He had a $15,000 nickel-and-silver coffin and flower stores were denuded of blooms to provide 38 carloads of flowers. Flags flew at half-staff and 250 cars followed through the streets of Brooklyn to Yale's resting place at Holy Cross Cemetery. At least 10,000 mourners, spectators and police watched the show. Among them were two women who it developed were married to Yale; each declared she was the rightful Mrs. Yale.

The *New York Daily News* rendered a final verdict, one that pacified local pride and would undoubtedly have pleased Yale himself. The newspaper declared the Yale funeral "was a better one than that given Dion O'Banion by Chicago racketeers in 1924."

YOUNGBLOODS: Sam Giancana's American-raised Chicago mafiosi

They represented in the 1930s a new phase in syndicated crime in America, an example of the ethnic reinforcements available to the new national crime syndicate in the ghettos. Organized crime continued under the increasing dominance of Italian and Jewish ethnic groups, reversing a trend of just prior to World War I when the more typical ghetto experience was one of social mobility and so had lead to the breakdown of the large Jewish and Italian gangs, specifically the Monk Eastman and Paul Kelly gangs.

These ethnic crime groupings revived under the big-money opportunities provided by Prohibition and so became America's first syndicate criminals, as distinguished from the more common ghetto criminals of the past. Young Turk elements began taking over the gangs, causing among the Italians, for example, a long-term bloody purging of the old-style, old-world mafiosi, replacing them with younger immigrants less "tainted" by the old crime rules and dominated by only one basic drive—the buck. Historically, a couple of decades should have been sufficient to move the ethnic Jewish and Italian gangs out of the ghettos and into a stratum of lower incidence of crime, even ethnic crime. But now the basically first-born ghetto youths were frozen into their locales by a second sociological force as powerful as Prohibition and its consequences—the Great Depression.

In the Chicago "Patch" area of the West Side, youth gangs saw only one future open to them after they passed the mindless age of juvenile crime. That future lay with the mob, the syndicate, the Capones—whatever one wished to call it.

The 42 Gang from the Patch spewed out a steady supply of mobsters-to-be, most prominent being Sam "Momo" Giancana, already at that age, to use a police description, "a snarling, sarcastic, ill-mannered, ill-tempered, sadistic psychopath." As Giancana moved up the syndicate ladder of success, he took with him a group of juvenile companions from the old 42 Gang who within the underworld became known as the "Youngbloods."

The Youngbloods later included other 42 Gang members, but their nucleus formed around such Patch graduates as Sam Battaglia, Milwaukee Phil Alderisio, Marshall Caifano, Sam DeStefano, Fifi Buccieri, Willie Daddano, Frank Caruso, Charles Nicoletti and Rocco Petenza. By the 1950s the Youngbloods were the mainstays of the Chicago Outfit. Many of the older Capone hands, those who had survived the violence of the preceding decades, were now starting to fall away under the ravages of age, men like Golf Bag Hunt, Terry Druggan, Phil D'Andrea, Jake Guzik, Little New York Campagna, Frank Diamond and Claude Maddox.

Even though Sam Giancana still took orders from the older hierarchy—including Tony Accardo and Paul Ricca, the latter elevated to near sainthood within the mob—the Youngbloods were the main muscle in the organization. Giancana kept his Youngbloods close to him, not assigning many to capo status with many soldiers to supervise and "feed," but appointing them instead to an elite corps of buttonmen serving directly under him and carving out large slices of mob profits for themselves.

The Youngblood reign lasted through the slow decline of Giancana in the late 1960s until his assassination in 1975. Within two years previous to that, Giancana had lost many of his most ardent Youngblood supporters. Men like Buccieri, Daddano and Battaglia died; others like DeStefano were murdered (DeStefano would have to go before Giancana could be taken out).

With Giancana's murder by the mob (unless one holds to the underworld charge that it was a CIA hit) the Youngblood element lost complete dominance although many remain to this day powerhouses within the Chicago Outfit. Like those they had previously replaced they are now the Oldbloods of the mob.

See also FORTY-TWO GANG

Z

ZANGARA, Joseph (1900–1933): Assassin

Joseph Zangara is always listed as and was executed as the would-be assassin of President-elect Franklin D. Roosevelt and the killer-by-mistake of Chicago mayor Anton Cermak. However, a strong minority view is that Zangara never wanted to kill FDR—contrary to his own later confession—but was a hired Mafia hit man assigned to shoot Mayor Cermak while he was with the president-elect in Miami in February 1933. Indeed, Judge John H. Lyle, generally held to be the most knowledgeable non-Mafia man on Chicago crime, stated categorically that "Zangara was a Mafia killer, sent from Sicily to do a job, and sworn to silence."

Cermak, elected as a "reformer," was anything but that. He waged war on the Capone Mob (at the time Big Al was already in prison) but not so much to clean up the city as to replace the Capones with his own gangsters, headed up by Teddy Newberry. He moved against Frank Nitti, Capone's at least titular successor, once Big Al was behind bars. In fact, court testimony later indicated that the mayor had dispatched some "tough cops" to erase Nitti, which they attempted to do after handcuffing the unarmed gangster. Nitti was shot three times in the back and neck but miraculously survived, whereupon the mayor of America's second city hurriedly left his bailiwick for Florida.

The way the theory goes, Nitti had Newberry killed and then sent a hit man—Zangara—to take care of the mayor. Considering the fact that the mayor had left Chicago on December 21, 1932, and was still in Florida on February 15, 1933, it is conceivable that he might not have been planning to return at all, figuring Florida sun was preferable to Windy City lead.

On February 15 Cermak was in an open car with FDR in Miami when Zangara opened fire, fatally shooting the "wrong man" Cermak. Yet Zangara had won several pistol-shooting awards when he was in the Italian Army. The fact that he of all people failed to hit the president-elect led some crime observers to believe that he might have hit his real target after all. Lingering in his deathbed for three weeks, Mayor Cermak declared he had no doubt that he had been Zangara's real target.

Why had Zangara missed FDR? According to press accounts, his failure was due to the alert reactions of fearless spectators who grabbed his arm and shoved it upward as he began to fire. Privately Zangara contradicted this version to his lawyers, saying his arm had not been seized until he had gotten off all his shots. A policeman who helped bring him down confirmed this version of the events. It made the theory that he had hit his target all the more plausible.

Zangara ranted and raved against capitalists, yet there was nothing on the record to indicate he was an anarchist, communist, socialist or even Fascist. Despite all his ravings previously against "capitalist presidents and kings," Zangara turned out to be a registered Republican.

Joseph Zangara was almost stripped of all his clothing after being seized in his unsuccessful attempt to assassinate President-elect Franklin D. Roosevelt. Some have insisted Zangara was a Mafia hit man who did get his actual target, Chicago mayor Anton Cermak.

For two years before the shooting Zangara had lived in Florida, his main occupation seeming to be betting on horses and dogs. One researcher on Zangara, the Reverend Elmer Williams, wrote that Zangara had worked in a syndicate "cutting plant" in Florida "convenient to a canal where the whisky was run in from the islands." Williams's thesis was that Zangara got in trouble with his underworld employers and was given the choice of being tortured and murdered himself or killing Cermak.

Of course Zangara went to the electric chair proclaiming his pride with his act, insisting he had wanted to kill FDR. He said of Cermak, "I wasn't shooting at him, but I'm not sorry I hit him."

Was that the real Zangara speaking or the Mafia hit man sticking to his cover story? If it was the lat-

ter, it was hardly unbelievable. The mob always could draw on such unlikely sources ready to lay down their lives in some secret agreement. In *The Godfather* Mario Puzo tells of the Bocchicchio family, which permitted one of its members to confess to a murder he hadn't committed and go to the chair for it. That was fiction but it was hardly outside the behavior patterns within certain Sicilian Mafia families. The family was made an offer, a reward, it couldn't refuse. Had Zangara got an offer he too could not refuse? The majority view says no, that he was a political assassin, period. There are those in law enforcement and the underworld who laugh at that.

See also NITTI, FRANK

ZERILLI, Joseph (1897–1977): Detroit crime family boss

When Joe Zerilli died on October 30, 1977, a high official declared he probably took more crime secrets to the grave with him than any boss who had died in the past decade, including Frank Costello.

In the early 1920s, Detroit was not a Mafia town. Instead, it belonged almost exclusively to the Jewish gangsters of the Purple Gang and to smaller Purple rivals, including the Little Jewish Navy. The name of the Detroit crime game was booze (although jewel robberies, hijacking and extortion were common as well), and the Purples were determined to control it. In the process, they committed upward of 500 gang murders, on a per capita basis probably far outdistancing Al Capone's gangland hits in Chicago.

The Purples had the ability to work well with mafiosi, and during the Detroit gang wars they imported Yonnie Licavoli and his gunners from St. Louis. They also worked well with Gaspar Milazzo and another fast-rising Sicilian gangster, Joseph Zerilli. The later Licavoli family split its time between Detroit and Cleveland (as did such Purples as Moe Dalitz). Milazzo was assassinated in 1930 by New York mafiosi fighting their own Old World wars. Zerilli rose to the top as the Purples pulled out from the local rackets to take far more lucrative positions in the national syndicate's gambling enterprises elsewhere.

Zerilli had come to the United States from Sicily at the age of 17 and started out as a pick-and-shovel laborer. Joining with the Purples in a number of criminal activities, he eventually built an illegal operation that ran up profits of $150 million a year from such enterprises as loan-sharking, extortion, narcotics, bookmaking and labor racketeering. Unlike some mafiosi, Zerilli did not turn his back on prostitution. Anything that made money Zerilli wanted.

As a Detroit citizen, Zerilli posed as a baker-businessman. He lived in a $500,000 home on a 20-acre suburban estate, quite an accomplishment for a breadmaker. As a Detroit don, Zerilli was personally involved in several murders, but, throughout his lifetime was convicted only twice, paying fines for such gross offenses as speeding and carrying concealed weapons.

Highly honored as a godfather, Zerilli was for a time one of only two non–New York members of the national commission. He did not play a role in the national organization of crime, however, because he respected the rights of other bosses to rule their own territories, and he always demanded that same right for Detroit.

Zerilli retired from control of the crime family business in his early 70s, successfully installing his son as his successor, something other dons have tried and failed to do. It was different in Detroit. The Zerilli touch had been perfect, and no one wanted to tamper with what old Joe Zerilli said would work. But in 1975, the elder Zerilli was forced to return to the helm, in part because his son received a four-year sentence for conspiring to obtain a hidden interest in a Las Vegas casino. Also pending was the very troublesome matter of Teamsters boss Jimmy Hoffa.

Hoffa was becoming hard-of-hearing. Zerilli through his top lieutenant, Tony Giacalone, as much as any mafioso had made Hoffa, and Detroit had informed the labor leader after his release from prison to cool it, that everyone was happy with Frank Fitzsimmons running the Teamsters. Unfortunately for Hoffa, he kept right on coming.

Exactly who was responsible for Jimmy Hoffa's disappearance and evident murder on July 30, 1975, is unknown. The conventional wisdom cites Pennsylvania–upstate New York boss Russ Bufalino and New Jersey mafioso Tony Provenzano as the likely assailants. However, the man Hoffa was slated to meet outside a Detroit-area restaurant was Zerilli aide Giacalone. Hoffa was snatched in Detroit and probably killed there.

If Joe Zerilli insisted on any one thing, it was control of his turf. Nothing was ever done in Detroit by other mafiosi without his approval, and he was never known to tolerate any outsiders handling rubouts in

his area. If a murder was done in Detroit, he not only had to be requested to allow it, but also had to handle it. Zerilli was the kind of old Don who insisted on such protocol.

Once, a Detroit mafioso, Nick Licata, fell into disfavor with Zerilli and fled to Los Angeles. Zerilli notified Jack and Tom Dragna that Licata was there. Acknowledging a sort of Golden Rule in crime, Zerilli would never have dreamed of going into L.A. territory in violation of the Dragna rights there. Instead, he suggested rather than requested (which would have been binding) that L.A. carry out the hit. Consequently, Zerilli did not object when the Dragnas decided against the hit, and even took Licata into the family. It was, Zerilli held, their right to do so. All he ever insisted on in return was that he decide on all hits in Detroit, and there are those observers who feel that the Hoffa matter was completely a Joe Zerilli operation.

The police never got a word out of the old man on the Hoffa disappearance.

ZIEGLER, Shotgun George (1897–1934): Public enemy and mob hit man

Shotgun George Ziegler was unique—a criminal who flourished in both organized crime and the more colorful world of the public enemy gangsters of the 1920s and 1930s.

Ziegler, whose real name was Fred Goetz, was just about the best-educated member of crimeland, having graduated from the University of Illinois where he had been a celebrated football player and a top golfer. Previously he had served as a second lieutenant and pilot during World War I. Famous FBI agent Melvin H. Purvis once wrote of Ziegler: "His character was one of infinite contradictions; well mannered, always polite, he was capable of generous kindnesses and conscienceless cruelty."

Arraigned as a youth on a rape charge, Ziegler's parents put up bail money before the trial. But, fearing he'd be convicted, Ziegler ran. Feeling guilty because his parents lost their money, he decided to pay them back the quick way. He held up a doctor who made a habit of carrying large sums of money. When the doctor drew a gun, Ziegler blew him away with a shotgun. It was the beginning of the career of Shotgun George Ziegler.

How and when he got there is not known, but Ziegler next turned up as part of the Capone Mob, becoming one of the gang leader's most-prized triggermen. There is considerable evidence that Ziegler became part of a special execution squad—à la Brooklyn's Murder, Inc., troop—that was employed by the Capone syndicate and some of its affiliated units. The team—Ziegler, Fred "Killer" Burke, Gus Winkler, "Crane Neck" Nugent and Claude Maddox—were said to be paid $2,000 a week (collectively) with expenses for travel and an occasional bonus tossed in. There is some reason to believe this unit, with others, may have handled the St. Valentine's Day massacre—certainly there is no doubt Burke was involved. Public enemy Creepy Karpis, who was well liked by Capone and later did time with Scarface Al in Alcatraz, insisted that the massacre was masterminded by Ziegler. Others do not accept this version, but agree that Ziegler probably handled at least 10 other killings for the Capones.

Ziegler was never happy being just a mob hit man, craving bigger rewards and, possibly more important, greater excitement. He joined the freelance Keating-Holden Gang of bank robbers. Then, suddenly, Ziegler disappeared from the crime scene and worked at his college-trained profession as an engineer. Then, just as suddenly, he would return to the Capones, go back to engineering, or pull a job with Keating-Holden.

In 1933, Ziegler joined the Barker-Karpis band of public enemies, and his superior intellect soon put him in a position of leading authority. He planned many of the gang's jobs and was the one who selected wealthy Edward George Bremer of St. Paul, Minnesota, as a kidnap target. Thanks to his foolproof planning, the job netted the gang $200,000. But the ransom money was too hot to dispose of, and the gang decided that Ziegler, whom all trusted implicitly, should take charge of hiding it for the time being.

In March 1934, Ziegler turned up in Cicero, Capone's captive city, where he went frequently to booze it up. Drinking was all fine and well, but Ziegler was talking wildly, bragging about all his crime capers—including the Bremer job. The Capone gangsters were upset—a man who talked about the exploits of the Barkers and Karpis might just as likely blab about the syndicate mobsters on other counts. In fact, Ziegler was in the process of losing his mind, which, however, in the underworld hardly represents extenuating circumstances.

On March 22, 1934, just two months after the Bremer job, Ziegler came strolling out of his favorite café in Cicero right into the blasts of four shotguns. Ninety percent of his head was blown away. It is not known for certain who was responsible. Four shotguns generally spelled the Capones, but there is a wider belief that the Barkers had pulled it off. If so, the Barkers had done so without first getting back the ransom money, but they sent Ma Barker to visit Ziegler's grieving widow. The old lady was able to convince Mrs. Ziegler that her husband had been killed either by the Capone forces or their enemies—and that Mrs. Ziegler should give back the $200,000. It is a matter of record that the Barkers neither lived long enough nor remained free to enjoy the loot.

As for Shotgun George Ziegler, his double career in syndicate and less-organized crime had been a relatively short one.

ZIPS: Sicilian Mafia imports

In the 1970s and 1980s, two groups of mad-dog killers became extremely powerful on the organized crime scene in New York. They were the Westies, Irish gangsters on Manhattan's West Side, and the so-called Zips—young mafioso gangsters imported from Sicily. Both groups caused severe problems for the established crime families. Neither could be trusted. Of the two the Zips were worse but were tolerated because they generated considerable amounts of money, many millions in fact, for the mob, especially for the Bonanno and later the Gambino crime families. Some of the Zips got so rich that they had to be rather inventive in spending their loot. One gave his young daughter a genuine fur coat for her Barbie doll.

Lefty Ruggiero, a Bonanno soldier once explained to undercover FBI agent "Donnie Brasco" (Joe Pistone) about the relationship between Carmine Galante, the head of the Bonannos, and the Zips: "Lots of people hate him [Galante]. . . . There's only a few people that he's close to. And that's mainly the Zips. . . . Those guys are always with him. He brought them over from Sicily, and he uses them for different pieces of work and for dealing all that junk. They're as mean as he is. You can't trust those bastard Zips. Nobody can. Except the Old Man."

Actually Galante was not the Zips' only sponsor. Carlo Gambino, head of the largest crime family at the time, also turned to the Zips when he needed reliable killers who could do a better job than the average Gambino soldier. Before his death, however, Gambino started having second thoughts about the Zips, and Galante took full control of the erratic Sicilians.

There is more than one explanation of how the Zips' name originated. One is that it was used pejoratively by other mobsters in reference to the Sicilians' passion for ziti. Another theory says it evolved from their use of silent, homemade zip guns. Other contemptuous underworld terms applied to them were Siggies and Geeps, never of course in face-to-face dealings.

The Zips' true power emanated not only from their cooperation with Galante but from their own parent organizations back in Sicily. The Sicilian Mafia cooperated with their American counterparts to import heroin to the United States. The Sicilians acquired the morphine base from the Middle East, refined the stuff in Sicily and shipped it to New York for distribution. The Zips were a vital cog in the operation and thus vital to Galante since he was determined to put all Mafia drug profits in America in his own coffers.

The American mob supplied support services and territories for distribution, for which the local families collected "rent." This was ideal for the local families since they profited from heroin without getting too involved in the deals.

As the heroin distribution grew, more and more Zips were needed, and Galante ordered reinforcements. By the late 1970s sales of heroin in this country probably topped $10 billion a year. Pressures mounted on the American mafiosi. Bosses had a hard time keeping their soldiers out of more active participation in drugs, and it looked like Galante might start recruiting mafiosi from other families, which would have gnawed away at the Mafia structure.

Just as important, the increasing narcotics traffic drew more attention from law enforcement and threatened the mobs' holds on more "wholesome" activities such as gambling, loan-sharking, construction shakedowns, massive auto thefts and so on, which frequently operated with a certain amount of law enforcement cooperation or at least benign neglect. These law enforcement figures found that narcotics dealings put too much pressure on them for it to be ignored.

In 1979 the only solution seemed to be the removal of Galante. He was assassinated in a spectacular hit in a Brooklyn restaurant. But before he could be killed, the Zips had to be "neutralized." This was done in typical Mafia style. The Zips were recruited to join in the Galante hit. The wild men did so since it clearly meant they would enjoy even greater profits thereafter.

Of course, the Mafia bosses were not trying to crimp the narcotics operation. They simply wanted a bigger slice for themselves and to run the operation less blatantly.

Paul Castellano, successor to the late Carlo Gambino, informed the Zips that most of the spoils had to be funneled to him and, allegedly, his family, despite a death sentence punishment hanging over any family member engaging in the drug trade. *That*, Castellano determined, did not apply to him—and he could exercise his usual greed and keep much of the profits for himself. The Zips, under their leader Sal "Toto" Catalano, agreed to the new deal.

It soon became clear, however, how little they respected the deal. The Zips started varied operations of their own in Gambino family territory without the godfather's consent, making it apparent that they really only felt obliged to answer to their bosses in Sicily. The Zips' power grew on their bloated drug profits. Castellano recognized the fact that the Zips were becoming more powerful in Brooklyn than were his own soldiers, who resented the Zips and their boss who was swallowing so much of the drug revenues. Something had to be done.

Many killings, carried out in Mafia crosscurrents of treachery took place before matters were settled. Soldiers on both sides died, but a new player entered the picture. Federal authorities started massive prosecutions that were to make the careers of future FBI director Louis Freeh and future New York mayor Rudy Giuliani. Numerous arrests were made in what became known as the Pizza Connection case. Some of the players died, primarily Catalano's top aide Cesare Bonventre, whose death may have been ordered by Catalano or Castellano or the pair operating together. The prosecutions resulted in wholesale convictions, Catalano drawing a 45-year sentence. Castellano was murdered in a plot masterminded by John Gotti.

The Zips were not completely eliminated, but their numbers were greatly reduced. And they did take some bad raps. Four months after Gotti seized leadership of the Gambinos, his top aide, Frank DeCicco, was killed in a car bombing. That attack, aimed at killing Gotti also, focused attention on the Zips, since the New York families long ago established a rule against such bombings in the city. Such murders produced too much heat if some soldiers' kin or some innocent bystander happened to be killed. However, the Zips came from Sicily where car bombings were a Mafia way of death.

As it turned out, the DeCicco killing was the work of Genovese crime boss Chin Gigante, who hoped the technique would shift suspicions to the Zips. It was one of the few times the Zips were "not guilty."

See also BONVENTRE, CESARE; CATALANO, SALVATORE "TOTO"

ZWILLMAN, Abner "Longy" (1899–1959): Crime syndicate founder and New Jersey boss

With the exception of Meyer Lansky, Abner "Longy" Zwillman was the most feared and respected member of the "Jewish Mafia," the tough, bright Jewish gangsters who played a key role, certainly the equal of the Mafia-bred mobsters under Lucky Luciano, in forming the national crime syndicate. Like Lansky, Zwillman sat in on the top council meetings of the syndicate, and there was no nonsense, as has been much perpetuated in recent years, that said only Italians could vote. Despite various descriptions of the national commission of the Mafia—which was actually limited in scope and authority—the ruling group of the syndicate was the so-called Big Six, equally divided between Italians and Jews. Members of this group (after the imprisonment of Luciano) who continued to rule into the early 1950s were Lansky, Zwillman, Frank Costello, Joe Adonis and Tony Accardo, and Greasy Thumb Guzik.

Zwillman worked closely with Lansky, Luciano, Costello and Willie Moretti in the early days. Moretti, an early boss of a tough Jersey crime family, was his junior partner and provided murder muscle when Zwillman needed it. Zwillman was one of the key figures in the new combination's successful efforts forcibly to absorb the Dutch Schultz empire. In the process, Zwillman became the undisputed boss of crime in New Jersey, in fact becoming identified as "the Al Capone of New Jersey."

His political power in New Jersey was awesome. Officials in many localities hopped to his tune, and,

in 1946, Republican governor Harold G. Hoffman personally solicited Zwillman's support. Three years later, the mobster passed the word to the Democratic candidate for the governorship, Elmer Wene, that he would contribute $300,000. All Zwillman wanted in return was the right to name the state's attorney general. Wene refused and lost the election.

The Zwillman-Moretti syndicate worked the state on a grand scale, and they operated a plush gambling casino in the Marine Room of the Riviera nightclub on the Palisades just above the George Washington Bridge. As a nightclub, the Riviera operated with star entertainers and was always mobbed by patrons eager to see the floor show. Entry to the Marine room, which was protected by guards, was much more difficult. As *New York Times* crime reporter Meyer Berger noted, "All players had to be known. Outsiders saw only the dining rooms."

Zwillman tried to maintain a respectable face. When the syndicate started getting heat in the 1932

Longy Zwillman, the "Al Capone of New Jersey," was an important member of the ruling body of the national syndicate and much honored by the boys for his torrid love affair with actress Jean Harlow. He died by hanging, perhaps a suicide, perhaps a mob execution.

hunt for the kidnapped Lindbergh baby, Zwillman relieved the pressure with a public relations coup, posting a large reward for the kidnapper. In the early 1950s, he invaded a number of legitimate businesses and sought the image of a civic-minded citizen, in one case donating $250,000 for a Newark slum clearance plan. However, that facade crumbled when in the late 1950s the McClellan Committee turned its rackets investigation spotlight on his activities. Subpoenaed by the committee and harassed by an IRS probe of his taxes, Zwillman started to take on a hangdog look.

At the same time, his problems within the syndicate increased. Zwillman incurred the wrath of Vito Genovese when he voted against that ambitious mobster who wanted to force Costello out of power. Then he guessed wrong by backing Albert Anastasia against Genovese. After Anastasia was murdered in 1957, other crime leaders began edging in on Zwillman's New Jersey rackets.

Given the sum total of the pressures on him, it did not seem especially surprising that Zwillman was said to have committed suicide on February 27, 1959, just before he was slated to appear before the McClellan Committee. There were, however, some troubling details about Zwillman's suicide. Apparently, he had managed to strangle himself with a plastic rope in the basement of his luxurious $200,000 mansion in West Orange, New Jersey. That clearly seemed to be a clumsy method of sui-

cide. Additionally, there were unexplained bruises on his body and strong indications that his hands had been tied with some kind of wire.

Whether or not Zwillman took his own life, his death must have been a great relief to members of the crime syndicate—especially Meyer Lansky, who feared Zwillman was growing too old to take the heat and might turn informer to avoid prison. In later years, Lansky insisted to Israeli biographers that he had not ordered Zwillman's death, that it had been decreed by Genovese. In exile in Italy, Luciano, who was critical of Lansky for not coming to the aid of an old comrade, said the job was done on orders of Carlo Gambino after Zwillman tried to put the bite on him following Genovese's imprisonment. However, no assassination of Zwillman could have taken place without Lansky's approval (just like a dozen years earlier, when Bugsy Siegel was dispatched).

The underworld version holds that Zwillman was killed, but with a measure of respect. The boys came to him and told him he had to go. Longy didn't want to die, but they explained patiently there was no other way. They even brought along a bottle of expensive brandy to ease the elderly hoodlum's passage. When he was feeling no pain, they trussed him up so that he would not flail wildly and suffer and then they hanged him from a water pipe in the basement of his house.

It was a clear case of suicide.

See also SEX AND THE MAFIA

Mafia Time Line

1878

The first major purge of the Mafia in Italy is launched by the government, causing many mafiosi to flee Sicily for North Africa, which becomes a way station for the promised land of America. Mafiosi settle in major American cities within Italian communities, such as New York, Boston, New Orleans, Chicago, Kansas City and St. Louis, to become bastions of Mafia power thereafter. New Orleans would become the first major home of Mafia power in the New World, aided by the area's longstanding tolerance of corruption.

1889

The first acknowledged Mafia killing in America occurs. A Neapolitan named Vincenzo Ottumvo is murdered in the middle of a card game. The crime goes unsolved and is followed over the next two years by at least 40 killings of rival mafiosi or Camorra Neapolitan gangs for control of waterfront rackets. This is a major criminal war, but the media and the authorities are not hip enough to give it an official name.

1891

New Orleans chief of police William Hennessey apparently sides with one major Mafia group and is murdered by the other major faction. Public outrage boils over, and a mob storms the prison protecting a number of Italians who were acquitted of the murder because none in the Italian community would testify. A total of 11 are lynched, two by hanging, the rest by an improvised firing squad. Later some of the media hint that the business community actively backed the lynching as a way to curb growing unionization moves by workers.

1892–1910

Following the murder of Chief Hennessey mafiosi in New Orleans stay undercover for a while, but other Mafia gangs elsewhere press their advantage over rivals including the Camorristas. The mafiosi usually win out due to sheer meanness and an ability to enforce omerta, or the rule of silence. For all its vaunted power the Camorra is too lenient by underworld standards. *New York Times* writer Nicholas Gage would later explain "that the Camorra punishment for a 'rat' was merely to slit his tongue before killing him, while the Mafia punishment was to cut off his genitals and jam them down his throat before execution."

1903

The general public is by now aware and frightened of La Mano Nera, or Black Hand—Italian terrorists or extortionists who commit murders under the motto of "pay or die."

1907

At the age of 10 Lucky Luciano starts his first racket, which the *New York Times*, quoting the *Mafia Encyclopedia*, would later call early networking in the Mafia: "For a penny or two a day, Luciano offered younger and smaller Jewish kids his personal protection against beatings on the way to school. If they didn't pay, he beat them up. One runty kid refused to pay, a thin little youngster from Poland, Meyer Lansky. Luciano attacked him and was amazed when Lansky gave as good as he got. They became bosom buddies after that."

1909

New York police form a covert branch under Lt. Joseph Petrosino to ferret out "Black Hand–Mafia" operations. Actually only a few mafiosi engage in Black Hand rackets, and indeed they often roust or kill Black Handers because the latter invite too much public scrutiny, which can interfere with major mafiosi activities.

1909

Lt. Petrosino, in Sicily to compare police records there with known New York criminals so as to have them deported back to Italy, is ambushed and killed in the main square of Palermo. The murder had been ordered by Mafia boss Paulo Marchese (a.k.a. Paul di Cristina), who later becomes a powerful Mafia figure in New Orleans.

1912

Owney "the Killer" Madden is shot six times by rivals at a New York dance but recovers. By the time he reaches crime czar status, Owney can brag that he has wiped out all his attackers.

1915

Al Capone joins the Five Points Gang and is recognized as the toughest of the toughest.

1916

The last of the great Mafia-Camorra wars in America erupts in New York, the Sicilians under Nicholas Morello, who controls much of Manhattan, and the Neapolitans under Don Pelligrino Morano, who runs the Brooklyn rackets. Morello dreams of a combination of the two forces. Morano feigns interest and invites Morello to a peace meeting in Brooklyn where the latter is assassinated. Morano believes he had permission from the authorities for the murder, the old country style, and is shocked when he is arrested. Eventually convicted, Morano is, reports the *Brooklyn Eagle*, "surrounded by a dozen Italians [who] showered kisses on his face and forehead. On the way to the jail other Italians braved the guard and kissed Morano's cheeks and forehead."

1920

Devoid of the leadership of Don Pelligrino Morano, who is serving a life sentence, the New York Camorristas are disorganized, and many members shift their allegiance to various Mafia outfits. Typical of these is a young Neapolitan named Vito Genovese who quickly climbs the ladder.

1920

The Prohibition era begins with the Eighteenth Amendment outlawing manufacturing, selling, distributing and transporting of alcoholic beverages. Prohibition alters organized crime, giving criminal gangs an alternative to violent crimes and serving as lackeys for politicians in electoral politics. There is much more money to be made sating the public's thirst for drink. As the criminals become richer they can no longer be bought by politicians but rather buy them.

1920

John Torrio, the chief aide to Big Jim Colosimo, becomes frustrated with Colosimo, who is satisfied being Chicago's millionaire pimp and has no ambitions for entering the booze racket. Torrio sends for his protégé, Al Capone, in New York, ostensibly to assist in the mob's sex rackets but actually to take care of Colosimo, which he does in May.

1924

In a move to lock up the entire booze racket in the Chicago area, Torrio and Capone import a tough New York gangster named Frankie Yale to hit Dion O'Banion, the head of the powerful North Side Gang. O'Banion does not know Yale and falls for a so-called handshake murder.

1925

Gang war rages between Hymie Weiss, O'Banion's successor, and other Torrio foes, and Chicago becomes a virtual battlefield. Finally Torrio himself is badly wounded. When he emerges from the hospital, he decides to take his $30 million and retire to the "sanity" of New York, leaving the entire operation to Capone.

1926

As the war continues, Weiss masterminds a daylight attack on Capone's headquarters at the Hawthorne Inn in Cicero. A caravan of cars passes the establishment and pours 1,000 rounds of machine-gun lead into the place; no one inside is killed, but a pedestrian dies in the attack. Vowing vengeance on Weiss, Capone finally eliminates his main rival by having him machine-gunned to death in front of the Holy Name Cathedral.

1927

Capone wins the so-called War of Sicilian Succession and installs Tony Lombardo as president, in the process wiping out most of the Genna Gang and the Aiello brothers who opposed him. But Lombardo is killed the following year, and Capone concentrates on eliminating the rest of the Aiellos. Finally the three brothers flee Chicago, one all the way back to Sicily.

1928

Arnold "the Brain" Rothstein, master criminal innovator who molded Lucky Luciano into a major crime leader, is murdered after welshing on a huge gambling debt. A month later, the National Crime Syndicate formed on Rothstein's blueprint is set up at a meeting at Cleveland's Statler Hotel. Luciano, not yet a top boss, is credited with pulling most of the strings.

1929

The St. Valentine's Day Massacre marks the bloody conclusion to Capone's battle for power in Chicago. Four killers dressed as Chicago policemen line up seven members of the Bugs Moran Gang, the last remnants of the O'Banion forces, and machine-gun them in a Chicago garage. Remarking that "only Capone kills like that," Moran goes into hiding.

1929

After the initial shock of the St. Valentine's Day Massacre, underworld leaders—Italians, Jews and Irish—hold a conclave in Atlantic City. The fall out includes the country being divided into separate territories, with all conflicts to be resolved by a nine-member national commission. At the meeting it was also decided Capone should agree to be arrested on a gun charge and take a one-year sentence to further defuse the massacre. Capone does not like the idea but agrees. It probably is a mistake since it demonstrated for the first time that Capone was not invulnerable.

1930–1931

While most of the mobsters around the country are satisfied by the national syndicate idea, the most unreconstructed elements are the two major factions of old-line mafiosi in New York led by Joe the Boss

Masseria and Salvatore Maranzano who were locked in the so-called Castellammarese War (named after the Castellammarese del Golfo area of Sicily). While the two sides vigorously kill each other, Luciano aligns himself with Masseria until the former arranges for his assassination. Luciano then joins the Maranzano group, waiting for the proper moment. Maranzano plots Luciano's demise at the same time. Luciano easily outmaneuvers his foe and emerges as the head of the American Mafia, becoming the so-called Boss of Bosses, a title he wisely rejects for the sake of unity although he clearly is the de facto head of the mafiosi.

1931

With the Mafia firmly in control, independent gangsters who won't play ball with the combination are eradicated, the notorious Jack "Legs" Diamond being the most prominent case in point.

1931

Luciano having brought the Italian elements into line, it becomes Meyer Lansky's job to whip the Jewish gangsters into accordance. This is accomplished by the Franconia conference in a New York hotel of that name. Jewish mobsters from around the nation attend and the convincing is done by Lansky and Moe Dalitz out of Cleveland and the Detroit Purple Gang. The triumphant decision of the conference is perhaps quaintly stated by Lansky's partner Bugsy Siegel: "The yids and the dagos would no longer fight each other." It is an agreement long adhered to with only minor exceptions, since even when Bugsy himself is later hit, it is with a combined vote of "yids and dagos."

1931

Al Capone is convicted on tax evasion charges and sentenced to 11 years in prison. He will never again return to mob leadership, ending up a hopeless paretic, a malady brought on by ravages of untreated syphilis contracted in his early whorehouse days.

1933

Prohibition ends, and many criminals are unable to make the transition to other criminal activities, although the Luciano-Lansky alliance thrives in gambling and the legal booze trade.

1935

Dutch Schultz is murdered in a New Jersey steakhouse on orders from the national commission because he insists on having special prosecutor Thomas E. Dewey murdered for prosecuting him. The other crime leaders fear such an assassination would produce a firestorm of heat. The boys also are worried Schultz will use the chaos to invade their rackets.

1936

Luciano, now the most powerful mobster in the nation, is convicted on compulsory prostitution charges and sentenced to 30 to 50 years, an incredible term at the time. The mob feels that it is a bad rap concocted by Dewey with the aid of perjurers because he cannot nab Luciano on more serious charges.

1936

"Machine Gun" Jack McGurn is shot dead in a Chicago bowling alley by unknown gunmen on the eve of the seventh anniversary of the St. Valentine's Day Massacre, for which he has long been regarded as a prime gunman.

1937

Lansky organizes the big Cuban hotel gambling casinos after showing dictator Fulgencio Batista the joys of depositing $2 million at a pop into secret Swiss bank accounts.

1940

Murder, Inc., turncoat Abe "Kid Twist" Reles informs on the crime syndicates with testimony that will wreck the assassination outfit's role as the killer troop enforcing the ruling commission's homicide decisions. Many killers are convicted, and some, doomed to the electric chair.

1941

Reles becomes known as the canary who couldn't fly when he plunges from the sixth floor of a Coney Island hotel where he has been held in protective custody in a room where six police officers had been required to be with him at all times. The public is left to judge whether he fell, jumped or was heaved out the window.

1942

During World War II Naval Intelligence, fearful of Nazi sabotage on the waterfront, solicits the cooperation of mob gangsters to secure the docks. The imprisoned Luciano approves the plan.

1944

Louis "Lepke" Buchalter dies in Sing Sing's electric chair. He becomes the only top mob figure to suffer that fate.

1946

Luciano is given a commutation of his prison term by Governor Dewey who says it is for his patriotic services during the war. Later the mob insists the Dewey campaign was given $90,000 in small bills for the governor's political war chest.

1946

After his deportation Luciano sneaks back into Cuba to preside over a major mob conference to settle syndicate affairs and decide what should be done about Bugsy Siegel, who is suspected of skimming off millions in construction costs while building the Flamingo, the mob's first major casino in Las Vegas. Bugsy is ordered to make up the money shortfall to stay alive. Luciano hopes to live in Havana and run American affairs from offshore. The Cuban government is friendly to the idea but is forced by the United States to deport Luciano to Italy once more.

1947

Bugsy Siegel relaxes when he learns he has been given more time but is then murdered while at ease.

1947

Having been released from prison in 1939, Al Capone is taken to his Florida mansion, living out his last eight years between periods of lucidity and mental inertia, totally unable to engage in mob activities.

1950–1951

The Kefauver Committee launches its investigation on organized crime with televised hearings that hold the audience enthralled by a parade of top mob figures, most of whom "take the fifth." In retrospect this does little to eliminate the Mafia, but public awareness forces J. Edgar Hoover to alter the Federal Bureau of Investigation's traditional attitude that the Mafia does not exist. Senator Estes Kefauver's fame wins him a vice presidential nomination, but he loses in the Eisenhower landslide.

1957

Bugs Moran, the last important surviving boss of the anti-Capone O'Banion gang, dies in prison. His power had waned after the 1929 St. Valentine's Day Massacre, and he was reduced to minor robberies that earned him two 10-year prison sentences. When he dies he does not get the usual O'Banion lavish mob funeral but a quickie burial in a potter's field outside prison walls.

1957

Albert Anastasia, so-called Lord High Executioner of Murder, Inc., is killed in a Manhattan barber shop. The crime is sponsored by a number of high-level mobsters, not because Anastasia is kill-crazy, but rather due to his attempt to cut himself in on part of the lucrative Cuban casino action. Clearly the main movers behind the killings are Luciano, Lansky, Genovese and Anastasia's underboss Carlo Gambino.

1957

Following the Anastasia murder a major underworld conference is held in Apalachin, New York. The conference is cut short by a law enforcement raid. The main suspects behind the raid again are Luciano, Lansky and Gambino, this time with the addition of Frank Costello. Their target is Genovese, who clearly wishes to gain ultimate power in the Mafia. He wants all of Costello's empire, but the other bosses decree that Costello can retire in peace. With the conference bust-up Genovese is in disgrace.

1959

The anti-Genovese plotters press their efforts by involving Genovese in a disastrous drug deal that lands him a 15-year prison term. (He will die behind bars in 1969.)

1960

The Gallo-Profaci war results in major bloodletting in Brooklyn. Boss Joe Profaci survives by splitting the Colombo faction from the Gallo brothers. A fragile peace finally is achieved, but the mob bosses suspect one another, rightly in great measure, of plotting against one another.

1962

The most important mafioso in America, Lucky Luciano, dies of a heart attack in exile in Italy. By then his power in the mob has been greatly reduced, and as he suspects, his longtime partner, Meyer Lansky, has been shorting tributes to him.

1963

The nation is once again enthralled by crime hearings by the U.S. Senate Subcommittee on Investigations in which informer Joseph Valachi reveals the standard procedures of many crime families. Although Valachi is less informed than he himself thinks, he has successfully absorbed much about "La Cosa Nostra." He reveals the rules followed by the crime commission that handles decisions involving multi-family disputes as well as the succession of new bosses.

1964

The "Banana War" roils the Mafia after Joseph Bonanno starts an ambitious plan to take over a king-sized portion of organizes crime. He plans to assassinate bosses Carlo Gambino and Tommy Lucchese in New York, another in Buffalo and another in Los Angeles, thus making Bonanno king of the hill. His plan is thwarted when his enemies are warned, and Bonanno flees to his strongholds in the West and in Canada. He finally surrenders to the law, claiming he had been kidnapped by his foes. Finally a compromise is worked out under which Bonanno agrees to retire and leave his son to take over his family. As a result Bonanno continues to pull the family strings until he does genuinely retire in 1968 following heart problems.

1966

Police raid a Forest Hills, Queens, restaurant named La Stella and arrest 13 important mobsters from around the country. The meeting is dubbed by the press as a "Little Apalachin" meeting. When the mobsters are released by the courts, they defiantly return to the same restaurant. Nothing of significance is learned by the law, but the *New York Times* dispatches its food critic, who accords La Stella an impressive two-star rating.

1967

The Justice Department sets up a special "strike force" in Buffalo to combat the Magaddino crime family. It is the first of its type and becomes the model of many others around the country.

1967

Longtime crime family boss Tommy Lucchese dies. Highly respected within the mob, he was not convicted of anything the last 44 years of his life.

1970

The Racketeer Influenced and Corrupt Organization Act, or RICO, is established. In following years it becomes the most vital tool in battling organized crime as the government wins the right to obtain long prison terms if a mafioso connection to a criminal "enterprise" can be proven. Mobsters are astonished by what the law can now do to them. When Frankie "the Beast" Falanga is hauled in by prosecutors and informed he would be indicted on RICO charges, he bounds out of his chair, screaming, "RICO? I don't even know any fucking RICO!" It is said he becomes so outraged that he drops dead just before going to trial.

1971

Crime boss Joseph Colombo is shot at an Italian-American Unity Day rally he has organized. The act, carried out by a black man, is recognized as having been sanctioned by the powerful Carlo Gambino who objects to the undue attention Colombo's antics have drawn toward the Mafia. Suffering severe brain damage, Colombo is left in a vegetative state for the last seven years of his life.

1972

Paul Ricca, along with Tony Accardo, the true leader of the Chicago Outfit, dies. The pair held the strings of power well over 30 years rather than such media-endowed chieftains as Frank Nitti and later Sam Giancana.

1972

"Crazy Joe" Gallo, much hunted by mafiosi, felt safe to celebrate his 43rd birthday at Umberto's Clam House, since a mob rule made Little Italy spots off limits for rubouts. In an exception, Gallo is shot down as a birthday surprise.

1973

Known as the "prime minister of the underworld" for his ability to spread bribes around the so-called upperworld for the benefit of the mobs, Frank Costello dies. In his later years, in retirement, he collected a number of press groupies and other admirers who insisted he was a major corrupter (he refers to a number of New York judges as "my boys") but not a murderer. Actually he laid out $100,000 to have Murder, Inc., canary Abe Reles "go out the window" while in protective custody. He never stopped saying the only way to put

an end to illegal gambling was to make it legal, parroting organized crime's favorite ploy, since mobsters know they can make more money than ever in a legal environment.

1975

Former Teamsters Union head Jimmy Hoffa disappears, or more likely is murdered by the mob, when he attempts to reassert his previous controls. Accounts of Hoffa's fate are offered in many forms, none very credible.

1975

Sam Giancana, ousted head of the Chicago Outfit (under controls by Paul Ricca and Tony Accardo), is murdered in the basement of his home. Giancana is about to face congressional grilling around his alleged CIA connections, the Castro assassination plots, and the murder of President John F. Kennedy.

1976

Carlo Gambino, the most powerful godfather in the nation and essentially the de facto "Boss of Bosses," dies in bed. In the last years of his rule, Gambino is preoccupied with leaving his mark on the Mafia, going so far as to kill leaders in other crime families to make sure they will have good leaderships from his hand-picked successors. In 1972, for example, Gambino had Tommy Eboli, the acting head of the Genovese crime family murdered and installed in his place a longtime friend and highly regarded mobster, Funzi Tieri. Clearly Gambino saw Tieri as the best don available in any crime family after Gambino himself is gone. Unfortunately, after Gambino goes, Tieri lasts only five years and most of that time faces legal problems.

1980

Genovese head Tieri is indicted and convicted of RICO charges, the first in the nation, but he dies in 1981 before he can be sent to prison.

1980

Philadelphia Mafia boss Angelo Bruno is murdered. Once called the "Gentle Don" for running one of the most peaceful crime families in the nation, he finds his domain changed when casino gambling is approved for Atlantic City. This attracts the major New York crime families, and Bruno must go when he tries to hold on to a tired old city no one had cared about for years.

1982

The use of RICO spreads around the country, and Cleveland boss James "Blackie" Licavoli becomes the first don to go to prison under the law's terms. He dies in 1985.

1983

Meyer Lansky dies. He created organized crime in its syndicate form, while Lucky Luciano created his part of the operation, the American Mafia. This latter portion survives to this day because it has an apparatus for vacancies being filled and because it remains a money-making machine. Lansky stands as the quintessential Jewish-American mobster, as most of them stayed in the syndicate until dying or selling out their positions in the rackets and retiring. Lansky, with no interest in creating a dynasty, reflects the Jewish mobster traditions, yet Lansky in large measure is the creator of the American Mafia and its real godfather.

1984

Nicholas Civella, the leader of the Kansas City crime family, is indicted under RICO and involvement in conspiracy and the skimming of the Las Vegas casinos, and thus a most important operative is taken down.

1985

Crime bosses in such cities as Kansas City, Chicago, Cleveland and Milwaukee are given long sentences for vast skimming of cash from Las Vegas casinos, which they control through Teamster pension funds.

1985

"Little Nicky" Scarfo, the boss of the Philadelphia Mafia, much-feared even by his own loyalists, is convicted and sent to prison for life.

1985

Paul Castellano, boss of the Gambino crime family, is murdered by John Gotti who takes over.

1987

The finis is written to the "Pizza Connection" case, with the convictions of about three dozen members in the New York and Sicilian Mafias.

1991

Major prosecutions in New England lead to guilty pleas by boss Raymond Patriarca and four others, decimating that Mafia family.

1992

The reign of the so-called Teflon Don, John Gotti, crashes down with a life sentence without parole. The prosecution case is greatly aided by the testimony of turncoat Sammy "the Bull" Gravano who wins a major reduction of prison time for himself, despite admitting to 19 murders by talking about Gotti's doings. Gotti tries to run the Gambino crime family through his son and later his older brother, but his own position deteriorates within the mob, and by the time he succumbs to cancer in 2002 the Gotti name has lost much influence.

1993

Carlos Marcello, reputed to be the powerful boss of the New Orleans crime family, dies. In actuality Marcello's reputation was at least partly hype, since he was long under the thumb of New York, which in many operations allowed him only a third of the revenues of certain rackets in his own family. The long-held theory that Marcello was linked with the Chicago mob to kill JFK overlooks the fact that New York would have been very annoyed.

1996

Turncoat Sammy "the Bull" Gravano drops out of the witness protection program, saying he does not fear mob vengeance for informing on John Gotti. Actually he doesn't want to be under the yoke of federal authorities and is eager to get back into the rackets. He is eventually convicted of jumping into the Ecstasy racket and is hit with a 20-year sentence with additional charges pending.

1997

Vincent "the Chin" Gigante is sentenced to 12 years on conviction for murder and racketeering activities. He has for years paraded around in public in a bathrobe talking to himself, pretending to be mentally incapable of standing trial. In 2003 he gives up the ghost and admits faking his dummy act as part of a plea bargain that adds only a small amount of time to his sentence and makes him eligible for parole in 2010.

2000

Anthony "Tony Ducks" Corallo, longtime head of the Lucchese family dies in prison, having served the last 13 years behind bars. He was previously called Tony Ducks for his ability to "duck" convictions.

2002

John Gotti dies in prison on a life sentence. He is regarded as the last crime boss with true charisma, if perhaps not up to par with real brains, a condition that left many of his minions in the Gambino family thinking rather ill of him.

2002

Joe Bonanno, the longest-living of the major mob bosses, dies at 97. He has been relatively inactive since 1968 when the other crime families forced him into retirement for having sought to kill several dons in order to establish himself as the foremost crime boss, virtually in control of the New York families. To prevent a major outbreak of fighting the bosses forced Bonanno to promise to step aside in favor of his son, who is unable to boss the family. Bonanno made rumbles several times of breaking his promises, something he was known to do on many occasions, but he failed to make a major comeback with his limited remaining muscle.

2004

The "Last Don," Bonanno boss Joseph Massino, is brought to trial. He is the final leader of the New York five families to face prosecution. It is said the government is much chagrined that Massino has eluded legal nets for well over 15 years. The government has indicated it may seek the death penalty for Massino, a fate never faced before by any Mafia godfather. Some see this merely as a ploy to force a guilty plea by Massino.

2004

There is little letup in the attempt to suppress the Gambino family, the nation's biggest even after the fall of John Gotti. Legal buzz persists that a new informer, Michael "Mikey Scars" DiLeonardo, will do more damage to the Mafia than squealers Joe Valachi, Jimmy "the Weasel" Fratianno, and Sammy "the Bull" Gravano put together. It is a given, say some legal sources, that Mikey Scars has named Joseph "JoJo" Corozzo, a former driver and lookout for John Gotti, as the real brains boss of the family, not the bland figurehead boss of the mob, Peter Gotti.

2005 and onward

The true test for the prosecution will not be whether some top Mafia bosses will be toppled but rather if the Mafia can be destroyed, something that has never been accomplished. Bosses come and go but the criminal combine survives with its ability to regenerate itself by making more money. In that sense it does what every successful corporation can do. That is the American dream in business, and for organized crime it will continue to maintain a hold on potential victims and in a perverse way will be recognized by the public in general as American as apple pie.

Photo Credits

(Numbers refer to page)

Agence France Presse/Corbis-Bettmann 158
AP/*The Record* 175A
AP Photo/Jane Rosenberg 334E
AP Photo/Elizabeth Williams 165D
AP Photo/U.S. Attorney's Office 249A
AP Photo/U.S. Department of Justice 334A
Associated Press/AP Photo 60C
Associated Press, Dade County Detention Center 316B
Associated Press, Hillsborough County 285D
Getty Images 281A
Horace Bristol/Corbis 390A

Illustrated American 211
National Archives 65, 212, 253, 274
New York Daily News 3, 10, 14, 28, 33, 42, 74, 78, 82, 87, 98, 99, 109, 110, 111, 118, 123, 145, 147, 157, 160, 171, 202, 223, 224, 232, 246, 248, 261, 267, 293, 312, 317, 321, 326, 328, 348, 356, 365, 367, 371, 373, 399
Scribner's Magazine 269
UPI/Corbis-Bettmann 163, 164, 165, 331
U.S. Coast Guard 322
Wide World 12, 89, 102, 120, 144, 176, 194, 203, 256, 279, 309, 325, 333, 364

All others: Author's collection

Index

Boldface page numbers indicate main entries. *Italic* page numbers indicate illustrations.